SECOND EDITION

INTRODUCTORY MANAGEMENT SCIENCE

G. D. EPPEN
University of Chicago

F. J. GOULD
University of Chicago

C. P. SCHMIDT
University of Alabama

Prentice-Hall, Inc., Englewood Cliffs, NJ 07632

Library of Congress Cataloging-in-Publication Data

EPPEN, GARY D., [date]
   Introductory management science.

   Bibliography: p.
   Includes index.
      1. Management—Mathematical models.   2. Management
science.   I. Gould, F. J. (Floyd Jerome), [date]
II. Schmidt, C. P.   III. Title.
HD30.25.E656 1987   658.4'033   86-17035
ISBN   0-13-501966-4

Editorial/production supervision: Susan Fisher
Interior and cover design: Suzanne Behnke
Manufacturing buyer: Ed O'Dougherty

To our parents and children.

Printed in the United States of America
10 9 8 7 6 5 4 3 2 1

ISBN 0-13-501966-4 01

Prentice-Hall International (UK) Limited, *London*
Prentice-Hall of Australia Pty. Limited, *Sydney*
Prentice-Hall Canada Inc., *Toronto*
Prentice-Hall Hispanoamericana, S.A., *Mexico*
Prentice-Hall of India Private Limited, *New Delhi*
Prentice-Hall of Japan, Inc., *Tokyo*
Prentice-Hall of Southeast Asia Pte. Ltd., *Singapore*
Editora Prentice-Hall do Brasil, Ltda., *Rio de Janeiro*

CONTENTS

PREFACE   **xvii**

1 **INTRODUCTION**   **1**

1.1   THE ROLE OF THIS BOOK   1
1.2   DIFFERENT TYPES OF MODELS AND WHAT THEY ARE ALL ABOUT   3
1.3   SPREADSHEET MODELS   8
1.4   A TAXONOMY OF MANAGEMENT SCIENCE MODELS   13
1.5   MODEL BUILDING   14
1.6   ON THE USE AND IMPLEMENTATION OF MODELING   16
1.7   CONSTRAINED OPTIMIZATION MODELS   18
1.8   WHY CONSTRAINTS ARE IMPOSED   22
1.9   INTUITIVE VERSUS FORMAL MODELING   25
1.10 SUMMARY   26
     MAJOR CONCEPTS QUIZ   26
     QUESTIONS FOR DISCUSSION   28
     COMPUTER PRINTOUTS: FIGURES 1.6, 1.7, 1.8, 1.9

2

LINEAR PROGRAMMING: FORMAL AND SPREADSHEET MODELS   30

APPLICATION CAPSULE: ALLOCATING A SCARCE RESOURCE

2.1   INTRODUCTION   31

2.2   PROTRAC, INC.   33

2.3   A SPREADSHEET REPRESENTATION OF PROTRAC E AND F   39

2.4   THE SPREADSHEET VERSUS THE FORMAL LP MODEL   44

2.5   CRAWLER TREAD: A BLENDING EXAMPLE   49

2.6   GUIDELINES AND COMMENTS ON MODEL FORMULATION   52

2.7   SUNK VERSUS VARIABLE COST   53

2.8   EXAMPLE 1: ASTRO AND COSMO (A PRODUCT-MIX PROBLEM)   55

2.9   EXAMPLE 2: BLENDING GRUEL (A BLENDING PROBLEM)   56

2.10   EXAMPLE 3: SECURITY FORCE SCHEDULING (A SCHEDULING PROBLEM)   51

2.11   EXAMPLE 4: A TRANSPORTATION MODEL   61

2.12   EXAMPLE 5: WINSTON-SALEM DEVELOPMENT CORPORATION (FINANCIAL PLANNING)   62

2.13   EXAMPLE 6: LONGER BOATS YACHT COMPANY—A VIGNETTE IN CONSTRAINED BREAK-EVEN ANALYSIS   64

2.14   EXAMPLE 7: MULTIPERIOD INVENTORY MODELS   65

2.15   EXAMPLE 8: THE BUMLES, INC., MINICASE (PRODUCTION AND INVENTORY CONTROL)   68

2.16   SUMMARY   72

2.17   KEY TERMS   72

MAJOR CONCEPTS QUIZ   73

PROBLEMS   77

CASE: RED BRAND CANNERS (FORMULATION)   93

CASE: AN APPLICATION OF SPREADSHEET ANALYSIS TO FOREIGN EXCHANGE MARKETS   97

COMPUTER PRINTOUTS: FIGURES 2.3, 2.4, 2.5, 2.6, 2.7, 2.18, 2.19, 2.27, 2.28, EXHIBITS 1, 2, 3, 4

3

LINEAR PROGRAMMING: GEOMETRIC REPRESENTATIONS AND GRAPHICAL SOLUTIONS   106

3.1   INTRODUCTION   106

3.2   PLOTTING INEQUALITIES AND CONTOURS   107

3.3   THE GRAPHICAL SOLUTION METHOD APPLIED TO PROTRAC, INC.   109

3.4   ACTIVE AND INACTIVE CONSTRAINTS   116

3.5   EXTREME POINTS AND OPTIMAL SOLUTIONS   120

3.6   SUMMARY OF THE GRAPHICAL SOLUTION METHOD FOR A MAX MODEL   122

3.7   THE GRAPHICAL METHOD APPLIED TO A MIN MODEL   122

3.8   UNBOUNDED AND INFEASIBLE PROBLEMS   124

3.9 SUMMARY   127

3.10 KEY TERMS   128

    MAJOR CONCEPTS QUIZ   129

    PROBLEMS   130

4 ANALYSIS OF LP MODELS: THE GRAPHICAL APPROACH   134

4.1 INTRODUCTION TO SENSITIVITY ANALYSIS (PROTRAC, INC., REVISITED)   134

4.2 CHANGES IN THE OBJECTIVE FUNCTION COEFFICIENTS   136

4.3 CHANGES IN THE RIGHT-HAND SIDES   138

4.4 TIGHTENING AND LOOSENING AN INEQUALITY CONSTRAINT   140

4.5 REDUNDANT CONSTRAINTS   141

4.6 WHAT IS AN IMPORTANT CONSTRAINT?   143

4.7 ADDING OR DELETING CONSTRAINTS   145

4.8 SUMMARY   146

4.9 KEY TERMS   147

    MAJOR CONCEPTS QUIZ   147

    PROBLEMS   149

5 LINEAR PROGRAMS: COMPUTER ANALYSIS, INTERPRETING SENSITIVITY OUTPUT, AND THE DUAL PROBLEM   152

    APPLICATION CAPSULE: AN INVENTORY OF TRUCKS   152

5.1 INTRODUCTION   153

5.2 THE PROBLEM THE COMPUTER SOLVES   153

5.3 THE COMPUTER ANALYSIS OF PROTRAC, INC.   162

5.4 THE CRAWLER TREAD OUTPUT: A DIALOGUE WITH MANAGEMENT (SENSITIVITY ANALYSIS IN ACTION)   174

5.5 A SYNOPSIS OF THE SOLUTION OUTPUT   183

5.6 THE DUAL PROBLEM   184

5.7 NOTES ON IMPLEMENTATION   195

5.8 SUMMARY   196

5.9 KEY TERMS   196

    MAJOR CONCEPTS QUIZ   197

    PROBLEMS   199

    APPENDIX 5.1 SOLVING AN LP WHEN NOT ALL VARIABLES ARE REQUIRED TO BE NONNEGATIVE   206

    APPENDIX 5.2 QUESTIONS BASED ON THE RED BRAND CANNERS CASE   206

    CASE: SAW MILL RIVER FEED AND GRAIN COMPANY   208

    CASE: KIWI COMPUTER   210

    CASE: PRODUCTION PLANNING AT BUMLES   214

DIAGNOSTIC ASSIGNMENT: CRAWLER TREAD AND A NEW ANGLE   217

COMPUTER PRINTOUTS: FIGURES 5.6, 5.11, 5.12, 5.14, 5.18, 5.20, 5.21

6   LINEAR PROGRAMMING: THE SIMPLEX METHOD   221

6.1   INTRODUCTION   221

6.2   THE ASTRO/COSMO PROBLEM REVISITED   223

6.3   TYPES OF SOLUTIONS TO THE ORIGINAL EQUATIONS   223

6.4   BASIC FEASIBLE SOLUTIONS AND EXTREME POINTS   227

6.5   TRANSFORMED EQUATIONS   229

6.6   THE CHARACTERIZATION OF ADJACENT EXTREME POINTS   231

6.7   THE INITIAL TABLEAU   232

6.8   INCREASING THE OBJECTIVE FUNCTION BY COMPUTING OPPORTUNITY COSTS   233

6.9   THE FULL TABLEAU REPRESENTATION   237

6.10   DETERMINING THE EXIT VARIABLE   239

6.11   UPDATING THE INITIAL TABLEAU   241

6.12   CONTINUING TO UPDATE SUCCESSIVE TABLEAUX   244

6.13   EXTENSIONS TO MORE GENERAL PROBLEMS   247

6.14   ALTERNATIVE OPTIMA   259

6.15   THE SIMPLEX METHOD FOR A MIN MODEL   259

6.16   NOTES ON IMPLEMENTATION   260

6.17   SUMMARY   260

6.18   KEY TERMS   261

MAJOR CONCEPTS QUIZ   262

PROBLEMS   264

APPENDIX 6.1 SENSITIVITY ANALYSIS: COMPUTING THE OPTIMAL DUAL VARIABLES   269

APPENDIX 6.2 SENSITIVITY ANALYSIS: COMPUTING ALLOWABLE CHANGES IN THE RHS   271

APPENDIX 6.3 SENSITIVITY ANALYSIS: COMPUTING ALLOWABLE CHANGES IN THE OBJECTIVE FUNCTION COEFFICIENT   275

COMPUTER PRINTOUT: FIGURE 6.25

7   LINEAR PROGRAMMING: SPECIAL APPLICATIONS   279

7.1   INTRODUCTION   279

7.2   THE TRANSPORTATION PROBLEM   280

7.3   SOLVING THE TRANSPORTATION PROBLEM   283

7.4   THE TRANSPORTATION MODEL: OTHER CONSIDERATIONS   300

7.5   THE ASSIGNMENT PROBLEM   306

7.6   SOLVING THE ASSIGNMENT PROBLEM: THE HUNGARIAN METHOD   310

7.7   THE ASSIGNMENT PROBLEM: OTHER CONSIDERATIONS   313

7.8   FINANCIAL AND PRODUCTION PLANNING   319

7.9 THE MEDIA SELECTION PROBLEM   323
7.10 SUMMARY   327
7.11 KEY TERMS   328
    MAJOR CONCEPTS QUIZ   328
    PROBLEMS   330
    COMPUTER PRINTOUTS: FIGURES 7.3, 7.31, 7.43, 7.48, 7.54

8 INTEGER AND QUADRATIC PROGRAMMING   336

    APPLICATION CAPSULE: SCHEDULING TRAINING AT AMERICAN AIRLINES   336
8.1 INTRODUCTION TO INTEGER PROGRAMMING   337
8.2 TYPES OF INTEGER LINEAR PROGRAMMING MODELS   338
8.3 GRAPHICAL INTERPRETATIONS   339
8.4 APPLICATIONS OF 0–1 VARIABLES   344
8.5 AN IP VIGNETTE: STECO'S WAREHOUSE LOCATION PROBLEM—FORMULATION AND COMPUTER ANALYSIS   349
8.6 THE ASSIGNMENT PROBLEM AND A SOCIAL THEOREM   353
8.7 THE BRANCH-AND-BOUND ALGORITHM   354
8.8 ILP AND MILP IN PRACTICE   362
8.9 NOTES ON IMPLEMENTATION OF INTEGER PROGRAMMING   364
8.10 SUMMARY OF IP   366
8.11 INTRODUCTION TO QUADRATIC PROGRAMMING   367
8.12 COMPUTER SOLUTION OF QP PROBLEMS   369
8.13 GEOMETRIC INTERPRETATION OF THE SENSITIVITY ANALYSIS   370
8.14 PORTFOLIO SELECTION   373
8.15 A PORTFOLIO EXAMPLE WITH LIVE DATA   376
8.16 KEY TERMS   380
    MAJOR CONCEPTS QUIZ   381
    PART 1. INTEGER PROGRAMMING QUESTIONS   381
    PART 2. QUADRATIC PROGRAMMING QUESTIONS   384
    PROBLEMS   386
    PART 1. PROBLEMS ON INTEGER PROGRAMS   386
    PART 2. PROBLEMS ON QUADRATIC PROGRAMS   391
    CASE: MUNICIPAL BOND UNDERWRITING   392
    DIAGNOSTIC ASSIGNMENT: ASSIGNING SALES REPRESENTATIVES   396
    COMPUTER PRINTOUTS: FIGURES 8.5, 8.6, 8.9, 8.20, 8.24, 8.35

9 NETWORK MODELS   400

    APPLICATION CAPSULE: A NETWORK MODEL AT AIR PRODUCTS AND CHEMICALS, INC.   400
9.1 INTRODUCTION   401
9.2 AN EXAMPLE: SEYMOUR MILES (A CAPACITATED TRANSSHIPMENT MODEL)   401

9.3   A GENERAL FORMULATION (THE CAPACITATED TRANSSHIPMENT MODEL)   404

9.4   THE SHORTEST-ROUTE PROBLEM   406

9.5   THE MINIMUM SPANNING TREE PROBLEM (COMMUNICATION LINKS)   413

9.6   THE MAXIMAL-FLOW PROBLEM   417

9.7   NOTES ON IMPLEMENTATION   423

9.8   SUMMARY   424

9.9   KEY TERMS   424

MAJOR CONCEPTS QUIZ   425

PROBLEMS   427

APPENDIX 9.1 A PC APPROACH TO NETWORK PROBLEMS   432

COMPUTER PRINTOUTS: FIGURES 9.40, 9.42, 9.44

10 PROJECT MANAGEMENT: PERT AND CPM   437

10.1   INTRODUCTION   437

10.2   THE GLOBAL OIL CREDIT CARD OPERATION   438

10.3   THE CRITICAL PATH—MEETING THE BOARD'S DEADLINE   443

10.4   VARIABILITY IN ACTIVITY TIMES   452

10.5   A MID-CHAPTER SUMMARY   456

10.6   CPM AND TIME-COST TRADE-OFFS   457

10.7   PROJECT COST MANAGEMENT: PERT/COST   463

10.8   NOTES ON IMPLEMENTATION   469

10.9   SUMMARY   470

10.10 KEY TERMS   471

MAJOR CONCEPTS QUIZ   472

PROBLEMS   474

APPENDIX 10.1 A PC APPROACH TO PERT/CPM   483

COMPUTER PRINTOUTS: FIGURES 10.13, 10.14, 10.16, 10.18, 10.24, 10.29, 10.43, 10.44, 10.46

11 INVENTORY CONTROL WITH KNOWN DEMAND   488

APPLICATION CAPSULE: COORDINATING DECISIONS FOR INCREASED PROFITS   488

11.1   INTRODUCTION   489

11.2   STECO WHOLESALING: THE CURRENT POLICY   491

11.3   THE ECONOMIC ORDER QUANTITY MODEL   495

11.4   QUANTITY DISCOUNTS AND STECO'S OVERALL OPTIMUM   505

11.5   THE EOQ MODEL WITH BACKLOGGING   508

11.6   THE PRODUCTION LOT SIZE MODEL: VICTOR'S HEAT TREATMENT PROBLEM   512

11.7   MATERIAL REQUIREMENTS PLANNING: FARMCRAFT MANUFACTURING CO.   515

11.8   SUMMARY   518

11.9 KEY TERMS   519
       MAJOR CONCEPTS QUIZ   519
       PROBLEMS   521
       APPENDIX 11.1 MATHEMATICAL DERIVATION OF EOQ RESULTS   525

12 INVENTORY MODELS WITH PROBABILISTIC DEMAND   527

12.1 INTRODUCTION   527
12.2 THE REORDER POINT-REORDER QUANTITY MODEL   528
12.3 THE APPLIANCE ANGLE PROBLEM   528
12.4 VICTOR'S CHOICE OF r: UNIFORM LEAD-TIME DEMAND   530
12.5 SELECTING A PROBABILITY OF STOCKING OUT   531
12.6 VICTOR'S CHOICE OF r: NORMAL LEAD-TIME DEMAND   533
12.7 EXPECTED ANNUAL COST OF SAFETY STOCK   535
12.8 ONE-PERIOD MODELS WITH PROBABILISTIC DEMAND
      (WILES' HOUSEWARES PROBLEM)   536
12.9 THE NEWSBOY PROBLEM   537
12.10 NOTES ON IMPLEMENTATION   540
12.11 SUMMARY   542
12.12 KEY TERMS   543
      MAJOR CONCEPTS QUIZ   543
      PROBLEMS   544
      DIAGNOSTIC ASSIGNMENT: INVENTORY TURNS PER YEAR   547

13 QUEUING MODELS   550

13.1 INTRODUCTION   550
13.2 THE BASIC MODEL   551
13.3 LITTLE'S FLOW EQUATION AND OTHER GENERALITIES   554
13.4 PROBLEM 1: A MULTISERVER QUEUE (HEMATOLOGY LAB)   556
13.5 A TAXONOMY OF QUEUING MODELS   559
13.6 ECONOMIC ANALYSIS OF QUEUING SYSTEMS   559
13.7 PROBLEM 2: THE M/G/s MODEL WITH BLOCKED CUSTOMERS CLEARED
      (WATS LINES)   561
13.8 PROBLEM 3: THE REPAIRPERSON PROBLEM   565
13.9 THE ROLE OF THE EXPONENTIAL DISTRIBUTION   567
13.10 QUEUE DISCIPLINE   568
13.11 NOTES ON IMPLEMENTATION   569
13.12 SUMMARY   569
13.13 KEY TERMS   570
      MAJOR CONCEPTS QUIZ   571
      PROBLEMS   572
      COMPUTER PRINTOUT: FIGURE 13.10

14 SIMULATION 575

APPLICATION CAPSULE: NAVAL SHIP PRODUCTION 575
APPLICATION CAPSULE: PLANNING TO GET THE LEAD OUT 576
14.1 INTRODUCTION 577
14.2 SIMULATION AND RANDOM EVENTS 581
14.3 AN INVENTORY CONTROL EXAMPLE: WILES' HOUSEWARES 583
14.4 GENERATING RANDOM EVENTS 586
14.5 COMPUTER SIMULATION OF WILES' PROBLEM 590
14.6 A SIMULATION STUDY: INVENTORY CONTROL AT PROTRAC 592
14.7 NOTES ON IMPLEMENTATION 596
14.8 SUMMARY 599
14.9 KEY TERMS 599
MAJOR CONCEPTS QUIZ 600
PROBLEMS 602
APPENDIX 14.1 A SPREADSHEET APPLICATION TO SIMULATION 607
DIAGNOSTIC ASSIGNMENT: SCHEDULING TANKER ARRIVALS 610
COMPUTER PRINTOUTS: FIGURES 14.14, 14.26, 14.27, 14.29

15 DECISION THEORY AND DECISION TREES 614

APPLICATION CAPSULE: DESIGNING A COMPLEX INTERCONNECTED SYSTEM 614
15.1 INTRODUCTION 615
15.2 THREE CLASSES OF DECISION PROBLEMS 616
15.3 THE EXPECTED VALUE OF PERFECT INFORMATION: NEWSBOY PROBLEM UNDER RISK 624
15.4 UTILITIES AND DECISIONS UNDER RISK 626
15.5 A MID-CHAPTER SUMMARY 630
15.6 DECISION TREES: MARKETING HOME AND GARDEN TRACTORS 631
15.7 SENSITIVITY ANALYSIS 635
15.8 DECISION TREES: INCORPORATING NEW INFORMATION 638
15.9 SEQUENTIAL DECISIONS: TO TEST OR NOT TO TEST 646
15.10 MANAGEMENT AND DECISION THEORY 649
15.11 NOTES ON IMPLEMENTATION 650
15.12 SUMMARY 651
15.13 KEY TERMS 652
MAJOR CONCEPTS QUIZ 653
PROBLEMS 654
APPENDIX 15.1 A PC APPROACH TO DECISION TREES 666
CASE: TO DRILL OR NOT TO DRILL 668
DIAGNOSTIC ASSIGNMENT: JOHNSON'S METAL 669

16 FORECASTING 671

16.1 INTRODUCTION 671
16.2 QUANTITATIVE FORECASTING 672
16.3 CAUSAL FORECASTING MODELS 673
16.4 TIME-SERIES FORECASTING MODELS 683
16.5 THE ROLE OF HISTORICAL DATA: DIVIDE AND CONQUER 697
16.6 QUALITATIVE FORECASTING 698
16.7 NOTES ON IMPLEMENTATION 700
16.8 KEY TERMS 702
MAJOR CONCEPTS QUIZ 702
PROBLEMS 704
APPENDIX 16.1 FITTING FORECASTING MODELS, THE DATA TABLE
SPREADSHEET COMMAND 706
COMPUTER PRINTOUTS: FIGURES 16.26, 16.27

17 HEURISTICS, MULTIPLE OBJECTIVES, AND GOAL PROGRAMMING 708

APPLICATION CAPSULE: NATIONAL CENTER FOR DRUG ANALYSIS 708
APPLICATION CAPSULE: MANAGEMENT OF COLLEGE STUDENT
RECRUITING ACTIVITIES 709
17.1 INTRODUCTION 709
17.2 FACILITY SCHEDULING (SEQUENCING COMPUTER JOBS) 711
17.3 SCHEDULING WITH LIMITED RESOURCES (WORKLOAD SMOOTHING) 714
17.4 MULTIPLE OBJECTIVES 720
17.5 NOTES ON IMPLEMENTATION 734
17.6 KEY TERMS 735
MAJOR CONCEPTS QUIZ 735
PROBLEMS 737
COMPUTER PRINTOUTS: FIGURES 17.16, 17.18, 17.19, 17.20, 17.21, 17.22

18 CALCULUS-BASED OPTIMIZATION AND AN INTRODUCTION TO NONLINEAR PROGRAMMING 743

18.1 INTRODUCTION 743
18.2 UNCONSTRAINED OPTIMIZATION IN ONE DECISION VARIABLE 744
18.3 UNCONSTRAINED OPTIMIZATION IN TWO DECISION VARIABLES 749
18.4 UNCONSTRAINED OPTIMIZATION IN n DECISION VARIABLES:
THE COMPUTER APPROACH 752
18.5 NONLINEAR OPTIMIZATION WITH CONSTRAINTS: A DESCRIPTIVE
GEOMETRIC INTRODUCTION 753

18.6 EQUALITY-CONSTRAINED MODELS AND LAGRANGE MULTIPLIERS   757
18.7 DIFFERENT TYPES OF NLP PROBLEMS AND SOLVABILITY   765
18.8 NOTES ON IMPLEMENTATION   770
18.9 KEY TERMS   771
     MAJOR CONCEPTS QUIZ   772
     PROBLEMS   774

ANSWERS TO ODD-NUMBERED PROBLEMS   777

**SELECTED ANSWERS TO MAJOR CONCEPTS
QUIZZES   817**

**TABLE T.1 AREAS FOR THE STANDARD NORMAL
DISTRIBUTION   822**

INDEX   823

VIGNETTES AND APPLICATIONS

CHAPTER ONE

1.2   Supply and Demand; Breakeven Analysis   3

1.3   Spreadsheet Models (Oak Products Production)   8

CHAPTER TWO

       APPLICATION CAPSULE: Allocating a Scarce Resource   30

2.2   PROTRAC, Inc. (formulation)   33

2.3   A Spreadsheet Representation of PROTRAC E & F   39

2.4   A Spreadsheet Parametric Analysis for PROTRAC E & F   44

2.5   Crawler Tread (formulation)   49

2.8   Astro and Cosmo (product mix)   55

2.9   Blending Gruel (blending problem)   56

2.10   Security Force Scheduling (scheduling problem and spreadsheet application)   57

2.11   Transportation Model   61

2.12   Winston-Salem Development Corporation (financial planning)   62

2.13   Longer Boats Yacht Company (constrained breakeven analysis)   64

2.15   Bumles, Inc., Minicase—Production and Inventory Control (a spreadsheet application)   68

       CASE: Foreign Exchange Markets (a spreadsheet application)   97

CHAPTER THREE	3.3	PROTRAC, Inc. (graphical analysis)	109

CHAPTER FOUR	4.1	PROTRAC, Inc. (graphical analysis)	134

CHAPTER FIVE

APPLICATION CAPSULE: An Inventory of Trucks 152
5.3 PROTRAC, Inc. (computer output) 162
5.4 Crawler Tread (computer output and sensitivity analysis) 174
5.6 Two Plants and Liquidation Prices 184
APPENDIX 5.2: Red Brand Canners Case (computer analysis) 206
CASE: Saw Mill River Feed and Grain Company 208
CASE: Kiwi Computer 210
CASE: Production Planning at Bumles 214
DIAGNOSTIC ASSIGNMENT: Crawler Tread and a New Angle 217

CHAPTER SIX

6.2 Astro/Cosmo (simplex application) 223
6.13 PROTRAC, Inc. (simplex application) 247

CHAPTER SEVEN

7.2 PROTRAC Distribution (diesels from harbors to plants) 280
7.5 PROTRAC-Europe's Auditing Problem 306
7.7 The Auditing Problem Reconsidered 313
7.8 Financial Planning 319
7.9 Media Selection 323

CHAPTER EIGHT

APPLICATION CAPSULE: Scheduling Training at American Airlines 336
8.3 PROTRAC, Inc. (integer program) 339
8.4 Capital Budgeting at PROTRAC (expansion decision) 344
8.5 An IP Vignette: Steco's Warehouse Location Problem 349
8.6 The Assignment Problem and a Social Theorem 353
8.9 Kelly-Springfield 364
Flying Tiger Line 365
Hunt-Wesson Foods 365
8.14 Portfolio Selection 373
CASE: Municipal Bond Underwriting 392
DIAGNOSTIC ASSIGNMENT: Assigning Sales Representatives 396

xiv

CHAPTER NINE

        APPLICATION CAPSULE: Air Products and Chemicals, Inc. 400
9.2 Seymour Miles (capacitated transshipment) 401
9.4 Aaron Drunner's Delivery Service; Equipment Replacement 406
9.5 Communication Link Project 413
9.6 Urban Development Planning Commission 417

CHAPTER TEN

10.2 Global Oil Credit Card Operation 438
10.3 Meeting the Board's Deadline 443
10.6 Financial Analysis for Retail Marketing 457
10.7 Planning Costs for Global Oil 463

CHAPTER ELEVEN

        APPLICATION CAPSULE: Coordinating Decisions for Increased Profits 488
11.2 Steco Wholesaling 491
11.4 Quantity Discounts and Steco's Overall Optimum 505
11.5 Selling Styrofoam 508
11.6 The Production Lot Size Model: Victor's Heat Treatment Problem 512
11.7 Material Requirements Planning: Farmcraft Manufacturing Co. 515

CHAPTER TWELVE

12.3 Appliance Angles 528
12.4 Victor's Choice of r: Uniform Lead-Time Demand 530
12.6 Victor's Choice of r: Normal Lead-Time Demand 533
12.8 Wiles' Housewares 536
12.9 The Newsboy Problem 537
12.10 Two Bin System 540
        DIAGNOSTIC ASSIGNMENT: Inventory Turns Per Year 547

CHAPTER THIRTEEN

13.1 St. Luke's Hematology Lab 550
      Buying WATS Lines 551
      Hiring Repairpeople 551
13.4 Hematology Lab 556
13.7 WATS Lines 561
13.8 Repairing Problem 565

CHAPTER FOURTEEN

        APPLICATION CAPSULE: Naval Ship Production 575
        APPLICATION CAPSULE: Planning to Get the Lead Out 576
14.2 Docking Facilities 581
      Inventory Control; Scheduling 582
14.3 Wiles' Housewares (inventory control) 583
14.5 Wiles' Problem (computer simulation) 590
14.6 Inventory Control at PROTRAC 592
        DIAGNOSTIC ASSIGNMENT: Scheduling Tanker Arrivals 610

CHAPTER
FIFTEEN

APPLICATION CAPSULE: Designing a Complex Interconnected System 614

15.3 The Expected Value of Perfect Information: Newsboy Problem Under Risk 624

15.6 Marketing Home and Garden Tractors 631

15.8 Marketing Research Example 638

CASE: To Drill or Not to Drill 668

DIAGNOSTIC ASSIGNMENT: Johnson's Metal 669

CHAPTER
SIXTEEN

16.3 Oil Company Expansion (curve fitting) 673

Quick and Dirty Fits 674

16.4 Application to Futures Prices 683

Forecasting Steco's Strut Sales (moving averages) 685

Application to Stock Prices 696

16.6 The Delphi Method 698

CHAPTER
SEVENTEEN

APPLICATION CAPSULE: National Center for Drug Analysis 708

APPLICATION CAPSULE: Management of College Student Recruiting 709

17.2 Sequencing Computer Jobs 711

17.3 Work-Load Smoothing 714

17.4 Swenson's Media Selection Problem (absolute priorities) 720

CHAPTER
EIGHTEEN

18.2 Perfume Production (marginal analysis) 744

18.3 Importing Coconut Oil (profit maximization) 749

18.6 Optimal Marketing Expenditures 757

PREFACE

The success of the first edition of this text, as measured by substantial adoptions over a wide range of schools, suggests that we have achieved a reasonable balance between a unique approach to the teaching of this subject and the presentation of traditional materials at the introductory level. In brief, the following characteristics of the first edition have been carried into this revision:

1. The role of the computer as part and parcel of the *application* of model-building is stressed. Throughout the text scenarios are presented, relevant models are discussed, and the model is then run on the computer. Highlighted printouts are discussed and interpreted in the context of the initial scenario.

2. Wherever possible, sensitivity analysis is stressed.

3. Wherever possible, the study of the model itself is from a geometric and intuitive point of view. Often the geometric analysis is discussed in tandem with the computer printout. The geometry is used to reveal the underlying structure of the model, and to show what the computer is saying.

4. For those who want to include introductions to various algorithms of management science, a first-level exposition of the usual techniques is included.

CHANGES IN THE SECOND EDITION

There are a number of major additions to the text. These are described below.

Spreadsheet and PC Applications

Spreadsheet models have become an accepted mode of analysis in a wide variety of business applications. Lotus 1–2–3 is now a standard part of the curriculum in many schools. Moreover, menu-driven problem-solving PC diskettes are becoming more and more available. Our response has been to create a substantial amount of new teaching material relating to these developments. Here is an overview of new spreadsheet and PC applications which appear in the text.

AN OVERVIEW OF SPREADSHEET AND PC APPLICATIONS

Specific Application	Technique	Section
Production at Oak Products	spreadsheet, spreadsheet optimizer	1.3
Protrac E & F	spreadsheet, spreadsheet optimizer	2.3, 2.4
Security Force Scheduling	spreadsheet, spreadsheet optimizer	2.10
Bumles, Inc., Minicase	spreadsheet, spreadsheet optimizer	2.15
Foreign Exchange Markets	spreadsheet, spreadsheet optimizer	CASE, Ch. 2
Network Problems (Shortest Route, Minimum Spanning Tree, Maximal Flow)	PC applications package	Appendix 9.1
PERT/CPM	PC applications package	Appendix 10.1
Simulation	spreadsheet	Appendix 14.1
Decision Trees	PC applications package	Appendix 15.1
Forecasting	spreadsheet	Appendix 16.1

Expanded Software Usage and Illustrations

In the first edition of the text, most of the computer printouts were produced by the LINDO code and these printouts related to LP and IP problems. In this new edition, examples of the use of LINDO (for LP and IP), GINO (for NLP), VINO (for spreadsheet optimization), LOTUS 1–2–3 (for spreadsheet modeling), What's*Best*! (for spreadsheet optimization), QSB (Quantitative Systems for Business, a general PC software package), and ARBORIST (for decision tree analysis) are given. Illustrating the use of these packages throughout the text should enhance the student's awareness of the increasing role that personal computers are playing in the implementation of management science models. Moreover, any of the software can be used in conjunction with the text. The student who develops "hands-on" experience in this way will have acquired a tool which could be useful at some later date for solving actual problems. The following list summarizes details about the software we've employed. (It should be noted that a number of PC application packages other than QSB are now being marketed and our use of QSB is not to be interpreted as a judgment of its merits relative to other available packages. Any such package can be used in conjunction with appropriate chapters of the text.) Any prices quoted are current as of April 1986.

1. GINO, LINDO and VINO
   Linus Schrage   Ph. 312/962-7449
   LINDO Systems, Inc.
   P.O. Box 148231
   Chicago, IL 60614

An educational package is available. A site license (costing about $2,000) includes the right to reproduce disks for use "inside the building" at no additional cost as well as individual copies for use "outside the building" for about $50 each. An individual program without a site license costs about $250. Larger versions for the PC as well as mainframe codes are also available.

2. What's*Best!*
   Sam Savage   Ph. 312/248-7300
   General Optimization, Inc.
   2251 N. Geneva Terrace
   Chicago, IL 60614

Copies of this package (including the floppy disks) can be obtained from Holden-Day for about $50. Programs with more capacity can be obtained from General Optimization, Inc.

3. Arborist
   Texas Instruments   Ph. 512/250-7357
   P.O. Box 2909, M/S 2151
   Austin, TX 78769

Suggested price is about $600. A quantity discount is offered for purchases of ten or more. A demonstration package is also available.

4. QSB
   College Marketing   Ph. 201/592-2000
   Prentice-Hall, Inc.
   Englewood Cliffs, NJ 07632

A site license is available for about $100. This license is free with an adoption of fifty or more copies of *Quantitative Concepts for Management* or *Introductory Management Science*, 2nd. edition. Individual disk packs can be ordered from most bookstores for about $15 under the *Quantitative Systems for Business* title, Prentice-Hall.

More Applications

Ten Application Capsules have been added to this edition. These provide snapshots of real world applications of management science. In addition, more applications have been introduced in the form of the FOREIGN EXCHANGE case (Chapter 2), the MUNICIPAL BOND UNDERWRITING case (Chapter 8), and in the new material on PORTFOLIO ANALYSIS (Sections 8.14 and 8.15).

Additional Teaching Aids

1. In the first edition there were three cases; there are now a total of eight. Alternative problem sets have been included for several of the cases from the previous edition, as well as for several new cases.

2. Major concepts quizzes have been refined, and selected answers appear at the end of the text.

3. Problem sets have been modified and expanded. Roughly half of the problems in most chapters are new.

4. A new student workbook has been developed. This contains solved problems and self-evaluation quizzes. Other accompanying materials are in the Instructor's Resource Manual, which includes answers to all problems, solutions to all cases and diagnostic assignments, and test banks.

Organization   The text is designed to permit a maximum degree of flexibility so that it will be useful in a wide variety of course configurations. Chapters 2 through 6 are sequential, although 5 and 6 can be interchanged. We have chosen to treat the mathematics of the simplex method (Chapter 6) after dealing with printout analysis and sensitivity interpretations (Chapter 5) because for many users of this text, Chapters 2 through 5 will be the appropriate LP material, and the more technical Chapter 6 will be omitted. The inventory chapters (11 and 12) are in sequence, but for all remaining chapters the sequence is relatively unimportant, as each is self-contained. The fact that most chapters are self-contained, and include a good supply of problems, makes it possible to accommodate almost any variety of introductory course. A course devoted to mathematical programming can be created by selecting Chapters 2 through 9, 17, and 18. To emphasize operations management topics, the instructor selects Chapters 10, 11, 12, 13, and 16. A course that concentrates on stochastic models would use Chapters 12, 13, 14, 15, and 16.

ACKNOWLEDGMENTS

We are indebted to those users of the text who have provided criticism and comment. At the University of Chicago we are especially indebted to Linus Schrage and Kipp Martin. We are grateful to Susan Fisher at Prentice-Hall for masterminding the production of this text.

1

INTRODUCTION

THE ROLE OF THIS BOOK

This book is about the use of quantitative models in solving management problems. The book has been written for two types of users: the general manager, or potential manager, who can profit from the use, or an understanding of the use, of quantitative modeling; and the student who is considering specializing in management science. Clearly, each type of user would have, at least to some extent, different requirements. The general manager requires an emphasis on topics that deal with the relationships between the model and the real-world problem, and how models fit into the process of solving such problems. On the other hand, the prospective specialist in management science requires a certain amount of technical enrichment, an exposure to various solution techniques, the so-called algorithms that management scientists develop and work with. Indeed, topics that are of great interest to the specialist may appear, to the general manager, to be sterile mathematical structures with little, if any, relevance to the real world. Because of these differences, one can well imagine that a book written exclusively for one type of user would look quite different from one written for the other.

Perhaps for this reason, one observes what might be considered two different approaches to the teaching of management science. One approach is slanted mainly to the specialist. It involves a presentation of various classes of models and then the teaching of the algorithms used to solve these models, usually with numerical examples suited to classroom use. These algorithms can be thought of as "the mathematical technology" that takes an input (a specific model) and creates an output (usually a computer printout). The other approach concentrates more on what has just been described as the input (the model) and the output (the printout). It is based on a view that, in the use of quantitative models, the crucial role of managers occurs during the formulation and implementation phases. It relegates to the computer the mathematical operations needed to solve models, and focuses on helping the manager to understand (1) what sorts of problems are amenable to modeling, (2) what the prospects are for obtaining a computer solution (within an affordable amount of time), and (3) what one can do to get the greatest possible value out of the model and the computer output.

Our goal has been to achieve, at the introductory level, an effective balance of these two approaches, to present an amount and mixture of material that serves well the interests of both users. We have tried to do this in such a way that either type of user will benefit from all the material. This, we feel, is possible because, in spite of the differences noted above, there is a common central thrust for each type of user: *an interest in real-world problem solving*. Without that, the management scientist would be a pure mathematician, and the manager would be without a job.

As a result of our "hybrid approach," what you will find in these chapters is a spectrum of information about a variety of quantitative models, how these models are formulated and solved, and how they are used to help managers attack real problems. The coverage in nearly every chapter can be broken down, generally speaking, into four categories: (1) *modeling* or *formulation*, the process of taking real-world problems and describing them in mathematical terms; (2) *solution techniques* or *algorithms*, the mathematical methods used to find answers from the models created in (1); (3) *computer solutions*, the use of standard computer programs to solve the models in (1); and (4) *philosophy*, a view of the relationships among the real-world problems, models, managers, and solutions. Each of these categories deserves at least brief comment.

Modeling and Formulation

In some senses, learning to model, or to think in terms of models, is one of the most important motives for studying management science. In nearly every chapter, and with the introduction of each new tool, details about modeling and problem formulation are discussed. Since the writing of the first edition of this text, an important new technique has appeared in the marketplace. This new technique is commonly referred to as the use of "what if" models, also termed computerized spreadsheet models. The computerized spreadsheet is a tool which in some sense "cuts across" many different types of formal mathematical models. The role of these spreadsheet models is illustrated at a very introductory level in this first chapter. More detailed examples, pertaining to a specific class of problems called **linear programs**, appear in the second chapter, which is entirely devoted to model formulation. And still other examples will be found in later material.

Algorithms

In this book, introductory forms of many of the usual management science algorithms (i.e. solution techniques) are given. For the most part, the presentation is standard and appears in conjunction with numerical examples. Appropriate chapters contain exercises in the use of these techniques.

Computer Solutions

In the real world the solution of a model is always performed on computers. In recognition of this fact, we have stressed computer solutions and their interpretation, and you will find a wealth of computer output throughout the text. Indeed, the interaction and interweaving of the symbolic model, numerical examples, geometric representations, and computer solutions is a distinguishing feature of our exposition. Experience has shown that this approach facilitates an insightful transition from student to real-world problem solver.

Philosophy In many of the chapters, when a new type of model is introduced, we stress the way in which that particular type of model fits into the overall role of the manager's decision-making function. Real-world contexts for actual usage, along with limitations, are emphasized.

Stemming from this philosophic stance—our desire to stress the way in which models fit into the process of solving problems—it has seemed to us appropriate that this first chapter be devoted to a general discussion of models and their use. In the following pages we consider such topics as the role of numerical data in quantitative models, model building, and the use and implementation of the output from models, from a general point of view. As mentioned above, "what if" models and the role of computerized spreadsheet models are introduced. We then turn our attention to the importance and use of constrained optimization models. You will find almost no equations in this chapter. We hope to establish firmly the notion that models exist to be used before you become immersed in the details of specific models. This attitude and a healthy skepticism are your best guarantee for getting the maximum amount of real benefit out of your study of management science.

Since we shall obviously be dealing with quantitative concepts, a word is in order regarding preparation. The level of mathematics required to work effectively with the material varies somewhat with the various chapters in this text. In terms of specific subject matter, a background in elementary algebra (i.e., the level commonly taught in high school) is sufficient for most chapters. However, the mathematical maturity that comes with a course in calculus will stand most students in good stead. It is especially useful to have been exposed to calculus before studying Chapters 12, 16, and 19. And if you already have managerial experience, that may serve you equally well.

———— 1.2
DIFFERENT TYPES OF MODELS AND WHAT THEY ARE ALL ABOUT

In our world, many kinds of models are associated with many kinds of activities. Engineers build model airplanes, urban planners build model cities, designers make model dresses, and stage managers make model sets. Physicists construct models of the universe, and economists build models of the economy. Business managers and corporate planners work with models of their own particular environments. Such an environment may be a complex multinational corporation or it may simply be a one-room shop where three products are assembled on four machines.

Despite the diversity of these models, they have one aspect in common. They are all idealized and simplified representations of reality. Another way of saying the same thing is that

A model is a selective abstraction of reality.

An artist looks at reality, filters it, and creates a selective representation. A modeler does the same thing.

Three Examples Based on observation, Sir Isaac Newton hypothesized the notion of gravitational force. Based on experimentation, Galileo quantified this model, stating that a falling body, no matter what its mass, falls a distance of

$$D = gt^2/2$$

FIGURE 1.1
Supply Function

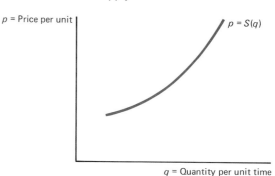

Gravity
feet in t seconds, where g is called the constant of acceleration. This quantitative statement is a **selective representation of reality** that explicitly describes the quantitative relation between distance D and time t. This equation, $D = gt^2/2$, is an excellent example of a model. It states an idealized numerical relationship. It is **idealized and simplified** because it ignores (or, putting it differently, "assumes away") everything else that is happening in the world and focuses only on a particular relationship between the two distinguished entities, D and t. Although the relationship set forth in the model is not *exactly* satisfied in any real situation (because for example, of air friction, windstorms, and other variable factors), the model is certainly useful, important, and simple. Its very simplicity represents a level of achievement often sought but seldom realized, for it is frequently the case that the best models are the simplest ones—those that are easiest to use and understand.

In economics, a well-known model describes the equilibrium price of a given commodity. This model is based on two functions: the supply function and the demand function. Figure 1.1 shows the supply function. It specifies the per unit price that must be offered to persuade suppliers to bring a quantity of the commodity to market.

Supply and
Demand
Note that

> Suppliers will ask a per unit price p to entice the production (per unit time) of the quantity q. As q increases, p will increase in accordance with the relationship $p = S(q)$.

The demand function is shown in Figure 1.2. It shows the price per unit that must hold in order for a total quantity q to be sold (per unit time). Note that

> A per unit price p must hold for a total quantity q to be purchased (i.e., demanded by buyers). If a larger total quantity is to be purchased, the unit price must fall. As q increases, p will decrease in accordance with the relationship $p = D(q)$.

A graphic view of the interaction between the supply function and the demand function is provided in Figure 1.3. We see that the equilibrium price, according to this model,

FIGURE 1.2

FIGURE 1.2
Demand Function

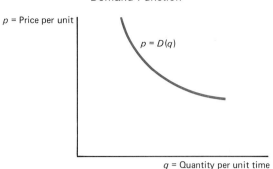

is that price at which the supply and demand curves intersect (i.e., the price where quantity supplied equals quantity demanded). In other words, at the equilibrium price, denoted p^*,

$$\text{quantity supplied by producers} = q^* = \text{quantity demanded by consumers}$$

or, more concisely,

$$\text{supply} = \text{demand}$$

This simple quantitative model is certainly a selective representation of reality. It ignores most of the world and describes only three entities of interest: price, quantity supplied, and quantity purchased. Price is related to supply. Price is related to demand. In equilibrium, says the model, price will find a level at which supply equals demand. It is a beautifully simple model, but it is also an idealization, for the world we live in is never truly in equilibrium. The price of an item varies from store to store, from day to day, from city to city, and from country to country. In the real world you cannot identify an equilibrium price. Nevertheless, the model has been found to be useful as a first approximation to reality and it is considered to be fundamental to the study of economics.

The model **supply = demand** has several features in common with the model $D = gt^2/2$. Both are extremely simple. Both are quantitative. That is, both models describe a **quantitative relationship** between entities of interest.

FIGURE 1.3
Market Equilibrium Model

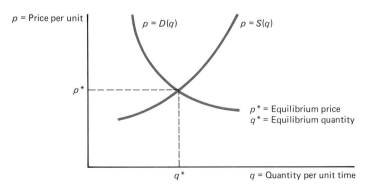

FIGURE 1.4
Break-Even Analysis Model

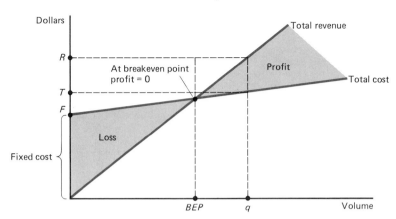

A third example of a simplified quantitative model is provided by **break-even analysis** (sometimes called cost–volume–profit analysis) for a firm. This model determines the **volume of sales** at which

$$\text{total revenue} = \text{fixed cost} + \text{variable cost}$$

Break-Even Analysis

This volume of sales is called the **break-even point** (BEP). Since at the break-even point, total revenue = total cost, it must be true that (1) at this point profit (i.e., revenue − cost) is zero; (2) for volumes less than BEP, the firm will incur a loss; and (3) for volumes that exceed BEP, the firm will accrue profits. These relationships are shown by the model represented in Figure 1.4. This simplified model shows some interesting quantitative relationships between various entities of interest. For example, because of previous commitments management may wish to focus on a sales volume of q units. You can conveniently read from Figure 1.4 that at this volume

$$\text{total cost} = T$$

$$\text{variable cost} = T - F$$

$$\text{total revenue} = R$$

$$\text{profit} = R - T$$

In the business environment, many of the useful models are quantitative in nature. **Our exclusive interest in this text is in quantitative models.** Unfortunately, most quantitative models in practice are much more complicated than the three examples given above. Although models used in business may become simpler in the future, it is notable that the trend has been in the opposite direction. While computation costs have been historically decreasing, those who work with quantitative models have been attacking problems with greater and greater complexity.

Models and Numbers

Quantitative models start with, operate on, and produce numbers. That is, numbers play many roles in the creation, solution, and use of quantitative models. Consider, for example, the fact that most models of interest to management are what we call **decision models**. Every decision model contains **decision variables**. The solution of the model yields numerical values for these decision variables. These values imply specific decisions.

It follows that selecting a decision amounts to determining numerical values for decision variables.

In the context of quantitative decision models, decisions are numbers.

In such models, it is also the case that

Decisions are based on an evaluation of numerical data.

Consider the following commonplace examples. A model to evaluate the alternatives of buying a house versus renting an apartment considers the down payments required, mortgage rates, cash flow, appreciation—in brief, numerical data. A model to help you decide whether to work for an MBA degree would consider length of time required, the tuition and other expenses, salary potential—numerical data. In short, numerical data are the guts of quantitative models.

We have seen that quantitative models are based on numerical data and that decision models produce numbers that are decisions. Models also serve as generators of numbers that are not, in their own right, decisions. For example, a model may reveal the maximum possible profit a certain enterprise can yield. In other words, what we have been saying is:

Models evaluate numerical data and they provide additional numerical data.

Indeed, models often do no more than refine, or evaluate, crude data in order to produce more useful data. In fact, the outputs of some models may be used as the inputs for other models. It is not atypical for models to be linked together, as illustrated in Figure 1.5. Notice, for example, that the marketing model has as its output a forecast of next year's demand, and this forecast is an input to the production model.

FIGURE 1.5
Analysts Use Models as Inputs to Other
Models

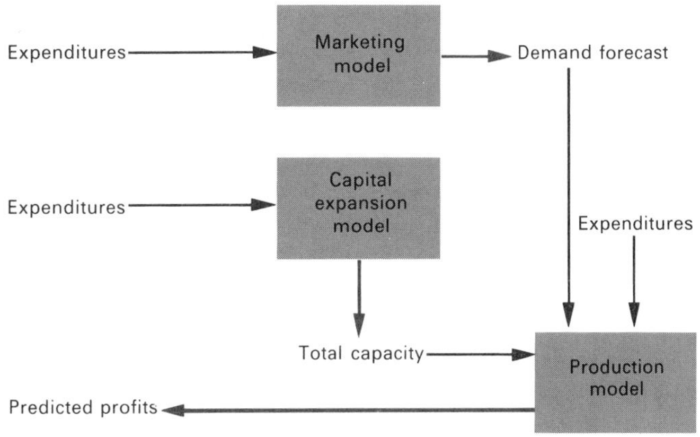

Objectives In order to evaluate data, most decision models contain, as well as decision variables, what we call an *objective*. The model symbolically specifies the ways in which various decisions will affect the objective. As simple illustrations of objectives, consider the following examples:

1. **Salesforce allocation model:** The decisions (i.e., decision variables) might be how many sales-people to assign to each territory. A typical objective might be to maximize sales revenues.
2. **Job-shop scheduling model:** The decisions (decision variables) might be how many hours to schedule given parts on given machines, and in what sequence. Alternative objectives might be to minimize costs, to minimize the total completion time for all parts, to minimize tardiness on deliveries, and so on.
3. **Cash-management model:** The decision variables might be the amount of funds to be held in each of several categories (cash, Treasury bills, bonds, stocks) each month. A typical objective might be to minimize the opportunity cost of holding more liquid assets.

A Framework and Classification All these examples of decision models fit into a general framework that we are beginning to establish, namely:

1. **Decision models selectively describe the environment.**
2. **Decision models designate decision variables.**
3. **Decision models designate objectives.**

We shall discuss these three points in more detail in the following pages and in other chapters. Before continuing with this general discussion, it will be useful at this time to introduce the concept of the **spreadsheet model**.

———— 1.3
SPREADSHEET MODELS

Computerized spreadsheet models, especially Lotus 1–2–3[1], have made quantitative models and decision models an everyday part of an enormous number of management activities. These models give managers a "user-friendly" technique for answering a wide range of so-called "what if" questions. These models appear to have met "the market test." Their popularity is a testimony to the value managers attach to their use.

"What If" Questions A "what if" question is exactly what the name suggests. The manager wants to know what happen to some quantity of interest if some characteristic of his operating environment changes in a specified way. Obviously, such questions are fundamental to any management task. The following simple production problem illustrates a spread-sheet format and shows how Lotus 1–2–3 can be used to answer "what if" questions.

Production at Oak Products, Inc. Oak Products, Inc. (OP) produces a line of high-quality solid oak chairs. There are six chairs in the product line: Captain, Mate, American High, American Low, Spanish King, and Spanish Queen. These chairs have been designed to use a number of inter-changeable component parts—long and short dowels, heavy and light seats, and heavy

[1] Lotus 1–2–3 is a trademark of Lotus Development Corporation.

FIGURE 1.6
The First OP Spreadsheet

	A	B	C	D	E	F	G	H	I	J	K
1	******************										
2	TOTAL PROFIT:										
3	8760										
4	******************										
5	Product		Capt	Mate	AmerHi	AmerLo	SpainK	SpainQ			
6	Profit\Unit		36	40	45	38	35	25			
7											
8	Quantity		40	40	40	40	40	40			
9	Produced										
10	--										
11			Product Resource Requirement						Total	Start	End
12									Usage	Inv.	Inv.
13	--										
14	Long Do		8	0	12	0	8	4	1280	1280	0
15	Short Do		4	12	0	12	4	8	1600	1900	300
16	Legs		4	4	4	4	4	4	960	1090	130
17	Heavy Se		1	0	0	0	1	1	120	190	70
18	Light Se		0	1	1	1	0	0	120	170	50
19	Heavy Ru		6	0	4	0	5	0	600	1000	400
20	Light Ru		0	4	0	5	0	6	600	1000	400
21	Capt Rail		1	0	0	0	0	0	40	110	70
22	Mate Rail		0	1	0	0	0	0	40	72	32
23	Amber Rail		0	0	1	1	0	0	80	93	13
24	Span Rail		0	0	0	0	1	1	80	85	5
25	--										

and light rungs. In addition, each type of chair has a distinguishing rail which caps the back. The interchangeable parts help protect OP against sudden shifts in demand. It is November 15 and Tom Burr, the plant manager, is set to meet James White from production control to finalize the production plan for the next two weeks. At OP, the finishing activity (i.e. sanding, spraying, and drying of the component parts) requires two weeks. For this reason, only components that are already on hand and finished can be used in chairs that will be produced in the next two weeks.

Using Lotus 1–2–3

Production planning at OP is done with Lotus 1–2–3. Jim White has run the Lotus 1–2–3 program on his PC. The result is the **spreadsheet** shown in Figure 1.6. A spreadsheet is a kind of representation of the problem. Jim has placed this representation of his problem on a grid with rows labeled 1 through 25 and columns labeled A through K. As you can see, Jim has placed text in many of the rows and columns. This text allows one to readily interpret the numbers in the spreadsheet. For example, the 4 in column C, row 15, is a piece of data indicating that 4 short dowels are used in producing one Captain chair. Also, Jim has placed his suggested production plan in row 8, columns C through H. Thus, Jim's proposal is to produce 40 chairs of each type. Row 3 shows that the total profit will be $8,760. The entries in row 15, columns I,J,K indicate that

1. Jim's production plan will use a total of 1600 short dowels.
2. The starting inventory of short dowels is 1900.
3. Jim's plan will leave a final inventory of 300 short dowels.

The production planning session proceeds as follows:

JIM: I've used the usual procedure to determine production, that is to make the same quantity of each product and maximize the total amount produced. This time we run out of long dowels first, but we do pretty well. We produce 40 of each chair and make $8,760.

TOM: I know that we've always produced equal quantities of each chair, but this time things are different. The president tells me that solid wood products are a hot item now and we will sell out no matter what we produce. He says to make as much profit as possible. What should we do?

JIM: I don't know the complete answer, but I do have an idea. American Highs are clearly our most profitable item, but notice that they also use the most long dowels and we're short of long dowels. If I give up 2 American Highs, I lose $90 of profit, but I gain 24 long dowels. I can use those dowels to make 3 Captains, in which case, I'll gain $108. So **what if** we make 100 Captains and no American Highs?

FIGURE 1.7
Jim's Revised Spreadsheet

	A	B	C	D	E	F	G	H	I	J	K
1	*****************										
2	TOTAL PROFIT:										
3	9120										
4	*****************										
5	Product		Capt	Mate	AmerHi	AmerLo	SpainK	SpainQ			
6	Profit\Unit		36	40	45	38	35	25			
7											
8	Quantity		100	40	0	40	40	40			
9	Produced										
10	-------										------
11			Product Resource Requirement						Total	Start	End
12									Usage	Inv.	Inv.
13	-------										-----
14	Long Do		8	0	12	0	8	4	1280	1280	0
15	Short Do		4	12	0	12	4	8	1840	1900	60
16	Legs		4	4	4	4	4	4	1040	1090	50
17	Heavy Se		1	0	0	0	1	1	180	190	10
18	Light Se		0	1	1	1	0	0	80	170	90
19	Heavy Ru		6	0	4	0	5	0	800	1000	200
20	Light Ru		0	4	0	5	0	6	600	1000	400
21	Capt Rail		1	0	0	0	0	0	100	110	10
22	Mate Rail		0	1	0	0	0	0	40	72	32
23	Amber Rail		0	0	1	1	0	0	40	93	53
24	Span Rail		0	0	0	0	1	1	80	85	5
25	-------										-----
26											

(Jim enters this new proposal into row 8, columns C through H. The Lotus 1–2–3 program automatically fills in new values for those grid cells that depend upon the production plan. The result is shown in Figure 1.7.)

TOM: Jim, that's great! You've increased profits by $360. I wonder if we can do better? I'm sure we can. In fact, I think we can use your idea again. Spanish Kings require 8 long dowels while Spanish Queens only require 4. I should be able to give up a King and lose $35, but make 2 Queens and gain $50. So, **what if** we make no Kings and a total of 120 Queens?

(The result is shown in Figure 1.8).

FIGURE 1.8
Tom's Revised Spreadsheet

```
         A       B   C     D     E      F      G      H     I      J     K
 1  ******************
 2  TOTAL PROFIT:
 3     9720
 4  ******************
 5     Product    Capt Mate AmerHi AmerLo SpainK SpainQ
 6  Profit\Unit    36   40    45     38     35     25
 7
 8  Quantity      100   40     0     40      0    120
 9  Produced
10  ---------------------------------------------------------------------------
11              Product Resource Requirement         Total Start  End
12                                                   Usage  Inv.  Inv.
13  ---------------------------------------------------------------------------
14  Long Do        8    0     12      0      8      4  1280  1280     0
15  Short Do       4   12      0     12      4      8  2320  1900  -420
16  Legs           4    4      4      4      4      4  1200  1090  -110
17  Heavy Se       1    0      0      0      1      1   220   190   -30
18  Light Se       0    1      1      1      0      0    80   170    90
19  Heavy Ru       6    0      4      0      5      0   600  1000   400
20  Light Ru       0    4      0      5      0      6  1080  1000   -80
21  Capt Rail      1    0      0      0      0      0   100   110    10
22  Mate Rail      0    1      0      0      0      0    40    72    32
23  Amber Rail     0    0      1      1      0      0    40    93    53
24  Span Rail      0    0      0      0      1      1   120    85   -35
25  ---------------------------------------------------------------------------
```

JIM: There's some good news and some bad news. The good news is that your economics was right. Profits increased by $600. The bad news is that we don't have the inventory to support this plan. The spreadsheet shows negative ending inventory for short dowels and a bunch of other things. This means that we have to use more short dowels than we have. It's just not possible.

TOM: I see what you mean. I clearly overshot the mark. I understand that we would decrease the production of Spanish Kings and increase the production of Spanish Queens somewhat and increase profits. With enough effort, I guess we could figure out how much we can push this trade-off before running out of inventory. But even so, how do we know it's a good solution? I really wonder **what's best**.

Tom is in luck. The Oak Products problem is a standard type of managerial planning problem, called a linear programming problem, and the best, or **optimal** solution is easily obtained. Indeed, there are several PC codes which take a linear programming problem, set up in a Lotus 1–2–3 spreadsheet format as above, and then optimize. Two such codes are VINO™[2] and What's*Best!*™[3]. When using either of these programs, only a few additional strokes at the keyboard are required to obtain the optimal plan. The result is shown in Figure 1.9. It is interesting to note that profit has increased by $1,174 over Jim's revised plan and that no Spanish style chairs are part of the optimal solution.

FIGURE 1.9
The Optimal Solution

	A	B	C	D	E	F	G	H	I	J	K
1	******************										
2	TOTAL PROFIT:										
3	10294										
4	******************										
5	Product	Capt	Mate	AmerHi	AmerLo	SpainK	SpainQ				
6	Profit\Unit	36	40	45	38	35	25				
7											
8	Quantity	100	72	40	53	0	0				
9	Produced										
10	--										
11		Product Resource Requirement							Total	Start	End
12									Usage	Inv.	Inv.
13	--										
14	Long Do	8	0	12	0	8	4	1280	1280	0	
15	Short Do	4	12	0	12	4	8	1900	1900	0	
16	Legs	4	4	4	4	4	4	1060	1090	30	
17	Heavy Se	1	0	0	0	1	1	100	190	90	
18	Light Se	0	1	1	1	0	0	165	170	5	
19	Heavy Ru	6	0	4	0	5	0	760	1000	240	
20	Light Ru	0	4	0	5	0	6	553	1000	447	
21	Capt Rail	1	0	0	0	0	0	100	110	10	
22	Mate Rail	0	1	0	0	0	0	72	72	0	
23	Amber Rail	0	0	1	1	0	0	93	93	0	
24	Span Rail	0	0	0	0	1	1	0	85	85	
25	--										

The above discussion only illustrates what a spreadsheet representation of a problem may look like, and what it can do. We've told you nothing about how to actually create a spreadsheet representation. You will see some of that in our discussion of model

[2] VINO is a trade mark of LINDO Systems, Inc.
[3] What's*Best!* is a trade mark of General Optimization Inc.

formulation in Chapter 2, where you'll also see several other specific spreadsheet examples, and more of the power that spreadsheets provide. At this point we return to our more broad discussion concerning models in general.

——— 1.4
A TAXONOMY OF MANAGEMENT SCIENCE MODELS

Management scientists work with **quantitative decision models**.

FIGURE 1.10

Decision Models by Uncertainty Class and
Corporate Use (D, Deterministic; P, Probabilistic; H, High; L, Low)

MODEL TYPE	UNCERTAINTY CLASSIFICATION	FREQUENCY OF CORPORATE USE
Linear Programming	D	H
Network (including PERT/CPM)	D, P	H
Inventory, Production, and Scheduling	D, P	H
Econometric, Forecasting, and Simulation	D, P	H
Integer Programming	D	L
Dynamic Programming	D, P	L
Stochastic Programming	P	L
Nonlinear Programming	D	L
Game Theory	P	L
Optimal Control	D, P	L
Queuing	P	L
Difference Equations	D	L

Formal Models Many models satisfy this description. In Figure 1.10, twelve different kinds of **formal mathematical models** are listed, all of which are used in real-world quantitative decision problems. The list is not exhaustive; it will simply give you an idea of the breadth of the field of quantitative modeling. Figure 1.10 also shows two other important features. The first is a classification scheme in terms of degree of uncertainty. Some of the models in management science are called **deterministic models**. This means that all the relevant data (i.e., data that the model will use or evaluate) are assumed to be known. Other types of models are **probabilistic** (also called **stochastic**) models. In such models, some of the relevant data (such as future demand, for example) are considered uncertain. In the latter type of model, probabilities may have to be specified for the uncertain data. Examples of both these types of models, deterministic and probabilistic, are treated in the text. Also, as you can see in Figure 1.10, some models, such as inventory and production, can be either of a deterministic or a probabilistic nature.

The second type of information provided by Figure 1.10 concerns **frequency of use** of these models in corporate settings. Based on three studies of this topic,[4] we have indicated, for each type of model, whether it tends to be used with high(H) or low(L)

---

[4] W. Ledbetter and J. F. Cox, "Are O.R. Techniques Being Used?", *Journal of Industrial Engineering*, 9 (February 1977), pp. 19–21; Efraim Turban, "A Sample Survey of Operations Research Activities at the Corporate Level," *Operations Research*, 20 (May–June 1972); F. C. Weston, "O.R. Techniques Relevant to Corporate Planning Function Practices: An Investigative Look," *Operations Research Bulletin* 19, Suppl. 2, (Spring 1971).

frequency by corporate managers. Such information was obtained by sampling large companies. You can see that, of the many different types of models, there are only four which seem to be frequently employed in applications. Twelve of the nineteen chapters in this text will deal with these four categories.

Spreadsheet Models

The list in Figure 1.10 is a list of **generic mathematical models** (sometimes called **formal models**) used by management scientists. Notice that spreadsheets are not on this list. A spreadsheet, *per se*, is not the same type of model as those on the list. A spreadsheet can be thought of as a **tool** for representing and manipulating a wide variety of mathematical models. As we saw with Oak Products, Inc., a linear programming model can be represented in a spreadsheet format. The same is true of inventory and production models, network models, and a variety of other models shown in Figure 1.10. Spreadsheet representations, in part, are a powerful tool precisely because of this general applicability. Throughout the text we shall conform to current usage, with terms such as "spreadsheet models," "spreadsheet representation," and "spreadsheet format" used interchangeably. The important point is that a spreadsheet is something that cuts across "model type." In a sense it stands on its own. It is a tool rather than a solution procedure.

> **The spreadsheet makes it easy to ask and answer "what if" questions about a real problem. To that extent, the spreadsheet must incorporate a selective representation of the problem, and from this point of view a spreadsheet is a model.**

——— 1.5
MODEL BUILDING

Whether a model is simple or complex, it is a representation that idealizes, simplifies, and selectively abstracts reality, and this representation is constructed by individuals. Unfortunately, the present technology is such that there are no easy rules or automatic methods for model building. The PC revolution and accompanying software developments may someday lead to user-friendly general model-building packages. Currently, however, model building involves a great deal of art and imagination as well as technical know-how.

In a business environment, quantitative modeling involves the specifications of interactions between many variables. In order to accomplish this "quantification," the problem must be stated in the language of mathematics. We shall see many examples of model building in the chapters to follow. Do not be misled by the specific examples in the text, for *in the complexity of real-world problems there is usually no single "correct way" to build a model. Different models may address the same situation in much the same way that paintings by Picasso and Van Gogh would make the same view look different.*

As an overall guide, we can break down the process of building a quantitative decision model into three steps:

1. The environment is studied.
2. A selective representation of the problem is formulated.
3. A symbolic (i.e., mathematical) expression of the formulation is constructed.

Let us now analyze the above breakdown in more detail. Then we will talk about the *use* of models.

Study the Environment

The first of the three model-building steps, a study of the environment, is easily under-valued by those new to modeling. The stated problem is often not the real problem. A variety of factors, including organizational conflicts, a difference between personal and organizational goals, and simply the overall complexity of the situation, may stand between the modeler and a clear understanding of the problem. Experience is probably the most essential ingredient for success—both experience in building models and a working experience in the environment to be studied.

Formulation

The second step, formulation, involves basic conceptual analysis, in which assumptions and simplifications usually have to be made. It is sometimes stated that **until a model can be formulated the very problem under consideration is unclear**. It has been said that without language we cannot think. In the same vein, it is often the case that without models we cannot make rational quantitative decisions. During the process of model formulation, pertinent relationships are conceptualized in much the same way that Galileo thought about the interactions among distance, time, and the rate of acceleration due to gravity in the falling-object problem. The process of formulation also requires the model builder to *select* or *isolate* from the total environment those aspects of reality relevant to the problem scenario. Since the problems we are concerned with involve decisions and objectives, these must be explicitly identified and defined. In some of the problems to be considered in future chapters it will become apparent that there are many applications in which the definition of the decision variables and the objective is a major task in itself. There may be various ways to define the decision variables, and the most appropriate definition may not be apparent initially. For example, it may be unclear whether a certain model should include amounts produced of every product or of only some subset of products. To keep the model suitably small for computational purposes, it may even be desirable to combine all products into one aggregate class. Moreover, the objectives may be unclear. Even the most capable managers may not know precisely what results they want to achieve. Equally problematic, there may be too many objectives to be satisfied, and it may be necessary to choose one out of many. (It will become evident that it is often impossible to optimize two different objectives at the same time, and thus, generally speaking, it is nonsensical to seek to obtain "the most return for the least investment.")

Once a logical formulation is accomplished (and this may be a verbal process), a symbolic form of the model must be constructed. In a sense, formulation and construction are integrated processes, with formulation the conceptual logical aspect and construction the expression of the logical relationships in the symbolic language of mathematics. All models are constructed of some medium. A dress designer constructs models out of fabric. The model city is made of clay. The conceptual formulation (a compact radial city with inner and outer hubs, underground parking, moving sidewalks, and so on) takes on a physical representation in the clay model. The conceptual and verbal relationships among distance, time, and acceleration due to gravity are represented via the medium of mathematical symbols in the statement $D = gt^2/2$.

Symbolic Construction

The interactions between formulation and the symbolic construction are usually critical. For example, a formulation of a corporate-planning model may involve a decision on whether to look 3, 5, or 10 years into the future. It may involve judgments on which divisions and subsidiaries to include. It may then turn out that the model as formulated is far too complex to be constructed in a way that can be useful. Perhaps the required data simply do not exist. Or perhaps the data can be found, but it turns out that with existing techniques it would take three days to run the model on the computer. This embarrassment can make the cost of using the model outweigh any potential gain. Unemployed management scientists can testify to the fact that, all too often, models are formulated that simply cannot be built.

Does this process of model building sound like too much for one person to accomplish? Often, it is. When operations research (for all practical purposes, today, the terms "operations research" and "management science" are synonymous) began, during World War II, logistic models were built by teams of mathematicians, statisticians, economists, physicists, engineers, and generalists. Today, the picture is not much different, except that econometricians, computer scientists, and management scientists have been added. Usually, management scientists train in the **theory and development of models**. They are also concerned with the **development of algorithms**, which are techniques for solving models. Thus, models are frequently built by heterogeneous and interdisciplinary teams of experts from various fields. A management scientist working alone has a very limited repertoire and limited capabilities.

———— 1.6
ON THE USE AND IMPLEMENTATION OF MODELING

Models are used in as many ways as there are people who build them. They can be used to sell an idea or a design, to order optimal quantities of nylon hosiery, to better organize our knowledge of the universe, or to better organize an economy or a firm.

Planning Models
In the firm, models are increasingly synonymous with executive planning. Planning models are used to forecast the future, to explore alternatives, to develop multiple-contingency plans, to increase flexibility and reaction time—in short, to provide planners with all sorts of data. However, although models are used for planning, it must be stated that

---

No model can ever be guaranteed to give a high-level planner the "best decision."

Models and Executive Judgment
In fact, as will be discussed in Section 1.7 the very notion of "best decision" is, strictly speaking, a mathematical rather than a real-world idea. You must remember that **a model is not reality. It is only a symbolic approximation, a selective approximation, of reality**. A model can produce a "best decision," but only within the limited context of the model. No model can completely capture the real world. Some considerations will always be left out. And because of the fact that no model can be guaranteed to produce a "best real-world decision," **the model is not a substitute for executive judgment and intuition**. But models do provide interesting data for executives to evaluate. They are, in the final analysis, used only as tools to aid in the decision-making process. Figure 1.11 shows one way of portraying the interaction between the model and the manager. You can see from this picture that

---

One aspect of the manager's role is to evaluate the model itself.

It is not unusual for the modern manager to be faced with a significant decision, after all is said and done, as to how much weight should be assigned to the recommendations

FIGURE 1.11
Feedback Interaction Between
Model and Manager

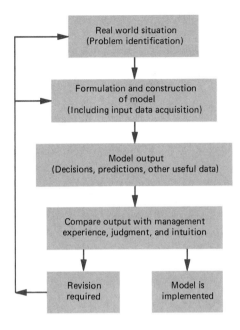

of a particular model. The need for managerial decisions may arise out of conflict or adversary confrontations, and quantitative models are often used as tools in this process. The manager's decision may well influence his or her career. This fact in itself provides a not insignificant incentive for the study of models and their proper employment in the managerial setting.

A Hierarchy of Models in the Firm
Concerning the use of models, it can also be said that models often play different roles at different levels of the firm. At the top levels, models more typically provide data and information, not decisions. They are useful as strategic planning tools. At lower levels, models are actually used to provide decisions. In many plants, for example, assembly-line operations are completely computerized. Decisions are produced by a model of the operation.

Models have different uses at different levels of the firm for a number of reasons. At progressively lower levels of an organization, alternatives and objectives are apt to become clearer. Interactions are easier to specify quantitatively. Data are often more available and the future environment more certain. For example, at the bottom of the hierarchy a decision may concern the scheduling of a particular machine. We know the products that will be run on it and the costs of changing the machine from the production of one product to any other product. The goal of the model may be to find a schedule that produces the necessary amounts by the due dates and minimizes changeover and storage costs.

Contrast the clarity and explicitness of that problem with a multibillion-dollar top-management decision between "invest and grow" and "produce and generate current earnings." Models can certainly be applied to such broad and fuzzy problems, but the models themselves are loaded with assumptions and uncertainties. In such cases, the validity of the model may be as difficult to determine as the appropriate decision.

In spite of these different uses of models at different levels of the firm, a few generalities apply to all quantitative-decision models. All such models provide a framework for logical and consistent analysis. More specifically, quantitative models are widely used for at least four reasons:

1. Models force managers to be explicit about objectives.
2. Models force managers to identify and record the types of decisions (decision variables) that influence objectives.
3. Models force managers to identify and record pertinent interactions and trade-offs between decision variables.
4. Models force managers to record constraints (limitations) on the values that the variables may assume.

It follows from these features that a model can be used as a **consistent tool** for evaluating different policies. That is, each policy or set of decisions is evaluated by the same objective according to the same formulas for describing interactions and constraints. Moreover, models can be explicitly adjusted and improved with historical experience.

A final point: Models provide the opportunity for a systematic use of powerful mathematical methods. They can handle a large number of variables and interactions. The mind is capable of storing only so much information.

> **Models allow us to use the power of mathematics hand in hand with the storage and speed of computers.**

—— 1.7
CONSTRAINED OPTIMIZATION MODELS

Many of the models studied in this text fall under the broad category of **constrained optimization models**. In this section we provide an overview of such models, emphasizing the concept of constrained optimization and some of the language used in dealing with constrained optimization models.

At the outset, it is to be noted that most people make many of their personal and professional decisions in situations where the set of allowable decisions has been restricted in some way. In the language of modeling, a restriction on the set of allowable decisions is called a *constraint*. Constraints may be self-imposed or dictated by others. A person with a strict budget must buy groceries for the week without spending too much money. A production manager must plan production schedules without exceeding the capacity of plant or equipment. A speculator is constrained in his or her trading by the amount of margin required to be on deposit with a broker. A parent of three teenagers can let only one of them take the family car on Saturday night. A plant superintendent can assign only unoccupied maintenance crews to unanticipated repairs. A member of Alcoholics Anonymous declines an invitation for cocktails. The list is endless. It is perhaps not surprising, therefore, that *constrained optimization*, which means achieving the best possible result considering the restrictions, has been the most active area of management-science research. Indeed, one of the most commonly employed management-science tools, linear programming, is a special model for carrying out constrained optimization. Since the Oak Products, Inc. model which we saw in Section 1.3 is a linear program, it is also a constrained optimization model.

Constrained optimization models, when solved, provide what are called *optimal deci-sions*, but this statement calls for the strongest possible caveat. *Optimization models pro-uce the optimal answer to a mathematical problem* posed by a model. This may or may not be a good (to say nothing of optimal) answer in the real context. Whenever we use words such as "real" or "true" we are referring to the real-world problem that underlies the mathematical model.

The term *optimality* is a theoretical (i.e., *mathematical*), as opposed to a real-world, concept.

The truth is that rarely is it meaningful to talk about optimal decisions for the complicated problems of business, and *one of the worst mistakes a manager can make is blindly to allow a model to make his or her decisions.* Rather than seeking the quantita-tively superior solution, the mature manager will often be more concerned with the op-timal political solution. This, however, does not by any means imply that quantitative models do not play an important role in the overall decision-making process. In order to appreciate this role, it is necessary to appreciate some of the relationships between the real problem, the problem analyst, the decision maker, and the model.

So, let us begin to explain the assertion that the complicated problems of business (and even more so, of government) have no optimal solution. There are always consider-ations that cannot be built into the model, for to include every potentially relevant con-sideration could easily complicate the model to the extent of making it impossible to solve. What do we mean by "complicate the model"? This will become clearer as we proceed. For now, it suffices to mention two major complicating factors: (1) form, or mathematical structure; and (2) size. For example, in terms of form it is, from a compu-tational point of view, desirable to keep all expressions in the model linear. But it simply may not be possible to capture some of the interactions with linear expressions, and consequently such interactions may not be included. In terms of size, models with too many constraints and too many variables cannot be solved even on high-speed com-puters. This consideration can also lead to simplifications, and a limited and incomplete representation of the real problem results. These facts help to amplify our earlier asser-tion that models are selective representations of reality. In any realistic application, the ultimate effect of this selectivity is the following truth:

The word "optimal" is strictly a mathematical notion. An "optimal (or best) decision" produced by a model should be interpreted, at best, as being a "good decision" for the real problem.

Consequently, as suggested by the schematic diagram in Figure 1.11, the decision maker has to "evaluate" the model. This means that she must blend the output of the model with her own experience and judgment, her personal interests, and her own perceptions about the nature and credibility of the model and its correspondence with the real prob-lem. And depending on the results of this "evaluation," the model, or even the perception of the problem, may have to be revised.

In fact, one important application of models is to provide reinforcement for the intuition of the decision maker. This reinforcement can be positive. It can provide quan-titative support and verification for the decision maker's own preconceived notions. It can bolster his confidence in his own intuition. It can show him explicitly how to go about implementing his preferred policy (regardless of the motivation for that policy) and what results, in quantitative terms, might be expected. On the other hand, the model's reinforcement can be negative. The results can challenge the intuition. Previously hidden or overlooked relations may become apparent. The decision maker may be forced to choose between intuition and the model. The better and more credible the model, the more difficult the choice.

Aside from these considerations there are also technical ways of determining how good a model may be and how relevant its recommendations may be for the real-world problem at hand. These technical aspects are in the realm of what is called "sensitivity analysis," and this will be emphasized in appropriate sections of the text.

At this point, let us explicitly show you the general form of a constrained optimization model.

General Formulation The terms *constrained optimization* and *mathematical programming* are often used to describe the same general model. Although the explicit meaning of this model can be described in words, the symbolic or mathematical representation is the most unambiguous way to depict all that it says. In its general symbolic form, the constrained optimization model is

$$
\text{maximize (or minimize) } f(x_1, x_2, \ldots, x_n)
$$
subject to the constraints that

$$
g_1(x_1, x_2, \ldots, x_n) \begin{array}{c} \leq \\ = \\ \geq \end{array} b_1
$$

$$
g_2(x_1, x_2, \ldots, x_n) \begin{array}{c} \leq \\ = \\ \geq \end{array} b_2
$$

$$
\vdots \qquad\qquad\qquad \vdots
$$

$$
g_m(x_1, x_2, \ldots, x_n) \begin{array}{c} \leq \\ = \\ \geq \end{array} b_m
$$

When all the functions in this model are linear, we will have the important special case of a *linear programming model*. In the next chapter we will begin to pay specific attention to linear programs, but for now the discussion is quite general.

The function f is called the *objective function*, or the *payoff function*, or simply the *return*. The model states that the problem is to make the value of this function as large (or as small) as possible, provided that the *constraints*, or restricting conditions, are also satisfied. The value of the objective function is often measured in such quantities as dollars of profit (in a maximization problem) or dollars of cost (in a minimization problem). The variables $x_1, x_2, \ldots, x_n$ are called *decision variables*. Recall our earlier definition that, for our purposes, decisions are numbers. The numerical values of the decision variables represent actions or activities to be undertaken at various levels. The decision maker has the values of these variables under his direct control. Any choice of these values indirectly assigns a numerical value to the objective function. The functions $g_1, \ldots, g_m$ are called *constraint functions.* Any selection of numerical values for the decision variables also indirectly assigns numerical values to the constraint functions. The model requires that each of these constraint function values must satisfy a condition expressed by a mathematical inequality or an equality. The first constraint, for example, is one and only one of the following conditions:

$$g_1(x_1, x_2, \ldots, x_n) \leq b_1$$

$$g_1(x_1, x_2, \ldots, x_n) = b_1$$

$$g_1(x_1, x_2, \ldots, x_n) \geq b_1$$

where b_1 is a parameter with a specified numerical value. In other words, in the language of models, *a constraint is a mathematical equality or inequality which must be satisfied.* The numbers b_i, $i = 1, 2, \ldots, m$, taken together are called the *right-hand sides* (abbreviated RHS). The number b_1 is called the right-hand side of the first constraint, and so on. The set of all m of the constraints taken together, that is, the group of relations

$$g_i(x_1, x_2, \ldots, x_n) \overset{\leq}{\underset{\geq}{=}} b_i, \qquad i = 1, \ldots, m$$

indirectly restricts the values that can be assigned to the decision variables.

For example, suppose the model contains the constraint

$$g_1(x_1, x_2, \ldots, x_n) \leq b_1$$

Consider a vector $x = (x_1, \ldots, x_n)$ of decisions which imply that

$$g_1(x_1, x_2, \ldots, x_n) > b_1$$

This choice of decisions will be forbidden by the model since it violates one of the constraints. The model will consider only those decisions that satisfy *all* the constraints.

Applications of Constrained Optimization Models

Constrained optimization models were first used in decision making in the 1940s. Among the major applications were logistic problems in World War II. The fields of operations research and management science arose from these early defense applications.

Now, applications of constrained optimization models range across all sorts of planning activities in both the public and private sectors. Applications in government are frequent. They have included modeling efforts in the areas of defense, health planning, transportation, energy planning, and resource allocation, to name only a few. In the private sector, applications vary from long-term planning to daily, or even hourly, scheduling of activities. Specific applications in long-term planning include capital budgeting, plant location, long-range marketing strategy, and long-range investment strategy. Shorter-term applications include production and work-force scheduling, inventory management, machine scheduling, aircraft routing, chemical blending, product design, media selection, statistical estimation, feed-mix blending, tanker scheduling, waste disposal, site selection, and project scheduling in the construction of nuclear submarines and major shopping centers. The list could go on and on.

In all these applications, there are decisions to be made in order to carry out an activity or collection of activities "optimally" according to some criterion (such as minimizing cost, time, waste, or delay, or maximizing profit or total amount shipped). Also, in all these applications, there are limitations imposed either by scarce resources that must be allocated or by certain requirements that must be satisfied, or a combination of both. These limitations or requirements place constraints on the decisions that can be made. Other constraints may exist in the form of logical relations or physical laws that must be satisfied by the decision variables. Thus, decisions must be found that optimize the objective subject to all the constraints.

1.8
WHY CONSTRAINTS ARE IMPOSED

The analyst confronts a real-world problem. His or her apparent goal is to construct a quantitative optimization model. A more correct description is: *The analyst's goal is to provide some quantitative rationale and support in the decision-making process.* In pursuit of this goal, analysts employ constraints for a variety of subtle reasons. The reasons generally have a great deal to do with *practicality*, and they may differ one from the other only in matters of degree or interpretation. We discuss next some of the considerations that lead to the use of constraints.

Immutable Short-Term Technology and the Laws of Nature   *In short-term planning situations, technological constraints may be inevitable.* Consider an equilibrium-pricing model that attempts to forecast average regional prices of wheat during a given crop year together with total net imports of wheat in that same period for a number of countries. The total global supply of wheat is fixed. In the real world, there is no way it can be changed until the next crop is harvested. In the short term, agricultural technology and botanical laws cannot be altered, no matter what price the planner would pay to do so. The same type of technological restrictions can occur in the steel industry. When a particular furnace or process has been shut down, say by a strike, a fixed amount of time may be required, for physical and chemical reasons, to start it up again. There may be no way to eliminate such a constraint, even for a price. Can you imagine other short-term models for which similar technological constraints cannot realistically be eliminated?

Bottlenecks   A steel strike has just occurred. There is no way we can increase our supplies for the next planning period. "Wrong," you say. "Pay a high enough price and you can import more supplies!" However, it turns out that import quotas exist, and so on. Bottlenecks such as this are a common cause for the appearance of constraints. Resources may genuinely be *scarce*.

Cost of the Search   *An important practical factor in problem solving involves the cost of finding the solution. Constraints are often used to reduce this cost.* Consider the parent whose child asks for help in using a book of state topography maps to locate the highest point in the United States. The problem could be tackled by an unconstrained search through the entire book. But with no more than an average knowledge of geography, the parent confidently ignores the maps of Ohio, Michigan, Indiana, Wisconsin, Iowa, Nebraska, and a host of others.

As another example, consider the U.S. distributor of a new French perfume. In making the product available to the public, the distributor wants to select an advertising campaign that maximizes the ratio

$$\frac{\text{total sales}}{\text{total advertising expenditure}}$$

The advertising options are numerous:

1. Advertising on buses in major cities.
2. Advertising on radio in major cities.
3. Advertising on network television.
4. Advertising in selected magazines.
5. Passing out handbills.

The distributor decides on the basis of educated intuition to eliminate the first, second, and fifth possibilities, and then sponsors a study to determine the best way to allocate dollars to specific advertisements within the remaining two categories. The funds for such a study are limited. By imposing constraints, the distributor is able to specialize the study, devoting more analysis to his two chosen categories, and hopefully obtaining better results.

Uncertainty, and Parametric Analysis   The attractiveness of many investment opportunities heavily depends on the future value of interest rates. Unfortunately these rates are notoriously difficult to forecast. If r_i is the interest rate in period i it may be possible to construct a model with constraints

$$L_i \leq r_i \leq U_i$$

Specific values are assigned to L_i and U_i and the model is solved. This yields the best solution if the interest rates fall into the prescribed range. Assigning different values to L_i and U_i and successively rerunning the model will provide results that indicate the extent to which the optimal solution is sensitive to interest rates. This technique is called "performing a parametric (or sensitivity) analysis on L_i and U_i." Such an analysis will enable us to say: "If the rates are allowed to vary in such and such an interval, then these are the results we can expect." This is one way of dealing with uncertainty.

Surrogate Objectives   We have seen, in our previous discussion, that in some sense *a model can be thought of as a "surrogate" or a replacement for reality.* Often this is particularly true of the objective function. Let us give an illustration. A study was to be undertaken for a client involved in several projects of interest to the old Department of Health, Education, and Welfare (HEW). The client wanted to determine the "optimal locations" for sixteen proposed health care clinics. The clinics were to have a modular design and were architecturally rather innovative. But what does it mean to "optimize locations"? What is the appropriate measure? Some suggestions are

1. Minimize the distances between locations and dense, low-income population areas.
2. Maximize the geographic coverage without regard to population density or income distribution.
3. Minimize the level of government subsidy required.
4. Maximize the aesthetic exposure (the visibility of the architect).

The alternatives are numerous. The problem in a study like this is not just how to quantify the objective. Actually, it is not even clear what HEW was looking for. Unless an appropriate objective function can be defined, *at least verbally*, it seems hopeless to embark on a quantitative study. But even when such a function is verbally stated, it may not be possible to quantify, and hence a **surrogate objective** may be employed. The objective of a defense planner may be to maximize "deterrence." This term, *per se*, is not possible to quantify. The defense planner may instead decide to maximize the number of submarine-based launchers. This would be a **surrogate** for his true objective.

Nest Feathering   On September 13, 1976, the editorial page of the *Wall Street Journal* featured a story on the new political power of a New York City councilman. The gist of the story was that the councilman used the federal antipoverty programs to build a powerful political machine for his own purposes. Whether funds were illegally used or not is unimportant to us. This item reports on a situation in which a subordinate achieves his own ends in spite of his boss. This situation is called the *underling problem*.

The underling's aspiration is that, like everyone else in life, he wants to maximize his own well-being. As a result, he has a personal objective function that differs in at least some respects from that of the organization (i.e., his boss). The underling's solution strategy is to disguise his own self-interest in a constraint and then argue for the constraint. The constraint looks innocuous to the boss—neither good nor bad. The underling's contrived justification seems plausible; so the boss innocently accepts the constraint, unaware of the full implications. The results of the constraint may be costly to the boss, but will benefit the underling.

In many cases, constraints of this nature impose a kind of prescreening in order to limit the alternatives that reach the final stage of the decision-making process. A prominent charitable foundation developed a program of fellowships to give management training in the United States to promising young civil servants from a developing African country. Dossiers were assembled for each candidate, and then a committee of representatives from the participating American universities selected the individuals to receive the fellowships. Ten winners were selected annually from a field of over 200 applicants, and everyone thought the program was a great success. A review of the program after several years revealed that unbeknown to the selection committee all fellowship winners (and indeed, all applicants) had been members of the same tribe (and political party). This tribe had traditionally held the important administrative positions in the colonial government, and thus controlled the application process. The group was in an ideal position to feather its own nest.

Or, for example, imagine how easy it is for a department head to draw up a job description that calls for a recent university graduate who majored in hieroglyphics, minored in engineering, and had work experience as a canoeing instructor. Would you be surprised to learn that her second cousin's son, with exactly those qualifications, was looking for a job?

The 1976 tax reform bill has been described as having at least sixty special-interest provisions. According to Senator Edward Kennedy (TIME, August 16, 1976), some of these provisions were so finely drawn that they resembled legislation for a "one-eyed bearded man with a limp." You are invited to speculate on the motivation for the inclusion of so many special provisions.

As a final and less specific example, notice that in large firms, major capital-investment decisions are typically made by the board of directors. They consider a group of alternatives that have reached them after passing a large number of reviews (departmental, divisional, regional, etc.). There are thus numerous opportunities for subordinates to impose various "nest feathering" constraints in order to influence the set of alternatives from which the final decision will be made.

Hierarchical Structure and the Delegation of Authority   Constraints seem to be an inherent part of organizational structure. *The necessity to delegate authority and responsibility for certain activities while maintaining overall responsibility for an entire op-*

eration almost always dictates the use of constraints and, consequently, the constrained optimization approach.

A good example is provided by the purchasing activity in multinational firms. When a firm has plants in several nearby countries, a question arises as to who should do the buying for each plant. In some multinational corporations, a centralized purchasing department buys for all plants. Many firms, however, use a decentralized system with a buying group for each plant. In this case, central management usually constrains the activities by insisting that all purchases be from centrally approved suppliers and that certain standard receiving and testing procedures be followed. The buyer at an individual plant then tries to minimize costs subject to the given constraints on delivery time, the quality of the material, and the set of possible suppliers.

The process of passing down constraints occurs at all levels in organizational hierarchies. The government constrains the corporation, which constrains its divisions, which constrain their plants, which constrain their departments, and so on. The net result is that most decision makers in organizations find themselves facing problems in contrained optimization. The constraints may change as firms reorganize to meet competition, and the variables may change for an individual as he or she progresses through an organization. But it is difficult to imagine a world in which the delegation of *limited* responsibility and authority is not a critical part of the management process.

Definition or Balance Equations   Often in a model certain relations between variables will be defined in the constraints. For example, in a model with inventory variables we may have a constraint that says

$$\begin{pmatrix} \text{inventory at} \\ \text{end of month } t \end{pmatrix} = \begin{pmatrix} \text{inventory at} \\ \text{beginning of month } t \end{pmatrix} + \begin{pmatrix} \text{production in} \\ \text{month } t \end{pmatrix} - \begin{pmatrix} \text{sales in} \\ \text{month } t \end{pmatrix}$$

As another example, a logistics model may have a "material balance" constraint that says

$$\text{amount entering a depot} = \text{amount leaving a depot}$$

Many examples of such constraints will be encountered.

—————— 1.9
INTUITIVE VERSUS FORMAL MODELING

In concluding this chapter, let us compare the type of formal quantitative models we have been discussing with what we wish to refer to as *intuitive* models. We believe that most decisions in life are made in accord with some internal and intuitive model of the problem at hand. Such models, although less formal than the ones we have considered, also try to capture certain trade-offs and interactions between variables. They may also be composed of objectives and constraints—the same fabric as formal models—but in mental rather than external symbolic form.

Within their structure, these internal models tend to incorporate diffuse, hard-to-quantify considerations that pertain to individual tastes and dispositions. To a degree, you are observing a person's outlook on life by seeing the reflection of his model in the way he searches for solutions and in the quality of the solutions he actually finds. The constraints in a formal model serve to define the environment within which we will seek to maximize our objective. The same is true of intuitive internal models.

As an illustration of the kinds of unquantifiable conditions or perceptions that are incorporated in intuitive models, consider the following quotations. Each statement suggests a way to constrain the search for wealth and success.

No man ever lost money underestimating the intelligence of the American people.

H. L. MENCKEN

There's a sucker born every minute.

P. T. BARNUM

These statements reflect a major difficulty with intuitive modeling. Intuitive models generally are not explicit. They are difficult to challenge, or criticize, or subscribe to because what such models say is ambiguous. Are the quotes assertions of fact? If so, how would you go about verifying either one beyond dispute? How would you obtain data to support such models? (Is a sucker really born "every minute," or would "every second" be a more precise assertion?)

By contrast, the formal model at least aspires to "laying it all out" and then, hopefully, "putting it all together." The objective can be disputed or accepted. It may not be the ideal, but it is what it is, and it may be manipulated and modified. The constraints are a matter of record. They can be challenged, modified, augmented, or eliminated. *Because of their explicit and unambiguous nature, formal models provide individuals and groups with a tool for eliminating inconsistency.* In this way, the use of formal models is an arm of rational behavior in the quest for good decisions.

—— 1.10
SUMMARY

This chapter has provided an overview on the use of quantitative decision-making models with special emphasis on their role as tools for the manager. The interaction between manager and model has been stressed, with attention given to the manager's role as an "evaluator" of models.

We proposed the concept that, from a quantitative point of view, decisions are numbers and the basis of decisions is the evaluation of quantitative data (i.e., the evaluation of numbers). We discussed the role of models in this process, emphasizing that the notion of "optimal" is a mathematical, as opposed to a real-world, concept. Models are a limited representation of reality, and for this reason a solution to a model is a solution to a "surrogate" for the real problem.

"What if" and constrained optimization models were discussed. The role of Lotus 1–2–3, VINO, and What's*Best!* in attacking these problems was introduced. Finally, numerous practical justifications were given for the appearance of constraints in models.

MAJOR CONCEPTS QUIZ _____

True–False

1. T **F** The more complicated the model, the more useful it generally is.
2. **T** F Models usually ignore most of the world.
3. **T** F Decision models produce numerical values for decision variables and hence, in this sense, decisions are numbers.

4. (T) **F** A decision model often captures interactions and trade-offs between certain variables or quantities of interest.

5. (T) **F** A model can be thought of as a "surrogate" for reality, and there is usually no single correct way to build a model of a realistic problem.

6. **T** (F) One advantage of the modeling approach is that it often eliminates the need to be very familiar with the environment being studied.

7. (T) **F** In practice, models are often built by teams of individuals drawn from different disciplines.

8. **T** (F) Optimization models provide the best decision for the real problem.

9. **T** (F) A model is a good substitute for executive judgment and experience.

10. (T) **F** An important role of management can be the evaluation of a model (determination of whether a model should be used and its results implemented).

11. **T** (F) Although Lotus 1–2–3 makes calculations easy, it has no real impact on creativity.

12. **T** (F) "What if" models are only useful for examining changes in the values of decision variables.

13. **T** (F) VINO and What's*Best!* can solve all mathematical programming problems.

14. **T** (F) You must understand the theory of linear programming to use VINO or What's*Best!*

Multiple Choice

15. A model is
  a. a selective representation of reality
  b. an abstraction
  c. an approximation
  d. an idealization
  (e.) all of the above

16. Decisions are often based on
  a. an evaluation of numerical data
  b. numbers produced by formal models
  c. the use of intuitive models that are never written down
  (d.) all of the above

17. Optimization models contain
  a. decision variables
  b. an objective function
  (c.) both of the above

18. An optimization model
  a. provides the best decision in a mathematical sense
  b. provides the best decision within the limited context of the model
  c. can provide a consistent tool for evaluating different policies
  (d.) all of the above

19. A model
  a. refines crude data in order to provide more useful data
  b. is a tool for the decision maker
  c. forces a manager to be explicit about objectives
  (d.) all of the above

20. A model
  a. forces a manager to identify explicitly the types of decisions that influence objectives
  b. forces a manager to identify interactions and trade-offs between decisions involving different entities (such as how much to produce of two different products that employ common resources)
  c. forces a manager to record explicitly constraints placed on the values that variables can assume
  (d.) all of the above

21. Models
   a. play different roles at different levels of the firm
   b. are rarely used even as inputs in the strategic planning process
   c. are a costly way of making routine daily decisions
   d. all of the above

22. Constrained optimization means
   a. that the underlying model is an extremely limited representation of reality
   b. achieving the best possible (mathematical) result considering the restrictions
   c. both of the above

23. A constraint
   a. is a mathematical equality or inequality that must be satisfied
   b. involves a constraint function and a right-hand side
   c. is formulated in terms of decision variables
   d. all of the above

24. Constraints are generally imposed
   a. because it is the only correct way to formulate the problem
   b. because of practical considerations
   c. to enable us to use the power tool of constrained optimization
   d. all of the above

25. Consider a prospective manager with interests and abilities that lie far from the quantitative techniques field. The point of her studying a quantitative modeling course might be
   a. to give her the opportunity of knowledgeably accepting or rejecting the use of quantitative tools
   b. to provide her with new ways of looking at the environment
   c. to give her more familiarity with the kind of assistance a computer might provide
   d. all of the above

26. With a "What if" analysis, we are sure to find
   a. an optimal solution
   b. a good solution
   c. a feasible solution (if one exists)
   d. none of the above

Answers

1. F	8. F	15. e	21. a
2. T	9. F	16. d	22. b
3. T	10. T	17. c	23. d
4. T	11. F	18. d	24. b
5. T	12. F	19. d	25. d
6. F	13. F	20. d	26. d
7. T	14. F		

QUESTIONS FOR DISCUSSION

1-1. "The hard problems are those for which models do not exist." Interpret this statement. Give some examples.

1-2. Suppose that you want to become a managerial decision maker but your special abilities and interests are far from the quantitative field. What is the point to your studying an introductory quantitative-modeling text?

1-3. What reasons can you think of to explain the fact that many models are built and never implemented? Does the absence of implementation mean that the entire model-development activity was a waste?

1-4. What is your interpretation of the phrase, "a successful application of a model"?

1–5. Profit maximization is commonly taken as the objective function for the firm. Is this a surrogate objective? Consider a firm such as ITT. Can you think of other objectives that might be appropriate? Do not worry about whether they are readily quantifiable.

1–6. We have said that there are no optimal decisions for the complex problems of business. Yet optimization models produce "optimal decisions." In what sense, then, are such decisions optimal?

1–7. Consider the following statement: "Our production policy should be to achieve maximum output at a minimum cost." Comment on this misunderstanding.

1–8. "An optimization problem has been solved but some of the constraints are violated." Discuss this assertion.

1–9. What is the meaning of a mathematical constraint when the data (parameter values) are not known with precision? What kinds of assumptions would tend to justify the use of models in such situations?

1–10. Discuss the meaning of the following.

    (a) A successful application.

    (b) A large problem versus a small problem.

    (c) An "important" constraint versus an "unimportant" constraint.

    (d) Solving a model.

2

LINEAR PROGRAMMING: FORMAL AND SPREADSHEET MODELS

ALLOCATING A SCARCE RESOURCE*

The 1973 world fuel crisis was a double whammy for the American airline industry: (1) The government restricted an airline's monthly fuel supply to a percentage of its 1972 monthly consumption, and (2) fuel prices for domestic trunk airlines jumped by more than 50% in the 5-month interval from December 1973 to May 1974. To add to the problem, fuel vendors were often unable to meet the airlines' demands at specific cities. The overall impact of these forces was canceled flights and exceptionally high prices paid for spot purchases. The airlines found themselves with record increases in operating costs, and fuel became the largest percentage of an airline's costs.

National Airlines constructed and implemented a linear programming model to attack this problem. The model took into account

1. The flight schedule.
2. The price and availability of fuel at each station.
3. The reserve requirement for each plane.

* Wayne D. Darnell and Carolyn Laflin, "National Airlines Fuel Management and Allocation Model," *Interfaces*, Vol. 7, No. 2, (February 1977), pp. 1–16.

4. The upper bound on weight for each plane.
5. The distance for each segment of a flight.
6. The fuel remaining when a plane arrives at a station.
7. Fuel consumption for each plane as a function of weight, flight altitude, weather, and speed.

It is interesting to note that it may not pay for a plane to take on extra fuel early in a flight even though the cost per gallon is relatively low. This is because the additional weight of the fuel can increase fuel consumption enough to produce a larger total cost.

National's LP model included 800 constraints and 2400 variables for a flight schedule of 350 flight segments, 50 station/vendor combinations, and multiple aircraft types. In the first month it was used, National's fuel costs dropped from an average of 16.35 cents per gallon to 14.43 cents. This was the largest percentage decrease realized by any of 11 domestic airlines during the same period. Indeed, 6 of the other 10 airlines suffered an increase in the average cost per gallon at that time. It is estimated that total fuel savings to National Airlines over a 2-year period was multimillions of dollars. In addition, sensitivity analyses available with the linear programming solution were most helpful in informing management as to when a change in policy might be required.

_____ 2.1
INTRODUCTION

We have seen in Chapter 1 that a model is an abstract representation, or a surrogate, for reality. In a decision-making environment, models are important because they capture the essence of many important problems. In a sense, the very notion of being able to *solve* a real-world business problem means that it is possible successfully to formulate the problem as a model. Thus, being able to formulate models—that is, to make the transition between real-world problem and quantitative model (the mathematical problem)—is an important first step in the use of modeling as a management tool.

Constraints For our purposes, a first step in model formulation will be the recognition of *constraints*. In Chapter 1 we saw numerous "generic" causes for the appearance of constraints. Constraints can be thought of as *restrictions* on the set of allowable decisions. Specific illustrations of such restrictions are particularly evident when dealing with the problems of management. For example

1. A portfolio manager has a certain amount of capital at his or her discretion. Investment decisions are restricted by the amount of that capital and the regulations of the SEC.
2. The decisions of a plant manager are restricted by the capacity of the plant and the availability of resources.
3. The staffing and flight plans of an airline are restricted by the maintenance needs of the planes and the number of employees on hand.
4. An oil company's decision to use a certain type of crude oil in producing gasoline is restricted by the characteristics of the gasoline (e.g., the octane rating and the antiknock capabilities).

In the context of mathematical modeling, a restriction, or constraint, on the allowable decisions is a concept of special importance. Constraints are often in one of two forms: *limitations* or *requirements*. In the examples listed above

1. The portfolio manager is constrained by *limitations* of capital and the *requirements* of the SEC.
2. Production decisions are constrained by *limitations* on capacity and resources.
3. The airlines are constrained by the *requirement* that a crew must spend at least 24 hours on the ground between flights.
4. The oil company is constrained by the *limitation* of the types of crude oil that are available and the *requirement* that the gasoline have at least a specified octane rating.

The Objective Function

All linear programming models have two important features in common. The first feature, illustrated in the examples above, is the existence of constraints. The second feature is that in every linear programming model there is some quantity to be maximized or minimized.

To show this, let us consider again the same four examples. The portfolio manager may want to maximize the return on the portfolio, and the production manager may want to satisfy the demand at minimum production cost. Similarly, the airline wants to meet a given schedule at the minimum cost and the oil company wants to use the available crude oil in such a way as to maximize profit.

Thus, you can see that in each of these examples there is some quantity that the decision maker desires either to maximize (typically profit, or return, or effectiveness) or to minimize (typically cost or time). In the language of modeling, this quantity is called the *objective function*.

Every linear programming problem has two important features in common: an *objective function* to be maximized or minimized, and *constraints*.

Linear programming provides an example of what is called a *constrained decision-making model*, also called a *constrained optimization model*. One common way of describing such a model is to refer to it as

---

the problem of allocating scarce resources in such a way as to optimize an objective of interest.

In this description, the phrase "scarce resources" means resources that are subject to constraints.

Although different and more general types of constrained decision-making models exist, it is nevertheless true that in applications linear programming is the most useful. It has been successfully applied to literally thousands of different types of managerial decision-making problems, and it is for this reason that we give considerable attention to the topic. We shall begin by presenting several specific numerical examples of linear programming formulations. Some of these examples will be illustrated in a spreadsheet format. Then, in the following chapters, it will be shown how linear programming can be used to solve these constrained decision-making problems.

PROTRAC, INC.

PROTRAC, Inc. produces two lines of heavy equipment. One of these product lines, termed earthmoving equipment, is essentially for construction applications. The other line, termed forestry equipment, is destined for the lumber industry. The largest member of the earthmoving equipment line (the E-9) and the largest member of the forestry equipment line (the F-9) are produced in the same departments and with the same equipment. Using economic forecasts for next month, PROTRAC's marketing manager has judged that during that period it will be possible to sell as many E-9s or F-9s as the firm can produce. Management must now recommend a production target for next month. That is, how many E-9s and F-9s should be produced?

In making this decision, the major factors to be considered are the following:

PROTRAC Data

1. PROTRAC will make a profit of $5000 on each E-9 that is sold and $4000 on each F-9.
2. Each product is put through *machining operations* in both department A and department B.
3. For next month's production, these two departments have 150 and 160 hours of available time, respectively. Each E-9 uses 10 hours of machining in department A and 20 hours of machining in department B, whereas each F-9 uses 15 hours in department A and 10 hours in department B. These data are summarized in Figure 2.1.

FIGURE 2.1
Protrac Machining Data

DEPARTMENT	HOURS		
	per E-9	per F-9	Total Available
A	10	15	150
B	20	10	160

4. In order to honor an agreement with the union, the total labor hours used in next month's *testing of finished products* cannot fall more than 10% below an arbitrated goal of 150 hours. This testing is performed in a third department and has nothing to do with the activities in departments A and B. Each E-9 is given 30 hours of testing and each F-9 is given 10. Since 10% of 150 is 15, the total labor hours devoted to testing cannot fall below 135. These data are summarized in Figure 2.2.

FIGURE 2.2
Protrac Testing Data

	1 E-9	1 F-9	REQUIREMENT ON TOTAL HOURS
Hours for Testing	30	10	135

5. In order to maintain the current market position, top management has decreed the operating policy that it is necessary to build at least one F-9 for every three E-9s produced.

6. A major customer has ordered a total of at least five E-9s and F-9s (in any combination whatever) for next month, and so at least that many must be produced.

Given these considerations, management's problem is to decide how many E-9s and how many F-9s to produce next month. In technical terms, management seeks to determine the *optimal product mix*, also called the *optimal production plan*. Let us now show how this problem can be expressed as a mathematical model, in particular as a linear program. To do so, we must identify the constraints and the objective function.

The Constraints   We have stated that in each department there is a limitation on the amount of time available for the machining operations in producing E-9s and F-9s. For example, from Figure 2.1 it is seen that for the time period under consideration no more than 150 hours is available in department A. This limited availability of hours is a constraint. To formulate the constraint concisely, let us begin by determining the number of hours that will be used in department A. Recall that both E-9s and F-9s must be machined in department A. From Figure 2.1 we know that each E-9 produced will use 10 hours of machining in department A. Each F-9 produced will use 15 hours in department A. Hence, for any particular production plan

**Dept. A
Constraint**   total hours used in dept. A = 10(no. E-9s produced) + 15(no. F-9s produced)

This can be expressed more easily if we introduce some simple notation. Let

$$E = \text{number of E-9s to be produced}$$

$$F = \text{number of F-9s to be produced}$$

Then the expression for the total hours used in department A becomes

$$\text{total hours used in dept. A} = 10E + 15F$$

But, as already stated, we also know from Figure 2.1 that at most 150 hours is available in department A. It follows that the unknowns E and F must satisfy the condition (i.e., the restriction)

$$10E + 15F \leq 150 \tag{2.1}$$

This is the constraint on hours used in department A. The symbol $\leq$ means *less than or equal to* and condition (2.1) is called an *inequality constraint*. The number 150 is called the *right-hand side* of the inequality. The left-hand side of the inequality clearly depends on the unknowns E and F, and is called a *constraint function*. The mathematical inequality (2.1) is a concise symbolic way of stating the constraint that the total number of hours used in department A to produce E units of E-9 and F units of F-9 must not exceed the 150 hours available.

**Dept. B
Constraint**   From Figure 2.1 we also see that each E-9 produced will use 20 hours of machining in department B and each F-9 produced will use 10 hours of machining in department B. Since there is at most 160 hours available in department B, it follows that the values of E and F must also satisfy

$$20E + 10F \leq 160 \tag{2.2}$$

Inequalities (2.1) and (2.2) represent two of the constraints in the current problem. Are there any others?

The foregoing discussion of major considerations indicates (i.e., major consideration 4) that there is also a union agreement to be honored. Figure 2.2 indicates that each E-9 produced will use 30 hours of testing, and each F-9 produced will use 10 hours of testing. Thus

$$\text{total hours used for testing} = 30E + 10F$$

Also from Figure 2.2 we see that the total labor hours used in testing cannot fall below 135 hours. Hence, we obtain the constraint

Testing Constraint

$$30E + 10F \geq 135 \tag{2.3}$$

The symbol $\geq$ means *greater than or equal to*, and condition (2.3) is also called an inequality constraint. Note that condition (2.3) is a mathematical inequality of the $\geq$ type (a requirement), as opposed to conditions (2.1) and (2.2), which are mathematical inequalities of the $\leq$ type (limitations).

Another constraint is that at least one F-9 must be produced for every three E-9s produced. This is stated in symbols as

Production Mix Constraint

$$E/3 \leq F$$

Since both sides of an inequality can be multiplied by the same positive number without changing the direction of the inequality, we can multiply both sides of this latter constraint by 3 to obtain

$$E \leq 3F$$

Later it will be seen that it is often convenient to express such an inequality with all of the unknowns on the left side (thereby forming the constraint function). Thus, in this case we transpose (subtract $3F$ from both sides) to obtain the convenient expression

$$E - 3F \leq 0 \tag{2.4}$$

The sixth major consideration states that at least 5 units must be produced next month, in any combination whatever. This constraint is simply stated as

Total Units Constraint

$$E + F \geq 5 \tag{2.5}$$

We have now specified in concise mathematical form five inequality constraints associated with **PROTRAC**'s production problem. Since it does not make physical sense to produce a negative number of E-9s or F-9s, we must include the two additional conditions

Nonnegativity

$$E \geq 0, \quad F \geq 0 \tag{2.6}$$

Conditions such as (2.6), which require E and F to be nonnegative, are called *nonnegativity conditions*. It is important to bear in mind that the term *nonnegative* is not the same as the term *positive*. The difference is that "nonnegative" allows for the possibility of the value zero, whereas the term "positive" forbids this value.

In summary, here are the constraints and the nonnegativity conditions for the **PROTRAC, Inc.** model:

$$10E + 15F \leq 150 \qquad (2.1)$$
$$20E + 10F \leq 160 \qquad (2.2)$$
$$30E + 10F \geq 135 \qquad (2.3)$$
$$E - 3F \leq 0 \qquad (2.4)$$
$$E + F \geq 5 \qquad (2.5)$$
$$E \geq 0, \qquad F \geq 0 \qquad (2.6)$$

In the model above, the choice of values for the pair of variables (E, F) is called a decision; E and F are thus called *decision variables* (i.e., the quantities that management controls). Clearly, in this problem a decision is a production mix. For example, $E = 6$, $F = 5$ is a decision to make six E-9s and five F-9s. Some nonnegative decisions will satisfy all of the constraints (2.1) through (2.5) of our model and some will not. For example, the decision $E = 6$, $F = 5$ can be seen to satisfy constraints (2.1), (2.3), (2.4), and (2.5) and to violate constraint (2.2). To see this, we substitute $E = 6$, $F = 5$ into constraints (2.1) through (2.5) and evaluate the results. Doing this, we obtain

Constraint 1

$$10E + 15F \leq 150$$
$$10(6) + 15(5) \leq 150$$
$$60 + 75 \leq 150$$
$$135 \leq 150 \qquad \text{true}$$

Hence, this constraint is satisfied when $E = 6$, $F = 5$.

Constraint 2

$$20E + 10F \leq 160$$
$$20(6) + 10(5) \leq 160$$
$$120 + 50 \leq 160$$
$$170 \leq 160 \qquad \text{false}$$

Hence, this constraint is violated when $E = 6$, $F = 5$.

In the same fashion, try to show for yourself that the decision $E = 6$, $F = 5$ satisfies constraints (2.3), (2.4), and (2.5).

Similarly, you can verify for yourself that the production mix $E = 5$, $F = 4$ does indeed satisfy all the constraints.

The mix, or decision, $E = 6$, $F = 5$ is not allowable because as we have just seen there are not enough hours available in department B (constraint 2) to support this decision. Another way of saying the same thing is that this decision is not allowable because it has violated one of the constraints. Of the infinitely many nonnegative pairs of numbers (E, F), some pairs, or decisions, will violate at least one of the constraints, and some will satisfy all the constraints. In our model, only nonnegative decisions that satisfy *all* the constraints are allowable. Such decisions are called *feasible decisions*.

Of all the allowable, or feasible, decisions, which one should be made? As we have noted earlier, every linear programming problem has a specific objective as well as constraints. The management of **PROTRAC**, Inc. would like to maximize profit, so this is the objective. **PROTRAC**'s profit clearly comes from two sources:

1. There is profit from the sale of E-9s.
2. There is profit from the sale of F-9s.

In our earlier discussion of major factors to be considered it was stated that the profit is $5000 for each E-9 and $4000 for each F-9. Since Protrac makes $5000 for each E-9 produced, and since E denotes the number of E-9s to be produced, we see that

$$5000E = \text{profit from producing } E \text{ units of E-9}$$

Similarly

$$4000F = \text{profit from producing } F \text{ units of F-9}$$

Thus, the decision to produce E units of E-9s and F units of F-9s results in a total profit given by

$$\text{total profit} = 5000E + 4000F \tag{2.7}$$

Of all the infinitely many decisions that satisfy all the constraints (i.e., of all feasible decisions), one that gives the largest total profit will be a *solution* to **PROTRAC**'s problem, or, as often referred to, an *optimal solution*. Thus, we seek a decision that will *maximize* total profit relative to the set of all possible feasible decisions. Such a decision is called an *optimal decision*. Since total profit is a *function* of the variables E, F, we refer to the expression $5000E + 4000F$ as the *objective function* and we want to find feasible values of E and F that *optimize* (which in this case means maximize) the objective function. Our objective, then, in mathematical terms, is stated concisely as

$$\text{maximize } 5000E + 4000F$$

or, even more simply, this is usually written as

$$\text{Max } 5000E + 4000F \tag{2.8}$$

It is important to bear in mind that the objective function is to be maximized *only* over the set of feasible decisions.

For instance, it was seen earlier that the decision $E = 5$, $F = 4$ is feasible because it satisfies all the constraints. Corresponding to this decision, the *objective value* would be

$$\text{total profit} = 5000E + 4000F$$

$$= 5000(5) + 4000(4) = 41,000$$

Associated with the decision $E = 6$, $F = 5$ the objective value would be

$$\text{total profit} = 5000E + 4000F$$

$$= 5000(6) + 4000(5) = 50,000$$

Although this objective value is larger than the previous one, and thereby more attractive, we recall that $E = 6$, $F = 5$ is not a feasible decision because it violates one of the constraints. Hence, **PROTRAC** is not able to consider this decision. It must be discarded. Can you find a *feasible* decision for which the objective value exceeds 41,000? Try, for example, the decision $E = 6$, $F = 3.5$. Verify that it satisfies all the constraints and that it yields an objective value of 44,000, which is clearly an improvement over 41,000. Do you believe that this production plan ($E = 6$, $F = 3.5$) is an optimal decision (i.e., a solution to our problem) or that, to the contrary, it is possible to do even better? Remember that only feasible decisions can be considered—that is, the production alternatives that satisfy *all* the constraints.

In the following chapters we shall see how to rigorously (i.e., without guesswork) solve this problem and many others like it. Also, we shall see how the computer is used to do much of the work for us. In the remainder of this chapter the goal is to give you more experience in the formulation of linear programming models, for model formulation is one of the early important steps in problem analysis. We shall also show how spreadsheet representations of an LP can be created and used. Let us first, however, take a moment to review the complete mathematical formulation of the **PROTRAC**, Inc. problem, and to make several observations on the form of this model.

**The Complete
Formulation of
the PROTRAC,
Inc. Problem**

In the preceding discussion we have translated a verbal description of a "real-world" problem into a complete mathematical model with an objective function and constraints. This model, which we call the *formal LP model*, is

$$\text{Max } 5000E + 4000F \quad \text{(objective function)}$$

subject to (s.t.)

$$10E + 15F \leq 150 \quad \text{(hours in department A)}$$
$$20E + 10F \leq 160 \quad \text{(hours in department B)}$$
$$30E + 10F \geq 135 \quad \text{(testing hours)}$$
$$E - 3F \leq 0 \quad \text{(mix constraint)}$$
$$E + F \geq 5 \quad \text{(total units requirement)}$$
$$E, F \geq 0 \quad \text{(nonnegativity conditions)}$$

Notice that in the formal LP model above, all the constraint functions (recall that the constraint functions are the left-hand sides of the inequality constraints) and the objective function are *linear functions* of the decision variables. As you may recall, the graph of a linear function of two variables is a straight line. In general, a linear function is one where each variable appears in a separate term together with its coefficient (i.e., there are no products or quotients of variables, no exponents other than 1, no logarithmic, exponential, or trigonometric terms). As you can see, this is true of each function in the model above. By contrast, $14E + 12EF$ is a nonlinear function because of the term $12EF$ involving a product of the variables. Also, $9E^2 + 8F$ is nonlinear because the variable E is raised to the power 2. Other examples of nonlinear functions are $6\sqrt{E} + F$ and $19 \log E + 12E^2F$.

**Linear
Functions**

As you might imagine, from the mathematical point of view, nonlinear functions are more difficult to deal with. The power of linear programming, in applications, stems from the power of linear mathematics, and from the fact that linear models can be readily used in real applications by managers and analysts with little or even no training in the underlying mathematics. For our purposes at this time the important facts to be remembered are

1. A linear program always has an objective function (to be either maximized or minimized) and constraints.
2. All functions in the problem (objective and constraints) are *linear functions*.

Integrality Considerations

In making a final observation, let us take another look at the complete formulation of the **PROTRAC**, Inc. model. It should be pointed out that unless we put in specific additional constraints, which force the decision variables to be integers, we must be prepared to accept fractional answers. In many LP models, such as in the **PROTRAC**, Inc. model, it will be true that fractional values for the decision variables do not have meaningful physical interpretations. For example, a solution that says "produce 3.12 E-9s and 6.88 F-9s" may not be implementable. On the other hand, there are many problems for which fractions obviously have meaning (e.g., "produce 98.65 gallons of crude oil"). In those cases where fractional answers are not meaningful, there are two possible recourses:

1. Add so-called *integrality conditions*, which force the decision variables to take on only integer values. This changes the problem to what is called an *integer program*. Integer programming models involve many additional considerations beyond the usual linear program. Integer programs are discussed at length in Chapter 8.
2. Solve the problem as an ordinary linear program and then round (e.g., to the nearest integer) any decision variable for which a fractional answer cannot be implemented. The advantages and disadvantages of this approach are also discussed in Chapter 8.

In practice, both of these approaches are adopted. For the present, it will suffice to assume that either fractional solutions are meaningful or else (for the purpose of implementation) they will be rounded to integers.

Before going on to a new formulation, let us show how the above formal LP model can be put on a spreadsheet. In the process we will be able to provide a balanced view of how the spreadsheet approach fits into the overall modeling context.

_____ 2.3
A SPREADSHEET REPRESENTATION OF PROTRAC E AND F

In the process of creating a spreadsheet representation the following facts are used:

Various Types of Cells

1. A spreadsheet is a grid, or matrix, with cells, which are the intersections of columns and rows. Letters are used to denote the columns, and numbers designate the rows. For example, C6 denotes the entry in column C and row 6. Each possible entry in the grid, such as C6, is called a cell. In referring to various cells it is customary to designate the column first (C) and then the row (6). In a typical spreadsheet many of the cells will be blank (i.e., unused), while other cells in the spreadsheet will contain various types of information.

Labels

2. In particular, some cells contain user-supplied **LABELS**. The labels are used in the same way that you would use labels to help read a table of data. Their purpose is to clarify the meaning of other entries in the spreadsheet.

Parameters and Decision Variables

3. Other cells contain user-supplied **NUMBERS**. Generally these numbers will represent
    a. The numeric value of **PARAMETERS**, which are the *data* for the given problem
    b. Numeric values for **DECISION VARIABLES**. These numeric values are called **DECISION VALUES**.

FIGURE 2.3

The Symbolic Spreadsheet for E & F

	A	B	C	D	E	F	G	H	I
1	Product		E	F					
2									
3	Quantity								
4	Profit/Unit		5000.00	4000.00					
5									
6	*************								
7	PROFIT								
8	+C4*C3+D4*D3								
9	**************								
10									
11			Resource Usage		Constraint Function		RHS		Slack
12			E	F					
13			----						
14	Dept A		10.00	15.00	(C14*C3) + (D14*D3)		150		+G14 − F14
15	Dept B		20.00	10.00	(C15*C3) + (D15*D3)		160		+G15 − F15
16	Test Hrs		30.00	10.00	(C16*C3) + (D16*D3)		135		−G16 + F16
17	Mix		1.00	3.00	− (C17*C3) + (D17*D3)†		0		−G17 + F17
18	Tot Units		1.00	1.00	(C18*C3) + (D18*D3)		5		−G18 + F18
19									
20									

Value for E to be Supplied by User

Value for F to be Supplied by User

---

† The careful reader will note that the formula in cell F17 represents $-E + 3F$. The mix constraint in the formal model was written as

$$E - 3F \leq 0 \qquad (2.4)$$

We have multiplied both sides by -1 to obtain

$$-E + 3F \geq 0$$

This was done in order to meet the requirement of VINO and What's *Best!* that the optimized value of a constraint function always be nonnegative. We hasten to add that this technicality has little to do with understanding the overall spreadsheet.

4. Still other cells contain user-supplied **FORMULAS**. For example, in the spreadsheet representation of an LP model, formulas are required to represent the objective function and the constraint functions. In some instances, there may be underlying formulas which determine the numeric value of various parameters in the model. Thus, for some parameters, as in 3(a) above, numeric values will be entered directly. Other parameters will be computed from formulas which the user has entered.

The above facts are used to create the spreadsheet shown in Figure 2.3. This spreadsheet is called the **SYMBOLIC SPREADSHEET** for the **PROTRAC** E and F problem.

Labels, Data, and Formulas in the E & F Spreadsheet

Let us summarize the way in which this spreadsheet has been created (and there are various ways to do this, according to the user's own taste). The first row consists of labels. The first row says that column C will refer to product *E* and column D to product *F*. Row 3 indicates that cell C3 will contain the quantity of *E* produced and *D*3 will contain the quantity of *F* produced. The blank tinted boxes appearing in C3 and *D*3 are simply our convention for drawing special attention to these cells. They are cells which, in a "what if" analysis, the user must manipulate by supplying specific numeric entries (in this case, specific decision values for the variables *E* and *F*). Alternatively, in a What'sB*est*! analysis, the computer will determine, and enter in C3 and *D*3, the optimal values for *E* and *F*.

In cells C4 and *D*4 parameter values have been entered. These are per unit profitabilities for *E* and *F*, respectively, as explained by the label in *A*4. In *A*8 we see a formula. This formula

$$+C4 * C3 + D4 * D3$$

represents the objective function for the **PROTRAC** E and F model. The formula indicates that profit will be computed by multiplying the contents of C3 by the contents of C4 (the "*" symbol means multiplication) and adding to it the contents of *D*3 multiplied by the contents of *D*4. The "+" symbol in front of C4 in the formula tells the spreadsheet program that it is indeed looking at a formula and not the text for a label.

Use a Plus to Begin a Formula

With the exception of column I, the other entries in the spreadsheet should be self-explanatory. You can see that the data in columns C and D, rows 14 through 18, come directly from the formal LP model for **PROTRAC** E and F. Although these data have been labeled as "resource usage," the only "resources" in this problem are labor hours in departments A and B, respectively, and hence, strictly speaking, the label is appropriate only for rows 14 and 15. There is, however, no need to be pedantic. In creating a spreadsheet, the user can choose any labeling scheme (or even none) that suits the purpose. Our purpose here is simply to illustrate the process.

Computing Slack

It remains to explain the entries, termed "slack," which appear in column I, rows 14 through 18. This term will be discussed at length in later portions of the text. For present purposes it suffices to state that

---

In the symbolic spreadsheet, *slack* is the difference between the constraint function and the right-hand side, computed so that it is nonnegative.

For example, look at the slack formula in cell I14. This slack value corresponds to the department A capacity constraint which is $10E + 15F \leq 150$. The spreadsheet shows the formula G14-F14 for the slack value. If we substitute the contents of G14 and F14, we see that $G14$-$F14$ is

$$150 - (C14 * C3 + D14 * D3)$$

which is the "right-hand side of the first constraint minus the left-hand side." Thus, the slack value for this constraint is unused capacity. Now consider the mix constraint, which we have rewritten as $-E + 3F \geq 0$. The entry in cell I17 of the spreadsheet shows that the slack formula for the mix constraint is the "left-hand side minus the right-hand side," which is the order of subtraction required to make this slack value nonnegative. What we have just illustrated is the following rule:

For a $\leq$ constraint, slack is the right-hand side minus the left-hand side. For a $\geq$ constraint, slack is the left-hand side minus the right-hand side.

This completes our discussion of the **symbolic spreadsheet** for **PROTRAC** E and F. But this is only the beginning of the story. A typical spreadsheet program allows you to look at two different spreadsheet representations of your model. The first, which we've just created, is the symbolic spreadsheet. The second, which we now discuss, is called the **VALUE SPREADSHEET**.

The Value Spreadsheet

To create the value spreadsheet, let us refer once again to Figure 2.3. We see that in this symbolic spreadsheet there are two distinguished cells that are waiting for specific

FIGURE 2.4
The Value Spreadsheet for $E = 2$, $F = 8$

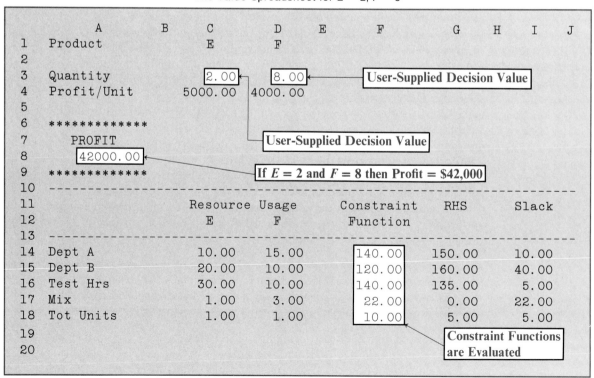

numeric values to be entered by the user. These are cells *C*3 and *D*3. If, for example, we enter the value 2 into *C*3 and 8 into *D*3 (meaning $E = 2$ and $F = 8$) then the spreadsheet program can (and will) compute ("evaluate") all of the formulas which have been entered in various cells, and these formulas will be replaced with their specific numeric values. The resulting **VALUE SPREADSHEET** appears in Figure 2.4.

Computing Value

Note that each cell which previously contained a formula now contains a number. For example, cell *F*14 now contains the number 140, which is the number of labor hours in department A when **PROTRAC** produces the mix ($E = 2$, $F = 8$). Corresponding to this constraint we see, from cell *I*14, that the slack value is 10, which is $150 - 140$. Hence there are 10 hours of unused labor in department A. If you were to enter different values for *E* and *F* the spreadsheet would recompute the values for cells such as *F*14 and *I*14 and the new results would appear. That is how the spreadsheet implements the "what if" analytic process which we described in Chapter 1.

Optimizing the Spreadsheet

If one is interested in the creation and use of spreadsheets for "what if" analyses only, then the above description covers the essentials of the process. However, when considering the spreadsheet representation of an LP, there is generally at least one more step of interest, which is the creation of the optimized spreadsheet. With either of the PC programs VINO or What's*Best!* the user can transform any value spreadsheet to an optimized spreadsheet with one additional stroke at the keyboard (and various graphics of interest can also be produced). Figure 2.5 shows the optimized spreadsheet for **PROTRAC** E and F.

FIGURE 2.5
The optimized Spreadsheet for E & F

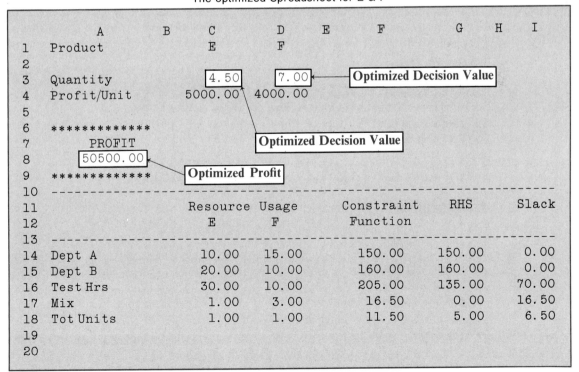

This optimized spreadsheet is a particular **value spreadsheet**, one in which the model has computed optimal values for the decision variables E and F. Thus, we see in Figure 2.5, reading cells $C3$ and $D3$, that the optimal decision values, which we denote as E^*, F^*, are ($E^* = 4.5$, $F^* = 7.0$). The spreadsheet also shows optimal numeric values in the "constraint function" and "slack" columns.

_____ **2.4**

THE SPREADSHEET VERSUS THE FORMAL LP MODEL

You have now seen how to capture the **PROTRAC** E and F linear programming problem in two forms:

1. The formal LP model
2. The spreadsheet representation

Which to Use? You may well be wondering, "What should I do? Do I need to do both? What are the relevant considerations?" The purpose of this section is to address such questions.

Let us begin with the advantages of a spreadsheet representation. First, as already discussed

---

The spreadsheet format is a convenient way to perform numerous "what if" analyses.

"But," we hear you say, "if our ultimate goal is to find **what's best**, do we really need to bother with the spreadsheet? Can't we just put the formal LP model on the PC and then optimize it? Wouldn't that be more efficient, since in any case it looks as if we more or less have to construct the formal LP model before creating the spreadsheet? Otherwise we wouldn't know the formulas for the objective function or the constraint functions, ..."

Another Level of "What If" As far as it goes, the above point of view is basically correct. But there is another level of "what if" potential associated with the spreadsheet concept that we have not yet exploited. Let us illustrate this with an example.

Suppose that in fact the total hours available in department A depend upon the number of workers scheduled to be on duty in the next two weeks. Suppose the dependency is expressed by the following formula:

$$\text{Total hours in dept. A} = 200(1 - e^{-(.05)MA}) \tag{2.9}$$

Converting Men to Total Hours where MA denotes the number of men scheduled to work in A. For example, if $MA = 28$ then there are 150.68 hours available. Let us assume that it is the numeric value for MA that the manager really has his hands on. We call this value **RAW DATA**, which means data which is readily available. Expression (2.9) transforms this raw data into the specific data required to formulate the model. Note that in the formal LP model we could not replace the right-hand side of the Dept. A constraint with the right-hand side of expression (2.9) without destroying the linearity of the problem (i.e. treating MA as a variable would make the problem nonlinear). It is precisely the nonlinearity of the formula that prevents us from using it directly in the problem formulated (see Question 28 in Section 2.18 at the end of this chapter).

Figure 2.6 shows a symbolic spreadsheet for the modified model.

FIGURE 2.6

The Symbolic Spreadsheet with a Formula
for Hours Available in Dept. A

	A	B	C	D	E	F	G	H	I
1									
2	Num Men								
3	Product		DptA						
4									
5	Quantity		E	F					
6	Profit/Unit		5000	4000					
7									
8	***************								
9	PROFIT								
10	+C6*C5 + D6*D5								
11	***************								
12	-----		-----			-----	-----		-----
13			Resource			Constraint	RHS		Slack
14			Usage			Function			
15	-----		E	F		-----	-----		-----
16	Dept A		10	15		(C16*C5) + (D16*D5)	200*(1 − @EXP(−0.05*C2))		+G16 − F16
17	Dept B		20	10		(C17*C5) + (D17*D5)	160		+G17 − F17
18	Test Hrs		30	10		(C18*C5) + (D18*D5)	135		−G18 + F18
19	Mix		1	3		−(C19*C5) + (D19*D5)	0		−G19 + F19
20	Tot Units		1	1		(C20*C5) + (D20*D5)	5		−G20 + F20

Raw Data to be Supplied by User

Decision Values to be Supplied by User

In cell $A2$ the label Num Men has been entered (for number of men). In cell $C2$ we see that the number of men is department A must be entered by the user. Thus, in this spreadsheet the user must provide specific values for the two decision variables (E and F) *and* for one parameter (MA). The formula entered in $G16$ represents the right-hand side of equation (2.9).

A value spreadsheet is obtained by entering specific numeric values for MA (cell $C2$), E(cell $C5$), and F(cell $D5$). The value spreadsheet Figure 2.7 was obtained by setting $MA = 28$, $E = 2$, $F = 8$. Note the similarity between Figure 2.4 and Figure 2.7.

FIGURE 2.7
The Value Spreadsheet for
$E = 2, F = 8, MA = 28$

	A	B	C	D	E	F	G	H	I
1			DptA						
2	Num Men		28.00						
3	Product		E	F					
4									
5	Quantity		2.00	8.00		User-Supplied			
6	Profit/Unit		5000.00	4000.00		Entries			
7									
8	*************								
9	PROFIT								
10	42000.00								
11	*************								
12	- -								
13			Resource Usage			Constraint	RHS		Slack
14			E	F		Function			
15	- -								
16	Dept A		10.00	15.00		140.00	150.68		10.68
17	Dept B		20.00	10.00		120.00	160.00		40.00
18	Test Hrs		30.00	10.00		140.00	135.00		5.00
19	Mix		1.00	3.00		22.00	0.00		22.00
20	Tot Units		1.00	1.00		10.00	5.00		5.00

A Parameter Analysis

In a typical real-world scenario the manager may, of course, wish to view the optimized spreadsheet for a problem. Actually, for a problem such as E and F, the manager may be thinking, "Well, it is true that I would like to see the optimized spreadsheet corresponding to my assignment of 28 men to MA. But **what if** I decide to put 26 men in department A? How would the optimized spreadsheet differ from the previous $MA = 28$ case? **What if** I then repeat this with 30 men, 32 men, etc.? In fact, my latest accounting run shows that the marginal cost of assigning one additional man to department A is 400 dollars. The same set of data shows that this cost of 400 dollars for each additional man is the same no matter how many men have been assigned to department A. I guess I should continue to assign workers to department A as long as the marginal return (i.e., the added return per worker) exceeds 400 dollars."

The spreadsheet optimizer is a tool that allows the manager to easily complete the analysis. The manager successively enters values for MA (cell $C2$) and obtains the optimal profit (cell $A10$) for each assignment. The result of this procedure, for values of MA ranging from 20 to 33, is the curve shown in Figure 2.8. (The data used to generate this curve show *diminishing returns to scale*).

FIGURE 2.8
Optimal Profit vs. Men in Dept. A

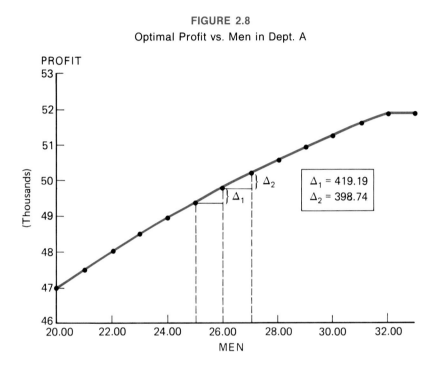

Graphs such as Figure 2.8 can be generated by the typical spreadsheet program. In our example, the analysis is completed by finding the leftmost point where adding an additional man produces less than $400 of additional profit. To the left of this point, the marginal return exceeds the marginal cost (of $400 per man) and to the right the marginal return is less than marginal cost. You can see that this occurs when MA is approximately 26. When MA is less than 26, the firm will make more money by assigning another man to department A. If MA is greater than 26, the firm will make money by removing a man from department A. The profit will be maximized when $MA = 26$.

The Real-World Situation

In typical real-world LP models, there may be many different parameters whose values, like the right-hand side of the department A constraint, are computed from rather complicated **NONLINEAR** formulas (e.g., expression (2.9) shows that the parameter "total hours in department A" is a nonlinear function of MA). Customarily, practitioners deal with this problem by writing a special "front end" program, called a **matrix generator**. The job of such a program is to take "raw data," such as a value for the term MA, and, using the appropriate formulas, transform these data into the inputs required by the LP model (the hours of capacity in department A). The matrix generator allows a user to solve many different LP's without needing to calculate transformed data by hand. The spreadsheet does the same job, but in a more "user-friendly"

Matrix Generators

environment. This discussion shows that

A powerful reason for using the spreadsheet approach is that it provides a convenient user-oriented way to generate the data required to formulate the LP. In many real-world applications, such data are generated by directly inputting readily available raw data. The spreadsheet then automatically computes the values for the transformed data.

Reasons for the Formal LP

Why then do we bother at all to write out the formal LP model? There are two reasons. As already mentioned, it is almost a prerequisite that in order to create the spreadsheet you must first formulate the problem as a formal LP model. The second reason is that in practice, regardless of which formulation we consider (i.e., spreadsheet vs. formal model), almost no one formulates a problem correctly on the first try. In other words, formulations often need to be debugged. We have two choices:

Debugging the Formal LP model

1. Write out the model as a formal LP and then try to solve it with one of many available interactive computer codes (in this text we use the LINDO code to solve an LP problem). If the model has been incorrectly formulated your first attempt to solve it will generally produce either a diagnostic indication or a nonsensical result. Proceed to debug, which means you examine your formulation and look for errors either in the logic of the formulation or in the way you typed the formulation into the computer.

Debugging the Spreadsheet Representation of the LP

2. Use the formal LP model as a guide in creating a symbolic spreadsheet representation. Try to optimize. An incorrectly formulated model will, as above, generally trigger some kind of fault indicator. Again, as above, you must now debug your work.

Although either of the above choices can lead to a correct formulation, experience suggests that the first route is easier. For a rather complicated model it is often easier to examine and analyze the formal LP model. Looking at all of the many formulas in the cells of the symbolic spreadsheet can be to say the least, confusing. The whole purpose of the spreadsheet approach is to get to the value spreadsheet, which the representation managers find easy to work with. But this can be created in a correct manner only after the formulation **has been debugged**. Thus

---

A Two-Stage Process

Writing the problem as a formal LP model, and then debugging the formulation, seems to be the easiest way to arrive at a correct model. After that, you may choose to create a spreadsheet representation for further manipulation and analysis in a convenient format.

The schematic diagram shown in Figure 2.9 summarizes some of the important differences between using the formal model in conjunction with an interactive code such as LINDO and using a spreadsheet optimizer.

For all of these reasons, the spreadsheet cannot be viewed as a replacement of the formal LP model, and programs which optimize spreadsheets cannot yet provide satisfactory replacements of interactive computer codes such as LINDO. More appropriately, we shall view the spreadsheet representation of an LP as another tool for the manager's use. It is a tool which in some ways enhances the manager's ability to have "hands-on contact" with the problem to be analyzed. The manager who wishes to use

FIGURE 2.9
A Comparison of Spreadsheet and
Formal Models

	FORMAL LP MODEL	SPREADSHEET REPRESENTATION
Matrix Generator:	Would be a separate computer program "not seen" by the manager.	The formulas for generating data are in the spreadsheet cells and can be viewed or modified by the manager.
"What If" Analyses:	Constraints and objective function values computed by hand.	All computations performed automatically on the spreadsheet.
Debugging the Problem Formulation:	Facilitated by looking at a listing of the formal model.	Not easily done with only the spreadsheet representation.

the tool effectively will want to understand a good deal about the structure of the underlying formal LP model. Why? Because it is that model and its properties that in fact we are really making use of, regardless of whether it is being represented on a spreadsheet. Elucidating the structure of the underlying LP model will occupy much of our attention for the next few chapters. Before that, however, we shall want to study several other examples, to gain experience both with model formulation and with creating spreadsheet representations.

_____ 2.5
CRAWLER TREAD: A BLENDING EXAMPLE

Although the **PROTRAC**, Inc. problem turned out to be a maximization model, many real-world problems occur in a minimization context. When profit is the objective, then clearly maximization is called for, but if, for example, cost is the objective, then minimization is called for. As an example of a minimization model, we consider the following Crawler Tread problem:

The Problem Statement   Iron ore from four different mines will be blended to make treads for a new product at **PROTRAC**, a medium-size crawler tractor, the E-6, designed especially to compete in the European market. Analysis has shown that in order to produce a blend with suitable tensile qualities, minimum requirements must be met on three basic elements, denoted for simplicity as A, B, and C. In particular, each ton of ore must contain at least 5 pounds of basic element A, at least 100 pounds of basic element B, and at least 30 pounds of basic element C. These data are summarized in Figure 2.10. The ore from each of the four different mines possesses each of the three basic elements, but in different

FIGURE 2.10
Requirements of Basic Elements
(pounds per ton)

BASIC ELEMENT	MINIMUM REQUIREMENT PER TON OF BLEND (lbs)
A	5
B	100
C	30

FIGURE 2.11

Compositions from Each Mine
(pounds per ton)

BASIC ELEMENT	MINE			
	1	2		
A	10	3	8	2
B	90	150	75	175
C	45	25	20	37

amounts. These compositions, in pounds per ton, are given in Figure 2.11. Notice that a ton of ore from the first mine contains 10 pounds of basic element A and hence satisfies the minimum requirement on this element of 5 pounds per ton. Similarly, this same ton of ore contains 90 pounds of basic element B and 45 pounds of basic element C, hence satisfying the requirement on basic element C but not on basic element B. Similarly, you can verify that a single ton of ore from the second mine will not satisfy the requirements on A or C. A single ton of ore from mine 3 will not satisfy requirements on B and C, and a single ton from mine 4 will not satisfy the requirement on A. However, many different blends can easily be found which will indeed satisfy the minimal requirements on all three basic elements. An example of such a blend would be a mixture composed of one-half ton from mine 1 and one-half ton from mine 4. The amount of basic element A in this blended ton is computed as follows:

$$\text{pounds of A} = (\text{pounds of A in 1 ton from 1})(\tfrac{1}{2}) + (\text{pounds of A in 1 ton from 4})(\tfrac{1}{2})$$

Hence

$$\text{pounds of A} = 10(\tfrac{1}{2}) + 2(\tfrac{1}{2}) = 5 + 1 = 6$$

Since $6 \geq 5$, the minimal requirement on basic element A is satisfied by this blend. Similarly, for the same blended ton, we can compute

$$\text{pounds of B} = (\text{pounds of B in 1 ton from 1})(\tfrac{1}{2}) + (\text{pounds of B in 1 ton from 4})(\tfrac{1}{2})$$

Hence

$$\text{pounds of B} = 90(\tfrac{1}{2}) + 175(\tfrac{1}{2}) = 132.5$$

In a similar fashion

$$\text{pounds of C} = 45(\tfrac{1}{2}) + 37(\tfrac{1}{2}) = 41$$

Feasibility

Comparing 132.5 with the requirement of 100, and 41 with the requirement of 30, it is seen that this blend of one-half ton from mine 1 and one-half ton from mine 4 easily satisfies all the minimal requirements, and hence this is said to be a **feasible blend**. There are many other possible blends of 1 ton which satisfy all the minimal requirements and hence which are also feasible. See if you can discover one or two. (Of course a spreadsheet representation would automatically do the calculations for you). However, since the ore from each mine has a different cost, different blends will also have different costs. The cost data are given in Figure 2.12. For example, from Figure 2.12 you can see that the

FIGURE 2.12

Dollar Cost per Ton from Each Mine

MINE	DOLLAR COST PER TON OF ORE
1	800
2	400
3	600
4	500

cost of the feasible blend one-half ton from mine 1 and one-half ton from mine 4 is

(cost per ton from mine 1)$(\frac{1}{2})$ + (cost per ton from mine 4)$(\frac{1}{2})$ = $800(\frac{1}{2})$ + $500(\frac{1}{2})$ = $650

Compare this cost with the cost of some of the other feasible blends which you may have discovered. The objective of management in the Crawler Tread problem is to discover a *least-cost feasible blend*. Let us see how this problem can be formulated as a linear programming model.

Since we are interested in finding an *optimal* 1-ton blend, we set up the *decision variables* as follows:

**Creating the
Formal LP
Model**

$$T_1 = \text{fraction of a ton to be chosen from mine 1}$$

$$T_2 = \text{fraction of a ton to be chosen from mine 2}$$

$$T_3 = \text{fraction of a ton to be chosen from mine 3}$$

$$T_4 = \text{fraction of a ton to be chosen from mine 4}$$

Then, using the numerical values given in Figure 2.11, the amounts of the basic elements in 1 ton of blend are calculated as follows:

$$\text{pounds of basic element A in 1 ton of blend} = 10T_1 + 3T_2 + 8T_3 + 2T_4 \quad (2.10)$$

$$\text{pounds of basic element B in 1 ton of blend} = 90T_1 + 150T_2 + 75T_3 + 175T_4 \quad (2.11)$$

$$\text{pounds of basic element C in 1 ton of blend} = 45T_1 + 25T_2 + 20T_3 + 37T_4 \quad (2.12)$$

We can now combine expressions (2.10), (2.11), and (2.12) with the minimal requirements designated in Figure 2.10 to obtain the three (requirement) constraints:

$$10T_1 + 3T_2 + 8T_3 + 2T_4 \geq 5 \quad (2.13)$$

$$90T_1 + 150T_2 + 75T_3 + 175T_4 \geq 100 \quad (2.14)$$

$$45T_1 + 25T_2 + 20T_3 + 37T_4 \geq 30 \quad (2.15)$$

Are there any other constraints in this model? Of course, we must include the usual nonnegativity conditions T_1, T_2, T_3, $T_4 \geq 0$, but there is still another important constraint which must be included. Since there are no other contributions to the 1 ton aside from the four mines, the fractional contributions from each mine must add up to 1. That is, we must include the constraint

$$T_1 + T_2 + T_3 + T_4 = 1 \quad (2.16)$$

The latter constraint, sometimes called a **balance condition**, is an **equality constraint**, and it restricts the values of the decision variables in such a way that the left-hand side *exactly* equals the right-hand side. This example shows that

> **The constraints in a linear programming model can be equalities as well as inequalities.**

Using the data in Figure 2.12, it is easy to see that the cost of any blend is given as follows:

$$\text{cost of 1 ton of blend} = 800T_1 + 400T_2 + 600T_3 + 500T_4$$

Noting that the objective is to minimize cost, we can now write the complete mathematical model for the Crawler Tread problem:

The Formal Crawler Tread Model

$$\text{Min } 800T_1 + 400T_2 + 600T_3 + 500T_4$$
$$\text{s.t. } 10T_1 + \quad 3T_2 + \quad 8T_3 + \quad 2T_4 \geq \quad 5$$
$$90T_1 + 150T_2 + 75T_3 + 175T_4 \geq 100$$
$$45T_1 + \quad 25T_2 + 20T_3 + \quad 37T_4 \geq \quad 30$$
$$T_1 + \quad T_2 + \quad T_3 + \quad T_4 = \quad 1$$
$$T_1, T_2, T_3, T_4 \geq 0$$

You should verify that all functions in this model are linear and consequently it is a linear programming problem.

Now that you have seen two very detailed examples of model formulation, along with a discussion of spreadsheet representations, we present a number of additional examples for you to work on. These examples will allow you to sharpen your formulation skills. You will also have more opportunities to create spreadsheet representations. Before presenting the examples, let us take a moment to give some loose guidelines on how to translate a word problem into a mathematical model.

_____ **2.6**

GUIDELINES AND COMMENTS ON MODEL FORMULATION

In translating a word problem into a formal model, you may find it helpful first to create a verbal model corresponding to the given problem. That is, you might proceed as follows:

1. Express each constraint in words; in doing this, pay careful attention to whether the constraint is a *requirement* of the form $\geq$ (at least as large as), a *limitation* of the form $\leq$ (no larger than), or $=$ (exactly equal to).
2. Then express the objective in words.

Steps 1 and 2 should then allow you to

3. Verbally identify the decision variables.

Often a careful reading of the problem statement will reveal that the decision variables and the objective are given to you (in the problem statement) in the exact form that you need. It is usually of great importance that your decision variables be correctly defined. Sometimes you may feel that there are several possible choices. For example, should they represent pounds of finished product or pounds of raw material? One guideline that is often useful is to ask yourself the question, *What decisions must be made in order to optimize the objective function?* The answer to this question will help lead you to identify the decision variables correctly.

Having accomplished steps 1 through 3, invent symbolic notation for the decision variables. Then

4. Express each constraint in symbols (i.e., in terms of the decision variables).
5. Express the objective function in symbols (in terms of the decision variables).

At this stage it is advisable to check your work for consistency of units. For example, if the coefficients in the objective function are in dollars per *pound*, the decision variables that appear in the objective function should be in pounds, not tons or ounces. Similarly, check that for each constraint the units on the right-hand side and the units on the left-hand side are the same. For example, if one of the constraints is a limitation of ≤ form on labor hours, the right-hand side will be labor hours. Then if, as above, the decision variables are pounds, the data for this constraint function (i.e., the numerical coefficients for each decision variable on the left-hand side of the constraint) should be in labor hours per pound. To put it quite simply, you do not want to end up with hours on one side and minutes or seconds or pounds or tons on the other.

At this point it would be a good idea to comment on one other aspect of model formulation. We have seen that inequality constraints may be of the form ≥ or ≤. Students often ask whether a linear programming problem can have a *strict inequality* constraint, such ask < or >. The answer is a resounding *no*. The reason for this is mathematical in nature. It is to assure that a well-formulated problem will have a solution. The mathematical details required to justify this assertion lie outside our scope of interest. This is not a costly prohibition, for in just about any real-world situation you can imagine involving inequality constraints, it is true that the ≤ or ≥ representation entirely captures the real-world meaning.

Let us now discuss one final aspect of model formulation. This deals with the nature of the cost data to be employed.

2.7

SUNK VERSUS VARIABLE COST

In many real-world problems there are often two types of costs: *fixed costs*, also referred to as *sunk costs*, and *variable costs*. Contrary to the first impressions that students sometimes have

---

It is only the variable costs that are relevant in optimization models.

The sunk, or fixed, costs have already been paid, which means that no future decisions can affect these expenditures. For example, suppose that 800 pounds and 500 pounds of two grades of aluminum (grade 1 and grade 2) have been purchased for future delivery, at specified prices, $5 and $10 per pound, respectively, and that the contract has been signed. Management's problem is, in part, to determine the optimal use of these 1300 pounds of aluminum so as, perhaps, to maximize profit obtained from producing aluminum knuckles and conduits. Associated with these two products there will be revenues and variable costs incurred in their production (costs of machining, stamping, etc.). In formulating this type of model the fixed, or sunk, costs of $9000 associated with the contracted purchase are irrelevant. This amount has already been spent and hence the *quantities to be purchased* are no longer variables. The variables will be how much product should be produced, and the relevant cost in this determination is only the variable cost. More specifically, the formulation corresponding to the description above might be as follows. Let

The Fixed Cost Can Be Ignored

$$K = \text{number of knuckles to be produced (decision variable)}$$

$$C = \text{number of conduits to be produced (decision variable)}$$

$$10 = \text{revenue per knuckle}$$

$$30 = \text{revenue per conduit}$$

$$4 = \text{cost of producing a knuckle (variable cost)}$$

$$12 = \text{cost of producing a conduit (variable cost)}$$

For each product we must calculate what accountants call the *unit contribution margin*, that is, the difference between per unit revenue and per unit variable cost. The unit contribution margins are

$$\text{for knuckles: } 10 - 4 = 6$$

$$\text{for conduits: } 30 - 12 = 18$$

Suppose that each knuckle uses 1 unit of grade 1 aluminum and 2 units of grade 2 aluminum. Each conduit uses 3 units of grade 1 and 5 units of grade 2. Then we obtain the following **formal linear programming model**:

$$\text{Max } 6K + 18C$$

$$\text{s.t.} \quad K + 3C \leq 800 \quad \text{(grade 1 limitation)}$$

$$2K + 5C \leq 500 \quad \text{(grade 2 limitation)}$$

$$K \geq 0, \quad C \geq 0$$

One way to see the irrelevance of the sunk cost is to note that the objective function in the formulation is the total contribution margin. The net income, or profit, would be

$$\text{net profit} = \text{contribution margin} - \text{sunk cost}$$

$$= 6K + 18C - 9000$$

However, finding feasible values of K and C that maximize $6K + 18C - 9000$ is the same as finding feasible values that maximize $6K + 18C$. The constant term of 9000 can therefore be ignored. The bottom line here is that maximizing a function plus a constant, or even a positive constant times a function, gives in either case the same result, in terms of optimal values of decision variables, that you would obtain without the constant. However, adding (or subtracting) the same constant to (or from) each coefficient in the objective function may change the result. This is all nicely illustrated in the Red Brand Canners case at the end of this chapter. This case is a good illustration of how both sunk and variable costs arise in real-world problems.

The remainder of this chapter contains examples of formulations that you can use to cement your ability to make the transition between the real-world problem and the mathematical model. This transition—the way in which the model has been set up, the way the constraints and the objectives have been formulated—is of prime importance.

Try to work the following problems on your own. Set them up as quickly as possible and **do not read more into a problem than precisely what is given**. Do not, for example, introduce additional constraints or logical nuances or flights of imagination of your own which might in your opinion make the model more realistic. Do not, for example, worry about "what happens next week" if the problem never refers to "next week." The problems that we pose are chosen to help you develop a facility for formulation. In order to do this, and so that you may check your work and gauge your progress, it must be true that within the described context the correct formulation should be unambiguous. In other words, there is a "right answer." Later, when your have more experience, the latitude for shades of interpretation and real-world subtleties will be broader. Because the topic of formulation is so important, and because practice is the only way to master this topic, an especially long list of problems appears at the end of this chapter.

One final word of advice: Do not simply read the problem and then immediately read the solution. That would be the best way to deceive yourself about what you understand. Do not read the solution until either (1) you are certain you have correctly solved the problem on your own or (2) you are absolutely convinced that you have hit an impasse.

———— 2.8
EXAMPLE 1: ASTRO AND COSMO (A PRODUCT-MIX PROBLEM)

A TV company produces two types of TV sets, the Astro and the Cosmo. There are two production lines, one for each set, and there are two departments, both of which are used in the production of each set. The capacity of the Astro production line is 70 sets per day. The capacity of the Cosmo line is 50 sets per day. In department A picture tubes are produced. In this department the Astro set requires 1 labor hour and the Cosmo set requires 2 labor hours. Presently in department A a maximum of 120 labor hours per day can be assigned to production of the two types of sets. In department B the chassis is constructed. In this department the Astro set requires 1 labor hour and the Cosmo also requires 1 labor hour. Presently, in department B a maximum of 90 labor hours per day can be assigned to production of the two types of sets. The profit contributions are 20 and 10 dollars, respectively, for each Astro and Cosmo set. These data are summarized in Figure 2.13.

FIGURE 2.13
Astro and Cosmo Data

	DAILY CAPACITY	LABOR UTILIZATION PER SET (hrs)		PROFIT PER SET
		DEPT. A	DEPT. B	
Astro	70	1	1	$20
Cosmo	50	2	1	10
Total Availability		120	90	

If the company can sell as many Astro and Cosmo sets as it produces, what should be the daily production plan (i.e., the daily production) for each set? Review the **PRO-TRAC**, Inc. E and F model and then try to formulate Astro and Cosmo as a linear program.

Solution to Example 1

$$A = \text{daily production of Astros} \quad \text{(sets/day)}$$

$$C = \text{daily production of Cosmos} \quad \text{(sets/day)}$$

**The Formal
LP Model For
Astro Cosmo**

$$\text{Max } 20A + 10C$$

$$\text{s.t.} \qquad A \le 70$$

$$C \le 50$$

$$A + 2C \le 120$$

$$A + C \le 90$$

$$A, C \ge 0$$

Note that in this model not all the decision variables appear in all the constraints. For example, the variable C does not appear in the constraint $A \le 70$. In general, not all the decision variables have to appear explicitly in every constraint.[1] Also, they need not all appear in the objective function.

———— **2.9**

EXAMPLE 2: BLENDING GRUEL (A BLENDING PROBLEM)

A 16-ounce can of dog food must contain protein, carbohydrate, and fat in at least the following amounts: protein, 3 ounces; carbohydrate, 5 ounces; fat, 4 ounces. Four types of gruel are to be blended together in various proportions to produce a least-cost can of dog food satisfying these requirements. The contents and prices for 16 ounces of each gruel are given in Figure 2.14.

FIGURE 2.14
Gruel Blending Data

GRUEL	CONTENTS AND PRICES PER 16 OZ OF GRUEL			
	PROTEIN CONTENT (OZ)	CARBOHYDRATE CONTENT (OZ)	FAT CONTENT (OZ)	PRICE
1	3	7	5	$4
2	5	4	6	6
3	2	2	6	3
4	3	8	2	2

[1] You may think of all decision variables being included, but with zero coefficients in places. Thus, the constraint $A \le 70$ is the same as $A + 0(C) \le 70$.

Review the Crawler Tread blending model and then formulate this gruel blending problem as a linear program. (HINT: Let x_i denote the proportion of gruel i in a 16-ounce can of dogfood, $i = 1, 2, 3, 4$.)

Solution to Example 2

The Formal LP Model For Blending Gruel

$$\text{Min } 4x_1 + 6x_2 + 3x_3 + 2x_4$$
$$\text{s.t.} \quad 3x_1 + 5x_2 + 2x_3 + 3x_4 \geq 3$$
$$7x_1 + 4x_2 + 2x_3 + 8x_4 \geq 5$$
$$5x_1 + 6x_2 + 6x_3 + 2x_4 \geq 4$$
$$x_1 + x_2 + x_3 + x_4 = 1$$
$$x_1, x_2, x_3, x_4 \geq 0$$

Note that in Example 1, from the point of view of implementation, fractional values for the decision variables would probably be unacceptable. In Example 2, however, fractional values would be expected and acceptable. Example 3 illustrates another setting where integer values would be needed.

_____ 2.10
EXAMPLE 3: SECURITY FORCE SCHEDULING (A SCHEDULING PROBLEM)

A personnel manager must schedule the security force in such a way as to satisfy the staffing requirements shown in Figure 2.15.

Officers work 8-hour shifts. There are 6 such shifts each day. The starting and ending times for each shift are given in Figure 2.16. The personnel manager wants to determine how many officers should work each shift in order to minimize the total number of officers employed, while still satisfying the staffing requirements. We can define the decision variables as follows:

$$x_1 = \text{number of officers working shift 1}$$
$$x_2 = \text{number of officers working shift 2}$$
$$\vdots$$
$$x_6 = \text{number of officers working shift 6}$$

FIGURE 2.15
Security Staffing Requirements

TIME	MINIMUM NUMBER OF OFFICERS REQUIRED
Midnight–4 A.M.	5
4 A.M.–8 A.M.	7
8 A.M.–Noon	15
Noon–4 P.M.	7
4 P.M.–8 P.M.	12
8 P.M.–Midnight	9

FIGURE 2.16
Shift Schedule

SHIFT	STARTING TIME	ENDING TIME
1	Midnight	8:00 A.M.
2	4:00 A.M.	Noon
3	8:00 A.M.	4:00 P.M.
4	Noon	8:00 P.M.
5	4:00 P.M.	Midnight
6	8:00 P.M.	4:00 A.M.

In formulating the objective function, note that the total number of officers is the sum of the number of officers assigned to each shift. Now write out the objective function, noting that the personnel manager wants to minimize this sum. The objective function is

$$x_1 + x_2 + x_3 + x_4 + x_5 + x_6$$

In formulating the constraints, you want to be sure that a particular set of values for $x_1, \ldots, x_6$ satisfies the staffing requirements. Some device is needed to see what officers are on duty during each of the 4-hour intervals prescribed in Figure 2.15. A tabular arrangement such as the one shown in Figure 2.17 is helpful in making this determination.

FIGURE 2.17
Officers on Duty in Each Interval

SHIFT	MIDNIGHT TO 4:00 A.M.	4:00 A.M. TO 8:00 A.M.	8:00 A.M. TO NOON	NOON TO 4:00 P.M.	4:00 P.M. TO 8:00 P.M.	8:00 P.M. TO MIDNIGHT
1	x_1	x_1				
2		x_2	x_2			
3			x_3	x_3		
4				x_4	x_4	
5					x_5	x_5
6	x_6					x_6
Requirements	5	7	15	7	12	9

Here we see that the officers who work shift 1 are on duty during each of the first two time intervals, and so on. Figure 2.17 also shows (adding down columns) how many officers work in each time interval (e.g., in the first time interval $x_1 + x_6$ officers are on duty; thus, we write the first constraint $x_1 + x_6 \geq 5$). Now try to write out the remaining constraints for this model. The complete solution is given below.

FIGURE 2.18
Symbolic Spreadsheet for Security Force
Scheduling

	A	B	C	D	E	F	G	H
1								
2	SECURITY STAFFING SPREADSHEET							
3								
4			Num	Num	Num	Xtra		
5		Start	Men	Men	Men	Men		
6	Shift	Time	Start	Work	Req'd			
7								
8	1	Mdngt		+C8+C13	5	+D8-E8		*******************************
9	2	4.am		+C8+C9	7	+D9-E9		Tot Men
10	3	8.am		+C9+C10	15	+D10-E10		Employed
11	4	Noon		+C10+C11	7	+D11-E11		+C8+C10+C9+C11+C12+C13
12	5	4.pm		+C11+C12	12	+D12-E12		*******************************
13	6	8.pm		+C12+C13	9	+D13-E13		
14								
15								
16								

Entries in this
Column are User-
Supplied Decision Values

Solution to Example 3

The Formal Security Force Scheduling Model

$$\text{Min } x_1 + x_2 + x_3 + x_4 + x_5 + x_6$$

$$\text{s.t. } x_6 + x_1 \geq 5$$

$$x_1 + x_2 \geq 7$$

$$x_2 + x_3 \geq 15$$

$$x_3 + x_4 \geq 7$$

$$x_4 + x_5 \geq 12$$

$$x_5 + x_6 \geq 9$$

$$x_i \geq 0, \qquad i = 1, 2, \ldots, 6$$

If you have access to a PC and Lotus 1–2–3 you can create a spreadsheet representation of this model. One possible symbolic spreadsheet is shown in Figure 2.18. Entering any set of decision values (i.e., numerical values for $x_1, \ldots, x_6$) produces a value spreadsheet. If you have access to a spreadsheet optimizer such as VINO or What's*Best!*, you can then proceed to optimize the value spreadsheet. This will produce Figure 2.19. This latter figure shows optimal values for the decisions x_1 through x_6.

The examples thus far have shown a product-mix model (Astro/Cosmo), a blending model (gruel), and a scheduling model (security force). These are all illustrations of *types* of LPs that you encounter in real-world problem solving. Here is another important type of LP, called a *transportation model*.

FIGURE 2.19
Optimized Spreadsheet for Security Force
Scheduling

	A	B	C	D	E	F	G	H	I	J
1										
2	SECURITY STAFFING SPREADSHEET									
3										
4			Num	Num	Num	Xtra				
5		Start	Men	Men	Men	Men		********		
6	Shift	Time	Start	Work	Req'd			Tot Men		
7	---							Employed		
8	1	Mdngt	0	5	5	0		32		Optimized
9	2	4.am	8	8	7	1		********		Objective
10	3	8.am	7	15	15	0				Value
11	4	Noon	0	7	7	0				
12	5	4.pm	12	12	12	0				
13	6	8.pm	5	17	9	8				
14	---									
15										
16			Optimized Decision Values							

EXAMPLE 4: A TRANSPORTATION MODEL

A company has two plants and three warehouses. The first plant can supply at most 100 units and the second at most 200 units of the same product. The sales potential at the first warehouse is 150, at the second warehouse 200, and at the third 350. The sales revenues per unit at the three warehouses are 12 at the first, 14 at the second, and 15 at the third. The cost of manufacturing one unit at plant i and shipping it to warehouse j is given in Figure 2.20. The company wishes to determine how many units should be shipped from each plant to each warehouse so as to maximize profit.

FIGURE 2.20
Manufacturing and Shipping Data

	WAREHOUSE		
PLANT	1	2	3
1	8	10	12
2	7	9	11

Solution to Example 4 Note that the proper choice of the decision variables is given to you in the problem statement itself. Models of this sort are often formulated with decision variables having two rather than a single subscript. Using this device, the decision variables are

$$x_{ij} = \text{units sent from plant } i \text{ to warehouse } j$$

and the model is

The Formal LP Transportation Model

$$\text{Max } 4x_{11} + 5x_{21} + 4x_{12} + 5x_{22} + 3x_{13} + 4x_{23}$$

$$\text{s.t.} \quad x_{11} + x_{12} + x_{13} \leq 100$$

$$x_{21} + x_{22} + x_{23} \leq 200$$

$$x_{11} + x_{21} \qquad \leq 150$$

$$x_{12} + x_{22} \qquad \leq 200$$

$$x_{13} + x_{23} \qquad \leq 350$$

$$x_{ij} \geq 0, \qquad \text{all } i, j$$

From the formulation above you can see that a transportation model has a very special form. For example, all the nonzero coefficients in the constraints are 1. In fact, a transportation model is an example of an entire class of linear programs called *network problems*. Other examples of transportation models will appear in Chapter 7, and Chapter 9 is devoted to network models.

EXAMPLE 5: WINSTON-SALEM DEVELOPMENT CORPORATION (FINANCIAL PLANNING)

Here is an interesting application of LP to financial planning. Winston-Salem Development Corporation (WSDC) is trying to complete its investment plans for the next two years. Currently, WSDC has $2,000,000 on hand and available for investment. In 6 months, 12 months, and 18 months, WSDC expects to receive an income stream from previous investments. The data are presented in Figure 2.21. There are two development projects in which WSDC is considering participation.

FIGURE 2.21
Income from Previous Investments

	6 MONTHS	12 MONTHS	18 MONTHS
Income	$500,000	$400,000	$380,000

1. The Foster City Development would, if WSDC participated at a 100% level, have the projected cash flow shown in Figure 2.22 (negative numbers are investment, positive numbers are income). Thus, in order to participate in Foster City at the 100% level, WSDC would immediately have to lay out $1,000,000. In 6 months there would be another outlay of $700,000, and so on.

FIGURE 2.22
Foster City Cash Flow

	INITIAL	6 MONTHS	12 MONTHS	18 MONTHS	24 MONTHS
Income	$ − 1,000,000	$ − 700,000	$1,800,000	$400,000	$600,000

2. A second project involves taking over the operation of some old Middle-Income Housing on the condition that certain initial repairs be made. The cash flow stream for this project, at a 100% level of participation, would be as shown in Figure 2.23.

FIGURE 2.23
Middle-Income Housing Cash Flow

	INITIAL	6 MONTHS	12 MONTHS	18 MONTHS	24 MONTHS
Income	$ − 800,000	$500,000	$ − 200,000	$ − 700,000	$2,000,000

Because of company policy, WSDC is not permitted to borrow money. However, at the beginning of each 6-month period all surplus funds (those not allocated to either Foster City or Middle-Income Housing) are invested for a return of 7% for that 6-month period. WSDC can participate in any project at a level less than 100%, in which case all of the cash flows of that project are reduced proportionately. For example, if WSDC were to opt for participation in Foster City at the 30% level, the cash flows associated with this decision would be 0.3 times the data in Figure 2.22. The problem currently facing WSDC is to decide how much of the $2,000,000 on hand should be invested in each of the projects and how much should simply be invested for the 7% semiannual return.

Management's goal is to *maximize the cash on hand at the end of 24 months.* Formulate this problem as an LP model.

Solution to Example 5   The constraints in this model must say that at the beginning of each of the 4 6-month periods

$$\text{money invested} = \text{money on hand}$$

Define the decision variables

$$F = \text{fractional participation in the Foster City project}$$

$$M = \text{fractional participation in the Middle-Income Housing project}$$

$$S_1 = \text{surplus initial funds (not invested in } F \text{ or } M \text{ initially)}$$
$$\text{to be invested at 7\%}$$

$$S_2 = \text{surplus funds after 6 months to be invested at 7\%}$$

$$S_3 = \text{surplus funds after 12 months to be invested at 7\%}$$

$$S_4 = \text{surplus funds after 18 months to be invested at 7\%}$$

Then the first constraint must say

$$\text{initial investment} = \text{initial funds on hand}$$

or

$$1{,}000{,}000F + 800{,}000M + S_1 = 2{,}000{,}000$$

Recognizing that because of the interest paid S_1 becomes $1.07S_1$ after 6 months, and similarly for S_2, S_3, and S_4, the remaining three constraints are

$$700{,}000F + S_2 = 500{,}000M + 1.07S_1 + 500{,}000$$

$$200{,}000M + S_3 = 1{,}800{,}000F + 1.07S_2 + 400{,}000$$

$$700{,}000M + S_4 = 400{,}000F + 1.07S_3 + 380{,}000$$

and the objective function is to maximize the cash on hand at the end of 24 months, which is

$$600{,}000F + 2{,}000{,}000M + 1.07S_4$$

We have thus derived the following model:

The Formal WSDC Model

$$\text{Max } 600{,}000F + 2{,}000{,}000M + 1.07S_4$$

$$
\begin{array}{llll}
\text{s.t.} & 1{,}000{,}000F + 800{,}000M + S_1 & = 2{,}000{,}000 \\
& \phantom{1{,}}700{,}000F - 500{,}000M - 1.07S_1 + S_2 & = \phantom{2{,}00}500{,}000 \\
& -1{,}800{,}000F + 200{,}000M - 1.07S_2 + S_3 & = \phantom{2{,}00}400{,}000 \\
& -400{,}000F + 700{,}000M - 1.07S_3 + S_4 & = \phantom{2{,}00}380{,}000 \\
& F \leq 1 \\
& M \leq 1
\end{array}
$$

$$F \geq 0, \qquad M \geq 0, \qquad S_i \geq 0, \qquad i = 1, 2, 3, 4$$

EXAMPLE 6: LONGER BOATS YACHT COMPANY—A VIGNETTE IN CONSTRAINED BREAK-EVEN ANALYSIS

The Longer Boats Yacht Company produces three high-performance racing sloops. These three boats are called the Sting, the Ray, and the Breaker. Figure 2.24 gives pertinent revenue and cost data for the next planning period.

FIGURE 2.24
Longer Boats' Data

SLOOP	SELLING PRICE PER UNIT	VARIABLE COST PER UNIT	FIXED COST
Sting	$10,000	$5,000	$5,000,000
Ray	7,500	3,600	3,000,000
Breaker	15,000	8,000	10,000,000

As you can see from these data, the *fixed cost* of each of these activities is considerable. As explained in Section 2.7, a "fixed cost" is a lump cost that is paid regardless of the quantity to be produced. Thus, the same fixed cost of $3,000,000 for Rays will occur whether the production run consists of 0 boats, 1 boat, or 40 boats. The high fixed costs include the costs of design modification, mold reconstruction, and yacht basin testing.

Break-even analysis was introduced in Chapter 1. Figure 2.25 shows a break-even analysis of the production of Stings. We see that if Longer Boats were to produce only Stings, it would have to produce at least 1000 boats to break even.

FIGURE 2.25
Break-Even Analysis for Stings

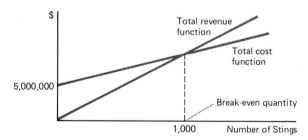

Longer Boats' problem is more complicated, however. First, for the next planning period management has already contracted to produce 700 Stings. Another customer has requested 400 Breakers, a request that management would like to honor. Longer Boats' marketing surveys have convinced management that at most 300 Rays should be produced. Management is still interested in how much it must sell to break even, but now there are three products as well as previous commitments or restrictions to take into consideration. Starting from basic principles, management notes that at break-even

$$\text{total revenue} = \text{total cost}$$

To obtain an expression of this fact in terms of the production quantities, the following decision variables are defined:

$$S = \text{number of Stings to produce}$$

$$R = \text{number of Rays to produce}$$

$$B = \text{number of Breakers to produce}$$

The break-even constraint, then, is

$$10,000S + 7500R + 15,000B = 5000S + 3600R + 8000B + 18,000,000$$

or

$$5000S + 3900R + 7000B = 18,000,000$$

We note that there is an infinite number of sets of values for S, R, and B that satisfy this constraint. Thus, in the multiproduct case, there are many break-even points, whereas in the single-product case (see Figure 2.25), there is only one. In the multi-product case, then, management must specify an additional restriction in order to iden-tify a particular break-even point of interest. Since Longer Boats is a relatively new company and is experiencing the cash flow problems associated with rapid growth, management would like to minimize the capital outflow. The fixed costs are of necessity incurred in their totality, and thus the goal becomes one of minimizing total variable costs. The total variable cost (the objective function) is

$$5000S + 3600R + 8000B$$

The complete model reflecting the break-even constraint, as well as the preestablished requirements and limits on demand, is as follows:

**The Formal
Longer Boats
LP Model**

$$\text{Min } 5000S + 3600R + 8000B$$
$$\text{s.t.} \quad 5000S + 3900R + 7000B = 18,000,000$$
$$S \geq 700$$
$$B \geq 400$$
$$R \leq 300$$
$$S \geq 0, \quad R \geq 0, \quad B \geq 0$$

―――― 2.14
EXAMPLE 7: MULTIPERIOD INVENTORY MODELS

This important class of models applies to inventories of materials, cash, and employees carried from one period to the next. Multiperiod models are sometimes referred to as **dynamic** problems. They reflect the fact that the decisions made in this period affect not only this period's returns (or costs) but the allowable decisions and returns in future periods as well. For this reason, multiperiod problems cannot be treated as if they were merely a collection of single-period problems. The topic of inventory management is considered in some detail in later chapters.

This is a classical, so-called deterministic, single-product inventory problem. It is called *deterministic* because we assume that the demand (i.e., number of orders to be satisfied) in each future period is known as the beginning of period 1. For example, a producer of polyurethane has a stock of orders for the next 6 weeks. Let d_i be a parameter that denotes this known demand (say, in terms of number of gallons that must be delivered to customers during week i), and assume that $d_i > 0$ for all i. Let C_i denote the cost of producing a gallon during week i, and let K_i denote the maximum amount that can be produced (because of capacity limitations) in week i. Finally, let h_i denote the per unit cost of inventory in stock at the end of week i. (Thus, the inventory is measured as the number of gallons carried from week i into week $i + 1$.) Suppose that the initial inventory (at the beginning of period 1 and for which no carrying charge is assessed) is known to be I_0 gallons. Find a production and inventory-holding plan that satisfies the known delivery schedule over the next 6 weeks at minimum total cost.

Before formulating the constrained optimization model, it will be useful to develop an expression for the inventory on hand at the end of each period. Since there is an inventory carrying charge, this quantity will clearly play a role in the objective function.

Let I_i be the inventory on hand at the end of week i. Define the decision variable x_i to be the gallons of polyurethane produced in week i. We note that

$$I_1 = I_0 + x_1 - d_1$$

That is, the inventory on hand at the end of week 1 is equal to the inventory on hand at the end of week 0 (the beginning of week 1) plus the production in week 1 minus the deliveries in week 1. (We are assuming that all demand must be satisfied. Hence, the known demand in week i, d_i, is by definition the amount delivered in week i.)

Similarly

$$I_2 = I_1 + x_2 - d_2$$

and, in general, the same reasoning yields, for any period t

$$I_t = I_{t-1} + x_t - d_t$$

This important inventory equation says that

inventory at end of t = inventory at beginning of t + production in t − demand in t

Note that if we substitute the known expression for I_1 into the equation for I_2, we obtain

$$I_2 = \underbrace{I_0 + x_1 - d_1}_{I_1} + x_2 - d_2 = I_0 + \sum_{i=1}^{2} x_i - \sum_{i=1}^{2} d_i$$

We could then substitute the foregoing expression for I_2 into the equation for I_3 to obtain

$$I_3 = I_0 + \sum_{i=1}^{3} x_i - \sum_{i=1}^{3} d_i$$

Repeating this procedure leads to an equivalent inventory equation

$$I_t = I_0 + \sum_{i=1}^{t} (x_i - d_i)$$

for any period t.

Note that this last expression relates the inventory at the end of period t to all previous production (the x values). The equation simply says that the inventory at the end of period t is equal to the initial inventory, plus the total production through period t, minus the total deliveries through period t. The variable I_t is sometimes referred to as a **definitional variable** because it is defined in terms of other decision variables (the x_i values) in the problem. The use of definitional variables sometimes makes it easier to see the proper formulation. Before writing the verbal model for this problem, we must figure out a way of saying that production in each period must be *at least* great enough so that demand (i.e., the delivery schedule) can be satisfied. In period 1 this means that $I_0 + x_1 \geq d_1$, or $I_0 + x_1 - d_1 \geq 0$. Since $I_0 + x_1 - d_1$ is the same as I_1, this is the same as saying that the inventory at the end of period 1 is nonnegative. Satisfying period 2 demand means that inventory at the beginning of period 2 (the end of period 1) plus period 2 production $\geq d_2$. That is

$$I_1 + x_2 \geq d_2 \qquad \text{or} \qquad I_1 + x_2 - d_2 \geq 0$$

which is the same as saying that the inventory at the end of period 2 is nonnegative. It should now be possible to see the pattern.

The condition that demand in period t must be satisfied is equivalent to the condition that inventory I_t at the end of period t must be nonnegative.

Solution to Example 7

Diagram

FIGURE 2.26

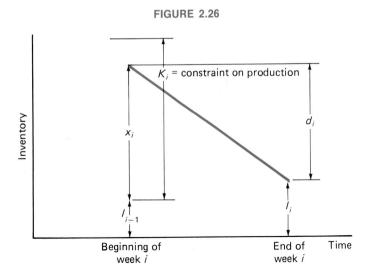

Verbal Model

Minimize   production cost + inventory cost

subject to

inventory at the end of week $t \geq 0$ $t = 1, 2, \ldots, 6$

production in week t $\leq K_t$ $t = 1, 2, \ldots, 6$

Decision Variables

$$x_t = \text{production in week } t$$

The Model

$$\text{Min} \sum_{t=1}^{6} C_t x_t + \sum_{t=1}^{6} h_t I_t$$

$$\text{s.t.} \quad I_t = I_{t-1} + x_t - d_t \quad t = 1, 2, \ldots, 6$$

$$x_t \leq K_t$$

$$x_t \geq 0 \qquad t = 1, 2, \ldots, 6$$

$$I_t \geq 0$$

In general, the structure of such models is fairly complex. That is, interactions are occurring between large numbers of variables. For example, inventory at the end of a given period t is determined by all production decisions in periods 1 through t. This is seen from the inventory equation

$$I_t = I_0 + \sum_{i=1}^{t} (x_i - d_i)$$

Therefore, the cost in period t is also determined by all production decisions in periods 1 through t. Finally, it is noted that the formulation above can be written in an equivalent form without the I_t variables appearing. Try to do this on your own.

─────── 2.15
EXAMPLE 8: THE BUMLES, INC. MINICASE (PRODUCTION AND INVENTORY CONTROL)

Bumles, Inc. uses part of its capacity to make hand-painted teapots. One teapot takes .5 hours of a painter's time. Bumles has 30 painters available. The plant is used for the teapots on Thursday, Friday and Saturday each week. During the remainder of the week the productive capacity is devoted to another product line. Not all of the 30 painters will necessarily be engaged, but each painter who is engaged is available to work any part of an 8-hour day, 2 days a week. A painter can be assigned to any 2-day schedule, and is paid for 16 hours of regular-time work, no matter what part of that time he actually spends producing teapots. If there is not enough production to keep all the workers assigned to a particular day busy for the entire day, the slack time is spent on cleaning the plant and similar activities.

If labor costs are not taken into account, the revenue from selling a teapot is $15. Demand must either be satisfied on the day on which it occurs or it is lost. Production on a given day can be used to satisfy demand that day or demand later in the week, i.e., teapots produced on Thursday can be used to satisfy demand on Friday or Saturday. However, because of the change of operations to hand-painted statues on Monday, Tuesday, and Wednesday, all teapots produced in a week must be shipped that week, i.e., there is never inventory on Thursday morning. Because of increased handling costs, it costs $.50 to carry a teapot in inventory from one day to the next. A unit of lost demand results in an all-inclusive penalty cost of $1 for a unit on Thursday, $3 on Friday, and $5 on Saturday. Painters are paid $8 per hour. Weekly demand for the teapots is 100 on Thursday, 300 on Friday, and 600 on Saturday.

Ignoring integrality conditions (i.e., allowing the possibility of fractional values of all decision variables), create an LP model that will schedule painters and production in such a way as to maximize revenue minus cost, where cost equals labor plus penalty and inventory-carrying costs. The model should be correct for any set of demands. In your formulation the first three constraints should be

$$DT = 100$$
$$DF = 300 \qquad \text{where } DT \text{ is the demand on Thursday, etc.}$$
$$DS = 600$$

In your formulation of the model, you must pay attention to relationships between production, sales, lost sales, demand, and inventory on any particular day. For example

> demand on day t = sales on day t + lost sales on day t

Solution to Example 8   In addition to the above relation between demand, sales, and lost sales, we also need the following relationship between production, inventory, and sales:

> production on day t = sales on day t + inventory at end of day t
> $-$ inventory at end of day $t - 1$

Let us define the variables:

$$St = \text{sales on day } t$$
$$Dt = \text{demand on day } t$$
$$Lt = \text{lost sales on day } t$$
$$Pt = \text{production on day } t$$
$$It = \text{inventory at end of day } t$$

FIGURE 2.27

Symbolic Bumles Spreadsheet

	A	B	C	D	E	F	G	H	I
1	BUMLES SPREADSHEET								
2									
3		Days	Thurs	Fri	Sat				
4		Demand	100	300	600				
5		Production							
6		Sales							
7		Lost Sales	+C4−C6	+D4−D6	+E4−E6				
8		End Inventory	+C5−C6	+C8+D5−D6	+D8+E5−E6				
9			TF	TS	FS				
10		Painters							
11		REVENUE−COST							
12	15*(C6+D)*								
13		------	------	------	------		------	------	------
14		TF	TS	FS			Used	Avail	Slack
15		Hrs/day			Hrs/Teapot.				
16		------	------	------	------		------	------	------
17	Prod-T	8	8		0.5		+C5	(1/E17)*(B17*C10+C17*D10)	+H17−G17
18	Prod-F	8		8	0.5		+D5	(1/E18)*(B18*C10+D18*E10)	+H18−G18
19	Prod-S		8	8	0.5		+E5	(1/E19)*(C19*D10+D19*E10)	+H19−G19
20	Workforce						+C10+D10+E10	30	+H20−G20

Decision Variables

* A12:   15*(C6+D6+E6) − 128*(C10+D10+E10) − 0.5*(C8+D8) − C7 − (3*D7) − (5*E7)

TF, TS, FS = number of painters assigned to Thursday-Friday, etc. Then the *formal LP model* is

```
MAX 15 ST + 15 SF + 15 SS − 128 TF − 128 TS − 128 FS − 0.5 IT
    − 0.5 IF − LT − 3 LF − 5 LS
SUBJECT TO
   DT = 100 ⎤
   DF = 300 ⎬ ←─────────────── demand constraints
   DS = 600 ⎦
    − 8 TF − 8 TS + 0.5 PT ≤ 0 ⎤
    − 8 TF − 8 FS + 0.5 PF ≤ 0 ⎬ ←───── production constraints
    − 8 TS − 8 FS + 0.5 PS ≤ 0 ⎦
   ST + IT − PT = 0 ⎤           inventory balance
   SF − IT + IF − PF = 0 ⎬      (defines inventory variables in
   SS − IF − PS + IS = 0 ⎦      terms of production and sales)
   IS = 0
   ST + LT − DT =  0 ⎤          demand sales relationship
   SF + LF − DF =  0 ⎬ ←─────── (defines lost sales in terms of
   SS + LS − DS =  0 ⎦          demand and sales)
   TF + TS + FS ≤ 30 ←───────── workforce constraint
```

Figures 2.27 and 2.28 show symbolic and optimized spreadsheets for the Bumles problem. In the spreadsheet representation we let the decision variables be sales on

FIGURE 2.28
Optimized Bumles Spreadsheet

	A	B	C	D	E	F	G	H	I
1	BUMLES SPREADSHEET								
2									
3	Days		Thurs	Fri	Sat				
4	Demand		100.00	300.00	600.00				
5	Production		60.00	420.00	480.00				
6	Sales		60.00	300.00	600.00				
7	Lost Sales		40.00	0.00	0.00		Optimal		
8	End Inventory		0.00	120.00	0.00		Decision Values		
9			TF	TS	FS				
10	Painters		0.00	3.75	26.25				
11	REVENUE-COST								
12	10460.00								
13	----								
14		TF	TS	FS			Used	Avail	Slack
15			Hrs/day		Hrs/Teapot				
16	----								
17	Prod-T	8.00	8.00		0.50		60.00	60.00	0.00
18	Prod-F	8.00		8.00	0.50		420.00	420.00	0.00
19	Prod-S		8.00	8.00	0.50		480.00	480.00	0.00
20	Workforce						30.00	30.00	0.00

each day, production on each day, and number of painters on each schedule. Then the lost sales on each day and ending inventory on each day are interpreted as definitional variables. Another way of saying this is that the inventory and lost sales are interpreted as dependent variables. The production and sales (as well as workers on each schedule) are interpreted as independent variables.

———— 2.16
SUMMARY

Constraints were defined to be mathematical conditions that rule out certain combinations of values for the decision variables, and **feasible** or **allowable decisions** were defined to be values of the variables that satisfy *all* the constraints. Linear programming was seen to involve **a search for a feasible decision which optimizes an objective function**. More specifically, linear programming was defined to be a mathematical model with the following properties:

1. There is a linear objective function which is to be maximized or minimized.
2. There are linear constraints, a constraint being a mathematical inequality (either $\leq$ or $\geq$) or an equality.
3. There are nonnegative decision variables.

Examples were given to show how a real-world "word problem" can be translated into a formal LP model. The examples illustrated that a profit objective leads to a Max model, whereas a cost objective gives a Min model. We also saw that a constraint of the "limitation" type is usually translated into a mathematical inequality of the $\leq$ form, and a constraint of the "requirement" type is usually translated into a $\geq$ inequality. In some situations, such as in blending problems, logical considerations will require the presence of equality constraints. Guidelines were also given on how to proceed with model formulation. **Spreadsheet representations** of an LP problem were shown, via specific examples, to have useful properties when the user is interested in manipulating the data in the model. Spreadsheet representations were compared with the **formal LP model**, and advantages of each were discussed.

———— 2.17
KEY TERMS

DECISION VARIABLES.   The variables under the decision maker's control. These are the variables that appear in the mathematical models which we have formulated in this chapter.

LINEAR FUNCTION.   A function where each variable appears in a separate term. There are no powers other than 1, and there are no logarithmic, exponential, or trigonometric terms.

OBJECTIVE FUNCTION.   Every linear program has a linear objective function which represents the goal to be either maximized or minimized.

CONSTRAINT.   A mathematical inequality (a inequality constraint) or equality (a equality constraint) that must be satisfied by the variables in the model.

CONSTRAINT FUNCTION.   The left-hand side of a constraint.

RIGHT-HAND SIDE.   The number on the right-hand side of a constraint.

LINEAR CONSTRAINT.   A constraint such that the constraint function is linear. Every linear program has linear constraints.

NONNEGATIVITY CONDITIONS.   Conditions in a model which stipulate that the decision variables can have only nonnegative (*positive* or *zero*) values.

OPTIMIZE.   To maximize or minimize.

DECISION.   A set of numerical values for the decision variables.

FEASIBLE DECISION.   A decision that satisfies *all* the constraints of a model, including the nonnegativity conditions. Feasible means allowable.

OPTIMAL DECISION.   A feasible decision that optimizes the objective function.

OPTIMAL PRODUCTION PLAN.   The optimal decision for a production model, that is, the optimal quantities of each product to be produced.

OPTIMAL PRODUCT MIX.   A synonym for optimal production plan.

CONSTRAINED OPTIMIZATION MODEL.   A model whose objective is to find values of decision variables that optimize an objective function subject to constraints.

LOTUS 1–2–3.   A spreadsheet program for the PC.

WHAT'SBEST!   A spreadsheet program which can also optimize the spreadsheet representation of an LP.

VINO.   A spreadsheet program which can also optimize the spreadsheet representation of an LP.

SPREADSHEET.   A grid whose cells contain labels, parameters, numbers, and formulas.

SYMBOLIC SPREADSHEET.   A spreadsheet representation with each formula explicitly shown.

VALUE SPREADSHEET.   A spreadsheet representation with all formulas numerically evaluated.

OPTIMIZED SPREADSHEET.   A value spreadsheet which is optimal.

FORMAL LP MODEL.   The mathematical representation of an LP problem.

SPREADSHEET REPRESENTATION.   The model is spreadsheet format.

MATRIX GENERATOR.   A computer program which transforms raw data into numbers to be directly employed in a model.

PARAMETER.   A number or symbol in a model, which must have a numerical value supplied by the user.

MAJOR CONCEPTS QUIZ

True–False

1. **T** F   In the context of modeling, restrictions on the allowable decisions are called constraints.
2. T **F**   Not every LP has to have constraints.
3. T **F**   Any model with an objective function, constraints, and decision variables is an LP.
4. T **F**   A limitation is expressed as a $\geq$ constraint.
5. T **F**   The nonnegativity conditions mean that all decision variables must be positive.
6. **T** F   Since fractional values for decision variables may not be physically meaningful, in practice (for the purpose of implementation) we often round the optimal LP solution to integer values.
7. T **F**   All the constraints in an LP are inequalities.
8. **T** F   Properly defining the decision variables is an important step in model formulation.
9. **T** F   The objective function of a cost-minimization model need only consider variable, as opposed to sunk, cost.
10. **T** F   The way in which a problem has been formulated as a model is of considerable interest to the manager, who may one day have to pass judgment on the validity of the model.

Multiple Choice

11. A constraint limits the values
    a. that the objective function can assume
    b. that the decision variables can assume
    c. neither of the above
    d. both a and b

12. Constraints may represent
    a. limitations
    b. requirements
    c. balance conditions
    d. all of the above

13. Linear programming is
    a. a constrained optimization model
    b. a constrained decision-making model
    c. a mathematical programming model
    d. all of the above

14. In an LP Max model
    a. the objective function is maximized
    b. the objective function is maximized and then it is determined whether this occurs at an allowable decision
    c. the objective function is maximized over the allowable set of decisions
    d. all of the above

15. The *distinguishing* feature of an LP (as opposed to more general mathematical programming models) is
    a. the problem has an objective function and constraints
    b. all functions in the problem are linear
    c. optimal values for the decision variables are produced

16. In translating a word problem into a formal model, it is often helpful to
    a. express each constraint in words
    b. express the objective in words
    c. verbally identify the decision variables
    d. all of the above

17. Model formulation is important because
    a. it enables us to use algebraic techniques
    b. in a business context, most managers prefer to work with formal models
    c. it forces management to address a clearly defined problem
    d. it allows the manager to better communicate with the management scientist and therefore to be more discriminating in hiring policies

18. The nonnegativity requirement is included in an LP because
    a. it makes the model easier to solve
    b. it makes the model correspond more closely to the real-world problem
    c. neither of the above
    d. both a and b

Questions 19 through 26 refer to the following problem:

Three Latvian terrorists, Lotta Crapp, Claire Voyante, and Fickle Finger, are en route to Hollywood to seek their fortune. The flight time is 40 hours at a fuel cost of $100 per gallon. In a Hollywood deli they strike up a quick friendship with the notorious Hymen Putter. Hymen's total income per year is $40,000—his alimony payments are $60,000. Knowing almost everyone in town, Hy is able to spin out a stairway to the stars for our three fortune seekers. They are now inspecting capsule medicine products by passing the capsules over a special lighting table where they visually check for cracked, partially filled, or improperly tinted capsules. Currently, any of our three moguls can be assigned to the visual inspection task. These ladies, however, differ in height, accuracy, and speed abilities. Consequently, their employer (Flora Fortune) pays them at slightly different wage rates. The significant differences are summed up in Figure 2.29.

FIGURE 2.29

INSPECTOR	SPEED (units/h)	ACCURACY (%)	HOURLY WAGE	HEIGHT
Lotta	300	98	$2.95	7 ft 2 in.
Claire	200	99	2.60	4 ft 8 in.
Fickle	350	96	2.75	5 ft 2 in.

Operating on a full 8-hour shift, Flora needs to have at least 2000 capsules inspected with no more than 2% of these capsules having inspection errors. In addition, because of the devastating Latvian autoimmune syndrome, no one lady can be assigned this task for more than 4 hours per day. Let

$$X_1 = \text{number of hours worked by Lotta}$$

$$X_2 = \text{number of hours worked by Claire}$$

$$X_3 = \text{number of hours worked by Fickle}$$

The objective is to minimize the cost of 8 hours of inspection. Assume that the inspection process must be in operation for all 8 hours. In other words, continuous production must occur during the 8-hour period. In addition, Lotta, Claire, and Fickle are the only inspectors, no more than one inspector can work at a time, and the plumber works at most 4 hours per day.

19. A correct accuracy constraint is
    a. $(0.98)(300)X_1 + (0.99)(200)X_2 + (0.96)(350)X_3 \geq 2000$
    b. $(0.02)(300)X_1 + (0.01)(200)X_2 + (0.04)(350)X_3 \leq (0.02)(2000)$
    c. $-2X_2 + 7X_3 \leq 0$
    d. none of the above
20. The production requirement constraint is correctly written as $300X_1 + 200X_2 + 350X_3 = 2000$.
    a. true
    b. false
21. Excluding the nonnegativity constraints, a proper formulation for this problem will contain six constraints.
    a. true
    b. false
22. It is possible that the correct formulation for this problem will have no feasible decisions. (Answer this question for the given data.)
    a. true
    b. false
23. If it were not for the accuracy requirement and the 4-hour limitation, the optimal solution would have only Fickle working.
    a. true
    b. false
24. The optimal solution will require that at least two of the three employees inspect.
    a. true
    b. false

25. A feasible policy is provided by
    a. 4 hours Claire, 4 hours Fickle
    b. 4 hours Lotta, 4 hours Claire
    c. both a and b

26. Let policy A be $x_1 = 4$, $x_2 = 4$, $x_3 = 0$. Let policy B be $x_1 = 3$, $x_2 = 4$, $x_3 = 1$. Note that each policy is feasible. Since A produces 2000 capsules and B produces 2050, A is preferred.
    a. true
    b. false

Questions 27 through 39 deal with spreadsheet concepts.

27. A parameter in a model can be a number or a symbol.
    a. T
    b. F

28. Consider the constraint $10E + 15F \le R$, where R is a parameter denoting hours in department A. Now suppose values of R are given by $(1 - e^{-(.05)MA})$. If we substitute this into the original constraint it becomes $10E + 15F \le 200 (1 - e^{-(.05)MA})$. This new constraint is linear in E, F, and the new parameter MA.
    a. T
    b. F

29. The symbolic spreadsheet is derived from a value spreadsheet.
    a. T
    b. F

30. One advantage of the spreadsheet representation is that it provides a convenient way to do parametric analysis.
    a. T
    b. F

31. In the symbolic spreadsheet representation of an LP, a constraint function is represented as a formula in a cell.
    a. T
    b. F

32. A spreadsheet representation can sometimes eliminate the need for a matrix generator and thereby enable the manager to directly manipulate raw data.
    a. T
    b. F

33. For feasible decisions, the slack cells in the value spreadsheet will contain nonnegative numbers.
    a. T
    b. F

34. Lotus 1–2–3 can be used to create a spreadsheet representation of an LP but it will *not* optimize the spreadsheet.
    a. T
    b. F

35. A parameter
    a. is a number in a model, or a symbol which is exogenous to the model (i.e., a symbol whose numerical value must be supplied to the model)
    b. may be represented by a symbol (such as "R") whose value must be determined by the model
    c. both of the above

36. A suggested way to create a spreadsheet representation of an LP is to first write out the formal LP model and then use this as a guideline to create a symbolic spreadsheet.
    a. T
    b. F

37. A spreadsheet representation of an LP can be useful because
   a. parameters representing raw data may enter into the model nonlinearly
   b. it makes the model easy to debug
   c. both of the above
38. A matrix generator
   a. transforms raw data into numbers which are needed in the LP
   b. is often employed in real-world problem solving
   c. is often fit in as a "front end" for traditional LP codes
   d. all of the above
39. A spreadsheet is a grid whose cells may contain
   a. labels
   b. numbers
   c. parameters
   d. formulas
   e. all of the above

Answers			
1. T	11. d	21. a	31. T
2. F	12. d	22. b	32. T
3. F	13. d	23. b	33. T
4. F	14. c	24. a	34. T
5. F	15. b	25. b	35. a
6. T	16. d	26. b	36. T
7. F	17. c	27. T	37. a
8. T	18. b	28. F	38. d
9. T	19. c	29. F	39. e
10. T	20. b	30. T	

PROBLEMS

2-1. Match each of the following terms with the most appropriate description below.

(a) Linear program.
(b) Requirement.
(c) Variable cost.
(d) Sunk cost.

(e) Decision variables.
(f) Constraint function.
(g) Restriction.
(h) Limitation.

1. The unknowns in an LP which represent decisions to be made.
2. Usually, a constraint of $\geq$ form.
3. A concept that is proper to include in the model.
4. Usually, not relevant to the model (break-even analysis would be an exception).
5. Usually, a constraint of $\leq$ form.
6. The left-hand side of the constraint.
7. Synonymous with constraint.
8. A special type of constrained optimization model.

2-2. Which of the following mathematical relationships could be found in a linear programming model? For those relationships that could not be found in an LP, state the reasons.

(a) $4x_1 + 12x_2 - \frac{3}{2}x_3 \leq 0$
(b) $-x_1 + 3x_2^2 - x_3 \leq 55$
(c) $2x_1 - 4x_3 \leq -12$
(d) $x_1 + 2x_1x_2 + x_3 = 43$
(e) $6x_1 + 4x_2 = 2\sqrt{x_3} - 5$
(f) $0x_1 + 0x_2 + x_3 = 22$

(g) $4x_1 + e^{x_2} + 4x_3 \leq 24$

(h) $20x_1 - 12x_2 + 1.414x_3 \geq 49$

2-3. *A Production Problem* (*see Example 1*) The Swelte Glove Company manufactures and sells two products. The company makes a profit of $12 for each unit of product 1 sold and a profit of $4 for each unit of product 2. The labor-hour requirements for the products in each of the three production departments are summarized in Figure 2.30. The supervisors of these departments have estimated that the following numbers of labor hours will be available during the next month: 800 hours in department 1, 600 hours in department 2, and 2000 hours in department 3. Assuming that the company is interested in maximizing profits, show the linear programming model of this problem.

FIGURE 2.30
Swelte Glove Company Production Data

	PRODUCT	
DEPARTMENT	1	2
1	1	2
2	1	3
3	2	3

2-4. *A Production Problem* (*see Example 1*) Wood Walker is a self-employed furniture maker. He makes three different style of tables, A, B, and C. Each model of table requires a certain amount of time for the cutting of component parts, for assembling, and for painting. Wood can sell all the units he makes. Furthermore, the model B may be sold without painting. Using the data in Figure 2.31, formulate an LP model that will help Wood determine the product mix that will maximize his profit.

FIGURE 2.31
Wood Walker Data

MODEL	CUTTING	TIME PER TABLE (hrs) ASSEMBLING	PAINTING	PROFIT PER TABLE
A	2	1	3	$40
B	3	3	5	55
Unpainted B	3	3	0	30
C	3	6	5	80
Capacity (hrs/month)	90	60	80	

2-5. *Financial Planning* Willie Maykit is president of a one-person investment firm that manages stock portfolios for a number of clients. A new client has just requested the firm to handle a $100,000 portfolio. The client would like to restrict the portfolio to a mix of the three stocks shown in Figure 2.32. Formulate an LP to show how many shares of each stock Willie should purchase to maximize the estimated total annual return.

FIGURE 2.32
Portfolio Mix

STOCK	PRICE PER SHARE	ESTIMATED ANNUAL RETURN PER SHARE	MAXIMUM POSSIBLE INVESTMENT
Gofer Crude	$60	$7	$60,000
Can Oil	25	3	25,000
Sloth Petroleum	20	3	30,000

2-6. *A Blending Problem (see Example 2)* Doug E. Starr, the manager of Heavenly Dog Kennels, Inc., provides lodging for pets. The kennel's dog food is made by mixing two soybean products to obtain a well-balanced dog diet. The data for the two products are shown in Figure 2.33. If Doug wants to be sure that his dogs receive at least 5 ounces of protein and 2 ounces of fat per day, what is the minimum cost mix of the two dog food products?

FIGURE 2.33
Well-Balanced Dog Diet

SOYBEAN PRODUCT	COST PER OUNCE	PROTEIN (%)	FAT (%)
1	$0.05	40	15
2	0.02	15	18

2-7. *A Blending Problem* McNaughton, Inc. produces two steak sauces, Spicy Diablo and mild Red Baron. These sauces are both made by blending two ingredients, A and B. A certain level of flexibility is permitted in the formulas for these products. The allowable percentages, along with revenue and cost data, are given in Figure 2.34. Up to 40 quarts of A and 30 quarts of B could be purchased. McNaughton can sell as much of these sauces as it produces. Formulate an LP whose objective is to maximize the net revenue from the sale of the sauces.

FIGURE 2.34
Allowable Percentages for McNaughton, Inc.

SAUCE	INGREDIENT A	INGREDIENT B	SALES PRICE PER QUART
Spicy Diablo	at least 25%	at least 50%	$3.35
Red Baron	at most 75%	*	2.85
Cost per Quart	$1.60	$2.59	

* No explicit maximum or minimum percentage.

2-8. *A Production Problem (see Example 1)* Cori Ander's Spice Company has a limited supply of two herbal ingredients that are used in the production of seasonings. Cori uses the two ingredients, HBO1 and HBO2, to produce either turmeric or paprika. The marketing department reports that although the firm can sell all of the paprika it can produce, it can only sell up to a maximum of 1200 bottles of turmeric. Unused herbal ingredients can be sold at $0.30 per ounce of HBO1 and $0.20 per ounce of HBO2. Additional data are shown in Figure 2.35. Formulate a revenue-maximizing LP.

FIGURE 2.35
Cori Ander's Spice Company

SEASONING	INGREDIENTS (oz/bottle) HBO1	HBO2	DEMAND (bottles)	SALES PRICE PER BOTTLE
Turmeric	4	1	1200	$2.60
Paprika	3	2	Unlimited	2.10
Availability (ounces)	8000	7000		

2-9. *Another Blending Problem* Guy Wires, superintendent of buildings and grounds at the University of Chicago, is planning to put fertilizer on the grass in the quadrangle area early in the spring. The grass needs nitrogen, phosphorus, and potash in at least the amounts given in Figure 2.36. Three kinds of commercial fertilizer are available; analysis and price are given in Figure 2.37. Guy can buy as much of each of these fertilizers as he wishes and mix them together before applying them to the grass. Formulate an LP model to determine how much of each fertilizer he should buy to satisfy the requirements at minimum cost.

FIGURE 2.36
Total Grass Requirements

MINERAL	MINIMUM WEIGHT (lb)
Nitrogen	10
Phosphorus	7
Potash	5

FIGURE 2.37
Fertilizer Characteristics (per 1000 lb)

FERTILIZER	NITROGEN CONTENT (lb)	PHOSPHORUS CONTENT (lb)	POTASH CONTENT (lb)	PRICE
I	25	10	5	$10
II	10	5	10	8
III	5	10	5	7

2-10. *Diet Planning (see Example 2)* Pearce Dears, former encounter group trainer, has turned into a feedlot operator. He desires to feed his animals in such a way as to meet their nutritional requirements at minimum cost. Pearce is considering the use of corn, soybeans, oats, and alfalfa. Figure 2.38 shows the relevant dietary information per pound of grain (e.g., 1 pound of corn provides 10 milligrams of protein). Formulate an LP model to determine a dietary mix that will satisfy the daily requirements at minimum cost.

FIGURE 2.38
Nutrients per Pound of Grain

NUTRIENT	CORN	SOYBEANS	OATS	ALFALFA	DAILY REQUIREMENT
Protein (mg)	10	9	11	8	Minimum of 40 mg
Calcium (mg)	50	45	58	50	Minimum of 120 mg
Fat (mg)	30	90	10	5	Maximum of 100 mg, Minimum of 20 mg
Calories	900	1200	1000	6000	Minimum of 4500 calories
Cost per Pound	60	30	35	85	

2-11. Two products are manufactured on each of three machines. A pound of each product requires a specified number of hours on each machine, as presented in Figure 2.39. Total hours available on machines 1, 2, and 3 are 10, 16, and 12, respectively. The profit contributions per pound of products 1 and 2 are 4 and 3, respectively. Define the decision variables and formulate this problem as a profit-maximizing linear program.

FIGURE 2.39
Machine-Time Data (hrs)

	PRODUCT	
MACHINE	1	2
1	3	2
2	1	4
3	5	3

2-12. *Capital Budgeting (see Example 5)*   An investment company must choose among four projects which are competing for a fixed investment budget of $1,200,000. The net investment and estimated returns for each project are shown in Figure 2.40. Each of these projects can be funded at any fractional level $\leq 100\%$. The company requires a 30% return, and wishes to minimize the risk. Assume the risk is additive. For example, the risk of funding Shale Oil at 20% and the office building at 50% will be $(0.2)(7) + (0.5)(3) = 0.29$. Formulate an LP model where the decision variables are the fraction of each project that should be undertaken.

FIGURE 2.40
Investment Projects

PROJECT	INVESTMENT	ESTIMATED RETURNS	RISK
Shopping Centers	$400,000	$575,000	5
Shale Oil	500,000	750,000	7
Office Buildings	350,000	425,000	3
Low-Income Housing	450,000	510,000	3

2-13. *Break-Even Analysis* (*see Example 6*)   Reese Eichler, a manufacturer of superfluous air filtration equipment, produces two units, the Umidaire and the Depollinator. Data pertaining to sales price and costs are shown in Figure 2.41. Reese's firm has already contracted to provide 500 Umidaires and would like to calculate the break-even quantities for both types of units. Formulate the cost-minimizing LP model.

FIGURE 2.41

Sales Price and Cost

PRODUCT	SELLING PRICE PER UNIT	VARIABLE COST PER UNIT	FIXED COST
Umidaire	$450	$240	$150,000
Depollinator	700	360	240,000

2-14. *A Production Problem* (*see Example 1*)   The per unit requirements and net revenues for forestry equipment and earthmoving equipment are given in Figure 2.42. Define the decision variables, and formulate a revenue-maximizing linear program.

FIGURE 2.42

Forestry and Earthmoving Equipment Data

EQUIPMENT	IRON (lbs)	LABOR (hrs)	REQUIREMENTS TRANSMISSIONS	HEAT TREATMENT (hrs)	NET REVENUE
Forestry	700	50	1	30	$802
Earthmoving	4200	110	1	12	660
Availability	680,000	21,000	290	6,000	

2-15. *Portfolio Planning*   An investment company currently has $10 million to invest. The goal is to maximize expected return earned over the next year. Their four investment possibilities are summarized in Figure 2.43. In addition, the company has specified that at least 30% of the funds must be placed in common stock and treasury bonds, and no more than 40% in money market funds and municipal bonds. All of the $10 million currently on hand will be invested. Formulate an LP model which tells how much money to invest in each instrument.

FIGURE 2.43

Summary of Investment Possibilities

INVESTMENT POSSIBILITY	EXPECTED EARNED RETURN (%)	MAXIMUM ALLOWABLE INVESTMENT (MILLIONS)
Treasury Bonds	8	$5
Common Stock	6	7
Money Market	12	2
Municipal Bonds	9	4

2-16. *Production Assignment*   A corporation has decided to introduce three new products. Two branch plants now have excess production capacity. Plant capacities and manufacturing costs are shown in Figure 2.44. Identify the decision variables and formulate an LP model that assigns production of the three products to the two plants so as to meet demand and minimize cost.

FIGURE 2.44
Manufacturing Costs per Unit

PLANT	PRODUCT A	PRODUCT B	PRODUCT C	CAPACITY
1	$7	$12	$13	200
2	14	9	8	250
Demand	120	90	180	

2-17. *Transportation Model (see Example 4)*   Bob Frapples packages holiday gift-wrapped exotic fruits. His packages are wrapped at two locations from which they are sent to five wholesalers. The cost of packaging his product at locations 1 and 2 is 5.25 and 5.70, respectively. Bob's forecasts for demand indicate that shipments must be as indicated in Figure 2.45. Wrapping capacity at location 1 is 20,000 packages and at location 2 is 12,000 packages. The distribution costs from the two locations to the five wholesalers are given in Figure 2.46. Formulate an LP model to determine how many packages Bob should send from each location to each wholesaler.

FIGURE 2.45
Wholesaler Demand

WHOLESALER	1	2	3	4	5
SHIPMENT REQUIRED	4000	6000	2000	10,000	8000

FIGURE 2.46
Distribution Costs

FROM LOCATION	TO WHOLESALER 1	2	3	4	5
1	0.06	0.04	0.12	0.09	0.05
2	0.15	0.09	0.05	0.08	0.08

**More
Challenging
Problems**

2-18. *A Scheduling Problem*   In a calculated financial maneuver, **PROTRAC** has acquired a new blast furnace facility for producing foundry iron. The company's management science group has been assigned the task of providing support for the quantitative planning of foundry activities. The first directive is to provide an answer to the following question: How many new slag-pit personnel should be hired and trained over the next six months? The requirements for trained employees in the pits and monthly wage rates for the next six months are given in Figure 2.47.

FIGURE 2.47

Labor Requirements and Wage Rates

	MONTH					
	JAN.	FEB.	MAR.	APR.	MAY	JUNE
Labor Requirements (hours)	8000	7000	8000	9000	11000	8000
Monthly Wage Rates	$800	$800	**$800**	$900	$900	$900

Trainees are hired at the beginning of each month. One consideration we wish to take into account is the union rule that it takes one month of classroom instruction before a worker can be considered well enough trained to work in the pits. Therefore, it is mandatory that a trainee be hired at least a month before a worker is actually needed. Each classroom student uses 100 hours of the time of a trained slag-pit employee so 100 less hours of the employee's time are available for work in the pit. We are also informed that, by contractual agreement, each trained employee can work up to 150 hours a month (total time, instructing plus in the pit). If the maximum total time available from trained employees exceeds a month's requirements, management may lay off at most 10% of the trained employees the beginning of the month. All employees are paid a full month's salary even if they are laid off. A trainee costs $400 a month in salary and other benefits. There are 60 trained employees available at the beginning of January. Formulate the hiring-and-training problem as a linear programming model. HINT: Let x_t denote the number of trained employees on hand at the beginning of month t before any layoffs, let y_t denote the number of trainees hired in month t, and let z_t denote the number of trained employee laid off at the beginning of month t.

2-19. *Farm Management*   A firm operates four farms of comparable productivity. Each farm has a certain amount of usable acreage and a supply of labor hours to plant and tend the crops. The data for the upcoming season are shown in Figure 2.48. The organization is considering three crops for planting. These crops differ primarily in their expected profit per acre and in the amount of labor they require, as shown in Figure 2.49.

FIGURE 2.48

Acreage and Labor Data by Farm

FARM	USABLE ACREAGE	LABOR HOURS AVAILABLE PER MONTH
1	500	1700
2	900	3000
3	300	900
4	700	2200

FIGURE 2.49

Acreage, Labor, and Profit Data by Crop

CROP	MAXIMUM ACREAGE	MONTHLY LABOR HOURS REQUIRED PER ACRE	EXPECTED PROFIT PER ACRE
A	700	2	$500
B	800	4	200
C	300	3	300

Furthermore, the total acreage that can be devoted to any particular crop is limited by the associated requirements for harvesting equipment. In order to maintain a roughly uniform work load among the farms, management's policy is that the percentage of usable acreage planted must be the same at each farm. However, any combination of the crops may be grown at any of the farms as long as all constraints are satisfied (including the uniform-work-load requirement). Management wishes to know how many acres of each crop should be planted at the respective farms in order to maximize expected profit. Formulate this as a linear programming model.

2-20. *A Blending Problem*   A vineyard wishes to blend four different vintages to make three types of blended wine. Restrictions are placed on the percentage composition of the blends (see Figure 2.50). Any amounts of Blend B and Blend C may be sold, but Blend A is considered a premium blend and therefore no more than 100 gallons are to be sold. Formulate an LP model that will make the best use of the vintages on hand.

FIGURE 2.50
Composition of Blends

BLEND	VINTAGE 1	2	3	4	SALES PRICE PER GALLON
A	at least 60% 1 & 2		*	at most 10%	$19
B	at least 40% 1 & 2		*	*	9
C	*	*	*	at most 60%	6
Supply (gallons)	150	300	300	500	

* Indicates no restriction.

2-21. *A Scheduling Problem (see Example 3)*   A certain restaurant operates 7 days a week. Waitresses are hired to work 6 hours per day. The union contract specifies that each waitress must work 5 consecutive days and then have 2 consecutive days off. Each waitress receives the same weekly salary. Staffing requirements are shown in Figure 2.51. Assume that this cycle of requirements repeats indefinitely, and ignore the fact that the number of waitresses hired must be an integer. The manager wishes to find an employment schedule that satisfies these requirements at a minimum cost. Formulate this problem as a linear program.

FIGURE 2.51
Waitress Staffing Requirements

DAY	MINIMUM NUMBER OF WAITRESS HOURS REQUIRED
Monday	150
Tuesday	200
Wednesday	400
Thursday	300
Friday	700
Saturday	800
Sunday	300

2-22. *A Production Problem*   A plant can manufacture four different products (A, B, C, D) in any combination. Each product requires time on each of four machines as shown in

Figure 2.52. Each machine is available 128 hours per week. Products A, B, C, and D may be sold at respective per pound prices of $5, $4, $3, and $4. Variable labor costs are $4 per hour for machines 1 and 2, and $3 per hour for machines 3 and 4. Material cost for each pound of product A is $2. The material cost is $1 for each pound of products B, C, and D. Formulate a profit-maximizing LP model for this problem.

FIGURE 2.52
Machine Time (Minutes per Pound of Product)

PRODUCT	MACHINE				MAXIMUM DEMAND
	1	2	3	4	
A	12	8	5	12	480
B	7	9	10	5	550
C	8	4	7	5	420
D	10	10	3	10	200

2-23. A manufacturer has four jobs, A, B, C, and D, that must be produced this month. Each job may be handled in any of three shops. The time required for each job in each shop, the cost per hour in each shop, and the number of hours available this month in each shop are given in Figure 2.53. It is also possible to split each job among the shops in any proportion. For example, one-fourth of job A can be done in 8 hours in shop 1, and one-third of job C can be done in 19 hours in shop 3. The manufacturer wishes to determine how many hours of each job should be handled by each shop in order to minimize the total cost of completing all four jobs. Identify the decision variables and formulate an LP model for this problem.

FIGURE 2.53
Job-Shop Data

SHOP	JOB				COST PER HOUR OF SHOP TIME	SHOP TIME AVAILABLE (hr)
	A	B	C	D		
1	32	151	72	118	$89	160
2	39	147	61	126	81	160
3	46	155	57	121	84	160

2-24. *Financial Planning* An investor has two money-making activities, coded Alpha and Beta, available at the beginning of each of the next four years. Each dollar invested in Alpha at the beginning of a year yields a return two years later (in time for immediate investment). Each dollar invested in Beta at the beginning of a year yields a return three years later. A third investment possibility, construction projects, will become available at the beginning of the second year. Each dollar invested in construction yields a return one year later. (Construction will be available at the beginning of the third and fourth years also.) The investor starts with $10,000 at the beginning of the first year and wants to maximize the total amount of money available at the end of the fourth year. The returns on investments are given in Figure 2.54.

(a) Identify the decision variables and formulate an LP model. HINT: Let M_i be the money available at the beginning of year i and maximize M_5 subject to the appropriate constraints.

(b) Can you determine the solution by direct analysis?

FIGURE 2.54
Return on Investment

ACTIVITY	RETURN PER DOLLAR INVESTED
Alpha	$1.40
Beta	1.80
Construction	1.20

2-25. *A Process Mix Problem* A small firm has two processes for blending each of two products, charcoal starter fluid and lighter fluid for cigarette lighters. The firm is attempting to decide how many hours to run each process. The inputs and outputs for running the processes for one hour are given in Figure 2.55. Let x_1 and x_2 be the number of hours the company decides to use process 1 and process 2, respectively. Because of a federal allocation program, the maximum amount of kerosene and benzene available is 300 units and 450 units, respectively. Sales commitments require that at least 600 units of starter fluid and 225 units of lighter fluid be produced. The per hour profits that accrue from process 1 and process 2 are p_1 and p_2, respectively. Formulate this as a profit-maximizing linear programming model.

(handwritten margin note: decision variables)

FIGURE 2.55
Units of Input and Output per Hour

PROCESS	INPUTS		OUTPUTS	
	KEROSENE	BENZENE	STARTER FLUID	LIGHTER FLUID
1	3	9	15	6
2	12	6	9	24

2-26. *A Scheduling Problem* While it is operating out of Stockholm, the aircraft carrier *Mighty* is on maneuvers from Monday through Friday and in port over the weekend. Next week the captain would like to give shore leave for Monday through Friday to as many sailors as possible. However, he must carry out the maneuvers for the week and satisfy navy regulations. The regulations are

(a) Sailors work either the A.M. shift (midnight to noon) or the P.M. shift (noon to midnight) any day they work, and during a week they must remain on the same shift every day they work.

(b) Each sailor who works must be on duty exactly four days, even if there is not enough "real work" on some days.

FIGURE 2.56
Sailors per Shift Day

	M	T	W	T	F
A.M.	900	300	700	750	500
P.M.	400	800	650	850	1000

The number of sailors required each shift of each day is shown in Figure 2.56. Formulate this problem as a linear programming problem. Define your variables in such a way that it is obvious how to implement the solution if one were to solve the LP you suggest (i.e., so that one would know how many sailors work on each day).

2-27. In the human diet, 16 essential nutrients have been identified. Suppose that there are 116 foods. A pound of food j contains a_{ij} pounds of nutrient i. Suppose that a human being must have N_i pounds of each nutrient i in the daily diet and that a pound of food j costs c_j cents. What is the least-cost daily diet satisfying all nutritional requirements? Use summation notation in the formulation of this problem. Aside from the question of palatability, can you think of an important constraint that this problem omits?

2-28. *An Arbitrage Problem* A speculator operates a silo with a capacity of 5000 bushels for storing corn. At the beginning of month 1, the silo contains 4000 bushels. Estimates of the selling and purchase prices of corn during the next four months are given in Figure 2.57. Corn sold during any given month is removed from the silo at the beginning of that month. Thus 4000 bushels are available for sale in month 1. Corn bought during any given month is put into the silo during the middle of that month, but it cannot be sold until the following month. Assume that the cost of storing the corn is based on average inventory and that it costs $.008 to store one bushel for one month. The storage cost for a month must be paid at the end of the month. All purchases must be paid for with cash by the delivery time. The speculator has $60 to invest and has no intention of borrowing to buy corn or pay storage costs. Therefore, if he has no cash at the beginning of a month, he must sell some of his stock to pay the storage charge at the end of the month and to pay for the corn if he purchases any. Given the sales and purchase prices and the storage cost, the speculator wishes to know how much corn to buy and sell each month so as to maximize total profits shortly after the beginning of the fourth month (which means after any sale that may occur in that month). Formulate an LP model for this problem. HINT: Let A_t denote bushels in the silo immediately after delivering the quantity sold in month t (x_t), and B_t bushels in the silo immediately after receiving the quantity purchased in month t (y_t), and P_t the cash position at the end of month t.

FIGURE 2.57
Selling and Purchase Price Data

MONTH	PURCHASE PRICE PER 1000 BUSHELS	SELLING PRICE PER 1000 BUSHELS
1	$40	$35
2	50	50
3	70	60
4	70	70

2-29. *Purchasing* Jack Bienstaulk is responsible for purchasing canned goods for GAGA food service at a large university. He knows what the demand will be over the course

FIGURE 2.58
Demand and Cost Data

	SEP.	OCT.	NOV.	DEC.	JAN.	FEB.	MAR.	APR.	MAY
Demand (cases)	1000	900	850	500	600	1000	1000	1000	500
Cost per Case	$20	$20	$20	$21	$21	$21	$22	$22	$22

of the school year and he has estimated purchase prices as well. These data are shown in Figure 2.58. He may purchase ahead of demand to avoid price increases, but there is a cost of carrying inventory of $0.20 per case per month applied to inventory on hand at the end of a month. Formulate a cost-minimizing LP that will help Jack determine the timing of his purchases. HINT: Let P_t be the number of cases purchased in month t and I_t be the number of cases in inventory at the end of month t.

Spreadsheet-Related Problems

2-30. *Portfolio Planning with the CAPM Model* An investment company currently has $10 million to invest. Its goal is to maximize expected return over the next year. The company wants to use the capital asset pricing model (CAPM) to determine each investment's expected return. The CAPM formula is:

$$ER = Rf + b * (Rm - Rf)$$

where
ER = expected return

Rf = risk-free rate

b = investment beta (market risk)

Rm = market return

The market return and risk-free rate fluctuate, and the company wants to be able to reevaluate its decision on a weekly basis. Its four investment possibilities are summarized in Figure 2.59. In addition, the company has specified that at least 30% of the funds must be placed in treasury bonds and money markets, and no more than 40% in common stock and municipal bonds. All of the $10 million currently on hand will be invested.

(a) Formulate this problem as an LP model using LOTUS 1–2–3 and VINO or What's*Best!* The spreadsheet should be constructed in such a way that the market return and the risk-free rate are entered directly and the appropriate LP model is generated.

(b) Optimize the model if the market return is 12% and the risk-free rate is 6%.

FIGURE 2.59

INVESTMENT POSSIBILITY	BETA	MAXIMUM ALLOWABLE INVESTMENT (MILLIONS)
Treasury Bonds	0	7
Common Stock	1	2
Money Market	$\frac{1}{3}$	5
Municipal Bonds	$\frac{1}{2}$	4

2-31. *Work Force and Production Planning* Review the PROTRAC E and F model discussed in Section 2.2 (See Figures 2.3 through 2.7). Now assume that the available production hours in departments A and B depend on the number of workers assigned to each department. Management decides that it is reasonable to approximate the capacity in these departments with the functions shown below:

$$\text{Capacity Dept. A} = 200(1 - e^{-.05(MA)})$$

$$\text{Capacity Dept. B} = 250(1 - e^{-0.8(MB)})$$

where MA and MB are the number of people assigned to departments A and B respectively. In the original version of this problem, it was assumed that 28 people were assigned to department A (i.e., $MA = 28$) and 13 were assigned to department B (i.e., $MB = 13$). Thus

$$\text{Capacity Dept. A} = 200(1 - e^{-1.4}) = 150.68$$

$$\text{Capacity Dept. B} = 250(1 - e^{-1.04}) = 161.64$$

The capacities were rounded to 150 and 160 respectively for that particular problem.

(a) Create a spreadsheet in which the number of people in departments A and B and the number of units of E and F can be entered directly. The resulting spreadsheet should include all of the information presented in the spreadsheet in Figure 2.6.

(b) Assume that 36 people are assigned to department A and 17 people are assigned to department B. Use your spreadsheet to determine if the plan $E = 6$ and $F = 9$ is feasible and what profit it would yield. Find the best solution you can in three attempts.

(c) Use VINO or What's*Best!* to find the optimal production policy when $MA = 36$ and $MB = 17$.

(d) Assume $MA = 28$. Plot the optimal profit as a function of MB for MB ranging from 10 to 30 in intervals of 2. To do this, your optimizer will have to be run 11 times and you then plot the data. Alternatively, after the 11 runs of data have been obtained, you may wish to use the graphics capabilities of LOTUS 1–2–3 to plot the data. What phenomenon does the graph of this optimal profit function illustrate?

**More Difficult
Spreadsheet
Exercises**

The following three problems are for those who wish to have more practice and depth in spreadsheet usage. The problems illustrate LOTUS 1–2–3 capabilities for "table lookups," use of a "SUM function," and use of the "If function." These features are explained in the LOTUS 1–2–3 manual. In the answers to these problems you will see a "$" symbol in some of the formulas. This symbol can be ignored in reading these formulas. The "$" symbol is yet another useful feature of LOTUS 1–2–3, one that makes it easier to construct and copy expressions. Your LOTUS 1–2–3 manual will explain this usage.

2-32. *Waitress Scheduling, Using Table Lookup (See Example 3 and Problem 2-21.)* In order to create the spreadsheet for this problem, you will need to use a "Table Lookup" command. This shows another versatile feature of spreadsheet usage. A certain restaurant operates 7 days a week. Waitresses are hired to work 6 effective hours per day. The restaurant attracts individuals and small groups, which we will call regular demand. In addition, the restaurant attracts a number of larger groups (Rotary, Lions, Quarterback Club, etc.) that schedule weekly meetings. The union contract specifies that each waitress must work 5 consecutive days and then have 2 consecutive days off. Each waitress receives the same weekly salary. The minimum required waitress hours is a function of the regular daily demand plus the waitress hours needed to staff the scheduled group meetings for the day. The regular daily demands (in waitress hours) and the number of group meetings currently scheduled each day are given in Figure 2.60. The manager uses the table in Figure 2.61 to determine the waitress hours required for the larger group meetings. The manager would like to find an employment schedule that satisfies required waitress hours at a minimum cost. Assume that this cycle repeats indefinitely, and ignore the fact that the number of waitresses hired must be an integer.

(a) Create a spreadsheet representation of this LP using LOTUS 1–2–3. Because demand may change from time to time, the spreadsheet should be constructed in such a way that the "Scheduled Larger Group Meetings" data and the "Regular Daily Demand" data are entered directly into their own cells. Note that the table shown in Figure 2.61 must also be entered. The spreadsheet should represent the appropriate LP for any set of these data.

FIGURE 2.60

	REGULAR DAILY DEMAND (WAITRESS HOURS)	SCHEDULED LARGER GROUP MEETINGS
Monday	125	1
Tuesday	200	0
Wednesday	350	1
Thursday	300	0
Friday	650	3
Saturday	725	4
Sunday	250	2

FIGURE 2.61

# GROUP MEETINGS/DAY	WAITRESS HOURS NEEDED
0	0
1	24
2	36
3	52
4	64
5	80

(b) Using VINO or What's*Best*!, optimize the spreadsheet for the data presented in Figures 2.60 and 2.61.

2-33. *Farm Management with the "SUM" Function (See Problem 2-19.)* A firm operates four farms of comparable productivity. Each farm has a certain amount of usable acreage and a supply of labor hours to plant and tend the crops. The data for the upcoming season are shown in Figure 2.62. The organization is considering three crops for planting. These crops differ in their expected profit per acre and in the amount of labor required, as shown in Figure 2.63. Also shown is the fact that each crop requires a different type of

FIGURE 2.62

FARM	USABLE ACREAGE	LABOR HOURS AVAILABLE PER MONTH
1	500	1700
2	900	3000
3	300	900
4	700	2200

FIGURE 2.63

CROP	MONTHLY LABOR HOURS REQUIRED PER ACRE	EXPECTED PROFIT PER ACRE	λ	n	HARV. MACHINE Cost/hr.
A	2	$500	.02	2	$15
B	4	200	.02	3	20
C	3	**300**	.03	1	20

harvester, with a different cost. The total acreage that can be devoted to any particular crop is limited by the firm's decision as to how many hours of harvesting equipment to rent. The firm has made a fixed investment of $19,000 in a harvesting equipment co-operative. For this investment, it can use any of the three types of harvesters at the costs given in Figure 2.63, up to the fixed $19,000. A harvester typically works at a slower rate when it is first put into operation on a farm. Each season, as the crew once again becomes familiar with the machine, and any small problems are worked out, the rate of production increases. This phenomenon is generally referred to as learning. In this case, the harvesting rate after t hours is given by the equation

$$\text{rate} = n * (1 - e^{-\lambda t}) \text{ acres per hour}$$

where
$$n = \text{long-run rate of harvesting, in acres per hour}$$
$$\lambda = \text{short-run adjustment factor}$$

The total acreage harvestable in a certain time period, say T hours, can then be found by integrating the rate with respect to time, i.e.,

$$\text{total acreage harvestable in } T \text{ hours} = \int_0^T n(1 - e^{-\lambda t})\,dt$$

$$= n * (T - 1/\lambda * (1 - e^{-\lambda T}))$$

The long-run rates and short-run adjustment factors for each type of equipment can be found in Figure 2.63. Management has decided to use 400, 315, and 335 harvesting machine hours for crops A, B, and C, respectively. In order to maintain a roughly uniform work load among the farms, management's policy is that the percentage of usable acreage planted must be the same at each farm. However, any combination of the crops may be grown at any of the farms as long as all constraints are satisfied (including the uniform-work-load requirement). Management wishes to know how many acres of each crop should be planted at the respective farms in order to maximize expected profit.

(a) Use LOTUS 1–2–3 and the "SUM function" in creating a spreadsheet representation of this LP. The spreadsheet should be constructed in such a way that the rental hours for each of the harvesting machines are entered directly. A cell should show the cost of the total hours requested. There should also be constraints that say, "the total acreage of each crop (across farms) cannot exceed total harvestable acreage for that crop."

(b) Optimize this model.

(c) Suggest another choice of harvesting machine hours that the farm could select. Does your choice yield a higher profit? Can you find a choice that does?

2-34. *Producing Forestry and Earthmoving Equipment, Using the "If Function"* Suppose that forestry equipment produces a net revenue of $802 per unit and requires 700 pounds of iron, 50 hours of labor, 30 hours of heat treatment, and 1 transmission per unit. Earthmoving equipment yields a net revenue of $660 per unit and requires 4200 pounds of iron, 110 hours of labor, 12 hours of heat treatment, and 1 transmission per unit. The company's capacity during this period is 680,000 pounds of iron, 21,000 hours of labor, and 6000 hours of heat treatment. Transmissions are supplied by a wholly-owned subsidiary that produces transmissions for the entire product line. The capacity for transmissions for forestry and earthmoving equipment is then determined by the number of production hours dedicated to their production at the subsidiary plant. Production of transmissions involves three phases: setup, startup, and regular production. The duration and production rates for these phases are given in Figure 2.64.

FIGURE 2.64

PHASES	DURATION (hrs)	TRANSMISSION (units/hr)
Setup	8	0
Startup	120	.5
Regular Production	—	1

(a) For example, if 10 hours are available at the subsidiary, 8 of these are required for setup, during which there is no production, and 2 are in the startup phase, during which 2(.5) = 1 transmission would be produced. If $H \geq 128$ hours are used, 120 of the hours will produce .5 transmission/hr., while $H - 128$ hours will produce one transmission/hr. Hence, the total transmissions produced would be $60 + H - 128 = H - 68$. Show the equations that determine the limit on transmissions capacity if T hours are available at the subsidiary for $T = 6$, $T = 108$, $T = 308$.

(b) Evaluate the equations you created in (a). Your answers should be 0, 50, 240.

(c) Define the decision variables and formulate this as a revenue-maximizing linear program using LOTUS 1–2–3 and VINO or *What'sBest!* The spreadsheet should be constructed in such a way that the number of labor hours in the subsidiary plant can be entered directly and the appropriate constraint will be created in the LP. HINT: In your spreadsheet manual, read how to use the built-in @If function. In this problem, you can nest the @If to determine which phase the scheduled hours will reach.

(d) Find the optimal solution if 358 hours of production time are available at the subsidiary plant.

CASE

RED BRAND CANNERS*

Here is a simple but interesting case that captures several points that are important in real-world problem formulation. In any real problem it is important for the manager to distinguish between those facts and data which are relevant and those which are not. This may be especially difficult because on occasion confused or incorrect concepts will be strongly held by members of the management team. This case is designed to reproduce such a setting. The present task will simply involve model formulation. You will deal with this case again, however, in Appendix 5.2, where you will be asked to produce solutions, analyses, critiques, and interpretations.

On Monday, September 13, 1965, Mr. Mitchell Gordon, vice-president of operations, asked the controller, the sales manager, and the production manager to meet with him to discuss the amount of tomato products to pack that season. The tomato crop, which had been purchased at planting, was beginning to arrive at the cannery, and packing operations would have to be started by the following Monday. Red Brand Canners was a medium-sized company which canned and distributed a variety of fruit and vegetable products under private brands in the western states.

---

* Reprinted with some modification and with permission of Stanford University Graduate School of Business, © 1965 by the Board of Trustees of the Leland Stanford Junior University.

Mr. William Cooper, the controller, and Mr. Charles Myers, the sales manager, were the first to arrive in Mr. Gordon's office. Dan Tucker, the production manager, came in a few minutes later and said that he had picked up Produce Inspection's latest estimate of the quality of the incoming tomatoes. According to their report, about 20 percent of the crop was grade "A" quality and the remaining portion of the 3,000,000-pound crop was grade "B."

Gordon asked Myers about the demand for tomato products for the coming year. Myers replied that for all practical purposes they could sell all the whole canned tomatoes they could produce. The expected demand for tomato juice and tomato paste, on the other hand, was limited. The sales manager then passed around the latest demand forecast, which is shown in Exhibit 1. He reminded the group that the selling prices had been set in light of the long-term marketing strategy of the company, and potential sales had been forecasted at these prices.

EXHIBIT 1
Demand Forecasts

PRODUCT	SELLING PRICE PER CASE	DEMAND FORECAST (CASES)
24–2½ Whole Tomatoes	$4.00	800,000
24–2½ Choice Peach Halves	5.40	10,000
24–2½ Peach Nectar	4.60	5,000
24–2½ Tomato Juice	4.50	50,000
24–2½ Cooking Apples	4.90	15,000
24–2½ Tomato Paste	3.80	80,000

Bill Copper, after looking at Myers's estimates of demand, said that it looked like the company "should use the entire crop for whole tomatoes and should do quite well (on the tomato crop) this year." With the new accounting system that had been set up, he had been able to compute the contribution for each product, and according to his analysis the incremental profit on the whole tomatoes was greater than for any other tomato product. In May, after Red Brand had signed contracts agreeing to purchase the growers' production at an average delivered price of 6 cents per pound, Cooper had computed the tomato products' contributions (see Exhibit 2).

Dan Tucker brought to Cooper's attention that, although there was ample production capacity, it was impossible to produce all whole tomatoes as too small a portion of the tomato crop was "A" quality. Red Brand used a numerical scale to record the quality of both raw produce and prepared products. This scale ran from zero to ten, the higher number representing better quality. Rating tomatoes according to this scale, "A" tomatoes averaged nine points per pound and "B" tomatoes averaged five points per pound. Tucker noted that the minimum average input quality for canned whole tomatoes was 8 points per pound, and for juice it was 6. Paste could be made entirely from "B" grade tomatoes. This meant that whole tomato production was limited to 800,000 pounds.

Gordon stated that this was not a real limitation. He had recently been solicited to purchased any amount up to 80,000 pounds of grade "A" tomatoes at $8\frac{1}{2}$ cents per pound and at that time had turned down the offer. He felt, however, that the tomatoes were still available.

EXHIBIT 2
Product Item Profitability

COSTS	24–2½ WHOLE TOMATOES	24–2½ CHOICE PEACH HALVES	24–2½ PEACH NECTAR	24–2½ TOMATO JUICE	24–2½ COOKING APPLES	24–2½ TOMATO PASTE
			PRODUCT			
Selling Price (per case)	$4.00	$5.40	$4.60	$4.50	$4.90	$3.80
Variable Costs						
Direct Labor	1.18	1.40	1.27	1.32	0.70	0.54
Variable Overhead	0.24	0.32	0.23	0.36	0.22	0.26
Variable Selling	0.40	0.30	0.40	0.85	0.28	0.38
Packaging Material	0.70	0.56	0.60	0.65	0.70	0.77
Fruit[a] (cost per case)	1.08	1.80	1.70	1.20	0.90	1.50
Total Variable Costs	3.60	4.38	4.20	4.38	2.80	3.45
Net Profit (per case)	0.40	1.02	0.40	0.12	2.10	0.35

[a] Product usage is as given below.

PRODUCT	POUNDS PER CASE
Whole Tomatoes	18
Peach Halves	18
Peach Nectar	17
Tomato Juice	20
Cooking Apples	27
Tomato Paste	25

EXHIBIT 3
Marginal Analysis of Tomato Products

Z = cost per pound of "A" tomatoes in cents

Y = cost per pound of "B" tomatoes in cents

(1) $(600,000 \text{ lb} \times Z) + (2,400,000 \text{ lb} \times Y) = (3,000,000 \text{ lb} \times 6)$

(2) $\dfrac{Z}{9} = \dfrac{Y}{5}$ $\dfrac{Z}{8} = \dfrac{Y}{5}$

Z = 9.32 cents per pound $Z = 8.32$

Y = 5.18 cents per pound $Y = 5.20$

PRODUCT	CANNED WHOLE TOMATOES	TOMATO JUICE	TOMATO PASTE
Selling Price	$4.00	$4.50	$3.80
Variable Cost (exluding Tomato Cost)	2.52	3.18	1.95
	$1.48	$1.32	$1.85
Tomato Cost	1.49	1.24	1.30
Marginal Profit	($0.01)	$0.08	$0.55

Myers, who had been doing some calculations, said that although he agreed that the company "should do quite well this year," it would not be by canning whole tomatoes. It seemed to him that the tomato cost should be allocated on the basis of quality and quantity rather than by quantity only, as Cooper had done. Therefore, he had recomputed the marginal profit on this basis (see Exhibit 3), and from his results, Red Brand should use 2 million pounds of the "B" tomatoes for paste, and the remaining 400,000 pounds of "B" tomatoes and all of the "A" tomatoes for juice. If the demand expectations were realized, a contribution of $48,000 would be made on this year's tomato crop.

Questions

1. Why does Tucker state that the whole tomato production is limited to 800,000 pounds (i.e., where does the number 800,000 come from)?

2. What is wrong with Cooper's suggestion to use the entire crop for whole tomatoes?

3. How does Myers compute his tomato costs in Exhibit 3? How does he reach his conclusion that the company should use 2,000,000 pounds "B" tomatoes for paste, the remaining 400,000 pounds of "B" tomatoes, and all of the "A" in juice? What is wrong with Myers's reasoning?

4. Without including the possibility of the additional purchases suggested by Gordon, formulate as an LP the problem of determining the optimal canning policy for this season's crop. Define your decision variables in terms of pounds of tomatoes. Express the objective function coefficients in cents per pound.

5. How should your model be modified to include the possibility of the additional purchases suggested by Gordon?

Alternate Questions for Red Brand Canners

Suppose Produce Inspection could use three grades to estimate the quality of the tomato crop. Grade "A" tomatoes average nine points per pound, "B" tomatoes average six points per pound, and "C" tomatoes average three points per pound. Using this system their report would indicate that 600,000 pounds are grade "A" quality, 1,600,000 pounds are grade "B", and the remaining 800,000 pounds are grade "C." Paste has no minimum average quality requirement.

6. What is the maximum production in pounds of canned whole tomatoes? Can Cooper's suggestion be implemented?

Myers extends his analysis to three grades in Exhibit 4.

Based on Exhibit 4, Myers recommends using all grade "C" tomatoes and 1,200,000 pounds of grade "B" tomatoes for paste, and all grade "A" tomatoes and all remaining grade "B" tomatoes for juice.

7. How does Myers compute his tomato costs in Exhibit 4? How does he reach his conclusion to use 800,000 pounds of grade "C" and 1,200,000 pounds of grade "B" for paste, and the rest of the tomatoes for juice? What is wrong with Myers's reasoning?

8. Without including the possibility of the additional purchases suggested by Gordon, formulate as an LP the problem of determining the optimal canning policy for this season's crop. Define your decision variables in terms of pounds of tomatoes. Express the objective function in cents.

9. How should your model be modified to include the possibility of the additional purchases suggested by Gordon?

EXHIBIT 4
Myers's Marginal Analysis

X = cost per pound of "C" tomatoes in cents

(1) $(600{,}000 \text{ lb} \times Z) + (1{,}600{,}000 \text{ lb} \times Y) + (800{,}000 \text{ lb} \times X) = (3{,}000{,}000 \text{ lb} \times 6)$

(2) $\dfrac{Z}{9} = \dfrac{Y}{6}$

(3) $\dfrac{Y}{6} = \dfrac{C}{3}$

Z = 9.31 cents per pound

Y = 6.21 cents per pound

X = 3.10 cents per pound

PRODUCT	CANNED WHOLE TOMATOES	TOMATO JUICE	TOMATO PASTE
Selling Price	$4.00	$4.50	$3.80
Variable Cost (excluding Tomato Cost)	2.52	3.18	1.95
	$1.48	$1.32	$1.85
Tomato Cost	1.49	1.24	.78
	($0.01)	$0.08	$1.07

CASE

AN APPLICATION OF SPREADSHEET ANALYSIS TO FOREIGN EXCHANGE MARKETS

The following case shows a more realistic and, as you might expect, more difficult, illustration of spreadsheet usage. The major purposes of this case are to show what the spreadsheet can do and to gain a more complete understanding of the logic captured by the spreadsheet through the formal LP model for this problem.

PROTRAC has manufacturing and sales operations in five major trading countries: United States, United Kingdom, France, Germany, and Japan. Due to the different cash needs in the various countries at various times, it is often necessary to move available funds from one country and denomination to another. In general, there will be numerous ways to rearrange funds so as to satisfy cash requirements out of availabilities. On this particular morning the divisions in France and Japan are short of cash. Specifically, the requirements are, respectively, 8 million francs and 1280 million yen. The divisions in the U.S., Britain, and Germany are long on cash. They have surpluses of 2 million dollars, 5 million pounds, and 3 million marks. Since there are many possible ways of redistributing the cash so as to satisfy the shortages out of the surpluses, the issue to be addressed is how one compares the possible conversion strategies. Because of high short-term U.S. interest rates, the firm has decided to evaluate its final cash position by this measure: the equivalent total dollar value of its final cash holdings.

On this morning, as usual, at 7:00 A.M. Jack Walker, the corporate treasurer, and Ezra Brooks, V.P. for overseas operations, meet at corporate headquarters to determine what funds, if any, should be moved. The conversation proceeds as follows:

EZRA: Good morning, Jack. I have something to show you. I've asked Fred to set this exchange problem up on a 1–2–3 spreadsheet. I think it will make our lives considerably easier.

JACK: I like the idea, but you will have to tell me how to use it.

EZRA: Sure, Jack. I think you will see that it contains all the usual information, but let's go through it step by step. The figures in the rectangle defined by Columns B through F and Rows 5 through 9 are the exchange rates. If we let a_{ij} be the rate in row i and column j, then one unit of currency i will exchange for a_{ij} units of currency j. In fact, these data reflect the bid-ask prices. For example, if we sell one pound we get 1.425 dollars, i.e., 1.425 is the bid price, in dollars, for a pound. On the other hand, if we sell one dollar we will receive 0.6998 pounds. This means we can buy a pound for $1/0.6998 = 1.429$ dollars (the asking price, in dollars, for a pound is 1.429). Hence the bid-ask spread is 1.425, 1.429. You can see that if we start with one dollar and buy as many pounds as possible and then use those pounds to buy dollars we end up with $0.6998 \times 1.425 = 0.9972$ dollars, i.e., we lose money.

JACK: That's the transaction cost. So obviously we want to minimize these transaction costs by not moving more money around than we have to. But where does this spreadsheet say something about our cash needs today?

EZRA: Our current cash holdings are shown in column B Rows 32 to 36. All figures are in millions; we have 2 million dollars, 5 million pounds and 3 million marks. Our requirements appear in column F in the same rows. You can see that we need 8 million French francs and 1280 million yen. As you know, our policy is to satisfy requirements in such a way that the dollar value of final holdings is maximized.

JACK: Great! So let's figure out what to do.

EZRA: That's the good part. We simply put our decisions in the appropriate cells in the section labelled "Currency Transactions" and the program does all the calculations. I've already entered what I think would be our typical decisions in this set of circumstances. Cells $B19$ through $B25$ show that I've sold 2.64 million marks and 4.00 million pounds in return for 6.70135 million dollars. I've then taken a million of those dollars and purchased 8.078 million francs, and with the remaining 5.70 million dollars I bought 1280.79 million yen. All of these numbers appear in cells $D19$, $F19$, $D25$, and $F25$ of the Currency Transactions section. For example you see in $D19$ that we used 1 million dollars to buy francs, and $D25$ shows that this purchase yielded 8.078 million francs. You can see by comparing $C32$ through $C36$ with $F32$ through $F36$ that we have satisfied our goals. Indeed, $G32$ through $G36$ show how much additional cash we have in each denomination. As you can see, the policy I've entered gives final holdings worth 10.24922 million dollars.

JACK: I see that we've met our cash requirements, and 1–2–3 certainly makes the calculations easier, but you know how I am, Ez. I'd feel that I understood better if I could see all of the formulas used to do the calculations.

EZRA: That's easy. I will simply print out the symbolic spreadsheet and you can look through it at your leisure!

JACK: (Some time later that morning.) All of this seems clear, Ez, but why did we follow such a complicated strategy?

EZRA: As you know, we have always run our exchange operation through Country Bank in New York, and this is their recommended strategy.

EXHIBIT 1

A Value Spreadsheet for Currency Trading

	A	B	C	D	E	F	G	H
1	CONVERSION STRATEGIES SPREADSHEET							
2	Can Sell a Pound for $1.425 = Bid Price				Can Buy a Pound for $1.429 = Ask Price			
3								
4		Dollar	Pound	Franc	Mark	Yen	"Dollar Value"	
5	Dollar	1.00000	0.69980	8.07800	2.62700	224.70	1.00000	
6	Pound	1.42500	1.00000	11.55000	3.75400	320.70	1.42699	
7	Franc	0.12340	0.08647	1.00000	0.32500	27.76000	0.12360	
8	Mark	0.37930	0.26620	3.07300	1.00000	85.51000	0.37998	
9	Yen	0.00443	0.00310	0.03586	0.01163	1.00000	0.00444	
10								
11								
12	************************************							
13	Dollar Value of Final Holding							
14	10.24922							
15	************************************							
16								
17	Currency Transactions							
18		Dollar	Pound	Franc	Mark	Yen	Total Currency Sold	
19	Dollar	0.00	0.00	1.00	0.00	5.70	6.70000	
20	Pound	4.00	0.00	0.00	0.00	0.00	4.00000	
21	Franc	0.00	0.00	0.00	0.00	0.00	0.00000	
22	Mark	2.64	0.00	0.00	0.00	0.00	2.64000	
23	Yen	0.00	0.00	0.00	0.00	0.00	0.00000	

$(1.425 + 1.429)/2$

This Row is Exchange Rates For 1 Franc

Dollars Sold

Sold

(Continued)

99

EXHIBIT 1 (Continued)

	A	B	C	D	E	F	G	H
24								
25	Currency Purchased	6.70135	0.00000	8.07800	0.00000		1280.79	

Dollars Bought · Francs Bought · Yen Bought

	A	B	C	D	E	F	G	H
26								
27	Balance Equations							
28								
29		Initial	Final	Amt	Amt	Cash	Excess	
30		Holding	Holding	Sold	Purch	Req'd	Held	
31								
32	Dollar	2.00000	2.00135	6.70000	6.70135	0.00000	2.00135	
33	Pound	5.00000	1.00000	4.00000	0.00000	0.00000	1.00000	
34	Franc	0.00000	8.07800	0.00000	8.07800	8.00000	0.07800	
35	Mark	3.00000	0.36000	2.64000	0.00000	0.00000	0.36000	
36	Yen	0.00000	1280.79	0.00000	1280.79	1280.00	0.79	
37								

Cash Available

Final Requirements are Satisfied

Cash Required

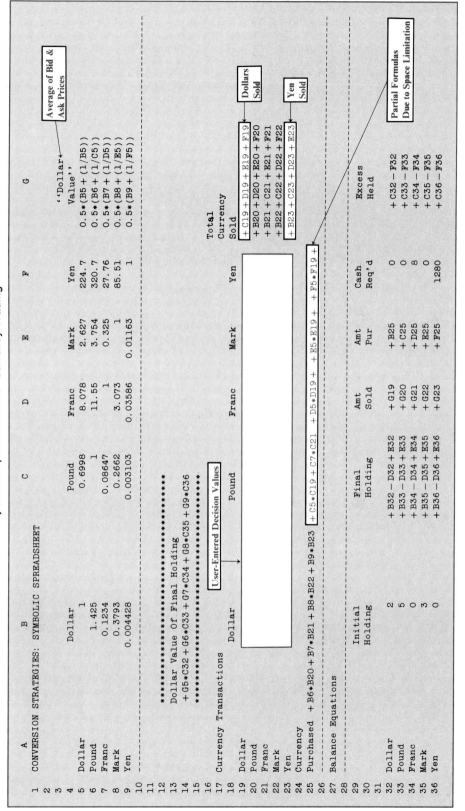

EXHIBIT 2

Symbolic Spreadsheet for Currency Trading

	A	B	C	D	E	F	G
1	CONVERSION STRATEGIES: SYMBOLIC SPREADSHEET						
2							
3							*Average of Bid & Ask Prices*
4		Dollar	Pound	Franc	Mark	Yen	'Dollar Value'
5	Dollar	1	0.6998	8.078	2.627	224.7	0.5*(B5+(1/B5))
6	Pound	1.425	1	11.55	3.754	320.7	0.5*(B6+(1/C5))
7	Franc	0.1234	0.08647	1	0.325	27.76	0.5*(B7+(1/D5))
8	Mark	0.3793	0.2662	3.073	1	85.51	0.5*(B8+(1/E5))
9	Yen	0.004428	0.003103	0.03586	0.01163	1	0.5*(B9+(1/F5))
10							
11	************************************						
12							
13	Dollar Value Of Final Holding						
14	+G5*C32+G6*C33+G7*C34+G8*C35+G9*C36						
15	************************************						
16							
17	Currency Transactions			*User-Entered Decision Values*			
18		Dollar	Pound	Franc	Mark	Yen	Total Currency Sold
19	Dollar						+C19+D19+E19+F19 (*Dollars Sold*)
20	Pound						+B20+D20+E20+F20
21	Franc						+B21+C21+E21+F21
22	Mark						+B22+C22+D22+F22
23	Yen						+B23+C23+D23+E23 (*Yen Sold*)
24	Currency						
25	Purchased	+B6*B20+B7*B21+B8*B22+B9*B23	+C5*C19+C7*C21+	+D5*D19+	+E5*E19+	+F5*F19+	*Partial Formulas Due to Space Limitation*
26							
27	Balance Equations						
28							
29		Initial	Final	Amt	Amt	Cash	Excess
30		Holding	Holding	Sold	Pur	Req'd	Held
31							
32	Dollar	2	+B32-D32+E32	+G19	+B25	0	+C32-F32
33	Pound	5	+B33-D33+E33	+G20	+C25	0	+C33-F33
34	Franc	0	+B34-D34+E34	+G21	+D25	8	+C34-F34
35	Mark	3	+B35-D35+E35	+G22	+E25	0	+C35-F35
36	Yen	0	+B36-D36+E36	+G23	+F25	1280	+C36-F36

JACK: I guess that seeing the problem in the spreadsheet representation makes it easier to think about the trading strategy. I sure would like to know if this really is a good approach.

EZRA: I worried about that for a while, too, but the foreign exchange market is very efficient for these major currencies, so it probably doesn't make much difference what strategy we follow.

JACK: I can't say that banal invocations of efficiency make me any more confident. As you know, I've made millions exploiting inefficiencies. Anyway, I don't have more time this morning to look for a better approach. Let's go with what we have.

As you are already aware, the foreign exchange problem presented in Exhibits 1 and 2 is an LP problem, and the optimal solution can be easily found with VINO or What'sBest! The spreadsheet for the optimal solution is shown in Exhibit 3. The optimal dollar value of the final cash positions is 10.26839, as compared with the 10.2492 that was obtained with Ezra's solution. We note that in some sense Ezra is right. The difference is less than .2%, i.e., $(10,268,390 - 10,249,220)/10,268,390 = .001867$. On the other hand, when large sums are being transferred even a small percentage can be a lot of money. In this example, the difference is $19,170, a handsome quantity that can be captured with almost no effort.

Questions

1. Write out the formal LP model for the foreign exchange problem. In your model use the following notation for the data given in the problem description:

a_{ij} = exchange rate from currency i into currency j (i.e., 1 unit of currency i will exchange for a_{ij} units of currency j)

$c_i = \frac{1}{2}(a_{i1} + 1/a_{1i})$ = "average dollar value" of currency i

b_i = initial holding in currency i

L_i = minimum amount of currency i required as final holding

Denote the decision variables, as follows:

X_{ij} = amount of currency i changed into currency $j, j \neq i$

Y_i = final holding in currency i

2. In the dialogue, Jack says, "We want to minimize these transaction costs by not moving more money around than we have to." Suppose we define

OV_1 = maximum "average dollar value" which can be generated from initial holdings

Note that finding the value of OV_1 requires more than simply evaluating each initial position in terms of average dollar value. For example, converting 1 pound to average dollar value gives $1.42699; converting 1 pound to 11.55 francs to average dollar value gives $(11.55)(.12360) = \$1.42758$. Thus it is preferable to convert initial holdings of pounds into francs rather than leaving the pound position intact. In fact, in order to find OV_1 one must solve a linear program. The solution is shown in Exhibit 4, which was created by setting the final cash requirement to zero and then optimizing the value of final holdings. We see that $OV_1 = 10.27773$. Now let OV_2 = maximum "average dollar value"

EXHIBIT 3
Optimized Spreadsheet for Currency Trading

	A	B	C	D	E	F	G	H
1	CONVERSION STRATEGIES: OPTIMIZED SPREADSHEET							
2								
3							"Dollar	
4		Dollar	Pound	Franc	Mark	Yen	Value"	
5	Dollar	1.00000	0.69980	8.07800	2.62700	224.70	1.00000	
6	Pound	1.42500	1.00000	11.55000	3.75400	320.70	1.42699	
7	Franc	0.12340	0.08647	1.00000	0.32500	27.76000	0.12360	
8	Mark	0.37930	0.26620	3.07300	1.00000	85.51000	0.37998	
9	Yen	0.00443	0.00310	0.03586	0.01163	1.00000	0.00444	
10	---							
11								
12		*****************************						
13		Dollar Value of Final Holding						
14		10.26839						
15		*****************************						
16							Total	
17	Currency Transactions						Currency	
18		Dollar	Pound	Franc	Mark	Yen	Sold	
19	Dollar	0.00	0.00	0.00	0.00	0.00	0.00000	
20	Pound	0.00	0.00	1.81	3.19	0.00	5.00000	
21	Franc	0.00	0.00	0.00	0.00	0.00	0.00000	
22	Mark	0.00	0.00	0.00	0.00	14.97	14.97000	
23	Yen	0.00	0.00	0.00	0.00	0.00	0.00000	
24	Currency							
25	Purchased	0.00000	0.00000	20.92168	11.97000	1280.08		
26	---							
27	Balance Equations							
28	---							
29		Initial	Final	Amt	Amt	Cash	Excess	
30		Holding	Holding	Sold	Purch	Req'd	Held	
31								
32	Dollar	2.00000	2.00000	0.00000	0.00000	0.00000	2.00000	
33	Pound	5.00000	.00000	5.00000	0.00000	0.00000	.00000	
34	Franc	0.00000	20.92168	0.00000	20.92168	8.00000	12.92168	
35	Mark	3.00000	.00000	14.97000	11.97000	0.00000	.00000	
36	Yen	0.00000	1280.08	0.00000	1280.08	1280.00	0.08	

```
A1:  'CONVERSION STRATEGIES
           A         B         C         D         E         F         G
 1    CONVERSION STRATEGIES
 2
 3                                                                     Dollar
 4              Dollar    Pound     Franc     Mark      Yen       Value
 5    Dollar         1    0.6998    8.078     2.627    224.7            1
 6    Pound      1.425        1     11.55     3.754    320.7     1.426989
 7    Franc     0.1234    0.08647       1     0.325     27.76    0.123596
 8    Mark      0.3793    0.2662    3.073         1     85.51    0.379981
 9    Yen      0.004428  0.003103  0.03586   0.01163       1     0.004439
10    ---------------------------------------------------------------------
11
12               ***********************************
13               Dollar Value Of Final Holding
14               10.27773
15               ***********************************
16                                                                   Total
17    Currency Transactions                                          Currency
18              Dollar    Pound     Franc     Mark      Yen       Sold
19    Dollar         0         0         0         0         0          0
20    Pound          0         0    5.798600       0         0    5.798600
21    Franc          0         0         0         0         0          0
22    Mark           0         3         0         0         0          3
23    Yen            0         0         0         0         0          0
24    Currency
25    Purchased      0    0.7986   66.97383       0         0
26    ---------------------------------------------------------------------
27    Balance Equations
28    ---------------------------------------------------------------------
29              Initial   Final     Amt       Amt       Cash      Excess
30              Holding   Holding   Sold      Pur       Req'd     Held
31
32    Dollar         2         2         0         0         0          2
33    Pound          5  -0.00000  5.798600    0.7986        0   -0.00000
34    Franc          0  66.97383        0   66.97383        0   66.97383
35    Mark           3         0         3         0         0          0
36    Yen            0         0         0         0         0          0
```

of final holdings subject to the cash requirements constraints. That is, OV_2 is the optimized objective value shown in Exhibit 3 ($OV_2 = 10.26839$).

In a case like this, as you will learn in Section 4.7, a more highly constrained LP cannot have a better OV than a less highly constrained LP, so it must always be true that $OV_2 \leq OV_1$. Let us define, for the problem,

$$\text{Transactions Costs} = OV_1 - OV_2$$

Using this definition, is the statement by Jack correct? That is, does the optimized solution in Exhibit 3 minimize transaction costs?

3. Recall the Conversion Strategies Spreadsheet presented in Exhibit 1. Use this spreadsheet and VINO or What's*BEST!* on your personal computer as required to answer the following questions:

   (i) Suppose that the exchange rates for two currencies (say the franc and the mark) are such that if we start with 1 franc and execute the trade 1 franc → marks → francs we end up with more than 1 franc. What would the optimal value of the objective function be under these circumstances? What economic term is used to describe this condition?

   (ii) Comment on the following statement: If **PROTRAC** has no specific cash requirements, the optimal solution would be to stand pat (i.e., in order to maximize "average dollar value" of final holdings, one should do no trading).

   (iii) Comment on the following statement: Because the foreign exchange market is efficient, we have seen that the best solution isn't much better (in percentage terms) than Ezra's solution. It is also true, for the same reason, that the worst solution isn't much worse (again in percentage terms) than Ezra's. (HINT: Find the solution that *minimizes* "average dollar value" of final holdings).

   (iv) Comment on the following statement: Consider a general problem like the **PROTRAC** problem. Such a problem might include hundreds of currencies. However, those currencies for which **PROTRAC** has no initial holding or no required cash position can be dropped from the formulation without affecting the optimal value of the objective function.

3

**LINEAR PROGRAMMING:
GEOMETRIC REPRESENTATIONS
AND GRAPHICAL SOLUTIONS**

INTRODUCTION

Two-dimensional geometry can be used as a "picture" to illustrate many of the important elements of linear programming models. Although two-dimensional geometry is a very special case, it is easy to work with, and many general concepts that apply to higher-dimensional models can be communicated with two-dimensional pictures. In particular, two-dimensional geometry is useful in providing the basis for the graphical solution approach. This is a simple way to solve a linear programming problem having only two decision variables. Although most real-world problems have more than two decision variables, and hence the graphical solution method will not be applicable, it nevertheless provides a good intuitive basis for much that follows. In other words, the purpose of this chapter is to provide graphical insights into the general LP model. This will provide a good foundation for the use of LP in a variety of real-world applications. Moreover, in our later discussions of computer printouts, the simplex method, and sensitivity analysis, we shall make frequent use of geometric illustrations.

At the outset we briefly recall the technique for plotting inequalities, for this technique provides the basis for the graphical analysis that follows.

107

CHAPTER 3
Linear Programming:
Geometric
Representations
and Graphical
Solutions

FIGURE 3.1
Plotting $2x_2 - x_1 \leq -2$

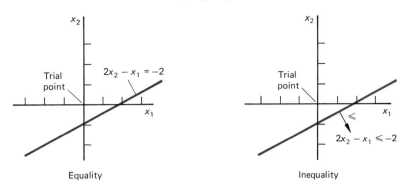

Equality   Inequality

3.2
PLOTTING INEQUALITIES AND CONTOURS

Let us begin by plotting the set of points (x_1, x_2) that satisfies the *inequality*

$$2x_2 - x_1 \leq -2 \tag{3.1}$$

Plotting
Inequalities

To accomplish this we will use the following general procedure for plotting inequalities:

■ *Step 1: Plot equality.*   Convert the inequality to an equality and plot the straight line that represents this equation. In our example the equality is $2x_2 - x_1 = -2$. The plot of this equation is shown in Figure 3.1.

■ *Step 2: Choose trial point.*   Choose any trial point that is not on the line. If the point $x_1 = 0$, $x_2 = 0$ is not on the straight line, then it is a convenient point. In our example, we select $x_1 = 0$, $x_2 = 0$ as the trial point. See Figure 3.1.

■ *Step 3: Evaluate left-hand side expression.*   Substitute the trial point into the expression on the left-hand side of the inequality. In the example, the expression is $2x_2 - x_1$. Substituting in the values $x_1 = 0$, $x_2 = 0$ yields a numerical value of 0.

■ *Step 4: Determine if the trial point satisfies the inequality.*
   a. If the trial point *satisfies* the original inequality, then the straight line plotted in step 1, and all points on the *same* side of the line as the trial point, satisfy the inequality.
   b. If the trial point *does not satisfy* the original inequality, then the straight line, and all points *not* on the same side as the trial point, satisfy the inequality.

In our example, since 0 *is not* ≤ -2, the trial point does *not* satisfy the inequality. Condition b above holds and the straight line and all points on the opposite side of the line from $(0, 0)$ satisfy the inequality. This set is shown in Figure 3.1. Note the convention of denoting the relevant side of the equality line with an arrow and $\leq$ or $\geq$, as appropriate.

An Incorrect
Method

Students often acquire the incorrect impression that the $<$ side of an inequality plot is always below the equality line. Hence, to plot the points satisfying a $\leq$ relation, they change the $\leq$ to $=$, graph the equality, and then hastily include all points that lie below the equality line. This may be incorrect, since the $<$ side can be above and

108

CHAPTER 3
Linear Programming:
Geometric
Representations
and Graphical
Solutions

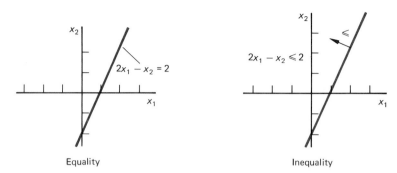

FIGURE 3.2.
Plotting $2x_1 - x_2 \le 2$

Equality   Inequality

not below. For example, let us graph the inequality $2x_1 - x_2 \le 2$. Following the procedure outlined above, we first plot the equation $2x_1 - x_2 = 2$ as shown in Figure 3.2. Now consider the trial point ($x_1 = 0$, $x_2 = 0$), which is *above* the line. At this point $2x_1 - x_2 = 2(0) - 0 = 0$ and, since 0 is less than 2, we have identified the $<$ side of the line in Figure 3.2. Hence, in this case, the points satisfying the $\le$ inequality are the points on the line along with all the points on the same side as ($x_1 = 0$, $x_2 = 0$), that is, points *on* and *above* the line. This is also shown in Figure 3.2. A comparison of Figures 3.1 and 3.2 should convince you that there is no general relationship between the sense of the inequality (i.e., $\le$ or $\ge$) and the *above* or the *below* side of the equality plot. The appropriate side can always be found using a trial point, as we have demonstrated.

The technique described above provides the basic tool for plotting the constraints in an LP, for recall that such constraints are always mathematical equalities or inequalities. In summary, to plot an inequality constraint of either the $\le$ or the $\ge$ type:

1. Change the inequality to equality, to obtain an equation, and then plot the straight line that represents this equation.

2. Choose any trial point that is not on this line. (If the point $x_1 = 0$, $x_2 = 0$ is not on the straight line, it is the easiest trial point.)

3. Substitute this trial point into the left side of the inequality constraint. Since the trial point is not on the line, the result is either less than the right-hand side or greater than the right-hand side. If the result is less than the right-hand side, the line and all points on the side containing the trial point satisfy the $\le$ inequality, and the line and all points on the other side satisfy the $\ge$ inequality. If the result is greater than the right-hand side, the conclusion is reversed.

Contour Lines   In concluding this review, it will be useful also to recall the notion of a *contour* (also called an *isoquant*) of a function. A *contour* of a function f of two variables is the set of all pairs (x_1, x_2) for which $f(x_1, x_2)$ takes on some specified *constant value*. When f is a profit function, the contours are often referred to as *isoprofit lines*, and when f is a cost function the contours represent *isocost lines*.

As an example of a contour, suppose that we are selling two products. The profit per unit of product 1 is $2 and the profit per unit of product 2 is $4. Then the total profit obtained from selling x_1 units of product 1 and x_2 units of product 2 is given by a function f of two variables defined by

$$\text{profit} = f(x_1, x_2) = 2x_1 + 4x_2$$

109

CHAPTER 3
Linear Programming:
Geometric
Representations
and Graphical
Solutions

Let us now plot all possible sales combinations of x_1 and x_2 for which we obtain $4 of profit. To do this we plot the equation

$$2x_1 + 4x_2 = 4 \tag{3.2}$$

The plot is shown by the lowest of the three lines in Figure 3.3 This line is called the 4-contour of the function f. In reality, since negative sales do not make sense, we would be interested in only that part of the 4-contour in Figure 3.3 which lies between the two distinguished points on the axes. Do not worry about this now. It will be dealt with in the next section.

FIGURE 3.3
4-, 6-, and 8-Contours of $2x_1 + 4x_2$

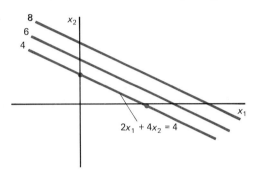

Clearly, we can replace the value 4 in the right-hand side of expression (3.2) with any other constant and then plot the result to obtain a different contour of f. Figure 3.3 also shows two other contours of f, those corresponding to right-hand sides, in expression (3.2), with values 6 and 8. You can readily see that these contours are parallel lines and you can deduce that in fact there are infinitely many such contours, one for each possible numerical value of the right-hand side in (3.2).

Plotting Contours and Inequalities The two concepts reviewed in this section, plotting equalities and plotting contours, will be employed to obtain graphical solutions of linear programming problems with two decision variables.

In summary:

Plotting contours reduces to plotting equalities. The contours of a linear function are a family of parallel lines. Plotting inequalities also reduces to plotting equalities, or contours, and then identifying the correct side.

3.3
THE GRAPHICAL SOLUTION METHOD APPLIED TO PROTRAC, INC.

The graphical solution method provides an easy way of solving linear programming problems with two decision variables. Since the **PROTRAC, Inc.** model from Chapter 2 has only two decision variables, E and F, we can employ that program to illustrate the graphical approach. The complete model for this problem is

$$\text{Max } 5000E + 4000F \qquad \text{(max profit)} \qquad (3.3)$$

$$\text{s.t.} \quad E + F \geq 5 \qquad \text{(minimal production requirement)} \qquad (3.4)$$

$$E - 3F \leq 0 \qquad \text{(market position balance)} \qquad (3.5)$$

$$+ 15F \leq 150 \qquad \text{(capacity in department A)} \qquad (3.6)$$

$$20E + 10F \leq 160 \qquad \text{(capacity in department B)} \qquad (3.7)$$

$$30E + 10F \geq 135 \qquad \text{(contractual labor agreement)} \qquad (3.8)$$

$$E, F \geq 0 \qquad \text{(nonnegativity conditions)} \qquad (3.9)$$

where we recall that the decision variables are defined as

$$E = \text{number of E-9s to be produced}$$

$$F = \text{number of F-9s to be produced}$$

The labels (3.3) through (3.9) have been used to distinguish the objective function and the constraints to facilitate future reference.

Plotting the Constraints Our first goal is to show how all the feasible decisions for this problem can be graphically portrayed. Let us first construct a coordinate system with values of E on the horizontal axis and values of F on the vertical. Thus, every point in the two-dimensional space is associated with a specific production alternative. For example, the point in Figure 3.4 is identified with the production alternative $E = 3$, $F = 4$. We now wish to see which of the possible combinations of (E, F) are feasible, that is, satisfy the restrictions (3.4) through (3.9).

Since the nonnegativity conditions (3.9) require $E \geq 0$ and $F \geq 0$, we need only consider the so-called nonnegative quadrant in looking for feasible production combinations, that is, feasible combinations of the decision variable (E, F). This is indicated in Figure 3.4. In this figure the arrows point in the direction of nonnegative values of E and F, and the nonnegative quadrant is shaded.

Clearly, not every point in the nonnegative quadrant is feasible. For example, consider the first constraint, labeled (3.4).

$$E + F \geq 5 \qquad (3.4)$$

FIGURE 3.4

Nonnegative Quadrant

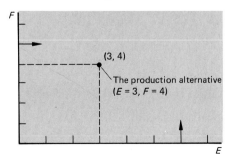

(3, 4)

The production alternative $(E = 3, F = 4)$

111

CHAPTER 3
Linear Programming:
Geometric
Representations
and Graphical
Solutions

Clearly, the combination ($E = 1$, $F = 1$), although corresponding to a point in the non-negative quadrant, violates this constraint. Obviously, we must further limit our graphic representation of the candidates for feasibility.

In order to depict accurately the feasible combinations, we must proceed by taking one constraint at a time. We begin with the first constraint,

$$E + F \geq 5 \tag{3.4}$$

The discussion in Section 3.2 indicated that to plot this constraint you should first plot the line $E + F = 5$ and then find the $>$ side, which in this case is seen to be all points above the diagonal line. Following this procedure you should verify that all points in the nonnegative quadrant which satisfy the first constraint are precisely those shown in the shaded region in Figure 3.5. This region represents nonnegative production plans that satisfy the one single constraint, (3.4), but not necessarily the others. For example, you can quickly verify that the plan ($E = 10$, $F = 10$) violates constraint (3.6). Clearly, we must still restrict the candidate decisions further, and as you might by now imagine, we are going to reapply the prescription just followed.

Thus, we now consider the second constraint,

$$E - 3F \leq 0 \tag{3.5}$$

In Figure 3.6 the plot of this condition appears together with condition (3.4). The production alternatives in the shaded region of Figure 3.6 satisfy

$$E + \quad F \geq 5 \tag{3.4}$$

$$E - 3F \leq 0 \tag{3.5}$$

$$E \geq 0, \qquad F \geq 0 \tag{3.9}$$

**Effect of
Adding
Constraints**

However, this shaded region will still contain some points that will violate some of the remaining constraints (3.6), (3.7), and (3.8). Thus, we must continue to superimpose one by one the remaining constraints. First, however, let us note that superimposing the second constraint (3.5) on the picture in Figure 3.5 has further restricted the decision variables and, graphically, has "trimmed down" the set of candidates for feasible decisions. As we continue to superimpose "tighter and tighter" conditions (i.e., more and

FIGURE 3.5
First Constraint

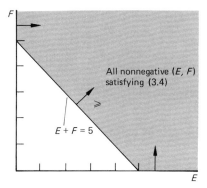

FIGURE 3.6
First Two Constraints, (3.4)
and (3.5)

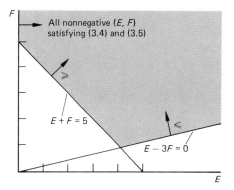

112

CHAPTER 3
Linear Programming:
Geometric
Representations
and Graphical
Solutions

more restrictions) on the decision variables, it should be clear that from the geometric point of view these restrictions will tend to trim down the constraint set even further. This phenomenon, the successive trimming down of the constraint set, illustrates the following important general principle. ("General" in this context means "also valid for problems with more than two decision variables.")

It will always be the case that adding more constraints either trims down the set of allowable decisions or, possibly, leaves the set unaffected. Adding additional constraints can never enlarge the set of allowable decisions.

The Feasible Set

The culmination of superimposing constraints (3.6), (3.7), and (3.8) on Figure 3.6 yields Figure 3.7, which is a graphic portrayal of all feasible values of the decision variables. This figure, with all five constraints plotted in the nonnegative quadrant, shows the set of production plans that *simultaneously* satisfies *all five* of the constraints, including the nonnegativity conditions. In linear programming terminology, this set is called the *feasible set*, or *feasible region*, or the *constraint set*. That is, the shaded region in Figure 3.7 is the constraint set for the **PROTRAC**, Inc. model.

The set of all nonnegative values of the decision variables that satisfies all the constraints simultaneously is called the constraint set, or the feasible set.

Can a Number Be Feasible?

In keeping with our definition of feasible set, any production plan [i.e., any pair of values for (E, F)] that satisfies all the constraints, including the nonnegativity conditions, is

FIGURE 3.7
Entire Feasible Set

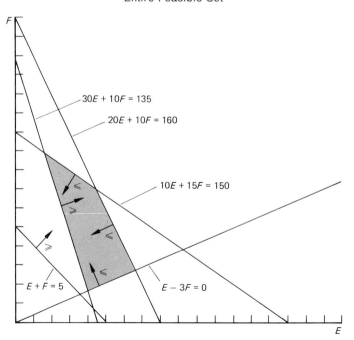

$30E + 10F = 135$

$20E + 10F = 160$

$10E + 15F = 150$

$E + F = 5$

$E - 3F = 0$

113

CHAPTER 3
Linear Programming:
Geometric
Representations
and Graphical
Solutions

said to be *feasible*. These feasible plans, or decisions, are the allowable production alternatives according to our model. Note that it is *incorrect* to speak of a feasible value of E separately, or a feasible value of F separately. Think carefully about this statement, for it is important to understand that *the term "feasible," in this two-dimensional illustration, always applies to a pair of numbers, not to a single number*.

To illustrate these feasible pairs geometrically, we have seen that you merely plot the constraint set. Although we have used several pictures to lead up to our graph of the entire constraint set, this was simply for illustrative purposes. In practice you would plot everything on the same picture, superimposing on the figure one constraint at a time. To accomplish this, for each constraint

1. Change the inequality to equality.
2. Plot the equality.
3. Identify the correct side for the original inequality. Having performed steps 1, 2 and 3 for each constraint, the feasible set is the region that, simultaneously, is on the correct side of all the lines.

Plotting the Objective Function

Obtaining a graphic portrayal of the constraint set is the first step in the graphical solution procedure. Now we want to use the graphic portrayal to find the optimal solution to the problem. Since we are dealing with a profit-maximization model, we must find a feasible production alternative that gives the highest possible value to the objective function

$$\text{profit} = 5000E + 4000F \tag{3.10}$$

If we begin to arbitrarily select feasible plans from Figure 3.7 and evaluate the objective function at each such point, trying to find the largest possible profit, we would soon realize that this process could be endless. There are infinitely many feasible pairs (E, F). How would this trial-and-error process ever terminate? We must find, systematically and quickly, a way to discover a profit-maximizing feasible plan.

In order to present a more robust approach, let us first redraw just the shaded feasible region on a new uncluttered graph, as shown in Figure 3.8. Now recall that, since in this case the objective function is a profit function, the contours of the objective

FIGURE 3.8
Constraint Set for PROTRAC, Inc.

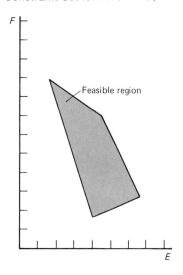

114

CHAPTER 3
Linear Programming:
Geometric
Representations
and Graphical
Solutions

function are called isoprofit lines, or, more simply, *profit lines.* Our next task is to super-impose on Figure 3.8 several arbitrary profit lines. For example, let us begin by setting expression (3.10) equal to 20,000 and superimposing on Figure 3.8 the corresponding profit line, as shown in Figure 3.9. We have restricted this line to the nonnegative quadrant because we are interested only in nonnegative values for E and F. Thus, any point on the line in Figure 3.9 corresponds to a production plan that will yield a profit of $20,000. You can see from this figure that there are an infinite number of nonnegative production plans that will yield a profit of $20,000. However, the fact that the profit line in Figure 3.9 does not intersect the shaded feasible region means that none of the production plans on this line are feasible.

Let us therefore experiment by selecting a different profit line to superimpose on Figure 3.9. For example, let us set expression (3.10) equal to 32,000 and plot the profit line

$$\text{profit} = 5000E + 4000F = 32,000$$

This is shown in Figure 3.10. You can see from Figure 3.10 that the 32,000-contour intersects the feasible region. Every production plan that lies on the intersection of this line with the feasible region is feasible, and yields a profit of $32,000. There are, as you can see, infinitely many such plans.

Our objective is to find a point in the feasible region that yields the highest profit. Are there any feasible plans that yield a higher profit than $32,000? Look at Figure 3.10 and see if you can answer this question.

The "Uphill" Direction   The key to correct identification of feasible plans with a profit greater than $32,000 lies in noting that the 32,000 profit line is parallel to the 20,000 profit line and lies above it (i.e., to the northeast). In general, as we increase profit, we increase the value of C in the profit equation

$$\text{profit} = 5000E + 4000F = C$$

and the profit line moves parallel to the 20,000 and the 32,000 profit lines. The direction of the motion is northeasterly because this is, in this particular example, the direction

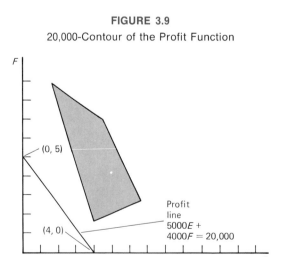

FIGURE 3.9

20,000-Contour of the Profit Function

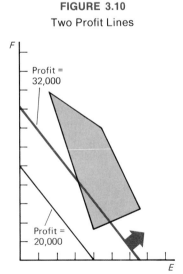

FIGURE 3.10

Two Profit Lines

in which profit increases. The direction of increasing contour values will be called the "uphill" direction. This direction is identified with an arrow in Figure 3.10.

Finding the Optimal Solution

Now that we have seen how to plot the feasible region and the objective function contours, we are armed with enough information to find the solution to the **PROTRAC**, Inc. model. As, in our mind's eye, we move, or "slide," the profit lines out to the northeast, without changing the tilt, we can identify feasible plans that yield higher and higher values for the objective function. At some point we will discover that any further movement in this direction will take the profit line beyond the feasible region, at which point all production plans on the line will be unacceptable. Can you now identify the position of the highest-valued contour that touches the feasible region in at least one point? Any feasible plan on this line will be an optimal solution to the **PROTRAC**, Inc. model.

Using either your imagination or a straight edge, and making a parallel outward displacement of the profit line in Figure 3.10, you will see that the highest-valued contour is the one shown in Figure 3.11. This is called the maximum profit line.

In this model it is seen that there is only one point in the feasible region which lies on the maximum profit line and hence this point is called a *unique optimal solution* to our problem. Although we have located our solution graphically, the accuracy with which we can determine the *optimal values* of the decision variables E and F would seem to depend on the accuracy of our graph. We shall see that this impression is incorrect. Also, we have not yet established the value of the maximum profit line (i.e., the maximum attainable profit). These two points are readily resolved by resorting to some easy algebra, as follows.

Figure 3.11 indicates that the optimal value of E is somewhere between 4 and 5, and the optimal value of F is approximately 7. Let us suppose that greater accuracy is desired. You can see in Figure 3.11 that the optimal solution occurs at *the intersection* of the two constraint lines

$$10E + 15F = 150 \qquad (3.11)$$

$$20E + 10F = 160 \qquad (3.12)$$

FIGURE 3.11
Optimality in the PROTRAC, Inc. Model

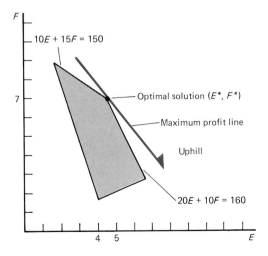

115

116

CHAPTER 3
Linear Programming:
Geometric
Representations
and Graphical
Solutions

Solving these two linear equations for the two unknowns E and F, we multiply the first equation (3.11) by 2 to obtain the new system:

$$2 \times (3.11): \quad 20E + 30F = 300 \tag{3.13}$$

$$20E + 10F = 160 \tag{3.12}$$

Then, subtracting (3.12) from (3.13), we find that

$$20F = 140$$

$$F = \tfrac{140}{20} = 7 \tag{3.14}$$

Substituting the value of F from (3.14) back into either (3.11) or (3.12), say (3.12), we obtain

$$20E + 10(7) = 160$$

$$E = \tfrac{90}{20} = 4.5 \tag{3.15}$$

Distinguishing the Optimal Solution Let us use the notation E^* and F^* to distinguish the optimal values of the decision variables, E and F, respectively. From (3.14) and (3.15) we have found the optimal production plan $E^* = 4.5$ and $F^* = 7$. This is the *optimal solution*, or, more simply, *the solution* to the **PROTRAC**, Inc. model. Using these optimal values ($E^* = 4.5$, $F^* = 7$) we can now compute the value of the maximum profit as follows:

$$\text{maximum profit} = 5000E^* + 4000F^*$$

$$= 5000(4.5) + 4000(7)$$

$$= 22{,}500 + 28{,}000 = 50{,}500$$

Optimal Solution and Optimal Value Are Different This is the value of the maximum profit contour in Figure 3.11 and is called the *optimal objective value* or, sometimes, merely the *optimal value*. Students are sometimes confused as to whether the term "solution" refers to the optimal values of the decision variables or the optimal value of the objective function. The important point to keep straight is that the term *solution*, or *optimal solution*, always refers to the optimal values of the decision variables. The term *optimal value* (singular), which we shall often call the OV, refers to the objective function evaluated at the solution. In the **PROTRAC**, Inc. model, the optimal production plan ($E^* = 4.5$, $F^* = 7$) is the solution; the optimal profit of $50,500 is the OV.

———— 3.4
ACTIVE AND INACTIVE CONSTRAINTS

In addition to the optimal production plan and the optimal profit, the management of **PROTRAC**, Inc. may want additional information about the solution. For example, management may ask

1. How many labor hours will the optimal solution use in department A?
2. How many labor hours will the optimal solution use in department B?
3. How many hours will the optimal solution use in testing?

117

CHAPTER 3
Linear Programming:
Geometric
Representations
and Graphical
Solutions

Recall that the labor hours used in department A are given by the left-hand side of the inequality (3.6). That is, referring back to the model, we see that

$$\text{hours used in department A} = 10E + 15F \qquad (3.16)$$

Since we are going to assign the optimal values $E = E^* = 4.5$, and $F = F^* = 7$, the expression (3.16) is evaluated as follows:

$$\text{hours used (at optimality) in department A} = 10E^* + 15F^*$$

$$= 10(4.5) + 15(7) = 150$$

This means that the answer to question 1 is 150, and we say that "at optimality, 150 hours are used in department A." In order to answer question 2 we recall that the labor hours in department B are given by the left-hand side of inequality (3.7). Hence, at optimality

$$\text{hours used in department B} = 20E^* + 10F^*$$

$$= 20(4.5) + 10(7) = 160$$

Finally, to answer question 3 we employ the left-hand side of inequality (3.8) to discover that, at optimality

$$\text{hours used in testing} = 30E^* + 10F^*$$

$$= 30(4.5) + 10(7) = 205$$

Let us now pursue these elaborations a bit further to introduce some important new terminology. We have just seen that the optimal production plan will consume 150 hours in department A. But we also recall from the model that 150 hours is the total amount of labor *available* in department A. Hence, for the optimal policy we see that

$$\text{hours of labor used} = \text{hours of labor available}$$

and the constraint is satisfied with *equality*. But how can that be, for the constraint on labor hours in department A is an *inequality* constraint, not an equality constraint? The answer is simple if you interpret the $\leq$ symbol correctly. Our $\leq$ constraint on labor in department A allows the use of labor to be either $<$ the amount *or* $=$ the amount available. Hence, equality is permissible. What is *not* permissible is for the labor usage to *exceed* the availability.

For this constraint, since there is no labor left unused, the constraint is said to be *active*, or equivalently, *binding*. Note that from management's point of view an active constraint plays a role of considerable importance. For example, if there were any further production of E-9s or F-9s, this active constraint would be violated. In this sense the active constraint prevents the earning of additional profits.

By applying analogous reasoning to the constraint on labor hours in department B you can easily verify that this constraint is also active.

Active Constraint   In Chapter 2 we saw that the constraints in a linear programming model are always of the form $=$, $\leq$, or $\geq$. *An equality constraint is always active. An inequality constraint, of either $\leq$ or $\geq$ type, is active only if, when evaluated at optimality, equality holds between the left-hand side and the right-hand side.*

Let us now consider the constraint on testing. Recall that this constraint requires, by a union agreement, that *at least* 135 hours (the right-hand side of the constraint) be used, whereas the answer to question 3 has shown that 205 hours (the left-hand side) will actually be used. Since we are using 70 hours in *excess* of what is required, there is said to be, at optimality, a *surplus* of 70 hours in this constraint. Here we have an example of an inequality constraint which is *not* active at optimality. As you might guess, such a constraint is said to be *inactive*.

The terms "active" and "inactive" are applicable to each constraint in the model. For example, if we evaluate, at optimality, the left-hand side of the constraint labeled (3.5), we see that

$$E - 3F = 4.5 - 3(7) = 4.5 - 21 = -16.5$$

Since constraint (3.5) stipulates that

$$E - 3F \leq 0$$

and since the actual value of the left-hand side is -16.5, we see that the left-hand side falls 16.5 units *below* the right-hand side. This constraint is said to have a *slack* of 16.5 units, and is also *inactive*.

Summarizing this terminology, we see that

1. If, at optimality (i.e., when evaluated at the optimal solution), the left-hand side of a constraint equals the right-hand side, that constraint is said to be *active*, or *binding*. Thus, an *equality* constraint is always active. An inequality constraint may or may not be active.

2. If a constraint is not active, it is said to be *inactive*. For a constraint of $\geq$ type, the difference between the left-hand side and the right-hand side (the excess) is called *surplus*. For a constraint of $\leq$ type, the difference between the right-hand side and the left-hand side (the amount unused) is called *slack*.

3. At optimality, each *inequality* constraint in a model has a slack or surplus value and for feasible decisions this value is always nonnegative. For a given constraint the slack or surplus value is zero if and only if that constraint is active.

We have seen how to identify algebraically those constraints which are active and those which are inactive, and hence have positive surplus or slack. We obtained this information by "plugging" the optimal values of the decision variables into the constraints. It will be useful to understand how the active and inactive constraints can also be easily identified from the graphical solution. To see this, let us recall the statement of the model:

$$\text{Max } 5000E + 4000F$$

$$
\begin{array}{llrcll}
\text{s.t.} & E + & F & \geq & 5 & \textcircled{1} \\
& E - & 3F & \leq & 0 & \textcircled{2} \\
& 10E + & 15F & \leq & 150 & \textcircled{3} \\
& 20E + & 10F & \leq & 160 & \textcircled{4} \\
& 30E + & 10F & \geq & 135 & \textcircled{5} \\
& & E, F & \geq & 0 & \textcircled{6}
\end{array}
$$

119

CHAPTER 3
Linear Programming:
Geometric
Representations
and Graphical
Solutions

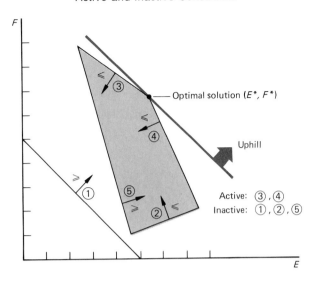

FIGURE 3.12
Active and Inactive Constraints

and let us again graph the constraints, but this time with each constraint line labeled. This is shown in Figure 3.12. The label ① is on the first line that we plotted, $E + F = 5$. The label ② is on the second line that we plotted, $E - 3F = 0$, and so on. That is, the line labeled ① is the first constraint in the model above, the line labeled ② is the second constraint, and so on. We have just seen that the third and fourth constraints, which represent labor capacity in departments A and B, are active in this model. From Figure 3.12 you can see that these constraints "pass through" the optimal solution. Stated equivalently, the optimal solution "lies on" these constraints. Although we did not use the term "active," we indeed solved for the values of E^* and F^* by implicitly recognizing that constraints ③ and ④ are active.

Identifying an Active Constraint

Geometrically, an active constraint is one that passes through the optimal solution.

We have seen that constraints ② and ⑤ are inactive. A quick check also shows that constraint ① is inactive. That is,

$$E^* + F^* = 4.5 + 7 = 11.5 > 5$$

Thus, we can see that

Identifying an Inactive Constraint

Geometrically, an inactive constraint is one that does not pass through the optimal solution.

The active and inactive constraints are easy to spot in the process of applying the graphical solution method. Indeed, that is the very goal of the graphical method, for once the active constraints are identified, as you have seen, we then solve simultaneous equations to obtain the optimal solution. Each inactive constraint will have surplus or slack, depending upon whether the corresponding inequality is $\geq$ or $\leq$. However, the numerical value of the surplus or slack cannot be read from the picture. It must be determined algebraically, as in the foregoing illustrations

_____ 3.5
EXTREME POINTS AND OPTIMAL SOLUTIONS

As you have seen, the solution to the **PROTRAC,** Inc. problem occurs at a corner of the feasible region—namely, at the corner where (what we have called) the third and fourth constraints intersect. In linear programming jargon the corners of the feasible region are called *extreme points*. The two terms, *extreme points* and *corners*, will be used interchangeably in our discussion.

A New
Objective
Function
To begin to understand the importance of the extreme points, let us imagine taking a different linear objective function, with the same constraint set, and solving the problem again. For example, suppose that we change the price of F-9s in such a way that the profitability is raised from $4000 to $10,000 per unit. Let us see how this change in the objective function affects the solution to the problem. First, since we have changed only the objective function, leaving the constraints as they were, the feasible region remains unchanged. All that is new is that the contours of the objective function will assume a new tilt. A profit line of this new objective function (the 50,000-contour) is shown in Figure 3.13. Sliding the new profit line uphill, the new optimal solution is found, as shown in Figure 3.13.

Note from Figure 3.13 that at the new optimal point the *active* constraints have changed. Now the third and fifth constraints are active, whereas previously the third

FIGURE 3.13
New Optimal Solution When the Objective
Function is 5000E + 10,000F

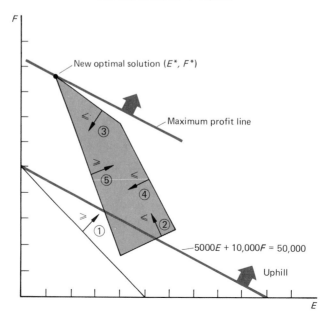

121

CHAPTER 3
Linear Programming:
Geometric
Representations
and Graphical
Solutions

and fourth were active. Thus, you can see that the change in the slope of the objective function has moved the optimal solution away from the previous corner, but it has moved to another *corner*, or extreme point. As previously, we can obtain the exact value of the new optimal policy by simultaneously solving the third and fifth constraint equations. Thus we have

$$10E^* + 15F^* = 150 \qquad \text{(third constraint)}$$

$$30E^* + 10F^* = 135 \qquad \text{(fifth constraint)}$$

A New Optimal Corner

Solving these equation yields $E^* = 1.5$ and $F^* = 9$. This is the new optimal policy. As you might have predicted, the new price structure, which has increased the relative profitability of F-9s, leads to an optimal production plan which specifies a cutback in E-9s and an increase in F-9s. You can also note from Figure 3.13 that at the new optimal solution there is now positive slack in labor in department B (constraint ④).

What we have seen is that with each of two different objective functions for **PROTRAC**'s problem we obtained an optimal corner solution. In fact, you can experiment for yourself to see that no matter how much you change the objective function, as long as it remains linear, there will always be an optimal corner solution. You can even change the constraint set and there will still always be an optimal corner solution, as long as everything is kept linear.

In Figure 3.14 you see an arbitrary six-sided constraint set and contours of three *different* objective functions, denoted f, g, and h. For each objective function the arrow indicates the direction in which we want to slide the plotted contour to optimize the objective function. Note that in each case there is an optimal solution at a corner. The objective function g in Figure 3.14 illustrates the interesting case in which *the optimal objective contour coincides with one of the constraint lines on the boundary of the feasible region. In this case there will be many optimal solutions, namely the corners B and C and all the boundary points in between.* This is called a case of *multiple optima*, or *alternative optima*. However, even in this case when there is not a *unique* optimal solution, it is still true that there is a corner solution which is optimal (in fact, there are two). Thus, the geometry illustrates an important fact about any LP problem with any number of decision variables:

In an LP problem, if there is an optimal solution, there is always at least one optimal corner solution.

FIGURE 3.14
You Always Get a Corner Solution

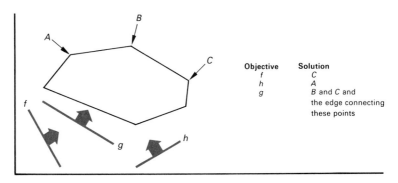

Objective	Solution
f	C
h	A
g	B and C and the edge connecting these points

122

CHAPTER 3
Linear Programming:
Geometric
Representations
and Graphical
Solutions

This result has a powerful implication in terms of using the graphical method for solving an LP. It means that you need not be overly meticulous in your plotting. Your diagram need only be sufficiently accurate to identify an optimal corner (i.e., the active constraints) of the feasible region. You then solve two equations in two unknowns to determine the exact optimal values of the decision variables.

In future chapters we will see other important implications of the fact that if there is an optimal solution, there will always be at least one at a corner.

3.6
SUMMARY OF THE GRAPHICAL SOLUTION METHOD FOR A MAX MODEL

Our discussion thus far has presented the following procedure for solving a linear programming problem in two decision variables:

1. Superimpose the graph of each constraint on the same nonnegative quadrant. The nonnegative values of the decision variables which simultaneously satisfy (lie on the correct side of) *all* the constraints form the *feasible region*, also called the *constraint set*.

2. Draw an arbitrary *profit line*, also called a *contour*, of the objective function to obtain the slopes of the objective function *contours*.

3. Determine the uphill direction by, for example, evaluating the objective function at any trial point that is not on the profit line you have just constructed.

4. Now, given the slope of the profit line from step 2, and the uphill direction from step 3, determine visually the corner of the constraint set which lies on the highest possible profit line that still intersects this set.

5. The values of the decision variables at this corner (i.e., the coordinates of the corner) give the solution to the problem. These values are found by identifying the active constraints and then simultaneously solving two linear equations in two unknowns. Thus, in order to implement the graphical method, your drawing need only be accurate enough to identify the active constraints.

6. The optimal value of the objective function (i.e., the maximum profit) is obtained by "plugging in" the optimal values for the decision variables and evaluating the objective function.

7. You have already identified the active constraints. The inactive constraints can also be read from your graph. They are those that do not pass through the solution.

3.7
THE GRAPHICAL METHOD APPLIED TO A MIN MODEL

The "Downhill" Direction

As we noted in Section 2.5, many real-world problems occur in a minimization context, and this was illustrated with the Crawler Tread problem. Thus far we have dealt only with the graphical representation of a Max model. The method applied to a Min model is quite similar, the only difference being that *the optimizing direction of the objective function* is now "downhill" rather than "uphill." Recall that in a Max model the objective function contours are often isoprofit lines or, more simply, profit lines. In a Min model, the objective function contours are often isocost lines or, more simply, cost lines. Our goal, in a Min model, is to determine a corner of the feasible region that lies on the *lowest-valued* objective function contour which still intersects the feasible region. As an example, let us apply the graphical method to the following simple minimization model in two-decision variables which we denote as x_1 and x_2.

123

CHAPTER 3
Linear Programming:
Geometric
Representations
and Graphical
Solutions

$$\text{Min } x_1 + 2x_2$$

$$\text{s.t.} \quad -3x_1 + 2x_2 \le 6 \qquad (1)$$

$$x_1 + x_2 \le 10.5 \qquad (2)$$

$$-x_1 + 3x_2 \ge 6 \qquad (3)$$

$$x_1, x_2 \ge 0$$

The feasible region for this problem is shown in Figure 3.15.

FIGURE 3.15

Feasible Region for the Min Model

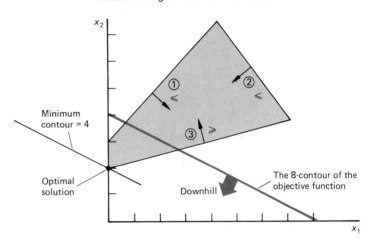

Finding the Optimal Solution

In order to find an optimal corner solution, we must

1. Plot a typical objective function contour to obtain the slope of such contours.
2. Determine the optimizing direction, which, since we are dealing with a Min model, is in this case the "downhill" direction.
3. With a parallel displacement of the objective function contour (from step 1), in the downhill direction (from step 2), determine which corner of the feasible region is optimal.
4. Solve the appropriate equations to obtain the exact optimal values of the decision variables. Then obtain the OV.

An Example

Let us now carry out these steps.

1. In Figure 3.15 we superimpose the contour, objective value = $x_1 + 2x_2 = 8$.
2. To determine the downhill direction, we evaluate the objective function at the trial point $(x_1 = 0, x_2 = 0)$. We obtain $x_1 + 2x_2 = 0 + 2(0) = 0$. Since 0 is less than 8, we see that the southwest side of our contour in Figure 3.15 is downhill.
3. By imagining a parallel displacement to the southwest, we obtain the optimal solution shown in Figure 3.15.
4. Note that the optimal solution lies on the intersection of the third constraint and the x_2 axis. The equation of the x_2 axis is $x_1 = 0$. Hence, the optimal solution is given by the two

124

CHAPTER 3
Linear Programming:
Geometric
Representations
and Graphical
Solutions

equations $x_1^* = 0$ and $-x_1^* + 3x_2^* = 6$. Thus, $x_1^* = 0$, and $x_2^* = 2$. The OV (optimal objective value) is obtained by evaluating the objective function at the optimal values for the decision variables.

$$OV = \text{optimal objective value} = x_1^* + 2x_2^*$$
$$= 0 + 2(2) = 4$$

The example above shows that the graphical analysis for a Min problem is exactly the same as that for a Max problem, as long as it is understood that the objective contours are always moved in the *optimizing direction*. We shall always represent this direction with an arrow and it is understood that the direction of the arrow is uphill in a Max **A Faulty** model, downhill in a Min model. We issue one caveat here which deserves emphasis. **Approach** Students on occasion fall into the trap of thinking that in a Max model the solution will always be the corner "farthest away" from the origin. And for a Min model, they instinctively feel that if the origin is feasible, it must be optimal. Otherwise, if the origin is not feasible, they feel that the corner "closest to" the origin will be optimal. Such reasoning may be false. The incorrect logic has to do with the false impression that the uphill direction is always outward from the origin (the northeast), and the downhill direction always inward toward the origin. This is analogous to the fact, discussed in Section 3.2, that there is no general relationship between the sense of an inequality ($\leq$ or $\geq$) and the above or below side of the equality plot in our graphical representation.

───────── 3.8
UNBOUNDED AND INFEASIBLE PROBLEMS

Thus far we have developed a geometric portrayal of LP problems in two decision variables. This portrayal has provided the basis for solving such problems and has also illustrated the important conclusion that "*if* there is an optimal solution, there will always be at least one at a corner." But how can an LP fail to have an optimal solution? In this section we use the geometric representation to see how that can occur.

Unbounded Recall the graphical display of the **PROTRAC**, Inc. model as shown in Figure 3.12, but
Problems let us now change the model by supposing that the constraints which we have labeled as ③ and ④ have been inadvertently omitted. Thus, we obtain the model

$$\text{Max } 5000E + 4000F$$

$$
\begin{aligned}
\text{s.t.} \quad & E + F \geq 5 & (1) \\
& E - 3F \leq 0 & (2) \\
& 30E + 10F \geq 135 & (5) \\
& E, F \geq 0
\end{aligned}
$$

The graphical analysis for this new problem is shown in Figure 3.16. You can see that the constraint set now extends indefinitely to the northeast and it is possible to slide the profit line arbitrarily far in this direction. Since for this particular problem the northeast is the optimizing direction, we can find allowable decisions which give arbitrarily large values to the objective function. In other words, we can obtain profits approaching in-

125

CHAPTER 3
Linear Programming:
Geometric
Representations
and Graphical
Solutions

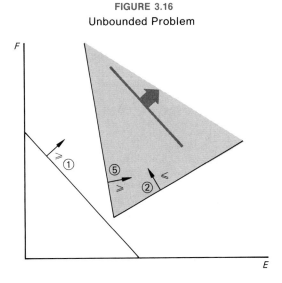

FIGURE 3.16
Unbounded Problem

finity. Such a problem has no solution, because for any set of allowable values for the decision variables we can always find other allowable values that improve the objective value. Problems of this type are termed *unbounded*. Unbounded problems are "pathological." They can arise, as in Figure 3.16, when one or more important constraints have been left out of the model, or possibly because of typing errors when entering a problem into the computer for solution. In real life no one has yet discovered how to obtain an infinite profit, and you can be assured that when a model is correctly formulated and correctly entered into the computer it will not be unbounded.

Unbounded Constraint Set   Students sometimes confuse the term "unbounded problem" with the concept of an "unbounded constraint set." The latter terminology refers to a feasible region in which at least one decision variable can be made arbitrarily large in value. If an LP is unbounded, the constraint set must also be unbounded, as illustrated by Figure 3.16. However, it is possible to have an unbounded constraint set without having an unbounded problem. This is illustrated graphically in Figure 3.17, which shows a hypothetical LP

FIGURE 3.17
Unbounded Constraint Set but a
Solution

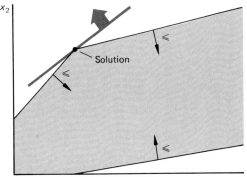

model in two decision variables, x_1 and x_2. The model has three constraints and an unbounded constraint set, but there is an optimal solution.

As we have said, an unbounded problem is considered to be pathological because there are no optimal values for the decision variables and there are no real-world realizations of such problems.

Infeasible Problems There is one other type of pathology to be aware of in linear programming. It is called *infeasibility* or, alternatively, *inconsistency*. This term refers to a problem with an empty constraint set; that is, there is no combination of values for the decision variables which simultaneously satisfies all the constraints. A graphical illustration of an infeasible problem is obtained by changing the first constraint in the **PROTRAC**, Inc. model to $E + F \leq 5$ instead of $E + F \geq 5$. This gives us the new model

An Infeasible LP

$$\text{Max } 5000E + 4000F$$

$$\text{s.t.} \quad E + F \leq 5$$

$$E - 3E \leq 0$$

$$10E + 15F \leq 150$$

$$20E + 10F \leq 160$$

$$30E + 10F \geq 135$$

$$E, F \geq 0$$

The constraint set for this LP is graphically represented in Figure 3.18 and you can see that there is no pair of values (E, F) that satisfies *all* the constraints.

As Figure 3.18 illustrates, *infeasibility depends solely on the constraints and has nothing to do with the objective function.* Obviously, an infeasible LP has no solution, but this pathology will not appear if the problem has been formulated correctly. In other words, in well-posed real problems, infeasibility always means that the model has been

FIGURE 3.18
Infeasible Model

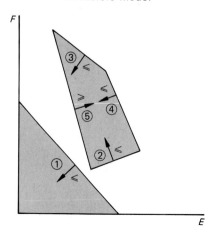

127

CHAPTER 3
Linear Programming:
Geometric
Representations
and Graphical
Solutions

incorrectly specified, either because of logical errors or because of typing errors when entering the problem into the computer. Logical errors may mean that either too many constraints, or the wrong constraints, have been included.

In summary:

Every linear program will fall into one of the following three nonoverlapping states:

1. **The problem has an optimal solution.**
2. **There is no optimal solution, because the problem is unbounded.**
3. **There is no optimal solution, because the problem is infeasible.**

In practice, a correctly formulated real-world LP will always have a solution. States 2 and 3 can arise only from (i) errors in model formulation, (ii) errors in entering the problem into the computer.

————— 3.9
SUMMARY

The powerful role of two-dimensional geometry in illustrating and motivating certain important concepts has been exploited in this chapter. In particular, we have used the geometric approach to solve linear programming problems in two-decision variables, to illustrate the meaning of active and inactive constraints, to show the important connection between optimal solutions and corners to the feasible region, and finally, to illustrate several pathological properties.

We saw that the graphical solution method involves two main steps: determining the set of feasible decisions and then selecting the best of these decisions. The underlying prerequisite for these steps is the ability to plot linear equalities and linear inequalities. The techniques needed were briefly reviewed in Section 3.2.

The task of determining the set of feasible decisions typically reduces to protraying the values of the decision variables that satisfy a collection of linear inequalities. (There could also be equalities in the system, but this merely means that the feasible decisions must also lie on each equality line.) In Section 3.3 we see that this set is determined by successively superimposing the plot of one inequality upon the other and then identifying the points that lie on the correct side of *all* the inequalities.

To find the best feasible decision, you plot a single objective function contour, identifying the optimizing direction (uphill for a Max model, downhill for a Min model), and then, with an imaginary parallel displacement of the contour in the optimizing direction, identify a corner solution. We saw in Section 3.5 that if an LP has an optimal solution, there will always be at least one optimal corner solution, also called an extreme point solution.

The graphical procedure is not limited by the necessity of creating a highly accurate picture, for it is only necessary to be able to identify the active constraints. Then, the optimal values of the decision variables are obtained by simultaneously solving these equations. From the geometric point of view, active constraints were defined as those that pass through the optimal corner of the feasible region. Algebraically, an active constraint is one for which the left-hand side, when evaluated at optimality, is equal to the

128

CHAPTER 3
Linear Programming:
Geometric
Representations
and Graphical
Solutions

right-hand side. "Surplus" and "slack" are terms used to denote the nonnegative difference between the two sides of an inequality constraint. The term "surplus" is used for a $\geq$ constraint, "slack" for a $\leq$ constraint.

Section 3.6 is devoted to a summary of the graphical solution method for a Max problem and in Section 3.7 we saw that the technique was easily extended to Min problems. The only necessary modification for a Min problem is to make sure that the contours of the objective contour are displaced in a downhill direction in the process of finding the best feasible decision.

Finally, Section 3.8 considered two pathological cases in which an LP model does not have an optimal solution. In an unbounded Max problem the objective function can assume arbitrarily large values (arbitrarily negative values in an unbounded Min problem). This typically implies that one or more important constraints have been omitted in formulating the model. An infeasible problem is one in which there are no feasible solutions; that is, the set of decision–variable values that satisfy all the constraints is empty. Such a result may occur because of incorrect formulation, such as insisting that two or more contradictory conditions must hold. Unbounded and infeasible problems can also occur as a result of transcription errors made when entering the model in the computer.

——— 3.10
KEY TERMS

CONTOUR. A contour of the function $f(x_1, x_2)$ is the set of all combinations of values for the variables (x_1, x_2) such that the function f takes on a specified constant value.

ISOPROFIT LINE. A contour of a profit function.

ISOCOST LINE. A contour of a cost function.

ISOQUANT. A synonym for contour.

GRAPHICAL SOLUTION METHOD. A two-dimensional geometric analysis of LP problems with two decision variables.

NONNEGATIVE QUADRANT. The northeast sector of the two-dimensional coordinate system in which both variables have nonnegative values.

FEASIBLE REGION. The set of combinations of values for the decision variables that satisfy the non-negativity conditions and *all* the constraints simultaneously, that is, the allowable decisions.

CONSTRAINT SET. A synonym for feasible region.

FEASIBLE SET. A synonym for feasible region.

FEASIBLE DECISION One that satisfies the nonnegativity conditions and all the constraints. Graphically, the feasible decisions are in one-to-one correspondence with the points in the feasible region.

MAXIMUM PROFIT LINE. The optimal contour of the objective function in a two-dimensional graphical analysis.

OPTIMIZING DIRECTION. The direction in which decisions with better objective function values lie.

UPHILL DIRECTION. The optimizing direction for a max model.

DOWNHILL DIRECTION. The optimizing direction for a min model.

OPTIMAL SOLUTION. A point in the feasible region that maximizes the objective function.

OPTIMAL VALUE. The optimal value of the objective function, that is, the value of the objective function when evaluated at the optimal solution. Abbreviated as OV.

OPTIMAL OBJECTIVE VALUE. A synonym for optimal value.

ACTIVE CONSTRAINT. A constraint for which, when evaluated at optimality, the left-hand side equals the right-hand side. Geometrically, this corresponds to a constraint line on which the optimal solution lies.

129

CHAPTER 3
Linear Programming:
Geometric
Representations
and Graphical
Solutions

BINDING CONSTRAINT. A synonym for active constraint.

INACTIVE CONSTRAINT. One that is not active. Consequently, an inactive constraint always has positive slack or surplus.

SLACK. The amount by which the left-hand side of a ≤ constraint, when evaluated at optimality, is less than the right-hand side. Slack is always nonnegative.

SURPLUS. The amount by which the left-hand side of a ≥ constraint, when evaluated at optimality, exceeds the right-hand side. Surplus is always nonnegative.

EXTREME POINT. Corner of the feasible region. If an LP has a solution, there is always at least one extreme point solution.

UNIQUE SOLUTION. Refers to the case in which an LP has one and only one optimal solution.

ALTERNATIVE OPTIMA. Refers to the case in which an LP has more than one optimal solution.

MULTIPLE OPTIMA. A synonym for alternative optima.

UNBOUNDED OBJECTIVE FUNCTION. An objective function which, over the feasible region, can be made arbitrarily large (positive) for a max model, arbitrarily negative for a min model.

UNBOUNDED CONSTRAINT SET. Constraint set in which at least one decision variable can be made arbitrarily large in value.

UNBOUNDED PROBLEM. An LP problem for which the objective function is unbounded. Such a problem has no solution.

INFEASIBLE PROBLEM. An LP problem with an empty feasible region. Such a problem has no solution.

INFEASIBILITY. A term referring to an infeasible problem.

INCONSISTENCY. A synonym for infeasiblity.

MAJOR CONCEPTS QUIZ

True–False

1. T **F** The feasible region is the set of all points that satisfy at least one constraint.

2. T **F** In two-dimensional problems, the intersection of any two constraints gives an extreme point of the feasible region.

3. T **F** An optimal solution uses up all of the limited resources available.

4. **T** F A well-formulated model will be neither unbounded nor infeasible.

5. **T** F Infeasibility, as opposed to unboundedness, has nothing to do with the objective function.

6. T **F** If an LP is not infeasible, it will have an optimal solution.

7. **T** F Consider any point on the boundary of the feasible region. Such a point satisfies all the constraints.

8. **T** F An active inequality constraint has zero slack or surplus, which means that the optimal solution satisfies the constraint with equality.

Multiple Choice

9. The graphical method is useful because
   a. it provides a general way to solve LP problems
   b. it gives geometric insight into the model and the meaning of optimality
   c. both a and b

10. The phrase "unbounded LP" means that
    a. at least one decision variable can be made arbitrarily large without leaving the feasible region
    b. the objective contours can be moved as far as desired, in the optimizing direction, and still touch at least one point in the constraint set
    c. not all of the constraints can be satisfied

11. Consider an optimal solution to an LP. Which of the following must be true?
    a. At least one constraint (not including nonnegativity conditions) is active at the point.
    b. Exactly one constraint (not including nonnegativity conditions) is active at the point.
    c. Neither of the above.

130

CHAPTER 3
Linear Programming:
Geometric
Representations
and Graphical
Solutions

12. Active constraints
a. are those on which the optimal solution lies
b. are those which, at optimality, do not use up all the available resources
c. Both a and b

13. An isoprofit contour represents
a. an infinite number of feasible points, all of which yield the same profit
b. an infinite number of optimal solutions
c. an infinite number of decisions, all of which yield the same profit

14. Which of the following assertions is true of an optimal solution to an LP?
a. Every LP has an optimal solution.
b. The optimal solution always occurs at an extreme point.
c. The optimal solution uses up all resources.
d. If an optimal solution exists, there will always be at least one at a corner.
e. All of the above.

15. Every corner of the feasible region is defined by
a. the intersection of two constraint lines
b. some subset of constraint lines and nonnegativity conditions
c. neither of the above

16. An unbounded feasible region
a. arises from an incorrect formulation
b. means the objective function is unbounded
c. neither of the above
d. a and b

Answers

1. F	5. T	9. b	13. c
2. F	6. F	10. b	14. d
3. F	7. T	11. c	15. b
4. T	8. T	12. a	16. c

PROBLEMS

3-1. Plot the set of points (x_1, x_2) that satisfy each of the following conditions:
(a) $2x_1 + 6x_2 = 12$
(b) $2x_1 + 6x_2 > 12$
(c) $2x_1 + 6x_2 \geq 12$
(d) $2x_1 + 6x_2 < 12$
(e) $2x_1 + 6x_2 \leq 12$

3-2. Plot the set of points (x_1, x_2) that satisfy each of the following conditions:
(a) $6x_1 + 2x_2 = 12$
(b) $6x_1 + 2x_2 > 12$
(c) $6x_1 + 2x_2 \geq 12$
(d) $6x_1 + 2x_2 < 12$
(e) $6x_1 + 2x_2 \leq 12$

3-3. (a) Plot the set of points that satisfy $-2x_1 - 6x_2 > -12$.
(b) Is this plot above or below the line $-2x_1 - 6x_2 = -12$?
(c) The plot is the same as which of the sets plotted in Problem 3-1?

3-4. (a) Plot the set of points that satisfy $-6x_1 - 2x_2 > -12$.
(b) Is this plot above or below the line $-6x_1 - 2x_2 = -12$?
(c) The plot is the same as which of the sets plotted in Problem 3-2?

131

CHAPTER 3
Linear Programming:
Geometric
Representations
and Graphical
Solutions

3-5. Claire Voyant, a colorful dealer in stereo equipment, puts together amps and preamps. An amp takes 12 hours to assemble and 4 hours for a high-performance check. A preamp takes 4 hours to assemble and 8 hours for a high-performance check. In the next month Claire will have 60 hours of assembly time available and 40 hours of high-performance check time available. Plot the combinations of amps and preamps that will satisfy

(a) The constraint on assembly time.

(b) The constraint on performance check time.

(c) Both constraints simultaneously.

3-6. Andre House is a fashion garment maker of customized jackets and trousers. Each jacket takes 3 hours for cutting and 5 hours for sewing. Each pair of trousers takes 1 hour for cutting and 5 hours for sewing. For the next month Andre has allocated 30 hours for cutting and 100 hours for needlework. Plot the combinations of jackets and trousers which Andre can make that will satisfy

(a) His constraints on cutting time.

(b) His constraints on sewing time.

(c) Both constraints simultaneously.

3-7. In Problem 3-5, suppose that Claire makes a profit of $10 on each amp and $5 on each preamp. Plot the $10, $20, and $60 profit contours.

3-8. In Problem 3-6, Andre makes $15 on each jacket and $10 on each pair of trousers. Plot the $150 and $300 profit contours.

3-9. Consider Claire's activity as described in Problems 3-5 and 3-7. Suppose that because of limitations on transistor availability she has determined that there are two additional constraints in her model. Namely, she can produce a maximum of 4 preamps and 6 amps in the next month. Taking all constraints into account,

(a) Find Claire's optimal (profit-maximizing) production plan, using graphical analysis.

(b) What is the OV?

(c) Which constraints are active?

(d) Which constraints are inactive, and what are their slack values?

3-10. Consider Andre House's activity as described in Problems 3-6 and 3-8. Suppose that because of demand constraints Andre must add two additional constraints to his model. He can sell a maximum of 8 jackets and 18 pairs of trousers in the coming month. Taking all constraints into account,

(a) Find Andre's optimal (profit-maximizing) production plan, using graphical analysis.

(b) What is the OV?

(c) Which constraints are active?

(d) Which constraints are inactive, and what are their slack values?

3-11. Could the omission of any two constraints make Claire Voyant's problem unbounded?

3-12. Could the omission of any two constraints make Andre House's problem unbounded?

3-13. Suppose that Claire's constraint on amps, $A \leq 6$, is replaced by $A \geq 6$. How does this affect the problem?

3-14. Suppose that Andre's constraint on jackets, $J \leq 8$, is replaced by $J \geq 12$. How does this affect the problem?

3-15. Consider the following LP:

$$\text{Max} \quad x_1 + x_2$$
$$\text{s.t.} \quad x_1 + 2x_2 \leq 6$$
$$3x_1 + 2x_2 \leq 12$$
$$x_1 \geq 0, \qquad x_2 \geq 0$$

132

CHAPTER 3
Linear Programming:
Geometric
Representations
and Graphical
Solutions

(a) Use the graphical method to find the optimal solution and the OV.

(b) Change the objective function to $2x_1 + 6x_2$ and find the optimal solution.

(c) How many extreme points does the feasible region have? Find the values of (x_1, x_2) at each extreme point.

3.16. Consider the following LP:

$$\text{Min } 2x_1 + x_2$$

$$\text{s.t.} \quad 4x_1 + x_2 \geq 8$$

$$2x_1 + 2x_2 \geq 10$$

$$x_1 \geq 0, \qquad x_2 \geq 0$$

(a) Use the graphical method to find the optimal solution and the OV.

(b) Change the objective function to $x_1 + 2x_2$ and find the optimal solution.

(c) How many extreme points does the feasible region have? Find the values of (x_1, x_2) at each extreme point.

3-17. Consider the following LP:

$$\text{Max } 3x_1 + 4x_2$$

$$\text{s.t.} \quad -2x_1 + 4x_2 \leq 16$$

$$2x_1 + 4x_2 \leq 24$$

$$-6x_1 - 3x_2 \geq -48$$

$$x_1, x_2 \geq 0$$

(a) Use the graphical method to find the optimal solution and the OV.

(b) Find the slack and surplus values for each constraint.

3-18. Consider the following LP:

$$\text{Min } 6x_1 + 4x_2$$

$$\text{s.t.} \quad 2x_1 + 2x_2 \geq 20$$

$$-4x_1 - 2x_2 \geq -24$$

$$x_2 \leq 4$$

$$x_1, x_2 \geq 0$$

(a) Use the graphical method to find the optimal solution and the OV.

(b) Find the slack and surplus values for each constraint.

3-19. Consider the following LP:

$$\text{Min } 5x_1 + 2x_2$$

$$\text{s.t.} \quad 3x_1 + 6x_2 \geq 18$$

$$5x_1 + 4x_2 \geq 20$$

$$8x_1 + 2x_2 \geq 16$$

$$7x_1 + 6x_2 \leq 42$$

$$x_1, x_2 \geq 0$$

133

CHAPTER 3
Linear Programming:
Geometric
Representations
and Graphical
Solutions

(a) Use the graphical method to find the optimal solution and the OV.

(b) Which constraints are active? Which are inactive?

(c) What are the slack and surplus values associated with each constraint?

(d) The feasible region has how many extreme points?

(e) Change the objective function to $15x_1 + 12x_2$. What are the alternative optimal corner solutions?

3-20. In Problem 3-19, change the objective function to Max $5x_1 + 2x_2$. Answer parts (a), (b), (c), and (d) for the new problem. In part (e) let the objective function be Max $15x_1 + 12x_2$ and identify the alternative optimal corner solutions.

More Challenging Problems

3-21. Consider the following LP model:

$$\text{Max } 600E + 1000F$$

$$\text{s.t.} \quad 100E + 60F \leq 21{,}000$$

$$4{,}000E + 800F \leq 680{,}000$$

$$E + F \leq 290$$

$$12E + 30F \leq 6{,}000$$

$$E, F \geq 0$$

(a) Let E be the horizontal axis, and F the vertical axis, and use graphical means to find the optimal solution to this problem and the OV. Label the corners of the constraint set as I, II, III, IV, and V, where I is on the vertical axis above the origin and you continue clockwise, ending with V at the origin.

(b) One of the constraints is redundant in the sense that it plays no role in determining the constraint set. Which one is it?

(c) What is the minimum change in the RHS of this constraint that would cause the constraint to become active?

(d) The coefficient of E in the third constraint is currently 1. What is the minimum increase in this coefficient that would cause the constraint to become active?

(e) Suppose that the coefficient of E, say c_E, in the objective function is increased, whereas the coefficient of F, say c_F, remains fixed. At what value for the coefficient of E would alternative optima first be encountered?

3-22. Consider the following problem:

$$\text{Min } -30E + 80F$$

$$\text{s.t.} \quad E \leq 3F$$

$$F \leq 3E$$

$$E + F \geq 4$$

$$2E + 3F \leq 24$$

$$3E + 2F \leq 24$$

(a) Use graphical means to find a solution and the OV.

(b) Create an objective function for a Min problem with the constraints given as above so that the optimal solution lies at the intersection of the lines $2E + 3F = 24$ and $3E + 2F = 24$. Find the exact value of the objective function at the solution.

(c) Replace the objective by Max $A_E E + A_F F$, where A_E and A_F are constants. What values of A_E and A_F make the optimal solution lie at the intersection of the lines $E = 3F$ and $E + F = 4$? Graphically show all the desired combinations.

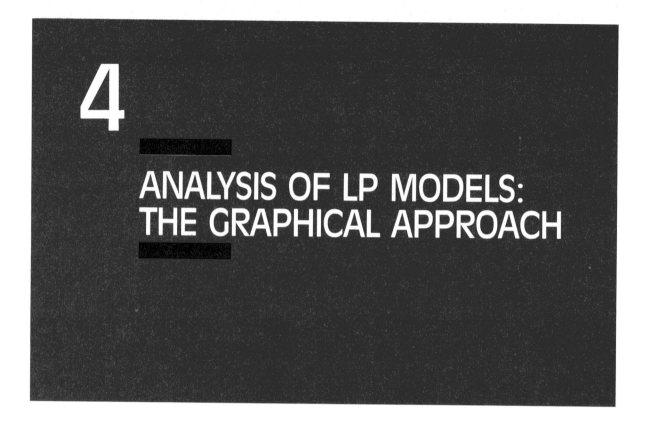

4

ANALYSIS OF LP MODELS: THE GRAPHICAL APPROACH

INTRODUCTION TO SENSITIVITY ANALYSIS (PROTRAC, INC. REVISITED)

Omitted Factors

The **PROTRAC**, Inc. model was formulated in Chapter 2 and solved in Chapter 3. You may well feel that if this were a real problem, management would now have a good solution to its real-world problem and would thus be free to turn attention to other matters. In many if not most cases this simply is not true. Often the solution to a model is only a starting point and is, in itself, the least interesting part of the analysis of the real problem. Remember that the model is an abstraction of the real problem. Typically a manager would need to ask numerous additional questions before she would be confident enough about the results to apply them to her real problem. For example, there may be rather significant considerations which because of their complexity have not been built into the model. To the extent that a model is a simplification of reality there will always be factors that are left out. Such factors may, for example, be of a political or ethical nature. Such considerations are usually difficult to quantify. Having solved her simplified model, the manager may now wish to know how well the optimal solution "fits in" with other considerations, which may not have been included.

Inexact Data

There may, as another example, be inexactitudes and uncertainty in some of the data that were used in the model. In real-world problem solving this is the norm rather than the exception. The motto is: "Do the best with what you have." In such cases, the manager will want to know: How *sensitive* is the optimal solution to the inexact data?

134

We may have an estimate of the absentee rate for next month's labor force, and the model has been run using this estimate. What happens to the optimal solution if we change the estimate by 5%, 10%, or even 15%? Will the OV (i.e., the optimal objective value) vary wildly, or will it remain more or less unchanged? Obviously, the answer to such questions will help to determine the credibility of the model's recommendations. For example, if the OV changes very little with large changes in the value of a particular parameter, we will not be concerned about uncertainty in that value. If on the other hand the OV varies wildly with small changes in that parameter, we cannot tolerate much uncertainty in its value. In this case either the model might be rejected or more resources might be committed to establishing a more precise value for the parameter in question.

Although some of the foregoing considerations can be dealt with only informally, we fortunately do have some rigorous and precise tools at our disposal. These tools are in the realm of *parametric analysis*, or *sensitivity analysis*, or *postoptimality analysis*. All of these terms mean essentially the same thing, and the topic is of such significance that an entire chapter (Chapter 5) is devoted to understanding the sensitivity information contained in the computer solution to an LP problem. Making good use of computer analysis is, of course, a problem faced by managers in the real world. In this chapter we lay some of the groundwork for being able to understand clearly the meaning of the computer results. The graphical approach which we worked with in Chapter 3 will make it relatively easy to do this. The ability to *see*, geometrically, how changes in the model affect the solution in the special two-decision-variable case makes it much easier to understand the changes that will occur in larger realistic models. In order to introduce the topic in a very specific way, let us again refer to our illustrative **PROTRAC**, Inc. model:

$$\text{Max } 5000E + 4000F \qquad \text{(max profit)}$$

$$\text{s.t.} \quad E + F \geq 5 \qquad \text{(minimal production requirement)}$$

$$E - 3F \leq 0 \qquad \text{(market position balance)}$$

$$10E + 15F \leq 150 \qquad \text{(capacity in department A)}$$

$$20E + 10F \leq 160 \qquad \text{(capacity in department B)}$$

$$30E + 10F \geq 135 \qquad \text{(contractual labor agreement)}$$

$$E, F \geq 0 \qquad \text{(nonnegativity conditions)}$$

Recall that the purpose of this model, as discussed in Chapter 2, is to recommend a production target *for next month*. Therefore, all the numerical data in the model are supposed to be pertinent to this period of interest, namely one month in the future.

A major application of linear programming involves planning models such as this, where future plans and policies are to be determined, and in such models future data are naturally required. Obviously in many real-world situations such data may not be known with complete certainty.

Uncertain Revenues and Costs   Suppose, for example, that the stated profitabilities of $5000 per E-9 and $4000 per F-9 are only estimates based on revenues and projected costs for next month, and that some of the costs of raw materials to be purchased next month are subject to change. Unfortunately, in order to achieve the lead time required in the planning process, the model must be run now, before the exact data are known. Thus, we must use the numbers above, which are our best current estimates, knowing full well that the actual profitabilities next month could differ. We might have some fairly solid ideas about the possible ranges in which the true values will lie, and the profitabilities of $5000 and $4000 might be our best estimates within such ranges. But how do we deal with the fact that the data are not known with complete certainty? That is one important topic covered in sensitivity analysis.

Uncertain RHS Data   Another possible concern may involve uncertainty in some of the constraint data. In linear programming, this type of uncertainty usually focuses on the right-hand sides of the constraints. For example, consider the number 135, which is the right-hand side of the contractual labor agreement constraint. It represents the minimal number of hours that must be spent on product testing next month. In a real-life application it is possible that such a number could also be uncertain. The actual minimal requirement that will be in force next month could be arrived at in a rather complicated way depending, for example, on the results of quality tests of this month's production, results that can only be *estimated* at the time the planning process occurs. Thus, the value of 135 is only a "best estimate." Again, management must cope with the uncertainty in such data.

These two examples reflect the major focus of sensitivity analysis and of the topics discussed in the following two sections. The first example, in which profitabilities are uncertain, illustrates what we call *changes in the objective function coefficients*. The second example illustrates changes in the *right-hand side*. In an LP model, the objective function coefficients and the right-hand sides are often called *parameters*, and for this reason the term "parametric analysis" is sometimes used for the investigation of the effects of changing the values of these parameters. Let us see how graphical analysis can provide insight into the effects of such changes.

_____ 4.2
CHANGES IN THE OBJECTIVE FUNCTION COEFFICIENTS

Suppose that the constraint data remain unchanged and only the objective coefficients are changed. Then the only effect on the model, from the geometric viewpoint, is that the slope of the profit lines is changed. We have, in fact, already seen an illustration of this phenomenon in Section 3.5. In Figure 3.13 all data in the **PROTRAC**, Inc. model remained unchanged except for the fact that the profitability of F-9s was raised from $4000 to $10,000 per unit. We saw that the effect of this change was to change the tilt of the profit lines to such an extent that a new corner solution was obtained. You can also quickly see that some changes in the objective function coefficients will *not* change the optimal solution, even though the profit lines will have a different slope. For example, let us replace the old objective function $5000E + 4000F$ with a new objective function $4000E + 5000F$. As we saw in Figure 3.11, the solution with the old objective function is $E^* = 4.5$, $F^* = 7.0$. The new objective function $4000E + 5000F$ assigns a lower profitability to E-9s and higher to F-9s. You might therefore expect to obtain an optimal solution calling for production of fewer than 4.5 E-9s and more than 7.0 of the more profitable F-9s. However, Figure 4.1 presents a graphical analysis which shows that this is not the case. In this figure there are three different objective functions:

$$5000E + 4000F$$

$$4000E + 5000F$$

$$5000E + 10,000F$$

FIGURE 4.1

PROTRAC, Inc. Model with Contours of Three
Different Profit Functions and the
Corresponding Solutions

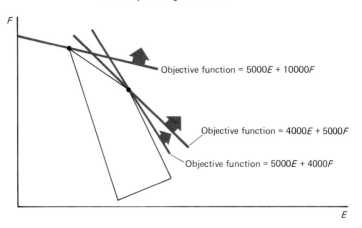

Same Solution   It is shown that the negative slopes of the contours associated with each of the three functions become progressively less steep (i.e., the contours become flatter) as the profitability of F-9s increases relative to E-9s [i.e., as the ratio (coefficient of F/coefficient of E) increases]. However, although the objectives $5000E + 4000F$ and $4000E + 5000F$ have contours with different slopes, *the slopes are not sufficiently different to give us a new corner solution.* For each of these two objectives the optimal solution is the same, namely $E^* = 4.5$ and $F^* = 7.0$.

Different OVs   On the other hand, it is important to note that in this case the optimal profits (i.e., the optimal objective values) will differ. In the former case we have

$$\text{optimal profit} = 5000E^* + 4000F^*$$

$$= 5000(4.5) + 4000(7) = 50{,}500$$

whereas in the latter case

$$\text{optimal profit} = 4000E^* + 5000F^*$$

$$= 4000(4.5) + 5000(7) = 51{,}200$$

In summary, what we have just seen is that

Changing the objective function coefficients changes the slopes of the objective function contours. This may or may not affect the optimal solution and the optimal value of the objective function.

This geometric analysis, although conducted on a two-dimensional problem, gives you good insight into more general problems, for even in models with more than two decision variables the summary statement above is correct. In the next chapter we will see how the computer can be used to provide for higher-dimensional models a wealth of sensitivity information on the effects of changes in the objective function coefficients. We shall also see how such information can be used to management's advantage.

———— 4.3
CHANGES IN THE RIGHT-HAND SIDES

Let us now ignore the objective function and focus on the right-hand sides of the constraint functions. Again, graphical analysis will nicely explain the effects of changes in these parameters. As a specific example, let us suppose that the fifth constraint of the **PROTRAC**, Inc. model

$$30E + 10F \geq 135 \qquad \text{(contractual labor)} \qquad (4.1)$$

is changed to

$$30E + 10F \geq 210 \qquad (4.2)$$

Parallel Shift in the Constraint Line and suppose that all other constraint data remain as they are given. Since 135 is a smaller number than 210, expression (4.1) is easier to satisfy than (4.2). For example, the pair $(E = 3, F = 5)$ satisfies (4.1) for

$$30E + 10F = 30(3) + 10(5) = 90 + 50 = 140$$

Since 140 is ≥ 135, (4.1) is satisfied. But 140 is less than 210 and hence the pair $(E = 3, F = 5)$ does *not* satisfy condition (4.2). Another way of saying this is that *fewer combinations of values for E and F will satisfy (4.2)*. Because of this fact, it would be reasonable to expect that the change from (4.1) to (4.2) might, in some sense, "shrink" the feasible region. From the geometric point of view, you can see that changing the right-hand side of a constraint creates a parallel shift in the constraint line. In this case, then, the reasoning above suggests that, in changing the RHS from 135 to 210, the fifth constraint line [corresponding to (4.1)] will shift in such a way as to eliminate some of the feasible region. Figure 4.2 shows the original constraint set with the constraints labeled ①

FIGURE 4.2
Graphical Analysis of the Original Model

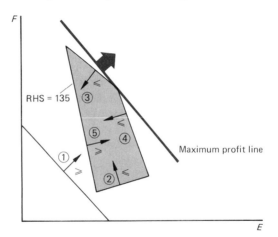

FIGURE 4.3

Graphical Analysis of the Model with New RHS
for the Fifth Constraint

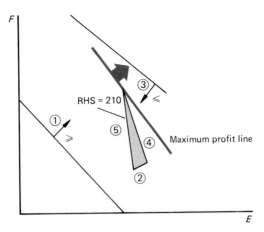

through ⑤. Figure 4.3 shows the new constraint set with the fifth constraint (4.1) replaced by (4.2).

Although, geometrically speaking, the constraint set in Figure 4.3 looks quite different from the one in Figure 4.2, all that has been done is to slide the constraint labeled ⑤ farther outward from the origin to its new position. You should experiment by assigning different values to this right-hand side, and to the other right-hand sides, to see the variety of different-looking feasible regions than can arise from such simple perturbations. One particularly interesting case arises if you further increase the right-hand side of the fifth constraint to 270, leaving all the other constraint data unchanged. You are asked in Problem 5 to show that in this case you will have created an inconsistent set of constraints. That is, the problem becomes infeasible.

Return now to Figure 4.3. The optimal solution is shown for the objective function $5000E + 4000F$. Comparing this with the graphical analysis for the original problem, Figure 4.2, you can see that the solution to the new problem is entirely different from the old. We have

> Old problem:
> > Active constraints: ③ and ④
> > Inactive constraints: ①, ②, and ⑤
> > Solution (by solving active constraints): $E^* = 4.5$, $F^* = 7$
> > Optimal profit = OV = 50,500

The New Solution

> New problem:
> > Active constraints: ④ and ⑤
> > Inactive constraints: ①, ②, and ③
> > Solution is computed as follows:

$$
\begin{array}{lrcr}
\text{Constraint ④:} & 20E + 10F & = & 160 \\
\text{Constraint ⑤:} & 30E + 10F & = & 210 \\
\hline
\text{Subtracting:} & -10E & = & -50 \\
& E & = & 5 \\
\text{Substituting:} & 20(5) + 10F & = & 160 \\
& F & = & 6
\end{array}
$$

Hence, $E^* = 5$, $F^* = 6$, and

$$\text{optimal profit} = \text{OV} = 5000E^* + 4000F^*$$
$$= 5000(5) + 4000(6) = 49{,}000$$

It should be clear from this analysis that changing even one right-hand-side value can have a profound effect on the solution. In Chapter 5 we shall develop additional tools for precisely determining the impact of certain RHS changes. Again, it will be shown that the computer can be used to provide sensitivity information on the effects of such changes. For now, we summarize what we have graphically seen in this section for two-dimensional models. These results, as with the previous results for changing an objective function coefficient, are also valid for problems with more than two decision variables.

> **Changing a right-hand-side value results in a parallel shift of the changed constraint. This *may* affect both the optimal solution and the OV (the optimal objective value). The effect will depend on exactly which right-hand-side values are changed, and by how much.**

4.4
TIGHTENING AND LOOSENING AN INEQUALITY CONSTRAINT

We conclude this discussion on parametric changes by making some general observations on the effects of right-hand-side changes for *inequality constraints*. This will lead us to several useful new terms.

In the discussion above we compared the two constraints

$$30E + 10F \geq 135 \tag{4.1}$$

and

$$30E + 10F \geq 210 \tag{4.2}$$

and noted that since each constraint is of $\geq$ form, and since the right-hand side of (4.2) is larger than the right-hand side of (4.1), the constraint (4.2) is more difficult to satisfy. This process of increasing the RHS of a $\geq$ constraint is called *tightening the constraint*. The constraint (4.2) is *tighter* than (4.1). Similarly, if the RHS of a $\leq$ constraint is decreased, the constraint becomes more difficult to satisfy and hence is tighter.

Tightening

> **Tightening an inequality constraint means making it more difficult to satisfy. For a $\geq$ constraint this means increasing the RHS. For a $\leq$ constraint this means decreasing the RHS.**

Suppose that instead of increasing the RHS of (4.1) we decrease it so that, for example, the constraint becomes

$$30E + 10F \geq 100 \tag{4.3}$$

You should be able to see that since the right-hand side has become a smaller number, and since (4.3) is a $\geq$ constraint, there are now *more* combinations of values for E and F that will satisfy the constraint. Thus, the constraint has become easier to satisfy. This process of decreasing the RHS of a $\geq$ constraint is called *loosening the constraint*. The constraint (4.3) is *looser* than (4.1). Similarly, if the RHS of a $\leq$ constraint is increased, the constraint becomes easier to satisfy and hence is looser.

Loosening

> **Loosening an inequality constraint means making it easier to satisfy. For a $\geq$ constraint this means decreasing the RHS. For a $\leq$ constraint this means increasing the RHS.**

The geometric effects of tightening and loosening are easily illustrated. Referring to Figures 4.2 and 4.3, we see that in moving from Figure 4.2 to Figure 4.3, constraint ⑤ has been tightened and the result is to contract the feasible region. If you move from Figure 4.3 to Figure 4.2, constraint ⑤ has been loosened and the effect is to expand the feasible region. These geometric results, that tightening contracts and loosening expands, are what you probably would have predicted, but there is another possibility that must be considered.

Consider constraint ①, $E + F \geq 5$. Note in Figure 4.2 that it currently plays no role in determining the shape of the feasible set. Also, with a suitably small change in the right-hand side, say from 5 to 5.1 or 4.9, the line will incur a small parallel displacement and still not intersect the original feasible set. Thus, in this case we see that a suitably small amount of tightening or loosening of constraint ① has no effect on the feasible set. We now summarize our observation on the geometric effects of tightening and loosening inequality constraints.

**Effect on
Constraint Set**

> **Tightening an inequality constraint either contracts the constraint set or, possibly, leaves it unaffected. Loosening an inequality constraint either expands the constraint set or, possibly, leaves it unaffected.**

These results are generally true for inequality constraints and do not depend on the dimension of the model (the number of decision variables) or on whether the constraint is of $\leq$ or $\geq$ form. It should be emphasized that in this analysis we have assumed that one constraint is manipulated while all the others remain fixed. The effects of tightening (loosening) several at a time are also to contract (expand) or, possibly, to leave the feasible region unchanged. However, if some constraints are tightened and others simultaneously loosened, there is little that can be categorically stated about the result. We conclude this section with the observation that tightening a constraint too much can produce infeasibility. For example, we saw that this occurred when the RHS of constraint ⑤ was increased to 270.

———— 4.5
REDUNDANT CONSTRAINTS

A constraint such as constraint ① in Figure 4.2 is termed *redundant*. Although there are five constraints plotted in this figure, only four of them are required to define the feasible region. This is because, as the picture clearly indicates, any combination of E and F

values that satisfies the constraints labeled ②, ③, ④, and ⑤ will automatically satisfy the constraint labeled ① as well. In this sense the first constraint is superfluous. Here is a precise definition:

A redundant constraint is one whose removal does not change the feasible region.

Since a redundant constraint could, by definition, be discarded without changing the feasible region, its elimination will also have no effect on the optimal solution to the problem, and you may well ask: "Why bother including such a constraint in the model?" There are two important responses to this question:

Keep Redundant Constraints

1. Redundant constraints are not generally very easy to recognize. Even in the simple case of problems with two decision variables, if you are looking only at the algebraic form of the mathematical model, the redundant constraints are not immediately spotted. For example, it is not obvious from the mathematical formulation that the constraint $E + F \geq 5$ is redundant in the **PROTRAC**, Inc. model. The graphical representation, of course, makes it clear for this two-dimensional problem. However, since graphical analysis is limited to two-dimensional problems, it is not useful for detecting redundancy in general real-world applications.

2. A constraint that is redundant today may not be redundant tomorrow. For example, suppose that the management of **PROTRAC**, Inc. decides to explore the effects of a new policy decision to produce at least seven, rather than five, units of E and F in total. Then the RHS of the first constraint changes to 7 instead of 5. The modified first constraint is plotted as a dashed line in Figure 4.4, and it is seen that the new constraint is no longer redundant. In other words, *tightening* the requirement from 5 to 7 forces us to cut off some previously allowable decisions.

It is quite possible that a constraint that is redundant for a given set of data may no longer be redundant when some of the data are changed.

It is often for this reason that a redundant constraint is in a model. It is common practice to solve planning models many times with different sets of data in order to gain in-

FIGURE 4.4
Tightening the First Constraint

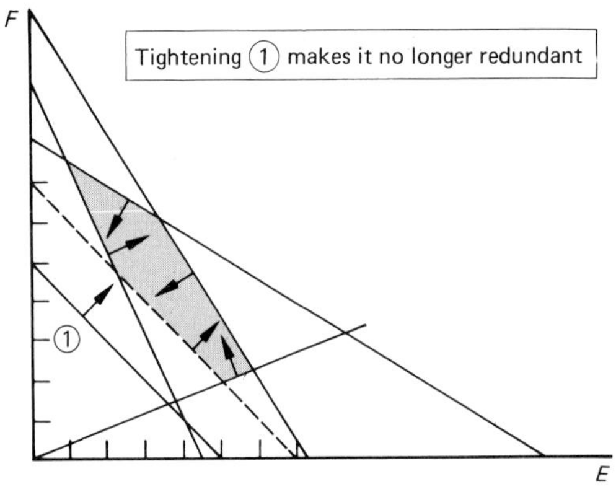

sight into possible future scenarios. The model builder may intuitively know that there are conditions of interest (values of the data) for which this constraint may become *important*, and that is why she included this constraint in her model.

_____ 4.6
WHAT IS AN IMPORTANT CONSTRAINT?

The concluding sentence of the preceding section suggests that there may be a distinction between "important" and "unimportant" constraints. Indeed, we have seen that, in general, an LP model may have numerous constraints. It would be of interest to know whether some of the many constraints may perhaps have special importance in the model. The management of **PROTRAC**, Inc. certainly has an interest in knowing which constraints are most restrictive in the sense of limiting the possibilities for greater profit.

Redundant
Least
Important
The discussion in the section above suggests that, *for a given set of data*, the redundant constraints (if there are any) are the least important. That is, we have already observed that constraint ① is redundant, which means that it can be ignored without changing the constraint set and hence without changing the optimal solution. Since it does not affect the solution, it is, *for the given set of data*, of little importance. But can we say more? Just in terms of what we have so far learned, can you identify other constraints in the model than seem to be "more important" than the others?

Then Inactive
In Figure 4.5 the graphical analysis of the **PROTRAC**, Inc. model is reproduced. This figure shows that there are indeed other constraints in the model that can be ignored without affecting the solution, namely, constraints ② and ⑤. The graphical analysis of the model with constraints ①, ②, and ⑤ deleted is given in Figure 4.6. Although the feasible region has become greatly enlarged, the optimal solution remains unchanged. Recall that in this problem constraints ①, ②, and ⑤ are the *inactive constraints*.

FIGURE 4.5
Graphical Analysis of PROTRAC, Inc.

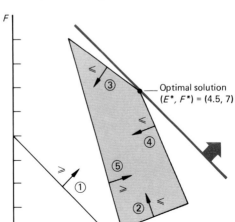

FIGURE 4.6

Graphical Analysis of PROTRAC, Inc. with
Constraits ①, ②, and ⑤ Deleted

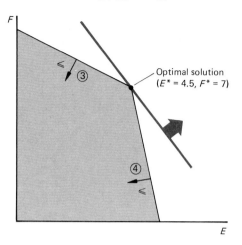

The phenomenon we have just observed is generally true, even in higher-dimensional problems.

> In any LP model, *for a fixed set of data*, the inactive constraints can be re-moved without affecting the optimal solution. The optimal solution is deter-mined entirely by the active constraints.

Active Most Important

Thus, for a given set of data it is the active constraints that are the important ones in the sense that they completely determine the solution. If we could only know in advance which constraints are active, the task of solving an LP would reduce to the relatively easy problem of solving a system of simultaneous linear equations, such as the equations for the lines labeled ③ and ④ in Figure 4.6. Thus, although we may agree that the active constraints are most important, this information becomes available only *after* the problem is solved, for unfortunately the modeler has no way of knowing, in advance, which of the inequality constraints will be active.[1] Consequently, a more complicated algorithm is needed to solve the general LP. This algorithm, called the simplex method, will be studied in Chapter 6.

In concluding this section, we wish to emphasize that when the data in a model change, the set of active and inactive inequality constraints can also change. *In other words, the unimportant (inactive) constraints for one set of data may become important (active) when the model is re-solved with different data.* You can think of a model as being "a logical framework or structure" that underlies the assigned numerical values of the parameters. This logical framework captures interactions among variables as well as requirements and limitations. The logical framework in a sense is independent of the actual values assigned to the parameters (i.e., the data). Different data values will give different realizations to the model. In this larger context it is not really meaningful to label some constraints as being more important than others. *The importance of the constraints is a relative question whose answer will depend on the values assigned to the data.*

---

[1] Recall that an equality constraint, by definition, is always active.

ADDING OR DELETING CONSTRAINTS

There is one final general observation which the graphical analysis immediately brings home. This concerns the effects of adding or deleting constraints. Comparing Figures 4.5 and 4.6 shows immediately what can happen when constraints are deleted. Deleting the constraint labeled ① (the redundant constraint) had no effect on the model. Deleting ② allows the feasible region to enlarge. Deleting ⑤ allows it to further enlarge, as represented in Figure 4.6. Thus, in general (i.e., for any LP problem)

Deleting constraints leaves the feasible region either unchanged or enlarged.

Effect on Feasible Region   We have previously observed the impact of adding constraints to a model. This impact was demonstrated during the course of plotting the constraint set for the **PROTRAC**, Inc. model. You will recall that superimposing successive constraints had the effect of "trimming down" the constraint set. Thus,

---

Adding constraints leaves the feasible region either unchanged or smaller.

Since adding constraints may have the effect of "trimming down" the feasible region, adding a new constraint to a model may happen to "trim off" a piece of the constraint set which contains the previous optimal solution. If this happens, the result may be a reduced OV (optimal objective value) for the new problem. This is shown in Figure 4.7, where a sixth inequality constraint has been added to the **PROTRAC**, Inc. model. The crosshatched region in Figure 4.7 portrays that part of the constraint set

FIGURE 4.7

Addition of a Sixth Constraint

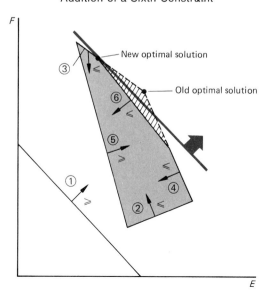

which is eliminated by the addition of the constraint labeled ⑥. The "uphill" direction in this diagram is to the northeast, and the new maximum profit line is not as far "uphill" as the former maximum profit line. Hence, the imposition of a new constraint has led to a reduction in the optimal profit. This is why management often prefers to operate with as few constraints as possible. *The larger the number of constraints, the greater the chance that the optimal objective value is less desirable.* The general result is that

Effect on OV

> **Adding constraints to a model will either impair the OV or leave it unchanged. Deleting constraints will either improve the OV or leave it unchanged.**

It can be observed in concluding that the results of adding and deleting constraints are analogous to the results of tightening and loosening inequality constraints, both in terms of effects on the feasible region and on the optimal objective value. Thus, in the above displayed result, the phrase "Tightening inequality constraints" could be substituted for "Adding constraints to a model." The phrase "Loosening inequality constraints" could be substituted for "Deleting constraints." The effects on the optimal objective value of tightening and loosening inequality constraints are explored in more detail in Chapter 5.

———— **4.8**

SUMMARY

This chapter has used graphical analysis on problems with two decision variables to introduce the topic of parametric analysis, which is also called sensitivity analysis or postoptimality analysis. The general approach in sensitivity analysis is to assume that an LP model has been solved and then investigate the effect of making various changes in the model. Typically, one is interested in the effect of the changes on the optimal solution and on the optimal value of the objective function.

In Section 4.2 we saw that changing the objective function coefficients changes the slope of the objective function contours. This may or may not affect the optimal solution and the optimal value of the objective function.

Sections 4.3 and 4.4 deal with changes in the right-hand side of the constraints. We first observed that changing a right-hand-side value results in a parallel shift of the changed constraint. This may affect both the optimal solution and the optimal objective value. The effect will depend on exactly which right-hand-side values are changed. Changes in the right-hand side of an inequality constraint can be thought of as tightening or loosening the constraint. Tightening a constraint means making it more difficult to satisfy. For a ≥ constraint this means increasing the RHS. For a ≤ constraint this means decreasing the RHS. Similarly, loosening a constraint means making it easier to satisfy. For a ≥ constraint this means decreasing the RHS. For a ≤ constraint this means increasing the RHS. From a geometric point of view, tightening an inequality constraint either contracts the constraint set, or, possibly, leaves it unaffected. Loosening an inequality constraint either expands the constraint set or, possibly, leaves it unaffected. From a practical point of view, these operations either further limit or further augment the options available to the decision maker.

Another way in which a model could be modified after its original formulation and solution is by adding or deleting constraints. The effect of these changes is investigated in Section 4.7. En route to this analysis it is useful to note that a redundant constraint is one whose removal does not change the feasible region. Also, as discussed in Section 4.6, an inactive constraint can be removed from the model without changing the optimal solution. One might therefore be tempted to remove redundant or inactive constraints from a model before solving it, if it were possible to identify such constraints. In fact, however, redundant constraints are usually not recognizable, and the inactive constraints are revealed only after the problem has been solved. Moreover, the concepts of redundant and inactive are data dependent. If you change the data, the redundant constraints, and the inactive constraints, may change. We find it productive to think of the model as being the "logical framework or structure" that describes the operation of the system under consideration, independently of the numerical values assigned to the parameters. Since constraints that are redundant or inactive for one set of parameter values may not remain in that status when the parameter values are changed, the notion of searching for redundant or inactive constraints seems as inappropriate as it is difficult. We conclude the discussion of this topic by observing that deleting constraints leaves the feasible region either unchanged or enlarged, whereas adding constraints leaves the feasible region either unchanged or smaller, and hence the effects of deleting and adding are analogous to the effects of loosening and tightening.

—————— 4.9
KEY TERMS

SENSITIVITY ANALYSIS. A California approach to management based on group phenomena and of particular interest to aspiring young models. In LP this has a more restricted meaning: Analyzing the effect on the problem, in particular the effect on the optimal solution and the optimal value of the objective function, of changes in various parameters.

PARAMETRIC ANALYSIS. A synonym for sensitivity analysis.

POSTOPTIMALITY ANALYSIS. Another synonym for sensitivity analysis.

PARAMETERS. A term referring to the numerical data in an LP model. The values of these parameters may change and the problem may be re-solved with these changed values.

TIGHTENING A CONSTRAINT. Refers to changes in the RHS of an inequality constraint which make the constraint more difficult to satisfy. This is accomplished by increasing the RHS of a $\geq$ constraint and decreasing the RHS of a $\leq$ constraint.

LOOSENING A CONSTRAINT. Refers to changes in the RHS of an inequality constraint which make the constraint easier to satisfy. This is accomplished by decreasing the RHS of a $\geq$ constraint and increasing the RHS of a $\leq$ constraint.

REDUNDANT CONSTRAINT. A constraint whose removal does not change the feasible region.

INACTIVE CONSTRAINT. An inequality constraint that does not pass through the optimal solution. Hence, for a given set of data, the removal of an inactive constraint will not change the optimal solution.

ACTIVE CONSTRAINT. A constraint that passes through the optimal solution. An equality constraint is always active. An inequality constraint is either active or inactive.

MAJOR CONCEPTS QUIZ ————————————————

True–False

1. (T) F   Sensitivity analysis greatly increases the possibility that a model can be useful to management.

2. T (F)   Consider a model in which, for some of the data, we know there is error. For example, some of the data represent estimates of future values for certain parameters. Suppose sensitivity analysis reveals that the OV is highly sensitive to these parameters. Such information provides more confidence in the recommendations of the model.

3. (T) F   Sensitivity analysis is a precise tool.

4. T (F)   Changing the RHS of a constraint changes its slope.

5. **T** (**F**) Changing a RHS cannot affect the set of inactive constraints.

6. (**T**) **F** Loosening an inequality constraint means changing the RHS to make it easier to satisfy.

7. (**T**) **F** A $\geq$ constraint is tightened by increasing the RHS.

8. **T** (**F**) Tightening a redundant inequality constraint cannot affect the feasible region.

9. (**T**) **F** For a given set of data, the inactive constraints are less important than the active ones.

10. **T** (**F**) Adding constraints to a model may help (i.e., improve) the OV.

Multiple Choice

11. Sensitivity analysis
    a. allows us to more meaningfully interpret the computer solution
    b. is done after the optimal solution is obtained, and is therefore called postoptimality analysis
    c. is sometimes called parametric analysis
    (d.) all of the above

12. Sensitivity analysis
    a. can be done graphically in two dimensions
    b. can increase our confidence in a model
    c. can weaken our confidence in the recommendations of a model
    (d.) all of the above
    e. a and b

13. The value of the geometric approach, in two dimensions, is
    a. to solve the problem quickly
    (b.) to understand what is happening in higher dimensions
    c. to better understand two-dimensional algebra

14. In LP, sensitivity analysis
    a. can deal with changes in the objective function coefficients
    b. can deal with changes in RHS
    (c.) both of the above

15. Changing an objective function coefficient
    a. produces a new optimal solution
    (b.) changes the tilt of the objective function contours
    c. gives a new OV
    d. all of the above

16. Tightening an inequality constraint
    a. improves the OV
    (b.) cannot improve the OV
    c. hurts the OV

17. A redundant constraint
    a. may not be easy to recognize
    b. should always be dropped from the model
    c. may not be redundant if the data are changed
    d. all of the above
    (e.) a and c
    f. a and b
    g. b and c

Answers

1. T	5. F	9. T	13. b
2. F	6. T	10. F	14. c
3. T	7. T	11. d	15. b
4. F	8. F	12. d	16. b
			17. e

PROBLEMS

4-1. In the **PROTRAC**, Inc. model, suppose that the objective function is changed to $5000E + 2000F$.

    (a) Use graphic analysis (e.g., Figure 4.1) to determine the effect on the optimal solution.

    (b) What is the effect on the OV?

4-2. In the **PROTRAC**, Inc. model, suppose that the objective function is changed to $2000E + 4000F$.

    (a) Use graphic analysis (e.g., Figure 4.1) to determine the effect on the optimal solution.

    (b) What is the effect on the OV?

4-3. Notice in Figure 4.1 the two objective functions

$$5000E + 4000F$$

$$5000E + 10,000F$$

The figure indicates that when the per unit profitability of F is increased from 4000 to 10,000, without changing the per unit profitability of E, the optimal value of E decreases. Why should the optimal value of E depend on the coefficient of F? Try to answer this question in words.

4-4. In the **PROTRAC**, Inc. model, suppose that the objective function is changed to $5000E + 2500F$.

    (a) Use graphic analysis to decide whether there will be a new optimal solution.

    (b) What is the effect on the OV?

4-5. In the **PROTRAC**, Inc. model, replace the RHS of the fifth constraint (contractual labor agreement), which is currently 135, with the value 270. State the effect on the constraint set.

4-6. In the **PROTRAC**, Inc. model, what is the smallest value of the RHS to make the first constraint be no longer redundant? How large can the RHS be made without destroying feasibility?

4-7. Consider the LP

$$\text{Max } 30x_1 + 10x_2$$

$$\text{s.t.} \quad 2x_1 + x_2 \leq 4$$

$$2x_1 + 2x_2 \leq 6$$

$$X_1 \geq 0, \qquad X_2 \geq 0$$

    (a) Solve graphically and state the optimal solution.

    (b) Keeping all other data as is, what per unit profitability should the product, whose current optimal value is zero, have in order that this product enter the optimal solution at a positive level?

    (c) How many optimal corner solutions exist after making the change described in part (b)? What are they?

    (d) In the original problem, how much can the RHS of the second constraint be increased (decreased) before the optimal solution is changed?

    (e) Answer part (d) for the RHS of the first constraint.

    (f) How do you explain the difference between parts (d) and (e)?

    (g) What will be the impact of adding the constraint $4x_1 + x_2 = 4$ to the original model?

    (h) What is the impact (on the optimal solution) of adding the constraint $3x_1 + 3x_2 \leq 15$ to the original model?

(i) Fill in the blanks in the following statement: The difference between parts (g) and (h) is that the original optimal solution already _____ the constraint in (h) but does not _____ the constraint in (g).

4-8. Consider the LP

$$\text{Max } 3x_1 + 9x_2$$

$$\text{s.t.} \quad 2x_1 + 3x_2 \leq 12$$

$$x_1 + x_2 \leq 6$$

$$x_1 \geq 0, \quad x_2 \geq 0$$

In terms of this model, answer (a)–(g) in Problem 7.

(h) What will be the impact of adding the constraint $X_1 + 2X_2 \leq 6$ to the original model?

(i) Explain the difference between parts (g) and (h).

4-9. Of the two constraints

$$-3x_1 + 2x_2 \geq -6$$

$$-3x_1 + 2x_2 \geq -10$$

which is tighter? Which of the constraints, if either, does the point $(x_1 = 2, x_2 = 1)$ satisfy? What about the point $(x_1 = 3, x_2 = 0)$?

4-10. Of the constraints

$$5x_1 - 12x_2 \geq 5$$

$$5x_1 - 12x_2 \geq -5$$

which is tighter? Which of the constraints, if either, does the point $(x_1 = 4, x_2 = 1)$ satisfy? What about the point $(x_1 = 2, x_2 = 1)$?

4-11. Of the two constraints in Problem 4-9, which is looser?

4-12. Of the two constraints in Problem 4-10, which is looser?

4-13. Fill in the blanks: Increasing the RHS of a $\leq$ constraint means that there will be _____ combinations of decision-variable values which satisfy the constraint. This means that one is _____ the constraint.

4-14. Fill in the blanks: Increasing the RHS of a $\geq$ constraint means that there will be _____ combinations of decision-variable values which satisfy the constraint. This means that one is _____ the constraint.

4-15. Using the words "enlarge," "diminish," "smaller," "larger," unchanged," fill in the blanks: Tightening a constraint cannot _____ the constraint set and may leave it _____ or _____.

4-16. Using the words supplied in Problem 15, fill in the blanks: Loosening a constraint cannot _____ the constraint set and may leave it _____ or _____.

4-17. In the **PROTRAC**, Inc. model, which constraint is redundant? Will this constraint remain redundant if its RHS value is increased by 10%, all other data held fixed?

4-18. In the **PROTRAC**, Inc. model, for what values of the RHS will the second constraint become redundant, assuming all other data are held fixed?

4-19. Suppose that you have created a model and that by some means you are able to identify a redundant constraint. Would you say it is generally true that such a constraint should be dropped from the model? Why? (Or why not?)

4-20. How would your answer to Problem 4-19 differ if the model is to be run one and only one time?

4-21. Suppose you know that in a given run of a model a particular constraint will be redundant. Does it follow that this constraint will also be inactive?

4-22. Discuss briefly the notion of "important" versus "unimportant" constraints.

4-23. Match up the two columns (one for one):

(a) Adding constraints   (1) May enlarge the feasible region
(b) Deleting constraints   (2) May make the feasible region smaller
(c) Important constraints   (3) Depend on the data set
(d) Tightening constraints   (4) May improve the OV
(e) Loosening constraints   (5) May hurt the OV

5

LINEAR PROGRAMS: COMPUTER ANALYSIS, INTERPRETING SENSITIVITY OUTPUT, AND THE DUAL PROBLEM

AN INVENTORY OF TRUCKS*

The Fleet Administration Division of North American Van Lines, Inc., has primary responsibility for planning and controlling the company's fleet of truck tractors. The task is complicated because drivers in the North American system are independent contractors. That is, they own, and are responsible for the maintenance of their tractor equipment, whose service is in turn leased to North American. In particular, Fleet Administration (1) recruits and trains owner-drivers; (2) buys new tractors from manufacturers and sells used tractors; (3) sells new tractors to drivers and buys used tractors from them; and (4) provides warranty, insurance, and financing arrangements to contract truckers.

Historically, Fleet Administration used a manual system to discharge its responsibilities. This system started with a forecast of demand for shipments which was translated into a forecast for the required number of new contract owners required during each remaining week of the fiscal year. This forecast, in turn, led to recruiting and training plans as well as plans for tractor purchases and sales. This process re-

* Dan Avramovich, Thomas M. Cook, Gary O. Langston, and Frank Sutherland, "A Decision Support System for Fleet Management: A Linear Programming Approach," *Interfaces*, Vol. 12, No. 3 (June 1982), pp. 1–9.

quired 120 labor hours of computational effort for each pass through the planning process. This implied both high costs and the lack of ability to evaluate alternative purchase and sales plans. In other words, the process simply evaluated the plan selected. It gave no information on what decisions could be made to improve it.

In the face of this situation North American created and implemented a decision support system with two main functions:

1. It used a large-scale LP model to determine a new/used, purchase/sales plan for tractors.
2. It used the LP results to generate a series of reports that illustrate the financial impact of the suggested plan.

The model has had an important effect on three areas within the firm. First, the average inventory has been reduced by 100 tractors, or approximately $3,000,000. This yields an approximate annual savings in inventory carrying costs of $600,000. Second, the ability to run up to three scenarios per day makes it possible for management to react quickly to changes in demand forecasts. Finally, the personnel used in the old manual system can be productively reassigned.

5.1
INTRODUCTION

In Chapter 4 we stated that the manager is typically interested in much more than simply the solution to an LP model. The analysis of a real-world problem often begins with the solution. We stated that the process of analyzing a model after the solution has been derived is termed *sensitivity analysis*, and we then dealt with some of the geometry that underlies sensitivity analysis. In this chapter we look in detail at how the manager might, in practice, use the wealth of information contained in the computer analysis of an LP. This can be an important, even daily, problem faced by managers in the real world—the problem of making good use of computer analysis. This discussion culminates in Section 5.4, in a realistic scenario involving the manager and the management scientist.

To begin the development of this chapter, it is important to understand the form of the LP model that the computer actually solves. This is called the *standard equality constraint form*. After illustrating some relevant properties of this form, we proceed to study the computer output for two problems already seen: **PROTRAC**, Inc. and Crawler Tread.

In concluding this chapter, we introduce a new topic, called *duality*, which is closely connected to sensitivity considerations, and which provides a more profound knowledge of the LP model. We discuss several aspects of the dual problem, highlighting its theoretic, computational, and economic significance.

5.2
THE PROBLEM THE COMPUTER SOLVES

We shall show that any linear program, regardless of the sense of the constraints (i.e., whether they are $\geq$, $=$, or $\leq$), can be transformed into an equivalent problem all of whose constraints are equalities. This step is accomplished with the use of *slack* and *surplus variables*.

154

CHAPTER 5
Linear Programs:
Computer Analysis,
Interpreting
Sensitivity Output,
and the Dual
Problem

FIGURE 5.1
$x_1 + x_2 = 5$, ≤ 5, and ≥ 5

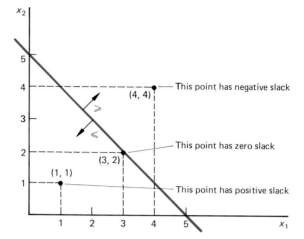

Slack and Surplus Variables

Let us begin by considering a single constraint, say

$$x_1 + x_2 \leq 5 \tag{5.1}$$

This is plotted in Figure 5.1, illustrating the constraint line, the $\leq$ side, and the $\geq$ side. The mechanics of plotting such a constraint were presented in Chapter 3. Recall that each point on the constraint line satisfies $x_1 + x_2 = 5$. All the points on one side of the line (in this case below the line) satisfy $x_1 + x_2 < 5$, and all the points on the other side satisfy the reverse inequality. We now point out that the inequality (5.1) can be transformed to an equality constraint as follows. First, we add a new variable, say s, called a *slack variable*, and rewrite (5.1) as

$$x_1 + x_2 + s = 5 \tag{5.2}$$

Now note that a point will satisfy (5.1) if and only if it satisfies (5.2) with s nonnegative. Consider, for example, the point $(x_1 = 1, x_2 = 1)$. This point satisfies (5.1). It also satisfies (5.2) with $s = 3$. By trying several pairs of values, such as (3, 2) and (4, 4) as illustrated in Figure 5.1, we are led to the following observations:

1. If a point (x_1, x_2) satisfies (5.1), it will, in Figure 5.1, lie on or below the plotted line, and *the value of the slack variable in (5.2) is nonnegative*. Thus, (5.1) is equivalent to the following *two conditions*:

$$x_1 + x_2 + s = 5$$
$$s \geq 0 \tag{5.3}$$

The nonnegativity of s ensures that the point (x_1, x_2) lies on the $\leq$ side of the line.

2. If a point (x_1, x_2) satisfies (5.1) with equality, the value of the slack variable in (5.2) is zero.

3. If the point (x_1, x_2) does not satisfy (5.1), it will lie strictly above the plotted line in Figure 5.1 [e.g., the point $(x_1 = 4, x_2 = 4)$]. In this case the value of the slack variable in (5.2) is negative, thereby violating (5.3).

155

CHAPTER 5
Linear Programs:
Computer Analysis,
Interpreting
Sensitivity Output,
and the Dual
Problem

We thus see that the slack variable s is the "slack," or extra amount that must be added to the left-hand side to turn the $\leq$ into $=$.

Now that we have used the notion of a slack variable to convert a single $\leq$ inequality constraint to an equality constraint, let us see what must be done to handle a *collection* of $\leq$ inequality constraints. Consider, for example, the three constraints

$$4x_1 - x_2 \leq 12$$
$$2x_1 + 6x_2 \leq 21$$
$$-3x_1 + 2x_2 \leq 6.5$$

In this case, converting to equalities requires the introduction of *three* new nonnegative slack variables, say x_3, x_4, x_5 (the three slacks could just as well be labeled as $s_1, s_2,$ and s_3). We then obtain the following equivalent system of equalities:

Adding Slack

$$4x_1 - x_2 + x_3 \qquad = 12$$
$$2x_1 + 6x_2 \qquad + x_4 \qquad = 21$$
$$-3x_1 + 2x_2 \qquad + x_5 = 6.5$$
$$x_3, x_4, x_5 \geq 0$$

Note that there is a *different* slack variable associated with each constraint.

We have now to consider the problem of converting a $\geq$ constraint into an equivalent equality. Let us take as an example

$$2x_1 + 4x_2 \geq 13$$

To convert this $\geq$ constraint to an equality, we *subtract* a nonnegative variable from the left-hand side and change the inequality to equality. This produces the two conditions

**Subtracting
Surplus**

$$2x_1 + 4x_2 - s = 13$$
$$s \geq 0$$

(5.4)

When a nonnegative variable is subtracted from a $\geq$ constraint, it is often termed a *surplus variable* (as opposed to a slack variable, which is added to a $\leq$ constraint). A surplus variable is the "surplus" that must be deducted from the left-hand side to turn the $\geq$ into $=$.

The foregoing discussion shows that

Any $\leq$ constraint can be converted to an equality by adding a new nonnegative slack variable to the left-hand side. Any $\geq$ constraint can be converted to an equality by subtracting a new nonnegative surplus variable from the left-hand side.

In solving linear programs, the computer uses an algorithm called the simplex method, which is designed to attack problems with only equality constraints. Given any LP, the discussion above shows how to convert it easily to the required form. As an illustration, recall the **PROTRAC**, Inc. model

$$\text{Max } 5000E + 4000F$$

$$
\begin{aligned}
\text{s.t.} \quad E + F &\geq 5 \\
E - 3F &\leq 0 \\
10E + 15F &\leq 150 \\
20E + 10F &\leq 160 \\
30E + 10F &\geq 135 \\
E, F &\geq 0
\end{aligned}
\tag{5.5}
$$

This LP problem has two variables and five constraints, two of them $\geq$ and three of them $\leq$. To convert this problem into an equivalent problem in *standard equality constraint form*, we must add slack variables to the second, third, and fourth constraints (the $\leq$ constraints) and subtract surplus variables from the first and fifth constraints (the $\geq$ constraints). Letting s_1, s_2, s_3, s_4, and s_5 denote the five new variables, we obtain

$$\text{Max } 5000E + 4000F$$

$$
\begin{aligned}
\text{s.t.} \quad E + F - s_1 &= 5 \\
E - 3F + s_2 &= 0 \\
10E + 15F + s_3 &= 150 \\
20E + 10F + s_4 &= 160 \\
30E + 10F - s_5 &= 135 \\
E, F, s_1, s_2, s_3, s_4, s_5 &\geq 0
\end{aligned}
\tag{5.6}
$$

This is the standard equality constraint form of the **PROTRAC**, Inc. model. This form of the problem still has five constraints, but the addition of slack and surpuls has increased the number of variables to seven instead of two. Notice that slack and surplus variables do not explicitly appear in the objective function. However, since

$$5000E + 4000F = 5000E + 4000F + 0s_1 + 0s_2 + 0s_3 + 0s_4 + 0s_5$$

it is acceptable to think of the surplus and slack variables as being included in the objective function, but with zero coefficients. In Chapter 3 we used the graphic solution method to show that $E^* = 4.5$ and $F^* - 7$ is the solution to the **PROTRAC**, Inc. inequality model (5.5). This means that the optimal values of the other variables (the slacks and surpluses) in the equality constraint model (5.6) are given by

$$s_1^* = E^* + F^* - 5 = 11.5 - 5 = 6.5$$

$$s_2^* = 0 - (E^* - 3F^*) = -(4.5 - 21) = 16.5$$

$$s_3^* = 150 - (10E^* + 15F^*) = 150 - (45 + 105) = 0$$

$$s_4^* = 160 - (20E^* + 10F^*) = 160 - (90 + 70) = 0$$

$$s_5^* = (30E^* + 10F^*) - 135 = (135 + 70) - 135 = 70$$

It would be useful at this point for you to review the material on active and in-active constraints in Section 3.4. We recall from that material: An *active* or *binding* constraint is one for which, *at optimality*, the left-hand side equals the right-hand side. From the geometric point of view, an active constraint is one on which the optimal solution lies. We saw that in the **PROTRAC, Inc.** model the active constraints are the third and fourth. The calculation above shows that their slack variables (s_3^* and s_4^*) are zero. On the other hand, the first, second, and fifth constraints are inactive, and their slack/surplus variables are positive. Thus, you can see that

---

Active constraints are precisely those for which the optimal values of the slack or surplus variables are zero. Inactive constraints are those for which the optimal values of the slack or surplus variables are positive.

It is not difficult to see that all of the discussion in Section 3.4 could be phrased in terms of these new entities, the slack and surplus variables. In particular, when at optimality a constraint has a zero value for the slack or surplus variable,[1] it means, geometrically speaking, that the solution to the problem lies on that constraint.

In order to check your understanding of the standard equality constraint form, try to convert the following model to one with only equality constraints.

$$\text{Max } x_1 + 3x_4$$

$$
\begin{aligned}
\text{s.t.} \quad & 2x_1 && + 3x_3 + && x_4 \le 12 \\
& x_1 + 13x_2 + 6x_3 + 0.5x_4 \le 41 \\
& \quad\quad 0.4x_2 + 2x_3 && \ge 22 \\
& -3x_1 && + 12x_4 = 15 \\
& x_1, x_2, x_3, x_4 \ge 0
\end{aligned}
$$

In this example there are four constraints and four decision variables.[2] Since only three of the constraints are inequalities we need to introduce only three new variables, in this case one surplus (for the third constraint) and two slacks (for the first and second constraints). The fourth constraint is already an equality, and hence *we do not introduce a*

---

[1] In the language of Chapter 3 we simply said that such a constraint has zero slack or surplus, without introducing the concept of a slack or surplus variable.

[2] Students are sometimes confused by a model such as this in which not all decision variables appear in the objective function and all the constraints, but this is perfectly valid. Think of the variables as being everywhere included but with zero coefficients in places.

158

CHAPTER 5
Linear Programs:
Computer Analysis,
Interpreting
Sensitivity Output,
and the Dual
Problem

slack or surplus variable for this equality constraint. Thus, the standard equality constraint form for the model above is

$$\text{Max } x_1 + 3x_4$$

$$\text{s.t.} \quad 2x_1 \qquad + 3x_3 + \quad x_4 + s_1 = 12$$
$$x_1 + 13x_2 + 6x_3 + 0.5x_4 + s_2 = 41$$
$$0.4x_2 + 2x_3 \qquad - s_3 = 22$$
$$-3x_1 \qquad + 12x_4 \qquad = 15$$
$$x_1, x_2, x_3, x_4, s_1, s_2, s_3 \geq 0$$

To summarize the discussion above, we have shown how slack and surplus variables are used to convert any LP problem into standard equality constraint form.

Geometry of the Standard Equality Constraint Problem

A brief look at the geometry of our new model will reveal a property which is important both in understanding the mechanics of the simplex algorithm (developed in Chapter 6) and in appreciating and correctly interpreting the information contained in the computer printout. This property has to do with the number of positive variables at any corner (and in particular at an optimal corner) of the constraint set.

In the preceding section we have seen that all variables (decision variables, slack and surplus variables) in the standard equality constraint problem [e.g., (5.6)] are required to be nonnegative (positive or zero). In this section we illustrate that at any corner of the constraint set (and in particular at an optimal corner), the maximum number of positive (*greater than zero*) variables, counting decision variables, slacks, and surpluses, is at most equal to the number of constraints in the model (not counting the "nonnegativity conditions").

To illustrate this "count property," consider the model shown in (5.7).

$$\text{Max } x_1 + x_2$$

$$\text{s.t.} \quad 8x_1 + \quad 7x_2 \leq \quad 56 \qquad ①$$
$$-6x_1 - 10x_2 \geq -60 \qquad ②$$
$$x_1 \qquad \leq \quad 6 \qquad ③$$
$$-x_1 + \quad x_2 \leq \quad 6 \qquad ④$$
$$x_1 \geq 0, \qquad x_2 \geq 0$$

(5.7)

The constraint set for this model is plotted in Figure 5.2, where the appropriate constraints are labeled ① through ④. Now consider the standard equality constraint form of the same model. It is

$$\text{Max } x_1 + x_2$$

$$\text{s.t.} \quad 8x_1 + \quad 7x_2 + s_1 \qquad = \quad 56 \qquad ①$$
$$-6x_1 - 10x_2 \qquad - s_2 \qquad = -60 \qquad ②$$
$$x_1 \qquad + s_3 \qquad = \quad 6 \qquad ③$$
$$-x_1 + \quad x_2 \qquad + s_4 = \quad 6 \qquad ④$$
$$x_1, x_2, s_1, s_2, s_3, s_4 \text{ all nonnegative}$$

(5.8)

159

CHAPTER 5
Linear Programs:
Computer Analysis,
Interpreting
Sensitivity Output,
and the Dual
Problem

FIGURE 5.2

Constraint Set for the Inequality
Constrained Model (5.7)

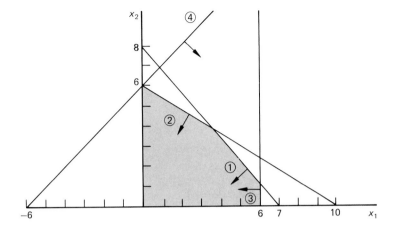

The original model had four constraints and two variables. The standard equality constraint form has the same number of constraints, but six variables. It is important to note that, when referring to the number of variables in the standard equality constraint model, *we count slack and surplus as well as decision variables*. Since (5.8) has two decision variables and four slack/surplus variables, there are six variables in this form of the model. Also, in referring to the number of constraints, *we do not count the nonnegativity conditions*.

Our geometric representation of (5.8) is nearly the same as for (5.7), the only difference being that each constraint will be labeled with its slack or surplus variable. This is shown in Figure 5.3, where for convenience we have labeled the five corners

FIGURE 5.3

Constraint Set for Standard Equality
Constraint Form (5.8)

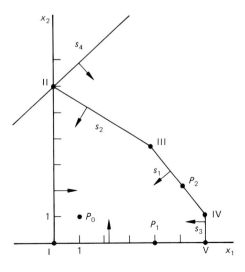

160

CHAPTER 5
Linear Programs:
Computer Analysis,
Interpreting
Sensitivity Output,
and the Dual
Problem

(with Roman numerals) and also identified several points which will be of interest. Labeling the constraints with the slack and surplus variables allows you to make the following "visual" observations:

1. At any point interior to the feasible region, all variables are positive. This is illustrated by point P_0 in Figure 5.3. At this point you can directly read $x_1 = 1$ and $x_2 = 1$. Using the values and the constraints in (5.8) you could explicitly calculate the values for $s_1, s_2, s_3,$ and s_4 at P_0, and you would see that these values are also positive. However, you need not perform this algebra, for the figure immediately shows us that all slacks and surpluses are positive at P_0.

2. At any point on the boundary, at least one variable will be zero. This is illustrated at points P_1 and P_2. At P_1, you can see that $x_2 = 0$; all other variables are positive.

Similarly, at P_2, which lies on the first constraint line, only s_1 is zero. Special boundary points of interest are the corners of the feasible region. For example, since the corner labeled III lies on the first and second constraint lines, the two variables s_1 and s_2 are zero at this corner, with all other variables positive. These examples show that the zero variables on the boundary could be decision variables as well as slack or surplus variables. Corner V, for example, shows that a decision variable (x_2) and a slack variable (s_3) can both be zero on the boundary.

Positive Variables and Corner Solutions

Based on such observations, we can now illustrate the main result of this section by counting the positive variables at each of the five corners of the constraint set. The result is shown in Figure 5.4.

FIGURE 5.4
Counting Positive Variables at Corners

CORNER	ZERO VARIABLES	POSITIVE VARIABLES	POSITIVE COUNT
I	x_1, x_2	s_1, s_2, s_3, s_4	4
II	x_1, s_2, s_4	x_2, s_1, s_3	3
III	s_1, s_2	x_1, x_2, s_3, s_4	4
IV	s_1, s_3	x_1, x_2, s_2, s_4	4
V	x_2, s_3	x_1, s_1, s_2, s_4	4

What this figure shows, quite simply, is *which* variables are positive at each corner, and, in addition, *how many* variables are positive at each corner. Remembering that there are four constraints in the model (5.8), Figure 5.4 illustrates the important general fact that

> **For any LP problem in standard equality constraint form, the number of positive variables at any corner is less than or equal to the number of constraints.**

This result has an important implication for the computer solution of an LP. You may recall from Section 3.5 that in an LP problem, if there is an optimal solution, there is always an optimal corner solution (there may be noncorner optima as well). As you will see in Chapter 6, the simplex method, which is the main algorithm used by computers to solve LP problems, always produces an optimal corner (assuming, of course,

161

CHAPTER 5
Linear Programs:
Computer Analysis,
Interpreting
Sensitivity Output,
and the Dual
Problem

that the problem is neither infeasible nor unbounded). Moreover, the simplex algorithm (as well as the computer) solves a problem in standard equality constraint form and, for such a problem, in accord with the conclusion displayed above, the number of positive variables at *any* corner (hence at an optimal corner) is less than or equal to the number of constraints. Thus, we can now see one reason why the above "count property" is of interest.

The computer solution to an LP problem always has at most *m* positive variables, where *m* is the number of constraints.

Our primary practical need for this last displayed conclusion is that

---

When the computer solution has less than *m* positive variables, the solution is called degenerate, and in this case special care will have to be taken in interpreting some of your computer output.

Degeneracy and Nondegeneracy

Since the ramifications of degeneracy are noteworthy, let us briefly pause to define the concept formally. We will then advance to the topic of computer analysis. A corner such as II in Figure 5.3, where the number of positive variables is *less than* the number of constraints, is termed a *degenerate corner*.[3] The remaining corners, I, III, IV, and V, where the number of positive variables is exactly equal to the number of constraints, are termed *nondegenerate corners*. If the optimal computer solution to an LP has less than *m* positive variables, it is termed a *degenerate solution* since it occurs at a degenerate corner. Analogously, a solution with exactly *m* positive variables is called a *nondegenerate solution*.

We have now become acquainted with the problem that the computer solves, namely the standard equality constraint model. We have seen an important property of this model, namely that any optimal solution produced by the computer will have at most *m* positive variables (exactly *m* meaning nondegenerate), where *m* is the number of constraints in the model; and we have learned that the correct interpretation of the printout will require the awareness of whether or not the optimal solution is nondegenerate. Let us now, in the following two sections, look at some actual computer output.

[3] Here is a subtle point for those who wish to descend slightly deeper into the pits of degeneracy. Figure 5.3 shows that the degenerate corner II has a redundant constraint passing through it (namely, the fourth constraint). Although this is true of any degenerate corner in two dimensions, do not conclude that this must always be the case. As a counterexample, visualize a three-dimensional constraint set which has the shape of a great pyramid standing inside the nonnegative orthant. This figure has four triangular sides and a base, corresponding to five inequality constraints. Thus, the original model has five inequality con-

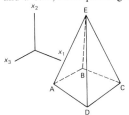

straints in three variables, and the corresponding standard equality constraint model will have five constraints and eight variables. At each of the four base corners, A, B, C, and D, three slack variables are zero and hence five variables are positive. Hence, since there are five constraints and at each of these corners five positive variables, these are nondegenerate corners. However, at corner E, four slacks are zero and hence only four variables are positive. Thus, corner E is degenerate but there are no redundant constraints. What this illustrates is the fact that in three or more dimensions, contrary to the two-dimensional case, a degenerate corner need not have a redundant constraint passing through it.

THE COMPUTER ANALYSIS OF PROTRAC, INC.

In this section we use the computer to analyze the **PROTRAC**, Inc. problem which we have already studied, from the geometric point of view, in Chapter 3. Your understanding of what you are reading on the computer printout will be deepened by relating, wherever possible, the concepts being presented to the geometric notions already developed.

For ease of reference let us reproduce the model here together with the graphical analysis displayed in Figure 3.11.

$$
\begin{array}{lllll}
\text{Max } 5000E + 4000F & & & \\
\text{s.t.} & E + F \geq 5 & \text{(total units requirement)} & ① \\
& E - 3F \leq 0 & \text{(market balance)} & ② \\
& 10E + 15F \leq 150 & \text{(department A)} & ③ & (5.5)\\
& 20E + 10F \leq 160 & \text{(department B)} & ④ \\
& 30E + 10F \geq 135 & \text{(contractual labor)} & ⑤ \\
& E, F \geq 0 & &
\end{array}
$$

As we have already observed, the graphical analysis produces the optimal solution $E^* = 4.5$, $F^* = 7.0$. In Chapter 3 we used the term "OV" to denote the optimal value of the objective function. For the model (5.5) we have

$$OV = \text{maximum profit} = 5000E^* + 4000F^*$$

$$= 5000(4.5) + 4000(7) = 50{,}500$$

as shown in Figure 5.5. We have also seen (see Section 3.4) that the two constraints on labor hours available in departments A and B are active at optimality. The three remaining constraints are inactive.

FIGURE 5.5.
Protrac, Inc. Revisited

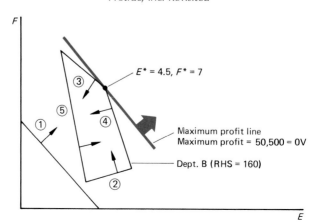

As we have already mentioned, the computer processes the standard equality constraint form of the model. However, as we have seen, the process of converting a problem to standard equality constraint form is quite mechanical. For this reason, most LP computer codes will accept, as input, your original model, which may have some inequality constraints, and then the computer will automatically change the model to standard equality constraint form before it solves the problem. Thus, we can input directly the original model, (5.5). There are, however, two important formalities to be observed when setting up a problem for the computer. First, *the simplex algorithm for solving linear programs requires that all variables be nonnegative.* Therefore, this must be true of the model that you input directly to the computer. However, since the computer always assumes that this is true, you do not need to write these nonnegativity conditions explicitly. In Appendix 5.1 we discuss the modifications you must perform on a problem in which not all of your decision variables are nonnegative. The second point is that *all variables in the constraints must appear on the left, with the constant terms on the right.* Of course, the model is the same whether or not all variables are on the left and all constants on the right, and in simply writing out the formulation of a model this formality need not be observed. But to satisfy the computer, the problem must be submitted in this form, and that is our present goal—to solve the problem on the computer. Let us now proceed to the task.

The Solution   We have solved the original **PROTRAC**, Inc. model (5.5) on our computer. The output appears in Figure 5.6.

We make the following observations:

1. This formulation of the model that was input appears at the top of the output. This is immediately followed by the OV of 50,500.
2. The optimal values of the decision variables are then shown in the "VALUE" column. There you see that $E^* = 4.5$, $F^* = 7.0$. In this column you find the optimal values of all variables which explicitly appear in the model that you input (we did not input slack or surplus variables, and hence they do not appear in this column).
3. The computer labels *rows* rather than constraints. It considers the objective function to be row 1, the first constraint to be row 2, and so on.
4. The "SLACK OR SURPLUS" column of the output gives the values of the slack and/or surplus variables. In the geometric analysis (Figure 5.5) we have seen that the constraints on departments A and B are active. All others are inactive. In the output, you can see that this shows up as zero slack values on rows 4 and 5 and positive slack or surplus on the remaining three rows.
5. The solution is nondegenerate. In Figure 5.5 only two lines intersect at the optimal corner. That is the geometric interpretation. In the output, nondegeneracy is revealed by the fact that there are five positive variables (E^*, F^*, and the slacks on rows 2, 3, and 6), which equals the number of constraints in the formulation at the top of the printout.

Sensitivity   Let us now move on to the portion of the output that deals with sensitivity analysis.
Analysis   It is important to note that *sensitivity analysis is based on the proposition that all data except for one number in the problem are held fixed*, and we ask for information about the effect of changing that one piece of data which is allowed to vary. The information we

FIGURE 5.6
Computer Output for PROTRAC, Inc.

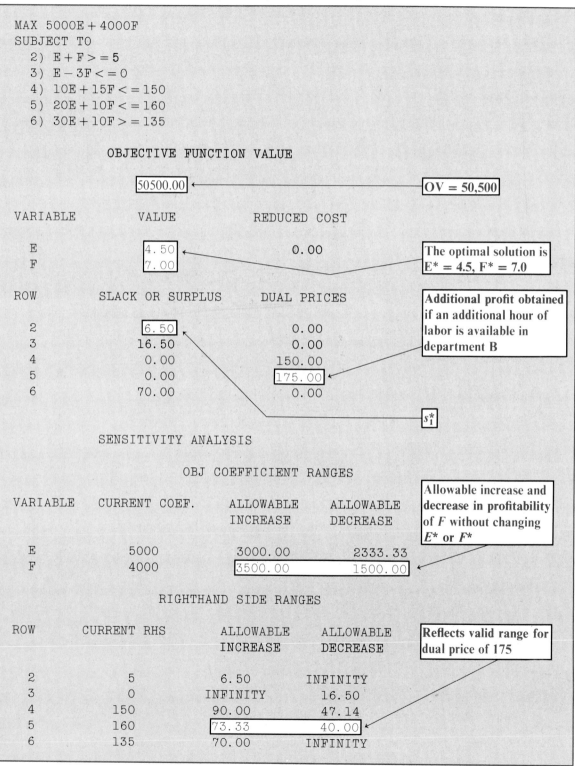

might be interested in could include (1) the effect on the OV (i.e., the maximum possible profit) and (2) the effect on the optimal policy E^*, F^*. In Section 5.4 you will see a realistic scenario in which sensitivity analysis is employed.

RHS Sensitivity First consider a situation in which we hold all numbers fixed except for the availability of labor hours in department B. What if, instead of having 160 hours available, we were to have 161 hours available? What would be the effect on the OV? Since this constraint on labor-hour availability is of the $\leq$ form, we can say, using the language of Section 4.4, that increasing the RHS amounts to "loosening" the constraint, which means making it easier to satisfy. Hence, you would certainly expect that the change from 160 to 161 will not decrease the OV. Will it, though, improve the OV; and if so, by how much? First, let us use the tools we have already acquired, namely geometric analysis, to answer our questions. Then we shall relate this analysis to the computer output. Let the symbol b denote the value of the RHS on the department B constraint. Thus, in Figure 5.5, $b = 160$. In Figure 5.7 we superimpose the department B constraint for the values $b = 161$, $b = 233\frac{1}{3}$, and $b = 250$. We know from the discussion in Section 4.3 that these three new values for b correspond, geometrically, to parallel displacements (away from the origin) of the constraint line. Also since an increase in b means that we are loosening this constraint, the geometric interpretation is that the constraint set, if it changes at all, will expand. The new constraint sets, together with the optimal solutions corresponding to the labor availabilities 161, $233\frac{1}{3}$, and 250, are shown in Figures 5.8, 5.9, and 5.10, respectively.

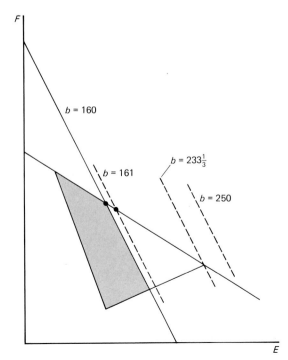

FIGURE 5.7
Three New Values for b

$b = 160$

$b = 233\frac{1}{3}$

$b = 161$

$b = 250$

FIGURE 5.8
$b = 161$

$b = 161$

Dept. A

166

CHAPTER 5
Linear Programs:
Computer Analysis,
Interpreting
Sensitivity Output,
and the Dual
Problem

FIGURE 5.9
$b = 233\frac{1}{3}$

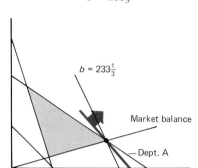

FIGURE 5.10
$b = 250$

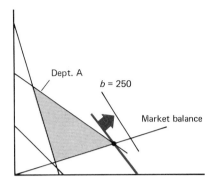

These figures reveal some interesting facts:

$b = 161$

1. When $b = 161$ the constraints on departments A and B continue to be active. This means that the new solution is given by the two equations

$$10E + 15F = 150$$
$$20E + 10F = 161$$

Solving, we obtain $E^* = 4.575$, $F^* = 6.95$.[4] The new maximum profit becomes

$$OV = 5000E^* + 4000F^*$$
$$= 5000(4.575) + 4000(6.95) = 50{,}675$$

Notice that

$$\Delta OV = \text{increase in profit} = (\text{profit when } b = 161) - (\text{profit when } b = 160)$$
$$= 50{,}675 - 50{,}500 = 175$$

and 175 is also, in the computer output shown in Figure 5.6, the dual price corresponding to row 5, the constraint on department B. What we have just illustrated is that

The Dual Price

On the computer printout, the dual price for the department B constraint shows the amount of improvement in the optimal objective value as the RHS of that constraint is increased a unit, with all other data held fixed.

$b = 233\frac{1}{3}$

2. Figure 5.9 shows that when $b = 233\frac{1}{3}$ the three constraints, department A, department B, and market balance are all active. The computer output for this problem is shown in Figure 5.11.

---

[4] Here is an interesting point. You might have intuitively supposed that adding another hour of labor to department B should lead to producing a little more E and a little more F in some appropriate mix, but we see that this is not what happens. Our new solution shows that the optimal policy gives 0.075 more E but 0.05 *less* F. The geometry (Figure 5.7) shows you why this happens.

FIGURE 5.11
Computer Output for $b = 233.33$

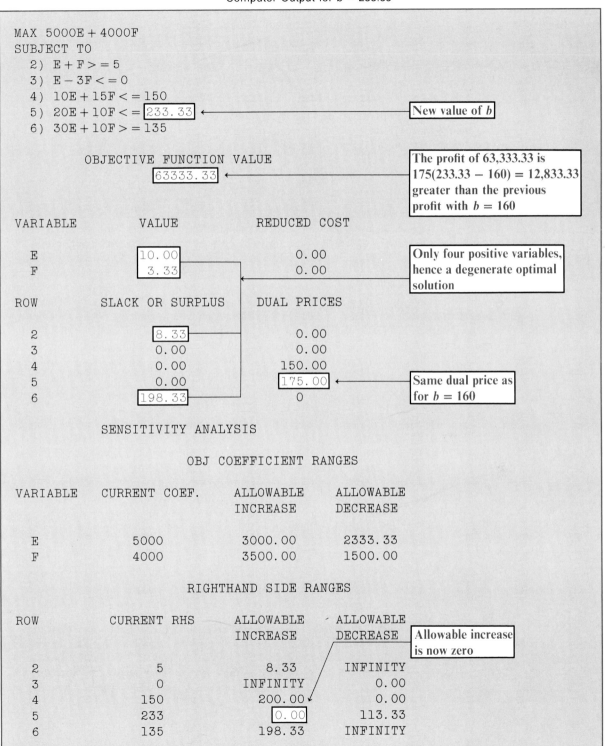

```
MAX 5000E + 4000F
SUBJECT TO
  2)  E + F > = 5
  3)  E − 3F < = 0
  4)  10E + 15F < = 150
  5)  20E + 10F < = 233.33          ← New value of b
  6)  30E + 10F > = 135
```

OBJECTIVE FUNCTION VALUE

63333.33   ← The profit of 63,333.33 is $175(233.33 − 160) = 12,833.33$ greater than the previous profit with $b = 160$

VARIABLE	VALUE	REDUCED COST
E	10.00	0.00
F	3.33	0.00

Only four positive variables, hence a degenerate optimal solution

ROW	SLACK OR SURPLUS	DUAL PRICES
2	8.33	0.00
3	0.00	0.00
4	0.00	150.00
5	0.00	175.00
6	198.33	0

Same dual price as for $b = 160$

SENSITIVITY ANALYSIS

OBJ COEFFICIENT RANGES

VARIABLE	CURRENT COEF.	ALLOWABLE INCREASE	ALLOWABLE DECREASE
E	5000	3000.00	2333.33
F	4000	3500.00	1500.00

RIGHTHAND SIDE RANGES

ROW	CURRENT RHS	ALLOWABLE INCREASE	ALLOWABLE DECREASE
2	5	8.33	INFINITY
3	0	INFINITY	0.00
4	150	200.00	0.00
5	233	0.00	113.33
6	135	198.33	INFINITY

Allowable increase is now zero

168

CHAPTER 5
Linear Programs:
Computer Analysis,
Interpreting
Sensitivity Output,
and the Dual
Problem

Figure 5.11 shows zero slack values on the three active constraints. There are only four positive variables. Since this problem has five constraints and since the optimal solution has only four positive variables, the solution is, according to the definition given in the preceding section, *degenerate*. Note on the output that the current solution is $E^* = 10$, $F^* = 3\frac{1}{3}$, Also,

$$OV = 5000E^* + 4000F^*$$
$$= 5000(10) + 4000(3\tfrac{1}{3}) = 63,333\tfrac{1}{3}$$

When $b = 233\frac{1}{3}$, the RHS on department B's labor constraint has been increased $73\frac{1}{3}$ units beyond the original value of 160. Consistent with the interpretation above of the dual price, which was 175, we see that the OV has increased by

$$\Delta OV = 63,333\tfrac{1}{3} - 50,500 = 12,833\tfrac{1}{3} = (175)(73\tfrac{1}{3})$$

$b > 233\frac{1}{3}$

3. When b increases up to and beyond the value $233\frac{1}{2}$, Figures 5.9 and 5.10 show that the labor constraint on department B becomes redundant. The values of E^* and F^* and the OV remain as in Figures 5.9 and 5.11. For example, the computer output corresponding to $b = 250$ appears in Figure 5.12. Note that the solution is once again nondegenerate, with the active constraints (0 slack) now being those on department A and market balance (compare with Figure 5.10). Also note that the dual price on the department B constraint has dropped from 175 to zero. This change in the dual price shows that the interpretation of its meaning given above must be restricted to a specific range in RHS values. The appropriate range appears on the computer output in the "RIGHTHAND SIDE RANGES" section under the "ALLOWABLE INCREASE" and "ALLOWABLE DECREASE" columns. Thus, Figures 5.6, 5.11, and 5.12 tell us that

a. When $b = 160$ (Figure 5.6) the dual price of 175 is valid for an allowable increase (in b) of $73\frac{1}{3}$ hours and an allowable decrease of 40 hours. Since $160 - 40 = 120$, and $160 + 73\frac{1}{3} = 233\frac{1}{3}$, we see that *for b values between 120 and $233\frac{1}{3}$ hours, the improvement in the OV for each unit of RHS increase, with all other data held fixed, is 175.*

b. When $b = 233\frac{1}{3}$ (Figure 5.11) the dual price remains at 175, but the allowable increase is 0, which means that the value 175 does not apply to RHS values any larger than $233\frac{1}{3}$ Indeed, the geometric analysis shows that the constraint becomes inactive and redundant when $b > 233\frac{1}{3}$. *Small changes in the RHS of an inactive constraint cannot affect the OV and hence for an inactive constraint the dual price will always be zero.*

c. When $b = 250$ (Figure 5.12) we see that now, with the relevant constraint inactive, the dual price is indeed zero and the allowable increase is infinite. That is, for any further increase in b the constraint will remain inactive and the dual price will remain at the value 0. In Figure 5.12 the allowable decrease of 16.66 will take the RHS back to $233\frac{1}{3}$. For values of b less than $233\frac{1}{3}$ we have seen in Figure 5.11 that the dual price is 175, not zero.

In summary,

**Dual Price
and the
Valid Range**

1. The dual price on a given constraint can be interpreted as the rate of improvement in OV as the RHS of that constraint increases (i.e., the improvement per unit increase in RHS) with all other data held fixed.[5] "Rate of improvement" means "rate of increase" for a Max model and "rate of decrease" for a Min model. If the RHS is decreased, the dual price is the rate at which the OV is *impaired*. This distinction is treated in more detail in Section 5.4. The interpretation of the dual price is valid only within a range for the given RHS. This range is specified by the

---

[5] The sensitivity output will not apply when more than one parameter is being changed.

FIGURE 5.12
Computer Output for $b = 250$

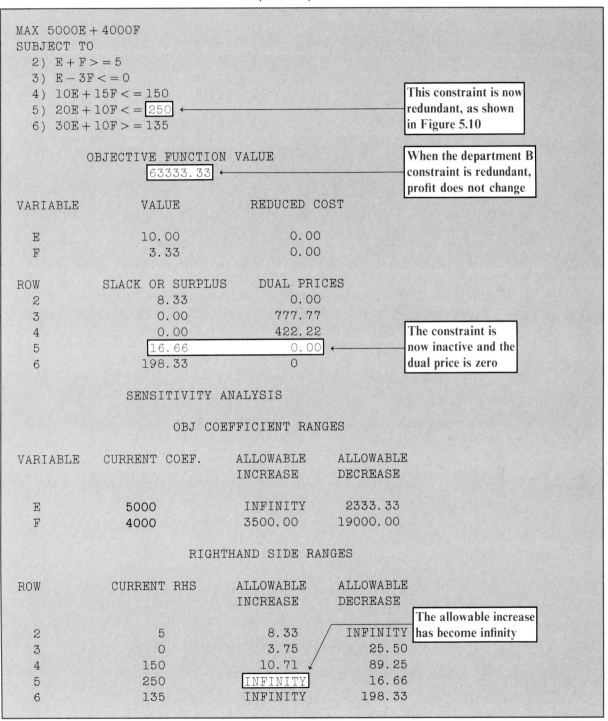

```
MAX 5000E + 4000F
SUBJECT TO
  2)  E + F > = 5
  3)  E − 3F < = 0
  4)  10E + 15F < = 150
  5)  20E + 10F < = 250
  6)  30E + 10F > = 135
```

This constraint is now redundant, as shown in Figure 5.10

OBJECTIVE FUNCTION VALUE
63333.33

When the department B constraint is redundant, profit does not change

VARIABLE	VALUE	REDUCED COST
E	10.00	0.00
F	3.33	0.00

ROW	SLACK OR SURPLUS	DUAL PRICES
2	8.33	0.00
3	0.00	777.77
4	0.00	422.22
5	16.66	0.00
6	198.33	0

The constraint is now inactive and the dual price is zero

SENSITIVITY ANALYSIS

OBJ COEFFICIENT RANGES

VARIABLE	CURRENT COEF.	ALLOWABLE INCREASE	ALLOWABLE DECREASE
E	5000	INFINITY	2333.33
F	4000	3500.00	19000.00

RIGHTHAND SIDE RANGES

ROW	CURRENT RHS	ALLOWABLE INCREASE	ALLOWABLE DECREASE
2	5	8.33	INFINITY
3	0	3.75	25.50
4	150	10.71	89.25
5	250	INFINITY	16.66
6	135	INFINITY	198.33

The allowable increase has become infinity

Dual Price and Inactive Constraints

2. According to the interpretation above, the dual price of an inactive constraint will always be zero.

Effect on Optimal Policy

3. Note that the RHS sensitivity information that the computer provides does not tell us how the optimal policy E^*, F^* changes. It merely explains the way in which the OV will change as the RHS changes.

Effect of Degeneracy

4. When we have a degenerate solution some of the dual prices will have either a zero allowable increase or zero allowable decrease. In this case we obtain in the printout only a limited amount of information. Nanely, we know only about the effect on the OV of one-sided changes in the RHS.

Objective Function Coefficient Sensitivity and Alternative Optima

Consider increasing the coefficient of F in the objective function, that is, increasing its per unit profitability, while holding the coefficient of E fixed. We have seen (in Figure 4.1) that the contours of the objective function will become flatter (have a less negative slope) as this coefficient increases. By referring to Figure 5.5 we see that the optimal solution remains at the corner $E^* = 4.5$, $F^* = 7.0$ until the coefficient of F increases enough that contours of the objective function are parallel to constraint ③. When the contours of the objective function are parallel to constraint ③, there are alternative optimal solutions, the current corner ($E^* = 4.5$, $F^* = 7.0$) and the corner determined by the intersection of constraints ③ and ⑤. If the coefficient of F continues to increase, the current solution ($E^* = 4.5$, $F^* = 7.0$) will no longer be optimal and the point determined by the intersection of constraints ③ and ⑤ will be the unique optimum. The allowable increase for the coefficient of F is thus determined by the increase in the coefficient that makes the contours of the objective function parallel to constraint ③. When, we may ask, does this occur?

The contours of the objective function are parallel to constraint ③ when both lines have the same slope, which means that the coefficients satisfy the following equality:

$$\frac{\text{coefficient of } E \text{ in } ③}{\text{coefficient of } F \text{ in } ③} = \frac{\text{coefficient of } E \text{ in objective}}{\text{coefficient of } F \text{ in objective}}$$

which implies that

$$\frac{10}{15} = \frac{5000}{\text{coefficient of } F \text{ in objective}}$$

which implies that

$$\text{coefficient of } F \text{ in objective} = (5000)(\tfrac{15}{10}) = 7500$$

The current coefficient of F in the objective function is 4000. It becomes parallel to ③, that is, alternative optima occur, if this value increases to 7500. Thus, the current optimal solution remains valid as long as the increase in F is ≤ 3500. *This is termed the allowable increase in the coefficient of F.* It is the value shown in Figure 5.6 under "ALLOWABLE INCREASE" for F. This combination of algebra and geometry explains both the meaning and the value of this entry on the printout. Further, by observing how the change in coefficients affects the slope of the objective function, we can make the following important generalizations:

Changing the objective function coefficients changes the slope of the objective function contours. This may or not affect the optimal solution and the optimal value of the objective function.

Now recall that as the coefficient of F increased (holding the coefficient of E fixed) we eventually obtained a new solution in which the optimal value of F increased. This agrees with your intuition since increasing the profitability of F would not cause you to produce F at a lower level! This illustrates the general concept that

**Effect on
Activity in a
Max Model**

In a Max model, increasing the profitability of an activity, keeping all other data unchanged, cannot reduce the optimal level of that activity.

The situation for a cost-minimization model is just reversed. Since we want to minimize total cost, we certainly would not expect that increasing the cost of an activity, while keeping all other data unchanged, could lead to a higher optimal level of that activity. This illustrates the general concept that

**Effect on
Activity in a
Min Model**

In a Min model, increasing the cost of an activity, keeping all other data unchanged, cannot increase the optimal level of that activity.

Let us now give a general statement of the facts concerning the "OBJ CO-EFFICIENT RANGES" of the printout. It is in interpreting this portion of the output that you must be careful to distinguish between the cases of a degenerate versus a non-degenerate solution.

For a nondegenerate solution

**Meaning of "OBJ
COEFFICIENT
RANGES" for a
Nondegenerate
Solution**

1. The columns "ALLOWABLE INCREASE" and "ALLOWABLE DE-CREASE," under the "OBJ COEFFICIENT RANGES" heading, tell you how much the coefficient of a given variable in the objective function may be increased or decreased without changing the optimal solution, where all other data are assumed to be fixed. Of course, as the profitability varies in this range the OV values are given by

$$OV = 5000E^* + (\text{profitability of } F) \cdot F^*$$

As an illustration of this, imagine that the coefficient of F is assigned the value 6000, which is within the allowable range shown in Figure 5.6. Then the

172

CHAPTER 5
Linear Programs:
Computer Analysis,
Interpreting
Sensitivity Output,
and the Dual
Problem

solution remains at $(E^* = 4.5, F^* = 7)$ and

$$OV = 5000E^* + 6000F^*$$
$$= 5000(4.5) + 6000(7) = 64,500$$

2. When a coefficient is changed by less than the allowable amounts, the current optimal solution remains the unique optimal solution to the model.

3. When a particular coefficient is increased by its allowable amount, there will be an alternative optimal solution with, for a Max model, a larger optimal value for the distinguished variable. (For a Min model, increasing a coefficient the allowable amount will produce an alternative optimum with a lower optimal value for the distinguished variable.)

4. When a variable's coefficient is decreased by its allowable amount, there will be another alternative optimal solution with the distinguished variable having a lower (higher) optimal value for a Max (Min) model.

Signal for Alternative Optima

There is one other fact of interest that applies to a *nondegenerate* solution. *When you see, for some variable in the "OBJ COEFFICIENT RANGES" section of the output, a zero entry under either of the columns "ALLOWABLE INCREASE" or "ALLOWABLE DECREASE," you know that there is at least one alternative optimal solution to the problem at hand.* Moreover, whenever there are alternative optima such a signal will appear. This is illustrated in Figure 5.13, a hypothetical maximization LP in two decision variables and three inequality constraints. The objective function contour is parallel to the second constraint (labeled ②) and in employing the graphic solution technique you can see that the corners labeled I and II are alternative optima for this problem. The computer, because of the algorithm it employs to solve the problem, will find only one of these corners as an optimal solution and the computer output applies only to that corner. Let us suppose that corner I is the solution found by the computer. The geometry in Figure 5.13 shows that any increase in the coefficient of x_1 will change the objective function contour to a tilt like that of the dashed line and corner II becomes the unique optimal solution. The computer output for the solution at corner I would have, as a

FIGURE 5.13
Alternative Optima

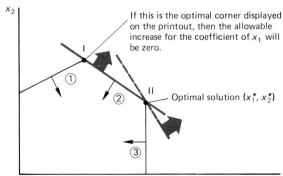

If this is the optimal corner displayed on the printout, then the allowable increase for the coefficient of x_1 will be zero.

Optimal solution (x_1^*, x_2^*)

signal for this phenomenon, a zero value next to x_1 under the "ALLOWABLE IN-CREASE" column.

Let us now consider the case of a printout showing a *degenerate optimal solution*. In this case two caveats must be observed.

Caveats for Degenerate Solutions

For a degenerate solution

1. The signals described above for alternative optima should ignored.

2. As long as an objective function coefficient is varied in the indicated range the optimal solution will not change. This was also true in the nondegenerate case. In the latter case, however, alternative optima were obtained when the coefficient was changed to the limit of its range, and then, as this direction of change continued, the original optimal solution dropped out. In the degenerate case this can no longer be guaranteed. All we can say is that any objective function coefficient must be changed by *at least, and possibly more than*, the indicated allowable amounts in order to produce a new optimal solution.

Reduced Cost

We have explained everything in our computer output except for the entries under the column "REDUCED COST." The following facts pertain to these entries. This is another instance where, in order to give a correct interpretation, you must first observe whether the optimal solution is nondegenerate.

Nondegenerate Case

1. In a *nondegenerate* optimal solution, the reduced cost of any particular decision variable is defined to be *the amount the coefficient of that variable in the objective function would have to change in order to have a positive optimal value for that variable*. Thus, if a variable is already positive at optimality, its reduced cost is zero (as in the case for both decision variables in Figures 5.6, 5.11, and 5.12). If the optimal value of a variable is zero, then from the definition of reduced cost you can see that the reduced cost is either the "ALLOWABLE INCREASE" or "ALLOWABLE DECREASE" which corresponds to the given variable (one of these values will be infinite; the other will be the reduced cost). For example, suppose that we change the data in the Protrac E and F model in such a way that the optimal value $E^* = 0$. Then the reduced cost of E is the amount its profitability (the coefficient of E in the objective function) would have to be *increased* in order to have an optimal solution with $E^* > 0$. This is precisely the entry that you would find corresponding to E in the "ALLOWABLE INCREASE" column. In this case, for any decrease in the coefficient of E (making E less profitable) the value E^* will remain at zero. Hence, the corresponding "ALLOWABLE DECREASE" would be infinite.

2. Another equivalent interpretation of reduced cost, for a nondegenerate solution, can be given. In a nondegenerate solution, the reduced cost of a decision variable (whose optimal value is currently zero) is the rate (per unit amount) at which the objective value is hurt as that variable is "forced into" (i.e., is forced to assume positive values in) an optimal solution. In the example above, with $E^* = 0$, the OV would decrease if we forced ourselves to find an optimal solution with the *additional* constraint that $E = 1$. (To see that the OV would *decrease* you need merely recognize that in the current model the optimal value of E is zero. Forcing E to be 1, then, can only yield us less return.) This *rate of decrease* as E^* is initially forced to be positive would be given by the reduced cost of E. Additional examples of the two interpretations above will appear in Section 5.4.

Degenerate Case

3. Now consider a *degenerate solution* with a decision variable whose optimal value is zero. The coefficient of that variable in the objective function must be changed by *at least, and possibly more than*, the reduced cost in order for there to be an optimal solution with that variable appearing at a positive level.

This completes our exploration of the meaning of each entry in the computer output. Although our discussion has been introductory, if you have mastered the material

174

CHAPTER 5
Linear Programs:
Computer Analysis,
Interpreting
Sensitivity Output,
and the Dual
Problem

presented from Chapter 2 up to this point, you are now able to use LP in practical situations: to formulate problems, solve them on a computer, and correctly interpret the output. The final sections of this chapter go in two different directions. Section 5.4 is intended to increase your familiarity with output interpretation by showing you how the printout might be employed in a realistic scenario. The orientation is managerial, with an emphasis on the sensitivity information and its use. In Section 5.5, we give a synopsis of how to interpret the sensitivity information on the printout. Then, in Section 5.6, the direction changes and the dual problem is discussed. It is a topic that is fundamental to a thorough knowledge of LP, and takes you deeper into several aspects of the subject.

_____ 5.4

THE CRAWLER TREAD OUTPUT: A DIALOGUE WITH MANAGEMENT (SENSITIVITY ANALYSIS IN ACTION)

This problem was introduced in Section 2.3. Recall that the ore from four different locations is blended to make crawler tractor treads. Each ore contains three essential elements, denoted for simplicity as A, B, and C, that must appear in the final blend at minimum threshold levels. Protrac pays a different price per ton for the ore from each location. The cost-minimizing blend is obtained by solving the following LP model, where T_i = the fraction of a ton of ore from location i in one ton of the blend.

$$
\begin{array}{lll}
\text{Min } 800T_1 + 400T_2 + 600T_3 + 500T_4 & & \text{(total cost)} \\
\text{s.t.} \quad 10T_1 + 3T_2 + 8T_3 + 2T_4 \geq 5 & & \text{(requirement on A)} \\
\phantom{\text{s.t.}} \quad 90T_1 + 150T_2 + 75T_3 + 175T_4 \geq 100 & & \text{(requirement on B)} \\
\phantom{\text{s.t.}} \quad 45T_1 + 25T_2 + 20T_3 + 37T_4 \geq 30 & & \text{(requirement on C)} \\
\phantom{\text{s.t.}} \quad T_1 + T_2 + T_3 + T_4 = 1 & & \text{(blend condition)} \\
\phantom{\text{s.t.}} \quad T_i \geq 0, \qquad i = 1, 2, 3, 4 & &
\end{array}
$$

Let us now discuss and analyze the computer output for the solution to this problem. Place yourself in the position of the manager who is responsible for planning future production. A number of questions are on the manager's mind. The modeler responds.

MANAGER: First of all, what is the solution to our problem?

I have run the problem on the computer, and here's the output [see Figure 5.14]. By "solution" I take it you mean the optimal values of the decision variables. These are printed in the section of output that I've labeled VARIABLES. The optimal values of the variables appear under the second column, headed VALUE. You can see that the rounded optimal values are

$$T1 = 0.26$$
$$T2 = 0.70$$
$$T3 = 0.04$$
$$T4 = 0.00$$

175

CHAPTER 5
Linear Programs:
Computer Analysis,
Interpreting
Sensitivity Output,
and the Dual
Problem

FIGURE 5.14
Output for Crawler Tread

```
MIN 800 T1 + 400 T2 + 600 T3 + 500 T4
SUBJECT TO
  2)  10 T1 + 3 T2 + 8 T3 + 2 T4 > = 5
  3)  90 T1 + 150 T2 + 75 T3 + 175 T4 > = 100
  4)  45 T1 + 25 T2 + 20 T3 + 37 T4 > = 30
  5)  T1 + T2 + T3 + T4 = 1
```

OBJECTIVE FUNCTION VALUE   OV

    1   511.111

VARIABLE	VALUE	REDUCED COST	
T1	0.259	0.000	
T2	0.703	0.000	Variables
T3	0.037	0.000	
T4	0.000	91.111	

ROW	SLACK OR SURPLUS	DUAL PRICES	
2	0.000	− 44.444	
3	31.666	0.000	Constraints
4	0.000	− 4.444	
5	0.000	−155.555	

SENSITIVITY ANALYSIS

OBJ COEFFICIENT RANGES

VARIABLE	CURRENT COEF.	ALLOWABLE INCREASE	ALLOWABLE DECREASE
T1	800.000	223.636	119.999
T2	400.000	66.847	299.999
T3	600.000	85.714	118.269
T4	500.000	INFINITY	91.111

RIGHTHAND SIDE RANGES

ROW	CURRENT RHS	ALLOWABLE INCREASE	ALLOWABLE DECREASE
2	5.000	2.375	0.250
3	100.000	31.666	INFINITY
4	30.000	0.714	7.000
5	1.000	0.250	0.043

176

CHAPTER 5
Linear Programs:
Computer Analysis,
Interpreting
Sensitivity Output,
and the Dual
Problem

MANAGER: How much does a ton of this blend cost?

The OV, which is the optimal value of the objective function, is also identified. You can see that the minimum cost is $511.11.

MANAGER: I'd like to keep my costs under $500 per ton. Isn't there any way I can do this?

It is impossible to find a lower-cost mixture that satisfies the constraints you have imposed.

MANAGER: You mean the requirements on essential elements?
Exactly.

MANAGER: Well, maybe I can modify those requirements. I really do want to keep my costs under $500 per ton.

Then you certainly will have to loosen your requirements. We can discuss how to do that.

MANAGER: All right. But first, I recall that the requirements were expressed as minimum threshold levels. Is there any way I can tell exactly how much of each essential element gets into the optimal mix?

That information is obtained from the second section of the output, which I've identified as CONSTRAINTS. The computer labels the four constraints of the problem as rows 2 to 5, respectively, since it regards the objective function as row 1. The first three constraints of the problem are the requirements on essential elements. This corresponds to the output labeled as rows 2, 3, and 4.

MANAGER: I see a column labeled SLACK OR SURPLUS and one labeled DUAL PRICES, but where are the amounts of the essential elements in the optimal blend?

This has to be deduced. Remember that before the inequality problem was solved, the computer had to transform it to standard equality constraint form. For this model, the column labeled SLACK OR SURPLUS is the optimal value of the surplus variable associated with each constraint in the transformed problem.

MANAGER: I think I see what you're getting at. The surplus in row 2 is zero. The first constraint is the requirement on A, which was 5 pounds. Since the original constraint is $\geq$, after conversion to equality form it must look like

$$10T1 + 3T2 + 8T3 + 2T4 - S1 = 5$$

Exactly.

MANAGER: Okay, and I understand what happens for rows 3 and 4. But the last constraint in the original model was an equality constraint. That means that it has neither a slack nor a surplus variable in standard form. Right?

Correct.

MANAGER: Then why is there a slack or surplus value of zero printed on the output for row 5? Doesn't that suggest there is a slack or surplus variable in that row?

You may be right, but the suggestion is unintended. For a constraint that was originally an equality the entry in this column is always zero. As you have correctly observed, the actual surplus variables in this problem are associated only with the first three constraints of the original model: That is, rows 2, 3, and 4.

MANAGER: Fine. Now let's return to the surplus variable on row 2. I see that its optimal value is zero. What does that have to do with the amount of essential element A in the final mix? I thought I saw the answer before, but now I'm confused.

It's easy. Since the optimal surplus value is zero, and since we know the other optimal values, it must be true that if we substitute the optimal values of all the variables into the equality form of the constraint we will obtain the following result:

$$10(0.25926) + 3(0.70370) + 8(0.03704) + 2(0.0000) - 0 = 5$$

177

CHAPTER 5
Linear Programs:
Computer Analysis,
Interpreting
Sensitivity Output,
and the Dual
Problem

In other words, since the optimal surplus value is zero, the optimal mix contains exactly 5 pounds of A.

MANAGER: I see. And since the surplus in row 4 is zero, the optimal mix must contain exactly 30 pounds of C. Is that right?

Precisely, and you can also figure out how much B there is.

MANAGER: Okay. For B, I have to look at row 3. Since the surplus is 31.6667 it must be true that

$$90(0.25926) + 150(0.70370) + 75(0.03704) + 175(0.0000) - 31.6667 = 100$$

But where do I go from here?

Well, your equation means that in the optimal mix the minimum requirement of 100 pounds is actually exceeded by 31.6667. That is, there are 131.6667 pounds of B actually included.

MANAGER: Isn't that odd? You'd think I could make a cheaper blend by using less B. Why should I use more than 100 pounds if I need only 100?

That is a very good question. You see, the combination of ores that satisfies the requirements on A and C at a minimum cost just happens to contain more than 100 pounds of B. Any combination of ores that includes less B will either not have enough of A and/or C, or, if it does have enough, it will cost more than $511.11 per ton. In other words, forcing yourself to include less of the excess amount of B while still satisfying the requirements on A and C will end up costing you more. You may have to think about that assertion, but it is exactly what the solution to the model is telling us.

MANAGER: Okay. I guess I can see your point. So how can I get my total cost down to $500 or less?

You will have to loosen your constraints. This means loosening the requirements on A or C.

MANAGER: Why not on B?

Because, in order to satisfy the requirements on A and C at minimum cost, you're already including over 100 pounds of B, which is more than your minimal threshold. In other words, the requirement on B is not active. You could loosen this requirement to a smaller number, such as 98, and the optimal mix would still contain the same composition and cost. Thus, loosening the requirement on B to a smaller number won't get us anywhere. You have to loosen one of the active requirements.

MANAGER: You mean one where there's zero surplus.

Precisely.

MANAGER: Okay. So I have to relax the requirement on A or C. But which one? And how much?

We can use the information under the DUAL PRICES heading to analyze these questions.

MANAGER: I was wondering what that column meant.

It means rate of improvement in the OV as we increase the right-hand side. Since we are interested in loosening a $\geq$ constraint, we will be decreasing the right-hand side. Now let's look at the dual price on row 2. It is -44.44. The negative sign means that as the right-hand side is *increased* the OV is "negatively improved," or hurt. Thus, as the right-hand side is loosened, or *decreased*, the OV is improved. What all of this boils down to is the common-sense idea that, as your requirement for A is loosened, your minimum cost will go down. The dual price tells us it goes down at the rate of $44.44 per pound.

MANAGER: Loosening the requirement for A must mean reducing it from 5 pounds to something less. Right?

Right.

178

CHAPTER 5
Linear Programs:
Computer Analysis,
Interpreting
Sensitivity Output,
and the Dual
Problem

MANAGER: And the dual price of -44.44 says that for each pound of reduction the cost goes down $44.44?

Right.

MANAGER: Great. This means if I require only 4 pounds per ton of A, instead of 5, the cost goes down to about $466.67 and I'm under $500. Right?

Well, not quite. But you're right in spirit. You have the correct rate of change, but this rate applies only to some *interval* of values around the original value of 5. The appropriate interval may not allow you to analyze the decrease of a whole unit—maybe only half a unit, for example.

MANAGER: Even so, if I cut the requirement to 4.5 pounds, I'd save $(\frac{1}{2})(44.44)$, which is over $22. My final cost would still be under $500!

True enough, but the allowable interval may not even include 4.5.

MANAGER: Obviously, we need to know that interval.

Right. And it appears on the bottom of the output under the section labeled RIGHTHAND SIDE RANGES.

MANAGER: I see. In the ALLOWABLE DECREASE column for row 2 we have 0.250. That must mean I can analyze a change from 5 down to 4.75. Right?

Right.

MANAGER: So my saving would be 0.25 (44.44), which is $11.11, and this gets me down exactly to $500. But what if I relaxed the requirement a little more, like to 4.50. Wouldn't that reduce the cost further?

Probably, but I can't tell you exactly how much because the rate of change may be different after a decrease of 0.25.

MANAGER: In technical language, that must mean the dual price may change.

Exactly.

MANAGER: Okay. Now just to see if I have it all straight, let me analyze the potential savings if I relax the requirement on C.

Go ahead.

MANAGER: The requirement on C is identified as row 4. The original right-hand side is 30. The output shows an allowable decrease of 7, so I can go down to 23. The dual price on row 4 is -4.44. This is my rate of savings as I decrease the right-hand side from 30. Hence, if I decrease the requirement to 23, I save

$$7(4.44) = \$31.08$$

This also gets me well under $500. In fact, if I cut down the requirement only 2.5 pounds, I can apply the same rate of change, and consequently I should save

$$(2.5)(4.44) = \$11.10$$

and this just about gets me down to a cost of $500. How am I doing?

Very well.

MANAGER: Okay. I see that I can get the cost per ton down to $500 if I relax the requirement on A to 4.75 pounds per ton *or* the requirement on C to 27.5 pounds per ton. But what if I relax both requirements on A and C, perhaps a little less but both at the same time? Then what?

Sorry, but again we don't have precise information on the output to that. The only way to tackle that question would be to rerun the model numerous times with different right-hand sides for A and C.

179

CHAPTER 5
Linear Programs:
Computer Analysis,
Interpreting
Sensitivity Output,
and the Dual
Problem

MANAGER: So when I use the dual price on one of the right-hand-side values, it's important to keep the others unchanged.

Correct.

MANAGER: So let me review this. I know that I can get my cost per ton down to $500 if I relax the requirement on A to 4.75 pounds per ton *or* the requirement on C to 27.5 pounds per ton. Which should I do?

The computer cannot give you a guideline on that. You might note that the required relaxation on A would be 0.25/5, or 5%, and on C it would be $2.5/30 = 8\frac{1}{3}\%$. But I don't know whether that is helpful. The point is that you, as the manager, have to decide on which change would do more harm to the properties of the blend. I think it probably boils down to an engineering question.

MANAGER: Yes, I think you are right, and I know who to talk with about that.

Good.

MANAGER: By the way, I've also been noticing the column of your printout that says ALLOW-ABLE INCREASE. I would guess that pertains to increases in the right-hand side.

Right again.

MANAGER: Would you just run through the analysis on the increase side to make sure that I'm with you?

Let's take row 2, the requirement on A. Suppose that you want to tighten this requirement.

MANAGER: Since we are dealing with a $\geq$ constraint, tightening would mean an increase in the right-hand side, which is the required amount of A.

Correct. Tightening a requirement can never help the OV and may hurt. In this case the dual price of -44.44 tells us that increasing the right-hand side will hurt. This means that the cost will go up. The allowable increase of 2.375 tells us that if we increase the original amount, 5, by any amount up to 2.375, the increase in cost is given by 44.44 times that amount.

MANAGER: In other words, the same dual price pertains to both increases and decreases in the right-hand side. The allowable increase and decrease are provided by the computer, and the dual price is the rate of improvement in the objective value as the right-hand side increases over that entire allowable range. If this rate is negative, it hurts the OV.

Right. And loosening a constant will always mean that the OV cannot be hurt and may be improved. Tightening means that the OV cannot be improved and may be hurt.

MANAGER: I even notice that the dual price on B is zero, which means that changes in the value of 100 don't have any effect. I guess that means we don't even need a constraint on B. Why is that?

Because, as I mentioned earlier, if you satisfy the requirements for A and C at a minimum cost, the requirement for B will be satisfied automatically.

MANAGER: So am I correct? Could the constraint on B be discarded?

I would think not. If you would ever want to change some of the data and then rerun the model, the constaint on B could become important. So I don't really want to say that it can be removed from the model.

MANAGER: Could you be a little more explicit, without getting into a lot of terminology?

All right. Just as an example, last week I heard from Mr. Shmootz that the cost of ore from location 2 might increase.

MANAGER: Mr. Shmootz?

Yes.

180

CHAPTER 5
Linear Programs:
Computer Analysis,
Interpreting
Sensitivity Output,
and the Dual
Problem

MANAGER: Well, I must admit that such a possibility is something I'm concerned about. But I don't see how we can take that kind of uncertainty into account.

This relates to your question. The cost of ore from location 2 is the coefficient of T2 in the objective function, namely 400. If this cost is increased, we would expect our OV to increase. If the cost of ore from location 2 goes up enough, we might even expect that less of it, or maybe even none of it, would be used in the optimal blend. This means more of the others must be used because the total amount used has to sum up to 1. This means that the relative importance of the constraints could change. Previous constraints that had been tight might not be, and vice versa. A lot of things can happen when you start playing with the data.

MANAGER: Tell me again what you mean by a tight constraint.

It means a constraint with an optimal slack or surplus value of zero. Such a constraint is also called *active*, or *binding*, or *effective*.

MANAGER: I'm glad you told me that. What about an equality constraint? Is it considered active or binding or whatever?

Yes. Always. In this terminology, although the constraint on B is currently inactive, it could become active if the data in the model are changed.

MANAGER: Fine. But I'm still confused. What does all this have to do with the cost of ore from location 2? Or is the whole thing just too complicated to explain?

Not at all. Let's look at the cost of ore from location 2. We can actually determine the range over which this cost can vary without influencing the optimal blend. In particular, look at the portion of output headed OBJ COEFFICIENT RANGES. In the row corresponding to T2 there are items called ALLOWABLE INCREASE and ALLOWABLE DECREASE. This gives the range in which the cost of T2 can vary.

MANAGER: You mean without changing the optimal mix?

Yes.

MANAGER: Okay. In other words, the cost of T2 is now $400 in our model. You mean that the output says it could be anywhere between $100 and $466.84 and the optimal mix stays the same?

Exactly.

MANAGER: I don't see how we can know that.

It's all in the mathematics.

MANAGER: I'll take your word for that. So if the cost increases from $400 to $450, we have nothing to worry about.

Well, I don't know about that. We know that the optimal mix will stay the same. This means that the optimal values of all the variables, including the slacks, stay the same. But our total cost will increase by 50 times the amount of T2 being used in the current solution.

MANAGER: I see. The OV will go from the old value, $511.11, to the new value

$$511.11 + 50(0.70370) = \$546.30$$

Yes. I see what you mean. Everything stays the same except the total cost. Did you say that even the surplus values stay the same?

Yes. If all the decision variables stay the same, you can see from either the geometry or the algebra that the surplus variables would have to also.

MANAGER: That must mean the constraints that are active also stay the same.

Good for you.

MANAGER: I see. By the way, what happens if the cost of T2 increases by more than the allowable amount?

181

CHAPTER 5
Linear Programs:
Computer Analysis,
Interpreting
Sensitivity Output,
and the Dual
Problem

Well, since we have a Min model I know that increasing the cost of an input cannot increase its use. Therefore, as the cost of T2 increases I know that the optimal value of T2 can never increase. In fact, since the current solution is nondegenerate I know that when the cost of T2 increases by more than the allowable amount, the optimal value of T2 will in fact surely decrease.

MANAGER: Wait a minute. Slow down. You said nondegenerate?

Yes. This simply means that in the computer output the number of variables with a positive optimal value, including both decision and slack or surplus variables, is equal to the number of constraints. Figure 5.14 shows that at optimality three decision variables and one surplus variable are positive. Thus there are four positive variables and four constraints, which means that we have a nondegenerate solution. This is a technicality but it is important in interpreting some of the output.

MANAGER: All right. Fine. So if the per unit cost of ore from mine 2 increases by more than its allowable amount, we will get an optimal solution with a smaller value of T2.

Yes. And not only that. The optimal values of some of the other variables may also change, but it isn't possible to say exactly which ones or how much. This means that a surplus that was positive could become zero, and hence a constraint that was inactive could become active, if you know what I mean.

MANAGER: Yes, I think I'm with you.

Good. And it could also mean that a constraint that previously had zero surplus could now become inactive in the sense that its surplus becomes positive. In other words, once the cost change exceeds the limit of the indicated range, all sorts of things can happen.

MANAGER: You're talking about a cost change that *exceeds* the allowable limit. What if it actually hits the limit?

Then, again since the current solution is nondegenerate, we know that there will be alternative optimal solutions, the current solution together with a new one which has less T2 in it.

MANAGER: Well, it seems to me that we have considerable information about the influence of uncertainty. That strikes me as remarkable.

I agree.

MANAGER: Okay, Thank you very much. I think I can do pretty well now on my own with the output analysis. We should really call it model analysis, shouldn't we?

I guess so.

MANAGER: Okay. Thanks again. I'm amazed at how much we can learn about the actual problem, above and beyond the solution.

Right. That is because of the relative simplicity of linear mathematics. By the way, do you mind if I ask you just one question to more or less check you out?

MANAGER: Okay. Shoot.

You have already noticed on the output that the optimal value of T4 is zero.

MANAGER: True.

I happen to know that ore from location 4 has some desirable tensile properties that haven't really been built into the model.

MANAGER: That is true.

Also, I understand from Mr. Shmootz that it isn't unreasonable to renegotiate the cost of T4 periodically.

MANAGER: Are you referring to the fact that **PROTRAC** has some family connections in the location 4 enterprise?

182

CHAPTER 5
Linear Programs:
Computer Analysis,
Interpreting
Sensitivity Output,
and the Dual
Problem

Something like that. But my point is this. How much would the cost of T4 have to decrease before you're willing to buy some?

MANAGER: Let's see. The current cost of T4 is $500 per ton. I think what you're trying to ask me is this: How much must this cost decrease before we obtain an optimal policy that uses T4? Is that your question?

Yes.

MANAGER: Okay. To find the answer I look at the SENSITIVITY ANALYSIS, where I see that if the cost of T4 decreases by less than $91.11 per ton, then, according to what you just said, the optimal value of this variable remains unchanged. That means it remains at zero. Consequently, taking into account what you just said about nondegeneracy, I know that if its cost is negotiated down to 408.89 or less, there will be an optimal solution with T4 positive. Right?

Correct. Now can you tell me what happens to the optimal objective value?

MANAGER: I guess I can figure that out. If the cost descreases as much as $91.11, no change occurs in the optimal values of any of the variables. In the objective function only the cost of T4 is changing. But since the value of T4 stays at zero, the OV won't change either. I guess it stays at $511.11 as long as the reduction in cost is less than $91.11.

Correct.

MANAGER: But what happens if the reduction exactly equals 91.11? You've told me that in this case the optimal value of T4 will become positive. Is that right?

Not quite. There will be two optimal solutions: the current one, and another one which has a positive optimal value of T4 and some new values for some of the other variables. But I don't know exactly how the others will change.

MANAGER: Okay, but does this mean that when the cost of T4 is reduced by exactly $91.11, the total cost suddenly drops down from $511.11?

No, since these are alternative optima the OV equals 511.11 at each.

MANAGER: Can we tell how much of T4 will be used in the alternative optimum?

I'm afraid not. All we know is that there will be some positive value for this variable.

MANAGER: And how do you know all that?

From the mathematics. And remember that these statements about alternative optimal solutions depend on the nondegeneracy of the current solution on the printout.

MANAGER: Okay. Great. And I suppose that if the decrease in the cost of T4 exceeds the allowable amount, the OV will then begin to decrease.

Again, this is true because of the nondegeneracy.

MANAGER: What if the nondegeneracy weren't satisfied?

Then we would have what is termed a degenerate solution. All we could say then is that the optimal solution will not change if the cost of T4 stays within the allowable range. Conceivably, the cost could decrease by *more than* 91.11 and we would still not get a new optimal solution. Thus you can see that in the degenerate case the output gives us somewhat less information.

MANAGER: Well, by now I think I know all that I need to about what's going on. Do you agree?

Yes. Shall we stop?

MANAGER: Really, since I'm doing so well, I have to ask one final question. What about that column in the first section of the output under the heading REDUCED COST?

It is really meaningful only for a decision variable whose optimal value is zero. It tells how much the per unit cost of that variable can be reduced before the optimal value of the variable will become positive.

183

CHAPTER 5
Linear Programs:
Computer Analysis,
Interpreting
Sensitivity Output,
and the Dual
Problem

MANAGER: We just answered that question about T4.

I know.

MANAGER: But we didn't use this column. We used the cost-sensitivity part of the output. In fact, I see that exactly the same value, 91.11, appears in both places.

Right.

MANAGER: So why bother with this reduced-cost column if the same value appears under the cost-sensitivity column?

Simply for convenience. The reduced cost pertains to variables whose optimal value is zero. You can easily spot these variables in the top section of the output. In the next column you can immediately read the reduced cost, which is a little easier than going down into the cost-sensitivity section. That's all there is to it.

MANAGER: Thank you. It's been very instructive!

My pleasure.

————— 5.5
A SYNOPSIS OF THE SOLUTION OUTPUT

When a linear program is solved, the computer output contains the following information:

Optimal Values
1. Optimal values are given for the decision variables, the slack and surplus variables, and the objective function. From the optimal value of the slack and surplus variables you can quickly deduce the value of the constraint functions (the amount of resources used, the levels of requirements satisfied, etc.) at an optimal solution. The constraints with zero slack or surplus are called *active*, *effective*, or *binding*. Those with positive slack or surplus are called *inactive*.

Dual Price and RHS Ranges
2. The dual price tells you the rate the improvement in the OV (optimal value of the objective function) as the right-hand side of a constraint increases. "Improvement" means increase in a Max model and decrease in a Min model. RIGHTHAND SIDE RANGES gives you an allowable range in right-hand-side (RHS) changes over which the dual price is valid. The dual price is also frequently referred to as a *dual variable*, a *shadow price*, or an *imputed price*.

Objective Coefficient Ranges
3. OBJ COEFFICIENT RANGES tells you the allowable changes that can be made in the objective function coefficients without changing the optimal solution (the optimal values of the variables). Under normal conditions (termed *nondegenerate*), if an objective function coefficient is changed by an amount that *equals* an allowable change, there will be an alternative optimal solution with new values for the variables. If the coefficient is changed by an amount that *exceeds* the allowable change, there will be a new (assuming nondegeneracy) optimal solution.

Reduced Cost
4. "Reduced cost output" applies to decision variables whose optimal value is zero. It provides the same information as the OBJ COEFFICIENT RANGES for these variables.

In concluding, it is to be noted that the format used for the solution of LP problems differs in minor details from one software package to another. However, a solid understanding of one system prepares you to deal with any system with a minimum of effort.

THE DUAL PROBLEM (SKIP)

Given any set of data for an LP model, we can use the same data to form a *different* LP model. The resulting problem is called the *dual* of the original problem. The dual has theoretic, economic, and computational importance which we shall discuss. First, let us see exactly how the dual problem is formed.

Transformation Rules In order to discuss duality theory in a satisfactory way we must drop the restriction that all variables in an LP model are nonnegative. For example, let us consider the following problem:

Problem (E1)

$$\text{Max } 3x_1 + 4x_2 - 2x_3 \qquad\qquad \textit{dual variables}$$

$$\text{s.t.} \quad 4x_1 - 12x_2 + 3x_3 \le 12 \qquad\qquad y_1$$

$$-2x_1 + 3x_2 + x_3 \le 6 \qquad\qquad y_2$$

$$-5x_1 + x_2 - 6x_3 \ge -40 \qquad\qquad y_3 \qquad\qquad \text{(E1)}$$

$$3x_1 + 4x_2 - 2x_3 = 10 \qquad\qquad y_4$$

$$x_1 \ge 0, \qquad x_2 \le 0, \qquad x_3 \text{ unconstrained in sign}$$

In this problem we see the appearance of each type of constraint ($\le$, $\ge$, and $=$). Moreover, we have dropped the requirement that all variables must be nonnegative. In this example we have required that only the variable x_1 be nonnegative. The variable x_2 is required to be nonpositive and x_3 is unconstrained in sign. (That is, the optimal value of x_3 can be positive, negative, or zero.) The dual of this problem (E1) is created by applying the following rules:

- **Rule 1:** The number of variables in the dual problem is equal to the number of constraints in the original problem. The number of constraints in the dual problem is equal to the number of variables in the original problem.

Since (E1) has four constraints and three variables, the dual to (E1) will have three constraints and four variables. We shall see that each of the four variables in the dual to (E1) will correspond to one of the constraints in (E1). For this reason we show the column of dual variables y_1, y_2, y_3, y_4 to the right of (E1).

- **Rule 2:** Coefficients of the objective function in the dual problem come from the right-hand side of the original problem.

Thus, according to Rule 2, the objective function for the dual problem is

$$12y_1 + 6y_2 - 40y_3 + 10y_4$$

- **Rule 3:** If the original problem is a Max model, the dual is a Min model. If the original problem is a Min model, the dual is a Max model.

Thus, since (E1) is a Max model the complete objective function for the dual problem is

$$\text{Min } 12y_1 + 6y_2 - 40y_3 + 10y_4$$

185

CHAPTER 5
Linear Programs:
Computer Analysis,
Interpreting
Sensitivity Output,
and the Dual
Problem

■ **Rule 4:** The coefficients for the first constraint function for the dual problem are the coefficients of the first variable in the constraints for the original problem, and similarly for the other constraints.

Thus, the first constraint function for the dual is

$$4y_1 - 2y_2 - 5y_3 + 3y_4$$

The second constraint function is

$$-12y_1 + 3y_2 + y_3 + 4y_4$$

Note that these constraints are obtained by reading "down" the rows of (E1). Using the same pattern, try to write out the third constraint function. (By Rule 1, there are only three constraints in the dual.) You should get

$$3y_1 + y_2 - 6y_3 - 2y_4$$

■ **Rule 5:** The right-hand sides of the dual constraints come from the objective function coefficients in the original problem.

Thus, by applying Rules 4 and 5 we have obtained the following constraint functions and respective right-hand sides for the dual

constraint function	RHS
$4y_1 - 2y_2 - 5y_3 + 3y_4$	3
$-12y_1 + 3y_2 + y_3 + 4y_4$	4
$3y_1 + y_2 - 6y_3 - 2y_4$	-2

■ **Rule 6:** The sense of the ith dual constraint is $=$ if and only if the ith variable in the original problem is unconstrained in sign.

Thus, since the third variable in the original problem (E1) is unconstrained in sign, the third dual constraint is an equality:

$$3y_1 + y_2 - 6y_3 - 2y_4 = -2$$

■ **Rule 7:** If the original problem is a Max (Min) model, then after applying Rule 6, assign to the remaining dual constraints a sense the same as (opposite to) the corresponding variable in the original problem.

To apply Rule 7, note that the first variable in the original (Max) model is ≥ 0 and the second is ≤ 0. This means that the first dual constraint is $\geq$ and the second dual constraint is $\leq$:

$$4y_1 - 2y_2 - 5y_3 + 3y_4 \geq 3$$

$$-12y_1 + 3y_2 + y_3 + 4y_4 \leq 4$$

186

CHAPTER 5
Linear Programs:
Computer Analysis,
Interpreting
Sensitivity Output,
and the Dual
Problem

Also, Rule 7 means that if (E1) had been written as a Min model the inequalities above would be written as ≤ 3 and ≥ 4, respectively.

■ **Rule 8:** The ith variable in the dual problem is unconstrained in sign if and only if the ith constraint in the original problem is an equality.

Since the fourth constraint in the original problem is $=$, Rule 8 dictates that the fourth dual variable, y_4, must be unconstrained in sign.

■ **Rule 9:** If the original problem is a Max (Min) model, then after applying Rule 8, assign to the remaining dual variables a sense opposite to (the same as) the corresponding constraint in the original problem.

Since the first and second constraints in the original Max problem are $\leq$, Rule 9 dictates that $y_1 \geq 0$, $y_2 \geq 0$. Since the third constraint in the original problem is $\geq$, we must have $y_3 \leq 0$.

Application to (E1) of the nine rules above has created the following dual problem:

**Dual of
Problem (E1)**

$$\text{Min } 12y_1 + 6y_2 - 40y_3 + 10y_4$$

$$\text{s.t.} \quad 4y_1 - 2y_2 - 5y_3 + 3y_4 \geq \quad 3$$

$$-12y_1 + 3y_2 + \quad y_3 + 4y_4 \leq \quad 4 \qquad \text{(E2)}$$

$$3y_1 + \quad y_2 - 6y_3 - 2y_4 = -2$$

$$y_1 \geq 0, \qquad y_2 \geq 0, \qquad y_3 \leq 0, \qquad y_4 \text{ unconstrained in sign}$$

You could now imagine that (E2) is the original problem. Let x_1, x_2, and x_3 be the variables in the problem that is dual to (E2), and you can verify that an application of the foregoing rules to (E2) will return us to (E1). This means that *taking the dual of the dual gives back the original problem.* We have called (E2) the dual of (E1), but it would be equally correct to call (E1) the dual of (E2). It just depends on which problem is considered the original one.

The rules above may at first seem like a lot to remember. However, compare Rules 6 and 8 and note that they are symmetric, merely stipulating that in either problem a variable that is unconstrained in sign corresponds to an equality constraint in the other problem. Similarly, Rules 7 and 9 are nearly symmetric. In schematic representation they say:

Max model		Min model
$x_i \geq 0$	$\Leftrightarrow$	ith constraint is $\geq$
$x_i \leq 0$	$\Leftrightarrow$	ith constraint is $\leq$
ith constraint is $\leq$	$\Leftrightarrow$	$y_i \geq 0$
ith constraint is $\geq$	$\Leftrightarrow$	$y_i \leq 0$

Here, now, are several examples of these rules.

Example 1

$$\text{Max } 3x_1 + 4x_2 \qquad\qquad \textit{dual variables}$$

$$\text{s.t.} \quad -2x_1 + 3x_2 \le \; 6 \qquad\qquad y_1$$

$$5x_1 - \; x_2 \le 40 \qquad\qquad y_2$$

$$x_1 + \; x_2 \le \; 7 \qquad\qquad y_3$$

$$x_1 \ge 0, \qquad x_2 \ge 0$$

The dual is

$$\text{Min } 6y_1 + 40y_2 + 7y_3$$

$$\text{s.t.} \quad -2y_1 + 5y_2 + y_3 \ge 3$$

$$3y_1 - \; y_2 + y_3 \ge 4$$

$$y_1 \ge 0, \qquad y_2 \ge 0, \qquad y_3 \ge 0$$

Notice how the dual constraint functions are formed by reading "down" the data in the original constraints. Incidentally, when, as in this example, the Max model has all constraints $\le$ with all variables nonnegative (and hence the Min model has all constraints $\ge$ with all variables nonnegative) the pair of problems carries the label *symmetric dual problems*.

Example 2

$$\text{Max } 19x_1 - 22x_2 \qquad\qquad \textit{dual variables}$$

$$\text{s.t.} \quad 4x_1 + 5x_2 = 12 \qquad\qquad y_1$$

$$x_1 \ge 0, \qquad x_2 \ge 0$$

The dual is

$$\text{Min } 12y_1$$

$$\text{s.t.} \quad 4y_1 \ge \quad 19$$

$$5y_1 \ge -22$$

$$y_1 \text{ unconstrained in sign}$$

Example 3

$$\text{Min } x_1 + 12x_2 - 2x_3 \qquad\qquad\qquad \textit{dual variables}$$

$$\text{s.t.} \quad 4x_1 + 2x_2 + 12x_3 \le \; 10 \qquad\qquad y_1$$

$$2x_1 - \; x_2 + 11x_3 \ge -2 \qquad\qquad y_2$$

$$x_1 \le 0, \qquad x_2 \text{ unconstrained in sign,} \qquad x_3 \ge 0$$

188

CHAPTER 5
Linear Programs:
Computer Analysis,
Interpreting
Sensitivity Output,
and the Dual
Problem

The dual is

$$\text{Max } 10y_1 - 2y_2$$

$$\text{s.t.} \quad 4y_1 + 2y_2 \geq 1$$

$$2y_1 - y_2 = 12$$

$$12y_1 + 11y_2 \leq -2$$

$$y_1 \leq 0, \qquad y_2 \geq 0$$

**Relations
between
Primal and
Dual**

In referring to a pair of dual problems it is often said that one of them (usually the original model) is the *primal* problem and the other is the *dual* problem. From an historical point of view, the term "primal" was invented by the mathematician Tobias Dantzig to denote the problem whose dual is a particular problem. The point to stress, however, is that duality is what is called a *symmetric* and *reflexive* relationship. This means that either problem may be considered to be the dual of the other, and whichever of the problems is designated as the primal,

The dual of the dual problem is again the primal problem.

For convenience, in this section let us adopt the convention that the Max model with, in general, m constraints and n variables, is the *primal*, and the Min model, with n constraints and m variables, is the *dual*.

The theoretic relationships between the primal and the dual are very simply stated, yet these relations have considerable importance in the theory of linear problems.

Let us say that a set of decision variable values is *feasible* for a given model if the set of values satisfies the constraints and sign requirements that are specified by the model. Moreover, we shall say that a specific set of decision variable values $(x_1, \ldots, x_n)$ is *primal feasible* if these values are feasible in the Max model, and similarly that a specific set of values $(y_1, \ldots, y_m)$ is *dual feasible* if these values are feasible in the Min model. The following result is important:

If $(x_1, \ldots, x_n)$ is any set of primal feasible values and $(y_1, \ldots, y_m)$ is any set of dual feasible values, the primal objective function (i.e., the function to be maximized) evaluated at x cannot exceed the dual objective function (i.e., the function to be minimized) evaluated at y.

**Objective
Function
Values**

As an example of this fact, let us refer to Example 1. The Max model is the primal and the Min model is the dual. Verify that the values (3, 2) are primal feasible (i.e., $x_1 = 3$, $x_2 = 2$) since they satisfy all the primal constraints and nonnegativity conditions. The associated primal objective value is

$$3x_1 + 4x_2 = 3(3) + 4(2) = 17$$

The values (0, 1, 6) are dual feasible (i.e., $y_1 = 0$, $y_2 = 1$, $y_3 = 6$) since they satisfy all the constraints and nonnegativity conditions of the dual problem. The associated objective

189

CHAPTER 5
Linear Programs:
Computer Analysis,
Interpreting
Sensitivity Output,
and the Dual
Problem

value is

$$6y_1 + 40y_2 + 7y_3 = 6(0) + 40(1) + 7(6) = 82$$

and since $82 > 17$, the dual objective value exceeds the primal value. You may wish to select other sets of primal feasible values and other dual feasible values. No matter what values are selected, as long as they are primal and dual feasible, the primal objective value will not exceed the dual value.

Now suppose that primal and dual feasible values are found that produce equal objective function values. If there were a different primal feasible value that produced a larger value for the primal objective function, it would also be larger than the dual objective value and this would contradict the foregoing result. Hence, there can be no primal feasible values for the decision variables that produce a larger value of the primal objective function. This means that the originally found primal feasible values are optimal. Similar reasoning applies to the dual. In other words, if primal and dual feasible values are found that produce equal objective function values, those decision variable values are optimal in their respective problems. In fact, an even stronger result links the primal and dual problems, namely,

1. Either of the two problems has a solution if and only if the other does.
2. When there is a solution, the optimal value of the objective function in the primal is the same as the optimal value of the objective function in the dual.

This elegant result says that solving either problem yields the same optimal objective value. It does *not* say that the *optimal solution* to each problem (i.e., the optimal values of the decision variables) is the same. Such a result would not be reasonable since the two problems are in spaces of different dimension. That is, there are n of the x variables (the primal variables) and m of the y variables (the dual variables). As an illustration of this, refer back to Example 1. There the primal variables are in two-dimensional space and the dual variables in three-dimensional space.

To explain the relations between the primal and dual problems more fully, it is necessary to recall from Section 3.8 the technical terms *infeasible* (or *inconsistent*) and *unbounded*. An LP problem is said to be *infeasible*, or *inconsistent*, if the constraints (including the nonnegativity conditions) cannot all be (simultaneously) satisfied. This means that the set of points described by the constraints is an empty set. An LP problem is said to be *unbounded* if the objective contour can be slid arbitrarily far in the desired direction without leaving the constraint set behind. This means that in a Max problem there are allowable decision variable values that make the value of the objective function arbitrarily large. The reverse interpretation holds for a Min problem.

It turns out that any linear program falls into one of the following three categories:

1. The problem has an optimal solution (This implies a finite optimal objective value.)
2. The problem is unbounded. (This implies consistent constraints but, if you like, an infinite—or negatively infinite, for a Min model—optimal objective value.)
3. The problem is infeasible. (This implies that there is no allowable choice for the decision variables.)

Although perfectly respectable as mathematical possibilities, the second and third phenomena are, in terms of applied problems, abnormal. Infinite profits do not exist, and a real-world problem, correctly formulated, cannot lead to an inconsistent model.

Using the foregoing terminology, we can now more completely characterize the relations between any pair of dual linear programs. These relations are known as the *dual theorem of linear programming*. This is the most important theoretic result in the study of LP problems. The dual theorem says that of the nine possible states for a pair of dual problems (e.g., one optimal, the other optimal; one optimal, the other unbounded; one optimal, the other infeasible; etc.), only four possibilities can actually occur.

Dual Theorem of LP

1. In any pair of dual linear programs, both may have optimal solutions, in which case the optimal objective values will be the same.
2. In any pair of dual linear programs, both may be inconsistent.
3. In any pair of dual linear programs, one may be unbounded and the other inconsistent.

The dual theorem states that these combinations are mutually exclusive and exhaustive. For example, the possibility that both the primal and the dual are unbounded is ruled out. The possibility is also ruled out that one problem can be unbounded while the other has an optimal solution. Thus, the dual theorem implies that if it is known that either problem is unbounded, the other *must* be inconsistent.

There is a final theoretic relationship between the primal and dual problems of considerable importance in applications. This is called the *principle of complementary slackness*, which can be stated as follows:

Consider an inequality constraint in any LP problem. If that constraint is inactive for any optimal solution to the problem, the corresponding dual variable will be zero in any optimal solution to the dual of that problem.

We have now presented essentially all the important theoretic relationships between pairs of dual linear programs. This theory is of considerable mathematical interest in its own right. In addition, the theory of duality has economic and computational significance. This will become apparent in the following sections.

Economic Significance of the Dual

From the point of view of applied analysis, the most important aspect of the dual problem is probably the associated economic interpretation. The fact is firmly established by the following relationships:

In a Max problem

> **dual price on printout = dual variable**

In a Min problem

> **dual price on printout = − dual variable**

191

CHAPTER 5
Linear Programs:
Computer Analysis,
Interpreting
Sensitivity Output,
and the Dual
Problem

Thus, all of the economic analysis in this chapter concerning changes in the RHS could have been presented in terms of *dual variables* rather than the *dual prices* in the printout. Indeed, the theory on which this analysis is based was originally developed in the context of the dual problem.

Rather than dwelling on how the change in the sign convention requires a somewhat different interpretation, we shall simply state that

1. The optimal value of the ith dual variable is the rate at which the primal optimal objective value will increase as b_i increases, assuming that all other data are unchanged; that is,

2. If an increase in the RHS increases (decreases) the optimal value, the dual variable is positive (negative), regardless of whether the primal is a Max or a Min problem.

Note that in discussing dual prices we used the term *rate of improvement*. In talking about dual variables we use the term *rate of increase*. These are the same for a Max model, opposite in sign for a Min model.

Evaluating a Resource

To illustrate the interpretation of the dual variables, let us imagine ourselves in a profit-maximization production context with constraints on the input resources. Suppose that aluminum is one of our resources and that the first constraint of our model is of $\leq$ form and represents a limitation on the availability of aluminum. Imagine that 8000 pounds of aluminum is currently in our stockpile, so we solve the model using the value 8000 for the first RHS, b_1. Let us suppose that in reading the computer output we find that the dual price for the first constraint is $16.50, which is the optimal value of y_1 in the dual problem. This means that the *marginal* contribution of aluminum (the value of the last, or the next, unit consumed) to the total profit is $16.50. Suppose the sensitivity information shows that this value of $16.50 holds for b_1 values between 7500 and 9000, and suppose the market price of aluminum is $20.00 per pound. Using the lower limit of 7500, and the fact that we have 8000 pounds in the stockpile, we can infer that each of our last 500 pounds of aluminum is yielding us less than the market value (the OV increases only $16.50 per unit, the market value is $20.00 per unit). In theory, then, we might sell 500 pounds on the market for a return of $(20)(500) = \$10,000$, whereas the cost, in terms of the output profit, would be $(16.50)(500) = \$8250$. The transaction would net us an additional $1750 above current profits.[6]

On the other hand, suppose that the market value of aluminum is only $14.00 per pound. In this case, the dual price of $16.50 indicates that we may want to consider purchasing an additional 1000 pounds of aluminum, for this would net us $16.50 - 14.00 = \$2.50$ per pound, or $2500 above and beyond the current profit.

The discussion above assumes the existence of a market for resources, and illustrates how the dual variables enable the planner to compare the market values with the value obtained from the consumption of those resources in his own operations. Although this discussion illustrates one possible economic interpretation of dual variables, one caveat should be issued. When a model includes constraints on resources, it generally implies that these resources are genuinely scarce over the planning period under consideration. This could occur, for example, because of bottlenecks, lead times to delivery, etc. In such a situation, there is, in essence, no market for the scarce resource.

---

[6] In a realistic situation the manager may not wish to exercise this option because he "may not be in the business of selling aluminum."

192

CHAPTER 5
Linear Programs:
Computer Analysis,
Interpreting
Sensitivity Output,
and the Dual
Problem

FIGURE 5.15
Factory 1 Data

RAW MATERIAL	INPUT PER LAWN MOWER	INPUT PER SPRINKLER	TOTAL AVAILABILITY
1	6	4	38
2	1	3	34
3	10	7	44
Per Unit Profitability	4	3	

Economic
Significance
of the Dual
Problem

Let us now focus for several minutes on the interpretation of the dual problem as a whole. Often, for example, the primal problem has the interpretation of finding profit-maximizing levels of production subject to constraints on scarce resources. How might we interpret the dual to this problem? Since the dual will be a Min model, we could say that it is a cost-minimization model. But it minimizes the cost of doing what? The following scenario will provide an answer to this question:

Suppose that a firm owns two factories in two different marketing districts. For simplicity, assume that each factory uses the same three scarce raw materials. Factory 1 makes two products, such as lawn mowers and sprinklers, in quantities x_1 and x_2. Factory 2 makes three different products, doorknobs, refrigerator handles, and cowbells, in quantities z_1, z_2, and z_3, and factory 2 uses precisely the same raw materials as factory 1. Let us imagine that the factory 1 data are as given in Figure 5.15. Then we obtain

Factory 1 Production Model

$$\text{Max } 4x_1 + 3x_2$$
$$\text{s.t.} \quad 6x_1 + 4x_2 \leq 38$$
$$x_1 + 3x_2 \leq 34 \qquad \text{(F1)}$$
$$10x_1 + 7x_2 \leq 44$$
$$x_1 \geq 0, \qquad x_2 \geq 0$$

The analogous data for factory 2 are presented in Figure 5.16. From Figure 5.16 we obtain

Factory 2 Production Model

$$\text{Max } 6z_1 + 2z_2 + z_3$$
$$\text{s.t.} \quad 4z_1 + 2z_2 + 7z_3 \leq 54$$
$$3z_1 + 9z_2 + 8z_3 \leq 126 \qquad \text{(F2)}$$
$$6z_1 + 5z_2 + 2z_3 \leq 33$$
$$z_1 \geq 0, \qquad z_2 \geq 0, \qquad z_3 \geq 0$$

What Is a
Fair Price?

Now recall our assumption that the same firm owns both of these factories and that the factories are located in different marketing districts. We also assume that the three

193

CHAPTER 5
Linear Programs:
Computer Analysis,
Interpreting
Sensitivity Output,
and the Dual
Problem

FIGURE 5.16
Factory 2 Data

RAW MATERIAL	INPUT PER DOORKNOB	INPUT PER REFRIGERATOR HANDLE	INPUT PER COWBELL	TOTAL AVAILABILITY
1	4	2	7	54
2	3	9	8	126
3	6	5	2	33
Per Unit Profitability	6	2	1	

raw materials are scarce in the sense of long lead times to delivery. Now we suppose that management obtains information indicating that for various economic reasons the prices (i.e., the profitabilities) in the factory 2 marketing district are going to increase drastically. It is not known exactly how much the prices will increase, but management is confident that the increase will be so large that it will be desirable for factory 2 to take over all production. Thus, all of the factory 1 stockpile of raw materials should be transferred to factory 2. However, management decides that factory 2 should pay factory 1 a "fair price" for the transfer of these raw materials. What is such a "fair price?" It seems intuitively clear that, at least from factory 1's point of view, a fair price would be one that is equal to the maximum possible profit factory 1 would make if it retained use of its resources that may now be shifted to factory 2. This is the factory 1 OV, and it would be a fair overall "lump-sum payment" for the three raw materials. The firm, however, needs to know more than the lump-sum payment. It must have per unit prices for each material. These prices are required for financial reporting (i.e., tax) purposes. All accounting for individual products is carried out on a per item basis. The firm thus must find "fair" unit prices that can stand the scrutiny of a careful review. In order to obtain "fair" per unit prices, we make the following observations. If factory 2 pays per unit prices of y_1, y_2, and y_3 for the three raw materials, then since factory 1 possesses 38, 34, and 44 units, respectively, of each raw material

$$\text{amount factory 2 pays} = 38y_1 + 34y_2 + 44y_3$$

Factory 2 wants to look as profitable as possible; thus, its goal is to

$$\text{Min } 38y_1 + 34y_2 + 44y_3$$

Factory 1, however, wants to make sure that it makes as much profit as it would if it remained in business for itself. From Figure 5.15 we see that if factory 1 had 6 units of raw material 1, 1 unit of raw material 2, and 10 units of raw material 3, it could produce one lawn mower for a profit of $4. Recall that y_i is the sales price of raw material i. Thus, factory 1 will insist that

$$6y_1 + y_2 + 10y_3 \geq 4$$

If this condition does not hold, factory 1 will choose not to sell its raw materials to factory 2. Making use of the raw materials to produce lawn mowers will be more profitable.

Similarly, factory 1 will insist that

$$4y_1 + 3y_2 + 7y_3 \geq 3$$

Otherwise, it is more profitable to make sprinklers than to sell the raw materials to factory 2.

In summary, then, the problem of determining fair prices is

$$\text{Min } 38y_1 + 34y_2 + 44y_3$$

$$\text{s.t. } 6y_1 + y_2 + 10y_3 \geq 4$$

$$4y_1 + 3y_2 + 7y_3 \geq 3$$

$$y_1, y_2 \geq 0$$

and this problem is the dual of (F1). Thus we have shown that the dual to the production problem has the following interpretation:

It provides "fair prices" in the sense of prices that yield the minimum acceptable liquidation payment.

When the simplex algorithm is used to solve an LP problem, it turns out that optimal solutions to both the original problem (which may be either a Max or Min model) and its dual are obtained. We have already seen this fact on the printout (subject to a possible sign change) and it will be demonstrated mathematically in Chapter 6.[7] Thus, if you want to solve a particular problem, you can, of course, go about it by solving the problem directly. Alternatively, you can take the dual of the original problem and then solve the dual problem on the computer. This will also provide a solution to the dual of the dual, which is the original problem. Since each of these possible routes leads to the same result, it is of interest, from the computational point of view, to inquire which procedure is more efficient.

To shed light on this question, we take note of the empirical fact that the amount of time required to solve a linear program depends more critically on the number of constraints than on the number of variables. If the original problem has m constraints and n variables, the dual problem has n constraints and m variables. It is then apparent that, *all other things being equal*, you should choose to solve the problem with fewer constraints.

Although the foregoing rule of thumb is a reasonably good general prescription, when you get into fairly large and structured models it may well break down, for in such cases, all other things may not be equal. Possible reasons for departure from this rule of thumb tend to become quite technical in nature. In some cases, irrespective of the number of constraints, one of the two problems, because of its form, may be solvable with a special code, such as what we call a *network code*, as opposed to a general-purpose LP code. The other problem, however, may not have the required special structure and hence may have to be solved with the general-purpose code. Since special structure codes tend to be computationally more efficient than general-purpose codes, this is an important consideration.

Other technical considerations have to do with the fact that even with a general LP code it may be easier to "get started" with one problem rather than the other. We

---

[7] It can also be shown that the same sensitivity information is produced on the output, whether one solves the primal or the dual.

195

CHAPTER 5
Linear Programs:
Computer Analysis,
Interpreting
Sensitivity Output,
and the Dual
Problem

will explain this startup procedure, sometimes called *phase I of the simplex method*, briefly in Chapter 6.

The choice between solving the original problem or its dual does not have much computational significance for small problems, say when either model has no more than several hundred constraints, since such problems can be handled with great speed on modern computing equipment. As the problems grow larger, into the ballpark of several thousand constraints, the choice between the original problem and its dual can become very important. On such occasions, technical consultation with a professional linear programmer may well be worthwhile.

_____ 5.7
NOTES ON IMPLEMENTATION

Batch
Processing
Mode versus
Conversational
Mode

In practice, linear programming has been and continues to be a very important tool. There are essentially two different ways that users work with the computer in solving LP problems: (1) the batch processing mode and (2) the conversational mode (often called the interactive mode). In batch processing the user submits previously prepared data, such as a deck of data cards or a magnetic tape of data, to a central computer center and then waits, perhaps for several hours or several days, to receive the output from the run. In the conversational mode, the user sits at a console, types in data, then runs the model and, typically, within seconds the output is printed on the console. The user may then modify the problem and rerun it. The advantages of the conversational mode are quick access to results, and the ability to manipulate the model (change data, change constraints, etc.), rerun it, access the output, and then, if desired, change and rerun again. The disadvantage is the work required to type in the data at the console. For such a reason, the conversational mode is not typically used for solving large-scale problems. For such problems the batch processing mode is considered more suitable. The relative disadvantage of the latter mode is longer turnaround time and the inability to manipulate the model "on line." That is, the benefits of direct interaction with the computer are lost.

Although LP is certainly the most widely used tool of management science, and although it has been applied to a very broad spectrum of problems, most of the real-world applications are probably clustered in the areas of distribution, transportation, and logistics planning. It has historically been true, and probably still is, that the biggest commercial users of LP are oil firms. In the petroleum industry LP is used in refinery processing and distribution planning.

Most of the latest-generation computers have their own LP batch software and the associated output will usually be more complicated than that associated with the (conversational mode) printouts seen in this chapter. Given your familiarity with the material in this chapter, not more than an hour or two of additional study would be required to digest the formats of other LP systems such as MPX (associated with IBM) or FMPS (associated with Univac).

Topics of importance in commercial applications of LP are matrix generation and report writing, both of which are too specialized to present in any detail in this text. Matrix generation involves writing subroutines which transform raw data into a format that is acceptable to a particular software system such as MPX. Report generation is a way to specify formats for output in ways that will be of specific interest to the user.

Where is LP used in the firm? It used to be the case that the management science group or the operations research department would be the only place in which terms such as "linear programming" or "optimization would even be understood. All of that

196

CHAPTER 5
Linear Programs:
Computer Analysis,
Interpreting
Sensitivity Output,
and the Dual
Problem

has changed. Recent surveys have shown that management science capabilities tend to be much more spread out within the firm. Today you might well find LP studies in the corporate planning department, in marketing, in operations, or in distribution.

As a final point, one great difference between textbook problems and real-world applications must be emphasized. In the textbook the data you need in order to solve a problem are always available. In real-world implementation, problems such as the reliability of one's data, even the existence of the needed data, are often a nightmare. Collecting needed data and forming and maintaining data banks—these activities can well determine the success or failure of an intended LP analysis

5.8 SUMMARY

The emphasis in this chapter has been on the interpretation of the computer output for an LP, as presented in Sections 5.3, 5.4, and 5.5. We have stressed the wealth of information available through sensitivity analysis on the right-hand sides and on the objective function coefficients. The role of degeneracy and signals for alternative optima were also discussed.

In the first part of this chapter (Section 5.2) we explored the role of slack and surplus variables and studied the construction and the geometry of the standard equality constraint form of an LP. Since the simplex algorithm, and thus computers, solve this form of an LP problem, this material provides a necessary introduction to the material that follows.

In concluding this chapter (Section 5.6) the role of the dual problem was presented in terms of its economic and computational importance.

5.9 KEY TERMS

SLACK OR SURPLUS VARIABLE.   Used to convert an inequality constraint to an equality constraint.

STANDARD EQUALITY CONSTRAINT FORM.   The form of the LP model that is solved by the computer.

DEGENERATE SOLUTION.   The number of variables in the standard equality form (counting decision variables, surpluses, and slacks) with positive optimal value is less than the number of constraints.

NONDEGENERATE SOLUTION.   The number of variables in the standard equality form (counting decision variables, surpluses, and slacks) with positive optimal value is equal to the number of constraints.

DUAL PRICE.   The ith dual price on the computer printout is the rate of improvement in OV as the ith RHS is increased.

DUAL VARIABLES.   The variables in the dual problem. The optimal value of the ith dual variable is the rate of increase in the OV as the ith RHS is increased.

ALLOWABLE RHS RANGE.   Range of RHS values for which the dual price (or dual variable) remains constant.

OBJECTIVE COEFFICIENT RANGES.   Gives ranges of objective function coefficients over which no change in the optimal solution will occur.

ALTERNATIVE OPTIMA.   The existence of more than one optimal solution.

PRIMAL PROBLEM.   The original LP.

DUAL PROBLEM.   A new LP, derived from the primal according to a set of transformation rules.

DUAL THEOREM OF LINEAR PROGRAMMING.   States a theoretic relationship between the primal and dual problems.

MAJOR CONCEPTS QUIZ

True–False

1. T **(F)** Any inequality constraint can be converted to an equivalent equality constraint by properly introducing slack or surplus variables which are unconstrained in sign.

2. **(T)** F Suppose that a $\leq$ constraint is converted to an equality. If a point does not satisfy the $\leq$ constraint, the associated slack value is negative.

3. T **(F)** In the standard equality form, inactive constraints, at optimality, have an optimal value of zero for the associated slack or surplus variables.

4. **(T)** F Degeneracy is important because we must give more restrictive interpretations to the computer output when the optimal solution is degenerate.

5. T **(F)** Dual price, for a given constraint, is the rate of change in OV as the RHS increases.

6. T **(F)** The dual price on the ith constraint is a nonconstant linear function of b_i over the range given by allowable decrease and allowable increase.

7. T F Assuming an optimal solution exists, the simplex method for a Max model produces optimal values for the variables in both the primal and the dual problem.

8. T F In most cases it is more efficient to solve the primal as opposed to the dual.

9. T F The optimal value of the ith dual variable is the rate of increase of OV as the RHS b_i increases.

10. T **(F)** Positive slack variables at optimality indicate redundant constraints.

11. **(T)** F A $\leq$ constraint with positive optimal slack will always have an infinite allowable increase for the RHS.

The following questions refer to the computer output shown in Figure 5.14:

12. T **(F)** If the requirements on A and C are each increased by 0.5 pound, sensitivity analysis tells us that the optimal cost will increase by $24.44.

13. T **(F)** The fact that the dual prices are all ≤ 0 is exclusively explained by the fact that we are dealing with a Min model.

Multiple Choice

14. Conversion to the standard equality constraint form
   a. is entirely automatic and hence can be done by the computer
   b. must be performed before the problem can be solved because this is the form of the problem solved by the simplex algorithm
   c. leads to an important observation about the number of positive variables in the computer solution
   d. all of the above

15. A degenerate optimal solution
   a. has less than m positive variables (where m is the number of constraints)
   b. provides no information on alternative optima
   c. may not provide information on the full range of allowable increase and allowable decrease in objective coefficients
   d. all of the above

16. "Improvement" means
   a. the OV is increased for a Max model
   b. the OV is decreased for a Min model
   c. both a and b

17. For a nondegenerate optimal solution to a Max model, if the objective function coefficient c_1 increases by (exactly) the allowable increase
   a. the OV may change
   b. the previous optimal solution remains optimal
   c. there will be a new optimal solution with a larger optimal value of x_1
   d. all of the above

198

CHAPTER 5
Linear Programs:
Computer Analysis,
Interpreting
Sensitivity Output,
and the Dual
Problem

18. We have just solved a cost Min model and $x_1^* = 0$. Management wants to know: "How much does the cost of x_1 have to be reduced before we will begin to use it at a positive level in an optimal solution?" The answer appears in which portion of the printout?
   a. values of variables
   b. allowable changes in RHS of first constraint
   c. allowable increase in the coefficient of x_1
   d. reduced cost

19. The primal is a Max model in m equality constraints and n nonnegative variables. The dual
   a. has n constraints and m nonnegative variables
   b. is a Min model
   c. both a and b

20. Consider any primal problem (P) and its dual (D).
   a. The OVs in (P) and (D) will be the same.
   b. (P) will have an optimal solution if and only if (D) does also.
   c. Both (P) and (D) cannot be infeasible.
   d. All of the above.

21. Let x be a nonoptimal feasible point in a maximization primal model. Let y be a dual feasible point. Then
   a. the primal objective value, at x, is greater than the dual objective value at y
   b. the primal objective value, at x, is less than the OV for the dual
   c. the primal objective value, at x could be greater than the dual onjective value at y

22. Consider the standard equality constraint form. Suppose that the first constraint, evaluated at a given point P_0, has a zero value for the slack variable. Then
   a. P_0 lies on the boundary of the feasible region
   b. P_0 lies on the first constraint line
   c. both a and b

23. A correct relationship is
   a. a constraint with zero dual price must be inactive
   b. a constraint with positive dual price must be active
   c. both a and b

The llowing questions refer to the computer output shown in Figure 5.14:

24. If the requirement on A is changed from 5 to 6.5
   a. the OV will decrease by $66.66
   b. the OV will improve by $66.66
   c. the OV will increase by $66.66
   d. the OV will not change

25. If the requirement on C is reduced from 30 to 20
   a. the OV will decrease by $44.44
   b. the OV will increase by $44.44
   c. the OV will improve by at least $31.00

26. If the cost of ore from location 2 is decreased to $300 per ton
   a. the OV will not change
   b. the optimal solution will not change
   c. neither a nor b
   d. both a and b

27. If the cost of ore from location 1 is reduced to $680 per ton
   a. there will be a new optimal solution with T1* > 0.25926
   b. there will be alternative optima
   c. the optimal solution above remains optimal
   d. all of the above

PROBLEMS

5-1. Use slack and surplus variables as required to convert the following problem to standard equality constraint form:

$$\text{Max } 3x_1 - 4x_2$$

$$\text{s.t.} \quad 8x_1 + 12x_2 \le 49$$

$$14x_1 - 6x_2 \le 29$$

$$3x_1 + 14x_2 \ge 12$$

$$x_1 + x_2 = 2$$

$$x_1 \ge 0, \qquad x_2 \ge 0$$

5-2. Use slack and surplus variables as required to convert the following problem to standard equality constraint form:

$$\text{Min } 14x_1 + 3x_2 + 29x_3$$

$$\text{s.t.} \quad 13x_1 + 32x_2 + 14x_3 \le 84$$

$$12x_1 - 48x_2 + 29x_3 \ge 49$$

$$6x_1 + 14x_2 - 18x_3 \le 22$$

$$2x_1 + x_2 + x_3 = 3$$

$$x_1 \ge 0, \qquad x_2 \ge 0, \qquad x_3 \ge 0$$

5-3. Consider the constraint

$$3x_1 + x_2 + s = 12$$

where s is a slack variable. What is the slack value associated with the points

(a) $x_1 = 4, x_2 = 0$?

(b) $x_1 = 1, x_2 = 3$?

(c) $x_1 = 5, x_2 = 2$?

5-4. Consider the constraint

$$12x_1 - x_2 - s = 10$$

where s is a surplus variable.

(i) What is the surplus value associated with the point

(a) $x_1 = 0, x_2 = 0$?

(b) $x_1 = 1, x_2 = 1$?

(c) $x_1 = 1, x_2 = 3$?

(ii) Determine feasibility of the points in part (i).

200

CHAPTER 5
Linear Programs:
Computer Analysis,
Interpreting
Sensitivity Output,
and the Dual
Problem

5-5. Consider an LP in 3 variables and 14 constraints. An optimal computer solution will have at most how many positive variables?

5-6. Consider an LP in 200 variables and 12 constraints.

 (a) An optimal nondegenerate computer solution will have how many positive variables?

 (b) An optimal degenerate computer solution will have how many positive variables?

5-7. Refer to the computer printout shown in Figure 5.6.

 (a) Suppose that 5 more hours of labor are made available in department A (row 4). What will be the change in the OV?

 (b) Suppose that 20 fewer hours of labor are available in department A. What will be the change in the OV?

 (c) The dual price on row 2 is valid for what range of values of the RHS?

5-8. The dual price on an inactive constraint always has what value? What can you say about the dual price on an active constraint?

5-9. Consider a constraint with a positive optimal slack value. What must the dual price be?

5-10. Refer to the computer printout shown in Figure 5.6.

 (a) Suppose that the right-hand side of the second constraint is changed to 25. What is the effect on the OV?

 (b) By how much can the constraint on labor hours in department A (row 4) be loosened before the dual price could possibly change?

 (c) Suppose that 90 more hours of labor are available in department A. By how much will the OV change?

5-11. Note that in Figure 5.11 there is an allowable increase of zero on row 5. What anomaly is responsible for this?

5-12. Refer to Figure 5.11. Is the exhibited solution degenerate or nondegenerate? Support your answer.

5-13. Refer to Figure 5.6. Suppose that the profitability of E is reduced to 4000 per unit.

 (a) What is the resulting optimal solution?

 (b) What is the *change* in the OV?

5-14. Refer to Figure 5.6. Suppose that the profitability of E is decreased to 3000 per unit.

 (a) What is the resulting optimal solution?

 (b) What is the *change* in the OV?

5-15. Refer to Figure 5.14.

 (a) How much would the price per ton of ore from location 4 have to decrease in order for it to become attractive to purchase it?

 (b) Suppose that the price of ore from location 1 decreases by $80 per ton. Is there any change in the optimal solution or in the OV?

 (c) Suppose that the price of ore from location 1 increases by $100 per ton. Is there any change in the optimal solution? What, if any, is the associated change in the cost of an optimally blended ton?

5-16. Refer to Figure 5.14.

 (a) Suppose that the price of ore from location 2 increases by $60 per ton. Is there any change in the optimal solution? What, if any, is the associated change in the cost of an optimally blended ton?

 (b) Analyze the main effect on the optimal solution of increasing the cost of ore from location 2 by exactly $66.847 per ton. (For example, does the present solution remain optimal? Is there an additional optimal solution, and if so how can it be characterized?)

 (c) For the change described above in part (b), what is the new OV?

201

CHAPTER 5
Linear Programs:
Computer Analysis,
Interpreting
Sensitivity Output,
and the Dual
Problem

5-17. You have just solved an LP model. You observe that you have a nondegenerate solution and for some objective function coefficient you see a zero entry under the "ALLOW-ABLE INCREASE" column. What does this tell you?

5-18. What LP problem will have the following dual?

$$\text{Min } 2y_1 + y_3 - 4y_4$$

$$\text{s.t.} \quad 2y_1 + y_2 + \qquad y_4 \le 15$$

$$-3y_1 + y_2 + y_3 - 2y_4 \ge 8$$

$$y_1 \ge 0, y_2 \le 0, y_3 \text{ unconstrained in sign}$$

$$y_4 \le 0$$

5-19. Find the dual to the following LP:

$$\text{Min } 4y_1 + 13y_2$$

$$\text{s.t.} \quad 18y_1 + 12y_2 \le 3$$

$$6y_1 + 2y_2 = 17$$

$$y_1 \ge 0, \qquad y_2 \ge 0$$

5-20. Explain how to use the reduced costs to know if there are alternative optimal solutions.

5-21. Suppose that the primal problem has 120 variables and 1500 constraints.

(a) How many variables are in the dual problem?

(b) How many constraints are in the dual problem?

(c) All other things equal, which problem should you prefer to solve (the primal or the dual)?

5-22. Change the data in Problem 5-21 to a primal problem with 1500 variables and 120 constraints and answer the same three questions.

5-23. Regarding Problem 5-21(c), give a reason why "all other things may not be equal."

5-24. "Except for a possible sign difference, the dual prices on the computer output are the same as the optimal values of the variables in the dual of the problem being solved." Answer True or False.

5-25. Employing the words "rate" and "OV," give the correct interpretation of

(a) Dual price on computer output.

(b) Optimal dual variable.

5-26. Let $c_1x_1 + c_2x_2 + \cdots + c_Kx_K$ denote the primal objective function (a Max model) and $b_1y_1 + b_2y_2 + \cdots + b_Ly_L$ the dual objective function.

(a) How many constraints are in the primal problem?

(b) How many constraints are in the dual problem?

(c) If $(u_1, \ldots, u_K)$ is primal feasible and $(v_1, \ldots, v_L)$ is dual feasible, what can you say about the two objective values?

5-27. Consider the following problem:

$$\text{Max } 4x_1 + x_2$$

$$\text{s.t.} \quad 3x_1 + 2x_2 - x_3 \le 0$$

$$x_1 - 3x_2 \qquad \ge 14$$

$$x_1, x_3 \ge 0$$

202

CHAPTER 5
Linear Programs:
Computer Analysis,
Interpreting
Sensitivity Output,
and the Dual
Problem

Thus, the variable x_2 is unconstrained in sign. As discussed in Appendix 5.1, replace x_2 with $y_1 - y_2$, $y_1 \geq 0$, and $y_2 \geq 0$ to convert this problem to an equivalent form in which all variables are nonnegative. Then convert the latter model to a problem in standard equality constraint form, with all variables denoted by the symbol z_j (replace x's, y's, and so on, with z's).

5-28. Consider the Buster Sod problem: Buster Sod operates a 1200-acre irrigated farm in the Red River Valley of Arizona. Sod's principal activities are raising wheat, alfalfa, and beef. The Red River Valley Water Authority has just given its water allotments for next year (Sod was allotted 2000 acre-feet) and Sod is busy preparing his production plan for next year. He figures that beef prices will hold at around $600 per ton and that wheat will sell at $1.60 per bushel. Best guesses are that he will be able to sell alfalfa at $34 per ton, but if he needs more alfalfa to feed his beef than he can raise, he will have to pay $36 per ton to get the alfalfa to his feedlot.

   Some technological features of Sod's operation are wheat yield, 50 bushels per acre; alfalfa yield, 3 tons per acre. Other features are given in Figure 5.17. Define the variables:

$$W = \text{wheat raised and sold (acres)}$$

$$A = \text{alfalfa raised (tons)}$$

$$B = \text{beef raised and sold (tons)}$$

$$A_3 = \text{alfalfa bought (tons)}$$

$$A_5 = \text{alfalfa sold (tons)}$$

FIGURE 5.17
Data for Buster Sod Problem

ACTIVITY	LABOR, MACHINERY, AND OTHER COSTS	WATER REQUIREMENTS (ACRE-FT)	LAND REQUIREMENTS (ACRES)	ALFALFA REQUIREMENTS (TONS)
1 acre of wheat	$8	1.5	1	
1 acre of alfalfa	30	2.5	1	
1 ton of beef	40	0.1	0.05	4

An LP formulation and solution to Buster Sod's problem are shown in Figure 5.18.

(a) Show calculations that explain the values of the coefficient of W in the objective function and the coefficients of A in the first and second constraints.

(b) How much water is being used?

(c) How much beef is being produced?

(d) Does Sod buy or sell alfalfa?

(e) How much should Sod pay to acquire another acre of land?

(f) Interpret the dual price on row 3.

(g) What happens to the optimal planting policy if the price of wheat triples? What happens to the OV?

(h) How much profit will Sod receive from the optimal operation of his farm?

(i) What happens to the optimal value of the objective function if the cost of alfalfa purchased increases from $36 to $37?

FIGURE 5.18

LP Formulation for Buster Sod Problem

```
MAX 72 W − 10 A + 560 B − 36 A3 + 34 A5
SUBJECT TO
   2) W + 0.333 A + 0.05 B < = 1200
   3) 1.5 W + 0.833 A + 0.1 B < = 2000
   4) −A + 4 B − A3 + A5 = 0
```

OBJECTIVE FUNCTION VALUE

8320000.00

VARIABLE	VALUE	REDUCED COST
W	0.00	6168.00
A	0.00	3439.27
B	20000.00	0.00
A3	80000.00	0.00
A5	0.00	2.00

ROW	SLACK OR SURPLUS	DUAL PRICES
2)	200.00	0.00
3)	0.00	4160.00
4)	0.00	36.00

SENSITIVITY ANALYSIS

OBJ COEFFICIENT RANGES

VARIABLE	CURRENT COEF	ALLOWABLE INCREASE	ALLOWABLE DECREASE
W	72.00	6168.00	INFINITY
A	−10.00	3439.27	INFINITY
B	560.00	INFINITY	411.20
A3	−36.00	2.00	100.21
A5	34.00	2.00	INFINITY

RIGHTHAND SIDE RANGES

ROW	CURRENT RHS	ALLOWABLE INCREASE	ALLOWABLE DECREASE
2	1200.00	INFINITY	200.00
3	2000.00	400.00	2000.00
4	0.00	80000.00	INFINITY

204

CHAPTER 5
Linear Programs:
Computer Analysis,
Interpreting
Sensitivity Output,
and the Dual
Problem

NOTE: The coefficient of A_3 is currently $-\$36$ and it will become $-\$37$. Thus the coefficient will *decrease* by $1.

(j) How much can the cost of buying alfalfa decrease before the current optimal planting policy will change?

FIGURE 5.19

Machine-time Data

	MACHINE		
PRODUCT	1	2	3
A	12	8	5
B	7	9	10
C	8	4	7
D	10	0	3
E	7	11	2

5-29. A plant can manufacture five different products in any combination. Each product requires time on each of three machines, as shown in Figure 5.19. All figures are in minutes per pound of product. Each machine is available 128 hours per week. Products A, B, C, D, and E are purely competitive, and any amounts made may be sold at respective per pound prices of $5, $4, $5, $4, and $4. Variable labor costs are $4 per hour for machines 1 and 2, and $3 per hour for machine 3. Material costs are $2 for each pound of products A and C, and $1 for each pound of products B, D, and E. You wish to maximize profit to the firm. The LP formulation and solution are shown in Figure 5.20.

(a) How many hours are spent on each of the three machines?

(b) What are the units of the dual prices on the constraints that control machine capacity?

(c) How much should the firm be willing to spend to obtain another hour of time on machine 2?

(d) How much can the sales price of product A increase before the optimal production plan changes? State your answer in the proper units.

More Challenging Problems

5-30. Note that the RHS of row 3, which is the market balance constraint, has an allowable increase of ∞ in Figure 5.11 and of 3.75 in Figure 5.12. Yet, as you can see by comparing Figures 5.9 and 5.10, the optimal corner is the same in both cases. Use the geometry to explain this difference in the values of allowable increase.

5-31. Why is the allowable decrease on the coefficient of F equal to 1500 in Figure 5.11 and 19,000 in Figure 5.12?

5-32. Suppose that you solve (P) on the computer and then solve (D). Can you explain why all sensitivity information for both problems appears on either printout?

5-33. Consider the problem

$$\text{Max } 2x_1 + x_2$$
$$\text{s.t.} \quad 4x_1 + 12x_2 \leq 100$$
$$19x_1 - 3x_2 \geq 6 \qquad \text{(P)}$$
$$x_1 \geq 10, \qquad x_2 \geq 10$$

Let D_1 be its dual. Now put (P) into standard equality constraint form and let D_2 be its dual. Show that D_1 and D_2 are equivalent.

FIGURE 5.20.

Solution for Five-Product,
Three-Machine Problem

```
MAX 1.416 A + 1.433 B + 1.85 C + 2.183 D + 1.7 E
SUBJECT TO
  2) 12 A + 7 B + 8 C + 10 D + 7 E < = 7680
  3)  8 A + 9 B + 4 C + 11 E < = 7680
  4)  5 A + 10 B + 7 C + 3 D + 2 E < = 7680
```

OBJECTIVE FUNCTION VALUE

1817.59

VARIABLE	VALUE	REDUCED COST
A	0.00	1.38
B	0.00	0.24
C	512.00	0.00
D	0.00	0.75
E	512.00	0.00

ROW	SLACK OR SURPLUS	DUAL PRICES
2	0.00	0.22
3	0.00	0.01
4	3072.00	0.00

SENSITIVITY ANALYSIS

OBJ COEFFICIENT RANGES

VARIABLE	CURRENT COEF.	ALLOWABLE INCREASE	ALLOWABLE DECREASE
A	1.41	1.38	INFINITY
B	1.43	0.24	INFINITY
C	1.85	0.09	0.04
D	2.18	0.07	INFINITY
E	1.70	0.11	0.08

RIGHTHAND SIDE RANGES

ROW	CURRENT RHS	ALLOWABLE INCREASE	ALLOWABLE DECREASE
2	7680.00	2671.30	2792.72
3	7680.00	4388.57	3840.00
4	7680.00	INFINITY	3072.00

SOLVING AN LP WHEN NOT ALL VARIABLES
ARE REQUIRED TO BE NONNEGATIVE

Suppose that, for logical reasons, some of the variables in your LP model are *not* required to be nonnegative. For example, suppose that in the particular LP model you have formulated there is a variable z such that when z is positive it denotes the quantity of an item sold, and when z is negative it represents the quantity bought. Thus, z may be positive, negative, or zero. In order to solve this LP on the computer it must be transformed into the standard form, in which *all* variables must be nonnegative.

To do this, introduce *two* new *nonnegative* variables, say z_1 and z_2, and let $z = z_1 - z_2$. Everywhere a z appears in your original model, simply replace it by $z_1 - z_2$ and rewrite the model.

For example, suppose that the original model is

$$\text{Max } 2x + 3z$$

$$\text{s.t.} \quad 4x + 5z \leq 30$$

$$x \geq 0, \qquad z \text{ not constrained in sign}$$

The equivalent LP problem with all variables nonnegative is

$$\text{Max } 2x + 3z_1 - 3z_2$$

$$\text{s.t.} \quad 4x + 5z_1 - 5z_2 \leq 30$$

$$x, z_1, z_2 \geq 0$$

We then solve this new problem on the computer to obtain optimal values x^*, z_1^*, and z_2^*. The optimal value of z in the original model is given by

$$z^* = z_1^* - z_2^*$$

It can be shown that the solution to the second model, which the simplex method obtains, will have the property that at most one of the pair z_1^*, z_2^* is positive. That is, at least one and possibly both have the value zero.

_____ **APPENDIX 5.2**

QUESTIONS BASED ON THE RED BRAND CANNERS CASE

We first saw the Red Brand Canners case in Chapter 2, where the model was formulated and assumptions were discussed. In the following questions, the analysis continues. You are asked to solve several formulations on the computer and then analyze the outputs.

1. Run on your own computer your LP formulation of the Red Brand Canners production problem. Do not include the option of purchasing up to 80,000 additional pounds of grade "A" tomatoes.

2. What is the net profit obtained after netting out the cost of the crop?

3. Myers has proposed that the net profit obtained from his policy would be $48,000. Is this true? If not, what is his net profit (taking into account, as in question 2, the cost of the crop).

207

CHAPTER 5
Linear Programs:
Computer Analysis,
Interpreting
Sensitivity Output,
and the Dual
Problem

4. Suppose Cooper suggests that, in keeping with his accounting scheme as advanced in Exhibit 2 on page 60, the crop cost of 6 cents per pound should be subtracted from each coefficient in the objective function. Change your formulation accordingly, and again solve the problem. You should obtain an optimal objective value which is greater than that obtained in question 2. Explain this apparent discrepancy (assume that unused tomatoes will spoil).

5. Suppose that unused tomatoes could be resold at 6 cents per pound. Which solution would be preferred under these conditions? How much can the resale price be lowered without affecting this preference?

6. Use the sensitivity output from question 1 to determine whether the additional purchase of up to 80,000 pounds of grade "A" tomatoes should be undertaken. Can you tell how much should be purchased?

7. Use a reformulated model to obtain an optimal product mix using the additional purchase option. The solution to your reformulated model should explicitly show how the additional purchase should be used.

8. Suppose that in question 1 the Market Research Department feels it could increase the demand for juice by 25,000 cases by means of an advertising campaign. How much should Red Brand be willing to pay for such a campaign?

9. Suppose in question 1 that the price of juice increased 10 cents per case. Does your computer output tell you whether the optimal production plan will change?

10. Suppose that RBC is forced to reduce the size of the product line in tomato-based products to 2. Would additional computer runs be required to tell which product should be dropped from the line?

11. Suppose that in question 1 an additional lot of grade "B" tomatoes is available. The lot is 50,000 pounds. How much should RBC be willing to pay for this lot of grade "B" tomatoes?

Alternate Questions on Red Brand Canners

For the following questions assume 3 grades of tomatoes, as in the alternate questions in Chapter 2.

12. Run on your own computer your LP formulation of Question 8 of the Alternate Questions for Red Brand Canners from Chapter 2.

13. What is the net profit obtained after netting out the cost of the crop?

14. Myers claims the net profit from his policy of producing 2,000,000 lb paste and 1,000,000 lb juice is $89,600. Is this correct? If not, what is his net profit (taking into account, as in question 13, the cost of the crop)?

15. Suppose Cooper suggests that, in keeping with his accounting scheme as advanced in Exhibit 2 on page 60, the crop cost per pound should be subtracted from each coefficient in the objective function. Change your formulation accordingly, and again solve the problem, assuming a crop cost of 7 cents per pound. You should obtain a solution that is different from that obtained in question 12. Which solution has a higher net profit (assume unused tomatoes will spoil)? Is it correct to include tomato costs in the objective function?

16. If in question 15 unused tomatoes could be resold for 7 cents a pound, which solution would be preferred? How much can the resale price be lowered without affecting this preference?

17. Use the sensitivity output from question 12 to determine whether the additional purchase of up to 80,000 pounds of grade "A" tomatoes should be undertaken. Can you tell how much should be purchased?

18. Use a reformulated model to obtain an optimal product mix using the additional purchase option. The solution to your reformulated model should explicitly show how the additional purchase should be used.

19. Suppose that in question 12 the Market Research Department feels they could increase the demand for paste by 3,000 cases by means of an advertising campaign. How much should Red Brand be willing to pay for such a campaign?

208

CHAPTER 5
Linear Programs:
Computer Analysis,
Interpreting
Sensitivity Output,
and the Dual
Problem

20. Suppose in question 12 that the price of canned whole tomatoes decreased by 16 cents per case. Does your computer output tell you whether the optimal production plan will change?

21. Suppose that the Market Research Department suggests that if the average quality of paste is below 4 the product will not be acceptable to customers. Would an additional computer run be necessary to determine the optimal production plan if this constraint were added to the model?

22. Suppose that in question 12 an additional lot of grade "C" tomatoes is available. The lot is 200,000 lb. How much would RBC be willing to pay for this lot of grade "C" tomatoes?

CASE

SAW MILL RIVER FEED AND GRAIN COMPANY

The purpose of this case is to exercise both judgmental and technical skills. You will have to decide, based on Mr. Overton's objectives, just what information you should provide him. You will then have to formulate an LP model (or models), run it (or them) on the computer, and present, in a summary report, the relevant results.

On Monday, August 28, 1986, Mr. Overton called in his sales manager and purchasing manager to discuss the company's policy for the coming month. Saw Mill had accepted orders from Turnbull Co. and McClean Bros. and had the option of accepting an order from Blue River, Inc. It also had the option of buying some additional grain from Cochrane Farm. Mr. Overton, managing director of Saw Mill, had to decide by the end of the week what action to take.

Usually, all purchases of grain are completed by the end of August. However, Saw Mill still has the possibility of an extra purchase of grain from Cochrane Farm. This commitment has to be made by September 1. The grain would be delivered to the Midwest Grain Elevator by the 15th of the month. This elevator acts simply as a storage facility for Saw Mill.

It is immutable company policy to charge a markup of 15% on the cost of the grain supplied to customers. Payments to the Midwest Grain Elevator are treated as an overhead and this is not to be challenged. Turnbull, McClean, and Blue River have agreed to pay, for their current orders, whatever price Saw Mill charges. However, Saw Mill realizes that if its price becomes too high, future business will be lost.

The details of the Turnbull, McClean, and Blue River orders are presented in Exhibit 1. The quantity, as well as the maximum moisture content, minimum weight

EXHIBIT 1
Data on Grain Orders

ORDERING COMPANY	QUANTITY (BUSHELS)	MAXIMUM PERCENT MOISTURE (per lb)	MINIMUM WEIGHT PER BUSHEL (LB)	MAXIMUM PERCENT DAMAGE (per lb)	MAXIMUM PERCENT FOREIGN MATERIAL (per lb)	DELIVERY DATE
Turnbull	40,000–45,000	13	56	2	2	9/20
McClean	32,000–36,000	15.5	54	5	3	9/22
Blue River	50,000–54,000	15	56	2	4	9/26

per bushel, maximum percentage damaged, and maximum percentage foreign material are presented.

The company has the option to supply any amount of grain that it wishes, within the specified range. It must, of course, satisfy the requirements. By September 4, Saw Mill must inform Turnbull and McClean how much grain they will receive. By the same date it must inform Blue River if it will accept its order and how much grain will be delivered if it accepts.

Saw Mill blends the grains that it owns to satisfy customer orders. On August 28 the company had 326,000 bushels of corn stored in the elevator. Obviously, it would be impossible to identify the exact composition of each kernel of corn that the Saw Mill River Feed and Grain Company delivered to the elevator. Hence, Exhibit 2 represents aggregated amounts and characteristics of different types of corn credited to Saw Mill River's account with the elevator. The 326,000 bushels are segregated into 11 types of corn, which differ according to (1) quantity available, (2) cost per bushel, (3) percentage moisture content, (4) weight per bushel, (5) percentage damaged, and (6) percentage foreign material.

EXHIBIT 2
Characteristics of Corn Types

TYPE OF CORN	QUANTITY (BUSHELS)	COST PER BUSHEL	PERCENT MOISTURE CONTENT	WEIGHT PER BUSHEL (LB)	PERCENT TOTAL DAMAGE	PERCENT FOREIGN MATERIAL
1	30,000	$1.45	12	57	2	1.5
2	45,000	1.44	15	57	2	1
3	25,000	1.45	12	58	3	3
4	40,000	1.42	13	56	4	2
5	20,000	1.38	15	54	4	2
6	30,000	1.37	15	55	5	3
7	75,000	1.37	18	57	5	1
8	15,000	1.39	14	58	2	4
9	16,000	1.27	17	53	7	5
10	20,000	1.28	15	55	8	3
11	10,000	1.17	22	56	9	5

The grain on offer from Cochrane Farm is one load of up to 50,000 bushels, with an average of 15% moisture, 3% damage, and 2% foreign material. The load has a density of 57 pounds per bushel, and Straddle (the purchasing manager) is convinced that the order can be obtained at a cost of $1.41 per bushel.

Use linear programming to help analyze Mr. Overton's problem. (Use notation T_i = bushels of corn type i to be sent to Turnbull. Similarly for B_i and M_i. Also let corn type 12 denote the corn from Cochrane Farm.) In no more than one page, labeled "Executive Summary," provide as concisely as possible information that will help Overton answer his questions. His main objectives are to maximize profit and to keep prices to the customers sufficiently low to attract future business. He can be expected to use his judgment to make the eventual decision; your job is to provide information that will enable him to look at the important trade-offs. You should also make your own recommendations.

Your presentation will be judged on the economy of your formulation (i.e., formulate your model, or models, *for the given set of data* as efficiently as possible) as well as on your recommendations concerning

(a) to buy or not to buy from Cochrane;
(b) to accept or not to accept the Blue River option;
(c) how much corn to supply to Blue River, Turnbull, and McClean.

CASE

KIWI COMPUTER

Kiwi Computer of Australia manufactures two types of personal computers: a portable model and a desktop model. Kiwi assembles the cases and printed circuit boards at its only plant, which also manufactures the cases and stuffs the circuit boards with components. Monthly production is limited by the following capacities:

Monthly Capacity

OPERATION	PORTABLE	DESKTOP
Case Production	4000	2000
Board Stuffing	2500	3000
Portable Assembly	2000	—
Desktop Assembly	—	1800

For example, 4000 portable cases can be produced in a month and no desktop cases, or no portable cases and 2000 desktop cases, or if equal time is devoted to both, 2000 portable and 1000 desktop cases can be produced. In order to be feasible, production of portable and desktop computers for a month must satisfy all the constraints simultaneously. The set of feasible production plans is the shaded area in Exhibit 1.

EXHIBIT 1

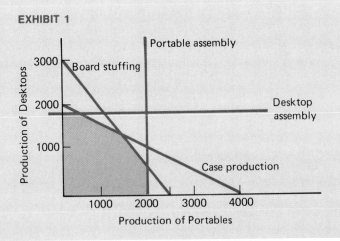

EXHIBIT 2

	DESKTOPS		PORTABLES	
Direct Materials		$ 800		$ 690
Direct Labor				
Case Production	$ 20		$15	
Board Stuffing	100		90	
Final Assembly	5	125	10	115
Fixed Overhead				
Case Production	$ 95		$ 95	
Board Stuffing	205		205	
Final Assembly	415	715	115	415
Total		$1640		$1220

The prices to retail computer stores are $1500 for the desktop and $1400 for the portable. In order to be competitive, Kiwi has to price its computers several hundred dollars below those of a very large and well-known computer manufacturer.

The entry of this manufacturer has caused a boom in the industry as the market has shifted from one aimed primarily at computer "hackers" to business professionals. Currently, Kiwi sells as many computers of either model as it produces. During the first quarter of the year Kiwi produced 2000 portables a month and 600 desktops. Both board stuffing and portable assembly were operating at capacity, but there was slack in case production and desktop assembly. Cost accountants determined standard costs and fixed overhead as shown in Exhibits 2 and 3. The fixed overhead data in Exhibit 2 are derived from the fixed overhead totals in Exhibit 3.

At a quarterly meeting of the company's executives, the sales manager pointed out that the desktop computer was not yielding a profit. He suggested that it be dropped from the company's product line.

The controller objected, saying, "If we produce more desktop computers, we can lower the fixed final assembly cost of $415. It's high now because we are producing so few units."

The production manager responded, "We can increase production if we subcontract out board stuffing. We could supply the boards and components and reimburse the subcontractor for its overhead and labor costs."

The president concluded the meeting by asking the sales manager, the controller, and the production manager to get together and come up with a recommendation concerning the company's product mix and subcontracting. He told them to assume that demand would remain high and current capacity would remain fixed.

EXHIBIT 3

	TOTAL FIXED OVERHEAD ($000)*	FIXED OVERHEAD PER UNIT
Case Production	$247	$95
Board Stuffing	533	205
Desktop Assembly	249	415
Portable Assembly	230	115
Total	$1259	

* Based on production of 600 desktop and 2000 portable computers per month.

Part A Subcontracting not allowed.

1. In Exhibit 2 the standard overhead cost assigned to desktop computers for final assembly is $415. Clearly indicate how this figure was derived.

2. (a) Do the desktop units make a contribution to profit? In other words, given that the overhead costs are fixed in the short run, is the company's profit higher than it would be if no desktop units were produced?

   (b) A correct computation of per unit profitabilities will show that the portable is more profitable than the desktop. Does this mean that more (or only) portables should be produced? Why?

3. In answering this question assume that boards cannot be stuffed by a subcontractor. Formulate a linear program for determining the optimal product mix.

4. Run your model using LINDO or whatever linear programming package is available and indicate the optimal mix of desktop and portable computers. Noninteger answers are acceptable for this problem.

5. Find the best feasible integer answer that can be achieved by rounding to adjacent integers your answers from question 4.

6. (a) Go back and recalculate the company's "standard costs" using your integer answers from question 5 and compare with those in Exhibit 2.

   (b) How much larger is the profit using the new mix (using the integer answers from question 5) compared to the old (i.e., 600 desktops, 2000 portables)?

Part B Subcontracting allowed.

We now allow some boards to be stuffed by subcontractors. Assume that production of a computer with a board stuffed by the subcontractor requires the same amount of time in case production and final assembly as production of a computer with a board stuffed at the factory.

7. Assume that the subcontractor is going to charge $110 for each desktop board stuffed and $100 for each portable board stuffed. Kiwi provides the subcontractor with the necessary materials. Should Kiwi employ the subcontractor to stuff boards? Argue why or why not without formulating and solving a new linear program.

8. Now formulate a linear program which includes subcontracting. In your formulation, distinguish between computers produced with internally and externally stuffed boards. Solve using LINDO or some other LP package.

9. Assume that in addition to the per board charge the subcontractor is now going to include a fixed charge for stuffing a batch of boards (same charge regardless of the number of boards or their type). For what fixed charge will Kiwi be indifferent between subcontracting and stuffing all boards internally?

Part C Sensitivity Analysis.

10. Refer to the linear programming formulation in question 8. Is the optimal solution degenerate? Explain.

11. Refer to the linear programming formulation in question 8. Do alternative optima exist? Explain.

12. Refer to the linear programming formulation in question 8. The subcontractor currently charges $110 for each desktop board stuffed. By how much would this charge have to decrease so that it would be optimal for Kiwi to have the subcontractor stuff desktop boards? Why?

13. Refer to the linear programming formulation in question 3. Assume Kiwi can increase the board stuffing capacity so that either 600 additional desktop boards or 500 additional portable boards or any equivalent combination can be stuffed. Should Kiwi increase the capacity if the cost would be $175,000 per month? Answer *without* resolving the linear program.

14. Refer to the linear programming formulation in question 3. Suppose a redesign of the desktop unit to use fewer chips reduces the cost of direct materials by $200. Does your computer output tell you whether the optimal production plan will change? Explain.

Alternative
Questions
on Kiwi
Computer

Kiwi is considering consolidating desktop assembly and portable assembly into one department. The new department would be capable of assembling 3000 portables in a month and no desktops, or no portables and 2200 desktops, or if equal time were devoted to both, 1500 portables and 1100 desktops could be assembled. They estimate that the monthly fixed overhead for this department would be less than $479,000, the current combined overhead for the desktop and portable assembly departments. In answering the following questions assume the departments will be combined.

Part A Subcontracting not allowed.

1. Let D,P equal the monthly production rate of desktops and portables, respectively, and F the fixed overhead of the new unified assembly department. Express total profit as a function of D,P, and F.

2. Must the value of F be known in order to determine the optimal product mix? Assume that fixed overhead is not affected by the values of D and P.

3. In answering this question assume that boards cannot be stuffed by a subcontractor. Formulate a linear program for determining the optimal product mix.

4. Run your model using LINDO or whatever linear programming package is available, and indicate the optimal mix of desktop and portable computers. Noninteger answers are acceptable for this problem.

5. Find the best feasible integer answer that can be achieved by rounding to adjacent integers your answers from question 4.

6. Suppose that the optimal profit (revenue minus *all* costs) is $330,286 if the two assembly departments are not combined. What is the largest that the fixed overhead of a combined assembly department could be and Kiwi still prefer to combine the departments?

Part B Subcontracting allowed.

7. Assume that the subcontractor is going to charge $150 for each desktop board stuffed and $135 for each portable board stuffed. Kiwi provides the subcontractor with the necessary materials. Should Kiwi employ the subcontractor to stuff boards? Argue why or why not without formulating and solving a new linear program.

8. Now formulate a linear program which includes subcontracting. In your formulation, distinguish between computers produced with internally and externally stuffed boards. Solve using LINDO or some other LP package.

9. Assume that in addition to the per board charge the subcontractor is now going to include a fixed charge for stuffing a batch of boards (same charge regardless of the number of boards or their type). For what fixed charge will Kiwi be indifferent between subcontracting and stuffing all boards internally?

10. Refer to the linear programming formulation in question 8. Is the optimal solution degenerate? Explain.

11. Refer to the linear programming formulation in question 8. Do alternative optima exist? Explain.

12. Refer to the linear programming formulation in question 8. The subcontractor currently charges $150 for each desktop board stuffed. Could the subcontractor lower his price enough so that it would be optimal for Kiwi to have him stuff desktop boards? Explain.

13. Refer to the linear programming formulation in question 3. Assume Kiwi can increase the board stuffing capacity so that either 600 additional desktop boards or 500 portable boards or any equivalent combination can be stuffed. Should Kiwi increase the capacity if the cost would be $175,000 per month? Answer *without* resolving the linear program.

14. Refer to the linear programming formulation in question 3. Suppose a redesign of the desktop unit to use fewer chips reduces the cost of direct materials by $200. Does your computer output tell you whether the optimal production plan will change? Explain.

CASE

PRODUCTION PLANNING AT BUMLES

(The Bumles problem was first discussed and solved in Chapter 2. Before attacking this case you will want to review the solution in Chapter 2, for the correct formulation of this problem will be similar.) Bumles, Inc. uses part of its capacity to make two types of hand-painted statues. The finished products can reasonably be grouped into two categories, A and B. A requires .5 hours of a painter's time and B requires .75 hours. Bumles has 45 painters available, but not all of these painters need to be used. The plant is used for hand-painted statues on Monday, Tuesday, and Wednesday each week. During the remainder of the week the productive capacity is devoted to another product line. Each painter who is engaged is available to work painting statues any part of an eight-hour day, two days a week. A painter can be assigned to any two-day schedule and is paid for 16 hours of regular-time work, no matter what part of that time he actually spends producing statues. If there is not enough production to keep all the workers assigned to a particular day busy for the entire day, the slack time is spent on cleaning the plant and similar activities. In addition, on any day, Bumles can request each working painter to work up to 4 hours of overtime (i.e., if Ed Jones normally works on Tuesday, Bumles can have him work 2, 3, or any other number between 0 and 4, hours of overtime on that day.

If labor costs are not taken into account, the revenue from selling an A is $21 and a B is $30. Demand must either be satisfied on the day on which it occurs or it is lost. Production on a given day can be used to satisfy demand that day or demand later in the week, i.e., statues produced on Monday can be used to satisfy demand on Monday, Tuesday, or Wednesday, and statues produced on Tuesday can be used to satisfy demand on Tuesday or Wednesday. However, because of the change of operations in production, all statues produced in a week must be shipped that week, i.e., there is never inventory on hand Monday morning. Because of increased handling costs, it costs $.25 to carry an A and $.30 to carry a B in inventory from one day to the next. A unit of lost demand results in an all-inclusive penalty cost of $2 for a unit of A on Monday, $4 on Tuesday, and $5 on Wednesday. The per unit penalty costs for B are $5 on Monday, $10 on Tuesday and $11 on Wednesday. Painters are paid $10 per hour of regular time and $15 per hour of overtime.

Demand varies significantly at Bumles. Management is considering two generic demand patterns.

Pre-Christmas Rush

	M	T	W
A	1500	1000	150
B	240	90	1100

After-Christmas Slump

	M	T	W
A	240	48	64
B	160	32	64

Bill Bumle, the Executive V.P., notes that A's yield a contribution of $21/.5 = \$42$ per labor hour, whereas B's yield a contribution of $30/.75 = \$40$ per labor hour. He also notes that the penalty for lost sales increases as the week goes on. He concludes that Bumles should first satisfy all demand for A's starting with Wednesday, then Tuesday, then Monday, and then use any leftover capacity to produce B's.

Specific Questions 1. Comment on the approach suggested by Bill Bumle.

2. Ignoring integrality conditions (i.e., allowing the possibility of fractional values of all decision variables), create an LP model that will schedule painters and production in such a way as to maximize revenue minus cost, where cost equals labor plus penalty and inventory-carrying costs. The model should be correct for any set of demands. In your formulation the first six constraints should be:

$$\text{(i)} \quad DAM =$$
$$\text{(ii)} \quad DAT = \qquad \text{where } DAM \text{ is the demand for A's}$$
$$\vdots \qquad\qquad \text{on Monday, etc.}$$
$$\text{(vi)} \quad DBW =$$

Thus, to solve the model for any set of demands one must only provide the RHS's for these constraints. In your formulation of the model, pay attention to relationships between production, sales, lost sales, demand, and inventory on any particular day. For example,

$$\text{demand on day } t = \text{sales on } t + \text{lost sales on } t$$

3. What are the decision variables? Define them carefully.
4. Show the formulation and briefly describe the purpose of each constraint.

For the above two specific demand patterns, solve the model. Then, in terms that would be understood by a general manager, state

5. How many items of what to produce each day.
6. How to schedule as many of the painters as you use, e.g., schedule 14.3 painters to work a Monday/Tuesday schedule, etc.
7. How many hours of overtime to use each day.
8. How much inventory of each product to carry each day.
9. How many units of lost sales to have each day.
10. Use your solutions to answer the following question: Assume that a year consists of 32 weeks of pre-Christmas rush demand and 18 weeks of after-Christmas slump demand. If Bumles wants each of the 45 painters to work an equal number of weeks, how many weeks will each painter work?

Additional Considerations

[The questions in this section should be answered by using the model created in question 2, with new parameters and performing additional analysis as needed.]

The painters' union has suggested a contract with a guaranteed annual wage (GAW) provision. In particular, this agreement specifies that a painter must be paid at least $11,500 per year for work on hand-painted statues. If, at the end of the year, the amount earned is less than $11,500, the firm simply gives the painter a check to make up the difference. Bumles plans to use all 45 painters even if the GAW provision is not accepted, but if it is all 45 painters will earn at least $11,500 per year.

To estimate the effect of this proposal on the Bumles operation, Bill assumes that 30 weeks of the 50-week year will have pre-Christmas rush demands and the other 20 weeks will have the demand schedule shown below.

	M	T	W
A	240	48	300
B	160	32	200

He also assumes that a detailed schedule can be worked out so that each painter earns the same pay during a year. Based on your LP model and Bill's assumptions

11. What is Bumles' total annual profit without the GAW provision?
12. Does your solution to question 11 satisfy the GAW provision? What effect will accepting the GAW provision have on Bumles' profitability (Increase, decrease, or no effect)? Show the calculations to support your answers. There is no need to solve another LP at this point.
13. How much would average wages have to be in the low demand weeks for the annual wage to be $11,500? For the low demand weeks, formulate an LP that Bumles could use

to find a production plan that would meet the GAW provision. Present a justification for your model and solve it.

14. Suppose the GAW provision is accepted. How much would Bumles save per year by using the plan found in question 13 compared with the plan of question 11 where additional payments would have to be made to the painters at the end of the year?

[These questions refer to the models you created to answer questions 1–10.]

15. In the current solution to the pre-Christmas problem, if we combine regular and overtime pay then each painter is paid $280/week. If another painter should become available, what is the maximum weekly amount that Bumles should pay him or her?

16. Suppose that, in the pre-Christmas problem, the demand for A on Monday increases by 10 units. What happens to the OV?

17. Answer question 16 for the post-Christmas problem.

18. What is responsible for the major difference in the answers to questions 16 and 17?

19. Suppose that, in the pre-Christmas problem, management's recent experience calls for an adjustment in the penalty cost for unsatisfied demand for A on Monday. The new value is set at $3. What happens to the optimal solution and the OV?

20. In question 19, suppose the new value is reset to $4. What is the effect on the optimal solution and the OV? (Give the best answer you can based on the computer output.)

21. Suppose that, in the pre-Christmas problem, the selling price of A is reduced to $15 and B is reduced to $20. Can you give a bound on the new OV?

DIAGNOSTIC ASSIGNMENT

CRAWLER TREAD AND A NEW ANGLE

In important respects, part of a manager's task invokes analysis and evaluation of the work of others as opposed to producing "from rock bottom" his or her own formulation and analysis. In this diagnostic role the manager will judge someone else's model. Have the correct questions been asked? Has a correct analysis been performed? The following vignette captures the spirit of such a situation. You are asked to comment on the analysis of a new opportunity.

Ralph Hanson has been the chief metallurgist at **PROTRAC**'s cast iron foundry for the last five years. He brings several important qualities to this position. First, he has an excellent technical background. He graduated from Case Western with an MMS (master of material science) and had five years' experience with U.S. Steel before joining **PROTRAC**. He has used this training and experience to implement several changes that have contributed to product quality and process efficiency. In addition, he has become an effective manager. Through a combination of formal course work and self-education, he has become familiar with many modern management techniques and approaches and has worked to see that these new methods are exploited whenever it is appropriate. Indeed, Ralph is responsible for introducing the use of LP models into the ore-blending and scrap-recycling activities at **PROTRAC**.

Ralph was the chief metallurgist when Crawler Tread, the first ore-blending application, was completed. By now both Ralph and Sam Togas, the plant manager, are comfortable with the use of LP models in the ore-blending area. Ralph typically formulates, solves and interprets the output himself. Currently, he is facing a new problem. The recession has seriously affected the demand for heavy equipment and **PROTRAC** has excess capacity in most departments, including the foundry. However, the defense industries are booming. A manufacturer of tanks requires a high-grade ore for producing tank treads. Indeed, the requirements are exactly the same as **PROTRAC** used in the Crawler Tread problem (see Section 5.4). The tank manufacturer is willing to pay **PROTRAC** $850 per ton of ore for up to 150,000 tons to be delivered within the next month. Ralph learns that he can have up to 98,000 tons of ore available. This is made up of 21,000 tons from mine 1; 40,000 from mine 2; 15,000 from mine 3; and 22,000 from mine 4.

Based on these data, Ralph formulates a new LP model. In this model, T_i is the number of tons of ore from mine i (for $i = 1, \dots, 4$) that are used in the blend and B is the number of tons of blended ore. He carefully annotates the formulation so that he can easily explain his analysis to Sam, the plant manager. The formulation and solution that Ralph used in his presentation are shown in Figure 5.21.

Sam was delighted with the project. It yielded a contribution margin of 30,500,000 and occupied resources (labor and machinery) that otherwise would have been idle. He immediately had the legal department draw up a contract for the sale of 98,000 tons of ore.

When Ralph arrived the next morning, Sam was waiting for him. The following discussion took place:

SAM: The contract is ready and I was about to call and confirm the arrangement, but there is a new development. We've just received a telex from mine 1. Due to the cancellation of another order, we can have up to another 3000 tons of ore at the standard price of $800 per ton if we want it. What should we do? Why don't you go back and re-solve your problem including the possibility of the additional 3000 tons from mine 1 and draw up a new contract if the new solution is better. Obviously, we can't do worse than we are doing now, and that's not bad.

FIGURE 5.21
Ralph's Formulation

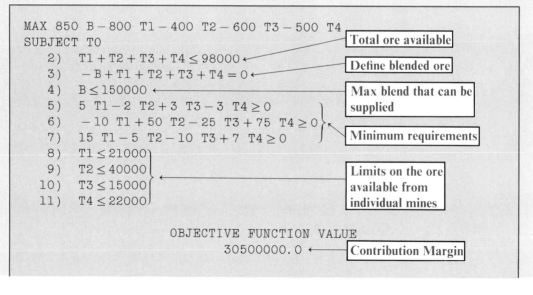

VARIABLE	VALUE	REDUCED COST
B	98000.00	0.00
T1	21000.00	0.00
T2	40000.00	0.00
T3	15000.00	0.00
T4	22000.00	0.00

ROW	SLACK OR SURPLUS	DUAL PRICES
2)	0.00	50.00
3)	0.00	−850.00
4)	52000.00	0.00
5)	4000.00	0.00
6)	3065000.00	0.00
7)	119000.00	0.00
8)	0.00	0.00
9)	0.00	400.00
10)	0.00	200.00
11)	0.00	300.00

SENSITIVITY ANALYSIS

OBJ COEFFICIENT RANGES

VARIABLE	CURRENT COEF.	ALLOWABLE INCREASE	ALLOWABLE DECREASE
B	850.00	INFINITY	50.00
T1	−800.00	200.00	50.00
T2	−400.00	INFINITY	400.00
T3	−600.00	INFINITY	200.00
T4	−500.00	INFINITY	300.00

RIGHTHAND SIDE RANGES

ROW	CURRENT RHS	ALLOWABLE INCREASE	ALLOWABLE DECREASE
2	98000.00	0.00	800.00
3	0.00	98000.00	52000.00
4	150000.00	INFINITY	52000.00
5	0.00	4000.00	INFINITY
6	0.00	3065000.00	INFINITY
7	0.00	119000.00	INFINITY
8	21000.00	INFINITY	0.00
9	40000.00	571.42	0.00
10	15000.00	2000.00	0.00
11	22000.00	500.00	0.00

RALPH: Actually, we don't have to do that. One of the great things about LP is that we can answer many questions involving changes from the original problem. In particular, the dual price on the amount of T_1 available (row 8) provides an upper bound on how much more we should pay to have the opportunity of buying an additional ton of ore from mine 1. If the dual price is positive, say $10, we should be willing to pay up to $10 more for the opportunity to buy another ton of ore (i.e., up to $810 for a ton of ore from mine 1). If it is zero, increasing the amount of ore that is available from mine 1 will not enable us to increase our profit.

A quick inspection of the solution reveals that the dual price on row 8 is zero.

RALPH: Since we can't increase our contribution margin, let's just leave the contract as it is and get back to work.

SAM: Damn it, Ralph, I don't understand this. We can buy the ore for $800 a ton and sell it for $850 a ton and you tell me we shouldn't do it.

RALPH: I know it's hard to see, but I know that if the right-hand side of row 8 is increased, the optimal value of the objective function will remain the same. This implies that additional tons of ore from mine 1 won't help us. I suppose it's because we can't add this additional ore to our blend and still satisfy the minimum elements requirements. Remember that the ore from mine 1 has only 90 pounds of element B per ton and the blend must have at least 100.

SAM: Look, Ralph, I have to meet with the grievance committee now. I just can't spend any more time on this project. I can't say I understand your answer, but you're the expert. Let's go with the current contract.

Questions

1. Is Ralph's interpretation of the numbers on the printout correct?
2. Is Ralph's response to the additional purchase opportunity correct? If you believe he has erred, where is the flaw?
3. Suppose row 2 were dropped from the model. What would be the dual price on row 8? On row 9?
4. Can you figure out what will happen to the OV if the RHS of row 9 is changed to 39,999?
5. Suppose the RHS of row 9 is increased to 40,001. What are the new optimal values of T_1, T_2, T_3, and T_4?
6. Figure out why the Allowable Increase on row 9 is 571.42.
7. Can you tell which constraint causes the degeneracy in Ralph's model?

6

LINEAR PROGRAMMING: THE SIMPLEX METHOD

6.1
INTRODUCTION

In Chapter 3 we studied the graphical method for solving an LP in two decision variables. The geometric presentation was useful in exploring important general properties of the LP model. However, since most real-world problems contain more than two decision variables, the graphical method is not generally applicable. Such problems are generally solved by using the simplex method, or simplex algorithm,[1] or some variation thereof. This method, which is described in this chapter, was created by George Dantzig in the late 1940s. Since then Dantzig and others have advanced its development, especially for special applications, some of which will be studied in later chapters.

Overview of the Simplex Method

The simplex method can be summarized briefly as follows: It is a systematic algebraic way of examining the corners (also called *vertices*, or *extreme points*) of an LP constraint set in search of an optimal solution. In particular, the algorithm first seeks an initial corner. This is called *phase I*. If the problem is *inconsistent*, phase I will discover this fact. Otherwise, the algebraic representation of an initial corner is found and phase I is complete. Then the algorithm proceeds to move along the constraint set from corner to *adjacent* corner. As we shall see, each corner of the LP constraint set can be represented

---

[1] An *algorithm* is a repetitive mathematical procedure designed to solve a particular problem, such as the algorithm for long division, or for taking square roots. In later chapters a variety of other algorithms are given for solving various models.

222

CHAPTER 6
Linear
Programming:
The Simplex
Method

algebraically as a particular kind of solution to a set of linear equations. Different solutions are generated in such a way as to produce a sequence of adjacent corners. Each move in the sequence (from corner to adjacent corner) is called an *iteration*, or *pivot*, and the move involves a manipulation on a linear system. The simplex algorithm is designed in such a way that the objective function will not decrease (increase) for a Max (Min) model and will generally increase (decrease) at each successive corner in the sequence. If the problem is unbounded, the algorithm will discover this during its execution. The mathematics of the uphill (or downhill for a Min model) move from one corner to an adjacent corner will be expressed in terms of a *pivoting operation* on a tableau of data. When an optimal corner has been reached, the algorithm recognizes this fact and terminates. Optimal solutions to both the primal and dual problems are provided.

From the description above, you can see that linear equations, and solutions to linear equations, play an important role. To understand the algorithm clearly, it is necessary to study this topic. It will occupy our attention in Section 6.3 through 6.6. We have, in previous chapters, learned a great deal about the geometric representation of LP models. In order to deepen your understanding of the current material, we will relate, whenever possible, the algebraic approach of this chapter to the geometry with which we are already familiar.

At the heart of the simplex algorithm is the algebraic representation of corners of the feasible region. We shall develop this representation in the context of a problem already encountered in Chapter 2.

FIGURE 6.1
Graphical Solution to Astro/Cosmo

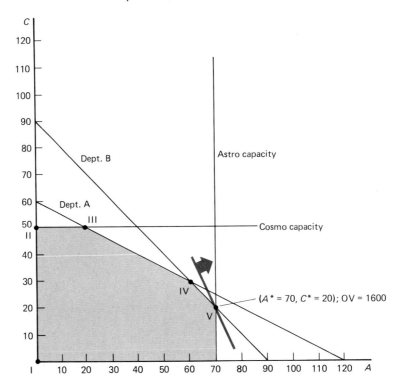

THE ASTRO/COSMO PROBLEM REVISITED

This model was presented as Example 1 in Section 2.8. The annotated model is

$$\text{Max } 20A + 10C \qquad \text{(profit)}$$

$$\text{s.t.} \quad A + 2C \le 120 \qquad \text{(labor constraint, department A)}$$

$$A + C \le 90 \qquad \text{(labor constraint, department B)}$$

$$A \le 70 \qquad \text{(Astro production line capacity)}$$

$$C \le 50 \qquad \text{(Cosmo production line capacity)}$$

$$A \ge 0, \quad C \ge 0$$

where A = units of Astro to be produced
C = units of Cosmo to be produced

The graphical representation of this problem is shown in Figure 6.1. Our first goal is to obtain an algebraic representation of the corners of the feasible region. To do this, the problem must first be converted to the equivalent standard equality constraint form. This is accomplished by adding a nonnegative slack variable to each $\le$ constraint and converting the $\le$ to $=$. In this way we obtain the problem

**"The Original
Equations"**

$$\text{Max } 20A + 10C$$

$$\text{s.t.} \quad A + 2C + s_1 \qquad\qquad = 120 \qquad \text{(department A)} \qquad (6.1)$$

$$A + C \quad + s_2 \qquad\quad = 90 \qquad \text{(department B)} \qquad (6.2)$$

$$A \qquad\qquad + s_3 \quad = 70 \qquad \text{(Astro capacity)} \qquad (6.3)$$

$$C \qquad\qquad\quad + s_4 = 50 \qquad \text{(Cosmo capacity)} \qquad (6.4)$$

Note that this problem has four equality constraints in the six variables A, C, s_1, s_2, s_3, and s_4. At the onset of our discussion we want to focus on the equations in the standard equality constraint form of the LP model. For convenience these are referred to as "*the original equations.*" We know from Chapter 5 that every nonnegative solution to these equations corresponds to a point in the feasible region, and vice versa. In particular, we need to identify the nonnegative solutions that correspond to the constraint set corners.

_____ 6.3

TYPES OF SOLUTIONS TO THE ORIGINAL EQUATIONS

Previously, the term "solution" has been used on occasion to denote a solution to the LP. From this point on we must be more precise with this term. *By "solution," we shall mean a solution to the original equations.* To eliminate confusion in terminology, the *LP solution is often referred to in the literature as an optimal solution.* Henceforth we shall

224

CHAPTER 6
Linear
Programming:
The Simplex
Method

conform to this usage. Thus, *a solution to the LP problem will be termed an optimal solution*. The unqualified term "solution" will refer to any set of values for the variables that satisfy the original equations.

There are, for our purposes, four types of solutions (in addition to optimal solutions) which must be distinguished. These are now defined:

Solutions

The term *solution* simply refers to *any* set of values for the six variables $(A, C, s_1, s_2, s_3, s_4)$ that satisfy equations (6.1) through (6.4), ignoring the nonnegativity conditions. In this problem there are an *infinite* number of solutions. One can see this in a variety of ways. For example, by a simple rearrangement of (6.1)–(6.4) we can solve for A, C, s_1, and s_2 in terms of s_3 and s_4 as follows:

$$A + 2C + s_1 \qquad = 120 \qquad\qquad (6.5)$$

$$A + \ C \qquad + s_2 = \ 90 \qquad\qquad (6.6)$$

$$A \qquad\qquad\qquad = \ 70 - s_3 \qquad\qquad (6.7)$$

$$C \qquad\qquad = \ 50 - s_4 \qquad\qquad (6.8)$$

Equations (6.5)–(6.8), which are equivalent to (6.1)–(6.4), show that we can find a solution to the original system by arbitrarily setting s_3 and s_4 equal to any values, then solving for A, C, s_1, and s_2. For example, if $s_3 = s_4 = 0$, we see that $(A = 70, C = 50, s_1 = -50, s_2 = -30, s_3 = 0, s_4 = 0)$ is a solution to the original equations. In a similar way it is clear that s_3 and s_4 could be arbitrarily set in an infinite number of ways, and (6.5)–(6.8) would determine a solution to the original equations.

How Many Solutions Are There?

In the general LP in standard equality constraint form there will be m equality constraints in n variables, with $m < n$. In this setting, (1) either there will be no solution (in which case the LP is infeasible), or (2) there will be an infinite number of solutions. This is illustrated by considering two linear equations in three unknowns. From a geometric point of view, the two equations represent two planes in three-dimensional space. If the planes do not intersect (which implies that they are parallel) the equations have no solution. Otherwise, the planes must intersect, which means that either they coincide or they determine a line. In either case there are infinitely many points in the intersection, which means that the two equations have an infinite number of solutions.

Feasible Solutions

This term refers to solutions that are *nonnegative*, which means that the values of all the variables (decision variables, slacks, and surplus) must be nonnegative. In other words, a feasible solution satisfies *all the constraints and the nonnegativity conditions of the model*. From the geometric point of view, a feasible solution to Astro/Cosmo is one that corresponds to a point in the shaded region of Figure 6.1.

Basic Solutions

We first define this concept in the Astro/Cosmo context. There are four equations and six variables in this problem. We used (6.5)–(6.8) to show that this set of equations will have an infinite number of solutions. We shall now focus on a particular kind of solution, obtained by setting $s_3 = s_4 = 0$ in (6.5)–(6.8). Note that when we do this we are left with four equations in four unknowns, and the solution to this square system, namely $(A = 70, C = 50, s_1 = -50, s_2 = -30)$ is *unique* (meaning that with $s_3 = s_4 = 0$, there is *one and only one* set of values for the remaining variables that will satisfy the equations).

In general, in (6.1)–(6.4), if any two variables are set equal to zero, they are, in principle, eliminated from the equations, leaving us with four rather than six variables.

225

CHAPTER 6
Linear
Programming:
The Simplex
Method

We shall see that *when certain pairs of variables are set equal to zero, the resulting system of equations (four equations in four unknowns) will have a unique solution.* Indeed, we have just shown that (s_3, s_4) is such a pair. This property cannot be guaranteed for all pairs, for the resulting 4×4 system may have no solutions or infinitely many solutions. However, when there *is* in fact a unique solution, the solution obtained thereby is called a *basic solution*. The two variables that were set equal to zero are called *nonbasic variables*, or sometimes, a *nonbasic set* (of variables). The remaining variables which can be solved for uniquely are called the *basic variables*, or sometimes, a *basic set* (of variables). Also, the set of basic variables is often referred to as a *basis*. Thus, we have shown that A, C, s_1, and s_2 are a basic set of variables and that s_3 and s_4 comprise a nonbasic set.

As another example, let us set the pair of variables (s_1, s_3) equal to zero (i.e., let $s_1 = 0$, and $s_3 = 0$). Doing this, the original equations (6.1)–(6.4) reduce to the following 4×4 system:

$$
\begin{aligned}
A + 2C &= 120 \\
A + C + s_2 &= 90 \\
A &= 70 \\
C + s_4 &= 50
\end{aligned}
$$

There is a *unique* (one and only one) solution to these equations, namely

$$A = 70, \qquad C = 25, \qquad s_2 = -5, \qquad s_4 = 25$$

Consequently, since this solution to the 4×4 system is unique, we say that

$$A = 70, \qquad C = 25, \qquad s_2 = -5, \qquad s_4 = 25, \qquad s_1 = 0, \qquad s_3 = 0$$

is a basic solution. The nonbasic variables are those which were set equal to zero, namely s_1 and s_3. The basic variables are A, C, s_2, and s_4, and these variables are said to form a basis. Note that *in the basic solution the values of both the basic and the nonbasic variables appear.*

How Many Basic Solutions Are There?

We have just seen two examples of basic solutions to the Astro/Cosmo equations (remember, we are for the time being ignoring the nonnegativity conditions and considering only the original equations). Since there are six variables in the original Astro/Cosmo equations, there are

$$\binom{6}{2} = \frac{6!}{4! \, 2!} = \frac{6 \cdot 5}{2} = 15$$

possible pairs of variables that can be formed.[2] This means that, conceivably, there could be 15 basic solutions. However, only 13 basic solutions exist and these are shown

---

[2] The symbol $\binom{6}{2}$ denotes the number of distinct pairs that can be taken out of six items. The factorial symbol ! is defined by $n! = n(n-1)(n-2) \cdots 1$. It is a convention that $0! = 1$. In general,

$$\binom{r}{s} = \frac{r!}{(r-s)! \, (s!)}$$

Also, it is true that

$$\binom{r}{s} = \binom{r}{r-s}$$

226

CHAPTER 6
Linear
Programming:
The Simplex
Method

FIGURE 6.2

13 Basic Solutions of Equations (6.1)–(6.4)

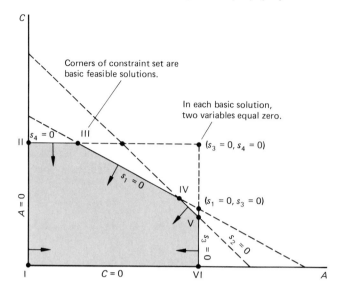

in Figure 6.2. To see why this occurs, note in Figure 6.2 that the pair $(s_3 = 0, A = 0)$ is *not* part of a basic solution. From the geometric point of view, this is because the lines in Figure 6.2 determined by $s_3 = 0$ and $A = 0$ are parallel. Hence, they do not intersect, which means that the original equations have *no solution* when $s_3 = 0$ and $A = 0$. This is also easily seen algebraically. If we set $A = 0$ and $s_3 = 0$, the original equations (6.1) through (6.4) reduce to four equations in four unknowns. One of the equations, namely (6.3), becomes

$$0 = 70$$

which shows that the resulting system is inconsistent.

Similar comments apply when we consider the pair $(s_4 = 0, C = 0)$. Thus two of the 15 possible pairs are eliminated. We are thus left with 13 basic solutions.

What we have just illustrated, with Astro/Cosmo, is the following general result:

**A General
Result
Concerning
Basic
Solutions**

Consider m simultaneous linear equations in n unknowns, with $m < n$. Either there is no solution or there are infinitely many solutions. In the latter case, *certain sets* (possibly all $\binom{n}{n-m}$), which equals $\binom{n}{m}$ sets) of $n - m$ of the unknowns can be set equal to zero and the resulting square system of m equations in m unknowns will have a unique solution.[3] Any set for which this is true provides what is termed a *basic solution*. The $n - m$ variables which were set to zero are called *nonbasic variables*. The remaining m variables are called *basic variables*. These m variables are said to form a *basis*. The term "basic solution" encompasses the values of *all* the variables: the nonbasic variables (which are all zero), and the basic variables (each of which may be positive, negative, or zero).

---

[3] To give a complete theoretic characterization of these sets requires the notion of linear independence, which takes us too far astray for our purposes.

The fourth, and for our purposes most important, type of solution is called a *basic feasible solution*. Recall from above that a feasible solution is a solution that satisfies all nonnegativity conditions of the model. Hence, *a basic feasible solution is, simply, a basic solution which is also feasible*, that is, *all* of whose variables are nonnegative. In a basic solution, by definition, the nonbasic variables are always at the value zero. Hence, *a basic solution is a basic feasible solution if and only if all the basic variables have non-negative values* (which means, as a special case, that some of them could be zero). If we look once more at Figure 6.2, we see that of the 13 basic solutions, only 6 are basic feasible, namely those labeled I through VI. We also see the striking fact that these are the corners of the Astro/Cosmo constraint set. In other words, we have found the algebraic representation of corners, which is what we had set out to do. This equivalence of basic feasible solutions and corners is the topic to be discussed next.

———— 6.4
BASIC FEASIBLE SOLUTIONS AND EXTREME POINTS

In this section we wish to examine further the relationship between the corners of the feasible set (a geometric concept) and basic feasible solutions (an algebraic concept introduced in the preceding section). We must consider two cases. In general, for an LP in standard equality constraint form with, say, m constraints (equations) and n unknowns, we learned in Chapter 5 that the number of positive variables (including slack and surplus) at any corner is *less than or equal to m*. These are the two possibilities to be considered:

Non-
degenerate
Corner
Case 1 The number of positive variables is exactly m. This is, by the definition given in Chapter 5, a nondegenerate corner. We can illustrate the important features of this case by referring to Figure 6.2, where the corners are labeled I through VI. First note that all of those corners are nondegenerate. Now consider any one of the corners—IV, for example. Since this point lies on constraints (6.1) and (6.2), we know that s_1 and $s_2 = 0$ at point IV. This fact uniquely determines the values of the other variables (i.e., $A = 60$, $C = 30$, $s_3 = 10$, $s_4 = 20$).

Since this corner corresponds to a solution with two variables at the value zero, and the others uniquely determined, it is, as we have discussed in the preceding section, a basic feasible solution to the original equations. Since the corner is nondegenerate, the basic feasible solution is termed nondegenerate. At any nondegenerate corner, such as IV, there is only one set of nonbasic variables (e.g., s_1 and s_2) and one set of basic variables (e.g., A, C, s_3, and s_4).

Degenerate
Corner
Case 2 The number of positive variables is less than m. This is, by definition, a degenerate corner. In this case the corner also corresponds to a basic feasible solution, but there will be more than one set of nonbasic (and hence basic) variables at such a corner.[4]

_____

[4] For this reason, some expositions state that "more than one basic feasible solution is associated with a degenerate corner." We find this potentially confusing, since any corner, degenerate or nondegenerate corresponds to a *unique solution* to the original equations. In the nondegenerate case, there is a single basic set associated with this solution. In the degenerate case, there are multiple basic sets, all associated with the same solution.

Since the corner is degenerate, the corresponding solution is also termed degenerate. This is illustrated by the following feasible region:

$$x + y \leq 10$$
$$x \quad \leq 5$$
$$y \leq 5$$
$$x, y \geq 0$$

Converting to equalities, we obtain

$$x + y + s_1 \qquad = 10$$
$$x \qquad + s_2 \qquad = 5$$
$$y \qquad + s_3 = 5$$
$$x, y, s_1, s_2, s_3 \geq 0$$

The geometric representation of the feasible set is shown in Figure 6.3. We note that, since corner A lies on the first, second, and third constraints, we have at that corner $s_1 = 0$, $s_2 = 0$, and $s_3 = 0$. Plugging these values into the equations implies that $x = 5$ and $y = 5$. Thus, corner A corresponds to the solution ($x = 5$, $y = 5$, $s_1 = 0$, $s_2 = 0$, $s_3 = 0$). Since there are only two positive variables and three constraints, corner A is degenerate. It is also a basic feasible solution since when, for example, s_1 and s_2 are set to zero, the values of the remaining variables are uniquely determined. Figure 6.4 shows the basic and nonbasic sets associated with the corners in Figure 6.3.

What Figure 6.4 reveals is that at the degenerate corner A there are three different sets of basic variables. Note that in each such set one of the basic variables has a zero value. At each of the other, nondegenerate, corners (B, C, and D) there is a unique set of basic variables. Moreover, the basic variables at corners B, C, and D are all positive. This is an illustration of the fact that, for a general model with m constraints, a degenerate basic feasible solution has $<m$ positive variables. A nondegenerate basic feasible solution has exactly m positive variables.

FIGURE 6.3
Degenerate Corner

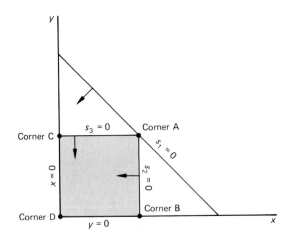

229

CHAPTER 6
Linear
Programming:
The Simplex
Method

FIGURE 6.4

Basic and Nonbasic Variables at the
Corners of Figure 6.3.

NONBASIC VARIABLES	BASIC VARIABLES AND VALUES	CORNER ON FIGURE 6.3
x, y	$s_1 = 10, s_2 = 5, s_3 = 5$	D
y, s_2	$x = 5, s_1 = 5, s_3 = 5$	B
s_1, s_2	$x = 5, y = 5, s_3 = 0$	A
s_1, s_3	$x = 5, y = 5, s_2 = 0$	A
s_2, s_3	$x = 5, y = 5, s_1 = 0$	A
x, s_3	$y = 5, s_2 = 5, s_1 = 5$	C

It turns out that, in fact, the correspondence between corners and basic feasible solutions is one to one. The general property is summarized as follows:

Correspondence Property

1. *Associated with every basic feasible solution to the original equations* is a unique corner (extreme point) of the constraint set. If the basic feasible solution is *nondegenerate*, so is the corner and there is, in this case, a unique set of basic variables associated with the corner. These are the positive variables at the corner. If the basic feasible solution is *degenerate*, so is the corner and there is, in this case, more than one set of basic variables associated with the corner. In each set, some basic variables will have a value of zero.

2. *Associated with every corner of the constraint set is* a unique basic feasible solution. If the corner is degenerate, so is the basic feasible solution, and there will be more than one associated set of basic variables. If the corner is nondegenerate, so is the basic feasible solution, and there will be exactly one associated set of basic variables.

The correspondence noted above is important because it ties together the geometry and the algebra. We know from geometric analysis that if an LP problem has an optimal solution, there is an optimal corner. This observation, plus the fact that every corner corresponds to a basic feasible solution, permits us to state:

> **If an LP has an optimal solution, there is a basic feasible solution that is optimal.**

The simplex algorithm searches among basic feasible solutions to find an optimal solution. In the next sections we see how this is done.

6.5

TRANSFORMED EQUATIONS

We have learned thus far that every constraint set corner (i.e., the values of the variables at the corner) is a basic feasible solution to the original equations. The simplex method will search corners by moving from one basic feasible solution to another. To accomplish this, the original equations will be recast into different but equivalent representations.

In particular

**Transformed
Equations
Corresponding
to a Corner**

Consider the feasible region for any LP model in standard equality constraint form. Corresponding to any corner of this feasible region is at least one (exactly one if the corner is nondegenerate) set of basic and nonbasic variables. Consider any such corner. Select any basic and associated nonbasic set corresponding to this corner. The original equations can be algebraically transformed into the following equivalent form:

> **Each basic variable appears in one and only one equation and, in that equation, its coefficient is $+1$** $\qquad$ (6.9)
>
> **Only constant terms are on the right side of the equations and these constant terms are nonnegative** $\qquad$ (6.10)

Such a representation of the original equations will be denoted as a *set of transformed equations corresponding to the corner under consideration*.

An Illustration

Let us illustrate these sets of transformed equations by referring to corners I and II in Figure 6.2. The original equations for Astro/Cosmo are

$$A + 2C + s_1 \qquad\qquad\quad = 120 \qquad (6.1)$$

$$A + C + s_2 \qquad\quad = 90 \qquad (6.2)$$

$$A + s_3 = 70 \qquad (6.3)$$

$$C + s_4 = 50 \qquad (6.4)$$

At corner I, the nonbasic variables are A and C (at corner I, $A = C = 0$). Hence, the basic variables are s_1, s_2, s_3, and s_4. Note that in (6.1)–(6.4) each basic variable appears in one and only one equation, and in that equation its coefficient is $+1$. Hence, (6.9) is satisfied. Similarly, you can see that (6.10) is satisfied. Thus, at corner I, (6.9) and (6.10) are satisfied by the original equations. What about corner II? We note that, at corner II, C, s_1, s_2, and s_3 are basic. We need to transform the original equations so that (6.9) and (6.10) are satisfied in terms of this basic set. We can proceed as follows: From (6.4) we obtain

$$C = 50 - s_4 \qquad (6.11)$$

Similarly, (6.3) yields

$$s_3 = 70 - A \qquad (6.12)$$

Substituting in (6.1) the expression for C given by (6.11) yields

$$A + 2(50 - s_4) + s_1 = 120$$

231

CHAPTER 6
Linear
Programming:
The Simplex
Method

or

$$A + s_1 - 2s_4 = 20 \tag{6.13}$$

Using the same approach on (6.2), we see that

$$A + (50 - s_4) + s_2 = 90$$

or

$$A + s_2 - s_4 = 40 \tag{6.14}$$

Thus, the transformed equations for the basic set at corner II are

**Transformed
Equations
for Corner II**

$$
\begin{align}
C \qquad\qquad + s_4 &= 50 \tag{6.4}\\
A \qquad\quad + s_3 \qquad\;\; &= 70 \tag{6.3}\\
A \quad + s_2 \qquad - s_4 &= 40 \tag{6.14}\\
A + s_1 \qquad\qquad - 2s_4 &= 20 \tag{6.13}
\end{align}
$$

Although, visually speaking, this set of equations do not "look like" the original set (6.1)–(6.4), they are indeed equivalent in the sense that they have precisely the same solutions. These transformed equations will reappear when we solve Astro/Cosmo with the simplex algorithm.

_____ 6.6
THE CHARACTERIZATION OF ADJACENT EXTREME POINTS

As already noted, the corners of the constraint set in Figure 6.2 are known as *extreme points*. There are six extreme points in this figure, which we have labeled as I through VI. Just as in the discussion in Chapter 5 on the geometry of the equality constraint model and as we did in Figure 6.4, we can with the aid of Figure 6.2 explicitly identify the positive variables and the zero variables at each corner (see Figure 6.5). Indeed, it is the corresponding zero variables that distinguish the different corners. For example, corner V is distinguished by the fact that at this point $s_2 = s_3 = 0$. These are the nonbasic variables at corner V. The basic variables at this corner, namely (s_1, s_4, A, C), are all

FIGURE 6.5
Basic and Nonbasic Variables at the Corners

CORNER	NONBASIC VARIABLES	BASIC VARIABLES	POSITIVE COUNT
I	A, C	s_1, s_2, s_3, s_4	4
II	A, s_4	s_1, s_2, s_3, C	4
III	s_4, s_1	A, s_2, s_3, C	4
IV	s_1, s_2	A, s_4, s_3, C	4
V	s_2, s_3	A, s_4, s_1, C	4
VI	s_3, C	A, s_4, s_1, s_2	4

positive. According to a previous definition, since there are four positive variables and four constraints in the model, this corner is nondegenerate.

As already stated, the simplex method will proceed by moving from corner to adjacent corner of the constraint set. The mathematics of this move, or pivot, is the essence of the algorithm. The mathematical procedure is based on an important fact. In moving, for example, from corner I to the adjacent corner II, you can see by comparing the two top rows of Figure 6.5 that the basic variable s_4 is exchanged with the nonbasic variable C (i.e., at corner II, C has become basic and s_4 has become nonbasic). Three of the four variables which were basic at corner I, namely s_1, s_2, and s_3, remain basic at corner II. One of the two variables which was nonbasic at corner I, namely A, remains nonbasic at corner II. Thus, there is a simple *exchange operation* in moving from corner I to corner II. You can verify that this fact characterizes the move between all adjacent corners in Figure 6.2. For example, in moving from corner III to adjacent corner IV, Figure 6.5 shows that the roles of s_2 and s_4 are exchanged.

We have now acquired all of the understanding necessary to apply the simplex algorithm to Astro/Cosmo.

Exchanging a Basic Variable with a Nonbasic Variable (margin heading)

_____ 6.7

THE INITIAL TABLEAU

The first part of the simplex algorithm, as mentioned earlier, is called phase I. Phase I *is designed to find a set of transformed equations corresponding to any initial corner of the constraint set.* In the Astro/Cosmo example, phase I is trivial, for we can arbitrarily select corner I in Figure 6.2 as the initial corner. As we have already noted, the transformed equations corresponding to corner I are precisely the original equations (6.1) through (6.4).

Corresponding to the initial corner we set up what is called an *initial tableau.* This is merely a convenient way of representing the transformed equations corresponding to the initial corner. For the Astro/Cosmo problem, taking corner I as the initial corner, the transformed equations are

Initial Tableau for Astro/Cosmo (margin heading)

$$A + 2C + s_1 \qquad\qquad = 120 \qquad (6.1)$$

$$A + \ C \qquad + s_2 \qquad\qquad = 90 \qquad (6.2)$$

$$A \qquad\qquad + s_3 \qquad = 70 \qquad (6.3)$$

$$C \qquad\qquad + s_4 = 50 \qquad (6.4)$$

The tableau representation of these equations is shown in Figure 6.6. Equations (6.1) through (6.4) are easily read from the tableau. The RHS appears under the "Value" column. Each row of the tableau represents an equation. The coefficient for each variable in the equation appears under the appropriate column in the tableau. The column headed "Basic Variable" simply identifies the basic set associated with these transformed equations. In particular, we see which variable is basic in each row. Thus, the first row of the tableau is read

$$1A + 2C + 1s_1 + 0s_2 + 0s_3 + 0s_4 = 120$$

233

CHAPTER 6
Linear
Programming:
The Simplex
Method

FIGURE 6.6
Tableau Representation of Transformed
Equations at Corner I

BASIC VARIABLE	A	C	s_1	s_2	s_3	s_4	VALUE
s_1	1	2	1	0	0	0	120
s_2	1	1	0	1	0	0	90
s_3	1	0	0	0	1	0	70
s_4	0	1	0	0	0	1	50

and this is precisely (6.1). Also, the "Basic Variable" column tells us that s_1 is the basic variable in the first equation. Read the remaining three rows of the tableau to verify that they represent (6.2), (6.3), and (6.4).

Given the initial corner of the feasible region and the associated tableau, phase I of the method is complete and phase II begins. In the first step of phase II we wish to move to an *adjacent* (and we wish to emphasize "adjacent") corner at which the value of the objective function is improved (in this case, since we are dealing with a Max model, we wish to increase the objective value). Note that at corner I the value of the objective function is zero.

From Figure 6.1 it is clear that either of the adjacent corners II or IV will give a higher value to the objective function. Moreover, this figure indicates that the path of adjacent corners, to the optimal solution (corner V), will be either the sequence I–II–III–IV–V or the sequence I–VI–V, depending on whether the first chosen is II or VI.[5] Figure 6.5 shows the sets of basic variables at any of the corners on the path. All of this information is visible from the geometric interpretation. Our goal now is to see how this information can be obtained algebraically, for remember that most real-world problems will not be two-dimensional and hence will not have nice geometric representations. Consequently, all aspects of their solution must be obtained by algebraic manipulations.

—————— 6.8
INCREASING THE OBJECTIVE FUNCTION BY COMPUTING OPPORTUNITY COSTS

Let us now recall the interpretations

$$A = \text{units of Astros produced}$$

$$C = \text{units of Cosmos produced}$$

$$s_1 = \text{labor slack in department A}$$

$$s_2 = \text{labor slack in department B}$$

$$s_3 = \text{slack in Astro production capacity}$$

$$s_4 = \text{slack in Cosmo production capacity}$$

[5] Since by stipulation the values of the objective function must be increasing from corner to adjacent corner, it should be clear that previously visited corners cannot be encountered again.

**Nonbasic
Columns**

Our desire to increase the objective function will be well served by giving physical interpretations to the *nonbasic columns* of the tableau. By *nonbasic columns* we mean those columns headed by the nonbasic variables. Since in Figure 6.6 A and C are nonbasic, there are two nonbasic columns, namely

$$A \text{ column} = \begin{pmatrix} 1 \\ 1 \\ 1 \\ 0 \end{pmatrix}$$

$$C \text{ column} = \begin{pmatrix} 2 \\ 1 \\ 0 \\ 1 \end{pmatrix}$$

We shall see that these columns reveal certain specific information about the Astro/Cosmo production technology.

To explain this, let us rewrite the transformation equations from Figure 6.6 in the form

$$s_1 = 120 - A - 2C \tag{6.15}$$

$$s_2 = 90 - A - C \tag{6.16}$$

$$s_3 = 70 - A \tag{6.17}$$

$$s_4 = 50 - C \tag{6.18}$$

**Incrementing
A by 1**

At corner I, since $A = C = 0$, there is no production of either Astros or Cosmos. The values of the variables s_1, s_2, s_3, and s_4 at corner I are 120, 90, 70, and 50, respectively. Equation (6.15) tells us that if we maintain Cosmo production at the level zero and increase the production of Astros to 1 unit, then in order to satisfy our constraints

- s_1, labor slack in department A, will *decrease* by a unit to 119. Similarly, from (6.16), (6.17), and (6.18).
- s_2, labor slack in department B, will *decrease* by a unit to 89.
- s_3, slack in Astro production capacity, will *decrease* by a unit to 69.
- s_4, slack in Cosmo production capacity, will be unaffected and hence remains at 50.

Now note that the data in the tableau (Figure 6.6) under column A are (1, 1, 1, 0). These data show the amount by which the current values of the basic variables must be *reduced* when (1) another unit of A is produced and (2) C is held at zero.

**Incrementing
C by 1**

Let us now consider the changes in the current values of the basic variables that would be incurred if C were incremented a unit while holding A at the value zero. You can see from (6.15)–(6.18) that the respective *reductions* in s_1, s_2, s_3, and s_4 are 2, 1, 0, and 1. Thus, the data in the tableau under column C, namely (2, 1, 0, 1), show the amounts by which the current values of the basic variables must be reduced when (1) another unit of C is produced and (2) A is held at zero. Because of these interpretations,

234

235

CHAPTER 6
Linear
Programming:
The Simplex
Method

the data in the nonbasic column are often referred to by the term *substitution coefficients*. Let us now see how this relates to the objective function.

The Astro/Cosmo objective function is

$$\text{profit} = 20A + 10C + 0s_1 + 0s_2 + 0s_3 + 0s_4 \qquad (6.19)$$

The basic variables at corner I are (s_1, s_2, s_3, s_4). The coefficients in the objective function that correspond to these basic variables are $(0, 0, 0, 0)$. These are called the *basic coefficients*. Thus, at corner I

**Basic
Coefficients
at Corner I**

$$\text{basic coefficients} = \begin{pmatrix} 0 \\ 0 \\ 0 \\ 0 \end{pmatrix}$$

Now suppose that C is held at zero and A is incremented a unit. We have seen that this will induce certain changes in the basic variables. That is, the values of the basic variables will be *reduced* by the coefficients in the A column, namely the amounts $(1, 1, 1, 0)$. Ignoring the *direct effect* (on the objective function) of increasing the nonbasic variable A, and taking into account only the *indirect effect* of the induced changes in the basic variables, the objective function will be *reduced* by

$$\text{(basic coefficients)} \cdot (A \text{ column})$$

This is a convenient shorthand notation to denote the operation of "adding the products of the corresponding terms" of the two columns. Thus, we see that when A is incremented by a unit, with C held at zero,

**Indirect Effect
on Objective
Function**

$$\textit{indirect decrease in profit} = \text{(basic coefficients)} \cdot (A \text{ column})$$
$$= 0(1) + 0(1) + 0(1) + 0(0) = 0$$
$$= \text{contribution due only to basic variable changes}$$

Thus, in this case, the resultant changes in the basic variables will not change the objective function. Let us now take the change in A (the *direct effect*) into account. You can see from (6.19) that if A is incremented by a unit, the *marginal contribution* to profit (i.e., not taking the indirect effects into account) will be to increase it by $20. Thus, we have shown that *having one more unit of A in the solution would net us a gain of $20*. In the language of economics this means that the *opportunity cost* of *not* having one more unit of A in the solution is

**Opportunity
Cost for A**

$$\text{opportunity cost} = \text{potential gain} - \text{potential decrease}$$
$$= \text{direct effect} - \text{indirect effect}$$
$$= 20 - 0 = 20$$

**Analysis of the
C Column**

Let us conduct the same analysis on the other nonbasic column of Figure 6.6, that headed by C. Since the column of substitution coefficients, the C column, is $(2, 1, 0, 1)$, we see that

236

CHAPTER 6
Linear
Programming:
The Simplex
Method

incrementing C by a unit while holding A at zero gives

$$\text{indirect decrease in profit} = (\text{basic coefficients}) \cdot (C \text{ column})$$

$$= 0(2) + 0(1) + 0(0) + 0(1) = 0$$

$$= \text{contribution due only to basic variable changes}$$

Also, from (6.19) we see that incrementing C by a unit will have a *direct effect*. Namely, this will cause a marginal contribution to the objective value of $+10$. In this case, then,

Opportunity Cost for C

$$\text{opportunity cost} = \text{potential gain} - \text{potential decrease}$$

$$= \text{direct effect} - \text{indirect effect}$$

$$= 10 - 0 = 10$$

Having computed the current opportunity costs *for all the nonbasic variables*, we have completed the algebra required in our search for an adjacent corner at which the objective function will improve. Recall from our discussion of Figure 6.5 that when moving from any corner to an adjacent corner, it must be true that only one of the currently nonbasic variables can be made basic. In other words, at an adjacent corner all of the currently nonbasic variables will remain at zero except for one, which will be incremented. What we have done in the discussion above is compute the *per unit change* in the objective function as each of the nonbasic variables, A and C, is incremented one at a time with the other held at zero. The term *per unit change* means change in profit per unit increase in the nonbasic variable. This is precisely the opportunity cost. *It follows that a desirable adjacent corner can be reached by increasing any current nonbasic variable with a positive opportunity cost.*

This gives us the algebraic rule for perceiving adjacent corners at which the objective function will increase. It is called the *enter rule*, and the variable that becomes positive is called the *enter variable*, since it is the variable chosen to become basic (i.e., to enter the basis).

The Enter Rule   For a general LP this rule can be stated as follows:

Increasing any nonbasic variable with a positive opportunity cost, keeping all other nonbasic variables at the value zero, will lead to an adjacent corner with a higher objective value. The variable chosen to be increased is called the enter variable. Usually, in order to have a systematic rule, the variable with the most positive opportunity cost is chosen to enter, but *any* variable with a positive opportunity cost will serve the purpose.

In the Astro/Cosmo model we have thus computed the result that the geometry in Figure 6.1 has already revealed. A move to either of the corners VI (i.e., increasing A) or II (i.e., increasing C) will improve the objective function. Before moving on to the next corner, let us take a moment to show how the initial tableau can be slightly expanded so as to facilitate the opportunity cost computations.

THE FULL TABLEAU REPRESENTATION

With each *nonbasic column* of the tableau in Figure 6.6, let us associate a so-called z_j value defined as follows:

z_j the Indirect Decrease

z_j = *indirect decrease* in the value of the objective function induced by bringing into the solution one unit of the variable above the jth nonbasic column of the tableau, keeping all other nonbasic variables at zero

If we let c_j denote the coefficient in the objective function corresponding to the jth nonbasic variable in the model, then

$$c_j - z_j = \text{direct effect} - \text{indirect effect}$$

$$= \text{opportunity cost}$$

For example, if we let A denote the first variable in the Astro/Cosmo model, then as we have computed in Section 6.8

$$z_1 = 0$$

$$c_1 = 20$$

$$c_1 - z_1 = 20 = \text{opportunity cost}$$

Similarly, if we let C denote the second variable in the model, then

$$z_2 = 0$$

$$c_2 = 10$$

$$c_2 - z_2 = 10 = \text{opportunity cost}$$

To represent these quantities in the tableau format, we proceed as follows:

1. Add a new leftmost column to the tableau. This column explicitly shows the coefficients in the objective function associated with each basic variable.

2. Add a new row above the tableau. This row shows the coefficients of *all* the variables in the objective function (including slack and surplus variables with zero coefficients).

3. Append two new rows to the bottom of the tableau. The first is the z_j row. The second is the $c_j - z_j$ row. This is the opportunity cost row.

Filling in the z_j Row

Let us illustrate by completing the tableau shown in Figure 6.6 in the prescribed manner. We show a partially completed tableau in Figure 6.7. To fill in the z_j row we use the data in Figure 6.7 as follows:

$$z_j = (\text{basic coefficients}) \cdot (j\text{th column of data})$$

238

CHAPTER 6
Linear
Programming:
The Simplex
Method

FIGURE 6.7
Partially Complete Tableau at Corner I

BASIC COEFFICIENT	BASIC VARIABLE	20	10	0	0	0	0	
		A	C	s_1	s_2	s_3	s_4	VALUE
0	s_1	1	2	1	0	0	0	120
0	s_2	1	1	0	1	0	0	90
0	s_3	1	0	0	0	1	0	70
0	s_4	0	1	0	0	0	1	50
	z_j							
	$c_j - z_j$							

Thus,

$$z_1 = 0(1) + 0(1) + 0(1) + 0(0) = 0$$

$$z_2 = 0(2) + 0(1) + 0(0) + 0(1) = 0$$

$$z_3 = 0(1) + 0(0) + 0(0) + 0(0) = 0$$

$$z_4 = 0(0) + 0(1) + 0(0) + 0(0) = 0$$

$$z_5 = 0(0) + 0(0) + 0(1) + 0(0) = 0$$

$$z_6 = 0(0) + 0(0) + 0(0) + 0(1) = 0$$

$z_j = c_j$ for Basic Variables   Although basic variables are never candidates for entry, notice that we have used the same equations to compute z_j values for the basic as well as the nonbasic columns. For basic variables the z_j value computed by this formula will always equal c_j and $c_j - z_j$ will be zero. Thus, the calculations are innocuous and it is merely for convenience of display that these entries are included in the tableau.

Notice also that the objective value at the current corner is easily calculated from the expanded tableau. The values of the basic variables at the current corner are given by the "Value" column of the tableau. The remaining variables, which are nonbasic at the current corner, have the value zero. Consequently, they make no contribution to the current value of the objective function. This shows that

Calculating the Current Objective Value

$$\text{current objective value} = (\text{basic coefficients}) \cdot (\text{values})$$

$$= 0(120) + 0(90) + 0(70) + 0(50)$$

$$= 0$$

The $c_j - z_j$ Row   Finally, the above z_j values are used in conjunction with the top row of c_j values to give

$$c_1 - z_1 = 20 - 0 = 20$$

$$c_2 - z_2 = 10 - 0 = 10$$

$$c_3 - z_3 = 0 - 0 = 0$$

$$c_4 - z_4 = 0 - 0 = 0$$

$$c_5 - z_5 = 0 - 0 = 0$$

$$c_6 - z_6 = 0 - 0 = 0$$

239

CHAPTER 6
Linear
Programming:
The Simplex
Method

FIGURE 6.8

Tableau at Corner I

		20	10	0	0	0	0	
BASIC COEFFICIENT	BASIC VARIABLE	A	C	s_1	s_2	s_3	s_4	VALUE
0	s_1	1	2	1	0	0	0	
0	s_2	1	1	0	1	0	0	
0	s_3	1	0	0	0	1	0	
0	s_4	0	1	0	0	0	1	
	z_j	0	0	0	0	0	0	
	$c_j - z_j$	20	10	0	0	0	0	0

The complete tableau at corner I is shown in Figure 6.8. Notice that the current objective function value is placed in the $c_j - z_j$ row under the "Value" column.

Beginning at corner I, the simplex method will produce a sequence of tableaux having the form of Figure 6.8. Each such tableau will correspond to a corner of the feasible region, representing the transformed equations at that corner and the appropriate opportunity costs.

We have already discussed the enter rule, which says that, at corner I, either A or C can be chosen to enter. Although A is the variable with most positive opportunity cost ($c_1 - z_1 = 20$), and hence might be the usual choice for entry, we shall for expository reasons choose to enter C into the basis. Geometrically, this will correspond in Figure 6.1 to a vertical move from corner I to corner II. Let us now examine the algebra associated with this move. *Enter the highest opportunity cost*

6.10
DETERMINING THE EXIT VARIABLE

We know from the corresponding value of $c_2 - z_2$, namely the value 10, that for each unit our enter variable C is incremented (holding the other nonbasic variable, A, at zero), the profit will increase by $10. We wish to increase C as much as possible, in order to increase the objective function as much as possible, but at the same time we do not want to violate any of the constraints in the model. With this proviso, let us see just how much C can be increased.

What Is the Maximum Increase of C? Recall that the first row of the current tableau (Figure 6.8) corresponds to the first constraint, (6.1), which is

$$A + 2C + s_1 = 120 \qquad \text{(department A)} \tag{6.1}$$

We see that each Cosmo produced uses 2 hours of labor in department A. Therefore, if we produce zero Astros and C Cosmos we will use $2C$ hours of labor in department A. Since we have only 120 hours available [the RHS of (6.1)], the maximum possible value of C, considering the labor constraint in department A, is calculated by solving the equation

$$2C = 120$$

Thus, there is enough department A labor available to produce only 60 Cosmos.

240

CHAPTER 6
Linear
Programming:
The Simplex
Method

Now consider the department B labor constraint given by the second row of the current tableau:

$$A + C + s_2 = 90 \qquad \text{(department B)} \qquad (6.2)$$

This shows that every Cosmo produced uses 1 hour of labor in department B. Thus, keeping Astro production at zero, the maximum number of Cosmos that could be produced while still satisfying the department B constraint is

$$C = 90$$

However, we know that it is impossible to produce 90 Cosmos because there is not enough labor available in department A. In fact, we saw that the department A labor constraint will allow a maximum of only 60 Cosmos to be produced. Thus, the value of $C = 60$ is the maximum production of Cosmos that will satisfy (6.1) and (6.2) simultaneously.

Proceeding with the remaining two rows in the body of the current tableau [those corresponding to constraints (6.3) and (6.4)], you should verify that (1) (6.3) places no constraint on the value of C and (2) (6.4) permits a maximum value of $C = 50$. Thus, the value $C = 50$ is the largest value of C (keeping A at the value zero) that will simultaneously satisfy all four constraints.

Geometric Interpretation
Let us now make the geometric interpretation. It is seen in Figures 6.1 and 6.2 that as C is increased, keeping A at the value zero, we will move upward from corner I, along the C axis, until reaching corner II, at which A and s_4 are nonbasic and at which C will have the value 50. Thus, at corner II the variables C and s_4 have exchanged roles. The variable C was nonbasic at corner I; at corner II it is basic. The variable s_4 was basic at corner I; at corner II it is nonbasic. For this reason s_4 is termed the *exit variable*. The other basic and nonbasic variables at corner II are the same as at corner I (which is not to imply that their *values* are the same, for clearly some of the basic variables at the two corners have different values).

We now show how the exit variable, s_4, and the largest possible value of C, computed as 50 in the discussion above, can be read from the tableau in Figure 6.8. To see this, we again look at (6.15)–(6.18), which express the basic variables at corner I in terms of the nonbasic variables.

$$s_1 = 120 - A - 2C \qquad (6.15)$$

$$s_2 = 90 - A - C \qquad (6.16)$$

$$s_3 = 70 - A \qquad (6.17)$$

$$s_4 = 50 - C \qquad (6.18)$$

At corner I we have $A = 0$, and in moving vertically upward to corner II A will remain at the value zero, since for this nonbasic pair only C will be increased. Thus, since throughout this move we have $A = 0$, we can rewrite (6.15)–(6.18) as

$$s_1 = 120 - 2C \qquad (6.15)$$

$$s_2 = 90 - C \qquad (6.16)$$

$$s_3 = 70 \qquad (6.17)$$

$$s_4 = 50 - C \qquad (6.18)$$

241

CHAPTER 6
Linear
Programming:
The Simplex
Method

You can see from these equations that in moving upward to corner II, as C gradually becomes positive the variable s_3 remains unchanged (from its value of 70 at corner I) and the variables s_1, s_2, and s_4 will decrease from their values at corner I (where $s_1 = 120$, $s_2 = 90$, $s_4 = 50$). You can also see that some simple algebra confirms our geometric observation that s_4 will be the first of these variables to hit zero. This is because

$$s_1 = 120 - 2C = 0 \quad \text{implies} \quad C = \tfrac{120}{2} = 60 \tag{6.20}$$

$$s_2 = 90 - C = 0 \quad \text{implies} \quad C = 90 \tag{6.21}$$

$$s_4 = 50 - C = 0 \quad \text{implies} \quad C = 50 \tag{6.22}$$

Relations (6.20), (6.21), and (6.22) show that as C increases from the value zero the variable s_4 will be the first basic variable to become zero, and this will occur when $C = 50$. Now, we can see from (6.20)–(6.22) how the exit variable and new value of C can be read from Figure 6.8. Notice that at corner II, C must be the minimum of the three ratios

$$\left\{ \tfrac{120}{2}, \tfrac{90}{1}, \tfrac{50}{1} \right\}$$

In Figure 6.8, these are the ratios of each number in the "Value" column to the corresponding number in the enter column (the C column) for which the number in the enter column is positive. That is, in (6.20) we compute the ratio of the first number in the "Value" column, namely 120, to the first number in the C column, namely 2; and similarly, for (6.21) and (6.22). For any row in which the enter column has a zero coefficient, such as the third row in the C column, which corresponds to (6.17), you can see that increasing C has no effect on the associated basic variable. That is, as C is increased (6.17) shows that the basic variable s_3 is unaffected. Also, it is not difficult to show that any row which has a negative entry in the enter column would have the property that the associated basic variable would *increase* as the enter variable increases. For example, if the first entry in the C column happened to be -2 instead of $+2$, the analog of (6.15) would be

$$s_1 = 120 - A + 2C$$

In this case it is clear that s_1 increases as C increases. Thus we need not consider either 0 entries or negative entries in the enter column. These observations lead to the following

The Exit Rule

EXIT RULE: **Consider the ratio of each number in the "Value" column to the corresponding number in the enter column, for which the number in the enter column is positive. The minimum ratio is the value of the enter variable at the next corner. The basic variable corresponding to the row with a minimum ratio is the exit variable.**

6.11
UPDATING THE INITIAL TABLEAU

Now that we have seen how to use the initial tableau, Figure 6.8, to determine algebraically the enter and exit variables, we must update the initial tableau to a new tableau that will correspond to corner II. The body of this tableau will represent the transformed

242

CHAPTER 6
Linear
Programming:
The Simplex
Method

equations corresponding to corner II. We have already seen (at the end of Section 6.5) that these equations are

$$C \qquad\qquad + \; s_4 = 50 \tag{6.4}$$

$$A \qquad\qquad + s_3 \qquad = 70 \tag{6.3}$$

$$A \qquad\quad + s_2 \qquad - \; s_4 = 40 \tag{6.14}$$

$$A \quad + s_1 \qquad\qquad - 2s_4 = 20 \tag{6.13}$$

Gaussian Elimination

Let us see how to operate on the initial tableau, Figure 6.8, to obtain these equations. The sequence of operations that we shall describe is called *Gaussian elimination*. Here are the first three steps:

STEP 1: **The entry in the enter column and the exit row of the current tableau (Figure 6.8) is called the *pivot element*. This is the circled element in Figure 6.8. Divide each entry in the exit row (the fourth row) by this element. In the "Basic Variable" column replace the exit variable with the entering variable and update the "Basic Coefficient" column as appropriate. This gives the row of the new tableau corresponding to the entering variable. Thus, the basic variable s_4 is replaced with C. Since the pivot element is 1, and since division by 1 produces no change, the entries in the fourth row stay the same. See the fourth row of Figure 6.9.**

FIGURE 6.9
Partial Update of Figure 6.8

BASIC COEFFICIENT	BASIC VARIABLE	20 A	10 C	0 s_1	0 s_2	0 s_3	0 s_4	VALUE
0	s_1			0	1	0	0	
0	s_2			0	0	1	0	
0	s_3			0	0	0	1	
10	C		0	1	0	0	0	1	50
z_j								
$c_j - z_j$								

Transformed exit row and basic columns

STEP 2: **The columns under each former basic variable other than the exit variable remain the same in all rows but the last two. Hence, the columns under s_1, s_2, and s_3 remain the same in the main body of the tableau. See this in Figure 6.9.**

STEP 3: **By virtue of step 1, the enter column already contains the number 1. Make the remaining entries zero in all rows except the last two.**

Following steps 1, 2, and 3 we obtain the partial tableau shown in Figure 6.9. All remaining entries in the main body of the tableau (all rows, including the "Value" col-

243

CHAPTER 6
Linear
Programming:
The Simplex
Method

umn, but the last two) can be obtained by the *pivot rule*, which works as follows: Suppose that we want the new entry in the s_2 row and the A column. You see in Figure 6.8 that the former entry was a 1. This number, together with the pivot element, defines a rectangle whose four corners are distinguished in Figure 6.8. (Note that any missing entry in the main body of Figure 6.9, together with the pivot element, will similarly define a unique rectangle.) The new entry in the s_2 row and the A column is given by a *pivoting operation* which consists of the following *opposite corner rule*:

Opposite Corner Pivot Rule

$$\text{new entry} = \text{old entry} - \frac{\text{product of opposite corners}}{\text{pivot element}}$$

Applying this rule, we obtain

$$\text{new entry} = 1 - \frac{(0)(1)}{1} = 1$$

Based on this pivoting operation, we can now state

STEP 4: **Apply the pivot rule to obtain all new entries for the remaining positions in the main body of the new tableau.**

We now use step 4 to obtain the appropriate entries. For example, the new entry in the s_1 row and the s_4 column is

$$\text{new entry} = 0 - \frac{(1)(2)}{1} = -2$$

The main body of the tableau, completed by applying step 4, is shown in Figure 6.10. Observe that we have indeed derived the transformed equations corresponding to corner II [i.e., (6.4), (6.3), (6.14), and (6.13)]. The tableau is completed by calculating the new

FIGURE 6.10
Main Body of the Tableau Corresponding
to Corner II

BASIC COEFFICIENT	BASIC VARIABLE	20 A	10 C	0 s_1	0 s_2	0 s_3	0 s_4	VALUE	
0	s_1	1	0	1	0	0	−2	20	
0	s_2	1	0	0	1	0	−1	40	
0	s_3	1	0	0	0	1	0	70	
10	C	0	1	0	0	0	1	50	
	z_j								
	$c_j - z_j$								

Updating by pivoting

FIGURE 6.11
Complete Tableau at Corner II

BASIC COEFFICIENT	BASIC VARIABLE	20	10	0	0	0	0		
		A	C	s_1	s_2	s_3	s_4	VALUE	
0	s_1	①	0	1	0	0	−2	20	
0	s_2	1	0	0	1	0	−1	40	
0	s_3	1	0	0	0	1	0	70	
10	C	0	1	0	0	0	1	50	
z_j		0	10	0	0	0	10		Last two rows are filled in
$c_j - z_j$		20	0	0	0	0	−10	500	

z_j's, $c_j - z_j$'s, and the new objective value. We obtain

$$z_1 = 0(1) \quad + 0(1) \quad + 0(1) + 10(0) = \quad 0; \qquad c_1 - z_1 = 20 - \quad 0 = \quad 20$$

$$z_2 = 0(0) \quad + 0(0) \quad + 0(0) + 10(1) = 10; \qquad c_2 - z_2 = 10 - 10 = \quad 0$$

$$z_3 = 0(1) \quad + 0(0) \quad + 0(0) + 10(0) = \quad 0; \qquad c_3 - z_3 = \quad 0 - \quad 0 = \quad 0$$

$$z_4 = 0(0) \quad + 0(1) \quad + 0(0) + 10(0) = \quad 0; \qquad c_4 - z_4 = \quad 0 - \quad 0 = \quad 0$$

$$z_5 = 0(0) \quad + 0(0) \quad + 0(1) + 10(0) = \quad 0; \qquad c_5 - z_5 = \quad 0 - \quad 0 = \quad 0$$

$$z_6 = 0(-2) + 0(-1) + 0(0) + 10(1) = 10; \qquad c_6 - z_6 = \quad 0 - 10 = -10$$

The new objective value, at corner II, is given by

$$(\text{basic coefficients}) \cdot (\text{values}) = 0(20) + 0(40) + 0(70) + 10(50) = 500$$

Inserting these new entries, the complete tableau for corner II is given in Figure 6.11. We have exercised

---

STEP 5: **Compute the values of z_j, $c_j - z_j$, and the current value of the objective function, and fill in the last two rows.**

_____ 6.12
CONTINUING TO UPDATE SUCCESSIVE TABLEAUX

The complete tableau at corner II, shown in Figure 6.11, shows that the current value of the objective function (meaning its value at corner II) is 500. This number appears in the last row of the "Value" column. We can also see that one of the currently nonbasic variables, namely A, has a positive opportunity cost, that is, the value of 20 which appears in the last row of the A column. This means that increasing the nonbasic variable A while keeping the other nonbasic variable, s_4, fixed at zero will further increase our objective value. Verify that increasing A while keeping s_4 at zero initiates in Figure 6.2 a move, or pivot, from corner II to corner III, where the variable s_1 becomes nonbasic. Any additional increase in A while keeping s_4 fixed at zero would force s_1 to become negative, which means we would be leaving the feasible region. Hence, we see

FIGURE 6.12
Tableau Corresponding to Corner III

| BASIC COEFFICIENT | BASIC VARIABLE | 20 | 10 | 0 | 0 | 0 | 0 | VALUE |
		A	C	s_1	s_2	s_3	s_4	
20	A	1	0	1	0	0	−2	20
0	s_2	0	0	−1	1	0	①	20
0	s_3	0	0	−1	0	1	2	50
10	C	0	1	0	0	0	1	50
z_j		20	10	20	0	0	−30	
$c_j - z_j$		0	0	−20	0	0	30	900

s_4 enters
s_2 exits

FIGURE 6.13

| BASIC COEFFICIENT | BASIC VARIABLE | 20 | 10 | 0 | 0 | 0 | 0 | VALUE |
		A	C	s_1	s_2	s_3	s_4	
20	A	1	0	−1	2	0	0	60
0	s_4	0	0	−1	1	0	1	20
0	s_3	0	0	1	−2	1	0	10
10	C	0	1	1	−1	0	0	30
z_j								
$c_j - z_j$								

Updating by pivoting

from the geometry that A should enter and s_1 should exit. Let us now apply the enter and exit rule to Figure 6.11 to obtain the same result.

Applying the Exit Rule   We have already noted that since the only positive entry in the last row is the value 20 under the A column, the enter rule says that A must enter the basis. To find the exit variable, we must check the ratios

$$\frac{20}{1}, \frac{40}{1}, \frac{70}{1}$$

The minimum ratio is $\frac{20}{1}$. Accordingly, the exit rule says that s_1 leaves the basic set, and 1 is the new pivot element, as indicated in Figure 6.11.

    Using the five steps outlined above, we obtain Figure 6.12. Try to derive this tableau on your own. If you have a problem, continue with the exposition. You will get more detail at the next step.

Pivoting From Corner III   The new tableau in Figure 6.12 indicates that s_4 should enter the basis because 30 is the only positive entry in the last row. The ratios

$$\frac{20}{1}, \frac{50}{2}, \frac{50}{1}$$

indicate that s_2 should leave the basic set because $\frac{20}{1}$ is the minimum ratio. The pivot element is 1, as indicated in Figure 6.12. This latest tableau shows that the value of the objective function has increased to 900 at corner III. The main body of this tableau is now updated to give Figure 6.13. To fill in the z_j row we use the data in Figure 6.13 as

246

CHAPTER 6
Linear
Programming:
The Simplex
Method

follows:

$$z_j = \text{(basic coefficients)} \cdot (j\text{th column of data})$$

Thus,

$$
\begin{aligned}
z_1 &= 20(1) &+ 0(0) &+ 0(0) &+ 10(0) &= &20 \\
z_2 &= 20(0) &+ 0(0) &+ 0(0) &+ 10(1) &= &10 \\
z_3 &= 20(-1) &+ 0(-1) &+ 0(1) &+ 10(1) &= &-10 \\
z_4 &= 20(2) &+ 0(1) &+ 0(-2) &+ 10(-1) &= &30 \\
z_5 &= 20(0) &+ 0(0) &+ 0(1) &+ 10(0) &= &0 \\
z_6 &= 20(0) &+ 0(1) &+ 0(0) &+ 10(0) &= &0
\end{aligned}
$$

Using these values in conjunction with the top row of c_j values, we compute

$$
\begin{aligned}
c_1 - z_1 &= 20 - &20 &= &0 \\
c_2 - z_2 &= 10 - &10 &= &0 \\
c_3 - z_3 &= 0 - (-10) &= &&10 \\
c_4 - z_4 &= 0 - &30 &= &-30 \\
c_5 - z_5 &= 0 - &0 &= &0 \\
c_6 - z_6 &= 0 - &0 &= &0
\end{aligned}
$$

Moreover, the objective function value at corner IV is also easily computed from the data in Figure 6.13.

$$
\begin{aligned}
\text{objective function value at corner IV} &= \text{(basic coefficients)} \cdot \text{(values)} \\
&= 20(60) + 0(20) + 0(10) + 10(30) \\
&= 1500
\end{aligned}
$$

FIGURE 6.14
Complete Tableau Corresponding to Corner IV

		20	10	0	0	0	0	
BASIC COEFFICIENT	BASIC VARIABLE	A	C	s_1	s_2	s_3	s_4	VALUE
20	A	1	0	-1	2	0	0	60
0	s_4	0	0	-1	1	0	1	20
0	s_3	0	0	①	-2	1	0	10
10	C	0	1	1	-1	0	0	30
z_j		20	10	-10	30	0	0	
$c_j - z_j$		0	0	10	-30	0	0	1500

s_1 enters
s_3 exits

247

CHAPTER 6
Linear
Programming:
The Simplex
Method

FIGURE 6.15

Tableau Corresponding to Corner V

BASIC COEFFICIENT	BASIC VARIABLE	20	10	0	0	0	0	VALUE
		A	C	s_1	s_2	s_3	s_4	
20	A	1	0	0	0	1	0	70
0	s_4	0	0	0	−1	1	1	30
0	s_1	0	0	1	−2	1	0	10
10	C	0	1	0	1	−1	0	20
z_j		20	10	0	10	10	0	
$c_j - z_j$		0	0	0	−10	−10	0	1600

Optimal tableau because all $c_j - z_j \leq 0$

Pivoting from Corner IV

Thus, the completed tableau at corner IV is shown in Figure 6.14. The tableau shown in Figure 6.14 shows that the value of the objective function has increased to 1500. The enter rule says that the objective function should further increase if s_1, the only nonbasic variable with a positive opportunity cost, now becomes basic.

The exit rule tells us to consider the ratios

$$\frac{10}{1}, \frac{30}{1}$$

and since $\frac{10}{1}$ is the minimum we must choose s_3 to exit. The pivot element is 1, as indicated in Figure 6.14. The complete tableau at corner V is shown in Figure 6.15. We now observe that this tableau is optimal because all the opportunity costs (the $c_j - z_j$ entries) are *negative*. This is a special case of the following *stopping rule*, also called the *optimality criterion*:

Optimality Criterion

When all opportunity costs are nonpositive, an optimal corner solution has been obtained.

The optimal solution is obtained by setting the nonbasic variables, in the optimal tableau, to zero and then reading the values of the basic variables (i.e., the "Value" column). Thus, reading from Figure 6.15, we see that

$$(A^* = 70, \quad C^* = 20, \quad s_1^* = 10, \quad s_2^* = 0, \quad s_3^* = 0, \quad s_4^* = 30)$$

and the OV is 1600. This coincides with the optimal solution produced by graphical analysis in Figure 6.1.

6.13
EXTENSIONS TO MORE GENERAL PROBLEMS

The essence of the simplex method, as described above, is:

1. Find any *corner* of the constraint set (which means, find the transformed equations corresponding to some corner). This will be *the initial corner*. Construct the tableau *corresponding to the initial corner*. This is called *phase I* of the method.

248

CHAPTER 6
Linear
Programming:
The Simplex
Method

2. Beginning at the initial corner, pivot from corner to adjacent corner in such a way that the value of the objective function improves at each iteration and so that, therefore, an optimal solution is obtained.

There are several possibilities that may interfere with the successful execution of these steps. These are *difficulties in phase I, infeasible problems, unbounded problems,* and *degenerate problems.* We shall address these circumstances in order.

Difficulties in Phase I/ Artificial Variables

Let us review some of what we have learned thus far. Phase I, as described above, amounts to finding some corner, indeed, *any* corner, for which we can construct the corresponding tableau. At any corner the main body of the tableau represents a special set of equations which are equivalent to the original equations. This special set of equations is what we have been calling the *transformed equations.* The important fact about these equivalent equations is this: They are in a form such that when the nonbasic variables at the corner being considered are set equal to zero, the values of the *basic variables* are obtained directly. From these data in the main body of the tableau we can easily construct the remainder of the tableau, that is the rows z_j and $c_j - z_j$ and the current objective value.

The reason that phase I was so easy for Astro/Cosmo is that the original equations (6.1) through (6.4) were already, without any modification, in the required form. That is

1. At corner I in Figure 6.2 the variables A and C are nonbasic.
2. When A and C are set equal to zero in (6.1)–(6.4), the values of the *basic variables* s_1, s_2, s_3, and s_4 are obtained directly without further manipulation. That is, they are simply read from the RHSs of the original equations. Review (6.1)–(6.4) to verify these statements.

In Astro/Cosmo there is a simple reason for the initial equations already being in the required form. The reason is that each constraint in the original model was of $\leq$ form, and all of the RHS values were nonnegative. This guaranteed that after adding the slack variables the required form was immediately at hand.

Not every set of equations in standard equality constraint form will be as nice as Astro/Cosmo. For example, consider the constraints

$$3x_1 + 4x_2 \geq 6$$
$$2x_1 - 6x_2 \leq 4$$
$$x_1 \geq 0, \qquad x_2 \geq 0$$

The standard equality constraint form contains $m = 2$ equations in $n = 4$ variables. The standard equality constraint form is

$$3x_1 + 4x_2 - s_1 \qquad = 6$$
$$2x_1 - 6x_2 \qquad + s_2 = 4$$
$$x_1 \geq 0, \qquad x_2 \geq 0, \qquad s_1 \geq 0, \qquad s_2 \geq 0$$

If the variables x_1 and x_2 are set equal to zero, we obtain a *unique* solution for the

249

CHAPTER 6
Linear
Programming:
The Simplex
Method

remaining variables, namely

$$s_1 = -6$$

$$s_2 = 4$$

The fact that $n - m$ of the variables could be set equal to zero to give a unique solution for the remaining m variables means, by definition, that the $n - m$ variables are a nonbasic set. That is, (x_1, x_2) are a set of nonbasic variables and (s_1, s_2) are a set of basic variables. Hence, the solution $(x_1 = 0, x_2 = 0, s_1 = -6, s_2 = 4)$ is a *basic solution*. But it is *not a basic feasible solution*, because s_1 is negative. Consequently, it cannot correspond to a corner. (Remember, corners correspond to basic feasible solutions!) Thus, for the equations above we cannot so easily construct an initial tableau.

In summary, then, the Astro/Cosmo example possesses the following *two key properties* which guarantee that the initial tableau can be easily constructed:

When Is Phase I Easy?

Property 1   This is essentially condition (6.9). It says that for a problem in standard equality constraint form, with n variables and m constraints, each constraint must contain a nonnegative variable with the coefficient *plus one* and that variable must appear only in that constraint. Any nonnegative variable with the property that it has coefficient *plus one* and appears in only one equation will, in our exposition, be referred to as a *distinguished variable*. If there are m distinguished variables, Property 1 will be satisfied. In (6.1)–(6.4) the variables s_1, s_2, s_3, and s_4 are *distinguished variables*. That is, the ith slack variable s_i appears in the ith and only in the ith equation and its coefficient in that equation is plus one. Since there are four such variables and four constraints, Property 1 is satisfied. Whenever Property 1 is satisfied, you can see that if we set the remaining (i.e., undistinguished) $n - m$ variables equal to zero, we obtain a *unique* solution for the m distinguished variables. By definition, this means that we have a *basic solution*. For example, consider again the foregoing system of constraints in standard equality form

$$3x_1 + 4x_2 - s_1 = 6$$

$$2x_1 - 6x_2 + s_2 = 4$$

$$x_1 \geq 0, \qquad x_2 \geq 0, \qquad s_1 \geq 0, \qquad s_2 \geq 0$$

A simple, almost trivial, transformation of this system will convert it into an equivalent system with two distinguished variables. See whether you can deduce how to do this. Here is the answer: Multiply the first of the two equations by -1 on both sides of the equality sign. You then obtain the equivalent system

A System with Property 1

$$-3x_1 - 4x_2 + s_1 = -6$$

$$2x_1 - 6x_2 + s_2 = 4$$

$$x_1 \geq 0, \qquad x_2 \geq 0, \qquad s_1 \geq 0, \qquad s_2 \geq 0$$

In this system s_1 and s_2 each have a coefficient of *plus one*. Each variable appears in only one equation and each equation contains one such variable. This means that s_1 and s_2 satisfy the definition of distinguished variables. Property 1 is satisfied. Property

250

CHAPTER 6
Linear
Programming:
The Simplex
Method

1 now allows us to easily find a basic solution. In this example, set the undistinguished variables x_1 and x_2 equal to zero. Then, as previously observed, we obtain the basic solution ($x_1 = 0$, $x_2 = 0$, $s_1 = -6$, $s_2 = 4$). But this is not a basic *feasible* solution. Because we must have a basic feasible solution we also need

Property 2 This is (6.10). It says that the values on the right-hand side of the equality constraints are *nonnegative*. If this property holds *simultaneously with Property 1*, the values of the basic variables (i.e., the distinguished variables) will be the RHS, and since this is nonnegative we will have a basic feasible solution and the initial tableau can be constructed.

Modifying Systems without Both Properties We must now show how a set of original equations that do not satisfy Properties 1 and 2, such as the example above, can be modified. To do this, let us look at another, slightly more complicated, illustration. For example, consider the following LP (a completely general system with $\leq$, $\geq$, $=$ constraints, as well as positive and negative RHSs):

The Original System

$$
\begin{aligned}
\text{Max } 12x_1 &+ 20x_2 + 8x_3 \\
\text{s.t.} \quad 3x_1 \quad &- 2x_3 \geq -2 \\
-4x_1 - x_2 &+ 12x_3 \geq 4 \\
-x_1 \quad &+ 3x_3 \leq -6 \\
3x_1 + 4x_2 &- 6x_3 = -12 \\
x_2 &+ 9x_3 = 31 \\
x_1 \geq 0, \quad x_2 \geq 0, &\quad x_3 \geq 0
\end{aligned}
$$

When this is converted to standard equality form we obtain

$$
\begin{aligned}
\text{Max } 12x_1 &+ 20x_2 + 8x_3 \\
\text{s.t.} \quad 3x_1 \quad - 2x_3 - s_1 \quad &= -2 \quad (6.23) \\
-4x_1 - x_2 + 12x_3 \quad - s_2 \quad &= 4 \quad (6.24) \\
-x_1 + 3x_3 \quad + s_3 &= -6 \quad (6.25) \\
3x_1 + 4x_2 - 6x_3 \quad &= -12 \quad (6.26) \\
x_2 + 9x_3 \quad &= 31 \quad (6.27)
\end{aligned}
$$

$$x_1 \geq 0, \quad x_2 \geq 0, \quad x_3 \geq 0, \quad s_1 \geq 0, \quad s_2 \geq 0, \quad s_3 \geq 0$$

This system of original equations does not satisfy either Property 1 or Property 2—certainly, then, not both properties simultaneously. To deal with such a system, we proceed as follows:

Satisfying Property 2 **Step 1** For each of the equality constraints with a negative RHS, multiply both sides by -1. This will guarantee that Property 2 is satisfied. For example, in the system above

251

CHAPTER 6
Linear
Programming:
The Simplex
Method

we must perform this transformation on (6.23), (6.25), and (6.26). We then obtain the *equivalent* problem:

$$\text{Max } 12x_1 + 20x_2 + 8x_3$$

$$
\begin{array}{llll}
\text{s.t.} & -3x_1 & + 2x_3 + s_1 & = 2 & (6.28) \\
& -4x_1 - x_2 + 12x_3 & - s_2 & = 4 & (6.24) \\
& x_1 \quad - 3x_3 & - s_3 = 6 & & (6.29) \\
& -3x_1 - 4x_2 + 6x_3 & = 12 & & (6.30) \\
& x_2 + 9x_3 & = 31 & & (6.27)
\end{array}
$$

$$x_1 \geq 0, \quad x_2 \geq 0, \quad x_3 \geq 0, \quad s_1 \geq 0, \quad s_2 \geq 0, \quad s_3 \geq 0$$

Satisfying Property 1

Step 2 Add what is termed a nonnegative *artificial variable* to each constraint that does not now, after multiplication by -1 as required in step 1, contain a distinguished variable. (Note that the order of these steps is important!) Each artificial variable is included in the objective function with a very large negative coefficient, denoted for convenience as $-M$. For example, think of $-M$ as meaning "minus a million." The reason for the large negative coefficient will become clear later. However, before pursuing this point, let us, as an example, refer back to the system (6.28), (6.24), (6.29), (6.30), (6.27). Equation (6.28) already contains a distinguished variable, namely s_1. The remaining equations contain no such variable. Why is x_2, which appears in the last equation with coefficient $+1$, not a distinguished variable? Here is the answer: because it appears in other equations as well. Since the last four equations contain no distinguished variables, we must add *an artificial variable* to each one. Doing this, and including the artificial variables, as prescribed, in the objective function, we obtain

The Modified System

$$\text{Max } 12x_1 + 20x_2 + 8x_3 - Ma_1 - Ma_2 - Ma_3 - Ma_4$$

$$
\begin{array}{lll}
\text{s.t.} & -3x_1 \quad + 2x_3 + s_1 & = 2 \quad (6.28) \\
& -4x_1 - x_2 + 12x_3 \quad - s_2 \quad + a_1 & = 4 \quad (6.31) \\
& x_1 \quad - 3x_3 \quad - s_3 \quad + a_2 & = 6 \quad (6.32) \\
& -3x_1 - 4x_2 + 6x_3 \quad + a_3 & = 12 \quad (6.33) \\
& x_2 + 9x_3 \quad + a_4 & = 31 \quad (6.34)
\end{array}
$$

$$x_1 \geq 0, \quad x_2 \geq 0, \quad x_3 \geq 0, \quad s_1 \geq 0, \quad s_2 \geq 0, \quad s_3 \geq 0,$$
$$a_1 \geq 0, \quad a_2 \geq 0, \quad a_3 \geq 0, \quad a_4 \geq 0$$

The artificial variables provide the needed distinguished variables for the last four equations. The initial *basic feasible solution* to this new system is

$$(x_1 = 0, \quad x_2 = 0, \quad x_3 = 0, \quad s_2 = 0, \quad s_3 = 0,$$
$$s_1 = 2, \quad a_1 = 4, \quad a_2 = 6, \quad a_3 = 12, \quad a_4 = 31)$$

252

CHAPTER 6
Linear
Programming:
The Simplex
Method

The five basic variables are the distinguished variables s_1, a_1, a_2, a_3, a_4 and the nonbasic variables are x_1, x_2, x_3, s_2, s_3. *This new problem is not the same as the original one. It is equivalent to the original problem only when all four artificial variables have the value zero.* If we were actually going to attempt to solve the original problem [with constraints (6.23)–(6.27)], we would first set up the initial tableau for the new problem [constraints (6.28) and (6.31)–(6.34)]. We would then pivot on this tableau with the hope that, after a sequence of pivots, all the artificial variables will be *nonbasic* (this is related to the motive for $-M$). Once they are nonbasic, their value is zero and we will then have a valid initial tableau for the original problem and phase I will have been successfully completed.

The Tableau for the Modified System

The initial tableau for the foregoing problem with artificial variables is given in Figure 6.16. Notice how the "Basic Coefficient" column now contains a coefficient $-M$ for each artificial variable in the basis. Also notice how the z_j and $c_j - z_j$ rows are computed using the symbols $-M$ just as if they stood for real numbers.

Given this initial tableau, the next step would be to perform a sequence of pivots in the attempt to drive all artificial variables out of the basis (thereby forcing their value to zero as desired). Since the terms $-M$ represent some very negative number such as "minus a million," and since the simplex method will at each iteration improve (in this example, increase) the value of the objective function whenever possible, the very large negative coefficients on the artificial variables in the objective function will guarantee that these will all be made nonbasic *if possible.*

Finding the Enter Variable

In Figure 6.16 note that the only positive opportunity cost is $8 + 24M$, which means that x_3 would be the enter variable. (The number M is assumed to be so large that any $c_j - z_j$ entry containing $+M$ is positive and any $c_j - z_j$ containing $-M$ is negative.) Now, in Figure 6.16 the exit variable would be obtained by finding the minimum of the ratios

$$\frac{2}{2}, \frac{4}{12}, \frac{12}{6}, \frac{31}{9}$$

Since the minimum is $\frac{4}{12}$, a_1 would be the exit variable and, as shown in Figure 6.16, 12 is the pivot element. From this point on we could follow the usual rules for updating

FIGURE 6.16
Initial Tableau with Artificial Variables

BASIC COEFFICIENT	BASIC VARIABLE	12 x_1	20 x_2	8 x_3	0 s_1	0 s_2	$-M$ a_1	$-M$ a_2	$-M$ a_3	$-M$ a_4	VALUE
0	s_1	-3	0	2	1	0	0	0	0	0	2
$-M$	a_1	-4	-1	(12)	0	-1	1	0	0	0	4
$-M$	a_2	1	0	-3	0	0	0	1	0	0	6
$-M$	a_3	-3	-4	6	0	0	0	0	1	0	12
$-M$	a_4	0	1	9	0	0	0	0	0	1	31
z_j		$6M$	$4M$	$-24M$	0	M	$-M$	$-M$	$-M$	$-M$	
$c_j - z_j$		$12 - 6M$	$20 - 4M$	$8 + 24M$	0	$-M$	0	0	0	0	$-53M$

Tableau with four artificial columns

successive tableaux. Now here is an important point:

The derivation of sensitivity information will be discussed in the appendices to this chapter, where it will be seen that the artificial columns play an important role, from the sensitivity point of view, in the final tableau. These sensitivity calculations are obviously important, but let us not lose sight of the fact that in real-world problem solving the computer does them for you. Of course, the computer does it all for you, including the addition of artificial variables as needed to perform phase I and then the sequence of pivots to optimality. The point here is that constraints on space do not allow us to give a detailed exposition of all aspects of the process. We have chosen to list the steps carefully from the initial problem to the optimal solution, including phase I as required. The appendices provide a more terse analysis of the *postoptimality*, or *sensitivity*, calculations. This does not reflect any attempt to give less emphasis to sensitivity *interpretations*, for as we have discussed at length in previous chapters, it is the sensitivity considerations that are often at the heart of managerial decision making. However, the purpose of this chapter is to understand the essentials of the simplex method per se, so it is these calculations that we describe in detail.

Now, proceeding with our main thrust, the goal, after setting up the initial tableau, is to drive all artificial variables out of the basis. When, and if, this is accomplished phase I will be complete and we will have an initial basic feasible solution to our original problem. The pivoting algorithm then continues to proceed as formerly described. Later in this section we will consider the possibility that *not all* of the artificial variables can be driven out of the basis. It will be shown that in this case the original problem is infeasible.

A Complete Example: PROTRAC, Inc. Revisited

Figure 6.16 has now served its purpose, namely to demonstrate the initial tableau for a problem with artificial variables. Rather than continuing to pivot on this tableau, we choose to return to a problem we have already visited—the **PROTRAC**, Inc. model. We shall carry out, by hand, the complete solution to this problem. This will give you the opportunity to check your understanding of how the simplex algorithm is applied to the general LP. Try to verify each step of the algorithm. The problem is

$$
\begin{aligned}
\text{Max } & 5000E + 4000F \\
\text{s.t.} \quad & E + F \geq 5 \\
& E - 3F \leq 0 \\
& 10E + 15F \leq 150 \\
& 20E + 10F \leq 160 \\
& 30E + 10F \geq 135 \\
& E, F \geq 0
\end{aligned}
$$

254

CHAPTER 6
Linear
Programming:
The Simplex
Method

We have previously discussed the graphic solution to this problem, shown in Figure 5.5, and the computer output is shown in Figure 5.6. Thus, doing the hand calculations will provide our third solution to this problem.

The first step in applying the simplex method is to convert to standard equality constraint form

$$
\begin{aligned}
\text{Max } & 5000E + 4000F \\
\text{s.t.} \quad & E + F - s_1 && = 5 \\
& E - 3F + s_2 && = 0 \\
& 10E + 15F + s_3 && = 150 \\
& 20E + 10F + s_4 && = 160 \\
& 30E + 10F - s_5 && = 135 \\
& E, F, s_1, s_2, s_3, s_4, s_5 \geq 0
\end{aligned}
$$

The RHS is nonnegative and hence Property 2 is already satisfied. However, in these original equations only the second, third, and fourth constraints contain distinguished variables. Therefore, to satisfy Property 1, we must add artificial variables to the first and last constraints. This gives

**Modified
Form for
Phase I**

$$
\begin{aligned}
\text{Max } & 5000E + 4000F - Ma_1 - Ma_2 \\
\text{s.t.} \quad & E + F - s_1 + a_1 && = 5 \\
& E - 3F + s_2 && = 0 \\
& 10E + 15F + s_3 && = 150 \\
& 20E + 10F + s_4 && = 160 \\
& 30E + 10F - s_5 + a_2 && = 135 \\
& E, F, s_1, s_2, s_3, s_4, s_5, a_1, a_2 \geq 0
\end{aligned}
$$

FIGURE 6.17
Initial Tableau for PROTRAC, Inc.

BASIC COEFFICIENT	BASIC VARIABLE	5000 E	4000 F	0 s_1	0 s_2	0 s_3	0 s_4	0 s_5	$-M$ a_1	$-M$ a_2	VALUE
$-M$	a_1	1	1	-1	0	0	0	0	1	0	5
0	s_2	①	-3	0	1	0	0	0	0	0	0
0	s_3	10	15	0	0	1	0	0	0	0	150
0	s_4	20	10	0	0	0	1	0	0	0	160
$-M$	a_2	30	10	0	0	0	0	-1	0	1	135
z_j		$-31M$	$-11M$	M	0	0	0	M	$-M$	$-M$	
$c_j - z_j$		5000 $+31M$	4000 $+11M$	$-M$	0	0	0	$-M$	0	0	$-140M$

FIGURE 6.18
First Updated Tableau

BASIC COEFFICIENT	BASIC VARIABLE	5000 E	4000 F	0 s_1	0 s_2	0 s_3	0 s_4	0 s_5	$-M$ a_1	$-M$ a_2	VALUE
$-M$	a_1	0	④	-1	-1	0	0	0	1	0	5
5000	E	1	-3	0	1	0	0	0	0	0	0
0	s_3	0	45	0	-10	1	0	0	0	0	150
0	s_4	0	70	0	-20	0	1	0	0	0	160
$-M$	a_2	0	100	0	-30	0	0	-1	0	1	135
z_j		5000	$-15,000$ $-104M$	M	5000 $+31M$	0	0	M	$-M$	$-M$	
$c_j - z_j$		0	$19,000$ $+104M$	$-M$	-5000 $-31M$	0	0	$-M$	0	0	$-140M$

FIGURE 6.19
Second Updated Tableau

BASIC COEFFICIENT	BASIC VARIABLE	5000 E	4000 F	0 s_1	0 s_2	0 s_3	0 s_4	0 s_5	$-M$ a_1	$-M$ a_2	VALUE
4000	F	0	1	$-\frac{1}{4}$	$-\frac{1}{4}$	0	0	0	$\frac{1}{4}$	0	$\frac{5}{4}$
5000	E	1	0	$-\frac{3}{4}$	$\frac{1}{4}$	0	0	0	$\frac{3}{4}$	0	$\frac{15}{4}$
0	s_3	0	0	$\frac{45}{4}$	$\frac{5}{4}$	1	0	0	$-\frac{45}{4}$	0	$\frac{375}{4}$
0	s_4	0	0	$\frac{70}{4}$	$-\frac{10}{4}$	0	1	0	$-\frac{70}{4}$	0	$\frac{290}{4}$
$-M$	a_2	0	0	㉕	-5	0	0	-1	-25	1	10
z_j		5000	4000	-4750 $-25M$	250 $+5M$	0	0	M	4750 $+25M$	$-M$	
$c_j - z_j$		0	0	4750 $+25M$	-250 $-5M$	0	0	$-M$	-4750 $-26M$	0	$95\,000/4$ $-10M$

Pivoting in Phase I We now have five distinguished variables, a nonnegative RHS (note that the zero value for the second RHS is permissible), and hence can easily construct the initial tableau as shown in Figure 6.17. The most positive opportunity cost is $5000 + 31M$, so we choose E to enter the basis. The minimum of the ratios

$$\frac{5}{1}, \frac{0}{1}, \frac{150}{10}, \frac{160}{20}, \frac{135}{30}$$

is $\frac{0}{1}$, which means that s_2 leaves the basis and hence 1 is the pivot element. The updated tableau is given in Figure 6.18. In Figure 6.18 the only positive opportunity cost is $19,000 + 104M$, which means that F enters the basis. The minimum of the ratios

$$\frac{5}{4}, \frac{150}{45}, \frac{160}{70}, \frac{135}{100}$$

is $\frac{5}{4}$, which means that a_1 leaves the basis, and hence 4 is the pivot element. The updated tableau is given in Figure 6.19. In this figure we could choose to omit the a_1 column since the artificial variable a_1 has now been driven to zero. However, in order to obtain sensitivity information we shall include the artificial variables in each successive tableau. The only positive opportunity cost is now $4750 + 25M$, which means that

256

CHAPTER 6
Linear
Programming:
The Simplex
Method

s_1 enters the basis. The minimum of the ratios

$$\left(\tfrac{375}{4}\right)/\left(\tfrac{45}{4}\right), \left(\tfrac{290}{4}\right)/\left(\tfrac{70}{4}\right), \tfrac{10}{25}$$

is $10/25$, which means that a_2 leaves the basis, and hence 25 is the pivot element. The updated tableau is given in Figure 6.20. At this point both artificial variables have been driven out of the basis and therefore phase I is complete. Since s_2 and s_5 are the nonbasic variables, this tableau corresponds to the southwest corner of the constraint set in Figure 5.5, at which the market balance (constraint ②), and contractual labor (constraint ⑤) constraints are active.

FIGURE 6.20

Phase I Is Complete

BASIC COEFFICIENT	BASIC VARIABLE	5000 E	4000 F	0 s_1	0 s_2	0 s_3	0 s_4	0 s_5	$-M$ a_1	$-M$ a_2	VALUE
4000	F	0	1	0	-0.30	0	0	-0.01	0	0.01	1.35
5000	E	1	0	0	0.10	0	0	-0.03	0	0.03	4.05
0	s_3	0	0	0	(3.5)	1	0	0.45	0	-0.45	89.25
0	s_4	0	0	0	1	0	1	0.70	0	-0.70	65.50
0	s_1	0	0	1	$-\tfrac{1}{5}$	0	0	$-\tfrac{1}{25}$	-1	$\tfrac{1}{25}$	0.40
z_j		5000	4000	0	-700	0	0	-190	0	190	
$c_j - z_j$		0	0	0	700	0	0	190	$-M$	-190	25,650

Pivoting in Phase II

The most positive opportunity cost is 700, so we choose s_2 to enter the basis. The minimum of the ratios—$4.05/0.10$, $89.25/3.5$, $65.5/1$—is $89.25/3.5$, which means that s_3 leaves the basis, and hence 3.5 is the pivot element. Thus, the new nonbasic variables are s_3 and s_5. This gives the corner in Figure 5.5 at which the contractual labor (constraint ⑤) and the department A (constraint ③) are active. The tableau is shown in Figure 6.21.

The only positive opportunity cost is 100, which means that s_5 enters the basis. The minimum of the ratios

$$9/(0.2/7), 25.5/(0.9/7), 40/\left(\tfrac{4}{7}\right)$$

FIGURE 6.21

Contractual Labor and Department A are Active

BASIC COEFFICIENT	BASIC VARIABLE	5000 E	4000 F	0 s_1	0 s_2	0 s_3	0 s_4	0 s_5	$-M$ a_1	$-M$ a_2	VALUE
4000	F	0	1	0	0	0.3/3.5	0	0.2/7	0	$-0.2/7$	9
5000	E	1	0	0	0	$-0.1/3.5$	0	$-0.3/7$	0	0.3/7	1.50
0	s_2	0	0	0	1	$-1/3.5$	0	0.9/7	0	$-0.9/7$	25.5
0	s_4	0	0	0	0	$-1/3.5$	1	(4/7)	0	$-4/7$	40
0	s_1	0	0	1	0	1/17.5	0	$-12.5/875$	-1	12.5/875	5.50
z_j		5000	4000	0	0	200	0	-100	0	100	
$c_j - z_j$		0	0	0	0	-200	0	$+100$	$-M$	$-M \to 100$	43,500

257

CHAPTER 6
Linear
Programming:
The Simplex
Method

is $40/(\frac{4}{7})$, which means that s_4 leaves the basis, and hence $\frac{4}{7}$ is the pivot element. Now that s_3 and s_4 are nonbasic, we know from Figure 5.5 that the optimal corner is obtained. The updated tableau is given in Figure 6.22.

The fact that there is no positive opportunity cost tells us that this tableau is optimal. Hence the optimal solution is

$$(F^* = 7, \qquad E^* = 4.5, \qquad s_2^* = 16.5, \qquad s_5^* = 70, \qquad s_1^* = 6.5, \qquad s_3^* = 0, \qquad s_4^* = 0)$$

and the OV is 50,500. This coincides with the information given on the computer printout shown in Figure 5.6.

The effort required to solve this problem by hand will lead you to appreciate the fact that computers routinely solve problems in thousands of variables and hundreds of constraints in seconds.

Infeasible Problems

A linear program is *infeasible* if there is no solution which simultaneously satisfies all the constraints and nonnegativity conditions. This means that the constraint set is empty. A geometric interpretation of infeasible problems has already been presented in Section 3.8. It would be well to review that discussion at this time.

In terms of the simplex procedure, if phase I can be successfully completed, the original problem cannot be infeasible, for completion of phase I produces an extreme point of the constraint set of the original problem. This implies that that constraint set cannot be empty.

The signal for infeasibility is that we obtain a tableau with the properties that

Signal for Infeasibility

1. All opportunity costs are *nonpositive* (i.e., the stopping, or *optimality*, *criterion*, has been encountered).
2. One or more artificial variables remains in the solution at a *positive level*. That is, one or more artificial variables remains in the basis and the associated entry in the "Value" column is positive.

It is worth pointing out that if all the constraints in the original problem are inequalities, and if (1) each $\le$ constraint has a nonnegative RHS and (2) each $\ge$ constraint has a nonpositive RHS, the problem cannot be infeasible, for the origin will satisfy all the constraints. For such a problem, after conversion to standard equality constraint form and then changing signs as required in step 1, the slack and surplus variables will

FIGURE 6.22
Optimal Tableau

BASIC COEFFICIENT	BASIC VARIABLE	5000 E	4000 F	0 s_1	0 s_2	0 s_3	0 s_4	0 s_5	$-M$ a_1	$-M$ a_2	VALUE
4000	F	0	1	0	0	0.1	-0.05	0	0	0	7
5000	E	1	0	0	0	-0.05	0.075	0	0	0	4.5
0	s_2	0	0	0	1	0.35	-0.225	0	0	0	16.5
0	s_5	0	0	0	0	-0.5	1.75	1	0	-1	70
0	s_1	0	0	1	0	0.05	0.025	0	-1	0	6.5
z_j		5000	4000	0	0	150	175	0	0	0	
$c_j - z_j$		0	0	0	0	-150	-175	0	$-M$	$-M$	50,500

258

CHAPTER 6
Linear
Programming:
The Simplex
Method

all be distinguished variables. Hence, for such a problem (as with Astro/Cosmo) the initial tableau can be directly set up without the inclusion of artificial variables.

As a final point, we recall from Section 3.8 that infeasibility is not a real-world phenomenon. That is, no correctly formulated real-world problem can be infeasible. Infeasibility is a mathematical anomaly introduced by the analyst. Either the constraints are too tight, so tight that not all of them can be simultaneously satisfied, or the analyst has made a clerical error in entering the data to the computer.

If you begin with an infeasible problem, then phase I of the simplex method will always detect this, and the computer will tell you that the problem is infeasible.

Unbounded Problems

A linear programming problem is *unbounded* if the objective function can be arbitrarily improved over the feasible region. This implies that the feasible region must also be unbounded.

Unbounded problems were also discussed in Section 3.8. There the geometric analysis was given and it was also stated that unboundedness is not a real-world phenomenon. No one has yet discovered a way to make infinite profits. Unboundedness is another mathematical anomaly introduced by either incorrect formulation (e.g., not enough constraints) or by errors in data entry.

Signal of Unboundedness

The simplex signal for an unbounded problem, when this is the case, occurs in phase II (i.e., after all artificial variables have been driven to zero). The signal is (1) a column with a positive opportunity cost and (2) all entries in the main body of the tableau, in that column, being ≤ 0. Suppose, for example, that the column headed by the variable x_j gives such a signal. Then statements (1) and (2) imply that as x_j (currently nonbasic, since all basic variables have zero opportunity cost) is made positive, holding all other nonbasic variables at zero, the objective function will be increased (at a constant rate given by the opportunity cost) while no basic variable will decrease. Thus, this can be done indefinitely without forcing any of the basic variables to zero.

Degenerate Problems

We know that a degenerate corner is one at which there are fewer than m positive basic variables, where m is the number of constraints in the model and hence the number of rows in the main body of the tableau. Thus, a degenerate corner will be encountered when the tableau shows a zero in the "Value" column. When this happens in the tableau, it is possible that the variable that we are trying to enter will come into the basis at zero level and hence in this pivot we remain at the same corner, merely changing the basic set, and the value of the objective function does not change. This is illustrated by the tableaux for the **PROTRAC**, Inc. model shown in Figures 6.17 and 6.18. At the corner corresponding to Figure 6.17 we see a degenerate solution, since at this corner the value of the basic variable s_2 is zero. The nonbasic variable E satisfies the entry criterion and s_2 with corresponding ratio zero is the exit variable. However, you can see in Figure 6.18 that E has entered at the level zero and the value of the objective function has not improved on this pivot. It has remained the same. A zero variable has left the basis, a new variable has entered at the level zero, and in short, the values of *all* variables have remained the same (hence, the corner has not changed). This phenomenon can occur for the reason that more than one set of basic variables is associated with a degenerate corner. This was discussed in connection with Figures 6.3 and 6.4.

In the case of the **PROTRAC**, Inc. model, although degeneracy was encountered, it did not cause a problem and the algorithm proceeded with no special provision for this phenomenon. What could happen in theory is that the algorithm could move back and forth among the several sets of basic variables at a degenerate corner, thus causing

259

CHAPTER 6
Linear
Programming:
The Simplex
Method

what is termed a cycling phenomenon. This rarely occurs in practice, although it is possible theoretically.

It has been shown that cycling can be avoided with certainty if the following provision is appended to the exit rule. Recall that the exit variable is identified by starting at the top of the "Value" column and computing prescribed ratios to determine a minimum ratio.

Whenever a tie occurs in the ratios for the exit variable, choose as the pivot row the first (i.e., the uppermost) row that produced the minimum ratio.

With this rule cycling will always be avoided and the simplex method becomes a perfect algorithm in the following sense. The simplex algorithm will always terminate in a finite number of steps in one of the following states:

1. You obtain an infeasibility signal.
2. You obtain an unbounded signal.
3. You obtain an optimal solution.

6.14
ALTERNATIVE OPTIMA

Recall that the optimality signal for the simplex tableau is that all entries in the last row (the opportunity costs) are ≤ 0.

When you encounter an optimal tableau with a zero entry in the last row, under a *nonbasic* column, that variable can be brought into the basis without changing the objective value. If the optimal solution is *nondegenerate*, the variable brought into the basis will be positive. This means that a new corner is obtained and hence an alternative optimal solution exists.

The geometric interpretation of alternative optima was discussed in Section 3.5. This phenomenon occurs when more than one corner of the feasible region lies on the optimal objective function contour. This implies that there is more than one optimal basic feasible solution and infinitely many nonbasic optimal solutions.

6.15
THE SIMPLEX METHOD FOR A MIN MODEL

All of the development in this chapter has pertained to solving a Max LP model. The modifications required to solve a Min model are very simple. Either of two possible approaches can be taken:

Approach 1   Take the negative of the objective function and solve the problem as though it were a Max model. This trick works because for any function $f(x)$, any point that minimizes $f(x)$ will also maximize $-f(x)$. Thus, by taking the negative of a Min objective function, and then solving as though it were a Max model, we obtain the correct optimal solution for the original Min model. To obtain the correct OV for the original Min model we multiply the OV for the Max model by -1.

Approach 2 Keep the Min objective as given, but artificial variables must appear in the objective function with coefficient $+M$. Also, reverse the entry rule and the stopping criterion. In other words, for a Min model enter the variable with the most negative opportunity cost. An optimal tableau is obtained when all opportunity costs are nonnegative.

_____ 6.16
NOTES ON IMPLEMENTATION

How Much Storage? The simplex algorithm as presented in this chapter gives, in most respects, the essential ideas originally employed in solving linear programs. However, iin current practice, some of the details have been considerably refined in order to produce greater computational efficiency, which generally means greater capabilities for the successful solution of larger and larger models. In particular, most LP software systems for today's modern computers employ what is called the "revised simplex method." The details of this are beyond our introductory scope, but it can be stated that the main difference between the procedure given in the text and the revised simplex method has to do with the way in which the tableau is represented in computer memory. The major reason for improving this representation is to exploit special structures in the LP data, such as sparsity of the data matrix. As an illustration, suppose that the problem has 500 rows (constraints) and 1000 columns (variables). If the original algorithm as herein presented is used, the tableau would require one coefficient for each variable in each constraint, a total of 500,000 numbers. But most of these coefficients are typically 0. It is not unusual for real problems of this size to have only about four nonzero entries per column, which implies there are only about 4000 pieces of nonzero data. It is this sort of special structure that is exploited in current software to cut down on storage requirements and hence to give greater computing power. As a result, modern batch processing codes can handle problems with thousands of rows and essentially an unlimited number of columns.

As this discussion suggests, the continuing development of sophisticated LP software is a special field in its own right and involves a solid background in both computer science and numerical analysis.

How Many Pivots? In concluding this section, we recall from Section 5.6 that, according to empirical folklore, the number of pivots required to solve an LP problem is roughly from m to $3m$, where m is the number of constraints. The number of pivots, of course, is a measure of how much computer time is involved in solving the problem. This "m to $3m$ rule" explains why, in practical applications, one typically attempts to formulate the LP model with as few constraints as possible, and with less concern given to the number of variables.

_____ 6.17
SUMMARY

In this chapter we have shown how the simplex method is used to solve an LP problem in standard equality constraint form (all constraints are equalities, all variables nonnegative). It was seen that the simplex method moves from corner to adjacent corner of the feasible region. Associated with each corner is a basic feasible solution and a simplex tableau which represents this solution, in terms of the transformed equations at the corner. The move from one corner to another is performed algebraically by performing the pivot operation on the tableau of data. In order to begin the method it may be necessary to add artificial variables to the problem.

Here is a detailed, step-by-step outline of how to apply the simplex method:

Steps of the Simplex Method

- **Step 1:** Cast the original problem into standard equality constraint form by introducing slack and surplus variables as required. If the original model is a Min problem, multiply the objective function by -1 and convert to Max.

- **Step 2:** Make all the right-hand sides nonnegative by multiplying both sides of the equalities by -1 wherever required.

- **Step 3:** Add artificial variables as necessary to obtain m distinguished variables. Each such variable, by definition, appears in only one constraint and has a coefficient, in that constraint, of $+1$. Each artificial variable is included in the objective function with coefficient $-M$, which stands for a very negative number ("minus a million").

- **Step 4:** Set up the main body of the initial tableau. This is simply a tabular representation of the equations coming out of step 3.

- **Step 5:** Compute the z_j row and the $c_j - z_j$ row, the latter being the opportunity costs of not having another unit of the variable x_j in the solution. Also compute the current value of the objective function. Now choose the entering nonbasic variable to be the one whose opportunity cost is most positive. (If there is no positive $c_j - z_j$, the current solution is optimal.)

- **Step 6:** The pivot column is defined in step 5. Choose the pivot row by finding the Min of the ratios of "Value" entries to positive entries in the pivot column. Then update the main body of the tableau by writing in the new basic variable, filling in the pivot row and the basic columns, and then pivoting on the remaining data.

- **Step 7:** Fill in the new z_j row, $c_j - z_j$ row, and the new value of the objective function.

- **Step 8:** Test for optimality: All data in the last row are ≤ 0.

- **Step 9:** If not optimal, update again. If optimal and at least one artificial variable remains in the basis at a positive level, the original problem is infeasible. If optimal and no artificial variables remain in the basis, you have the optimal solution to the original problem. As soon as all artificial variables have been removed from the basis, phase I is complete.

- **Step 10:** As each iteration after phase I is complete, test for an unbounded problem: a positive entry in the last row and all elements ≤ 0 in the corresponding column of the main body of the tableau.

The sequence of operations described above will lead you to the solution of any LP problem. In concluding, however, let us mention the fact that the efficient computational implementation of the simplex method is quite complicated and is a topic worthy of study in its own right. Nevertheless, at the heart of the simplex method is the above-described tabular representation of extreme points and the concept of pivoting in order to update from one basic feasible solution to another.

6.18
KEY TERMS

VERTEX. A corner of an LP constraint set.

EXTREME POINT. A brash or zealous assertion made for rhetorical purposes; in the LP context extreme point and vertex are synonymous.

PHASE I. The first part of the simplex method, designed to find the transformed equations corresponding to any initial corner of the constraint set of the given problem.

ITERATION. In the simplex method, the move from one corner to an adjacent corner.

PIVOT. Synonymous with iteration.

ORIGINAL EQUATIONS. The m constraint equations in the standard equality constraint form of the original problem with n variables, including decision variables, surplus variables, and slack variables, and where $m < n$.

262

CHAPTER 6
Linear
Programming:
The Simplex
Method

OPTIMAL SOLUTION. A solution that is optimal for the given problem.

SOLUTION. Although in many contexts the terms "solution" and "optimal solution" are synonymous, in the study of the simplex method the term "solution" means any solution (i.e., set of values for the n variables), not necessarily optimal, to the original equations.

FEASIBLE SOLUTION. A solution for which all variables are nonnegative.

BASIC SOLUTION. A solution to m simultaneous linear equations in n unknowns, $m < n$, with the property that $n - m$ of the variables have the value zero and the values of the remaining m variables are uniquely determined; obtained when a set of nonbasic variables are assigned the value zero.

BASIC FEASIBLE SOLUTION. A basic solution for which the values of all variables are nonnegative; corresponds to a corner of the LP feasible region.

NONBASIC VARIABLES. A set of $n - m$ variables such that, when these variables are set equal to zero, the values of the remaining variables are uniquely determined.

BASIC VARIABLES. Given a set of $n - m$ nonbasic variables, the remaining m variables are termed basic.

BASIC SET. A set of basic variables (refers to the set of variables, not their values).

NONBASIC SET. A set of nonbasic variables (refers to the set of variables).

NONDEGENERATE BASIC FEASIBLE SOLUTION. A basic feasible solution with exactly m positive variables (hence exactly $n - m$ zero variables).

DEGENERATE BASIC FEASIBLE SOLUTION. A basic feasible solution with fewer than m positive variables (hence more than $n - m$ zero variables).

TRANSFORMED EQUATIONS. Corresponding to each corner of the feasible region is a set of "transformed equations" which represent the basic feasible solution at that corner. These equations are equivalent to the original equations and have the following special form: (1) Each basic variable appears in one and only one equation and in that equation its coefficient is $+1$, and (2) Only constant terms are on the right-hand side of the equalities and they are nonnegative.

SUBSTITUTION COEFFICIENTS. The data in a nonbasic column which shows the reductions that must occur (so that the original equations remain satisfied) in the current values (at a given corner) of the basic variables when the nonbasic variable is incremented a unit and all other nonbasic variables held fixed at zero.

TABLEAU. A tabular representation of the transformed equations plus an opportunity cost row; there is a tableau corresponding to each corner of the feasible region.

BASIC COEFFICIENTS. The coefficients in the objective function which correspond to a set of basic variables.

OPPORTUNITY COST. A term applying to the nonbasic variables at each corner; it is the cost of *not* incrementing a nonbasic variable by a unit (while keeping all other nonbasic variables at zero and allowing basic variables to adjust appropriately); this is equivalent to the improvement in OV obtained per unit increment in the nonbasic variable.

ENTER VARIABLE. At the current corner, the nonbasic variable that is chosen to become basic in the move to the next corner.

EXIT VARIABLE. At the current corner, the basic variable that is chosen to become nonbasic at the next corner.

OPTIMALITY CRITERION. The criterion for recognizing the tableau corresponding to an optimal corner, this is, for a Max problem, all opportunity costs ≤ 0.

DISTINGUISHED VARIABLE. A nonnegative variable that appears in only one constraint and has coefficient $+1$.

ARTIFICIAL VARIABLE. In phase I, a variable added to a constraint lacking a distinguished variable.

MAJOR CONCEPTS QUIZ ————————————————

True–False   **1. T   F**   Every basic solution to the original equations corresponds to a corner of the constraint set.

2. T   F   At a nondegenerate corner there will be more than one set of basic variables.

263

CHAPTER 6
Linear
Programming:
The Simplex
Method

3. T F At a degenerate corner the basic variables are all positive.

4. T F Basic solutions that are not feasible will never be encountered in phase II of the simplex method.

5. T F Each constraint in the standard equality form model (excluding nonnegativity conditions) is represented by a row of the simplex tableau.

6. T F Since the z_j row gives the *loss* of profit (in a Max model) resulting from adding one unit of the column variable to the current solution, we can select the best variable to add to the current solution by choosing any column with a negative z_j value.

7. T F For a Max LP model, it is the enter rule that guarantees a nondecreasing objective function in each move.

8. T F The enter rule can be modified to prevent cycling.

9. T F In solving a Min model, as opposed to a Max model, the enter rule and optimality criterion are the only differences.

10. T F You can solve either the primal or the dual with the simplex method, but not both.

11. T F Degeneracy will result whenever a tie occurs in the minimum ratio for the enter rule.

12. T F An unbounded problem is discovered in phase I.

Multiple Choice

13. Every simplex iteration for a Max problem replaces a variable in the current basis with another variable which has
    a. a larger per unit profitability as shown in the c_j (i.e., objective function coefficient) row
    b. a positive $c_j - z_j$ value
    c. the smallest $c_j - z_j$ value
    d. any negative $c_j - z_j$ value

14. Every tableau in the simplex method
    a. exhibits a solution to the original equations
    b. exhibits a basic feasible solution to the equations in the standard equality form of the model
    c. corresponds to an extreme point of the constraint set
    d. exhibits a set of transformed equations
    e. all of the above

15. Artificial variables
    a. are used to aid in finding an initial solution
    b. are used in phase I
    c. can be used to find optimal dual prices in the final tableau
    d. all of the above

16. The signal for optimality in a Max model is
    a. $c_j - z_j \leq 0$, for all j
    b. $z_j \leq 0$, for all j
    c. $c_j - z_j > 0$, for all j

17. Suppose that in a nondegenerate optimal tableau a slack variable s_2 is basic for the second constraint, whose RHS is b_2. This means that
    a. the original problem is infeasible
    b. all of b_2 is used up in the optimal solution
    c. both the dual price and the optimal value of the dual variable, for the second constraint, are zero
    d. a better OV could be obtained by increasing b_2

18. Which of the following is not true of the simplex method?
    a. At each iteration, the objective value either stays the same or improves.
    b. It indicates an unbounded or infeasible problem.
    c. It signals optimality.
    d. It converges in at most m steps, where m is the number of constraints.

264

CHAPTER 6
Linear
Programming:
The Simplex
Method

19. Infeasibility is discovered
   a. in computing the enter variable
   b. in computing the exit variable
   c. in phase I

20. Cycling
   a. can always be prevented
   b. is a real-world concern
   c. will cause more pivots to occur before termination

Answers

1. F	**6.** F	**11.** F	**16.** a
2. F	**7.** T	**12.** F	**17.** c
3. F	**8.** F	**13.** b	**18.** d
4. T	**9.** T	**14.** d	**19.** c
5. T	**10.** F	**15.** d	**20.** a

PROBLEMS

6-1. Consider, as appropriate, (i) a system of m linear equations in n unknowns and (ii) an LP. Pertaining to the appropriate system, match each of the following terms with the correct definition below.

(a) Feasible region.

(b) Solution.

(c) Basic variables.

(d) Basis.

(e) Feasible solution.

(f) Nonbasic variables.

(g) Basic feasible solution.

(h) Substitution coefficient.

(i) Basic solution.

(j) Artificial variable.

(k) Opportunity cost.

(1) A set of m variables whose values (in order that the equations be satisfied) are uniquely determined when the values of the remaining variables are set to zero.

(2) A variable added to a constraint in order to obtain easily an initial tableau.

(3) The solution (to the equations) obtained when the nonbasic variables are set equal to zero.

(4) The set of points that satisfies all the constraints and nonnegativity conditions for the original problem.

(5) A basic solution in which no variable has a negative value.

(6) Any set of values of the n variables such that the equations are satisfied.

(7) A set of basic variables.

(8) The trade-off between an entering nonbasic variable and a basic variable.

(9) Any set of nonnegative values of the n variables such that the equations are satisfied.

(10) Improvement in OV obtained per unit increase in a nonbasic variable.

(11) $n - m$ variables which, when assigned values of zero, uniquely determine the values of the remaining variables (such that the equations are satisfied).

6-2. Consider the partial initial simplex tableau shown in Figure 6.23 for a Max model.

(a) Write the original LP corresponding to this tableau.

(b) Complete the tableau.

265

CHAPTER 6
Linear
Programming:
The Simplex
Method

FIGURE 6.23

BASIC COEFFICIENT	BASIC VARIABLE	4 x_1	22 x_2	26 x_3	0 s_1	0 s_2	0 s_3	VALUE
		2	1	0	1	0	0	38
		0	3	1	0	1	0	32
		3	0	−1	0	0	1	16
z_j								
$c_j - z_j$								

(c) What is the initial set of basic variables?

(d) What is the initial set of nonbasic variables?

(e) Give the coordinates of the corner of the feasible region that corresponds to the initial basic feasible solution.

(f) What is the enter variable?

(g) What is the exit variable?

(h) What is the pivot element?

(i) Solve the problem using the simplex method.

6-3. Consider the partial simplex tableau shown in Figure 6.24 for a Max model.

(a) Write the transformed equations corresponding to this tableau.

(b) What are the basic variables?

(c) What are the nonbasic variables?

(d) Complete the tableau.

(e) Is the current solution optimal? If not, which variable should enter and which should exit?

(f) Use the simplex method to finish solving the problem.

6-4. Consider the following LP:

$$\text{Max } 3x_1 + 4x_2$$

$$\text{s.t.} \quad 2x_1 + 4x_2 \leq 12$$

$$6x_1 + 4x_2 \leq 24$$

$$x_1 \geq 0, \qquad x_2 \geq 0$$

FIGURE 6.24

BASIC COEFFICIENT	BASIC VARIABLE	20 x_1	30 x_2	25 x_3	0 s_1	0 s_2	0 s_3	VALUE
		3	0	1	1	−2	0	100
		1	1	0	0	1	0	200
		−5	0	0	−2	4	1	400
z_j								
$c_j - z_j$								

266

CHAPTER 6
Linear
Programming:
The Simplex
Method

(a) Either by algebraic or geometric analysis, find all basic solutions.

(b) Which of these correspond to extreme points of the feasible region?

6-5. Consider the following LP:

$$\text{Max } 5x_1 + 6x_2$$

$$\text{s.t.} \quad 3x_1 + 6x_2 \le 8$$

$$6x_1 + 4x_2 \le 24$$

$$x_1 \ge 0, \qquad x_2 \ge 0$$

(a) By either algebraic or geometric analysis, find all basic solutions.

(b) Which of these correspond to extreme points of the feasible region?

6-6. Consider an LP in standard equality constraint form. There are three constraints and four variables.

(a) What is the maximum number of basic solutions to this problem?

(b) Need it be true that there are, in fact, this number of basic solutions?

(c) Suppose that the problem has an optimal solution. Can you say anything about the number of basic feasible solutions?

HINT: Can you give an upper and a lower bound?

6-7. Answer parts (a), (b), and (c) of Problem 6-6 for an LP in two constraints and four variables.

6-8. Each of the following tableaux is associated with a Max model. One or more of the following descriptions applies to each tableau: (1) optimal; (2) shows problem is unbounded; (3) shows problem is infeasible; (4) current corner is degenerate; (5) there are alternative optima; (6) the problem is feasible and the current corner is not optimal. Label each tableau with the applicable descriptor.

(a)

BASIC COEFFICIENT	BASIC VARIABLE	9 x_1	6 x_2	0 s_1	0 s_2	VALUE
9	x_1	1	$\frac{1}{3}$	$\frac{1}{3}$	0	10
0	s_2	0	3	$-\frac{1}{2}$	1	12
	z_j	9	3	3	0	
	$c_j - z_j$	0	3	-3	0	90

feasible not optimal enter x_2

(b)

BASIC COEFFICIENT	BASIC VARIABLE	3 x_1	6 x_2	8 x_3	0 s_1	0 s_2	0 s_3	VALUE
6	x_2	$\frac{1}{2}$	1	0	$-\frac{1}{2}$	0	$\frac{2}{3}$	100
8	x_3	0	0	1	$\frac{1}{2}$	0	$-\frac{1}{4}$	100
0	s_2	0	0	0	$-\frac{1}{2}$	1	$-\frac{1}{3}$	200
	z_j	3	6	8	1	0	2	
	$c_j - z_j$	0	0	0	-1	0	-2	1400

alternative optimal solution x_1 is NBV may be entered into sol. & obj value will so unchanged

267

CHAPTER 6
Linear
Programming:
The Simplex
Method

(c)

degenerate opt sol.
By $s_2 = 0$

BASIC COEFFICIENT	BASIC VARIABLE	3 x_1	6 x_2	8 x_3	0 s_1	0 s_2	0 s_3	VALUE
6	x_2	$\frac{1}{3}$	1	0	$-\frac{1}{2}$	0	$\frac{2}{3}$	100
8	x_3	0	0	1	$\frac{1}{2}$	0	$-\frac{1}{4}$	200
0	s_2	0	0	0	$-\frac{1}{2}$	1	$-\frac{1}{3}$	0
	z_j	2	6	8	1	0	2	
	$c_j - z_j$	-1	0	0	-1	0	-2	2200

(d)

infeasible
all $C_j - Z_j \leq 0$
artificial var. remains
in basis

BASIC COEFFICIENT	BASIC VARIABLE	4 x_1	10 x_2	0 s_1	$-M$ a_2	$-M$ a_3	VALUE
0	s_1	0	12	1	0	-12	10
4	x_1	1	1	0	0	1	4
$-M$	a_2	0	-1	0	1	0	3
	z_j	4	$4+M$	0	$-M$	4	
	$c_j - z_j$	0	$6-M$	0	0	$-4-M$	$16-3M$

(e)

unbounded
var X_2 to enter basis
all coeff. in col for $X_2 \leq 0$

BASIC COEFFICIENT	BASIC VARIABLE	9 x_1	6 x_2	0 s_1	0 s_2	VALUE
9	x_1	1	$-\frac{1}{3}$	$\frac{1}{3}$	0	10
0	s_2	0	-3	$-\frac{1}{2}$	1	12
	z_j	9	-3	3	0	
	$c_j - z_j$	0	9	-3	0	90

(f)

optimal

BASIC COEFFICIENT	BASIC VARIABLE	9 x_1	6 x_2	0 s_1	0 s_2	VALUE
9	x_1	1	0	$\frac{2}{3}$	$\frac{1}{3}$	10
6	x_2	0	1	$-\frac{1}{2}$	$\frac{2}{3}$	12
	z_j	9	6	3	7	
	$c_j - z_j$	0	0	-3	-7	162

6-9. Use the simplex method to solve

$$\text{Max } 40x_1 + 60x_2 + 50x_3$$

$$\text{s.t.} \quad 10x_1 + 4x_2 + 2x_3 \leq 950$$

$$2x_1 + 2x_2 \qquad \leq 410$$

$$x_1 \qquad + 2x_3 \leq 610$$

$$x_1 \geq 0, \qquad x_2 \geq 0, \qquad x_3 \geq 0$$

268

CHAPTER 6
Linear
Programming:
The Simplex
Method

6-10. Use the simplex method to solve

$$\text{Max } 5x_1 + x_2 + 3x_3$$

$$\text{s.t.} \quad 2x_1 - x_2 + 2x_3 \leq 4$$

$$x_1 + x_2 + 4x_3 \leq 4$$

$$x_1 \geq 0, \qquad x_2 \geq 0, \qquad x_3 \geq 0$$

6-11. Use the simplex method to solve

$$\text{Max } 25x_1 + 50x_2$$

$$\text{s.t.} \quad 2x_1 + 2x_2 \leq 1000$$

$$3x_1 \quad\ \leq\ 600$$

$$x_1 + 3x_2 \leq\ 600$$

$$x_1 \geq 0, \qquad x_2 \geq 0$$

6-12. Consider the following problem:

$$\text{Min } 3x_1 + 5x_2 + x_3$$

$$\text{s.t.} \quad 4x_1 + 2x_2 + x_3 \geq 8$$

$$x_i \geq 0, \qquad i = 1, 2, 3$$

(a) How many basic variables are there at each corner of the feasible region?
(b) Write the dual of the problem.
(c) Solve both of the problems with the simplex method.
(d) Change the objective function coefficient of x_1 to 4. Solve both the primal and dual problems by the simplex method. What can you say about the results?
(e) Change the objective function coefficient of x_3 in the original problem to -1, and solve both the primal problem and its dual by the simplex method. What can you say about the results?

6-13. Use the simplex method to solve

$$\text{Min } 6x_1 + 8x_2 + 16x_3$$

$$\text{s.t.} \quad 2x_1 + x_2 \qquad \geq 5$$

$$x_2 + 2x_3 \geq 4$$

$$x_1, x_2, x_3 \geq 0$$

6-14. Use the simplex method to solve

$$\text{Min } x_1 + 3x_2 + 2x_3$$

$$\text{s.t.} \quad x_1 + 4x_2 \geq\ 8$$

$$2x_1 + \quad x_3 \geq 10$$

$$2x_1 + 3x_2 \leq 15$$

$$x_1, x_2, x_3 \geq 0$$

269

CHAPTER 6
Linear
Programming:
The Simplex
Method

6-15. Use artificial variables and set up the initial tableau for

$$\text{Min } 6x_1 + x_2 + 3x_3 - 2x_4$$

$$\text{s.t.} \quad x_1 + x_2 \qquad\qquad \leq 42$$

$$2x_1 + 3x_2 - x_3 - x_4 \geq 10$$

$$x_1 \qquad + 2x_3 + x_4 = 30$$

$$x_1, x_2, x_3, x_4 \geq 0$$

6-16. Consider the following problem:

$$\text{Min } 3x_1 - 5x_2 + 4x_3$$

$$\text{s.t.} \quad 4x_1 - 2x_2 + x_3 = 20$$

$$3x_1 + 4x_3 \geq 12$$

$$-2x_2 + 7x_3 \geq 7$$

$$x_1, x_2, x_3 \geq 0$$

(a) Write the dual problem.
(b) Set up the initial tableau for the dual problem.

More Challenging Problems

6-17. Use artificial variables and the simplex method to solve

$$\text{Min } -2x_1 - x_2 - 4x_3 - 5x_4$$

$$\text{s.t.} \quad x_1 + 3x_2 + 2x_3 + 5x_4 \leq 20$$

$$2x_1 + 16x_2 + x_3 + x_4 \geq 4$$

$$3x_1 - x_2 - 5x_3 + 10x_4 \leq -10$$

$$x_1, x_2, x_3, x_4 \geq 0$$

6-18. Write the dual to Problem 6-14 and use the optimal tableau from Problem 6-14 to obtain the optimal values of the dual variables.

6-19. Compute all sensitivity information (all allowable increases and decreases) from the optimal tableau to Problem 6-17. (See footnote 8, Appendix 6.3.)

6-20. Refer to Figure 6.3.

(a) What is the theoretic limit on the number of nonbasic sets this model can have?
(b) How many nonbasic sets are there? Which pairs of variables do not form a nonbasic set?
(c) How many distinct basic solutions are there?
(d) How many basic feasible solutions are there?

———————— **APPENDIX 6.1**

SENSITIVITY ANALYSIS: COMPUTING THE OPTIMAL DUAL VARIABLES

In Chapter 5 we discussed the fact that corresponding to any LP there is another LP, called the dual problem. We stated that either of these two problems will have an optimal solution if and only if the other one does also, and in this case the two optimal objective

270

CHAPTER 6
Linear
Programming:
The Simplex
Method

values are equal. As an example, consider the **PROTRAC**, Inc. model solved with the simplex method in Section 6.13 (the computer output for the solution appears in Figure 5.6). The model is

$$
\begin{array}{lllll}
\text{Max } 5000E + 4000F & & & \\
\text{s.t.} & E + F \geq 5 & \text{(total units requirement)} & \text{①} \\
& E - 3F \leq 0 & \text{(market balance)} & \text{②} \\
& 10E + 15F \leq 150 & \text{(department A)} & \text{③} & (P) \\
& 20E + 10F \leq 160 & \text{(department B)} & \text{④} \\
& 30E + 10F \geq 135 & \text{(contractual labor)} & \text{⑤} \\
& E \geq 0, \quad F \geq 0 &
\end{array}
$$

The dual of this problem is[6]

$$
\begin{array}{ll}
\text{Min } 5y_1 + 150y_3 + 160y_4 + 135y_5 & \\
\text{s.t.} \quad y_1 + y_2 + 10y_3 + 20y_4 + 30y_5 \geq 5000 & \\
\quad\quad y_1 - 3y_2 + 15y_3 + 10y_4 + 10y_5 \geq 4000 & (D) \\
\quad\quad y_1, y_5 \leq 0; \quad\quad y_2, y_3, y_4 \geq 0 &
\end{array}
$$

Recall that for a Max model the dual prices on the computer printout are the same as the optimal values of the variables in the dual problem. For a Min model dual prices and optimal dual variables are the same in magnitude (absolute value) but opposite in sign. Since the **PROTRAC**, Inc. problem is a Max model, the dual prices and the optimal solution to the dual problem are the same. Thus, we can read from the "DUAL PRICES" column of Figure 5.6 to obtain

$$
y_1^* = 0, \quad y_2^* = 0, \quad y_3^* = 150, \quad y_4^* = 175, \quad y_5^* = 0
$$

The following result shows where the optimal values of the dual variables are located in the tableau:

Locating Dual Variables in the Optimal Tableau

For either a Max or a Min model, the optimal value of the kth dual variable can be found in the z_j row of the optimal tableau, in the column headed by the distinguished variable in the kth constraint (the variable in the original standard equality constraint form which appears only in the kth constraint and has coefficient $+1$).

[6] If the primal problem (P) is written in standard equality constraint form, the dual problem, let us call it (D′), would have five variables free in sign, seven rather than two constraints, and hence would look different from (D). However, you may wish to verify for yourself, by writing out (D′), that in fact the difference is in appearance only. The extra five constraints in (D′) are the five sign conditions that appear in (D).

271

CHAPTER 6
Linear
Programming:
The Simplex
Method

It is beyond the scope and intent of this text to give a formal proof of this result. However, it can be intuitively motivated as follows. Consider, for example, the labor constraint in department B (constraint ④). In the standard equality form, the slack variable on this constraint is s_4. Since constraint ④ is a $\leq$ constraint, we also know that s_4 is the distinguished variable associated with this constraint. As seen in Figure 6.22, s_4 is nonbasic (i.e., has the value zero) at the optimal corner. We know, also from Figure 6.22, that the opportunity cost of s_4 is the entry in the s_4 column in the $c_j - z_j$ row, namely -175. This means that if s_4 were increased by a unit, then the value of the objective function would decrease by \$175. But increasing s_4 a unit is tantamount to decreasing by 1 unit the availability of labor in department B. Thus, 1 less hour of labor availability in department B decreases profit by \$175, and we interpret this to mean also that 1 more hour of labor would increase profit by \$175, which is the negative of the entry in the $c_j - z_j$ row, the s_4 column. That is, $175 = z_j - c_j$ and, since c_j is zero because s_4 is a slack variable, we have $175 = z_j$ (i.e., 175 is the entry in the s_4 column in the z_j row). This is y_4^*.

Let us further illustrate the rule above in terms of Figure 6.22. Recall that the variables s_2 and s_3 are the distinguished variables for the second and third constraints, respectively. Therefore, the values of y_2^* and y_3^* noted above are found in the z_j row of Figure 6.22, in the columns headed by s_2 and s_3, respectively. The distinguished variables for the first and fifth constraints are a_1 and a_2 and consequently the y_1^* (y_5^*) noted above is found in the z_j row under the a_1 (a_2) column. Thus, you see that all dual prices can be obtained from the optimal tableau, with the caveat that

> **If you wish to obtain the dual prices from the tableau, you should keep (at each iteration) all columns corresponding to any artificial variables that had to be added to the model.**

Sensitivity analysis is also referred to as postoptimality analysis. This is for two reasons. First the *interpretations* are always with reference to a current optimal solution. Second, most of the *computations* are performed after the optimal tableau is obtained. In the discussion above you saw that the dual prices can in fact be read directly from the optimal tableau. In the following two appendices you will see that the remainder of the sensitivity analysis is obtained with additional computation based on data in the optimal tableau.

APPENDIX 6.2

SENSITIVITY ANALYSIS: COMPUTING ALLOWABLE CHANGES IN THE RHS[7]

In Appendix 6.1 it was seen that the z_j row of the distinguished variable columns gives the dual prices. Let b_i denote the current (original) value of the ith RHS and let b_i' denote a different value. Let d_i denote the dual price on the ith constraint. In the discussion of

[7] The discussion in this section is equally applicable to a Max or a Min model.

272

CHAPTER 6
Linear
Programming:
The Simplex
Method

sensitivity analysis in Chapter 5 it was stated that *for some limited range of values b'_i,* the product

$$(b'_i - b_i)d_i$$

gives the improvement in OV as b_i is changed to b'_i, with all other data held fixed. Let us see how to compute this range.

At the current optimal corner solution there is a set of current basic and nonbasic variables. Suppose that in the original equations you change b_i to b'_i, leaving all other data fixed, and then consider the new basic solution to these equations, in terms of the current set of basic and nonbasic variables. Changing b_i to b'_i, will change the values of at least some basic variables. *The allowable values for b'_i are precisely those values for which the new basic solution remains feasible* (i.e., for which the values of the basic variables remain nonnegative). This is because the change from b_i to b'_i has no effect on substitution coefficients, or z_j's, or $c_j - z_j$'s, and hence an optimal tableau for the new problem will be precisely the same as the current optimal tableau except for new non-negative numbers in the "Value" column (i.e., the numbers giving the new values for the basic variables and for the objective function).

Consider, for example, the RHS, b_i, associated with an *inactive constraint.* The optimal value of the corresponding slack or surplus variable, call it s_i^*, is positive, and therefore s_i is basic. Consider the sets of basic and nonbasic variables at an optimal basic feasible solution. As b_i changes, the only basic variable to change value will be s_i. For example, in Figure 5.5 verify that when the RHS of the market balance constraint is changed, then in the current optimal solution only the value of the slack variable, s_2, will change. All other basic variables will retain their current values and the current nonbasic variables of course remain at zero. The current value of s_2 is 16.5, as shown in the optimal tableau, Figure 6.22. This is the amount the RHS can be decreased without destroying the feasibility of the current optimum. If b_2 is decreased by more than 16.5 units, the slack value s_2, at the current optimum, will be negative. We also observe that the RHS can be arbitrarily increased.

Rule for Inactive Constraints

Thus, *for an inactive constraint the RHS can be tightened by an amount equal to the optimal slack value (found in the optimal tableau) without destroying feasibility. It can be arbitrarily loosened.* This dictates the "allowable increase" and "allowable decrease" values for such right-hand sides (i.e., for inactive constraints). As specific cases, note in Figure 5.6 that on the market balance constraint, a $\leq$ constraint, the allowable increase (loosening) is infinite and the allowable decrease (tightening) is s_2^*, namely 16.5. Since the first constraint is of $\geq$ form, and since its optimal surplus value is 6.5, the allowable decrease (loosening) is infinite while the allowable increase (tightening) is s^*, namely 6.5.

Now consider the RHS, b_i, associated with *an active constraint.* As this RHS changes, the values of the basic variables, in the basic solution, will also change. Whenever one of them becomes negative the allowable range will have been exceeded.

To calculate the allowable range we must first identify the distinguished variable associated with the constraint under consideration. Suppose that, in the **PROTRAC**, Inc. model, we are interested in constraint ③ (i.e., in the equality $10E + 15F + s_3 = 150$). We identify s_3 as the distinguished variable and note that since the constraint is active, we have $s_3^* = 0$. Now rewrite the equation as $10E + 15F = 150 - s_3$. We see then that as far as the basic variables E and F are concerned, increasing s_3 is equivalent to decreasing the RHS value 150 by the same amount, and decreasing s_3 is equivalent to increasing the RHS value 150 by the same amount.

273

CHAPTER 6
Linear
Programming:
The Simplex
Method

Thus, the following two questions are equivalent:

1. Given the optimal solution, how much can the RHS of constraint ③ be decreased before one of the currently nonnegative basic variables becomes negative?
2. Given the optimal solution, how much can s_3 be increased before one of the currently nonnegative basic variables becomes negative?

However, we have answered a question just like question 2 each time we have pivoted a nonbasic variable into the basic feasible solution. Thus, we can now use the same process to achieve our goal of finding an answer to question 1. As before, the answer is determined by the following calculation: Let k be the column identified by the distinguished variable, i be an index indicating a row in the optimal tableau, V_i be the entry in the value column of row i, and a_{ik} the substitution coefficient in row i, column k.

Allowable Decrease for Active Constraint

Allowable decrease in RHS equals minimum over all i for which $a_{ik} > 0$ of V_i/a_{ik}.

Returning to our example of constraint ③ in the **PROTRAC**, Inc. model, we have already identified the slack variable s_3 as the distinguished variable. According to our prescription the allowable decrease should be equal to the minimum of $\{7/0.1, 16.5/0.35, 6.5/0.05\}$. The minimum ratio is $16.5/0.35 = 47.14$. You can see in the computer output, Figure 5.6, that indeed this is the allowable decrease for the RHS of the third constraint.

Using the same type of reasoning allows us to derive the following rule for determining the allowable increase:

Allowable Increase for Active Constraint

The allowable increase in the RHS equals the minimum over all i for which $a_{ik} < 0$ of $-V_i/a_{ik}$.

Continuing our example of constraint ③, we see that the allowable increase in the RHS of constraint ③ equals the minimum of $\{-4.05/-0.05, -70/-0.5\}$, which is $-4.5/-0.05$ or 90. Again the computer output verifies that this is indeed the allowable increase.

Performing the same calculations for constraint ④, we obtain

$$\text{allowable decrease} = \text{Min } \{4.5/0.075, 70/1.75, 6.5/0.025\}$$
$$= \text{Min } \{60, 40, 260\} = 40$$
$$\text{allowable increase} = \text{Min } \{7/0.05, 16.5/0.225\}$$
$$= \text{Min } \{140, 73.33\} = 73.33$$

Verify that these are the numbers that appear in Figure 5.6.

274

CHAPTER 6
Linear
Programming:
The Simplex
Method

FIGURE 6.25
Printout for Astro/Cosmo, Revised

```
MAX 20 A + 10 C
SUBJECT TO
   2) A + 2 C <= 120
   3) A + C <= 60
   4) A <= 70
   5) C <= 50
```

New value
for capacity in
department B

```
1)              OBJECTIVE FUNCTION VALUE

                1200.00

VARIABLE            VALUE            REDUCED COST

   A                60.00                0.00
   C                 0.00               10.00

ROW          SLACK OR SURPLUS        DUAL PRICES

   2                60.00                0.00
   3                 0.00               20.00
   4                10.00                0.00
   5                50.00                0.00


             SENSITIVITY ANALYSIS

           OBJ COEFFICIENT RANGES

VARIABLE      CURRENT      ALLOWABLE      ALLOWABLE
              COEF         INCREASE       DECREASE

   A          20.00        INFINITY        10.00
   C          10.00         10.00         INFINITY

           RIGHTHAND SIDE RANGES

ROW           CURRENT      ALLOWABLE      ALLOWABLE
              RHS          INCREASE       DECREASE

   2          120.00       INFINITY        60.00
   3           60.00        10.00          60.00
   4           70.00       INFINITY        10.00
   5           50.00       INFINITY        50.00
```

Min {10, 20}

$z_j - c_j$ in
C column,
Figure 6.24

SENSITIVITY ANALYSIS: COMPUTING ALLOWABLE CHANGES IN THE OBJECTIVE FUNCTION COEFFICIENT[8]

In Chapter 5 it was shown how the computer output provides, for each objective function coefficient, a range of values such that the coefficient may be varied within that range without changing the optimal solution. We also used the geometry to interpret these ranges and to show how these values could be determined in a problem with two decision variables. Recall that the *interpretation always assumes that all other data in the model are unchanged.*

In this appendix we show how the objective function coefficient ranges that appear on the computer output can be derived from the optimal tableau. The discussion is motivated by a somewhat altered version of the Astro/Cosmo problem. The formulation and computer solution are presented in Figure 6.25. The only change between the original problem and this revised version is that the total capacity in department B is reduced from 90 to 60. In other words, the RHS of the second constraint is now 60. To obtain the standard equality form of this model, we simply add a slack variable to each constraint as follows:

$$
\begin{aligned}
\text{Max } 20A &+ 10C \\
\text{s.t.} \quad A &+ 2C + s_1 && = 120 \\
A &+ C \phantom{{}+{}} + s_2 && = 60 \\
A &\phantom{{}+ 2C + s_1 + s_2} + s_3 && = 70 \\
&\phantom{+{}}C \phantom{{}+ s_1 + s_2 + s_3} + s_4 &&= 50
\end{aligned}
$$

The simplex algorithm is now applied to this problem. The optimal tableau is shown in Figure 6.26.

From both Figures 6.25 and 6.26 we see that the optimal solution to the problem is $A^* = 60$, $C^* = 0$, $s_1^* = 60$, $s_2^* = 0$, $s_3^* = 10$, $s_4^* = 50$. Further, we note in Figure 6.26 that s_1, A, s_3, and s_4 are basic variables, whereas C and s_2 are nonbasic. We now turn our attention to determining the allowable increase and allowable decrease for each coefficient in the objective function. There are two different cases to consider: (1) coefficients for nonbasic variables and (2) coefficients for basic variables.

In the following discussion it may be helpful to visualize the geometric analysis of the problem. This is produced in Figure 6.27.

Coefficients of Nonbasic Variables

Consider the variable C. We have already noted that it is nonbasic. That is, $C^* = 0$ in the optimal solution. Decreasing the coefficient of C in the objective function makes it an even less profitable product, and hence, since this is a Max model, it is intuitively clear that decreasing this coefficient could not possibly persuade us to start producing C. This intuitive argument is consistent with the fact that the "ALLOWABLE DECREASE" for

---

[8] The discussion in this section applies to a Max model. If your initial problem is a Min model, you could proceed as follows: (1) multiply the objective function by -1, and compute the simplex solution to the Max problem; (2) use the optimal tableau to compute allowable increases and decreases in objective coefficients, as described in this appendix; and (3) interchange the terms "allowable increase" and "allowable decrease." That is, the allowable increase computed for the Max model turns out to be the allowable decrease for the Min model.

276

CHAPTER 6
Linear
Programming:
The Simplex
Method

FIGURE 6.26
Optimal Tableau for Astro/Cosmo, Revised

BASIC COEFFICIENT	BASIC VARIABLE	20 A	10 C	0 s_1	0 s_2	0 s_3	0 s_4	VALUE
0	s_1	0	1	1	−1	0	0	60
20	A	1	1	0	1	0	0	60
0	s_3	0	−1	0	−1	1	0	10
0	s_4	0	1	0	0	0	1	50
	z_j	20	20	0	20	0	0	
	$c_j - z_j$	0	−10	0	−20	0	0	1200

FIGURE 6.27
Geometric Analysis of Astro/Cosmo, Revised

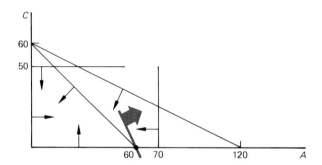

the coefficient of C presented in Figure 6.25 is "INFINITY." The geometric support for this argument is that as the coefficient of C decreases, the objective function contour in Figure 6.27 rotates clockwise, approaching, but never attaining, a horizontal position.

Now consider increasing the coefficient of C in the objective function. Referring to Figure 6.26, we recall that the current solution remains optimal as long as all values of $c_j - z_j$ remain ≤ 0. Suppose that the coefficient of C is increased from 10 to 12. Only two numbers in the optimal tableau change and both changes occur in the C column. In the top row, the value of the coefficient increases from 10 to 12, and in the last row, the value of $c_j - z_j$ increases from -10 to -8. Thus, an increase of 2 in c_j increased $c_j - z_j$ by 2. We see then if the coefficient of C increases by more than the current magnitude (absolute value) of $c_j - z_j$ in the C column, the new value of $c_j - z_j$ in the C column will be positive and the current solution is no longer optimal. This explains the allowable increase of 10 shown for the coefficient of C in Figure 6.25. From the geometric point of view (Figure 6.27) an increase of 10 in the coefficient C will rotate, the objective function contour counterclockwise, so that it is parallel to the constraint $A + C \leq 60$. At this point there are two optimal corners.

The discussion above illustrates the following general fact:

For a nonbasic variable in a Max model,

> allowable decrease = infinity
>
> allowable increase = value of $z_j - c_j$ in the optimal tableau

FIGURE 6.28
Changing the Coefficient of A

BASIC COEFFICIENT	BASIC VARIABLE	$20 + \Delta C_A$ A	10 C	0 s_1	0 s_2	0 s_3	0 s_4	VALUE
0	s_1	0	1	1	-1	0	0	60
$20 + \Delta C_A$	A	1	1	0	1	0	0	60
0	s_3	0	-1	0	-1	1	0	10
0	s_4	0	1	0	0	0	1	50
z_j		$20 + \Delta C_A$	$20 + \Delta C_A$	0	$20 + \Delta C_A$	0	0	
$c_j - z_j$		0	$-10 - \Delta C_A$	0	$-20 - \Delta C_A$	0	0	$1200 + 60\,\Delta C_A$

Coefficients of Basic Variables

The procedure for basic variables is more complicated, since the coefficient of a basic variable plays a role in determining the value of z_j for all of the *nonbasic* columns in the model. For example, in Figure 6.26 you can see that the coefficient of A influences the value of z_j in the C and s_2 columns. From the geometry (Figure 6.27) you can see that as the coefficient of A is increased, the objective function contour rotates clockwise, approaching, but never reaching, a slope of $-\infty$. Thus, the allowable increase should be infinity, as indeed it is in the computer printout (Figure 6.25). Moreover, as the coefficient of A is decreased, the objective contour becomes less steep. As soon as the coefficient has decreased 10 units the objective contour is parallel to the constraint $A + C \leq 60$, at which point there will be two optimal corners. Again, this allowable decrease of 10 agrees with the information provided in the output. Our goal now is to see how these values are obtained algebraically from the optimal tableau (Figure 6.26).

In order to study the effect of changes in the coefficient of A, let us change the current value, 20, to some new value, say $20 + \Delta C_A$. If $\Delta C_A < 0$, the coefficient of A decreases. If $\Delta C_A > 0$, it increases. Let us now see what happens to the optimal tableau (Figure 6.26) when this change is made. The new tableau is given in Figure 6.28. Note that the change ΔC_A has affected the values of $c_j - z_j$ only for the nonbasic variables C and s_2. It has also affected the z_j values in the A, C, and s_2 columns, and the objective function value.

The optimal solution from Figure 6.26 will remain optimal if all $c_j - z_j \leq 0$ in Figure 6.28. Since the $c_j - z_j$'s for basic columns remain unchanged, we need examine only the nonbasic columns. Thus, we see that

$$-10 - \Delta C_A \leq 0 \qquad \text{if and only if} \qquad -10 \leq \Delta C_A$$
$$-20 - \Delta C_A \leq 0 \qquad \text{if and only if} \qquad -20 \leq \Delta C_A$$

This shows that the coefficient of A can be decreased by as much as Min $\{10, 20\} = 10$ units without destroying the optimality of the solution in Figure 6.26. It can be arbitrarily increased. This explains how the allowable increase and allowable decrease are determined algebraically from the optimal tableau. The general rule for determining the allowable changes for coefficients of basic variables is derived from reasoning entirely analogous to that presented above. In order to present this rule, let i be the row in the optimal tableau associated with the basic variable of interest; let j be a nonbasic column, and a_{ij} the value of the substitution coefficient in row i, column j of the optimal tableau.

278

CHAPTER 6
Linear
Programming:
The Simplex
Method

Then

$$\text{allowable increase} = \text{Min}\left(\frac{c_j - z_j}{a_{ij}}\right) \text{ for those nonbasic columns}$$

where $a_{ij} < 0$

$$\text{allowable decrease} = \text{Min}\left(\frac{-(c_j - z_j)}{a_{ij}}\right) \text{ for those nonbasic columns}$$

where $a_{ij} > 0$

Returning to Figure 6.26 and the variable A and applying the general rule, we note that there are no negative entries in the A row and thus there is no limit on the allowable increase in the coefficient of A (i.e., no $a_{Aj} < 0$). Similarly, we see that the allowable decrease must equal the minimum of $-(-\frac{10}{1})$ and $-(-\frac{20}{1})$ or 10, which is the value we already computed.

For more practice with this rule, refer to the **PROTRAC**, Inc. Problem in Figure 6.22. Concerning the coefficient for F

$$\text{allowable increase} = \text{Min}\left(\frac{-175}{-0.05}\right) = 3500$$

$$\text{allowable decrease} = \text{Min}\left(\frac{-(-150)}{0.1}\right) = 1500$$

Similarly, for the coefficient for E

$$\text{allowable increase} = \text{Min}\left(\frac{-150}{-0.05}\right) = 3000$$

$$\text{allowable decrease} = \text{Min}\left(\frac{-(-175)}{0.075}\right) = 2333.33$$

Verify that these are indeed the values provided in the computer output in Figure 5.6.

7

LINEAR PROGRAMMING: SPECIAL APPLICATIONS

———— 7.1
INTRODUCTION

Linear programming is the workhorse of the world of quantitative models. The ability to handle hundreds of constraints, thousands of decision variables, and the incredible number of interactions that these numbers imply makes LP an important tool in a wide variety of problems.

In this chapter we concentrate on some special applications of linear programming. In particular, we consider four specific models. Sections 7.2 through 7.4 are devoted to the transportation problem. In this problem, management must determine how to allocate products from its various warehouses to its customers in order to satisfy demand at the lowest possible cost. This model is important because of its successful applications and because it can be solved quickly and efficiently with special algorithms. These algorithms are presented in Section 7.3.

Sections 7.5 through 7.7 are devoted to the assignment problem. This model enables management to determine the optimal assignment of salespeople to districts, jobs to machines, or editors to manuscripts. The model itself is a special type of transportation problem. It can be solved with a special algorithm, the Hungarian method, which is presented in Section 7.6.

A financial and production planning model is presented in Section 7.8. Although it is small and relatively simple by the standards of actual applications, it illustrates how more complicated planning models can be constructed and solved. Finally, Section 7.9 considers an important marketing problem. The problem, called the media selection

280

CHAPTER 7
Linear
Programming:
Special
Applications

problem, is concerned with designing an effective advertising campaign. More precisely, management must decide how many ads to place in each of several possible advertising media. The decision is constrained by an overall budget allocation, the number of openings for ads in the various media, and rules of thumb insisted on by management. The media selection problem is a specific example of an important class of management problems. These are profit-maximization problems in which a decision variable yields declining marginal profits for increased values of the variable.

—————— 7.2
THE TRANSPORTATION PROBLEM

PROTRAC's Distribution Problem: Sending Diesels from Harbors to Plants

PROTRAC has four assembly plants in Europe. They are located in Leipzig, East Germany (1); Nancy, France (2); Liege, Belgium (3); and Tilburg, the Netherlands (4). The engines used by these plants are produced in the United States and shipped to Europe. Engines arrive at the harbors in Amsterdam (A), Antwerp (B), and LeHavre (C).

Production plans for the third quarter, July through September, have been set. The *requirements* (the *demand* at *destinations*) for E-4 diesel engines are as follows:

PLANT	NUMBER OF ENGINES
(1) Leipzig	400
(2) Nancy	900
(3) Liege	200
(4) Tilburg	500
	2000

The *available* number of E-4 engines at harbors (the *supply* at *origins*) in time to be used in the third quarter are shown below.

HARBOR	NUMBER OF ENGINES
(A) Amsterdam	500
(B) Antwerp	700
(C) LeHavre	800
	2000

Note that this is a balanced problem in the sense that the total supply of engines available equals the total number required. Figure 7.1 illustrates the problem. In this figure the number above the harbors indicates the supply available and the number above the plants indicates the quantity demanded. The lines indicate the possible delivery routes.

PROTRAC must decide how many engines to send from each harbor to each plant. The engines are transported by common carrier and charges are on a per engine basis. The relevant costs are given in Figure 7.2. For ease of presentation, we will refer to the harbors with letters and the plants with numbers, as indicated in the supply and demand information above.

281

CHAPTER 7
Linear
Programming:
Special
Applications

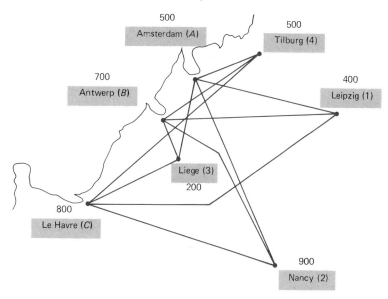

FIGURE 7.1
PROTRAC's Transportation Problem

FIGURE 7.2
Cost to Transport an Engine from an Origin
to a Destination

FROM ORIGIN	TO DESTINATION			
	1	2	3	4
A	12	13	4	6
B	6	4	10	11
C	10	9	12	4

The LP Formulation and Solution

PROTRAC's goal is to minimize the total cost of transporting the E-4 engines from the harbors to the plants. Since the transportation cost for any specific harbor–plant combination (e.g., Antwerp–Nancy) is directly proportional to the number of engines sent from the harbor to the plant ($4 per engine in the Antwerp–Nancy example), we can formulate this problem as an LP model. To do so, we let

The Decision Variables

x_{ij} = number of engines sent from harbor i to plant j

$i = A, B, C$

$j = 1, 2, 3, 4$

Thus, x_{C4} is the number of engines sent from C, LeHavre, to 4, Tilburg. With this definition, the total transportation cost, which is our objective function, becomes

The Objective

$$12x_{A1} + 13x_{A2} + \cdots + 4x_{C4}$$

The problem has two general types of constraints:

1. The number of items shipped from a harbor cannot exceed the number that are available. For example,

$$x_{A1} + x_{A2} + x_{A3} + x_{A4}$$

FIGURE 7.3
PROTRAC's Transportation Problem

```
MIN   12 XA1 + 13 XA2 + 4 XA3 + 6 XA4 + 6 XB1 + 4 XB2 + 10 XB3
      + 11 XB4 + 10 XC1 + 9 XC2 + 12 XC3 + 4 XC4
SUBJECT TO
   2)  XA1 + XA2 + XA3 + XA4 <= 500
   3)  XB1 + XB2 + XB3 + XB4 <= 700
   4)  XC1 + XC2 + XC3 + XC4 <= 800
   5)  XA1 + XB1 + XC1 = 400
   6)  XA2 + XB2 + XC2 = 900
   7)  XA3 + XB3 + XC3 = 200
   8)  XA4 + XB4 + XC4 = 500

         OBJECTIVE FUNCTION VALUE

              12000.00

  VARIABLE          VALUE          REDUCED COST

     XA1            300.00             0.00
     XA2              0.00             2.00
     XA3            200.00             0.00
     XA4              0.00             0.00
     XB1              0.00             1.00
     XB2            700.00             0.00
     XB3              0.00            13.00
     XB4              0.00            12.00
     XC1            100.00             0.00
     XC2            200.00             0.00
     XC3              0.00            10.00
     XC4            500.00             0.00

   ROW             SLACK          DUAL PRICES

     2               0.00             0.00
     3               0.00             7.00
     4               0.00             2.00
     5               0.00           - 12.00
     6               0.00           - 11.00
     7               0.00           - 4.00
     8               0.00           - 6.00
```

283

CHAPTER 7
Linear
Programming:
Special
Applications

is the total number of engines shipped from A. Since only 500 engines are available at A, the constraint is

$$x_{A1} + x_{A2} + x_{A3} + x_{A4} \leq 500$$

A similar constraint is required for each origin.

2. Demand at each plant must be satisfied. For example,

$$x_{A1} + x_{B1} + x_{C1}$$

is the total number of engines sent to plant 1. Since 400 engines are demanded at plant 1, the constraint is

$$x_{A1} + x_{B1} + x_{C1} = 400$$

A similar constraint is required for each plant.

The complete formulation and solution to **PROTRAC**'s transportation problem are presented in Figure 7.3. In this figure we see that 6 of the 12 possible routes are used (6 x_{ij} are positive) and that the minimum possible transportation cost is $12,000.

— **7.3**
SOLVING THE TRANSPORTATION PROBLEM

We have just used a general-purpose linear programming code based on the simplex algorithm to solve a transportation problem. The fact that this works is not surprising, since the simplex algorithm can be used to solve any LP problem and the transportation problem is an LP problem. However, because of the special structure of the transportation problem, we can use other algorithms that are designed to exploit the unique characteristics of this class of problems. In general, these algorithms make it possible to solve very large problems in a fraction of the time that would be required with the simplex algorithm.

In particular, we will discuss four specific algorithms: the northwest corner rule, Vogel's approximation method, the stepping-stone method, and MODI (the modified distribution method). These algorithms serve two different purposes. The northwest corner rule and Vogel's approximation method are alternative methods of finding an initial feasible solution. The stepping-stone method and MODI are alternative methods of proceeding from an initial feasible solution to the optimal solution. As this discussion suggests, the first step in solving the transportation problem is to find an *initial feasible solution*. A *feasible solution*, by definition, is any allocation of supplies that satisfies all demand (i.e., a set of x_{ij}'s that satisfies all the constraints).

Once an initial feasible solution has been obtained, the algorithm proceeds in a step-by-step manner. At each step the goal is to find a feasible solution with a "better" (smaller) value for the objective function. When no better feasible solutions are available, the optimal solution has been found. An *optimal solution* is a cost-minimizing feasible solution. We see, then, that the transportation problem algorithm uses the same general approach as the simplex algorithm that was discussed in Chapter 6. In this case, however, the calculations are much simpler.

The Transportation Tableau
It is convenient to illustrate how these algorithms work by employing tableaux. Figure 7.4 shows the appropriate tableau for **PROTRAC**'s transportation problem. This tableau indicates the supply at each origin (e.g., 500 at A) and the demand at each destination (e.g., 200 at 3). We note that total supply equals total demand. Each cell represents a route from an origin to a destination and the number in the upper righthand

284

CHAPTER 7
Linear
Programming:
Special
Applications

FIGURE 7.4
Transportation Tableau for PROTRAC'S
Transportation Problem

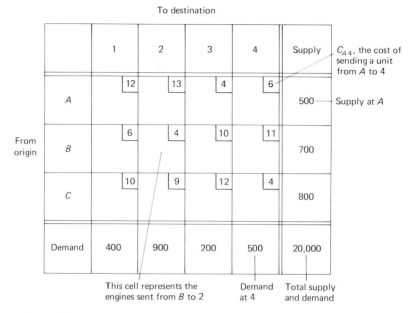

corner of the cell is the per unit cost of sending an engine along that route (e.g., 4 is the cost to send an engine from B to 2). Our goal is to find a way to use the given supplies to satisfy the demands at the minimum transportation cost.

We will now show two different methods of finding an initial feasible solution, the northwest corner rule and Vogel's approximation method.

FIGURE 7.5
First Allocation

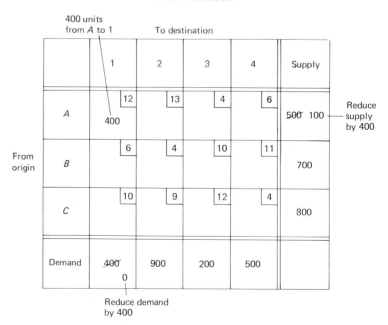

The northwest corner rule starts in the northwest corner (the upper left-hand cell, route A1), and allocates *as many units as possible* to that route. In our example, 400 units are demanded at 1 and 500 are available at A. The entire demand at 1 is thus allocated from A and our tableau is modified as shown in Figure 7.5.

Further allocations are then made either by moving to the right or by moving down. Demands are satisfied by moving sequentially from left to right and supplies are allocated by moving from the top to the bottom. In the example, since all the demand at destination 1 was satisfied, and since there is positive supply remaining at origin A, we remain in the same row and move to the right to consider the demand at destination 2, which is 900 engines. To satisfy this we allocate the 100 units still available at A, and then needing more supply, we move down to use the 700 units available at B, and then down once again to use 100 of the 800 units available at C. With these allocations the tableau appears as shown in Figure 7.6. Continuing in this manner, a move to the right to destination 3 leads us to allocate 200 of the 700 units still available at C to 3 and finally the remaining 500 units to 4. The resulting tableau is shown in Figure 7.7. This tableau exhibits an initial feasible solution. We note that all demands are satisfied and that all supplies are exhausted.

The value of the objective function for the initial feasible solution produced by the northwest corner rule is shown in Figure 7.8.

The northwest corner rule has the advantage that it is extremely easy to use and yields an initial feasible solution quickly with a minimum of computational effort. On the other hand, there is no reason to believe that it will yield a good feasible solution, that is, one for which the value of the objective function is close to the optimal value. Indeed, we note that the northwest corner rule does not even consider costs in the process of allocating supplies. Thus, this procedure will yield a good feasible solution only as a matter of chance.

Vogel's Approximation Method

Vogel's approximation method (VAM) uses cost information by employing the concept of an opportunity cost to determine an initial feasible solution. Consider, for example, origin A. The cheapest route emanating from origin A is the route to destination 3,

FIGURE 7.6

Next Three Allocations

To destination

		1	2	3	4	Supply
		12	13	4	6	500̶ 100̶
	A	400	100			0
		6	4	10	11	700̶ 0
From origin	B		700			
		10	9	12	4	800̶ 700
	C		100			
	Demand	400̶	900̶	200	500	
		0	0			

286

CHAPTER 7
Linear
Programming:
Special
Applications

FIGURE 7.7

Initial Feasible Solution

To destination

		1	2	3	4	Supply
From origin	A	12 400	13 100	4	6	500 100 0
	B	6	4 700	10	11	700 0
	C	10	9 100	12 200	4 500	800 700 500 0
	Demand	400 0	900 0	200 0	500 0	

FIGURE 7.8

Total Cost for the Northwest Corner
Rule Solution

ROUTE	NUMBER OF ENGINES	COST PER ENGINE	COST
A1	400	$12	$4,800
A2	100	13	1,300
B2	700	4	2,800
C2	100	9	900
C3	200	12	2,400
C4	500	4	2,000
Total Cost			$14,200

which has a cost of $4 per engine. The next cheapest route emanating from A is the route to 4, with a cost of $6 per engine. Roughly, then, any engine at A that is not sent to 3 will incur an additional cost of *at least* $2 = $6 − $4. VAM thus assigns a penalty cost (opportunity cost) of $2 to the first row (origin A). We emphasize that this is the penalty based on *not* using the best route in that row. A penalty cost is calculated for each row and each column in a similar fashion. The results of these calculations are shown in Figure 7.9.

VAM proceeds by attempting to avoid large penalties. The first step is to locate the largest of all the row and column penalties, and then make an allocation which avoids that penalty. In this case, we see that the third column (destination 3) has the largest penalty, namely 6. To avoid this penalty we must use the cheapest available route (find the best origin) for that column. We thus allocate as many units as possible to A3, the cheapest route in column 3. Since demand at 3 is 200 and the supply at A is 500, 200 units are allocated to route A3. This allocation is represented in Figure 7.10. The following steps are then employed to update the values for supply, demand, and

287
CHAPTER 7
Linear
Programming:
Special
Applications

FIGURE 7.9
Row and Column Penalties

	To destination		Smallest in row A	2nd smallest in row A		
	1	2	3	4	Supply	Row penalties
A	12	13	4	6	500	2 — Calculated by 6 − 4
B	6	4	10	11	700	2
C	10	9	12	4	800	5
Demand	400	900	200	500		
Column penalties	4	5	6	2		

From origin

Largest penalty

FIGURE 7.10
Allocation and New Penalties

Assign max possible to minimum cost cell

	To destination					
	1	2	3	4	Supply	Row penalties
A	12	13	4 / 200	6	500 300	6 — New row penalty
B	6	4	10	11	700	2
C	10	9	12	4	800	5
Demand	400	900	200 / 0	500		
Column penalties	4	5	0	2		

From origin

the penalties, taking into account the allocation we have just made of 200 units to A3:

Updating the Tableau

1. The allocation of 200 to route A3 reduces the supply at A and the demand at 3. The supply becomes 300 and the demand is now 0.

2. Since the demand at 3 is now satisfied, no additional engines will be sent to this destination. Column 3 is shaded out to indicate that the costs in this column should not be used to calculate new penalty costs. Thus, the routes in column 3 are now considered "unavailable."

3. Column and row penalties are calculated for this tableau as before. For example, in the first row, since A4 is the cheapest *available* route, with a cost of 6 and A1 is the next cheapest *available* route, with a cost of 12, the penalty for row A is $12 - $6 = $6. We also note that since a column (column 3) was removed from use in further calculations, the value of the column penalties for the remaining columns did not change from the first to the second tableau.

In summary, then, we see that a four-step process was used to move from the first tableau to the second. In particular, VAM

1. Identifies the row or column with the largest penalty.
2. Makes the largest possible allocation to the unused route with the minimum cost in the row or column selected in step 1. (Ties may be broken arbitrarily.)
3. Adjusts the appropriate supply and demand in view of this allocation.
4. Eliminates any column with 0 remaining demand (or row with 0 remaining supply) from further consideration.
5. Calculates new penalty costs.

VAM continues to apply this process in a sequential manner until an initial feasible solution is obtained.

Applying the four-step process to the second tableau yields the result shown in Figure 7.11. Note that, in this case, the largest penalty, 6 units, was on the first row of Figure 7.10. Since all of the remaining 300 units of supply were sent to A4, the first row

FIGURE 7.11

Two Allocations

To destination

	1	2	3	4	Supply	Row penalties
A	12	13	4 / 200	6 / 300	5̶0̶0̶ 3̶0̶0̶ 0	
B	6	4	10	11	700	2
C	10	9	12	4	800	5
Demand	400	900	2̶0̶0̶ 0	5̶0̶0̶ 200		
Column penalties	4	5		7		

From origin

288

289

CHAPTER 7
Linear
Programming:
Special
Applications

FIGURE 7.12

Three Allocations

To destination

	1	2	3	4	Supply	Row penalties
A	12	13	4 200	6 300	500 ~~300~~ 0	
B	6	4	10	11	700	2
C	10	9	12	4 200	800 ~~600~~ 	1
Demand	400	900	~~200~~ 0	~~500~~ ~~200~~ 0		
Column penalties	4	5				

was eliminated. The same four-step procedure is now applied to Figure 7.11. Since destination 4 now has the largest penalty (7), an allocation of 200 units is made to route C4, the cheapest route in that row. The next tableau is shown in Figure 7.12. Continuing as before yields the tableau shown in Figure 7.13.

At this point there is only one possible way to allocate the 600 units available at C to obtain a feasible solution. We must allocate 400 units to C1 and 200 units to C2. This yields the final tableau shown in Figure 7.14.

FIGURE 7.13

Four Allocations

To destination

	1	2	3	4	Supply	Row penalties
A	12	13	4 200	6 300	~~500~~ ~~300~~ 0	
B	6	4 700	10	11	~~700~~ 0	
C	10	9	12	4 200	~~800~~ 600	1
Demand	400	~~900~~ 200	~~200~~ 0	~~500~~ ~~200~~ 0		

290

CHAPTER 7
Linear
Programming:
Special
Applications

FIGURE 7.14

Initial Feasible Solution

To destination

		1	2	3	4	Supply
From origin	A	12	13	4 200	6 300	500 300 0
	B	6	4 700	10	11	700 0
	C	10 400	9 200	12	4 200	800 600 0
	Demand	400 0	900 200 0	200 0	500 200 0	

The initial feasible solution produced by VAM is presented and evaluated in Figure 7.15. VAM clearly requires more computational work than the northwest corner rule. The hope is that it will yield a better initial feasible solution, that is, one close to the optimal solution. In this case we see that the value of the objective function is $12,000, compared with a cost of $14,200 that was produced by the northwest corner solution (see Figure 7.8). This is a substantial improvement. Indeed, if we refer to Figure 7.3, we see that the optimal value of the objective function is $12,000. Thus, *in this case* Vogel's approximation method produced an optimal solution. But this will not occur frequently. There are two important points to make at this time:

Will the Solution Be Optimal?

1. In general, neither Vogel's approximation method nor the northwest corner rule is guaranteed to yield *directly* an optimal solution. They simply yield an *initial feasible solution.*
2. Even in those cases when these procedures yield an optimal solution, *you would not know that it was optimal.*

FIGURE 7.15

Total Cost for Vogel's
Approximation Method

ROUTE	NUMBER OF ENGINES	COST PER ENGINE	COST
A3	200	$4	$800
A4	300	6	1,800
B2	700	4	2,800
C1	400	10	4,000
C2	200	9	1,800
C4	200	4	800
Total Cost			$12,000

Thus, we clearly need a procedure whereby we can move from an initial feasible solution to the optimal solution. The stepping-stone method is such a procedure and it is the next topic to consider. Before turning to a new topic, however, it is useful to summarize the material on finding initial feasible solutions.

Summary of Procedures for Finding Initial Feasible Solutions

Northwest Corner Rule

1. Start in the upper left-hand corner (origin A, destination 1) and allocate as many units as possible to this cell. That is, use as much supply from origin A as possible, to satisfy demand at destination 1. This means that the amount allocated is the minimum of supply at A and demand at 1.
2. Reduce the available supply at the current origin and unsatisfied demand at the current destination by the amount of the allocation.
3. Identify the first origin with available supply. This is either the current origin or the one directly below it.
4. Identify the first destination with unsatisfied demand. This is either the current destination or the one immediately to the right of it.
5. Allocate, as in step 1, as many items as possible to the route associated with the origin-destination combination identified in steps 3 and 4.
6. Return to step 2.

Vogel's Approximation Method

1. For each row with an available supply and each column with an unfilled demand, calculate a penalty cost by subtracting the smallest entry from the second smallest entry.
2. Identify the row or column with the largest penalty cost. (Ties may be broken arbitrarily.)
3. Allocate the maximum amount possible to the available route with the lowest cost in the row or column selected in step 2.
4. Reduce the appropriate supply and demand by the amount allocated in step 3.
5. Remove any rows with zero available supply and columns with zero unfilled demand from further consideration.
6. Return to step 1.

Stepping-Stone Method

The stepping-stone method is a sequential procedure that starts with an initial feasible solution to a transportation problem (e.g., one produced by the northwest corner rule or Vogel's approximation method) and finds the optimal solution. At each step this procedure attempts to send items along one route *that is unused* in the current feasible solution, while eliminating the use of one of the routes that is currently being used. This changing of routes is done so as to (1) maintain a feasible solution and (2) improve (decrease, in the current context) the value of the objective function. The procedure stops when there is no changing of routes that will improve the value of the objective function. The solution that has this property is the optimal solution. Let us turn immediately to our example problem. The initial feasible solution produced by the northwest corner rule is reproduced in Figure 7.16. We begin with

Finding the Marginal Costs

Step 1 Use the current feasible solution to evaluate the marginal cost of sending material over each of the unused routes, that is, each of the unoccupied cells.

Consider, for example, the currently unused route A3. We wish to determine the marginal cost of using route A3 (i.e., the cost of sending one unit along this route) if

292

CHAPTER 7
Linear
Programming:
Special
Applications

FIGURE 7.16

Initial Feasible Solution Produced
by the Northwest Corner Rule

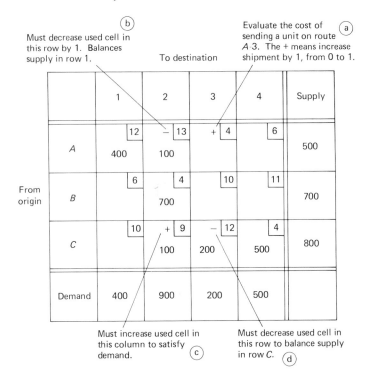

we adjust *only* the other currently *used* routes in such a way as to maintain a feasible solution. The adjustment proceeds as follows:

a. Increase the number of units in cell A3 by 1. This is indicated by a + in the A3 cell.

b. An increase in A3 of 1 unit necessitates a decrease in a used cell in the same row (A1 or A2) of 1 unit. Otherwise, we would exceed the supply of 500 items at A. Suppose that we choose A2. This is indicated by a − in the A2 cell.

c. A decrease of 1 unit in A2 necessitates an increase of 1 unit in a used cell of column 2 (either B2 or C2). Otherwise, we will not satisfy the demand of 900 at 2. Suppose that we choose C2. This is indicated by a + in the C2 cell.

d. An increase of 1 unit in C2 necessitates a decrease of 1 unit in a used cell in row C (C3 or C4). Otherwise, we would exceed the supply of 800 at C. Suppose that we choose C3. This is indicated by a − in the C3 cell.

e. The decrease of 1 unit in C3 is balanced by the increase (step a) in A3. Thus, no further changes are required.

In steps a–e we have found a way to increase A3 by a unit and to adjust the *currently used routes* to maintain a feasible solution.

This process is the heart of the stepping-stone process and thus of this subsection. The example, however, may be misleadingly simple. Complications can occur in attempting to apply it to other problems or even other unused routes in this problem. At this point it is useful to make several comments about the adjustment process in general terms.

Degenerate Solutions	**1.** Suppose that, in the general problem, there are m origins and n destinations. In the present example, $m = 3$ and $n = 4$. If a feasible solution uses less than $m + n - 1$ routes ($3 + 4 - 1 = 6$ routes in this example) the problem is termed degenerate. Special adjustments must be made to use the stepping-stone method on a degenerate problem. This topic is discussed in Section 7.4.	
"Dead Ends"	**2.** The determination of the appropriate path is more complicated than merely jumping from the cell of interest to *any* used cell in the same row or column. "Dead ends" may be encountered, in which case you must make another try. For example, suppose that we had chosen A1 in step b. Then we would have found no occupied cell in column 1 to balance the decrease in A1. This would also have been true if we had chosen B2 in step c. Similarly, it would not have been possible to choose C4 in step d.	
Number of Cells in a Path	**3.** The "stepping-stone" path obtained in steps a through e above contains four cells (including the initial unused cell). The fact that any row or column with a $+$ must also have a $-$ dictates this fact. Although there must always be at least four cells, the path may require more than four.	

Let us summarize the process:

a. Put a $+$ in the unoccupied cell of interest (A3 in the example).
b. Put a $-$ in a used cell in the same row (A2 in the example).
c. Put a $+$ in a used cell in the column determined in step b (C2 in the example).

Stopping Conditions for a Stepping-Stone Path	The process continues by altering $+$'s and $-$'s as well as rows and columns until a sequence of cells is established that satisfies two conditions:

1. It has a $+$ in the original unused cell of interest.
2. Any row (or column) that has a $+$ placed in it also has a $-$, and vice versa. |

The sequence of steps with these properties is called a *stepping-stone* path.

We now return to the example problem and calculate the marginal cost of introducing, as above, the use of route A3.

ACTION	ROUTE	EFFECT ON THE OBJECTIVE FUNCTION
Increase 1 Unit	A3	$+4$
Decrease 1 Unit	A2	-13
Increase 1 Unit	C2	$+9$
Decrease 1 Unit	C3	-12
Marginal Cost		-12

We see, then, that every time we increase by 1 unit the quantity shipped from A to 3 by making the adjustments indicated in our calculation, the value of the objective function will decrease by 12.

It is now obvious that the initial feasible solution is not optimal and that we will want to find a new solution. To do so, we evaluate, in an analogous way, the marginal cost of using each of the other currently unused routes. Let us look at cell A4. In Figure 7.17, the $+$'s in cells A4 and C2 and the $-$'s in cells A2 and C4 are provided to illustrate how the value -2 was calculated. This number results from the following calculation. (The numbers in diamonds below correspond to the numbers in diamonds

294

CHAPTER 7
Linear
Programming:
Special
Applications

FIGURE 7.17

Marginal Cost of Unused Routes

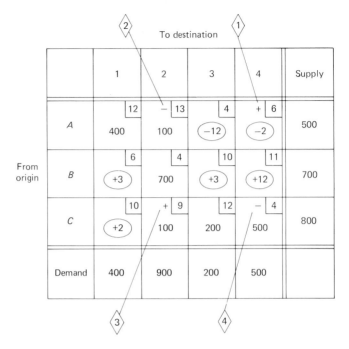

in Figure 7.17 and indicate the sequence in which the route to evaluate cell A4 was constructed.)

SEQUENCE	ACTION	ROUTE	EFFECT ON THE OBJECTIVE FUNCTION
①	Increase 1 Unit	A4	+6
②	Decrease 1 Unit	A2	−13
③	Increase 1 Unit	C2	+9
④	Decrease 1 Unit	C4	−4
	Marginal Cost		−2

You should evaluate the other unused cells to check your understanding. The results are indicated by the encircled numbers in Figure 7.17.

Choosing an Unused Route

Step 2 If all the marginal costs are greater than or equal to zero, stop; you have an optimal solution. If not, select that cell with the most negative marginal cost. In the example, cell A3 has the most negative value, −12.

Generating the New Tableau

Step 3 Determine the maximum number of items that can be allocated to the *route* selected in step 2 (cell A3) and adjust the allocations appropriately. The following table can be used to determine the number of units to allocate to cell A3 in the example:

295

CHAPTER 7
Linear
Programming:
Special
Applications

ACTION	ROUTE	NUMBER AVAILABLE IN DECREASING CELLS
Increase 1 Unit	A3	
Decrease 1 Unit	A2	100
Increase 1 Unit	C2	
Decrease 1 Unit	C3	200

Here we see that the procedure that yields a marginal cost of -12 can be followed only 100 times. After the process has been performed 100 times the solution will have a zero in cell A2 (i.e., no items being shipped from A to 2). In other words, at this point the shipments from A to 2 cannot be further reduced. Thus, in moving from the current solution (the initial feasible solution in this case) to the next solution, we increase the $+$ cells (A3 and C2) by 100 units and decrease the $-$ cells (A2 and C3) by 100 units. This yields the tableau shown in Figure 7.18.

Repeat Steps Until Optimal

Step 4 Return to step 1. Thus, we must reevaluate the marginal cost of introducing each of the currently unused routes. For example, the numbers in diamonds in Figure 7.18 show the stepping-stone path required to evaluate cell B1. This path, which contains six cells, illustrates the above-mentioned possibility that more than four cells may be required.

The evaluation of each currently unused route produces the circled numbers in Figure 7.18. These are the marginal costs of using each of these routes.

Proceeding to step 2 we see that the greatest improvement will be obtained by using route C1, since its marginal cost is the lowest. In step 3 we determine that at

FIGURE 7.18
Improved Solution

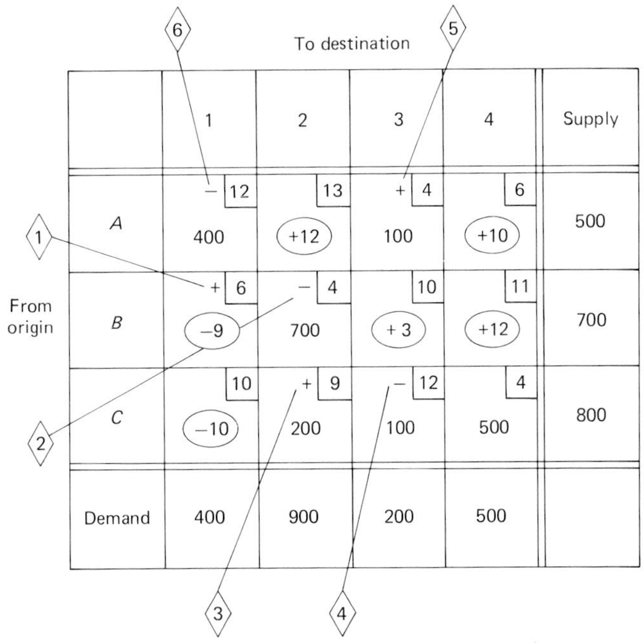

296

CHAPTER 7
Linear
Programming:
Special
Applications

FIGURE 7.19
Optimal Solution

To destination

		1	2	3	4	Supply
	A	12 300	13 (+2)	4 200	6 (0)	500
From origin	B	6 (+1)	4 700	10 (+13)	11 (+12)	700
	C	10 100	9 200	12 (+10)	4 500	800
	Demand	400	900	200	500	

most 100 units can be allocated to this route. (The current value of 100 in cell C3 determines this value.) The adjusted tableau and the marginal costs that result from it are shown in Figure 7.19. Since all of the marginal costs are now greater than or equal to zero, we know that we have found an optimal solution. The optimal value of the objective function can be calculated as shown in Figure 7.20.

FIGURE 7.20
Optimal Solution for PROTRAC's
Transportation Problem

ROUTE	NUMBER OF ENGINES	COST PER ENGINE	COST
A1	300	$12	$3,600
A3	200	4	800
B2	700	4	2,800
C1	100	10	1,000
C2	200	9	1,800
C4	500	4	2,000
Total Cost			$12,000

Comparison with Computer Solution

Let us now compare the final transportation tableau for this problem with the solution the computer produced with the simplex algorithm in Figure 7.3. We note that both approaches yield the same value for the objective function and the same solution. In addition, we see that what we have called marginal costs for the unused cells (the numbers in circles on the final transportation tableau) have the same values as reduced costs produced by the computer. This is reassuring, since both entities have the same interpretation, that is, the marginal cost of increasing the value of a particular variable.

We have already seen that the initial feasible solution produced by Vogel's approximation method is also optimal, because the total cost is $12,000. Comparing Figures 7.19 and 7.14, it is seen that the two solutions are different, even though the objective values are the same. Thus, for this problem, VAM produced an alternative optimal solution to the one we found by using the northwest corner rule and the stepping-stone method. Had we started with VAM, we would have known that we had an optimal solution after the first time we evaluated the marginal costs of the unused routes. When we started with the solution produced by the northwest corner rule, a series of three evaluations was required to find an optimal solution.

As a final point, we note that, in using the stepping-stone method, the existence of an alternative optimum can be recognized by the appearance of a zero marginal cost in the optimal tableau. Thus, in Figure 7.19 the zero marginal cost on the unused cell A4 means that this route could be introduced without increasing the cost. You should verify that introducing this route gives the VAM solution of Figure 7.14.

The stepping-stone method is a useful way to present the computation of marginal costs, since there is a physical interpretation that is easy to follow. There is, however, an easier way to compute these values. It is the modified distribution (MODI) method.

**The Modified
Distribution
(MODI)
Method**

The MODI method is a two-step procedure for finding the marginal costs. Again, we will assume that *each feasible solution encountered uses $m + n - 1$ routes.*

Step 1 Determine an index for each row (u_i for row i) and an index for each column (v_j for column j) such that $u_i + v_j = c_{ij}$ for every *used* cell where c_{ij} is the cost of sending a unit from origin i to destination j. If we start with the initial feasible solution produced by the northwest corner rule (see Figure 7.16), we must select the u_i's and v_j's to satisfy the following constraints:

ROUTE BEING USED	COST PER ENGINE	EQUATION
A1	$12	$u_A + v_1 = 12$
A2	13	$u_A + v_2 = 13$
B2	4	$u_B + v_2 = 4$
C2	9	$u_C + v_2 = 9$
C3	12	$u_C + v_3 = 12$
C4	4	$u_C + v_4 = 4$

Since there are seven variables and only six equations, we can arbitrarily select the value of one of these variables and then use the equations to solve for the other values. For example, if we let $u_A = 0$, we can substitute this value into the first equation and then determine the following index values by working our way down the system of equations. In each case we can substitute a numerical value for one of the variables in an equation.

$$v_1 = 12, \qquad v_2 = 13, \qquad u_B = -9, \qquad u_C = -4, \qquad v_3 = 16, \qquad v_4 = 8$$

It is particularly easy to make these calculations on a transportation tableau, as shown in Figure 7.21. Setting $u_A = 0$ forces v_1 to be 12 since A1 is occupied and $c_{A1} = 12$. With the same logic we see that v_2 must equal 13. This, in turn, implies that $u_B = -9$,

298

CHAPTER 7
Linear
Programming:
Special
Applications

FIGURE 7.21
Row and Column Indices

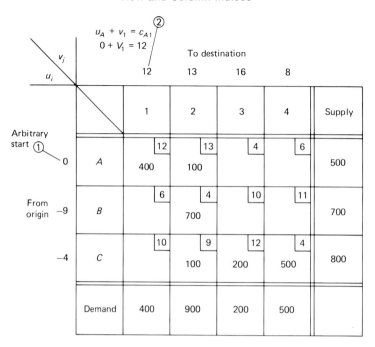

and so on. Now, having determined the u_i's and the v_j's for the occupied cells, we are ready for step 2.

Step 2   Calculate the marginal costs for the *unused* cells. If i, j is an *unused* cell, the marginal cost of using it (call the marginal cost e_{ij}) is given by the equation

$$e_{ij} = c_{ij} - (u_i + v_j)$$

In our example, cell A3 is unoccupied. We see that $u_A = 0$, $v_3 = 16$ and $c_{A3} = 4$. Thus

$$e_{A,3} = 4 - (0 + 16) = -12$$

The same process is used to determine e_{ij} for every unused cell, and the results are shown in Figure 7.22. Comparing this with Figure 7.17 reveals that the e_{ij} values in Figure 7.22 are exactly the same as the marginal cost figures produced by the stepping-stone method. However, they are much easier to find since it is not necessary to find the stepping-stone path for every unused route.

Once the MODI method is used to compute the marginal costs, the system of solving the transportation problem is the same as for the stepping-stone method. In particular, the next step is to select which of the unused routes, if any, to start using. When a cell is selected, it is then necessary to determine how many items to allocate to that cell. To answer that question it is necessary to locate the stepping-stone route for that particular cell. To clarify the similarities and differences between the stepping-stone method and the MODI method of solving a transportation problem, the two approaches are summarized in the following section.

299

CHAPTER 7
Linear
Programming:
Special
Applications

FIGURE 7.22
Marginal Costs of Unused Routes

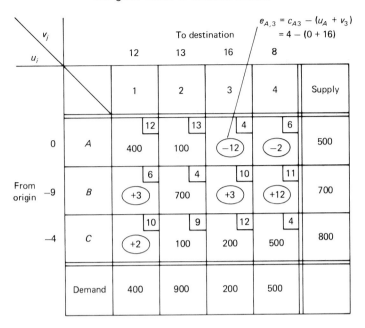

For each of the two methods we will assume that the procedure starts with an initial feasible solution that has $m + n - 1$ routes (used cells), each used cell representing an x_{ij} variable at a positive level.

Stepping-Stone Method

1. Use the current solution to create a unique stepping-stone path for each unused cell. Use these paths to calculate the marginal cost of introducing each unused route into the solution.
2. If all the marginal costs are greater than or equal to zero, stop; you have the optimal solution. If not, select that cell with the most negative marginal cost. (Ties may be broken arbitrarily.)
3. Using the stepping-stone path, determine the maximum number of items that can be allocated to the route selected in step 2 and adjust the allocation appropriately.
4. Return to step 1.

MODI Method

1. Use the current solution and operations (a) and (b) below to evaluate the marginal cost of sending material over each of the unused routes.
   a. Set $u_1 = 0$. Find row indices $u_2, \ldots, u_m$ and column indices $v_1, \ldots, v_n$ such that $c_{ij} = u_i + v_j$ for every *used* cell.
   b. Let $e_{ij} = c_{ij} - (u_i + v_j)$ for every *unused* cell; e_{ij} is the marginal cost of introducing cell i, j into the solution.

Steps 2 through 4 are the same as in the stepping-stone method.

THE TRANSPORTATION MODEL: OTHER CONSIDERATIONS

This section is devoted to extensions of the basic transportation problem introduced in Section 7.2 and to a discussion of special problems that can occur in applying the stepping-stone or MODI solution algorithms. In particular, we will consider

1. Solving max transportation problems.
2. The case when supply exceeds demand.
3. Eliminating unacceptable routes.
4. Degeneracy in transportation problems.
5. Special properties of the transportation model.

Solving Max Transportation Problems

Suppose that in the example problem your goal was to maximize the value of the objective function rather than minimize it. You could use the same solution procedure with one small, but fundamental, change. Think of the marginal values as returns rather than costs. You would thus want to allocate units to the cell with the *largest* marginal value and the procedure would terminate when all the unused routes had *negative* marginal values.

When Supply Exceeds Demand

Suppose that in the example problem the supply at A was 600 engines rather than 500. Then, when all demand is satisfied, the sum, over the three origins, of the engines left over will be 100. In the computer solution to the model, as formulated in Figure 7.3, this causes no special problems. The supply that was not allocated at each origin would appear as a slack variable for that origin. In order to solve the problem by hand using the tableau methods discussed in the preceding section, you must add a dummy destination to the transportation tableau. The modified tableau is shown in Figure 7.23. Note that the cost of supplying the dummy destination, from any origin, is set at zero, and the demand at the dummy destination is set equal to the total excess supply (100 units). Hence, in the solution to this problem, a total of 100 items will be sent to the dummy destination. In reality, any items sent to the dummy destination remain at the origin and thus incur a transportation cost of 0.

We note that if demand exceeds supply, the real problem has no feasible solution. Management might, however, be interested in supplying as much demand as possible at minimum cost. To solve this problem we append a dummy origin with supply equal to the difference between total actual demand and total actual supply. The cost of supplying any destination from this origin is zero. Any supply allocated from the dummy origin to a destination is interpreted as unfilled demand.

Eliminating Unacceptable Routes

Assume that certain routes in a transportation problem are unacceptable. Organizational constraints such as regional restrictions or delivery time could indicate that certain origins could not serve certain destinations. (For example, assume that route A3 could not be used.) This fact is handled in formulating transportation problems by assigning an arbitrarily large cost identified as M to that cell. M is so large that M plus or minus a finite number is still larger than any other number in the tableau. This would then automatically eliminate the use of cell A3 since the cost of doing so would be very large.

The same general approach was used in Section 6.13 to eliminate artificial variables from the basis when using the simplex algorithm to solve LP problems.

301

CHAPTER 7
Linear
Programming:
Special
Applications

FIGURE 7.23

Adding Dummy Destinations

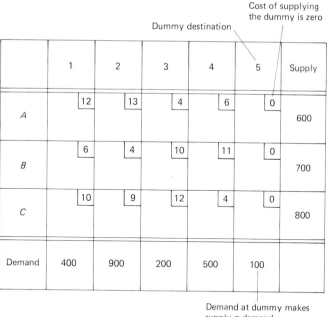

	1	2	3	4	5	Supply
A	12	13	4	6	0	600
B	6	4	10	11	0	700
C	10	9	12	4	0	800
Demand	400	900	200	500	100	

Degeneracy in Transportation Problems

The initial feasible solution, produced by either the northwest corner rule or VAM, and all subsequent feasible solutions encountered with either the stepping-stone method or MODI, will have *at most* $m + n - 1$ positive variables (used cells). When there are less than $m + n - 1$ used cells, that feasible solution is termed *degenerate*. This condition may arise either in the initial feasible solution or at some intermediate feasible solution. Since both the stepping-stone and the MODI methods, as represented above, require $m + n - 1$ used cells (we have not carefully explained *why* this is true, but we have stated it as an assumption), we need a procedure to handle the cases when degeneracy occurs. Consider as an example the **PROTRAC** transportation problem wiith a small modification. Assume that demand at destination 2 is 800 units and demand at destination 4 is 600 units. The initial feasible solution produced by applying the northwest corner rule is shown in Figure 7.24. Since there are only five used cells, this feasible solution is degenerate. With some reflection, you may see that this situation arose because the allocation to route B2 simultaneously exhausted the supply at origin B and satisfied the remaining demand at destination 2. Whenever such a phenomenon occurs, in the application of the northwest corner rule, you will end up with fewer than $m + n - 1$ used routes, and hence degeneracy.

Problems Determining Marginal Costs

Now, beginning with the degenerate initial feasible solution (Figure 7.24), let us attempt to determine the marginal cost for each unused cell. Let us take the MODI approach, which means that we need to find row and column indices such that

$$u_A + v_1 = 12, \qquad u_A + v_2 = 13, \qquad u_B + v_2 = 4, \qquad u_C + v_3 = 12, \qquad u_C + v_4 = 4$$

We start by setting $u_A = 0$. This implies that $v_1 = 12$ and $v_2 = 13$. This, in turn, implies that $u_B = -9$. At this point the process breaks down. We have three unknowns in the last two equations. The system, thus, is not entirely determined, as it was in our earlier example. This situation occurs because the feasible solution is degenerate. If you tried

302

CHAPTER 7
Linear
Programming:
Special
Applications

FIGURE 7.24

Degenerate Solution

To destination

u_i \ v_j		12 (1)	13 (2)	(3)	(4)	Supply
0	A	12 / 400	13 / 100	4	6	500
-9	B	6	4 / 700	10	11	700
	C	10	9	12 / 200	4 / 600	800
	Demand	400	800	200	600	

to calculate marginal costs by using stepping-stone paths, the method, in this degenerate case, would also fail because there would be cells for which a stepping-stone path did not exist. This is true, for example, of cell B3. Can you find others?

The Remedy   The process of solving a transportation problem in which degeneracy occurs consists of employing one of the unused cells as what might be called "*an artificial used*

FIGURE 7.25

Solving a Degenerate Problem

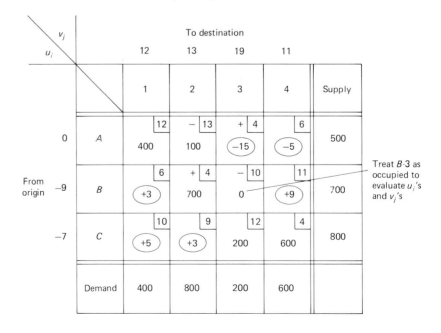

Treat *B*-3 as occupied to evaluate u_i's and v_j's

303

CHAPTER 7
Linear
Programming:
Special
Applications

cell." We simply select any unused cell that will permit us to find the values for u_i and v_j. In our example problem there are several such cells. In particular, if A3, B3, A4, B4, or C2 were used, values for v_3, v_4, and u_C could be found. We proceed by selecting cell B3. As you see in Figure 7.25, a value of 0 is placed in this cell. That is, it is being used "artificially" at the level zero. The explicit assignment of "zero use" is made simply to remind us to treat cell B3 as *used*. (You can think of the zero as actually representing an infinitesimally small positive quantity whose presence, though, gives us $m + n - 1$ used cells.) Let us now follow the MODI method:

- **Step 1:** The values of u_i and v_j are determined as usual. These, in turn, are used to calculate the marginal cost for each unoccupied cell. The marginal costs are circled.
- **Step 2:** We wish to introduce cell A3.
- **Step 3:** To determine how many units can be sent on route A3, we must determine the stepping-stone route. This is indicated by the +'s in cells A3 and B2 as well as the −'s in cells A2 and B3. We then use the following table to determine the number of units to allocate to A3.

ACTION	ROUTE	NUMBER AVAILABLE IN DECREASING CELLS
Increase	A3	
Decrease	A2	100
Increase	B2	
Decrease	B3	0

Since B3 has 0 items available, this is the amount that we can transfer into A3 and B2. The transfer of 0 to A3 allows us now to treat A3 as used (whereas in Figure 7.25 A3 is unused). Thus, we obtain the tableau and the new values for u_i and v_j shown in Figure 7.26.

FIGURE 7.26
Zero Transfer

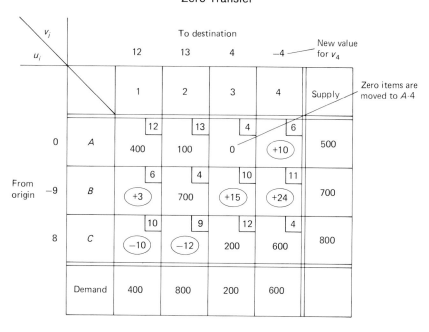

304

CHAPTER 7
Linear
Programming:
Special
Applications

FIGURE 7.27
Transfer into C2

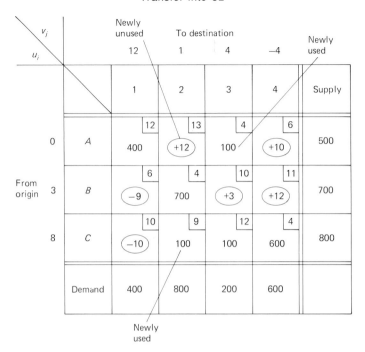

Since cells C1 and C2 have negative marginal costs, the current solution is not optimal. We choose to use route C2. The stepping-stone path for this cell is indicated by the +'s and −'s on the tableau. The maximum amount that can be reallocated is determined by the 100 unit allocation in cell A2. The new tableau and the values for u_i and v_j are shown in Figure 7.27. Note that the solution is no longer degenerate. The last application of the MODI method moved 100 units into two previous unused cells (A3 and C2) while setting only one cell (A2) to zero. The solution of this problem is achieved in one more application of the MODI method. The final tableau appears in Figure 7.28.

In summary, we see that degeneracy in the initial feasible solution is easily handled. If the number of used cells, say u, is less than $m + n - 1$, we simply locate $(m + n - 1) - u$ of the unused cells to treat as being "artificially used" for purposes of calculating the values of u_i and v_j.

In a degenerate problem we see that it is possible to pass through an iteration of the MODI method (or the stepping-stone method) without improving the value of the objective function. This occurs when 0 items are reallocated. This phenomenon occurred in passing from the first to the second tableau in the example just completed.

In concluding this discussion, we state that degeneracy may suddenly occur with an intermediate feasible solution. In the adjustment process, when decreasing the − cells on the stepping-stone path, two or more of these could conceivably become zero. When this happens a degenerate feasible solution results. Suppose, for example, that three − cells simultaneously became zero. Then place 0 in *two* of the cells that have just been decreased to zero. That is, two of these cells are treated as being artificially used. We then continue as previously.

305

CHAPTER 7
Linear
Programming:
Special
Applications

FIGURE 7.28
Optimal Solution

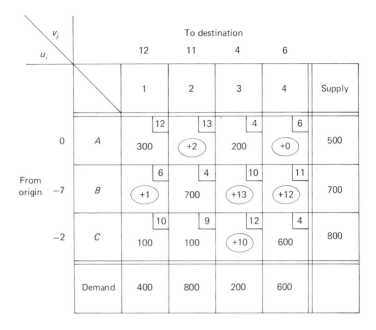

Special
Properties
of the
Transportation
Model

Two aspects of the transportation model and the algorithms used to solve it deserve special mention. First, note that, in addition to employing the simplex method, four special algorithms have been presented: the northwest corner rule, Vogel's approximation method, the stepping-stone method, and the MODI method. Addition and subtraction are the only arithmetic operations used in each of these special algorithms. Contrast this with the simplex algorithm, which also requires division in its implementation.

The fact that the solution algorithms only require addition and subtraction is one of the reasons that transportation problems can be solved so rapidly. This characteristic is shared by some other network algorithms. This topic is discussed in Chapter 9. Thus, our first observation is

> **It is possible to solve the transportation problem with algorithms that use only addition and subtraction.**

The second observation is concerned with the fact that the transportation model has integer solutions under quite general conditions. From earlier chapters we know that, in general, LP models do *not* produce integer solutions. Even general LP models in which all of the parameters are integer (e.g., the **PROTRAC**, Inc. problem) do not necessarily produce integer solutions. The transportation model is an exception. In particular

> **If all of the supplies and demands in a transportation problem have integer values, the optimal value of the decision variables will also have integer values.**

306

CHAPTER 7
Linear
Programming:
Special
Applications

This result is interesting in its own right, and explains why, at the outset, the simplex method produced integer solutions to **PROTRAC**'s problem in Figure 7.3.

The special algorithms specifically designed for the transportation problem make it possible to solve large transportation models quickly, often more quickly than with a general-purpose LP code based on the traditional simplex algorithm. However, the use of a general-purpose LP routine offers the advantage of flexibility in model formulation. For example, using the general LP approach, upper and lower bounds can be placed on route usage (i.e., on the x_{ij}'s) and/or more general linear constraints can be enforced. In order to handle such generalizations conveniently, and due to the widespread availability of general LP codes, the general simplex approach is not an uncommon way, in practice, of solving "transportation-like" models.

Let us now turn to an important special case of the transportation model. This is *the assignment problem.*

7.5

THE ASSIGNMENT PROBLEM

PROTRAC-Europe's Auditing Problem

The assignment problem occurs in many management contexts. In general, it is the problem of determining the optimal assignment of n "*indivisible*" agents or objects to n tasks. For example, management might have to assign salespeople to sales territories or servicereps to service calls or editors to manuscripts or commercial artists to advertising copy. The agents or objects to be assigned are indivisible in the sense that no agent can be divided among several tasks. The important constraint, for each agent, is that *he or she be assigned to one and only one task.* Let us illustrate the assignment model with a particular problem facing the president of **PROTRAC**-Europe. **PROTRAC**'s European headquarters is in Brussels. This year, as part of his annual audit, the president has decided to have each of the four corporate vice-presidents visit and audit one of the assembly plants during the first two weeks in June. As you recall, the assembly plants are located in Leipzig, East Germany; Nancy, France; Liege, Belgium; and Tilburg, the Netherlands.

There are a number of advantages and disadvantages to various assignments of the vice-presidents to the plants. Among the issues to consider are:

1. Matching the vice-presidents' areas of expertise with the importance of specific problem areas in a plant.
2. The time the audit will require and the other demands on each vice-president during the two-week interval.

FIGURE 7.29
Assignment Costs for Every
Vice-President–Plant Combination

	PLANT			
V.P.	LEIPZIG (1)	NANCY (2)	LIEGE (3)	TILBURG (4)
Finance (F)	24	10	21	11
Marketing (M)	14	22	10	15
Operations (O)	15	17	20	19
Personnel (P)	11	19	14	13

307

CHAPTER 7
Linear
Programming:
Special
Applications

3. Matching the language ability of a vice-president with the dominant language used in the plant.

Attempting to keep all these factors in mind and arrive at a good assignment of vice-presidents to plants is a challenging problem. The president decides to start by estimating the cost to **PROTRAC** of sending each vice-president to each plant. The data are shown in Figure 7.29. With these costs, the president can evaluate any particular assignment of vice-presidents to plants. For example, if he chooses the assignment

ASSIGNMENT		COST
V.P.	PLANT	
F	1	24
M	2	22
O	3	20
P	4	13
Total Cost		79

he incurs a total cost of 79.

Solving by Complete Enumeration

One way to find an optimal solution is to list all possible solutions, calculate the cost of each solution, and pick the best. This process is called *complete enumeration*. Let us see how many solutions there are to this problem. Consider assigning the vice-presidents in the order F, M, O, P. We have the following steps:

1. F can be assigned to any of four plants.
2. Once F is assigned, M can be assigned to any of the three remaining plants.
3. Similarly, O can be assigned to any of the two remaining plants.
4. P must be assigned to the only available plant.

There are, thus, $4 \times 3 \times 2 \times 1 = 24$ possible solutions. In general, if there were n vice-presidents and n plants, there would be $n(n-1) \times \cdots \times 2 \times 1$ solutions. This series of multiplications is represented by the symbol $n!$ and called n factorial. As n increases, $n!$ increases even more rapidly. In particular, here is the relation between n and $n!$ for (integral) values of n between 1 and 10:

n	1	2	3	4	5	6	7	8	9	10
$n!$	1	2	6	24	120	720	5040	40,320	362,880	3,628,800

Thus, if the president were currently worrying about which of his 10 salespeople to assign to each of the 10 sales districts, it is clear that complete enumeration would not be a reasonable approach.

Relation to the Transportation Problem

An effective way of representing **PROTRAC**'s assignment problem is with a tableau of the type shown in Figure 7.30. In this figure we note that there is only one of each type of vice-president available (the supply) and one vice-president is required at each plant

308

CHAPTER 7
Linear
Programming:
Special
Applications

FIGURE 7.30

PROTRAC's Assignment Problem

Plants V.P.'s j	Leipzig 1	Nancy 2	Liege 3	Tilburg 4	Number of V.P.'s available
Finance (F)	24	10	21	11	1
Marketing (M)	14	22	10	15	1
Operations (O)	15	17	20	19	1
Personnel (P)	11	19	14	13	1
Number of V.P.'s required	1	1	1	1	4

This cell represents
assigning P to 2

Total V.P.'s available
and required

(the demand). Also, it is a balanced problem in the sense that the total number of vice-presidents available equals the total number required. Each cell represents the assignment of a specific vice-president to a specific plant. The number in the upper right-hand corner is **PROTRAC**'s cost for that assignment.

This hauntingly familiar representation is, of course, reminiscent of the standard transportation problem tableau of the sort introduced in Figure 7.4. There is only one difference. In the assignment problem, we must respect the additional feature that supply cannot be distributed to more than one destination. That is, as previously mentioned, each unit of supply (each agent) must go to one and only one destination. An answer that sent three-fourths of a vice-president to Leipzig and the remaining one-fourth to Liege would not be meaningful and is, therefore, prohibited. Let us now recall the discussion under the heading "Special Properties of the Transportation Model" at the end of Section 7.4. There we learned that, if all the supplies and demands are integers, the optimal allocations will also be integers. In the assignment problem, all supplies and demands are one; and hence integer. Thus, we can be assured that we will not obtain fractional allocations. Thus, we can see that

---

The *assignment problem* can be solved as a *transportation problem* in which the supply at each origin and the demand at each destination is equal to 1.

The LP Formulation and Solution

Since the assignment problem is a special kind of transportation problem, it can be formulated as an LP problem. To create this formulation we use the same definition of variables as we used for the transportation problem. In particular, we let

$$x_{ij} = \text{number of vice-presidents of type } i \text{ assigned to plant } j;$$
$$i = \text{F, M, O, P}; j = 1, 2, 3, 4$$

The formulation and solution are shown in Figure 7.31. In this formulation the first constraint (row 2) states that the number of vice-presidents sent from F must be less

309

CHAPTER 7
Linear
Programming:
Special
Applications

FIGURE 7.31
LP Formulation and Solution of
PROTRAC's Assignment Problem

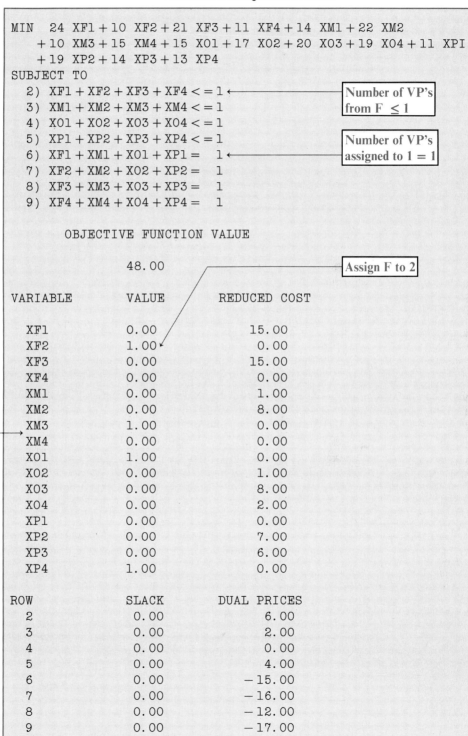

```
MIN   24 XF1 + 10 XF2 + 21 XF3 + 11 XF4 + 14 XM1 + 22 XM2
      + 10 XM3 + 15 XM4 + 15 XO1 + 17 XO2 + 20 XO3 + 19 XO4 + 11 XPI
      + 19 XP2 + 14 XP3 + 13 XP4
SUBJECT TO
   2)  XF1 + XF2 + XF3 + XF4 < = 1
   3)  XM1 + XM2 + XM3 + XM4 < = 1
   4)  XO1 + XO2 + XO3 + XO4 < = 1
   5)  XP1 + XP2 + XP3 + XP4 < = 1
   6)  XF1 + XM1 + XO1 + XP1 =   1
   7)  XF2 + XM2 + XO2 + XP2 =   1
   8)  XF3 + XM3 + XO3 + XP3 =   1
   9)  XF4 + XM4 + XO4 + XP4 =   1


            OBJECTIVE FUNCTION VALUE

                 48.00

   VARIABLE          VALUE           REDUCED COST

      XF1            0.00              15.00
      XF2            1.00               0.00
      XF3            0.00              15.00
      XF4            0.00               0.00
      XM1            0.00               1.00
      XM2            0.00               8.00
      XM3            1.00               0.00
      XM4            0.00               0.00
      XO1            1.00               0.00
      XO2            0.00               1.00
      XO3            0.00               8.00
      XO4            0.00               2.00
      XP1            0.00               0.00
      XP2            0.00               7.00
      XP3            0.00               6.00
      XP4            1.00               0.00


   ROW             SLACK           DUAL PRICES
    2               0.00               6.00
    3               0.00               2.00
    4               0.00               0.00
    5               0.00               4.00
    6               0.00             - 15.00
    7               0.00             - 16.00
    8               0.00             - 12.00
    9               0.00             - 17.00
```

> Number of VP's
> from F ≤ 1

> Number of VP's
> assigned to 1 = 1

> Assign F to 2

Note:
**Optimal Decision
Variables all 0
or 1; see discussion
under "Special
Properties"**

310

CHAPTER 7
Linear
Programming:
Special
Applications

than or equal to 1. Rows 3 through 5 place similar restrictions on vice-presidents M, O, and P, respectively. Row 6 requires 1 vice-president to be assigned to plant 1. Rows 7 through 9 place a similar requirement on plants 2, 3, and 4, respectively.

In the optimal solution part of Figure 7.31 we see that all decision variables are 0 or 1 and the optimal assignment is

ASSIGNMENT		COST
V.P.	PLANT	
F	2	10
M	3	10
O	1	15
P	4	13
Total Cost		48

Also, the optimal value of the objective function is 48.

7.6
SOLVING THE ASSIGNMENT PROBLEM: THE HUNGARIAN METHOD

Since the assignment problem is an LP problem, it can be solved with the simplex algorithm. That was the approach used to obtain the solution presented in Figure 7.31. Further, since the assignment problem is a special variety of transportation problem, we could use the approach presented in Section 7.3 (e.g., a combination of the VAM and MODI algorithms) to find the optimal assignment.

However, the special structure of the assignment problem has enabled mathematicians to devise a particularly simple algorithm for solving this problem. This algorithm, which is called the *Hungarian method*, will be illustrated in the context of **PROTRAC**'s assignment problem. The general approach of this algorithm is to "reduce" the cost matrix by a series of arithmetic operations. These reductions are used to create "reduced" costs of zero in the cost matrix. The optimal assignment is achieved by selecting among the cells with a zero "reduced" cost. Let us start, however, at the beginning. We start with the cost matrix shown in Figure 7.32 and move to the Hungarian method.

FIGURE 7.32
Cost Matrix

V.P.	PLANT			
	1	2	3	4
F	24	10	21	11
M	14	22	10	15
O	15	17	20	19
P	11	19	14	13

311

CHAPTER 7
Linear
Programming:
Special
Applications

FIGURE 7.33
Row Reductions

| V.P. | PLANT | | | | ROW |
	1	2	3	4	REDUCER
F	14	0	11	1	10 ← Subtracted from row F in Figure 7.32
M	4	12	0	5	10
O	0	2	5	4	15
P	0	8	3	2	11

Step 1: Row Reduction   Create a new cost matrix by selecting the minimum cost in each row and subtracting it from every cost in that row. For example, subtracting 10 from each cell in row F yields the following revised row:

| V.P. | PLANT | | | |
	1	2	3	4
F	14	0	11	1

Changing the cost coefficients in this way will have no affect on the optimal solution, for F must still be assigned to one of the four plants, and each such assignment has been reduced by *the same constant*. This means that, were we to use the new costs above, the optimal value of the objective function (i.e., the minimum total cost) would be 10 units less than had we used the original costs. We now apply the same procedure (i.e., subtracting the minimum cost in the row from each element) to the remaining rows. The result is shown in Figure 7.33. As above, this change in costs will not affect the optimal solution to the problem. That is, using the costs from Figure 7.33 produces the same optimal assignment as that obtained by using the original costs (Figure 7.32). However, with the new costs the optimal objective value will be $10 + 10 + 15 + 11 = 46$ less than with the original costs.

Step 2: Column Reduction   Select the minimum-cost entry in each column and subtract it from every entry in that column. This step yields the matrix in Figure 7.34.

FIGURE 7.34
Column Reduction

| V.P. | PLANT | | | |
	1	2	3	4
F	14	0	11	0
M	4	12	0	4
O	0	2	5	3
P	0	8	3	1
Column Reducer	0	0	0	1

Subtracted from column 4 in Figure 7.33

312

CHAPTER 7
Linear
Programming:
Special
Applications

Again, this will not affect the optimal solution. The new optimal objective value will now be 47 units less than previously.

Step 3: Determine if Matrix is Reduced   Find the minimum number of row and column straight lines necessary to cover all the zeros in Figure 7.34. If the minimum number equals the number of rows (or columns), the matrix is termed *reduced*; go to step 5. If the number of lines is less than the number of rows (or columns), go to step 4. In our example, only three lines, as shown in Figure 7.35, are required to cover all the zeros. Thus, the matrix is not reduced and we go to step 4.

FIGURE 7.35
Covering Zeros

V.P.	PLANTS				
	1	2	3	4	
F	14	0	11	0	← Covering zeros in row F
M	4	12	0	4	
O	0	2	5	3	
P	0	8	3	1	

Step 4: Further Reductions   Find the minimum uncovered (unlined) cell. Subtract the value of this cell from every uncovered cell. Add it to the value of the cell at every intersection of the lines drawn in step 3. Leave other cells unchanged. Return to step 3. Thus, since the 1 in cell P4 is the smallest uncovered cost, this operation yields the matrix shown in Figure 7.36.

Step 3 (again)   It now takes four lines to cover all the zeros. One possible set of covering lines is shown on the matrix in Figure 7.36. Note that there are other such sets of four lines. We now go to step 5.

Step 5: Locate the Optimal Solution   It is now possible to find an assignment using only cells with a zero cost. We wish to assign one vice-president to each plant. In terms of the cost matrix, this means that we must choose one and only one cell in each column and in each row. To have an optimal assignment, we must select cells with a zero cost. The solution to **PROTRAC**'s assignment problem is shown in Figure 7.37. The cells with zero cost that are part of the solution are indicated by putting an × across the cell. Note that cell P1 has a cost of 0. It, however, cannot be part of an optimal solution. If P is assigned to plant 1, this eliminates row P and column 1 from further use. (Recall

FIGURE 7.36
Further Reductions

V.P.	PLANT			
	1	2	3	4
F	15	0	12	0
M	4	11	0	3
O	0	1	5	2
P	0	7	3	0

313

CHAPTER 7
Linear
Programming:
Special
Applications

FIGURE 7.37
Optimal Solution

V.P.	PLANT			
	1	**2**	**3**	**4**
F	15	⊠	12	0
M	4	11	⊠	3
O	⊠	1	5	2
P	0	7	3	⊠

that we can use only one cell in each row and column.) Since column 1 is eliminated, we are unable to assign vice-president O at a zero cost (i.e., the only zero in row O occurs in column 1). The value of the objective function can be found by referring to the original cost matrix:

ASSIGNMENT		COST
V.P.	**PLANT**	
F	2	10
M	3	10
O	1	15
P	4	13
Total Cost		48

> Cost of assigning F to 2(see Figure 7.32)

Note that this cost is the sum of all reductions that have been applied. We see, then, that the Hungarian method provides a simple algorithm for solving the assignment problem. Again, we note that addition and subtraction are the only arithmetic operations required by this method.

——— 7.7
THE ASSIGNMENT PROBLEM: OTHER CONSIDERATIONS

PROTRAC's assignment problem is a minimization problem in which the number of vice-presidents equals the number of plants and every possible assignment is acceptable. In this section we consider "assignment-like" problems in which all these conditions do not hold. In particular, we consider problems where (1) there is an unequal number of "persons" to assign and "destinations" needing assignees, (2) there is a maximization problem, and (3) there are unacceptable assignments.

Unequal Supply and Demand: The Auditing Problem Reconsidered

We wish to consider two cases. First, assume that supply exceeds demand. In particular, assume that the president himself decides to audit the plant in Tilburg. He must then decide which of the four vice-presidents to assign to each of the three remaining plants. His problem is represented by the matrix in Figure 7.38.

To solve this problem with the simplex algorithm we would simply drop the constraint that required a vice-president at plant 4, that is, the last constraint (row 9) in Figure 7.31. The result of this change is that the slack variable in one of the four first

314

CHAPTER 7
Linear
Programming:
Special
Applications

FIGURE 7.38
Supply Exceeds Demand

| | | PLANT | | | NUMBER OF V.P.'S |
V.P.		1	2	3	AVAILABLE
F		24	10	21	1
M		14	22	10	1
O		15	17	20	1
P		11	19	14	1
NUMBER OF V.P.'S REQUIRED		1	1	1	3 4

constraints would be 1 in the optimal solution to our modified LP problem. In other words, one vice-president would not be assigned to a plant.

Adding a Dummy Plant

The Hungarian method requires an equal number of vice-presidents and plants. In order to adapt the president's new problem to this requirement, we simply add a "dummy" plant to the problem. The appropriate cost matrix is shown in Figure 7.39. Note that the cost of assigning any vice-president to the dummy plant is zero. In the optimal solution to this problem, one of the vice-presidents will be assigned to the dummy plant. This, of course, implies that in the real problem he is not assigned to a plant.

We now consider the case where demand exceeds supply. For example, assume that the vice-president of personnel had to visit the International Headquarters in East Moline, Illinois, during the first two weeks in June and is thus unable to participate in the management audit. The president's problem is then represented by the cost matrix in Figure 7.40.

Adding a Dummy Vice-President

In this form the problem is infeasible. It is clearly impossible to satisfy the demand for four vice-presidents with a supply of three. If the president wanted to find which three plants to audit in order to minimize his cost, he could add a dummy vice-president as shown in the cost matrix in Figure 7.41.

FIGURE 7.39
Adding a Dummy Plant

| | | PLANT | | | | NUMBER OF V.P.'S |
V.P.		1	2	3	Dummy	AVAILABLE
F		24	10	21	0	1
M		14	22	10	0	1
O		15	17	20	0	1
P		11	19	14	0	1
NUMBER OF V.P.'S REQUIRED		1	1	1	1	4

There is no cost to satisfy demand at the dummy

Dummy demand; now supply = demand

315
CHAPTER 7
Linear
Programming:
Special
Applications

FIGURE 7.40
Demand Exceeds Supply

V.P.	PLANT				NUMBER OF V.P.'S AVAILABLE
	1	2	3	4	
F	24	10	21	11	1
M	14	22	10	15	1
O	15	17	20	19	1
NUMBER OF V.P.'S REQUIRED	1	1	1	1	4 3

FIGURE 7.41
Adding a Dummy Vice-President

V.P.	PLANT				NUMBER OF V.P.'S AVAILABLE
	1	2	3	4	
F	24	10	21	11	1
M	14	22	10	15	1
O	15	17	20	19	1
Dummy	0	0	0	0	1 ← Dummy supply; now supply = demand
NUMBER OF V.P.'S REQUIRED	1	1	1	1	4

Zero cost to assign the dummy

The problem could now be solved by any of the methods we have discussed. In the solution, the dummy vice-president would be assigned to a plant. In reality, this plant would not be audited. The optimal solution is the solution that minimizes the cost of the audits undertaken by F, M, and O. The president should make sure that this is the problem he wants solved, however. It might make more sense to think that **PROTRAC** would incur some cost if a plant was not audited by a vice-president and that this cost could vary from plant to plant. Under these assumptions the new row of the matrix could be labeled "not audited" and the appropriate cost should be entered in each cell. At any rate, when demand exceeds supply, one or more new rows of supply, with appropriate costs, must be appended to the cost matrix before a feasible solution can be found.

Maximization Problems

Consider an assignment problem in which the response from each assignment is a profit rather than a cost. For example, suppose that **PROTRAC** must assign new salespeople to sales territories. Four trainees are ready to be assigned and three territories require a new salesperson. One of the salespeople will have to wait until another territory becomes available before he or she can be assigned. The effect of assigning any salesperson to a territory is measured by the anticipated marginal increase in net profit due to the assignment. Naturally, **PROTRAC** is interested in maximizing total net profit. The *profit* matrix for this problem is presented in Figure 7.42. The only new feature of this figure is that the number in each cell represents a profit rather than a cost.

316

CHAPTER 7
Linear
Programming:
Special
Applications

FIGURE 7.42

Maximization Assignment Problem

SALESPERSON	TERRITORY			NUMBER OF SALESPEOPLE AVAILABLE
	1	2	3	
A	40	30	20	1
B	18	28	22	1
C	12	16	20	1
D	25	24	27	1
NUMBER OF SALESPEOPLE REQUIRED	1	1	1	3
				4

Profit if A is assigned to 3

Only one change is required to create the LP formulation of this problem. The word "Max" now precedes the objective function. The formulation is shown in Figure 7.43. We see that this problem can be solved with the simplex algorithm. An optimal solution could also be found by using transportation algorithms presented earlier in the chapter.

Using the Hungarian method to solve the problem is somewhat more complicated, however. First, since we have more salespeople than districts, a dummy district, as in the preceding section (Figure 7.39), must be added to the matrix. This change is shown in the matrix in Figure 7.44.

Since the number of salespeople now equals the number of territories, we have satisfied one of the requirements of the Hungarian method. However, a more fundamental problem remains. The assignment problem is by definition a minimization problem and the Hungarian method is designed to solve this minimization problem. We now wish to use it to solve our Max problem. Our problem is thus to convert the Max problem into a Min problem in such a way that the optimal solution to the Min problem is also the optimal solution to the original Max problem. There are a variety of ways to accomplish this.

Calculating the Equivalent Cost Matrix

One approach is to subtract each entry in a column from the maximum value in that column. We note that 40 is the largest value in column 1. Subtracting each value from 40 yields the following new column of "costs":

SALESPERSON	TERRITORY 1
A	40 − 40 = 0
B	40 − 18 = 22
C	40 − 12 = 28
D	40 − 25 = 15

Following this procedure for each column yields the cost matrix in Figure 7.45.

To understand the rationale behind this procedure, it is perhaps easiest to think of the cost matrix as representing *opportunity costs*. For example, we know that we must select one cell in column 1. Suppose that no assignments had been made; that is, we could select any row we wanted. If we were maximizing profit, we would, in Figure 7.44, select row 1 since 40 is the largest profit. If we were minimizing opportunity cost we would

FIGURE 7.43
The LP Formulation of a Max
Assignment Problem

```
MAX 40 XA1 + 30 XA2 + 20 XA3 + 18 XB1 + 28 XB2 + 22 XB3
    + 12 XC1 + 16 XC2 + 20 XC3 + 25 XD1 + 24 XD2 + 27 XD3
SUBJECT TO
  2)  XA1 + XA2 + XA3 < = 1
  3)  XB1 + XB2 + XB3 < = 1
  4)  XC1 + XC2 + XC3 < = 1
  5)  XD1 + XD2 + XD3 < = 1
  6)  XA1 + XB1 + XC1 + XD1 = 1
  7)  XA2 + XB2 + XC2 + XD2 = 1
  8)  XA3 + XB3 + XC3 + XD3 = 1
```

Profit if A is assigned to 3

```
        OBJECTIVE FUNCTION VALUE

                    95.00 ←          This is the Optimal Profit
VARIABLE          VALUE          REDUCED COST

   XA1            1.00              0.00
   XA2            0.00              0.00
   XA3            0.00              4.00
   XB1            0.00             20.00
   XB2            1.00              0.00
   XB3            0.00              0.00
   XC1            0.00             24.00
   XC2            0.00             10.00
   XC3            0.00              0.00
   XD1            0.00             18.00
   XD2            0.00              9.00
   XD3            1.00 ←            0.00
```

Assign D to 3

```
 ROW             SLACK          DUAL PRICES

   2             0.00              4.00
   3             0.00              2.00
   4             1.00              0.00
   5             0.00              7.00
   6             0.00             36.00
   7             0.00             26.00
   8             0.00             20.00
```

also select row 1 since 0 is the smallest cost (see Figure 7.45). Now assume that salesperson A had already been assigned, that is, that row 1 was not available. Then if we were maximizing profit, still wishing to assign to column 1, we would select row D because 25 is the largest available profit (see Figure 7.44). If we were minimizing opportunity costs, we would also select row D because 15 is the lowest available cost (see Figure 7.45).

318

CHAPTER 7
Linear
Programming:
Special
Applications

FIGURE 7.44
Adding a Dummy Territory to the
Max Problem

SALESPERSON	TERRITORY				NUMBER OF SALESPEOPLE AVAILABLE
	1	2	3	Dummy	
A	40	30	20	0	1
B	18	28	22	0	1
C	12	16	20	0	1
D	25	24	27	0	1
NUMBER OF SALESPEOPLE REQUIRED	1	1	1	1	4

FIGURE 7.45
Equivalent Cost Matrix

Column entries = 40 − entry in Figure 7.44	SALESPERSON	TERRITORY			
		→1	2	3	4
	A	0	0	7	0
	B	22	2	5	0
	C	28	14	7	0
	D	15	6	0	0

This example illustrates why minimizing opportunity costs yields a solution that maximizes profits.

At this point the Hungarian method can be applied to this matrix in the usual fashion. Doing so yields the optimal solution shown in Figure 7.46. This solution is the same as the solution presented in Figure 7.43. Here we note that salesman C is assigned to the dummy territory; that is, he is not assigned. In Figure 7.43 this conclusion is shown by the fact that XC1, XC2, and XC3 are all zero.

Note that the optimal solution is found by applying the Hungarian method to the equivalent opportunity cost matrix. Finding the correct value for the optimal value of the objective function requires us to combine the optimal solution produced by the Hungarian method with the profit figures in the original problem formulation.

FIGURE 7.46
Optimal Solution by the Hungarian Method

	ASSIGNMENT		PROFIT	
	SALESPERSON	TERRITORY		Profit from original problem, Figure 7.44
Optimal solution derived from equivalent cost matrix, Figure 7.45	A	1	40	
	B	2	28	
	C	4	0	
	D	3	27	
	Total Profit		95	

Suppose that you are solving an assignment problem and you know that certain assignments are simply unacceptable. For example, assume that because of a strong personality conflict the president of **PROTRAC**–Europe is sure that he does not want to have the vice-president of operations (O) audit the assembly plant at Nancy (2). To achieve this goal, he simply assigns an arbitrarily *large cost*, represented by the letter M, to the cell in row O column 2. M is such a large number that subtracting any finite number from M still leaves a value of M that is larger than other relevant numbers. Such an assignment will automatically eliminate the assignment of vice-president O to 2.

This is, of course, the same general approach used to ensure that unacceptable routes are not part of the optimal solution in a transportation problem and to eliminate artificial variables from the solution to LP problems.

7.8
FINANCIAL AND PRODUCTION PLANNING

The Production Problem

The **PROTRAC**, Inc. model was introduced in Chapter 2. It is a product-mix problem, that is, a problem in which **PROTRAC** is deciding how many E-9s and F-9s to make in the coming month, in view of a number of constraints. Recall that E is the number of E-9s to produce and F is the number of F-9s. The complete model is

$$\text{Max } 5000E + 4000F$$

$$\begin{array}{llll} \text{s.t.} & E + F \geq 5 & \text{(total unit requirements)} \\ & E - 3F \leq 0 & \text{(mix requirements)} \\ & 10E + 15F \leq 150 & \text{(hours in department A)} \\ & 20E + 10F \leq 160 & \text{(hours in department B)} \\ & 30E + 10F \geq 135 & \text{(testing hours)} \\ & E, F \geq 0 \end{array}$$

The production manager is satisfied that from his perspective this model captures the essence of the problem. He sends to the management committee a proposal that the recommendations of the model be considered for implementation.

Financial Considerations

When the management committee reviews the activities that are proposed for the coming month, it soon becomes clear that the **PROTRAC** production model captures only a part of **PROTRAC**'s real situation. In particular, certain important financial considerations have been ignored. Specifically, **PROTRAC** must incur material and direct labor costs in the next month, whereas payments from the eventual customers will not be forthcoming for another three months. The current formulation ignores the fact that **PROTRAC** will have to borrow funds to cover at least part of the current expenditures.

The data in Figure 7.47 are relevant to the financial considerations. **PROTRAC** has budgeted $100,000 of cash on hand to cover the current material and labor costs and plans to borrow any additional funds needed for these material and labor costs. **PROTRAC** can borrow money at an annual interest rate of 16%, but in order to hedge against downside risks, the bank has limited the total due to the bank (principal plus interest) to be no more than two-thirds of the sum of **PROTRAC**'s cash on hand and

320

CHAPTER 7
Linear
Programming:
Special
Applications

FIGURE 7.47

Financial Data

PRODUCT	PER UNIT MATERIAL AND LABOR COSTS	PROFIT CONTRIBUTION	SALES PRICE
E	$75,000	$5,000	$80,000
F	20,000	4,000	24,000

accounts receivable. The management committee is concerned that the time value of money has been ignored in calculating the profit contributions. It feels that if present value of net cash flow is maximized fewer E-9s and more F-9s will be produced, because of the relatively high material and labor costs of the E-9s. The committee cannot agree, however, on what the proper discount rate should be. Some members argue for a 12% annual discount rate, others for a 16% rate, and a few for a 20% rate.

The Combined Model

PROTRAC's problem is to formulate a new objective function, determine how much to borrow (if any), and devise a production plan incorporating this new information. To solve this problem, it is convenient to introduce a variable. Let

$$D = \text{debt (i.e., total dollars borrowed), in thousands of dollars}$$

The net cash flow next month will be $1,000D - 75,000E - 20,000F$, while (since payments will not be forthcoming for another three months) the net cash flow three months later will be $80,000E + 24,000F - 1,040D$. The coefficient 1,040 is derived from the above statement that **PROTRAC** can borrow at 16% per annum, and hence at 4% for three months. Define the discount factor, α, based on the annual discount rate, R, as

$$\alpha = \frac{1}{1 + R/4}$$

The objective is to maximize present value of net cash flow, so the objective function becomes

The Objective Function

$$\text{Max } 1,000D - 75,000E - 20,000F + \alpha(80,000E + 24,000F - 1,040D)$$

For example, if $R = 20\%$, $\alpha = .952381$, and the objective function becomes

$$\text{Max } 1190.48E + 2857.14F + 9.52381D$$

Note that D actually has a positive coefficient here, because **PROTRAC** is assuming it can earn 20% on its investments, but only has to pay back 16% interest on borrowed funds. If $R = 16\%$ or $R < 16\%$, then the coefficient of D would be zero or negative, respectively. Additional constraints are also required:

1. PROTRAC must borrow enough so that it is able to cover the material and labor costs associated with production. In general terms, the appropriate inequality is

Minimum Debt Constraint

$$\text{debt} + \text{cash on hand} \geq \text{material and labor costs}$$

321

CHAPTER 7
Linear
Programming:
Special
Applications

To expand this expression, we note that **PROTRAC** has $100,000 of cash on hand. In addition, from Figure 7.47 we see that total material and labor costs are $75,000 for each E and $20,000 for each F. Thus, our equation becomes, expressing everything in thousands,

$$D + 100 \geq 75E + 20F$$

or in computer-acceptable format

$$D - 75E - 20F \geq -100$$

2. The bank requires that the total amount due the bank (i.e., debt plus interest) must be no greater than two-thirds of **PROTRAC**'s cash on hand plus the accounts receivable. In other words

**Maximum
Debt
Constraint**

$$\tfrac{2}{3}(\text{cash on hand} + \text{accounts receivable}) \geq \text{debt} + \text{interest}$$

From Figure 7.47 we see that each E sells for $80,000 and each F sells for $24,000. Thus, in thousands, the total accounts receivable is

$$80E + 24F$$

and the constraint becomes

$$100 + 80E + 24F \geq 1.5(1.04D)$$

or in computer-acceptable format

$$80E + 24F - 1.56D \geq -100$$

Note that the lower bound on the value of D (implicit in the first of the above constraints) depends upon the cost of labor and materials, whereas the upper limit on D (implicit in the last of the above constraints) is based on the sales prices. The complete formulation and solution for the case $R = 20\%$ is shown in Figure 7.48.

In the solution we see that $D = 279.4872$. Since this variable is in thousands of dollars, we know that **PROTRAC** must borrow $279,487.20. The surplus variables for rows 7 and 8 indicate that (since row 8 is active) **PROTRAC** will borrow as much as possible, which (since row 7 has positive surplus) is more than is required to finance material and labor costs. This occurs because the model assumes that excess funds can be invested to earn 20% interest, while the cost of those funds is only 16%.

**Effect of
Financial
Considerations** Finally, we note that inserting the financial considerations in the pure production model leads to quite a different plan from the one determined on the basis of only the production constraints. Figure 7.49 summarizes the results for the pure production model and the model with financial constraints for three different values of the discount rate, R. The optimal value of the objective function is less in the production and finance models because future cash flows are discounted and interest costs are included. In the production and finance model the optimal production plan does not depend on the value of the discount rate within the observed range of 12% to 20%. The optimal debt does, but in a simple manner. If $R < 16\%$, borrow as little as possible, namely $192,500. If $R > 16\%$, borrow as much as possible, namely $279,487.20. If $R = 16\%$ there are alternative optimal solutions where D lies between $192,500 and $279,487.20.

FIGURE 7.48
E and F Financial and Production
Planning Model

```
MAX       1190.47998 E + 2857.14014 F + 9.52381 D
SUBJECT TO
    2)      10 E + 15 F <= 150
    3)      20 E + 10 F <= 160
    4)      30 E + 10 F >= 135
    5)         E -  3 F <=   0
    6)         E +    F >=   5
    7)    - 75 E - 20 F + D >= - 100
    8)      80 E + 24 F - 1.56 D >= - 100


                OBJECTIVE FUNCTION VALUE
```

	This compares with 50,500 for the Pure Production Problem

```
    1)              30161.7700
```

```
    VARIABLE          VALUE          REDUCED COST
```

These compare with $E = 4.5$, $F = 7.0$ in the Pure Production Problem	E	1.500000	.000000
	F	9.000001	.000000
	D	279.487200	.000000

```
    ROW          SLACK OR SURPLUS          DUAL PRICES

    2)                .000000              209.488600
    3)              40.000000                .000000
    4)                .000000             - 13.866840
    5)              25.500000                .000000
    6)               5.500000                .000000
    7)              86.987180                .000000
    8)                .000000             - 6.105007
```

FIGURE 7.49
Results from Models With and Without
Financial Considerations

	PURE PRODUCTION	PRODUCTION AND FINANCE		
		R = 12%	R = 16%	R = 20%
E	4.5	1.5	1.5	1.5
F	7.0	9.0	9.0	9.0
D	—	192.5	192.5	279.4872
OV	50,000	31,844.65	30,576.90	30,161.77

THE MEDIA SELECTION PROBLEM

The Problem in General

The media selection problem is faced by a firm or advertising agency as they try to develop an effective promotional campaign. Basically, the question is how many "insertions" (ads) the firm should purchase in each of several possible media (e.g., radio, TV, newspapers, and magazines). The goal, in a not very specific sense, is to have the advertising campaign be as effective as possible. As we shall see, the explicit objective we will adopt is subjective. Constraints on the decision maker are typically provided by the total advertising budget and the number of opportunities to place an ad that are available in each of the media. Management may further constrain the decision by insisting on various rules of thumb. For example, it migl.t be insisted that at least a certain dollar amount be spent on a specific medium (e.g., at least $10,000 must be spent on newspaper advertising). Alternatively, it might be stipulated that no more than a certain percentage of the budget (say 50%) be spent on any one medium.

Finally, the decision may be influenced by "the law of diminishing returns"; that is, management may believe that the effectiveness of an ad decreases as the number of exposures in a medium increases during a specified period of time. For example, the tenth exposure of a TV ad in a given week would typically not have the same impact on the audience as the first or second exposure.

We present a media selection problem in detail in the following subsection. It is at first, however, interesting to point out that the model has an unusual objective function. Clearly, management would like to select its advertising campaign to maximize demand. Conceptually, then, the model should find the advertising campaign that maximizes demand and satisfies the budget and other constraints. Unfortunately, the link between demand and the advertising campaign is sufficiently vague so that it has proved difficult to construct a useful model based on this approach. The approach that is used is to measure the response to a particular ad in a particular medium in terms of what are called *exposure units*. This is a subjective measure based on management's assessment of the quality of the particular ad, the desirability of the potential market, and so on. In other words, it is an arbitrary measure of the "goodness" of a particular ad. An exposure unit can be thought of as a kind of utility function. Maagement's problem then becomes one of maximizing total exposure units, taking into account other properties of the problem (e.g., cost per number of potential customers reached, etc.). A specific example follows.

Promoting PROTRAC's New Product

The small-tractor division at **PROTRAC** has decided to enter the recreational vehicle market with the Rover, a motorcycle-like machine with three oversized tires. Since this is a new product line, a rather extensive advertising campaign is planned during the introductory month and a budget of $72,000 is set up to fund the campaign.

PROTRAC decides to use daytime radio, evening TV, and daily newspaper ads in its advertising campaign. Data concerning the cost per ad in each of these media and the number of purchasing units reached by each ad are provided by **PROTRAC**'s advertising agency. The data are summarized in Figure 7.50.

We have already mentioned that the effectiveness of an ad is measured in exposures. Management arbitrarily selects a scale from 0 to 100 for each offering of an ad. In particular, it is assumed that each of the first 10 radio ads has a value of 60 exposure units and each radio ad after the first 10 is rated as having 40 exposures. Figure 7.51 shows a plot of total exposures as a function of the number of daytime radio ads during the month.

324
CHAPTER 7
Linear
Programming:
Special
Applications

FIGURE 7.50
Media Data

ADVERTISING MEDIUM	NUMBER OF PURCHASING UNITS REACHED PER AD	COST PER AD
Daytime Radio	30,000	$1700
Evening TV	60,000	2800
Daily Newspaper	45,000	1200

FIGURE 7.51
Total Exposures versus Number of Radio Ads.

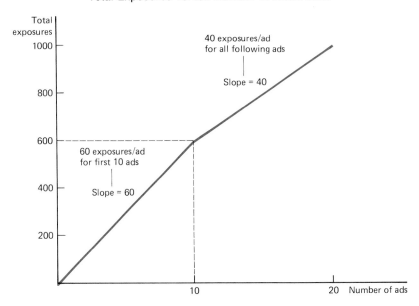

Note that in this figure, since each of the first 10 radio ads is rated as having 60 exposures, the slope of the first line segment is 60. After the first 10 ads, since each radio ad is rated as having 40 exposures, the slope of the second line segment is 40. Radio ads, then, suffer from diminishing returns. It is management's subjective evaluation that the first ads are more effective than later ones. This evaluation is based primarily on the assumption that a large proportion of those who see the later ads in a given medium will also have seen the earlier ones.

PROTRAC's analysts feel that the same situation will occur with TV and newspaper ads; that is, they, too, will suffer from diminishing returns. Indeed, they assume

FIGURE 7.52
Exposures Per Ad

ADVERTISING MEDIUM	FIRST 10 ADS	ALL FOLLOWING ADS
Daytime Radio	60	40
Evening TV	80	55
Daily Newspaper	70	35

325

CHAPTER 7
Linear
Programming:
Special
Applications

that in all three cases the slope (i.e., the exposures per ad) will change at the tenth ad. The exposures per ad (i.e., the slope of the two line segments), however, vary with the particular medium. The data are summarized in Figure 7.52.

The total exposures as a function of the number of ads in each medium are plotted in Figure 7.53.

Management wants to ensure that the advertising campaign will satisfy certain criteria that it feels are important. In particular: (1) no more than 25 ads should appear in a single medium, (2) a total number of 1,800,000 purchasing units must be reached across all media, and (3) at least one-fourth of the ads must appear on evening TV. To model **PROTRAC**'s media selection problem as an LP problem, we let

The Decision Variables

$x_1 =$ number of radio ads up to the first 10

$y_1 =$ number of radio ads after the first 10

$x_2 =$ number of TV ads up to the first 10

$y_2 =$ number of TV ads after the first 10

$x_3 =$ number of newspaper ads up to the first 10

$y_3 =$ number of newspaper ads after the first 10

With this notation we note that $60x_1$ is the total exposures from the number of "first 10" radio ads and $40y_1$ is the total exposures from the remaining radio ads. Thus,

FIGURE 7.53

Total Exposures versus Number of Ads.

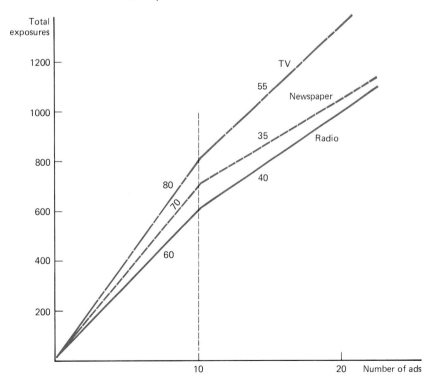

the objective function is

$$\text{Max } 60x_1 + 40y_1 + 80x_2 + 55y_2 + 70x_3 + 35y_3$$

Turning to the constraints, we note that

$$x_1 + y_1 = \text{total radio ads}$$

$$x_2 + y_2 = \text{total TV ads}$$

$$x_3 + y_3 = \text{total newspaper ads}$$

Referring to Figure 7.50, we see that each radio ad costs \$1700. The expression for the total spent on radio ads is $1700(x_1 + y_1)$. Since TV ads cost \$2800 each and newspaper ads cost \$1200 each, the total advertising expenditure is $1700(x_1 + y_1) + 2800(x_2 + y_2) + 1200(x_3 + y_3)$. **PROTRAC** has allocated \$72,000 for the promotional campaign. This constraint is enforced by the following inequality:

$$1700x_1 + 1700y_1 + 2800x_2 + 2800y_2 + 1200x_3 + 1200y_3 \leq 72{,}000$$

The constraint that no more than 25 ads appear on daytime radio is imposed by the inequality $x_1 + y_1 \leq 25$. A similar constraint is required for each medium.

Referring again to Figure 7.50, we see that each radio ad reaches 30,000 purchasing units. Thus, the total number of purchasing units reached by radio ads is $30{,}000(x_1 + y_1)$. The requirement that the entire campaign reach at least 1,800,000 purchasing units is imposed by the inequality

$$30{,}000x_1 + 30{,}000y_1 + 60{,}000x_2 + 60{,}000y_2 + 45{,}000x_3 + 45{,}000y_3 \geq 1{,}800{,}000$$

Finally, the constraint that at least one-fourth of the ads must appear on evening TV is guaranteed by the constraint

$$\frac{x_2 + y_2}{x_1 + y_1 + x_2 + y_2 + x_3 + y_3} \geq \frac{1}{4}$$

or

$$-x_1 - y_1 + 3x_2 + 3y_2 - x_3 - y_3 \geq 0$$

The complete formulation is presented in Figure 7.54. Note that the last three constraints enforce the definition of the variables x_1, x_2 and x_3. There is, however, one additional point to be noted. According to the definitions x_1 is the number of radio ads up to the first 10 and y_1 is the number of radio ads after the first 10. Let x_1^* and y_1^* be the optimal values of these variables. Clearly it would not make sense to have an optimal solution with $x_1^* < 10$ and $y_1^* > 0$, that is, it does not make sense to have placed ads after the first 10 when not all of the first 10 have been placed. Nothing in the constraints prevents this. However, it will not occur. The reason is that the marginal contribution of x_1, in the objective function, is larger than that of y_1. If $x_1 < 10$ and $y_1 > 0$ is feasible, you can see from the constraints that the values $x_1 + E$ and $y_1 - E$ will also be feasible, where E is a very small positive number. Moreover, in the objective function, since the coefficient of x_1 is larger than the coefficient of y_1, this substitution

FIGURE 7.54
Formulation of the Media Selection Problem

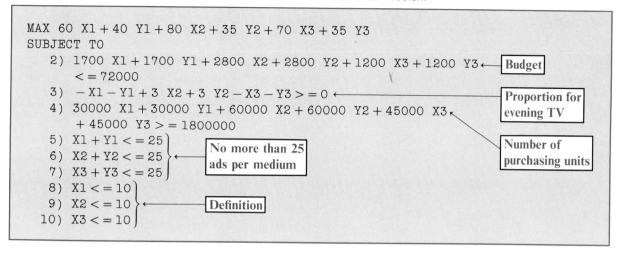

```
MAX  60 X1 + 40 Y1 + 80 X2 + 35 Y2 + 70 X3 + 35 Y3
SUBJECT TO
    2) 1700 X1 + 1700 Y1 + 2800 X2 + 2800 Y2 + 1200 X3 + 1200 Y3    Budget
       < = 72000
    3) − X1 − Y1 + 3 X2 + 3 Y2 − X3 − Y3 > = 0                      Proportion for
    4) 30000 X1 + 30000 Y1 + 60000 X2 + 60000 Y2 + 45000 X3         evening TV
       + 45000 Y3 > = 1800000
    5) X1 + Y1 < = 25 ⎤                                             Number of
    6) X2 + Y2 < = 25 ⎬   No more than 25                           purchasing units
    7) X3 + Y3 < = 25 ⎦   ads per medium
    8) X1 < = 10 ⎤
    9) X2 < = 10 ⎬    Definition
   10) X3 < = 10 ⎦
```

will give an improved objective value. In prosaic terms, the maximization will push x_1 to its limit (10 ads) before making y_1 greater than zero. Analogous comments apply to x_2, y_2 and x_3, y_3.

_____ 7.10
SUMMARY

This chapter is devoted to special applications of the linear programming model. Four models are presented in some detail.

Sections 7.2 through 7.4 are devoted to the transportation problem. The generic problem is one of determining the least-cost method of satisfying demands at a number of destinations by shipping materials from supplies available at several origins. This problem is motivated by a specific problem faced by **PROTRAC**–Europe. In Section 7.2 this problem is formulated as an LP problem and solved on the computer. Section 7.3 presents two algorithms for finding an initial feasible solution, the northwest corner rule and Vogel's approximation method, as well as two algorithms for moving from an initial feasible solution to the optimal solution, the stepping-stone method and MODI, the modified distribution method. The final section in this group, Section 7.4, covers a pot-pourri of topics related to the transportation problem. The first four subsections discuss the adaptations that are necessary in order to use the algorithms (those given in Section 7.2) for solving the transportation problem when the models differ from the original model. Finally, we see that the transportation problem has two special properties. First, if all supplies and demands are integer quantities, there is an optimal integer solution. Second, the algorithms for solving the transportation problem use only addition and subtraction. This fact helps explain why the special algorithms are able to obtain optimal solutions so quickly.

Sections 7.5 through 7.7 treat the assignment problem following the pattern of the preceding three sections. The generic assignment problem is one of assigning n persons to n tasks in order to minimize the total cost of the assignments. This problem is again motivated by a specific problem faced by **PROTRAC**–Europe. The problem is formulated

328

CHAPTER 7
Linear
Programming:
Special
Applications

as an LP problem and solved on the computer. In this process we note that the assignment problem is a special type of transportation problem in which all supplies and demands equal 1. Section 7.6 presents the Hungarian method, an efficient algorithm for solving the assignment problem. Finally, Section 7.7 treats a variety of special subjects dealing with the use of the Hungarian algorithm.

Section 7.8 discusses and formulates examples of several other important classes of LP models used for financial and production planning. Media selection in the marketing context is discussed in Section 7.9.

———— 7.11
KEY TERMS

TRANSPORTATION PROBLEM.   An LP model to find the least expensive way of satisfying demands at n destinations with supplies from m origins.

ORIGIN.   A source of material in a transportation problem.

DESTINATION.   A location with a demand for material in a transportation problem.

NORTHWEST CORNER RULE.   An algorithm that finds an initial feasible solution to a transportation problem by satisfying demands and exhausting supplies in a prescribed order.

VOGEL'S APPROXIMATION METHOD (VAM).   An algorithm that finds an initial feasible solution to a transportation problem by considering the "penalty cost" of not using the cheapest available route.

TRANSPORTATION TABLEAU.   A table used to display the parameters for a transportation problem and to provide a convenient way of applying the solution algorithms.

STEPPING-STONE METHOD.   A sequential algorithm that starts with a feasible solution and produces an optimal solution to a transportation problem.

STEPPING-STONE PATH.   A series of adjustments in a feasible solution to a transportation problem that incorporates a new route and retains a feasible solution.

MODIFIED DISTRIBUTION METHOD (MODI).   A simpler way of calculating the parameters needed in the stepping-stone method.

DEGENERACY.   A condition indicated in a transportation problem by the fact that less than $m + n - 1$ routes are being used.

CELL.   The rectangle in a transportation tableau used to identify the route between an origin and a destination.

DUMMY ORIGIN.   An imaginary source that is added to a transportation problem so that total supply equals total demand. Used in the algorithms specifically designed for the transportation problem.

DUMMY DESTINATION.   An imaginary destination that is added to a transportation problem so that total supply equals total demand. Used in the algorithms specifically designed for the transportation problem.

HUNGARIAN METHOD.   An algorithm specifically designed to solve the assignment problem.

MATRIX REDUCTION.   The process used in the Hungarian method to convert the original cost matrix to one in which the optimal assignment is selected from assignments with a cost of zero.

EXPOSURE UNITS.   An arbitrary measure of the "goodness" of an ad used in solving media selection problems.

MAJOR CONCEPTS QUIZ ————————————

True–False   1. **T   F**   The coefficient of x_{ij} in the objective function of a transportation problem is the cost of sending a unit from i to j.

2. **T   F**   Vogel's approximation method is based on the concept of a break-even quantity.

3. **T   F**   The stepping-stone method requires a feasible solution as a starting point.

329

CHAPTER 7
Linear
Programming:
Special
Applications

4. **T F** In the MODI method you must determine an index for each row (u_i for row i) and an index number of each column (v_j for column j) such that $u_i + v_j = x_{ij}$ for every used cell.

5. **T F** To solve a Max transportation problem you terminate when all the unused routes have negative marginal values.

6. **T F** If total supply exceeds total demand in a transportation problem, to find a solution you should add a dummy destination with a transportation cost of zero from every origin.

7. **T F** A transportation problem cannot have an optimal integer solution unless all of the supplies, demands, and transportation costs are integers.

8. **T F** One way to transform a Max assignment problem into a problem that can be solved with the Hungarian algorithm is to subtract each entry in a column from the maximum value in that column.

Multiple Choice

9. The northwest corner rule
   a. is used to find an initial feasible solution
   b. is used to find an optimal solution
   c. is based on the concept of minimizing opportunity cost
   d. none of the above

10. In Vogel's approximation method the opportunity cost associated with a row is determined by
    a. the difference between the smallest cost and the next smallest cost in that row
    b. the difference between the smallest unused cost and the next smallest unused cost in that row
    c. the difference between the smallest cost and the next smallest unused cost in the row
    d. none of the above

11. The maximum number of items that can be allocated to an unused route with the stepping-stone algorithm is
    a. the maximum number in any cell
    b. the minimum number in any cell
    c. the minimum number in an increasing cell
    d. the minimum number in a decreasing cell on the stepping-stone path for that route

12. The MODI method uses the stepping-stone path
    a. to calculate the marginal cost of unused cells
    b. to determine how many items to allocate to the selected unused cell
    c. to determine the values of the row and column indexes
    d. not at all

13. Degeneracy occurs in a transportation problem when
    a. demand exceeds supply
    b. exactly one used cell becomes unused while moving items to a currently unused cell
    c. less than $m + n - 1$ cells are used
    d. none of the above

14. The assignment problem
    a. is a special case of the transportation problem
    b. can be solved with the simplex algorithm
    c. always has an optimal integer solution when treated as an LP
    d. all of the above

Answers

1. T	5. T	9. a	12. b
2. F	6. T	10. b	13. c
3. T	7. F	11. d	14. d
4. F	8. T		

PROBLEMS

(7-1) Consider the transportation tableau in Figure 7.55.
  (a) Find an initial feasible solution and evaluate its cost with
      (i) The northwest corner rule.
      (ii) Vogel's approximation method.
  (b) Comment on the relative quality of the solutions determined in part (a).

FIGURE 7.55

Origins \ Destinations	1	2	3	Supply
A	10	8	4	45
B	9	5	7	50
C	3	6	9	45
D	5	7	6	30
Demand	90	30	50	

7-2. Consider the transportation tableau in Figure 7.56.
  (a) Find an initial feasible solution and evaluate its cost with
      (i) The northwest corner rule.
      (ii) Vogel's approximation method.
  (b) Comment on the following statement: Vogel's approximation method always yields a better initial feasible solution than the northwest corner rule because it considers costs in making its allocation decisions.

FIGURE 7.56

Origin \ Destinations	1	2	3	Supply
A	96	85	144	60
B	66	48	62	30
C	108	72	60	45
Demand	45	75	15	

(7-3) Consider the transportation problem presented in Problem 7-1. Find the optimal solution by
  (a) Starting with the solution produced by the northwest corner rule and then using the stepping-stone method. Specify the optimal value of the objective function.

331

CHAPTER 7
Linear
Programming:
Special
Applications

(b) Starting with the solution produced by Vogel's approximation method and using the MODI method, specify the optimal value of the objective function.

(c) What is the additional cost if management insists on sending at least 10 units from C to 1?

(d) What is the additional cost if management insists on sending 10 units from C to 2?

7-4. Consider the transportation problem presented in Problem 7-2. Find the optimal solution by

(a) Starting with the solution produced by the northwest corner rule and then using the MODI method, specify the optimal value of the objective function.

(b) Starting with the solution produced by Vogel's approximation method and using the stepping-stone method, find the optimal value of the objective function.

(c) What is the additional cost if management insists on sending at least 30 units from A to 1?

(d) What is the additional cost if management insists on sending 10 units from C to 1?

7-5. What additional cost will management incur in Problem 7-3 if 15 units are sent from D to 3?

7-6. What additional cost will management incur in Problem 7-4 if no item can be sent from B to 2?

7-7. Use the northwest corner rule and the stepping-stone method to find the optimal solution to the *maximization* transportation problem shown in Figure 7.57. State the optimal value of the objective function.

FIGURE 7.57

	1	2	3	Supply
A	5	7	10	400
B	4	9	6	300
C	8	3	2	200
Demand	150	500	250	900

7-8. Use Vogel's approximation method and the MODI method to find the optimal solution to the *maximization* problem shown in Figure 7.58. State the optimal value of the objective function.

FIGURE 7.58

	1	2	3	Supply
A	10	7	5	400
B	6	9	4	300
C	2	3	8	200
Demand	150	500	250	900

332

CHAPTER 7
Linear
Programming:
Special
Applications

7-9. Use the northwest corner rule and the stepping-stone method to solve the transportation problem shown in Figure 7.59. State the optimal value of the objective function. Note that supply exceeds demand.

FIGURE 7.59

	1	2	Supply
A	7	5	200
B	4	8	100
C	5	6	300
Demand	200	300	

7-10. Use Vogel's approximation method and the MODI method to solve the transportation problem shown in Figure 7.60. State the optimal value of the objective function. Are there alternative optimal solutions?

FIGURE 7.60

	1	2	3	Supply
A	2	6	3	200
B	5	1	9	300
C	7	9	8	100
Demand	300	200	100	

7-11. Johnson Electric produces small electric motors for four appliance manufacturers in each of its three plants. The unit production costs vary with the locations because of differences in the production equipment and labor productivity. The unit production costs and monthly capacities (supplies) are shown in Figure 7.61. The customer orders that must be produced next month are shown below.

CUSTOMER	DEMAND
1	300
2	500
3	400
4	600

The cost of supplying these customers varies from plant to plant. The unit transportation costs in dollars are given in Figure 7.62. Johnson must decide how many units to produce in each plant and how much of each customer's demand to supply from each plant. It

333

CHAPTER 7
Linear
Programming:
Special
Applications

FIGURE 7.61

PLANT	UNIT PRODUCTION COST	MONTHLY PRODUCTION CAPACITY
A	$17	800
B	20	600
C	24	700

FIGURE 7.62

FROM	TO			
	1	2	3	4
A	3	2	5	7
B	6	4	8	3
C	9	1	5	4

wishes to minimize total production and transportation costs. Formulate Johnson's problem as a transportation problem and show the original tableau.

7-12. Fernwood Lumber produces plywood. The cost to produce 1000 board feet of plywood varies from month to month because of the variation in handling costs, energy consumption, and raw materials costs. The production cost per 1000 board feet in each of the next 6 months is shown below.

MONTH	1	2	3	4	5	6
PRODUCTION COST (DOLLARS)	950	1000	1200	1100	850	900

Demand for the next 6 months is as follows:

MONTH	1	2	3	4	5	6	Total
DEMAND	50	80	100	90	60	70	450

Fernwood can produce up to 90,000 board feet per month. It also has the option of carrying inventory from one month to the next for a carrying cost of $25 per 1000 board feet per month. For example, 1000 board feet produced in month 1 for demand in month 2 incurs a carrying charge of $25. Furthermore, unsatisfied demand in one month can be filled in later periods at the cost of $40 per 1000 board feet per month-delay. Fernwood would like to know how much to produce each month and how much inventory to carry in order to satisfy demand at minimum cost. Formulate Fernwood's problem as a transportation problem and show the original transportation tableau.

334

CHAPTER 7
Linear
Programming:
Special
Applications

7-13. A partner at Foot, Thompson and McGrath, the advertising agency, is trying to decide which of four account executives to assign to each of four major clients. The estimated costs of each assignment for each executive are presented in Figure 7.63. Use the Hungarian method to find the optimal solution to this problem. State the optimal value of the objective function.

FIGURE 7.63

	ACCOUNT			
EXEC.	1	2	3	4
A	15	19	20	18
B	14	15	17	14
C	11	15	15	14
D	21	24	26	24

7-14. Sam has four different repair bays in the maintenance shop and three jobs to assign to them. Because of differences in the equipment available, the people assigned to each bay, and the characteristics of the job, each job requires a different amount of time in each bay. The estimated times for each job in each bay are shown in Figure 7.64. Sam would like to minimize the total time required. Use the Hungarian method to obtain the optimal solution to this problem. State the optimal value of the objective function. Are there alternative optimal solutions?

FIGURE 7.64

	JOB		
BAY	1	2	3
A	17	29	16
B	15	28	11
C	18	26	11
D	13	25	11

7-15. **PROTRAC** is deciding which of four salespeople to assign to each of four midwestern sales districts. Each salesperson is apt to achieve a different sales volume in each district. The estimates are shown in Figure 7.65. Protrac would like to maximize total sales volume. However, it is impossible to assign salesperson B to district 1 or salesperson A to district 2 since these assignments would violate personnel rotation policies. Use the Hungarian method to solve this problem. State the optimal value of the objective function.

FIGURE 7.65

	DISTRICT			
SALESPERSON	1	2	3	4
A	65	73	55	58
B	90	67	87	75
C	106	86	96	89
D	84	69	79	77

335

CHAPTER 7
Linear
Programming:
Special
Applications

7-16. A realtor plans to sell four plots of land and has received individual bids from each of five developers. Because of the amount of capital required, these bids were made with the understanding that no developer would purchase more than one plot. The bids are shown in Figure 7.66. The realtor wants to maximize total income from these bids. Solve this problem using the Hungarian method. State the value of the objective function.

FIGURE 7.66

PLOT	DEVELOPER				
	1	2	3	4	5
A	16	15	25	19	20
B	19	17	24	15	25
C	15	15	18	0	16
D	19	0	15	17	18

8

INTEGER AND QUADRATIC PROGRAMMING

APPLICATION CAPSULE

SCHEDULING TRAINING AT AMERICAN AIRLINES*

Each month between 500 and 600 crew members from 10 different crew bases are scheduled to receive a short course in the recurrent training program. The recurrent training is given at the American Airlines Flight Academy at Dallas/Fort Worth Airport. A variety of rules govern (a) when a crew member is due to receive recurrent training (in order to remain qualified to fly on a particular type of equipment); and (b) the pay a crew member is entitled to receive during the recurrent training period (the pay depends on whether the crew member is trained on free time or is relieved of an assignment). The scheduling must satisfy a variety of constraints. For example, there must be enough people available in reserve to replace those trainees relieved of a flying assignment. A manual procedure had previously been used for the scheduling. In an attempt to redress numerous problems associated with the manual system, the American Airlines Operations Research group undertook an effort to model the system. A major component of the overall model was an integer linear program involving more than 26,000 variables and 500 constraints. Because of the need for quick turn-

* Shapiro, Monroe, "Scheduling Crewmen for Recurrent Training," *Interfaces*, 11, no. 3 (June 1981) 1–8.

around in solving this problem, a 3-phase heuristic approach was devised. The system was implemented in 1977 and became an integral component of the crew-scheduling procedure. By conservative estimates the program saved $250,000 per year in crew costs.

━━━━ 8.1
INTRODUCTION TO INTEGER PROGRAMMING

The first half of this chapter is devoted to problems that could be formulated and solved as linear programming problems except for the unpleasant nuance that some or all of the variables are required to assume integer values. Such problems are called IP (integer programming) problems. Integer programming has become a very important specialized area of management science. In this introductory chapter, it will be possible only to scratch the surface—to illustrate the importance of the topic, as well as one of the most useful solution methods. At the outset, let us recall from previous chapters that in a linear programming problem the variables are permitted to take on fractional values, such as 6.394, and in keeping with the principle that "whatever is allowed will occur," fractional answers must be expected.[1] In spite of this, actual (real-world) decision vari-

A Practical Approach
ables often must be integers. For example, a firm produces bags of cattle feed. A solution that requires them to make 3000.472 bags does not make sense. In such situations a noninteger solution is often adapted to the integer requirement by simply rounding the results to a neighboring integer. This produces what we call "a rounded solution." Using such a solution is acceptable to management in those situations where, in a significant practical sense, the rounding simply does not matter. For example, there is no significant difference either in the objective function or in the constraints between producing 19,283.64 and 19,283 bags of Big Bull cattle feed. Indeed, there are probably enough approximations used in assembling the data for the model that management would be content with any production figure near the 19,000-bag level.

There are, however, a number of important problems where this rather cavalier attitude toward the integer requirements of the real problem just does not work. This complication can be caused by the scale of the variables under consideration. For example, if the solution to an LP model suggested that Boeing should build 11.6 747's and 6.8 727's, management probably would not be comfortable just going ahead and

When Integer Solutions Matter
deciding to build 11 747's and 6 727's, or, for that matter any other rounded combination. The magnitude of the return and the commitment of resources associated with each unit of this problem make it advisable to determine the best possible *integer solution*. As another example, it will be seen that many models use integer variables to indicate logical decisions. For example, we will see problems where we want X_7 to equal 1 if we should build a warehouse in Kansas City and X_7 to equal 0 if we should not. Suppose that the solution to an LP version of this problem yielded a noninteger value (e.g., $X_7 = 0.38$). We shall see that this value contains no useful information about the solution to the real problem. Clearly, we cannot build 0.38 of a warehouse. We certainly could select warehouses of different sizes, but nevertheless, either we have a warehouse

---

[1] An exception to this is described in Chapter 7. Transportation models with integral supplies and demands will always produce integer-valued optimal solutions. As will be seen in Chapter 9, this remarkable property is true of a more general class of models called network models. Transportation models are a special type of network models.

in Kansas City or we do not. You might guess that, in a case such as this, rounding to the nearest integer (0 in this case) would be a way to approach this difficulty. Unfortunately, that is not guaranteed to give a good (to say nothing of optimal) solution. Indeed, we shall see that rounding may not even lead to a feasible solution in cases such as these.

The bottom line is that there are many important management problems which would be linear programming problems except for the requirement of integer values for some of the decision variables, where you *cannot* find a good solution by using the simplex method and then rounding off the resulting optimal values of the decision variables. These problems must be solved with algorithms designed especially to solve **integer programming problems**.

Management scientists have been aware of the importance of integer linear programming problems for years, and a great deal of time and effort has been devoted to research on the solution of these problems. These efforts have returned some dividends and marked progress has been made in this area over the last 10 years. It should be also noted that the great strides in computer technology have made a crucial contribution to the increased ability to solve integer linear programming problems.

LP vs. IP   In spite of the impressive improvement in our ability to solve integer programming problems, the technology is still quite different from what we have available to attack programming problems in which the decision variables need not be integer. Many problems that can be solved easily as LP problems become unsolvable for practical purposes if the decision variables are required to be integers (i.e., the time and cost needed to compute a solution are too large).

In the following sections we first describe two general classes of integer linear programming models and use **graphical analysis** to illustrate the relationship between linear programming, integer linear programming, and the process of rounding LP solutions to obtain a possible solution to the IP. This graphical approach will provide an intuitive feeling for the nature of the problem we are confronting. We then turn our attention to a special variety of integer programs in which the integer variables are restricted to the values of 0 or 1. Using such "indicator" or "Boolean" variables allows us to **formulate** a variety of logical conditions which are not otherwise easily captured. A number of important practical problems involve such conditions, and several of these formulations are discussed. We then turn to the topic of **solving** integer linear programs. First we consider the **branch-and-bound algorithm** that is used to solve these problems. Then our attention turns to the topic of integer linear programming in practice, emphasizing **strategic considerations** as well as discussing possibilities for **sensitivity analysis**.

In real applications, integer programs are never solved by hand. In order to convey the context of how you would, in practice, deal with such problems we have provided in this chapter, as in others, several computer printouts. Some of these are annotated in order to highlight the interpretation of various numbers. In looking over these printouts, review the problem and the formulation; ask yourself whether the solution is intuitively plausible and, if not, try to explain why. This type of analytic thinking can be developmental; it plays a useful role in the management function.

_____ 8.2
TYPES OF INTEGER LINEAR PROGRAMMING MODELS

Integer programming is a general term for mathematical programming models with **integrality conditions** (conditions stipulating that some or all of the decision variables must have integer values). We have already pointed out that **integer linear programming**

models are linear programming models with the additional characteristic that some of the decision variables are required to take on integer values. There are several classifications within this category of models.

All-Integer Programs

An **all-integer model** (ILP) is, as the name suggests, a problem in which all of the decision variables are required to be integers. For example

$$\text{Min } 6x_1 + 5x_2 + 4x_3$$

$$\text{s.t.} \quad 108x_1 + 92x_2 + 58x_3 \geq 576$$

$$7x_1 + 18x_2 + 22x_3 \geq 83 \tag{8.1}$$

$$x_1, x_2, x_3 \geq 0 \text{ and } integer$$

is an all-integer model. Without the additional constraints x_1, x_2, x_3 integer (i.e., the integrality conditions), this problem is an LP problem.

A problem in which only some of the variables are restricted to integer values and others can assume any nonnegative number (i.e., *any continuous value*) is referred to as a **mixed integer linear program** (MILP). For example, suppose that in the previous problem only x_1 and x_2 were required to be integer and x_3 was not. This problem then becomes

Mixed Integer Programs

$$\text{Min } 6x_1 + 5x_2 + 4x_3$$

$$\text{s.t.} \quad 108x_1 + 92x_2 + 58x_3 \geq 576$$

$$7x_1 + 18x_2 + 22x_3 \geq 83$$

$$x_1, x_2, x_3 \geq 0; \quad x_1 \text{ and } x_2 \text{ integer}$$

0–1 Integer Programs

In some problems the integer variables are restricted to the values 0 or 1. Such problems are called **binary or 0–1 integer linear programs.** These problems are particularly important because the 0–1 variables may be used to represent dichotomous decisions (yes/no decisions). A variety of scheduling, plant location, production planning, and portfolio construction problems are 0–1 integer linear programming problems. They are discussed in some detail in Section 8.4. As we shall see, 0–1 variables can be found in IP's and in MILP's.

In this chapter we often consider the linear programming problem (LP) that results if we start with an ILP or an MILP and ignore the integer restrictions. This LP problem is referred to as **the LP relaxation** of the ILP or the MILP. For example, if we remove the phrase "and integer" from the ILP presented in (8.1), the resulting LP is the LP relaxation of the original integer program.

———— **8.3**

GRAPHICAL INTERPRETATIONS

In Chapter 4 we saw that it is possible to gain substantial insight into the nature and the solution of LP problems by examining the graphical analysis of a problem with two decision variables. The same approach is useful for an IP problem and we now turn our attention to that topic.

Consider a modified version of the **PROTRAC** E and F problem discussed in Chapters 2 through 5. In particular, consider the problem

$$
\begin{array}{lrll}
\text{Max } 18E + 6F & & & \\
\text{s.t.} & E + \quad F \geq & 5 & (1) \\
& 42.8E + 100F \leq & 800 & (2) \\
& 20E + \quad 6F \leq & 142 & (3) \\
& 30E + \quad 10F \geq & 135 & (4) \\
& E - \quad 3F \leq & 0 & (5) \\
& E, F \geq 0 \text{ and integer} & &
\end{array}
$$

(8.2)

For a detailed description of the original problem, see Section 2.2. In brief, E is the number of E-9s and F is the number of F-9s that **PROTRAC** decides to produce. The objective function is the profit as a function of the production decision. Constraint (1) reflects a need to meet previous commitments. Constraints (2) and (3) are production time restrictions in departments A and B, respectively. Constraint (4) represents part of a union agreement, and constraint (5) is imposed because of management's attitude

FIGURE 8.1
Feasible Set for **PROTRAC** ILP

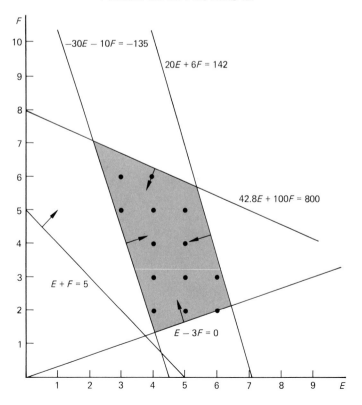

about the appropriate product mix. The only important change between (8.2) and the LP problem in Section 2.2 is the word "integer." As we shall see shortly, the impact of this single word is profound.

To solve this problem with a graphical approach, we prescribe three steps:

1. Find the feasible set for the LP relaxation of the ILP problem.
2. Identify the integer points inside the set determined in step 1.
3. Find, among those points determined in step 2, one that optimizes the objective function.

The first two steps have been accomplished in Figure 8.1. The shaded region is the feasible set for the LP relaxation and the dark dots are the integer points contained in this set. This set of integer points is the set of feasible solutions to the ILP. In other words, there are only 13 feasible solutions to the ILP problem. They are the points (3, 6), (4, 6), (3, 5), (4, 5), (5, 5), (4, 4), (5, 4), (4, 3), (5, 3), (6, 3), (4, 2), (5, 2), and (6, 2).

To solve the problem, we must now determine which of the feasible points yields the largest value of the objective function. We proceed as in an LP problem, that is, by moving a contour of the objective function in an *uphill direction* (since we are dealing with a Max model) until it is not possible to move it farther and still intersect a feasible point.

The result of this process is shown in Figure 8.2. We see that the optimal solution to the ILP is the point $E = 6$ and $F = 3$. Since the objective function is $18E + 6F$, this solution yields an optimal value of the objective function of $18(6) + 6(3) = 126$.

FIGURE 8.2
Graphical Solution to **PROTRAC** ILP

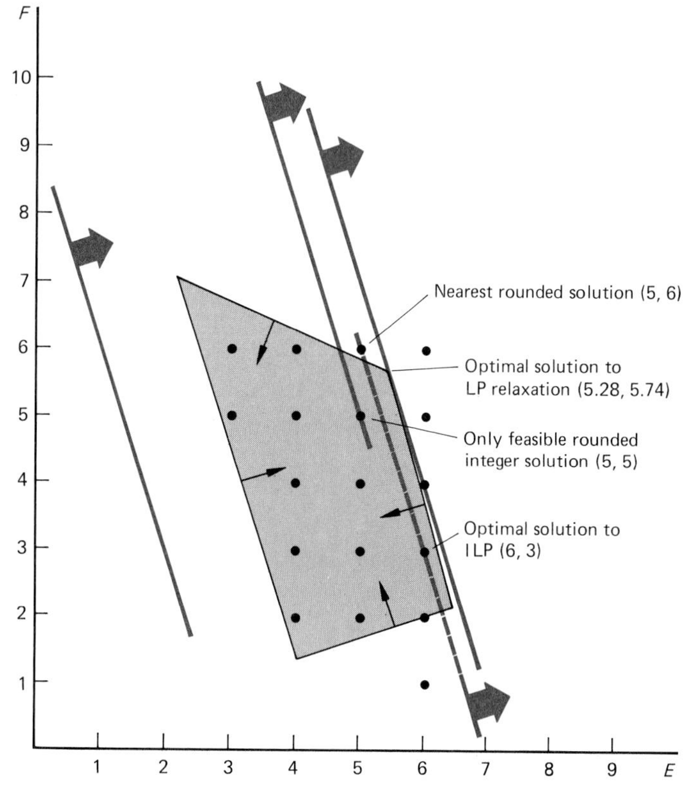

We can use Figure 8.2 to illustrate some important facts about the LP relaxation. We first note that the optimal solution to the LP relaxation occurs at the intersection of lines $42.8E + 100F = 800$, $20E + 6F = 142$.

This result is obtained by pushing, uphill, the contour of the objective function as far as possible and still have it intersect the feasible set for the LP relaxation. Since the intersection of the two constraints does not occur at an integer point, the optimal solution to the LP relaxation is not feasible for the ILP. To find the optimal solution (i.e., the optimal values of the decision variables) for the LP relaxation, we solve for the intersection of the two binding constraints. Solving these two equations in two unknowns yields $E^* = 5.28$, $F^* = 5.74$. Thus, the optimal value of the objective function, *termed the OV*, for the LP relaxation is $18(5.28) + 6(5.74) = 129.48$.

Comparing these two optimal values (126—ILP and 129.48—LP relaxation), we see that the OV for the LP relaxation is larger than for the original ILP. This fact is a special case of a phenomenon that we observed in our earlier discussions of linear programming. Think of creating an ILP or an MILP by starting with the LP relaxation and adding the integer restrictions. We know that *in any mathematical programming problem, adding constraints cannot help and may hurt the optimal value of the objective function.* Thus, our optimal value decreases with the addition of the integer constraint. With this observation we are prepared to make the following comments:

1. In a **Max** problem the OV of the LP relaxation always provides an **upper bound** on the OV of the original ILP or MILP. Adding the integer constraints either hurts, or leaves unchanged, the OV for the LP. In a Max problem, hurting the OV means making it smaller.

2. In a **Min** problem the OV of the LP relaxation always provides a **lower bound** on the OV of the original ILP or MILP. Again, adding the integer constraints either hurts, or leaves unchanged, the OV for the LP. In a Min problem, hurting the OV means making it larger.

Rounded Solutions

We have observed that the optimal solution to the LP relaxation is $E^* = 5.28$, $F^* = 5.74$. Each of these variables could be rounded up or down and hence there are four rounded solutions $[(5, 5), (5, 6), (6, 5), (6, 6)]$ that neighbor the optimal solution to the LP relaxation. The general fact is that with two decision variables there are four rounded neighbor solutions; with n decision variables there could be 2^n such points.

Let us now examine in more detail some of the potential problems that can arise when using a rounded solution. Refer to Figure 8.2. If we solve the LP relaxation and round each variable to the nearest integer, we obtain (5, 6), which is infeasible. In this case the point (5, 5) is the *only* feasible point that can be obtained by rounding (5.28, 5.74). The other candidates, (5, 6), (6,6), and (6, 5), are all infeasible.

This problem illustrates two important facts about rounded solutions:

1. **A rounded solution need not be optimal.** In this case the value of the objective function at the only feasible rounded solution is

$$18(5) + 6(5) = 120$$

This compares to a value of 126 for the optimal value of the ILP. We see, then, that a proportional loss of $\frac{6}{126}$, or almost 5%, is incurred by using this rounded solution rather than the optimal solution.

2. A rounded solution need not be near the optimal IP solution. Students often have an intuitive idea that even though a rounded solution may not be optimal, it should be "near" the optimal IP solution. Referring again to Figure 8.2, we see that the rounded solution is not one of the immediate integer neighbors of the optimal IP solution. Indeed, only four points in the feasible set [(3, 6), (4, 6), (3, 5), and (4, 5)] are further from the optimal solution than the rounded solution. It seems hard to claim that in this example the rounded solution is "near" the optimal IP solution.

In Figure 8.3 we introduce another ILP that illustrates an additional and even more drastic problem associated with rounded solutions. In this figure the shaded area is the feasible set for the LP relaxation, the dots are integer points, and the circled dot is the only feasible solution to the ILP. The optimal solution to the LP relaxation is indicated at the tip of the wedge-shaped feasible set. Notice that if we start with the optimal solution to the LP [roughly (3.3, 4.7)] and then round this to any of the four neighboring integer points, we obtain an infeasible point. That is, for this example, **no manner of rounding can produce feasibility**.

In summary, we have noted that an intuitively appealing way of attacking an ILP is to solve the LP relaxation of the original problem and then round the solution to a neighboring integer point. We have seen that this approach can have certain problems. In particular

1. None of the neighboring integer points may be feasible.
2. Even if one or more of the neighboring integer points is feasible
    a. Such a point need not be optimal for the IP.
    b. Such a point need not be even "near" the optimal IP solution.

Enumeration The graphical approach is used to illustrate some important ideas about ILP's. However, sometimes a figure like Figure 8.1 gives students the wrong perspective about the difficulty of solving an ILP. Since there are only 13 feasible points for the PROTRAC

FIGURE 8.3
All Rounded Solutions Are Infeasible

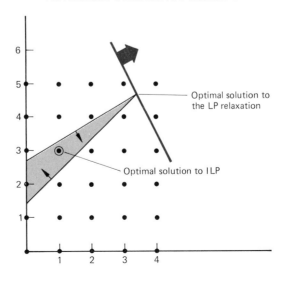

ILP, a student may get the impression that one can reasonably list all the feasible points, evaluate the objective function at each of them, and select the best one, that is, solve the problem by **complete enumeration**. In this case, one could do that. Unfortunately, however, complete enumeration is not a reasonable solution procedure for most ILP's. Suppose, for example, that we had an ILP with one hundred 0–1 variables. In this case there could be up to 2^{100}, which is 1.27×10^{30}, feasible points. The time required to enumerate all of these points would exceed a lifetime, even with the fastest computer.

It is interesting to compare the enumeration method for ILP's with the simplex algorithm for LP's. As we have seen, the simplex method can be viewed as a way of visiting corners of the constraint set and evaluating the objective function at the corners visited. It is also true that there can be billions of corners on the constraint set of a large LP. The important point, however, is that *not all corners are visited*. Indeed, the simplex algorithm is very efficient. It proceeds in such a way as to improve the value of the objective function at each successive corner. Once no improvement is possible, the procedure stops and indicates that an optimal solution has been reached. At this time there is no comparable algorithm for ILP's. There are methods (to be discussed later) that are better than complete enumeration, but they are not able to eliminate large numbers of alternative solutions as quickly and efficiently as the simplex algorithm does for LP's.

8.4
APPLICATIONS OF 0–1 VARIABLES

Binary, or 0–1, variables play an especially important role in the applications of ILP's and MILP's. These variables make it possible to incorporate "yes or no decisions," sometimes called "dichotomous decisions," into a mathematical programming format. Two quick examples will illustrate what we mean:

1. In a plant location problem we let $x_j = 1$ if we choose to have a plant at location j and $x_j = 0$ if we do not.
2. In a routing problem we let $x_{ijk} = 1$ if truck k goes from city i to city j and $x_{ijk} = 0$ if it does not.

Thus, you can see from these examples that the use of 0–1 variables provides us with a new "formulational tool." In this section we will see some examples of how 0–1 variables are used to make dichotomous decisions in several different applications. We will also see how they can be manipulated to enforce various types of logical conditions.

Capital Budgeting: An Expansion Decision

Many firms make decisions on capital investments on an annual basis. In large firms the decisions are often the culmination of a long process that starts with recommendations from individual departments and continues through various firm-wide and division-wide competitions. It is not unusual to have the final selection among major alternatives rest with the board of directors. In smaller firms the process is not so elaborate, but the capital budgeting decision is still a fundamental part of an annual evaluation of the firm's future.

In its simplest form, the capital budgeting decision is a matter of choosing among n alternatives in order to maximize the return subject to constraints on the amount of capital invested over time. As a particular example, suppose that **PROTRAC**'s board of directors faces the problem summarized in Figure 8.4. The dollar amounts in this figure

FIGURE 8.4

Capital Budgeting Problem

ALTERNATIVE (*j*)	PRESENT VALUE OF NET RETURN	CAPITAL REQUIRED IN YEAR *i* BY ALTERNATIVE *j*				
		1	2	3	4	5
Expand Belgian Plant	40	10	5	20	10	0
Expand Small Machine Capacity in U.S.	70	30	20	10	10	10
Establish New Plant in Chile	80	10	20	27	20	10
Expand Large Machine Capacity in U.S.	100	20	10	40	20	20
Capital Available in Year *i*	b_i	50	45	70	40	30

are in thousands. The board must select one or more of the alternatives. If they decide to expand the Belgian plant, the present value of the net return to the firm is $40,000. This project requires $10,000 of capital in the first year, $5000 in the second, and so on. The board has previously budgeted up to $50,000 for all capital investments in year 1, up to $45,000 in year 2, and so on.

An ILP Model for Capital Budgeting at PROTRAC

This problem can be modeled as an ILP in which all the variables are 0–1 variables. This is called a 0–1 ILP. In particular, let $x_i = 1$ if project i is accepted and $x_i = 0$ if project i is not accepted. The problem then becomes

$$\text{Max } 40x_1 + 70x_2 + 80x_3 + 100x_4 \quad \leftarrow \boxed{\text{Present value from accepted projects}}$$

$$\text{s.t.} \quad 10x_1 + 30x_2 + 10x_3 + 20x_4 \leq 50$$

$$\boxed{\text{Capital required in year 2}} \rightarrow \boxed{5x_1 + 20x_2 + 20x_3 + 10x_4} \leq 45 \quad \leftarrow \boxed{\text{Capital available in year 2}}$$

$$20x_1 + 10x_2 + 27x_3 + 40x_4 \leq 70$$

$$10x_1 + 10x_2 + 20x_3 + 20x_4 \leq 40$$

$$10x_2 + 10x_3 + 20x_4 \leq 30$$

$$x_i = 0 \text{ or } 1; \quad i = 1, \ldots, 4$$

Here the objective function is the total present value of the net returns and each constraint controls the amount of capital used in each of the five periods.

The LP Relaxation

Let us approach this problem by first solving the LP relaxation. The formulation and solution are shown in Figure 8.5. Note that in working with the LP relaxation to a 0–1 ILP, we ignore the constraints $x_i = 0$ or 1. Instead, we add the constraints $x_i \leq 1$, $i = 1, 2, 3, 4$ (as shown in Figure 8.5). Of course, in an LP, each x_i is always nonnegative. Thus, in the relaxation, instead of $x_i = 0$ or 1, we have x_i constrained to an interval (i.e., $0 \leq x_i \leq 1$). It would be nice if in the optimal solution each x_i were, fortuitously, to take one extreme or the other of these allowable values (either 0 or 1), for then the original ILP would be solved. Unfortunately, as Figure 8.5 shows, this happened only with x_4; the values of x_1, x_2, and x_3 are fractional. Since x_3 should equal 1 if **PROTRAC**

FIGURE 8.5

LP Relaxation of **PROTRAC's** Capital
Budgeting Problem

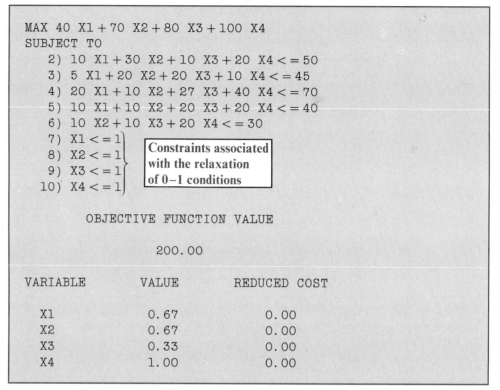

```
MAX 40 X1 + 70 X2 + 80 X3 + 100 X4
SUBJECT TO
    2) 10 X1 + 30 X2 + 10 X3 + 20 X4 < = 50
    3) 5 X1 + 20 X2 + 20 X3 + 10 X4 < = 45
    4) 20 X1 + 10 X2 + 27 X3 + 40 X4 < = 70
    5) 10 X1 + 10 X2 + 20 X3 + 20 X4 < = 40
    6) 10 X2 + 10 X3 + 20 X4 < = 30
    7) X1 < = 1
    8) X2 < = 1
    9) X3 < = 1
   10) X4 < = 1
```

Constraints associated
with the relaxation
of 0–1 conditions

```
        OBJECTIVE FUNCTION VALUE

                200.00

VARIABLE          VALUE         REDUCED COST

    X1            0.67             0.00
    X2            0.67             0.00
    X3            0.33             0.00
    X4            1.00             0.00
```

establishes a plant in Chile and 0 if it does not, the result $x_3 = 0.33$ is not meaningful. We also note that attempting to find a solution to the ILP problem by solving the LP relaxation and then rounding does not work very well. Standard "nearest integer" rounding rules (i.e., round numbers ≤ 0.499 to 0 and numbers ≥ 0.500 to 1) yield the solution $x_1 = 1, x_2 = 1, x_3 = 0, x_4 = 1$. A quick check reveals that this solution is infeasible since it grossly violates the first constraint.

The Optimal **All-Integer Solution** To obtain the optimal IP solution for the **PROTRAC** capi-
IP Solution tal budgeting problem, we must turn to *an integer programming code*—in this case, a computer program that employs an algorithm specifically designed to solve the 0–1 ILP. The formulation and solution of the ILP are shown in Figure 8.6.

Note that the four constraints that require the x_i's to be ≤ 1 have been dropped. In this particular program (LINDO), the phrase "integer-variables = 4" indicates that all four of the variables are 0–1 variables.

The solution shows that management should accept the first three alternatives; x_4 is now zero, whereas in the LP relaxation it was 1. Note also that the objective function is now 190. This is a reduction of 10 (5%) from the optimal value of the objective function for the LP relaxation. In practice, one may well be interested in solving integer programs with hundreds of 0–1 variables. After seeing the analysis of this small example and the problems associated with the relaxation approach, you can well appreciate the even greater importance, in larger and more complex applications, of having special algorithms to solve the IP problem.

FIGURE 8.6
ILP Model of **PROTRAC's** Capital
Budgeting Problem

```
MAX 40 X1 + 70 X2 + 80 X3 + 100 X4
SUBJECT TO
   2)  10 X1 + 30 X2 + 10 X3 + 20 X4 < = 50
   3)   5 X1 + 20 X2 + 20 X3 + 10 X4 < = 45
   4)  20 X1 + 10 X2 + 27 X3 + 40 X4 < = 70
   5)  10 X1 + 10 X2 + 20 X3 + 20 X4 < = 40
   6)        10 X2 + 10 X3 + 20 X4 < = 30

INTEGER — VARIABLES = 4

             OBJECTIVE FUNCTION VALUE

                      190.00

    VARIABLE         VALUE         REDUCED COST

       X1            1.00            - 15.00
       X2            1.00              0.00
       X3            1.00              0.00
       X4            0.00            - 50.00
```

Logical Conditions   An important use of 0–1 variables is to impose constraints which arise from logical conditions. Several examples are cited below.

No More Than k of n Alternatives   Suppose $x_i = 0$ or 1, for $i = 1, \ldots, n$. The constraint

$$x_1 + x_2 + \cdots + x_n \le k$$

implies that at most k alternatives of n possibilities can be selected. That is, since each x_i can be only 0 or 1, the above constraint says that not more than k of them can equal 1. For the data in Figure 8.4, assume that **PROTRAC** feels that not more than one foreign project can be accepted. For this reason, the board wants to rule out a decision that includes both the Belgian expansion and a new plant in Chile. Adding the constraint

$$x_1 + x_3 \le 1$$

to the ILP in Figure 8.6 implies that the solution can contain at most one of the overseas alternatives.

Dependent Decisions   You can use 0–1 variables to force a dependent relationship on two or more decisions. Suppose, for example, that management does not want to select alternative k unless it first selects alternative m. The constraint

$$x_k \le x_m \qquad\qquad (8.3)$$

or

$$x_k - x_m \leq 0$$

enforces this condition. Note that if m is *not* selected, then $x_m = 0$. Equation (8.3) then forces x_k to be 0 (i.e., alternative k is not selected). Alternatively, if m is selected, $x_m = 1$; then (8.3) becomes $x_k \leq 1$. This leaves the program free to select $x_k = 1$ or $x_k = 0$.

As an example, again consider Figure 8.4, and suppose that **PROTRAC**'s management feels that, if they are going to expand within the United States, their competitive position implies that they must definitely expand the large machine capacity. Adding the constraint

$$x_2 - x_4 \leq 0$$

to the ILP in Figure 8.6 assures that the model cannot select "expand small machine capacity" unless "expand large machine capacity" is also selected.

Similarly, suppose the board decided, "If we're going to expand our domestic capacity, we're going to expand both lines." Adding the constraint

$$x_4 - x_2 = 0$$

to the ILP in Figure 8.6 would enforce this condition since it implies that x_4 and x_2 must take the same values.

Lot Size Constraints   Consider a portfolio manager with the following constraints: (1) If he purchases security j, he must purchase at least 20 shares; and (2) he may not purchase more than 100 shares of security j. Let x_j be the number of shares of security j purchased. The constraint that *if* j is purchased, then at least 20 shares must be purchased, is called a "minimum lot size" or "batch size" constraint. Note that we cannot create such a constraint in an LP model. The constraints

$$20 \leq x_j \leq 100$$

do not do the job since they insist that x_j always be at least 20. We want the conditions either $x_j = 0$ or $20 \leq x_j \leq 100$. To achieve this we will make use of a 0–1 variable, say y_j, for security j. The variable y_j has the following interpretation:

- If $y_j = 1$, then purchase security j.
- If $y_j = 0$, do not purchase security j.

Now consider the two constraints

$$x_j \leq 100 y_j \qquad (8.4)$$

$$x_j \geq 20 y_i \qquad (8.5)$$

We see that if $y_j = 1$, then (8.4) and (8.5) imply that $20 \leq x_j \leq 100$. On the other hand, if $y_j = 0$, then (8.4) implies that $x_j \leq 0$. Similarly, (8.5) implies that $x_j \geq 0$. These two inequalities together imply that $x_j = 0$. Thus, if $y_j = 1$ when we purchase j, and 0 when we do not, we have the proper conditions on x_j.

How can we be sure that $y_j = 1$ if we purchase security j? The inequality (8.4) $(x_j \leq 100 y_j)$ guarantees it. We see that in this inequality you cannot have both $x_j > 0$ and $y_j = 0$. Thus, if $x_j > 0$, y_j must equal 1. We see then that inequalities (8.4) and (8.5) together guarantee the "minimum lot size" constraint.

***k* of *m* Constraints**   Michi Gaas, an exchange student from the Middle East, came to the university for graduate work. He was told by his advisor that anyone intending to earn a Ph.D. degree in history had to satisfy at least 2 of the following criteria: "You must be single, rich, or crazy." Unfortunately Michi was destitute and married. In fact, before entering into matrimony, he spent years looking for a bride who was tall, dark, beautiful, and rich. Finally in frustration he said to himself, "Three out of four ain't bad;" and the woman he chose (who chose him) was not rich. These are examples of problems in which k of m constraints must be satisfied. In general notation, let the "superset" of m constraints be

$$g_i(x_1, \ldots, x_n) \leq b_i, \qquad i = 1, \ldots, m$$

Now introduce m new 0–1 variables y_i and let U be chosen so large that, for each i, $g_i(x_i, \ldots, x_n) \leq U$ for every x satisfying any set of k inequalities taken from the above m. Then the following $m + 1$ constraints express the desired condition:

$$\sum_{i=1}^{m} y_i = k$$

$$g_i(x_1, \ldots, x_n) \leq b_i y_i + (1 - y_i)U, \qquad i = 1, \ldots, m$$

Note that $\sum_{i=1}^{m} y_i = k$ forces k of the y_i variables to have the value 1. This means that exactly k of the above inequalities are equivalent to

$$g_i(x_1, \ldots, x_n) \leq b_i.$$

The remaining inequalities are equivalent to

$$g_i(x_1, \ldots, x_n) \leq U$$

and by the assumption on the choice of U such a constraint is redundant.

───── 8.5
AN IP VIGNETTE: STECO'S WAREHOUSE LOCATION PROBLEM—
FORMULATION AND COMPUTER ANALYSIS

In order to conserve capital, Steco, the steel wholesaler, leases its regional warehouses. It currently has a list of three warehouses it can lease. The cost per month to lease warehouse i is F_i. Also, warehouse i can handle a maximum of T_i trucks per month.

There are four sales districts and the typical monthly demand in district j is d_j truckloads. The average cost of sending a truck from warehouse i to district j is c_{ij}. Steco wants to know which warehouses to lease and how many trucks to send from

FIGURE 8.7

Warehouse Location Problem

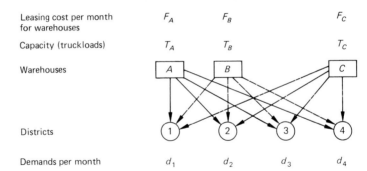

each warehouse to each district. A schematic representation of the problem is illustrated in Figure 8.7. The data for this problem are presented in Figure 8.8.

In this table we see, for example, that it costs $7750 to lease warehouse A for a month and that up to 200 trucks can be dispatched from this warehouse. Also, the monthly demand in sales district 1 is 100 trucks. The numbers in the body of the table are the costs of sending a truck from warehouse i to sales district j (e.g., the cost of sending a truck from B to 3 is $100).

Modeling Considerations

If you want to attack this problem with a mathematical programming model, you must first decide which variables (if any) you will treat as integers and which (if any) you will treat as continuous variables.

The decision to lease a particular warehouse or not seems to require a 0–1 variable since the cost of leasing warehouse i does not vary with the level of activity (i.e., with the number of trucks sent from it). We will thus let

$$y_i = 1 \quad \text{if we lease warehouse } i, \qquad y_i = 0 \quad \text{if we do not}$$

At first glance it also seems appropriate to treat the number of trucks sent from a warehouse to a district as an integer variable. Trucks are, after all, integer entities and it does not make sense to talk about sending one-third of a truck from here to there. There are, however, several factors that could persuade us to treat the number of trucks

FIGURE 8.8

Warehouse Location Data

WAREHOUSE	COST PER TRUCK ($c_{i,j}$) SALES DISTRICT				MONTHLY CAPACITY (NUMBER OF TRUCKS)	MONTHLY LEASING COSTS
	1	2	3	4		
A	$170	$ 40	$ 70	$160	200	$7750
B	150	195	100	10	250	4000
C	100	240	140	60	300	5500
MONTHLY DEMAND (TRUCK LOADS)	100	90	110	60		

as a continuous variable. In particular

1. This is a planning model, not a detailed operating system. In actual operation the demands in the districts will vary. Management will have to devise methods of handling this uncertainty. Trucks assigned to a specific warehouse might be allocated among adjacent districts on a daily-as-needed basis or Steco might use common carriers to satisfy excess demand. At any rate, the number of trucks that the solution to our mathematical programming problem says should go from warehouse i to district j is only an *approximation* of what will actually happen on any given day. Thus, treating these entities as continuous variables and rounding to the nearest integer to determine how many trucks to assign to each warehouse should provide a useful answer and a good approximation of the *average* monthly operating cost.

2. Treating the number of trucks as integer variables may make the problem much more diffi-cult to solve. This is simply a reflection of the general fact that the greater the number of integer variables, the more difficult it is to solve an ILP.

3. It certainly costs much more to lease one of the warehouses than to send a truck from a warehouse to a sales district. The relative magnitude of these costs again implies that it is relatively more important to treat the "lease or not lease" decision as an integer variable, as opposed to the trucks. To illustrate this point, note that it costs $5500 per month to lease warehouse C and $60 to send a truck from warehouse C to sales district 4. Suppose that we modeled the problem as an LP. If $y_3 = 0.4$ in the optimal solution, rounding to 0 causes a $2,200 change in the OV (optimal value of the objective function), whereas if $x_{C4} = 57.8$, rounding either up or down has less than a $60 effect.

In summary, there are, in this example, arguments that suggest little advantage to treating the number of trucks as integers. We thus proceed to formulate Steco's ware-house location problem as an MILP, and we will have a pleasant surprise.

The Mixed ILP Model   To model Steco's problem as an MILP, we will let

$$y_i = 1 \quad \text{if lease warehouse } i, \qquad y_i = 0 \quad \text{if not;} \qquad i = A, B, C$$

$$x_{ij} = \text{the number of trucks sent from warehouse } i \text{ to district } j;$$

$$i = A, B, C; \qquad j = 1, \ldots, 4$$

We shall now construct the model by developing each of its component parts. First consider the objective function. The expression

$$170x_{A1} + 40x_{A2} + 70x_{A3} + \cdots + 60x_{C4}$$

is the total cost associated with the trucks and

$$7750y_A + 4000y_B + 5500y_C$$

is the total leasing cost. Thus, the objective function is

$$\text{Min } 7750y_A + 4000y_B + 5500y_C + 170x_{A1} + \cdots + 60x_{C4}$$

Now consider the constraints. We must consider both demand and capacity. The follow-ing constraint guarantees that demand will be satisfied at sales district 1:

$$x_{A1} + x_{B1} + x_{C1} = 100$$

Four constraints like this (one for each district) are required to guarantee that demand is satisfied.

The constraint

$$x_{A1} + x_{A2} + x_{A3} + x_{A4} \le 200y_A \quad \text{or} \quad x_{A1} + x_{A2} + x_{A3} + x_{A4} - 200y_A \le 0$$

serves two purposes. It guarantees that capacity at warehouse A is not exceeded and it forces us to lease warehouse A if we want to send anything out of this warehouse. To see this, recall that y_i, or in this case y_A, must equal 0 or 1. First, assume that $y_A = 1$. The inequality above then becomes

$$x_{A1} + x_{A2} + x_{A3} + x_{A4} \le 200$$

FIGURE 8.9

Steco's Warehouse Location Problem

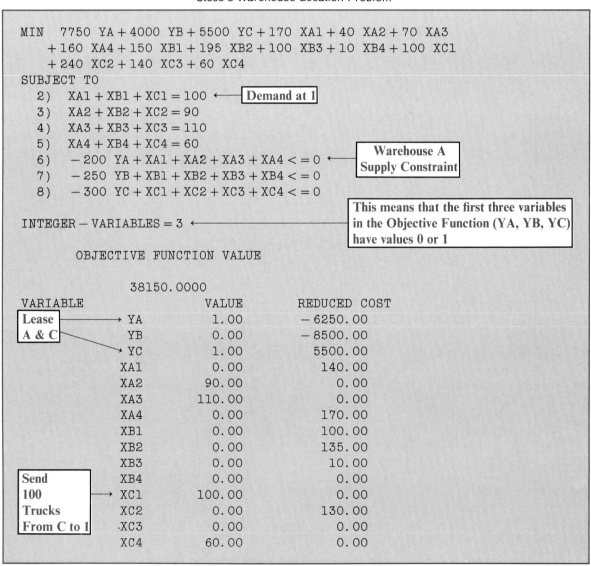

that is, no more than a total of 200 trucks can be sent out of warehouse A. This is a type of capacity constraint that you have previously seen in transportation models. Now consider the case when y_A is 0. Then the inequality becomes

$$x_{A1} + x_{A2} + x_{A3} + x_{A4} \leq 0$$

that is, no items can be sent out of warehouse A. This constraint then guarantees that nothing can be sent out of warehouse A unless $y_A = 1$. Note that when $y_A = 1$, the term $7750y_A$ in the objective function equals 7750. Thus, we see that nothing is sent out of warehouse A unless we incur the monthly leasing cost for that particular warehouse. Three such constraints, one for each warehouse, are needed in the model.

The complete model and its solution are shown in Figure 8.9.

Output Analysis   A quick glance at the output shows that the optimal values of all truck allocations are integer, even though we decided in the formulation to allow these variables to be continuous. Was this just fortuitous? The answer is no. Here is the reason. We started with a warehouse location problem. Note that once we have decided which warehouse to lease, the problem of finding the optimal allocation of trucks is an LP problem called the transportation problem. In Chapter 7 we saw that if the supply available at each warehouse and the demand at each district are integers, then the optimal solution to the transportation problem will be all integers.

We now have enough information to conclude that the optimal solution to the above warehouse location problem with integer supplies and demands will always include an integer allocation of trucks. The argument involves two steps: (1) The optimal solution must lease some set of warehouses and (2) Every possible set of leased warehouses yields an integer allocation of trucks.

For this problem, then, we now see that it would have been naive and costly to require as additional constraints that the x_{ij}'s be integer. The word is "Never pay for a free good."

8.6
THE ASSIGNMENT PROBLEM AND A SOCIAL THEOREM

The assignment problem has been discussed in Sections 7.5, 7.6 and 7.7. Here is an application:

Let there be n men and n women and let c_{ij} be a measure (say on a scale of one to ten) of the mutual pleasure the ith man and the jth woman derive, on the average, per unit of time (e.g., per day) spent together. Let x_{ij} be the fraction of his time that man i spends with woman j. Suppose the men and women do nothing but spend time together. To maximize total happiness, solve

$$\text{Max} \sum_{i=1}^{n} \sum_{j=1}^{n} c_{ij}x_{ij},$$

$$\text{s.t.} \quad \sum_{j=1}^{n} x_{ij} = 1, \qquad i = 1, \ldots, n$$

$$\sum_{i=1}^{n} x_{ij} = 1, \qquad j = 1, \ldots, n$$

$$x_{ij} \geq 0, \qquad i, j = 1, \ldots, n$$

Note the meaning of the constraints:

1. The first n constraints say that each man's time is completely taken up by women:
2. The next n constraints say that each woman's time is completely taken up by men.

In Chapter 7 it was stated that since the assignment problem is a special case of the transportation model, and since the right-hand side data is integral, there will be an all-integer optimal solution to the assignment problem (as there was for the transportation model in the Steco example). Hence our mating problem has an optimal solution with each $x_{ij} = 0$ or 1, which means that, at optimality, each man is matched with a woman, and vice versa. Thus we have a proof that monogamy is an optimal social arrangement. But be careful. If we replace "Max" with "Min" in the objective function, we obtain an optimal 0–1 solution! (The "integrality property" has nothing to do with whether the objective function is maximized or minimized.) Thus we have also proved that monogamy *minimizes* total happiness!

———— 8.7
THE BRANCH-AND-BOUND ALGORITHM

The General Approach The branch-and-bound approach is currently the most efficient general-purpose method of solving ILP's and MILP's. Actually, branch and bound is *not* a specific algorithm assigned to solve a specific problem. Rather it is a general approach to problem solving, an approach that must be adapted to a specific setting. The general idea is to partition the set of all feasible solutions to a given problem into smaller and nonoverlapping subsets. Bounds on the value of the best solution in each subset are then computed. Then the branch-and-bound algorithm cleverly allows one to eliminate certain subsets from consideration. In this way one is said to *partially* (as opposed to completely) *enumerate* all of the possible feasible solutions.

An ILP Example Let us begin with a specific problem, which for convenience we refer to as (P1):

$$
\begin{aligned}
&\text{Max } x_1 + 5x_2 \qquad\qquad\qquad \text{(P1)}\\
&\text{s.t.} \quad 11x_1 + 6x_2 \le 66\\
&\qquad\quad 5x_1 + 50x_2 \le 225\\
&\qquad x_1, x_2 \ge 0 \text{ and integer}
\end{aligned}
$$

In the following discussion, it will be helpful to use the graphical method discussed in Section 8.3.

Step 1 The first step is to solve the LP relaxation of (P1). If luck is with us, we may have an optimal solution right away, since it is always true that if the solution to the LP relaxation satisfies the integer restriction, it is the optimal solution. We will now use the graphical solution technique to solve the LP relaxation of (P1) and test our luck. Figure 8.10 shows (by shading) the feasible set for the LP relaxation of (P1). The **Solving the LP Relaxation** dots in the shaded region are the feasible points which also satisfy the integrality con-

FIGURE 8.10

LP Relaxation of (P1)

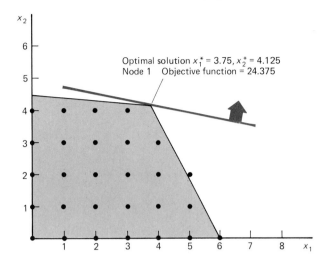

Optimal solution $x_1^* = 3.75$, $x_2^* = 4.125$
Node 1   Objective function = 24.375

ditions. Note that there are 27 such points, including the points on the axes such as $(0, 4)$ and $(4, 0)$, which are feasible. Figure 8.10 also shows the optimal corner for the LP. To find the optimal numerical values for the decision variables we solve for the point where the two active constraints intersect; that is, we solve

$$11x_1 + 6x_2 = 66 \qquad \text{and} \qquad 5x_1 + 50x_2 = 225$$

for x_1 and x_2. This yields $x_1^* = 3.75$, $x_2^* = 4.125$. Since these values are not integers, we have *not* solved (P1). We have obtained some information about the problem, however. In particular

1. Recall that the symbol OV stands for optimal value of the objective function. When we find the OV for the LP relaxation, we establish an upper bound for the OV of (P1). Let us call this upper bound U. Thus, since the objective function is $x_1 + 5x_2$, we know that

$$\text{OV for (P1)} \leq 3.75 + 5(4.125) = 24.375 = U$$

2. As you can see in Figure 8.10, if we take the optimal solution to the relaxed problem and round it down to $x_1 = 3$, $x_2 = 4$, (truncate the fractional portion), we obtain a feasible solution to (P1). Now evaluating the objective function at this point (or at any other *feasible* point), we establish a *lower bound* for the OV of (P1). Let us call this value F. Hence,

$$\text{OV for (P1)} \geq 3 + 5(4) = 23 = F$$

The value of F (i.e., 23) may or may not be the OV for (P1). At present, we cannot tell. All we now know is that $23 \leq \text{OV} \leq 24.375$. We must find out whether a better solution can be found. To do this, we *branch*.

The information about a branch-and-bound solution is typically summarized in a "tree-like" diagram. The first node in such a diagram is shown in Figure 8.11. This node will look somewhat different from the other nodes in our tree since we place the values for our *current* best upper bound (CBUB) on the OV and our current best lower bound (CBLB) on the OV above this node.

FIGURE 8.11

Node Corresponding to (P1)

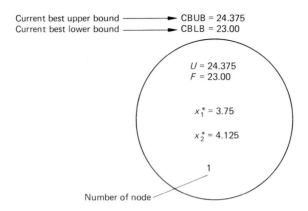

Current best upper bound ———————▶ CBUB = 24.375
Current best lower bound ———————▶ CBLB = 23.00

$U = 24.375$
$F = 23.00$

$x_1^* = 3.75$

$x_2^* = 4.125$

1

Number of node

Step 2 We proceed by dividing (P1) into two smaller problems. In this example, we will branch on x_1. This is an arbitrary choice. We could just as well have branched on x_2. The branching process makes use of the fact that in the optimal solution to (P1), either $x_1 \leq 3$ or $x_1 \geq 4$. Why is this true? Because there are no integer values for x_1 in the region eliminated by forcing x_1 to be ≤ 3 or x_1 to be ≥ 4. The values of x_1 that are eliminated are $3 < x_1 < 4$. Since x_1 must be an integer, we have not eliminated any feasible points from the feasible set for (P1). We have, however, eliminated points (i.e., noninteger values) from the feasible set of the LP relaxation of (P1). Indeed, we see that the optimal value of x_1, in the LP relaxation of (P1), is neither ≤ 3 nor ≥ 4 and hence the current optimal point (intentionally) has been eliminated by the branching process. This process creates one of its two new problems by appending the constraint $x_1 \leq 3$ to (P1). The other new problem is created by appending the constraint $x_1 \geq 4$ to (P1). We thus have

Branching

$$\text{Max } x_1 + 5x_2 \qquad \text{(P2)}$$
$$\text{s.t.} \quad 11x_1 + 6x_2 \leq 66$$
$$5x_1 + 50x_2 \leq 225$$
$$x_1 \quad \leq \quad 3$$
$$x_1, x_2 \geq 0 \text{ and integer}$$

and

$$\text{Max } x_1 + 5x_2 \qquad \text{(P3)}$$
$$\text{s.t.} \quad 11x_1 + 6x_2 \leq 66$$
$$5x_1 + 50x_2 \leq 225$$
$$x_1 \quad \geq \quad 4$$
$$x_1, x_2 \geq 0 \text{ and integer}$$

These two problems are shown in Figure 8.12.

FIGURE 8.12
Problems (P2) and (P3)

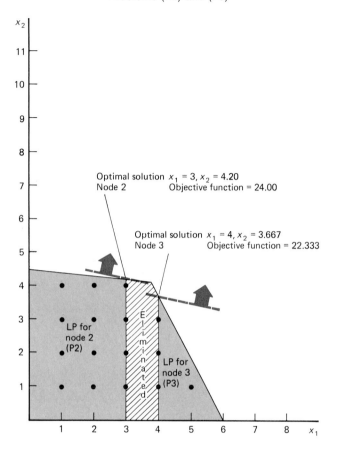

Figure 8.12 reveals two interesting facts:

1. We have split the (P1) feasible set into two pieces and eliminated from consideration a region containing no integer points. The eliminated region is crosshatched. The boundary lines are *not* in the region eliminated.

2. All of the feasible *integer* solutions to (P1) are now contained in either (P2) or (P3). Since the objective functions for (P1), (P2), and (P3) are identical, it follows that *either the optimal solution to (P2) or the optimal solution to (P3) must be the optimal solution to (P1)*, the original ILP. Thus, we may forget (P1), and consider only (P2) and (P3).

The branch-and-bound approach proceeds by solving the LP relaxations for problems (P2) and (P3). The optimal solutions are shown in Figure 8.12. In problem (P2) the value of U is provided by the optimal value of the objective function for the LP relaxation (namely 24.00). For (P3), we obtain $U = 22.333$. We have already observed that the optimal solution to (P1) is either in (P2) or (P3); thus the OV for (P1) must be $\leq$ the Max of the values of U provided by these two nodes. Since node 2 yields a U of 24.00 and node 3 yields a U of 22.333, our *current* best upper bound is 24.00. We thus change the value of CBUB above node 1. To change the value of CBLB, we would have to have obtained a point that is feasible in (P1) and yields a value of the objective function > 23.00, our CBLB. Since neither node 2 nor node 3 has an all-integer solution, we have not obtained a new feasible solution. [Although in this problem we could round down at nodes 2 and 3 to obtain new feasible solutions to (P1), in general the search for feasible points may be difficult, and therefore we wish to present a procedure that does not include a new feasible solution at each node.] Thus the value of CBLB remains as it was.

Creating a Tree

Figure 8.13 incorporates the information from (P2) and (P3) into a decision diagram called a *tree*. To determine what to do next we consider the nodes at the bottom of our tree, nodes 2 and 3 in this case. We note that the upper bound on node 3 is 22.333 and the current value of CBLB is 23.00. We have thus *already found a better solution than we can possibly obtain in the feasible set for (P3)*. Therefore, *we can ignore (P3) and concentrate our efforts on (P2)*. To indicate that (P3) has now been eliminated from consideration, we place in Figure 8.13 a T below (P3) which means that *that particular branch of the tree is now terminated*. In general, if, after calculating the value of U for a node, we find that $U \leq$ CBLB, then this node can be eliminated from further consideration. We do this by writing a T below the node, indicating that this branch of the tree has been terminated.

FIGURE 8.13

Tree with Three Nodes Corresponding to
(P1), (P2), and (P3)

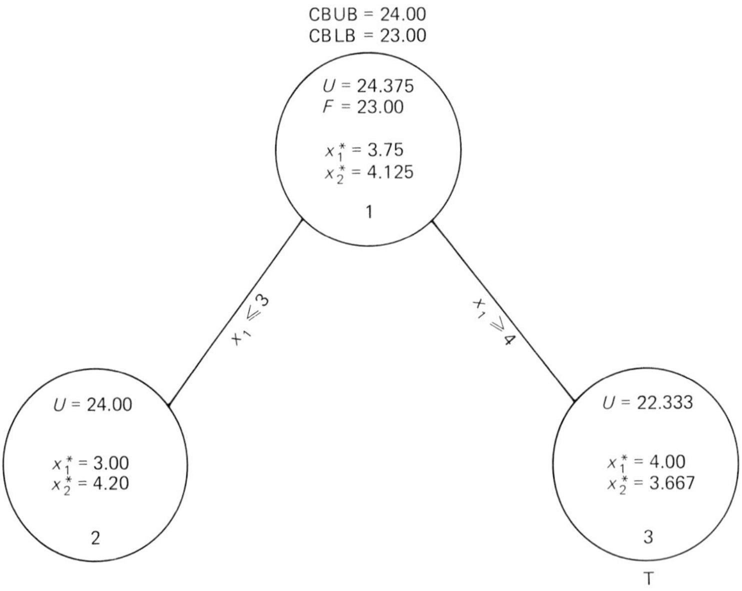

CBUB = 24.00
CBLB = 23.00

$U = 24.375$
$F = 23.00$

$x_1^* = 3.75$
$x_2^* = 4.125$

1

$x_1 \leq 3$

$x_1 \geq 4$

$U = 24.00$

$x_1^* = 3.00$
$x_2^* = 4.20$

2

$U = 22.333$

$x_1^* = 4.00$
$x_2^* = 3.667$

3

T

Let us now continue by considering (P2). We still do not know the optimal solution to (P2), for we still have a noninteger value for x_2^*. Since (P2) is an ILP, we attack it with branch and bound, and to do this we must branch again. The variable x_1 is integer in the optimal solution to (P2). Hence we must branch on x_2, which we do by using the constraints $x_2 \leq 4$ or $x_2 \geq 5$. Doing this, we replace (P2) with the problems

$$\text{Max } x_1 + 5x_2 \qquad \text{(P4)}$$
$$\text{s.t.} \quad 11x_1 + 6x_2 \le 66$$
$$5x_1 + 50x_2 \le 225$$
$$x_1 \le 3$$
$$x_2 \le 4$$
$$x_1\ x_2 \ge 0 \text{ and integer}$$

$$\text{Max } x_1 + 5x_2 \qquad \text{(P5)}$$
$$\text{s.t.} \quad 11x_1 + 6x_2 \le 66$$
$$5x_1 + 50x_2 \le 225$$
$$x_1 \le 3$$
$$x_2 \ge 5$$
$$x_1\ x_2 \ge 0 \text{ and integer}$$

Note that the constraints for (P4) are the constraints for (P1); that is,

$$11x_1 + 6x_2 \le 66$$

$$5x_1 + 50x_2 \le 225$$

plus the constraint that was appended to define (P2) (i.e., $x_1 \le 3$), plus the new constraint that is appended to define (P4) (i.e., $x \le 4$). A similar interpretation can be given to (P5). The result of this branch is shown in Figure 8.14 and the new tree is shown in Figure 8.15.

FIGURE 8.14
Problems (P3), (P4), and (P5)

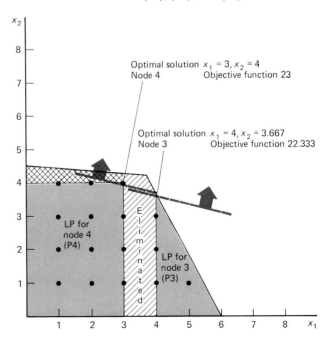

FIGURE 8.15
The Completed Tree

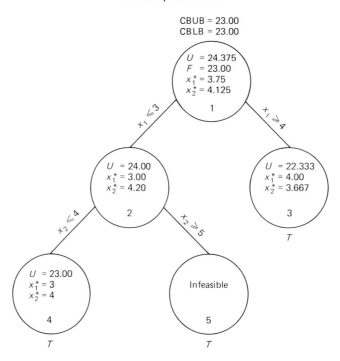

The Final Tree   In comparing Figures 8.14 and 8.12, there are several important features to be noted:

1. Problem (P3) remains unchanged (exactly as it was in Figure 8.12).

2. An additional set of noninteger points, including the optimal solution to the LP relaxation of (P2), has been eliminated from consideration. All of the newly eliminated area that was in the feasible set of the LP relaxation of (P1) is double-crosshatched.

3. The constraint set for the LP relaxation of (P5) is empty. There are no points that satisfy the constraints $5x_1 + 50x_2 \le 225$, $x_1 \ge 0$, $x_2 \ge 5$. This also means that (P5) has no feasible solution, which means that we may now forget about (P5). This is indicated by placing, in Figure 8.15, a T below node 5, which terminates another branch of the tree. We now see that there are two causes for termination: Terminate a node when

1. Its U is $\le$ CBLB or
2. It represents an infeasible problem.

Thus, we need only concentrate on (P4), and solving the LP relaxation of that problem, as shown in Figure 8.14, reveals that the optimal solution to the relaxation of (P4), namely $(x_1^* = 3,\ x_2^* = 4)$, is all-integer. This means that $(x_1^* = 3,\ x_2^* = 4)$ is the optimal solution to (P4). For this reason, (P4) is another terminal node on our tree and, in Figure 8.15, we have accordingly placed a T under that node. Thus, we have an illustration of the third cause for termination. In summary, terminate a node when

1. Its U is $\le$ CBLB,
2. It represents an infeasible problem, or
3. The LP relaxation provides a solution to the integer problem represented by that node.

Referring again to Figure 8.15, we note that the value of CBUB has changed from the value it held in Figure 8.13. The branch on node 2 yielded an infeasible problem (node 5) and a problem (node 4) with a U of 23.00. Thus the current best upper bound (CBUB) is reduced from 24.00 to 23.00. In node 4, we also have an all-integer solution. This point is thus a feasible solution to (P1). It yields a value of 23.00 for the objective function. Since our current best lower bound is 23.00, we do not change the CBLB.

In general, **when all nodes have been terminated, the branch-and-bound method is complete**. The optimal solution to the original problem (P1) is the solution which established the CBLB. In this case CBLB is 23.00 and thus $(x_1^* = 3, x_2^* = 4)$ is the optimal solution to (P1). Upon termination, as in Figure 8.15, it will always be the case that CBLB = CBUB.

MILP's The branch-and-bound procedure described above can be easily modified to work on MILP's. Consider a small modification of the ILP analyzed above. In particular, assume that the problem is

$$\text{Max } x_1 + 5x_2$$

$$\text{s.t.} \quad 11x_1 + 6x_2 \leq 66$$

$$5x_1 + 50x_2 \leq 225$$

$$x_1 \geq 0 \text{ and integer,} \qquad x_2 \geq 0$$

The only change from the previous problem is that x_2 is no longer required to be an integer (i.e., x_2 can be any nonnegative number). To solve this problem, we start as before with the LP relaxation in Figure 8.10. Since x_1^* is not integer (it assumes the value 3.75), we obtain the initial value of F by rounding x_1^* down to 3. The value of x_2 is permitted to remain fractional at 4.125. Thus, we obtain $F = 3 + 5(4.125) = 23.625$. As before, CBUB = 24.375, but now CBLB = 23.625. Now we branch, as previously, on x_1 by introducing the constraints $x_1 \leq 3$ or $x_1 \geq 4$. This yields Figure 8.12. The following information can be read from this figure:

1. Node 2 yields a U of 24.00 and node 3 yields a U of 22.333; thus the CBUB becomes 24.00.
2. The optimal solution to node 2 has an integer value for x_1; thus this is a feasible solution to (P1). It follows that
   a. We achieve a new current best lower bound of 24.00.
   b. Node 2 can be terminated.
3. At node 3 $U \leq$ CBLB; thus node 3 can be terminated.

Since both nodes have been terminated, the optimal solution is the solution that yielded the CBLB. Thus, $x_1^* = 3.00$ and $x_2^* = 4.20$ is the optimal solution.

Summary of Branch and Bound We summarize the application to ILP. The adaption for MILP should be obvious. In what follows, the phrase "solve a node" means solve the LP relaxation of the LP corresponding to the node. A "solved node" is one for which this has been done. Otherwise, the node is "unsolved."

1. Draw a node corresponding to the original IP, and solve the node. The OV for the relaxation is the value of U at the node. If the optimal solution is all-integer, it is optimal for the IP.

Otherwise, use any method to find a feasible point for the IP, and let F denote the objective value at this point. Set the current best upper bound (CBUB) equal to U and the current best lower bound (CBLB) equal to F.

2. Commence with any solved node that has not been terminated. From this node (the parent) *branch* so as to create two new unsolved nodes (the successors) with the property that the optimal solution to one of the successor IP's will be the optimal solution to the parent IP. The branching may be accomplished by taking any fractional component, say x_i^*, of the optimal solution to the parent's relaxation. Let $[x_i^*]$ be the truncation of x_i^* to its integer part. Then $[x_i^*] + 1$ is the next integer larger than x_i^*. One successor will be the parent's problem augmented by the constraint $x_i \leq [x_i^*]$. The other successor is formed by augmenting the parent's problem with $x_i \geq [x_i^*] + 1$. Then either pick another solved node and repeat, or go to step 3.

3. Commence with any unsolved node and attempt to *solve*. The OV for the relaxation is the value of U at the node. Write a T under the node, and terminate this branch, if the LP relaxation is infeasible or if $U \leq$ CBLB or if the optimal solution is all-integer. If the optimal solution is all-integer, evaluate the objective function at this point; call the value F. Compare CBLB with F. If $F >$ CBLB, set CBLB = F. If the branch is not terminated, either repeat step 3 or go to step 2. If the node is terminated, go to step 4.

4. If all nodes are terminated, the optimal solution to the original IP is the all-integer solution that produced the value CBLB.

It is appropriate, at this point, to make the observation that for very large problems the branch-and-bound method can be stopped before all nodes have been terminated. The node producing the CBLB will provide an *approximate solution* to the original ILP. In this case CBLB will be less than the value CBUB, and the difference CBUB–CBLB indicates the closeness of the approximation.

Finally, let us comment on the application of the branch-and-bound technique to special ILP's with 0–1 variables. In this case, suppose that one is branching on the 0–1 variable y_1. Then one successor will have $y_1 = 0$. The other will have $y_1 = 1$. It should be mentioned that for the ILP in 0–1 variables there is another type of branch-and-bound application, sometimes called **partial enumeration**, which has enjoyed considerable success. Also, for the general ILP there are other methods which have been applied. These include **cutting-plane methods** and **Lagrangian relaxation**. As stated at the outset of this chapter, our introductory discussion merely touches the surface of this intricate topic.

————— 8.8
ILP AND MILP IN PRACTICE

Strategic Considerations in Solving IP Problems

As the summary above shows, there is considerable flexibility in the use of branch and bound. For example, after solving the original relaxation, and then branching, one could solve the two successors. Alternatively, you might choose to solve just one of the successors and then immediately branch again on that node. Elaborating on this, one possible strategy is a "horizontal attack." One proceeds through the tree according to the sequence of nodes shown in Figure 8.16. To execute this strategy, one solves the original node and then iterates in the following pattern: branch on 1, solve 2, solve 3, branch on 2, solve 4, solve 5, branch on 3, solve 6, solve 7, branch on 4, solve 8, solve 9, and so on. In this way one moves horizontally through the entire tree at each particular level.

At the other extreme, Figure 8.17 shows a strategy based on a "vertical attack." These two approaches illustrate just one of the several ways that judgment enters into the solution of ILP problems. Although the details of such strategic considerations

FIGURE 8.16
Horizontal Attack

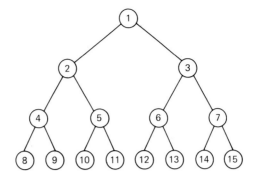

FIGURE 8.17
Vertical Attack

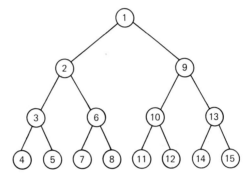

become too specialized for this introductory discussion, it is well to understand that in practice there is often considerable room for choice and ingenuity in the application of branch and bound.

Sensitivity We have seen that the branch-and-bound method uses *numerous* applications of the simplex method to solve an integer program. Thus it is, in general, much more time-consuming to solve ILP's and MILP's than LP's. Unfortunately, it is also true that the solution to an ILP or MILP contains much less information than the solution to an LP. In particular, *the solution to an ILP or MILP does not contain sensitivity information.* No information concerning the sensitivity of the OV (i.e., the optimal value of the objective function) to changes in the RHS of a constraint, or to a change in the value of an objective function coefficient, is produced. In other words, **an IP solution does not include information that is equivalent to the dual price and cost sensitivity information in an LP**. This does not imply that changes in the RHS, or in a cost coefficient, do not affect the solution to an IP. They do. Indeed, the solutions to ILP's can be extremely sensitive to changes in parameter values.

The following somewhat unrealistic, but for the present purpose illustrative, capital budgeting example will illustrate these points:

$$\text{Max } 10x_1 + 100x_2 + 1000x_3$$

$$\text{s.t.} \quad 29x_1 + 30x_2 + 31x_3 \le b_1$$

$$x_1, x_2, x_3 \text{ are 0 or 1}$$

FIGURE 8.18

Sensitivity Data

	OPTIMAL SOLUTION			
b_1	x_1	x_2	x_3	OV
29	1	0	0	10
30	0	1	0	100
31	0	0	1	1000

The problem is easily solved by inspection. The table in Figure 8.18 shows the optimal solution and the optimal value of the objective function (OV) for various values of the parameter b_1. From the data in Figure 8.18 we note that a change in 1 unit in the right-hand side of the constraint (say from 29 to 30) increases the OV by a factor of 10 (from 10 to 100). Clearly, if the manager were aware of such an opportunity, he or she would be anxious to make such a change.

Unfortunately, no such sensitivity information is produced when you solve an ILP or an MILP. You can only receive the optimal solution and the OV. Sensitivity information such as that shown in Figure 8.18 can be achieved only by repeatedly solving the model with new parameter values. When the model has a number of constraints, using this approach to generate useful sensitivity data for an ILP can require the analyst to run a large number of alternative programs. This can be an expensive and time-consuming activity.

One final word on sensitivity. Many ILP computer codes are part of LP packages. Thus, they may produce sensitivity data as part of their solution reports, in spite of the fact that these data have no meaning in the ILP context. This is true of LINDO, which is the ILP and LP code used in this text.

Heuristic Algorithms

Because of the importance of the applications, IP is currently an active area of research. As a final comment, it should be noted that much of this research is in the area of heuristic algorithms. These are algorithms designed to efficiently produce "good," although not necessarily optimal, solutions. It should be clear by now that

> From the viewpoint of the manager, a heuristic procedure may certainly be as acceptable as, and possibly even preferable to, a "more exact" algorithm that produces an optimal solution. The dominant considerations should be the amount of insight and guidance the model can provide, and the cost of obtaining these.

8.9
NOTES ON IMPLEMENTATION OF INTEGER PROGRAMMING

Integer solutions are an important, indeed essential, condition for the application of mathematical programming models to many important real-world problems. Recent advances in research and computer technology have made it possible to make real progress on problems that involve variables that must be treated as integers. An example appeared in the Application Capsule at the beginning of this chapter. Other examples follow.

Kelly-Springfield

The Kelly-Springfield Tire Company has a model-based system to coordinate sales forecasting, inventory control, production planning, and distribution decisions. One crucial link in this system is the production planning model. Central to this problem is the effect of setup time. In the manufacture of each particular line of tires a machine is "set up" by installing a piece of equipment (called a die) particular to that line. It takes a fixed amount of time (and thus a fixed cost) to remove one die from a machine and insert another. In other words, there is a fixed "changeover" or "setup" cost of moving from the production of one line of tires to another, no matter how many tires you decide to produce after the machine is set up. The decision to set up (i.e., to produce a particular line in a given production period) or not, is treated as a 0–1 variable in the MILP used to attack this problem. The total integrated system (including the production planning system) is credited with impressive results. The system implemented in 1970 is estimated to have yielded savings of $500,000 a year. Since an improved system was installed in 1976, average unit inventory decreased by 19%, customer service improved, productivity increased, and additional savings totaling $7.9 million annually resulted. For more details, see "Co-ordinated Decisions for Increased Profits," *Interfaces* 10, December 1980.

Flying Tiger Line

Another interesting application concerns the use of integer programming by the Flying Tiger Line (an all-cargo airline) in approaching two strategic questions: the design of their service network, and the selection and deployment of their aircraft fleet. The size of the MILP used to attack this problem and the cost of solving it are staggering when your primary exposure has been to classroom problems. One model for 33 cities, 8 hubs (locations where cargo can be interchanged), and 10 aircraft types included 843 constraints, 3807 continuous variables, and 156 integer (aircraft selector) variables. No explicit cost savings are included in the presentation of this application. Management's satisfaction with the project, however, is obvious from the ongoing nature of the investigation. For a detailed account, see "A Mixed-Integer Programming Approach to Air Cargo Fleet Planning," *Management Science*, November 1980.

Hunt-Wesson Foods

A third application is a major distribution-system study for Hunt-Wesson Foods, Inc. The problem is to select sites for regional distribution centers and to determine what customer zones each distribution center should serve, as well as which of several plants should supply the distribution centers. The problem is an MILP with two types of integer variables:

$y_k = 1$ if site k is used for a distribution center and 0 if it is not

$y_{kl} = 1$ if customer district l is served by the warehouse at site k and 0 if it is not

The quantities of material shipped are continuous variables.

The problem involves 17 commodity classes, 14 plants, 45 possible distribution center sites, and 121 customer zones. The MILP model used to attack it had 11,854 rows, 727 0–1 integer variables, and 23,513 continuous variables. A special algorithm was constructed to solve the problem. In the article describing this problem the authors state that the realizable annual cost savings produced by the study are estimated to be in the low-seven figures. For more details, see "Multicommodity Distribution System Design by Benders Decomposition," *Management Science*, January 1974.

The three studies cited here have a number of features in common:

1. Each attacked a major problem of strategic importance to a firm.
2. Each made a significant contribution to successfully dealing with the problem.
3. Each included a large-scale MILP.
4. Clever modeling and/or special algorithms were required in each application.
5. Each project required a major commitment of funds and managerial talent.

The examples illustrate that a good model may enable management to achieve a level of analysis and performance that might otherwise be impossible, but such models are costly to develop, and often require an ongoing and time-consuming input from management. In all of the examples the authors (of the articles) stressed a close working-relationship between the analysts (modelers) and management. In the case of Kelly-Springfield, the current model has evolved over a 15-year horizon with two major efforts. We see, then, that the use of quantitative models to solve important problems may well entail a serious commitment to a long process. Small tactical problems may be successfully subdued with a quick "off the shelf" treatment. Fundamental strategic problems are seldom that obliging.

—————— **8.10**

SUMMARY OF IP

The introduction points out that integer programming (IP) is an important and developing area of constrained optimization. Section 8.2 identifies all-integer models (ILP) and mixed-integer models (MILP) as the two main types of integer linear programs. In MILP's only some of the decision variables are restricted to integer values, whereas the integer restriction applies to all decision variables in ILP's. Further, the importance of problems involving integer variables that are restricted to the values 0 or 1 is discussed. Finally, the LP relaxation is defined. Section 8.3 uses a graphical approach to solve an ILP with two decision variables. This approach is then used to investigate the conceptual relationships between an ILP and its LP relaxation. We saw that

1. In a *Max* problem the OV of the LP relaxation always provides an *upper bound* on the OV of the original IP.
2. In a *Min* problem the OV of the LP relaxation always provides a *lower bound* on the OV of the original IP.

In Section 8.3 we also defined the term "rounded solution." This is any rounding of the optimal solution to the LP relaxation. Thus, there are many rounded solutions. In some applications, as discussed in Section 8.1, any rounded solution may be an acceptable substitute for the true ILP solution. In other cases, no rounded solution will be acceptable. We saw in Section 8.3 that, in general,

3. It may be that no rounded solution is near the IP optimum.
4. It may be that no rounded solution is feasible (i.e., satisfies the constraints of the LP relaxation).

Sections 8.4 and 8.5 consider the use of 0–1 variables in a variety of applications. In particular, models for a capital budgeting problem and a warehouse location problem are considered in some detail. Section 8.6 contains an application of the fact that certain LP's always have all-integer solutions. Section 8.7 explains the branch-and-bound approach used to solve ILP's and MILP's. The graphical approach is used to show that branching is a matter of dividing the feasible set for a problem into disjoint subsets. Bounding uses the optimum value of the LP relaxation to eliminate subproblems from consideration. Section 8.8 deals with two important topics concerning the real-world use of ILP's and MILP's. First, we point out the importance of "tree-pruning strategies" in implementing the branch-and-bound approach. Second, we see that sensitivity data are not produced as a natural by-product of the solution to an ILP and MILP. Further, it was illustrated that ILP's may be inconsistent and erratic in their sensitivity to changes in parameter values. These two facts combine to establish the necessity of using multiple computer runs with different parameters to produce sensitivity information in the IP setting. This is often an important part of attacking a real problem with an IP model. In the final section, 8.9, several major applications of IP are cited.

_____ 8.11
INTRODUCTION TO QUADRATIC PROGRAMMING

Quadratic programming (QP), like linear integer programming, is a first cousin of linear programming. Compare the following:

Linear Programming Problem

Maximize or minimize the value of *LINEAR* objective function subject to a set of linear equality and inequality constraints as well as nonnegativity conditions on the values of the decision variables.

Quadratic Programming Problem

Maximize or minimize the value of a *QUADRATIC* objective function subject to a set of linear equality and inequality constraints as well as nonnegativity conditions on the values of the decision variables.

Obviously, the only difference in these two problems is in the functional form of the objective function. We know about linear functions. Here are some examples of quadratic functions:

Quadratic Functions

$$9x_1^2 + 4x_1 + 7$$

$$3x_1^2 - 4x_1x_2 + 15x_2^2 + 20x_1 - 13x_2 - 14$$

These functions are the sum of terms involving the squares of variables (e.g., $3x_1^2$), cross products (e.g., $4x_1x_2$), linear functions (e.g., $20x_1$), and constants (e.g., 14). In general a quadratic function in N variables can be written in the form

A General Quadratic in N Variables

$$\sum_{i=1}^{N} A_i x_i^2 + \sum_{i=1}^{N-1} \sum_{j=i+1}^{N} B_{ij} x_i x_j + \sum_{i=1}^{N} C_i x_i + D$$

Note that when all of the coefficients A_i and B_{ij} are zero then the function is linear. Hence, a linear function is a special case of a quadratic function.

Changing from a linear to a quadratic objective function means that a new algorithm is required to solve the problem. This change also implies that many of the facts we have learned about linear programming problems no longer hold. The following example illustrates some of the differences between quadratic programming problems and linear programming problems. The formal QP model is

$$\text{Min } (x_1 - 6)^2 + (x_2 - 8)^2$$

$$\text{s.t.} \quad x_1 \leq 7$$

$$x_2 \leq 5$$

$$x_1 + 2x_2 \leq 12$$

$$x_1 + x_2 \leq 9$$

$$x_1, x_2 \geq 0$$

A geometric representation of this problem appears in Figure 8.19. The constraint set, of course, is the same as for an LP and thus needs no new explanation. In order to see that the objective function is a special case of our previous quadratic function, it can be rewritten in the form $x_1^2 - 12x_1 + 36 + x_2^2 - 16x_2 + 64$. You may also recognize the expression

$$(x_1 - 6)^2 + (x_2 - 8)^2 = k$$

as the equation of a circle with radius $\sqrt{k}$ and center at the point (6, 8). Thus, as shown in Figure 8.19, the contours of the objective function are concentric circles around the point (6, 8). Since these contours increase in value as the radius k increases, and since the above problem is a minimization problem, the optimal solution in Figure 8.19 occurs at the point (4, 4). This can be roughly described as the point where the contour "first touches" the feasible set. In this example that "touch" is a point of tangency, though in other cases a solution could occur at a corner, just as in LP. The optimal value of

FIGURE 8.19
Graphical Solution for the QP Example

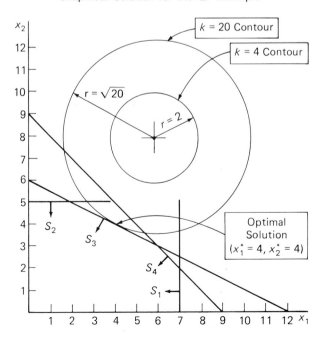

FIGURE 8.20
Solving a QP with GINO

```
MODEL:
   1) MIN = (X1 − 6)^2 + (X2 − 8)^2;
   2) X1 < 7;
   3) X2 < 5;
   4) X1 + 2*X2 < 12;
   5) X1 + X2 < 9;
END


SOLUTION STATUS: OPTIMAL TO TOLERANCES. DUAL CONDITIONS: SATISFIED.

              OBJECTIVE FUNCTION VALUE

      1)            20.000000

   VARIABLE          VALUE          REDUCED COST
      X1           4.000000           0.000001
      X2           4.000000           0.000000

      ROW    SLACK OR SURPLUS           PRICE
      2)          3.000000           0.000000
      3)          1.000000           0.000000
      4)          0.000000           3.999999
      5)          1.000000           0.000000
```

the objective function (i.e. its value at the point (4, 4)) is $(4 − 6)^2 + (4 − 8)^2 = 20$. This example clearly indicates that, in contrast to linear programming,

Comparison to LP

1. There need not be an optimal corner solution. An algorithm like the simplex, which searches for the best corner, thus cannot be used to solve this problem.

2. As a direct result of 1, there may be more positive variables in the optimal solution than there are constraints. For the example problem there are 5 positive variables (x_1, x_2, s_1, s_2, s_4) and only 4 constraints.

—— 8.12
COMPUTER SOLUTION OF QP PROBLEMS

Real-world QP problems are solved with computers. There are two approaches: One is to use a general nonlinear programming code like GINO[2] and the other is to use a specially written quadratic programming code. We will restrict our attention to the first approach.

For the example in the previous section, Figure 8.20 shows the input and solution for the GINO code. Except for minor conventions like * for multiplication and ^ for

[2] GINO, which stands for General Interactive Nonlinear Optimizer, much like LINDO, is a user-friendly code for solving NLP problems. There is also a diskette available for personal computer use. For information on either the micro or mainframe versions, interested readers should contact Professor Linus Schrage, Graduate School of Business, University of Chicago, 1101 East 58th Street, Chicago, IL 60637.

exponentiation, the GINO input reads like the mathematical formulation of the formal QP model.

In the next section the "PRICE" column of the computer printout is interpreted with a geometric analysis. For the present, concerning the sensitivity output in Figure 8.20, we simply state the following facts:

1. Consider the number in the "PRICE" column corresponding to the ith constraint. Just as in LP (e.g. the LINDO output) this represents the rate of improvement in OV as the ith RHS is increased, with all other data unchanged.

2. The "REDUCED COST" applies to a variable whose optimal value is zero. For such a variable, the reduced cost is the rate at which the objective value is "hurt" as that variable is forced to assume positive values in an optimal solution.

—————— **8.13**

Geometric Interpretation of the Sensitivity Analysis

Let us now consider what happens to the optimal solution and the optimal value of the objective function as the RHS of the 3rd constraint, i.e., the binding constraint, changes. We will refer to the value of the RHS of the 3rd constraint as R. In the current problem $R = 12$. The analysis is geometric and is tied to Figure 8.21. For convenience

FIGURE 8.21
The Solution Path as R Varies

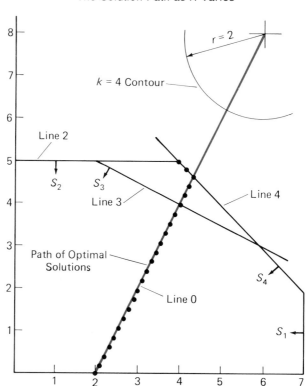

of exposition let

$$\text{Line 2 be the line} \qquad x_2 = 5$$

$$\text{Line 3 be the line } x_1 + 2x_2 = 12$$

$$\text{Line 4 be the line} \quad x_1 + x_2 = 9$$

Each of these lines is identified in Figure 8.21.

Tracing the Optimal Solution We first note that as R decreases the 3rd constraint will move to the southwest parallel to Line 3. Similarly, as R increases the 3rd constraint moves to the northeast parallel to Line 3. From geometry we recall the fact that any tangent to a circle is perpendicular to a line connecting the point of tangency and the center. Hence, as R is increased or decreased (within limits), the optimal solution to the problem lies on the line joining the points $(x_1 = 4, x_2 = 4)$ and $(x_1 = 6, x_2 = 8)$. The equation of this line is $2x_1 - x_2 = 4$ and it is identified as Line 0 in Figure 8.21.

Changing the RHS

From Figure 8.21 we now see that as R decreases the optimal solution moves down Line 0 until it reaches the axis (the nonnegativity constraint on x_2). At this point $x_1 = 2$ and $x_2 = 0$ and thus $x_1 + 2x_2 = 2$. Similarly, as R increases the optimal solution moves up along Line 0 until R assumes a value such that the 3rd constraint passes through the intersection of Line 4 and Line 0. This value is determined by solving the equations $x_1 + x_2 = 9$ and $2x_1 - x_2 = 4$ for x_1 and x_2 to obtain the point $(x_1 = 4\frac{1}{3}, x_2 = 4\frac{2}{3})$. Substituting these values in the equation $x_1 + 2x_2 = R$ yields $R = 13\frac{2}{3}$.

As R assumes values greater than $13\frac{2}{3}$, the optimal solution moves along Line 4 until R assumes a value such that the 3rd constraint passes through the intersection of Line 2 and Line 4. This intersection occurs at the point $(x_1 = 4, x_2 = 5)$ and since $x_1 + 2x_2 = R$, the 3rd constraint intersects this point when $R = 14$. As R becomes larger than 14, the 3rd constraint becomes redundant and the optimal solution remains at the point $(x_1 = 4, x_2 = 5)$. We have now traced the path of the optimal solutions for all possible values of $R \geq 2$. To find the optimal solution for a specific value of R it is only necessary to solve the appropriate two simultaneous linear equations.

A Path of Solutions

The Optimal Value of the Objective Function (OV)

Once you have the optimal solution, say (x_1^*, x_2^*), the optimal value of the objective function (OV) is obtained by evaluating the expression $(x_1^* - 6)^2 + (x_2^* - 8)^2 = \text{OV}$. We now wish to develop an expression for the OV as a function of R. This function will be identified by the notation $\text{OV}(R)$. In particular we will restrict our attention to values of R between 2 and $13\frac{2}{3}$, i.e., to those values of R for which the optimal solution lies on Line 0.

When the optimal solution lies on Line 0, it lies at the intersection of the lines

$$2x_1 - x_2 = 4 \qquad \text{Line 0}$$

$$x_1 + 2x_2 = R \qquad \text{3rd Constraint}$$

Solving for x_1 and x_2 in terms of R we obtain

$$x_1 + 2(2x_1 - 4) = R$$

or

$$x_1^* = \frac{R + 8}{5} \qquad \text{and} \qquad x_2^* = 2\left(\frac{R + 8}{5}\right) - 4 = \frac{2R - 4}{5}.$$

Note when $R = 12$, $x_1^* = 4$ and $x_2^* = 4$ which is our original result. Since the objective function is $(x_1 - 6)^2 + (x_2 - 8)^2$ its value at x_1^*, x_2^* is

$$\left(\frac{R+8}{5} - 6\right)^2 + \left(\frac{2R-4}{5} - 8\right)^2$$

or

$$OV(R) = \frac{R^2 - 44R + 484}{5}$$

The function $OV(R)$, over the range $2 \le R \le 13\frac{2}{3}$, is plotted in Figure 8.22. Note that over this range the OV function is quadratic. Also note that when $R = 12$ the objective function value is 20, the same as the value produced by the computer in Figure 8.20.

Improvement vs. Change

Recall that the definition of the dual price on the 3rd constraint is the rate of improvement of the OV as the RHS of the 3rd constraint (i.e. R) is increased. Recall from our discussion of LP that the "rate of improvement" always has the same magnitude (absolute value) as the "rate of change." In a Min problem, however, a negative rate of change (the OV getting smaller) is a positive rate of improvement. Thus in our example problem if we can determine the rate of change we can determine the rate of improvement simply by changing the sign. We observe this somewhat inconvenient distinction because the geometric analysis proceeds naturally in terms of rate of change while both LINDO and GINO produce, in the sensitivity analysis, the rate of improvement.

In geometric terms the rate of change in the function $OV(R)$ at some point, say $R = \hat{R}$, is the slope of the tangent to the graph of the function at the point $(\hat{R}, OV(\hat{R}))$. In the language of calculus, the rate of change at $\hat{R}$ is the first derivative of $OV(R)$ evaluated at $\hat{R}$. This entity is denoted $OV'(\hat{R})$. Figure 8.22 shows the tangent to the

FIGURE 8.22
OV(R) vs R

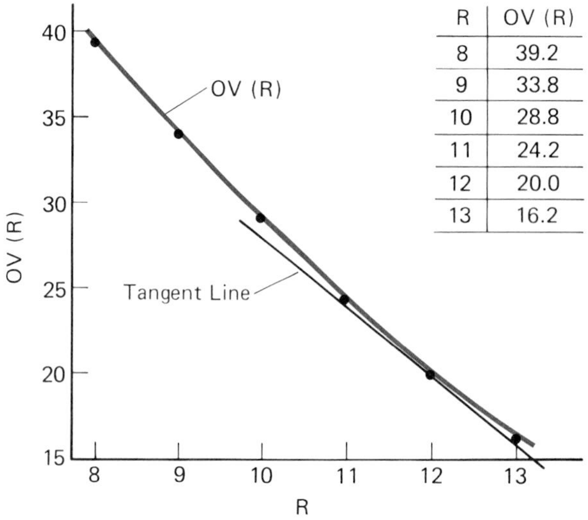

R	OV (R)
8	39.2
9	33.8
10	28.8
11	24.2
12	20.0
13	16.2

graph at the point ($R = 12$, $OV = 20$). To deduce the slope, one can take the first de-rivative to obtain $OV'(R) = \dfrac{2R - 44}{5}$ and thus $OV'(12) = -4$. We have already noted that since the rate of change is -4, the rate of improvement (i.e., the dual price) in this Min model must be 4. This result is exactly what we see in the computer output in Figure 8.20.

An important fact to note is that in Figure 8.22 the slope of the tangent is *different* for every value of R. Thus, comparing QP to LP, we find the following major difference:

3. In general for a QP problem there is no allowable increase and decrease in the RHS of a constraint for which the dual price remains the same.

Now let us consider what happens as we change a coefficient of a term in the objective function.

(a) If we change the coefficient on some x_j variable we relocate the center of the concentric circles. For example, in the previous objective function let us change the coefficient of x_1 from the value -12 to -18, to obtain the new objective

$$x_1^2 - 18x_1 + 36 + x_2^2 - 16x_2 + 64$$

This can be rewritten as

$$(x_1 - 9)^2 + (x_2 - 8)^2 - 45$$

which shows that the center of the concentric circles is relocated from the point ($x_1 = 6$, $x_2 = 8$) to the point ($x_1 = 9$, $x_2 = 8$). This relocation also produces a new optimal solution.

(b) Changing a coefficient on one of the x_j^2 terms in the previous objective function will change the shapes of the contours from circles to ellipses. Rather than dwelling on this more complicated geometry, it should already be apparent that, in contrast to LP

4. In general, for a QP problem, for a coefficient in the objective function, it is not possible to give a range of values such that the optimal solution does not change.

This completes the general discussion of quadratic programming. In the next section we turn to a specific application.

_____ 8.14
PORTFOLIO SELECTION

Portfolio selection is a fundamental problem in modern finance. In reality there are enough aspects to portfolio analysis to fill up a book, and indeed volumes have been written on the topic. Our discussion will provide only a brief glimpse into this fascinating practice.

The problem can be stated as follows: An investor has \$P to invest in a set of n stocks and would like to know how much to invest in each stock. The chosen collection is called the investor's portfolio. The investor has conflicting goals: He or she would like a portfolio with both a large expected return and a small risk. These goals are con-flicting because most often, in the real world, portfolios with high expected return also have high risk.

Here is an example of what we mean by the term *return*. Suppose an investment of D_i dollars is put into asset i and suppose that over some specified time period this D_i dollars grows to $1.3D_i$. Then we would say that the *return* over that period is

$\dfrac{1.3D_i - D_i}{D_i} = .3$. The concept of risk is more subtle and more difficult to elaborate on. For the purpose of this discussion we will assume that *risk is measured by the variance of the return on the portfolio.* Actually, this is consistent with the way that most portfolio analysts would measure risk.

Now, since the portfolio manager seeks low risk and high expected return, one way to frame the problem is to minimize the variance of the return (i.e. minimize risk) subject to a lower bound on expected return. There may also be some constraints on the proportion of the portfolio devoted to particular individual stocks.

This problem turns out to be a quadratic programming problem. In formulating this model, one can let x_i be the proportion of the portfolio invested in stock i. For example, in a two-stock model if we have P dollars to invest and if the optimal solution were $x_1 = .7$ and $x_2 = .3$ we would then invest a total of $.7P$ dollars in stock 1, and the remaining $.3P$ dollars would go to stock 2.

Formulating the Portfolio Model

Let us now write out the general model for a two-asset problem. We shall use the following notation:

$$\sigma_i^2 = \text{variance of yearly returns from stock } i,\ i = 1, 2$$

$$\sigma_{12} = \text{covariance of yearly returns from stocks 1 and 2}$$

$$R_i = \text{expected yearly return from stock } i,\ i = 1, 2$$

$$G = \text{lower bound on expected yearly return from total investment}$$

$$S_i = \text{upper bound on investment in stock } i,\ i = 1, 2$$

For the present purposes we simply accept the following facts:

1. The *variance of the yearly returns from stock i* is a number describing the "variability" of these returns from year to year. This will be made more precise in the next section.

2. The *covariance of the yearly returns from stocks 1 and 2* is a number which describes the extent to which the returns of the two stocks move up or down together. This also will be made more precise in the next section.

3. The *expected return of the portfolio* is defined to be the number $x_1 R_1 + x_2 R_2$.

4. The *variance of the portfolio* is defined to be the number $\sigma_1^2 x_1^2 + 2\sigma_{12} x_1 x_2 + \sigma_2^2 x_2^2$.

From these definitions it follows that, for the two-stock example, the portfolio problem takes the form

The Formal Portfolio Model— Two Assets

$$\text{Min } \sigma_1^2 x_1^2 + 2\sigma_{12} x_1 x_2 + \sigma_2^2 x_2^2 \qquad \text{(Variance of Return)}$$

$$\text{s.t. } x_1 + x_2 = 1 \qquad \text{(All funds must be invested)}$$

$$x_1 R_1 + x_2 R_2 \geq G \quad \longleftarrow \quad \boxed{\begin{array}{l}\text{Lower bound on the}\\ \text{expected return of the portfolio}\end{array}}$$

$$\left.\begin{array}{l} x_1 \leq S_1 \\ x_2 \leq S_2 \end{array}\right\} \quad \longleftarrow \quad \boxed{\begin{array}{l}\text{Upper bounds on investments}\\ \text{in individual stocks}\end{array}}$$

$$x_1, x_2 \geq 0$$

FIGURE 8.23
The Portfolio Selection Problem

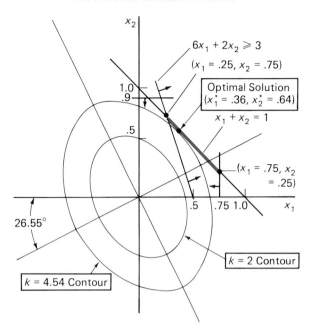

To create a specific numerical example let

$$\sigma_1^2 = .09 \qquad R_1 = .06 \qquad S_1 = .75 \qquad G = .03$$
$$\sigma_2^2 = .06 \qquad R_2 = .02 \qquad S_2 = .9 \qquad \sigma_{12} = .02$$

The feasible set for this problem is shown in Figure 8.23, where for convenience the objective function and both sides of row 3 have been multiplied by 100. Because of the equality constraint ($x_1 + x_2 = 1$) the feasible set is the heavy line segment connecting the points (.25, .75) and (.75, .25). Each contour of the objective function is an ellipse with its center at the origin and its minor axis lying on a line that forms a 26.55° angle with the x_1 axis. The 2 and 4.54 contours are shown in Figure 8.23.

Note that as the value of the contour increases, the general shape of the ellipse remains the same, but it increases in size. The problem is to select the smallest value for the contour so that the ellipse just touches the feasible set. As indicated in Figure 8.23, the 4.54 contour touches the feasible set at the point ($x_1^* = .36, x_2^* = .64$) which is the optimal solution.

It is not important for you to know how to construct these contours. Real problems are after all solved with the computer, not graphically. The geometric representation, however, is a useful way to understand the model and is helpful in interpreting properties of the solution.

The GINO solution to the above example is shown in Figure 8.24. Note that only the first constraint (Row 2) is binding. This, of course, was seen in the geometric representation in Figure 8.23. Since the slack in the expected return constraint (Row 3) is .454, we know that the expected return from this portfolio is 3.454. Comparing the optimal values of x_1^* and x_2^*, we see that the optimal portfolio contains more of the security

FIGURE 8.24
Gino Solution to the Portfolio
Selection Problem

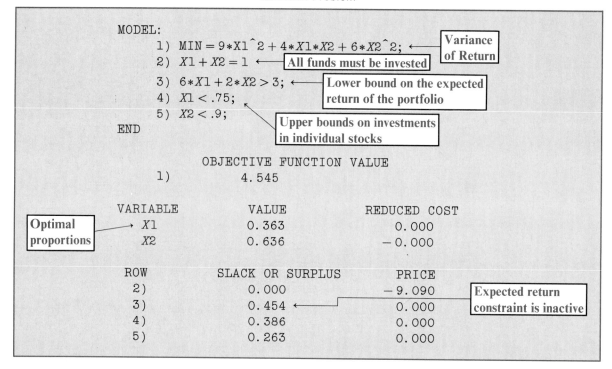

```
MODEL:
     1)  MIN = 9*X1^2 + 4*X1*X2 + 6*X2^2;    ← | Variance
     2)  X1 + X2 = 1   ← | All funds must be invested | of Return
     3)  6*X1 + 2*X2 > 3;   ← | Lower bound on the expected
     4)  X1 < .75;              return of the portfolio |
     5)  X2 < .9;
END                     | Upper bounds on investments
                          in individual stocks |

              OBJECTIVE FUNCTION VALUE
     1)           4.545


        VARIABLE          VALUE          REDUCED COST
          X1              0.363            0.000
          X2              0.636           -0.000


        ROW           SLACK OR SURPLUS        PRICE
         2)               0.000            -9.090
         3)               0.454   ←          0.000     | Expected return
         4)               0.386             0.000        constraint is inactive |
         5)               0.263             0.000
```

Optimal proportions → X1

with the lower expected yearly return (i.e., security 2). The reason is that the variance of security 2 is lower than that of security 1. The optimal mix is one that minimizes the portfolio variance while guaranteeing an expected portfolio return of at least 3%.

_____ 8.15

A PORTFOLIO EXAMPLE WITH LIVE DATA

In this section we turn to a three-asset example. Actual data will be used to estimate the parameters in the model. The problem will then be solved by computer and we will discuss the solution. In this section the three assets will be designated, at the outset, as x, y, and z. Let

$$X = \text{fraction of asset } x \text{ in the portfolio}$$

$$Y = \text{fraction of asset } y \text{ in the portfolio}$$

$$Z = \text{fraction of asset } z \text{ in the portfolio}$$

The terminology "asset i" will be used to refer to asset x, or asset y, or asset z.

In the previous sections the portfolio model was presented as if the parameters that describe the distribution of future returns were known, i.e., it was assumed that the expected returns, variances, and covariances were known. In the real world these parameters must be estimated with historical data. In general if n periods (years) of data are available, there will be, for each asset i, an actual historical return R_i^t associated with each period t where t ranges from 1 to n. In other words, each asset will have n historical returns. The expected periodic return from asset i is estimated with $\bar{R}_i = \dfrac{1}{n} \sum_{t=1}^{n} R_i^t$, which is the average of the asset's historical returns. The periodic historical returns R_i^t are also used to estimate variances and covariances. The appropriate formulas are

$$\text{Estimate of the variance of return for asset } i = \frac{1}{n} \sum_{t=1}^{n} (R_i^t - \bar{R}_i)^2$$

$$\text{Estimate of the covariance of returns for assets } i \text{ and } j = \frac{1}{n} \sum_{t=1}^{n} (R_i^t - \bar{R}_i)(R_j^t - \bar{R}_j).$$

As before, we also define

$$G = \text{lower bound on expected return of the portfolio}$$

$$S_i = \text{upper bound on the fraction of asset } i \text{ that can be in the portfolio}$$

In terms of the parameters, the quadratic programming formulation of the three-asset problem is

**The Formal
Portfolio
Model
Three
Assets**

$$\text{Min } \sigma_x^2 X^2 + \sigma_y^2 Y^2 + \sigma_z^2 Z^2 + 2\sigma_{xy}XY + 2\sigma_{xz}XZ + 2\sigma_{yz}YZ\} \qquad \text{quadratic objective}$$

$$\text{s.t. } R_x X + R_y Y + R_z Z \geq G$$
$$X + Y + Z = 1$$
$$X \leq S_x$$
$$Y \leq S_y \qquad \text{feasible region is same as in LP}$$
$$Z \leq S_z$$
$$X, Y, Z \geq 0$$

The objective function is the variance of the portfolio return, which, as stated in Section 8.14, is commonly considered to be the risk of the portfolio. (The rationale for this definition of risk, as well as the derivation of the objective function, is in the domain of statistics and is beyond our scope.) The first constraint expresses the lower bound on the expected return of the portfolio. The second constraint says that the fractions add to one, and the remaining constraints are upper bounds.

When a portfolio is allowed to be constructed from more than three assets the expected return is defined to be $\sum_{i=1}^{n} X_i R_i$. As before, R_i is the expected return from asset i, and X_i is the fraction of asset i in the portfolio. In this general case of N assets, the variance of the return of the portfolio is defined as[3]

$$\sum_{i=1}^{N} X_i^2 \sigma_i^2 + 2 \sum_{i=1}^{N-1} \sum_{j=i+1}^{N} X_i X_j \sigma_{ij}$$

[3] In matrix notation the variance of the portfolio return is written as $X^T Y X$, where X is the vector $(X_1, \ldots, X_N)$ and Y denotes the symmetric "covariance matrix" whose (i,j)th entry is σ_{ij} (and where $\sigma_{ii} = \sigma_i^2$).

After numerical estimates are substituted for the parameters, this quadratic programming problem can be solved with GINO. As a specific example let us now consider three stocks and historical returns from 1943–54. The three stocks chosen are AT&T, General Motors, and US Steel. The returns for 1943–1954 are (data from H. M. Markowitz, *Portfolio Selection*, Yale University Press, 1959)

Actual Returns

ROW	ATT	GM	USS
1	0.300	0.225	0.149
2	0.103	0.290	0.260
3	0.216	0.216	0.419
4	−0.046	−0.272	−0.078
5	−0.071	0.144	0.169
6	0.056	0.107	−0.035
7	0.038	0.321	0.133
8	0.089	0.305	0.732
9	0.090	0.195	0.021
10	0.083	0.390	0.131
11	0.035	−0.072	0.006
12	0 176	0.715	0.908

Definition of Return

In this table the return in year n is defined by

$$\frac{(\text{closing price, } n) - (\text{closing price, } n - 1) + (\text{dividends, } n)}{(\text{closing price, } n - 1)}$$

where closing prices and dividends are expressed in dollars/share.[4]

Next, we meet the covariance matrix. Using the above estimation formulas, the result of the calculations is

Estimated Variances and Covariances

	ATT	GM	USS
ATT	1.08075E-02		
GM	1.24072E-02	5.83917E-02	
USS	1.30751E-02	5.54264E-02	9.42268E-02

Finally, we need to calculate the average return for each stock. The result is

Average Returns

STOCK	AVERAGE RETURN
ATT	8.90833E-02
GM	0.213667
USS	0.234583

---

[4] Note the following unsatisfactory implication of averaging this definition: Suppose there are no dividends, that in year 1 the stock goes from 1.0 to 1.5 (with a return of .5) and in year 2 the stock goes from 1.5 to 1 (with a return of −.33). The average 2-year return is .17/2. Would you agree? This shows that estimating expected returns (and covariances) can be a delicate issue. It should be emphasized that this illustration is very introductory in nature.

Now suppose that you wish to minimize the variance of the return of the portfolio, subject to a 15% expected return and a restriction that no more than 75% of the portfolio can be in any individual stock. The quadratic program of interest and GINO solution are given below:

Computer Solution to THREE-ASSET Model

```
MODEL:
  1) MIN = 0.0108075*X^2 + 0.0583917*Y^2 + 0.0942268*Z^2 +
     0.0248144*X*Y + 0.0261502*X*Z + 0.1108528*Y*Z;
  2) 0.089*X + 0.21*Y + 0.23*Z > 0.15;
  3) X + Y + Z = 1;
  4) X < 0.75;
  5) Y < 0.75;
  6) Z < 0.75;
END

            OBJECTIVE FUNCTION VALUE

        1)          0.023107


VARIABLE          VALUE          REDUCED COST
      X          0.514878          0.000000
      Y          0.368962          0.000000
      Z          0.116060          0.000000


    ROW    SLACK OR SURPLUS              PRICE
    2)          0.000000          -0.375298
    3)         -0.000100           0.010082
    4)          0.235122           0.000000
    5)          0.381038           0.000000
    6)          0.633940           0.000000
```

Note that the solution to the above problem specifies a portfolio of 51.5% ATT, 36.9% GM, and 11.6% US Steel. Since row 2 is active, the expected yearly return is exactly 15%. The optimal objective value indicates that the variance of yearly return is about .023, which means the standard deviation is $\sqrt{.023} = 15\%$. If in 1955 in one had believed in the validity of this model, and if one had further assumed (in addition to the validity of the model) that the portfolio returns are normally distributed with mean 15% and standard deviation of 15%, then according to statistical theory one might reasonably have expected that such a portfolio, in 1955 and ensuing years, would have produced returns roughly between -15% and $+45\%$. In fact, the returns in 1955–57 for the three assets were

	1955	1956	1957
ATT	.103	.039	.030
GM	.512	-0.50	-.200
USS	.647	.322	-.266

FIGURE 8.25
The Efficient Frontier

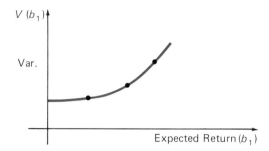

Hence, using the above optimal fractions, the portfolio returns would have been

	1955	1956	1957
	31.7%	3.9%	−8.9%

In concluding this section, we observe that the dual price on row 2 indicates that a 1% increase in expected return (an increase of .01 in the RHS of row 2) would lead to *roughly* an *increase* of .00375 in variance (i.e., since increasing the RHS of row 2 will hurt the OV, and since we have a Min model, the OV will increase). Hence the new variance would be about .0268, with the standard deviation equal to $\sqrt{.0268} = 16\%$. These numbers are approximate because for a nonlinear program the slopes of $V(b_1)$ are instantaneous (rather than constant in intervals as is the case with LP). This fact was discussed in terms of a general quadratic program in Section 8.13. For the portfolio model, it is reflected by the general shape for $V(b_1)$ as shown in Figure 8.25. (Note that the graph shows that tightening the constraint—i.e., increasing b_1—hurts the OV more and more.)

In the language of finance, this graph is called the efficient frontier, and its properties are studied in finance courses. For our purposes we merely observe that it is a piecewise quadratic convex function. To find any point on the graph of this function, one simply selects a value for the RHS of the constraint that sets a lower bound on the expected return (the first constraint), and solves the problem.

8.16
KEY TERMS

INTEGER LINEAR PROGRAMS.   Problems that satisfy all the conditions of a linear program except that some or all of the variables are required to be integers.

ILP.   An integer linear program in which all the decision variables are required to be integers.

MILP (MIXED INTEGER LINEAR PROGRAM).   An integer linear program in which only some of the variables are required to be integers.

LP RELAXATION.   An LP problem that is derived from an ILP or an MILP by ignoring the integrality constraints.

ROUNDED SOLUTION.   A feasible solution to an ILP or MILP found by solving the LP relaxation and rounding each of the integer variables either up or down.

OPTIMAL VALUE. Short for the optimal value of the objective function.

OV. An abbreviation for the optimal value of the objective function.

OPTIMAL SOLUTION. The value of the decision variables in the optimal solution.

COMPLETE ENUMERATION. Solving an ILP by listing all the feasible points, evaluating the objective function at each of them, and selecting the best solution.

BRANCH AND BOUND. A solution technique used on ILP's and MILP's based on dividing the original problem into mutually exclusive parts and employing the OV from the LP relaxations to obtain bounds.

QUADRATIC PROGRAMS. Problems that maximize or minimize the value of a quadratic objective function subject to linear constraints and nonnegativity conditions.

PORTFOLIO ANALYSIS. The problem of minimizing the variance of return subject to a requirement on expected return.

EFFICIENT FRONTIER. The OV function of a portfolio analysis QP.

VARIANCE. A statistical measure of risk.

STANDARD DEVIATION. The square root of variance.

COVARIANCE. A statistical measure of the extent to which random quantities are correlated.

MAJOR CONCEPTS QUIZ

Part 1. Integer Programming Questions

True–False

1. **T F** Rounding LP solutions to meet the real-world requirement for integer decision variables is a common practice.

2. **T F** In general, it is no more difficult to solve an IP than an LP.

3. **T F** The binary variable in an IP may be used to represent dichotomous decisions.

4. **T F** In a *Max* problem, the OV of the LP relaxation always provides a *lower bound* on the OV of the original ILP or MILP.

5. **T F** The first step in obtaining a rounded solution to an MILP is to solve its LP relaxation.

6. **T F** Solving an ILP by complete enumeration involves evaluating the objective function at all corners of the feasible set of the LP relaxation.

7. **T F** In the LP relaxation of the ILP capital budgeting problem there are as many constraints as there are periods.

8. **T F** In an ILP with n binary decision variables, each of which indicates the selection (or not) of an alternative, the condition that no more than k alternatives be selected can be imposed with the constraint $x_1 + x_2 + \cdots x_n \leq k$.

9. **T F** In Steco's warehouse location problem, the optimal number of trucks to send from each warehouse to each plant was an integer because after the warehouses are selected the problem is a transportation problem with integer supplies and demands.

10. **T F** Suppose x_1 and x_2 are both binary variables where $x_i = 1$ has the interpretation of building a plant in location i. The condition "a plant can be built in location 2 only if the plant in location 1 is also built" is captured with the constraint $x_1 \leq x_2$.

11. **T F** Consider a transportation model with integer supplies and demands and where, in addition, integrality conditions are imposed on the x_{ij}'s. Since this makes the problem an integer program, it must be solved with special IP codes.

Multiple Choice

12. In an ILP
   a. ignoring integrality restrictions, all constraint functions are linear
   b. all decision variables must be integers
   c. all decision variables must be nonnegative
   d. all of the above

13. In an MILP
    a. the objective function is linear
    b. all decision variables must be integers
    c. some coefficients are restricted to be integers, others are not
    d. all of the above

14. The LP relaxation of an ILP
    a. permits a nonlinear objective function
    b. ignores the integrality restrictions on the decision variables
    c. relaxes the nonnegativity restrictions on the decision variables
    d. all of the above

15. A rounded solution to a Max ILP may not be feasible because
    a. it violates the integrality constraints
    b. it violates the nonnegativity constraints
    c. its OV is smaller than the OV of the LP relaxation
    d. none of the above

16. If x_k and x_m are 0–1 variables (the value 1 meaning select) for projects k and m, respectively, the constraint $x_k + x_m \leq 0$ implies that
    a. k cannot be selected unless m is selected
    b. k must be selected if m is selected
    c. m cannot be selected unless k is selected
    d. none of the above

17. Suppose a product can be manufactured either not at all or else in lot sizes $\geq L$ and let x be the quantity of the product produced. The following two constraints are appropriate:
    a. $x + Uy \leq 0; x - Ly \geq 0$
    b. $x - Uy \geq 0; x - Ly \geq 0$
    c. $x - Uy \leq 0; x - Ly \geq 0$
    d. $x - Uy \leq 0; x - Ly \leq 0$
    where U is an arbitrarily large number and y is a 0–1 variable.

18. In solving a Max ILP a lower bound for the OV of the original problem can always be found by
    a. solving the LP relaxation of the ILP and using the OV of the LP
    b. finding a feasible solution to the ILP by any available means and evaluating the objective function
    c. solving the LP relaxation and then rounding fractions <0.5 down, those ≥ 0.5 up, and evaluating the objective function at this point
    d. none of the above

19. In the branch-and-bound approach to a Max ILP, a node is terminated when
    a. its $U < CBLB$
    b. the LP relaxation is infeasible
    c. the LP relaxation provides a solution to the integer problem represented by that node
    d. any of the above

20. The computer solution to an MILP
    a. contains no sensitivity information
    b. contains sensitivity information on only the noninteger variables
    c. contains sensitivity information only on right-hand sides
    d. contains sensitivity information only on the objective function

More Challenging Problem

The next 10 questions are based on the following problem:

   A firm has 10 outlets that must be supplied with a certain product. The demands (all positive) at the outlets are $d_1, \ldots, d_{10}$, and these demands must be *exactly* satisfied (i.e., not more than d_i units can be distributed to outlet i). The firm may supply these demands by having a supplier deliver directly to each outlet. The supplier charges $50 for each unit delivered, independent of the outlet location. The supplier would charge only $35 per unit for any location if the location would order at least D units. Since each of the $d_i < D$, the firm can make no use of the discount. The firm is considering leasing a centrally located warehouse for $K > 0$ dollars and using this warehouse as an intermediary depot. The depot could order any quantity and could distribute to any number of outlets. It has been agreed that the depot would pay the same as the outlets ($50 per unit if $<D$ units are ordered; $35 per unit if the total order is at least D units).

The cost of sending a unit from the warehouse to outlet i is $C_i > 0$, $i = 1, \ldots, 10$. Assume that $D < \sum_{i=1}^{10} d_i$. Management would like to know

1. Should the warehouse be leased?
2. If so, which outlets should be served by the warehouse and which should be supplied directly by the supplier?

In formulating a model to answer these questions, let

$$x_i = \text{quantity sent directly from supplier to location } i$$

$$y_i = \text{quantity sent from warehouse to location } i$$

$$z = \text{quantity sent from supplier to warehouse}$$

A correct set of constraints for this model is

$$x_i + y_i = d_i, \qquad i = 1, \ldots, 10$$

$$\sum_{i=1}^{10} y_i - z \le 0$$

$$z - tD \ge 0$$

$$z - t \sum_{i=1}^{10} d_i \le 0$$

$$x_i, y_i \ge 0, \qquad i = 1, \ldots, 10; \qquad z \ge 0, \qquad t \text{ is 0 or 1}$$

21. The correct objective function is
    a. Min $\sum_{i=1}^{10} 50x_i + \sum_{i=1}^{10} C_i y_i$
    b. Min $\sum_{i=1}^{10} 50x_i + \sum_{i=1}^{10} (C_i + 35)y_i + tK$
    c. Min $\sum_{i=1}^{10} 50x_i + 35z + \sum_{i=1}^{10} C_i y_i + tK$
    d. Min $\sum_{i=1}^{10} (50x_i + C_i y_i) + 35D$
    e. none of the above

22. For the problem as stated, there will never be an optimal solution in which the depot orders a positive amount but less than D units.
    a. True
    b. False

23. Management should lease the warehouse if
   a. the optimal value of D is positive
   b. the optimal value of t is positive
   c. the optimal value of z is positive
   d. all of the above
   e. b and c

24. Consider location k such that $35 + C_k > 50$. Since the marginal cost of shipping directly to k from the supplier is less than the marginal cost of going through the warehouse, there will be no optimal solution in which this outlet (the kth) receives products both from the warehouse and directly from the supplier.
   a. True
   b. False

25. There always will exist an optimal solution in which no outlet receives deliveries from both the supplier (directly) and the warehouse.
   a. True
   b. False

26. Suppose $35 + C_i = 50$, $i = 1, \ldots, 10$. Then $t^* = 0$ in any optimal solution.
   a. True
   b. False

27. This model may have an optimal solution in which the total quantity ordered from the supplier exceeds $\sum_{i=1}^{10} d_i$.
   a. True
   b. False

28. If the optimal value $z^* = \sum_{i=1}^{10} d_i$, then it is certain that the optimal solution will be $x_i^* = 0$, $i = 1, \ldots, 10$, $y_i^* = d_i$, $i = 1, \ldots, 10$, and $t^* = 1$.
   a. True
   b. False

29. This model will allow the possibility of having inventory left at the warehouse after all demands are satisfied.
   a. True
   b. False

30. Suppose each $C_i \geq 15$.
   a. Then the optimal solution to the model is obviously $x_i^* = d_i$, $y_i^* = 0$, $i = 1, \ldots, 10$, $z^* = 0 = t^*$.
   b. For some values of the parameters d_i the solution may differ, and hence it is wisest to run the model.

Part 2. Quadratic Programming Questions

True–False

31. **T F**   A quadratic programming program may have quadratic constraint functions.

32. **T F**   Maximizing or minimizing any nonlinear objective function subject to a set of linear equality and inequality constraints, as well as nonnegativity conditions on the values of the decision variables, is a quadratic programming problem.

33. **T F**   Any LP problem can be solved with a QP code.

34. **T F**   It is not possible to characterize extreme points of the feasible region of a QP.

35. **T F**   The optimal solution to a QP problem need not be a corner solution.

36. **T F**   The optimal solution to a QP problem must include at least as many positive variables as there are constraints.

37. **T F**   Loosening a constraint in a QP will either not change or improve the OV.

38. **T F**   In a Max problem the rate of improvement of OV is the negative of the rate of change.

39. **T   F**   The slope of the tangent to the graph of the function OV(R) at the point $(\hat{R}, OV(\hat{R}))$ is the rate of change in the function OV(R) at $R = \hat{R}$.

40. **T   F**   Changing a coefficient of a term in the objective function of a QP always changes the optimal solution.

41. **T   F**   The variance of the return from a portfolio is a linear function of the amount invested in each stock in the portfolio.

42. **T   F**   If there are three stocks in the portfolio, the feasible region will lie on a plane.

43. **T   F**   The portfolio problem includes a lower bound on the expected return. In general this constraint need not be binding.

Multiple Choice

44. The definition of a QP problem does not include
    a. nonnegativity conditions
    b. quadratic constraint functions
    c. linear equality constraints
    d. nonlinear terms in the objective function

45. In a QP problem in n variables $(x_1, \ldots, x_n)$, the objective function may not include terms of the form
    a. x_j^2
    b. $x_i x_j$
    c. $x_i^2 \cdot x_j$
    d. $9x_i$

46. An LP is a special case of a QP because
    a. the LP feasible region is a special case of a QP feasible region
    b. the LP constraint functions are a special case of the QP constraint functions
    c. nonnegativity conditions are special to an LP
    d. the LP objective function is a special case of the QP objective function

47. The optimal solution to a QP problem with n constraints may not have
    a. negative values for some decision variables
    b. more than n positive decision variables
    c. less than n positive decision variables
    d. zero values for some decision variables

48. The optimal solution to a QP problem
    a. must lie on a corner of the feasible set
    b. cannot be on a corner of the feasible set
    c. is always nondegenerate
    d. none of the above

49. In the optimal solution for a QP problem, slack and surplus variables
    a. have no meaning even though they appear on the computer solution
    b. have the same meaning as in an LP problem
    c. have a different meaning than in an LP problem
    d. are unrestricted in sign

50. GINO can be used to solve
    a. general nonlinear programming problems
    b. QP's
    c. LP's
    d. all of the above

51. Loosening a constraint in a portfolio problem
    a. must increase the dual price on that constraint
    b. must decrease the dual price on that constraint
    c. may change the sign of the dual price on that constraint
    d. cannot increase the objective function

Answers

1. T	14. b	27. T	40. F
2. F	15. d	28. T	41. F
3. T	16. d	29. T	42. T
4. F	17. c	30. a	43. T
5. T	18. b	31. F	44. b
6. F	19. d	32. F	45. c
7. F	20. a	33. T	46. d
8. T	21. c	34. F	47. a
9. T	22. T	35. T	48. d
10. F	23. e	36. F	49. b
11. F	24. F	37. T	50. d
12. d	25. F	38. F	51. d
13. a	26. T	39. T	

Part 1. Problems on Integer Programs

8-1. A firm produces two products, A and C. Capacity on the A line is 7 units per day. Each unit of C requires 4 hours of drying time, and a total of 22 drying hours per day is available. Also, each unit of A requires 2 hours of polishing and each unit of C requires 3 hours of polishing. A total of 19 hours of polishing time is available each day. Each unit of A yields a profit of $1, whereas each unit of C yields a profit of $3. The firm wants to determine a daily production schedule to maximize profits. A and C can only be produced in integer amounts.

(a) Formulate this problem as an ILP.

(b) Use a graphical approach to find the optimal solution to the LP relaxation.

(c) Find the optimal solution to the ILP.

(d) Find an integer solution by rounding each value in the answer to part b to its integer part. Is this solution feasible?

(e) How much profit would the firm lose by adopting the latter rounded solution?

8-2. Consider the following ILP:

$$\text{Max } 2x_1 + 3x_2$$

$$\text{s.t.} \quad x_1 - x_2 \geq 0$$

$$x_1 + 2x_2 \leq 6$$

$$2x_1 + x_2 \leq 8$$

$$x_1, x_2 \geq 0 \text{ and integer}$$

(a) Use a graphical approach to find the optimal solution to the LP relaxation.

(b) How many feasible points are there?

(c) Using a graphical approach, find the optimal solution to the ILP.

(d) Find an integer feasible solution by rounding the answer to part (a). Is the rounded solution optimal?

8-3. Consider a minimization ILP. Does the optimal value for the LP relaxation provide an upper or a lower bound for the optimal value of the ILP? Explain your answer.

8-4. Consider a minimization ILP. Does the value of the objective function at a feasible rounded solution provide an upper or a lower bound for the optimal value of the ILP? Explain your answer.

8-5. Consider a maximization ILP. Does the optimal value of the LP relaxation of this problem provide an upper or a lower bound for the optimal value of the ILP? Explain your answer.

8-6. Consider a maximization ILP. Does the value of the objective function at a feasible rounded solution provide an upper or a lower bound for the optimal value of the ILP? Explain your answer.

8-7. *Investment Problem* A portfolio manager has just been given $100,000 to invest. She will choose her investments from a list of 20 stocks. She knows that the net return from investing one dollar in stock i is r_i. (Thus, if she invests x_i dollars in stock i she will end up with $(1 + r_i)x_i$ dollars.) In order to maintain a balanced portfolio, she adopts the following two rules of thumb:

1. She will not invest more than $20,000 in a single stock.
2. *If* she invests anything in a stock, she will invest at least $5000 in it.

The manager would like to maximize her return subject to these rules of thumb. Formulate this problem as an MILP. Define your decision variables carefully.

8-8. *Airline Scheduling* Alpha Airline wishes to schedule no more than one flight out of Chicago to each of the following cities: Columbus, Denver, Los Angeles, and New York. The available departure slots are 8 A.M., 10 A.M. and 12 noon. Alpha leases the airplanes at the cost of $3,000 before and including 10 A.M. and $1,500 after 10 A.M., and is able to lease at most 2 per departure slot. The expected profit contribution before rental costs per flight is shown in Figure 8.26. Formulate a model for a profit-maximizing schedule. Define your decision variables carefully.

FIGURE 8.26
Expected Profit Contribution (thousands)

	TIME SLOT 8	10	12
Columbus	8	4	4
Denver	8	7	8
Los Angeles	11	10.5	9.5
New York	17	16	15

8-9. *A Start-up Problem* A problem faced by an electrical utility each day is that of deciding which generators to start up. The utility in question has three generators with the characteristics shown in Figure 8.27. There are two periods in a day and the number of megawatts needed in the first period is 2900. The second period requires 3900 megawatts. A generator started in the first period may be used in the second period without incurring an additional startup cost. All major generators (e.g., A, B, and C above) are turned off at the end of each day. Formulate this problem as an MILP.

FIGURE 8.27

GENERATOR	FIXED STARTUP COST	COST PER PERIOD PER MEGAWATT USED	MAXIMUM CAPACITY IN EACH PERIOD (MW)
A	$3000	$5	2100
B	2000	4	1800
C	1000	7	3000

8-10. *Production Planning*   A certain production line makes two products. Relevant data are given in Figure 8.28. Total time available (for production and setup) each week is 40 hours. The firm has no inventory of either product at the start of week 1 and no inventory is allowed at the end of week 3. The cost of carrying a unit of inventory from one week to the next is $3 for each product. One unit of unsatisfied demand costs $6 for product A and $9 for product B. Demand data are given in Figure 8.29. The line is shut down and cleaned each weekend. As a result, if either product is produced in a week the appropriate setup time cost is incurred. Note that it is possible to produce both products in the same week. If both are produced, both setup times and costs are incurred. No production can take place during the time that the line is being set up. Formulate this 3-week planning problem as an MILP. The objective is to maximize the profit over a 3-week period. Define your notation carefully and use summation notation in your formulation.

FIGURE 8.28

	PRODUCT	
	A	B
Setup Time	6 hours	8 hours
Per Unit Production Time	0.5 hour	0.75 hour
Setup Cost	$120	$160
Per Unit Production Cost	$6	$8
Selling Price	$15	$20

FIGURE 8.29

	WEEK		
PRODUCT	1	2	3
A	28	34	10
B	6	8	16

8-11. The board of directors of a large manufacturing firm is considering the set of investments shown in Figure 8.30. Let R_i be the total revenue from investment i and C_i be the cost to make investment i. The board wishes to maximize total revenue and invest no more than a total of M dollars. Formulate this problem as an ILP. Define your decision variables.

FIGURE 8.30

INVESTMENT	CONDITION
1	None
2	Only if 1
3	Only if 2
4	Must if 1 *and* 2
5	Not if 1 *or* 2
6	Not if 2 *and* 3
7	Only if 2 *and not* 3

FIGURE 8.31

Investment Restrictions

PROJECT	CONDITION
A	None
B	Not if C and only if E
C	Not if B
D	Only if A
E	Not if F and only if C
F	Not if E and only if C
G	Only if A and B

8-12. *Investment Selection* A real estate developer is considering several closely interrelated projects. Certain projects may be undertaken only if certain conditions are met (see Figure 8.31). Let R_i be the total revenue from project i and C_i be the cost to undertake project i. The developer wishes to maximize total revenue and invest no more than a total of M dollars. Formulate this problem as an ILP. Define your decision variables.

8-13. Use a graphical approach and the branch-and-bound algorithm to solve the ILP presented in Problem 8-1. Branch first on A, present each new problem in the process together with its solution, and express the analysis in a decision diagram.

8-14. Use a graphical approach and the branch-and-bound algorithm to solve the ILP presented in Problem 8-2. Branch first on x_1. For each new problem state what constraint you would add to what problem to create the new problem; for example, a phrase like "Add constraint $x_1 \leq 2$ to problem 1." Express the analysis in a decision diagram like those in the text.

8-15. Consider the following formulation of Problem 8-1:

$$\text{Max } A + 3C$$

$$\text{s.t.} \quad A \quad\quad\quad \leq 7$$

$$4C \leq 22$$

$$2A + 3C \leq 19$$

$$A \geq 0 \text{ and integer}, \quad\quad C \geq 0 \text{ and integer}$$

Plot the optimal objective value as a function of the RHS of the second constraint as the value of the RHS ranges between 0 and 24.

HINT: Use the graphical approach and the figure prepared in the solution to Problem 8-1.

8-16. Consider the ILP presented in Problem 8-2. Plot the optimal objective value as a function of the RHS of the constraint

$$x_1 + 2x_2 \leq \text{RHS}$$

for $0 \leq \text{RHS} \leq 7$.

8-17. Consider the following ILP:

$$\text{Min } 4x_1 + 5x_2$$

$$\text{s.t.} \quad 3x_1 + 6x_2 \geq 18$$

$$5x_1 + 4x_2 \geq 20$$

$$8x_1 + 2x_2 \geq 16$$

$$7x_1 + 6x_2 \leq 42$$

$$x_1 \geq 0 \text{ and integer}, \quad\quad x_2 \geq 0 \text{ and integer}$$

(a) Find the optimal solution to the LP relaxation.

(b) List all the feasible points.

(c) Find the optimal solution to the ILP.

(d) Find a feasible rounded solution.

(e) Is the latter optimal?

(f) How large is the cost of using the rounded solution identified above relative to the optimal solution?

8-18. Consider the ILP presented in Problem 8-17.

Plot the optimal objective value as a function of the RHS of the constraint

$$3x_1 + 6x_2 \geq \text{RHS}$$

for $0 \leq \text{RHS} \leq 40$.

8-19. Consider the printout shown in Figure 8.9. Given the optimal values of YA, YB, and YC, write out the transportation model that the optimal truck allocations solve.

8-20. Use a graphical approach and the branch-and-bound algorithm to solve the ILP presented in Problem 8-17. Branch first on x_2. For each new problem state what constraint you would add to what problem to create the new problem; for example, a phrase like "Add constraint $x_2 \geq 2$ to problem 1." Express the analysis in a decision diagram like those in the text.

8-21. *Capacity Expansion* An electric utility is planning the expansion of its generation capacity for the next five years. Its current capacity is 800 MW, but based on its forecast of demand it will require additional capacity as shown in Figure 8.32. The utility can increase its generation capacity by installing 10, 50, or 100 MW generators. The cost of installing a generator depends on its size and the year it is brought on line. See Figure 8.33. Once a generator is brought on line its capacity is available to meet demand in succeeding years. Formulate an ILP that minimizes the cost of bringing generators on line while satisfying the minimum capacity requirements. HINT: Let x_t, y_t, and z_t be the number of 10, 50, and 100 MW generators brought on line in year t and c_t the total capacity in year t after these generators have been brought on line.

FIGURE 8.32

Capacity Requirements

YEAR	MINIMUM CAPACITY (MW)
1	880
2	960
3	1050
4	1160
5	1280

FIGURE 8.33

Cost of Bringing Generators on Line
(Thousands)

GENERATOR SIZE	YEAR				
	1	2	3	4	5
10 MW	$300	$250	$208	$173	$145
50	670	558	465	387	322
100	950	791	659	549	458

8-22. Norco Home Cosmetics Sales is just moving into a six-county region of southern Utah. The map below shows the location of the counties and their populations, P_i. Norco plans to assign two salespersons to this region. The company assigns two counties to each salesperson, a base county and an adjacent county. Counties are adjacent if they share a common *side*; a common corner is *not* sufficient.

P_1 1	P_2 2	P_3 3
P_4 4	P_5 5	P_6 6

For example, in the map above, counties 1 and 2 are adjacent, but 1 and 5 are not. Norco's objective is to maximize the total population of the assigned counties. A feasible solution is to make 4 a base with 1 as the assigned adjacent and also make 3 a base with 2 as the assigned adjacent. The value of the objective function for this solution is $P_1 + P_2 + P_3 + P_4$.

Define

$$B_j = \begin{array}{l} 1 \text{ if county } j \text{ is used as a base} \\ 0 \text{ if not, } j = 1, \ldots, 6 \end{array}$$

$$A_{ij} = \begin{array}{l} 1 \text{ if county } i \text{ is used as a county adjacent to base } j \\ 0 \text{ if not, } j = 1, \ldots, 6; i \text{ adjacent to } j \end{array}$$

Thus the variables are $B_1, B_2, B_3, B_4, B_5, B_6, A_{21}, A_{41}, A_{12}, A_{52}, A_{32}, A_{23}, A_{63}$, etc.

(a) In the model for this problem, double counting must not occur (i.e., a county must not be used as both a base and an assigned adjacent). Write a constraint that assures no double counting for county 1.

(b) Write a constraint that says "if any salesperson is assigned to county 2 as a base then a salesperson must also be assigned to an appropriate adjacent county."

(c) Write a constraint that says "if either county adjacent to 1 is scheduled (as an adjacent to 1) then 1 must be used as a base."

(d) This model can be written with 12 inequality constraints and 1 equality constraint. True or False.

(e) This model can be written with 7 equality constraints and 6 inequality constraints. True or False.

8-23. Refer to the problem description that precedes problem 21. Assume in addition to the conditions described there, that there is a fixed cost of $R > 0$ dollars assigned to each shipment that leaves the supplier. This implies, for example, that if the supplier makes direct shipments to locations 3, 5, and 8 and to the warehouse then an additional cost of $4R$ dollars is incurred.

Formulate this problem as an MILP, using the notation introduced earlier and whatever additional notation is required.

Part 2. Problems on Quadratic Programs

8-24. "If *at least one* of the stocks in the portfolio has an expected return greater-than-or-equal-to the required return on the entire portfolio, then this formulation will never be infeasible." Under what conditions will this statement be true?

8-25. Consider the problem solved in Section 8.15. The current solution to this problem is $(X = 0.515, Y = 0.369, Z = 0.116)$. Is this point an extreme point of the feasible region? Why or why not?

8-26. Consider the problem solved in Section 8.15. Assume you are considering adding the stock of the IMCRZY corporation to your portfolio selection model. This stock has a *negative* expected return. Under what conditions might the model select stock from IMCRZY to be in the portfolio?

8-27. Consider the problem solved in Section 8.15. What is the allowable decrease on the constraint which limits the investment of stock Y to 75 percent of the portfolio?

8-28. As with pure LP analysis, there is sensitivity analysis output associated with QP. Would you expect this QP sensitivity analysis to include allowable increases and decreases on the RHS?

8-29. Consider the problem solved in Section 8.15. Assume your objective is to maximize return subject to the constraint that the variability of the portfolio cannot exceed V. Reformulate the problem with this modification.

8-30. Refer to question 8-29. Set $V = 0.023107$. If there are no alternative optima in the original problem, what is the maximum expected return in your reformulated model? Explain.

CASE

MUNICIPAL BOND UNDERWRITING*

The municipal bond market is tough and aggressive, which means that a successful underwriter must be at the state-of-the-art in terms of competitive bidding. Bond markets often change from hour to hour. An active underwriter may bid on several issues each day with as little as 15 to 20 minutes to prepare a bid. This case has two objectives: (1) The student is familiarized with some of the mechanics of an important financial market; (2) The student will develop an IP model with real world importance. A variant of this model is actually used by several banks and investment bankers. In practice, bids are routinely prepared in a minute of CPU time on an IBM 370/168 for problems involving as many as 100 maturities and 35 coupon rates.

───── 1

BASIC SCENARIO

Each year billions of dollars of tax-exempt debt securities are offered for sale to the public. This is usually done through an underwriter acting as a broker between the issuer of the security and the public. The issuing of the securities to the underwriter is usually done through a competitive bid process. The issuer will notify prospective underwriters in advance of the proposed sale and invite bids which meet constraints set forth by the issuer. In constructing a proposed sale, the issuer divides the total amount to be raised (say $10,000) into bonds of various maturities. For example, to raise $10,000, the issuer might offer a one year bond with face value of $2,000, a two-year bond with face value of $3,000, and a three year bond with face value of $5,000.

───────

* This modeling approach was derived from the discussion in Nauss and Keeler, *Management Science*, Vol. 27, No. 4, April 1981, pp. 365–376. This CASE was initially formulated by Professor K. Martin.

At maturity, the face value of these bonds would be paid to the buyer. Thus in this example, the issuers would pay the buyers $2,000 in principal at the end of year one, and so on.

A bid by an underwriter (to the issuer) has three components:

1. An agreement to pay the issuer the face value of all of the bonds at the issue date. ($10,000 in our example).
2. A premium paid to the issuer at the issue date. (More on this later).
3. An annual interest rate for each of the bonds cited in the proposal. These rates are called the coupon rates and determine the amount of interest the issuer must pay the buyers each year. Suppose that the underwriter proposed the following coupon rates for our example.

MATURITY DATE	RATE %
1 year	3
2 years	4
3 years	5

The interest to be paid by the issuer would then be calculated as follows:

$$\text{Year } 1 = 2{,}000(.03) + 3{,}000(.04) + 5{,}000(.05) = 430$$

$$\text{Year } 2 = \phantom{2{,}000(.03) + {}} 3{,}000(.04) + 5{,}000(.05) = 370$$

$$\text{Year } 3 = \phantom{2{,}000(.03) + 3{,}000(.04) + {}} 5000(.05) = 250$$

Historically, the net interest cost (NIC) is the criterion most often employed by the issuer in evaluating bids. The NIC is the sum of interest payments over all years for all maturities minus any premium offered by the underwriter. The winning bid is the one with the minimum NIC. The time value of money is ignored in calculating the NIC. Even though the bid with the lowest NIC may not be best for the issuer when present values are considered, this is immaterial to the underwriter since the bid is evaluated according to the NIC.

The profit of the underwriter is the difference between what the buyer pays him and what he (the underwriter) pays the issuer. That is,

Profit = [Total Selling Price to Public] − [Total Face Value + Premium].

Thus, in preparing a bid the underwriter must

1. determine the coupon (interest) amounts the issuer will pay on each maturity,
2. for each maturity, estimate the selling price (i.e., the underwriter's selling price to the public) for bonds of each coupon rate. (The selling price for bonds need not be the same as the face value of the bond.)

The underwriter has two conflicting objectives. Higher coupon rates imply the bonds will have a higher selling price to the public and hence more money to the underwriter which can be used both as premium and profit. Thus the coupon rates must be set large enough so that if the bid is accepted the underwriter makes a reasonable profit. But higher coupon rates affect the interest the issuer will have to pay (higher coupon rates imply more interest) as well as the premium which the underwriter can offer the issuer. This tradeoff between premium and interest may imply that lower coupon rates will decrease the cost to the issuer and hence increase the chances of winning the bid.

The approach we take is to incorporate the underwriter's profit as a constraint and then minimize NIC (the cost to the issuer) in order to maximize the chances of winning the bid.

————2
DATA FOR A SPECIFIC SCENARIO

The city of Dogpatch is going to issue municipal bonds in order to raise revenue for civic improvements. Sealed bids will be received until 5:00 p.m. on February 7, 1973 for $5,000,000 in bonds dated March 1, 1973. The bid represents an offer from the underwriter to (i) pay $5,000,000 to Dogpatch, (ii) pay an additional (specified) premium to Dogpatch, (iii) an interest schedule which Dogpatch will pay to the bond holders. The interest is payable on March 1, 1974 and annually thereafter. The bonds become due (i.e. Dogpatch must pay off the face value, without option for prior payment) on March 1 in each of the maturity years in Table 1 below and in the amounts indicated. That is, Table 1 indicates Dogpatch's obligation (in terms of principal) to the bondholders.

TABLE 1

YEAR (MATURITY)	AMOUNT (× $1000)
1975	$250
1976	425
1977	1025
1978	1050
1979	1100
1980	1150

The bonds will be awarded to the bidder on the basis of the minimum NIC. No bid will be considered with an interest rate greater than 5% or less than 3% per annum. Bidders must specify interest rates in multiples of one-quarter of one percent per annum. Not more than three different interest rates will be considered (a repeated rate will not be considered a different rate). The same rate must apply to all bonds of the same maturity.

Estimating selling prices of various maturities as a function of coupon rates is a complicated process depending upon available markets and various parameters. For the sake of this example, take the data in Table 2 as given. Note that the underwriter may sell bonds to the public at more or less than the face value.

TABLE 2
Estimated Selling Price (× 1000)

FACE VALUE	250	425	1025	1050	1100	1150
PERCENT	1975	1976	1977	1978	1979	1980
3	245	418	1015	1040	1080	1130
$3\frac{1}{4}$	248	422	1016	1042	1084	1135
$3\frac{1}{2}$	250	423	1017	1044	1085	1140
$3\frac{3}{4}$	251	424	1025	1046	1090	1150
4	253	430	1029	1050	1095	1155
$4\frac{1}{4}$	255	435	1035	1055	1096	1160
$4\frac{1}{2}$	256	437	1037	1060	1105	1165
$4\frac{3}{4}$	257	440	1038	1062	1110	1170
5	258	441	1040	1065	1115	1175

_____ 3

Example (A sample bid)

Assume an underwriter establishes the following coupon rates for each maturity.

TABLE 3

MATURITY	COUPON RATE	TOTAL INTEREST (+ $1000)
1975	3%	$15.00
1976	$4\frac{1}{2}$%	57.375
1977	$4\frac{3}{4}$%	194.75
1978	$4\frac{1}{2}$%	236.25
1979	$4\frac{1}{2}$%	297.00
1980	$4\frac{1}{2}$%	362.25

Given these coupon rates the bonds would be sold to the public (see estimates in Table 2) for $5,050,000. Assume the underwriter's spread or profit requirement is $8.00 per $1,000 of face amount of bonds. For a $5,000,000 issue this will be $40,000. Thus the premium paid to Dogpatch by the underwriter for this bid is

$$\text{premium} = \$5,050,000 - \$5,000,000 - \$40,000$$

$$= \$10,000.$$

_____ 4

Questions

1. Calculate Dogpatch's NIC for the example given in Section 3.
2. Suppose, as in Table 2, the underwriter has a choice between selling a 1975 bond at $4\frac{1}{4}$ percent for $255,000 or a 1975 bond at $4\frac{1}{2}$ percent for $256,000. Just in terms of minimizing

NIC (ignoring other possible constraints), which would the underwriter prefer to offer. Suppose that in either case the underwriter's profit is the same.

3. In Table 2, consider the 1975 maturity at 5%. Suppose that you as an investor can with certainty receive 5% interest on money invested on March 1, 1974. What compounded yearly rate of interest would you be receiving if you pay $258,000 for the 1975 bond and use the above investment opportunity with your first receipt of interest?

4. Formulate a constrained optimization model for solving the underwriter's problem. This formulation should minimize the NIC of the underwriter's bid subject to the underwriter receiving an $8 margin per $1000 of face amount and the other constraints given in Section 2. Be very clear and concise in defining any notation you use and indicate the purpose of each constraint in your formulation.

5. Solve your constrained optimization model using LINDO.

6. Bid requests often include additional constraints. Assume that one such additional restriction is that coupon rates must be nondecreasing with maturity. Add the necessary constraint(s) to enforce this condition. You do not need to resolve with LINDO.

7. Next assume that the maximum allowed difference between the highest and lowest coupon rates is one percent. Add the necessary constraint(s) to enforce this condition. You do not need to resolve with LINDO.

8. Refer to your formulation in question 4. If the bonds (regardless of maturity and coupon value) could never be sold in excess of face value will your formulation have a feasible solution? Why or why not?

9. Assume your formulation in question 4 has a feasible solution. Is it possvile that the addition of the constraint(s) from question 6 or the constraint(s) from question 7 (or both taken together) make the formulation infeasible?

A word of advice: One danger of misformulating a rather large integer programming model, and then attempting to run it on a computer, is that you may waste a great deal of computer time (this of course could be true of any large model). Your solution to question 5 above, using a correctly formulated model, should take no more than one minute of *CPU time* on any machine as fast as a DEC 2050. Your model, although rather large, should take no more than an hour to correctly type-in at a console.

DIAGNOSTIC ASSIGNMENT

ASSIGNING SALES REPRESENTATIVES

One of the main themes in the text is that the manager plays the role of the intermediary between the real problem and the model. The manager must decide if the assumptions are appropriate and if the solution produced by the model makes sense in the context of the real problem.

Sally Erickson is midwest sales director for Lady Lynn Cosmetics. Lady Lynn is a rapidly expanding company that sells cosmetics through representatives. These representatives originally contact most of their customers through house parties. At these parties, the representative demonstrates the products and takes orders. The guests have an opportunity to win some samples of the products and to order products. The hostess receives "gifts" depending on the volume of orders.

FIGURE 8.34

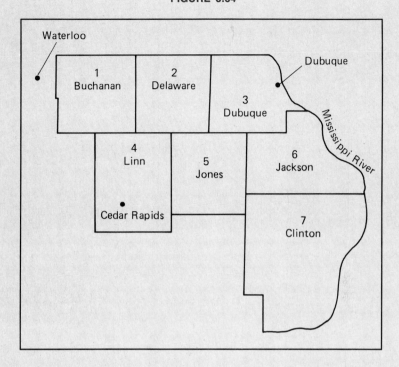

Sally is in the process of assigning representatives to the seven eastern Iowa counties shown in Figure 8.34. Actually, she has only two trained representatives to assign at this time. The policy at Lady Lynn is to assign a representative to a base county and one adjacent county. Actual practice is based on a heuristic which assigns representatives sequentially. The county with the largest population is selected as the base for the first representative and the adjacent county with the largest population is also assigned to her. The unassigned county with the largest population is assigned as the next base and so on. The populations of the counties are shown below.

1. Buchanan   16,000
2. Delaware   15,000
3. Dubuque   98,000
4. Linn   109,000
5. Jones   4,000
6. Jackson   6,000
7. Clinton   100,000

Using this scheme, the first representative would be assigned to Linn County as a base. As the map shows, Buchanan, Delaware, and Jones are the adjacent counties. Since Buchanan has the largest population of these three counties it would be the assigned adjacent county. The second representative would be based in Clinton with Jackson as the assigned adjacent county. Sally realizes that the goal is to maximize the total population assigned to representatives. She is concerned that, since Dubuque County is nearly as large as Clinton, the proposed solution may not be optimal, and after a moment's thought she can see that it clearly is not: The pair Dubuque and Delaware beat Clinton and Jackson. She decides to abandon the traditional heuristic approach and to model the problem as an IP. Although this particular problem is quite simple, she believes that if she can create a successful model it could then be appropriately modified to assign the company's 60 midwest representatives to well over 300 counties. In formulating the problem, she lets

$$y_i = 1 \quad \text{if county } i \text{ is a base}$$

$$= 0 \quad \text{if not}$$

$$x_{ji} = 1 \quad \text{if adjacent county } j \text{ is assigned to base } i$$

$$= 0 \quad \text{if not}$$

The formulation and solution are shown in Figure 8.35. Sally has used an IP code to solve the problem.

The solution shows that y_4 and $y_1 = 1$; thus, Linn and Buchanan counties are selected as the base counties. It also shows that the optimal value of the objective function is 250, which implies that 250,000 people will be served by the two representatives. Sally thus is pleased to have discovered that the solution suggested by the standard heuristic is incorrect before she implemented that solution. She is a bit surprised that the optimal solution does not involve either Dubuque or Clinton

FIGURE 8.35

```
MAX   16 Y1 + 15 Y2 + 98 Y3 + 109 Y4 + 4 Y5 + 6 Y6 + 100 Y7
    + 15 X21 + 109 X41 + 16 X12 + 98 X32 + 109 X42 + 4 X52
    + 15 X23 + 4 X53 + 6 X63 + 16 X14 + 15 X24 + 4 X54 + 15 X25
    + 98 X35 + 109 X45 + 6 X65 + 100 X75 + 4 X56 + 98 X36
    + 100 X76 + 4 X57 + 6 X67
SUBJECT TO
   2)  - Y1 + X21 + X41 = 0
   3)  - Y2 + X12 + X32 + X42 + X52 = 0
   4)  - Y3 + X23 + X53 + X63 = 0
   5)  - Y4 + X14 + X24 + X54 = 0
   6)  - Y5 + X25 + X35 + X45 + X65 + X75 = 0
   7)  - Y6 + X56 + X36 + X76 = 0
   8)  - Y7 + X57 + X67 = 0
   9)    Y1 + Y2 + Y3 + Y4 + Y5 + Y6 + Y7 = 2

INTEGER - VARIABLES = 29

    LP OPTIMUM FOUND AT STEP 15

    OBJECTIVE FUNCTION VALUE

        250.000000
```

(Continued)

FIGURE 8.35 (Continued)

VARIABLE	VALUE	REDUCED COST
Y1	1.00	0.00
Y2	0.00	0.00
Y3	0.00	0.00
Y4	1.00	0.00
Y5	0.00	0.00
Y6	0.00	0.00
Y7	0.00	0.00
X21	0.00	94.00
X41	1.00	0.00
X12	0.00	94.00
X32	0.00	12.00
X42	0.00	1.00
X52	0.00	106.00
X23	0.00	12.00
X53	0.00	23.00
X63	0.00	21.00
X14	1.00	0.00
X24	0.00	1.00
X54	0.00	12.00
X25	0.00	106.00
X35	0.00	23.00
X45	0.00	12.00
X65	0.00	115.00
X75	0.00	21.00
X56	0.00	115.00
X36	0.00	21.00
X76	0.00	19.00
X57	0.00	21.00
X67	0.00	19.00

Counties, but she feels sure that the IP code provides the optimal solution to her model and thus she is determined to implement it.

Questions

1. Sally's solution is obviously wrong. Find, by inspection of the data, a correct optimal solution. How many alternative optima are there?

2. What is wrong with Sally's model? Write out seven additional constraints which will give a correct formulation.

9

NETWORK MODELS

A NETWORK MODEL AT AIR PRODUCTS AND CHEMICALS, INC.

Air Products and Chemicals, Inc., of Allentown, Pennsylvania, has developed and implemented a large mathematical model to control deliveries of liquid oxygen and nitrogen to customers at minimum cost and with improved reliability. It is estimated that the system saves Air Products over $2 million annually.

With annual sales exceeding $1.5 billion, Air Products is one of the three largest manufacturers and distributors of industrial gases in North America. In particular, oxygen and nitrogen are manufactured in highly automated plants and transported as liquids at a temperature of $-320°F$ using a fleet of more than 500 tractor-trailer trucks. Storage tanks at customer sites are provided by Air Products under long-term contracts, and inventories are monitored and replenished.

Air Products has made a quantum leap from manual order generation and scheduling to the use of an advanced state-of-the-art on-line constrained optimization model. The computer solves daily a mathematical problem involving 800,000 variables and 200,000 constraints.

The first implementation was at Wharton, New Jersey, in October 1981. The system has since been implemented in nine additional depots and continues to be expanded. It has been saving the company between 6% and 10% of operating costs.

Other benefits are its significant impact on the management of the distribution function and the opportunities it has created to piggyback other applications onto the on-line network. It has changed decision making from a reactive to an active mode. The system is being presented to customers as a competitive advantage in providing better service.

——— 9.1
INTRODUCTION

Throughout this text the introduction to each chapter has been used as a preview of topics covered in the chapter. In the case of networks, we depart from this practice and turn immediately to an example of an important class of management problems. With this example in hand we will be in a position to consider the network model and its importance in both theory and practice, as well as several special forms of the model and the algorithms used to solve them.

Much of what would normally appear in the introduction is contained in Section 9.3.

——— 9.2
AN EXAMPLE: SEYMOUR MILES (A CAPACITATED TRANSSHIPMENT MODEL)

Seymour Miles is the distribution manager for Zigwell Inc., **PROTRAC**'s largest midwestern distributor. Zigwell distributes its crawler tractors in five midwestern states. Currently, Seymour has 10 E–9s *in situ* at what we shall designate as site ①. These crawlers must be delivered to two major construction sites denoted as sites ③ and ④. Three E–9s are required at site ③ and 7 are required at site ④. Because of prearranged schedules concerning driver availability, these crawlers may be distributed only according to any of the alternative routes shown in Figure 9.1, called a *network diagram*.

In Figure 9.1, each of the arrows between sites is termed an *arc*, or *branch*, of the network. The arc from ② to ④ is sometimes denoted symbolically by the pair (2, 4). Each site is termed a *node* of the network. The figure shows a +10 identified with site

FIGURE 9.1

Network Diagram for Seymour's Problem

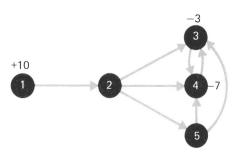

FIGURE 9.2
Capacities and Costs Appended

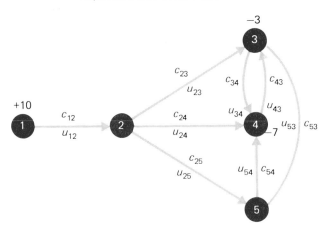

Network Terminology

①. This means that 10 E–9s (items of *supply*) are available at this site. The identifiers -3 and -7 attached to sites ③ and ④, respectively, denote the *requirements* or *demands* at these two sites. The figure also indicates that E–9s may be delivered to site ③ via any of the alternative routings ① → ② → ③, ① → ② → ④ → ③, ① → ② → ⑤ → ④ → ③, or ① → ② → ⑤ → ③. Which of the allowable routes is ultimately selected will be determined by the associated *costs* of traversing the routes and *capacities* along the routes. These additional data are shown in Figure 9.2. For convenience the costs and capacities are represented in symbolic (i.e., parametric) notation. The costs c_{ij} are *per unit costs*. For example, the cost of traversing arc (5, 3) is c_{53} per crawler. These costs are primarily due to fuel, tolls, and the cost of the driver for the average time it takes to traverse the arc. Because of preestablished agreements with the Teamsters, Zigwell must change drivers at each site it encounters on a route. Because of limitations on the current availability of drivers, there is an upper bound on the number of crawlers that may traverse any given arc. Thus, as an example, u_{53} is the upper bound or capacity on arc (5, 3).

Seymour's problem is to find a shipment plan that satisfies the demands at minimum cost, subject to the capacity constraints. You can now appreciate the trade-offs facing Seymour. For example, if $c_{25} + c_{53}$ is less than c_{23}, the route ① → ② → ⑤ → ③ will have a total cost which is less than the total cost of route ① → ② → ③, and hence ① → ② → ⑤ → ③ is preferred to ① → ② → ③. However, the maximum number of E–9s that can be sent across the preferred route is Min $\{u_{12}, u_{25}, u_{53}\}$. If this number is less than 3, the number of E–9s required at 3, all of the shipment cannot be accomplished via ① → ② → ⑤ → ③. This is a problem in only five nodes and eight arcs and even in a simplified example such as this the optimal solution may not be obvious. Imagine such a problem with 30 or 40 nodes and many more arcs.

Seymour's problem is called *a capacitated transshipment model*. We now show that this problem can easily be expressed as an LP. First, define the decision variables

$$x_{ij} = \text{total number of E–9s sent on arc } (i, j)$$

$$= \text{flow from node ① to node ⓙ}$$

LP Formulation of the Problem

Then the problem is

$$\begin{aligned}
\text{Min } & c_{12}x_{12} + c_{23}x_{23} + c_{24}x_{24} + c_{25}x_{25} + c_{34}x_{34} + c_{43}x_{43} + c_{53}x_{53} + c_{54}x_{54} \\
\text{s.t. } & +x_{12} = 10 \\
& -x_{12} + x_{23} + x_{24} + x_{25} = 0 \\
& -x_{23} - x_{43} - x_{53} - x_{34} = -3 \\
& -x_{24} + x_{43} - x_{34} - x_{54} = -7 \\
& -x_{25} + x_{53} + x_{54} = 0 \\
& 0 \le x_{ij} \le u_{ij}, \quad \text{all arcs } (i, j) \text{ in the network}
\end{aligned}$$

There are now a number of observations to be made about this model.

Properties of the LP

1. The problem is indeed an LP. There is one variable x_{ij} associated with each arc in the network (Figure 9.2). There are 8 arcs in this network and thus 8 corresponding variables, x_{12}, x_{23}, x_{24}, x_{25}, x_{43}, x_{53}, x_{34}, and x_{54}. The objective is to minimize total cost.

2. There is one equation associated with each node in the network. The first equation says that the total flow *out of* node ① is 10 units. Recall that this is the total supply at node ①. The second equation says that the total flow *out of* node ② (namely, $x_{23} + x_{24} + x_{25}$) minus the total flow *into* node ② (namely, x_{12}) is zero. In other words, the total flow out of node ② must equal the total flow into node ②. The third equation says that the total flow *out of* node ③ (namely, x_{34}) must be 3 units less than the total flow *into* node ③ (namely, $x_{23} + x_{43} + x_{53}$). This is the mathematical way of expressing the requirement for a *net delivery* of 3 units to node ③. The equations for nodes ④ and ⑤, respectively, have similar interpretations. Thus, the equation for each node expresses a *flow balance* and takes into account the fact that the node may be either a supply point or a demand point or neither. Intermediate nodes (such as ② and ⑤ in Figure 9.1) which are neither supply points nor demand points are often termed *transshipment nodes.*

3. The positive right-hand sides correspond to nodes that are net suppliers (origins). The negative right-hand sides correspond to nodes that are net destinations. The zero right-hand sides correspond to nodes that have neither supply nor demand. The sum of all right-hand-side terms is zero, which means that the total supply in the network equals the total demand.

Special Structure of LP

4. The *special structure* of this network model is revealed by placing the data of the constraints in the tableau format shown in Figure 9.3, called a *node–arc incidence matrix.* Each row of Figure 9.3 corresponds to a node and contains the data of the corresponding constraint in the LP.

FIGURE 9.3

Node–Arc Incidence Matrix

	ARC								
NODE	**(1, 2)**	**(2, 3)**	**(2, 4)**	**(2, 5)**	**(4, 3)**	**(5, 3)**	**(3, 4)**	**(5, 4)**	**RHS**
1	+1	0	0	0	0	0	0	0	10
2	−1	+1	+1	+1	0	0	0	0	0
3	0	−1	0	0	−1	−1	+1	0	−3
4	0	0	−1	0	+1	0	−1	−1	−7
5	0	0	0	−1	0	+1	0	+1	0

FIGURE 9.4
Transportation Tableau for Seymour's
Problem

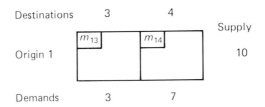

Each column of Figure 9.3 corresponds to an arc (or a variable). Since there are 8 arcs in the model, there are 8 corresponding columns in the tableau. The key to the *special structure* of this network model is the fact that in each column of the node–arc incidence matrix there is a $+1$ and a -1 and the remaining terms are zero. The $+1$ is in the row corresponding to the node at which the arc originates. The -1 is in the row corresponding to the node at which the arc terminates. In Figure 9.3, consider the column under arc (2, 5). Since this arc originates at node ②, there is a $+1$ in row 2. Since the arc terminates at node ⑤, there is a -1 in row 5. All other entries in this column are zero. It should be noted that the node–arc incidence matrix can be created directly from Figure 9.1 without first writing down the LP. Similarly, Figure 9.1 could be constructed from the data in Figure 9.3 (or from the LP). In other words, Figures 9.1 and 9.3 are equivalent ways of communicating the network structure of Seymour's problem.

5. Since Seymour's problem is an LP it could be solved with the simplex method like any other LP. In the special case in which the capacity limits u_{ij} are infinitely large, the special network structure can be exploited in the following way: Compute the least cost, say m_{ij}, of distributing a single unit of flow from origin i to destination j. For Seymour's problem the only origin is node ① and the destinations are ③ and ④. Thus we obtain Figure 9.4.

For example, m_{13} denotes the least-cost way of distributing a unit of flow from node ① to node ③. In Section 9.5 we present an algorithm for easily computing these values m_{ij}, given the data of the original problem. These computations involve repeated applications of what is termed *the shortest route algorithm*. For now, the point is that by performing such computations we have been able to reduce the transshipment problem to a standard transportation problem, which can then be solved with the algorithms given in Chapter 7.

9.3
A GENERAL FORMULATION (THE CAPACITATED TRANSSHIPMENT MODEL)

The Model   Seymour's problem is a special case of the following general symbolic form of a network model. Again, the decision variables x_{ij} will denote the "flow" from node i to node j across the arc connecting these two nodes.

$$\text{Min} \sum_{(i,j)} c_{ij} x_{ij}$$

$$\text{s.t.} \quad \sum_{k} x_{jk} - \sum_{k} x_{kj} = L_j, \qquad j = 1, \ldots, n$$

$$0 \le x_{ij} \le u_{ij}, \qquad \text{all } (i, j) \text{ in the network}$$

Let us observe that

1. The sum $\sum_{(i,j)} c_{ij}x_{ij}$ in the objective function is understood to be over all arcs in the network. Thus, the objective is to minimize the total cost of the flow.

2. Consider the jth constraint, for some fixed value of j. The sum $\sum_k x_{jk}$ is understood to be over all k for which arc (j, k), with j fixed, is in the network. Thus, $\sum_k x_{jk}$ is the total flow *out of* the specified node j. Similarly, $\sum_k x_{kj}$ is over all k for which arc (k, j), with j fixed, is in the network. Thus, $\sum_k x_{kj}$ is the total flow *into* node j. Thus, the jth constraint says

$$\text{total flow out of node } j - \text{total flow into node } j = \text{supply at } j$$

where negative supply (i.e., $L_j < 0$) represents a requirement. Nodes with negative supply are called *destinations*, *sinks*, or *demand points*. Nodes with positive supply (i.e., $L_j > 0$) are called *origins*, *sources*, or *supply points*. Nodes with zero supply are called *transshipment points*.

3. For simplicity it is assumed that $\sum_{j=1}^n L_j = 0$ (i.e., total supply = total demand) and all $c_{ij} \geq 0$.

4. The last set of constraints places *capacities* on the flows x_{ij}. As a special case some of the u_{ij} could be infinitely large, meaning that these are arcs with no capacity constraints. Setting a zero value for a u_{ij} would be equivalent to eliminating arc (i, j) from the network.

5. The given data for the model are the c_{ij}'s, the L_j's, and the u_{ij}'s.

Its Importance   The capacitated transshipment model (often called *the* network model) is important because several important management decision problems are special cases. In particular the transportation problem, assignment problem, and shortest-route problem are special cases of the capacitated transshipment model, and the maximal flow problem is closely related.

There are two advantages in being able to identify a problem as a special case of *the* network (or capacitated transshipment) model. First, theoretical results that are established for the general model apply automatically to the specific cases. The outstanding example of this phenomenon is the integer property of *the* network model. The integer property is that

---

Integer Optimal Solutions

If all terms L_j and u_{ij} are integers in the capacitated transshipment model, there will always be an integer-valued optimal solution to this problem.

From earlier chapters you know that LP models do not in general yield optimal solutions that have integer-valued variables. The network model with integer values for all L_j and u_{ij} does. This has an important implication on the usefulness of the various special versions of the network model.

The second reason it is useful to identify a problem as a special case of the capacitated transshipment model is that the *special structure* of this model typically makes it possible to find a special algorithm that solves the problem more easily than applying the general simplex algorithm. The transportation and assignment problems discussed in Chapter 7 are two good examples of this phenomenon. The MODI method and the Hungarian algorithm presented there illustrate how management scientists have used the special structure of the network model to create superior ways of attacking the transportation and assignment models, respectively.

The impact of some of the superefficient codes derived from the special structure of the network model is rather amazing. Recently, the Internal Revenue Service constructed a network model with 50,000 constraints and 60 million variables. Only one hour of high-speed computer time was required to solve the problem. It turns out that in such a problem it can require less time to obtain the optimal solution than to read the output.

The transportation and assignment problems and the special algorithms used to solve them have been discussed at length in Chapter 7. In Problems 19 and 20 you will be asked to demonstrate that each of these problems is a special case of the capacitated transshipment model.

Sections 9.4, 9.5, and 9.6 are devoted to the shortest-route problem, the minimum spanning tree problem, and the maximal flow problem, respectively. In each case the problem is represented with a network diagram, and a special algorithm for solving the problem is presented. In Problem 21 you are asked to demonstrate that the shortest-route problem is another special case of the capacitated transshipment model.

The minimum spanning tree problem is *not* a special case of the capacitated transshipment model. It is an important problem in its own right and illustrates that network diagrams are useful in representing a large variety of problems.

_____ 9.4
THE SHORTEST-ROUTE PROBLEM

The shortest-route problem refers to a network for which each arc (i, j) has an associated number c_{ij} which is interpreted as the distance (or possibly the cost, or time) from node i to node j. A *route*, or a *path*, between two nodes is any sequence of arcs connecting the two nodes. The objective is to find the shortest (or least-cost or least-time) routes from a specific node to each of the other nodes in the network.

Aaron's
Delivery
Service

As an illustration, Aaron Drunner makes frequent wine deliveries to seven different sites. Figure 9.5 shows the seven sites together with the possible travel routes between sites. Note that here, unlike the transshipment model, the arcs are *nondirected*. That is, on each arc, flow is permitted in either direction. Each arc in Figure 9.5 has been labeled with the distance between the nodes the arc connects. The home base is denoted H. Aaron feels that his overall costs will be minimized by making sure that any future delivery to any given site is made along the shortest route to that site. Thus, his objective is to specify the seven shortest routes from node H to each of the other seven nodes. Note that in this problem, as stated, the task is not to find optimal x_{ij}'s. The task is to find an optimal set of routes.

406

FIGURE 9.5
Aaron's Network of Sites

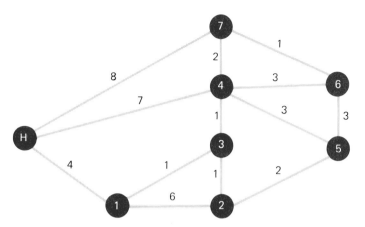

**The
Shortest-Route
Algorithm**

The algorithm for solving this problem will assume that all c_{ij} are nonnegative. The algorithm will find the shortest paths from H to all other nodes in the network. The resulting arcs form what is termed a *shortest-path tree*.[1] The algorithm will take $n - 1$ steps, where n is the number of nodes in the network. For Aaron's problem there are seven potential delivery sites and a home base. Hence, there are eight nodes in his network and $n = 8$. The algorithm will take $n - 1 = 7$ steps.

Labels

The algorithm employs what is called a *labeling procedure*. As the algorithm progresses a label for each node will be determined. This label will be a pair of numbers in parentheses. For a particular node, the first number in the label represents a distance from H to that node, along a specific route, and the second number represents the node that precedes the node in question on the specified route. Initially, the labels on nodes other than H are called *temporary labels*. When the shortest distance (i.e., the best route) from H to a given node has been determined, the temporary label on that node becomes a *permanent label*.

The algorithm begins by labeling node Ⓗ with the *permanent label* (0, H), where 0 simply means that the shortest route from Ⓗ to itself has length 0, and the H simply identifies this as the starting node.

Next, all nodes that can be reached *directly* (i.e., by traversing a single arc) from node Ⓗ are assigned temporary labels. In Aaron's problem, as shown in Figure 9.5, these are nodes ①, ④, and ⑦. Each node is labeled with the direct distance from node Ⓗ and with the previous node on the route, which is merely Ⓗ. These labels are shown in Figure 9.6. For example, node ⑦ is a distance of 8 units from node Ⓗ. Hence, the label is (8, H). Similarly, the labels on nodes ④ and ① are (7, H) and (4, H), respectively.

**Site 1
Permanently
Labeled**

Next, of the nodes just labeled, we identify the one with the smallest distance value in its label (ties may be broken arbitrarily). This will identify the node closest to Ⓗ. In Figure 9.6 this is node ①. Since any other route to node ① must pass through nodes ⑦ or ④, the route Ⓗ–① is clearly the shortest route to node ①. For this reason the label (4, H) on node ① becomes a permanent label. The permanently labeled nodes will

---

[1] A *tree* in an n-node network is defined to be $n - 1$ arcs, with the property that every pair of nodes in the network is connected by some sequence of these arcs.

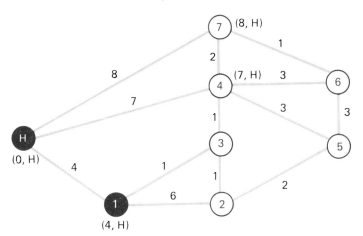

FIGURE 9.6
Initial Assignment of Labels

be shaded in the network diagrams. In Figure 9.6 nodes H and ① are shown with their permanent labels. Nodes ④ and ⑦ have temporary labels. This completes step 1, and we now have one of the seven sites with a permanent label.

The next step begins by branching outward from the last permanently labeled node. We first assign temporary labels to all nodes that can be reached directly from the last permanently labeled node, which is node ①. Thus, we focus on nodes ② and ③. Since the permanent label on node ① indicates that the shortest distance to node ① is 4, and since the direct distance from node ① to node ② is 6 [i.e., the distance on arc (1, 2) is 6], we deduce that by traveling through the last permanently labeled node the distance to node ② is $4 + 6 = 10$ units. For this reason the temporary label on node ② is assigned a distance entry of 10 units. Since this distance is incurred on the route H–①–②, node ① is the predecessor of node ② and the complete temporary label assigned to node ② is therefore (10, 1). Similarly, the temporary label on node ③ is (5, 1). As shown in Figure 9.7, the nodes with labels are now H, ①, ②, ③, ④, and ⑦.

FIGURE 9.7
Second Assignment of Labels

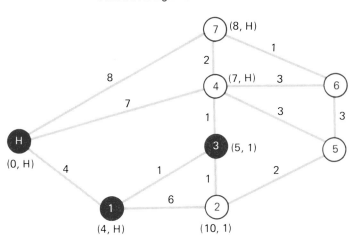

We now focus on the nodes with temporary labels, namely ②, ③, ④, and ⑦. First, consider nodes ② and ③. It is clear that since the distance label of 5 on node ③ is less than the distance label of 10 on node ②, the route Ⓗ–①–③ is shorter than any route to ③ commencing with the sequence Ⓗ–①–②. There remain still other possible routes to node ③, but any such route must commence either with the sequence Ⓗ–④ or the sequence Ⓗ–⑦. Since such routes will have distances of at least 7 or 8 units, respectively (because of the labels on nodes ④ and ⑦), the route Ⓗ–①–③ is the shortest path from Ⓗ to node ③. Consequently, the label on node 3 becomes permanent, as indicated by the shading in Figure 9.7. This completes step 2, and we now have two sites with permanent labels, namely site ①, which is closest to Ⓗ, and site ③, which is the next closest to Ⓗ.

The discussion above indicates that, *upon the completion of each step, the temporary label with the smallest distance component is declared permanent and this becomes the next closest node to the starting node.*

Since node ③ was the last permanently labeled node, we next branch outward from this node to consider its "neighbors," nodes ② and ④. Travel to node ② through node ③ can, according to Figure 9.7, be accomplished in 6 units of distance. Hence, the temporary label on ② is changed from (10, 1) to (6, 3). Similarly, the temporary label on node ④ is revised to (6, 3). The nodes with temporary labels are now ②, ④, and ⑦. As shown in Figure 9.8, nodes ② and ④ are tied for having the smallest distance component in the label. We break the tie by arbitrarily selecting node ④ to be the one declared permanent. The updated assignment at the end of the third step, with permanent labels on sites ①, ③, and ④, is shown in Figure 9.8.

FIGURE 9.8
Third Assignment of Labels

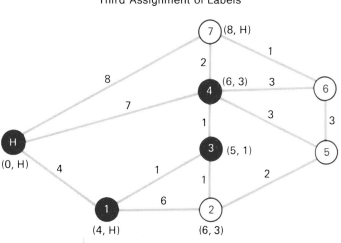

The next (fourth) step is to branch out from node ④. Nodes ⑤ and ⑥ are assigned temporary labels, (9, 4) and (9, 4), respectively (see Figure 9.9). Node ⑦ can be reached through 4 in a distance of 8 units, which is the same as the distance component on the current label. It is arbitrary whether we leave the label at (8, H) or change it to (8, 4). We choose the former. The nodes with temporary labels are now ②, ⑤, ⑥, and ⑦. Among these, node ② has the smallest distance component. Hence, it is now declared permanent, as shown in Figure 9.9.

FIGURE 9.9
Fourth Assignment of Labels

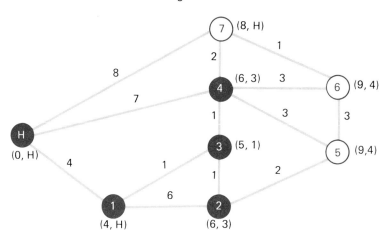

The next (fifth) step branches out from ②. Node ⑤ becomes permanently labeled with (8, 2). In the sixth step, the label (8, H) becomes permanent on node ⑦, and in the final (seventh) step the label (9, 4) becomes permanent on node ⑥. The result is shown in Figure 9.10.

The permanent labels in Figure 9.10 now allow us to find the shortest route from H to any of the sites. For example, consider node ⑥. The permanent label (9, 4) tells us that the shortest route from Ⓗ to ⑥ has a distance of 9 units. To find the route that will

Backtracking

take us from Ⓗ to ⑥ in 9 units, we use the labels to *backtrack* from node ⑥. The label on ⑥ tells us that we reach ⑥ from ④. Moving back to node ④, its label tells us that we reach ④ from ③. Continuing backward, we reach ③ from ①, and ① from Ⓗ. Thus, we see that the shortest route from node Ⓗ to node ⑥ is Ⓗ–①–③–④–⑥. The same approach will produce the shortest routes to all of Aaron's sites. These are identified in Figure 9.11.

FIGURE 9.10
All Nodes Permanently Labeled

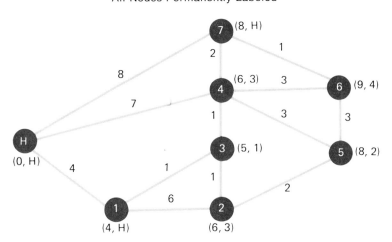

FIGURE 9.11
Shortest Routes to All Sites

NODE	SHORTEST ROUTE FROM NODE H	DISTANCE
2	H–1–3–2	6
3	H–1–3	5
4	H–1–3–4	6
5	H–1–3–2–5	8
6	H–1–3–4–6	9
7	H–7	8

The data in Figure 9.11 are used to produce Figure 9.12, in which the shortest route from H to every other node is traced. Any arc that is used in one or more of these routes is indicated with boldface. The set of boldface arcs is the *shortest-path tree* for Aaron's problem. As defined in footnote 1, a tree in an n-node network consists of a set of $n − 1$ arcs (in this case 7 arcs) which connect every pair of nodes. The shortest path from H to any node will traverse only a subset of arcs on the tree.

The algorithm we have presented may seem to require many steps, and indeed for a problem as simple as Aaron's you may well have been able to solve it by inspection. The reason is that with so few nodes there are few alternative routes. However, problems encountered in practice could well involve hundreds or even thousands of nodes. Problems of this size would generally be impossible to solve by inspection. For such problems a systematic method such as the above labeling algorithm is required, and we note that this algorithm is easily implemented on the computer.

Summary of Steps Let us summarize the method we have presented.

■ **Step 1:** Consider all nodes that are directly connected (i.e., by a single arc) to the origin. The distance component of the label on each such node is set equal to its distance from the origin. The predecessor component is the origin. These nodes now have temporary labels.

FIGURE 9.12
Shortest-Path Tree for Aaron's Network

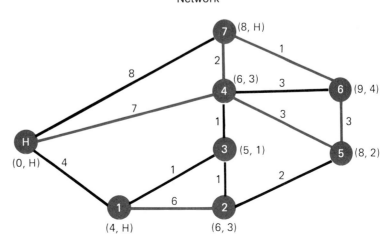

■ **Step 2:** Of all nodes with temporary labels, choose one whose distance component is minimal, and declare that node to be permanently labeled. Any ties, at any point in the algorithm, may be arbitrarily broken. As soon as all nodes have permanent labels, go to step 4.

■ **Step 3:** Each node which currently is not permanently labeled is either unlabeled or has a temporary label. Let l denote the last node whose label has been declared permanent. Consider all nodes that are neighbors of l (i.e., directly connected to l with a single arc). For each such node compute the sum of (its distance to l) plus (the distance component of the label on l). If the node in question is unlabeled, assign a temporary label consisting of this distance and l as predecessor. If the node in question already has a temporary label, give it a new one only if the newly calculated distance is less than its current distance component. If this is the case, the label consists of this distance, with l as predecessor. Now return to step 2.

■ **Step 4:** The pemanent labels indicate the shortest distance from the origin to each node in the network. Permanent labels also indicate the preceding node on the shortest path to each node. To find the shortest path to a given node, start at that node and move backward to its preceding node. Continue with this backward movement until arriving at the origin. The sequence of nodes traced forms the shortest route between the origin and the node in question.

**An Application:
Equipment
Replacement**

Lisa Carr is responsible for obtaining reproduction equipment (Xerox-like machines) for **PROTRAC**'s secretarial service. She must choose between leasing newer equipment at high rental cost but low maintenance cost or more-used equipment with lower rental costs but higher maintenance costs. Lisa has a four-period time horizon to consider. Let c_{ij} denote the cost of *leasing* new equipment at the beginning of period i, $i = 1$, 2, 3, 4, and maintaining it to the beginning of period j, where j can take on the values $2, \ldots, 5$. If the equipment is maintained only to the beginning of period j, for $j < 5$, new equipment must again be leased at the beginning of j. For example, several alternative feasible policies are

1. Lease new equipment at the beginning of each time period. Presumably, such a policy would involve the highest leasing charges and the minimum maintenance charges. The total (leasing + maintenance) cost of this policy would be $c_{12} + c_{23} + c_{34} + c_{45}$.

2. Lease new equipment only at the beginning of period 1 and maintain it through all successive periods. This would undoubtedly be a policy of minimum rental cost but maximum maintenance. The total (leasing + maintenance) cost of this policy would be c_{15}.

3. Lease new equipment at the beginning of periods 1 and 3. The total cost would be $c_{13} + c_{35}$.

FIGURE 9.13

Network for Lisa's Decision

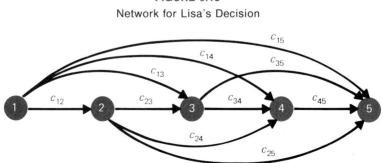

Of all feasible policies, Lisa desires one with a minimum cost. The solution to this problem is obtained by finding the shortest (i.e., in this case, minimum-cost) route from node 1 to node 5 of the network shown in Figure 9.13. Each node on the shortest route denotes a replacement, that is, a period at which new equipment should be leased.

9.5
THE MINIMUM SPANNING TREE PROBLEM (COMMUNICATION LINKS)

A communication link must be installed between 12 cities. The costs of the possible direct links between *permissible* pairs of cities are identified in Figure 9.14. Each unit of cost represents 10,000 dollars. The network in Figure 9.14 simply identifies *possible* direct links and their costs. For example, it shows that no direct link is possible between city 1 and city 6. There is a direct link possible between city 1 and city 5, at a cost of 1 unit; and so on. These cost are also reproduced in tabular form in Figure 9.15, where the blank entries correspond to impermissible links. Note that, when there is a possible link between city i and city j, it is true that $c_{ij} = c_{ji}$. This is reflected by the data in Figure 9.15.

The task is to construct a *tree* that connects all nodes of the network at minimum total cost. This is called a *minimum spanning tree*. In Section 9.4 a tree was defined to be $n - 1$ arcs, in an n-node network, which connect every pair of nodes. Indeed, in that section you saw that the shortest-route algorithm produced a particular tree in the network it addressed. Here we construct another type of tree.

FIGURE 9.14
Costs of Possible Links

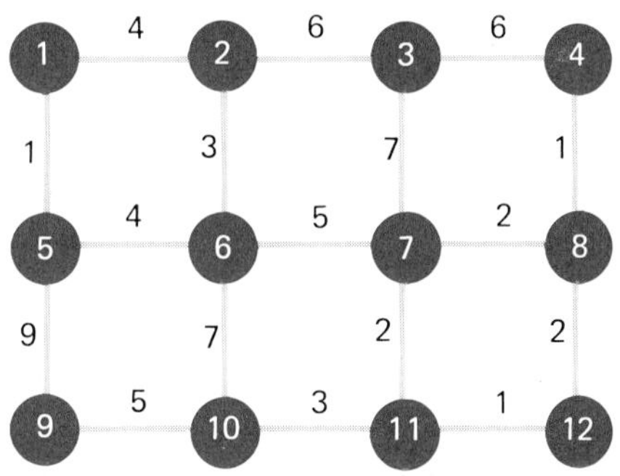

The Greedy Algorithm

The algorithm for solving this problem is extremely simple. We shall give two forms for essentially the same algorithm. The first form, the *graphic method*, is particularly easy to implement by hand on a graphic display such as Figure 9.14.

Graphic Method

■ **Step 1:** Arbitrarily begin at any node. Pick the cheapest arc leading out of that node. This is the first link. It forms a *connected* segment of two nodes. The remaining nodes are termed *unconnected*.

■ **Step 2:** Consider all arcs leading from the connected segment to the unconnected nodes. Select the cheapest to be the next link. Break ties arbitrarily. This adds a new node to the connected segment. Repeat this step until all nodes are connected, which requires $n - 1$ steps.

FIGURE 9.15

Cost Table for Communication Links

FROM CITY	TO CITY											
	1	2	3	4	5	6	7	8	9	10	11	12
1		4			1							
2	4		6			3						
3		6		6			7					
4			6					1				
5	1					4			9			
6		3			4		5			7		
7			7			5		2			2	
8				1			2					2
9					9					5		
10						7			5		3	
11							2			3		1
12								2			1	

This is called a *greedy algorithm* because at each step the best possible choice is made. This is one of the few problems in management science where the greedy algorithm is guaranteed to produce an optimal solution. The use of the greedy algorithm as a heuristic is discussed in Chapter 18.

Greedy Algorithm Applied

Let us apply the graphic method to the network shown in Figure 9.14. We are allowed to begin at any node. We arbitrarily select node ①. According to Figure 9.14, the cheapest arc emanating from node ① is the arc (1, 5). This is the first link, as shown in Figure 9.16. Nodes ① and ⑤ are now connected. The cheapest arc emanating from either of these has a cost of 4. Either of the arcs (1, 2) or (5, 6) can be chosen as the next link. Let us choose (5, 6). Now nodes ①, ⑤, and ⑥ are connected. Next in succession the arcs (6, 2), (6, 7), (7, 8), (8, 4), (7, 11), (11, 12), (11, 10), (10, 9), (4, 3) are selected.

FIGURE 9.16

Picking the First Link in the Graphic Method

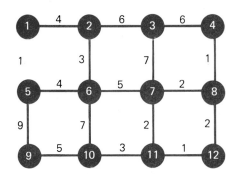

FIGURE 9.17
Minimum-Cost Spanning Tree Produced by
the Graphic Method

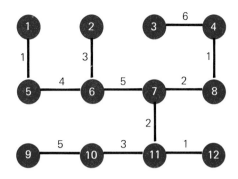

The final tree is shown in Figure 9.17. The minimum total cost of connecting all nodes of the network is obtained by adding the costs on the arcs in the minimum spanning tree. In this case the minimum cost is 33 units.

The second form of the greedy algorithm for this problem is more suited to be implemented directly on the tabular data in Figure 9.15, without resorting to the network diagram. This is the form that the computer would employ.

Tabular Method

■ *Step 1:* Arbitrarily begin with any node. Designate this node as connected and place a √ beside the row corresponding to this node. Cross out the column label corresponding to this node.

■ *Step 2:* Considering all rows with a √, find the smallest value in columns with labels not crossed out, and circle this value. Ties are arbitrarily broken. The column containing this circled element designates the new connected node. Cross out this column label and place a check in the row corresponding to this node. Repeat this step until all nodes are connected.

■ *Step 3:* After all nodes are connected, the minimum-cost spanning tree is identified by the circled elements.

Tabular Method Applied

As an illustration, let us apply the algorithm to the data in Figure 9.15. We begin arbitrarily the algorithm with node ①, placing a check next to row 1 and crossing out column 1. Step 2 requires us to identify the smallest value in row 1, which is 1 under column 5. Thus, we circle the value 1, cross out column 5, and put a check next to row 5. At this point nodes ① and ⑤ are connected and Figure 9.15 has been revised to look like Figure 9.18.

Continuing the algorithm, the minimum value in rows 1 and 5, considering the columns not crossed out, is 4 in column 6 (alternatively, the 4 in column 2 could be selected). Thus, nodes ①, ⑤, and ⑥ are now connected. A check is placed next to row 6 and column 6 is crossed out. Continuing this way, we terminate with Figure 9.19. Reading across the rows of this figure, we see that

■ Node ① connects to 5.
■ Node ④ connects to 3.
■ Node ⑤ connects to 6.
■ Node ⑥ connects to 2 and 7.
■ Node ⑦ connects to 8 and 11.

FIGURE 9.18
Nodes 1 and 5 Are Connected

FROM CITY	1	2	3	4	5	6	7	8	9	10	11	12
✓ 1		4			①							
2	4		6			3						
3		6		6			7					
4			6					1				
✓ 5	1					④			9			
6		3			4		5			7		
7			7			5		2			2	
8				1			2					2
9					9					5		
10							7		5		3	
11							2			3		1
12								2			1	

FIGURE 9.19
Final Tableau

FROM CITY	1	2	3	4	5	6	7	8	9	10	11	12
✓ 1		4			①							
✓ 2	4		6			3						
✓ 3		6		6			7					
✓ 4			⑥					1				
✓ 5	1					④			9			
✓ 6		③			4		⑤			7		
✓ 7			7			5		②			②	
✓ 8			①				2					2
✓ 9					9					5		
✓ 10							7		⑤		3	
✓ 11							2			③		①
✓ 12								2			1	

- Node ⑧ connects to 4.
- Node ⑩ connects to 9.
- Node ⑪ connects to 10 and 12.

Figure 9.20 shows the graphic realization of these connections. You can see that we have obtained precisely the same tree as we obtained using the graphic method (Figure 9.17). This is because, in each application, ties that occurred were broken in the same fashion.

FIGURE 9.20

Minimum-Cost Spanning Tree Produced by
the Tabular Method

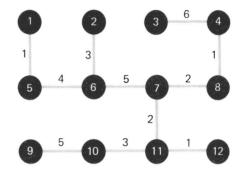

Other Applications

In the minimum spanning tree problem the c_{ij} terms could represent distances as well as costs, and the applications include the design of transportation systems (the nodes are terminals and the arcs are highways, pipelines, air routes, etc.) as well as communications systems. Nodes could also represent interfacing satellite computer terminals located at various distances from one another. Imagine a system for which communication lines must be installed to connect these terminals. The objective might be to connect all nodes in such a way as to minimize the total length of the communication lines. The solution to this problem would be the minimum spanning tree.

———— 9.6
THE MAXIMAL-FLOW PROBLEM

In this problem there is a single *source* node (the input node) and a single *sink* node (the output node). The problem is to find the maximum amount of total flow (petroleum, cash, messages, traffic, etc.) that can be routed through the network (from source to sink) in a unit of time. The amount of flow per unit time on *each arc* is limited by *capacity restrictions*. For example, pipeline diameters limit the flow of crude oil on the links of a distribution system. Flow capacities for nodes are not specified. The only requirement here is that for each node (other than the source or the sink) the balance relation

$$\text{flow out of the node} = \text{flow into the node}$$

must be satisfied.

Formally, letting node ① be the source and n be the sink, the problem is,

$$
\begin{aligned}
&\text{Max } f \\
&\text{s.t.} \quad \sum_j x_{ij} - \sum_j x_{ji} =
\begin{cases}
f, & \text{if } i = 1 \\
-f, & \text{if } i = n \\
0, & \text{otherwise}
\end{cases} \\
&\quad\quad 0 \le x_{ij} \le u_{ij}, \quad \text{all } (i, j) \text{ in the network}
\end{aligned}
$$

We observe that

1. The variables x_{ij} denote the flow per unit time across the arc (i, j) connecting node ⓘ and node ⓙ.

2. Consider the ith constraint, for some fixed value of i. The sum $\sum_j x_{ij}$ is over all j for which arc (i, j), with i fixed, is in the network. Thus, $\sum_j x_{ij}$ is the total flow *out of* node ⓘ. Similarly, the sum $\sum_j x_{ji}$ is over all j for which there is an arc (j, i) in the network (where i is fixed). Thus, $\sum_j x_{ji}$ is the total flow *into* node i.

3. The symbol f is a variable denoting the total flow through the network per unit time. By definition this is equal to the flow per unit time leaving the source, node ① (the first contraint). This is also equal to the flow per unit time entering the sink, node ⓝ (the second constraint). The objective is to maximize this quantity.

4. The u_{ij}'s denote the capacities on the flows per unit time across the various arcs.

This problem, together with the shortest-path problem, is of interest in its own right. It also appears as a subproblem in solving other, more complicated, models. For such reasons, as well as because of some of the theoretic underpinnings (which go beyond our present scope of interest), it is sometimes stated that these two problems (shortest path and max flow) are of central importance in network theory.

The Urban Development Planning Commission

Here is an example of the maximal-flow problem. Gloria Stime is in charge of the UDPC (Urban Development Planning Commission) ad hoc special interest study group. This group's current responsibility is to coordinate the construction of the new subway system with the highway maintenance department. Due to the construction of the new subway system in the proximity of the city's beltway, the eastbound traffic on the beltway must be detoured. The planned detour actually involves a network of alternative routes which have been proposed by the highway maintenance department. Different speed limits and traffic patterns produce different flow capacities on the various arcs of the proposed network. This is shown in Figure 9.21.

Node ① denotes the beginning of the detour, that is, the point at which the eastbound traffic leaves the beltway. Node ⑥ is the point at which the detoured traffic reenters the beltway. Also, in Figure 9.21, the flow capacities depend on the direction of the flow. The symbol 6 on arc (1, 3) denotes a capacity of 6000 vehicles per hour in the $1 \rightarrow 3$ direction. The symbol 0 on the same arc means that a zero capacity exists

FIGURE 9.21

Proposed Network and Flow Capacities
(Thousands of Vehicles Per Hour)

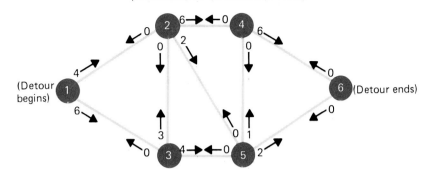

in the $3 \to 1$ direction. This is because the indicated arc (1, 3) denotes a one-way street from ① to ③. In this example it is seen that each of the other arcs denotes one-way travel. (The algorithm to be presented will also apply to problems with arcs permitting positive levels of flow in each direction.)

In the following section we present an algorithm for determining the maximum number of vehicles per hour which can flow through the proposed detour network. We also compute, more specifically, how much flow should traverse each link (arc) to achieve the overall maximal flow.

A Maximal-Flow Algorithm

In order to have a better feeling for the algorithm, let us first consider a path of flow from node ① to node ⑥. There are, of course, many such paths. As an example, let us arbitrarily consider ① → ② → ⑤ → ⑥. A quantity of flow along such a path is said to be *feasible* if

Feasible Flow

1. On no arc of the path does the quantity exceed the arc capacity.
2. With the exception of nodes ① and ⑥, the flow at each node obeys the *conservation condition*

flow entering the node = flow leaving the node

It is important to note the following implication of condition 1:

The maximum amount that can flow from source to sink along a given path is equal to the minimum of the arc capacities on the path.

Flow Capacity

Thus for the path ① → ② → ⑤ → ⑥ a flow of, for example, 1 unit on each arc is *feasible* since it obeys the conservation condition and does not exceed any arc capacity. Is this the maximum flow along this path? Since the minimum of the arc capacities on the path is 2, we know that another feasible flow is 2 units on each arc, and this is the *flow capacity along this particular path*.

In the maximal-flow algorithm, various trial flows are sequentially considered. The algorithm will revise the trial flows in order to increase the overall flow through the network. In this process it is useful to employ the following procedure. Whenever we assign a flow to a particular arc, we shall adhere to the rules

1. *Reduce* the capacity *in the direction of the assigned flow* by the amount of the flow.
2. *Increase* the capacity in the opposite direction by the amount of the flow.

For example, consider arc (1, 2) in Figure 9.21. This arc is

with a capacity of 4 in one direction and 0 in the other. Suppose, as in the above discussion, that we wish to assign 2 units of flow to this arc. Then, according to rules 1 and 2 of the stated procedure, we will revise the flow capacities as follows:

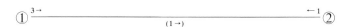

Undoing Trial Flows   The $(2\rightarrow)$ which appears below the arc indicates that 2 units of flow have been assigned in the $1 \rightarrow 2$ direction. We have decreased the capacity in the $1 \rightarrow 2$ direction by $4 - 2 = 2$ units. This is the remaining capacity available for flow (considering this arc alone) in the $1 \rightarrow 2$ direction. We have at the same time increased flow in the $2 \rightarrow 1$ direction by 2 units. This provides a "fictitious capacity" in the $2 \rightarrow 1$ direction. It is "fictitious" because any future flow assigned in the $2 \rightarrow 1$ direction will merely cancel out some of the $1 \rightarrow 2$ flow already assigned. Thus, if at some future point in the course of the algorithm, we should decide to send a single unit of flow in the $2 \rightarrow 1$ direction, it would be necessary (again according to rules 1 and 2) to subtract a unit from the fictitious $2 \rightarrow 1$ capacity and add a unit to the $1 \rightarrow 2$ capacity. Doing this, we would obtain the newly revised capacities.

$$\textcircled{1} \overset{3\rightarrow}{\underset{(1\rightarrow)}{\rule{8cm}{0.4pt}}} \overset{\leftarrow 1}{} \textcircled{2}$$

Thus, rules 1 and 2 provide a device that allows us to "undo" previously assigned trial flows. Since we have "sent back" one of the two initially assigned units, there is now a flow of 1 unit in the $1 \rightarrow 2$ direction, with a remaining capacity of 3 units in this direction. The remaining 1 unit of "fictitious capacity" in the $2 \rightarrow 1$ direction allows us to undo this single unit of $1 \rightarrow 2$ flow, in which case there is no flow on the arc.

We are now in a position to give the steps of the maximal-flow algorithm.

- ■ *Step 1:* Find any path from source to sink that has positive flow capacity. That is, considering all arcs on the path, the minimum of the capacities in the direction of flow (source → sink) must be positive. If no such path is available, the optimal solution has been found.
- ■ *Step 2:* Let c_{Min} denote the minimum-flow capacity of all arcs on the path selected in step 1. Increase the existing flow through the network by sending an additional flow of c_{Min} over this path.
- ■ *Step 3:* For this same path, decrease the capacities in the direction of flow, on each arc, by c_{Min}. Increase the capacities in the opposite direction by c_{Min}, for all arcs in the path.

Let us apply the algorithm to Gloria Stime's problem (Figure 9.21).

Iteration 1   We arbitrarily begin with path $1 \rightarrow 3 \rightarrow 5 \rightarrow 6$. On this path, $c_{\text{Min}} = 2$, the flow capacity in the $5 \rightarrow 6$ direction (i.e., the direction of flow from source to sink) on arc (5, 6). Thus, all capacities in the direction of flow are reduced by 2 units. Capaci-

FIGURE 9.22
Gloria's First Update

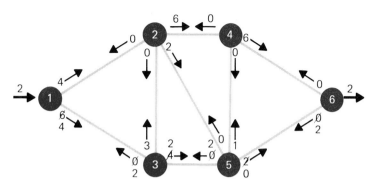

ties in the opposite direction are increased by 2 units. Note that (5, 6) will now have a capacity of zero in the $5 \rightarrow 6$ direction, which means that the *path* $1 \rightarrow 3 \rightarrow 5 \rightarrow 6$ *now* has zero capacity. The revised network appears in Figure 9.22. In Figure 9.22, the arrow leading into node ① indicates a total flow of 2 units entering the network. This is also, as shown, the amount of flow leaving node ⑥. That is, we now have 2000 vehicles per hour being transported across the network. Is this a maximal flow? The answer is no, because there are remaining paths from source to sink with a positive capacity (e.g., $1 \rightarrow 2 \rightarrow 4 \rightarrow 6$ in Figure 9.22).

Solving Gloria's Problem

Iteration 2   Reapplying step 1, we select the path $1 \rightarrow 2 \rightarrow 4 \rightarrow 6$. The value of c_{Min}, determined by arc $1 \rightarrow 2$, is 4 units. The revised network appears in Figure 9.23. Note that the total flow through the network is now 6 units, which is the sum of the c_{Min} values from the first two iterations.

Iteration 3   We now select the path $1 \rightarrow 3 \rightarrow 2 \rightarrow 4 \rightarrow 6$. The value of c_{Min} is 2 units and the revised network appears in Figure 9.24. Note that both arcs leading into node ⑥ now have a capacity of 0 in the direction of node ⑥. Thus, there are no remaining paths from node ① to node ⑥ with positive capacity on all arcs of the path. Figure 9.24 shows that the maximal flow for this network is 8000 vehicles per hour. Let us now show how to compute the amount and direction of flow on each arc so that this total flow of 8000 vehicles per hour can be achieved.

FIGURE 9.23
Gloria's Second Update

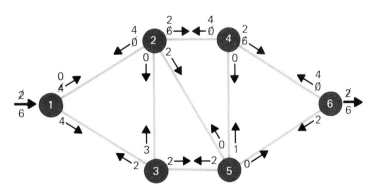

FIGURE 9.24
Gloria's Third Update

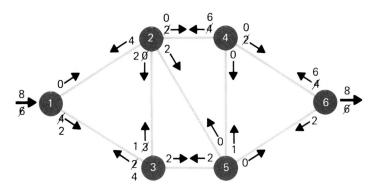

Determining the Final Flows

The final flow on each arc is determined by comparing the final arc capacity with the initial arc capacity. The rule is, for each arc,

---

If final capacity is *less than* initial capacity, compute the difference. That difference is the amount of flow traversing the arc.

For example, Figure 9.21 shows that on arc (3, 5) the initial capacities were

Initial: ③ $\xrightarrow{4\rightarrow}$ ————————————————————————— $\overset{\leftarrow 0}{}$ ⑤

The final capacities, shown in Figure 9.24, are

Final: ③ $\underset{2\rightarrow}{}$ ————————————————————————— $\underset{\leftarrow 2}{}$ ⑤

Since the final capacity in the $3 \rightarrow 5$ direction is 2 units less than the initial capacity in that direction, the difference $4 - 2 = 2$ is the final *flow* over this arc and it is in the $3 \rightarrow 5$ direction.

Applying this rule to all arcs in the network produces the maximal flow pattern shown in Figure 9.25.

FIGURE 9.25
Maximal-Flow Pattern for Gloria's Problem

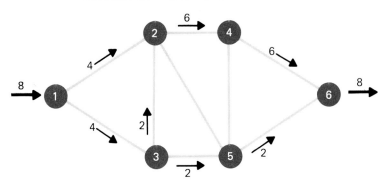

One of the key theoretic results in network theory relates to the maximal-flow problem. The result, called the Max flow/Min cut theorem, is very simple to state. We first define the notion of a *cut* and a *cut capacity*.

■ **Cut:** A partition of the nodes into two disjoint classes, say C_1 and C_n, where the source is in C_1 and the sink is in C_n.

■ **Cut Capacity:** Consider all arcs that directly connect a node in C_1 to a node in C_n. The sum of the capacities on these arcs, in the $C_1 \rightarrow C_n$ direction, is called the cut capacity.

In Gloria's network, Figure 9.21, there are many possible cuts. Several are shown in Figure 9.26.

FIGURE 9.26
Illustrative Cuts and Cut Capacities

C_1	C_n	CUT CAPACITY
①, ②, ③, ⑤	④, ⑥	9
①, ②, ③	④, ⑤, ⑥	12
①	②, ③, ④, ⑤, ⑥	10
①, ②, ③, ④, ⑤	⑥	8
①, ②	③, ④, ⑤, ⑥	14

To calculate the cut capacity of the first cut in Figure 9.26 we must sum up the capacities on each of the arcs connecting a node in C_1 with a node in C_n. In this case we must sum the capacities on arcs (2, 4), (5, 4), and (5, 6). Since these capacities are 6, 1, and 2, respectively, the cut capacity is 9. Other cut capacities are calculated in a similar manner.

You can see in Figure 9.26 that the smallest of the cut capacities is 8, which, as we have seen, is the maximal flow in Gloria's network. The max flow/min cut theorem states that this equality will always be true. Intuitively, it generalizes the concept that the maximal flow on any *path* is equal to the Min of the capacities on the path. Thus, we have

MAX FLOW/MIN CUT THEOREM: **The maximal flow in any network is equal to the minimal-cut capacity.**

_____ **9.7**
NOTES ON IMPLEMENTATION

Network models and algorithms are among the most important applications of management science, and specialization in this topic has become a career path in the field. Along this line, in recent years we have seen the appearance of a number of consulting firms that deal exclusively with network applications. The main emphasis of such firms is often on strategic planning problems from the point of view of "distribution" studies, where the term "distribution" is taken in a quite general sense: flow of physical product, information, vehicles, cash, and so on.

The software libraries for most of the large computer systems include packages for solving various network problems. Some of the "state of the art" software for very large-scale applications must be purchased from private vendors.

The application of network models to real problems involves considerable skill and experience in casting problems, which initially may not appear to be network models, into a network representation. For example, an LP model for a problem of interest may not be a network problem, but its dual may in fact have a network structure; or the network structure may emerge in the dual only after some clever manipulation of the original problem. To capitalize on the advantages of the network structure, it is often worth the price of "straining" the initial formulation to cast it (or its dual) into a network representation.

As a final note, as stated in the text, it is worth emphasizing that many real problems contain subproblems which may have a network form.

9.8
SUMMARY

Network problems are important for several reasons. These problems have such a simple special linear form that special superefficient algorithms can be applied to obtain optimal solutions. Also, under mild restrictions on the data it will always be true that integral-valued optimal solutions exist and are provided by the network algorithms. Finally, all of this is of interest because a wide variety of real-world problems can be cast as network problems. The flows may represent physical quantities, paperwork, cash, vehicles, and so on. The type of problem amenable to the network approach is often very large in scale. One can imagine, for example, a network model of an international enterprise involved in paper production. The network might depict the overall multiperiod distribution system from the forest through lumber storage, a variety of paper mills, widely distributed warehouses, and even wholesalers in numerous marketing districts. A model for such a vast operation offers the potential of creating considerable savings in the firm's global operations. The potential size of such models leads one to appreciate the importance of speed in the solution algorithm.

Often the crucial element in network modeling is the analyst's ingenuity in being able to cast the original complex problem into the network format. Usually, this is far from a trivial exercise in "model formulation," and considerable "on-site" experience inside the operation being modeled is often a prerequisite.

Of course, all network models can be solved with an LP algorithm, but in this chapter we have studied special-purpose algorithms for solving three specific network problems of interest: shortest route, minimal spanning tree, and maximal flow. These algorithms are of interest in their own right, as well as being useful in solving subproblems of larger or more complex problems.

9.9
KEY TERMS

NETWORK DIAGRAM.   A schematic representation consisting of nodes and arcs over which flows may occur.

ARC.   A connection between two nodes in a network.

BRANCH.   A synonym for arc.

NODE.   An element in a network.

CAPACITATED TRANSSHIPMENT MODEL.   A network model with supplies at specified origins, demands at specified destinations, and shipment alternatives through intermediate nodes on capacitated routes from origins to destinations.

ORIGIN.   A node in a network with positive supply.

DESTINATION.   A node in a network with positive demand.

NODE–ARC INCIDENCE MATRIX.   A tableau format for the constraint data in a network model. Corresponding to each arc of the network is a column of the tableau. Corresponding to each node is a row of the tableau. Each column has only two nonzero entries, $+1$ and -1. The $+1$ (-1) is in the row corresponding to the node at which the arc originates (terminates).

SHORTEST-ROUTE PROBLEM.   The problem of finding shortest routes from a specified node (the origin) to each of the other nodes in a network.

TEMPORARY LABEL.   Intermediate label on a node in the shortest-route algorithm.

PERMANENT LABEL.   In the shortest-route algorithm, the permanent label on a node shows the shortest distance from origin to the node and shows the predecessor node on the shortest route.

TREE. $(n - 1)$ arcs, in an n-node network, which connect all pairs of nodes.

SHORTEST-PATH TREE.   The shortest path from origin to any node will traverse a subset of the arcs on this tree.

MINIMUM SPANNING TREE.   A tree that connects all nodes of a network at minimum total cost.

MAXIMAL-FLOW PROBLEM.   The problem of routing the maximal amount of flow through a network.

CUT.   A partition of the nodes of a network into two disjoint classes, say C_1 and C_n, where the source is in C_1 and the sink is in C_n.

CUT CAPACITY.   The sum of the capacities in the $C_1 \rightarrow C_n$ direction over all arcs that directly connect a node in C_1 to a node in C_n.

NETWORK PROBLEM.   Generally refers to the capacitated transshipment model or one of its special forms.

MAJOR CONCEPTS QUIZ _____

True–False

1. **T F**   A capacitated transshipment problem has one variable for each node.

2. **T F**   A node–arc incidence matrix for the network problem has a $+1$, a -1, and all other entries 0 in each column.

3. **T F**   If the right-hand side of any arc capacity inequality in a capacitated transshipment problem is zero, the problem is infeasible.

4. **T F**   In the shortest-route problem a temporary label on a node becomes a permanent label when the node of interest becomes a closest temporary labeled node to the base node.

5. **T F**   The minimum spanning tree connects all nodes of a network at minimum total cost.

6. **T F**   In the minimum spanning tree problem the greedy algorithm is a useful heuristic but is not guaranteed to find an optimal solution.

7. **T F**   The maximal-flow algorithm requires the construction and direct evaluation of every path from the source to the sink.

8. **T F**   The maximal flow through any path in a network is equal to the minimum arc capacity on that path.

9. **T F**   In the maximal-flow problem a cut is *any* two disjoint sets of nodes.

Multiple Choice

10. A positive right-hand side in a flow balance equation of a capacitated transshipment problem indicates that
    a. the node is an origin
    b. the node is a destination
    c. the node is a transshipment node
    d. none of the above

11. Which of the following is a condition which assures that there is an optimal integer solution to a capacitated transshipment problem?

   a. the right-hand side of all flow equations (the L_j's) be integer

   b. the arc capacities (the u_{ij}'s) be integer

   c. either a or b

   d. both a and b

12. In the shortest-route problem, the first number in a permanent label on the node

   a. is the minimum distance between the base and that node

   b. is the minimum distance between the base and that node on any path that passes through the node indicated by the second number in the label

   c. is the minimum distance between that node and a specified destination

   d. both a and b

13. The shortest-path tree

   a. connects every pair of nodes

   b. is the set of all arcs used in tracing the shortest paths from a base H to every other node

   c. both a and b

14. In the maximal-flow problem the maximized flow is equal to

   a. the flow over an arbitrary cut

   b. the maximal capacity over all cuts

   c. the minimal cut capacity

   d. none of the above

Questions 15 through 19 refer to the following problem: A company has two plants and three warehouses. The first plant can supply at most 500 pounds of a particular product, and the second plant at most 200 pounds. The demand at the first warehouse is 150, at the second warehouse 200, and at the third warehouse 350. The cost of manufacturing one pound at plant i and shipping it to warehouse j is given below:

	WAREHOUSE		
PLANT	1	2	3
1	8	10.2	12.6
2	7	9	11.8

Suppose the problem is to determine a shipping schedule which satisfies demand at minimum cost.

15. This problem is

   a. a network model

   b. a transportation model

   c. an integer program

   d. all of the above

   e. a and b

16. Let x_{ij} denote the amount sent from plant i to warehouse j. The demand constraint for the first warehouse is properly written as

   a. $x_{11} + x_{21} = 150$

   b. $x_{11} + x_{21} \geq 150$

   c. Both a and b are correct (i.e., it does not matter whether $=$ or $\geq$ is used).

17. Let x_{ij} denote the amount sent from plant i to warehouse j. In symbols, the supply constraints can be written as

  a. $\sum_{i=1}^{3} x_{ij} \leq s_j, j = 1, 2$

  b. $\sum_{i=1}^{3} x_{ij} = s_j, i = 1, 2$

  c. $\sum_{j=1}^{3} x_{ij} = s_j, i = 1, 2$

  d. none of the above

  e. Both a and b are correct (i.e., it does not matter whether $=$ or $\leq$ is used).

18. The simplex method will always find an integer solution to this problem.

  a. True

  b. False

19. Since total supply $=$ total demand, all constraints (supply and demand) must be written as equalities.

  a. True

  b. False

Answers

1. F	6. F	11. d	16. c
2. T	7. F	12. d	17. d
3. F	8. T	13. c	18. a
4. T	9. F	14. c	19. b
5. T	10. a	15. e	

PROBLEMS

9-1. Consider the following linear constraints of a transshipment model. Construct the corresponding incidence matrix and the associated network diagram, labeling each node with its supply or demand.

$$x_{13} + x_{12} + x_{14} = 2$$
$$-x_{12} + x_{24} = 1$$
$$-x_{13} + x_{35} = 0$$
$$-x_{24} - x_{14} + x_{46} + x_{45} = 0$$
$$-x_{35} + x_{56} - x_{45} = 0$$
$$-x_{46} - x_{56} = -3$$
$$x_{ij} \geq 0, \quad \text{all } (i, j)$$

9-2. Consider the following constraints:

$$x_{12} + x_{13} + x_{14} = 4$$
$$-x_{12} + x_{23} + x_{25} = -2$$
$$-x_{13} - x_{23} + x_{34} = 0$$
$$-x_{14} - x_{34} + x_{45} = 0$$
$$-x_{25} - x_{45} = -2$$

Construct the corresponding incidence matrix and network diagram.

FIGURE 9.27

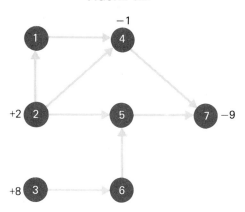

9-3. Write the linear constraints corresponding to the transshipment network of Figure 9.27.

9-4. Write the linear constraints corresponding to the transshipment network of Figure 9.28.

FIGURE 9.28

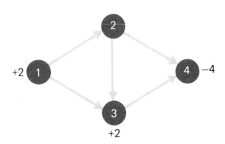

9-5. Construct the incidence matrix for the network shown in Problem 9-4.

9-6. For the problem faced by Aaron Drunner, find another shortest-path tree.

9-7. Algorithms were presented in this chapter for determining two types of trees: the shortest-path tree and the minimum spanning tree. Each algorithm can be applied to the same problem, that is, the same network with the same arc parameters. The question arises as to whether the two algorithms produce the same tree. Apply the minimum spanning tree algorithm at Aaron's problem to show that this algorithm can produce the same tree as the shortest-path tree. Construct a simple three-node example to show that in general the two algorithms will produce different trees.

9-8. Consider the distribution network shown in Figure 9.29. Find the shortest route from node ① to all other nodes in the network.

FIGURE 9.29

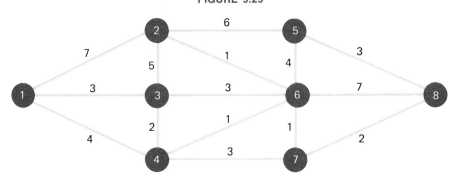

FIGURE 9.30

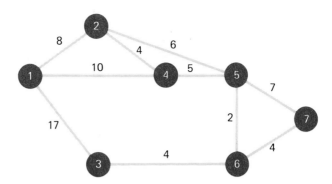

9-9. Consider the distribution system shown in Figure 9.30. Find the shortest path from node ① to each of the other nodes.

9-10. Find the minimum spanning tree for the distribution network in Problem 9-8.

9-11. Find the minimum spanning tree for the distribution system in Problem 9-9.

9-12. Mr. Crimmage is operating the Chicago Health Club with leased equipment and space. Recently, his landlord suggested long-term leasing. Based on the long-term lease plan, he obtained Figure 9.31, which displays the expected net profit if he leases from the beginning of year i to the beginning of year j (in hundreds of dollars). Mr. Crimmage wishes to know when and how long to lease so as to maximize the profit over the next 4 years. Formulate his problem with a network representation and solve it.

FIGURE 9.31

		j			
		2	**3**	**4**	**5**
i	1	9	16	20	32
	2		10	16	23
	3			12	20
	4				7

9-13. *Smoke Detector Layout*   Peter Dout is designing the layout of a new coordinated smoke detector system in a warehouse. The required locations as indicated by the insurance company are shown in Figure 9.32. The arcs represent feasible lengths for the electronic connections. The numbers on the arcs represent linear feet. What layout will connect all detectors and use the least total length of electronic connections?

FIGURE 9.32

9-14. *Radar Towers*   Faye Saver is laying cable between six radar towers in Montana in order that any tower can communicate with any other. The matrix of distances between towers is shown in Figure 9.33. What connections should be made to minimize total cable length?

FIGURE 9.33

	TO TOWER					
FROM TOWER	1	2	3	4	5	6
1		15	14	35	32	25
2	15		20	23	22	25
3	14	20		30	26	21
4	35	23	30		13	22
5	32	22	26	13		18
6	25	25	21	22	18	

9-15. *Crude Distribution*   Lindsay Doyle is responsible for the transport of crude oil to several storage tanks. A portion of the pipeline network is shown in Figure 9.34. What is the maximal flow from node ① to node ⑦?

FIGURE 9.34

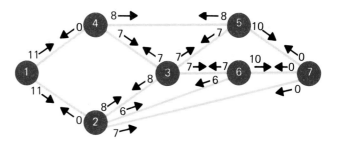

9-16. For the network shown in Problem 9-15, Lindsay is planning to double the capacity of the pipeline connecting tanks 1 and 4.

(a) What will be the new maximal flow?

(b) Let the capacities on the arcs be in units of hundreds of gallons per day. How many days will he save by his new plan in transporting 500,000 gallons from node 1 to node 7?

9-17. Determine the maximal flow from node ① to node ⑥ across the highway network shown in Figure 9.35.

FIGURE 9.35

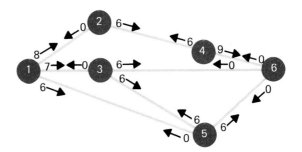

9-18. Consider the network shown in Figure 9.36. First find the maximal flow, and then find the cut with capacity equal to the maximal flow. Assume ① is the source and ⑦ the sink.

FIGURE 9.36

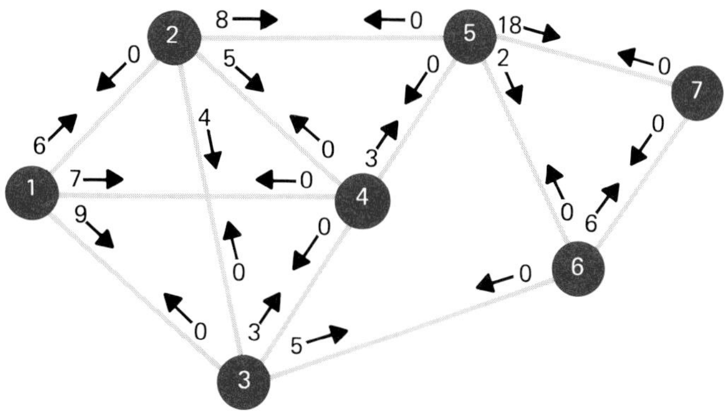

9-19. Demonstrate that the transportation problem with S origins and D destinations is a special case of the capacitated transshipment model.

9-20. Demonstrate that the assignment problem is a special case of the capacitated transshipment model.

9-21. Demonstrate that the problem of determining the minimum-cost route from one node to another specific node can be expressed as a special case of the capacitated transshipment model.

9-22. Consider the following transportation tableau (Figure 9.37) which represents the cost, c_{ij}, required to move one unit from origin i to destination j.

(a) Draw a network diagram corresponding to the tableau.

(b) Construct the incidence matrix for the network.

FIGURE 9.37

To Destination

		1	2	3	4	Supply
	A	18	9	16	∞	100
From Origin	B	∞	5	3	4	150
	C	7	9	∞	8	100
	Demand	80	50	100	120	350

9-23. Consider the transshipment network of Figure 9.38. Nodes 1 and 5 are the plant sites. The plants produce 200 and 150 truckloads, respectively. Nodes 3, 6 and 9 are the outlet sites. The outlets demand 50, 250, and 50 truckloads, respectively. The number on arc (i, j) indicates costs of transporting one truckload from i to j. Assume the cost from i to j is the same as the cost from j to i.

FIGURE 9.38

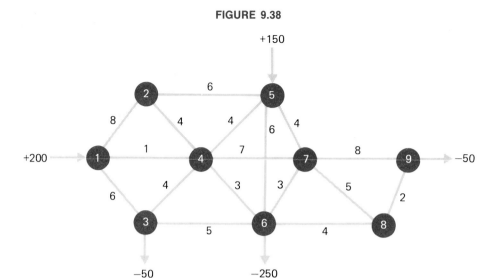

(a) How many variables does the LP formulation of this problem have?

(b) How many constraints does the LP formulation of this problem have?

(c) Find the least costs of moving one truckload from 1 to 3, 6, and 9.

(d) Find the least costs of moving one truckload from 5 to 3, 6, and 9.

(e) Construct the transportation tableau.

(f) Solve the problem with one of the algorithms given in Chapter 7.
What is the total cost?

9-24. Suppose that you were asked to evaluate a proposal of moving the plant at node 1 to node 7 in Figure 9.38. The moving expense is estimated to be 150. What is your recommendation? To answer this question, first find the least costs from 7 to 3, 6, and 9, and then construct a transportation tableau and apply one of the algorithms in Chapter 7.

_____ **APPENDIX 9.1**

A PC APPROACH TO NETWORK PROBLEMS

Chapter 9 includes a discussion of three specific network problems and the algorithms used to solve them. It is not surprising that software has been developed to solve these three classes of problems on the personal computer. This appendix illustrates the use of the QSB system on examples of problems from the text.

The Shortest-Route Problem

A shortest-route problem is defined in Figure 9.12. This figure is reproduced in Figure 9.39 with two modifications: The nodes have been renumbered starting by assigning the number 1 to node H since QSB does not accept 0 as a node number, and for ease of translation Figure 9.39 was produced by adding 1 to each node number in Figure 9.12. Also a name, such as "B1," has been appended to each branch. QSB calls for a branch name, and the selected name has been added to the figure for clarity.

The input and solution from the QSB system are presented in Figure 9.40. A quick check reveals that the solution presented here corresponds to the result shown in Figure 9.11.

FIGURE 9.39
A Shortest-Path Tree

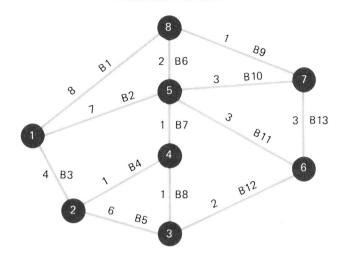

FIGURE 9.40
Solving a Shortest-Route Problem
with QSB

```
Branch        Branch         Start       End        Distance
Number         Name          Node        Node
   1         〈B1    〉       〈1  〉      〈8  〉     〈 8.00000〉
   2         〈B2    〉       〈1  〉      〈5  〉     〈 7.00000〉
   3         〈B3    〉       〈1  〉      〈2  〉     〈 4.00000〉
   4         〈B4    〉       〈2  〉      〈4  〉     〈 1.00000〉
   5         〈B5    〉       〈2  〉      〈3  〉     〈 6.00000〉
   6         〈B6    〉       〈5  〉      〈8  〉     〈 2.00000〉
   7         〈B7    〉       〈4  〉      〈5  〉     〈 1.00000〉
   8         〈B8    〉       〈3  〉      〈4  〉     〈 1.00000〉
   9         〈B9    〉       〈8  〉      〈7  〉     〈 1.00000〉
  10         〈B10   〉       〈5  〉      〈7  〉     〈 3.00000〉
  11         〈B11   〉       〈5  〉      〈6  〉     〈 3.00000〉
  12         〈B12   〉       〈3  〉      〈6  〉     〈 2.00000〉
  13         〈B13   〉       〈6  〉      〈7  〉     〈 3.00000〉


                    Optimal Solution


Node      Distance        Shortest Route from Node 1


 2           4            1- 2 (B3)
 3           6            1- 2- 4- 3 (B3-B4-B8)
 4           5            1- 2- 4 (B3-B4)
 5           6            1- 2- 4- 5 (B3-B4-B7)
 6           8            1- 2- 4- 3- 6 (B3-B4-B8-B12)
 7           9            1- 2- 4- 5- 7 (B3-B4-B7-B10)
 8           8            1- 8 (B1)
```

Data for a minimum spanning tree problem were originally presented in Figure 9.14. This figure is reproduced in Figure 9.41 where two additional pieces of information are introduced: Each branch is given a name, like "B1," since QSB calls for a branch name, and the arcs in the optimal solution produced by QSB are indicated by heavy lines.

FIGURE 9.41
A Minimum Spanning Tree Problem

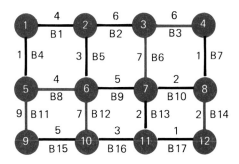

FIGURE 9.42
Solving a Minimum Spanning Tree
Problem with QSB

Branch Number	Branch Name	Start Node	End Node	Distance
1	⟨B1 ⟩	⟨1 ⟩	⟨2 ⟩	⟨ 4.00000⟩
2	⟨B2 ⟩	⟨2 ⟩	⟨3 ⟩	⟨ 6.00000⟩
3	⟨B3 ⟩	⟨3 ⟩	⟨4 ⟩	⟨ 6.00000⟩
4	⟨B4 ⟩	⟨1 ⟩	⟨5 ⟩	⟨ 1.00000⟩
5	⟨B5 ⟩	⟨2 ⟩	⟨6 ⟩	⟨ 3.00000⟩
6	⟨B6 ⟩	⟨3 ⟩	⟨7 ⟩	⟨ 7.00000⟩
7	⟨B7 ⟩	⟨4 ⟩	⟨8 ⟩	⟨ 1.00000⟩
8	⟨B8 ⟩	⟨5 ⟩	⟨6 ⟩	⟨ 4.00000⟩
9	⟨B9 ⟩	⟨6 ⟩	⟨7 ⟩	⟨ 5.00000⟩
10	⟨B10 ⟩	⟨7 ⟩	⟨8 ⟩	⟨ 2.00000⟩
11	⟨B11 ⟩	⟨5 ⟩	⟨9 ⟩	⟨ 9.00000⟩
12	⟨B12 ⟩	⟨6 ⟩	⟨10 ⟩	⟨ 7.00000⟩
13	⟨B13 ⟩	⟨7 ⟩	⟨11 ⟩	⟨ 2.00000⟩
14	⟨B14 ⟩	⟨8 ⟩	⟨12 ⟩	⟨ 2.00000⟩
15	⟨B15 ⟩	⟨9 ⟩	⟨10 ⟩	⟨ 5.00000⟩
16	⟨B16 ⟩	⟨10 ⟩	⟨11 ⟩	⟨ 3.00000⟩
17	⟨B17 ⟩	⟨11 ⟩	⟨12 ⟩	⟨ 1.00000⟩

FIGURE 9.42 (CONTINUED)

```
Optimal Solution

Branch on the Tree               Distance

        1 - 2 (B1)                   4
        1 - 5 (B4)                   1
        2 - 3 (B2)                   6
        2 - 6 (B5)                   3
        6 - 7 (B9)                   5
        7 - 8 (B10)                  2
        7 - 11 (B13)                 2
        8 - 4 (B7)                   1
        10 - 9 (B15)                 5
        11 - 10 (B16)                3
        11 - 12 (B17)                1

        Total distance = 33
```

Figure 9.42 presents the input data and the optimal solution for this problem. Comparing the results with those shown in Figure 9.20 reveals that QSB has produced an alternative optimal solution.

The Maximal-Flow Problem

Data for a maximal-flow problem were presented in Figure 9.21. This figure is reproduced in Figure 9.43 where two additional pieces of information have been appended: Each branch is given a name, like "B1," since QSB calls for branch names, and the optimal solution produced by QSB is indicated by the bold arcs, arrow heads, and arc flows.

FIGURE 9.43
A Max-Flow Problem

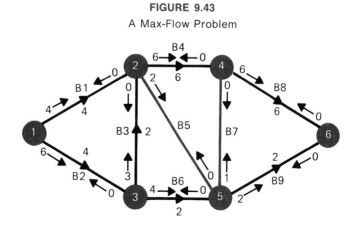

The input for QSB and the corresponding solution are shown in Figure 9.44.

FIGURE 9.44

Solving a Max-Flow Problem

Branch Number	Branch Name	Start Node	End Node	Flow Capacity From Start Node	Flow Capacity From End Node
1	⟨B1 ⟩	⟨1 ⟩	⟨2 ⟩	⟨ 4.00000⟩	⟨ ⟩
2	⟨B2 ⟩	⟨1 ⟩	⟨3 ⟩	⟨ 6.00000⟩	⟨ ⟩
3	⟨B3 ⟩	⟨2 ⟩	⟨3 ⟩	⟨ ⟩	⟨ 3.00000⟩
4	⟨B4 ⟩	⟨2 ⟩	⟨4 ⟩	⟨ 6.00000⟩	⟨ ⟩
5	⟨B5 ⟩	⟨2 ⟩	⟨5 ⟩	⟨ 2.00000⟩	⟨ ⟩
6	⟨B6 ⟩	⟨3 ⟩	⟨5 ⟩	⟨ 4.00000⟩	⟨ ⟩
7	⟨B7 ⟩	⟨4 ⟩	⟨5 ⟩	⟨ ⟩	⟨ ⟩
8	⟨B8 ⟩	⟨4 ⟩	⟨6 ⟩	⟨ 6.00000⟩	⟨ ⟩
9	⟨B9 ⟩	⟨5 ⟩	⟨6 ⟩	⟨ 2.00000⟩	⟨ ⟩

Solution

The Final Flow for maxflo   Page: 1

```
                    Branch    End Node           Net Flow    From Start Node
                                                             To End Node
Start
Node                     1 - 2 (B1)                 4
                         1 - 3 (B2)                 4
                         2 - 4 (B4)     Branch       6
                         3 - 5 (B6)     Name         2
                         3 - 2 (B3)                 2
                         4 - 6 (B8)                 6   Max-Flow thru
                         5 - 6 (B9)                 2   Network

                    Maximal total flow = 8
```

We observe that QSB produces the same optimal solution that was shown in Figure 9.25.

10

PROJECT MANAGEMENT: PERT AND CPM

10.1
INTRODUCTION

**Projects:
Ancient and
Modern**

The task of managing major projects is an ancient and honorable art. In about 2600 B.C., the Egyptians built the Great Pyramid for King Khufu. The Greek historian Herodotus claimed that 400,000 men worked for 20 years to build this structure. Although these figures are now in doubt, there is no question about the enormity of the project. The Book of Genesis reports that the Tower of Babel was not completed because God made it impossible for the builders to communicate. This project is especially important, since it establishes an historical precedent for the ever-popular practice of citing divine intervention as a rationale for failure.[1]

Modern projects ranging from building a suburban shopping center to putting a man on the moon are amazingly large, complex, and costly. Completing such projects on time and within the budget is not an easy task. In particular, we shall see that the complicated problems of scheduling such projects are often structured by the interdependence of activities. Typically, certain of the activities may not be initiated before others have been completed. In dealing with projects possibly involving thousands of such dependency relations, it is no wonder that managers seek effective methods of analysis.

---

[1] The *Chicago Tribune* (August 5, 1977) noted the following comment concerning the blackout in New York in July of that year: "Con Ed called the disaster an act of God."

Some of the key questions to be answered in this chapter are

1. What is the expected project completion date?
2. What is the potential "variability" in this date?
3. What are the scheduled start and completion dates for each specific activity?
4. What activities are *critical* in the sense that they must be completed exactly as scheduled in order to meet the target for overall project completion?
5. How long can *noncritical* activities be delayed before a delay in the overall completion date is incurred?
6. How might I effectively concentrate resources on activities in order to speed up project completion?
7. What controls can be exercised on the flows of expenditures on the various activities throughout the duration of the project in order that the overall budget can be adhered to?

Origins of PERT and CPM

PERT and CPM, acronyms for Program Evaluation Review Technique and Critical Path Method, respectively, will provide answers to these questions. Each of these approaches to scheduling represents a project as a network, and hence the material in this chapter, although self-contained, can be viewed as a natural extension of the network approach as discussed in Chapter 9.

PERT was developed in the late 1950s by the Navy Special Projects Office in cooperation with the management consulting firm of Booz, Allen, and Hamilton. The technique received substantial favorable publicity for its use in the engineering and development program of the Polaris missile, a complicated project that had 250 prime contractors and over 9000 subcontractors. Since that time, it has been widely adopted in other branches of government and in industry and has been applied to such diverse projects as construction of factories, buildings, and highways, research management, product development, the installation of new computer systems, and so on. Today, many firms and government agencies require all contractors to use PERT.

CPM was developed in 1957 by J. E. Kelly of Remington Rand and M. R. Walker of DuPont. It differs from PERT primarily in the details of how time and cost are treated. Indeed, in actual implementation, the distinctions between PERT and CPM have become blurred as firms have integrated the best features of both systems into their own efforts to manage projects effectively.

In keeping with our philosophy throughout the text, we approach the topic of project management on two levels. First, the essential techniques will be developed in an easily grasped illustrative example. Second, the use of the computer will be illustrated to indicate how one would handle the techniques in a large-scale, real-world application.

———— 10.2
THE GLOBAL OIL CREDIT CARD OPERATION

No one would claim that it is like building the Great Pyramid, but the impending move of the credit card operation to Des Moines, Iowa, from the home office in Dallas is an important project for Rebecca Goldstein and Global Oil. The board of directors of Global has set a firm deadline of 22 weeks for the move to be accomplished. Becky is a manager in the Operations Analysis Group. She is in charge of planning the move, seeing that everything comes off according to plan and making sure that the deadline is met.

The move is difficult to coordinate because it involves many different divisions within the company. Real estate must select one of three available office sites. Personnel has to determine which employees from Dallas will move, how many new employees to hire, and who will train them. The systems group and the treasurer's office must organize and implement the operating procedures and the financial arrangements for the new operation. The architects will have to design the interior space and oversee needed structural improvements. Each of the sites that Global is considering is an existing building with the appropriate amount of open space. However, office partitions, computer facilities, furnishings, and so on, must all be provided.

A second complicating factor is that there is an interdependence of activities. In other words, some parts of the project cannot be started until other parts are completed. Consider two obvious examples: Global cannot construct the interior of an office before it has been designed. Neither can it hire new employees until it has determined its personnel requirements.

The Activity List for Global Oil

Becky knows that PERT and CPM are specifically designed for projects of this sort and she wastes no time in getting started. The first step in the process is to define the activities in the project and to establish the proper precedence relationships. This is an important first step since errors or omissions at this stage can lead to a disastrously inaccurate schedule. Figure 10.1 shows the first *activity list* that Becky prepares for the move (the columns labeled "Time" and "Resources" are indications of things to come).

Immediate Predecessors of an Activity

Conceptually, Figure 10.1 is straightforward. Each activity is placed on a separate line and its *immediate predecessors* are recorded on the same line. The immediate predecessors of an activity are those activities that must be completed prior to the start of the activity in question. For example, in Figure 10.1 we see that Global cannot start activity C, determine personnel requirements, until activity B, create the organizational and financial plan, is completed. Similarly, activity G, hire new employees, cannot begin until activity F, select the Global personnel that will move from Texas to Iowa, is completed. This activity, F, in turn, cannot start until activity C, determine personnel requirements, is completed.

The activity list with immediate predecessors, and the yet-to-be-obtained time estimates will provide the essential ingredients to answer the first five questions at the start of this section and we shall shortly see how PERT and CPM are used to produce these answers. In practice, however, another graphical approach, the Gantt Chart, also is used

FIGURE 10.1
First Activity List

ACTIVITY	DESCRIPTION	IMMEDIATE PREDECESSORS	TIME	RESOURCES
A	Select Office Site	—		
B	Create Organizational and Financial Plan	—		
C	Determine Personnel Requirements	B		
D	Design Facility	A, C		
E	Construct Interior	D		
F	Select Personnel to Move	C		
G	Hire New Employees	F		
H	Move Records, Key Personnel, etc.	F		
I	Make Financial Arrangements with Institutions in Des Moines	B		
J	Train New Personnel	H, E, G		

commonly to attack such problems. We thus make a slight detour to consider this precursor of the network approaches (PERT and CPM) before returning to the main thrust of the chapter.

The Gantt Chart

The Gantt chart was developed by Henry L. Gantt in 1918 and remains a popular tool in production and project scheduling. Its simplicity and clear graphical display have established it as a useful device for simple scheduling problems. The Gantt chart for Becky's problem is shown in Figure 10.2. Each activity is listed on the vertical axis. The horizontal axis is time and the anticipated as well as actual duration of each activity is represented by a bar of the appropriate length. The chart also indicates *the earliest possible starting* time for each activity. For example, activity C cannot start before time 5 since, according to Figure 10.1, activity B must be completed before activity C can begin. As each activity (or part thereof) is completed the appropriate bar is shaded. At any point in time, then, it is clear which activities are on schedule and which are not. The Gantt chart in Figure 10.2 shows that as of week 13 activities D, E and H are behind schedule, while G has actually been entirely completed (because it is all shaded) and hence is ahead of schedule.

Weaknesses of Gantt Charts

This simple example shows how the Gantt chart is mainly used as a record-keeping device for following the progression in time of the subtasks of a project. As Figure 10.2 shows, we can see which individual tasks are on or behind schedule. It seems important to note at this point that in the Gantt chart context the phrase "on schedule" means "it has been completed no later than the earliest possible completion time." Thus Figure 10.2 shows that D and H could have been completed, *at the earliest*, by week 12. Since they are not completed by week 13 they are, in this sense, behind schedule. As we shall see, this is too simple a concept for whether an activity is on schedule. The appropriate point of view should be whether *the overall project* is being delayed in terms of a target

FIGURE 10.2
A Gantt Chart

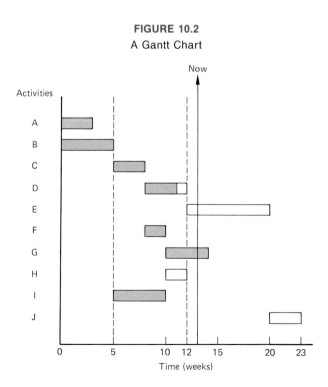

440

completion date. The Gantt chart fails to reveal some of the important information needed to attack this question. For example, the Gantt chart fails to reveal which activities are *immediate predecessors* of other activities. In Figure 10.2 it may appear that F and I are immediate predecessors of G since G can start at 10 and F and I can each finish at 10. In fact, however, Figure 10.1 tells us that only F is an immediate predecessor of G. A delay in I would *not* affect the potential starting time of G, or for that matter of any other activity. It is this type of "immediate predecessor" information that must be used to deduce the impact on completion time for the overall project. This latter type of information is of obvious importance to the manager. The overall weakness of Gantt charts is reflected by their uselessness in making such inferences. We shall now see that the network representation contains the immediate predecessor information that we need.

The Network Diagram

In a PERT network diagram each activity is represented by an arrow that is called a *branch* or an *arc*. The beginning and end of each activity is indicated by a circle that is called a *node*. The term *event* is also used in conjunction with the nodes. An event represents the completion of the activities that lead into a node. Referring to the activity list in Figure 10.1, we see that "select office site" is termed activity A. When this *activity* is completed, the *event* "office site selected" occurs.

Constructing the Network Diagram

Figure 10.3 shows a network diagram for activities A through C. We emphasize at the outset that the numbers assigned to the nodes are arbitrary. They are simply used to identify events and do not imply anything about precedence relationships. Indeed, we shall renumber the node that terminates activity C several times as we develop the network diagram for this project, but correct precedence relationships will always be preserved. In the network diagram each activity must start at the node in which its immediate predecessors ended. For example, in Figure 10.3, activity C starts at node ③ because its immediate predecessor, activity B, ended there. We see, however, that complications arise as we attempt to add activity D to the network diagram. Since both A and C are immediate predecessors to D, and since we want to show any activity such as D only once in our diagram, nodes ② and ④ in Figure 10.3 must be combined and D should start from this new node. This is shown in Figure 10.4. Node ③ now represents the event that both activities A and C have been completed. Note that activity E, which

FIGURE 10.3
Network Diagram for Activities A through C

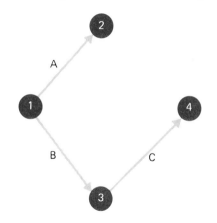

FIGURE 10.4
A Partial Network Diagram

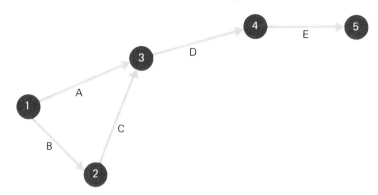

has only D as an immediate predecessor, can be added with no difficulty. However, as we attempt to add activity F, a new problem arises. Since F has C as an immediate predecessor, it would emanate from node ③ (of Figure 10.4). We see, however, that this would imply that F also has A as an immediate predecessor, which is incorrect.

The Use of Dummy Activities

This diagramming dilemma is solved by introducing a *dummy activity* which is represented by a dashed line in the network diagram in Figure 10.5. This dummy activity is fictitious in the sense that it requires no time or resources. It merely provides a pedagogical device that enables us to draw a network representation that correctly maintains the appropriate precedence relationships. Thus, Figure 10.5 indicates that activity D can begin only after both of the activities A and C have been completed. Similarly, activity F can occur only after activity C is completed.

Figure 10.6 shows the network diagram for the first activity list as presented in Figure 10.1. We note that activities G and H both start at node ⑥ and terminate at node ⑦. This does not present a problem in portraying the appropriate precedence relationships, since only activity J starts at node ⑦. This might, however, create a problem for certain computer programs used to solve PERT and CPM problems. In some of these programs, each activity is identified by the number of its *starting and ending* node. If such a program is to be used, the representation of G and H in Figure 10.6 would lead the computer to regard them as the same activity. This would be incorrect, since in fact activities G and H are not the same. A dummy activity can be used to cure this condition.

FIGURE 10.5
Introducing a Dummy Activity

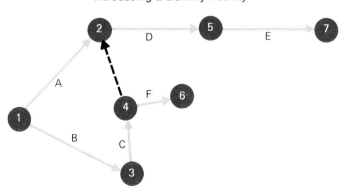

FIGURE 10.6
Network Diagram for the First Activity List
for the Move to Des Moines

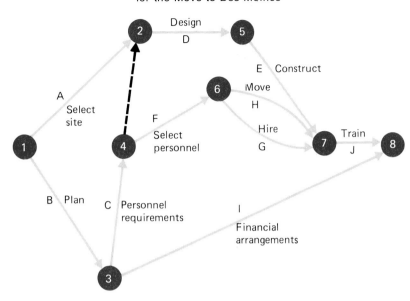

Figure 10.7 illustrates the procedure. Since the dummy activity requires no time, the correct time and precedent relationships are maintained. This new representation has been introduced into Figure 10.9. The computer code which we will employ does not require that these dummy activities be input. Thus, for our purposes, they serve mainly the pedagogical goal of correctly portraying the precedence relations (i.e., as used in Figure 10.5).

FIGURE 10.7
Introducing a Second Dummy Activity

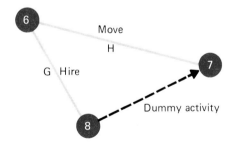

——— 10.3
THE CRITICAL PATH–MEETING THE BOARD'S DEADLINE

The activity list and an appropriate network diagram are useful devices for representing the precedence relationships among the activities in a project. Recall that the board has set a firm goal of 22 weeks for the overall project to be completed. Before Becky can tell if she can meet this goal, she will have to incorporate time estimates into the process.

FIGURE 10.8
First Activity List with Expected Activity
Times in Weeks

ACTIVITY	DESCRIPTION	IMMEDIATE PREDECESSORS	EXPECTED ACTIVITY TIME (WKS)	RESOURCES
A	Select Office Site	—	3	
B	Create Organizational and Financial Plan	—	5	
C	Determine Personnel Requirements	B	3	
D	Design Facility	A, C	4	
E	Construct Interior	D	8	
F	Select Personnel to Move	C	2	
G	Hire New Employees	F	4	
H	Move Records, Key Personnel, etc.	F	2	
I	Make Financial Arrangements with Institutions in Des Moines	B	5	
J	Train New Personnel	H, E, G	3	

Time Assignments

The PERT–CPM procedure requires management to produce an estimate of the expected time it will take to complete each activity on the activity list. Let us assume that Becky has worked with the appropriate departments at Global to arrive at the expected time estimates (in weeks) shown in Figure 10.8. (In Section 10.4 we shall discuss in more detail the way in which these time estimates were produced.) Figure 10.9 shows the network diagram with the expected activity times appended in brackets.

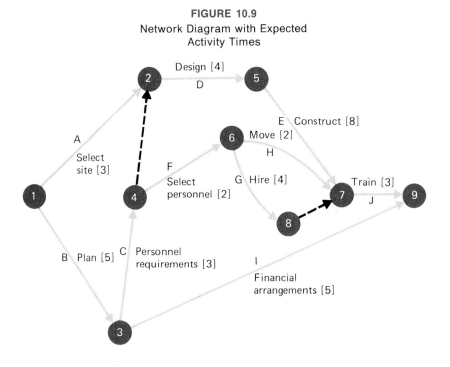

FIGURE 10.9
Network Diagram with Expected
Activity Times

From Figure 10.8 you can see (by adding up the separate expected activity times) that the total working time required to complete all the individual activities would be 39 weeks. However, the total calendar time required to complete the entire project can clearly be less than 39 weeks, for many activities can be performed simultaneously. For example, Figure 10.9 shows that activities A and B can be initiated at the same time. Activity A takes 3 weeks and B takes 5 weeks. If management arranges to begin both activities at the same time (at calendar time = 0), both will be completed by calendar time = 5. To obtain a prediction of the minimum calendar time required for overall project duration, we must find what is referred to as a *critical path* in the network. A *path* can be defined as a sequence of connected activities that leads from the starting node ① to the completion node ⑨. For example, the sequence of activities B–I requiring 10 weeks to complete, is a path. So is the sequence B–C–D–E–J requiring 23 weeks to complete. You can identify numerous other paths in Figure 10.9. To complete the project, the activities *on all paths* must be completed. In this sense we might say that "all paths must be traversed." Thus, we have just seen that our project will take *at least* 23 weeks to complete, for the path B–C–D–E–J must be traversed. However, numerous other paths must also be traversed, and some of these may require even more time. Our task will be to analyze the total amount of calendar time required in order that all paths should be traversed. Thus, we wish to determine the *longest path* from start to finish. This path, called the *critical path*, will determine the overall project duration, because no other path will be longer. If activities on the longest path are delayed, then, since these activities must be completed, the entire project will be delayed. For this reason the activities on the critical path are called the *critical activities* of the project. It is this subset of activities that must be kept on schedule.

We now specify the steps employed in finding a critical path. Fundamental in this process will be the *earliest start time* for each activity. To illustrate this idea, consider activity D, "design the facility." Now assume that the project starts at time zero and ask yourself: "What is the earliest time at which activity D can start?" Clearly, it cannot start until activity A is complete. It thus cannot start before time = 3. However, it also cannot start before the dummy activity (that requires 0 time) is complete. Since the dummy cannot start until B and C are complete (a total of 8 weeks), we see that D cannot start until 8 weeks have passed. In this calculation, it is crucial to note that activities A and B both start at time 0. After 3 weeks A is complete, but B still requires another 2 weeks. After a total of 5 weeks, B is complete and C can start. After another 3 weeks, a total of 8 from the start, C is completed. Thus, after 8 weeks, both A and C are complete and D can start. In other words,

$$\text{earliest start time for activity D} = 8 \text{ weeks}$$

Another important concept is *earliest finish time* for each activity. If we let

$$\text{ES} = \text{earliest start time for a given activity}$$

$$\text{EF} = \text{earliest finish time for a given activity}$$

$$t = \text{expected activity time for the given activity}$$

then, for a given activity, the relation between earliest start time and earliest finish time is

$$\text{EF} = \text{ES} + t$$

FIGURE 10.10
Earliest Start Time Rule

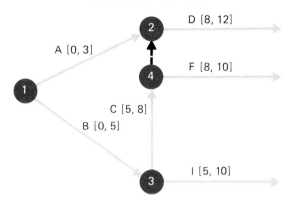

For example, we have just shown that for activity D we have ES = 8. Thus, for activity D,

$$EF = ES + t$$
$$= 8 + 4 = 12$$

We now recall that each activity begins at a node. We know that a given activity leaving a node cannot be started until *all* activities leading into that node have been finished. This observation gives the following

---

EARLIEST START TIME RULE: **The ES time for an activity leaving a particular node is the largest of the EF times for all activities entering the node.**

Let us apply this rule to nodes ①, ②, ③, and ④ of Becky's network, Figure 10.9. The result is shown in Figure 10.10. We write in brackets the earliest start and earliest finish times for each activity next to the letter of the activity, as shown in Figure 10.10. Note that the earliest start time rule applied to activity D says that ES for activity D is equal to the largest value of the EF times for the two precedent activities C (via the dummy) and A. Thus, the ES for D is the largest of the two values [8, 3], which is 8.

Forward Pass Completed
Continuing to each node in a *forward pass* through the entire network, the values [ES, EF] are easily computed for each activity. The result is shown in Figure 10.11. Note that the earliest finish time for J is 23 weeks. This means that the earliest completion time for the entire project is 23 weeks. This answers the first of the questions itemized in Section 10.1: "What is the expected project completion date?" In order to answer the third, fourth, and fifth questions, we now proceed with the algorithm for finding the critical path. Having gone through the above *forward pass*, the next step is to make a *backward pass* calculation.

Backward Pass Begun
The *backward pass* begins at the completion node, node ⑨. We then trace back through the network computing what is termed a latest start and latest finish time for each activity. In symbols,

Latest Start and Latest Finish Times

LS = latest start time for a particular activity

LF = latest finish time for a particular activity

FIGURE 10.11
Global Oil Network With Earliest Start
and Earliest Finish Times Shown

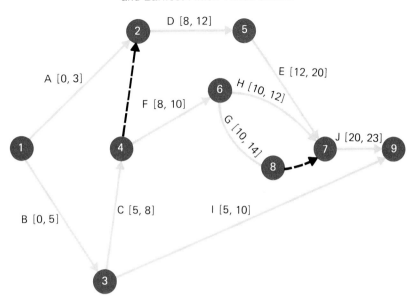

The relation between these quantities is

$$LS = LF - t$$

For activity J we define the latest finish time to be the same as its earliest finish time, which is 23. Hence, for activity J,

$$LS = LF - t = 23 - 3 = 20$$

To determine the latest finish time for activity H, as well as for all other activities in the network, the following rule is applied:

LATEST FINISH TIME RULE: **The LF time for an activity entering a particular node is the smallest of the LS times for all activities leaving that node.**

Thus, for activity H, which enters node ⑦, we apply the rule to see that LF = 20 because J is the only activity leaving node ⑦ and we have already stated that LS = 20 for activity J. Also, for activity H we can then compute

$$LS = LF - t = 20 - 2 = 18$$

The complete network with the LS and LF entries is shown in Figure 10.12. These entries appear on the arc for each activity in brackets, directly under the ES and EF times.

FIGURE 10.12
Global Oil Network with LS and LF
Times Shown Below Activities

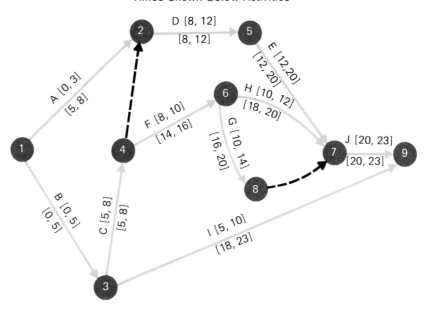

**Slack and the
Critical Path**

Based on Figure 10.12, the next step of the algorithm is to identify another important value, the amount of slack or free time associated with each activity. *Slack* is defined to be the amount of time an activity can be delayed without affecting the completion date for the overall project. For each activity, the slack value is computed as

$$\text{slack} = \text{LS} - \text{ES} = \text{LF} - \text{EF}$$

For example, the slack for activity G is given by

$$\text{slack for G} = \text{LS for G} - \text{ES for G}$$
$$= 16 - 10$$
$$= 6$$

and the same value is given by

$$\text{LF for G} - \text{EF for G} = 20 - 14 = 6$$

This means that activity G could be delayed up to 6 weeks beyond its earliest start time without delaying the overall project. On the other hand, the slack associated with activity C is

$$\text{slack for C} = \text{LS for C} - \text{ES for C}$$
$$= 5 - 5$$
$$= 0$$

FIGURE 10.13
Summary Scheduling

ACTIVITY	EARLIEST START	EARLIEST FINISH	LATEST START	LATEST FINISH	SLACK
A	0	3	5	8	5
B	0	5	0	5	*****
C	5	8	5	8	*****
D	8	12	8	12	*****
E	12	20	12	20	*****
F	8	10	14	16	6
G	10	14	16	20	6
H	10	12	18	20	8
I	5	10	18	23	13
J	20	23	20	23	*****

Thus, activity C has no slack and must begin as scheduled at week 5. *Since this activity cannot be delayed without affecting the entire project, it is a critical activity and is on the critical path.*

The critical path activities are those with zero slack.

A computer printout of relevant data for this project is shown in Figure 10.13. This is the type of output you would be likely to see in a real study. Note that asterisks are printed for those activities with zero slack. Thus, we can see from this computer output that the critical path for Becky's project is B–C–D–E–J. The minimum overall completion time is 23 weeks, which is the sum of the times on the critical path, as well as the earliest finish time for the last activity (J). Figure 10.13 also provides the answers to questions 3, 4, and 5 raised in Section 10.1. In other words, we have, up to this point, answered the following questions from that section.

1. What is the expected project completion date?
   Answer: 23 weeks.

3. What are the scheduled start and completion dates for each specific activity?
   Answer: An activity may be scheduled to start at any date between "earliest start" and "latest start." The scheduled completion date will be "start date + expected activity time." For example, activity G can be scheduled to start anywhere between time = 10 and time = 16. As shown in Figure 10.8, the expected activity time is 4 weeks. Hence, the scheduled completion date will be "start date + 4."

4. What activities are *critical* in the sense that they must be completed exactly as scheduled in order to meet the target for overall project completion?
   Answer: The activities on the critical path: namely, B, C, D, E, J.

5. How long can *noncritical* activities be delayed before a delay in the overall completion date is incurred?
   Answer: Any activity may be started as late as the "latest start" date without delaying the overall project completion.

Three questions, namely 2, 6, and 7, remain to be answered. But first, before proceeding further, let us take an overview of what we have learned. It is clear from the critical path analysis that Becky has a problem. The board of directors wants the credit-card operation to start operating in Des Moines in 22 weeks, and with the current plan 23 weeks are required. Obviously, something must change if this goal is to be met. There are two basic ways to proceed:

Ways of Reducing Project Duration

1. *A strategic analysis:* Here the analyst asks: "Does this project have to be done the way it is currently diagrammed?" In particular, "Do all of the activities on the critical path have to be done in the specified order?" Can we make arrangements to accomplish some of these activities in a different way not on the critical path?

2. *A tactical approach:* In this approach the analyst assumes that the current diagram is appropriate and works at reducing the time of certain activities on the critical path by devoting more resources to them. The current expected times assume a certain allocation of resources. For example, the 8 weeks for construction (activity E) assumes a regular 8-hour workday. The contractor can complete the job more rapidly by working overtime, but at increased costs.

FIGURE 10.14
Computer Input for Redefined Activity List

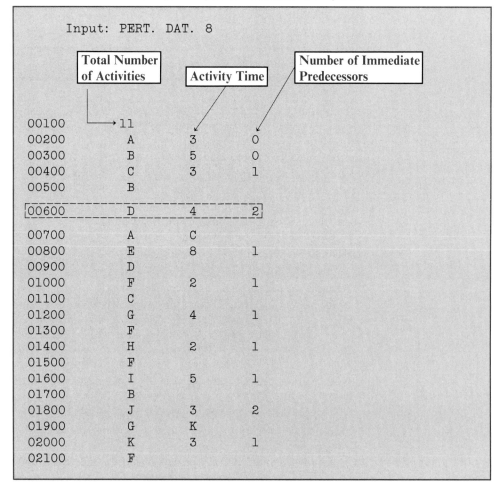

The tactical approach will get us more into CPM considerations, to be discussed in Section 10.6. For now, let us deal with the so-called strategic questions.

A Strategic Analysis

Becky starts with a strategic analysis, since she is anxious to keep the cost of the move as low as possible. After some study she suddenly realizes that the current network assumes that activity J, the training of new employees, must be carried out in the new building (after E is complete), and after records and key personnel have been moved (after H is complete). After reconsidering, she believes that these requirements can be changed. First of all, J can be accomplished independently of H. The previous specification that H should be an immediate predecessor of J was simply incorrect. Moreover, she believes that she can secure an alternative training facility by arranging to use surplus classroom space in Des Moines at a minimal cost. She can then have the new employees trained and ready to start the moment that construction ends. On the other hand, she has to add another activity to the activity list: Secure a training facility (to be denoted as activity K). Although she feels that such a rearrangement may be helpful, it is possible that in this redefined network she may have created a new critical path with a still unsatisfactory minimum time (i.e., one greater than 22 weeks).

Computer Output for the Redefined Network

Figure 10.14 shows the redefined activity list in the form in which Becky submits the problem to her on-line computer. In the input which she is required to provide, the dummy activities are never employed. Line 100 specifies the total number of activities, 11. To understand the rest of the format, consider line 600. This tells us that the activity D (design facility) has an expected completion time of 4 weeks and that it has 2 immediate predecessors. The next line, 700, shows that these 2 predecessors are A (select office site) and C (determine personnel requirements). In lines 2000 and 2100 we see that the new activity, K (secure training facility) takes 3 weeks and has 1 immediate predecessor, F (select personnel). Also note how the input for activity J (line 1800) shows that activity H is no longer one of its immediate predecessors. Figure 10.15 shows the network diagram for the redefined project.

FIGURE 10.15
Network Diagram for the Redefined Project

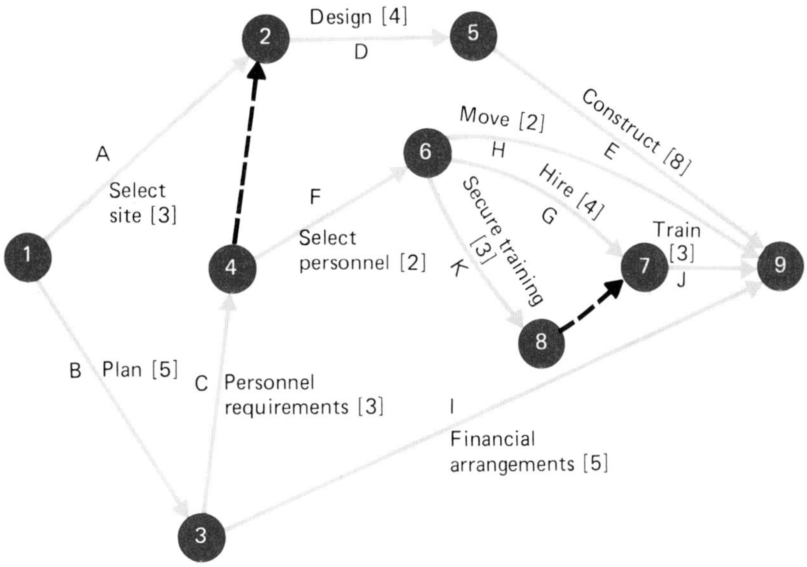

FIGURE 10.16
Computer Solution for the Redefined Project

```
NAME OF INPUT FILE =
PERT. DAT

PROJECT LENGTH = 20.00
```

ACTIVITY	TIME	EARLIEST START	LATEST START	EARLIEST FINISH	LATEST FINISH	SLACK
B	5.00	0.00	0.00	5.00	5.00	********
A	3.00	0.00	5.00	3.00	8.00	5.00
C	3.00	5.00	5.00	8.00	8.00	********
I	5.00	5.00	15.00	10.00	20.00	10.00
F	2.00	8.00	11.00	10.00	13.00	3.00
D	4.00	8.00	8.00	12.00	12.00	********
K	3.00	10.00	14.00	13.00	17.00	4.00
G	4.00	10.00	13.00	14.00	17.00	3.00
H	2.00	10.00	18.00	12.00	20.00	8.00
E	8.00	12.00	12.00	20.00	20.00	********
J	3.00	14.00	17.00	17.00	20.00	3.00

Although this diagram is useful for pedagogical reasons, it is not an important part of solving the problem. Indeed, Becky skips this step and asks the computer to solve the problem. The computer solution is shown in Figure 10.16. Here we see that the redefined project can be completed in 20 weeks (the sum of the times on the critical path) and hence the board's deadline can be met. It is also seen that the activity "train" (J) is no longer on the critical path. In spite of the fact that 3 weeks is needed to secure a training facility, activity J has a slack of 3 weeks. The computer solution shows that the critical path for the redefined project is B–C–D–E. (Recall that ***** in the SLACK column indicates that an activity is on the critical path.)

Let us now consider the second question raised in the introduction: "What is the potential variability in the expected project completion date?"

10.4
VARIABILITY IN ACTIVITY TIMES

So far, we have been acting as though the activity times and the derived values for ES, LS, EF, and LF were all deterministic. This may not be strictly correct, for in reality the activity times are often not known in advance with certainty. In view of this fact, PERT employs a special formula for estimating activity times. We shall now present the details, and in so doing it will be seen that the PERT approach can also be used to calculate the probability that the project will be completed by any particular time.

The PERT system of estimating activity times requires someone who understands the activity in question well enough to produce three estimates of the activity time:

1. *Optimistic time* (denoted by a): the minimum time. Everything has to go perfectly to achieve this time.

2. *Most probable time* (denoted by m): the most likely time. The time required under normal circumstances.

3. *Pessimistic time* (denoted by b): the maximum time. One version of Murphy's Law is that if something can go wrong, it will. The pessimistic time is the time required when Murphy's Law is in effect.

Consider, for example, activity E, construct the interior. Becky and the general contractor carefully examine each phase of the construction project and arrive at the following estimates:

$$a = 4$$

$$m = 7$$

$$b = 16$$

The relatively large value for b is caused by the possibility of a delay in the delivery of the air-conditioning unit for the computer. If this unit is delayed, the entire activity is delayed. Moreover, in this case, since E is on the critical path, a delay in this unit will delay overall project completion.

In the original uses of the PERT approach (i.e., late 1950s), the procedures for estimating the expected value and standard deviation of the activity times were motivated by the assumption that activity time is a random variable which has a unimodel beta probability distribution. A typical beta probability distribution is shown in Figure 10.17.

Estimating the Expected Activity Time   The estimate of the expected activity time for each activity is based on the values of a, b, and m. The formula is

$$\text{estimate of expected activity time} = \frac{a + 4m + b}{6} \qquad (10.1)$$

Thus for activity E,

$$\text{estimate of expected activity time} = \frac{4 + 4(7) + 16}{6} = 8$$

FIGURE 10.17
Unimodal Beta Distribution

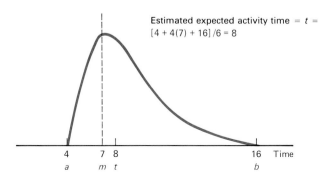

Estimated expected activity time $= t =$
$[4 + 4(7) + 16]/6 = 8$

By working with the appropriate individuals in Global Oil, Becky used (10.1) to estimate each of the expected activity times that were presented in Figure 10.8 and subsequently used in the critical path analysis.

Estimating the Standard Deviation of an Activity Time

The standard deviation of an activity time is estimated by assuming that there are 6 standard deviations between the optimistic and pessimistic times:

$$\text{estimate of the standard deviation of activity time} = \frac{b - a}{6} \tag{10.2}$$

Thus, for activity E,

$$\text{estimate of standard deviation} = \frac{16 - 4}{6} = 2$$

Figure 10.18 shows the three estimates (a, m, b), the expected activity times, the standard deviation of the activity times, and the variance of the activity times for the redefined activity list. The variance is simply the square of the standard deviation. It is useful to record the variance of each activity since these values will be used in making statements about the probability of completing the overall project by a specific date.

In any application, it is of course possible to use any procedure that seems appropriate to estimate the expected value and standard deviation of the activity time. Indeed, in some circumstances data may be available and various statistical procedures can be used to estimate these parameters of the model.

Probability of Completing the Project on Time

The fact that activity times are random variables implies that the completion time for the project is also a random variable. That is, there is a potential variability in the overall completion time. Even though the redefined project has an *expected* completion time of 20 weeks, there is no guarantee that it will actually be completed within 20 weeks. If *by chance* various activities take longer than their expected time, the project might not be completed within the desired 22-week schedule. In general, it would be useful to know the probability that the project will be completed within a specified time. In particular,

FIGURE 10.18
Time Estimates

ACTIVITY	a	m	b	$(a + 4m + b)/6$ (EXPECTED VALUE)	$(b - a)/6$ (STD. DEV.)	$[(b - a)/6]^2$ (VARIANCE)
A	1	3	5	3	$\frac{2}{3}$	$\frac{4}{9}$
B	3	4.5	9	5	1	1
C	2	3	4	3	$\frac{1}{3}$	$\frac{1}{9}$
D	2	4	6	4	$\frac{2}{3}$	$\frac{4}{9}$
E	4	7	16	8	2	4
F	1	1.5	5	2	$\frac{2}{3}$	$\frac{4}{9}$
G	2.5	3.5	7.5	4	$\frac{5}{6}$	$\frac{25}{36}$
H	1	2	3	2	$\frac{1}{3}$	$\frac{1}{9}$
I	4	5	6	5	$\frac{1}{3}$	$\frac{1}{9}$
J	1.5	3	4.5	3	$\frac{1}{2}$	$\frac{1}{4}$
K	1	3	5	3	$\frac{2}{3}$	$\frac{4}{9}$

Becky would like to know the probability that the move will be completed within 22 weeks.

The analysis proceeds as follows:

1. Let T equal the total time that will be taken by the activities on the critical path.

2. Find the probability that the value of T will turn out to be less than or equal to any specified value of interest. In particular, for Becky's project we would find Prob $\{T \leq 22\}$. A good approximation for this probability is easily found if two assumptions hold.

   a. *The activity times are independent random variables.* This is a valid assumption for most PERT networks and seems reasonable for Becky's problem. There is no reason to believe that the time to construct the interior should depend on the design time, etc.

   b. *The random variable T has an approximately normal distribution.* This assumption relies on the *central limit theorem*, which in broad terms states that the sum of independent random variables is approximately normally distributed.

Now recalling that our goal is to find $P\{T \leq 22\}$, where T is the time along the critical path, we will want to convert T to a standard normal random variable and use Table T.1 at the end of the text to find $P\{T \leq 22\}$. The first step in this process is to find the standard deviation of T. To do this we need the variance of T. When the activity times are independent, we know that the variance of the total time along the critical path equals the sum of the variances of the activity times on the critical path. Thus, for Becky's problem

$$\text{var } T = \begin{pmatrix} \text{variance for} \\ \text{activity B} \end{pmatrix} + \begin{pmatrix} \text{variance for} \\ \text{activity C} \end{pmatrix} + \begin{pmatrix} \text{variance for} \\ \text{activity D} \end{pmatrix} + \begin{pmatrix} \text{variance for} \\ \text{activity E} \end{pmatrix}$$

Using the numerical values in Figure 10.18 yields

$$\text{var } T = 1 + \tfrac{1}{9} + \tfrac{4}{9} + 4 = \tfrac{50}{9}$$

Finally,

$$\text{std. dev. } T = \sqrt{(\text{var } T)} = \sqrt{50}/3 = 2.357$$

We now proceed to convert T to a standard normal random variable in the usual way. Recalling that 20 weeks is the mean (i.e., the expected completion time), we see that the distance from the mean to 22 weeks is

$$(22 - 20)/2.357 = 0.8485$$

standard deviations. If we consult Table T.1 at the end of the text for the area under a normal curve from the left-hand tail to a point 0.8485 standard deviations above the mean, we find that the answer is about 0.80. Thus, there is about an 80% chance that the critical path will be completed in less than 22 weeks.

This analysis shows how to shed light on the second of the questions asked in the introduction. In particular, it shows how to find the probability that the *critical path* will be finished by *any* given time. It illustrates the importance of considering the variability in individual activity times when considering overall project completion times. The analysis for Becky's problem indicates that, using expected time as our "real-world forecast," the expected project duration will be 20 weeks and, if so, it will be completed 2 weeks ahead of the desired date. The analysis of uncertainty above sheds additional light on this estimate. It shows a significant probability (i.e., $0.2 = 1 - 0.8$) that *the critical path* will not be completed by the desired completion date. The implication is that there is *at least* a probability of 0.2 that the overall project may not be completed by the desired date. The modifier "at least" has been employed because of the following complicating factor: Because of randomness, some other path, estimated as being non-critical, may in reality take longer to complete than the purported critical path.

——— 10.5
A MID-CHAPTER SUMMARY

Required PERT Inputs

Using the PERT approach the analyst must provide the following inputs:

1. A list of the activities that make up the project.
2. The immediate predecessors for each activity.
3. The expected value for each activity time [using $t = (a + 4m + b)/6$].
4. The standard deviation for each activity time [using $t = (b - a)/6$].

The PERT estimation procedure uses pessimistic, most likely, and optimistic estimates of the activity time to obtain the expected value and the standard deviation for each activity. The standard deviation is required only if the analyst wishes to make probability statements about completing the project by a certain date.

The analysis uses the inputs listed above to

PERT Outputs

1. Calculate the critical path.
2. Calculate the minimum expected time in which the project can be completed.
3. Show slack values for each activity, together with the latest expected time that any activity can start (or finish) without delaying the project.
4. Calculate the probability that the current critical path will be completed by a specified date if estimates of the standard deviation are provided.

If the project cannot (or is unlikely to) be completed by a desired date, the project must be redefined either by

PERT and Planning

1. Strategic analysis, in which the project network is modified by introducing new activities or changing the relationships between existing activities, or
2. Tactical analysis, in which activity times are changed by the application of additional resources.

PERT and Control

Finally, we can observe that PERT is not only a planning system. You can now see that it can also be used to monitor the progress of a project. Management can compare the actual activity times as they occur with those that were used in the planning process. If, for example, activity B took 6 or 7 weeks, rather than the 5 weeks used in the network diagram, Becky would know that the project is behind schedule. This would give her the opportunity to arrange to assign more resources to some other activity on the critical path in an effort to shorten that activity and hopefully meet the desired overall due date.

Identification of the critical path and prompt reporting give management a powerful tool to deal with the difficult problem of bringing a complicated project in on schedule.

CPM AND TIME–COST TRADE-OFFS

As we have just seen, PERT provides a useful approach to the analysis of scheduling problems in the face of *uncertainty about activity times*. Such uncertainty will often be the case with new or unique projects where there is little previous time and cost experience to draw upon. In other types of projects there may be considerable historical data with which one may make good estimates of time and resource requirements. In such cases it may be of interest to deal more explicitly with costs in the sense of analyzing possibilities to shift resources in order to reduce completion time. The concept that there is a trade-off between the time that it takes to complete an activity and the cost of the resources devoted to that activity is the basis of a model that was originally part of the CPM method.

The model assumes that cost is a linear function of time. Consider, for example, Figure 10.19. This figure illustrates that management has the opportunity to aim at an activity time anywhere between a minimum value and a maximum value. The choice of an activity time implies an activity cost as specified by the diagram.

Given the availability of such a time–cost trade-off function for each activity in the project, management has the opportunity to select each activity time (within limits) and incur the associated cost. Clearly, the choice of individual activity times affects the project completion time. The question becomes: "What activity times should be selected to yield the desired project completion time at minimum cost?" The CPM approach to answering this question will be presented in the context of the creation of a financial analysis package by the Operations Analysis Group at Global.

A Financial Analysis Project for Retail Marketing

In addition to the move to Des Moines, Becky is responsible for a new financial analysis package that will be used in the retail marketing section of Global. The program is used in evaluating potential outlets (gas stations) in terms of location and other characteristics. The systems design is complete. The computer programming must still be done and the package must be introduced to the retail marketing section.

Figure 10.20 shows the activity list and network diagram for this project. The time shown is termed the *normal time*. This corresponds to the maximum time shown in Figure 10.19. Recall that we are here assuming that activity times can be estimated with good accuracy, and hence "normal time" is a known quantity. From Figure 10.20 it is

FIGURE 10.19
Time–Cost Trade-Off Function

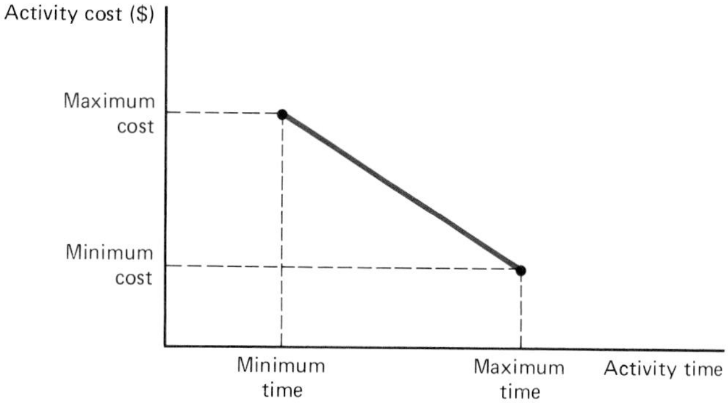

FIGURE 10.20

Activity List and Network Diagram for the
Financial Analysis Project

ACTIVITY	IMMEDIATE PREDECESSOR	NORMAL TIME (HR)
DIP (Design Information Processor)	—	32
WIP (Write Information Processor)	DIP	40
DAP (Design Analysis Package)	—	50
WAP (Write Analysis Package)	DAP	24
INT (Introduce System)	WIP, WAP	120

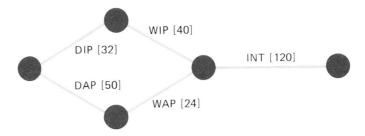

clear that the longest path through the network is DAP–WAP–INT and hence this is
the critical path. The earliest completion time for the project is 194 hours.

The CPM system is based on four pieces of input data for each activity:

**Required
Activity Data**

1. *Normal time:* the maximum time for the activity.
2. *Normal cost:* the cost required to achieve the normal time.
3. *Crash time:* the minimum time for the activity.
4. *Crash cost:* the cost required to achieve the crash time.

These data for the financial analysis project are presented in the first four columns
of Figure 10.21. The fifth column shows the maximum crash hours, defined by

$$\text{Max crash hours} = \text{normal time} - \text{crash time}$$

FIGURE 10.21

Time–Cost Data for the Financial
Analysis Project

ACTIVITY	(1) NORMAL TIME	(2) NORMAL COST	(3) CRASH TIME	(4) CRASH COST	(5) MAXIMUM CRASH HOURS	(6) COST PER CRASH HOUR
DIP	32	$640	20	$800	12	$13.33
WIP	40	480	30	720	10	24.00
DAP	50	1000	30	1200	20	10.00
WAP	24	288	15	360	9	8.00
INT	120	4800	70	5600	50	16.00
TOTAL		$7208				

FIGURE 10.22

Time–Cost Trade-Off Function for DIP

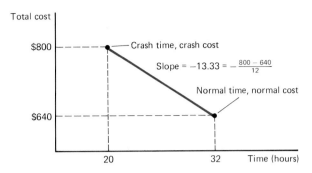

Figure 10.22 shows how these data are used to create the time–cost trade-off function for activity DIP, design the information processor.

Note that, according to Figure 10.21, using all normal times leads to a total project cost of $7208. Also note that the last column in Figure 10.21 shows how much it costs per hour (as computed in Figure 10.22) to reduce each activity time beneath its normal time. In CPM jargon, the process of reducing an activity time is called *crashing*. For example, management could choose to have DIP completed in 31 hours, rather than the normal 32 hours, for a marginal cost of $13.33. The normal time of 32 hours costs $640 and a time of 31 hours would therefore cost $640 + 13.33 = $653.33.

Crashing the Project

We have noted that, using only the normal time for each activity, the earliest completion time for this project is 194 hours (along the critical path DAP–WAP–INT). Management is now in a position to determine the minimum-cost method of reducing this time to specified levels. To reduce the project time to 193, Becky would crash an activity on the critical path by 1 hour. Since it costs less per hour to crash WAP than either of the other two activities on the critical path ($8 < $10 and $8 < $16), Becky would first crash WAP by 1 hour. This decision yields a project time of 193 hours, a critical path of DAP–WAP–INT, and a total project cost of $7216 = $7208 + $8. If Becky wants to achieve a time of 192 hours, exactly the same analysis would apply and she would crash WAP by another hour and incur a marginal cost of $8.

Crashing to 192 Hours

If Becky has crashed WAP by 2 hours to achieve a project time of 192 hours, and still wants to crash the project by another hour (to achieve 191), the analysis becomes more complicated. Figure 10.23 shows the situation. The dollar figure in the diagram is

FIGURE 10.23

Marginal Costs of Crashing the
Financial Analysis Project

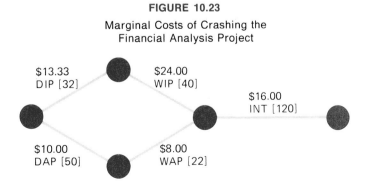

the marginal cost of crashing. Note that there are now two critical paths, DIP–WIP–INT and DAP–WAP–INT, and that both require 192. Crashing one of the four activities (DIP, WIP, DAP, or WAP) by 1 hour would bring one path down to 191 hours, but would still leave the project time at 192, since there would still be a critical path of 192 hours. A time of 191 could only be obtained by crashing activities on both paths. If Becky crashed DIP and WAP by 1 hour each it would reduce both paths to 191 hours and it would cost her \$13.33 + \$8.00 = \$21.33. Alternatively, INT could be crashed by 1 hour for a cost of \$16.00. Can you see that there are other alternatives to consider?

Crashing below 192 Hours

Although it is possible to do this sort of marginal cost analysis in any CPM network, it is clear that it would be difficult and tedious to carry it out in a complicated network. This consideration leads us to an LP formulation of the problem.

A Linear Programming Model

The problem of obtaining a specific project time at minimum cost can be formulated as a linear programming problem. Figure 10.24 shows the formulation of the financial analysis problem with a limit of 184 hours on the project time. To understand this formulation, let

The Decision Variables

$$\text{CWIP} = \text{hours crashed on activity WIP}$$

$$\text{ESWIP} = \text{earliest start time for activity WIP}$$

$$\text{EFINT} = \text{earliest finish time for activity INT}$$

The other decision variables follow this same pattern. From these definitions it follows that

The Objective Function

1. The objective function is the total cost of crashing the network. This is the appropriate objective. The cost of completing the project on normal time is already determined. You can think of management's problem as deciding how much (and where) to crash to obtain the desired earliest finish time at minimum additional cost.

2. Rows 2 through 5 establish limits for the earliest start time for activities WIP, WAP, and INT. For example, rewriting row 2 yields

$$\text{ESWIP} \geq 32 - \text{CDIP}$$

We note that since 32 is the normal time for DIP and CDIP is the amount that DIP is crashed, the right-hand side is the time that activity DIP will take after it is crashed. Thus, this constraint states that the earliest start time for WIP must be $\geq$ the modified activity time for DIP. Since DIP is *the only* predecessor for WIP, we know that the earliest start time for WIP is exactly this modified activity time of DIP. You will thus expect to see

$$\text{ESWIP} = 32 - \text{CDIP}$$

The Constraints

A $\geq$ constraint is used rather than an = constraint because, in general, there could be several paths leading into a node and the earliest start time of an activity leaving that node is determined by the entering path that takes the longest time. This is illustrated by rows 4 and 5. Rewriting these constraints yields

$$\text{row 4} \quad \text{ESINT} \geq 40 - \text{CWIP} + \text{ESWIP}$$

$$\text{row 5} \quad \text{ESINT} \geq 24 - \text{CWAP} + \text{ESWAP}$$

Row 4 states that INT cannot start until WIP is complete and row 5 makes a similar statement for WAP. It will often be the case that only one of these will be active in an optimal solution.

FIGURE 10.24

LP Solution of the Financial
Analysis Problem

```
MIN 13.33 CDIP + 24 CWIP + 10 CDAP + 8 CWAP + 16 CINT
SUBJECT TO
    2)  CDIP + ESWIP > = 32
    3)  CDAP + ESWAP > = 50
    4)  CWIP − ESWIP + ESINT > = 40
    5)  CWAP − ESWAP + ESINT > = 24
    6)  CINT − ESINT + EFINT = 120
    7)  CDIP < = 12
    8)  CWIP < = 10
    9)  CDAP < = 20
   10)  CWAP < = 9
   11)  CINT < = 50
   12)  EFINT < = 184


        OBJECTIVE FUNCTION VALUE

            144.000000


VARIABLE          VALUE          REDUCED COST

   CDIP            0.00              5.33
   CWIP            0.00             16.00
   CDAP            0.00              2.00
   CWAP            2.00              0.00
   CINT            8.00              0.00
   ESWIP          32.00              0.00
   ESWAP          50.00              0.00
   ESINT          72.00              0.00
   EFINT         184.00              0.00


ROW               SLACK          DUAL PRICES

    2              0.00             − 8.00
    3              0.00             − 8.00
    4              0.00             − 8.00
    5              0.00             − 8.00
    6              0.00             −16.00
    7             12.00              0.00
    8             10.00              0.00
    9             20.00              0.00
   10              7.00              0.00
   11             42.00              0.00
   12              0.00             16.00
```

FIGURE 10.24 *(continued)*

```
                    SENSITIVITY ANALYSIS
                   OBJ COEFFICIENT RANGES

    VARIABLE     CURRENT      ALLOWABLE     ALLOWABLE
                  COEF        INCREASE      DECREASE

        CDIP     13.33        INFINITY        5.33
        CWIP     24.00        INFINITY       16.00
        CDAP     10.00        INFINITY        2.00
        CWAP      8.00          2.00          5.33
        CINT     16.00          5.33          8.00
       ESWIP      0.00          5.33          8.00
       ESWAP      0.00          2.00          8.00
       ESINT      0.00          5.33          8.00
       EFINT      0.00         16.00        INFINITY


                   RIGHTHAND SIDE RANGES

    ROW          CURRENT      ALLOWABLE     ALLOWABLE
                  RHS         INCREASE      DECREASE

        2         32.00         2.00          7.00
        3         50.00         7.00          2.00
        4         40.00         2.00          7.00
        5         24.00         7.00          2.00
        6        120.00        42.00          8.00
        7         12.00       INFINITY       12.00
        8         10.00       INFINITY       10.00
        9         20.00       INFINITY       20.00
       10          9.00       INFINITY        7.00
       11         50.00       INFINITY       42.00
       12        184.00         8.00         42.00
```

3. Row 6 is the definition of earliest finish time for activity INT:

$$EFINT = ESINT + \underbrace{120 - CINT}_{\substack{\text{activity time for} \\ \text{INT after crashing}}}$$

4. Rows 7 through 11 limit the amount of crashing on each activity. The limit is given by column (5) in Figure 10.21 "Maximum Crash Hours."

5. Row 12 sets an upper limit on the project time we want to achieve. This constraint depends on the fact that the finish time for activity INT determines the finish time for the overall project. In general, a similar constraint would be required for each activity leading into the terminal node. Here we have only one such activity, INT.

The Solution   The solution shows that WAP should be crashed by 2 hours and INT by 8 hours to achieve a minimum cost reduction of 10 hours in the project completion time (i.e., the optimal value of EFINT is 184 and this is the project completion time). As usual with LP output, however, this is only a small part of the information available. For example, the dual price on row 12 tells us that it will cost $16 to crash the network for 1 additional hour. The right-hand-side ranges show that this rate of $16 per hour holds for another 42 hours. In this simple problem you can see that this next 42 hours of crashing (beyond the first 10) should be done on INT. In general this type of LP sensitivity information can provide useful guidance to management in the attempt to control the progress of large projects.

In concluding this section, we recall the sixth of the questions raised in Section 10.1: "How might I effectively concentrate resources on activities in order to speed up project completion?" In this section we have seen that in a context where time and costs are suitably defined, as in the CPM model, *project crashing* allows management to answer this question.

We now proceed to discuss the final question raised in Section 10.1: "What controls can be exercised on the flows of expenditures on the various activities throughout the duration of the project in order that the overall budget can be adhered to?"

—— 10.7
PROJECT COST MANAGEMENT: PERT/COST

The desirability of a project typically depends on its total costs and revenues. (Discounting may be necessary to express costs and/or returns in current dollars if the project is of long duration.) Once a project has been selected, effective cost management includes two important functions: planning and control.

Planning Costs for the Credit Card Project: the PERT/Cost System

Large projects can strongly influence the financial situation within a firm. The need to pay for the various activities creates a demand on both the firm's overall budget and the daily cash flow. Obviously, the times at which activities are scheduled determines when budget demands occur.

It is important for a firm to be able to anticipate budget demands in order to be able to handle them economically and effectively. The PERT/Cost system is specifically designed to help management anticipate such demands in a clear and consistent manner. PERT/Cost is essentially an alternative approach to cost accounting. Typically, cost accounting systems are organized on a cost center basis (e.g., by departments). The PERT/Cost system is organized on a project basis, where the basic elements of control are the activities.

In order to apply the PERT/Cost system to the project of moving the credit card operation to Des Moines, Becky must now complete Figure 10.8 by filling in the final column, titled "Resources." This is an estimated or "expected" total cost of completing each activity. These expected activity costs, together with the expected activity times, the earliest start time, and the latest start time, are presented in Figure 10.25 for the redefined credit card project. The earliest start and latest start data are taken from the computer solution, Figure 10.16.

Uniform Expenditure Assumption

The goal of the PERT/Cost system is to construct a graph of budget demands over time. This requires knowledge of how funds will be spent throughout the life of an activity. For example, the demands on the budget are different if the $32,000 for activity E, construct the interior, is due at the beginning of the 8-week activity time or at the end of it. PERT/Cost makes the assumption that expenditures occur uniformly

FIGURE 10.25

Resource Requirements for the
Redesigned Project

ACTIVITY	EXPECTED TIME	EARLIEST START	LATEST START	TOTAL RESOURCES REQUIRED
A	3	0	5	$ 2,100
B	5	0	0	5,000
C	3	5	5	1,800
D	4	8	8	4,800
E	8	12	12	32,000
F	2	8	11	1,000
G	4	10	13	2,800
H	2	10	18	7,000
I	5	5	15	4,000
J	3	14	17	30,000
K	3	10	14	1,500
Total				$92,000

End of Week Assumption

throughout the life of the activity; that is, for E a budget demand of $4000 occurs during each of the 8 weeks.

Figure 10.26 shows the budget demands by time if all activities start at their *earliest start time*. This table is constructed by assigning a row to each activity and recording the budget demands for that activity in the appropriate column (week) as determined by the earliest start time. In forming this table, "earliest start" times are interpreted as referring to the end of the appropriate week. Thus activity B starts at time 0 (the end of week 0 = beginning of week 1) and requires 5 weeks to complete. This means that activity C, as shown in Figure 10.26, cannot start until the end of week 5. It lasts 3 weeks and makes a budget demand of $600 per week. This information is summarized in the third row of Figure 10.26.

The total weekly cost is determined by adding down a column, that is, by adding the budget demands during the week from all the activities. For example, the budget demand during the thirteenth week is $5200, the sum of $4000 from E, $700 from G, and $500 from K.

The total project cost is found by cumulating the weekly costs from the beginning of the project. For example, note that the weekly cost is $1700 for each of the first 3 weeks. The total project cost after 3 weeks is therefore $5100. The total cost at the end of the project (week 20) must, of course, be the total cost for the entire project.

Figure 10.27 creates the profile of budget demands over time if each activity starts at its *latest start time*.

The information from Figures 10.26 and 10.27 is combined in Figure 10.28. The upper line is a plot of the earliest start time costs from Figure 10.26 and the lower line is a plot of the latest start time costs from Figure 10.27. The shaded area between the lines shows the area of feasible cumulative budgets for total project costs if the project is completed on time. The fact that the actual budget demands must fall within the envelope created by the earliest start time and the latest start time makes it easy for management to anticipate its cumulative expenditures. For example, Becky can see that by the end of week 12 Global Oil will have to have spent between $14,200 and $28,100.

We have progressed step-by-step through the budget calculations for the PERT/Cost planning system because this is a useful exercise from the pedagogical point of

FIGURE 10.26

Budget Demands: Earliest Start Time

ACTIVITY	WEEK																			
	1	2	3	4	5	6	7	8	9	10	11	12	13	14	15	16	17	18	19	20
A	700	700	700																	
B	1,000	1,000	1,000	1,000	1,000															
C						600	600	600												
D									1,200	1,200	1,200	1,200								
E													4,000	4,000	4,000	4,000	4,000	4,000	4,000	4,000
F									500	500										
G											700	700	700	700						
H											3,500	3,500								
I						800	800	800	800	800										
J															10,000	10,000	10,000			
K											500	500	500							
Weekly Cost	1,700	1,700	1,700	1,000	1,000	1,400	1,400	1,400	2,500	2,500	5,900	5,900	5,200	4,700	14,000	14,000	14,000	4,000	4,000	4,000
Cumulative Project Cost	1,700	3,400	5,100	6,100	7,100	8,500	9,900	11,300	13,800	16,300	22,200	28,100	33,500	38,000	52,000	66,000	80,000	84,000	88,000	92,000

465

FIGURE 10.27
Budget Demands: Latest Start Time

ACTIVITY	1	2	3	4	5	6	7	8	9	10	11	12	13	14	15	16	17	18	19	20
A						700	700	700												
B	1,000	1,000	1,000	1,000	1,000															
C						600	600	600												
D									1,200	1,200	1,200	1,200								
E													4,000	4,000	4,000	4,000	4,000	4,000	4,000	4,000
F												500	500							
G														700	700	700	700			
H																			3,500	3,500
I																800	800	800	800	800
J																		10,000	10,000	10,000
K															500	500	500			
Weekly Cost	1,000	1,000	1,000	1,000	1,000	1,300	1,300	1,300	1,200	1,200	1,200	1,700	4,500	4,700	5,200	6,000	6,000	14,800	18,300	18,300
Cumulative Project Cost	1,000	2,000	3,000	4,000	5,000	6,300	7,600	8,900	10,100	11,300	12,500	14,200	18,700	23,400	28,600	34,600	40,600	55,400	73,700	92,000

WEEK

FIGURE 10.28
Cumulative Budget Demands Versus Time

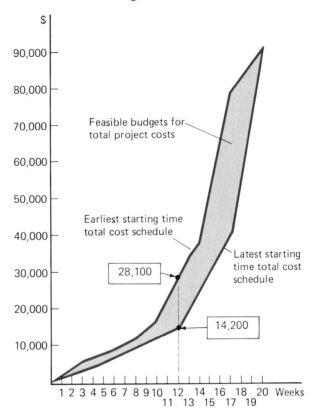

view. In practice these calculations are typically done on a computer. Figure 10.29 shows the computer output that corresponds to Figures 10.26 and 10.27.

Controlling Project Costs

The concept behind any control system is to compare the *actual performance* with *planned performance* and to take remedial action if it is necessary. The thermostat in your house is a control system that operates continuously in time by comparing the actual temperature to the desired temperature and turning the furnace (air conditioner) off or on as necessary.

The PERT/Cost system compares actual project costs to budgeted project costs at regular intervals so that management has an early indication if the project is not proceeding according to plan. Management is then in a position to take appropriate action.

The PERT/Cost Control Report

Figure 10.30 is a PERT/Cost *control report* prepared 11 weeks after the start of the redefined project to move the credit card operation to Des Moines. The labels on the columns indicate how the report is prepared. Column (4), the actual cost, and column (3), the budgeted cost, provide the basic information used in the control function. The actual cost, column (4), is self-explanatory. *The budgeted cost, column (3), is calculated on the assumption that the percentage of budget used up by an activity is the same as the percentage of that activity that is completed.* Thus, when an activity is 50% complete, its budgeted cost is 50% of the entire budget [column (2)] for that activity. Note that

FIGURE 10.29
Computer Analysis of Budget Demands

RESOURCE USAGE PROFILE ACCORDING TO EARLIEST START TIME

TIME INTERVAL   RESOURCE USAGE

FROM END OF WEEK	TO END OF WEEK	WEEKLY	CUMULATIVE
0.00 →	3.00	1700.00	5100.00
3.00 →	5.00	1000.00	7100.00
5.00 →	8.00	1400.00	11300.00
8.00 →	10.00	2500.00	16300.00
10.00 →	12.00	5900.00	28100.00
12.00 →	13.00	5200.00	33300.00
13.00 →	14.00	4700.00	38000.00
14.00 →	17.00	14000.00	80000.00
17.00 →	20.00	4000.00	92000.00

RESOURCE USAGE PROFILE ACCORDING TO LATEST START TIME

TIME INTERVAL   RESOURCE USAGE

FROM END OF WEEK	TO END OF WEEK	WEEKLY	CUMULATIVE
0.00 →	5.00	1000.00	5000.00
5.00 →	8.00	1300.00	8900.00
8.00 →	11.00	1200.00	12500.00
11.00 →	12.00	1700.00	14200.00
12.00 →	13.00	4500.00	18700.00
13.00 →	14.00	4700.00	23400.00
14.00 →	15.00	5200.00	28600.00
15.00 →	17.00	6000.00	40600.00
17.00 →	18.00	14800.00	55400.00
18.00 →	20.00	18300.00	92000.00

if an activity is completed, the entry in column (1) is 100 and this means the entry in column (3) will be the same as the entry in column (2). Consider, for example, activity A, "select office site." We see from column (1) of Figure 10.30 that this activity, by the end of week (11), is 100% complete. Thus, its budgeted cost, column (3), is equal to its entire budget [column (2)] of $2100. Since its actual cost is $2300, there is a cost overrun of $200. This number is recorded in the last column. A similar interpretation applies to activity I, "make financial arrangements." It is 20% complete and has a budget of $4000; thus, its budgeted cost is $800 ($800 = 0.20 × $4000). Since only $500 has been spent, there is a budget surplus of $300. The parentheses in the last column indicate a budget surplus.

FIGURE 10.30
Project Costs After 11 Weeks

ACTIVITY	(1) PERCENT COMPLETE	(2) BUDGET	(3) [(1)/100] × (2) BUDGETED COST TO DATE	(4) ACTUAL COST TO DATE	(5) (4)−(3) COST OVERRUN TO DATE
A	100	2,100	2,100	2,300	200
B	100	5,000	5,000	4,900	(100)
C	100	1,800	1,800	1,800	0
D	75	4,800	3,600	4,600	1,000
E	0	32,000	0	0	0
F	100	1,000	1,000	1,200	200
G	25	2,800	700	1,400	700
H	50	7,000	3,500	5,400	1,900
I	20	4,000	800	500	(300)
J	0	30,000	0	0	0
K	0	1,500	0	0	0
Total		92,000	18,500	22,100	3,600

In this situation, since activities A and F are already completed, their cost overruns cannot be corrected. However, activities D, G, and H, none of which are yet complete, are showing significant overruns to date and these activities should be promptly reviewed. This type of periodic managerial intervention is often required to keep the total project cost within the budget.

Potential Implementation Problems

Although PERT/Cost can provide an effective control procedure, it is well to be aware of potential implementation problems. For example, the required recording of data can involve significant clerical effort, especially when many projects with many activities are underway. Moreover, some costs, such as overhead, may be common to several activities. The allocation of such common costs can be problematic. Finally, as we mentioned at the beginning of Section 10.7, the PERT/Cost system differs in organization from typical cost accounting systems. The typical departmental cost center orientation needs to be substantially revised to handle the PERT/Cost activity–oriented system. Such redesign may be politically as well as materially expensive.

10.8
NOTES ON IMPLEMENTATION

Some 25 years after its inception, the critical path concept is an important part of current practice. Almost anytime you have a large project with a number of interrelated activities, you will find a network-based planning and reporting system being used. Over time, the distinctions between PERT and CPM have become blurred. Firms have developed their own internal computer-based models incorporating those features of the original PERT and CPM systems that are important to their specific activity.

It is common to think of using critical path methods on large one-of-a-kind projects (e.g., the U.S. space shuttle). However, the methods can and do apply to activities that occur at quite regular intervals. A good example of such an activity is the major overhaul of the dragline in a particular coal mining operation. This maintenance must be performed on a fairly regular schedule and is of major importance because when the dragline is not operating, the mine is not operating. The firm can and does use the network for the previous overhaul in planning for an upcoming overhaul. The network plays an important role in assuring that all those involved understand the various steps and their interrelationship, as well as ensuring that all of the requisite parts and materials are available when they are needed. Given the turnover in personnel, and human frailties, the network serves as a convenient way to capture past experience. The activities associated with the overhaul vary from time to time, so the chart must be reworked, but the previous version generally provides a good starting point.

For our example firm, estimating time variability is not an important part of creating their PERT–CPM network. Indeed, they rely on a single best estimate rather than the three that are part of the PERT approach. The crucial element in developing an economical plan for the overhaul is the availability of various craftsmen (electricians, pipefitters, etc.). Each time an overhaul is to be performed, the tasks vary somewhat and thus the demand for various craftsmen varies from year to year. In addition, the supply of available craftsmen within the firm varies from time to time depending on the level of other activities. The planning operation typically involves running the model under a variety of assumptions. Alternatives might include regular employees working regular time, regular employees doubling up (i.e., working two shifts), bringing in outside workers, and so on. Such calculations can make it clear that it pays to spend $20,000 in overtime for electricians if it puts the mine back in operation a day earlier.

Impact of the Computer

The computer has had a major impact on the use of CPM and PERT. Large construction projects may require 1000 or more nodes. In the 1960s it was not unusual to find the network diagram for such a project spread out over three walls of a room that was dedicated to that purpose for the duration of the project. Major changes in the plan were a major pain in their own right and communication among the multiple contractors was cumbersome. The computer has changed all of that. The analysis is now done on a computer. Multiple runs spanning the life of the project are the order of the day. In the early phases it is important to ensure that orders for major components are placed early enough. Complicated systems (i.e., generators, furnaces, etc.) may have a delivery time of several years. Regular updating based on supplier reports enables management to see when it is necessary to expedite an order. New information is fed into the model and the program rerun on a weekly basis. Obviously, the information obtained from such runs influences the allocation of resources. It may even affect the design of the project. If a cost control report more or less like the one shown in Figure 10.30 indicates serious cost overruns early enough, later parts of the project may be redesigned. For example, one firm reported reworking the heating plant design based on one boiler rather than two after the cost of excavation and driving piles ran far ahead of budget. This change enabled the firm to bring the project in on time *and* budget.

10.9
SUMMARY

This chapter deals with the role of PERT and CPM in project management. The fundamental concept is to represent a project as a network. Section 10.2 shows how to use an activity list to construct a network diagram for a project, where the activity list identifies each activity in the project and its immediate predecessors. Section 10.3 shows how the network diagram and the expected activity times are used to determine the critical path, which is a longest path through the network. In the process, the terms "earliest start time," "earliest finish time," "latest start time," "latest finish time," and "slack" are defined.

Section 10.4 introduces the notion of variability in activity times. It deals with two main topics: the PERT system of estimating times and the probability that all the activities on the critical path will be completed by a specified date. The PERT system of estimating time is based on the assumption that activity time has a beta distribution. It uses an optimistic, a most probable, and a pessimistic time estimate to derive the expected activity time and the standard deviation of the activity time.

Management would like to know the probability that the project under consideration will be completed by a specific date. If one assumes that activity times are independent and that the sum of the activity times on the critical path has a normal distribution, it is a straightforward exercise to calculate *the probability that the critical path will be completed by a specified date*. This is not the probability that the project will ultimately be completed by the specified date, for the effect of randomness could turn a supposedly noncritical path into a critical one. However, this does give us an upper estimate for the probability that the overall project will be completed by a specific date.

Section 10.6 presents the CPM framework for analyzing the problem of time–cost trade-offs. The amount of time that an activity takes is determined by the level of resources devoted to that activity. The model in this section employs the notion of project crashing. The model is intended to help management select a completion time for each activity so as to achieve a specified completion date for the overall project at minimum cost. The basic input for the model is a set of functions, one for each activity. Each function portrays the activity cost as a linear function of activity time within specified limits on the time. These data are then used either in a marginal cost analysis or in a linear programming model to select the best activity times.

Section 10.7 considers project cost management via the PERT/Cost system. It deals with both a cost planning and a cost control model. The planning model produces a graph of the feasible budget demands as a function of time. This graph is constructed from the resource usage profiles based on the earliest start time and the latest start time.

The project cost control model is a system of comparing actual costs to budgeted costs. The budgeted cost model uses the assumption that for partially completed activities the budgeted cost is equal to the budget for the completed activity multiplied by the proportion of the activity that has been completed. The model allows management to recognize cost overruns on various activities before they are completed.

_____ 10.10
KEY TERMS

PERT. An acronym for Program Evaluation Review Technique, a method for scheduling and controlling projects.

CPM. An acronym for Critical Path Method, a method for scheduling and controlling projects.

ACTIVITY. A job that must be completed as part of a project, signified by a branch in a PERT network.

EVENT. The completion of all activities leading into a node in a PERT network.

NODE. A circle in a PERT network indicating the completing of certain activities and the initiation of others.

BRANCH. A line in a PERT network indicating an activity.

PATH. A sequence of activities leading from one node to another.

CRITICAL PATH. A sequence of activities that determines a longest path through the network. which yields the minimum time in which an entire project can be completed.

IMMEDIATE PREDECESSORS.   Those activities that must be completed immediately prior to the start of the activity in question.

ACTIVITY LIST.   A list of the jobs in a project with their immediate predecessors, expected times, and resources required.

NETWORK DIAGRAM.   A graphical method of representing a project with nodes and arcs.

DUMMY ACTIVITY.   An imaginary activity that requires no time and is used either (i) to maintain the appropriate precedence relationships in a PERT network diagram, or (ii) as required by some computer programs when two activities both leave the same node and then both terminate at another node.

EARLIEST START TIME.   In a PERT network, the earliest moment at which an activity can start.

LATEST START TIME.   In a PERT network, the latest moment at which an activity can start without delaying completion of the overall project.

EARLIEST FINISH TIME.   In a PERT network, the earliest moment at which an activity can be completed.

EARLIEST FINISH TIME.   00:01 A.M.

LATEST FINISH TIME.   The latest time at which an activity can be completed without delaying the completion of the overall project.

SLACK.   The time that an activity can be delayed beyond its earliest start time without delaying the completion of the overall project.

OPTIMISTIC TIME.   The time required to complete an activity if everything goes perfectly.

MOST PROBABLE TIME.   The time required to complete an activity under normal circumstances.

PESSIMISTIC TIME.   The time required to complete an activity under the most unfavorable conditions.

BETA DISTRIBUTION.   A probability distribution used to model the activity times in PERT.

CRASHING.   A term in the CPM method describing the process of reducing the time required to complete an activity.

PERT/COST.   A system for determining the feasible patterns of cash flow during a project.

NORMAL TIME.   In CPM, the maximum time for completion of an activity, corresponding to minimal resource usage.

CRASH TIME.   In CPM, the minimum possible time for completion of an activity, corresponding to maximal resource concentration.

MAJOR CONCEPTS QUIZ _____

True–False

1. **T F**   In a PERT network diagram, each activity is represented by a circle called a node.

2. **T F**   The term "event" is used to refer to nodes in a PERT network.

3. **T F**   A dummy activity is required in a correct network representation of the following activity list.

ACTIVITY	IMMEDIATE PREDECESSORS
1	—
2	—
3	1
4	2, 3
5	2
6	5

4. **T F**   The earliest finish time for an activity depends on the earliest finish time for the project.

5. **T F** The latest finish time for an activity depends on the earliest finish time for the project.

6. **T F** All activities on the critical path have their latest finish time equal to their earliest start time.

7. **T F** A strategic analysis of a PERT network concentrates on the allocation of resources to reduce the time on the critical path.

8. **T F** The probability of completing the project by time T is equal to the probability of completing the critical path by time T.

9. **T F** The standard deviation of an activity time is estimated as $(b - a)/6$, where b is the pessimistic and a is the optimistic time.

10. **T F** The CPM approach to time–cost trade-offs assumes that cost is a linear function of time.

11. **T F** The LP formulation of the network crashing problem minimizes the total cost of crashing subject to an upper bound on project duration.

12. **T F** In the PERT/Cost model the earliest starting time total cost schedule always is less than or equal to the latest starting time total cost schedule.

13. **T F** Time variabilities leading to a longer-than-expected total time for the critical path will always extend the project completion date.

14. **T F** If a noncritical activity is delayed more than its slack time, all other factors unchanged, then the project completion date will be extended.

15. **T F** Gantt charts provide useful immediate predecessor information.

Multiple Choice

16. Of all paths through the network, the critical path
   a. has the maximum expected time
   b. has the minimum expected time
   c. has the maximum actual time
   d. has the minimum actual time

17. The earliest start time (ES) for an activity leaving node C
   a. is the Max of the earliest finish times for all activities entering node C
   b. equals the earliest finish time for the same activity minus its expected activity time
   c. depends on all paths leading from the start through node C
   d. all of the above

18. The latest finish time for an activity entering node H
   a. equals the Max of the latest start times for all activities leaving node H
   b. depends on the latest finish time for the project
   c. equals the latest start time minus the activity time for the same activity
   d. none of the above

19. The slack for activity G
   a. equals EF for G − ES for G
   b. equals LF for G − ES for G
   c. equals LS for G − ES for G
   d. none of the above

20. Estimating expected activity times in a PERT network
   a. makes use of three estimates
   b. puts the greatest weight on the most likely time estimate
   c. is motivated by a beta distribution
   d. all of the above

21. The calculation of the probability that the critical path will be completed by time T
   a. assumes that activity times are statistically independent
   b. assumes that total time of the critical path has approximately a beta distribution
   c. requires knowledge of the standard deviation for all activities in the network
   d. all of the above

22. In the CPM time–cost trade-off function
   a. the cost at normal time is 0
   b. within the range of feasible times, the activity cost increases linearly as time increases
   c. cost decreases linearly as time increases
   d. none of the above

23. The marginal cost of crashing a network could change when
   a. the activity being crashed reaches its crash time
   b. the activity being crashed reaches a point where another path is also critical
   c. both a and b

24. Fundamental ideas in the LP network crashing models are
   a. activity time equals normal time + crash time
   b. earliest start time for an activity leaving a node equals the Max of the earliest finish times for activities leaving that node
   c. earliest finish time equals latest finish time minus activity time
   d. none of the above

25. The PERT/Cost model assumes that
   a. each activity achieves its optimistic time
   b. the costs are uniformly distributed over the life of the activity
   c. that activity times are statistically independent
   d. none of the above

26. The PERT/Cost control report
   a. requires a budget for each activity
   b. requires a report on the percentage of completion of each activity
   c. calculates cost overruns
   d. all of the above

Answers							
1. F		8. F		15. F		22. c	
2. T		9. T		16. a		23. c	
3. T		10. T		17. d		24. d	
4. F		11. T		18. b		25. b	
5. T		12. F		19. c		26. d	
6. F		13. T		20. d			
7. F		14. T		21. a			

PROBLEMS

10-1. The Build-Rite Construction Company has identified 10 activities that take place in building a house. They are
   1. Walls and Ceiling (erect the wall frames and ceiling joists).
   2. Foundation (pour the foundation slab).
   3. Roof Timbers (put up the roof timbers).
   4. Roof Sheathing (install roof sheathing over the timbers).
   5. Electrical Wiring (install the electrical wiring).
   6. Roof Shingles (shingle the roof).
   7. Exterior Siding (put on the exterior siding).
   8. Windows (install the window units).
   9. Paint (paint the interior and exterior).
   10. Inside Wall Board (hang the inside wall board).

In addition, the following customs are typically observed:

1. Wiring is done from the interior side of the wall, while the window unit is mounted after the wall frame has been erected.
2. Inside wall board and exterior siding are installed over the window unit.
3. Painting is not begun until the house is watertight.

Make a list showing each activity and its immediate predecessors.

10-2. Quacker Mills hires engineering undergraduates and moves them through six management experiences (activities) to prepare them to be plant managers. There are three disciplines and two positions (starting and advanced) in each discipline. These six activities are shown in Figure 10.31. Further, a person who has not been a production line engineer cannot be a department head, nor can someone who has not been a foreperson be a product line scheduler. Make an activity list showing each activity and its immediate predecessors.

FIGURE 10.31

	DISCIPLINE		
	PLANT ENGINEERING	**LINE SUPERVISION**	**PRODUCTION PLANNING**
Starting	Production Line Engineer ^{1}	Foreperson ^{2}	Assistant Product Line Scheduler ^{3}
Advanced	Plant Engineer ^{4}	Department Head ^{5}	Product Line Scheduler ^{6}

10-3. Construct the network diagram for the house construction system used by Build-Rite Construction Company in Problem 10-1.

10-4. Construct a network diagram for the activities given in Figure 10.32.

FIGURE 10.32

ACTIVITY	IMMEDIATE PREDECESSORS
1	—
2	—
3	1
4	1
5	1
6	2, 5
7	2, 4, 5
8	3
9	6
10	7, 8, 9
11	6
12	7, 8, 9, 11

10-5. Build-Rite has estimated the times given in Figure 10.33 as necessary to complete each of the tasks involved in building a house.

FIGURE 10.33

ACTIVITY NUMBER	ACTIVITY	IMMEDIATE PREDECESSORS	EXPECTED TIME (DAYS)
1	Walls and Ceiling	2	5
2	Foundation	—	3
3	Roof Timbers	1	2
4	Roof Sheathing	3	3
5	Electrical Wiring	1	4
6	Roof Shingles	4	8
7	Exterior Siding	8	5
8	Windows	1	2
9	Paints	6, 7, 10	2
10	Inside Wall Board	8, 5	3

For each activity, define

(a) Earliest start time.

(b) Earliest finish time.

(c) Latest start time.

(d) Latest finish time.

(e) Slack.

In addition, identify the critical path.

10-6. As a project manager, you are faced with the activity network and estimated activity times shown in Figure 10.34. For each activity, define

(a) Earliest start time.

(b) Earliest finish time.

(c) Latest start time.

(d) Latest finish time.

(e) Slack.

In addition, identify the critical path.

FIGURE 10.34

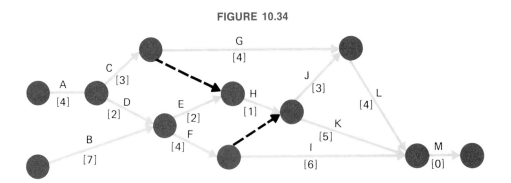

10-7. You are called in as a production consultant. The plant currently uses a PERT–CPM approach to a production run described by the activity network of Figure 10.35.

FIGURE 10.35

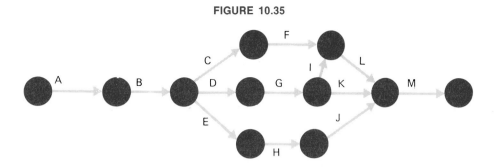

Based on your evaluation, however, the immediate predecessors of each activity are as follows:

ACTIVITY	IMMEDIATE PREDECESSORS
A	—
B	—
C	A
D	B
E	B
F	C
G	D
H	E
I	G
J	E
K	H
L	F
M	L, I, K, J

(a) Draw the revised activity network.

(b) Compute earliest and latest start and finish times for the revised network based on the assumption that each activity takes 1 hour longer than its alphabetic predecessor (i.e., A = 1 hour, B = 2 hours, etc.). Find the slack of each activity. Identify the critical path. How much less time does the production run take under this revised activity network than it did with the original network?

10-8. Consider the network and activity times shown in Figure 10.36. You would like to reduce the minimum time to complete the project. Suppose that you can reduce an activity time as much as you like as long as you increase some other activity or activities by the same amount. For example, you can reduce G by 1 hour if you increase C and D by $\frac{1}{2}$ hour each. Assume that activity times of zero are permissible.

(a) Find the current critical path and the minimum time required to complete the project.

(b) Reallocate times to achieve the minimum possible time to complete the project. Note that in this network, the total of all activity times must equal the current total 20 hours.

FIGURE 10.36

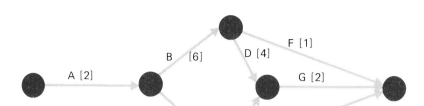

10-9. Based on company history, Build-Rite's management has determined that the optimistic, most probable, and pessimistic times for each activity are as follows:

ACTIVITY NUMBER	ACTIVITY	OPTIMISTIC TIME (DAYS) a	MOST PROBABLE TIME (DAYS) m	PESSIMISTIC TIME (DAYS) b
1	Walls and Ceiling	3	5	7
2	Foundation	2	3	4
3	Roof Timbers	1	2	3
4	Roof Sheathing	1	2	9
5	Electrical Wiring	4	4	4
6	Roof Shingles	4	8	12
7	Exterior Siding	1	3	17
8	Windows	1	2	3
9	Paint	2	2	2
10	Inside Wall Board	2	3	4

Compute the expected activity time and the standard deviation for each activity.

10-10. Based on the activity network shown in Figure 10.37 and the associated activity times given below, compute the expected value and the standard deviation for each activity time. Find the earliest start times, earliest finish times, latest start times, latest finish times, and slack for each activity. Specify the critical path.

FIGURE 10.37

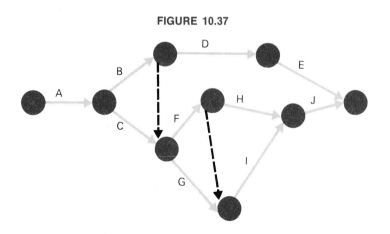

ACTIVITY	OPTIMISTIC	MOST PROBABLE	PESSIMISTIC
A	1	2	3
B	1	3	5
C	2	3	10
D	2	5	8
E	1	2	3
F	1	1	1
G	1	1	1
H	1	3	5
I	2	4	6
J	1	5	9

10-11. Assume that activity times in Build-Rite's activity network (see Problem 10-9) are independent of each other and that the sum of any combination of activity times is normally distributed. What is the probability that all the activities on the current critical path will be completed within 12 days? Within 25 days? Is this the same as the probability that a house will be completed in 25 days? Comment.

10-12. As a project manager, you are faced with the activity network of Figure 10.38 and the associated estimates of optimistic, most probable, and pessimistic activity times shown below.

(a) Compute the expected activity time and standard deviation for each activity time, assuming a unimodal beta probability distribution for each activity time. Identify the critical path and expected time for completion of the project.

(b) Under the usual assumptions find the probability that the activities on the critical path will be completed within 17 weeks.

(c) How many weeks should be allowed to give a 90% probability of completing the critical path on time?

FIGURE 10.38

ACTIVITY	OPTIMISTIC (WEEKS)	MOST PROBABLE (WEEKS)	PESSIMISTIC (WEEKS)
A	2	4	6
B	1	2	3
C	2	4	12
D	1	4	7
E	1	1	1
F	1	3	5
G	2	4	5
H	1	6	11
I	2	2	2

10-13. Build-Rite's engineers have calculated the cost of completing each activity in both normal time and crash time, where the values for normal time and crash time, respectively, correspond to the estimates of expected time and optimistic time from Problem 10-9. Their results follow:

NUMBER	ACTIVITY	NORMAL COST ($)	CRASH COST ($)
1	Walls and Ceiling	50	72
2	Foundation	20	30
3	Roof Timbers	15	30
4	Roof Sheathing	8	20
5	Electrical Wiring	30	30
6	Roof Shingles	13	21
7	Exterior Siding	65	45
8	Windows	45	52
9	Paint	40	40
10	Inside Wall Board	22	34

(a) Specify the normal time, normal cost, crash time, crash cost, maximum crash days, and cost per crash day for each activity. Assume linear cost relationships.

(b) Compute the expected cost of the project (based on normal time).

(c) Suppose that the company has to reduce the completion time by 7 days. How much would this reduction cost? How much would it cost to reduce the completion time by 11 days?

10-14. Consider the activity network in Problem 10-10. The following are estimates of costs for completion in crash time and normal time, where the times correspond to the optimistic and expected time, respectively:

ACTIVITY	CRASH COST ($)	NORMAL COST ($)
A	60	40
B	20	12
C	60	48
D	30	24
E	20	10
F	25	25
G	18	18
H	72	46
I	44	30
J	37	25

(a) Prepare a table showing the normal time, normal cost, crash time, crash cost, maximum crash hours, and cost per crash hour for each activity.

(b) What would be the minimum cost of the project if it were to be completed in
  (i) 15 hours?
  (ii) 12 hours?
  (iii) 10 hours?

(c) Formulate a linear programming model that will assess the additional cost of reducing the completion time to 9 hours.

10-15. Refer to Problem 10-13 and formulate a linear programming model that would allow Build-Rite to assess the cost of crashing its activity network by x hours.

10-16. Consider the activity network and normal activity times shown in Figure 10.39, as well as the following data:

(a) Find the critical path and the minimum time required to complete the project.

(b) Plot a graph showing the required additional costs as project length decreases.

FIGURE 10.39

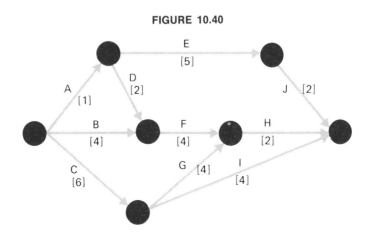

ACTIVITY	COST/CRASH UNIT	MAX. CRASH UNITS
A	10	1
B	—	0
C	5	10
D	10	2
E	20	5
F	10	1

10-17. Use the normal costs from Problem 10-13 and the time data from Problem 10-5 to construct early-start and late-start cost tables and the graph of cumulative expenditures versus time for Build-Rite.

10-18. Figure 10.40 shows the activity network for the Molotov Explosives Company (activity times shown in brackets). Daily activity costs for Molotov Explosives' production process

FIGURE 10.40

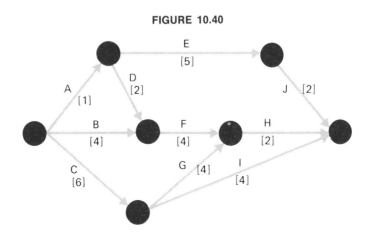

follow:

ACTIVITY	DAILY COST ($)
A	45
B	55
C	70
D	32
E	53
F	27
G	13
H	10
I	15
J	15

Construct early-start and late-start cost tables and a graph of budget demands versus time for a production run. Assume that costs are incurred linearly for each activity.

10-19. Build-Rite's record of historical expenditures at the end of Day 15 is as follows:

ACTIVITY NUMBER	ACTIVITY	COST INCURRED TO DATE ($)
2	Foundation	22
1	Walls and Ceiling	46
3	Roof Timbers	15
4	Roof Sheathing	10
6	Roof Shingles	4.50
5	Electrical Wiring	20
8	Windows	22.50
10	Inside Wall Board	20
7	Exterior Siding	40
9	Paint	0

Evaluate the current project costs based on the assumption that

(a) All activities begin on the earliest possible date and that the expected value is the time required.

(b) All activities begin on the latest possible start date and that the expected value is the time required.

In both cases, assume that budgeted cost is equal to the budget for the completed activity multiplied by the proportion of the activity that is complete.

10-20. Review the data for Molotov Explosives (Problem 10-18). Prepare an analysis of the current production costs if the figures below represent costs incurred at the end of the seventh unit of time. Assume that the budgeted cost is equal to the budget for the completed activity multiplied by the proportion of the activity that is complete. Assume further that all activities are proceeding along the earliest start schedule.

ACTIVITY	COST INCURRED TO DATE ($)
A	$40
B	240
C	450
D	64
E	250
F	115
G	22
H	0
I	10
J	10

10-21. This is a more complex version of Problem 10-8. As the production foreman for the Hurricane Fan Company, you have used PERT–CPM techniques to schedule your production runs. Your current activity network and activity times are shown in Figure 10.41. A production consultant has pointed out that, due to the similarity in job skills needed for each activity, resources are perfectly transferable between activities (i.e., the time required to do an activity can be reduced by any amount by increasing the time required for another job by the same amount). If the consultant is correct, how much can the time needed for each production run be reduced?

FIGURE 10.41

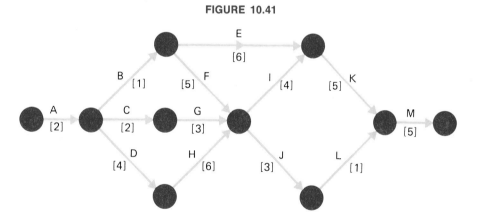

━━━━━━━ APPENDIX 10.1
THE PC APPROACH TO PERT/CPM

The Critical Path Chapter 10 illustrated a computer-based approach to PERT and CPM with systems that are resident on the main frame computer at the University of Chicago. There are a number of PC software packages that can also be used to perform the numerical calculations that accompany a PERT and/or CPM project. This appendix illustrates the use of the QSB software package on these problems. In particular we use QSB to analyze the redefined relocation project as presented in Figure 10.15. The first step is to construct the PERT diagram, and thus Figure 10.15 is reproduced in Figure 10.42 with one important change: In the QSB approach, each activity is defined by the numbers of the nodes at its beginning and end. The software requires that the ending node have a larger number than the starting node. Since this condition is not satisfied in the original definition of the project, the nodes have been renumbered in Figure 10.42.

FIGURE 10.42
Network Diagram for Redefined Project

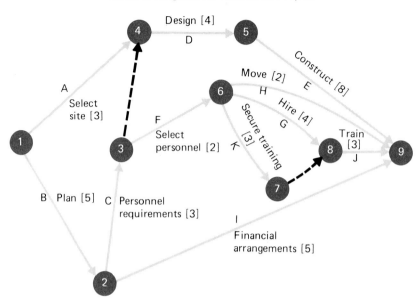

FIGURE 10.43
The QSB Solution

		PERT ANALYSIS FOR GLOBAL						
ACTIVITY NO. NAME		ACTIVITY EXP. TM. VAR.		EARLIEST START	LATEST START	EARLIEST FINISH	LATEST FINISH	SLACK LS-ES
1	B	5.0000	1.0000	0	0	5.0000	5.0000	Critical
2	A	3.0000	0.4444	0	5.0000	3.0000	8.0000	5.0000
3	C	3.0000	0.1111	5.0000	5.0000	8.0000	8.0000	Critical
4	I	5.0000	0.1111	5.0000	15.000	10.000	20.000	10.000
5	D1	0	0	8.0000	8.0000	8.0000	8.0000	Critical
6	F	2.0000	0.4444	8.0000	11.000	10.000	13.000	3.0000
7	D	4.0000	0.4444	8.0000	8.0000	12.000	12.000	Critical
8	E	8.0000	4.0000	12.000	12.000	20.000	20.000	Critical
9	K	3.0000	0.4444	10.000	14.000	13.000	17.000	4.0000
10	G	4.0000	0.6944	10.000	13.000	14.000	17.000	3.0000
11	H	2.0000	0.1111	10.000	18.000	12.000	20.000	8.0000
12	D2	0	0	13.000	17.000	13.000	17.000	4.0000
13	J	3.0000	0.2500	14.000	17.000	17.000	20.000	3.0000

Expected completion time = 20

Critical paths for Global with completion time = 20

CP # 1 : (with variance = 5.555555)

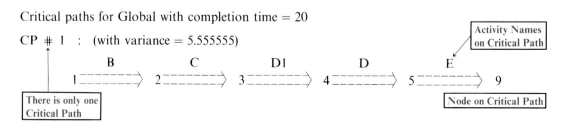

The input and output for the critical path calculation are shown in Figure 10.43. The input and output are easy to read, and no further explanation is required.

Probability of Completing the Project

In order to compute the probability that the critical path will be completed by a specific time with QSB, you are only required to input the expected completion time and the specific completion time. The input and computer output for the redefined Global Oil Project when the specified completion time is 22 weeks are shown in Figure 10.44. Note that the output includes a statement of the conditions under which the probability calculation holds. The probability that the project will be completed in this time is .802. The same results were presented in Section 10.4.

FIGURE 10.44

The QSB Probability Calculation

```
The following probability calculations assume that activities are
independent and that all paths are also independent. They also assume
that your network has a large enough number of activities so as to
enable use of the normal distribution. Therefore, when the activities
are not independent or the number of activities is not large, the
following analysis may be highly biased.
```
                                    You enter
                                    these numbers
```
Expected completion time = 20

What is your project schedule time (type 0 to end analysis)? 22

   On CP # 1 :     Variance = 5.555555    Standard deviation = 2.357023
       Probability of finishing within  22  is  .8019281

The probability of finishing the whole project within 22 is .8019281

Do you want to enter a new scheduled completion time (Y/N)?
```

Crashing

QSB also includes a heuristic approach to the problem of crashing a CPM network. That is, it includes an approach based on an intuitively appealing rule of thumb. This program is used to attack the financial analysis project introduced in Figure 10.20 of Section 10.6. QSB again requires that the nodes be numbered in such a way that each activity is defined by a pair of increasing numbers. Figure 10.45 is a reproduction of Figure 10.20 in which the nodes have been appropriately numbered.

FIGURE 10.45

A Crashing Problem

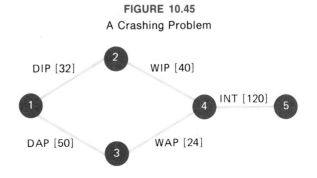

FIGURE 10.46
The QSB Crashing Solution

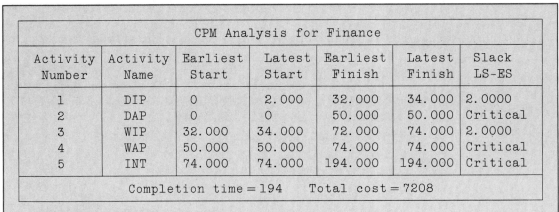

CPM Analysis for Finance						
Activity Number	Activity Name	Earliest Start	Latest Start	Earliest Finish	Latest Finish	Slack LS-ES
1	DIP	0	2.000	32.000	34.000	2.0000
2	DAP	0	0	50.000	50.000	Critical
3	WIP	32.000	34.000	72.000	74.000	2.0000
4	WAP	50.000	50.000	74.000	74.000	Critical
5	INT	74.000	74.000	194.000	194.000	Critical
Completion time = 194 Total cost = 7208						

Critical paths for Finance with completion time = 194
Total cost = 7208

```
CP #  1     :
      DAP            WAP            INT
    1=======> 3=======> 4=======> 5
```
Unique Critical Path

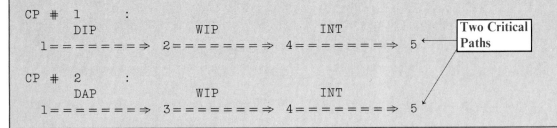

CPM Analysis for Finance						
Activity Number	Activity Name	Earliest Start	Latest Start	Earliest Finish	Latest Finish	Slack LS-ES
1	DIP	0	0	24.000	24.000	Critical
2	DAP	0	0	49.000	49.000	Critical
3	WIP	24.000	24.000	64.000	64.000	Critical
4	WAP	49.000	49.000	64.000	64.000	Critical
5	INT	64.000	64.000	184.000	184.000	Critical
Completion time = 184 Total cost = 7396.667						

Critical paths for Finance with completion time = 184
Total cost = 7396.667

```
CP #  1     :
      DIP            WIP            INT
    1=======> 2=======> 4=======> 5
```
Two Critical Paths
```
CP #  2     :
      DAP            WIP            INT
    1=======> 3=======> 4=======> 5
```

Figure 10.46 shows the input and output from QSB for project completion times of 194 and 184. Recall that 194 is the earliest completion time for the project. We see that the QSB produces a normal cost of $7208 for the project. This corresponds to the result shown in Figure 10.21. However, when the project is crashed to yield a completion time of 184, the heuristic solution used by QSB produces a cost of $7396.67.

The minimum cost to achieve a completion time of 184 is provided by the solution to the LP crashing model presented in Figure 10.24. Here we see that the crashing cost is $144. Adding this amount to the normal cost of $7208 yields a total cost of $7352, which is less than the $7396.67 obtained by QSB. This example thus provides a clear reminder that heuristic approaches are useful rules of thumb and are not guaranteed to yield the optimal solution.

11

INVENTORY CONTROL WITH KNOWN DEMAND

COORDINATING DECISIONS FOR INCREASED PROFITS*

Kelly-Springfield is a major manufacturer of auto and truck tires. This firm operates four factories and produces tires for its own house brands as well as for some 20 private-label customers (department store chains, petroleum companies, auto supply chains, and tire wholesalers). From 1976 to 1979 Kelly expanded its share of the 140-million-unit replacement auto tire industry by nearly 1% and achieved a full 1% increase in the 32-million-unit truck-tire replacement market.

This achievement results in no small part from the improved service provided by a management-science based production and inventory control system. Kelly measures service in terms of the percentage of units shipped within 24 hours of receipt of an order for passenger tires. This percentage steadily increased from 78.5% in 1975 to 85.3% in 1979. This improvement was achieved while average inventory expressed in days' supply decreased from 94.7 days to 78.8 days. Although customer service remained static for truck tires, average inventory decreased from 76.0 to 52.2 days.

* R. H. King, and R. R. Love, Jr., "Coordinating Decisions for Increased Profits," *Interfaces*, 10, no. 6 (December 1980), 4–19.

Assuming a 15% prime and 1978 product prices, total inventory reduction generated annual savings of $2.2 million.

These remarkable results were achieved with a computer and management-science-based "total system" that includes four major components: sales forecasting, inventory control, production planning, and distribution determination. This complex system has been constructed in two major versions over a 12-year horizon. In the second (current) version forecasting for each of the 26,000 stocking units for up to 23 months is done on a top-down manner. In other words Kelly-Springfield sales potential is an assumed share of the projected replacement market, which in turn depends on the national economy, and so on. The inventory control section is based on the reorder point, reorder quantity model with a safety stock. The production planning system uses both linear programming and dynamic programming. The distribution system uses a heuristic based on the transportation model of linear programming to determine factory-to-warehouse shipments and transshipments among warehouses to eliminate critical inventory imbalances.

The total benefits from the system come from many sources. The annual savings of $2.2 million reduced inventory investment was mentioned above. Other annual returns are due to increased productivity ($4.2 million), reduced scrap ($860,000), reduced transfer tonnage ($500,000), and reduced personnel ($175,000). Thus, the total system yields benefits totaling $8.4 million annually. As discussed above, the improved service due to the system has enabled Kelly-Springfield to expand its market share.

———— 11.1
INTRODUCTION

Steco is the country's second largest steel wholesaler. Its main function is to supply various items to customers. In order to do this the key operations are (1) buying items from the producer; (2) holding these items in inventory; and (3) marketing, selling, and distributing these items in response to demand.

Victor Kowalski is a success at Steco. After 18 years in marketing Victor was recently promoted to vice-president of operations. The purchasing, inventory control, and marketing functions are now his responsibility. He is confident of his ability to handle the marketing aspects of his new position, but he feels less secure in his knowledge of inventory control. Since the holding of inventory is a critical part of Steco's business, Victor's inventory-related decisions will have an important effect on his firm's performance and his own career.

From his favorite management science text, Victor learns

What Are Inventories?

1. Inventories are defined as *idle goods in storage*, waiting to be used.

2. There are many types of inventories; for example, inventories of raw materials, inventories of in-process materials, inventories of finished goods, inventories of cash, and even inventories of individuals.

3. Inventories are held for many reasons. Some distributors hold inventory in order to fill quickly an order placed by a customer. Otherwise, in many cases, the customer would order from a competitor. This, however, is only one reason why inventories are held. They are, in fact, held for any of the following reasons:

   a. Inventories smooth out the time gap between supply and demand. For example, the corn crop is harvested in September and October, but user demand for corn (as a raw material for animal feed, corn oil, etc.) is steady throughout the year. Thus, the harvest must be stored in inventory for later use. Users are willing to pay others to worry about storing for the convenience of having the crop available when they need it.

b. The possibility of holding inventory often contributes to lower production costs, for it is more economical to produce some items in large batches even though immediate orders for the items may not exist. One chooses to store the excess in inventory as opposed to producing in a more costly way—that is, a lower but more continuous rate in time.

c. Inventories provide a disguised way of storing labor. For example, in dynamic production problems the availability of labor may be a binding constraint in some later time period but slack in the earlier periods. The possibility of producing excess output in these earlier periods, and carrying the product forward in inventory frees labor in the later periods for alternative uses.

d. Finally, as in Steco's case, inventory is a way of providing quick customer service at the time an item is needed, and customers are willing to pay for this convenience.

4. There are generally three types of costs associated with the inventory activity: *holding costs, ordering costs,* and *stockout costs.*

a. *Holding costs:* One of the smaller items stocked by Steco is a piece of $\frac{3}{10}$-inch-thick high-carbon steel called an "appliance angle." Victor currently observes that there are 3000 appliance angles in stock. Each angle costs Steco $8. Thus, Steco currently has

$$(8) \times (3000) = \$24,000$$

tied up with the inventory of this item. Suppose that Steco were to reduce this inventory to only 1000 items. Instead of $24,000, the investment would be reduced to $8000. It would then be possible to invest some of the $16,000 which is released—in other words, by holding inventory Steco forgoes the opportunity to make other investments. This so-called *opportunity cost* is perhaps the most important contribution to inventory holding cost. The magnitude of this cost is closely tied to the interest rate. As an indication of its importance, consider that since 1970 the prime interest rate has always been above 5% and that in the early 1980s it hovered near 20%.

There are other holding costs, such as breakage, pilferage, insurance, and special handling requirements. *The larger the inventories, the larger the inventory holding costs.*

b. *Ordering costs:* Each time Steco places an order to replenish its inventories an ordering cost is incurred. *This cost is independent of the quantity ordered.* It is related to the amount of time required for paperwork and accounting when an order is placed and is a direct function of the salaries of involved personnel.

c. *Stockout costs:* A stockout means that the firm runs out of inventory. In most technical uses, the term "stockout" refers to the more specific phenomenon that orders arrive after inventory has been depleted. There are, at least in the context of a model, two ways to treat such orders. One way is to save up the orders and fill them later after the inventory has been replenished. This is called *backlogging.* (Note that this is really an *assumption* in a model. In the real world, customers usually get to vote on whether they are willing to wait. The extent to which customers are willing to accept backlogging could be a major factor in determining the appropriateness of a model that makes a backlogging assumption.) Another way to deal with stockouts is simply not to accept any orders received when there is no inventory on hand. Thus, the study of inventory includes models that deal with the possibility of stocking out, and in such a case some models assume backlogging; others assume no backlogging. In either case there is a cost of stocking out. This cost could include the lost profit from not making the sale (in the no-backlogging case); or late delivery (the backlogging case); as well as discounts for a number of more intangible factors, such as the cost of possibly losing the customer, of losing goodwill, and of establishing a poor record of service. In the case of stockouts with no backlogging, we generally use the term *penalty cost*, which means the per unit cost of unsatisfied demand. In the case of stockouts with backlogging we speak of a *backlogging cost*, which means the per unit cost of backlogging demand.

It is obvious to Victor that, for a company such as Steco, with hundreds of thousands of dollars tied up in inventory, there must be a right way and a wrong way to manage the inventory function. The main trade-offs are clear: On one hand, it is good to have inventory on hand to make sure that customers' orders can be satisfied (i.e., to avoid *stockout costs*). On the other hand, carrying inventory implies a *holding cost*. This can be reduced by ordering smaller quantities more often, but this means increased *ordering costs*. These three cost factors must be balanced against each other.

Once the fundamental question of what items to order has been determined, the questions to be answered are the same for all inventory control systems. For every type of item held in inventory, someone must decide (1) *when* a replenishment order should be placed and (2) *how much* should be ordered; that much is easy. Finding good answers to these questions is not. A multitude of factors combine to make this a difficult problem. Some of the most important considerations are

1. The extent to which future demand is known.
2. The cost of stocking out, and management's policy (backlogging or not).
3. The inventory holding and ordering costs.
4. The possibility of long lead times–the period of time between when an order is placed and when the material actually arrives.
5. The possibility of quantity discount purchasing plans.

Victor realizes that he has his work cut out for him and decides to give high priority to a review of Steco's inventory system.

_____ 11.2

STECO WHOLESALING: THE CURRENT POLICY

In getting started, Victor decides to focus on a small but tractable problem, the current inventory policy for appliance angles. This is what he learns: These angles (used in constructing the frames for many home appliances, such as stoves, refrigerators, freezers, etc.) are a high-volume item for Steco. Figure 11.1 shows the monthly demand for appliance angles during the preceding year.

The term *demand* means "orders received." It is not necessarily the same as *sales*. For example, in January of last year 5300 items were demanded. If *at least* 5300 items were in inventory, then sales equaled demand (i.e., sales were 5300). If fewer than 5300 items were in inventory, say only 5000, then sales were 5000, which is less than the demand of 5300, and consequently a stockout occurred.

As a matter of fact, over a period of several years the demand for appliance angles has remained at a steady rate of about 5000 items per month. Based on this fact, management's policy last year was to add 5000 angle irons to inventory each month. Since demand is expected to hold at about the same level in the future, this is the current policy as well. Victor's question remains: "Is this a good policy?"

One way to attempt to answer this question would be to see how well the policy did last year. This turns out *not* to be an easy task. The answer depends on a considerable amount of information that Victor does not have. Consider:

1. Was there a shortage in January? Demand (5300) is larger than the amount ordered (5000). Thus there might have been. But if Steco had at least 300 angles on hand on January 1, there would not have been. Right? Not necessarily! What if the January replenishment of 5000 angles did not show up until January 10 and there was an order for 300 angles on January 5?

FIGURE 11.1
Monthly Appliance Angle Demand

MONTH	DEMAND (UNITS)
January	5,300
February	5,100
March	4,800
April	4,700
May	5,000
June	5,200
July	5,300
August	4,900
September	4,800
October	5,000
November	4,800
December	5,100
Total Annual Demand	60,000
Average Monthly Demand	5,000

2. Holding costs are equally confusing. Suppose that in March the 5000 angles from the producer arrived on March 1 and an order from one of Steco's customers, for 4800 angles, arrived on March 2. The holding cost was very small. On the other hand, if the customer order for the 4800 angles had occurred on March 31, the holding cost would have been much larger.

Victor quickly gives up the task of calculating last year's actual cost. He simply does not have enough information. Instead, he decides to see what the policy of ordering 5000 angles each month *would* cost in an *abstract, idealized* world. In this world Victor assumes that

Simplifying Assumptions

1. Shipments always arrive on the first day of the month.
2. Demand is known and occurs at a constant rate of 5000 units per month.
3. All demand will be satisfied with no backlogging. In other words, stockouts are forbidden.

Victor's incentive for using this *model* is provided by his colleagues. They assure him that *on the average* these assumptions describe rather well the actual circumstances at Steco. He thus decides to use them, realizing that he may have to take the complicating factors of variability and uncertainty into account later. With these assumptions Victor can make a plot of the inventory on hand at any time. Such a plot is shown in Figure 11.2.

FIGURE 11.2
Inventory on Hand, 5000 Order Quantity

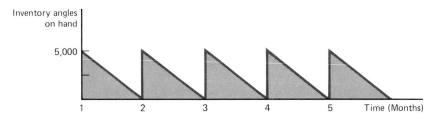

Notice how the inventory jumps up by 5000 units at the beginning of each month when a shipment arrives, and decreases continuously at a constant rate of 5000 items per month (the constant monthly rate of demand). Also notice that a shipment from the producer arrives at the instant the inventory on hand hits zero. Thus, no stockouts occur. Given assumptions 1, 2, and 3, the cost of operating the system shown in Figure 11.2 depends only on *how much new stock is ordered* and on the *holding and ordering costs*. Since in this ideal world there are no stockouts, Victor need not worry about stockout costs. Let us see how the operating cost arises.

Calculating Annual Ordering and Holding Costs

In cooperation with his accountants Victor learns that (1) it costs $25.00 to place an order and (2) it costs $1.92 to hold an angle in inventory for a year. Given his assumptions, Victor is now in a good position to compute, within his model, the annual cost of *ordering 5000* items per month. Since orders are placed with suppliers once a month

$$\text{annual ordering cost} = 12(25) = \$300$$

To calculate the annual holding cost, Victor uses the following logic:

$$\text{average time each item remains in inventory} = \tfrac{1}{2} \text{ month}$$

Expressed in terms of years, then, for each batch

$$\text{average time each item remains in inventory} = \tfrac{1}{24} \text{ year}$$

Since the cost to hold 1 item for 1 year is $1.92, it must follow that for each batch

$$\text{cost to hold 1 item for } \tfrac{1}{24} \text{ year} = (1.92)(\tfrac{1}{24})$$

Thus, for each batch of 5000 items

$$\text{holding cost per batch} = 5000(1.92)(\tfrac{1}{24})$$

Since 12 of these batches are ordered each year

$$\text{annual holding cost} = (12)(5000)(1.92)(\tfrac{1}{24})$$
$$= (2500)(1.92)$$
$$= \$4800$$

Victor's simplifying assumptions and calculations in the idealized world have produced an annual holding cost of $4800. Another derivation may be more intuitive. First note that the average inventory level is one-half of the maximum inventory level when demand is constant (see Figure 11.3). Thus, over the year the average inventory level is

FIGURE 11.3
Inventory on Hand, 5000 Order Quantity

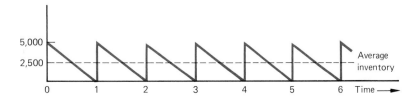

2500 units, and we have

$$\text{annual holding cost} = (\text{average inventory level}) \cdot (\text{holding cost per item per year})$$

$$= (2500) \cdot (1.92) = \$4800$$

Now combining the yearly holding and ordering costs, Victor computes that, in terms of his model, the annual inventory costs for appliance angles are

Total Annual Cost

$$\text{total annual cost} = \text{annual holding cost} + \text{annual ordering cost}$$

$$= 4800 + 300$$

$$= \$5100$$

As we have pointed out, this figure is based on the policy of ordering 5000 items each month. Suppose that he had placed larger orders, say for 10,000 items each time an order was placed. The effects of this change can be seen by comparing Figures 11.3 and 11.4. Note that an order would now be placed every 2 months (i.e., 6 per year) and that the average inventory is 5000 items. The total annual cost would then be computed as follows:

$$\text{total annual cost} = \text{annual holding cost} + \text{annual ordering cost}$$

$$= (5000)(1.92) + 6(25)$$

$$= 9600 + 150$$

$$= \$9750$$

Note that *increasing* the order quantity *increased* the annual holding cost and *decreased* the annual ordering cost.

In contrast, suppose that a policy of ordering 2500 items twice a month was followed. Then the average inventory is 1250 items and 24 orders would be placed each year. In this case

$$\text{total annual cost} = \text{annual holding cost} + \text{annual ordering cost}$$

$$= (1250)(1.92) + (24)(25)$$

$$= 2400 + 600$$

$$= 3000$$

FIGURE 11.4
Inventory on Hand, 10,000 Order Quantity

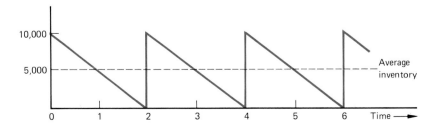

Note that *decreasing* the order quantity *decreased* the annual holding cost and *increased* the annual ordering cost.

Victor now clearly understands the general effect of changing the amount that is ordered. What he wonders is whether the policy followed last year by Steco, and currently being followed, is optimal in the *idealized model*. This policy is to order 5000 units per month. It would appear from the last calculation above that a policy of ordering 2500 items twice a month would be superior. Is there even a better policy?

In his search for the answer to this question, Victor comes across a computer-based inventory control system called ICON.[1] This system is designed to answer two key questions: (1) when to order[2] and (2) how much to order. With reference to the appliance angle policy, this is just what Victor wants to know. When should orders be placed? How much should be ordered?

He decides to explore further this ICON system. He is amazed to discover that this system is based in part on an adaptation of a simple model that he recalls having studied as an undergraduate almost 20 years ago, the *economic order quantity [EOQ] model*. Victor had always thought of it as a textbook model with unrealistic assumptions, a model selected to give a simple and easily taught result. In part, Victor was correct. The EOQ model does ignore a number of important factors. He was, however, wrong in his estimate of its usefulness. This model attempts to balance the cost of placing orders with the cost of holding inventory. In the present appliance angle context, that is just what Victor is looking for. In a larger context, the EOQ model forms the backbone for most of the commercially available computer-based inventory control systems.

As Victor is soon to learn, the ICON system is able to use the EOQ model because it follows a two-step process. First, it uses the EOQ model to answer the "when" and "how much" questions, with or without quantity discounts, and then it modifies these answers to allow for variabilities in demand. The latter topic will be discussed in Chapter 12.

Victor decides to see how this system works by first applying the EOQ model to the trial problem posed above. Would any improvements have been obtained?

———— 11.3
THE ECONOMIC ORDER QUANTITY MODEL

Developing the Model

The EOQ model in its simplest form assumes that

1. No stockouts are allowed. That is, each new order arrives (in totality) as soon as the inventory level hits zero.

EOQ Assumptions

2. There is a constant rate of demand.
3. The relevant costs are ordering and holding costs.

Victor notes that these three assumptions are precisely the assumptions he has already made in his calculation (i.e., using his model) that Steco's annual inventory cost

---

[1] This is a hypothetical system in our scenario that resembles several currently available commercial systems.

[2] We have already seen that, assuming a known rate of demand (5000 items per month), as soon as we choose an order quantity we also implicitly determine how often we order (e.g., once a month, once every 2 months, etc). The "when to order" question has not yet been addressed. It asks *when* we should order, in terms of the level of the current inventory on hand. This will be seen to depend on lead time to delivery.

is $5100. Recall that this cost is based on a policy of adding to the stock 5000 angles each month. The EOQ model will give Victor some feeling for the "goodness" of that policy, for it will calculate the *optimal order quantity*, which is defined to be the quantity that under the three assumptions above *minimizes the total cost per year of ordering appliance angles and holding them in inventory*. It is based on

   1. *Ordering cost = C_0:*   Every time an order is placed, the purchasing department must contact the supplier to determine the current price and delivery time, complete and mail the order form, enter the order into the inventory control system, and initiate the receiving and stock-keeping records. When the order arrives, the receiver must complete the receiving and stock-keeping records and update the order status in ICON. All of this costs money. As we have already seen, Steco estimates the cost of placing an order for appliance angles, *regardless of the number of units ordered*, to be $25. This includes two thirds of an hour of clerk-category labor at $18 per hour for wages and fringe benefits, one third of an hour of an assistant purchasing agent's time at $24 per hour, plus $5 in material, phone, and mailing costs. Thus,

$$C_0 = \tfrac{2}{3}(18) + \tfrac{1}{3}(24) + 5 = \$25$$

   2. *Inventory carrying cost = C_h:*   Every dollar invested in inventory could be put to use elsewhere by Steco. For example, it could be put in a bank or invested in Treasury bills and earn interest for Steco. When a dollar is tied up in inventory, Steco loses the opportunity to invest it elsewhere. This lost opportunity is called the "opportunity cost." Typically, the opportunity cost accounts for a large part of the cost of holding inventory. In addition, there are overhead costs such as rent, light, and insurance that must be allocated to the items in inventory.

   The cost of holding inventory is typically expressed as the cost of holding one unit for one year and is calculated as a percentage of the cost of the item. Steco estimates that the cost of holding an appliance angle in inventory for one year is 24% of its purchase price. The 24% figure can be subdivided into an opportunity cost of 20% plus an overhead allocation per item of 4%. Since each angle costs $8, the cost of holding each item in inventory for one year is

$$C_h = 0.24 \times \$8.00 = \$1.92$$

which is the figure Victor used in his calculations.

The Annual Holding and Ordering Cost   The first step in calculating the optimal (i.e., cost minimizing) order quantity is to derive an expression for the annual holding and ordering cost (AHO) as a function of the order quantity. It consists of two parts, annual ordering cost and annual holding cost.

$$\text{annual ordering cost} = C_0 \cdot (\text{number of orders per year}) \qquad (11.1)$$

Victor notes that if the order quantity is 5000 units, he will place 12 orders a year since the model assumes a total demand of 60,000, and $60,000/5000 = 12$. This leads him to the general formula

$$N = D/Q \qquad (11.2)$$

where N = number of orders per year
         D = annual demand
         Q = order quantity

Thus, in general

$$\text{annual ordering cost} = C_0 N = C_0 D/Q \tag{11.3}$$

To compute the annual holding cost Victor makes use of two facts: (1) the annual holding cost is equal to C_h times the average inventory and (2) the average inventory is equal to one-half of the maximum inventory when demand occurs at a constant rate. Since the order quantity is also the maximum amount of inventory on hand (see Figures 11.3 and 11.4), it follows that

$$\text{annual holding cost} = C_h Q/2 \tag{11.4}$$

If we add together expressions (11.3) and (11.4), we see that the assumptions of the EOQ model have enabled Victor to obtain the following expression for the annual holding and ordering cost as a function of the order quantity Q:

AHO

$$\text{AHO}(Q) = C_0 D/Q + C_h Q/2 \tag{11.5}$$

Since demand occurs at the rate of D units per year, we know that these Q units will be depleted in Q/D years, which is precisely when the inventory level hits the value zero. For example, when $Q = 5000$ and $D = 60,000$, the order of 5000 units is depleted in $5000/60,000 = \frac{1}{12}$ year $= 1$ month, as we have already seen (Figure 11.3). For appliance angles, the relevant values of C_0, D, and C_h can be plugged into expression (11.5) to give annual holding and ordering cost

$$= \text{AHO}(Q) = \$25(60,000/Q) + \$1.92(Q/2) = (1,500,000/Q) + 0.96Q \tag{11.6}$$

When $Q = 5000$ it is seen that

$$\text{AHO}(5000) = \$300 + \$4800 = \$5100$$

which is exactly the result Victor obtained in the previous section. Now, however, using (11.6), Victor can represent the annual holding and ordering cost for angles as a function of the order quantity Q in graphical form. The result is shown in Figure 11.5.

From this graph it is clear that the optimal order quantity [the one that minimizes $\text{AHO}(Q)$] is somewhat larger than 1000 items. Victor is amazed at how much this differs from the current policy of 5000 items per month. If he felt like it, Victor could find a good value for the order quantity by trial and error, that is, by plugging in for Q in (11.6) various values around 1100 or 1200 until he was satisfied that he was close enough to the optimum.

The EOQ Formula

It is not necessary to rely on trial and error to find Q^*, the optimal order quantity. (The asterisk indicates the value of Q that is the optimal solution to the model.) A formula can be derived to calculate its value as a function of the parameters in the problem. One way to derive this equation is to note that the optimal value of Q occurs where the annual ordering cost equals the annual holding cost (see Figure 11.5). Note that both are around $1200. Following this approach yields

$$\text{annual holding cost} = \text{annual ordering cost}$$

$$C_h \cdot Q^*/2 = C_0 D/Q^* \tag{11.7}$$

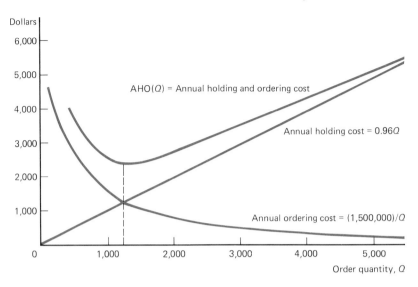

FIGURE 11.5

Graph of Annual Holding and Ordering
Costs as a Function of Order Quantity

or

$$Q^{*2} = 2C_0 D / C_h \qquad (11.8)$$

or

The Formula

$$Q^* = \sqrt{\frac{2DC_0}{C_h}} \qquad (11.9)$$

Alternatively, this formula can be derived by using differential calculus to minimize the function $AHO(Q)$ presented in (11.5) (see Appendix 11.1). An alternative form of (11.9) that is sometimes used is

**An Alternate
Form**

$$Q^* = \sqrt{\frac{2DC_0}{iP}} \qquad (11.10)$$

where P = purchase price ($8 for angles)
i = fraction of P that is used to calculate C_h (0.24 for angles)

This quantity Q^* is often termed the *economic order quantity*, and it should be noted that it is expressed in terms of the input parameters C_0, C_h, and D. By substituting the appliance angle values for D, C_0, and C_h into (11.9), Victor can find the optimal order quantity for his problem:

$$Q^* = \sqrt{\frac{2 \times 60{,}000 \times 25}{1.92}} = 1250$$

Plugging this value into the expression for the annual holding and ordering cost for angles [equation (11.6)] yields

$$AHO(Q^*) = AHO(1250) = (1,500,000)/1250 + (0.96)(1250)$$

$$= \$1200 + \$1200 = \$2400$$

The calculation above illustrates the fact that when Q equals Q^*, the associated annual holding cost $(C_h Q^*/2)$ and the annual ordering cost $(C_0 D/Q^*)$ are equal. This fact is rigorously proved in Appendix 11.1.

Victor has already observed that the policy of ordering 5000 units at a time produces in the model a total annual cost of \$5100. If the quantity 1250 were to be used instead, the cost in the model would be \$2400, resulting in over a 50% savings. Victor is convinced that the idealized economic order quantity model is a good enough representation of Steco to make these results quite interesting.

Related Expressions

Although Victor is happy to learn of the optimal order quantity and the savings that come with it, he is not satisfied. He realizes there are other questions yet to be resolved. For example, he is curious to know the optimum number of times appliance angles should be ordered each year and the *cycle time*, which is defined as the interval between the arrival of two consecutive orders.

He has already used the fact that $N = D/Q$ to calculate the annual ordering cost. Thus, N^*, the optimal number of times to order each year, is given by the expression

$$N^* = D/Q^* \tag{11.11}$$

For angles, this yields a result of $N^* = 60,000/1250 = 48$. Recall that with the current policy Steco places only 12 orders per year. The new result is quite different.

Victor has also noted that the cycle time, the time required to use up an order, is Q/D years. Letting T^* denote the optimal cycle time, we see that

$$T^* = Q^*/D = 1250/60,000 = 0.020833 \tag{11.12}$$

which implies that Steco should order angles every 0.25 month since $(0.020833)(12) = 0.25$. Note that when the cycle time is 0.25 month he must order 4 times per month and thus 48 times per year. This is the same as the value for N^* above. Note that expression (11.5) for $AHO(Q)$ depends on the given parameters C_0, C_h, and D, as well as the variable Q. It is possible to obtain an expression for the *optimal value* of AHO, in terms of only the input parameters C_0, C_h, and D (i.e., eliminating Q) as follows: Substitute the expression for Q^* [expression (11.9)] into (11.5) to obtain

$$AHO^* = AHO(Q^*) = C_0(D/Q^*) + C_h(Q^*/2)$$

$$= C_0 \left(D \middle/ \sqrt{\frac{2DC_0}{C_h}} \right) + C_h \left(\sqrt{\frac{DC_0}{2C_h}} \right)$$

$$= C_0 D \sqrt{\frac{C_h}{2DC_0}} + C_h \sqrt{\frac{DC_0}{2C_h}} \tag{11.13}$$

$$= \sqrt{\frac{C_0 DC_h}{2}} + \sqrt{\frac{C_0 DC_h}{2}} = \sqrt{2C_0 DC_h}$$

FIGURE 11.6
When-to-Order Decision

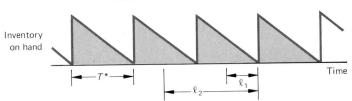

For angles this becomes $AHO^* = \sqrt{2 \times \$25 \times 60{,}000 \times \$1.92} = \$2400$, a value that Victor has previously calculated.

Lead Times and When-to-Order Under the assumptions of the EOQ model, the "how-much-to-order" decision is provided by the derived quantity Q^*. The number of orders per year is given by $N^* = D/Q^*$. The remaining basic question is "when-to-order." The answer to this question is straight-forward, but it depends on the *lead time to delivery*. Under the assumptions of the EOQ model, the entire order quantity Q^* arrives in a single batch precisely when the inventory level hits zero. Thus, if it takes ℓ days for an order to arrive, the order should be placed ℓ days before the end of each cycle. This is illustrated for two different values of ℓ in Figure 11.6. Here T^* is the optimal cycle length, i.e., the cycle length that arises from ordering Q^* items, and ℓ_1 and ℓ_2 are two examples of lead times. If the order is to arrive at time A and the lead time is ℓ_1, the order should be placed at time $A - \ell_1$. If the order is to arrive at time A and the lead time is ℓ_2, the order should be placed at time $A - \ell_2$. In practice, the actual demand will not strictly obey the constant rate assumption shown in Figure 11.6. For this reason, in reality, point A may not be well defined, and hence "order at time $A - \ell_1$" is not a suitable rule. Rather, in practice, the when-to-order rule is typically stated as follows:

WHEN-TO-ORDER RULE: **An order should be placed when the *inventory position* equals the demand during the lead time.**

Inventory Position Defined

where by definition

inventory position = inventory on hand + inventory on order

In the case in which demand is at a constant rate, this rule is equivalent to the more intuitive timing rule; that is, order ℓ days before you want the order to arrive.

We first note that there are 240 working days in a year at Steco. Since yearly demand, D, for angles is 60,000 items, assumed to occur at a constant rate, this implies that d, the daily demand, is

$$d = D/240 = 60{,}000/240 = 250 \text{ per day}$$

We have seen in (11.12) that the optimal cycle time T^* is $1250/60{,}000$ years. Since there are 240 days per year, this becomes

$$T^* = \frac{1250}{60{,}000} \times 240 = 5 \text{ days}$$

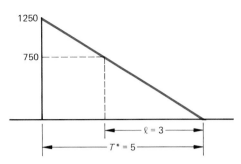

FIGURE 11.7
When-to-Order if $\ell < T^*$

**Why the
When-To-
Order Rule
Works**

We first consider a case in which the lead time (ℓ) is less than the optimal cycle time T^*. In particular, let $\ell = 3$. The timing rule says to order 3 days before you want an order to arrive. Thus 2 days after an order of 1250 angles arrives (3 days before the next order) an order for 1250 angles is placed. The situation is illustrated in Figure 11.7. Note that when the order is placed there are no other orders outstanding (no items on order) and since daily demand is $1250/5 = 250$, the order is placed when there are 750 items on hand. Since

$$\text{inventory position} = \text{inventory on hand} + \text{inventory on order}$$
$$= \qquad 750 \qquad + \qquad 0$$
$$= \qquad 750$$

and

$$\text{demand over the lead time} = 3 \text{ days} \times 250 \text{ items/day} = 750 \text{ items}$$

we can therefore state that the reorder point is when

$$\text{inventory position} = \text{demand over the lead time}$$

Now consider a case where ℓ is greater than T^*. In particular, suppose that $\ell = 8$, $T^* = 5$ and you want the order to arrive on day 30. Then as shown in Figure 11.8, the

FIGURE 11.8
When-to-Order if $\ell > T^*$

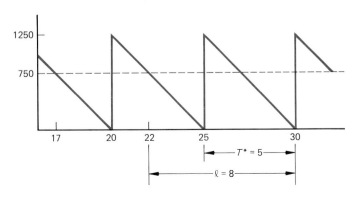

order must be placed 8 days (on day 22) before you want it to arrive. Note in Figure 11.8 that at time 22

$$\text{inventory on hand} = 750$$

Further, the order that will arrive at time 25 was placed at time 17 because the lead time is 8. This order is still outstanding. It is the only order outstanding. Thus,

$$\text{inventory on order} = 1250$$

Again by definition,

$$\text{inventory position} = \text{inventory on hand} + \text{inventory on order}$$
$$= 750 + 1250$$
$$= 2000$$

The demand during the lead time is given by the calculation

$$8 \text{ days} \times 250 \text{ items/day} = 2000$$

Once again we see that the rule "*order when the inventory position equals the demand during the lead time*" yields the same result as the timing rule.

How the Rule Works

The when-to-order rule based on inventory position may seem needlessly complicated. In practice, however, it is easy to implement. The inventory clerk simply keeps a running total of the inventory position for each item. *When an order is placed* (not when an order arrives), *he adds the order quantity to the inventory position.* When an order arrives there is no change in inventory position, for this is merely a transfer of Q^* items from inventory on order to Q^* items on hand. *When an order is sent to a customer, the clerk must subtract the amount from the inventory position.* When the inventory position reaches a specified precomputed number, the demand during the lead time, an order is placed.

In a system where there is uncertainty in demand, we shall see that the concept of safety stock can be easily incorporated within the inventory position rule. This provides a simple and effective inventory control procedure.

Sensitivity

Victor now feels that he understands the application of the EOQ model to angles quite well. But let us at this point very carefully and clearly summarize exactly what he has shown:

1. Using the company's current policy of ordering 5000 items each time an order is placed, the inventory costs in the model are $5100.
2. If the company would use the optimal EOQ policy of ordering 1250 items each time an order is placed, the inventory costs from the model would be $2400.

Whether the optimal EOQ policy should be used in the future depends on the realism of the assumptions. After all, the EOQ model, like any other model, is idealized. It is no more than a selective representation of reality: an abstraction and an approximation. In this case, as with all models, the main question is: "How sensitive are the results of the model to the assumptions and the data?"

Victor has already determined that the assumptions (no stockouts are allowed, all goods arrive in a batch, the only relevant costs are ordering and holding costs, demand is on average 5000 items per month) are realistic in terms of Steco's policies and operations. Since the model is fairly realistic, it seems reasonable that the inventory costs obtained within the model are fairly good estimates of the costs that Steco is actually incurring. Therefore, using a policy that is optimal in the model (order quantity of 1250) seems preferable to the traditional policy of ordering 5000. However, Victor must still be concerned about how sensitive the optimal order quantity and, more important, the optimal annual cost are to the data. After all, each of the parameters C_0 and C_h is in itself an estimate. He is worried about how sensitive the EOQ results might be to the estimates for these parameters. If he errs in estimating these parameters, how much effect will that have on the difference between the calculated Q^* and AHO* and the true Q^* and AHO*? If the results are highly sensitive to the values of the estimates, it is not clear whether the optimal policy for the model should actually be implemented by Steco. Moreover, Victor's overall task is to deal with the inventory control on all of Steco's thousands of products. Substantial resources will be needed to estimate the parameters for all the products with great accuracy, if that is required.

Let us therefore consider how the EOQ results might vary with changes in our estimated holding and ordering costs. Recall that Victor assumed that $C_h = 1.92$ and $C_0 = \$25$. We will consider four cases in which the true parameters are different from the values selected by Victor. These "true values" are shown in the first two columns of Figure 11.9. In case (i) Victor has overestimated both cost parameters by about 10% each. Had he estimated the parameters correctly he would have ordered 1267 items and incurred an annual holding and ordering cost of $2179. Because of his estimation errors he orders 1250. In order to find out what costs he will actually incur, Victor must evaluate the AHO equation with its true parameter values [$C_h = 1.72$ and $C_0 = 23$ in case (i)] and the value of Q determined by his estimates (1250). This calculation follows:

$$AHO(Q) = C_0 D/Q + C_h Q/2$$
$$= 23(60{,}000/1250) + 1.72(\tfrac{1250}{2})$$
$$= 23(48) + 1.72(625)$$
$$= 1104 + 1075$$
$$= 2179$$

This number is shown as Victor's Cost in column (5). We thus see that if Victor underestimates the two cost parameters as shown, it has no effect on the annual holding and

FIGURE 11.9
Sensitivity to C_h and C_0

(1) TRUE PARAMETERS		(2) OPTIMAL Q	(3) MINIMUM COST	(4) VICTOR'S DECISION[a]	(5) VICTOR'S COST	(6) LOSS (%)
C_h	C_0					
(i) 1.72	23	1267	$2179	Q = 1250	$2179	0
(ii) 1.72	27	1372	2361	Q = 1250	2371	0.42
(iii) 2.12	23	1141	2419	Q = 1250	2429	0.41
(iv) 2.12	27	1236	2621	Q = 1250	2621	0

[a] Based on $C_h = 1.92$, $C_0 = 25$.

ordering cost (to the nearest dollar). The other three cases show that the effect on the annual holding and ordering cost of any combination of 10% errors in the estimates of C_0 and C_h is negligible.

Precise Estimates not Required

Our analysis suggests that in Victor's case the EOQ model is insensitive even to approximately 10% variations or errors in the cost estimates. It turns out that this is a property enjoyed by EOQ models in general. Thus, Victor concludes that if he can obtain at least reasonable estimates of ordering and holding costs, the value of Q thereby obtained by will yield an AHO very close to the true minimum.

Managerial Considerations

If future demand were known with complete certainty and were truly at a constant monthly rate, then under the other assumptions, that ordering and holding costs are the only relevant costs, and no stockouts are allowed, it is true that the values Q^* and $AHO(Q^*)$ as produced by the idealized EOQ model would indeed be optimal, not just in the model but in the real problem as well. However, in practice, as we repeatedly emphasize, the real-wold problem rarely satisfies the assumptions of the model exactly. For example, in most real-world contexts it would be unlikely that future demand would be known with complete certainty. It is even more unlikely that it would occur at a constant monthly or daily rate. Indeed, in the appliance angle context, as Figure 11.1 shows, last year's demand rate of 5000 items per month is only an average. There was no constant monthly rate. And what about the future? This value of 5000 per month is only an estimate of the rate of demand in the future. In Chapter 12 Victor will enlarge his perspective to see how the ICON system deals with uncertainty in future demand in formal ways.

Protecting Against Uncertain Lead Time Demand

As a first step, however, he as the manager might feel that the EOQ assumptions, together with the estimated demand of 5000 items per month, are realistic enough to make the model directly useful as is. On the other hand, he must recognize that using the previously derived reorder point of 750 items (for 3-day lead times) will almost surely lead to some stockouts. A stockout will, in fact, occur whenever the demand during the 3-day lead time (i.e., the 3-day period which commences when the reorder point is achieved) exceeds 750 items. Another possible cause for a stockout could be the occurrence of a longer lead time for unforeseen reasons. The job of the manager is to deal successfully with uncertainty. In the Steco context, if stockouts are truly to be avoided, then Victor as manager may choose to increase the reorder point (leaving the reorder quantity unchanged). He may, for example, choose to reorder when 1000 items are on hand. What would he achieve with such a change?

Since, during the expected 3-day lead time, 750 items are estimated to be demanded (assuming that the constant demand rate holds), we see that 250 items will still remain in inventory when the order arrives. This extra 250 units serves as a precaution against larger-than-expected demand or a delay in the scheduled delivery. It is called a safety or buffer stock.

A safety stock is the difference between the reorder point and the expected lead-time demand.

In the appliance angle example, carrying a safety stock of 250 items would raise the average inventory level by 250 items. This would affect only the yearly carrying charge, which would increase by

$$C_h(250) = (1.92)(250) = \$480$$

and hence the only effect of the 250-item buffer stock is to raise the annual cost estimate from $2400 to $2880, still a considerable savings over the current policy. (This statement ignores any changes in costs due to stockouts.)

Thus, as a first-order consideration, possible uncertainties in demand, or in lead time, can be treated with a managerial judgment on a suitable safety stock level. This is handled by simple modification of the reorder point rule. Whether a simple modification should be made is in itself a matter of managerial judgment. It is a question of the extent to which stockouts are to be avoided, and a question of whether a deeper treatment should be undertaken. After all, the question of what a suitable safety stock level is remains unanswered. In Chapter 12 this question will be analyzed in greater depth.

Other variations in the basic model might be called for to capitalize on the opportunity to get quantity discounts. This is treated in the following section.

—— 11.4
QUANTITY DISCOUNTS AND STECO'S OVERALL OPTIMUM

The EOQ model that Victor has been working with minimizes the annual holding and ordering cost. There was previously no need to take into account the cost of purchasing the product, for the per item cost to Steco was assumed to be a constant independent of Q. Victor now learns that Steco's supplier will make a special offer as an incentive for more business. The supplier has agreed to offer a $0.10 discount on every angle purchased if Steco orders in lots of at least 5000 items. Of course, higher order quantities will also reduce the number of orders placed, and hence the annual ordering cost. However, as already discussed (compare Figures 11.3 and 11.4), a high order quantity leads to a higher average inventory level and hence higher holding costs. Whether the discount will, on balance, be advantageous to Steco is not obvious.

Victor decides to proceed as before, that is, to develop an annual cost curve and then find the order quantity that minimizes it. His annual total cost [ATC(Q)] is the sum of the annual holding and ordering cost [AHO(Q)] and the annual purchase cost [APC], that is,

$$\text{ATC}(Q) = \text{AHO}(Q) + \text{APC}$$

From previous results [equation (11.5)] Victor knows that

$$\text{AHO}(Q) = C_0 D/Q + iPQ/2$$

Note that since C_h depends on the unit price P, the expression for AHO also involves P. The annual purchase cost is simply the unit price times annual demand. Thus,

Annual Purchase Cost

$$\text{APC} = PD$$

It follows that

Annual Total Cost

$$\text{ATC}(Q) = C_0 D/Q + iPQ/2 + PD$$

Victor wishes to evaluate this function for two different prices, the regular price of $8.00 per unit and the potential discounted price of $7.90 per unit. He obtains the following

FIGURE 11.10
Annual Total Cost for Regular and
Discount Prices

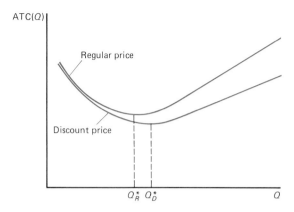

two functions:

Regular price equation:

$$\text{ATC}(Q) = \frac{25 \times 60{,}000}{Q} + (0.24)(8.00)(Q/2) + (8.00)(60{,}000)$$

Discount price equation:

$$\text{ATC}(Q) = \frac{25 \times 60{,}000}{Q} + (0.24)(7.90)(Q/2) + (7.90)(60{,}000)$$

The general shape of these curves is shown in Figure 11.10. There are several facts to notice.

1. The discount curve lies below the regular cost curve. This is so since each term in the regular price $\text{ATC}(Q)$ is greater than or equal to the corresponding term in the discount price $\text{ATC}(Q)$.

2. The value of Q, say Q_D^*, that minimizes the discount price $\text{ATC}(Q)$ is larger than the value of Q, say Q_R^*, that minimizes the regular price $\text{ATC}(Q)$. This is true because, using (11.10),

$$Q_D^* = \sqrt{\frac{2 \times 25 \times 60{,}000}{(0.24) \times (7.90)}} > \sqrt{\frac{2 \times 25 \times 60{,}000}{(0.24) \times (8.00)}} = Q_R^*$$

Obviously, Victor would like to minimize his annual total cost, $\text{ATC}(Q)$. If he could get the discount price regardless of the order quantity, he would of course order Q_D^*. However, assume that the discount price holds only if he orders at least B items at a time. Two situations could arise. These are illustrated in Figure 11.11.

The shaded curves in these figures indicate the actual cost function that Victor faces. They illustrate that the regular price curve must be used for order quantities of B or less and that the discount price curve can be used for order quantities greater than B.

We see that if $B \leq Q_D^*$, Victor will achieve the minimum cost by ordering Q_D^*. If, however, $B > Q_D^*$, the optimal decision, in general, is not immediately obvious. The

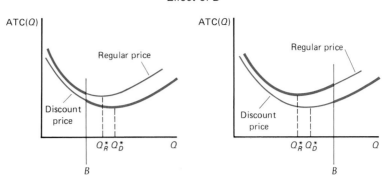

FIGURE 11.11
Effect of B

best Victor can do on the regular price curve is to order Q_R^*. The best he can do on the discount price curve is to order B. (He cannot order less than B and get the discount price, and ordering more than B increases ATC.) To determine which of these is optimal he must calculate the ATC(Q) at these two points and compare them. The general rule then is

The Optimal Order Quantity

If $B \leq Q_D^*$, order Q_D^*.

If $B > Q_D^*$, order $\begin{cases} Q_R^* & \text{if regular price} \leq \text{discount price} \\ & \text{ATC}(Q_R^*) \qquad \text{ATC}(B) \\ B & \text{if not} \end{cases}$

Applying the Rule

To apply this rule, Victor notes that he must order at least 5000 items to get the discount. Thus $B = 5000$. To calculate Q_D^* he uses the EOQ formula as follows:

$$Q_D^* = \sqrt{\frac{2 \times 25 \times 60{,}000}{(0.24)(7.90)}} = 1257.9 \sim 1258 \tag{11.14}$$

Since $Q_D^* = 1258 < 5000 = B$, he must compare two alternatives to determine the optimal order quantity. From his previous calculations [those following (11.10)] he knows that Q_R^* equals 1250. Thus, the value ATC(Q_R^*) is calculated by the regular price equation above.

$$\text{ATC}(Q_R^*) = \frac{25 \times 60{,}000}{1250} + (0.24)(8.00)\frac{1250}{2} + (8.00)(60{,}000)$$

$$= 1200 + 1200 + 480{,}000 = 482{,}400$$

Similarly, the value ATC(B) is calculated by the discount price equation.

$$\text{ATC}(B) = \frac{25 \times 60{,}000}{5000} + (0.24)(7.90)\frac{5000}{2} + (7.90)(60{,}000)$$

$$= 300 + 4740 + 474{,}000 = 479{,}040$$

These calculations show that Victor should order 5000 items to take advantage of the quantity discount. This decision saves

$$\$482,400 - \$479,040 = \$3360$$

per year over the next best decision (ordering Q_R^*). What this discussion suggests is that quantity discounts can play an important role in determining the optimal inventory policy. Indeed, this is so important that Steco's ICON system has been designed to deal with the problem. ICON first solves the basic EOQ model, and then in a second stage, when quantity discounts are available, the system runs through the calculations that Victor has just made.

_____ 11.5
THE EOQ MODEL WITH BACKLOGGING

One of the important functions of inventory is to protect against stockouts. We have already seen earlier in this chapter how a manager will add a safety stock to the reorder point to decrease the likelihood of stockouts with an EOQ model. However, in some cases it may be advantageous to both the buyer and the seller if not all orders are satisfied out of inventory on hand. Indeed, the seller sometimes plans on running out and knows that there will be some demand when there is no inventory on hand. Holding this demand in abeyance and then satisfying it out of later inventory is called *backlogging demand*.

We thus wish to drop the no-stockout assumption in the basic model and examine the implications of doing so. The essence of backlogging in the EOQ context is illustrated in Figure 11.12.

Much of Figure 11.12 is familiar. An order for Q items arrives every T days. The order arrives all at once (in a batch), at which time the inventory on hand jumps up by Q items. Between the arrival of orders inventory depletes at a constant rate, reflecting the fact that demand is occurring at a constant rate. The new wrinkle is the fact that not all demand is satisfied out of inventory on hand. Certain customers are asked to wait and their demand is satisfied when the next order arrives. In a strict sense those customers whose orders arrive during the first t_1 days of an inventory cycle have their demand satisfied out of inventory on hand. Those whose orders arrive during the rest of the cycle (t_2) wait until the next replenishment to receive their goods. The process of asking customers to wait (or backlogging) is indicated in Figure 11.12 as a negative value of inventory on hand.

Costs of Backlogging   Typically, the supplier must offer some sort of financial incentive to his customers to accept a waiting period. This incentive might take the form of financial considerations;

FIGURE 11.12
EOQ Model with Planned Backorders

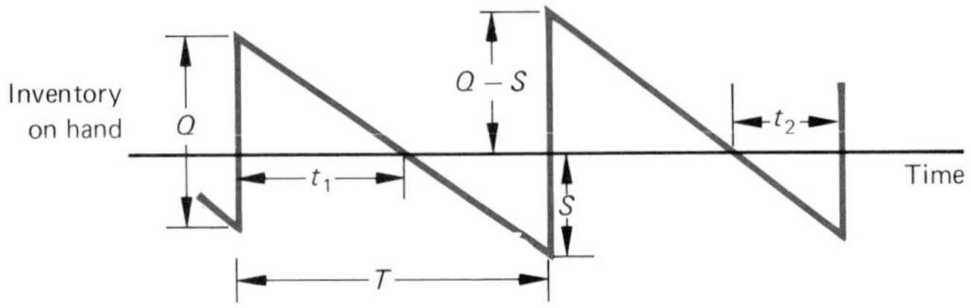

that is, the supplier might accept payment up to 90 days after delivery at no extra charge, whereas immediate delivery implies immediate payment or the addition of finance charges. Another approach is simply to offer a price reduction for backlogged orders. The point is that the supplier typically incurs a cost for these items, but sometimes it is sensible to incur these costs intentionally.

Returning to Figure 11.12, note that during the cycle time (T) the firm holds inventory during t_1 and accepts backorders (i.e., backlogged demand) during t_2 when the inventory has been depleted. Clearly,

$$t_1 + t_2 = T$$

The symbol S indicates the total number of units backlogged during a cycle, that is, the total number of units of unsatisfied demand accumulated during t_2. We see then that, with an order size of Q, the maximum level of inventory on hand is $Q - S$, since S items from each new order must be used to fill previously backlogged orders and the remaining $Q - S$ are placed in inventory.

In the basic EOQ model management has to make one decision, the value of Q, since this determines the cycle time and the entire policy. When backorders are permitted, management must select both Q and S. As before, Q, together with the constant rate of demand D, determines T, the cycle length, but S must be specified before it is clear how many units will be backlogged on each cycle and how much inventory will be held.

The Decision Variables The values of the decision variables Q and S are selected to minimize the sum of the annual ordering, holding, and backlogging costs. Backlogging costs are assessed in exactly the same manner as holding costs; that is, the cost to backlog an item for a year must be specified, and the cost per cycle is built up from this quantity. The cost per cycle is used in turn to calculate the annual cost. A detailed development follows.

The Annual Cost Expression Let AHOB(Q, S) be the annual holding, ordering, and backlogging cost as a function of Q and S. Also, let C_b be the cost of backlogging an item for a year. We now proceed to develop the cost of a cycle.

1. *Ordering cost:* Since one order is placed each cycle, this is simple. The ordering cost equals C_0.

2. *Holding cost:* The maximum inventory level is $Q - S$. Demand occurs at the constant rate of D items per year. If follows that the quantity ($Q - S$) will last for a time (in years) given by

$$t_1 = \frac{Q - S}{D}$$

if it is consumed at the *rate D*. The average time (in years) that a unit is held in inventory is $t_1/2$, and ($Q - S$) items are held. Thus, the holding cost per cycle is

$$C_h(Q - S)t_1/2 = C_h(Q - S)(\tfrac{1}{2})[(Q - S)/D]$$

$$= \frac{C_h}{2}\frac{(Q - S)^2}{D}$$

3. *Backlogging cost:* A maximum of S units are backlogged. Since backlogging occurs at the rate of demand D, the time for backlogging must be

$$t_2 = S/D$$

A total of S items are backlogged for an average of $t_2/2$ years; thus, the backlogging cost per cycle is

$$C_b S t_2/2 = C_b S(\tfrac{1}{2})(S/D)$$

$$= \frac{C_b}{2}\frac{S^2}{D}$$

The annual holding, ordering, and backlogging cost, AHOB(Q, S), can now be obtained by adding the costs from 1, 2, and 3 above to obtain the cost per cycle and then multiplying by the number of cycles per year. As in the basic EOQ model there are D/Q cycles per year [equation (11.2)]. Thus,

Annual Cost

$$\text{AHOB}(Q, S) = D/Q\left[C_0 + \frac{C_h}{2}\frac{(Q-S)^2}{D} + \frac{C_b}{2}\frac{S^2}{D}\right] \quad (11.15)$$

Management can now use (11.15) to calculate the annual holding, ordering, and backlogging cost for any choice of the decision variables Q and S. With differntial calculus one can also use the same equation to derive the expressions for Q^* and S^*, the optimal values of Q and S. The results of this derivation are presented in (11.16) and (11.17).

Optimal Values of Q, S

$$Q^* = \sqrt{\frac{2C_0 D}{C_h}\left(\frac{C_h + C_b}{C_b}\right)} \quad (11.16)$$

$$S^* = Q^*\left(\frac{C_h}{C_h + C_b}\right) \quad (11.17)$$

Plugging the expressions for Q^* and S^* into (11.15) yields AHOB(Q^*, S^*), the minimum annual holding, ordering, and backlogging cost. The result is shown in (11.18).

$$\text{AHOB}(Q^*, S^*) = \left[2C_0 D C_h\left(\frac{C_b}{C_h + C_b}\right)\right]^{1/2} \quad (11.18)$$

It is interesting to compare these expressions to those for Q^* and AHO(Q^*) in the basic EOQ model. Recall that in the basic model (11.9)

$$Q^* = \sqrt{\frac{2C_0 D}{C_h}}$$

and (11.13)

$$\text{AHO}(Q^*) = (2C_0 D C_h)^{1/2}$$

First compare (11.16) and (11.9). We first note that since $(C_h + C_b)/C_b \geq 1$, the optimal order quantity in the backlogged case is at least as large as the optimal order quantity in the basic model. Similarly, by comparing (11.18) and (11.13) we see that since $C_b/(C_b + C_h) \leq 1$, the annual cost for the backlogged model is at most as large as the annual cost in the basic model.

Backlogging as a Profitable Opportunity Suppose that the cost of backlogging an item for a year is twice as large as the cost of holding the same item for a year; that is, assume that $C_b = 2C_h$. Does your intuition tell you that you would never choose a backlog in this case? If it does you have learned again how easily we are misled by our intuition. From (11.17) we see that since $C_h/(C_h + C_b) = \frac{1}{3}$,

$$S^* = Q^*(\tfrac{1}{3})$$

which implies that one-third of the orders will be backlogged. Now from (11.18) and the facts that

$$\frac{C_b}{C_h + C_b} = \tfrac{2}{3} \quad \text{and} \quad \left(\frac{C_b}{C_h + C_b}\right)^{1/2} = 0.816$$

we conclude that the annual cost in the backlogged model is only 0.816 times as much as the annual cost in the basic model. In other words, what to many people seems like an unattractive alternative (backlogging when it is twice as expensive as holding inventory) turns out to play an important role in the optimal inventory policy. One-third of the orders are backlogged. This policy has an important effect on the costs (approximately a 20% reduction).

One way to think about the basic model is to assume that backlogging is allowed, but that since C_b is extremely large (infinite) no orders are ever backlogged. It is reassuring to note that if C_b is set equal to infinity in (11.16), (11.17), and (11.18), then $S^* = 0$, and Q^* and AHOB(Q^*, S^*) reduce to the appropriate expressions for the no-backlog case.

Selling Styrofoam

Suppose that a supplier of styrofoam is faced with the following situation for his styrofoam panels, which are 2 feet by 8 feet by 2 inches thick:

$$D = 50{,}000 \text{ panels per year}$$

$$C_h = \$4 \text{ per year}$$

$$C_b = \$8 \text{ per year}$$

$$C_0 = \$25 \text{ per order}$$

From (11.16) we see that

$$Q^* = \sqrt{\frac{2C_0 D}{C_h}\left(\frac{C_h + C_b}{C_b}\right)} = \sqrt{\frac{2(25)(50{,}000)}{4}\left(\frac{4+8}{8}\right)} = 968 \text{ panels}$$

Equation (11.17) shows that

$$S^* = Q^*\left(\frac{C_h}{C_h + C_b}\right) = 968\left(\frac{4}{4+8}\right) = 322 \text{ panels}$$

Finally, (11.18) yields

Cost with Backlogging

$$\text{AHOB}(Q^*, S^*) = \left[2C_0 DC_h\left(\frac{C_b}{C_b + C_h}\right)\right]^{1/2}$$

$$= \left[2(25)(50{,}000)(4)\left(\frac{8}{8+4}\right)\right]^{1/2} = \$2580$$

If the firm had not taken advantage of the opportunity to backlog orders, then the optimal order quantity would be calculated as follows:

$$Q^* = \sqrt{\frac{2C_0D}{C_h}}$$

$$= \sqrt{\frac{2(25)(50,000)}{4}} = 790$$

Similarly, the minimum annual holding and ordering cost would be

**Cost without
Backlogging**

$$\text{AHO}(Q^*) = [2C_0DC_h]^{1/2}$$

$$= [2(25)(50,000)(4)]^{1/2} = \$3162$$

These calculations provide a specific example of the general case described above and illustrate again the importance of using the opportunity to backlog orders if the characteristics of the market make that alternative possible. It is important to note that the "when-to-order rule" must be modified when backlogging is permitted. The proper modification is noted in Problem 15.

—————— **11.6**

THE PRODUCTION LOT SIZE MODEL: VICTOR'S HEAT-TREATMENT PROBLEM

Although Steco is primarily a steel wholesaler, it does have some productive capacity. In particular, it has an extensive and modern heat-treatment facility which it uses to produce a number of items that it then holds in inventory. The heat-treatment facility has two important characteristics: There is a large setup cost associated with producing each product, and once the setup is complete, production is at a steady and known rate.

The setup cost, which is analogous to the ordering cost in the EOQ model, is incurred because it is necessary to change the chemicals and the operating temperature in the heat-treatment facility to meet the specifications set forth by the metallurgical laboratory. Also, each item must spend a specified time at a specific temperature in each of several chemical baths. Thus, an order quantity of heat-treated steel does not arrive in inventory all at once. Rather, it arrives steadily over a period of several days. This change requires a modificattion in the EOQ formula, even if the assumptions of a constant rate of demand and the inventory carrying cost being equal to C_h times the average inventory are maintained.

It is usually more convenient to work with this model in terms of daily production and demand rates. Thus, consider a product in which

**Parameters
of the Model**

d = number of units demanded each day

p = number of units produced each day during a production run

C_0 = setup cost that is independent of the quantity produced

C_h = cost per *day* of holding inventory
    (note the change in notation to emphasize holding cost per day)

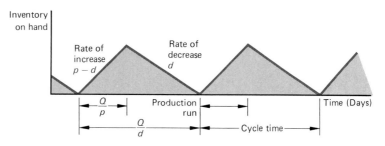

FIGURE 11.13

Inventory on Hand for the
Production Lot Size Model

It is obvious that p must be greater than d for the problem to be interesting. If $p < d$, demand is greater than Steco's ability to produce, and holding inventory is the least of their problems.

Figure 11.13 presents a plot of what the inventory on hand would look like if Steco decided to produce in lots of Q items each.

There are several aspects of this graph that must be noted in order to calculate the average holding and setup and cost per day.

1. During a production run items are added to inventory at a rate of p units per days and removed at the rate of d per day. The net effect is an increase at the rate of $p - d$ units per day.
2. At other times, items are removed from inventory at a rate of d items per day.
3. Since Q items are produced in a run, at the rate of p items per day, each production run is Q/p days long.
4. Since Q items are produced in a run, and d is the daily demand rate, each cycle time is Q/d days long.

Facts 1 and 3 can be used to find the maximum amount of inventory on hand (see Figure 11.13).

$$\text{maximum inventory} = (p - d)Q/p$$

Since the average inventory equals one-half of the maximum inventory, it follows that

$$\text{average inventory} = 1/2(p - d)Q/p$$

Rearranging the terms in the expression above, we obtain

$$\text{average inventory} = Q/2(1 - d/p)$$

$$\text{holding cost per day} = C_h Q/2(1 - d/p)$$

Similarly, since there is one setup every cycle and a cycle lasts Q/d days,

$$\text{setup cost per day} = \frac{C_0}{Q/d} = C_0 \frac{d}{Q}$$

Thus, the daily holding and setup cost, denoted DHS(Q), is given by the expression

$$\text{DHS}(Q) = C_0 \frac{d}{Q} + C_h \frac{Q}{2}\left(1 - \frac{d}{p}\right)$$

If you think of $C_h(1 - d/p)$ as a constant, this expression takes the same form as given by (11.5), the expression for the annual holding and ordering cost in the EOQ model.

It follows, then, that the value of Q that minimizes DHS(Q) will be given by the EOQ equation (11.9) with C_h appropriately modified. Thus, for the production lot size model,

**Optimal
Lot Size**

$$Q^* = \sqrt{\frac{2dC_0}{C_h(1 - d/p)}} \tag{11.19}$$

The result could also be derived with differential calculus, analogous to the derivation in Appendix 11.1.

To apply this analysis to any particular product, Victor must estimate the various parameters for that product and then evaluate (11.19) to obtain Q^*. Thus, once the parameters are estimated, finding Q^* is reduced to a matter of "plug and chug."

Just to confirm his understanding of the production lot size model, Victor decides to work his way through the calculations for a $\frac{3}{8}$-inch hardened reinforcing rod, a product used in reinforced concrete construction.

The demand for this product averages 200 rods per day. It costs $100 to set up to heat treat the rods and they can be produced at a rate of 400 rods per day. Victor estimates the holding cost per day as ($1)(0.24)/240 = 0.001, where $1 is the cost of the rod and 0.24 is the annual interest rate used by Steco for all products. The figure 240 is the assumed number of working days per year.

The optimal production lot size for this product, then, is

$$Q^* = \sqrt{\frac{2 \times 200 \times 100}{0.001(1 - \frac{200}{400})}} = 8944$$

A production run of this size yields a supply of rods large enough to satisfy demand for

$$\frac{8944}{200} = 44.72 \text{ days} \qquad \cdot$$

In practice, Victor might adjust this quantity to take into account the fact that a number of other products also have to make use of the heat-treatment facility. He would perhaps add a safety stock to allow for the possibility that demand might run ahead of production at the beginning of a production run. Quantity discounts would probably not play a role in his decision since the rods that are heat treated are drawn from Steco's general inventory of $\frac{3}{8}$-inch high–carbon steel rods. These rods are used for a number of purposes and their purchase must be determined by total demand.

MATERIAL REQUIREMENTS PLANNING: FARMCRAFT MANUFACTURING CO.

The directors of Steco have recently approved the purchase of Farmcraft Manufacturing Co., a major producer of planting equipment. As a manufacturer, Farmcraft maintains inventories of intermediate goods which are to be used in producing finished products. During a major restudy of Farmcraft's inventory management, Victor is called in as a consultant. He quickly learns that his experience at Steco has little direct application. Steco maintains finished product inventories to satisfy consumer demand. There is a big difference between this activity and that which occurs at Farmcraft.

In a typical manufacturing process certain parts and subassemblies are used in a number of finished products. For a firm like Farmcraft you would expect to see basic parts like bolts and nuts, custom parts like wheels and treads, and subassemblies like transmissions and engines used in a number of finished products. We shall use the term *intermediate goods* to refer to all parts and subassemblies.

It is, of course, clear that the demand for intermediate goods is generated by the demand for the finished product. The question to be asked is: "What levels of intermediate good inventories are required to assure that finished product demand will be satisfied?" We shall see that the relationships between intermediate goods and final product, if properly taken into account, can lead to important efficiencies in establishing appropriate inventory levels. *Material requirements planning*, abbreviated MRP, is an important technique to deal with dependencies in demand. Let us use a simple example to explain the approach.

In Figure 11.14 we see a display of some of the requirements for a 12-row beet and bean planter. The flow in this figure illustrates that the gearbox must be available in order to produce the transmission, for indeed the gearbox is part of the transmission. Moreover, the transmission must be available in order to produce the power train, for it is part of the power train, and this power train in turn goes into the final product. Thus, Figure 11.14 gives you an indication of some of the dependencies among intermediate goods. It is this type of dependency that will be used in the MRP analysis of required inventory levels.

Proceeding, suppose that Farmcraft's production schedule calls for 1000 units of finished product (12-row planters) to be assembled by April 1 of next year. In order to meet this schedule the power train, wheel assembly, and earth turning units must be

FIGURE 11.14
Material Input List

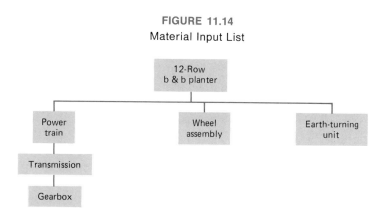

FIGURE 11.15
Current Inventory for Farmcraft

COMPONENT	UNITS CURRENTLY IN INVENTORY
Power Train	360
Transmission	250
Gearbox	400

completed by March 15, allowing 2 weeks for the final assembly. Let us now focus on the inventory control aspects of the power train. The number of units currently in inventory are shown in Figure 11.15. The first question to be asked is: "How many units of each component will ultimately be required in inventory to fulfill the requirement that 1000 units of finished product must be assembled by April 1?"

You may believe that the answer is obvious: namely, 1000 units of each component are required. Therefore, you may say that the *additional requirements*, above and beyond current inventory levels, are obtained by subtracting current levels from 1000, as shown in Figure 11.16. The problem with this answer is that it does not take into account the dependencies revealed in Figure 11.14. It ignores the facts that gearboxes are already installed in the 250 transmissions on hand, and transmissions are already installed in the 360 power trains on hand. Taking these facts into account, the MRP analysis of additional requirements would proceed as follows:

The Correct Analysis of Requirements

units of finished product to be assembled	1000
total requirement for power trains	1000
power trains in current inventory	360
additional power trains required	640

Now since each additional power train will require a transmission, we have

total requirement for transmissions	640
transmissions in current inventory	250
additional transmissions required	390

Similarly, since each of the additional transmissions will require a gearbox, one obtains

total requirement for gearboxes	390
gearboxes in current inventory	400
additional gearboxes required	0

FIGURE 11.16
Additional Requirements: A Wrong Answer

COMPONENT	NUMBER REQUIRED TO MEET DEMAND FOR 1000 PLANTERS	NUMBER IN INVENTORY	ADDITIONAL REQUIREMENT
Power Train	1000	360	640
Transmission	1000	250	750
Gearbox	1000	400	600

FIGURE 11.17

Comparison of Results

COMPONENT	ADDITIONAL REQUIREMENTS WITHOUT DEPENDENCY (FIGURE 11.16)	ADDITIONAL REQUIREMENTS TAKING DEPENDENCY INTO ACCOUNT
Power Train	640	640
Transmission	750	390
Gearbox	600	0

FIGURE 11.18

Additional Requirements and Lead Times
for the Power Train Assembly

COMPONENT	ADDITIONAL REQUIREMENTS	LEAD TIME (WORKING DAYS)
Power Train	640	20
Transmission	390	5
Gearbox	0	0

You can now see how MRP was used to take the dependency of intermediate goods into account and to produce an improved list of additional requirements as given in Figure 11.17. The analysis using MRP clearly leads to lower inventory levels and hence lower inventory charges.

Since each component of the power train requires production and assembly time, some planning must be done in order to deliver the 640 additional power trains on schedule. The necessary information is given in Figure 11.18. The lead time in this context is the amount of time it will take to produce the additional requirements, given that all components are available at the start of the process. For example, it requires 20 working days to produce 640 power trains once the 640 transmissions (250 from inventory and 390 newly produced), as well as all of the other materials in the power train, are available.

With the information in Figure 11.18 we can construct the time line shown in Figure 11.19. As previously stated, the 1000 complete planters are due on April 1, the sixtieth working day of the year. This data marks the end of the production and assembly process and the start of our calculation. It was also previously stated that the power trains must be available on March 15, to allow the 10 working days required to assemble final components into the planters. Figure 11.19 was constructed by starting at the desired completion time and working backward. This process is often called *time phasing* or

**Timing of
Requirements**

FIGURE 11.19

Time Phasing Planter Production

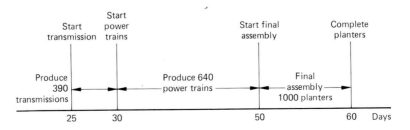

lead-time offsetting. We see from this construction that the process of producing the 390 additional transmissions must be started on the twenty-fifth working day (roughly February 5; the exact date, of course, depends on the year). If Farmcraft did not already have at least 390 gearboxes in inventory, the date at which the entire process of producing power trains started would have been even earlier.

The popularity of MRP in real applications is partly due to its conceptual simplicity.

To apply MRP, start backward from the finished product and successively compute net additional requirements for the dependent intermediate goods.

However, in spite of its simplicity an enormous volume of calculations must be performed to apply MRP in most real manufacturing environments. Consequently, the success of MRP is to a large extent due to the capabilities of large-scale computers.

11.8
SUMMARY

This chapter is devoted primarily to the basic EOQ model (economic order quantity) and its various modifications. The model assumes a constant known rate of demand, with no stockouts, and the relevant costs are those of ordering and holding. A policy with frequent orders give a high ordering cost and low holding cost. Infrequent orders give a low ordering cost and high holding cost. The EOQ formula determines an order quantity Q^* that balances these two costs, that is, minimizes annual holding and ordering costs. Given Q^*, the number of orders per year is D/Q^*, where D is annual demand, and the amount of time it takes to deplete the quantity Q^*, called the cycle time, is Q^*/D.

After developing the EOQ formula and related expressions [i.e., AHO(Q^*)], our attention turns to the question of when to order. The concept of a reorder point is introduced, and inventory position, the sum of inventory on hand and inventory on order, is introduced as the appropriate quantity to use in establishing the reorder point. The rule, in the absence of a safety stock is: "Reorder when the inventory position equals lead-time demand." In the remainder of Section 11.3 we consider the sensitivity of the model to changes in the values of the cost parameters and the use of safety stocks to allow for uncertainty in demand or in lead time. With a safety stock, the reorder point rule is: "Reorder when inventory position equals lead-time demand plus safety stock."

Other sections of this chapter deal with modifications of the basic model that are important in applications. For example, Section 11.4 shows how the optimal order quantity must be modified in the face of a quantity discount. Section 11.5 investigates the advantages of backlogging demand (delivering orders late) when the market is such that this procedure will work. Section 11.6 treats the case in which items are not ordered from an outside source, but are produced internally. In such cases the quantity of material ordered typically does not arrive all at one time in a single batch. Its arrival is spread out over an interval of time. The basic model must be modified to take this fact into account.

The last section in this chapter goes more deeply into the problem of inventory control in a production facility as compared to a retail or a wholesale firm. The MRP, material requirements planning, technique is introduced. This technique is specifically designed to take into account the interdependencies in the inventories of assembled products. It is also used to plan the time at which various functions must be started in order to satisfy the demand for completed projects (finished product).

LEAD TIME.   The period of time between when an order is placed and when it actually arrives.

QUANTITY DISCOUNT.   A purchase plan under which the seller offers a special price to the buyer if he or she purchases a specified quantity or more.

ECONOMIC ORDER QUANTITY.   The optimal order quantity for a particular inventory control model with constant rate of demand, and where relevant costs are those of ordering, holding, and possibly those of backlogging demand.

ORDERING COST.   One of the cost parameters in the EOQ model. The marginal cost of placing an order.

INVENTORY CARRYING COST.   One of the cost parameters in the EOQ model. The cost of holding an item in inventory for a specified time.

CYCLE TIME.   The interval between the arrival of the two consecutive orders.

INVENTORY POSITION.   Inventory on hand plus that on order.

SAFETY STOCK.   Additional items that are added to the reorder point in order to protect against stockouts due to uncertainty in demand over the lead time.

PRODUCTION LOT SIZE MODEL.   A modification of the EOQ model that allows for a finite rate of receiving materials.

INVENTORY.   Units of goods, money, or individuals held in anticipation of future needs.

BUFFER STOCK.   A synonym for safety stock.

BACKLOGGING.   The practice of delivering goods to customers some time after the order has been received rather than immediately upon receipt of the order.

OPPORTUNITY COST.   If taking one action (say A) implies that another action (say B) cannot be taken, the net return associated with action B is an opportunity cost of taking action A.

COST OF BACKLOGGING.   One of the cost parameters in the EOQ model expanded to allow for backlogging. The cost of backlogging an item for a specified time.

STOCKOUT.   Not having enough inventory on hand to satisfy demand.

ICON.   A hypothetical inventory control system in this text. Its characteristics are similar to many commercial packages.

DEMAND.   The number of items ordered. Because of stockouts, this may be different from the number of items sold.

REORDER POINT.   Part of a reorder point–reorder quantity inventory control system. When the inventory position reaches this number, an order should be placed.

ORDER QUANTITY.   Part of an inventory control system. The number of items that are ordered when an order is placed.

MATERIAL REQUIREMENTS PLANNING.   An inventory control system for manufactured products involving assemblies.

TIME PHASING.   The process of determining when production or purchasing activities should begin in an MRP system.

PENALTY COST.   The loss in a no-backlogging model when it is not possible to satisfy demand; usually stated as a per unit cost of unsatisfied demand.

STOCKOUT COST.   Stated in terms of either penalty cost or backlogging cost.

MAJOR CONCEPTS QUIZ ————————————

True–False

1. **T   F**   The opportunity cost segment of the holding cost is determined by factors such as breakage, pilferage, and insurance.

2. **T   F**   Demand is always greater than or equal to sales.

3. **T   F**   In the EOQ model the annual ordering cost is directly proportional to the order quantity.

4. **T   F**   If the lead time is smaller than the cycle time, an order should be placed when the inventory on hand equals the demand during the lead time (assuming zero safety stock).

5. T F In the EOQ model the annual holding and ordering cost is reasonably insensitive to errors in estimating the cost parameters.

6. T F The safety stock is the difference between the reorder point and the actual demand over the lead time.

7. T F For any set of demand and cost parameters, the minimum annual holding and ordering cost (backlogging not permitted) is never smaller than the minimum annual holding, ordering, and backlogging cost (backlogging permitted).

8. T F In the production lot size model, since production is at a steady rate, no setup cost is included in the model.

9. T F Material requirements planning takes the dependency of intermediate goods into account to determine the additional requirements of component parts.

Multiple Choice

10. The following are some of the reasons inventory is held:
    a. protect against uncertainty in demand
    b. lower production costs
    c. store labor
    d. all of the above

11. Important considerations in deciding *when* and *how much* to order include all factors except
    a. the lead time
    b. the proportion of the holding cost that is due to the opportunity cost
    c. the possibility of quantity discounts
    d. the extent to which future demand is known

12. In the EOQ model
    a. shipments arrive in a batch
    b. demand is known and occurs at a constant rate
    c. all demand must be satisfied
    d. all of the above

13. In the EOQ model if the price of the item increases and all other parameters remain the same, the optimal order quantity will typically
    a. increase
    b. decrease
    c. stay the same

14. In the EOQ model the optimal number of orders per year
    a. increases directly with
    b. increases as the square root of
    c. decreases directly with
    d. does not change with
    the annual rate of demand.

15. Consider an EOQ model with a quantity discount where a smaller per unit price applies to all units if B or more units are purchased. If Q_D^* minimizes AHO assuming the smaller price, and Q_R^* minimizes AHO assuming the regular price, and $Q_D^* > B$, the optimal order quantity is always
    a. Q_D^*
    b. either Q_R^* or B, depending on which yields the smaller annual total cost
    c. Q_R^*
    d. B

16. In the EOQ model with backlogging the optimal number of orders to backlog is
    a. directly proportional to
    b. directly proportional to the square root of
    c. not dependent on
    d. directly proportional to the reciprocal of
    the annual rate of demand.

17. In the production lot size model, increasing the rate of production
   a. increases
   b. does not influence
   c. decreases
   the optimal number of orders to place each year.

Answers			
1. F	5. T	9. T	13. b
2. T	6. F	10. d	14. b
3. F	7. T	11. b	15. a
4. T	8. F	12. d	16. b
			17. a

PROBLEMS

11-1. A local hardware store sells 364,000 pounds of nails a year. It currently orders 14,000 pounds of nails every 2 weeks at a price of $0.50 per pound. Assume that

1. Demand occurs at a constant rate.
2. The cost of placing an order is $50 regardless of the size of the order.
3. The annual cost of holding inventory is 12% of the value of the average inventory level.
4. These factors do not change over time.

   (a) What is the average inventory level?
   (b) What is the annual holding cost?
   (c) What is the annual ordering cost?
   (d) What is the annual holding and ordering cost?
   (e) What is the annual total cost?
   (f) Would it be cheaper for the owner to order in larger lots (and less frequently) or smaller lots (and more frequently)?

11-2. The campus ice cream store sells 120 quarts of vanilla ice cream each month. The store currently restocks its inventory at the beginning of each month. The wholesale price of ice cream is $2 per quart. Assume that

1. Demand occurs at a constant rate.
2. The annual cost of holding inventory is 25% of the value of the average inventory level.
3. Last year the annual total cost was $3030.
4. These factors do not change over time.

   (a) Compute average inventory level.
   (b) Compute annual holding cost.
   (c) Compute annual ordering cost C_0.
   (d) Plot a graph of annual holding costs and annual ordering costs as a function of order quantity.
   (e) Graphically show at what point the AHO is minimized. How much can the ice cream store save if it uses the optimal order quantity?

11-3. A local entrepreneur and renowned visionary sells pencils at a constant rate of 25 per day. Each pencil costs $0.05. If ordering costs are $5 and inventory holding costs are 20% of the cost of the average inventory, what are the optimal order quantity and the optimal number of orders that should be placed each year?

11-4. Threadbare Haberdashery sells suits at a constant rate of 20 per day. Assume 300 days in a year. Suits cost $100 each and the annual inventory carrying costs are 20% of the cost of average inventory. It costs $54 to place an order. What are the values for Q*, N*, T*, and AHO(Q*)?

11-5. Specific Electric is a giant manufacturer of electrical appliances in the United States. It uses electric motors that it purchases from another firm at a constant rate. Total purchase costs during the year are $2,400,000. Ordering costs are $100 and annual inventory holding costs are 20% of the cost of the average inventory.

(a) What is the dollar value of the optimal order quantity?

(b) How many times a year should SE order?

(c) What is the optimal cycle time in years and in days if there are 250 working days per year?

HINT: If P is the cost per unit to Specific Electric and $Q*$ is the optimal quantity, $PQ*$ is the dollar value of the optimal order quantity.

11-6. Suppose that the actual holding cost in Problem 11-5 is 10% of the cost of average inventory and the ordering cost is $150. Find the ratio R defined as

$$R = \frac{\text{actual } AHO(Q^0)}{AHO(Q^*)}$$

where $AHO(Q)$ = Annual holding and ordering cost for a policy Q

Q^0 = Optimal policy with original parameter values.

Q^* = Optimal policy with new parameter values.

Assume that Specific Electric uses the optimal policy derived in Problem 11-5.

11-7. Strumm and Howell is a local record store that specializes in country music. The store has been quite successful in recent years, with retail sales of $400,000 per year. Sales occur at a constant rate during the year. S and H buys its records from a major recording company. The retail sales price equals $\frac{5}{3}$ times the cost to S and H. The ordering cost for each shipment of orders is $75, independent of the size of the order. Annual inventory holding costs are 10% of the cost of the average inventory level.

(a) What is the dollar value of the optimal order quantity?

(b) How often should S and H order each year?

(c) What is the optimal cycle time in years?

HINT: If P is the cost per unit to S and H and $Q*$ is the optimal order quantity, $PQ*$ is the dollar value of the optimal order quantity.

11-8. The cost estimates for the ordering and holding cost in Problem 11-7 may vary in a range of 20%. Find the maximum value of R defined in Problem 11-6. The two cost variables may have a positive or negative covariance. In which case would S and H need more precise estimates?

11-9. The Waukon, Iowa, outlet of Cheap Cheep Chicks orders baby chickens from the firm's central incubator in Des Moines. Ten dozen chicks are demanded each day of the 250-workday year. It costs $40 to process an order independent of the number of chicks ordered and $80 to hold a dozen chicks in inventory for a year. Assume that Cheap Cheep calculates inventory holding costs based on the average inventory level. The incubation period for eggs is 20 days, and thus it takes 20 days between the time an order is placed and the time the chicks are delivered.

(a) What is the optimal order quantity?

(b) How many orders should be placed each year?

(c) What is the optimal cycle time in years? In working days?

(d) What is the lead time?

(e) What is the inventory position at each order point?

(f) What is the demand during the lead time?

11-10. Suppose that the Waukon, Iowa, outlet of Cheap Cheep Chicks (see Problem 11-9) had its own incubator and could get same-day delivery of fresh eggs. These eggs must be placed in the incubator the day they arrive, and they are guaranteed to hatch in 20 days. It costs $40 to process an order for eggs independent of the number of eggs ordered. All other facts about the operation are the same as in Problem 11-9.

(a) What is the optimal order quantity for eggs?

(b) How many orders should be placed each year?

(c) What is the optimal cycle time in years? In work days?

(d) What is the lead time?

(e) What is the inventory position at each order point?

(f) What is the demand during the lead time?

11-11. Bed Bug, a local manufacturer of orthopedic mattresses, currently satisfies its constant production requirements of 500 coiled springs per day by using an EOQ model based on an ordering cost of $90, a product cost of $1 per spring, and an inventory holding cost of 15% of the cost of average inventory. Springy Steel, its supplier, has recently offered a 0.5% discount if Bed Bug orders in quantities of at least 20,000 springs, or a 0.7% discount if it orders quarterly. Assume 240 workdays per year.

(a) Find Q^*, T^*, N^*, and the annual total cost under the current cost assumptions.

(b) Calculate annual total cost for each of the discount alternatives.

(c) What should Bed Bug do?

11-12. Hong Kong's leading optical products center, I. Kant C. U., experiences demand for its eyeglasses at a constant annual rate of 5000 pairs. The store sells the glasses for $9 a pair, which is 150% of their cost. The ordering costs are $100 and annual inventory holding costs are 10% of the cost of average inventory. Currently, the center orders once a month. If it uses an optimal policy how much can the center discount the selling price without reducing its profit?

11-13. The Reefer Tobacco Company, the nation's largest distributor of California-grown smoking products, has a constant demand of 192 packs per month for its most popular product, Wachy Tabachy. Its ordering cost is $100, annual holding costs are 25% of the average inventory (due to the high risk of seizure), and the product costs $200 per pack. Currently, it does not backlog demand and follows the optimal ordering policy. Recently, a local consultant recommended that the company backlog demand. This requires a price discount. Reefer feels that it must offer a discount of $0.20 per day. Allowing for vacations and religious holidays, there are 200 days per year.

(a) Under the current policy (no backlogging), find Q^*, N^*, T^*, and AHO(Q^*).

(b) What is the value for C_b, the cost of backlogging a unit for a year?

(c) For the suggested backlogging policy, find Q^*, S^*, N^*, T^*, and AHOB(Q^*).

(d) Which policy should Reefer implement?

11-14. The demand for general books at the University Bookstore occurs at a constant rate of 25,000 books per year. The manager satisfies this demand without backlogging. He calculates the optimal order quantity based on ordering costs of $25 and an annual holding cost of $5 per book. Orders are delivered 7 days after they are received by telephone. Assume 250 days per year.

(a) What are the values for Q^*, N^*, T^*, and AHO*?

(b) When an order is placed, what is the level of
   (i) Inventory on hand?
   (ii) Inventory on order?
   (iii) Inventory position?

(c) What is the demand during the lead time?

11-15. Suppose that in Problem 11-14 the bookstore has the option of backlogging orders and that it costs $1.667 to backlog a unit of demand for a year. (When backlogging is permitted inventory position is defined as inventory on hand plus inventory on order plus S^*).

(a) What are the values for Q^*, N^*, T^*, S^*, and $AHOB^*$?

(b) When an order is placed, what is the level of
   (i) Inventory on hand?
   (ii) Inventory on order?
   (iii) Inventory position?

(c) What is the demand during the lead time?

(d) Should the bookstore backlog orders?

11-16. XXX Distillery, a major producer of arthritis and nerve medicine in the Southeast, produces its stock in batches. In order to begin each run, the company owners must select a suitable location and assemble the equipment. The cost of this operation is $750. Production yields 48 gallons of product each day, each of which costs $0.05 per day to hold in inventory. Demand is constant at 600 gallons per month. Assume 12 months, 300 days per year, and 25 days per month.

(a) Find Q^*, N^*, and T^* for the optimal production lot size.

(b) Find the maximum inventory and the length (in days) of each production run for the optimal production lot size.

(c) Find $AHO(Q^*)$.

11-17. Because of the importance of business confidentiality, XXX Distillery in Problem 16 decides to make four production runs per year.

(a) Find the production order quantity, Q^*, cycle time (in days), length of production run, and maximum inventory level.

(b) Find AHO for the policy in part (a).

11-18. Consider Problem 11-16.

(a) Suppose that XXX Distillery purchased rather than produced its product and that the cost of placing an order is $750. Find Q^* and $AHO(Q^*)$.

(b) How does $AHO(Q^*)$ in part (a) compare with $AHO(Q^*)$ when there is a production rate of 48 gallons per day? Explain this relationship.

(c) Plot the $AHO(Q^*(p))$ as a function of the daily production rate, p.

(d) Due to the economies of scale, unit production costs decrease as p goes up. The exact relationship is $C(p) = 30/p$ where $C(p)$ is the unit production cost when the daily production rate is p. Find the minimum value of the sum of AHO and annual production costs for $p = 24$ and $p = 48$.

11-19. Due to technical obsolescence of its equipment, XXX Distillery (Problem 11-16) stops producing and functions only as a marketing organization. It now purchases its product from another producer. XXX must buy at least 1200 gallons per order to qualify for a quantity discount. What is the smallest discount per gallon that would persuade XXX to order 1200 gallons?

11-20. The Clunker Car Company (CCC) produces automobiles based on the latest Model T technology. Some of the materials used in its newest line of import-competing automobiles, the C-Cars, are shown in Figure 11.20. CCC's current inventory levels include 300 throats, 200 butterfly valves, 250 spark plug sets (1 set per engine), 50 carburetors, and 75 engines.

525

FIGURE 11.20

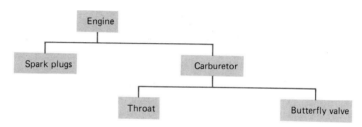

(a) What additional amounts of each part will be needed to satisfy an order for 375 engines?

(b) Assume that the lead time for assembly is 10 days for engines and 5 days for carburetors. Assume further that the lead time for ordering throats is 3 days, butterfly valves is 2 days, and spark plugs is 6 days. Find the ordering and assembly schedule for an order due in 30 days.

11-21. Solve Problem 11-20 with the following data:

Current inventory
150 throats
100 butterfly valves
125 spark plug sets
90 carburetors
130 engines
Assembly time
Engines, 8 days
Carburetors, 6 days
Ordering time
Throats, 5 days
Butterfly valves, 3 days
Spark plugs, 5 days

What is the date that the first action must be taken? Which action is it?

——————— APPENDIX 11.1

MATHEMATICAL DERIVATION OF EOQ RESULTS

The EOQ
Model

To derive expression (11.9), the optimal value of Q in the EOQ model, you must find the value of Q that minimizes expression (11.5), the annual holding and ordering cost.

$$\text{AHO} = C_0 \left(\frac{D}{Q} \right) + C_h \left(\frac{Q}{2} \right)$$

Taking the first derivative with respect to Q yields

$$\frac{d}{dQ} \text{AHO} = \frac{-C_0 D}{Q^2} + \frac{C_h}{2}$$

Setting this result equal to zero and solving for Q gives

$$Q^* = \sqrt{\frac{2C_0D}{C_h}}$$

which is (11.9).

To demonstrate that Q^* yields a minimum, you take the second derivative of AHO with respect to Q and determine if it is positive:

$$\frac{d^2}{dQ^2} \text{AHO} = \frac{2C_0D}{Q^3}$$

Since the result is positive for all $Q > 0$, you can conclude that Q^* yields a minimum.

Equality of the Annual Holding and Ordering Cost

It is useful to show that

$$C_0\left(\frac{D}{Q^*}\right) = C_h\left(\frac{Q^*}{2}\right)$$

that is, that the optimal order quantity yields equal values for the annual holding and annual ordering costs.

The demonstration is achieved by substituting the expression for Q^* into the left-hand side of the inequality and obtaining the right-hand side.

$$C_0\left(\frac{D}{Q^*}\right) = C_0\frac{D}{(2C_0D/C_h)^{1/2}}$$

$$= C_0\left(\frac{2}{2}\right)\frac{DC_h^{1/2}}{(2C_0D)^{1/2}}\left(\frac{C_h}{C_h}\right)^{1/2}$$

$$= C_h\frac{1}{2}\left(\frac{2C_0D}{C_h}\right)^{1/2}$$

$$= C_h\left(\frac{Q^*}{2}\right) \qquad\qquad \text{Q.E.D.}$$

12

INVENTORY MODELS WITH PROBABILISTIC DEMAND

———— 12.1
INTRODUCTION

Dealing with Uncertainty   There are many sources of uncertainty in a typical production and distribution system. There is uncertainty as to how many items customers will demand during the next week, month, or year. There is uncertainty about delivery times. If one of your suppliers says that you will receive your order before January 5, can you rely on it or will your order arrive weeks or months later? There is uncertainty in the production processes. What happens to your production and delivery plans if a worker is sick or if a critical machine breaks down? Uncertainty exacts a toll from management in a variety of ways. A spurt in demand or a delay in production may lead to stockouts with the potential for lost revenue and customer dissatisfaction. Alternatively, a firm might react to a current or anticipated stockout by expediting orders, placing special orders with a supplier, or working overtime. All of these activities can be costly.

Firms typically hold inventory to provide protection against uncertainty. Clearly, a cushion of inventory on hand allows management to face unexpected demands or delays in delivery with a reduced chance of incurring a stockout. We have, however, already observed that holding inventory is not free. The question, then, is: "How much inventory should a firm hold to provide reasonable protection against uncertainty?"

In previous chapters we have seen that management attempts to deal with such questions about uncertainty in a variety of ways. For example, in LP models, sensitivity analysis is typically used to assure management that its decisions are not vulnerable to changes in the parameters of the model. This chapter considers uncertainty in a more formal fashion. It looks at models in which uncertainty is dealt with explicitly by incorporating a *probability distribution of demand* into the evaluation of the various alternative inventory control schemes.

The chapter has two main divisions. The first deals with the *reorder point–reorder quantity* models that were introduced in the preceding chapter. The new twist is that a distribution for lead-time demand will be introduced. Also, no backlogging will be allowed. The second division introduces *one-period inventory models*. These models are appropriate for situations in which only one ordering decision is to be made in anticipation of future demand. Such models are directly applicable to purchase decisions involving, for example, style goods or perishable products. The rationale for these models also provides the basis for more complex models involving a sequence of ordering decisions.

———— 12.2
THE REORDER POINT–REORDER QUANTITY MODEL

In the preceding chapter we have seen Victor Kowalski develop a reorder point–reorder quantity model to control the inventory of appliance angles. There are three main points to review:

1. *The rule itself:*   The operating rule in a reorder point–reorder quantity model is specified by two parameters: the reorder point (r) and the reorder quantity (Q). The operating rule states that when the inventory position[1] equals r, an order for Q items should be placed. Because this model is defined by its two parameters, it is commonly referred to as an (r, Q) model. We will adopt this notation.

2. *Determining Q:*   The reorder quantity, Q, is determined using the EOQ (economic order quantity) model. This model must be modified to take quantity discounts and backlogging into account when such factors are appropriate.

3. *Determining r:*   The reorder point, r, is chosen to protect the firm from running out of stock during the lead time. If demand is known with certainty, then r is set equal to the demand during the lead time.

———— 12.3
THE APPLIANCE ANGLE PROBLEM

Let us review some of the details of Victor's problem and the EOQ model that he used to solve it. The model assumed that demand occurred at a constant and known rate of 5000 items per month. The cost of placing an order and the annual holding cost per item were specified as $25.00 and $1.92, respectively. Steco purchased items from the mill at $8.00 each unless orders were placed in lots of at least 5000 items, in which case the price was $7.90 per unit. Under these conditions Victor discovered, using the EOQ formulas, that an order quantity of 5000 items minimized the annual total cost (ATC), defined as the sum of the purchase, ordering, and inventory costs during the year.

Under the assumption that demand is known and occurs at a constant rate, we saw that the reorder point r, as noted in point 3, should be set equal to the demand

---

[1] Inventory position is defined as inventory on hand plus that already on order.

FIGURE 12.1

(r, Q) Model with Known Demand

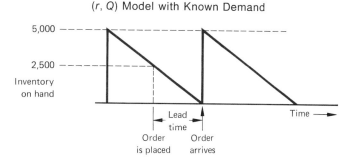

during the lead time. Since demand was assumed to be 5000 items per month, if the lead time was one-half month, Victor would select the reorder point of 2500 angles (i.e., $r = 2500$). With these assumptions, inventory would run out at just the instant the order arrived (see Figure 12.1).

We also noted in Chapter 11 that in reality demand is almost never known with certainty. We saw that in such a case the reorder point r, as described above, can result in a stockout. To illustrate the last point, suppose that in the angle problem the actual demand during the 2-week lead time turned out to be more than the 2500 units implied by the assumption of a constant rate of 5000 per month. Since only 2500 units are on hand at the beginning of the 2-week lead time, and since no new units arrive until the end, if demand during that 2-week period exceeds 2500, there will be a stockout, which means, by definition, that orders arrive but inventory has been depleted. For example, suppose that there is a demand for 2550 items rather than 2500. This is a small percentage error, but still Victor would be unable to fill 50 orders at the time they were demanded. Each unfilled order could represent a serious loss to Steco. If the customer was not willing to wait for a late delivery (i.e., demand cannot be backlogged), Steco would lose the profit from this potential sale. In addition, the customer might choose to do business in the future with a firm that could provide better service.

One obvious way to reduce the chance of running out of stock is to increase the value of r. This was also discussed in Chapter 11. If Victor had reordered when there were 2750 items on hand, he clearly would not run out if the demand were 2550 or 2650 or even 2750. There is another side to this story, however. Increasing r increases on the average the amount of inventory that Steco will hold. If Victor increases r to 2750 and the average demand is 2500, then clearly, on the average, he will have 250 items on hand when the next order arrives. Holding inventory is not free. Indeed, one of the two cost components considered in the EOQ model is the cost of holding inventory. Victor is thus faced with a classical management problem. If he increases r, the reorder point, he decreases the chance that he will run out of stock, but he increases his average inventory holding cost. If he decreases r, he increases the chance of running out, but decreases the average inventory holding cost. The question is: "How large should r be to achieve the proper balance between these two factors?" In the preceding chapter it was suggested that a manager might *intuitively* add an appropriate safety stock to the average lead-time demand to solve this problem. In this chapter we give a formal framework for thinking about the choice of r. It will be seen that this framework can assist management in making a more informed decision.

**How Large
Should r Be?**

VICTOR'S CHOICE OF r: UNIFORM LEAD-TIME DEMAND

The analytic approach that is commonly used to determine the reorder point is to assume that the probability distribution of demand during the lead time is known. In other words, it is not assumed that demand is exactly known but, rather, the probabilities with which it might assume various values are assumed to be known. For example, rather than assuming that demand during the lead time is 2500 units, it might be assumed that demand would equal 2475 with probability one-half and 2525 with probability one-half. Indeed, the term "decisions under risk" is used by many authors to indicate a situation in which the probabilities of the uncertain events are known.

Victor knows something about the demand for angles from his experience in sales. It seems to him that the demand during the $\frac{1}{2}$-month lead time is never more than 3000 items or less than 2001. Between these two extremes one level of demand seems about as likely as the next. Since there are 1000 numbers in this interval, this implies that the probability that demand equals 2482 or 2535 or any other number in the interval is $\frac{1}{1000}$. In other words, Victor initially approaches the problem of choosing r by assuming that lead-time demand is uniformly distributed over the interval from 2001 to 3000. With this assumption, Victor can easily control the probability of a stockout. Consider the following examples:

1. If Victor sets r equal to any value larger than 3000, he will never run out during the lead time. For example, if he sets r equal to 3010, he will always have at least 10 angles on hand when the next order arrives. Since demand during the lead time is ≤ 3000 and he starts with 3010 on hand, he must have at least 10 on hand at the end of the lead time.
2. If an r of 2995 is selected, a stockout will occur if demand is 2996, 2997, 2998, 2999, or 3000. Since the probability of each of these quantities is $\frac{1}{1000}$, the probability of a stockout is $\frac{5}{1000} = 0.005$.

$p(s)$, the Probability of a Stockout

These examples indicate how the probability of a stockout can be controlled by the choice of r. Generalizing this discussion, we see that if the reorder point is r, with $r < 3000$, then a stockout will occur if demand is $r + 1, r + 2, \ldots, 3000$. If we let $p(s)$ be the probability of a stockout, then if $r \geq 3000$, $p(s)$ is zero. If $r < 3000$, then

$$p(s) = \frac{3000 - r}{1000}$$

Some values of $p(s)$ and r are shown in Figure 12.2.

Figure 12.2 illustrates the intuitively appealing fact that as r increases, $p(s)$ decreases. It also establishes the idea that specifying $p(s)$ dictates a value for r. To see this you must simply read Figure 12.2 from right to left. If Victor wants the probability of stocking out to equal 0.05, then he must choose $r = 2950$. Similarly, a $p(s)$ of 0.13 implies an r of 2870.

Victor now understands that choosing $p(s)$ implies a value for r, and vice versa. He still does not know how to choose a "good" value for r, or $p(s)$. One approach would be to assign a "penalty cost" per unit stockout. Victor would then choose r to minimize the expected holding and penalty cost during the lead time. One problem with this would be that penalty costs can be difficult to assess. In any case, an example of this type of approach is presented in the second half of this chapter in connection with the discussion of one-period inventory models.

FIGURE 12.2

r, the Reorder Point, Versus p(s), the
Probability of a Stockout, Assuming
Uniform Lead-Time Demand

r	p(s)
3010	0
3000	0
2950	0.05
2920	0.08
2870	0.13
2750	0.25
2500	0.50

Another way to determine r, or $p(s)$, is to intuitively balance several implications. This is discussed in the next three sections.

12.5
SELECTING A PROBABILITY OF STOCKING OUT

We have just illustrated the fact that choosing the reorder point r is equivalent to choosing $p(s)$, the probability of stocking out during the lead time to delivery. In thinking about the appropriate value for $p(s)$ in the case of appliance angles Victor considers the following facts:

1. Appliance angles are carried by all steel wholesalers.
2. The lead time for delivery from the steel mill is 2 weeks. Thus, Steco cannot quickly replenish its supply.

The result of these two facts is that if Steco is unable to fill an order when it is placed, the customer will almost always go to another supplier. Victor thus wants to make sure that Steco does not run out very often. Consequently, he wants to select a small value for $p(s)$.

To get a feeling for the effects of a particular choice of $p(s)$, he might ask: "Suppose I choose $p(s) = 0.05$. How often will I stock out *during a year*?" There is no certain numerical answer to Victor's question. We can, however, make the following observations:

1. Since the order quantity Q is 5000, and since annual demand is 60,000, there are 12 orders placed per year. Thus, during each year there are 12 lead times, which means 12 opportunities to stock out. This is the maximum number of stockouts that can occur.
2. During *each* lead time Steco will stock out with a probability of $p(s)$. This is independent of whether a stockout occurred during any previous lead time.

Average Stockouts Per Year   Thus, if $p(s) = 0.05$ for *each* lead time, and we have 12 lead times a year, there will be, on the average, $(0.05)(12) = 0.6$ stockout per year, which means about 6 stockouts every 10 years. Victor may well be willing to select a value for $p(s)$ on the basis, as above, of *average stockouts per year*. But he can also obtain more specific information.

The two observations above imply that the *binomial distribution* can be used to calculate the probability of incurring any specific number of stockouts during a year.

In general terms, the binomial distribution assumes two inputs: (1) an event that has a probability, say α, of occurring at a given trial and (2) a sequence of n independent trials. Then[2]

$$\text{The probability of having the event occur exactly } x \text{ times in } n \text{ trials}$$

$$= \frac{n!}{x!\,(n-x)!}\,\alpha^x(1-\alpha)^{n-x} \qquad \text{for } x = 0, 1, 2, \ldots, n \qquad (12.1)$$

The Binomial Distribution and the Number of Stockouts

In the angles example the interpretation of a "trial" would be "lead time," and the "event" under consideration would be "a stockout during a lead time." Thus, $\alpha = p(s)$. Since there are 12 lead times per year, we would have $n = 12$. Choosing, as above, $p(s) = 0.05$, we can compute the probability of exactly x stockouts from the expression

$$\frac{12!}{x!\,(12-x)!}\,(0.05)^x(0.95)^{n-x}$$

Victor can use this expression to calculate the probability of any specific number of stockouts in a year. For example, he computes that the probability of zero stockouts is 0.54, and there will be exactly 1 stockout (in a year) with probability 0.34. Although he now has the possibility of deriving considerable specific information, he would like a simple statistic to use in comparing the effects of alternative values of $p(s)$. Since he does not want to stock out "very often," he decides to compute the probability that he will stock out more than once during a year.

He makes use of the following relationship:

Prob {more than one stockout} = $1 - $ {Prob [zero stockouts] + Prob [one stockout]}

$$(12.2)$$

In particular, when $p(s) = 0.05$,

$$P\{\text{more than one stockout}\} = 1 - \{0.54 + 0.34\} = 0.12$$

where, as given above, Prob {0 stockouts} = 0.54, and Prob {1 stockout} = 0.34. Similar analysis can be used to construct a table such as the one shown in Figure 12.3. This table incorporates two implications which follow from a choice of $p(s)$ or r: (1) probability of more than one stockout in a year and (2) average number of stockouts per year.

In concluding this section, two points should be emphasized:

1. The first two columns of Figure 12.3 [i.e., the relation between r and $p(s)$] depend on the probability distribution of demand during the lead time. Recall in the discussion above that Victor assumed a probability of $\frac{1}{1000}$ for all integer demands from 2001 to (and including) 3000.

---

[2] The term $n! = n(n-1)(n-2)\cdots 1$. For example, $4! = 4 \cdot 3 \cdot 2 \cdot 1 = 24$. By convention, $0!$ is assigned the value 1.

FIGURE 12.3
Data When Demand Is Uniform

$p(s)$	r	PROBABILITY OF MORE THAN ONE STOCKOUT PER YEAR	AVERAGE NUMBER OF STOCKOUTS PER YEAR
0	3000	0	0
0.02	2980	0.03	0.24
0.05	2950	0.12	0.6
0.10	2900	0.34	1.2
0.25	2750	0.84	3
0.50	2500	0.997	6

2. The last two columns of Figure 12.3 have nothing to do with the probability distribution of lead time demand. They are based on
   a. The probability of a stockout during *each* lead time [the value of $p(s)$]
   b. The number of orders placed each year (the value of n, which is determined by Q)

Effect of Order Size on Stockouts

To emphasize the last point, recall that Victor selected an order quantity Q of 5000 items. Since his model anticipates an annual demand of 60,000 items, $n = 12$ (i.e., 60,000/5000) orders are planned for each year. Suppose that, instead of 5000, an order quantity of $Q = 10,000$ items had been selected. In this case only 6 orders would be planned each year; that is, there would be 6 times throughout the year during which a stockout could occur. Then, with $p(s) = 0.05$ and $n = 6$, expression (12.1) produces

$$\text{probability of no stockouts} = \frac{6!}{0!\,6!}(0.05)^0(0.95)^6 = 0.735$$

$$\text{probability of one stockout} = \frac{6!}{1!\,5!}(0.05)^1(0.95)^5 = 0.232$$

Thus, the probability of more than one stockout during the year becomes $1 - (0.735 + 0.232) = 0.033$. This compares with 0.12 for the case of 12 orders per year. Also note that, with 6 orders per year there are, on the average, 0.3 stockouts per year, as opposed to 0.6 in the previous case. We see, then, that only Q and $p(s)$ play a role in determining the last two columns of Figure 12.3.

_____ 12.6
VICTOR'S CHOICE OF r: NORMAL LEAD-TIME DEMAND

Victor assumed that demand during lead time was uniformly distributed between 2001 and 3000. Many of the commercial inventory control systems find it useful to assume that the demand during the lead time has a normal probability distribution. This assumption is popular for two main reasons:

1. It is a good enough approximation to reality to yield useful results.
2. The normal probability distribution is completely characterized by two parameters: the mean, μ, and the standard deviation, σ. Since only two numbers are required to specify the demand for each product, it is easy to store in a computer the probability distribution for many products (in some cases, thousands). Think how much space would be required if yoɹ had to specify, for each product, a different probability distribution with 1000 possible outcomes.

FIGURE 12.4

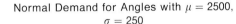

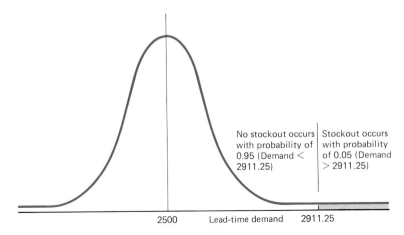

FIGURE 12.4
Normal Demand for Angles with $\mu = 2500$, $\sigma = 250$

Victor has just learned that ICON, the inventory control system used at Steco, assumes that demand during the lead time has a normal distribution. Since the inventory of angles will actually be controlled by this system, Victor decides to find out how this system would select r. He learns that by using past demands, the system has estimated that the demand during the lead time has a mean, μ, of 2500 and standard deviation, σ, of 250. A diagram of this distribution is shown in Figure 12.4.

Finding r
Given $p(s)$
The assumption that demand during the lead time has a normal distribution with $\mu = 2500$ and $\sigma = 250$ makes it possible for Victor to find the appropriate r for any value of $p(s)$, the probability of a stockout during a lead time, that he chooses. For example, suppose that he wants to have, as previously, $p(s) = 0.05$. Refer to Table T.1 on page 822, and you will see that an r value that is 1.645 standard derivations above the mean corresponds to a $p(s)$ of 0.05. It follows that for the assumed normal distribution with $\mu = 2500$ and $\sigma = 250$, as shown in Figure 12.4, the reorder point r is given by $r = 2500 + 1.645(250) = 2911.25$. Similar calculations, using different values for $p(s)$, yield the data shown in Figure 12.5.

These data should be compared with Figure 12.3. You can see that for the same values of $p(s)$ the two figures give different values for r. This shows how changing the distribution of lead-time demand changes the relation between r and $p(s)$. However, since the order quantity Q is 5000 and thus there are 12 orders per year, the last two columns of Figure 12.5 remain the same as in Figure 12.3.

FIGURE 12.5
Data When Demand Is Normal with $\mu = 2500$, $\sigma = 250$

$p(s)$	r	PROBABILITY OF MORE THAN ONE STOCKOUT PER YEAR	AVERAGE NUMBER OF STOCKOUTS PER YEAR
0.02	3013.5	0.03	0.24
0.05	2911.2	0.12	0.6
0.10	2820.2	0.34	1.2
0.25	2668.5	0.84	3
0.50	2500.0	0.997	6

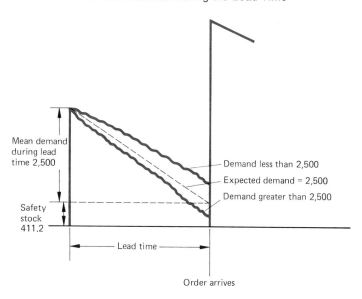

FIGURE 12.6
Random Demand During the Lead Time

12.7
EXPECTED ANNUAL COST OF SAFETY STOCK

We have discussed several implications of selecting a particular value for the reorder point, r. One is the average number of stockouts per year. Another is the probability of stocking out more than once during a year. Associated with various choices for r will be a safety stock, and a consideration of importance is the expected annual holding cost that is associated with keeping this safety stock. Recall that the *safety stock* has been defined as the quantity that is added to the expected demand during the lead time to protect against uncertainty. Thus,

$$\text{safety stock} = r - \text{expected demand during the lead time}^{3}$$

Average Inventory Increased by Safety Stock
  It is a fact that the average inventory on hand during a year is increased by an amount equal to the safety stock. To understand this, recall that if Victor selected a $p(s) = 0.05$, the appropriate value of r using the normal distribution for lead-time demand is 2911.2 (see Figure 12.5). Since the expected demand during the lead time is the mean of our normal distribution, namely 2500, we see that the safety stock, in this instance is 411.2 units. This situation is shown in Figure 12.6. Here we see that sometimes demand is less than and sometimes greater than the mean demand (2500). On the average, however, demand will equal 2500 units and thus Steco will have increased the average amount of inventory on hand by the safety stock. Recall from Chapter 11 that C_h, Steco's cost of holding an angle in inventory for a year, is \$1.92. Then

$$\text{expected annual cost of safety stock} = C_h \cdot (\text{safety stock}) = 1.92(411.2) = 789.50$$

Other costs could be calculated for other values of r. These calculations are combined with previous calculations in Figure 12.5 to yield Figure 12.7.

---

[3] Expected demand during the lead time is the mean of the lead-time demand distribution.

FIGURE 12.7
Characteristics When Demand is Normal
with $\mu = 2500$, $\sigma = 250$

$p(s)$	r	SAFETY STOCK	PROBABILITY OF MORE THAN ONE STOCKOUT PER YEAR	AVERAGE NUMBER OF STOCKOUTS PER YEAR	EXPECTED ANNUAL COST OF SAFETY STOCK
0.02	3013.5	513.5	0.03	0.24	$985.92
0.05	2911.2	411.2	0.12	0.6	789.50
0.10	2820.2	320.2	0.34	1.2	614.78
0.25	2668.5	168.5	0.84	3	323.52
0.50	2500	0	0.997	6	0

Managerial Judgment Needed   This table makes it easier for management to understand the trade-off between holding inventory and stocking out, and provides the basis for at least a partially enlightened choice for the reorder point, r. Management can compare, for example, the case when $p(s) = 0.05$ and $r = 2911$ with the no-safety-stock situation, $p(s) = 0.5$ and $r = 2500$. Here it costs $789.50 to decrease the probability of more than 1 stockout per year from 0.997 to 0.12 (also, to decrease the average number of stockouts per year from 6 to less than 1). Rather than asking himself, "Do I prefer a $p(s)$ of 0.50 to one of 0.05?" a manager can ask, "Is it worth about $789.50 to decrease the probability of more than 1 stockout per year from 0.997 to 0.12?" With $p(s) = 0.50$ he would expect to stock out more than once essentially every year, whereas with $p(s) = 0.05$ he would expect to stock out more than once (during the year) only about once in every 8 years ($\frac{1}{8} = 0.125$). A table like Figure 12.7 provides an excellent example of how management can typically make use of formal models. The models are used to generate data, such as those shown in the table. Based on these data, and his own experience, the manager uses his judgment in making his decision.

12.8
ONE-PERIOD MODELS WITH PROBABILISTIC DEMAND (WILES' HOUSEWARES PROBLEM)

Peggy McConnel is the chief buyer for housewares at Wiles, Chicago's leading retailer. The chief buyer's role is important in a retail organization like Wiles. Peggy is responsible for designing the overall retailing strategy and operating procedures for her area. She also supervises a group of buyers who make specific purchase decisions.

Certain sections of the housewares department have just suffered their second consecutive bad year. Competing shops, such as Box and Barrel, which specialize in imported cooking and dining articles, have made serious inroads into Wiles' once secure position. The gourmet cooking, glassware, stainless flatware, and contemporary dishes sections of Wiles are not generating enough revenue to justify the amount of floor space currently committed to them.

Peggy plans to meet this challenge head-on. She has reorganized the sections that are in trouble to create a store within a store. To achieve the same ambience as her competitors, she has adopted display techniques that feature natural wood and modern lighting. She has essentially created a specialty shop, like her competitors, within the housewares department. With these changes, plus the store's reputation for quality and service, she feels that Wiles can effectively compete.

To introduce the new facility at Wiles, Peggy decides to make the month of October "International Dining Month." This promotion will feature a sale on five special articles, each from a different country. These articles will be especially made for Wiles and include a copper omelet pan from France, a set of 12 long-stem wine glasses from Spain, and so on. Each of the items has been selected by a buyer on Peggy's staff. The design and price are agreed on. The items have to be ordered at least 6 months in advance and they will not become part of Wiles' regular product line. Any items left at the end of October will be sold to a discount chain at a reduced price. In addition, Wiles has adopted the policy that if it runs out of the special sale items, a more expensive item from its regular line of merchandise will be substituted at the sale price. It is all part of the "once in a lifetime" promotion.

The Essence of the Problem

Peggy and her buyers must decide how many of these items to order now, 6 long months before the sale takes place in October. If demand were known, the decision would be easy: Order the quantity demanded. But demand is uncertain. *If they order too many, excess items will be sold at a loss. If they order too few, substitute items must be sold at a loss.* Unfortunately, they cannot find help by examining the (r, Q) inventory system that Wiles uses for stock items in housewares. This problem does not fit that mold. The (r, Q) model balances reorder costs and inventory holding costs. Here the ordering cost is not in question. Each item will be ordered once. Peggy needs to balance the cost of ordering too much against the cost of ordering too little. A new approach is required.

——— 12.9
THE NEWSBOY PROBLEM

The problem faced by Peggy and her staff is a classic management science problem known as the newsboy problem. In this problem the newsboy buys Q papers from the delivery truck driver at the beginning of the day. During the day he sells papers. How many he will sell is unknown in advance. At the end of the day the papers are worthless. If he buys more than he sells, he loses the money associated with the leftover papers. If he does not buy enough, he loses the potential profits from additional sales.

Suppose that he pays C dollars for each paper and sells them for S dollars each. Let $C = \$0.10$ and $S = \$0.25$. The model is built on three components:

Components of the Newsboy Problem

1. The holding cost, h, is the cost per unit to the newsboy of each leftover paper. In this example

$$h = C = \$0.10$$

2. The penalty cost, p, is the profit that the newsboy "loses" with each paper that could have been sold but was not because he had run out. In this example,

$$p = S - C$$
$$= \$0.25 - \$0.10$$
$$= \$0.15$$

3. The probability distribution of demand.

The information about the probability that demand takes on particular values is contained in the probability distribution of demand. One would expect this distribution to be different for different products, times, and so on. Indeed, the form of the distribution can change. In some cases a normal distribution is appropriate. Other distributions may be more realistic in other cases. In this example, suppose, for simplicity, that the newsboy employs a *uniform* distribution. In particular, he believes that any demand between 1 and 100 is equally likely. Thus,

$$\text{Prob }\{\text{demand} = 1\} = \tfrac{1}{100}$$

$$\text{Prob }\{\text{demand} = 23\} = \tfrac{1}{100}$$

$$\text{Prob }\{\text{demand} = \text{any integer from 1 through 100}\} = \tfrac{1}{100}$$

Therefore,

$$\text{Prob }\{\text{demand} \leq 5\} = \tfrac{5}{100} = 0.05$$

$$\text{Prob }\{\text{demand} \leq 23\} = \tfrac{23}{100} = 0.23$$

Generalizing this reasoning, we see that

$$\text{Prob }\{\text{demand} \leq x\} \begin{cases} = 0 & \text{where } x \leq 0 \\ = x/100 & \text{where } x = 1, 2, \ldots, 100 \\ = 1 & \text{where } x \geq 100 \end{cases}$$

The Optimal Order Quantity The three components (p, h, and the probability distribution of demand) come together in the following equation to determine Q^*, the optimal (i.e., *cost minimizing*) order quantity.[4]

$$Q^* \text{ is the smallest integer such that } P\{\text{demand} \leq Q^*\} \geq \frac{p}{p + h} \qquad (12.3)$$

In our example, $p = \$0.15$, $h = \$0.10$, and

$$P\{\text{demand} \leq x\} = \frac{x}{100} \qquad \text{for } x = 1, 2, \ldots, 100$$

Substituting these values into (12.3) yields

$$P\{\text{demand} \leq Q^*\} \geq \frac{p}{p + h}, \qquad \text{which means}$$

$$\frac{Q^*}{100} \geq \frac{0.15}{0.15 + 0.10} = 0.60$$

$$Q^* = 60$$

---

[4] The derivation of this result would require a technical discussion which we have chosen to omit because of constraints on both space and level of treatment.

If Peggy is to fit her problem into the newsboy model, she must specify each of the three components. Consider the copper omelet pan. Wiles will buy these pans for $22 each and will sell them for $35. Any pans left at the end of the sale will be sold to Clampton's Discount Chain for $15 each. If Wiles runs out of these pans, it will substitute one of its regular copper omelet pans and sell it for the sale price of $35. These regular pans cost $32 each and normally sell for $65. These data provide the basis for calculating the cost parameters in the newsboy problem.

Specifying the Components

1. Let us first determine the holding cost, h. Since Wiles pays $22 for each pan and sells each leftover pan for $15, the store loses $7 on each pan not sold during the sale. Thus, $h = \$7$.

2. Next, let us look at the penalty cost, p. Each time a regular pan is substituted for a sale pan to satisfy excess demand, Wiles gains $3 ($35 − $32). If a sale pan had been available, Wiles would have gained $13 ($35 − $22). Taking into account this "forgone gain," and treating it as an "opportunity cost," we see that the cost per unit of running out of sale omelet pans is $10 ($13 − $3).

3. Peggy must also specify the probability distribution of demand. This is not easy. There are no directly applicable historical data. Wiles has not tried exactly this promotion before. There is, however, information about the results of other sales. In addition, Peggy has opinions and information about the state of the economy, the desirability of this particular item, and so on.

Faced with the fact that she must specify a probability distribution, she uses the following approach:

 a. Her best guess for demand during the sale is 1000 pans. She feels it is equally likely that actual demand may exceed or fall short of this best guess.

 b. She feels confident that demand will not be less than 700 pans or more than 1300.

 c. A demand near 1000 seems much more likely than one near 700 or 1300.

Based on these three observations, Peggy decides on the following model:

1. Demand is normal.
2. The mean, μ, equals her best estimate of demand, $\mu = 1000$.
3. The standard deviation, σ, is given by the calculation

$$\sigma = \frac{1300 - 700}{6} = 100$$

This calculation is based on the observation that an interval 3 standard deviations above and 3 standard deviations below the mean includes almost all possible outcomes. In other words, the distance between the largest and the smallest potential outcomes is $3 + 3 = 6$ standard deviations. This distribution is shown in Figure 12.8.

FIGURE 12.8
Normal Distribution with $\mu = 1000$ and $\sigma = 100$

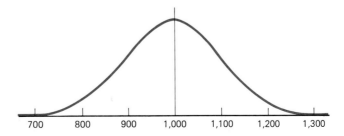

Computing the Order Quantity With the assumption that demand is normal with $\mu = 1000$ and $\sigma = 100$, and using the values determined above for h and p, the optimal order quantity Q^* is found by solving equation (12.3). Peggy must select Q^* such that

$$P\{\text{demand} \leq Q^*\} \geq \frac{p}{p + h} = 0.588$$

We see from Table T.1 on page 822 that 0.588 of the area under the curve for a normal distribution lies to the left of a point that is about 0.22 standard deviation above the mean. Since Peggy has assumed a mean of 1000 and a standard deviation of 100,

$$Q^* = 1000 + 0.22(100) = 1022$$

In other words, given her specification of h, p, and the probability distribution of demand, the newsboy model indicates that Peggy should order 1022 omelet pans.

Importance of the Choice of Distribution Let us now suppose that Peggy changes her distribution. Instead of using the normal, suppose that she were to assume a uniform distribution on the interval from 700 to 1300. In this case,

$$P\{\text{demand} \leq x\} = \frac{x - 700}{600} \qquad \text{for } x = 701, 702, \ldots, 1300$$

and solving (12.3) for Q^* gives

$$P\{\text{demand} \leq Q^*\} = \frac{Q^* - 700}{600} \geq 0.588$$

$$Q^* \geq 600(0.588) + 700 = 1052.8$$

and hence $Q^* = 1053$. With the normal assumption she orders 1022. Had she used the uniform distribution, she would order 1053. You can see that the assumption about the distribution of demand can be of considerable importance. It is typical of probabilistic inventory models that assumptions about the distribution of demand can greatly affect the recommended decision. That is why care must be exercised to find a distribution that best approximates reality. You can think of the distribution itself as a model of reality—a model that we then use in another model to recommend a decision.

12.10
NOTES ON IMPLEMENTATION

The "Two-Bin" System Inventory control is one of the oldest and most common applications of quantitative models. In manufacturing companies, the most popular implementation of inventory control models has been historically the "two-bin" inventory system. In this system a certain number of items are set aside, in bin 1, so to speak. All other items are held in another location, bin 2. Items are removed from bin 2 in order to satisfy demand. When bin 2 is empty and the stock clerk starts to use items from bin 1, this is the signal to place an order for a predetermined quantity of items. In the 1950s a computer card would be attached to bin 1. When the clerk removed the first item from bin 1 he or she also removed the computer card and sent it to inventory control. This card initiated the order for the item.

The two-bin system is a method of implementing the reorder point–reorder quantity model. The age of cheap computing and remote terminal entry has made this system less important. In more current versions, the process of billing a customer will often automatically adjust the inventory level. For example, the cash register in a department store, as well as itemizing your bill, will often make a record of the item you purchased. This information is fed to a computer, which adjusts the inventory level and triggers a reorder when appropriate. The data accumulated with such devices can also be used in evaluating the success of a product line and forecasting future demand.

Software Packages

A number of computer manufacturers offer an inventory control package as a standard part of their software package. Packages of some long standing include IBM's IMPACT, Honeywell's PROFIT, and RCA's WISDOM. IBM also has a more recent entry in the field entitled INFOREM, *In*ventory *Fo*recasting and *R*eplenishment *M*odels.

To the extent that one can generalize, these packages are based on the use of exponential smoothing (see Chapter 18) for forecasting and a reorder point–reorder quantity model as the inventory control mechanism. Each package has its own features, and we do not intend to go into detail here. It is, however, interesting to note that simulation (see Chapter 14) is an option in certain cases. This makes it possible to evaluate the operation of the system under various sets of parameters (e.g., reorder point, reorder quantity, or demand distribution) or to compare the operations of different types of systems. The very existence of these different packages indicates the importance of the inventory management function.

In some industries (or activities) inventory control has a special significance and the assumptions underlying the standard packages (IMPACT, etc.) do not fit very well. In such cases it pays for the organization to develop its own inventory control system. One example is provided by the steel wholesaling business (like Steco). Here, for certain products, the idiosyncrasies of the supplier, the steel manufacturers, make it difficult to use a standard approach. Certain types of steel are produced in large batches (heats) on a schedule that is known a year or so in advance. The wholesaler must determine if it wishes to buy part of a particular heat. Once a heat is sold out, prospective buyers must wait for the next heat. This uncertainty in supply must be reflected in the inventory control system for these items.

Another example, where organizations may need to develop their own self-tailored systems, is provided by the inventory of replacement parts for complicated systems. The military services have an enormous number of items of this sort. Consider an electric generator that is an important part of a nuclear sub. The number of such items in service is small and they fail infrequently. Since they are expensive, the inventory carrying cost is high. One thus would like to hold a minimal inventory. On the other hand, the penalty cost of running out is also high. Losing the service of a multimillion dollar sub for several weeks while a new generator is built has high opportunity costs. In many such cases, the following type of rule is employed. "Order an item for inventory each time an item is withdrawn."

The bottom line is that inventory control is an important management function and that quantitative models have made and are making an important contribution in this area. Although the mathematics may vary from one specific model to another, the concept of balancing ordering, holding, and stockout costs remains valid across many applications. General managers should understand the assumptions and operating implications of their own system. The blind assumption that because an inventory control system is large, complex, and computerized, it therefore cannot be understood, and/or must be all right, is a large first step in the wrong direction.

SUMMARY

This chapter considers two important inventory control models: (1) reorder point–reorder quantity, (r, Q), models in which backlogging is not permitted and demand during the lead time is specified with a probability distribution; and (2) one-period problems in which demand is specified with a probability distribution.

In Chapter 11 we learned about the (r, Q) model in a deterministic setting (meaning a known constant rate of demand). We saw how Q was chosen, using the EOQ formula, to balance ordering and holding costs. The value of r was set equal to the demand that would occur during the lead time.

It can be shown that the introduction of uncertainty in demand does not greatly affect the appropriate choice for Q. Uncertainty, however, does imply that we must give more attention to the choice of r. Because of uncertain demand over the lead time, the value of r computed from the deterministic model may result in stockouts, which may be costly via the loss of future commerce. To reduce the probability of stocking out, management uses a safety stock, but this increases annual holding costs. The trade-off is as follows: Not ordering enough may lead to too many stockouts and large stockout costs; ordering too much, although reducing stockout costs, will lead to inordinately high holding costs. In this chapter some formal tools are given to help management make a decision that balances the holding and stockout costs.

A quantity of interest is $p(s)$, the probability of incurring a stockout during a lead time. This is obviously related to r, the quantity on hand when we reorder at the beginning of the lead time. The relation between $p(s)$ and r is through the distribution of lead-time demand. Given a distribution, r determines $p(s)$, and vice versa. We used, in this chapter, two illustrative distributions, the uniform and the normal.

Several implications of a given value of $p(s)$ are given.

1. $p(s)$ and Q determine the average number of stockouts per year.
2. $p(s)$ and Q determine the probability of stocking out more than once in a year.
3. $p(s)$ and the distribution for lead-time demand determine r, and this quantity determines the safety stock level with its holding cost.

The discussion of (r, Q) models culminates in Figure 12.7. This figure provides a framework in which a manager can gauge his or her intuition about the appropriate probability of stocking out. For the case of normal lead-time demand and several values of the reorder point r, the probability of more than one stockout per year, the average number of stockouts per year, and the associated expected annual cost of safety stock are shown. This makes it possible for the manager to see how much he or she must pay to reduce the number of stockouts per year. Selecting the appropriate trade-off is left to managerial judgment.

Consideration of one-period models with probabilistic demand starts in Section 12.8 with the introduction of the Wiles housewares problem. In Section 12.9 it is established that Wiles' problem is a special case of a classic management science problem known as the newsboy problem. The solution to the newsboy problem is presented and then Wiles' problem is solved within this context.

PROBABILISTIC DEMAND. Models in which the demand for the item under consideration is specified by a probability distribution.

$p(s)$. The probability of a stockout during a lead time.

BINOMIAL DISTRIBUTION. A probability distribution with two parameters: the probability that an event occurs at a given trial and the number of independent trials.

EXPECTED ANNUAL COST OF SAFETY STOCK. The amount by which the expected annual holding cost is increased by using a safety stock.

ONE-PERIOD MODEL. A problem in which there is one opportunity to order an item and this occurs before a random demand occurs.

NEWSBOY PROBLEM. A classic management science problem. A one-period inventory model with linear holding and penalty costs.

NORMAL DISTRIBUTION. A probability distribution with two parameters: μ, the mean, and σ, the standard deviation.

OPPORTUNITY COST. A concept of "forgone profit" used in defining the penalty cost in a newsboy model.

UNIFORM DISTRIBUTION. The probability of any event in the specified range is equally likely.

STOCKOUT. Not having enough inventory on hand to satisfy demand.

MAJOR CONCEPTS QUIZ ————————————————

True–False

1. **T F** In probabilistic inventory models, larger holding costs are typically used to prevent ordering too frequently.

2. **T F** The reorder point must be chosen to balance the number of stockouts versus holding cost.

3. **T F** The expected annual cost of a safety stock depends on only three quantities: r, the mean of the lead-time demand distribution, and the holding cost C_h.

4. **T F** For different lead-time demand distributions, as long as $p(s)$ is the same, the safety stock level will also be the same.

5. **T F** Q plays an important role in determining the average number of stockouts per year.

6. **T F** The tools developed in this chapter serve to automate the choice of r.

7. **T F** In the newsboy model, the proper definition of penalty cost involves the concept of forgone profit, or so-called "opportunity" cost.

8. **T F** Suppose that known annual demand is 60,000, and each order is for 15,000 items. Then a maximum of 4 stockouts per year can occur.

Multiple Choice

9. Given the probability of a stockout during a lead time, the probability of incurring exactly 2 stockouts in a given year can be determined by using
   a. the uniform distribution
   b. the normal distribution
   c. the binomial distribution
   d. all of the above

10. The correspondence between $p(s)$ and r depends on
   a. the average number of stockouts in a year
   b. the lead-time demand distribution
   c. the safety stock level

11. The choice of $p(s)$, as well as the number of orders placed per year, determine
   a. average number of stockouts per year
   b. the probability of more than 1 stockout in a year

c. parameters for the binomial distribution

d. all of the above

e. none of the above

12. The normal distribution is convenient to work with because

  a. It is specified by only two parameters, μ and σ

  b. the same table is used no matter how one chooses μ and σ (i.e., for *any normal distribution*)

  c. it is often a good approximation of reality

  d. all of the above

  e. none of the above

13. The newsboy model

  a. balances holding and penalty costs for a one-period problem

  b. minimizes ordering, holding, and penalty costs for a one-period problem

  c. applies only to problems for which there is a uniform or normal distribution of demand

  d. all of the above

14. Consider the smallest value of Q^* that satisfies

$$P\{\text{demand} \leq Q^*\} \geq \frac{p}{p + h}$$

  a. This value will depend on the assumed distribution of demand.

  b. This value provides the optimal order quantity for the newsboy model.

  c. This value minimizes the sum of expected holding and penalty costs in the newsboy model.

  d. All of the above.

15. The assumption about the lead-time demand distribution

  a. can affect the cost of keeping a given safety stock level

  b. will typically affect the choice of a safety stock level

  c. will affect the average number of stockouts per year

  d. both a and b

Answers

1. F	5. T	9. c	13. a
2. T	6. F	10. b	14. d
3. T	7. T	11. d	15. b
4. F	8. T	12. d	

PROBLEMS

12-1. At **PROTRAC**'s Seattle outlet the demand during a week for the overhaul kit for small marine engines is a random variable with the following distribution:

$p(0) = 0.01$	$p(7) = 0.13$
$p(1) = 0.03$	$p(8) = 0.11$
$p(2) = 0.06$	$p(9) = 0.09$
$p(3) = 0.06$	$p(10) = 0.06$
$p(4) = 0.11$	$p(11) = 0.03$
$p(5) = 0.13$	$p(12) = 0.01$
$p(6) = 0.14$	

The kits cost $166.67 each, the cost of placing an order is $50, the cost of holding a kit in inventory for a year is 20% of the purchase price, and delivery lead time is 1 week. Assume 50 weeks per year and derive an (r, Q) model with a probability of 0.04 of stocking out during a cycle.

12-2. Pierce Dears, the lead salesman for **PROTRAC**'s Seattle outlet, has just negotiated a contract to sell 18 overhaul kits per week to Goal, the discount chain store, for the foreseeable future. Since this demand is deterministic Pierce decides to adjust the inventory control policy as shown in Figure 12.9.

FIGURE 12.9

CHARACTERISTIC	PARAMETERS FOR THE INVENTORY POLICY IN PROBLEM 12-1	PARAMETERS FOR THE INVENTORY POLICY IN PROBLEM 12-2
Order Quantity	Q^*	$Q^* + 18T^*$
Cycle Time (Weeks)	T^*	T^*
Reorder Point	r^*	r^*

In words, he has simply increased the order quantity to cover the demand during the cycle time. Since the additional demand is deterministic he says there is no need to change r.

(a) Is this a good policy? Explain your answer.

(b) What policy would you recommend if Pierce wanted to maintain a 0.04 probability of stocking out during an inventory cycle?

(c) Management at **PROTRAC**'s Seattle outlet decided that the 0.10 probability of a stockout per cycle would be best for them. Find Q^* and r^*.

(d) What is the probability of more than 1 stockout during the year?

12-3. Assume that **PROTRAC**'s Seattle outlet uses the optimal policy in Problem 12-1.

(a) What is the probability of exactly 2 stockouts during the year?

(b) What is the probability of more than 1 stockout during the year?

12-4. Suppose the delivery lead-time has been changed from 1 week to 2 weeks in Problem 12-1. All other data are the same. Assume the demands are independent from week to week.

(a) What is the probability of 20 demands during the lead time?

(b) What is the probability of 22 or more demands during the lead time?

(c) Find Q^* and r^*.

12-5. Increasing Q, the order quantity, will have what effect on

(a) The probability of a stockout *during an inventory cycle*?

    (i) Increase it?

    (ii) Decrease it?

    (iii) Leave it unchanged?

    Explain your choice.

(b) The probability of more than 1 stockout per year?

    (i) Increase it?

    (ii) Decrease it?

    (iii) Leave it unchanged?

    Explain your choice.

12-6. Increasing r, the reorder point, will have what effect on

(a) The probability of a stockout *during an inventory cycle?*
    (i) Increase it?
    (ii) Decrease it?
    (iii) Leave it unchanged?
Explain your choice.

(b) The probability of more than 1 stockout per year?
    (i) Increase it?
    (ii) Decrease it?
    (iii) Leave it unchanged?
Explain your choice.

12-7. At Steco the weekly demand for high-titanium rods is normally distributed with mean 100 and standard deviation 5. These rods cost $5 each and the cost of holding a rod in inventory for a year is equal to 20% of its cost. The cost of placing an order is $25 independent of the quantity ordered. Delivery lead time is 1 week. Management wants a 0.06 probability of stocking out during an inventory cycle. Assume 50 weeks per year. What (r, Q) system would you recommend?

12-8. Consider the data presented in Problem 12-7. Now assume that increased demand has forced Steco's supplier to increase the delivery lead time for high-titanium rods from 1 week to 4 weeks. HINT: Demand during the lead time is the sum of the demands during each of the four weeks. The demand each week has a normal distribution and it is reasonable to assume that demands are independent from week to week.)

The following information is useful in solving Problem 12-8. Assume that X is normally distributed with mean μ_X and standard deviation σ_X and Y is also normally distributed with mean μ_Y and standard deviation σ_Y. Let $Z = X + Y$ and assume X and Y are independent. Then Z is normally distributed with mean $\mu_Z = \mu_X + \mu_Y$ and standard deviation $\sigma_Z = \sqrt{\sigma_X^2 + \sigma_Y^2}$

(a) What (r, Q) policy would you recommend in view of this change?

(b) What effect has the change in delivery lead time had on the value for Q? Explain why.

(c) Does r increase
    (i) Less rapidly than
    (ii) At the same rate as
    (iii) More rapidly than
the lead time? Explain why.

12-9. What is the expected annual cost of the safety stock associated with the (r, Q) policy you recommended in Problem 12-7?

12-10. What is the expected annual cost of the safety stock associated with the (r, Q) policy you recommended in Problem 12-8?

12-11. The regional distribution center of Deuce Hardware sells small window air conditioners for $250 each. These units cost $200. All units not sold by September 1 are sold for one-half of the retail price in an end-of-the-season sale. Assume that demand for this air conditioner during the season is normally distributed with a mean of 600 and a standard deviation of 100.

(a) How many air conditioners should Deuce order at the beginning of the season?

(b) What is the probability that Deuce will not satisfy all demand during the season? The management of Deuce decides to select the order quantity so that the probability of a stockout is 0.10.

(c) How many air conditioners should be ordered at the beginning of the season?

(d) What "cost of goodwill" has to be added implicitly to the financial penalty cost to justify this decision?

12-12. The question the concessionaire must answer is how many soft pretzels to buy for the Great Fond du Lac Boat Race. The pretzels cost 15 cents and sell for 25 cents. Unsold pretzels can be returned to the supplier for an 8-cent refund. (The supplier then sells them in its Day Old Shoppe for 15 cents.) Demand is normal with a mean of 2000 and a standard deviation of 250.

   (a) How many pretzels should be ordered?

   (b) Suppose demand has a standard deviation of 500. How many pretzels should be ordered? What can you say about the relationship between the order quantity and the standard deviation?

   (c) The concessionaire decides to set the probability of a stockout at 0.20. How many pretzels should be ordered? σ is now 500.

   (d) What additional cost of a lost sale must implicitly be added to the financial loss to justify this decision?

DIAGNOSTIC ASSIGNMENT

INVENTORY TURNS PER YEAR

Introduction   Contributing to the operation of an enterprise through its various committees is an important part of the managerial function. This vignette attempts to capture some of that experience. Assume the role of Larry Luchek. You will attend the next meeting of the management committee as a replacement for Victor Kowalski. Be prepared to make a presentation to the group on the topic of inventory turns if you feel there is more to be said. Remember that the other members of the committee are not necessarily experts in up-to-date inventory control technology, so if you have a point to make you should be prepared to illustrate it with numerical examples. As you will see, such arguments are the medium of exchange in the committee under consideration.

A Management Committee Meeting   Steco's management committee is having its biweekly meeting. Frank Watson, the president; Jayne Frazier, the treasurer; and Tom Galanti, vice-president of marketing; are all assembled in the conference room. Victor Kowalski, vice-president of operations, is on a tour of West Coast facilities and cannot attend the meeting. He is represented by his assistant, Larry Luchek. The discussion proceeds as follows:

FRANK: This probably isn't the best time to raise the topic since Vic isn't here, but I want to mention it anyway so that it will be on the agenda for the next meeting. I was just reading in *Business Week* that the Japanese are beating our pants off in inventory control methods. Since inventory is our main business we have to be sure that we are doing as well as possible.

JAYNE: I read the same article and frankly it wasn't very clear to me. The entire discussion was in terms of "turns." I'm quite familiar with our system and that isn't a term we use. At any rate the bottom line of the article is that the Japanese are doing so much better because they have many more inventory turns than the typical U.S. firm, and I inferred that more turns means you pay less inventory charges. As I recall, the typical Japanese firm averaged about 20 turns whereas the U.S. average was about six. The article also mentioned that European firms on the average have even a smaller number of turns; I think the average was about two turns. Whatever all of that proves.

LARRY: I'm sure that Vic could give you a more complete analysis of the situation than I can because I'm rather new to this assignment. However, I may be able to shed some light on the subject. Turns are defined as

$$\text{turns} = \text{annual demand/average inventory.}$$

Jayne, your remarks are right on target. For a given annual demand, more turns means lower average inventory and, hence, lower holding costs. However, since average inventory is a function of the order quantity and our order quantities are determined by the EOQ formula, the number of turns that we have for our products must be optimal. Let's look at a specific example. We assume that demand in each month for reinforced appliance angles is a normal random variable with a mean of 50 and a standard deviation of 15. Note that this assumption yields an annual demand of 12(50) equals 600. The typical lead time is one month and, as you know, Steco's standard practice is to have a stockout probability of 0.05. We have estimated an ordering cost of $25.00 and a holding cost of $1.92 per unit per year. By using the EOQ formula we can verify that Q^*, the optimal order quantity, is 125. The average inventory is one-half of the order quantity, or 62.5 angles. This yields 9.6 turns per year. Here, I'll put the calculations on the board.

$$\text{Annual demand} = D = 600 \text{ angles}$$

$$\text{Ordering cost} = C_0 = \$25.00$$

$$\text{Holding cost} = C_h = \$1.92 \text{ per angle per year}$$

$$\text{Optimal order quantity} = Q^* = \sqrt{2C_0 D/C_h} = 125$$

$$\text{Average inventory} = Q^*/2 = 62.5$$

$$\text{Turns} = D/(Q^*/2) = 9.6$$

$$\text{Orders per year} = N^* = D/Q^*$$

therefore

$$\text{Turns} = 2N^*$$

JAYNE: Are you sure about that, Larry? I understand your calculations, but, as I recall, our inventory audit shows a larger average inventory.

LARRY: There may be some random fluctuations, but we use an (r, Q) model and on average it will indicate how the system works. In particular, these calculations form the basis for two observations. First we see that the number of turns (9.6) that results from our calculations is indeed smaller than the figure of 20 that you cite for Japanese firms. However, the number of turns is optimal given our current costs. In order to change the number of turns we must change the costs. Next we see that the number of turns is simply two times the number of orders we place during a year. Thus, to increase the optimal number of orders without increasing the annual cost, we would have to lower the cost of placing an order. Since our system is already computerized, this doesn't sound very promising to me. Frankly, I don't see that there is a lot of room for improvement.

TOM: Larry, this situation reminds me of the nonreinforced appliance angle problem. I remember discussing that order with Vic because it was the case he used to learn about ICON, our inventory control system. It seems to me that because of quantity discounts we increased our order quantity from 1250 to 5000. Obviously this large increase in the order quantity would cause a large decrease in the number of turns. If I understood your formulae correctly, increasing the order quantity by a factor of four would reduce the number of turns by the same factor, four. So it is obvious that quantity discounts can play an important role in determining the number of turns. I suppose that it is possible that suppliers in the United States are more able than their Japanese competitors to demand larger order quantities in order to obtain quantity discounts, and thus the number of turns on the average is smaller here. I must say that does not sound like a reasonable hypothesis to me. There must be another explanation.

FRANK: I think that we have devoted as much time to this topic as we should in Vic's absence. We'll put it on the agenda for the next meeting. I now want to bring your attention to our current cash flow problems. The combination of slow payment by our customers and the high interest costs are causing serious problems. . . .

Questions

1. What main point has Larry omitted from his analysis and how (if at all) would this affect his calculation for the number of turns?

2. Larry has correctly pointed out that ordering cost will affect the number of turns. Tom has correctly pointed out that quantity discounts play a role. As a result of your analysis, what other features might management consider?

QUEUING MODELS

INTRODUCTION

Monte Jackson might not subscribe to the notion that all of life is a queue, but as administrative director of St. Luke's Hospital in Philadelphia, he must deal with a number of situations that can be described as queuing problems. Briefly, a queuing problem is one in which you have a sequence of items (such as people) arriving at a facility for service, as shown in Figure 13.1. At this moment, Monte is concerned about three particular "queuing problems."

Problem 1:
St Luke's
Hematology
Lab

St. Luke's treats a large number of patients on an outpatient basis; that is, there are many patients who come to the hospital to see the staff doctors for diagnosis and treatment who are not admitted to the hospital. Outpatients plus those admitted to the 600-bed hospital produce a large flow of new patients each day. Most new patients must visit the hematology laboratory as part of the diagnostic process. Each such patient has to be seen by a technician. The system works like this: After seeing a doctor, the

FIGURE 13.1
General Queuing Problems

Arrivals

FIGURE 13.2
Some Queuing Problems

PROBLEM	ARRIVALS	SERVICE FACILITY
1	Patients	Technicians
2	Telephone Calls	Switchboard
3	Broken Equipment	Repairpeople

patient arrives at the laboratory and checks in with a clerk. Patients are assigned on a first-come, first-served basis to test rooms as they become available. The technician assigned to that room performs the tests ordered by the doctor. When the testing is complete, the patient goes on to the next step in the process (perhaps X-ray) and the technician sees a new patient.

Monte must decide how many technicians to hire. Superficially, at least, the trade-off is obvious. More technicians mean more expense for the hospital and quicker service for the patients.

Problem 2: Buying WATS Lines

As part of its remodeling process, St. Luke's is designing a new communications system. Monte must decide how many WATS lines the hospital should buy. He knows that when people pick up the phone, they want to get through without having to try several times. How many lines he needs to achieve that result at a reasonable cost is not so clear.

Problem 3: Hiring Repairpeople

St. Luke's hires repairpeople to maintain 20 individual pieces of electronic equipment. The equipment includes measuring devices like the electrocardiogram machine, small dedicated computers like the one used for lung analysis, and equipment like the CAT scanner. If a piece of equipment fails and all the repairpeople are occupied, it must wait to be repaired. Monte must decide how many repairpeople to hire. He must balance their cost against the cost of having broken equipment.

As Figure 13.2 indicates, all three of these problems fit the general description of a queuing model. Monte will resolve these problems by using a combination of analytic and simulation models. However, before we reach the level of sophistication required to deal with Monte's specific problems, it is necessary for us to spend some time with the basic queuing model. In the process we will learn some terminology and we will see the type of analytic results that are available.

——— 13.2
THE BASIC MODEL

Consider the Xerox machine located in the fourth-floor secretarial service suite. Assume that users arrive at the machine and form a single line. Each arrival in turn uses the machine to perform a specific task. These tasks vary from obtaining a copy of a 1-page letter to producing 100 copies of a 25-page report. This system is called a single-server (or single-channel) queue. Questions about this or any other queuing system center on four quantities:

1. The number of people in the system: the number of people currently being served, as well as those waiting for service.
2. The number of people in the queue: the number of people waiting for service.

3. The waiting time: the interval between when an individual enters the system and when he or she leaves the system. Note that this interval includes the service time.

4. The waiting time in the queue: the time between entering the system and the beginning of service.

To answer questions about these quantities, it is necessary to make some basic assumptions about particular aspects of the system. In the basic model the following assumptions are made:

Assumptions of the Basic Model

Arrival Process   Each arrival will be called a "job." Since the time between arrivals is not known with certainty, we will need to specify a probability distribution for it. In the basic model a particular distribution called the *exponential distribution* (sometimes called the *negative exponential distribution*) is used. This distribution plays a central role in many queuing models. It provides a reasonable representation of the arrival process in a number of situations and its so-called lack of memory property makes it possible to obtain analytic results. The words "Poisson input" are also used to describe the arrival process when the time between arrivals has an exponential distribution. This is because of the relationship between the exponential distribution and the Poisson distribution. In particular, if the interarrival time has an exponential distribution, the number of arrivals in a specified length of time (say, three hours) has a Poisson distribution. But we digress. The exponential distribution and its relationship to the Poisson is discussed in some detail in Section 13.9. At this point, it is only necessary to understand that the exponential distribution is completely specified by one parameter. This parameter, called λ, is the *mean arrival rate*, i.e., how many jobs arrive (on the average) during a specific period of time. In a moment we will consider an example where

$$\lambda = 0.05 \text{ jobs per minute}$$

This implies that *on the average* five hundredths of a job arrives every minute. It is probably more natural to think in terms of a longer time interval. An equivalent statement is that *on the average* one job arrives every 20 minutes. Using more technical terms, we say that *the mean interarrival time* is 20 minutes. Mean interarrival time is the average time between two arrivals. Thus, for the exponential distribution

$$\text{average time between jobs} = \text{mean interarrival time} = 1/\lambda \qquad (13.1)$$

Thus, if $\lambda = 0.05$,

$$\text{mean interarrival time} = 1/\lambda = 1/0.05 = 20$$

Service Process   In the basic model, the time that it takes to complete a job (the service time) is also treated with the exponential distribution. The parameter for this exponential distribution is called μ. It represents the *mean service rate* in jobs per minute. In other words, μT is the number of jobs that would be served (on the average) during a period of T minutes if the machine were busy during that time. In the upcoming example we will assume that $\mu = 0.10$. This implies that on the average 0.10 of a job is completed each minute. An equivalent statement is that on the average one job is completed every 10 minutes. The *mean, or average, service time* (the average time to complete a job) is $1/\mu$. When μ, the mean service rate, is 0.10, the average service time is 10 since $1/\mu = 1/0.10 = 10$.

Queue Size   There is no limit on the number of jobs that can wait in the queue. The queue is said to be infinite.

FIGURE 13.3
Operating Characteristics for the Basic Model

CHARACTERISTIC	SYMBOL	FORMULA
Expected number in system	L	$\dfrac{\lambda}{\mu - \lambda}$
Expected number in queue	L_q	$\dfrac{\lambda^2}{\mu(\mu - \lambda)}$
Expected waiting time (includes service time)	W	$\dfrac{1}{\mu - \lambda}$
Expected time in queue	W_q	$\dfrac{\lambda}{\mu(\mu - \lambda)}$
Probability that the system is empty	P_0	$1 - \lambda/\mu$

Queue Discipline Jobs are served on a first-come, first-served basis, that is, in the same order as they arrive at the queue.

Time Horizon The system operates as described continuously over an infinite horizon.

Consider these assumptions in the context of the Xerox problem. Suppose that the average arrival time between jobs is 20 minutes. As we have seen, the fact that the interarrival time has an exponential distribution [see (13.1)] means that $1/\lambda = 20$, and thus $\lambda = 0.05$, or that the jobs arrive at the rate of 0.05 job per minute. Similarly, if the average time to complete a job is 10 minutes, we know that $1/\mu = 10$, $\mu = 0.10$, and that jobs are completed at the rate of 0.10 job per minute when the machine is operating.

Formulas Assume $\lambda < \mu$ The values of these two parameters (together with the assumptions) are all that is needed to calculate several important characteristics of the basic model. The necessary formulas are presented in Figure 13.3. WARNING! The formulas in Figure 13.3 hold only if $\lambda < \mu$. If this condition does not hold (i.e., if $\lambda > \mu$), the number of people in the queue will grow without limit. Consider, for example, a specific case where $\lambda = 0.25$ and $\mu = 0.10$. Remember that $1/\lambda$ is the average interarrival time. Thus, since $1/\lambda = 1/0.25 = 4$, on the average a job arrives every 4 minutes. Similarly, $1/\mu$ is the average time it takes to complete a job. Since $1/\mu = 1/0.10 = 10$, on the average it takes 10 minutes to complete a job. It seems clear that in this case the service operation will get further behind (the queue will grow longer) as time goes by.

Now return to the Xerox problem, in which $\lambda < \mu$ and the formulas in Figure 13.3 hold. Plugging the numerical values from the Xerox problem, $\lambda = 0.05$ and $\mu = 0.10$, into the formulas yields the results presented in Figure 13.4.

These numbers require some interpretation. L, for example, is the expected number of people in the system (those being served plus those waiting) after the queue has reached **Formulas Give Steady State Results** *steady state*. In this sentence, the phrase "steady state" means that the probability that you will observe a certain number of people (say 2) in the system does not depend on the time at which you count them. If a steady state has been achieved, the probability that there are two people using and/or waiting for the Xerox machine should be the same at 2:30 P.M. and at 4:00 P.M.

The other characteristics presented in Figures 13.3 and 13.4 have a similar interpretation. Thus, in a steady state, (1) the system is empty with a probability of one-half ($P_0 = 0.5$); (2) on the average there is 0.5 person in the queue ($L_q = 0.5$); (3) on the average

FIGURE 13.4

Evaluating the Operating Characteristics of the
Basic Model when $\lambda = 0.05$, $\mu = 0.10$

expected number in system

$$L = \frac{\lambda}{\mu - \lambda} = \frac{0.05}{0.10 - 0.05} = 1$$

expected number in queue

$$L_q = \frac{\lambda^2}{\mu(\mu - \lambda)} = \frac{0.0025}{0.10(0.10 - 0.05)} = 0.5$$

expected waiting time

$$W = \frac{1}{\mu - \lambda} = \frac{1}{0.10 - 0.05} = 20$$

expected time in queue

$$W_q = \frac{\lambda}{\mu(\mu - \lambda)} = \frac{0.05}{0.10(0.10 - 0.05)} = 10$$

probability that the system is empty

$$P_0 = 1 - \frac{\lambda}{\mu} = 1 - \frac{0.05}{0.10} = 0.5$$

an arrival must wait 10 minutes before starting to use the machine ($W_q = 10$); and (4) on the average an arrival will spend 20 minutes in the system ($W = 20$).

Using the Results
These results hold for the basic model and the particular values for the parameters ($\lambda = 0.05$ and $\mu = 0.10$). They provide information that is useful to management in analyzing this service facility. Suppose, for example, that management makes the following calculations: Since $\lambda = 0.05$, on the average five hundredths of a job arrives each minute. During each 8-hour day there are $8 \times 60 = 480$ minutes. Thus during each day there is on the average a total of

$$(0.05)(480) = 24$$

arrivals. From the calculations in Figure 13.4 we know that on the average each person spends 20 minutes in the system ($W = 20$). Thus, a total of (24 arrivals per day) (20 minutes per arrival) = 480 minutes or 8 hours is spent at this facility. Management might well feel that this is too long. A variety of steps might be taken.

1. A new machine might be purchased with a smaller mean service time.
2. Another machine might be purchased and both machines used to satisfy the demand. This would change the system to a two-server queue.
3. Some personnel might be sent to a different and less busy copying facility. This would change the arrival process.

Management might select one of these alternatives, or perhaps some other option. But in any case, management must balance the cost of providing service against the cost of waiting. The results in Figure 13.4 and similar results for other systems would be a central part of the analysis. These ideas will be developed in more detail in the context of Monte Jackson's problems.

───── 13.3

LITTLE'S FLOW EQUATION AND OTHER GENERALITIES

It has been proven that in a steady-state queuing process

The Flow Equation
$$L = \lambda W \tag{13.2}$$

This result states that L, the expected number of people in the system, equals λ, the arrival rate, times W, the expected waiting time. To perform a quick numerical check, see if the numbers derived for the Xerox problem (Figure 13.4) satisfy (13.2). The calculation is shown in (13.3).

$$L = 1.0 = 0.05 \times 20 = \lambda W \tag{13.3}$$

Intuitive Derivation

To understand the intuitive foundation for this result, consider the diagram in Figure 13.5. In Scene 1 our hero arrives and joins the queue. In Scene 2 he has just completed service. Assume the system is in steady state. Since in this case the average number of people in the system is independent of time, let us measure this quantity when our hero completes being served. At this time, the number of people in the system is precisely the total number who arrived after he did (i.e., the individuals who arrived during his waiting time). Therefore, if W is his waiting time and people arrive at a rate of λ, we would expect L, the average number in the system, to equal λW.

Equation (13.2) is often called Little's flow equation. Note that it applies to any steady-state queuing process and is thus applicable to a wide variety of problems. The proof used to establish (13.2) also shows that

A Similar Equation

$$L_q = \lambda W_q \tag{13.4}$$

A numerical check for the Xerox problem shows that

$$L_q = 0.5 = 0.05 \times 10 = \lambda W_q$$

which again agrees with the result in Figure 13.4. One must take some care in applying this result in more complicated cases. It is essential that λ represents the rate at which arrivals *join* the queue. This may be different from the rate at which people "arrive." Consider, for example, a queue with an upper limit on the number of items that can wait in the queue. A modern phone system that will hold a certain number of calls (say 10) in a queue until a service representative becomes available provides a good example. In such a system a person who calls and finds the system full simply receives a busy signal—in other words, is sent away. He or she does not join the queue. Thus, if $\lambda = 0.25$ (the arrival rate) and the mean time between calls is 4 minutes, this is *not* the rate that people *join*. Thus, the relationship $L = 0.25W$ will not hold for this system.

Another important general result depends on the observation that

expected waiting time = expected waiting time in queue + expected service time

For the basic model we have already made use of the fact that

$$\text{expected service time} = 1/\mu$$

FIGURE 13.5
Little's Flow Equation

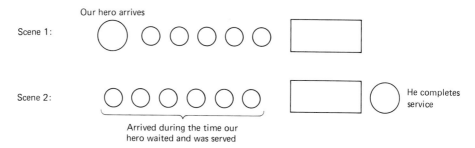

Putting the general result in symbols yields

$$W = W_q + 1/\mu \qquad (13.5)$$

For the Xerox problem we have

$$W = 20 = 10 + 1/0.10 = W_q + 1/\mu$$

Not only does this hold for the basic model, but the general result [equation (13.5)] holds for any queuing model in which a steady state occurs.

Solving the Three Equations   Equations (13.2), (13.4), and (13.5) make it possible to compute the four operating characteristics L, L_q, W, and W_q once one of them is known. To illustrate this fact, let us start the Xerox problem over again. We begin as last time using the first formula in Figure 13.3 to calculate L:

$$L = \frac{\lambda}{\mu - \lambda} = \frac{0.05}{0.10 - 0.05} = 1$$

Now rather than using the other formulas in Figure 13.3 that are specifically for the basic model, we will use the two general results that we have just presented. First from Little's flow equation (13.2) we know that

$$L = \lambda W$$

Thus, knowing $L = 1$ and $\lambda = 0.05$, we obtain $W = L/\lambda = 20$. Then, turning to (13.5), we see that

$$W = W_q + 1/\mu$$
$$W_q = W - 1/\mu = 20 - 1/0.10 = 10$$

Finally, (13.4) shows that

$$L_q = \lambda W_q = 0.05 \times 10 = 0.5$$

This alternative method of obtaining numerical results will turn out to be most useful when analyzing more complicated systems.

───── 13.4
PROBLEM 1: A MULTISERVER QUEUE (HEMATOLOGY LAB)

Recall that as we started this chapter, our stated goal was to attack three particular problems at St. Luke's with queuing models. In the preceding two sections we have laid the groundwork for this process. We have introduced, defined, and illustrated the characteristics of the systems that we will consider (e.g., expected number in queue, expected waiting time, etc.). We have also made some general results such as Little's flow equation available for use in future analysis. We are now in a position to turn our attention to Monte Jackson's problems.

The system described in Problem 1 of Section 13.1, the blood-testing problem, is illustrated in Figure 13.6. Note that each patient joins a common queue and, on arriving

FIGURE 13.6

Multiserver Queue

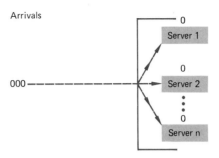

at the head of the line, enters the first examining room that becomes available. This type of system must not be confused with a system in which a queue forms in front of each server as in the typical grocery store.

Assume that the interarrival time is given by an exponential distribution with parameter $\lambda = 0.20$. This implies that a new patient arrives every 5 minutes on the average, since

$$\text{mean interarrival time} = 1/\lambda = 1/0.20 = 5$$

Also, assume that each server is identical and that each service time is given by an exponential distribution with parameter $\mu = 0.125$. This implies that the mean service time is 8 minutes, since

$$\begin{array}{c}\text{mean service time for}\\ \text{an individual server}\end{array} = 1/\mu = 1/0.125 = 8$$

Requirement for Steady State

Note that if there were only one server, the queue would grow without limit, since $\lambda > \mu$ ($0.20 > 0.125$). For a multiserver queue, however, a steady state will exist as long as $\lambda < s\mu$, where s is the number of servers. For example, if we have two servers, $0.20 < 2(0.125)$ or $0.20 < 0.25$.

As before, we want to find values L, L_q, W, and W_q. However, since this is a multiserver queue (not a single-server queue as in the Xerox problem), we must use different formulas. To evaluate these formulas it is convenient to start with the expression for P_0, the probability that the system is empty. For this model

$$P_0 = \cfrac{1}{\displaystyle\sum_{n=0}^{s-1} \frac{(\lambda/\mu)^n}{n!} + \frac{(\lambda/\mu)^s}{s!}\left(\cfrac{1}{1-(\lambda/s\mu)}\right)} \tag{13.6}$$

The Key Equations

and L_q, the expected number of people in the queue, is

$$L_q = P_0\left[\frac{\lambda^{s+1}}{\mu^{s-1}(s-1)!\,(\mu s - \lambda)^2}\right] \tag{13.7}$$

Equations (13.6) and (13.7) and the general results in (13.2), (13.4), and (13.5) make it possible to calculate values for W_q, W, and L for any specified parameter values (μ and λ) and any number of servers (value of s).

Assume, for example, that Monte decided to hire two technicians. Then, since $s = 2$, $\lambda = 0.20$, and $\mu = 0.125$, we see that $\lambda/\mu = 0.20/0.125 = 1.6$, and $\lambda/s\mu = 0.20/2(0.125) = 0.8$. Equation (13.6) becomes[1]

$$P_0 = \cfrac{1}{1 + 1.6 + \cfrac{(1.6)^2}{2}\left(\cfrac{1}{1 - 0.8}\right)} = 0.11$$

and the probability that the system is empty is 0.11. We can now use this result in (13.7) to find L_q.

$$L_q = 0.11\left[\frac{0.2^3}{0.125 \times 1 \times (0.250 - 0.20)^2}\right] = 2.82$$

That is, the expected number of people in the queue is somewhat less than 3.
From (13.4), Monte knows that $L_q = \lambda W_q$. Thus,

$$W_q = \frac{L_q}{\lambda} = \frac{2.82}{0.20} = 14.10$$

or, on the average, a patient waits for 14.10 minutes before entering an examining room.
Let us now look at the general observation that

expected waiting time = expected waiting time in queue + expected service time

We note that the expected service time in this expression is the expected time an individual will spend being served. This does not depend on the number of servers. It depends only on the amount of time an individual server takes to do the job. In this case all servers are the same. Each has a mean service time of $1/\mu$. Since

$$W = \text{expected waiting time}$$

$$W_q = \text{expected time in queue}$$

$$1/\mu = \text{expected service time}$$

we have

$$W = W_q + 1/\mu$$

$$= 14.10 + 1/0.125$$

$$= 14.10 + 8$$

$$= 22.10$$

On the average, then, a patient spends 22.10 minutes in the hematology area, waiting for a technician and having tests.
These calculations make the decision easy for Monte. With one technician, since $\lambda > \mu$, the system is unstable and the queue will steadily grow. This could be considered irresponsible. With two technicians, the average waiting time in the queue is less than

---

[1] To evaluate this expression, you must use the facts that $0! = 1$ and $(1.6)^0 = 1$.

15 minutes. By current hospital standards, this is a small and acceptable value. If, in some cases, the queue gets uncomfortably long (remember that W_q is an expected value and the actual time in the queue will vary), the supervisors of the hematology laboratory can temporarily move one of the blood analysts to a technician's position. Monte thus feels comfortable with the idea of hiring two full-time technicians without performing a detailed cost analysis.

_____ 13.5
A TAXONOMY OF QUEUING MODELS

There is a large number of possible queuing models. For example, if the interarrival time in the basic model had been given a different distribution (not the exponential) we would have a different model, in the sense that the expressions for L, L_q, and so on, would no longer hold. To facilitate communication among those working on queuing models, D. G. Kendall proposed a taxonomy based on the following notation:

The Notation
$$A/B/s$$

where A = arrival distribution
B = service distribution
s = number of servers

Different letters are used to designate certain distributions. Placed in the A or the B position, they indicate the arrival or the service distribution, respectively. The following conventions are in general use:

Some Conventions

M = exponential distribution

D = deterministic number

G = any (a general) distribution of service times

GI = any (a general) distribution of arrival times

We can see, for example, that the Xerox problem is an $M/M/1$ model, that is, a single-server queue with exponential interarrival and service times. Also, the solution that Monte chose for Problem 1, the hematology lab problem, is an $M/M/2$ model, that is, a two-server queue with exponential interarrival times and exponential service times for each server.

_____ 13.6
ECONOMIC ANALYSIS OF QUEUING SYSTEMS

Monte selected the number of lab technicians to hire by looking at the probabilities and using his judgment. This is not an unusual approach in queuing models and is especially common in the not-for-profit sector. Monte realizes that he is balancing the cost of hiring more technicians against the costs he incurs by forcing the patients to wait. The cost of hiring additional technicians is fairly clear. The waiting cost is not.

Monte first notes that the cost to the patient is irrelevant to his decision, except as it affects the patient's willingness to use the hospital. It really does not matter who is waiting—a tax lawyer who charges $200 per hour for his services or an unemployed person with no opportunity cost—unless the waiting time persuades the patient to use another health facility. This observation explains why certain monopolies like government bureaus and utilities can be so casual about your waiting time. There is no place else to go!

Besides the possible effect on demand, the hematology lab could cost the hospital money if it reduced the output of the hospital. Suppose, for example, that the outpatient clinics could process 50 new patients each day, but that the hematology lab could only handle 10. (This is clearly an extreme example to establish a point.) In this case, the hospital would be wasting a valuable resource, the doctors and other staff in the clinics, because of a bottleneck in the hematology lab. However, having stated this, it still is not easy to assess an explicit cost of a patient waiting.

If you are willing and able to estimate certain costs, you can build expected cost models of queuing systems. Consider, for example, the hematology lab problem (in general terms any multiserver queue with exponential interarrival and service times) and suppose that management is willing to specify two costs:

Cost Parameters

$$C_S = \text{cost per hour of having a server available}$$

$$C_W = \text{cost per hour of having a person wait in the system}$$

With these it is possible to calculate the total costs associated with the decision to use any particular number of servers. Let us start by calculating the total cost of hiring 2 servers for an 8-hour day. There are two components:

$$\text{server cost} = (C_S)(2)(8)$$

where C_S is the cost per hour for 1 server, 2 is the number of servers, and 8 is the number of hours each server works, and

$$\text{waiting cost} = (C_W)(L(2))(8)$$

This calculation may not be as obvious, but the rationale is the same as for the server cost. If there are, on the average, $L(2)$ people waiting when the system has 2 servers, then $L(2)$ times 8 is the average number of "waiting hours" per day. Hence, $(C_W)(L(2))(8)$ is the average waiting cost for the 8-hour day.

If we wanted to calculate the total cost of using 4 servers for a 6-hour day, we would take

$$(C_S)(4)(6) + (C_W)(L(4))(6)$$

or

$$[(C_S(4) + (C_W)(L(4))]6$$

The term in square brackets, $[(C_S)(4) + (C_W)(L(4))]$, then, is the total cost per hour of using 4 servers. We now define

$$\text{TC}(s) = \text{total cost per hour of using } s \text{ servers}$$

and we see that

The Total Cost per Hour

$$\text{TC}(s) = (C_S)(s) + (C_W)(L(s))$$

Our goal is to choose s, the number of servers, to minimize this function.

FIGURE 13.7

Costs in an *M/M/s* Queue

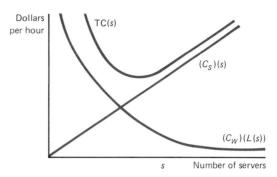

Figure 13.7 shows the general shape of the function TC(s). This function is determined by plotting the two component parts, (C_S)(s) and (C_W)($L(s)$), and adding them together.

We see that TC(s) assumes a minimum for some value s. Unfortunately it is not possible to derive a formula that gives the optimal value of s. (This is in contrast to the EOQ model, where we can find the optimal order quantity, Q^*, with the equation $Q^* = \sqrt{2DC_0/C_h}$ as in Chapter 11.)

It is, however, a relatively easy matter to attack a specific problem numerically, that is, by trying several values for s and selecting the value that yields the minimum total cost. Rather than pursuing this further, let us complete our examination of the hematology lab problem with these observations: We have seen how to find values for L, L_q, W, and W_q. These values were then used to select the appropriate number of technicians (servers). This decision might be made on intuitive grounds or on the basis of an explicit economic analysis. We now move on to Monte's second problem.

———— 13.7
PROBLEM 2: THE *M/G/s* MODEL WITH BLOCKED CUSTOMERS CLEARED (WATS LINES)

Do not be misled by the title of this section. It is devoted to Problem 2, Monte's attempt to select the appropriate number of WATS lines for St. Luke's. Fortunately, in this case he can expect help from the telephone company. They have a great deal of expertise in such matters, since queuing models have found extensive use in the field of telephone traffic engineering. The problem of how many lines are needed by a switchboard is typically attacked by using the *M/G/s* model, "with blocked customers cleared." You already know that this model is a multichannel queue with s servers (s lines), exponential interarrival times for the calls, and a general distribution for the service time, which in this case is the length of each call. The phrase "blocked customers cleared" is queuing jargon. It means that *when an arrival finds all of the servers occupied (all of the lines busy), he or she does not get in a queue but simply leaves.* This phrase clearly describes the behavior of the traditional telephone switchboard. More sophisticated systems now provide for queuing of a finite number of customers, in some cases even providing the lucky customer the opportunity to enjoy a Muzak version of "You Light Up My Life," or "As Time Goes By."

The problem of selecting the appropriate number of lines (servers) is attacked by computing the steady-state probability that exactly j lines will be busy. This, in turn, will be used to calculate the steady-state probability that all s lines are busy. Clearly, if you have s lines and they are all busy, the next caller will not be able to place a call.

The steady-state probability that there are exactly j busy servers and that there are s lines (servers) available is given by the expression

Probability of j Busy Servers

$$P_j = \frac{(\lambda/\mu)^j/j!}{\sum_{k=0}^{s} (\lambda/\mu)^k/k!} \tag{13.8}$$

where λ = arrival rate (the rate at which calls arrive)
   $1/\mu$ = mean service time (the average length of a conversation)
   s = number of servers (lines)

The expression is called the *truncated Poisson distribution* or the *Erlang loss distribution*. It is noteworthy that although we are considering a general service-time distribution, the value P_j defined by (13.8) depends only on the mean of this distribution.

Consider a system in which $\lambda = 1$ (calls arrive at the rate of 1 per minute) and $1/\mu = 10$ (the average length of a conversation is 10 minutes). Here $\lambda/\mu = 10$. Suppose that we have 5 lines in the system ($s = 5$) and want to find the steady-state probability that exactly 2 are busy ($j = 2$). From (13.8) we see that

$$P_2 = \frac{(\lambda/\mu)^2/2!}{\sum_{k=0}^{5} (\lambda/\mu)^k/k!}$$

$$= \frac{(10)^2/2 \cdot 1}{1 + 10^1/1 + 10^2/2 \cdot 1 + 10^3/3 \cdot 2 \cdot 1 + 10^4/4 \cdot 3 \cdot 2 \cdot 1 + 10^5/5 \cdot 4 \cdot 3 \cdot 2 \cdot 1}$$

$$= \frac{50}{1 + 10 + 50 + 166.67 + 416.67 + 833.33}$$

$$= \frac{50}{1477.67} = 0.034$$

In other words, on the average, 2 lines wouuld be busy 3.4% of the time.

The more interesting question is: "What is the probability that all of the lines are busy?" since in this case a potential caller would not be able to place a call. To find the answer to this question, we simply set $j = s$ in (13.8). In our example $s = 5$ and we obtain

$$P_5 = \frac{(\lambda/\mu)^5/5!}{\sum_{k=0}^{5} (\lambda/\mu)^k/k!}$$

Using values that we calculated in our evaluation of P_2, we see that

$$P_5 = \frac{833.33}{1477.67}$$

$$= 0.564$$

or on the average the system is totally occupied 56.4% of the time.

The probability that the system is totally occupied (all servers are busy) is important enough that its value has been calculated for a large range of values for λ/μ and s
and the results recorded in graphs. The notation $B(s, \lambda/\mu)$ is used for this probability,
and its values for a variety of values of s and λ/μ are presented in Figure 13.8. Let us use
this figure to find $B(5, 10)$, the steady-state probability that the system is busy if there are

FIGURE 13.8

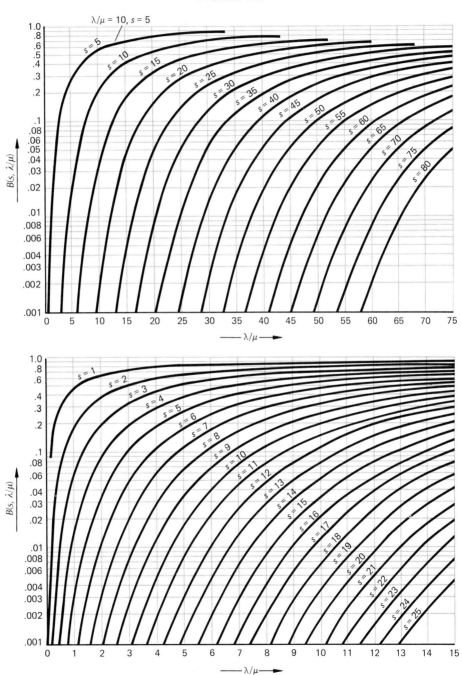

Reprinted with permission of Macmillan Publishing Company from *Introduction to Queuing Theory* by
Robert B. Cooper. Copyright © 1972 by Robert B. Cooper.

FIGURE 13.9

$B(s, 10)$ for $s = 0, \ldots, 10$

s	$B(s, 10)$	DECREASE IN $B(s, 10)$[a]
0	1.000	
1	0.909	0.091
2	0.820	0.089
3	0.732	0.088
4	0.647	0.085
5	0.564	0.083
6	0.485	0.079
7	0.409	0.076
8	0.338	0.071
9	0.273	0.065
10	0.215	0.058

[a] The decrease in $B(s, 10)$ is defined as $B(s - 1, 10) - B(s, 10)$. It is the reduction in the probability of finding a busy system, caused by adding the sth line.

5 lines and $\lambda/\mu = 10$. We proceed as follows:

1. Find the value $\lambda/\mu = 10$ on the horizontal axis.
2. Follow this line up until it intersects with the curved contour $s = 5$.
3. Finally, read on the vertical axis the value of $B(s, \lambda/\mu)$ that corresponds to this intersection.

In this case ($s = 5$, $\lambda/\mu = 10$) the value of $B(5, 10)$ is approximately 0.56. We thus have obtained the same result with significantly less effort.

Purchasing additional lines obviously decreases the probability of finding the system busy, making $B(s, \lambda/\mu)$ smaller. Values of $B(s, 10)$ with 1 to 10 servers are recorded in Figure 13.9. Here it is clear that the marginal effect of adding more servers decreases. For example, adding a second line when there was one in service decreases the probability of the system being busy by 0.089, whereas adding the tenth line when there were already nine in service decreases this probability by 0.058.

Another interesting and useful quantity in the design of phone installations is the average number of busy lines. This quantity is called the *carried load* in queuing jargon. If $\bar{N}$ is the average number of busy servers, then

Average Number of Busy Servers

$$\bar{N} = (\lambda/\mu)[1 - B(s, \lambda/\mu)] \qquad (13.9)$$

Assume now that in Monte's problem with WATS lines for St. Luke's, $\lambda = 1$ and $\mu = 10$. Thus, if he purchases 10 lines, we see in Figure 13.9 that $B(10, 10) = 0.21$. It follows from (13.9) that

$$\bar{N} = 10(1 - 0.21) = 7.9$$

In other words, the system will be busy with probability 0.21 or about one-fifth of the time and, on the average, almost 8 lines will be busy. Monte feels that this is a reasonable compromise. There does not seem to be a great deal of excess capacity, but, on the other hand, the probability of finding the system busy is in a region that he feels is appropriate for the hospital. If he is uncomfortable with this solution, based on a subjective balancing of the number of lines and the probability of finding the system busy, and is willing to specify a cost for each time a caller finds the system busy, he can select the number of lines to minimize the expected cost per hour. He would proceed in the same manner as in the $M/M/s$ system in Section 13.6.

─── 13.8
PROBLEM 3: THE REPAIRPERSON PROBLEM

In this problem Monte must decide how many repairpersons to hire to maintain 20 pieces of electronic equipment. Repairpersons deal with machines on a first-come (perhaps first-failed is more accurate), first-served basis.

A single repairperson treats each broken machine. You can thus think of the failed machines as forming a queue in front of multiple servers (the repairpersons).

This is another $M/M/s$ problem but it differs in a fundamental way from the $M/M/s$ system (the blood-testing problem) considered in Section 13.4. In this problem there is a limited number of items (20) which can join the queue, whereas in the hematology lab problem an unlimited number could potentially join the queue.

A queuing problem, like the repairperson problem, in which only a finite number of "people" are eligible to join the queue is said to have a *finite calling population*. Problems with an unlimited number of possible participants are said to have an *infinite calling population*.

Consider the problem with 20 machines and 2 repairpersons. Assume that when a machine is running, the time between breakdowns has an exponential distribution with parameter $\lambda = 0.25$, that is, the average time between breakdowns is $1/\lambda = 4$ hours. Similarly, assume that the time it takes to repair a machine has an exponential distribution and that the mean repair time is 0.50 hour (i.e., $1/\mu = 0.50$). This problem is an $M/M/2$ problem with a maximum of 18 items in the queue (20 including the 2 in service) and a finite calling population. In this case the general equations for the steady-state probability that there are n jobs in the system is a function of λ, μ, R (the number of repairpersons) and M (the number of machines). In particular,

Probability of
n Jobs in
the System

$$P_n = \frac{M!}{n!(M-n)!} (\lambda/\mu)^n P_0 \quad \text{for } 0 \leq n \leq R$$

$$P_n = \frac{M!}{(M-n)! \, R! \, R^{n-R}} (\lambda/\mu)^n P_0 \quad \text{for } R < n \leq M$$

These equations plus the fact that

$$\sum_{n=0}^{M} P_n = 1$$

make it possible (if painful) to calculate values of P_n for any particular problem.

There are, however, no simple expressions (even by these standards) for the expected number of jobs (broken machines) in the system or waiting. If the values for P_n are computed, then it is (truly) a simple task to find a numerical value for the expected number in the system. You must just calculate

$$\text{Expected number in system} = \sum_{n=0}^{M} nP_n$$

FIGURE 13.10
Computer Analysis of the
Repairperson Problem

```
HOW MANY SERVERS AND HOW MANY SPACES?
(SPACES MUST AT LEAST EQUAL SERVERS)
2,20

INDICATE SERVICE TIME DISTRIBUTION TYPE
E (EXPONENTIAL) OR C (CONSTANT):
E

POPULATION SIZE (ENTER 0 IF INFINITE) =
20

ARRIVAL RATE AND MEAN SERVICE TIME
0.25, 0.5

NO.-IN-SYS.         PROBABILITY        CUMULATIVE-PROB

       0               0.033              0.033
       1               0.083              0.116
       2               0.099              0.215
       3               0.111              0.326
       4               0.118              0.444
       5               0.118              0.563
       6               0.111              0.673
       7               0.097              0.770
       8               0.079              0.849
       9               0.059              0.908
      10               0.041              0.948
      11               0.025              0.974
      12               0.014              0.988
      13               0.007              0.995
      14               0.003              0.998
      15               0.001              1.000
      16               0.000              1.000
      17               0.000              1.000
      18               0.000              1.000

AVG.-NO.-IN-SYS. = 5.198
AVG.-NO.-WAITING = 3.348
PROBABILITY ALL SPACES FULL = 0.000
PROBABILITY FREE SERVER AVAILABLE = 0.116
AVG.-TIME-IN-SYS. FOR THOSE WHO GET SERVED = 1.405
AVG.-NO.-BUSY-SERVERS = 1.850
STOP
```

FIGURE 13.11

Models in the Computer-Based System

QUEUING SYSTEM	QUEUE SIZE	CALLING POPULATION
$M/M/s$	Any specified number	Infinite
$M/M/s$	$N - s$	Finite, Say N
$M/G/\infty$	0	Infinite
$M/G/1$	Infinite	Infinite
$M/M/s$	0	Finite
$M/D/1$	0	Finite
$M/G/s$	0	Infinite
$M/D/s$	Infinite	Infinite

Computers Are for Calculating

If God had intended man to perform this kind of calculation by hand, He would not have let computers be invented. Figure 13.10 shows the output of a computer routine that can be used to compute values of P_n, the expected number in the system, and the expected number waiting, for a variety of different systems. As shown, the user enters the system parameters and the computer does the rest. In this case, "the rest" consists of numerically evaluating the equations for P_n and using these results to find the expected number in the system. As you see in Figure 13.10, the computer stopped evaluating the number in the system at 18, since the probability was zero for any larger number. The summary data show that for this system, L_q, the average number of machines waiting for service, is 3.348 and W, the expected time in the system, is 1.405.

An on-line computer program such as the one used for the repairperson problem is a convenient way to obtain quick numerical results for a number of queuing systems. Indeed, it could also have been used to solve Problems 1 and 2. Figure 13.11 shows the models that can be evaluated with this particular program.

———— 13.9
THE ROLE OF THE EXPONENTIAL DISTRIBUTION

There is an enormous body of literature concerning queuing systems and it is virtually impossible for a manager to be aware of all the results. There are, however, some general considerations that are useful in helping a manager think about the use of queuing models. One such consideration is the role of the exponential distribution in analytic queuing models.

Possibility of Analytic Results

There are essentially no analytic results for queuing situations that do not involve the exponential distribution either as the distribution of interarrival times or service times or both. This fact makes it important for a manager to recognize the set of circumstances in which it is reasonable to assume that an exponential distribution will occur. The following two properties of the exponential distribution help to identify it:

Properties of the Exponential Distribution

1. *Lack of memory:* In an arrival process this property implies that the probability that an arrival will occur in the next few minutes is not influenced by when the last arrival occurred; that is, the system has no memory of what has just happened. This situation arises when (1) there are many individuals who could potentially arrive at the system, (2) each person decides to arrive independently of the other individuals, and (3) each individual selects his or her time of arrival completely at random. It is easy to see why the assumption of exponential arrivals fits the telephone system so well.

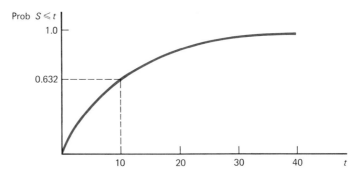

FIGURE 13.12
A High Probability of Short Service Times

2. *Small service times:* With an exponential distribution, small values of the service time are common. This can be seen in Figure 13.12. This figure shows the graph of the probability that the service time S is less than or equal to t (Prob $\{S \leq t\}$) if the mean service time is 10, i.e., $\mu = 0.1$ and $1/\mu = 10$. Note that the graph rises rapidly and then slowly approaches the value 1.0. This indicates a high probability of having a short service time. For example, when $t = 10$, the probability that $S \leq t$ is 0.632. In other words, more than 63 percent of the service times are smaller than the average service time. This compares to a normal distribution where only 50 percent of the service times are smaller than the average. The practical implication of this fact is that an exponential distribution can best be used to model the distribution of service times in a system in which a large proportion of jobs take a very short time and only a few run for a long time.

3. *Relation to the Poisson distribution:* While introducing the basic model (Section 13.2) we noted the relationship between the exponential and Poisson distributions. In particular, if the time between arrivals has an exponential distribution with parameter λ, then in a specified period of time (say, T) the number of arrivals will have a Poisson distribution with parameter λT. Then, if X is the number of arrivals during the time T, the probability that X equals a specific number (say n) is given by the equation

$$\text{Prob}\,\{X = n\} = \frac{e^{-\lambda T}(\lambda T)^n}{n!}$$

This equation holds for any integer value of n, i.e., $n = 0, 1, 2,$ and so on.

The relationship between the exponential and the Poisson distributions plays an important role in the theoretical development of queuing theory. It also has an important practical implication. By comparing the number of jobs that arrive for service during a specific period of time with the number that the Poisson distribution suggests, the analyst is able to see if his or her choice of a model and parameter values for the arrival process is reasonable.

13.10
QUEUE DISCIPLINE

In the previous sections we have specified the arrival distribution, the service distribution, and the number of servers to define a queuing system. Queue discipline is still another characteristic that must be specified in order to define a queuing system. In all of the models that we have considered so far, we have assumed that arrivals were served on a first-come, first-served basis (often called FIFO, for "first-in, first-out"). This is certainly an appropriate assumption for telephone systems and for many systems where people are the arrivals. This is not necessarily the case for other systems, however. In an elevator the last person in is often the first out (LIFO). And in the repairperson model, there is really no reason to fix the machines in the same order as they break down. If a certain machine can be returned to production in 5 minutes, it seems like a good idea to do it first, rather than making it wait until a 1-hour job on a machine that broke down earlier is completed.

Adding the possibility of selecting a good queue discipline makes the queuing models more complicated. Problems of this sort are often referred to as scheduling problems and there is an extensive literature that deals with them.

13.11
NOTES ON IMPLEMENTATION

Queuing problems are everywhere. This fact is obvious even to the most casual observer. Airplanes "queue up" in holding patterns, waiting for a runway so they can land and then they line up again to take off. People line up for tickets, to buy groceries, and, if they happen to live in England, for almost everything else. Jobs line up for machines, orders line up to be filled, and so on.

The models discussed in this chapter are useful representatives of only a small portion of the broad expanse of queuing problems. The results presented here in general require that either the time between arrivals, the service time, or both have an exponential distribution. They are important because they yield tight analytic results and because, in many circumstances, it is reasonable to assume that the arrival process is a Poisson process. In particular, we have noted that a large (essentially infinite) calling population in which individual members of the population decide at random to arrive at service facilities generates an exponential distribution for the time between arrivals. It is not surprising then that the analytic models are often used on systems with this type of arrival mechanism. Communication networks (especially the telephone system) and traffic control systems are two important examples of such systems.

Digital simulation is a popular approach for studying queuing problems that do not fit the analytic mold. Indeed, current programs such as GPSS (IBM's General Purpose Systems Simulator) have been created to facilitate the simulation process. A general discussion of simulation along with some specific comments on queuing simulators is included in the next chapter.

13.12
SUMMARY

This chapter provides an introduction to the subject of queuing. It points out that many interesting problems can be cast in the arrival/service mode of a queuing model.

Section 13.4 considers a multiserver queue. Some new formulas are presented. tial interarrival times and service times. Four system characteristics—expected number in system, L; expected number in queue, L_q; expected waiting time, W; and expected time in queue, W_q—are defined. Formulas are presented for these characteristics as a function of the parameters of the arrival and service processes. A numerical example is presented.

Little's flow equation, $L = \lambda W$, is presented in Section 13.3. This equation plus the general fact that

$$W = W_q + \text{expected service time}$$

are offered as alternative means for computing queue characteristics.

Section 13.4 considers a multiserver queue. Some new formulas are presented. These formulas are combined with results from the preceding section to compute numerical results for a staffing problem in a hematology lab. Section 13.5 briefly introduces a system of notation for describing queuing systems. This notation is exploited in Section 13.6, which is devoted to an economic analysis of the staffing problem in the hematology lab.

Sections 13.7 and 13.8 continue the consideration of multiserver queues. Section 13.7 is devoted to an $M/G/s$ system, in which customers who arrive and find the queue full do not wait, but simply leave. This model is particularly useful in the design of telephone systems. A specific example of this type is presented.

Section 13.8 considers the repairperson problem, an $M/M/s$ system with a finite calling population. It also illustrates the use of computers in obtaining numerical results for a particular problem.

Section 13.9 describes the importance of the exponential distribution in the analytic analysis of queuing systems. It also presents two characteristics of the exponential distribution, the lack of memory property and the high probability of small values.

Section 13.10 briefly considers the topic of queue discipline.

____ 13.13
KEY TERMS

QUEUING THEORY.   The study of waiting lines.

INTERARRIVAL TIME.   The amount of time between two consecutive arrivals at a service facility. Typically a random quantity.

SERVICE TIME.   The amount of time that it takes an item to pass through the service facility. Typically a random quantity.

QUEUE DISCIPLINE.   The rule used by the service facility to determine which items to serve. First-come, first-served is a typical example.

CHANNEL.   A synonym for server in queuing jargon (e.g., a single-channel queue is a queue with a single server).

ARRIVAL PROCESS.   That part of a queuing model that determines the arrival pattern.

SERVICE PROCESS.   That part of a queuing model that determines the service time for each item.

QUEUE SIZE.   The limit on the number of items that are permitted to wait in line for service.

STEADY STATE.   A condition in which the probability of viewing a certain situation (e.g., an empty queue) does not depend on the time at which you look.

OPERATING CHARACTERISTICS.   Quantities such as the expected number in queue that describe the operation of the queuing system.

CALLING POPULATION.   The number of items that might call on the system for service; thus, a factor in determining the arrival process.

LACK OF MEMORY.   A characteristic of the exponential distribution that makes it possible to derive analytic results for many queuing models.

MAJOR CONCEPTS QUIZ

True–False

1. **T F** The number of people in the system means the number waiting in line.
2. **T F** The waiting time includes the service time.
3. **T F** The exponential distribution is described by a mean and a standard deviation.
4. **T F** The mean interarrival time is the reciprocal of the mean arrival rate, and the mean service time is the reciprocal of the mean service rate.
5. **T F** The basic model is $M/M/1$.
6. **T F** As the number of servers increases, the cost of waiting generally increases.
7. **T F** The assumption that the mean service rate is less than the mean arrival rate is enough to eliminate the formation of infinitely long queues.
8. **T F** Little's flow equation states a directly proportional relationship between expected waiting time and expected number of people in the system.
9. **T F** The notation $G/M/2$ means the service distribution is general, the arrival distribution is exponential, and there are two parallel servers.

Multiple Choice

10. Which of the following does not apply to the basic model?
    a. exponentially distributed arrivals
    b. exponentially distributed service times
    c. finite time horizon
    d. unlimited queue size
    e. the discipline is first-come, first-served

11. A major goal of queuing is to
    a. minimize the cost of providing service
    b. provide models which help the manager to trade off the cost of service
    c. maximize expected return
    d. optimize system characteristics

12. Characteristics of queues such as "expected number in the system"
    a. are relevant after the queue has reached a steady state
    b. are probabilistic statements
    c. depend on the specific model
    d. all of the above

13. In Little's flow equation, which of the following is *not* true?
    a. λ is the constant of proportionality between expected number in the queue and expected time in the queue.
    b. λ is the constant of proportionality between expected number in the system and expected time in the system.
    c. λ is the arrival rate, including those arrivals who choose not to join the system.

14. The most difficult aspect of performing a formal economic analysis of queuing systems is
    a. estimating the service cost
    b. estimating the waiting cost
    c. estimating use

15. In a multiserver system with blocked customers cleared, which one of the following does not apply?
    a. When all servers are busy, new arrivals leave.
    b. Interesting characteristics are the probability that all servers are busy and the average number of busy servers.
    c. One would never do an expected-cost-per-hour analysis.

16. For the exponential distribution, which of the following is *not* a characteristic?
    a. lack of memory
    b. typically yields service times greater than the mean
    c. a single parameter

PROBLEMS

13-1. Barges arrive at the La Crosse lock on the Mississippi River at an average rate of one every 2 hours. If the interarrival time has an exponential distribution

  (a) What is the value of λ?

  (b) What is the mean interarrival time?

  (c) What is the mean arrival rate?

13-2. On the average a car arrives for a complete tune-up every 20 minutes. If the interarrival time has an exponential distribution

  (a) What is the value of λ?

  (b) What is the mean arrival rate?

13-3. An immigration agent at Heathrow Airport in London could on the average process 120 entrants during her 8 hours on duty if she was busy all of the time. If the time to process each entrant is a random variable with an exponential distribution

  (a) What is the value of μ?

  (b) What is the mean service time?

  (c) What is the mean service rate?

13-4. Joe's Service Station served 88 cars during an 8-hour period with no idle time. Assume that the service time is a random variable with an exponential distribution and use the given information to estimate

  (a) The value of μ.

  (b) The mean service time.

  (c) The mean service rate.

13-5. Consider the immigration officer mentioned in Problem 13-3. Assume that the basic model is a reasonable approximation of her operation. Recall that if she was busy all the time she could process 120 entrants during her 8-hour shift. If on the average an entrant arrives at her station once every 6 minutes, find

  (a) The expected number in the system.

  (b) The expected number in the queue.

  (c) The expected waiting time.

  (d) The expected time in queue.

  (e) The probability the system is empty.

13-6. Consider the La Crosse lock mentioned in Problem 13-1. Assume that the basic model is a reasonable approximation of its operation. The new estimate of the mean interarrival for the coming season is 40 minutes for barges, and on the average it takes 20 minutes to move a barge through the lock. Find

  (a) The expected number in the system.

  (b) The expected number in the queue.

  (c) The expected waiting time.

  (d) The expected time in queue.

  (e) The probability that the system is empty.

  (f) The longest average service time for which the expected waiting time is less than 30 minutes.

572

13-7. Consider a single-channel queue. Assume that the basic model is a reasonable approximation of its operation. Comment on the following scheme to estimate λ:

1. Let N equal the number of arrivals between 8:00 A.M. and 4:00 P.M.
2. Set $\lambda = 8/N$.

13-8. Consider a single-channel queue. Assume that the basic model is a reasonable approximation of its operation. Comment on the following scheme to estimate μ:

1. Let M equal the number of customers served between 8:00 A.M. and 4:00 P.M.
2. Set $\mu = M/8$.

13-9. Consider the basic model. Let $\mu = 10$ and plot the probability that the system is empty for $\lambda = 0, 1, \ldots, 10$.

13-10. Consider the basic model. Let $\lambda = 10$ and plot the expected number in the system for $\mu = 10, 11, \ldots, 20$.

13-11. Use Little's flow equation and the fact that $L = \lambda/(\mu - \lambda)$ in the basic model to derive the expression for W.

13-12. Use Little's flow equation, the expression for the mean service time, and the fact that $L = \lambda/(\mu - \lambda)$ in the basic model to derive the expression for W_q.

13-13. At the Homeburg Savings and Loan, customers who wish to buy certificates of deposit form a single line and are served on a first-come, first-served basis by a specific bank officer. Service time is normally distributed with a mean of 5 minutes and a standard deviation of 1 minute. Customers arrive at the rate of 1 every 8 minutes. A time study shows that customers spend an average of 10 minutes in the system (i.e., waiting and being served). What is the average number of people in the system?

13-14. A doctor schedules his patients to arrive at the rate of 3 per hour and treats them on a first-come, first-served basis. On the average he spends 10 minutes with each patient, but this time can vary anywhere from 5 to 40 minutes. On the average there are 3 patients in his office (2 waiting and 1 being served).

(a) How long on the average does a patient spend at the doctor's office?

(b) Suppose the interarrival and service times follow an exponential distribution. The average service time and the average number in the office are accurate. What should be the average arrival rate?

13-15. Assume that it was stated in Problem 13-14 that patients arrive at the rate of 7 per hour. Comment on this problem.

13-16. Assume that it was stated in Problem 13-13 that the mean service time was 10 minutes rather than 5. Comment on this problem.

13-17. The Homeburg Savings and Loan uses 3 tellers on Saturdays. The interarrival time and the service time for customers each has an exponential distribution. Customers arrive at the rate of 20 per hour and the mean service time is 6 minutes. Customers form a single queue and are served by the first available teller. Under steady-state conditions, find

(a) The probability that no customers are waiting or being served.

(b) The expected number of people in the queue.

(c) The expected waiting time in the queue.

(d) The expected waiting time.

(e) The expected number of people in the system.

13-18. The Business School reserves five ports on its on-line computer for faculty use. If a faculty member attempts to log on and all the ports are occupied he receives a busy signal and must try to log on at a later time. To estimate the system characteristics, the head of the computation center wants to know the steady-state values of the characteristics assuming an infinite calling population, an infinite queue, exponential interarrival times, and service times where jobs arrive at the rate of 6 per hour and the mean service time is 30 minutes. Find

(a) The probability that all ports are open.

(b) The expected number of people in the queue.

(c) The expected waiting time in the queue.

(d) The expected waiting time.

(e) The expected number in the system.

13-19. Describe a $M/D/3$ queuing system in words.

13-20. Describe a $GI/M/4$ queuing system in words.

13-21. Steco has 100 sales representatives in the United States. They call orders into a central office where an office worker using the central inventory control system confirms product availability, price, and delivery date. The representative calls directly from the customer's office before signing a contract. Calls are held in a queue and served by the first available office worker on a first-come, first-served basis. Calls arrive at the rate of 40 per hour and the mean service time is 6 minutes. Management estimates that it costs $20 per hour to have a sales representative wait and $12 per hour to employ an office worker. Model this situation as an $M/M/s$ queue with an infinite calling population and calculate the expected total cost per hour if Steco hires 5 office workers.

13-22. Find the expected total cost per hour for the system in Problem 13-21 if Steco hires 6 office workers.

13-23. Use the solutions to Problems 13-21 and 13-22 to determine the value for the ratio C_S/C_W for which Steco is indifferent between having 5 or 6 office workers.

13-24. Determine the value for the ratio C_S/C_W for which Steco is indifferent between 4 and 5 office workers.

13-25. A telephone exchange has 7 lines. Calls arrive at the rate of 2 per minute and the interarrival time has an exponential distribution. Conversations have a normal distribution with mean of 5 and a standard deviation of 1. When all 7 lines are occupied, the caller simply receives a busy signal.

(a) What is the probability that exactly 3 lines are busy?

(b) What is the probability that the system is totally occupied?

(c) What is the average number of busy servers?

13-26. A market research group has 4 interviewers located in adjacent booths in a suburban shopping mall. A contact person meets people walking in the mall and asks them if they are willing to be interviewed. They estimate that customers willing to agree to the interview arrive at the rate of 6 per hour and the interarrival time has an exponential distribution. On the average the interview takes 30 minutes. If all booths are occupied, a person who has agreed to be interviewed will not wait and simply goes about his or her business.

(a) Comment on the following statement: Since $\lambda > \mu s$, this system will grow without bound.

(b) Calculate the probability that exactly 1 interviewer is occupied.

(c) Find the probability that all 4 interviewers are occupied.

(d) Find the average number of busy interviewers.

14

SIMULATION

NAVAL SHIP PRODUCTION*

Ingalls Shipbuilding, a division of Litton Industries, Inc., is one of the largest shipyards in the world. From 1974 through 1977 the division's sales ranged from $500 million to $800 million with employment of approximately 20,000.

In 1969 and 1970 Ingalls was awarded Total Package Procurement contracts for five amphibious assault ships (LHAs) and 30 DD963 destroyers. These were firm-fixed-price contracts in which Ingalls received performance specifications and assumed sole responsibility for system design, detailed design, material procurement, planning, testing, and construction.

These contracts led to unanticipated cost overruns of $500 million dollars and a claim for this amount against the Navy. The basis for this claim rested on Ingalls' contention that Navy-responsible delays and design changes had created disruptions which had spread difficulties throughout the system and eventually produced the cost overruns. Although detailed data were submitted with the claim the difficulty of estimating the costs of second- and third-order "ripple effects" led to an adversary

* Kenneth G. Cooper, "Naval Ship Production: A Claim Settled and a Framework Built," *Interfaces*, 10, no. 6 (December 1980), 20–30.

relationship between Ingalls and the Navy. This relationship endangered not only Ingalls' current profit position but the potential for future business.

To clarify its claim, Litton had a simulation program constructed to correctly quantify Navy-responsible delay and disruption costs and to demonstrate the ripple effects. Simulation was selected because it permitted

1. Direct answering of "what if" questions; in particular, what if the Navy-initiated delays had not occurred?
2. A more complete and realistic representation of the system.
3. Clear and defensible attribution of impacts to specific sources.

The short-run impact of the model was to obtain a $447 million settlement for Ingalls from the Navy. Since the claim was settled out of court both the direct cost of further litigation (perhaps from $170 million to $350 million) and a vast amount of managerial and professional time and talent were saved.

Perhaps the long-run effects are more important. Since its original application eight different shipbuilding programs totaling 55 ships and approximately $7 billion of business have been modeled. In these applications the model is used to estimate the effect of various actions in scheduling or managing resources, as well as the impact of a multitude of exogenous factors.

APPLICATION CAPSULE

PLANNING TO GET THE LEAD OUT*

In the mid-1970s concern over the use of tetraethyl lead (TEL), as well as the amount of sulfur, in automobile gasoline became a topic of national concern. One result was that the California legislature passed a law requiring a scheduled lead and sulfur phase-down. Under this law the maximum TEL content had to be decreased in phased steps from 1.4 to 0.4 grams per gallon over a 3-year horizon.

This law presented a major challenge to Exxon's Benicia Refinery since it fundamentally changed the way in which gasoline was produced. Gasoline production is performed in two steps: refining, in which crude oil is separated into various components that are stored in large (component) tanks; and blending, in which the components are mixed together to produce finished products which are stored in (finished-product) tanks. TEL was an important part of this process because of the flexibility it provided. If a batch of gasoline did not meet the octane specification a little more TEL could be added to bring it up to standard.

Reducing the use of TEL had a particularly dramatic influence on the storage of components and finished products. Without the ability to enhance octane ratings with TEL it was necessary to expand the inventory of higher-octane components or blended products or perhaps both to ensure an adequate supply of the full range of

* Lewis Golovin, "Product Blending: A Simulation Case Study in Double-Time," *Interfaces*, 9, no. 5 (November 1979), 64–76.

finished products. Preliminary calculations indicated at least two new component tanks and one or two new finished-product tanks would be needed. At a cost of over $1 million per tank this was clearly a problem that deserved careful attention.

Exxon constructed a discrete time simulator to analyze this problem. The program simulates the operation of the gasoline production facilities on an hour-to-hour basis. The simulator had several advantages: Gathering of input data was easy and straightforward, management became involved in determining the blending strategy used in the simulation, and results were produced on operations reports very similar to those in actual use. Each of these factors make the results more "believable" to management and thus made the recommendations more acceptable.

As a result of the analysis, Exxon management decided to change the way in which components and final products were stored and to authorize the construction of one additional component tank and one additional finished-product tank. Thus the company was able to reduce its planned capital expenditure by at least one tank—an estimated savings of at least $1.4 million.

14.1
INTRODUCTION

Many people believe that "experience is the best teacher." Unfortunately, it is often too costly (in time or money) to obtain real experience. These two statements supply a primary motivation for the use of simulation.

The Basic Idea of Simulation

The basic idea of simulation is to build an experimental device that will "act like" (simulate) the system of interest in certain important respects.

The goal is to create an environment in which it is possible to obtain information about alternative actions via experimentation. The use of simulation is fundamental to many applied experiments; for example:

1. Testing of medicines on laboratory animals. In this case the animal responses *simulate* human responses.
2. Driving automobiles on test tracks. Here the test track *simulates* the environment the auto will face.
3. Testing wing designs for airplanes in wind tunnels. The wind tunnel *simulates* flight conditions.
4. Training airline pilots in actual cabins under *simulated* conditions.

In the context of quantitative analysis, simulation has come to mean experimentation based on a mathematical model. This concept is illustrated in Figure 14.1. Note that *in a simulation the analyst supplies (as input) the decisions and the system parameters and receives (as output) some measure or multiple measures of effectiveness*, such as profit, or cost, or measures of attainment of any other goals of interest. It is interesting to contrast a simulator with an optimization model.

FIGURE 14.1
Typical Simulator

Input: Decisions and parameter values

Simulator

Output: Measures of effectiveness

As shown in Figure 14.2, in an optimization model we input *parameter values*. The output is an *optimal decision* and the optimal value of the measure of effectiveness (the OV). In a simulation the decision is part of the input and the output is simply a value (not necessarily optimal), or values, of the measures of effectiveness. Consider a modified version of the **PROTRAC** E and F problem from Chapters 2, 3, 4, and 5. In particular, assume that **PROTRAC**'s production problem is expressed as the following mathematical programming model:

The Modified PROTRAC Model

$$\text{Max } 100{,}000(1 - e^{-0.1E}) + 80{,}000(1 - e^{-0.3F})$$

$$\begin{aligned}
\text{s.t.} \qquad\qquad E + F &\geq 5 && \text{(total production)}\\
E - 3F &\leq 0 && \text{(product mix)}\\
3\delta(E) + 10E + 2\delta(F) + 15F &\leq 150 && \text{(time in department A)}\\
4\delta(E) + 20E + 3\delta(F) + 10F &\leq 160 && \text{(time in department B)}\\
30E + 10F &\geq 135 && \text{(labor for product testing)}\\
E, F &\geq 0
\end{aligned}$$

where we employ the notation

$$\delta(E) = 1 \quad \text{if } E > 0 \qquad \text{and} \qquad \delta(E) = 0 \quad \text{if } E = 0$$
$$\delta(F) = 1 \quad \text{if } F > 0 \qquad \text{and} \qquad \delta(F) = 0 \quad \text{if } F = 0$$

FIGURE 14.2
Optimization Model

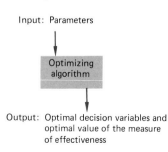

Input: Parameters

Optimizing
algorithm

Output: Optimal decision variables and
optimal value of the measure
of effectiveness

FIGURE 14.3
Returns from Production of E's

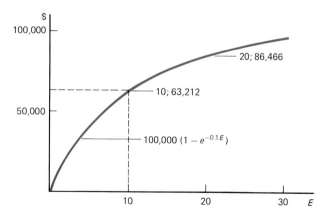

The original model has been modified to take two facts into account:

1. The market for E's and F's is not unlimited, and thus the objective function has been adjusted to include diminishing returns. A plot of the returns from making E's $[100,000(1 - e^{-0.1E})]$ is shown in Figure 14.3. Here we see that manufacturing E clearly yields diminishing marginal and average returns. The marginal returns are diminishing because the slope of the graph is decreasing (such a function is termed concave). To see that the average returns are decreasing, note that the first 10 E's yield a total return of \$63,212, which gives an average return of \$6321 per E. The second 10 yield an increase of only \$23,254 (\$86,466 − \$63,212), an average of \$2325 per E.

2. The time required in departments A and B has been adjusted to include setup times. By definition, $\delta(E) = 1$ if $E > 0$. Thus, if **PROTRAC** decides to produce any E's (i.e., $E > 0$) the term $\delta(E)$ equals 1. This implies that $3\delta(E) = 3$, and thus there are only 147 hours (150 − 3) available to produce E's and F's. You can think of the 3 hours as the setup time, the time it takes to prepare to produce E's no matter how many are produced. A similar interpretation holds for the term $2\delta(F)$ in the department A constraint, as well as the term $4\delta(E)$ and $3\delta(F)$ in the department B constraint.

The problem is like the **PROTRAC** E and F problem considered in Chapters 3, 4, and 5 except for the differences stated above. The original model, an LP, was simple to solve. The modified problem is clearly not an LP, and thus the simplex algorithm cannot be used. Indeed, there is no conveniently available algorithm to attack the problem in this form.

Now suppose that you were asked to find a solution to the actual **PROTRAC** E and F problem (i.e., the real-world problem faced by the manager) and you feel that the mathematical programming formulation shown above would give a useful answer. Unfortunately, we are not able to find a computer code to locate an optimal solution and thus another approach must be found. One way to proceed is to use the mathematical programming *formulation* of the problem to *simulate* the operation of the production facility, that is, use the mathematical programming *formulation* as an experimental device in order to select good values for E and F. You might, for example, follow the flowchart in Figure 14.4.

Simulating the PROTRAC Production Operation   To use the flowchart in Figure 14.4, you must first select values for E and F. Suppose, for example, that you first choose $E = 5$ and $F = 10$. We now move to box ②. Constraints 1 and 2 are clearly satisfied, but consider the third constraint. If our choice of values is feasible, the inequality

$$3\delta(E) + 10E + 2\delta(F) + 15F \leq 150$$

FIGURE 14.4
Simulating the Modified *E* and *F* Problem

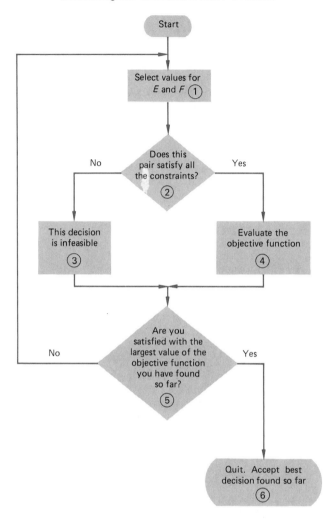

must hold. Substituting $E = 5$ and $F = 10$ into the left-hand side of this expression yields

$$3\delta(5) + 10(5) + 2\delta(10) + 15(10) = 3 + 50 + 2 + 150 = 205$$

Thus, the model tells us that the solution $E = 5$, $F = 10$ violates the third constraint and is infeasible. We thus move to box ③ in Figure 14.4 and then on to box ⑤. Since we have not yet found a feasible solution to the problem, the response to the question in box ⑤ has to be "no" and we go back to pick another pair of values for E and F.

Suppose this time that we select $E = 4$ and $F = 3$. In box ② we determine that this choice satisfies all the constraints (i.e., it is feasible). We thus move to box ④ and evaluate the objective function as follows:

$$100{,}000(1 - e^{-0.1(4)}) + 80{,}000(1 - e^{-0.3(3)})$$

$$= 100{,}000(1 - 0.670320) + 80{,}000(1 - 0.406570)$$

$$= \$32{,}968 + \$47{,}474 = \$80{,}442$$

Now entering box ⑤, we have a question to answer. Are we satisfied with our best (and only) feasible answer so far? If the answer is yes, we go to box ⑥; that is, we accept the solution $E = 4$, $F = 3$ as the best we are going to find and quit. If the answer is no, we return to ① and pick another decision (another pair of values for E and F).

What Is a Simulation Model? If this were a real problem, there would be many questions to ask; for example: Is there a good way to choose the trial decisions? How do you know when the decision is "good enough?" For the moment, our goal has been served—namely, to illustrate a type of simulation model. In particular, by "simulation model" we mean

---

a series of logical and mathematical operations that provide a measure of effectiveness for a particular set of values of the parameters and decisions.

14.2
SIMULATION AND RANDOM EVENTS

Simulation models are often used to analyze a decision under uncertainty, that is, a problem in which the behavior of one or more factors can be represented by a probability distribution. This type of simulation is sometimes called a *Monte Carlo method*. Let us turn to several examples of this approach.

Design of Docking Facilities A typical problem is illustrated in Figure 14.5. Here trucks, perhaps of various sizes carrying different types of loads, arrive at a warehouse to be unloaded. The amount of time between truck arrivals is *random*.

There are a variety of design questions:

1. How many docks should be built?
2. What type and quantity of materials handling equipment is required?
3. How many personnel are required over what periods of time?

FIGURE 14.5

Truck Docking Problem

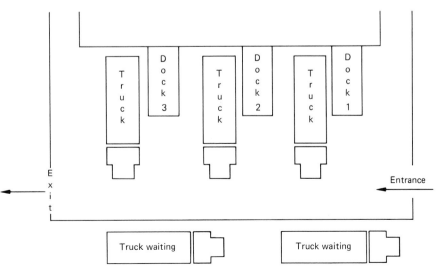

Management must balance the cost of acquiring and using the various resources (docks, materials handling equipment, and people) against the cost of having trucks wait to be unloaded.

A similar problem of designing docking facilities for oil tankers is important to the oil companies because of the high cost of having a supertanker full of oil waiting for an open dock (see the "special diagnostic vignette" at the end of this chapter).

Such problems are in the formal domain of "queuing models" as described in Chapter 13. They are often attacked with simulation when analytic results are difficult to obtain.

Determination of Inventory Control Policies

Simulation can be and is used to study a variety of problems in this general area. One such problem is illustrated in Figure 14.6. In this system, the factory produces goods that are sent to the warehouses to satisfy customer demand. Assume that demand at each warehouse is *random*. Management must answer such questions as

1. Is a *pull system* (in which warehouses order from the factory) or a *push system* (in which the factory decides how much to send to each warehouse) preferred?
2. Is it useful to have a central warehouse that receives orders from all other warehouses?
3. Is it useful to have a *transshipment system* (in which one warehouse can order goods from another warehouse)? If so, what are the appropriate operating rules for such a system?

Such problems can be and often are attacked with simulation.

Scheduling Problems

Consider an important production facility that produces several different products. The examples of this situation include most assembly lines and highly automated pieces of manufacturing equipment, such as blast furnaces, automatic screw machines, and photographic film-coating machines.

In all cases the question is how much of which product to make in view of uncertain future demand for each of the products. Such problems can be attacked with simulation.

When Should Simulation Be Used?

The problems we have just discussed are related to problems presented and solved by analytic means in earlier chapters. Natural questions are: What is the difference, if any, between these problems and those in the earlier chapters? When do I use analytic means and when do I use simulation to attack a model? To answer these questions, it is useful to understand simulation involving random events.

Our discussion of simulation with random events is based on illustrative problems. Two problems from Chapter 12, the omelet pan problem featuring Peggy McConnel from Wiles department store, and the (r, Q) inventory model faced by Victor Kowalski, form the basis of the discussion. As we saw in Chapter 12, these problems can be attacked

FIGURE 14.6
Distribution System

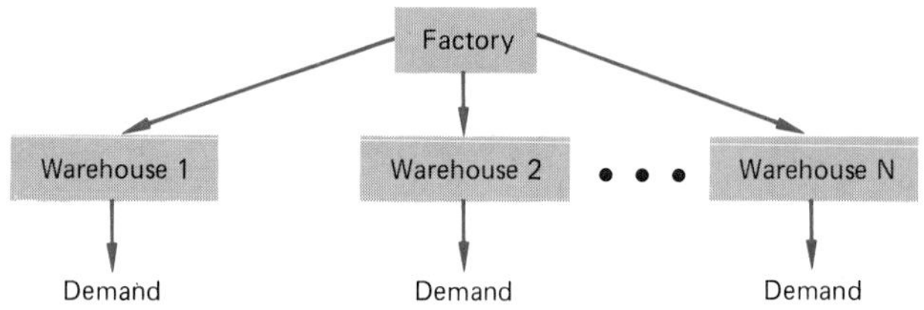

with analytic methods. As a matter of fact, this would be the preferred approach for those specific examples. However, the pedagogical advantages of being able to compare the analytic and simulation approaches on the same problem motivate us to base our presentations on these models. As we shall see later, in the real world simulation is typically used when it is impossible or too expensive to obtain analytic results.

——— 14.3
AN INVENTORY CONTROL EXAMPLE: WILES' HOUSEWARES

Consider the omelet pan problem described in (Section 12.8). In this problem Peggy McConnel, the chief buyer for housewares at Wiles Department Store, is trying to decide how many special omelet pans to order for a promotion. Wiles will buy the special pans for $22 and will sell them for $35. Any pans left at the end of the sale will be sold to Clampton's Discount Chain for $15 each. We thus see that Wiles will lose $7 for each special pan left unsold at the end of the promotion. This per unit amount, for each unsold special pan, is defined as the per unit holding cost, h. Thus, $h = \$7$.

As part of the promotion, Peggy has decided to use regular omelet pans to satisfy demand if she runs out of the special pans. Regular pans cost $32 each. In this case, then, the per unit cost of running out of special pans (i.e., the per unit penalty cost) consists entirely of forgone revenue (also called "opportunity cost"). If Peggy is out of special pans and a customer orders one, she will sell for $35 a regular pan that costs $32, and enjoy a contribution margin of only $3 ($35 − $32). However, if a special pan had been available, she would have sold this pan that cost $22 for $35, and thereby enjoyed a contribution margin of $13. She thus incurs a $10 ($13 − $3) "opportunity loss" (decline in contribution margin) for stockouts of special pans. This loss is referred to as the per unit penalty cost, p. Note that Peggy's calculations assume that using regular pans to satisfy the promotional demand will *not* create any unsatisfied regular demand. Because of the location of her regular pan supplier, the supply is large enough that this complication need not be considered.

The problem facing Peggy is how many special pans to order in view of an uncertain demand. We will see how to attack this question with simulation, beginning with an illustrative simple example. Later, in Section 14.5, we will invoke the assumption of a normal demand distribution ($\mu = 1000$, $\sigma = 100$) which is the situation treated in Chapter 12. Let us now assume that demand has the following probability distribution. These demands have been chosen artificially small in order to simplify the example. Let us, for the moment, also assume that we know how to "generate a random demand" from this probability distribution. The technique of doing this will be explicitly treated in the next section.

Simplified Demand Distribution

prob {demand = 8} = 0.1

prob {demand = 9} = 0.2

prob {demand = 10} = 0.3

prob {demand = 11} = 0.2

prob {demand = 12} = 0.1

prob {demand = 13} = 0.1

FIGURE 14.7

Simulating the Cost of Ordering y Pans

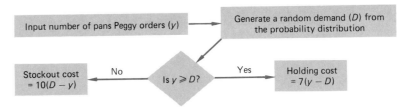

With this demand information Peggy could construct the simulator shown in Figure 14.7. To see how the simulator works, assume that Peggy decides to order 11 omelet pans. Then $y = 11$. If the random demand turns out to be 9, then $y > D$ and the simulator takes the "yes" branch in the flowchart. The cost of this *simulated* promotion is $7(11 - 9) = \$14$. This, of course, is the appropriate cost since, if Peggy ordered 11 pans and only 9 were sold, Wiles would have 2 left over. Since the per unit holding cost is $7, this implies a cost of $14.

Estimating Expected Cost   In this simple example Peggy could analytically calculate the *expected cost* of ordering 11 pans. Before doing so, let us use the simulator to estimate this value. We must make a number of trials, setting $y = 11$ and generating a new demand on each trial. The cost that results on any given trial depends, of course, on the value of demand that was generated on that particular trial. The *average cost* over all trials, then, is an estimate of the expected cost. This process, for 10 trials, is illustrated in Figure 14.8. Since the total cost for the 10 trials is $96, the average cost is $96/10 = \$9.60$. Thus, based on these 10 trials, Peggy's best estimate of the expected cost of ordering 11 pans is $9.60.

Determining the Order Quantity   If Peggy wanted to use simulation to determine how many pans to order, she would

1. Select an order size (in the example above, the order is 11).
2. Run a number of trials (say 10).
3. Calculate the average cost.
4. Repeat steps 2 and 3 for a different order size.
5. Select the order size with the smallest cost.

FIGURE 14.8

Ten Simulated Trials

TRIAL NUMBER	QUANTITY ORDERED	RANDOM DEMAND	PANS LEFT OVER	PANS SHORT	COST
1	11	9	2		7 × 2 = 14
2	11	13		2	10 × 2 = 20
3	11	10	1		7 × 1 = 7
4	11	10	1		7 × 1 = 7
5	11	9	2		7 × 2 = 14
6	11	12		1	10 × 1 = 10
7	11	11	0		7 × 0 = 0
8	11	12		1	10 × 1 = 10
9	11	11	0		7 × 0 = 0
10	11	9	2		7 × 2 = 14
				Total Cost	$96

It is worth noting that, since the demand is random, the average cost is also random. This means that if Peggy ran another set of 10 trials with the same order size of 11 pans, the simulator would generate a different series of demands and thus would most likely obtain a different average cost. This fact leads to the following important observation:

> **Suppose that, in a decision under uncertainty, management would like to make that decision that minimizes expected cost or maximizes expected profit. With simulation, it is *impossible to guarantee* that this decision can be identified.**

Suppose, for example, that Peggy now uses algebra to calculate the expected cost of ordering 11 pans. The calculation is shown below.

$$\text{expected cost} = 10(13 - 11) \, \text{Prob} \, \{D = 13\} + 10(12 - 11) \, \text{Prob} \, \{D = 12\}$$
$$+ \, 7(11 - 11) \, \text{Prob} \, \{D = 11\} + 7(11 - 10) \, \text{Prob} \, \{D = 10\}$$
$$+ \, 7(11 - 9) \, \text{Prob} \, \{D = 9\} + 7(11 - 8) \, \text{Prob} \, \{D = 8\}$$

or

$$\text{expected cost} = 20(0.1) + 10(0.1) + 0(0.2) + 7(0.3) + 14(0.2) + 21(0.1) = 10$$

It is no surprise that the average cost generated by one run of the simulator ($9.60) does not equal the expected cost ($10) since, according to the remarks above, different runs will produce different values for the average. The implication of this fact on the process of making a decision is interesting. Figure 14.9 shows the algebraically computed expected cost and a simulated average cost, based on order sizes of 9, 10, 11, and 12 pans.

Here we see that if Peggy were to base her decision on the simulated average costs the cost-minimizing decision would be to order 11 pans, whereas to minimize the expected cost she should order 10 pans. This is, of course, a deliberately oversimplified example, but it is an excellent illustration of the fact that simulation, in general, does not achieve optimality. We should at this point reemphasize that in a real problem you would not both calculate the expected cost and use simulation to calculate an average cost. Simulation is used when it is computationally impractical or even not possible to calculate the expected cost associated with the alternative decisions. This simple example serves to illustrate relationships between simulation and analytic models.

FIGURE 14.9
Expected Costs and Simulated Average Costs

NUMBER ORDERED	EXPECTED COST	SIMULATED AVERAGE COST BASED ON 10 TRIALS
9	$14.70	$16.00
10	9.80	11.10
11	10.00	9.60
12	13.60	11.50

Recapitulation   The next section deals with the technique of generating random events such as the number of omelet pans demanded. First, let us summarize and comment on several aspects of what we have seen to date.

1. A simulator takes parameters and decisions as inputs and yields a measure (or measures) of effectiveness as output.

2. If the simulator contains random events, each pass through the simulator (for the same parameters and decisions) will generally yield a different value for the measure of effectiveness.

3. In Peggy's problem the measure of effectiveness for an order of size 11, in each trial, was taken to be cost (each row of Figure 14.8). The 10 trials taken together combine to produce another measure of the goodness of order size—namely, average cost. It is to be noted that even more information is available. Figure 14.8 shows a 30% probability of obtaining a shortage (this occurred in 3 of the 10 trials). This is additional data with which to assess the "goodness" of ordering 11 pans, and it shows how, with simulation, numerous "measures of effectiveness" can be produced. There is another important property of simulation that is illustrated by Figure 14.8. The 10 trials have actually produced a distribution of costs. They vary from 7 to 20 and the mean is 9.6. This provides some indication as to the *variability* associated with the policy being measured (order 11 pans). Indicators of variability are important products of simulation studies. Management usually seeks policies for which the potential outcome is highly predictable, which means low variability.

4. If the simulator contains random events, then increasing the number of passes through the simulator (for the same parameters and decisions) will, "on the average," improve the accuracy of the estimate of the expected value of the measure of effectiveness (see Figure 14.15 and the subsequent discussion). In other words, if Peggy had used 100 or 1000 trials in Figure 14.9, the average cost for each order quantity would "on the average" be closer to the corresponding expected cost.

5. In a simulator we can never be sure that we have found the optimal decision. We can simply identify the best decision among those evaluated.

6. Management must assess four main factors in a simulation study:
   a. Does the model capture the essence of the real problem? See Section 14.7 for more discussion of this point.
   b. Are the data being presented in such a way that the results represent the actual situation? See Section 14.6 for a specific example.
   c. Have enough trials been performed for each decision so that the average value of the measure (or measures) of performance is a good indication of the expected value?
   d. Have enough decisions and the right decisions been evaluated so that we can believe that the best answer found is "close enough" to the optimum?

We will embellish the factors b and c later in the chapter.

——— 14.4
GENERATING RANDOM EVENTS

Using Random   In our simulation of the omelet pan problem, it was necessary to generate a random
Numbers   demand, D, from a specified probability distribution. To do this we need a device that generates an 8 with probability of 0.1, a 9 with a probability of 0.2, and so on.

It is easy to think of a physical device that would serve that purpose. We could, for example,

1. Place 10 identical balls in an urn. Label 1 ball with an 8, 2 balls with a 9, 3 balls with a 10, 2 balls with an 11, 1 ball with a 12, and 1 ball with a 13.

2. Shake up the urn and draw a ball at random.

In this process we sometimes say that "we wish to *draw a random sample* of the distribution of demand" as a synonym for "we wish to generate a random demand from the specified distribution." We will use both expressions in our discussion of simulation.

The process of drawing balls from an urn to generate random quantities is easy to visualize. However, you will not be surprised to learn that this is not the system this is typically used.

The generation of random events by hand typically involves the use of a table of random numbers. One such table is presented in Figure 14.10. This table is the result of a random sample of the integers 00 through 99 (a total of 100 numbers) where each number is equally likely. You thus can think of each number in the table as being the

FIGURE 14.10
Table of Random Digits

	1	2	3	4	5	6	7	8	9	10
1	97	95	12	11	90	49	57	13	86	81
2	02	92	75	91	24	58	39	22	13	02
3	80	67	14	99	16	89	96	63	67	60
4	66	24	72	57	32	15	49	63	00	04
5	96	76	20	28	72	12	77	23	79	46
6	55	64	82	61	73	94	㉖	18	37	31
7	50	02	74	70	16	85	95	32	85	67
8	29	53	08	33	81	34	30	21	24	25
9	58	16	01	91	70	07	50	13	18	24
10	51	16	69	67	16	53	11	06	36	10
11	04	55	36	97	30	99	80	10	52	40
12	86	54	35	61	59	89	64	97	16	02
13	24	23	52	11	59	10	88	68	17	39
14	39	36	99	50	74	27	69	48	32	68
15	47	44	41	86	83	50	24	51	02	08
16	60	71	41	25	90	93	07	24	29	59
17	65	88	48	06	68	92	70	97	02	66
18	44	74	11	60	14	57	08	54	12	90
19	93	10	95	80	32	50	40	44	08	12
20	20	46	36	19	47	78	16	90	59	64
21	86	54	24	88	94	14	58	49	80	79
22	12	88	12	25	19	70	40	06	40	31
23	42	00	50	24	60	90	69	60	07	86
24	29	98	81	68	61	24	90	92	32	68
25	36	63	02	37	89	40	81	77	74	82
26	01	77	82	78	20	72	35	38	56	89
27	41	69	43	37	41	21	36	39	57	80
28	54	40	㊂	04	05	01	45	84	55	11
29	68	03	82	32	22	80	92	47	77	62
30	21	31	77	75	43	13	83	43	70	16
31	53	64	54	21	04	23	85	44	81	36
32	91	66	21	47	95	69	58	91	47	59
33	48	72	74	40	97	92	05	01	61	18
34	36	21	47	71	84	46	09	85	32	82
35	55	95	24	85	84	51	61	60	62	13
36	70	27	01	88	84	85	77	94	67	35
37	38	13	66	15	38	54	43	64	25	43
38	36	80	25	24	92	98	35	12	17	62
39	98	10	91	61	04	90	05	22	75	20
40	50	54	29	19	26	26	87	94	27	73

FIGURE 14.11

Associating Random Numbers with Demands

RANDOM NUMBERS	PROPORTION OF TOTAL NUMBERS ASSIGNED	DEMAND FOR OMELET PANS	PROBABILITY
00–09	0.10	8	0.1
10–29	0.20	9	0.2
30–59	0.30	10	0.3
60–79	0.20	11	0.2
80–89	0.10	12	0.1
90–99	0.10	13	0.1

result of drawing a ball from an urn that contains 100 balls (numbered 00–99) where each ball is equally likely to be drawn.

Assigning Random Numbers to Events

With this interpretation, all that is needed to generate random demands for omelet pans is to assign to each random number (00–99) a particular demand. The only requirement for a correct assignment is that the proportion of total numbers assigned to a demand must equal the probability of that demand. A correct assignment is shown in Figure 14.11. Note that a demand of 8 pans is assigned to the numbers 00–09 (10 numbers). Thus $\frac{10}{100} = 0.1$ of the numbers are associated with this demand, and 0.1 is the previously specified probability that the demand for omelet pans will equal 8. A moment's thought should convince you that this assignment is correct. If each number (00–99) is equally likely, the probability that one of the numbers 00–09 would result is 0.10, the desired value. It should also be clear that this is not the only correct assignment. We could assign a demand of 8 to any 10 numbers (e.g., 49, 13, 26, 27, 50, 93, 96, 72, 02, 06) and have a correct assignment. The assignment shown in Figure 14.11 is convenient in the sense that contiguous values of the random numbers are associated with the same value of demand. It is also the assignment scheme which we used to generate the demand sequence shown in the simulation in Figure 14.8.

Let us now see how we generated this sequence of demands. The first step is to select an arbitrary place in the table (Figure 14.10) to begin. We start in row 6, column 7. We observe that the random number is 26. Referring to Figure 14.11, we see that a random number of 26 implies a demand of 9. We proceed by reading down the table. The second random number is 95, which, in Figure 14.11, implies a demand of 13. Another 8 observations are produced by continuing to read down the table. The results are the demands shown in Figure 14.8.

We now consider another illustration of how the table of random numbers can be used to simulate random events.

Simulating the Rolling of a Fair Die

Since the die is fair, each of the faces with the numbers 1, 2, . . . , 6 is equally likely; that is, each face occurs with probability $\frac{1}{6}$. Figure 14.12 shows one way in which the random numbers can represent the faces of the die. For example, the figure shows that if the random number 49 is drawn, this simulates a roll of the die which gives the face with 4 dots. Similarly, a 45 gives a roll of 3. Note that, in Figure 14.12, the 4 numbers 96–99 are discarded so that the probabilities of faces 1, 2, and so on, can be exactly $\frac{1}{6}$. That is, 16 out of a total of 96 numbers are assigned to each face of the die.

The Normal Distribution

The normal distribution plays an important role in many analytic and simulation models. In simulation, we often assume that random quantities are normally distrib-

FIGURE 14.12

Identifying the Faces of a
Die with Random Numbers

RANDOM NUMBERS	FACE
00–15	1
16–31	2
32–47	3
48–63	4
64–79	5
80–95	6
96–99	a

[a] Ignore this result; go to next random number.

uted. To illustrate, we return to Peggy McConnel and Wiles' omelet pan problem. This problem was introduced in Section 12.8 and reviewed in Section 14.3. In the problem she actually faced, Peggy assumed that a normal distribution with a mean of 1000 and a standard deviation of 100 described the demand that would occur. She then used this distribution to determine the optimal number of pans to order.

Suppose that she had chosen to use simulation to estimate the expected cost associated with any particular order quantity (the approach described in Section 14.3). In order to accomplish this, on each simulation trial she would have to draw a random demand from a normal distribution with a mean μ of 1000 and a standard deviation σ of 100. This is a two-step process:

Generating a Random Demand

1. Take a number from the random number table and divide by 100. For example, suppose that we arbitrarily start in row 28, column 3, of Figure 14.10 and obtain the number 0.76.
2. Use Table T.1 on page 822 to find the number (say v) such that the area under the normal curve to the left of v equals the number selected in 1. In this example we must find v such that the area under the normal curve to the left of v equals 0.76. From Table T.1 we see that v must be 0.706 standard deviation to the right of the mean. Thus, $v = \mu + 0.706\sigma = 1000 + 0.706(100) = 1070.6$. This is the first randomly generated demand.

To generate another demand, we would take the next random number (82) from Figure 14.10 and start the process over again.

Other Distributions

The general concept of the two-step process used to generate normally distributed random quantities can be used for any other distribution. The process is illustrated in Figure 14.13 where W denotes a random quantity such as demand. The crucial element is a plot of the Prob $\{W \leq w\}$. The figure shows a typical function of this type, namely, one that goes from 0 to 1 and is nondecreasing. We should stress that Figure 14.13

A General Method

motivates the *concept* underlying the technique of generating an arbitrary random quantity. In practice, the process is typically performed in the computer with either a tabular or analytic representation of a graph like Figure 14.13. The process starts as before, by selecting a number, say 80, from the random number table. The value of this random number is then located on the vertical axis (or, in the computer, in an appropriate table). You then read from the graph (or the computer does a "table lookup") to obtain the value of the random quantity (approximately 5.1 in Figure 14.13). This is exactly how we used Table T.1 to generate normally distributed random quantities.

FIGURE 14.13
Generating Random Quantities

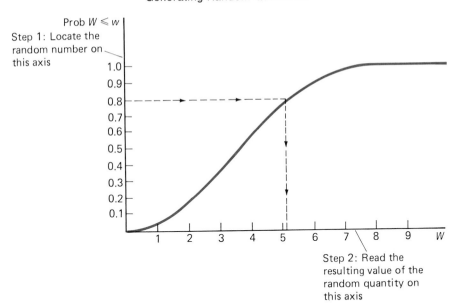

Step 1: Locate the random number on this axis

Prob $W \leqslant w$

Step 2: Read the resulting value of the random quantity on this axis

————— **14.5**

COMPUTER SIMULATION OF WILES' PROBLEM

Simulation by hand is time-consuming and tedious (to put it kindly) even for simple models like the omelet pan problem. For more complicated models, these characteristics are exacerbated and, in addition, it becomes increasingly difficult to avoid making logical and/or computational errors. On the other hand, computers are specifically designed to perform a large number of logical and numerical operations rapidly and accurately. In addition, computers can be easily programmed to generate random quantities from any specific distribution. The process is essentially the one described in the preceding section. The random numbers are produced internally by the computer and used to obtain the appropriate random quantity. In most computer simulation packages it is possible to request observations from one of a number of standard probability distributions simply by stating what distribution you want and providing the parameters for that distribution. For all of these reasons, almost all simulations are performed on computers. Indeed, a number of general-purpose simulation packages are used to investigate inventory and queuing problems. Some of these packages are commercially available and others exist in specific firms or universities.

One such package is used for research on multiechelon inventory systems at the University of Chicago. It is an on-line system that can be used to study a great variety of inventory systems. Indeed, the following discussion shows how it could be used to study Peggy McConnel's omelet pan problem. In particular, the system is used to *estimate* the expected holding and penalty cost if 1022 pans are ordered. The analytic analysis in Chapter 12 revealed that, assuming a normal distribution of demand (with $\mu = 1000$, $\sigma = 100$), 1022 is the optimal number of pans.

Figure 14.14 shows the input and the output for a set of 1000 trials on this problem. To use this system the user must input various parameters. In this particular set of experiments we used the same parameters that were used in the analytic solution in

FIGURE 14.14
Computer Simulation of Wiles' Problem

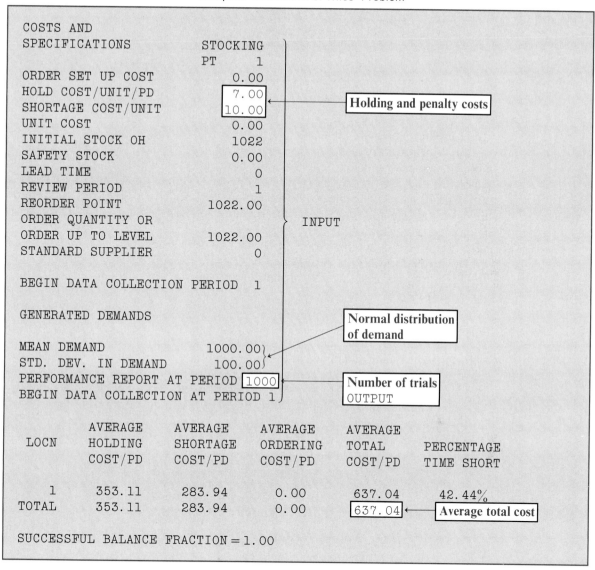

```
COSTS AND
SPECIFICATIONS            STOCKING
                          PT    1
ORDER SET UP COST             0.00
HOLD COST/UNIT/PD             7.00     ◄──  Holding and penalty costs
SHORTAGE COST/UNIT           10.00
UNIT COST                     0.00
INITIAL STOCK OH             1022
SAFETY STOCK                  0.00
LEAD TIME                        0
REVIEW PERIOD                    1
REORDER POINT              1022.00
ORDER QUANTITY OR                      }  INPUT
ORDER UP TO LEVEL          1022.00
STANDARD SUPPLIER                0

BEGIN DATA COLLECTION PERIOD   1

GENERATED DEMANDS                        Normal distribution
                                         of demand
MEAN DEMAND              1000.00 }
STD. DEV. IN DEMAND       100.00
PERFORMANCE REPORT AT PERIOD  1000  ◄──  Number of trials
BEGIN DATA COLLECTION AT PERIOD 1        OUTPUT

        AVERAGE   AVERAGE   AVERAGE   AVERAGE
LOCN    HOLDING   SHORTAGE  ORDERING  TOTAL     PERCENTAGE
        COST/PD   COST/PD   COST/PD   COST/PD   TIME SHORT

  1     353.11    283.94     0.00     637.04    42.44%
TOTAL   353.11    283.94     0.00     637.04    ◄── Average total cost

SUCCESSFUL BALANCE FRACTION = 1.00
```

Chapter 12. Note, for example, that the per unit holding cost is $7 and the per unit penalty cost is $10. Also note that many features of the program, such as multiple stocking points, order setup costs, safety stocks, and lead times, are not part of Peggy's problem.

Adapting the Model to the Problem

Our goal is to simulate 1000 trials. Of course, Peggy's problem is a one-period model (formally, in Chapter 12, called the newsboy model). Our simulator is for a multi-period inventory system. How can we adapt this to Peggy's problem? In Figure 14.14 we see that the value 1022 is entered for the *initial inventory* (initial stock OH) and for both the *order-up-to-level* and the *reorder point*. Consider for a moment what happens in the simulation. The inventory model will consider 1000 periods. Each period will simulate a random demand for Peggy's problem. The initial inventory (inventory on hand at the beginning of period 1) is 1022. During the first period our normal distribution is used to generate a random demand that must be satisfied out of initial inventory.

FIGURE 14.15
Costs for the Omelet Pan Problem if 1022 Pans
are Ordered

	AVERAGE COST NUMBER OF TRIALS			
	500	1000	10,000	EXPECTED COST
	$648.46	$637.04	$661.09	$662.00

Thus, inventory on hand at the end of the first period (the beginning of period 2) is less than 1022, which is the *reorder point*. Therefore, an order is placed to bring the inventory up to the *order-up-to-level*, 1022. Since the lead time is zero, the order arrives instantaneously, and thus the inventory on hand at the beginning of period 2 is 1022. This process is repeated 1000 times in the simulation. We thus have a sample of 1000 periods in which the inventory on hand at the beginning of each period is 1022. This can be interpreted as simulating 1000 trials in Peggy's scenario.

The output shows that the average total cost per period is $637.04. Similar experiments were performed with 500 and 10,000 trials. The average costs are shown in Figure 14.15. The expected cost that was calculated using analytic techniques not covered in this text is also shown.

The Random Nature of the Output
It is interesting to note that a sample of 500 trials yielded a "better" estimate of the expected cost than the sample of 1000 trials. Although one expects to get "better" results with larger samples, this example drives home the fact that results from a simulation of this sort are indeed random, and thus we cannot be assured that with any particular sample the average cost will be closer to expected cost just because we take a larger sample. All we can say is that "on the average," larger samples will get us closer (see the concluding comments in Section 14.3). Thus, when 10,000 trials were taken, the average cost was, as we would expect, closer to the true expected cost. In some sense, then, the result with 1000 trials is a fluke. But that is the point. When a simulator contains random events, the output is random and your results must be interpreted accordingly.

14.6

A SIMULATION STUDY: INVENTORY CONTROL AT PROTRAC

The customer service division of **PROTRAC** holds inventories of literally thousands of different replacement parts. Their inventory control system is based on *monthly inspections* (this is called periodic review) with a reorder point (r), reorder quantity (Q) for each product. Although we have considered reorder point–reorder quantity (r, Q) inventory control models in Chapter 12, we had no method of finding values for r and Q that minimized the expected cost per unit of time, given that demand is uncertain. The selection of Q was based on the EOQ model, which assumes a constant and known rate of demand. (Thus, this model serves as only a rough approximation for problems such as the current one where demand is uncertain.) The value of r was selected independently of Q to yield a subjectively chosen probability of a stockout. Finally, the (r, Q) model in Chapter 12 assumes *continuous review*; that is, we were aware of the instant that the inventory position reached r. In the model we are now considering, the status of the system is determined only at the beginning of each month. For this reason the inventory position could well be less than r when an order is placed. Simulation will provide a tool for selecting r and Q for this new system on a cost-efficient basis. In the context of

FIGURE 14.16

Cost and Demand Data for Pistons

cost of placing an order (K) = $90
unit cost = $60
cost to hold a unit for a year (h) = $12
cost per unit of unsatisfied demand = $19
delivery lead time = 4 months
monthly demand: normal ($\mu = 20$, $\sigma = 5$)

PROTRAC's customer service department, consider a particular part, the piston for the tread control unit for the D-9 crawler tractor (a $60 item). The inventory control system works as follows:

1. The first day of each month the inventory position for these pistons is determined where

$$\text{inventory position} = \text{inventory on hand} + \text{inventory on order}$$

2. If the inventory position is greater than r, no order is placed.
3. If the inventory position is less than or equal to r, Q items are ordered.

A review of the cost and demand data associated with pistons yields the information shown in Figure 14.16. All of the numbers in Figure 14.16 are estimates. The costs are provided by the accounting group and the assumptions about demand were developed by analyzing past data, incorporating subjective judgments, and ultimately specifying a reasonable and conveniently available probability distribution. At any rate, **PROTRAC**'s inventory control manager would be happy if he could choose inventory control parameters (values of r and Q) that yield a low average cost per period (i.e., per month) when the calculations are based on the data in Figure 14.16.

Preliminary Analytic Analysis   At this point **PROTRAC** could immediately turn to a simulation study; that is, the analyst could experiment to find "good values" for r and Q. However, in many simulation projects it is useful to do some analytic analysis *before* starting the simulation. This analysis typically suggests good starting values for the decision variables (r and Q in this problem) and can significantly reduce the amount of experimentation (simulation) that must be performed to find an acceptable answer.

In this particular problem **PROTRAC** can use models from the chapters on inventory control to provide some guidance in choosing reasonable values of r and Q to start the simulation study. None of these models will fit this problem exactly. If they did, we would not need the simulation study. We could use the analytic result. The fundamental concept is that the models provide a better idea of appropriate experimental values for r and Q in the simulation study.

The approach **PROTRAC** uses is similar to the one proposed for the continuous review inventory control system discussed in Chapter 12. This approach consists of two steps.

1. *Finding a value for Q:*   In this step **PROTRAC** ignores the variability of demand in the real problem and uses the EOQ formula (see Section 11.3 for a discussion of this model) to determine Q. Thus, Q is obtained from the expression

$$Q = \sqrt{2KD/h} \qquad (14.1)$$

where K = fixed cost of placing an order
    = \$90
D = expected annual demand
    = 12 months $\times$ 20 pistons/month
    = 240
h = cost of holding a unit in inventory for a year
    = \$12

The values for these parameters were taken from Figure 14.16. Making the appropriate numerical substitutions into (14.1) yields

$$Q = \sqrt{\frac{2 \times 90 \times 240}{12}} = \sqrt{3600} = 60$$

2. *Finding a value for r:* The discussion in Chapter 12 suggested that **PROTRAC** should select r to protect against stockouts during the lead time. To get a rough estimate of r, we note that expected demand during the 4-month lead time is equal to

4 months $\times$ 20 pistons/month = 80 pistons

Since demand is random, it will certainly be greater than 80 some of the time. To protect against stockouts, it seems reasonable to start the simulation study with values for r in the vicinity of 90 or 100.

It is possible to do a more detailed analysis that exploits the fact that monthly demand has a normal distribution, but we choose to emphasize the simulation study, and thus we proceed directly to it.

Getting Started

Using experimental (in this case simulation) results to evaluate alternative decisions or systems must be done with care if you are going to obtain valid results. Without attention to detail it is easy to perform experiments that are worse than worthless, for they may yield misleading information. In a simulation study, the way the simulation is started can sometimes determine if the results are meaningful or not. This is particularly true if a small sample is taken.

Sensitivity to Initial Conditions and Small Samples

To illustrate this point, suppose that we want to estimate the average cost per period (per month) when $r = 90$ and $Q = 60$ and that we plan to take a sample of 10 periods (i.e., run the simulator for 10 months). In case 1 we set the initial inventory equal to 150 and in case 2 we set the initial inventory to 0. We ask the computer to generate 10 demand observations from a normal distribution with $\mu = 20$ and $\sigma = 5$. The same sequence of random numbers, and hence demands, is used in both case 1 and case 2. The results of the two simulations (using the same simulator that produced Figure 14.14) are summarized in Figure 14.17. We see that widely disparate results occur.

FIGURE 14.17
Simulation Results with Different Starting Conditions

CASE	INITIAL INVENTORY	AVERAGE HOLDING COST PER PERIOD	AVERAGE SHORTAGE COST PER PERIOD	AVERAGE ORDERING COST PER PERIOD	AVERAGE TOTAL COST PER PERIOD	PERCENTAGE OF PERIODS SHORT
1	150	38.71	56.62	30.00	125.33	33.33
2	0	7.02	531.15	40.00	578.17	66.67

FIGURE 14.18
Average Total Cost per Period

r	40	60	80	100	110
			Q		
90	105.60	82.02	78.48	76.48	81.08
95	88.64	72.51	71.72	73.42	
100	79.55	(68.85)	69.49		
110	77.91	71.86	70.01		
120	85.77				

These data demonstrate, for a multiperiod problem, the fact that *with a small number of periods* (in this case 10) *the results of a simulation can be very sensitive to the initial conditions.* Since the initial conditions may be highly arbitrary, it is difficult to have confidence in results that are heavily dependent on them. There are two common tactics for dealing with this problem. One is to *average over a large rather than small number of periods*, the motive being to run the simulator long enough that the effects of the initial conditions will have dissipated. Another tactic is to use a large number of periods and then discard results from the earlier periods. In our simulation we opt for the latter approach. Thus the simulation will run for 1000 periods and we will not start to gather data until period 101. Before turning to the results of the simulation study, we conclude this subsection with the general observation that

> **Simulation results are useful only when care is taken in the experimental design to eliminate extraneous effects such as starting or ending conditions.**

Simulation Results

Figure 14.18 summarizes the results of **PROTRAC**'s piston simulation study. In this figure the numbers in the body of the table are the average total cost per period. For example, we see that when $r = 90$ and $Q = 60$ the simulation yielded an average cost per period of $82.02. It is worth noting that neither case 1 nor case 2 in the preceding subsection yielded an average cost close to this figure. This illustrates more vividly the combined effects of arbitrary starting conditions and a small sample on the results generated by a simulator.

Each entry in Figure 14.18 is an average obtained from doing one trial of 1000 periods. An alternative approach would have been to do 10 trials of 100 periods, thereby obtaining 10 values for average total cost per period. Averaging each such set of 10 should provide about the same numbers as those recorded in Figure 14.18. However, the latter approach would have provided information on variability (for a given choice of r and Q) which Figure 14.18 does not provide.

The data in Figure 14.18 suggest that among the alternatives examined, **PROTRAC** should select $r = 100$ and $Q = 60$, since this combination yields the smallest average cost per month, $68.85.[1] These values are close to those suggested by our preliminary analytic analysis. Indeed, the value of Q is precisely the one suggested by the EOQ model.

---

[1] Had we done the alternative analysis of 10 trials, 100 runs each, for each (r, Q) pair, we might have seen a higher variability, hence higher risk, associated with the $r = 100$, $Q = 60$ policy. For this reason the manager might have opted for an (r, Q) choice producing a somewhat higher but less variable average monthly cost. Limitation of space prevents us from doing a more detailed analysis of this particular example.

These observations support the notion that in some cases the approximate models that are used to select values for r and Q are quite good. In more complicated (and more realistic) problems where the demand distribution may vary from month to month, and where the lead time may also be random, simulation would provide an even more useful follow-on to the analytic analysis.

_____ 14.7
NOTES ON IMPLEMENTATION

Simulation is a powerful and flexible analytic tool that can be used to study a wide variety of management problems. It is generally used in cases where a good analytic model either does not exist or is too complicated to solve. This description encompasses a large segment of real-world problems and, as a result, surveys of the use of management science techniques typically put simulation at or near the top. However, there are a number of important factors for management to consider before making a commitment to a simulation study.

Simulation as a Tool of Last Resort

Although the language varies from source to source, there is general agreement that simulation is a last-resort technique. In other words, as stated above, simulation is frequently used when no convenient analytic model is available. With an analytic model the laws of mathematics can be used, often to obtain optimal decisions and sometimes sensitivity data, provided, of course, that the analysis is not so complex as to be prohibitive. In a simulation with random events, optimality is out of the question. Often a number of runs are required just to get a good estimate of the "goodness" of a particular decision.

In a simulation study, it is often necessary to use some sort of search procedure to find a good decision. This can be a formidable task. Suppose, for example, that there are 10 decision variables, each of which can assume 10 different values. There are then 10^{10} (10 billion) possible decisions to consider. For the sake of calculation, assume that it is necessary to evaluate only 1% of the possible decisions in order to be confident that a good decision has been reached and that 20 trials are required to get a good estimate of an expected value of the measure of effectiveness for each particular decision. In this case, $(0.01)(10^{10})(20) = 2 \times 10^9$ (2 billion) passes through the simulator would be required.

In such a case, the moral is clear. Do not simulate unless you have to.

Designing a Simulator

The acronym KISS for "Keep It Simple, Stupid" is popular among professionals in the quantitative analysis business. The idea applies with special force to simulation. A common and often fatal error of simulation studies is that they are too complicated. This may be an overreaction to the freedom gained by moving from analytic models to simulation models. Analytic models are often quite restrictive in their assumptions. Once we depart from linear functions or very simplistic assumptions, the mathematics gets harder by an order of magnitude. The result is that many of the popular analytic models have limited applicability.

Simulation can be much more permissive about functional forms. Since we are typically just generating an observation from a function (not solving a set of equations), linear functions do not command the same premium in simulation as they do in analytic models.

Whatever the motivation, there is typically a strong urge to include many factors in a simulation model. For example, it may not seem difficult to add a customer return feature to an inventory control model. In essence, all that is required is some additional computer code to generate this feature and incorporate it into the model. "There is no theoretic barrier, so why not do it?" This impression can be seriously wrong.

Why Keep It Simple?
Large complicated simulations incorporating a large number of "lifelike" features are at first blush appealing to management. However, they suffer from at least three serious problems:

1. They are often expensive to write and document.

2. They are an expensive experimental device. In the first place, the computer code may become so complex that each run is time consuming and therefore expensive. Moreover, the more complex the simulation, the more runs one generally wants to make. Consider a very simple model with two parameters and one decision (e.g., Peggy McConnel's problem). Suppose that we wish to simulate the effect of five different decisions (e.g., five order sizes). For each decision we run 10 trials. Thus, for each set of specified values for the parameters, we make $5(10) = 50$ runs. If we want to explore this system with 3 different sets of values for each parameter ($3^2 = 9$ combinations), we must make $9(50) = 450$ runs. Suppose that in a more complex model there are 10 instead of 2 parameters, and again each parameter may assume (because, say, of uncertainty) 3 different values ($3^{10} = 59,049$ combinations). In this case we must make $(59,049)50 = 2,952,450$ runs! In multiplying the number of parameters by 5 we multiplied the number of runs by 6561. Since increasing complexity invariably leads to increasing the number of parameters, you can see how troublesome this can become.

3. Complex simulations often produce so much data that the results are difficult to interpret.

Lean abstract models that capture the essence of the real problem and set encumbering details aside are as important to successful simulation studies as they are to good analytic models. Casual observation suggests that more simulation projects have died from too grand an original conception than from any other disease.

Running a Simulator
It seems almost innocuous to say that simulation studies should be carefully planned before they are run. But this planning can be intricate and may well require statistical expertise. Should we do 1 trial of 1000 periods or 10 trials of 100 periods each? In other words, the analyst must decide how much and what kind of sampling to do with each decision and how many different decisions to try. Management's problem can be conceptually illustrated in Figure 14.19, where we imagine that simulation is being used to

FIGURE 14.19
When is Enough Enough?

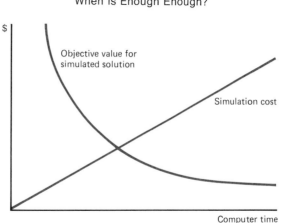

find a low-cost decision for a particular problem. The notion is that by increasing the cost of experimentation (i.e., the amount of computer time), a better simulated solution can be found.

Search Strategies

Although this concept has merit, the application is not easy. The shape of the "objective value for simulated solution" function is not well known. It is just not clear how much the solution can be expected to improve with increased experimentation. In view of this fact, two general strategies are useful:

1. Search in a sequential manner; that is, use the results of earlier simulations to suggest the next decision to try.
2. Use a relatively small number of trials for each decision in an attempt to locate the general area in which the decisions are good. Then increase the number of trials to obtain more precision within this area.

Simulation Languages

The importance and widespread use of simulation has led to the creation of special simulation languages. In general, these languages are intended to

1. Facilitate model formulation
2. Be easy to learn
3. Provide good debugging and error diagnostics
4. Be flexible enough to use on a wide range of problems

Different languages have different strengths and are intended for different types of simulation studies. A detailed examination of these languages is beyond the scope of this book. It is useful, however, to know of some of the more popular entries in this field.

GPSS (General-Purpose Systems Simulator) was developed in the early 1960s. Flowchart concepts provide the underlying rationale for this language. SIMSCRIPT 2.5 and GASP II are both based on the FORTRAN IV computer language. Both were developed in the early to mid-1960s. The former was developed by H. M. Markowitz at the Rand Corporation and the latter by A. Alan B. Pritsker.

Pritsker and N. Hurst produced GASP IV in 1973. It incorporates the features of GASP II, and provides a number of new and attractive features as well.

Even this brief comment on programming languages suggests that programming computer simulators is an arcane subject and managers will have to rely on expert guidance both in the formulation and experimentation phases. All managerial concerns about the use of experts apply *a fortiori* to simulation projects.

Two guidelines that are useful in all quantitative studies are especially important in simulation studies.

Documentation

Insist on good documentation. A new manager (in contrast to an analyst) should be able to understand the input required, the assumptions of the model, and the meaning of the output with a reasonable amount of effort. This requires clear documentation. Too often the usefulness of a simulation program effectively ends with the tenure of the originator. The only reasonable cure for this problem is good documentation. It is difficult to overemphasize the importance of this guideline.

Group Dynamics

All quantitative modeling efforts require intensive interaction and communication between the modeler and the user. This is particularly true of simulation projects. The users must understand how to enter decisions and parameters and how to analyze the output. The firsthand knowledge of the users is essential in making sure that the simulation captures the essence of the real problem. Also, the fact that the user has an intimate knowledge of the real problem can be an important part of the search for good solutions.

Good documentation and group dynamics are closely interrelated and are an important part of managing any project based on quantitative modeling and analysis.

——— 14.8
SUMMARY

Section 14.1 points out that the use of experimentation to evaluate alternatives is an important part of applied science and that computer-based simulation is the most common experimental approach to management problems.

Section 14.2 discusses the use of simulation on decisions under uncertainty, that is, on problems in which the behavior of one or more factors can be represented by a probability distribution. Several examples are presented.

An inventory example is used in Section 14.3 to illustrate how random events are incorporated into a simulation study. This example is used to drive home the fact that experimental results will not necessarily lead to the same decision that would be derived if one could use the analytic criterion of minimizing the expected cost. By its very nature the output from a simulator with random components is random. "On the average" using a large number of trials will make the simulated average cost closer to the theoretic expected cost. The example in Section 14.3 also showed how multiple measures of effectiveness can be produced and, very important, how simulation with multiple trials provides an indication of the variability with a given policy.

Section 14.4 presents the details as to how a table of random numbers can be used to generate observations from an arbitrary probability distribution. The normal distribution is presented as a special case. Random numbers are at the basis of the technique of simulating random events.

Sections 14.5 and 14.6 use an existing University of Chicago computer simulation package to examine two inventory control problems. In the process a number of important topics are considered. These include the use of analytic models in determining an appropriate starting place for a simulation study, and the effect of arbitrary starting conditions and of sample size on the results.

The final section is devoted to the topic of implementation. The discussion takes a general management point of view and considers such topics as designing a simulator, running a simulator, good documentation, and group dynamics. A brief introduction to the extensive subject of simulation languages is also included.

——— 14.9
KEY TERMS

SIMULATOR. An experimental device that in important respects acts like a system of interest.

SIMULATION MODEL. A series of logical and mathematical operations that provides a measure of effectiveness for a particular set of values of the parameters and decisions.

MONTE CARLO METHOD. A type of simulation that uses probability distributions to determine whether random events occur.

SIMULATED RANDOM DEMAND. Demand that is drawn from a probability distribution.

TRIAL. A single run of a simulation model (i.e. a single pass through the simulator).

MULTIPLE TRIALS. Multiple passes through the simulator, each pass using the same values for decisions and parameters, but a different series of random numbers and hence possibly different outcomes for random events.

RANDOM NUMBER TABLE. A random sampling of integers in a given range (say from 0 to 99) where each integer is equally likely to occur.

PROBABILITY DISTRIBUTION. A means of depicting the likelihood of an uncertain quantity.

PENALTY COST. A per unit cost of unsatisfied demand.

HOLDING COST. A per unit cost of having excess at the end of a period.

PERIODIC REVIEW. A policy of determining inventory level at specific points in time (such as at the end of every week).

CONTINUOUS REVIEW. Knowledge of the inventory level at any instant of time (real-time updating as depletions occur).

EXPECTED VALUE. A statistical concept referring to the expected value, or mean, or some random quantity with a specified probability distribution.

VARIABILITY. In simulation, a reference to the amount of fluctuation in measures of effectiveness as numerous trials are performed.

MAJOR CONCEPTS QUIZ

True–False

1. **T F** The basic concept of simulation is to build an experimental device that will "act like" the system of interest in important respects.

2. **T F** A deterministic model (one with no random elements) can be used as a simulation model.

3. **T F** If a simulator includes random elements, two successive trials with the same parameter values will produce the same value for the measure of effectiveness.

4. **T F** In a simulation with random elements it is impossible to guarantee that the decision that maximizes expected profit has been selected.

5. **T F** In real-world problems it is common practice to compare the expected cost associated with a decision with the average cost for that decision produced by a simulator.

6. **T F** In a simulation with several distinct random outcomes a correct association of random numbers and events implies that each random number must represent one of the outcomes.

7. **T F** With small sample sizes the results of a simulation can be very sensitive to the initial conditions.

8. **T F** Simulation is sometimes described as a last-resort technique since it is generally not employed until analytic approaches have been examined and rejected.

9. **T F** A common error in designing a simulator is to use such restrictive assumptions that the model fails to capture the essence of the problem.

10. **T F** Additional experimentation with a simulator is sure to increase the simulation cost but may also improve the quality of the solution.

Multiple Choice

11. In a typical simulation model input provided by the analyst includes
   a. values for the parameters
   b. values for the decision variables
   c. a value for the measure of effectiveness
   d. all of the above
   e. both a and b

12. An advantage of simulation, as opposed to optimization, is that
   a. often multiple measures of goodness can be examined
   b. some appreciation for the variability of outcomes of interest can be obtained

    c. more complex scenarios can be studied

    d. all of the above

13. Consider a simulator with random elements which uses profit as a measure of effectiveness. For a specified assignment of parameter values

    a. the average profit over a number of trials is used as an estimate of the expected profit associated with a decision

    b. the average profit is always closer to the expected profit as the number of trials increases

    c. the average profit over 10 trials is always the same

    d. none of the above

14. A random number refers to

    a. an observation from a set of numbers (say the integers 0–99) each of which is equally likely

    b. an observation selected at random from a normal distribution

    c. an observation selected at random from any distribution provided by the analyst

    d. none of the above

15. The random number 0.63 has been selected. The corresponding observation, say v, from a *normal* distribution is determined by the relationship:

    a. v is "the probability that the normally distributed quantity is ≤ 0.63"

    b. v is the number such that "the probability that the normally distributed quantity is $\leq v$" equals 0.63

    c. v is the number such that "the probability that the normally distributed quantity equals v" is 0.63

    d. none of the above

16. Analytic results are sometimes used before a simulation study

    a. to identify "good values" of the system parameters

    b. to determine the optimal decision

    c. to identify "good values" of the decision variables for the specific choices of system parameters

    d. all of the above

17. To reduce the effect of initial conditions in a simulation study one can

    a. vary the values of the system parameters

    b. increase the number of alternative decisions studied

    c. increase the sample size and ignore data from a number of the first runs for each set of parameters and decisions

    d. all of the above

18. If both an analytic model and a simulation model could be used to study a problem including random events, the analytic model is often preferred because

    a. the simulator generally requires a number of runs just to get a good estimate of the objective value (such as expected cost) for a particular decision

    b. the analytic model may produce an optimal decision

    c. the simulation study may require evaluating a large number of possible decisions

    d. all of the above

19. Large complicated simulation models suffer from the following problems:

    a. Average costs are not well defined.

    b. It is difficult to create the appropriate random events.

    c. They may be expensive to write and to use as an experimental device.

    d. All of the above.

20. In performing a simulation it is advisable to

    a. use the results of earlier decisions to suggest the next decision to try

    b. use the same number of trials for each decision

    c. simulate all possible decisions

    d. none of the above

PROBLEMS

In the following problems you will be asked to perform a number of simulations. In all cases, assign consecutive random numbers to each event and assign smaller values of random numbers to smaller numerical values of the event. For example:

EVENT (DEMAND)	PROBABILITY	PROPER ASSIGNMENT	IMPROPER ASSIGNMENT
3	0.2	00–19	30–49
4	0.7	20–89	00–29 and 60–99
5	0.1	90–99	50–59

In each simulation problem a row and column will be indicated. Select the first random number at this position in Figure 14.10 and read as instructed in the problem statement. Following this procedure will enable you to check your answers with those in the back of the book.

14-1. Cite examples of the use of simulation (in the broad sense) by the military.

14-2. Cite examples of the use of simulation (in the broad sense) in professional sports.

14-3. Consider the Astro/Cosmo production problem that was presented as Example 1 in Section 2.8. The LP formulation of this model is

$$\text{Max } 20A + 30C$$

$$\text{s.t.} \qquad A \leq 70$$

$$C \leq 50$$

$$A + 2C \leq 120$$

$$A, C \geq 0$$

(a) Construct a flowchart showing how to approach this problem as a simulation.

(b) Use the flowchart to evaluate the two potential solutions: $(A = 40, C = 30)$ and $(A = 50, C = 30)$.

14-4. Consider the following LP problem:

$$\text{Min } 50X + 30Y$$

$$\text{s.t.} \quad 3X + Y = 25$$

$$X + Y \geq 15$$

$$X, Y \geq 0$$

(a) Construct a flowchart and use it to select the best of the three alternatives for X given by

4, 5, and 6.

(b) Is it profitable to reduce the RHS requirement of the first constraint to 23 at a cost of 10? Use the flow-chart and alternative values for X in part (a).

14-5. Comment on the following statement: The simplex algorithm is a type of simulation, since it has to evaluate a number of alternative solutions enroute to finding the optimal solution.

14-6. Consider the **PROTRAC** E and F problem first seen in Chapter 2. The LP formulation is

$$\text{Max } 5000E + 4000F$$

$$
\begin{aligned}
\text{s.t.} \quad E + F &\geq 5 \\
10E + 15F &\leq 150 \quad \text{(time used in department A)} \\
20E + 10F &\leq 160 \quad \text{(time used in department B)} \\
-30E - 10F &\leq -135 \\
E - 3F &\leq 0 \\
E, F &\geq 0
\end{aligned}
$$

The manager has the opportunity to expand the total capacity in departments A and B by up to 100 hours at a cost of $140 per hour of capacity in either plant. He plans to make his decision by sequentially trying about 20 different RHS combinations and selecting the combination that yields the largest net profit. "Since this procedure is based on the simplex algorithm, it is not a simulation." Comment on the last sentence.

14-7. **PROTRAC** has a cash management problem. In this problem **PROTRAC**'s cash balance is determined each morning. The change in the cash balance from one morning to the next is a random variable. In particular, it increases by $10,000 with probability 0.3, decreases by $10,000 with probability 0.2, and remains the same with probability 0.5. Associate random numbers with these events so as to accurately reflect the correct probability in a simulation study.

14-8. Consider the following brand-switching problem. In this problem probabilities are used to describe the behavior of a customer buying beer. Three particular beers (B, M, and S) are incorporated in the model. Customer behavior is summarized in Figure 14.20. Thus, we see in the first row that a customer who buys beer B in week 1 will buy the same beer in week 2 with probability 0.85, will buy beer M with probability 0.10, and will beer S with probability 0.05. A similar interpretation holds for the other rows. Consider a customer who buys beer B in week 1. Assume that you wish to simulate his behavior for the next 10 weeks. We know that in week 2 he would buy beers B, M, and S with probabilities 0.85, 0.10, and 0.05. If in week 2 he bought beer M, he would buy beers B, M, and S with probability 0.08, 0.85, and 0.07, respectively. Define the events you would need and associate random numbers with these events so as to accurately reflect the correct probabilities.

FIGURE 14.20

BEER PURCHASED IN WEEK i	PROBABILITY OF PURCHASE IN WEEK $i + 1$		
	B	M	S
B	0.85	0.10	0.05
M	0.08	0.85	0.07
S	0.13	0.17	0.70

14-9. Assume that you want to generate a sample from a normal distribution that has a mean of 100 and a standard deviation of 10. If the number you obtain from the table of random numbers is 94, what is the value of the normal random variable?

14-10. Assume that you want to generate a sample from a normal distribution that has a mean of 50 and a standard deviation of 100. If the number you obtain from the table of random numbers is 5, what is the value of the normal random variable?

14-11. The probability that $W \leq x$ is plotted in Figure 14.21. Use this function to generate three sequential observations of the random variable W. Start in row 17, column 4 of Figure 14.10 and read down.

FIGURE 14-21

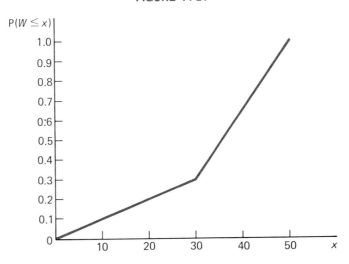

14-12. The probability mass function of the Poisson distribution is given by

$$p(x \mid \lambda) = \frac{\lambda^x}{x!} e^{-\lambda}, \qquad x = 0, 1, \ldots$$

Let $\lambda = 2$ and calculate the probability you observe x, $x = 0, 1, \ldots, 5$. What are the observations for the random numbers 40, 60, 80?

14-13. Simulate a sample of 10 periods for the omelet pan problem described in this chapter. Assume that you have 10 pans on hand at the beginning of each period. Use the random numbers starting in row 20, column 8, reading down Figure 14.10. Use the association of random numbers with demand given in Figure 14.11.

(a) Calculate the average cost per period.

(b) Record the number of stockouts (count a stockout as occurring when demand > 10).

14-14. The weekly demand for milk for the last 50 weeks at the All-Ways-Open convenient market is shown in Figure 14.22.

(a) Assign random numbers to demands so that the probability of a particular demand in the simulation is equal to the relative frequency of that demand over the last 50 weeks.

(b) The store orders 20 cases every week. What are the average shortage and average excess inventory for 10 weeks? Begin in row 1, column 1 of Figure 14.10 and read down.

(c) What are the expected shortage and the expected excess inventory?

FIGURE 14.22

SALES (CASES)	NUMBER OF WEEKS
18	2
19	8
20	15
21	15
22	5
23	5
Total	50

14-15. The number of disk brake jobs performed by the service department of the Green Cab Company during each of the last 30 weeks is shown in Figure 14.23.

(a) Assign random numbers to the number of brake jobs performed so that the probability of a particular number of jobs in the simulation is equal to the relative frequency of that number of jobs over the last 30 weeks.

(b) Simulate 10 weeks of demand. Begin in row 5, column 3 of Figure 14.10 and read down.

FIGURE 14.23

NUMBER OF BRAKE JOBS	NUMBER OF WEEKS
5	3
6	8
7	9
8	6
9	4
Total	30

14-16. Steco currently carries inventory for stainless steel sheets in 2 nearby cities, L and A. Weekly demands (in trucks) and the probabilities for each city are shown in Figure 14.24. Assume that the demands are independent. L starts each week with 8 trucks of inventory on hand. A starts each week with 10 trucks of inventory on hand.

FIGURE 14.24

DEMAND	PROBABILITY L	PROBABILITY A
5	0.10	
6	0.10	
7	0.60	0.10
8	0.10	0.10
9	0.10	0.40
10		0.20
11		0.20

(a) Simulate 20 weeks of demand at L and record the number of stockouts. Begin in row 21, column 6 of Figure 14.10 and read down.

(b) Start in row 1, column 7 and read down to simulate 20 weeks of demand at A and record the number of stockouts.

Suppose that Steco centralized its stainless steel sheet inventory and satisfied all demand from L and A out of 1 new warehouse (call it LA).

(c) If LA started each week with 18 trucks of inventory on hand, would you expect the number of stockouts to increase, decrease, or remain the same as compared to when L and A operated independently? Why?

(d) Use the same sequence of demands you used in parts (a) and (b) to simulate 20 weeks of operation for the new warehouse, LA. Record the number of stockouts. Does this result agree with your answer to part (c)?

14-17. The time between arrivals at the drive-up window of the Slippery Savings and Loan is shown in Figure 14.25. All customers form a single line and are served in the order of arrival. Assume that it takes 8 minutes to serve each customer. Also assume that no one is being served or waiting to be served when the first customer arrives. Simulate the arrival of 16 customers and record the number of customers who have to wait. Begin in row 1, column 1 of Figure 14.10 and read down.

FIGURE 14.25

TIME BETWEEN ARRIVALS (MIN)	PROBABILITY
5	0.25
10	0.50
15	0.25

14-18. The Homeburg Volunteer Fire Department makes an annual door-to-door solicitation for funds. There are 20,000 households to solicit. The department asks households to be supporters (a $5 donation) or patrons (a $10 donation). An analysis of data from previous years indicates that

1. No one is home at 20% of the homes visited. If no one is home, the home is *not* revisited, and thus no donation is obtained. When someone is home, 70% of the time a woman answers the door and 30% of the time a man answers the door.

2. 20% of the women make a contribution. 40% of them are supporters and 60% are patrons.

3. 25% of the men make a contribution. 55% of them are supporters and 45% are patrons.

(a) What is the expected value of the return from the solicitation?

(b) Make a flowchart for this process. The output should be the contribution that occurs from calling on a house.

(c) Use the flowchart in part (b) to simulate 5 visits and record the total contribution from these 5 visits. Begin in row 5, column 5 of Figure 14.10 and read down. What is your estimate of the return from the annual solicitation based on this simulation?

(d) Simulate 10 visits to answer the same question as in part (c). Begin in row 27, column 9 of Figure 14.10 and read down.

FIGURE 14.26
The annotated simulation spreadsheet

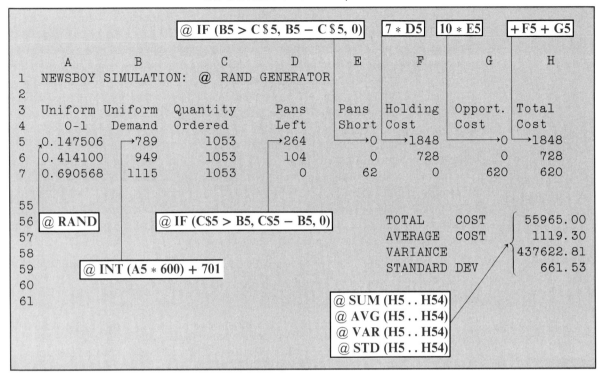

APPENDIX 14.1
A SPREADSHEET APPLICATION TO SIMULATION

The ability of spreadsheet programs to perform arithmetic operations easily, to copy formulas, and to present results in a readable form makes them a natural tool for certain simulations. In this appendix we illustrate the use of Lotus 1–2–3 to simulate the Wiles omelet pan problem that was originally presented in Section 12.8 and was further discussed at length in this chapter. We will assume that

$$\text{Prob} \{\text{Demand} = x\} = \tfrac{1}{600} \qquad \text{for } x = 701, 702, \dots, 1300,$$

i.e. that it is equally likely that the number of pans demanded is any integer between 701 and 1300. In Section 12.9 we showed that when this assumption was made, Wiles would minimize the expected cost by ordering 1053 pans.

We now use Lotus 1–2–3 to simulate the effect of this decision. The goal of this simulation is to estimate the expected value and the standard deviation of the actual cost that Wiles will incur if 1053 pans are ordered. There will be 50 independent trials in the simulation. In each trial we will: (1) draw a random observation from the demand distribution, (2) calculate the number of pans left over or the number of units of unsatisfied demand, and (3) calculate the appropriate holding or opportunity (penalty) cost. The sample mean and sample standard deviation of these fifty trials will then be used to estimate the expected value and standard deviation of the population of costs. Figure 14.26 is an annotated version of part of the spreadsheet used in the simulation. We have omitted rows 8 through 54 since they are simply additional examples of the formulas and calculations shown in rows 5, 6, and 7.

In Figure 14.26 each row is a simulation trial. To understand the calculations consider the entries in row 5, columns B through H. Cell C5 shows that there were 1053 pans on hand at the beginning of the period. The demand (cell B5) was 789. Thus there were 264 pans left over (cell D5 = 264) and there were no units of unsatisfied demand (cell E5). Since there were 264 pans left over, the holding cost is $7 \times 264 =$ $1848 (cell F5). The shortage of 0 pans generated an opportunity cost of $0 (cell G5). The total cost which is the sum of the holding and opportunity cost is thus $1848.00 (cell H5).

The formulas that would be entered in the symbolic spreadsheet and are here shown in the annotations are quite obvious for columns F, G, and H and need no special comment other than the reminder that the holding cost is $7 per pan left over and the opportunity (penalty) cost is $10 per unit of unsatisfied demand. The If functions in columns D and E are used to determine if demand is greater or less than the quantity ordered so that the correct cost can be assessed. The entry in D5 says that if C5 > B5 (supply is greater than demand) then enter the quantity $\{C5 - B5\}$ in D5 (pans left over); otherwise enter 0. The entry is E5 says that if B5 > C5 (demand is greater than supply), then enter the quantity $\{B5 - C5\}$ in E5 (pans short); otherwise enter 0. Note that either D5 or E5 must be zero. Creating the formulas for columns B through H and copying them as often as desired (once for each trial) is rather a straightforward task in Lotus 1–2–3.

Generation of the appropriate random demand is also quite simple in this example. The RAND function that is part of the Lotus 1–2–3 software is used in column A to generate a random variable that is uniformly distributed between 0 and 1. The formula in column B transforms the variable in column A into a new variable (the demand) with the desired characteristics, i.e. that each integer from 701 through 1300 is equally likely. The transformation proceeds as follows:

■ **Step 1:** The observation from column A is multiplied by 600. This produces a number between 0 and 600 and each number in this interval is equally likely to occur. For example in Row 5, 600(0.147506) = 88.5036.

■ **Step 2:** The integer function which is part of Lotus 1–2–3 then takes the integer part of this number; e.g. in Row 5 in integer function changes the number from 88.5036 to 88. Note that the result of steps (1) and (2) is to produce, with equal likelihood, any integer between 0 and 599.

■ **Step 3:** The number that is produced by the integer function is then added to 701 to yield the observed demand. Continuing with the illustration, 88 + 701 = 789, the entry in B5.

The result of this process is an entry in column B which is, with equal likelihood, any integer from 701 through 1300. The careful reader may have observed that the process used to generate the demand in column B could produce a value of 1301. If the random number in column A was 1.00000 the demand would be 1301 which is, of course, not possible in Wiles problem. We chose to ignore this possibility since the probability of this event is zero. Further, in a reasonably sized sample the effect of a demand of 1301 (as compared to 1300) on the simulation results would be negligible. If the designer of the simulation felt strongly, the possibility of a demand of 1301 could be eliminated with the If function.

Computing the summary statistics for the simulation is a simple task with Lotus 1–2–3. You only have to enter the appropriate function and specify the desired range.

FIGURE 14.27
Simulation Results

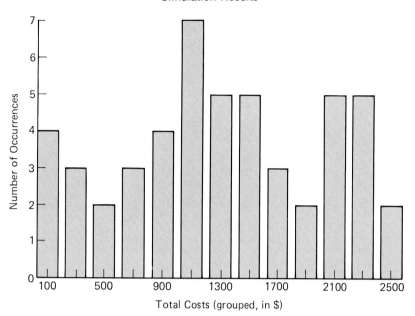

The numerical results and the formulas used to produce them are shown in cells H56 through H59. Note that the average cost is $1119.30 and that the standard deviation is 661.53. Assuming that the distribution of costs is approximately normal implies that the probability is .5 that the cost is more than 1119.30 and .16 that it is greater than $1780.83 ($1119.30 + $661.53 = $1780.83). The magnitude of these costs suggest that it would be useful to understand if the costs are particularly sensitive to the demand distribution. Simulation could be used to investigate this question. The information generated might result in more effort devoted to estimating the distribution of demand or indeed to questioning the value of the planned promotion.

Although the summary statistics are useful, the cliche that a picture is worth a thousand words has real truth in simulation studies. Figure 14.27 shows a histogram of the costs from the simulation. The sample distribution is distinctly not normal. Note that in 14 of the 50 trials, costs of more than $1,800 were incurred. This represents 28 percent of the sample observations. Using the sample mean and standard deviation and a normal approximation yielded the result that costs greater than $1,781 should occur with probability .16. In other words the histogram of sample costs suggests that a normal approximation is probably not very good and that such an approximation understates the level of risk in this promotion. The data in the histogram might well lead Wiles Management to reconsider the promotion. Lotus 1–2–3 makes it easy to generate graphics like Figure 14.27. Such presentations are clearly management friendly.

Certainly this simple example does not deal with many of the questions that can come up when simulation is used to analyze a problem in the real world. Questions of generating the same sequence of random numbers in order to use them in comparing alternatives or of generating observations from general distributions come quickly to mind. These software specific questions fall outside the purview of this text. Our purpose was simply to illustrate the possibility of using spreadsheet software to perform simulations and that goal has been accomplished with the current example.

SCHEDULING TANKER ARRIVALS

Simulation is a popular method for studying systems with random components. It follows that managers are often placed in the position of accepting or rejecting recommendations based on simulation studies, or perhaps recommending additional analysis. This vignette illustrates such a situation.

David O'Brien is the manager of Global Oil's St. Croix refinery. This refinery was built in 1954 and is served by a dock facility designed to handle 250,000-barrel tankers. Tankers arrive at the dock and unload into a 700,000-barrel storage tank at the rate of 400,000 barrels per day. The refinery itself accepts oil from the storage tank at the rate of 250,000 barrels per day. This is called the input pipeline capacity. The storage tank thus serves as a buffer storage facility, allowing the tankers to unload more rapidly. If the storage tank is full, however, the rate at which tankers can unload decreases to 250,000 barrels per day.

Global installed the storage tank because the firm must pay a penalty cost, a so-called demurrage fee, if a tanker has to wait too long before it is able to start unloading its oil. In particular, a demurrage fee of $1400 per day is charged if a 250,000-barrel tanker must wait more than 2 days to start unloading. The charge is a pro-rata charge, so if a tanker waits 3.5 days, for example, before the start of unloading, then its total fee is $(3.5 - 2.0) \times \$1400$ or $2100.

Global is considering servicing the St. Croix refinery with its fleet of new 500,000-barrel supertankers. The harbor is deep and can easily accommodate the new tankers, but because of the limited unloading capacity, demurrage charges are a concern. A 500,000-barrel tanker incurs demurrage fees at the rate of $3000 per day if it must wait more than 2 days to start unloading.

Currently, 1 250,000-barrel tanker arrives every 1.5 days on the average, that is, at a rate of $\frac{2}{3}$ tankers per day, or 166,667 barrels of oil per day. Dave has proposed that if Global moves to the 500,000-barrel tankers, demurrage charges should remain about the same as long as the average daily arrival of oil is held constant. He therefore decides that the supertankers should arrive at the rate of $\frac{1}{3}$ tanker per day or 1 every 3 days, since 500,000-barrels/tanker $\times$ $\frac{1}{3}$ tanker/day equals 166,667 barrels/day.

Dave learns that if the 500,000-barrel tankers are used, Global in fact is willing to incur a small increase in the total annual demurrage charges. This is because 1 supertanker requires less crew than 2 of the current tankers. However, the firm would not like to see a large increase in these charges.

To check his intuitive notion that the effects of doubling the tanker size and cutting the arrival rate in half should cancel each other, Dave decides to use Tanker, Global's on-line simulator, which was written to aid him in operating the dock. This simulator assumes that the arrivals are drawn from an exponential distribution (see Chapter 13) with a user-specified mean. The item of interest is the total annual demurrage charges. The simulation will provide two ways to estimate this quantity:

1. *Average cost per tanker method* Use the simulated results to compute the average cost per tanker as

$$\frac{\text{total demurrage fees}}{\text{number of tankers}}$$

and multiply this figure by the average number of tankers per year. Since supertankers arrive at the rate of 1 every 3 days, this implies 120 per year (assuming a 360-day year). Thus, for supertankers we obtain the estimate

$$\text{total annual cost} = (\text{average cost per tanker}) \times (120)$$

2. *Average cost per day method* Use the simulated results to compute the average cost per day as

$$\frac{\text{total demurrage fees}}{\text{number of days}}$$

and multiply this figure by 360, the number of days in a year. Using this method, we obtain the estimate (for either type of tanker)

$$\text{total annual cost} = (\text{average cost per day}) \times (360).$$

Actually Dave decides to run two simulations: one with parameters describing the currrent situation and the other with parameters describing the proposed situation. In each case he decides to sample roughly 2 months of data. He thus plans to simulate the arrival and unloading of 44 of the 250,000-barrel tankers (an expected duration of 44 × 1.5 or 66 days) and 22 of the 500,000-barrel tankers (an expected duration of 22 × 3.0 or 66 days). The simulation with current parameters is used as a test to see if the results are a reasonable approximation of the current situation.

The results of the simulations are shown in Figures 14.28 and 14.29.

The relevant data are summarized in Figure 14.30.

FIGURE 14.28

250,000-Barrel Tankers

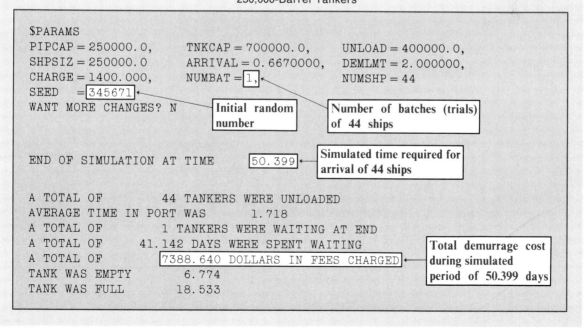

```
$PARAMS
PIPCAP = 250000.0,     TNKCAP = 700000.0,     UNLOAD = 400000.0,
SHPSIZ = 250000.0      ARRIVAL = 0.6670000,   DEMLMT = 2.000000,
CHARGE = 1400.000,     NUMBAT = 1,            NUMSHP = 44
SEED   = 345671
WANT MORE CHANGES? N
```

Initial random number

Number of batches (trials) of 44 ships

```
END OF SIMULATION AT TIME       50.399
```

Simulated time required for arrival of 44 ships

```
A TOTAL OF        44 TANKERS WERE UNLOADED
AVERAGE TIME IN PORT WAS       1.718
A TOTAL OF         1 TANKERS WERE WAITING AT END
A TOTAL OF     41.142 DAYS WERE SPENT WAITING
A TOTAL OF      7388.640 DOLLARS IN FEES CHARGED
TANK WAS EMPTY       6.774
TANK WAS FULL       18.533
```

Total demurrage cost during simulated period of 50.399 days

FIGURE 14.29
500,000-Barrel Tankers

```
$PARAMS
PIPCAP = 250000.0,    TNKCAP = 700000.0,    UNLOAD = 400000.0,
SHPSIZ = 500000.0,    ARIVAL = 0.3330000,   DEMLMT = 2.000000,
CHARGE = 3000.000,    NUMBAT = 1,           NUMSHP = 22,
SEED   = 345671
WANT MORE CHANGES? N


END OF SIMULATION AT TIME    52.192


A TOTAL OF       22   TANKERS WERE UNLOADED
AVERAGE TIME IN PORT WAS         1.915
A TOTAL OF        3   TANKERS WERE WAITING AT END
A TOTAL OF      12.364  DAYS WERE SPENT WAITING
A TOTAL OF     3982.445  DOLLARS IN FEES CHARGED
TANK WAS EMPTY      10.992
TANK WAS FULL        6.035
```

FIGURE 14.30
Summary Data

TANKER SIZE	250,000	500,000	TANKER SIZE	250,000	500,000
(a) Total demurrage charges	$7388.640	$3982.445	(e) = (a)/(c) Average cost per day	$146.60	$76.304
(b) Number of tankers unloaded	44	22	(f) Expected tankers per year	240	120
(c) Number of days	50.399	52.192	(g) = (d) × (f) Tanker-based cost per year	$40,301.52	$21,722.40
(d) = (a)/(b) Average cost per tanker	$167.923	$181.020	(h) = (e) × 360 Day-based cost per year	$52,776.00	$27,469.44

Dave finds the data in Figure 14.30 to be interesting from several points of view. First, concerning the results from the 250,000-barrel tankers (i.e., the current situation), experience has shown that, over the last several years of operation, more than half of the time no demurrage charge has been incurred during a 2-month interval. However, a $7000 charge for a 2-month period in which a charge is incurred is not rare. Dave thus feels that the simulator is by chance giving a conservative estimate (in the sense of an overestimate) of the average demurrage charges and it should thus be a good test of the proposed system.

Second, he is surprised that 500,000-barrel tankers yield a considerably lower annual cost with both estimation techniques. His intuition had suggested that the costs for the two systems would be about equal. However, he knows that the difference could easily be a random event, because this particular result is, of course, based on a sample. The good news, however, is that there is nothing in the data to suggest that the demurrage charges would be significantly larger with the 500,000-barrel tankers.

The mark of a good manager is to know when to decide as well as what to decide. With the simulation analysis for back-up, Dave confidently recommends that Global switch to the 500,000-barrel tankers with a 0.333 rate of arrival.

Questions

1. Explain the cause of the difference Dave encountered with the two methods of estimating total annual demurrage fees in the simulation with 500,000-barrel tankers.

2. Do you believe the results of the study? Comment on Dave's recommendation and study.

15

DECISION THEORY AND DECISION TREES

━━━━━━━━━━ **APPLICATION CAPSULE**

DESIGNING A COMPLEX INTERCONNECTED SYSTEM*

The Palo Verde Nuclear Generating Station near Phoenix, Arizona, is one of the world's largest power facilities. This plant, which is located in the Arizona desert, requires 90 million gallons of cooling water per day. Wastewater from Phoenix is used to meet this need. However, to serve this purpose, the wastewater must be transported some 39 miles to the plant site, treated, stored, used, recycled, and the residue disposed of. Indeed, the water supply system can be thought of as having five major components: conveyance, treatment, cooling, storage, and residue disposal. Each of these components could have been designed in several different ways. For example

1. The water could have been transported in a single or dual line with one or several pumping stations.
2. The water could have been treated with any of several methods like bionitrification or reverse osmosis.

* Carl W. Hamilton and G. William Bingham, "Management Science Applications in the Planning and Design of a Water Supply System for a Nuclear Power Plant," *Interface*, Vol. 9, No. 5, (November 1979), pp. 50–62.

3. The water could have been used for one or more cycles in the cooling process. More cycles means that less water is required, but there is an increased probability of fouling the unit because of residue in the water.

The design problem was difficult not only because of the large number of alternatives, but because of the high level of interdependence. For example

1. If dual supply lines were selected, a smaller reservoir could have been chosen since the supply would have been more secure.
2. The quality of material needed in the condenser depended on the quality of water being emitted from the treatment phase.
3. The residue in the water after cooling depends both on the quality of the incoming water and the number of cycles in the cooling process.

Decision trees were a particularly useful device for analyzing this problem. They allowed engineers and managers to incorporate uncertainty directly in the decision process. Perhaps more important, they provided a valuable device for visualizing and communicating the complex structure of the system.

15.1
INTRODUCTION

Decision theory provides a framework for analyzing a wide variety of management problems. The framework establishes (1) a system of classifying decision problems based on the amount of information about the problem that is available and (2) a decision criterion, that is, a measure of the "goodness" of a decision for each type of problem.

In the first part of this chapter we will present the decision theory framework and relate it to models previously discussed. The second half of the chapter is devoted to decision trees. Decision trees apply decision theory concepts to sequential decisions that include uncertain events. They are a pragmatic and practical aid to managerial decision making.

Decision against Nature
In general terms, decision theory treats decisions against nature. This phrase refers to a situation where the result (return) from a decision depends on the action of another player (nature). For example, if the decision is to carry an umbrella or not, the return (get wet or not) depends on what action nature takes. It is important to note that in this model the returns accrue only to the decision maker. Nature does not care what the outcome is. This condition distinguishes decision theory from game theory. In game theory both players have an economic interest in the outcome.

In decision theory problems, the fundamental piece of data is a payoff table like Figure 15.1. In this figure the alternative decisions are listed along the side of the table and the possible states of nature are listed across the top. The entries in the body of the table are the payoffs for all possible combinations of decisions and states of nature. The decision process proceeds as follows:

1. You, the decision maker, select one of the alternative decisions $d_1, \ldots, d_n$. Suppose that you select d_1.
2. After your decision is made, a state of nature occurs. Suppose that state 2 occurs.

FIGURE 15.1
Payoff Table

FIGURE 15.1
Payoff Table

DECISION	STATE OF NATURE			
	1	2	$\cdots$	m
d_1	r_{11}	r_{12}	$\cdots$	r_{1m}
d_2	r_{21}	r_{22}	$\cdots$	r_{2m}
$\vdots$	$\vdots$	$\vdots$	$\vdots$	$\vdots$
d_n	r_{n1}	r_{n2}	$\cdots$	r_{nm}

3. The return you receive can now be determined from the payoff table. Since you made decision 1 and state of nature 2 occurred, the return is r_{12}.

In general terms the question is: "Which of the decisions should we select?" We would like as large a return as possible, that is, the largest possible value of r_{ij}. It is obvious that the decision we should select will depend on our belief concerning what nature will do, that is, on which state of nature will occur. If we believe state 2 will occur, we select the decision associated with the largest number in column 2, and so on.

In the following section we will consider different assumptions about nature's behavior. Each assumption leads to a different *criterion* for selecting the "best" decision, and hence to a different procedure.

_____ 15.2
THREE CLASSES OF DECISION PROBLEMS

This section deals with three classes of decision problems against nature. Each class is defined by an assumption about nature's behavior. The three classes are decisions under certainty, decisions under risk, and decisions under uncertainty.

Decisions Under Certainty

A decision under certainty is one in which you know which state of nature will occur. Alternatively, you can think of it as a case with a single state of nature. Suppose, for example, that in the morning you are deciding whether to take your umbrella to work and you know *for sure* that it will be raining when you leave work in the afternoon. The payoff table for this problem, Figure 15.2, is where $7 is the cost of having your suit cleaned if you get caught in the rain. It enters the table with a minus sign since it is a table of returns. Obviously, the optimal decision is to take the umbrella.

All linear programming models, integer programming models, and many other deterministic models such as the EOQ model can be thought of as decisions against nature in which there is only one state of nature. This is so because we are sure (within the context of the model) what return we will get for each decision we make. For a con-

FIGURE 15.2

	RAIN
Take Umbrella	0
Do not	-7.00

crete example, consider the **PROTRAC** E and F model of Chapter 2:

$$
\begin{array}{ll}
\text{Max } 5000E + 4000F \\
\text{s.t.} \quad 10E + 15F \leq 150 \\
\qquad 20E + 10F \leq 160 \\
\qquad 30E + 10F \geq 135 \\
\qquad E - 3F \leq 0 \\
\qquad E + F \geq 5 \\
\qquad E, F \geq 0
\end{array}
$$

Figure 15.3 presents this problem in the form of a payoff table. In this table, a return of $-\infty$ is assigned to any infeasible decision. For example, since $E = 0$, $F = 0$ violates the third and fifth constraints, the associated return is defined to be $-\infty$. For any feasible pair (E, F) the return is defined to be the objective function value—namely, $5000E + 4000F$. For this model we know exactly what return we get for each decision (each choice of the pair E, F). We can thus list all returns in one column and think of it as representing one state of nature that we are sure will occur.

Finding the Optimal Decision May Be Difficult
    Conceptually, it is easy to solve a problem with one state of nature. You simply select the decision that yields the highest return. In practice, as opposed to "in concept," finding such a decision may be another story. Since E and F can take on an infinite number of values, there will be an infinite number of rows for this problem (see Figure 15.3). Even in this simple problem, enumerating the alternatives and selecting the best of them is not possible. Additional mathematical analysis (in this case, the simplex algorithm) is needed to find the optimal decision.

Decisions Under Risk
A lack of certainty about future events is a characteristic of many if not most management decision problems. Consider how the decisions of the financial vice-president of an insurance company would change if she were to know exactly what changes were to occur in the bond market. Imagine the relief of the head buyer at Bloomingdale's if he were to know exactly how many full-length mink coats would be purchased in his store this year. This relief would be shared in part by the manufacturers of mink coats and even the operators of mink farms.

FIGURE 15.3
Payoff Table for the **PROTRAC**
E and F Problem

DECISION	STATE OF NATURE
$E = 0, F = 0$	$-\infty$
$E = 5, F = 4$	41,000
$\vdots$	$\vdots$
$E = 6, F = 3.5$	44,000
$\vdots$	$\vdots$

It thus seems clear that numerous decision problems are characterized by a lack of certainty. It is also clear that those who deal effectively with these problems, through either skill or luck, are often handsomely rewarded for their accomplishments. In the first book of the Old Testament, Joseph is promoted from slave to assistant Pharaoh of Egypt by accurately forecasting seven years of feast and seven years of famine.[1]

In quantitative modeling, the lack of certainty can be dealt with in various ways. For example, in a linear programming model, some of the data may be an estimate of a future value. In the above **PROTRAC** E and F model, next month's capacity (availability of hours) in department A (the right-hand side of the first constraint) may depend on factors that will occur next week, but the production plans, let us say, must be spelled out today. As previously described in Chapter 5, management might deal with this lack of certainty by estimating the capacity as 150 and then performing sensitivity analysis.

Definition of Risk

Decision theory provides alternative approaches to problems with less than complete certainty. One such approach is called "decisions under risk." In this context, the term "risk" has a restrictive and well-defined meaning. When we speak of decisions under risk, we are referring to a class of decision problems for which there is more than one state of nature and for which we make the assumption that **the decision maker can arrive at a probability estimate for the occurrence for each of the various states of nature**. Suppose, for example, that there are $m > 1$ states of nature, and let p_j be the probability estimate that state j will occur. We can then use equation (15.1) to calculate ER_i, the expected return if we make decision i.

$$ER_i = \sum_{j=1}^{m} r_{ij} \cdot p_j = r_{i1}p_1 + r_{i2}p_2 + \cdots + r_{im}p_m \tag{15.1}$$

For this type of problem, *management should then make the decision that maximizes the expected return.*[2] In other words, $i*$ is the optimal decision where

Optimality Criterion

$$ER_{i*} = \text{maximum over all } i \text{ of } ER_i$$

The newsboy (or omelet pan) problem discussed in Section 12.9 is an example of such a problem. Recall that the newsboy could buy papers for 10 cents each and sell them for 25 cents. However, demand was not known with certainty. He assumed that any demand between 1 and 100 papers was equally likely. More specifically, letting state j be the event that demand is j items, he assumed that for each integer j, $1 \leq j \leq 100$, $p_j = 0.01$. For illustrative purposes and ease of computation, suppose he had assumed, instead, the following probability distribution for demand:

$$P_0 = \text{Prob } \{\text{demand} = 0\} = \tfrac{1}{10}$$

$$P_1 = \text{Prob } \{\text{demand} = 1\} = \tfrac{3}{10}$$

$$P_2 = \text{Prob } \{\text{demand} = 2\} = \tfrac{4}{10}$$

$$P_3 = \text{Prob } \{\text{demand} = 3\} = \tfrac{2}{10}$$

---

[1] As well as being an accurate forecaster, by virtue of his skill in successfully interpreting Pharaoh's dreams, Joseph has been called the first psychoanalyst. Less well known is the fact that Joseph was also the first management scientist. In anticipation of the famine, he advised Pharaoh to build storage facilities to hold inventories of grain. When it was all over and the famine had been survived, Joseph was asked how he had come to acquire such wisdom and knowledge. "Lean-year programming," was his reply.

[2] It will be shown that this is equivalent to another criterion: minimizing expected regret.

FIGURE 15.4

Payoff Table (Net Cash Flows)
for the Newsboy Problem

	STATE OF NATURE (DEMAND)			
DECISION	0	1	2	3
0	0	0	0	0
1	−10	15	15	15
2	−20	5	30	30
3	−30	−5	20	45

The Payoff Table   In this problem, each of the four different values for demand is a different state of nature and the number of papers ordered is the decision. The returns, or payoffs, for this problem are shown in Figure 15.4.

The entries in this figure represent the net cash flow associated with each combination of number ordered and number demanded. These entries are calculated with the expression

$$\text{payoff} = 25 \text{ (number of papers sold)} - 10 \text{ (number of papers ordered)}$$

where 25 cents is the selling price per paper and 10 cents is the cost of buying a paper. It is important to note that in this model sales and demand need not be identical. Indeed, sales is the minimum of the two quantities {number demanded, number ordered}. For example, when no papers are ordered, then clearly none can be sold, no matter how many are demanded. Thus, for all entries in the first row the above expression for payoff gives $25(0) - 10(0) = 0$. If 1 paper is ordered and none are demanded, then none are sold, and the payoff is $25(0) - 10(1) = -10$, which is the first entry in row 2. However, if 1 paper is ordered and 1 or more are demanded, then exactly 1 will be sold and the payoff becomes $25(1) - 10(1) = 15$. This explains the other three entries in row 2. Can you verify that the remaining values in the body of Figure 15.4 are correct?

Once all the data are assembled for Figure 15.4, the process of finding the optimal decision is strictly mechanical. You use (15.1) to evaluate the expected return for each decision (ER_i for $i = 0, 1, 2, 3$) and pick the largest. For example, if you order two papers,

$$ER_2 = -20(\tfrac{1}{10}) + 5(\tfrac{3}{10}) + 30(\tfrac{4}{10}) + 30(\tfrac{2}{10}) = 17.5$$

The first term is the return if we order 2 papers and zero are demanded multiplied by the probability that 0 are demanded. The second term is the return if we order 2 papers and 1 is demanded (see Figure 15.4) times the probability that 1 paper is demanded. The other terms are similarly defined. The expected returns for all of the decisions are calculated as follows:

$$ER_0 = 0(\tfrac{1}{10}) + 0(\tfrac{3}{10}) + 0(\tfrac{4}{10}) + 0(\tfrac{2}{10}) = 0$$

Expected Returns

$$ER_1 = -10(\tfrac{1}{10}) + 15(\tfrac{3}{10}) + 15(\tfrac{4}{10}) + 15(\tfrac{2}{10}) = 12.5$$

$$ER_2 = -20(\tfrac{1}{10}) + 5(\tfrac{3}{10}) + 30(\tfrac{4}{10}) + 30(\tfrac{2}{10}) = 17.5$$

$$ER_3 = -30(\tfrac{1}{10}) - 5(\tfrac{3}{10}) + 20(\tfrac{4}{10}) + 45(\tfrac{2}{10}) = 12.5$$

Since ER_2 is the largest of these four values, the optimal decision is to order 2 papers. With this example, we have now illustrated another class of decision problems (decisions under risk) and the associated decision criterion (maximize the expected return).

Although it was easy to find the optimal decision in the previous example, this is not necessarily always the case. For example, imagine that the demand for papers could be any integer between 1 and 1000. The tabular representation of the problem would then have 1000 columns and 1000 rows. Finding the optimal decision by calculating each of 1000 expected returns and then choosing the largest of these values is tedious at best. As a final comment, we note that although this formulation of the Newsboy problem may appear to differ from the formulation in Section 12.9, it can be shown that either formulation leads to the same optimal order quantity. These are two equivalent ways of viewing the same problem.

Decisions Under Uncertainty

In this case we again have more than one possible state of nature, but now the decision maker is unwilling or unable to specify the probabilities that the various states of nature will occur. There is a long-standing debate as to whether such a situation should exist; that is, should the decision maker always be willing to at least subjectively specify the probabilities even when he or she does not know very much (anything) about what state of nature is apt to occur? Leaving this debate to the philosophers, we turn to the various approaches suggested for this class of problem.

Laplace Criterion

This approach interprets the condition of "uncertainty" as equivalent to assuming that all states of nature are equally likely. This is the point of view: "If I know nothing, then anything is equally likely." For example, in the newsboy problem, we had the payoff table shown in Figure 15.5.

FIGURE 15.5

DECISION	STATE OF NATURE			
	0	1	2	3
0	0	0	0	0
1	−10	15	15	15
2	−20	5	30	30
3	−30	−5	20	45

Assuming all states of nature to be equally likely means, since there are four states, that each state occurs with probability 0.25. Using these probabilities converts the problem to a decision under risk and one could then compute the expected return. You can easily verify that, using these probabilities, expected return would again be maximized by decision 2.

Although in some situations this "equally likely" approach may produce acceptable results, in other settings it would be inappropriate. For example, consider your friend from Yugoslavia, about to watch the football game between Notre Dame and USC in a year in which one team was experiencing a bad season and the other was thus heavily favored in the betting. Although your friend knows nothing about football and has no knowledge about the probability of either team winning, these probabilities clearly exist and are *not* equal. In other words, even though one has "no knowledge," there may be underlying probabilities on the various states of nature, and these probabilities may in no way be consistent with the "equal likelihood" assumption. With this realization, there may be contexts in which you would not wish to use the criterion of expected return based on the equal-likelihood assumption (i.e., the Laplace criterion). For such cases, there are three different criteria which can be used to make decisions under uncertainty: *maximin*, *maximax*, and *minimax regret*. All of these criteria can be used without specifying probabilities. The discussion will be illustrated with the newsboy problem. Look at the earlier payoff table for a moment and think what criterion you might use to make a decision. By this we mean, think of a rule that you could describe to a friend. It has to be a general rule so that your friend could apply it to any payoff table and come up with a decision. Remember, you are willing to make no assumptions about the probabilities on states of nature. Now consider the following criteria.

**Maximin
Criterion**

This is an extremely conservative, or perhaps pessimistic, approach to making decisions. It evaluates each decision by the worst thing that can happen if you make that decision. In this case, then, it evaluates each decision by the *minimum* possible return associated with the decision. In the newsboy example the minimum possible return if 3 papers are ordered is -30; thus, this value is assigned to the decision "order 3 papers." Similarly, we can associate with each other decision the minimum value in its row. Following this rule enables the decision maker to prepare a table as shown in Figure 15.6.

FIGURE 15.6

DECISION	MINIMUM RETURN
0	0
1	-10
2	-20
3	-30

The decision that yields the maximum value of the minimum return (hence, maximin) is then selected. In this case, then, the newsboy should order 0 papers.

This result is not intuitively appealing. The realist wonders how any activity would ever be initiated with this criterion. Those who "believe in" the maximin criterion might argue that this example is not appropriate, since the newsboy would not contemplate buying papers unless something was known about the distribution of demand. Maximin is often used in situations where the planner feels he or she cannot afford to be wrong. Defense planning might be an example. The planner chooses a decision that does as well as possible in the worst possible (most pessimistic) case.

It is, however, easy to create examples in which most people would not accept the decision selected with the maximin criterion. Consider, for example, the payoff table in Figure 15.7. Most people would prefer decision 1. It is much better than decision 2 for all states of nature except state 3, and then it is only slightly worse. Nevertheless, the maximin criterion would select decision 2. If you are among those who strongly

FIGURE 15.7
Payoff Table: Maximin Example

DECISION	STATE OF NATURE								
	1	2	3	4	5	6	7	8	9
1	100	100	2.9	100	100	100	100	100	100
2	3	3	3	3	3	3	3	3	3

prefer decision 1 in this example, you must then ask yourself the following question: "If the maximin criterion provides an answer that I don't like in this simple example, would I be willing to use it on more complicated and important problems?" There is no correct answer to this question. The answer depends on the taste of the decision maker.

Maximax Criterion

This criterion is as optimistic as maximin is pessimistic. It evaluates each decision by the best thing that can happen if you make that decision. In this case, then, it evaluates each decision by the maximum possible return associated with that decision. In particular, refer again to the payoff table for the newsboy problem. If the newsboy ordered 2 papers, the best possible outcome would be a return of 30. This value is thus assigned to the decision, "order 2 papers." In other words, for each decision we identify the maximum value in that row. Using this rule, the decision maker prepares a table as shown in Figure 15.8.

FIGURE 15.8

DECISION	MAXIMUM RETURN
0	0
1	15
2	30
3	45

The decision that yields the maximum of these maximum returns (hence, maximax) is then selected. In this case, then, the newsboy should order 3 papers.

The maximax criterion is subject to the same type of criticism as maximin; that is, it is easy to create examples where using the maximax criterion leads to a decision that most people find unacceptable. Consider the payoff table presented in Figure 15.9, for example. Most people prefer decision 1 since it is much better than decision 2 for every state of nature except state 3, and then it is only slightly worse. The maximax criterion, however, selects decision 2.

FIGURE 15.9
Payoff Table: Maximax Example

DECISION	STATE OF NATURE								
	1	2	3	4	5	6	7	8	9
1	100	100	100	100	100	100	100	100	100
2	3	3	101.1	3	3	3	3	3	3

Regret and Minimax Regret

Regret introduces a new concept for measuring the desirability of an outcome; that is, it is a new way to create the payoff table. So far, all the decision criteria have been used on a payoff table of dollar returns as measured by net cash flows. In particular, each entry in Figure 15.4 shows the net cash flow for the newsboy for every combination of decision (number of papers ordered) and state of nature (number of papers demanded). Figure 15.10 shows the regret for each combination of decision and state of nature. It is derived from Figure 15.4 by

1. Finding the maximum entry in each column (e.g., 30 is the largest entry in the third column, the column under State of Nature "2").

FIGURE 15.10
Regret Table for the Newsboy Problem

	STATE OF NATURE			
DECISION	0	1	2	3
0	0	15	30	45
1	10	0	15	30
2	20	10	0	15
3	30	20	10	0

2. Calculating the new entry by subtracting the current entry from the maximum in its column. Thus, the new entry in row 2, column 3 is

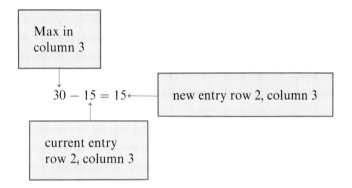

In each column, these new entries, called regret, indicate how much better we can do. In other words, "regret" is synonymous with "opportunity cost" of not making the best decision for a given state of nature. It follows that the decision maker would like to make a decision that minimizes regret, but (same old story) he does not know which state of nature will occur. If he knew a probability distribution on the state of nature, he could minimize the expected regret. (In the next section, we will see that this is equivalent to maximizing expected net cash flow.) If he does not know the probability, the typical suggestion is to use the conservative *minimax criterion*, that is, to select that decision that does the best in the worst case (the decision which has the smallest maximum regret).

For example, consider the regret table for the newsboy problem shown in Figure 15.10. If 1 paper is ordered, the maximum regret of 30 occurs if 3 papers are demanded. The value 30 is thus associated with the decision "order 1 paper." In other words, the maximum value in each row is associated with the decision in that row. Following this rule produces the table in Figure 15.11.

FIGURE 15.11

DECISION	MAXIMUM REGRET
0	45
1	30
2	20
3	30

The decision maker then selects the decision that minimizes the maximum regret. In this case, the minimax regret criterion implies that the newsboy should order 2 papers. Our newsboy example illustrates that, when making decisions without using probabilities, the three criteria, maximin cash flow, maximax cash flow, and minimax regret, can lead to different "optimal" decisions.

——— 15.3
THE EXPECTED VALUE OF PERFECT INFORMATION: NEWSBOY PROBLEM UNDER RISK

Let us return to the newsboy problem under risk (i.e., with a probability distribution on demand). Recall that, in this case, the optimal policy was to order 2 papers and that the expected return was 17.5. It is useful to think about this problem in a very stylized fashion in order to introduce the concept of the expected value of perfect information. In particular, let us assume that the sequence of events in the newsboy's day (the "current sequence of events") proceeds as follows:

1. The devil, by drawing from the demand distribution for papers, determines the number of papers that will be demanded.
2. The newsboy, not knowing what demand had been drawn, but knowing the distribution of demand, orders his papers.
3. The demand is then revealed to the newsboy and he achieves an *actual* (as opposed to expected) return determined by his order-size decision and the demand.

Now consider a new scenario. The newsboy has an opportunity to make a deal with the devil. (If you think this is silly, remember that Faust is equally improbable.) Under the new deal the sequence of events proceeds as follows:

1. The newsboy pays the devil a fee.
2. The devil determines the demand as above.
3. The devil tells the newsboy what the demand will be.
4. The newsboy orders his papers.
5. The newsboy achieves the return determined by the demand and the number of papers he ordered.

The question is: "What is the largest fee the newsboy should be willing to pay in step 1?" This fee is called the *expected value of perfect information*. In general terms,

$$\text{fee} = \left(\begin{array}{c} \text{expected return} \\ \text{with new deal} \end{array} \right) - \left(\begin{array}{c} \text{expected return with} \\ \text{current sequence of events} \end{array} \right)$$

With the new deal the newsboy, in step 4, will always order the number of papers that will give him the maximum return for the state of nature that will occur. However, the payment in step 1 must be made *before* he learns what the demand will be. Referring to Figure 15.4 we see that if 0 papers will be demanded, he will order 0 papers and enjoy the maximum return of 0. Since the devil is drawing from the distribution of demand, there is a probability of $\frac{1}{10}$ that what the newsboy will learn from the devil is that demand will in fact be zero. Similarly, he will learn with a probability of $\frac{3}{10}$ that 1 paper will be demanded. If this occurs, he will order 1 paper and enjoy the maximum return of 15. Following this reasoning, his expected return under the new deal is

$$ER(new) = 0(\tfrac{1}{10}) + 15(\tfrac{3}{10}) + 30(\tfrac{4}{10}) + 45(\tfrac{2}{10}) = 25.5$$

We have already seen that in the absence of perfect information his optimal decision (order 2 papers) gives an expected return of 17.5. Thus, if EVPI stands for the expected value of perfect information, we can calculate it as follows:

EVPI for Newsboy

$$EVPI = 25.5 - 17.5 = 8.0$$

This is the maximum amount our vendor should be willing to pay in step 1 for the deal with the devil. Although the story we have used to develop the concept is far-fetched, the expected value of perfect information (EVPI) has important practical significance. It is an upper bound on the amount that you should be willing to pay to improve your knowledge about what state of nature will occur. Literally millions of dollars are spent on various market research projects and other testing devices (geological tests, quality control experiments, etc.) to determine what state of nature will occur in a wide variety of applications. The expected value of perfect information indicates the expected amount to be gained from any such endeavor and thus places an upper bound on the amount that should be spent in gathering information.

When Does EVPI = Expected Regret?

The expected value of perfect information is always equal to the expected regret of the optimal decision under risk (the decision that maximizes expected return). We will show that this fact holds in the newsboy example.

When the probabilities on the states of nature are specified, it is a straightforward task to compute the expected regret for each decision. Using the previous probability distribution of demand and the regret table (Figure 15.10), the calculation for expected regret if 0 papers are ordered is

$$\text{expected regret }(0) = 0(\tfrac{1}{10}) + 15(\tfrac{3}{10}) + 30(\tfrac{4}{10}) + 45(\tfrac{2}{10}) = 25.5$$

The first term is the regret if 0 papers are demanded times the probability that 0 papers are demanded. The second term is the regret if 1 paper is demanded times the probability that 1 paper is demanded, and so on.

The expected regret for the other possible order quantities is computed in a similar fashion:

$$\text{expected regret }(1) = 10(\tfrac{1}{10}) + 0(\tfrac{3}{10}) + 15(\tfrac{4}{10}) + 30(\tfrac{2}{10}) = 13.0$$
$$\text{expected regret }(2) = 20(\tfrac{1}{10}) + 10(\tfrac{3}{10}) + 0(\tfrac{4}{10}) + 15(\tfrac{2}{10}) = 8.0$$
$$\text{expected regret }(3) = 30(\tfrac{1}{10}) + 20(\tfrac{3}{10}) + 10(\tfrac{4}{10}) + 0(\tfrac{2}{10}) = 13.0$$

We see that ordering 2 papers yields the minimum expected regret. But ordering 2 papers was also the optimal decision when the criterion was to maximize the expected net dollar return.

It is always the case that, in decision making under risk, these two criteria (minimize expected regret, maximize expected net dollar return) will prescribe the same decision as optimal.

Also

The expected regret of the optimal decision under risk (i.e., the minimum expected regret) equals the expected value of perfect information.

_____ 15.4
UTILITIES AND DECISIONS UNDER RISK

Utility is an alternative way of measuring the attractiveness of the result of a decision. In other words, it is an alternative way of finding the values to fill in a payoff table. Up to now we have used net dollar return (net cash flow) and regret as two measures of the "goodness" of a particular combination of a decision and a state of nature.

Utility suggests another type of measure. Our treatment of this topic includes three main sections:

1. A rationale for utility (i.e., why using net cash flow can lead to unacceptable decisions).
2. How to use a utility function.
3. Creating a utility function.

The Rationale for Utility In the preceding section we saw that the maximin and maximax decision criteria could lead to unacceptable decisions in simple illustrative problems. We now point out that the criterion of maximizing expected net cash flow in a decision under risk can also produce unacceptable results. For example, consider an urn that contains 99 white balls and 1 black ball. You are offered a chance to play a game in which a ball will be drawn from this urn. Each ball is equally likely to be drawn. If a white ball is drawn, you must pay $10,000. If the black ball is drawn, you receive $1,000,000. You must decide whether to play. The payoff table based on net cash flow is shown in Figure 15.12.

FIGURE 15.12
Payoff Table (Net Cash Flows)

DECISION	STATE OF NATURE	
	WHITE BALL	BLACK BALL
Play	−10,000	1,000,000
Do Not Play	0	0

We now use the information in this table, together with the facts that the probabilities of a white and a black ball are, respectively, 0.99 and 0.01, to calculate the expected return for each decision (play or do not play) in the usual way.

$$ER(play) = -10,000(\tfrac{99}{100}) + 1,000,000(\tfrac{1}{100})$$

$$= -9900 + 10,000 = 100$$

$$ER(do\ not\ play) = 0(\tfrac{99}{100}) + 0(\tfrac{1}{100}) = 0$$

Since ER(play) > ER(do not play), we should play if we apply the criterion of maximizing the expected net cash flow.

Now step back and ask yourself if you would decide to play this game. Remember that the probability is 0.99 that you will lose $10,000. Many people simply find this large "downside risk" to be unacceptable; that is, they are unwilling to accept the decision based on the criterion of maximizing the expected net cash flow. Thus, once again we see a simple example which shows a need to take care in selecting an appropriate criterion. This is all the more true in dealing with complicated real-world problems.

Fortunately, it is not necessary to reject the concept of maximizing expected returns. To adapt the expected return criterion to general decisions under risk it is only necessary to recognize that net dollar returns do not always accurately reflect the "attractiveness" of the possible outcomes of decisions. To show what this means, ask yourself if you would be willing to win or lose 10 cents depending on the flip of a fair coin. (Most people would say yes.) How about winning or losing $10,000, depending on a flip of the same coin? (Here most people would say no.) What is the difference? A 10-cent gain seems to balance a 10-cent loss. Why does a $10,000 gain not balance a $10,000 loss? The answer is that in the latter situation most people are "risk averse," which means they would feel that the loss of $10,000 is more painful than the benefit obtained from a $10,000 gain.

Decision theory deals with this problem by introducing a function that measures the "attractiveness" of money. This function is called a *utility function*, where for the sake of this discussion the word "utility" can be thought of as a measure of "satisfaction." A typical "risk-averse" utility function is shown in Figure 15.13. Two characteristics of this function are worth noting:

1. It is nondecreasing, since more money is always at least as attractive as less money.
2. It is concave. An equivalent statement is that the marginal utility of money is nonincreasing. To illustrate this phenomenon, let us examine Figure 15.13.

First suppose that you have $100 and someone gives you an additional $100. Note that your "utility" increases by

$$U(200) - U(100) \simeq 0.680 - 0.525 = 0.155$$

FIGURE 15.13

Typical (Risk-Averse) Utility Function

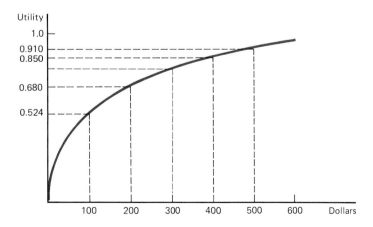

FIGURE 15.14

Some Utility Functions

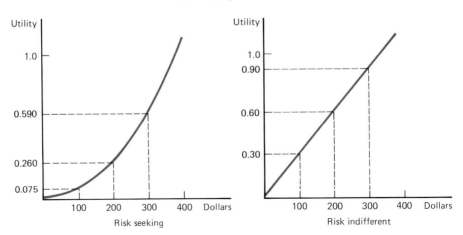

Risk seeking

Risk indifferent

Now suppose that you start with $400 and someone gives you an additional $100. Now your utility increases by

$$U(500) - U(400) \simeq 0.910 - 0.850 = 0.060$$

In other words, 100 additional dollars is less attractive to you if you have $400 on hand than it is if you start with $100. Another way of describing this phenomenon is that the increase of a specified amount of dollars increases utility less than the loss of the same amount of dollars decreases utility.

Risk Seeking   Figure 15.14 shows two other general types of utility functions. The first is a *risk-seeking* (convex) function, where a gain of a specified amount of dollars increases the utility more than a loss of the same amount of dollars decreases the utility. For example, if you start with $200 and increase your holding by $100 to $300, your utility increases by

$$U(300) - U(200) \simeq 0.590 - 0.260 = 0.330$$

whereas if you start with $200 and decrease your holding by $100 to $100, your utility decreases by

$$U(200) - U(100) \simeq 0.260 - 0.075 = 0.185$$

Thus, with a risk-seeking utility function an increase of $100 increases your utility more than a decrease of $100 decreases it. As we saw, exactly the opposite statement holds for a risk-averse (concave) function like the one shown in Figure 15.13.

Risk Indifferent   For the risk-indifferent function shown in Figure 15.14, a gain or a loss of a specified dollar amount produces a change of the same magnitude in your utility.

Using a Utility Function   In the next section we will worry about how you go about creating a utility function. For the meantime, assume that somehow one has been created. Using this function to make decisions when the probabilities of the states of nature are known is a straightforward process. To be specific, you simply redo the payoff table, substituting the utility of the net cash flow for that cash flow, and proceed as before. Consider, for example, the

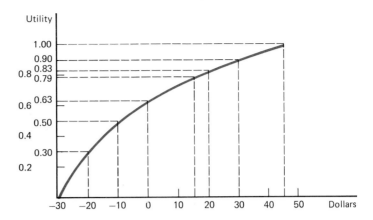

FIGURE 15.15
Newsboy's Utility Function

newsboy problem, where we let Figure 15.15 represent the newsboy's utility for money. The newsboy can use this figure and the payoff table of net cash flows (Figure 15.4) to create a new payoff table where the entries are the utility of the net cash flow associated with each combination of a decision and a state of nature. For example, row 4, column 3 in Figure 15.4 shows a net cash flow of 20. Figure 15.15 translates this into a utility of about 0.83, which becomes the new entry in row 4, column 3. The complete table is presented in Figure 15.16. The newsboy now proceeds as before; that is, he calculates the expected utility for each decision. Using the previously employed probabilities $(\frac{1}{10}, \frac{3}{10}, \frac{4}{10}, \frac{2}{10})$, and letting EU_i be the expected utility for decision i, the calculations are

$$EU_0 = 0.63(\tfrac{1}{10}) + 0.63(\tfrac{3}{10}) + 0.63(\tfrac{4}{10}) + 0.63(\tfrac{2}{10}) = 0.63$$

$$EU_1 = 0.50(\tfrac{1}{10}) + 0.79(\tfrac{3}{10}) + 0.79(\tfrac{4}{10}) + 0.79(\tfrac{2}{10}) = 0.761$$

$$EU_2 = 0.30(\tfrac{1}{10}) + 0.69(\tfrac{3}{10}) + 0.90(\tfrac{4}{10}) + 0.90(\tfrac{2}{10}) = 0.777$$

$$EU_3 = 0(\tfrac{1}{10}) \quad + 0.57(\tfrac{3}{10}) + 0.83(\tfrac{4}{10}) + 1(\tfrac{2}{10}) \quad = 0.703$$

Based on a criterion of maximizing the expected utility, the newsboy would order 2 papers. Referring to the discussion of decisions under risk in Section 15.2, we see that if the newsboy based his decision on maximizing the expected net cash flow, he would also order 2 papers. It is not always true that the decisions which has the largest expected cash flow will also have the largest expected utility. The fact that this phenomenon

FIGURE 15.16
Newsboy Payoff Table (Utilities)

DECISION	STATE OF NATURE			
	0	1	2	3
0	0.63	0.63	0.63	0.63
1	0.50	0.79	0.79	0.79
2	0.30	0.69	0.90	0.90
3	0	0.57	0.83	1.00

occurred in this particular example does not imply that it will occur in general. A different utility function could yield a different decision.

Creating a Utility Function

One system of creating a utility function like the one shown in Figure 15.15 requires the decision maker, in our case the newsboy, to make a series of choices between a sure return and a lottery. In more formal language, the decision maker is called on to create an "equivalent lottery." This, however, is the second step. Let us start at the beginning.

The newsboy can arbitrarily select the end points of his utility function. It is a convenient convention to set the utility of the smallest net dollar return equal to 0 and the utility of the largest net return equal to 1. Since in the newsboy example the smallest return is -30, and the largest is $+45$, he sets $U(-30) = 0$ and $U(45) = 1$. Note that these values are used in Figure 15.15. These two values play a fundamental role in finding the utility of any quantity of money between -30 and 45. It is perhaps easiest to proceed by example.

Assume that the decision maker starts with $U(-30) = 0$ and $U(45) = 1$ and wants to find the utility of 10 [i.e., $U(10)$]. He proceeds by selecting a probability p such that he is indifferent between the following two alternatives:

An Equivalent Lottery

1. Receive a payment of 10 for sure.
2. Participate in a lottery in which he receives a payment of 45 with probability p or a payment of -30 with probability $1 - p$.

Clearly if $p = 1$, the decision maker prefers alternative 2, since he prefers a payment of 45 to a payment of 10. Equally clear, if $p = 0$, he prefers alternative 1, since he prefers a payment of 10 to a loss of 30 (i.e., a payment of -30). It follows that somewhere between 0 and 1 there is a value for p such that the decision maker is indifferent between the two alternatives. This value will vary from person to person depending on how attractive the various alternatives are to them. We call this value of p the utility for 10. We obviously have not *proved* that using the probability p to define an equivalent lottery is a meaningful way to construct a utility function. An understandable discussion of why this approach works would carry us far beyond the scope of this text. We must be content to stop with the how and leave the why to other courses.

———— 15.5
A MID-CHAPTER SUMMARY

The preceding three sections provide the theoretical foundation on which the rest of the chapter is based. The ensuing sections are devoted to procedures that play an important role in solving real-world problems. It is useful to summarize what we have achieved before moving ahead.

Section 15.2 provided a general framework for a class of problems identified as decisions against nature. In this framework, the problem can be described by a payoff table in which the returns to the decision maker depend on the decision selected and the state of nature that occurs. Three specific cases were identified:

1. *Decisions under certainty:* The decision maker knows exactly what state of nature will occur. His "only" problem is to select the best decision. Deterministic problems such as linear programming, integer programming, and the EOQ model fall in this category.

2. *Decisions under risk:* A probability distribution is specified on the states of nature. The decision maker may use the following criteria to select a "best decision":

   a. Maximize expected return as measured by net dollar return
   b. Maximize expected return as measured by utility
   c. Minimize expected regret (opportunity cost)

We saw that criteria a and c always lead to the same decision. Many inventory control and queuing problems fall into the category of decisions under risk.

3. *Decisions under uncertainty:* Here it is assumed that the decision maker has no knowledge about which state of nature will occur. The decision maker might apply the Laplace criteria, that is, assign equal probabilities to the various states of nature and then choose a decision that maximizes expected return. Alternatively, the decision maker may attack the problem without using probabilities. In this case, we discussed three different criteria for making a "best decision":

   a. Maximize minimum net dollar return
   b. Maximize maximum net dollar return
   c. Minimize maximum regret

Each of these criteria will, in general, lead to different decisions.

Section 15.3 was devoted to the concept of the expected value of perfect information (EVPI). This entity plays an important role by establishing an upper bound on the amount you should pay to gain new information about what state of nature will occur. We saw that EVPI is equal to the optimal (Min) value of expected regret.

Finally, in Section 15.4 we discussed utility as an alternative measure of the attractiveness of each combination of a decision and a state of nature. The desire to use a utility function is motivated by the fact that in some cases, for example because of the magnitudes of the potential losses, the decision that maximizes the expected net dollar return is not the decision that you would want to select.

The remaining sections in this chapter will deal with extensions of the model for decisions under risk. They consider decision trees, a technique of significant practical importance, and introduce two important concepts: the use of new information in decision making and the analysis of sequential decision problems.

───── 15.6
DECISION TREES: MARKETING HOME AND GARDEN TRACTORS

A *decision tree* is a graphical device for analyzing decisions under risk, that is, problems in which the probabilities on the states of nature are specified. More precisely, decision trees were created to use on problems in which there is a sequence of decisions, each of which could lead to one of several uncertain outcomes. For example, a concessionaire typically has to decide how much to bid for each of several possible locations at the state fair. The result of this decision is not certain, since it depends on what the competitors decide to bid. Once the location is known, the concessionaire must decide how much food to stock. The result of this decision in terms of profits is also not certain since it depends on customer demand.

Our discussion of decision trees is organized in the following manner: In this section we introduce the basic ideas. Section 15.7 examines the sensitivity of the optimal decision to the assessed values of the probabilities. Section 15.8 shows how Bayes Theorem is used to incorporate new information into the process, and Section 15.9 considers a sequential decision problem. The entire discussion is motivated by the following marketing problem faced by the management of **PROTRAC**.

The design and product testing phase has just been completed for **PROTRAC**'s new line of home and garden tractors. Top management is attempting to decide on the appropriate marketing and production strategy to use for this product. Three major alternatives are being considered. Each alternative is identified with a single word.

1. *Aggressive* (*A*): This strategy represents a major commitment of the firm to this product line. A major capital expenditure would be made for a new and efficient production facility. Large inventories would be built up to guarantee prompt delivery of all models. A major marketing campaign involving nation-wide sponsorship of television commercials and dealer discounts would be initiated.

2. *Basic* (*B*): In this plan, production of E-4 (the small crawler tractor) would be moved from Joliet to Moline. This move would phase out the trouble-plagued department for adjustable pelican and excavator production. At the same time, the E-4 line in Joliet would be modified to produce the new home and garden product. Inventories would be held for only the most popular items. Headquarters would make funds available to support local or regional advertising efforts, but no national advertising campaign would be mounted.

3. *Cautious* (*C*): In this plan, excess capacity on several existing E-4 lines would be used to produce the new products. A minimum of new tooling would be developed. Production would be geared to satisfy demand, and advertising would be at the discretion of the local dealer.

Management decides to categorize the condition of the market (i.e., the level of demand) as either strong (S) or weak (W). Figure 15.17 presents the payoff table and management's best estimate of the probability of a strong or a weak market. The payoffs in the body are the net profits measured in millions of dollars. They were generated by carefully calculating the sales, revenues, and costs associated with each decision–state of nature combination. It is interesting to note that a cautions (C) decision yields a higher profit with a weak market than it does with a strong market. If there is a strong market and **PROTRAC** is cautious, not only will the competition capture the small tractor market, but as a result of the carryover effect of these sales, the competition will seriously cut into **PROTRAC**'s current market position for accessories and other home products.

We are dealing here with what we have termed "decisions under risk" and it is, of course, possible to calculate the expected return for each decision and select the best one, just as we did in Section 15.2. The calculations follow:

$$ER(A) = 30(0.45) - 8(0.55) = 9.10$$

$$ER(B) = 20(0.45) + 7(0.55) = 12.85$$

$$ER(C) = 5(0.45) + 15(0.55) = 10.50$$

The optimal decision is to select (B), the basic production and marketing strategy.

FIGURE 15.17

Payoffs (Millions of Dollars) and
Probabilities for the Basic Marketing Problem

	STATE OF NATURE	
	STRONG, S	WEAK, W
	PROBABILITY	
DECISION	0.45	0.55
Aggressive (A)	30	−8
Basic (B)	20	7
Cautious (C)	5	15

FIGURE 15.18

First Step in Creating a Decision Tree
for the Home and Garden Tractor Problem

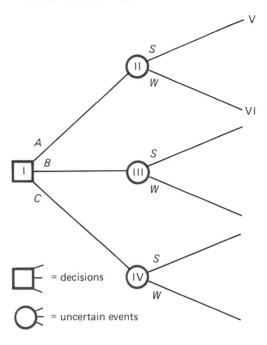

<table>
</table>

Creating a Decision Tree

This marketing problem can also be represented by a decision tree. The first step in creating it is shown in Figure 15.18. In our exposition of decision trees, a *square node* will represent a point at which a decision must be made, and each line leading from a square will represent a possible decision. The *circular nodes* will represent situations when the outcome is not certain. Each line leading from a circle represents a possible outcome. The term *branches* will be employed for the lines emanating from the nodes, whether square or circular.

For the home and garden tractor problem, the decision tree in Figure 15.18 shows the initial node, labeled I. Since it is square, a decision must be made. Thus, management must choose one of the strategies A, B, or C. Depending on which decision is selected, a new position will be attained on the tree. For example, selecting strategy A leads us from node I to node II. Since II is a circle, the next branch that will occur is not known with certainty. If the market condition turns out to be strong, position V is attained. If, instead, the market proves to be weak, position VI is attained. Since they represent the end of the decision process, positions such as V and VI are referred to as *terminal positions*. Also, since nodes II, III, and IV are not followed by other nodes, they are called *terminal nodes*.

Appending the Probabilities and Terminal Values

The decision tree presented in Figure 15.18 provides an efficient way for management to visualize the interactions between decisions and less than certain events. However, if management wishes to use the decision tree to select an optimal decision, some additional information must be appended to the diagram. In particular, one must assign the return associated with each terminal position. This is called the *terminal value*. One must also assign a probability to each branch emanating from each circular node. For the basic model this is a simple task, and performing it yields the decision tree presented in Figure 15.19. You can see that the appended terminal values and branch probabilities are taken directly from Figure 15.17.

FIGURE 15.19
Complete Decision Tree for Home and
Garden Tractor Problem

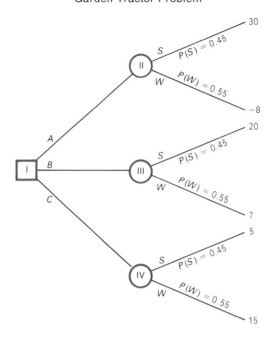

Folding Back

Using a decision tree to find the optimal decision is called solving the tree. To solve a decision tree one works backward or, in the jargon of the trade, by *folding back* the tree. First, the terminal branches are *folded back* by calculating an expected value for each terminal node. For example, consider node II. The calculation to obtain the expected value for this node is

$$\text{expected terminal value} = 30(0.45) + (-8)(0.55) = 9.10$$

In other words, the expected value to be obtained if one arrives at node II is 9.10. Now the branches emanating from the node are folded back (i.e., eliminated) and the expected value of 9.10 is assigned to the node, as shown in Figure 15.20.

Reduced Decision Tree

Performing the same calculations for nodes III and IV yields what is termed the *reduced decision tree*, shown in Figure 15.21. Note that the expected terminal values on nodes II, III, and IV are identical to the expected returns computed earlier in this section for decisions A, B, and C, respectively. Management now faces the simple problem of

FIGURE 15.20
Folding Back Terminal Branches

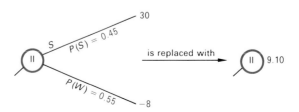

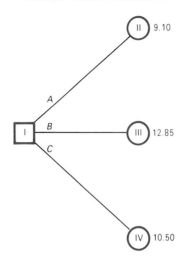

choosing the alternative that yields the highest expected terminal value. In this case, as we have seen earlier, the choice is alternative B.

The above discussion provides a simple illustration of how the basic model can be analyzed with a decision tree. In Sections 15.8 and 15.9 you will see the use of decision trees in more structured scenarios. However, this introductory discussion illustrates an important point: *For the basic model a decision tree simply provides another, more graphic, way of viewing the same problem.* Exactly the same information is utilized, and the same calculations are made whether one uses the steps described in Section 15.2 or a decision tree to solve the problem.

——— 15.7
SENSITIVITY ANALYSIS

Expected
Return as a
Function
of *P*(S)

Before proceeding to the next main topic, a model in which new information becomes available concerning the likelihood of the uncertain events, it will be useful to consider again the expected return associated with each of the decisions in our previous example. We have already noted that to calculate the expected return of stategy A, one uses the relationship

$$\text{ER(A)} = (30)P(S) + (-8)P(W)$$

where $P(S)$ is the probability of strong and $P(W)$ is the probability of weak. We also know that

$$P(S) + P(W) = 1 \quad \text{or} \quad P(W) = 1 - P(S)$$

Thus

$$\text{ER(A)} = 30P(S) - 8[1 - P(S)] = -8 + 38P(S)$$

This expected return, then, is a linear function of the probability that the market response is strong.

A similar function can be found for alternatives B and C since

$$ER(B) = 20P(S) + 7[1 - P(S)] = 7 + 13P(S)$$

and

$$ER(C) = 5P(S) + 15[1 - P(S)] = 15 - 10P(S)$$

**Plotting
Expected
Return**
Eventually we are going to plot each of these three functions on the same set of axes. We start in Figure 15.22 with the expected return for decision A, ER(A). The vertical axis is expected return and the horizontal axis is $P(S)$, the probability that the market is strong. Note that when $P(S) = 0$, then $ER(A) = -8$. To see that this makes sense, recall that when $P(S) = 0$, we are sure that the market will be weak and Figure 15.17 shows that if the market is weak and we make decision A the return is -8.

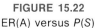

FIGURE 15.22
ER(A) versus $P(S)$

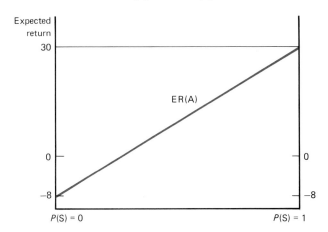

A similar argument shows that ER(A) should be 30 when $P(S) = 1$ since in this case we are sure that the market is strong. The fact that a straight line connects these two points follows from the fact that

$$ER(A) = -8 + 38P(S)$$

which is a linear function of $P(S)$. In Figure 15.23, ER(A), ER(B), and ER(C) are all plotted on the same set of axes.

Since the criterion for making a decision when you have decisions under risk is to select the decision with the highest expected return, Figure 15.23 shows which decision is optimal for any particular value of $P(S)$. For example, if as in Figure 15.17, the value of $P(S)$ is 0.45, then Figure 15.23 shows that ER(B) > ER(C) > ER(A). Hence, as we have already computed, for this value of $P(S)$ the optimal decision is B. On the

FIGURE 15.23
Expected Return as a Function of $P(S)$

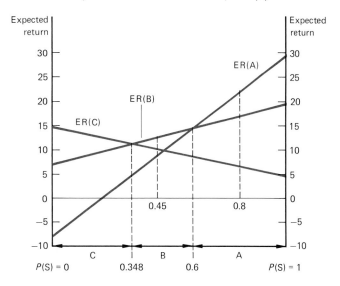

other hand, if $P(S) = 0.8$, we see that $ER(A) > ER(B) > ER(C)$ and thus A is the optimal decision.

In more general terms we see that if $P(S)$ is larger than the value of $P(S)$ at which the graphs of $ER(A)$ and $ER(B)$ cross, strategy A should be selected. The $P(S)$ value at which strategy A becomes optimal can be found by setting $ER(A)$ equal to $ER(B)$ and solving for $P(S)$; that is

$$ER(A) = ER(B)$$

$$-8 + 38P(S) = 7 + 13P(S)$$

$$25P(S) = 15$$

$$P(S) = 0.6$$

**The Optimal
Policy Is
Not Very
Sensitive**
In a similar way, it is easily determined that the graphs of $ER(C)$ and $ER(B)$ cross when $P(S) = 0.348$. Thus, Figure 15.23 indicates that **PROTRAC** should select the basic production and marketing strategy (i.e., decision B) if $P(S)$ is larger than 0.348 and smaller than 0.6. This is consistent with what we already computed under the assumption that $P(S) = 0.45$. However, the analysis of Figure 15.23 provides considerably more information than we had previously. It is now clear, for example, that the optimal decision in this case is not very sensitive to the precision of our estimate for $P(S)$. The same strategy, B, remains optimal for an increase or decrease of more than 0.10 in the previously estimated probability of 0.45.

Although a diagram such as Figure 15.23 can only be used when there are two possible states of nature, it provides a useful pedagogical device for illustrating the sensitivity of the optimal solution to the estimate of probabilities. For higher dimensions, generalizations of this approach exist, but such a discussion would go beyond the introductory level of this chapter.

DECISION TREES: INCORPORATING NEW INFORMATION

A Market Research Study for Home and Garden Tractors

The management of **PROTRAC**'s domestic tractor division was just on the verge of recommending the basic marketing and production strategy (B) when the board of directors insisted that a market research study had to be performed. Only after such a study would the board be willing to approve the selection of a marketing and production strategy. As a result of the board's decision, management consulted the corporate marketing research group at **PROTRAC** headquarters. It was agreed that this group would perform a market research study and would report within a month on whether the study was encouraging, E, or discouraging, D. Thus, within a month the new-product planners would have this additional information. This new information should obviously be taken into account before making a decision on the marketing and production strategy.

Management could treat the new information informally; that is, once the test results were available, management's estimate of $P(S)$, the probability that the market would be strong, could be updated. If the study turned out to be encouraging, E, presumably management would want to increase the estimate of $P(S)$ from 0.45 to 0.50, 0.60, or maybe more. If the study results were discouraging, D, then $P(S)$ should be decreased.

The question is: How should the updating be accomplished? There is a formal way to do this, based on the concept of *conditional probability*. Before presenting this method we will pause to introduce the concept of conditional probability and the mechanics of working with these quantities. Even if you have had a course in probability or statistics, you may wish to review the following subsection.

Conditional Probability and Bayes Theorem

Consider the following two-stage process:

1. A fair die is thrown.
2. A ball is chosen at random from one of three urns. Each urn contains 100 balls, but with a different number of white (W) and black (B) balls. The result of stage 1 determines which urn will be used. Details are presented in Figure 15.24.

In this figure we see that if a 1 is thrown, we draw a ball from urn 1. Since we are throwing a fair die, the probability that we draw a ball from urn 1 is $\frac{1}{6}$; that is, $P(1) = \frac{1}{6}$. Similarly, if we throw a 2 or 3, we will draw a ball from urn 2. This implies that $P(2) = \frac{2}{6}$. Finally, if a 4, 5, or 6 is thrown, we draw a ball from urn 3 and thus $P(3) = \frac{3}{6}$.

FIGURE 15.24
Two-Stage Process

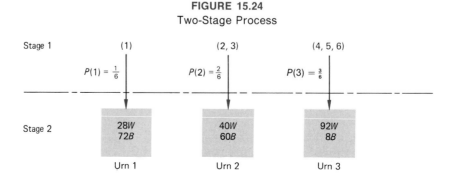

The symbol $P(W|1)$ signifies a *conditional probability*. The vertical line is read as "given." Thus, $P(W|1)$ is read "the probability of W given 1." It means the probability of drawing a white ball (W) assuming that the drawing is made from urn 1. Recall that once an urn is selected, a ball is chosen at random, which means that each ball in the urn is equally likely to be drawn. Looking at Figure 15.24, we see that

$$P(W|1) = 0.28 \quad \text{and} \quad P(B|1) = 0.72$$

$$P(W|2) = 0.40 \quad \text{and} \quad P(B|2) = 0.60$$

$$P(W|3) = 0.92 \quad \text{and} \quad P(B|3) = 0.08$$

We would like to use the probabilities just presented to find $P(1|B)$. We have just seen that this means the probability that the ball was drawn from urn 1 given that we know it is black. To clarify this, assume that a friend goes through the two-stage process in the next room. He then comes in and reports that the ball is black. He then asks, "What is the probability that it came from urn 1?"

Before answering that question, suppose he had asked, "What is the probability that the ball I drew came from urn 1?" and he did *not* tell you the color of the ball. In this case all you know is that he would have drawn from urn 1 if he had thrown a 1 with his fair die. Thus, the *unconditional probability* that the ball came from urn 1 is $P(1) = \frac{1}{6}$.

Now that you know the ball is black and that urn 1 has the highest percentage of black balls, your intuition probably suggests that the probability of urn 1 has increased. If so, your intuition is correct. We will now use conditional probabilities to lend some precision to that intuitive feeling.

Joint Probability In order to calculate $P(1|B)$, we use the following relation, which is developed in courses dealing with probability and statistics. Let I denote any urn (e.g., $I = 1$). Then

$$P(I \text{ and } B) = P(B \text{ and } I) = P(B|I)P(I) = P(I|B)P(B) \quad (15.2)$$

where $P(B \text{ and } I)$ is called the joint probability that both B and I occur. For example, if $I = 1$, then $P(B \text{ and } 1)$ is the probability that the ball is black and was drawn from urn 1. We will also use the fact that

$$P(B) = P(B|1)P(1) + P(B|2)P(2) + P(B|3)P(3) \quad (15.3)$$

We have now developed all the expressions we need to derive an expression for $P(1|B)$. From the last two expressions in (15.2) we obtain

$$P(I|B) = \frac{P(B|I)P(I)}{P(B)} \quad (15.4)$$

Bayes Theorem Then, substituting 1 for the value of I, and substituting the right-hand side of (15.3) for $P(B)$, expression (15.4) becomes

$$P(1|B) = \frac{P(B|1)P(1)}{P(B|1)P(1) + P(B|2)P(2) + P(B|3)P(3)} \quad (15.5)$$

Equation (15.5) is called *Bayes' Rule* or *Bayes' Theorem*. Since all terms on the right-hand side of (15.5) are known, Bayes' Rule provides a way to compute $P(1|B)$. Let us now apply this rule to the set of data at hand. We have previously determined that $P(B|1) = 0.72$ and $P(1) = \frac{1}{6}$. Hence

$$P(B|1)P(1) = (\tfrac{72}{100})(\tfrac{1}{6}) = 0.12$$

This gives us the numerator. For the denominator, again using the given data,

$$P(B) = (\tfrac{72}{100})(\tfrac{1}{6}) + (\tfrac{60}{100})(\tfrac{2}{6}) + (\tfrac{8}{100})(\tfrac{3}{6}) = 0.36$$

Thus, we obtain, using (15.5) and the calculations above,

$$P(1|B) = \frac{0.12}{0.36} = \frac{1}{3} \tag{15.6}$$

Recall that the unconditional probability (i.e., with no additional information) that the ball was drawn from urn 1 is $\frac{1}{6}$. Once we are told that the ball is black, the probability that it came from urn 1 increases. In this particular case it doubles.

A Tabular Approach The tabular display in Figure 15.25 is a convenient way to display the data required to compute all conditional probabilities.

FIGURE 15.25
Marginal and Joint Probabilities

		ROLL THE DIE			MARGINAL PROBABILITY
		URN 1	URN 2	URN 3	
Draw a ball	B	$P(B \& 1) = \frac{72}{600}$	$P(B \& 2) = \frac{120}{600}$	$P(B \& 3) = \frac{24}{600}$	$P(B) = \frac{36}{100}$
	W	$P(W \& 1) = \frac{28}{600}$	$P(W \& 2) = \frac{80}{600}$	$P(W \& 3) = \frac{276}{600}$	$P(W) = \frac{64}{100}$
Marginal Probability		$P(1) = \frac{1}{6}$	$P(2) = \frac{2}{6}$	$P(3) = \frac{3}{6}$	

The six entries $P(B \& 1)$, $P(W \& 1)$, $P(B \& 2)$, and so on are called *joint probabilities*. They were computed using (15.2) and the already available data. For example

$$P(B \& 1) = P(B|1)P(1) = (\tfrac{72}{100})(\tfrac{1}{6}) = \tfrac{72}{600}$$
$$P(W \& 1) = P(W|1)P(1) = (\tfrac{28}{100})(\tfrac{1}{6}) = \tfrac{28}{600}$$

Marginal Probabilities and so on. The values on the lower and right rim of Figure 15.25 are called *marginal probabilities*, which is simply another term for what we have referred to as *unconditional probabilities*. You can see that each marginal probability is the sum of the joint probabilities in the appropriate row or column. For example, we see that

$$P(B) = P(B \& 1) + P(B \& 2) + P(B \& 3)$$
$$= \tfrac{72}{600} + \tfrac{120}{600} + \tfrac{24}{600} = \tfrac{36}{100}$$

Now let us see how Figure 15.25 can be used to calculate conditional probabilities. To do this, we simply use expression (15.2). For example, suppose we wish to calculate

$P(B|1)$. Using (15.2) we see that

$$P(B \ \& \ 1) = P(B|1)P(1)$$

which yields

$$P(B|1) = P(B \ \& \ 1)/P(1)$$

You can see that the data required to evaluate the right side of this equality are available in Figure 15.25. Thus

$$P(B|1) = P(B \ \& \ 1)/P(1) = (\tfrac{72}{600})/(\tfrac{1}{6}) = 0.72$$

Similarly, to calculate $P(1|B)$ we again use expression (15.2) as follows:

$$P(B \ \& \ 1) = P(1|B)P(B)$$

or

$$P(1|B) = P(B \ \& \ 1)/P(B)$$

Again, the data to evaluate the right side of this equality are available in Figure 15.25. Thus

$$P(1|B) = P(B \ \& \ 1)/P(B) = (\tfrac{72}{600})/(\tfrac{36}{100}) = \tfrac{2}{6}$$

Prior and Posterior Probabilities

Note that this agrees with the result we derived in (15.6) by applying Bayes' Theorem. In summary, expression (15.2), along with a table of marginal and joint probabilities such as Figure 15.25, allows us to compute all conditional probabilities. We conclude this subsection by introducing the language that is typically used to describe the type of process just presented. The original probabilities $P(1) = \tfrac{1}{6}$, and so on, are referred to as *prior probabilities* (i.e., before the new information that the ball is black). The updated conditional probabilities [e.g., $P(1|B)$] are called *posterior probabilities* (i.e., after the new information).

The Market Research Example Continued

Recall that the management of **PROTRAC**'s domestic tractor division had all but decided to implement the basic (B) marketing and production strategy for the new line of home and garden tractors. The analysis was based on the assessment that $P(S) = 0.45$, that is, the probability of a strong market is 0.45. The board of directors has now ordered them to have a marketing research study taken before deciding which strategy (A—aggressive, B—basic, C—cautious) to select. In this subsection we will see how to use Bayes' Theorem to incorporate the results of the marketing research study into the decision process. The end result will be an updating for the values of $P(S)$ and $P(W)$.

The marketing research group has agreed to report within a month whether according to their study the test is encouraging (E) or discouraging (D). We now assume that the marketing research group is able to state the following indication of reliability: "The past results with our test have tended to be in the right direction. If a market has been strong, the test results have been encouraging 60% of the time and discouraging 40% of the time. If a market has been weak, the test results have been discouraging

70% of the time and encouraging 30% of the time." Management can use this information to assess the conditional probabilities of the test results given the market conditions. This assessment is

Reliability of the Test

$$P(E|S) = 0.6 \qquad P(E|W) = 0.3$$
$$P(D|S) = 0.4 \qquad P(D|W) = 0.7$$

We now represent management's problem with the decision tree presented in Figure 15.26. The first node (I) corresponds to performing the marketing research. The node is circular because the outcome is not certain. There are two possible results. Either the test is encouraging (E) or discouraging (D); $P(E)$ and $P(D)$ represent the probabilities of these two outcomes.

FIGURE 15.26
Decision Tree with Test Results

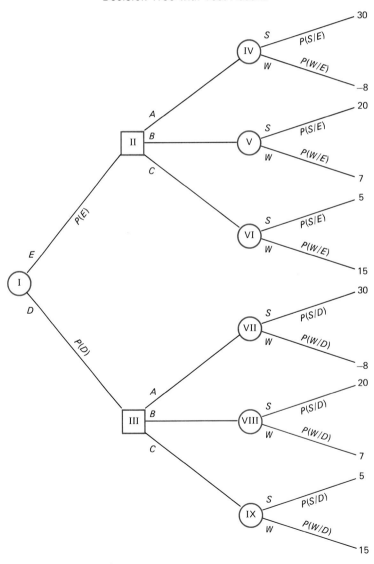

If the test is encouraging, we proceed to node II, which is square because a decision must be made. Management must decide to select A or B or C. Suppose that management selects A. We are then led to node IV, another situation with two possible outcomes, namely whether the market is strong (S) or weak (W). If it turns out to be strong, **PROTRAC** will enjoy a net return of 30, which is the terminal value on the branch.

It is important to note that the tree is created in the chronological order in which information becomes available and decisions are required; that is

Importance of Chronological Order

1. Test result.
2. Make decision.
3. Market condition.

In order to solve this tree we must find the values for $P(S|E)$, $P(W|E)$, $P(S|D)$, $P(W|D)$, $P(E)$, and $P(D)$. This is accomplished by using Bayes' Theorem with the data $P(E|S) = 0.6$, $P(D|S) = 0.4$, $P(E|W) = 0.3$, $P(D|W) = 0.7$, $P(S) = 0.45$, and $P(W) = 0.55$. Adapting (15.3) to this problem, we see that

$$P(E) = P(E|S) \cdot P(S) + P(E|W) \cdot P(W)$$

$$= (0.6)(0.45) + (0.3)(0.55) = 0.435$$

Thus, the probability that the marketing research study will be encouraging is 0.435. This implies that the probability that it is discouraging must be 0.565. Thus, $P(D) = 0.565$. In this setting, (15.4) becomes

$$P(S|E) = \frac{P(E|S)P(S)}{P(E)} = \frac{(0.6)(0.45)}{0.435} \approx 0.621$$

Updating $P(S)$

Thus, the event of an encouraging test result, and the use of Bayes' Theorem, allows us to update the prior value of $P(S)$, namely 0.45, to a higher value, $P(S|E) = 0.621$. Similar calculations yield $P(W|E) = 0.379$, $P(S|D) = 0.318$, and $P(W|D) = 0.682$.

In Figure 15.27 the probabilities are attached to the decision tree. The first step in solving the tree is to fold it back to the terminal nodes.

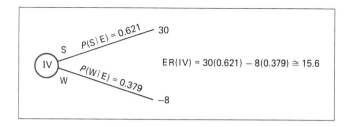

For example, node IV is folded back by calculating its expected return and assigning it to the node. Figure 15.28 shows the tree after the first step. This figure can be used to determine the optimal decisions. We see that if the test is encouraging (E), we arrive at node II. Then to maximize the expected return, we should take action A, that is, follow the aggressive production and marketing strategy. Similarly, if the test result is discouraging, we should take action C. Why? Because 11.81 is the largest possible expected return when the test is discouraging.

FIGURE 15.27
Decision Tree with New Information

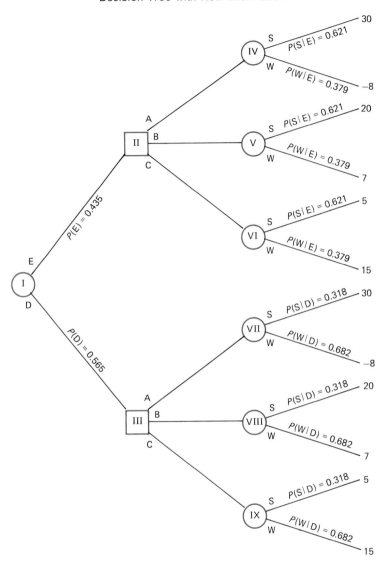

The Expected Value of Sample Information Suppose that we use the optimal decisions determined above to fold back the decision tree shown in Figure 15.28 one more step. We obtain

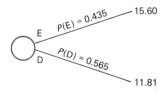

The expected return then is

$$ER = 15.60(0.435) + 11.81(0.565) \approx 13.46$$

FIGURE 15.28

Decision Tree After One Foldback

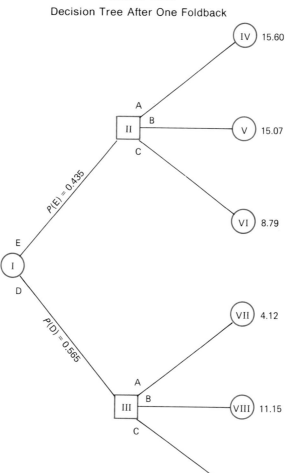

This value is the expected return of performing the market test and making optimal decisions.

In Section 15.6 we saw that if the market test is not performed, the optimal decision is to select B, the basic strategy, and that this decision has an expected return of 12.85. Clearly then, performing the market test increases **PROTRAC**'s expected return **EVSI** by $13.46 - 12.85 = 0.61$. Appropriately enough, this quantity is called the *expected value of sample information* (EVSI). In general terms

$$\text{EVSI} = \begin{pmatrix} \text{maximum possible} \\ \text{expected return} \\ \text{with sample} \\ \text{information} \end{pmatrix} - \begin{pmatrix} \text{maximum possible} \\ \text{expected return} \\ \text{without sample} \\ \text{information} \end{pmatrix}$$

Let us now calculate the expected value of *perfect* information. Recall from Section 15.3 that this is the amount that management would be willing to pay for perfect information. The payoff table originally presented in Figure 15.17 is reproduced on the next page for your convenience (Figure 15.29).

FIGURE 15.29

	STATE OF NATURE	
	S	W
	PROBABILITY	
DECISION	0.45	0.55
A	30	−8
B	20	7
C	5	15

EVPI and EVSI Compared If it were sure that the market would be strong, management would pick decision A and enjoy a return of 30. Similarly, if it were sure that the market would be weak, management would pick decision C and enjoy a return of 15. How much would management pay for perfect information? Since perfect information will reveal a strong market with probability 0.45, and a weak market with probability 0.55, we see that

$$\text{EVPI} = (30)(0.45) + (15)(0.55) - 12.85 \approx 8.90 \qquad (15.7)$$

Equation (15.7) tells us that perfect information will bring us an expected increase of 8.90 over the previous expected return. This is the maximum possible increase in the expected return which can be obtained from new information. The expected value of sample information EVSI is the increase in the expected return that was obtained with the information produced by the market test. Since EVPI = 8.9 and EVSI = 0.61, we see that the market test is not very effective. If it were, the value for EVSI would be much closer to EVPI.

_____ 15.9
SEQUENTIAL DECISIONS: TO TEST OR NOT TO TEST

In the preceding section, we assumed that the board of directors had decided to have a market research study done. We then considered the question of how the management of **PROTRAC**'s domestic tractor division should use the information generated by the study to update the decision model. Let us step back for a moment. It seems clear that the decision to have a market study done is in essence no different from the decision to adopt one marketing and production strategy or another. Management must carefully weigh the cost of performing the study against the gain that might result from having the information that the study would produce. It is also clear that the decision on whether to have a market research test is not an isolated decision. If the test is given, management must still select one of the marketing and production strategies. Thus, the value of performing the test depends in part on how **PROTRAC** uses the information generated by the test. In other words, the value of an initial decision depends on a *sequence* of decisions and uncertain events that will follow the initial decision. This is called a *sequential*

Sequential Decision Problems *decision problem.*

This is an extremely common type of management problem and is actually the kind of situation that decision trees are designed to handle. It is in situations where there are a number of interrelated decisions and events with more than one possible outcome that the ability to display the problem graphically is especially useful.

FIGURE 15.30

Test or No-Test Tree with Returns
and Probabilities Assigned

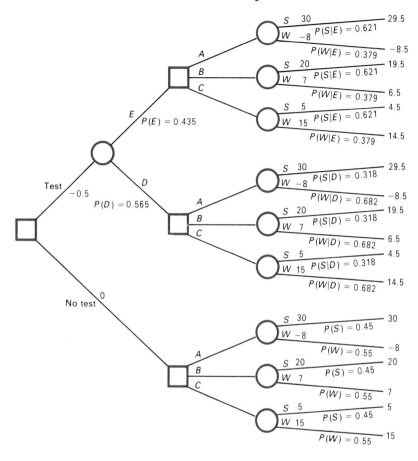

Figure 15.30 shows the test or no-test tree. In terms of structure and the probabilities, you see that the upper (test) branch is the tree from Figure 15.27 and the lower (no test) branch is the tree from Figure 15.19.

The terminal values merit some discussion. They are determined in a two-step process:

Determination of Terminal Values

1. Assign the appropriate cash flow to each decision and uncertain event. In this problem we have assumed that the market test costs $500,000. Since all costs and returns are measured in millions, a figure of -0.5 is placed by the test branch and a figure of 0 is placed by the no-test branch. Similarly, a figure 30 is placed on the upper branch since this is the profit if **PROTRAC** selects A and the market is strong.

2. Determine a particular terminal value by adding the cash flows on all branches between the first node and the terminal position. For example, the number 29.5 on the uppermost terminal position comes from adding the costs on the path Test–E–A–S (i.e., costs of $-0.5 + 0 + 0 + 30 = 29.5$).

You solve this tree by folding it back. You fold back a circular node by calculating the expected returns. You fold back a square (decision) node by selecting the decision

FIGURE 15.31
Solving the Test or No-Test Tree

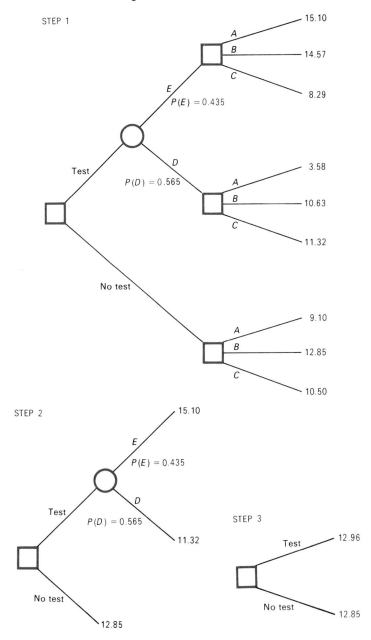

that yields the highest expected return. Three steps are required to solve the test or no-test tree. They are shown in Figure 15.31.

The Optimal Strategy   The *optimal strategy* is a complete plan for the entire tree. It specifies what action to take no matter which of the uncertain events occurs. To determine the optimal strategy for the test or no-test tree, we refer to Figure 15.31. From step 3 we see that since 12.96 > 12.85, **PROTRAC** should have the market test. From step 1 we see that if the result of the test is encouraging (E), then A is the best decision since it yields the largest expected return. Similarly, if the result of the test is discouraging (D), then C is the best decision.

MANAGEMENT AND DECISION THEORY

A typical management decision has the following characteristics:

1. It is made once and only once (e.g., should I buy one hundred shares of IBM stock today or not?)
2. The return depends on an uncertain event that will occur in the future (e.g., the price of IBM stock will go up or down), and we have no historical information about this event.

We know about related events that may tell us something about the likelihood of the various outcomes (e.g., the behavior of the price of IBM stock last week). But we cannot perform an experiment to provide a good, reliable estimate of the relevant probabilities (e.g., we cannot perform an experiment that tells us about the price of IBM stock next week.)

Reviewing the Conceptual Framework

What does the material in this chapter contribute to our understanding of how to attack this problem? In brief, this chapter recommends the following conceptual framework:

1. For each decision, determine the utility of each possible outcome.
2. Determine the probability of each possible outcome.
3. Calculate the expected utility of each decision.
4. Select the decision with the largest expected utility.

Once the first two steps are completed the next two steps are easy, at least conceptually. But how can you *know* the probabilities and the utilities?

Probabilities and Utilities are Subjective Assessments

The answer is that there are no values to *know*. These are not entities, the "true" value of which can be revealed by experimentation or further analysis. Indeed, these two quantities, *probabilities* and *utilities*, are *subjective* and represent the *best judgment and taste of the manager*. Certainly the manager's evaluation of these two quantities can be influenced by study, but there is no opportunity for direct experimentation with the underlying phenomena, as there would be, for example, in physical or biological science.

There is, nevertheless, some structure to cling to in this sea of subjectivity. The structure is provided by a logical device called an *equivalent lottery*. This concept gives one a *consistent framework* for quantifying both probabilities and utilities. We will first show how a manager can use an equivalent lottery to create a utility function.

The Equivalent Lottery

At the outset, the manager can arbitrarily select the end points of the utility function. It is a convenient convention to set the utility of the smallest net dollar return equal to 0 and the utility of the largest net return equal to 1. Consider an example with possible returns of -30, 10, and 45. If the function $U(x)$ specifies the utility of x dollars, then the manager sets $U(-30) = 0$ and $U(45) = 1$. To assess $U(10)$, the utility of 10, he proceeds by selecting a probability of p such that he is indifferent between the following two alternatives:

Alternative 1. **Receive a payment of 10 for sure (with certainty).**

Alternative 2. **Participate in a lottery in which the payoff is 45 with a probability p or -30 with a probability $1 - p$.**

Clearly if $p = 1$, the manager prefers alternative 2, since a payment of 45 is preferable to a payment of 10. Equally clear, if $p = 0$, the manager prefers alternative 1, since a payment of 10 is preferable to a loss of 30 (i.e., a payment of -30). It seems reasonable, then, to assert that somewhere between 0 and 1 there is a value for p such that the decision maker is indifferent between the two alternatives. We call this value of p *the utility for 10.*

Assessing Subjective Probabilities

The manager can use this approach to assess a subjective probability. Suppose, for example, that on this date you wish to assess the probability that George Bush will be the Republican candidate for President in 1988. The first step is to think of two games. In game 1 you receive $100 if Bush is the candidate and $0 if he is not. In game 2 you receive $100 with probability p and $0 with probability $1 - p$. You now adjust the value of p until you are indifferent between the two games. The resulting value of p is *your* subjective probability that Bush will be the Republican candidate in 1988. It is clear that your assessment may be different from that of Barbara Bush or Tip O'Neil.

We have argued that the equivalent lottery allows one to quantify both subjective probability and utility. We now stress again that the values obtained through this process are personal and a matter of judgment, and thus by definition they will vary from person to person. Certainly, then, two individuals, each of whom is facing the same decision and using the recommended approach, may arrive at different decisions. And why not! The recommended approach allows the decision maker to incorporate personal knowledge (and experience), and surely there is no reason to believe that everyone will "know" the same things at the moment of decision.

The Advantage of the Lottery Approach

However, a cynic might ask, "Why bother with all this machinery?" If judgment and taste play such an important role in these assessments, isn't it better to use judgment in a holistic approach and simply select the alternative that intuitively seems best? What do we gain from assessing probability and utility separately? The reply is that separating the two assessments makes it possible for a manager to concentrate attention on each of these entities (probability and utility), one at a time. The problem with a simple intuitive approach is that we humans have a hard time thinking about more than one thing at a time. While thinking about payoffs, it is hard at the same time to be thinking about likelihoods and then to combine them in one's head. In other words, the simple, intuitive approach makes it too easy to put heavy emphasis on a particularly awful outcome (or a particularly attractive outcome) and not enough weight on the fact that this outcome may be extremely unlikely. As an example, look at the number of people who won't fly in an airplane, but will drive in a car. *Separating the assessments of probabilities and utilities forces a manager to give appropriate and separate consideration to each entity before combining the two to determine the final decision.*

PC Software

The revolution in personal computing and the explosion in software that has accompanied it has had an impact on decision analysis. A few years ago, general-purpose decision analysis programs from commercial software suppliers were not widely available. Some companies created programs for their own purposes, but these were not available to the general public. At this writing at least three microcomputer packages (Arborist, Riskcalc, and Supertree) are similar in the sense that each enables the user to use the power of the personal computer to carry out the various tasks associated with decision trees.

_____ **15.11**

NOTES ON IMPLEMENTATION

In practice, the material in this chapter is included under the more general heading of "decision analysis." Ralph Keeney, a leading scholar in the field, defines decision analysis as "a formalization of common sense for decision problems which are too complex for informal use of common sense." Decision analysis, which is based on axioms originally stated by von Neumann and Morgenstern, involves assigning probabilities and utilities to possible outcomes and maximizing expected utility. This approach is applied to highly complex problems that are typically sequential in nature. It can be thought of as having four parts: (1) structuring the problem, (2) assessing the probability of the possible outcomes, (3) determining the utility of the possible outcomes, and (4) evaluating alternatives and selecting a strategy.

Much of the material in this chapter concerns item 4, the technical process of evaluating alternatives and selecting a strategy. This is appropriate since this is the conceptual heart of decision analysis. In practice, however, this is the easy part of the problem. A significantly greater proportion of effort is spent on the other three areas. Structuring the problem, which involves generating alternatives and specifying objectives in numerically measurable terms, is a particularly unstructured task. In some of the applications, objectives have been quantified in the areas of environmental impact, public health and safety, and so on.

Role of Personal Judgment

It is important to understand that decision analysis does *not* provide a completely objective analysis of complicated problems. Many aspects of a decision analysis require personal judgment—whether it be structuring the problem, assessing probabilities, or assigning utilities. In many important complex problems there simply are not enough empirical data to provide a basis for complete analysis. Nevertheless, experience has shown that the framework provided by decision analysis has been useful.

In the early 1960s decision analysis began to be successfully applied to a number of problems in the private sector. These include problems of gas and oil exploration as well as capital investment. Although developments have continued on private sector problems, two other general problem areas have witnessed a wide variety of applications of decision analysis. In the health care field, decision analysis has been applied to such diverse problems as the evaluation of new drugs, the analysis of treatment strategies for diseases, and the selection of medical technology for a particular facility. The second problem area concerns applications in the government. In particular, decision analysis has been applied to everything from the seeding of hurricanes, to the negotiation of international oil tanker standards, to the choice between coal and nuclear technology for large-scale power plants. A readable overview of decision analysis with an extensive bibliography is available in "Decision Analysis: An Overview," *Operations Research*, September–October 1982.

15.12
SUMMARY

The first part of this chapter deals with the fundamentals of decision theory. A summary of this material is provided in Section 15.5. The following four sections are devoted to decision trees, a graphical device for attacking problems in which a sequence of decisions must be made, and these decisions are interspersed with events that have several possible outcomes. It is typically true that square nodes are used to represent decisions and round nodes are used to represent events. The branches emanating from a square node are the possible decisions and the branches emanating from a round node are the possible outcomes. When a decision tree has been completed, a path from the start of the tree to a terminal node represents a specific sequence of decisions and uncertain events. The complete tree represents all possible such sequences.

Solving a decision tree is a sequential process that starts at the terminal nodes and proceeds back to the start of the tree in a process that is described as "folding back."

The process includes two steps: The branches emanating from a round node are folded back by assigning to the node the expected value of the chance events; branches emanating from a decision node are folded back by selecting the alternative with the maximum expected return and assigning this value to the decision node. The solution of a decision tree yields an optimal strategy; that is, it specifies what sequence of actions should be taken for any of the possible sequences of chance events.

Bayes' Theorem plays an important role in the construction of decision trees, because this is the device that makes it possible to incorporate new information into the decision process in a formal way. Bayes' Theorem is based on the concept of conditional probability, and thus some time is devoted to that general topic.

The expected value of sample information is a measure of the value of incorporating sample information into a decision under uncertainty. The expected value of perfect information is an upper bound on the value of sample information.

───── 15.13
KEY TERMS

PAYOFF TABLE. A table showing the returns for each possible state of nature–decision combination in a decision against nature.

DECISION UNDER CERTAINTY. A decision against nature in which the state of nature is known with certainty.

DECISION UNDER RISK. A decision against nature in which a probability distribution on the states of nature is known.

DECISION UNDER UNCERTAINTY. A decision against nature with no knowledge about the likelihood of the various states of nautre.

MAXIMIN. A conservative decision criterion of maximizing the minimum return.

MAXIMAX. A optimistic decision criterion of maximizing the maximum return.

REGRET. A measure of how much better the decision maker could have done had he or she known the state of nature (the opportunity cost of not making the best decision for a given state of nature).

EXPECTED VALUE OF PERFECT INFORMATION. An upper bound on the value of new information.

UTILITY. In this chapter, a measure of the "value" of money to an individual.

RISK AVERSE. A preference to avoid downside risks, precisely reflected in a concave utility function.

RISK SEEKING. A preference for upside returns, precisely reflected in a convex utility function.

RISK INDIFFERENT. Reflected by a linear utility function.

EQUIVALENT LOTTERY. A device for creating a utility function.

DECISION TREE. A graphical device for analyzing decisions under risk.

CIRCULAR NODE. Indicates a nondeterministic event on a decision tree.

BRANCH. The lines emanating from the nodes in a decision tree.

FOLDING BACK. The process of solving a decision tree by working backward.

TERMINAL POSITION. The end of a branch emanating from a terminal node.

TERMINAL NODE. A node in a decision tree that is not succeeded by other nodes.

TERMINAL VALUE. The net return associated with a terminal position.

PRIOR PROBABILITIES. The originally assessed values for probabilities.

POSTERIOR PROBABILITIES. An updated probability. The updating combines the prior probabilities and new information with Bayes law.

DECISION STRATEGY. A plan that prescribes which decision to take for any possible series of outcomes.

CONDITIONAL PROBABILITY. The probability of an event (say, B) given that another event (say, A) occurs; denoted $P(B|A)$ and defined $P(B|A) = P(B \text{ and } A)/P(A)$.

SQUARE NODE. A node showing a marked lack of social development and abusively used in certain decision tree diagrams. Or: a point at which a decision must be made.

MAJOR CONCEPTS QUIZ

True–False

1. **T F** Decision trees involve sequences of decisions and random outcomes.
2. **T F** In decision theory, returns are dependent on the actions of an indifferent adversary termed "nature."
3. **T F** One underlying aspect of decision theory is that, regardless of what we assume about nature, in terms of whether we know probabilities of various states, we are led to the same criterion for selecting a "best decision."
4. **T F** Many deterministic optimization models can be thought of as decision making under certainty, where there is only one state of nature and one selects a decision that maximizes returns.
5. **T F** One way to deal with decision making in the "uncertainty" context is to treat all states of nature as equally likely and maximize expected return.
6. **T F** The computation of the value of perfect information is based on the concept that all randomness has been eliminated.
7. **T F** Maximizing expected net dollar return always yields the same optimal policy as minimizing expected regret.
8. **T F** A risk-averse utility function is convex.
9. **T F** Decision trees are solved by folding forward.
10. **T F** Bayes Theorem provides a formula for how one can use new information to update a prior probability assessment.

Multiple Choice

11. Decision theory is concerned with
    a. the amount of information that is available
    b. criteria for measuring the "goodness" of a decision
    c. selecting optimal decisions in sequential problems
    d. all of the above
12. Concerning decision making under risk, which of the following is not true?
    a. We assume that the decision maker knows the probability with which each state of nature will occur.
    b. We use the criterion of maximizing return.
    c. We use the criterion of maximizing expected return.
    d. We use the criterion of minimizing expected regret.
13. Which of the following criteria does *not* apply to decision making under uncertainty?
    a. maximin return
    b. maximax return
    c. minimax regret
    d. maximize expected return
14. Maximin return, maximax return, and minimax regret are criteria that
    a. lead to the same optimal decision
    b. can be used without probabilities
    c. both a and b
15. The expected value of perfect information (EVPI)
    a. places two-sided bounds (upper and lower) on how much should be spent in gathering information

b. can be determined without using probabilities

c. refers to the utility of additional information

d. equals the expected regret of the optimal decision under risk

16. The concept of utility is a way to

  a. measure the attractiveness of money

  b. take into account aversion to risk

  c. take into account inclination to take risk

  d. a and b

  e. a, b, and c

17. Which of the following does not apply to a decision tree?

  a. A square node is a point at which a decision must be made.

  b. A circular node represents an encounter with uncertainty.

  c. One chooses a sequence of decisions which has the greatest probability of success.

  d. One attempts to maximize expected return.

18. The expected value of perfect information (EVPI)

  a. shows the cost necessary to produce perfect information about the future.

  b. shows the maximum possible increase in expected return with sample information

  c. shows the expected increase in information required to select the optimal decision

  d. all of the above

19. When computing the expected value of perfect information (EVPI) it is important that the payment is made

  a. in advance of receiving the information

  b. after receiving the information

  c. in an irrevocable way

  d. both (a) and (c)

20. When decisions are made sequentially in time

  a. decision trees cannot be employed

  b. Bayes Theorem must be used

  c. the terminal value at the end of each sequence of branches is the net of the cash flows on that sequence

  d. the terminal value at the end of each sequence of branches is an expected net cash flow

Answers

1. T	6. F	11. d	16. e
2. T	7. T	12. b	17. c
3. F	8. F	13. d	18. b
4. T	9. F	14. b	19. d
5. T	10. T	15. d	20. c

PROBLEMS

15-1. Consider the payoff table shown in Figure 15.32, in which the entries are net dollar returns. Assume that this is a decision with no knowledge about the states of nature.

FIGURE 15.32

DECISION	STATE OF NATURE			
	1	2	3	4
1	35	22	25	12
2	27	25	20	18
3	22	25	25	28
4	20	25	28	33

(a) What is the optimal decision if the Laplace criterion is used?

(b) What is the optimal decision if the maximin criterion is used?

(c) What is the optimal decision if the maximax criterion is used?

(d) Create the payoff table in which the entries are regret.

(e) What is the optimal decision if the criterion of minimax regret is used?

15-2. Consider the payoff table shown in Figure 15.33, in which the entries are net dollar returns. Assume that this is a decision with no knowledge about the states of nature.

FIGURE 15.33

	STATE OF NATURE		
DECISION	1	2	3
1	6	0	9
2	5	6	3
3	2	8	7

(a) What is the optimal decision if the Laplace criterion is used?

(b) What is the optimal decision if the maximin criterion is used?

(c) What is the optimal solution if the maximax criterion is used?

(d) Create the payoff table in which the entries are regret.

(e) What is the optimal decision if the criterion of minimax regret is used?

15-3. Consider the payoff table in Figure 15.32. Assume that the following probabilities are specified for the states of nature:

$$P(1) = 0.1, \qquad P(2) = 0.4, \qquad P(3) = 0.3, \qquad P(4) = 0.2$$

(a) Find the decision that maximizes the expected net dollar return.

(b) Find the decision that minimizes the expected regret.

(c) Comment on the relationship between the answers to parts (a) and (b).

15-4. Consider the payoff matrix in Figure 15.33. Assume that the probabilities of the states of nature are as follows:

$$P(1) = \tfrac{1}{4} \qquad P(2) = \tfrac{1}{2} \qquad P(3) = \tfrac{1}{4}$$

(a) Find the decision that maximizes the expected net dollar return.

(b) Find the decision that minimizes the expected regret.

Suppose that $P(1)$ and $P(2)$ are not known, but $P(3)$ is estimated to be $\tfrac{1}{4}$.

(c) Plot expected net dollar return versus $P(2)$ for the three decisions in the same graph, and find the range for $P(2)$ for which each decision is optimal.

(d) Plot expected regret versus $P(2)$ for the three decisions in the same graph, and find the range for $P(2)$ for which each decision is optimal.

(e) What did you find in the above two answers?

15-5. Phil Johnson of Johnson's Printing in Chicago must decide either to accept a contract for a government form printing job or fly to L.A. to bid on a brochure. Capacity constraints prohibit him from doing both jobs and he must decide on the government contract before the bidding process starts. He estimates the payoff table in terms of net dollar return as shown in Figure 15.34.

FIGURE 15.34

	STATE OF NATURE	
DECISION	DO NOT GET BROCHURE JOB, NJ	GET BROCHURE JOB, J
Accept Government Contract, G	1000	1000
Accept Brochure Job, B	−1000	4000

(a) What is the optimal decision based on the maximin criterion?

(b) If the probability that he gets the brochure job is $\frac{1}{3}$, which decision will maximize his expected net dollar return?

(c) Let $P(J)$ be the probability that he gets the brochure job. Plot the expected return for each decision as a function of $P(J)$ on the same axis.

(d) What is the smallest value of $P(J)$ for which Phil Johnson should decide to go to L.A. if he wishes to maximize his expected net dollar return?

(e) What is the optimal decision if minimax regret is the decision criterion?

(f) What is the optimal decision if minimize expected regret is the decision criterion and $P(J) = \frac{1}{3}$?

(g) Assume that the purchasing agent for the brochure job has already decided who will receive the bid but Phil doesn't know the result. If Phil believes that $P(J) = \frac{1}{3}$, what is the maximum amount that Phil should pay to have this information?

(h) What would you call the quantity calculated in part (g)?

15-6. A souvenir vendor discovers that sales in July depend heavily on the weather. Products must be ordered in January. The wholesaler offers small, medium, and large variety packs at special prices, and the vendor must decide to buy one of them. The payoff table in terms of net dollar return is shown in Figure 15.35.

FIGURE 15.35

	STATE OF NATURE			
DECISION	COLD	COOL	WARM	HOT
Small	0	1000	2000	3000
Medium	−1000	0	3000	6000
Large	−3000	−1000	4000	8000

The utility function for money is presented in Figure 15.36. If the vendor believes that each state of nature is equally likely

(a) Which decision maximizes the expected net dollar return?

(b) Which decision maximizes the expected utility?

(c) Explain the relationship between the answers to parts (a) and (b).

15-7. Phil Johnson of Johnson's Printing (see Problem 15-5) has decided to use the utility function shown in Figure 15.36 to determine if he should bid on the brochure job.

FIGURE 15.36

Utility Function

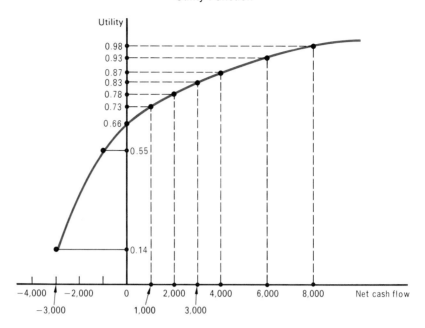

(a) What is the optimal decision if the decision criterion is to maximize the expected net dollar return and the probability of getting the brochure job is $\frac{1}{3}$? What is the expected net dollar return of the optimal decision?

(b) Would you expect the decision to change if the decision criterion is to maximize the expected utility? Discuss.

(c) What is the expected utility of the optimal decision?

(d) What is the utility of the expected dollar return from submitting a bid for the brochure?

(e) What is the expected utility of submitting a bid for the brochure?

(f) Are the answers to parts (d) and (e) the same? Should they be?

15-8. Assign a utility of 0 to a net cash flow of $-\$20,000$ and a utility of 1 to a net cash flow of $\$50,000$. Create your own utility function by the following steps:

(a) Find equivalent lotteries for net cash flows of $0 and $20,000.

(b) Plot the four points on your utility function and connect them with straight lines.

(c) Based on this utility function, are you risk averse, risk seeking, risk indifferent, or none of the above?

15-9. Assume you are risk averse and have assigned the following two end points on your utility function:

$$U(-30) = 0$$

$$U(70) = 1$$

(a) What is a lower bound on $U(30)$?
Suppose that you are indifferent between a sure payment of 30 and a lottery with a probability of 0.7 of winning 70 and a probability of 0.3 of losing 30.

(b) What is a lower bound on your utility for a sure payment of 50?

(c) What is the smallest upper bound of your utility for a sure payment of 10?

HINT: Recall that a utility function is nondecreasing and if the decision maker is risk averse, it is concave.

15-10. Assume that you have assigned the following two end points on your utility function:

$$U(-30) = 0$$

$$U(70) = 1$$

Suppose that you are indifferent between a sure payment of 30 and a lottery with a probability of 0.3 of winning 70 and a probability of 0.7 of losing 30. Furthermore, you feel that a sure payment of 10 is equivalent to a gamble with a probability of 0.9 of losing 30 and a probability of 0.1 of winning 30.

(a) How can you describe your utility function? Are you a risk-lover?

(b) What are upper and lower bounds on $U(50)$?

(c) What are upper and lower bounds on $U(25)$?

15-11. The customer service manager for **PROTRAC** is responsible for expediting late orders. To do the job effectively, when an order is late the manager must determine if the lateness is caused by an ordering error or a delivery error. If an order is late, one or the other of these two types of errors must have occurred. Because of the way in which this system is designed, both errors cannot occur on the same order. From past experience, the manager knows that an ordering error will cause 8 out of 20 deliveries to be late, whereas a delivery error will cause 8 out of 10 deliveries to be late. Historically, out of 1000 orders, 30 ordering errors and 10 delivery errors have occurred. Assume that an order is late. If the customer service manager wishes to look first for the type of error that has the largest probability of occurring, should it be an ordering error or a delivery error?

15-12. The Scrub Professional Cleaning Service receives preliminary sales contracts from two sources: (1) its own agent and (2) building managers. Historically, $\frac{3}{8}$ of the contracts have come from Scrub agents and $\frac{5}{8}$ from building managers. Unfortunately, not all preliminary contracts result in actual sales contracts. Actually, only $\frac{1}{2}$ of those preliminary contracts received from building managers result in a sale, whereas $\frac{3}{4}$ of those received from Scrub agents result in a sale. The net return to Scrub from a sale is $1600. The cost of processing and following up on a preliminary contract that does not result in a sale is $160.

(a) What is the probability that a preliminary contract leads to a sale? What is the expected return associated with a preliminary sales contract?

(b) Which party, agents or building managers, contributes more to the expected return?

Scrub keeps all of its sales filed by the source of reference; that is, it maintains one file for sales resulting from preliminary contracts submitted by Scrub agents and another for sales resulting from preliminary contracts submitted by building managers. Scrub knows that John Jones holds one of its sales contracts and it wishes to have more information about him.

(c) Which file should it search first to have the higher probability of finding his name?

15-13. Clyde's Coal Company sells coal by the $\frac{1}{2}$-ton, 1-ton, or 2-ton load. The probability is 0.20 that an order is from town A; 0.30 for town B; and 0.50 from town C. The relative frequency of the number of orders of each size from each town is shown in Figure 15.37.

(a) What is the probability that an order will be for $\frac{1}{2}$ ton?

(b) If an order is for $\frac{1}{2}$ ton, what is the probability that it came from town A?

Clyde makes a different amount of profit on each type of load of coal in each city. The profit figures are shown in Figure 15.38.

(c) Find the expected profit per load for Clyde.

FIGURE 15.37

Relative Frequencies of Number
of Orders for Each Town

TOWN	LOAD SIZE (TONS)		
	$\frac{1}{2}$	1	2
A	0.50	0.00	0.50
B	0.00	0.50	0.50
C	0.25	0.75	0.00

FIGURE 15.38

Profit in Dollars per Load

TOWN	LOAD SIZE (TONS)		
	$\frac{1}{2}$	1	2
A	100	190	370
B	90	200	360
C	70	130	270

15-14. Walter's Dog and Pony Show is scheduled to appear in Cedar Rapids on July 14. The profits obtained are heavily dependent on the weather. In particular, if the weather is rainy, the show loses $15,000, and if sunny the show makes a profit of $10,000. (We assume that all days are either rainy or sunny.) Walter can decide to cancel the show, but if he does he forfeits a $1000 deposit he put down when he accepted the date. The historical record shows that on July 14 it has rained $\frac{1}{4}$ of the time in the last 100 years.

(a) What decision should Walter make to maximize his expected net dollar return?

(b) What is the expected value of perfect information?

15-15. Consider the problem faced by Walter in Problem 15-14. Walter has the option to purchase a forecast from Victor's Weather Wonder. Victor's accuracy varies. On those occasions when it has rained, he has been correct (i.e., he predicted rain) 90% of the time. On the other hand, when it has been sunny, he has been right (i.e., he predicted sun) only 80% of the time.

(a) If Walter had the forecast, what strategy should he follow to maximize his expected net dollar return?

(b) How much should Walter be willing to pay to have the forecast?

15-16. A gambler has an opportunity to play the following two-stage game. At stage 1 he pays $10 and draws a ball at random from an urn containing 45 white and 55 red balls. The balls are identical except for color. The player may now quit or move on to play stage 2 at the cost of an additional $10. In stage 2, if a white ball was drawn in stage 1, the player draws a ball at random from a white urn that contains 15 blue and 95 green balls. If a red ball was drawn in stage 1, the player draws a ball at random from a red urn that contains 70 blue and 30 green balls. If in stage 2 the player draws a blue ball, the house pays him $50. If he draws a green ball, the house pays him $0. Use a decision tree to determine the optimal strategy for the gambler.

15-17. A certain retail firm places applicants for credit into two categories, bad risks and good risks. Statistics indicate that 10% of the population would be classified as a bad risk by the firm's standards. The firm uses a credit-scoring device to decide whether credit should be granted to an applicant. Experience suggests that if a good risk applies, the person will get credit 90% of the time. If a bad risk applies, credit will be granted 20% of the time. Management believes that it is reasonable to assume that the persons who apply for credit are selected at random from the population. What is the probability that a person granted credit will be a bad risk? (Use Bayes' Theorem.)

15-18. At **PROTRAC**'s Moline plant, crankshafts are produced on each of two large automatic machines. The newer of the two machines is both faster and more reliable than the older machine. Out of a lot size of 1000 crankshafts, 800 would be produced on the new machine. The new machine produces defective crankshafts at the rate of 1 per 100, whereas the old machine produces defects at the rate of 5 per 100.

(a) How many defectives do you expect out of 1000 crankshafts?

(b) What is the probability that a defective piece selected at random was produced on the new machine?

15-19. Johnson's Metal (JM), a small manufacturer of metal parts, is attempting to decide whether to enter the competition to be a supplier of transmission housings for **PRO-TRAC**. In order to compete, the firm must design a test fixture for the production process and produce 10 housings that **PROTRAC** will test. The cost of development, that is, designing and building the fixture and the test housings, is $50,000. If JM gets the order, an event estimated as occurring with probability 0.4, it will be possible to sell 10,000 items to **PROTRAC** for $50 each. If JM does not get the order, the development cost is essentially lost. In order to produce the housings, JM may either use its current machines or purchase a new forge. Tooling with the current machines will cost $40,000 and the per unit production cost is $20. However, if JM uses its current machines, it runs the risk of incurring overtime costs. The relationship between overtime costs and the status of JM's other business is presented in Figure 15.39. The new forge costs $260,000, including tooling costs for the transmission housings. However, with the new forge, JM would certainly not incur any overtime costs, and the production cost will be only $10 per unit. Use a decision tree to determine the optimal set of actions for JM.

FIGURE 15.39
Cost and Probability Data for Johnson's Metal Problem

OTHER BUSINESS	PROBABILITY	OVERTIME COST TO JM
Heavy	0.2	$200,000
Normal	0.7	100,000
Light	0.1	0

15-20. It is January 1 and Justin Case, chief counsel for Chemgoo, is faced with a difficult problem. It seems that the firm has two related lawsuits for patent infringement. For each suit, the firm has the option of going to trial or settling out of court. The trial date for one of the suits, which we will cleverly identify as suit 1, is scheduled for July 15 and the second (suit 2, of course) is scheduled for January 8, next year. Preparation costs for either trial are estimated at $10,000. However, if the firm prepares for both trials, the preparation costs of the second trial will be only $6000. These costs can be avoided by settling out of court. If the firm wins suit 1, it pays no penalty. If it loses, it pays a $200,000 penalty. Lawyers for the firm assess the probability of winning suit 1 as 0.5. The firm has the option to settle out of court for $100,000. Suit 2 can be settled out of court for a cost of $60,000. Otherwise, a trial will result in one of three possible outcomes: (1) the suit is declared invalid and the firm pays no penalty; (2) the suit is found valid but with no infringement, and the firm pays a penalty of $50,000; or (3) the suit is found valid with infringement, and the firm pays a penalty of $90,000. The likelihood of these outcomes depends in general on the result of suit 1. The judge will certainly view suit 1 as an important precedent. The lawyers' assessment of the probability of the three possible outcomes of suit 2 under three sets of possible conditions (relating to suit 1) are presented in Figure 15.40.

FIGURE 15.40

OUTCOMES	NO INFORMATION CONCERNING SUIT 1[a]	FIRM WINS SUIT 1	FIRM LOSES SUIT 1
Invalid	0.3	0.7	0.1
Valid, No infringement	0.3	0.2	0.5
Valid, Infringement	0.4	0.1	0.4

[a] That is, suit 1 is settled out of court.

(a) Represent the firm's problem with a decision tree.

(b) Solve the decision tree and find the optimal strategy for the firm.

(c) What is the expected loss that the firm will incur if it follows the optimal strategy?

(d) What decisions would be made if the firm treated each suit independently, ignoring any interactions between the two? What is the expected savings from the decision analysis of this scenario?

HINT: Since all the figures are costs, you may find it easier to work with the cost figures and minimize the expected cost.

15-21. Olive Branch is a writer of romance novels. A movie company and a TV network both want exclusive rights to one of her most popular works. If she signs with the network she will receive a single lump sum, but if she signs with the movie company the amount she will receive depends on the market response to the movie. Olive's payoffs are summarized in Figure 15.41.

FIGURE 15.41

| | STATE OF NATURE | | |
DECISION	SMALL BOX OFFICE	MEDIUM BOX OFFICE	LARGE BOX OFFICE
Sign with movie company	$200,000	$1,000,000	$3,000,000
Sign with TV network	900,000	900,000	900,000

If the probability estimates for the states of nature are $P(\text{Small}) = 0.3$, $P(\text{Medium}) = 0.6$, $P(\text{Large}) = 0.1$, to whom should Olive sell the rights? What is the most Olive should be willing to pay to learn what the size of the box office would be before she decides with whom to sign?

15-22. Kelly Construction wants to get in on the boom of student condominium construction. The company must decide whether to purchase enough land to build a 100-, 200-, or 300-unit condominium complex. Many other complexes are currently under construction, so Kelly is unsure how strong demand for its complex will be. If the company is conservative and builds only a few units, it loses potential profits if the demand turns out to be high. On the other hand, many unsold units would also be costly to Kelly. Figure 15.42 has been prepared, based on three levels of demand:

FIGURE 15.42

| | DEMAND | | |
DECISION	LOW	MEDIUM	HIGH
Build 100	$500,000	$500,000	$500,000
Build 200	0	1,000,000	1,000,000
Build 300	−700,000	400,000	1,500,000

(a) What is the optimal decision if the maximin criterion is used?

(b) What is the optimal decision if the maximax criterion is used?

(c) What is the optimal decision if the criterion of minimax regret is used?

(d) If $P(\text{Low}) = 0.3$, $P(\text{Medium}) = 0.5$, and $P(\text{High}) = 0.2$, which decision will maximize the expected net dollar return?

(e) What is the expected value of perfect information?

15-23. Marple Manufacturing is planning the introduction of a new product. The cost to set up to manufacture one of the product's components is very high, so Marple is considering purchasing that component rather than manufacturing it. Once set up to manufacture the component, however, Marple's variable cost per unit would be low in comparison to the purchase price of the component. Marple's materials manager has calculated the net profit in thousands of dollars for three different levels of demand in Figure 15.43:

FIGURE 15.43

	DEMAND		
DECISION	LOW	MEDIUM	HIGH
Make component	11	32	53
Buy component	15	30	45

The states of nature have probabilities $P(\text{Low}) = 0.4$, $P(\text{Medium}) = 0.3$, and $P(\text{High}) = 0.3$. Draw a decision tree and use it to decide whether Marple should make or buy the component.

15-24. Chuck drives to a consulting job in Palo Alto on Wednesdays. He returns to San Jose the same day right at the evening rush hour. If he takes Route 280 home he has observed that his travel time is highly variable from one week to the next, but if he takes El Camino his travel time is relatively constant. Based on his experience, Chuck has set up the payoff table shown in Figure 15.44 which gives his travel time in minutes.

FIGURE 15.44

	STATE OF NATURE	
DECISION	LIGHT TRAFFIC	HEAVY TRAFFIC
Take 280	30	70
Take El Camino	40	40

(a) Chuck estimates that about 80% of the time the traffic will be light. Which route should he take?

(b) Chuck's wife Boots gets very worried if he is even a little late in coming home. Which route would you recommend he take now? Explain.

15-25. A small hospital in rural Greene County buys blood each month from a distant blood bank. A certain rare blood type must be restocked each month because its shelf life is only one month long. If the order is placed one month in advance the cost to the hospital is $10 per unit. If the demand for the rare blood type during the month exceeds the supply it must be special-ordered at a cost of $100 per unit. The demand for the past 3 years is shown in Figure 15.45.

FIGURE 15.45

DEMAND	FREQUENCY
0	24 months
1	8
2	4
Total	36 months

(a) Develop a payoff table for the hospital.

(b) How many units should the hospital order each month?

15-26. Martin Gale, head of quality control at Marple Manufacturing, must decide whether to inspect shipments of a particular purchased component. To achieve a quantity discount, Marple buys the components in lots of 1000 units. If the lot is 100% inspected by Quality Control the cost is $500. If the lot is not inspected and it contains defective components, then Marple will incur a cost of $20 per defective component. This cost is incurred when Quality Control does final inspection of the product containing the component and the product must be scrapped because it contains a defective component. Based on a similar component supplied by the same manufacturer, Martin estimates the probabilities shown in Figure 15.46.

FIGURE 15.46

PERCENT DEFECTIVE IN LOT	PROBABILITY
1	0.40
2	0.30
3	0.20
4	0.10

(a) Develop a payoff table where the alternatives are either 100% inspection or no inspection. Assume that with 100% inspection if defective components are found the supplier will replace them with good components at no additional charge.

(b) Should the components be inspected?

15-27. Rick O'Shea is an independent trucker operating out of Tucson. He has the option of either hauling a shipment to Denver or hauling a different shipment to Salt Lake. If he chooses the shipment to Denver, he has a 90% chance of finding there a return shipment to Tucson. If he does not find a return shipment he will return to Tucson empty. If he chooses the shipment to Salt Lake, he has a 50% chance of finding a return shipment to Tucson. His payoffs are shown in Figure 15.47.

FIGURE 15.47

	RETURN SHIPMENT	NO RETURN
Salt Lake	$4000	$3500
Denver	3850	3350

(a) Draw the decision tree for this problem.

(b) Using the criterion of expected net dollar return, to which city should Rick go?

15-28. Olive Branch's payoff table (problem 15-21) is given in Figure 15.48.

FIGURE 15.48

	STATE OF NATURE		
DECISION	SMALL BOX OFFICE	MEDIUM BOX OFFICE	LARGE BOX OFFICE
Sign with movie company	$200,000	$1,000,000	$3,000,000
Sign with TV network	900,000	900,000	900,000
Probability	0.3	0.6	0.1

She may hire a market research firm to conduct a survey at a cost of $200,000. The result of the survey would be either a favorable (F) or unfavorable (U) public response to the movie. The firm's ability to assess the market as measured by conditional probabilities is

$$P(F|\text{Small}) = .2 \qquad P(U|\text{Small}) = .8$$

$$P(F|\text{Medium}) = .5 \qquad P(U|\text{Medium}) = .5$$

$$P(F|\text{Large}) = .9 \qquad P(U|\text{Large}) = .1$$

(a) Draw the decision tree for this problem.

(b) Should Olive have the survey conducted? How should she use the results of the survey?

(c) What is the EVSI? What is the most Olive should be willing to pay for the survey?

15-29. Kelly Construction (problem 15-22) wants to reduce the uncertainty about the number of units it should build. It has decided to conduct a survey which will result in one of three measures of demand: M_1, weak, M_2, moderate, M_3, strong. The payoff table is shown in Figure 15.49.

FIGURE 15.49

	DEMAND		
DECISION	LOW, D_1	MEDIUM, D_2	HIGH, D_3
Build 100, B_1	$500,000	$500,000	$500,000
Build 200, B_2	0	1,000,000	1,000,000
Build 300, B_3	−700,000	400,000	1,500,000
Probability	0.3	0.5	0.2

The conditional probabilities are given in Figure 15.50.

FIGURE 15.50

	$P(M_j \mid D_i)$		
	M_1	M_2	M_3
D_1	.7	.2	.1
D_2	.3	.4	.3
D_3	.1	.3	.6

(a) Draw the decision tree for this problem.

(b) What is Kelly's optimal strategy?

(c) What is the EVSI? Compare it to the EVPI by computing the ratio EVSI/EVPI and noting that the most this ratio could be is 1.

15-30. The payoff table for the hospital in Greene County (problem 15-25) is given in Figure 15.51.

FIGURE 15.51

ORDER QUANTITY	DEMAND		
	0, D_1	1, D_2	2, D_3
0, Q_1	0	100	200
1, Q_2	10	10	110
2, Q_3	20	20	20
Probability	$\frac{2}{3}$	$\frac{2}{9}$	$\frac{1}{9}$

The hospital administrator has decided to check the scheduled surgeries each month to see if there will be any operations requiring the rare blood type. He may find that there are no scheduled surgeries, S_1, one scheduled surgery, S_2, or two scheduled surgeries, S_3, requiring the rare blood type. The conditional probabilities are:

FIGURE 15.52

	$P(S_j \mid D_i)$		
	S_1	S_2	S_3
D_1	.95	.04	.01
D_2	.05	.8	.15
D_3	.02	.08	.9

(a) Draw the decision tree for this problem.

(b) What is the EVSI?

(c) How much can the administrator expect to save each month by checking the surgery schedule?

THE PC APPROACH TO DECISION TREES

Construction and Analysis of a Decision Tree

In Section 15.10 we mentioned that the software package Arborist can be used in the construction and analysis of a decision tree. Here we briefly illustrate some of the features of this approach in the context of the test or no-test tree shown in Figure 15.30. For convenience of reference this figure is reproduced in Figure 15.53.

The nodes have been numbered to facilitate the discussion. Arborist uses a divided screen to make it possible for you to view simultaneously both the entire tree and a small segment where you are currently working. It also has the ability to copy specific branches of the tree. Note in this example that once the no-test branch is completed, it is a great convenience to produce the branches emanating from nodes 3 and 4 simply by copying the branch emanating from node 5 and changing the probabilities. These features help to simplify the construction process.

The analysis, and particularly the ability to perform sensitivity analysis, is enhanced by the ability to represent each terminal value as a formula. In general the proce-

FIGURE 15.53
Test or No-Test Tree with Returns
and Probabilities Assigned, and
Nodes Numbered

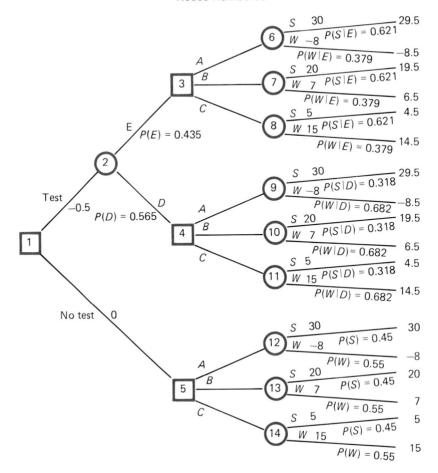

dure is to assign a variable name to each cash flow as it is entered on a branch. The formula for the terminal value at a particular terminal position is simply the appropriate arithmetic combination of the variables that lie on the path from the root of the tree to that terminal position. For example, suppose that in Figure 15.53 a variable called *Cost*, with a current value of -0.5, is assigned to the test branch emanating from node 1, and a variable called *Return*, with a current value of 30, is assigned to the strong branch emanating from node 6. Then the formula for the uppermost terminal position could be written as

$$\text{Profit} = \text{Return} - \text{Cost}.$$

If this approach were used throughout the tree, then to calculate the effect of an increase in the cost of the test you would simply have to enter a new value for "Cost," and Arborist would calculate a complete new set of terminal values. Once the tree is constructed, the optimal policy is determined as the result of a single command.

Risk Analysis

Arborist makes it easy to produce the probability distribution of terminal values (profits in this example). This feature, along with the split screen capabilities of Arborist, is illustrated in Figure 15.54.

FIGURE 15.54
Arborist Output

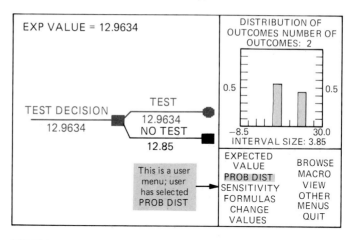

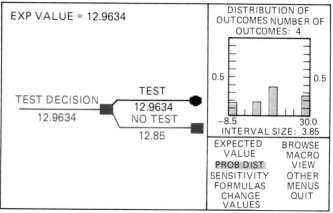

Referring back to Figure 15.31, we note that the correct expected returns, and thus the correct decision (i.e. test), is also shown in this figure. The upper panel shows a histogram of the probability distribution that results from the *no-test* decision. It shows that values between 6.9 and 10.75 occur with a probability that appears to be equal to about 0.55 and values between 18.45 and 22.30 occur with the remaining probability, a value that appears to be about 0.45. The interval size of 3.85 was automatically selected by Arborist once the number of desired intervals was specified (in this case the user specified 10 intervals). The lower panel presents similar results for the *test* decision. Consider the importance of this information to a manager. As we know, the *test* decision is optimal if a criterion of expected return is used. In this case, however, the expected return of *test* is only slightly larger (12.96 − 12.85 = 0.11) than the *no-test* alternative; and it is much riskier. Selecting the *test* decision and the ensuing optimal decision yields a return between −8.5 and −4.65 with a probability that appears to equal about 0.16. On the other hand there is a probability that appears to be about 0.26 of realizing a return in the interval between 26.15 and 30.00. It is not hard to imagine that under these circumstances the risk-averse manager would select the no-test branch. It will not surprise you to learn that it is not necessary to attempt to read the probabilities from these histograms. Printouts with the exact intervals and probabilities are available from Arborist on request. Experience has shown, however, that the graphical display does a better job of capturing the overall sense of the situation for many managers. It is important to recall that subjective probabilities are used to construct most decision trees and therefore it is often not reasonable to assume great precision for these estimates.

CASE

TO DRILL OR NOT TO DRILL

Terri Underhill has recently been assigned to the economic analysis section of Global Oil. Prescot Oil has just offered to buy the Burns Flat lease from Global for $15,000 and Terri has been assigned the task of preparing Global's response. The Burns Flat lease gives Global the right to explore for oil under 320 acres of land in western Oklahoma. Terri must recommend either to sell the lease or to drill.

If Global drills, the results are uncertain. Based on drilling records in western Oklahoma, and on current market prices, Terri prepares a table showing the possible outcomes, the probability of each outcome, and the net return to Global (Exhibit 1).

EXHIBIT 2

POSSIBLE OUTCOMES	PROBABILITY	NET RETURN
Dry Well	0.2	−100,000
Gas Well	0.4	40,000
Oil and Gas	0.3	90,000
Oil Well	0.1	200,000

1. On the basis of these data, should Global drill or sell the lease?
2. What is the most that Global should pay in advance to know what the outcome of drilling would be?

Terri, however, knows that she does not have to make the decision simply on the basis of historical records. DRI, Drilling Resource, Inc., which is Etto Oxstein's company, will perform a test for $6000 to determine the underground formation of the Burns Flat terrain. The test will indicate which of three categories (plate, varied, or ridge) best describes the underground structure. The conditional probabilities of the possible outcomes vary with the underground structure. Exhibit 2 shows the results of the last 50 tests.

EXHIBIT 2

TEST RESULT/OUTCOME	PLATE	VARIED	RIDGE	TOTAL
Dry	8	2	0	10
Gas	2	16	2	20
Gas & Oil	0	14	1	15
Oil	0	0	5	5
	10	32	8	50

If the test is taken, the opportunity to sell the lease is forfeited. The market for oil leases understands that a decision to sell after the test indicates that drilling does not appear to be profitable.

3. Use a decision tree to determine the optimal strategy for Global.
4. What is the expected return associated with the optimal policy?
5. What is the maximum *additional* amount that Global should be willing to pay DRI for the test?

DIAGNOSTIC ASSIGNMENT

JOHNSON'S METAL

Shirley Johnson, president of Johnson's Metal (JM), is facing the decision presented in Problem 15-19, but a new element has entered the picture. Shirley has the opportunity to hire Compal, a consulting firm that does what it calls "competitive analysis." In particular, in this situation Compal offers to do a detailed study of the other firms which will compete to supply transmission housings to **PROTRAC**. After the analysis, Compal will report to JM that conditions for JM to get the contract are either encouraging or discouraging.

Compal states that, if conditions are encouraging, then JM will get the **PROTRAC** contract with probability equal to 0.5. On the other hand, Compal states that if conditions are unfavorable the probability that JM will get the **PROTRAC** contract is only 0.35. At this time Compal states that the probability of encouraging and discouraging conditions are equally likely. Compal charges $1000 for its services.

Shirley asks Aline Drawer, her assistant, to determine if JM should hire Compal. Indeed she asks Aline to determine the optimal strategy.

Aline prepares the decision tree for the problem and by working back through it, determines that the optimal strategy is

1. Hire Compal
2. If conditions are encouraging
   a. Build the test fixture
   b. If JM gets the order, use current tools
3. If conditions are discouraging
   a. Build the test fixture
   b. If JM gets the order, use current tools

He makes an appointment to discuss the results with Shirley. The meeting proceeds as follows:

SHIRLEY: Aline! I see the decision tree and I'm duly impressed, but the result doesn't make any sense. Why should I pay Compal $1000 if we take the same action no matter what they say?

ALINE: Surely, Shirley, you don't mean that the analysis did not make a difference. I understand that your statement holds now that the analysis is complete, but how would you have known what strategy to follow without the decision tree?

SHIRLEY: Aline! You missed my point! No matter what costs or probabilities are involved, I say that we should build the test fixture, and then use the current tools if we get the order. This simply has to be a better strategy than to hire Compal and then do the same thing no matter what they say.

ALINE: I understand, but I know I've done the decision tree right, so I don't know what to tell you.

SHIRLEY: I don't have the time or interest to check the details of your analysis. All I know is that I want to make a decision about Compal tomorrow morning and I want to have an answer that makes sense. Your job is to provide me with that answer.

Questions

1. Is Shirley right; that is, is it impossible for Aline's strategy to be optimal?
2. Is Aline right; that is, is his analysis correct given the data at his disposal?
3. Assume Aline's role; that is, it is now your job to provide Shirley with an answer that makes sense.

16

FORECASTING

_____ **16.1**

INTRODUCTION

The date is June 15, 1941. Joachim von Ribbentrop, Hitler's special envoy, is meeting in Venice with Count Ciano, the Italian foreign minister, whereupon von Ribbentrop says: "My dear Ciano, I cannot tell you anything as yet because every decision is locked in the impenetrable bosom of the Führer. However, one thing is certain: If we attack, the Russia of Stalin will be erased from the map within eight weeks."[1] Nine days later, Nazi Germany launched operation Barbarossa and declared war on Russia. With this decision a chain of events that led to the end of the Third Reich had been set in motion and the course of history was dramatically changed.

Although few decisions are this significant, it is clearly true that many of the most important decisions made by individuals and organizations crucially depend on an assessment of the future. Predictions or forecast with greater accuracy than that achieved by the German General Staff are thus fervidly hoped for and in some cases diligently worked for.

Economic forecasting considered by itself is an important activity. Government policies and business decisions are based on forecasts of the GNP, the level of unemployment, the demand for refrigerators, and so on. Among the major insurance companies, one is hard-pressed to find an investment department that does not have a contract with some expert or firm to obtain economic forecasts on a regular basis. Billions of dollars

[1] A. L. C. Bullock, *Hitler: A Study in Tyranny* (New York: Harper & Row, 1962).

of investments in mortgages and bonds are influenced by these forecasts. Over 2000 people show up each year at the Annual Forecast Luncheon sponsored by the University of Chicago to hear the views of three economists on the economic outlook. The data are overwhelming. Forecasting is playing an increasingly important role in the modern firm.

Not only is forecasting increasingly important, but quantitative models are playing an increasingly important role in the forecasting function. There is clearly a steady increase in the use of quantitative forecasting models at many levels in industry and government. A conspicuous example is the widespread use of inventory control programs which include a forecasting subroutine. For economic entities such as the GNP or exchange rates many firms now rely on econometric models for their forecasts. These models, which consist of a system of statistically estimated equations, have had a significant impact on the decision processes in both industry and government.

There are numerous ways to classify forecasting models and the terminology varies with the classification. For example, one can refer to "long-range," "medium-range," and "short-range" models. There are "regression" models, "extrapolation" models, and "conditional" or "precedent-based" models, as well as "nearest-neighbor" models. The major distinction we employ will be between *quantitative* and *qualitative forecasting techniques.*

───── 16.2
QUANTITATIVE FORECASTING

Quantitative forecasting models possess two important and attractive features:

Advantages of Quantitative Forecasting Models

1. They are expressed in mathematical notation. Thus, they establish an unambiguous record of how the forecast is made. This provides an excellent vehicle for clear communication about the forecast among those who are concerned. Furthermore, it provides an opportunity for systematic modification and improvement of the forecasting technique. In a quantitative model coefficients can be modified and/or terms added until the model yields good results. (This assumes that the relationship expressed in the model is basically sound.)

2. With the use of computers, quantitative models can be based on an amazing quantity of data. For example, a major oil company was considering a reorganization and expansion of its domestic marketing facilities (gasoline stations). Everyone understood that this was a pivotal decision for the firm. The size of the proposed capital investment alone, not to mention the possible influences on the revenue from gasoline sales, dictated that this decision be made by the board of directors. In order to evaluate the alternative expansion strategies, the board needed forecasts of the demand for gasoline in each of the marketing regions (more than 100 regions were involved) for each of the next 15 years. Each of these 1500 estimates was based on a combination of several factors, including the population and the level of new construction in each region. Without the use of computers and quantitative models a study involving this level of detail would generally be impossible. In a similar way, inventory control systems which require forecasts that are updated on a monthly basis for literally thousands of items could not be constructed without quantitative models and computers.

The technical literature related to quantitative forecasting models is enormous and a high level of technical, mainly statistical, sophistication is required to understand the intricacies of the models in certain areas. In the following two sections we summarize some of the important characteristics and the applicability of such models. We shall distinguish two categories based on the underlying approach. These are *causal models* and *time-series models.*

CAUSAL FORECASTING MODELS

In a causal model, the forecast for the quantity of interest "rides piggyback" on another quantity or set of quantities. In other words, our knowledge of the value of one variable (or perhaps several variables) enables us to forecast the value of another variable. In more precise terms, let y denote the true value for some variable of interest, and let $\hat{y}$ denote a predicted or forecast value for that variable. Then, in a causal model,

$$\hat{y} = f(x_1, x_2, \ldots, x_n)$$

where f is a forecasting rule, or function, and $x_1, x_2, \ldots, x_n$ is a set of variables.

In this representation the x variables are often called *independent variables*, whereas $\hat{y}$ is the *dependent or response variable*. The notion is that we know the independent variables and use them in the forecasting model to forecast the dependent variable. Consider the following examples:

1. If y is the demand for baby food, then x might be the number of children between 7 and 24 months old.
2. If y is the demand for plumbing fixtures, then x_1 and x_2 might be the number of housing starts and the number of existing houses, respectively.
3. If y is the traffic volume on a proposed expressway, then x_1 and x_2 might be the traffic volume on each of 2 nearby existing highways.
4. If y is the yield of usable material per pound of ingredients from a proposed chemical plant, then x might be the same quantity produced by a small-scale experimental plant.

For a causal model to be useful, the independent variables must either be known in advance or it must be possible to forecast them more easily than $\hat{y}$, the dependent variable. For example, knowing a functional relationship between the pounds of sauerkraut and the number of bratwurst sold in Milwaukee in the same year may be interesting to sociologists, but unless sauerkraut usage can be easily predicted, the relationship is of little value for anyone in the bratwurst forecasting business.

To use a causal forecasting model, then, requires two conditions.

Requirements for Use

1. A relationship between values of the independent and dependent variables such that the former provides information about the latter.
2. The values for the independent variables must be known and available to the forecaster at the time the forecast must be made.

One commonly used approach, in creating a causal forecasting model, is called *curve fitting*.

Curve Fitting: An Oil Company Expansion

The fundamental ideas of curve fitting are easily illustrated by a problem in which one independent variable is used to predict the value of the dependent variable. As a specific example, consider an oil company that is planning to expand its network of modern self-service gasoline stations. It plans to use traffic flow (measured in the average number of cars per hour) to forecast sales (measured in average dollar sales per hour).

The firm has had five stations in operation for more than a year and has used historical data to calculate the averages shown in Figure 16.1.

These data are plotted in Figure 16.2. Such a plot is often called a *scatter diagram*. We now wish to use these data to construct a function that will enable us to forecast

FIGURE 16.1
Sales and Traffic Data

STATION	CARS PER HOUR	SALES PER HOUR ($)
1	150	220
2	55	75
3	220	250
4	130	145
5	95	200

the sales at any proposed location by measuring the traffic flow at that location and plugging its value into the function we construct. In particular, suppose that the traffic flow at a proposed location in Buffalo Grove is 183 cars per hour. How might we use the data in Figure 16.2 to forecast the sales at this location?

A Subjective Method

Quick and Dirty Fits A method that is commonly used when there is a single independent variable and a need to produce a forecast quickly is to fit a particular type of curve to the data "by eye." The goal is to find a "curve" that comes close enough to the points in the scatter diagram to satisfy the person who needs the forecast. We note that in this process it is not necessary to "touch" any data point, but the line could pass through a point if it yields a good fit.

A straight line is the type of curve most commonly selected. This process is illustrated in Figure 16.3. The line shown has no special properties except that it appears (at least to the authors) to lie close to the data. Once the line is drawn, one can read from the graph a forecast of sales for any particular traffic flow. The figure shows that this particular line yields a forecast of $202.50 for a traffic flow of 183.

The better-equipped office is not limited to fitting a straight line by eye. A French curve enables the decision maker to select a function that lies closer to the data. Figure 16.4 illustrates this point. Again, a forecast for a traffic flow of 183 is shown.

FIGURE 16.2
Sales Versus Traffic

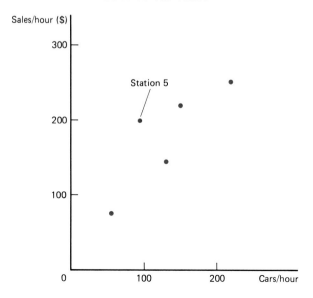

FIGURE 16.3
Fitting a Line by Eye

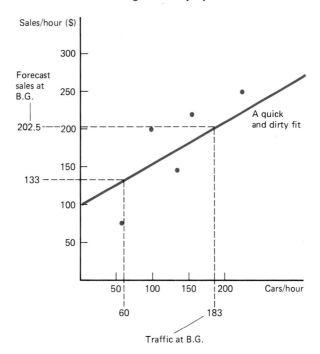

FIGURE 16.4
Fitting a Curve by Eye

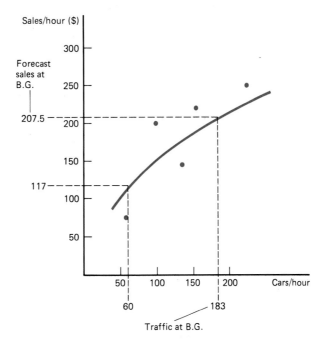

The straight line and the curve selected in Figures 16.3 and 16.4 yield approximately the same forecast for demand (sales/hr) when the traffic flow is 183. A larger difference, both in absolute and relative terms, would occur if these figures were used to forecast demand at a location with a traffic flow of 60. The straight line yields a forecast of 133, whereas the curve yields a forecast of 117. So which model is right?

There is no black and white answer to that question at the time the company must decide whether to build the station in Buffalo Grove. Forecasting models, like all other models, require the final step of managerial approval. *Based on judgement, which may be strongly influenced by direct experience with a forecasting model, the manager must decide whether to accept a particular forecast or to devote more resources to obtaining a better forecast (i.e., one in which he has more confidence).*

Deficiencies of the Quick and Dirty Method

The quick and dirty method just described has two major deficiencies.

1. It is impossible to extend to problems with more than one independent variable. Think of trying to use this approach if you were given historical values of sales, traffic flow, *and* the number of competing stations in a 3-mile radius. It quickly becomes clear that a ruler and/or a French curve will not provide enough help.

2. There is no measure of what a "good fit" means. Once a manager has chosen a specific functional form (say a straight line), there is no automatic way to select one line that is better than other possible lines. Sure, the manager can look at them and pick the one he likes. However, if he can specify a measure of goodness, the process of curve fitting can be reduced to a standard and more objective technical operation.

An Objective Method

Least-Squares Fits   The method of least squares is a formal procedure for curve fitting that overcomes the two deficiencies just discussed. It is a two-step process.

1. Select a specific functional form (e.g., a straight line).
2. Within the set of functions specified in step 1, choose the specific function that minimizes the sum of the squared deviations between the data points and the function values. We hasten to illustrate this idea:

Consider the sales–traffic flow example. In step 1, assume that we select a straight line; that is, we restrict our attention to functions of the form $y = a + bx$. Step 2 is illustrated in Figure 16.5. Here values for a and b were chosen, the appropriate line $y = a + bx$ was drawn, and the deviations between observed points and the function are indicated. For example,

$$d_1 = y_1 - [a + bx_1] = 220 - [a + 150b]$$

where y_1 = actual (observed) sales/hr at location 1 (i.e., 220)
x_1 = actual (observed) traffic flow at location 1 (i.e., 150)
a = intercept (on the vertical axis) for function in Figure 16.5
b = slope for the function in Figure 16.5

The value d_1^2 is a measure of how close the value of the function $[a + bx_1]$ is to the observed value, y_1; that is, it indicates how well the function fits at this one point.

We want the function to fit well at all points. One measure of how well it fits overall is the sum of the squared deviations, which is $\sum_{i=1}^{5} d_i^2$. Let us now consider a general problem with n as opposed to 5 observations. Then, since each $d_i = y_i -$

FIGURE 16.5

Method of Least Squares

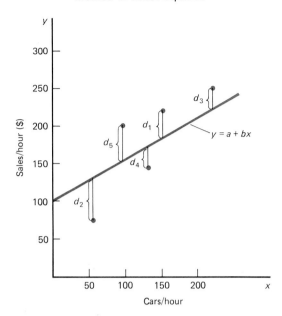

$(a + bx_i)$, the sum of the squared deviations can be written as

$$\sum_{i=1}^{n} (y_i - [a + bx_i])^2 \tag{16.1}$$

Using the method of least squares, we select a and b so as to minimize the sum shown in expression (16.1). The rules of calculus can be used to determine the values of a and b that minimize this sum. The procedure is to take the partial derivative of the sum in expression (16.1) with respect to a and set the resulting expression equal to zero. This yields one equation. A second equation is derived by following the same procedure with b. The equations that result from this procedure are

$$\sum_{i=1}^{n} -2(y_i - [a + bx_i]) = 0 \quad \text{and} \quad \sum_{i=1}^{n} -2x_i(y_i - [a + bx_i]) = 0$$

Recall that the values for x_i and y_i are the observations and our goal is to find the values of a and b that satisfy these two equations. The solution can be shown to be

**The Minimizing
Values of
a and b**

$$b = \frac{\sum_{i=1}^{n} x_i y_i - \dfrac{1}{n} \sum_{i=1}^{n} x_i \sum_{i=1}^{n} y_i}{\sum_{i=1}^{n} x_i^2 - \dfrac{1}{n} \left(\sum_{i=1}^{n} x_i \right)^2} \tag{16.2}$$

$$a = \frac{1}{n} \sum_{i=1}^{n} y_i - b \frac{1}{n} \sum_{i=1}^{n} x_i$$

**Calculating
a and b**

The next step is to determine the values for $\sum x_i, \sum x_i^2, \sum y_i, \sum x_i y_i$. Note that these quantities depend only on the data we have observed and that we can find them with simple arithmetic operations. The table in Figure 16.6 is devoted to this purposes.

FIGURE 16.6
Least-Squares Calculations: The Linear Case

i	x_i (CARS/HR)	y_i (SALES/HR)	$x_i y_i$	x_i^2
1	150	220	33,000	22,500
2	55	75	4,125	3,025
3	220	250	55,000	48,400
4	130	145	18,850	16,900
5	95	200	19,000	9,025
Σ	650	890	129,975	99,850

Plugging the numerical values into the equations shown in expression (16.2), and setting $n = 5$, yields

$$b = 0.93$$

$$a = 57.1$$

The resulting least-squares line is shown in Figure 16.7 as a solid line. The quick and dirty line from Figure 16.3 is shown as a dashed line. This figure suggests that at least some individuals (e.g., the authors) are not too good at selecting by eye a line that well fits the data (by the least–squares criterion).

The example above has shown how to make *linear fits* for the case of one independent variable. But the method of least squares can be used with any number of independent variables and with any functional form. As an illustration, suppose that we wish to fit a quadratic function of the form

$$y = a_0 + a_1 x + a_2 x^2$$

FIGURE 16.7
Least-Squres Line

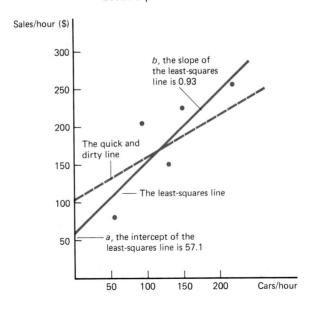

to our previous data with the method of least squares. Our goal, then, is to select a_0, a_1, and a_2 in order to minimize the sum of squared deviations, which is now

$$\sum_{i=1}^{5} (y_i - [a_0 + a_1 x_i + a_2 x_i^2])^2 \tag{16.3}$$

We proceed by setting the partial derivatives with respect to a_0, a_1, and a_2 equal to zero. This gives the equations

$$5a_0 + (\sum x_i)a_1 + (\sum x_i^2)a_2 = \sum y_i$$
$$(\sum x_i)a_0 + (\sum x_i^2)a_1 + (\sum x_i^3)a_2 = \sum x_i y_i \tag{16.4}$$
$$(\sum x_i^2)a_0 + (\sum x_i^3)a_1 + (\sum x_i^4)a_2 = \sum x_i^2 y_i$$

Finding the numerical values of the coefficients is a straightforward task. We proceed in the same tabular manner as in Figure (16.6) Indeed, we need all of the values calculated there. To conserve space, we use scientific notation and express numbers in powers of 10. For example, we will write 22,500 as 2.25×10^4. The calculations, to two decimals of accuracy, are shown in Figure 16.8.

The numerical values from Figure 16.8 can now be plugged into the equations presented in expression (16.4) to yield

$$5a_0 + 650a_1 + 99,800a_2 = 890 \tag{16.5}$$

$$6.50a_0 + 998a_1 + 172,600a_2 = 1300 \tag{16.6}$$

$$9.98a_0 + 1726a_1 + 322,500a_2 = 2153 \tag{16.7}$$

Both sides of (16.6) have been divided by 10^2 and both sides of equation (16.7) have been divided by 10^4 to obtain the form shown.

We are now left with the straightforward but tedious task of solving three linear equations in three unknowns. Completing this exercise yields

$$a_0 \approx -65.726$$

$$a_1 \approx 3.015$$

$$a_2 \approx -0.0074$$

FIGURE 16.8
Least-Squares Calculations: The
Quadratic Case

i	$x_i \times 10^2$	$y_i \times 10^2$	$x_i y_i \times 10^4$	$x_i^2 \times 10^4$	$x_i^3 \times 10^6$	$x_i^3 \times 10^8$	$x_i^2 y_i \times 10^6$
1	1.50	2.20	3.30	2.25	3.38	5.06	4.95
2	0.55	0.75	0.41	0.30	0.17	0.09	0.23
3	2.20	2.50	5.50	4.84	10.65	23.43	12.10
4	1.30	1.45	1.89	1.69	2.20	2.86	2.45
5	0.95	2.00	1.90	0.90	0.86	0.81	1.80
Σ	6.50	8.90	13.00	9.98	17.26	32.25	21.53

FIGURE 16.9

Evaluating the Quadratic Function

x	$-65.726 + 3.015x - 0.0074x^2$
0	-65.726
50	66.46
100	161.52
200	240.22

FIGURE 16.10

Quadratic Least-Squares Function

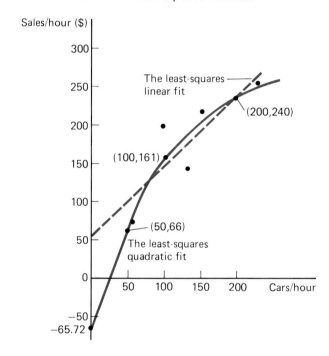

To plot this function, we first evaluate it for four values of x as shown in Figure 16.9.[2]

These points are plotted in Figure 16.10 and a curve is drawn through them. The linear least-squares fit is also shown. The quadratic function appears to fit the data better, but beware. As we have seen in the use of quick and dirty methods, the eye is not always a reliable guide to what is happening.

Comparing the Linear and Quadratic Fits

A Good Fit? In the method of least squares, we have selected the sum of the squared deviations as our measure of "goodness of fit." We can thus compare the linear and the quadratic fit with this criterion. The calculations are shown in Figure 16.11, where columns (1) and (2) are the actual historical data from Figure 16.1, column (3) is the least-squares linear fit, and the column identified as (4) is the least-squares quadratic fit.

[2] One can use differential calculus to show that the function has a maximum value at

$$x = -a_1/2a_2 \approx 241.3$$

FIGURE 16.11
Sum of the Squared Deviations

i	(1) x_i	(2) y_i	(3) $a + bx_i$	$[(2) - (3)]^2$ d_i^2	(4) $a_0 + a_1x_i + a_2x_i^2$	$[(2) - (4)]^2$ d_i^2
1	150	220	196	576	220.57	0.32
2	55	75	108	1089	77.64	6.96
3	220	250	262	144	261.87	140.85
4	130	145	178	1089	200.71	3104
5	95	200	145	3025	246.31	2145
Σ				5923		5398

We see that the sum of the squared deviations for the quadratic function is indeed smaller than that for the linear function (i.e., 5398 < 5923). Indeed, the quadratic gives us roughly a 10% decrease in the sum of squares. The general result has to hold in this direction; that is, the quadratic function must always fit better than the linear function. A linear function is, after all, a special type of a quadratic function (one in which $a_2 = 0$). It follows then that the best quadratic function must be at least as good as the best linear function. This concept seems to have some general merit. Why not choose an even more general form, such as a cubic or a quartic, thereby getting an even better fit? In principle the method can be applied to any specified functional form. In practice, functions of the form (again using only a single independent variable for illustrative purposes)

$$y = a_0 + a_1x + a_2x^2 + \cdots + a_nx^n$$

Is a Perfect Fit the Best? are often suggested. Such a function is called a polynomial of degree n and it represents a broad and flexible class of functions (for $n = 2$ we have a quadratic, $x = 3$ a cubic, $n = 4$ a quartic, etc.). One can obtain an amazing variety of curves with polynomials, and thus they are popular among curve fitters. One must, however, proceed with caution when fitting data with a polynomial function. Under quite general conditions it is possible, for example, to find a $(k - 1)$-degree polynomial that will perfectly fit k data points. To be more specific, suppose that we have on hand seven historical observations, denoted (x_i, y_i), $i = 1, 2, \ldots, 7$. It is possible to find a sixth-degree polynomial

$$y = a_0 + a_1x + a_2x^2 + \cdots + a_6x^6$$

that exactly passes through each of these seven data points (see Figure 16.12).

This perfect fit (giving zero for the sum of squared deviations), however, is deceptive, for it does not imply as much as you may think about the predictive value of the model. For example, refer again to Figure 16.12. When the independent variable (at some future time) assumes the value x_8, the true value of y might be given by y_8, whereas the predicted value is $\hat{y}_8$. Despite the previous perfect fit, the forecast is very inaccurate. In this situation a linear fit (i.e., a first-degree polynomial) such as the one indicated in Figure 16.12 might well provide more realistic forecasts for the future, although by the criterion of least squares it does not "fit" the historical data nearly as well as the sixth-degree polynomial. Also, note that the polynomial fit has hazardous extrapolation properties. That is, the polynomial "blows up" at its extremes; x values only slightly larger than x_6 produce very large predicted y's. Looking at Figure 16.12, you can understand why high-order polynomial fits are referred to as "wild."

FIGURE 16.12
A Sixth-Degree Polynomial
Produces a Perfect Fit

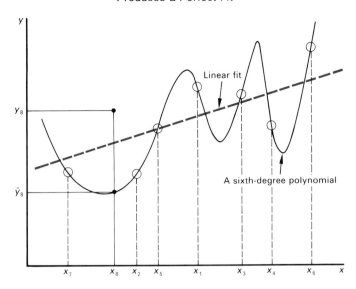

The intent of the paragraph above is to suggest that a model which has given a good fit to historical data may provide a terrible fit to future data. That is, a good historical fit may have poor predictive power. So what is a good fit?

What is a Good Fit?
The answer to this question involves considerations both philosophic and technical. The answer to the question depends, first, on whether one has some idea about the underlying real-world process which relates the y's and the x's. To be an effective forecasting device, the forecasting function must to some extent capture important features of that process. The more one knows, the better one can do. To go very far into this topic, one must employ a level of statistics that would extend well beyond this introductory coverage. For our purposes it suffices to state that knowledge of the underlying process is typically phrased in statistical language. For example, linear curve fitting, in the statistical context, is called *linear regression analysis*. If the statistical assumptions about the linear regression model are precisely satisfied, then in a precise and well-defined sense statisticians can prove that the linear fit is the "best possible fit." But in a real sense, this begs the question. In the real world one can never be completely certain about the underlying process. It is never "served to us on a platter." One only has some (and often not enough) historical data to observe. The question then becomes: How much confidence can we have that the underlying process is one that satisfies a particular set of statistical assumptions? Fortunately, quantitative measures do exist. Statistical analysis, at least for simple classes of models like linear regression, can reveal how well the historical data do indeed satisfy those assumptions.

And what if they do not? One tries a different model. Let us regress (digress) for a moment to recall some of the philosophy involved with the use of optimization models. There is an underlying real-world problem. The model is a selective representation of that problem. How good is that model, or representation? One usually does not have precise measures, and many paragraphs in this text have been devoted to the role of managerial judgment and sensitivity analysis in establishing a model's credibility. Ideally, to test the goodness of a model, one would like to have considerable experience with its use. If, in repeated use, we observe that the model performs well, then our

Validating Models

confidence is high.[3] However, what confidence can we have at the outset, without experience? One benchmark, which brings us close to the current context, is to ask the question: Suppose the model had been used to make past decisions; how well would the firm have fared? This approach "creates" experience by *simulating* the past. This is often referred to as *validating* the model. One way to use this approach, in the forecasting context, is called "divide and conquer" and is discussed at some length in Section 16.5. Typically, one uses only a portion of the historical data to create the model—for example, to fit a polynomial of a specified degree. One can then use the remaining data to see how well the model would have performed. This procedure is specified in some detail in Section 16.5. At present, it suffices to conclude by stressing that in curve fitting the question of "goodness of fit" is both philosophic and technical, and you do not want to lose sight of either issue.

The Role of the Computer

These few examples of causal forecasting models demonstrate that even in simple problems the required calculations are tedious. In most problems of an interesting size, it is impractical to perform the calculations by hand. This is especially true in problems where there are several independent variables. Fortunately, this is not a serious problem. The wide availability of computers and the steadily decreasing cost of computing have reduced the problem of performing the necessary calculations so that, at least in many applications, it is insignificant. The important questions are: What model, if any, can do a reliable job of forecasting, and are the data required for such a model available and reliable?

Summary Comments

A causal forecasting model uses one or more independent variables to forecast the value of a dependent or response variable. The model is often created by fitting a curve to an existing set of data and then using this curve to determine the response associated with new values of the independent variable(s). The method of least squares is a particularly useful method of fitting a curve. We have illustrated the general concept of this method and considered the specific problems of fitting a straight line, a quadratic function, and higher-order polynomials to a set of data. For simplicity, all of our illustrations have involved a single independent variable but the same techniques, except for quick and dirty, apply to problems with many variables.

In concluding, we have discussed both philosophic and technical issues which the "curve fitter" must address. Comments on the role of causal models in managerial decision making are reserved for Section 16.7. We now turn our attention to time-series analysis.

——— 16.4
TIME-SERIES FORECASTING MODELS

Extrapolate Historical Behavior

Another class of quantitative forecasting techniques comprises the so-called *time-series models*. These models produce forecasts by *extrapolating the historical behavior of the values of a particular single variable of interest*. For example, one may be interested in the sales for a particular item, or a fluctuation of a particular market price with time.

---

[3] No matter how much observation seems to substantiate the model, we can never conclude that the model is "true". Recall the high degree of "substantiation" of the flat earth model: "If you leave port and sail westward you will eventually fall off the earth and never be seen again."

Time-series models use a technique to *extrapolate* the historical behavior into the future. Figuratively, the series is being lifted into the future "by its own bootstraps."

In order to provide several examples of bootstrap methods, let us suppose that we have on hand the daily closing prices of a January soybean futures contract for the past 12 days, including today, and that from this past stream of data we wish to predict tomorrow's closing price. Several possibilities come to mind:

Several Possible Approaches

1. If it is felt that all historical values are important, and that all have equal predictive power, we might take the *average* of the past 12 values as our best forecast for tomorrow.
2. If it is felt that today's value (the twelfth) is far and away the most important, this value might be our best prediction for tomorrow.
3. It may be felt that in the current "fast-trending market" the first 6 values are too antiquated, but the most recent 6 are important and each has equal predictive power. We might then take the average of the most recent 6 values as our best estimate for tomorrow.
4. It may be felt that *all* past values contain useful information, but today's (the 12th observation) is the most important of all, and, in succession, the 11th, 10th, 9th, and so on, observations have decreasing importance. In this case we might take a *weighted average* of all 12 observations, with increasing weights assigned to each value in the order 1 through 12 and with the 12 weights summing to 1.
5. We might actually.plot the 12 values as a function of time and then draw a linear "trend line" which lies close to these values. This line might then be used to predict tomorrow's value.

Let use now suppose that tomorrow's actual closing price is observed and consider our forecast for the day after tomorrow, using the 13 available historical values. Methods 1 and 2 can be applied in a straightforward manner. Now consider method 3. In this case we might take tomorrow's actual observed price, together with today's and the previous 4 prices, to obtain a new 6-day average. This technique is called *a simple 6-period moving average*, and it will be discussed in more detail in the following sections.

Let us now refer to method 4. In this instance, since we employ all past values, we would be using 13 rather than. 12 values, with new weights assigned to these values. An important class of techniques called *exponential smoothing models* operate in this fashion. These models will also be explored in the ensuing discussion.

Finally, we shall explore in the more detail the technique mentioned in item 5. This provides another illustration of forecasting by a *curve-fitting method*.

We mention at this point that whenever we have values for a particular (single) variable of interest, which can be plotted against time, these values are often termed a *time series*, and any method used to analyze and extrapolate such a series into the future falls within the general category of *time-series analysis*. This is currently a very active area of research in statistics and management science. We will be able to barely scratch the surface in terms of formal development. Nevertheless, some of the important concepts, from the manager's viewpoint, will be developed.

Curve Fitting

We have already considered this topic in the discussion of causal models. In using curve fitting in the time-series context the main difference is that in this situation the independent variable is time. The historical observations of the dependent variable are plotted against time and a curve is then fit to these data. The curve is then extended into the future to yield a forecast. In this context, extending the curve simply means evaluating the derived function for larger values of t, the time. This procedure is illustrated for a straight line in Figure 16.13.

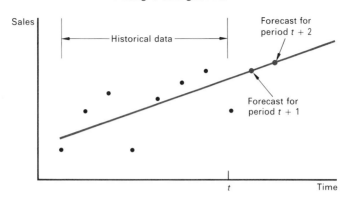

FIGURE 16.13
Fitting a Straight Line

The use of time as in independent variable has more serious implications than altering a few formulas, and a manager should understand the important difference between a causal model using curve fitting and a time-series model using curve fitting.

A Different Rationale
The mathematical techniques for fitting the curves are identical, but the rationale, or philosophy, behind the two models is basically quite different. To understand this difference, think of the values of y, the variable of interest, as being produced by a particular underlying process or system. The causal model assumes that as the underlying system changes to produce different values of y, it will also produce corresponding differences in the independent variables and thus, by knowing the independent variables, a good forecast of y can be deduced. The time-series model assumes that the system that produces y is essentially *stationary* (or *stable*) and will continue to act in the future as it has in the past. Future patterns in the movement of y will closely resemble past patterns. This means that time is a surrogate for many factors which may be difficult to measure but which seem to vary in a consistent and systematic manner with time. If the system that produces y significantly changes (e.g., because of changes in environment, technology, or government policy) then the assumption of a *stationary process* is invalid and consequently a forecast based on time as an independent variable is apt to be badly in error.

Just as for causal models, it is, of course, possible to use other than linear functions to extrapolate a series of observations (i.e., to forecast the future). As you might imagine, one alternative that is often suggested in practice is to assume that y_t is a higher-order polynomial in t, that is,

$$y_t = b_0 + b_1 t + b_2 t^2 + \cdots + b_k t^k$$

As before, appropriate values for the parameters $b_0, b_1, \ldots, b_k$ must be mathematically derived from the values of previous observations. The high-order polynomial, however, suffers from the pitfalls described earlier. That is, perfect (or at least extremely good) historical fits with little or no predictive power may be obtained.

Moving Averages: Forecasting Steco's Strut Sales
The assumption behind models of this type is that the average performance over the recent past is a good forecast of the future. It is perhaps surprising that these "naive" models are extremely important in applications. Almost all of the inventory control packages include a forecasting subroutine based on a particular type of moving average called exponentially weighted moving averages. On the basis of a criterion such as

"frequency of use," the method of moving averages is surely an important forecasting procedure.

One person who is deeply concerned about the use of simple forecasting models is Victor Kowalski, the new vice-president of operations of Steco. His introduction to inventory control models is discussed in Chapter 11. Since he is responsible for the inventory of thousands of items, simple (i.e., inexpensive) forecasting models are important to him. In order to become familiar with the various models he decides to "try out" different models on some historical data. In particular he decides to use last year's monthly sales data for stainless steel struts to learn about the different models and to see how well they would have worked if Steco had been using the models last year. He is performing what is called a *validation* study.

A Common Notation   The forecasting models are presented, of course, in symbols. Victor feels that it would be useful to use a common notation throughout his investigation. He thus decides to let

$$y_{t-1} = observed\ sales\ of\ struts\ in\ month\ t - 1$$

$$\hat{y}_t = forecast\ of\ sales\ for\ struts\ in\ period\ t$$

He is interested in forecasting the sales one month ahead; that is, he will take the known historical values $y_1, \ldots, y_{t-1}$ (demand in months 1 through $t - 1$) and use this information to produce $\hat{y}_t$, the forecast for y_t. In other words, he will take the actual past sales, through May, for example, and use them to forecast the sales in June, then he will use the sales through June to forecast sales in July, and so on. This process produces a sequence of $\hat{y}_t$ values. By comparing these values with the observed y_t values, one obtains an indication of how the forecasting model would have worked, had it actually been in use last year.

Simple *n*-Period Moving Average   The simplest model in the moving-average category is the *simple n-period moving average*. In this model the average of a fixed number (say *n*) of the most recent observations is used as an estimate of the next value of *y*. For example, if *n* equals 4, then after we have observed the value of *y* in period 15, our estimate for period 16 would be

$$\hat{y}_{16} = \frac{y_{15} + y_{14} + y_{13} + y_{12}}{4}$$

In general,

$$\hat{y}_{t+1} = \frac{1}{n}(y_t + y_{t-1} + \cdots + y_{t-n+1})$$

The application of a three-period and a four-period moving average to Steco's strut sales data is shown in Figure 16.14.

We see that the three-month moving average forecast for sales in April is the average of January, February, and March sales, $(20 + 24 + 27)/3$ or 23.67. *Ex post* (that is, after the forecast) actual sales in April were 31. Thus, in this case the sales forecast differed from the actual sales by $31 - 23.67$, or 7.33.

Inspection of the data in Figure 16.14 suggests that neither forecasting method seems particularly accurate. It is, however, useful to replace this *qualitative impression*

FIGURE 16.14
Three- and Four-Month Simple
Moving Averages

MONTH	ACTUAL SALES (THOUSANDS)	THREE-MONTH SIMPLE MOVING AVERAGE FORECAST	FOUR-MONTH SIMPLE MOVING AVERAGE FORECAST
Jan.	$20		
Feb.	24		
Mar.	27		
Apr.	31	(20 + 24 + 27)/3 = 23.67	
May	37	(24 + 27 + 31)/3 = 27.33	(20 + 24 + 27 + 31)/4 = 25.50
June	47	(27 + 31 + 37)/3 = 31.67	(24 + 27 + 31 + 37)/4 = 29.75
July	53	(31 + 37 + 47)/3 = 38.33	(27 + 31 + 37 + 47)/4 = 35.50
Aug.	62	(37 + 47 + 53)/3 = 45.67	(31 + 37 + 47 + 53)/4 = 42.00
Sept.	54	(47 + 53 + 62)/3 = 54.00	(37 + 47 + 53 + 62)/4 = 49.75
Oct.	36	(53 + 62 + 54)/3 = 56.33	(47 + 53 + 62 + 54)/4 = 54.00
Nov.	32	(62 + 54 + 36)/3 = 50.67	(53 + 62 + 54 + 36)/4 = 51.25
Dec.	29	(54 + 36 + 32)/3 = 40.67	(62 + 54 + 36 + 32)/4 = 46.00

with some *quantitative measure* of how well the two methods performed. A commonly used measure of comparison is the average of the squared errors, where

A Measure of Forecast Performance

$$\text{average squared error} = \frac{\sum\limits_{\text{all forecasts}} (\text{forecast sales} - \text{actual sales})^2}{\text{number of forecasts}}$$

The average squared error is calculated for the three-month (beginning with April) and four-month (beginning with May) moving average forecast in Figure 16.15. Since the three-month moving average yields an average squared error of 195.78, whereas the four-month moving average yields an average squared error of 267.21, it seems (at least

FIGURE 16.15
Average Squared Error

MONTH	ACTUAL SALES (THOUSANDS)	THREE-MONTH SIMPLE MOVING AVERAGE FORECAST	SQUARED ERROR	FOUR-MONTH SIMPLE MOVING AVERAGE FORECAST	SQUARED ERROR
Apr.	$31	23.67	53.73		
May	37	27.33	93.51	25.50	132.25
June	47	31.67	235.01	29.75	297.55
July	53	38.33	215.21	35.50	306.25
Aug.	62	45.67	266.67	42.00	400.00
Sept.	54	54.00	0	49.75	18.06
Oct.	36	56.33	413.31	54.00	324.00
Nov.	32	50.67	348.57	51.25	370.56
Dec.	29	40.67	136.19	46.00	289.00
Total			1762.20		2137.67
Average			195.78		267.21

historically) that including more historical data harms rather than helps the forecasting accuracy.

The simple moving average has two shortcomings, one philosophical and the other operational. The *philosophical* problem centers on the fact that in calculating a forecast (say $\hat{y}_8$), the most recent observation (y_7) receives no more weight or importance than an older observation such as y_5. This is because each of the last n observations is assigned the weight $1/n$. This procedure of assigning equal weights stands in opposition to one's intuition that in many instances the more recent data should tell us more than the older data about the future. Indeed, the analysis in Figure 16.15 suggests that better predictions for strut sales are based on the most recent data.

The second shortcoming, which is *operational*, is that if n observations are to be included in the moving average, then $(n - 1)$ pieces of past data must be brought forward to be combined with the current (the nth) observation. These past data must be stored in some way, in order to calculate the forecast. This is not a serious problem when a small number of forecasts are involved. The situation is quite different for the firm that needs to forecast the demand for thousands of individual products on an item-by-item basis. If, for example, Steco is using 8-period moving averages to forecast demand for 5000 small parts, then for each item 7 pieces of data must be stored for each forecast. This implies that a total of 35,000 pieces of data must be stored. In such a case storage requirements, as well·as computing time, may become important factors in designing a forecasting and inventory control system.

Weighted *n*-Period Moving Average The notion that recent data are more important than old data can be implemented with a *weighted n-period moving average*. This generalizes the notion of a simple n-period moving average, where, as we have seen, each weight is $1/n$. In this more general form, taking $n = 3$ as a specific example, we would set

$$\hat{y}_7 = \alpha_0 y_6 + \alpha_1 y_5 + \alpha_2 y_4$$

where the α's (which are called weights) are nonnegative numbers which are chosen so that smaller weights are assigned to more ancient data and all the weights sum to 1. There are, of course, innumerable ways of selecting a set of α's to satisfy these criteria. For example, if as above the weighted average is to include the last three observations (a weighted 3-period moving average), one might set

$$\hat{y}_7 = \tfrac{3}{6} y_6 + \tfrac{2}{6} y_5 + \tfrac{1}{6} y_4$$

Alternatively, one could define

$$\hat{y}_7 = \tfrac{5}{10} y_6 + \tfrac{3}{10} y_5 + \tfrac{2}{10} y_4$$

In either of these expressions we have decreasing weights that sum to 1. In practice, the proper choice of weights could well be a study in itself. Rather than discussing the rationale for various choices of weights, our desire is to illustrate the use of the model.

To get some idea about its performance, Victor applies the 3-month weighted moving average with weights 3/6, 2/6, 1/6 to the historical stainless strut data. The forecasts and the average squared error are shown in Figure 16.16.

Comparing the average squared errors of the 3-month simple moving average (195.78), the 4-month simple moving average (267.21), and the 3-month weighted moving

FIGURE 16.16

Three-Month Weighted Moving Average

MONTH	ACTUAL SALE (THOUSANDS)	THREE-MONTH WEIGHTED MOVING-AVERAGE FORECAST	SQUARED ERROR
Jan.	$20		
Feb.	24		
Mar.	27		
Apr.	31	$[(3 \times 27) + (2 \times 24) + (1 \times 20)]/6 = 24.83$	38.07
May	37	$[(3 \times 31) + (2 \times 27) + (1 \times 24)]/6 = 28.50$	72.25
June	47	$[(3 \times 37) + (2 \times 31) + (1 \times 27)]/6 = 33.33$	186.87
July	53	$[(3 \times 47) + (2 \times 37) + (1 \times 31)]/6 = 41.00$	144.00
Aug.	62	$[(3 \times 53) + (2 \times 47) + (1 \times 37)]/6 = 48.33$	186.87
Sept.	54	$[(3 \times 62) + (2 \times 53) + (1 \times 47)]/6 = 56.50$	6.25
Oct.	36	$[(3 \times 54) + (2 \times 62) + (1 \times 53)]/6 = 56.50$	420.25
Nov.	32	$[(3 \times 36) + (2 \times 54) + (1 \times 62)]/6 = 46.33$	205.35
Dec.	29	$[(3 \times 32) + (2 \times 36) + (1 \times 54)]/6 = 37.00$	64.00
Total			1323.91
Average			147.10

average (147.10) confirms the suggestion, based on Figure 16.15, that recent sales results are a better indicator of future sales than are older data. Although the weighted moving average places more weight on more recent data, it does not solve the operational problems of data storage since $n - 1$ pieces of historical sales data must still be stored. We now turn to a weighting scheme that cleverly addresses this problem.

Opertional Objection Removed

Exponential Smoothing: The Basic Model   We saw that, in using a weighted moving average, there are many different ways to assign decreasing weights that sum to 1. One way is called exponential smoothing, which is a shortened name for an *exponentially weighted moving average.* This is a scheme that weights recent data more heavily than past data, with weights summing to 1, but it avoids the operational problem just discussed. In this model, for any $t \geq 1$ the forecast for period $t + 1$, denoted $\hat{y}_{t+1}$, is a weighted sum (with weights summing to 1) of the actual *observed sales in period t* (i.e., y_t) and *the forecast for period t* (which was $\hat{y}_t$). In other words,

Forecast for $t + 1$	Observed in t	Forecast for t

$$\hat{y}_{t+1} = \alpha y_t + (1 - \alpha)\hat{y}_t \qquad (16.8)$$

where α is a user-specified constant such that $0 < \alpha < 1$. Thus, to compute $\hat{y}_{t+1}$, only $\hat{y}_t$ need be stored (together with the value of α). As soon as the actual y_t is observed, we compute $\hat{y}_{t+1} = \alpha y_t + (1 - \alpha)\hat{y}_t$. If Steco wanted to forecast demand for 5000 small parts, in each period, then 5001 items would have to be stored (the 5000 $\hat{y}_t$ values, and the value of α), as opposed to the previously computed 35,000 items needed to implement an 8-period moving average.

In order to obtain more insight into the exponential smoothing model, let us note that when $t = 1$ the expression used to define $\hat{y}_2$ is

$$\hat{y}_2 = \alpha y_1 + (1 - \alpha)\hat{y}_1$$

FIGURE 16.17
Exponential Smoothing ($\alpha = 0.6$)

MONTH	ACTUAL SALES (THOUSAND)	$\hat{y}_t$	$\alpha y_t + (1 - \alpha)\hat{y}_t$	SQUARED ERROR
Jan.	$20	40	$0.6 \times 20 + 0.4 \times 40 = 28.00$	
Feb.	24	28	$0.6 \times 24 + 0.4 \times 28 = 25.60$	
Mar.	27	25.60	$0.6 \times 27 + 0.4 \times 25.60 = 26.44$	
Apr.	31	26.44	$0.6 \times 31 + 0.4 \times 26.44 = 29.18$	20.79
May	37	29.18	$0.6 \times 37 + 0.4 \times 29.18 = 33.87$	61.21
June	47	33.87	$0.6 \times 47 + 0.4 \times 33.87 = 41.75$	172.39
July	53	41.75	$0.6 \times 53 + 0.4 \times 41.75 = 48.50$	126.60
Aug.	62	48.50	$0.6 \times 62 + 0.4 \times 48.50 = 56.60$	182.27
Sept.	54	56.60	$0.6 \times 54 + 0.4 \times 56.60 = 55.04$	6.76
Oct.	36	55.04	$0.6 \times 36 + 0.4 \times 55.04 = 43.62$	362.52
Nov.	32	43.62	$0.6 \times 32 + 0.4 \times 43.62 = 36.65$	134.93
Dec.	29	36.65		58.47
Total				1125.94
Average				125.10

In this expression $\hat{y}_1$ is an "initial guess" at the value for y in period 1, and y_1 is the observed value in period 1. At this point Victor decides to select an α of 0.6 and a $\hat{y}_1$ of 40 and to apply the model to the stainless steel strut data. His efforts are shown in Figure 16.17. As this figure shows, Victor has actual and estimated sales for 12 months. However, before beginning his computations he decides that he will calculate the average squared error for only the last 9 months (April through December). This, he believes, will give a better comparison with the results obtained from the other models (see Figures 16.15 and 16.16).

Victor is delighted with the results. The average squared error is smaller than what he obtained with the previous three models and the calculations are simple. From a computational view it is reasonable to consider exponential smoothing as an affordable way to forecast the sales of the thousands of products that Steco holds in inventory.

Although the results obtained from the exponential smoothing model are impressive, it is clear that the particular numerical values that appear in Figure 16.17 depend on the values selected for the smoothing constant α, and the "initial guess" $\hat{y}_1$.

The Forecast Gives Weight to All Past Observations Because of the importance of the basic exponential smoothing model, it is worth exploring in more detail how it works and when it can be successfully applied to real problems. We will now examine some of its properties. To begin, note that if $t \geq 2$ it is possible to substitute $t - 1$ for t in (16.8) to obtain

$$\hat{y}_t = \alpha y_{t-1} + (1 - \alpha)\hat{y}_{t-1}$$

Substituting this relationship back into the original expression for $\hat{y}_{t+1}$ [i.e., into (16.8)] yields for $t \geq 2$,

$$\hat{y}_{t+1} = \alpha y_t + \alpha(1 - \alpha)y_{t-1} + (1 - \alpha)^2 \hat{y}_{t-1}$$

By successively performing similar substitutions one is led to the following general expression for $\hat{y}_{t+1}$:

$$\hat{y}_{t+1} = \alpha y_t + \alpha(1 - \alpha)y_{t-1} + \alpha(1 - \alpha)^2 y_{t-2} + \cdots + \alpha(1 - \alpha)^{t-1} y_1 + (1 - \alpha)^t \hat{y}_1$$

$$(16.9)$$

For example,

$$\hat{y}_4 = \alpha y_3 + \alpha(1-\alpha)y_2 + \alpha(1-\alpha)^2 y_1 + (1-\alpha)^3 \hat{y}_1$$

Since $0 < \alpha < 1$, it follows that $0 < 1 - \alpha < 1$. Thus,

$$\alpha > \alpha(1-\alpha) > \alpha(1-\alpha)^2$$

The Weights Are Declining Exponentially

In other words, in the previous example y_3, the most recent observation, receives more weight than y_2, which receives more weight than y_1. This illustrates the general property of an exponential smoothing model—that *the coefficients of the y's decrease as the data become older.* It can also be shown that *the sum of all of the coefficients (including the coefficient of $\hat{y}_1$) is 1*; that is in the case of $\hat{y}_4$, for example,

$$\alpha + \alpha(1-\alpha) + \alpha(1-\alpha)^2 + (1-\alpha)^3 = 1$$

We have thus seen in expression (16.9) that the general value $\hat{y}_{t+1}$ is a weighted sum of *all previous observations* (including the last observed value, y_t). Moreover, the weights sum to 1 and are decreasing as historical observations get older. The last term in the sum, namely $\hat{y}_1$, is not a historical observation. Recall that it was a "guess" at y_1. We can now observe that as t increases, the influence of $\hat{y}_1$ on $\hat{y}_{t+1}$ decreases and in time beomes negligible. To see this, note that the coefficient of $\hat{y}_1$ in (16.9) is $(1-\alpha)^t$. Thus, the weight assigned to $\hat{y}_1$ decreases exponentially with t. Even if α is small [which makes $(1-\alpha)$ nearly 1] the value of $(1-\alpha)^t$ decreases rapidly. For example, if $\alpha = 0.1$ and $t = 20$, then $(1-\alpha)^t = 0.12$. If $\alpha = 0.1$ and $t = 40$, then $(1-\alpha)^t = 0.015$. Thus, as soon as enough data have been observed, the value of $\hat{y}_{t+1}$ will be quite insensitive to the choice for $\hat{y}_1$.

Obviously, the value of α, which is a parameter input by the analyst, affects the performance of the model. As you can see explicitly in (16.8), it is the weight given to the data value (y_t) most recently observed. This implies that the larger the value of α, the more strongly the model will react to the last observation. This, as we will see, may or may not be desirable. Figure 16.18 shows values for the weights (in expression 16.9) when $\alpha = 0.1$, 0.3, and 0.5. You can see that for the larger values of α (e.g., $\alpha = 0.5$) more

FIGURE 16.18

Weights for Different Values of α

VARIABLE	COEFFICIENT	$\alpha = 0.1$	$\alpha = 0.3$	$\alpha = 0.5$
y_t	α	0.1	0.3	0.5
y_{t-1}	$\alpha(1-\alpha)$	0.09	0.21	0.25
y_{t-2}	$\alpha(1-\alpha)^2$	0.081	0.147	0.125
y_{t-3}	$\alpha(1-\alpha)^3$	0.07290	0.10290	0.0625
y_{t-4}	$\alpha(1-\alpha)^4$	0.06561	0.07203	0.03125
y_{t-5}	$\alpha(1-\alpha)^5$	0.05905	0.05042	0.01563
y_{t-6}	$\alpha(1-\alpha)^6$	0.05314	0.03530	0.00781
y_{t-7}	$\alpha(1-\alpha)^7$	0.04783	0.02471	0.00391
y_{t-8}	$\alpha(1-\alpha)^8$	0.04305	0.01729	
y_{t-9}	$\alpha(1-\alpha)^9$	0.03874	0.01211	
y_{t-10}	$\alpha(1-\alpha)^{10}$	0.03487	0.00847	
Sum of the Weights		0.68619	0.98023	0.99610

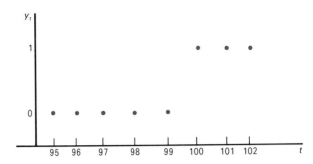

FIGURE 16.19
System Change When $t = 100$

relative weight is assigned to the more recent observations and the influence of older data is more rapidly diminished.

To illustrate further the effect of choosing various values for α (i.e., putting more or less weight on recent observations), we consider three specific cases.

Response to a Sudden Change

■ **Case 1:** Suppose that at a certain point in time the underlying system experiences a rapid and radical change. How does the choice of α influence the way in which the exponential smoothing model will react? As an illustrative example consider an extreme case in which

$$y_t = 0 \qquad \text{for } t = 1, 2, \ldots, 99$$
$$y_t = 1 \qquad \text{for } t = 100, 101, \ldots$$

This situation is illustrated in Figure 16.19. Note that in this case if $\hat{y}_1 = 0$, then $\hat{y}_{100} = 0$ for any value of α, since we are taking the weighted sum of a series of zeros.

Thus, at time 99 our best estimate of y_{100} is 0, whereas the actual value will be 1. At time 100 we will first see that the system has changed. The question is: How quickly will the forecasting system respond as time passes and the information that the system has changed becomes available?

To answer this question, we plot $\hat{y}_{t+1}$ for $\alpha = 0.5$ and $\alpha = 0.1$ in Figure 16.20. Note that when $\alpha = 0.5$, $\hat{y}_{106} = 0.984$; thus at time 105 our estimate of y_{106} would be 0.984, whereas the true value will turn out to be 1. When $\alpha = 0.1$ our estimate of y_{106} is only 0.468.

We see then that a forecasting system with $\alpha = 0.5$ responds much more quickly to changes in the data than does a forecasting system with $\alpha = 0.1$. The manager would thus prefer a relatively large α if the system is characterized by a low level of random behavior, but is subject to occasional enduring shocks. (Case 1 is an extreme example of this situation.) However, suppose that the data are characterized by large random errors but a stable mean. Then if α is large, a large random error in y_t will throw the forecast value, $\hat{y}_{t+1}$, way off. Hence, for this type of process a smaller value of α would be preferred.

Response to a Steady Change

■ **Case 2:** As opposed to the rapid and radical change investigated in Case 1, suppose now that a system experiences a *steady* change in the value of y. An example of a steady growth pattern is illustrated in Figure 16.21. This example is called a *linear ramp*. Again the question is: How will the exponential smoothing model respond and how will this response be affected by the choice of α?

FIGURE 16.20
Response to a Unit Change in y_t

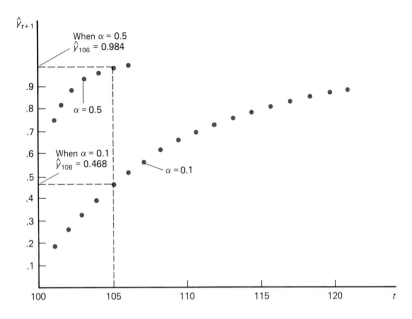

FIGURE 16.21
Steady Increasing Values of y_t (a Linear Ramp)

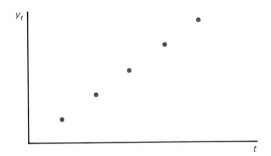

In this case, recall that

$$\hat{y}_{t+1} = \alpha y_t + \alpha(1 - \alpha)y_{t-1} + \cdots$$

Since all previous y's $(y_1, \ldots, y_{t-1})$ are smaller than y_t and since the weights sum to 1, it can be shown that, for any α between 0 and 1, $\hat{y}_{t+1} < y_t$. Also, since y_{t+1} is greater than y_t, we see that $\hat{y}_{t+1} < y_t < y_{t+1}$. Thus our forecast will always be too small. Finally, since smaller values of α put more weight on older data, the smaller the value of α, the worse the forecast becomes. But even with α very close to 1 the forecast is not very good if the ramp is steep. The moral for managers is that exponential smoothing (or indeed any weighted moving average), without an appropriate modification, is not a good forecasting tool in a rapidly growing market. The model could be adjusted to include a trend, but this topic lies beyond the introductory scope of this chapter.

FIGURE 16.22
Seasonal Pattern in y_t

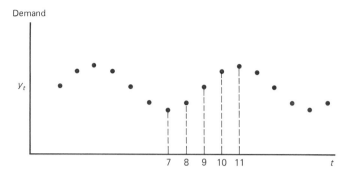

■ **Case 3:** Suppose that a system experiences a regular *seasonal pattern* in y (such as would be the case if y represents, for example, the demand in the city of Chicago for swimming suits). How then will the exponential smoothing model respond, and how will this response be affected by the choice of α? Consider, for example, the seasonal pattern illustrated in Figure 16.22, and suppose it is desired to extrapolate *several periods forward*. For example, suppose we wish to forecast demand in periods 8 through 11 based only on data through period 7. Then

$$\hat{y}_8 = \alpha y_7 + (1 - \alpha)\hat{y}_7$$

Now to obtain $\hat{y}_9$, since we have data only through period 7, we assume that $y_8 = \hat{y}_8$. Then

$$\hat{y}_9 = \alpha y_8 + (1 - \alpha)\hat{y}_8 = \alpha\hat{y}_8 + (1 - \alpha)\hat{y}_8 = \hat{y}_8$$

Similarly, it can be shown that $\hat{y}_{11} = \hat{y}_{10} = \hat{y}_9 = \hat{y}_8$. In other words, $\hat{y}_8$ is the best estimate of all future demands. Now let us see how good these predictions are. We know that

$$\hat{y}_{t+1} = \alpha y_t + \alpha(1 - \alpha)y_{t-1} + \alpha(1 - \alpha)^2 y_{t-2} + \cdots$$

Suppose that a small value of α is chosen. By referring to Figure 16.18 we see that when α is small (say 0.1) the coefficients for the most recent terms change relatively slowly (i.e., they are nearly equal to each other). Thus, $\hat{y}_{t+1}$ will resemble a simple moving average of a number of terms. In this case the future predictions (e.g., $\hat{y}_{11}$) will all be somewhere near the average of the past observations. The forecast thus essentially ignores the seasonal pattern. If a large value of α is chosen, $\hat{y}_{11}$, which equals $\hat{y}_8$, will be close in value to y_7, which is obviously not good. In other words, the model fares poorly in this case regardless of the choice of α.

The exponential smoothing model $\hat{y}_{t+1} = \alpha y_t + (1 - \alpha)\hat{y}_t$ is intended for situations in which the behavior of the variable of interest is essentially stable, in the sense that deviations over time have nothing to do with *time*, per se, but are caused by *random effects* which do not follow a regular pattern. This is what we have termed the *stationarity* assumption. Not surprisingly, then, the model has various shortcomings when it is used in situations (such as swimming suit demand) that do not fit this prescription. Although this statement may be true, it is not very constructive. What approach should a manager take when the exponential smoothing model as described above is not appropriate? In the case of a seasonal pattern a naive approach would be to use the exponential smoothing model on "appropriate" past data. For example, to forecast sales in June one might take a smoothed average of sales in previous Junes. This approach has two problems. First, it ignores a great deal of useful information. Certainly sales from last July through this May should provide at least a limited amount of information about the likely level of sales this June. Second, if the cycle is very long, say a year, this approach means that very old data must be used to get a reasonable sample size. The above assumption, that the system or process producing the variable of interest is essentially *stationary* over time, becomes more tenuous when the span of time covered by the data becomes quite large.

If the manager is convinced that there is either a trend (Case 2) or a seasonal effect (Case 3) in the variable being predicted, a better approach is to develop modified exponential smoothing models that incorporate these features. References to models of this sort exist in the technical literature and the models are not exceptionally complicated. Presentation of these developments, however, carries us too far into the realm of a quite special technique and too far from our goal in this chapter of presenting mainly the basic concepts.

The Random Walk

The moving-average techniques discussed above are examples of what are called time-series models. Recently, much more sophisticated methods for time-series analysis have become available. These methods, based primarily on developments by G. E. P. Box and G. M. Jenkins[4] in the late 1960s, have already had an important impact on the practice of forecasting, and indeed the Box–Jenkins approach is incorporated in certain computer packages.

These time-series forecasting techniques are based on the assumption that the true values of the variable of interest, y_t, are generated by a stochastic (i.e., probabilistic) model. Introducing enough of the theory of probability to enable us to discuss these models in any generality seems inappropriate, but one special and very important (and very simple) process, called a *random walk*, serves as a nice illustration of a stochastic model. Here the variable y_t is assumed to be produced by the relationship

$$y_t = y_{t-1} + \varepsilon$$

where the value of ε is determined by a random event. To illustrate this process even more explicitly, let us consider a man standing at a street corner on a north-south street. He flips a fair coin. If it lands with a head showing, he walks one block north. If it lands with a tail showing, he walks one block south. When he arrives at the next corner (whichever one it turns out to be) he repeats the process. This is the classic example of a random walk. To put this example in the form of the model, label the original corner zero. We shall call this the value of the first observation, y_1. Starting at this point, label successive corners going north $+1, +2, \ldots$. Also starting at the original corner label successive corners going south $-1, -2, \ldots$ (see Figure 16.23). These labels that describe the location of our random walker are the y_t's.

In the model, $y_t = y_{t-1} + \varepsilon$, where (assuming a fair coin) $\varepsilon = 1$ with probability $\frac{1}{2}$ and $\varepsilon = -1$ with probability $\frac{1}{2}$. If our walker observes the sequence H, H, H, T, T, H, T, T, T, he will follow the path shown in Figure 16.23.

Forecasts Based on Conditional Expected Value

Suppose that after our special agent has flipped the coin nine times (i.e., he has moved nine times, and we have, starting with corner 0, 10 observations of corners) we would like to forecast where he will be after another move. This is the typical forecasting problem in the time-series context. That is, we have observed $y_1, y_2, \ldots, y_{10}$ and we need a good forecast $\hat{y}_{11}$ of the forthcoming value y_{11}. In this case, according to a reasonable criterion, the best value for $\hat{y}_{11}$ is the *conditional expected value* of the random

[4] G. E. P. Box and G. M. Jenkins, *Time Series Analysis, Forecasting and Control* (San Francisco: Holden-Day, Inc., 1970).

FIGURE 16.23
Classic Random Walk

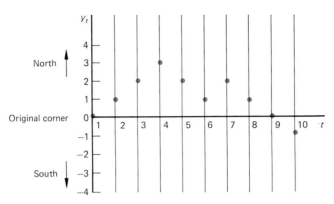

quantity y_{11}. In other words, the best forecast is the expected value of y_{11} given that we know $y_1, y_2, \ldots, y_{10}$. From the model we know that y_{11} will equal $y_{10} + 1$ with a probability equal to $\frac{1}{2}$ and y_{11} will equal $y_{10} - 1$ with a probability equal to $\frac{1}{2}$. Thus, $E(y_{11}|y_1, \ldots, y_{10})$, the conditional expected value of y_{11} given $y_1, y_2, \ldots, y_{10}$, is calculated as follows:

$$E(y_{11}|y_1, \ldots, y_{10}) = (y_{10} + 1)\tfrac{1}{2} + (y_{10} - 1)\tfrac{1}{2} = y_{10}$$

Thus we see that for this model the data $y_1, \ldots, y_9$ are irrelevant and *the best forecast of the random walker's position one move from now is his current position.* It is interesting to observe that the best forecast of y_{12} given $y_1, \ldots, y_{10}$ is also y_{10}. Indeed, the best forecast for any future value of y, given this particular model, is its current value.

Seeing What Isn't There   This example is not as silly as it may seem at first glance. Indeed, there is a great deal of evidence that supports the idea that stock prices behave like a random walk and that the best forecast of a future stock price is its current value. Not surprisingly, this conclusion is not warmly accepted by research directors and technical chartists who make their living forecasting stock prices. One reason for the resistance to the random walk hypothesis is the almost universal human tendency when looking at a set of data to observe certain patterns or regularities, no matter how the data are produced. Consider the time-series data plotted in Figure 16.24. It does not seem unreasonable to

FIGURE 16.24
Time-Series Data

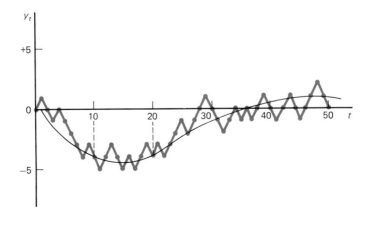

believe that the data are following a sinusoidal pattern as suggested by the smooth curve in the figure. In spite of this impression, the data were in fact generated by the random walk model presented earlier in this section. This illustrates the tendency to see patterns where there are none. In Figure 16.24, any attempt to predict future values by extrapolating the sinusoidal pattern would have no more validity than flipping a coin.

In concluding this section we should stress that it is *not* a general conclusion of time-series analysis that the best estimate of the future is the present [i.e., that $\hat{y}_{t+1} = y_t$]. This result holds for the particular random walk model presented above. The result depends crucially on the assumption that the expected or mean value of ε, the random component, is zero. If the probability that ε equals 1 had been 0.6 and the probability that ε equals -1 had been 0.4, the best forecast of y_{t+1} would not have been y_t. To find this forecast one would have had to find $E(y_{t+1} | y_1, \ldots, y_t)$. Such a model is called a *random walk with a drift*.

_____ 16.5
THE ROLE OF HISTORICAL DATA: DIVIDE AND CONQUER

Historical data play a critical role in the construction and testing of forecasting models. Hopefully, a rationale precedes the construction of a quantitative forecasting model. There may be theoretical reasons for believing that a relationship exists between some independent variables and the dependent variable to be forecast and thus that a causal model is appropriate. Alternatively, one may take the time-series view that the "behavior of the past" is a good indication of the future. In either case, however, if a quantitative model is to be used, the parameters of the model must be selected. For example:

1. In a causal model using a linear forecasting function, $y = a + bx$, the values of a and b must be specified.
2. In a time-series model using a weighted n-period moving average, $\hat{y}_{t+1} = \alpha_0 y_t + \alpha_1 y_{t-1} + \cdots + \alpha_{n-1} y_{t-n+1}$, the number of terms, n, and the values for the weights, $\alpha_0, \alpha_1, \ldots, \alpha_{n-1}$, must be specified.
3. In a time-series model using exponential smoothing, $\hat{y}_{t+1} = \alpha y_t + (1 - \alpha)\hat{y}_t$, the value of α must be specified.

Estimating Parameters and Testing the Model

In any of these models, in order to specify the parameter values, one typically must make use of historical data. A useful guide in seeking to use such data effectively is to "divide and conquer." More directly, this means that it is often a useful practice to use part of the data to estimate the parameters and the rest of the data to test the model.

For example, suppose that a firm has weekly sales data on a particular product for the last two years and plans to use an exponential smoothing model to forecast sales for this product. The firm might use the following procedure:

1. Pick a particular value of α and compare the values of $\hat{y}_{t+1}$ to y_{t+1} for $t = 25$ to 75. The first 24 values are not compared, so as to negate any initial or "startup" effect, that is, to nullify the influence of the initial guess, $\hat{y}_1$. The analyst would continue to select different values of α until the model produces a satisfactory fit during the period $t = 25$ to 75.
2. Test the model derived in step 1 on the remaining 29 pieces of data. That is, using the best value of α from step 1, compare the values of $\hat{y}_{t+1}$ and y_{t+1} for $t = 76$ to 104.

If the model does a good job of forecasting values for the last part of the historical data, there is some reason to believe that it will also do a good job with the future. On the other hand, if by using the data from weeks 1 through 75, the model cannot perform well in predicting the demand in weeks 76 through 104, the prospects for predicting the future with the same model seem dubious. In this case, another forecasting technique might be applied.

A Null Test   The same type of divide-and-conquer strategy can be used with any of the forecasting techniques we have presented. This approach amounts to *simulating* the model's performance on past data. It is a popular method of testing models. It should be stressed, however, that this procedure represents what is termed a "null test." If the model fails on historical data, the model probably is not appropriate. If the model succeeds on historical data, *one cannot be sure that it will work in the future.* Who knows, the underlying system that is producing the observations may change. It is this type of sober experience that causes certain forecasters to be less so.

—— 16.6
QUALITATIVE FORECASTING

Expert Judgment   Many important forecasts are not based on formal models. This point seems obvious in the realm of world affairs—matters of war and peace, so to speak. Perhaps more surprisingly it is also often true in economic matters. For example, during the high-interest-rate period of 1980 and 1981, the most influential forecasters of interest rates were not two competing econometric models run by teams of econometricians. Rather, they were Henry Kaufman of Salomon Brothers and Albert Wojnilower of First Boston, the so-called Doctors Doom and Gloom of the interest-rate world. These gentlemen combined relevant factors such as the money supply and unemployment, as well as results from quantitative models, in their own intuitive way (their own "internal" models) and produced forecasts that had widespread credibility and impact on the financial community.

The moral for managers is that qualitative forecasts can well be an important source of information. Managers must consider a wide variety of sources of data before coming to a decision. Expert opinion should not be ignored. A sobering and useful measure of all forecasts—quantitative and qualitative—is a record of past performance. Good performance in the past is a sensible type of null test. An excellent track record does not promise good results in the future. A poor record, however, hardly creates enthusiasm for high achievement in the future. Managers should thus listen to experts cautiously and hold them to a standard of performance.

There is, however, more to qualitative forecasting than selecting "the right" expert. Techniques exist to elicit and combine forecasts from various groups of experts and we now turn our attention to these techniques.

The Delphi Method and Consensus Panel   The Delphi Method confronts the problem of obtaining a combined forecast from a group of experts. One approach is to bring the experts together in a room and let them discuss the event until a consensus emerges. Not surprisingly, this is called a *consensus panel*. This approach suffers because of the group dynamics of such an exercise. One strong individual can have an enormous effect on the forecast because of his or her personality, reputation, or debating skills. Accurate analysis may be pushed into a secondary position.

The Delphi Method was developed by the Rand Corporation to retain the strength of a joint forecast, while removing the effects of group dynamics. The method uses a

FIGURE 16.25
Delphi Method

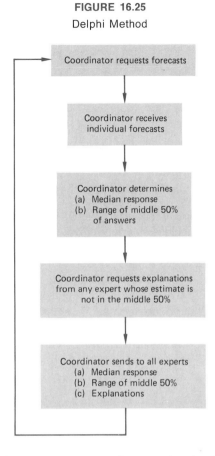

coordinator and a set of experts. No expert knows who else is in the group. All communication is through the coordinator. The process is illustrated in Figure 16.25.

After three or four passes through this process, a consensus forecast typically emerges. The forecast may be near the original median, but if a forecast that is an outlier in round 1 is supported by strong analysis, the extreme forecast in round 1 may be the group forecast after three or four rounds.

Grass Roots Forecasting and Market Research

Other qualitative techniques focus primarily on forecasting demand for a product or group of products. They are based on the concept of asking either those who are close to the eventual consumer, such as salespeople or consumers themselves, about a product or their purchasing plans.

Consulting Salesmen   In grass roots forecasting, salespeople are asked to forecast demand in their districts. In the simplest situations, these forecasts are added together to get a total demand forecast. In more sophisticated systems individual forecasts or the total may be adjusted on the basis of the historical correlation between the salesperson's forecasts and the actual sales. Such a procedure makes it possible to adjust for an actual occurrence of the stereotyped salesperson's optimism.

Grass roots forecasts have the advantage of bringing a great deal of detailed knowledge to bear on the forecasting problem. The individual salesperson who is keenly aware of the situation in his or her district should be able to provide better forecasts than more aggregate models. There are, however, several problems:

1. *High cost:* The time salespeople spend forecasting is not spent selling. Some view this opportunity cost of grass roots forecasting as its major disadvantage.

2. *Potential conflict of interest:* Sales forecasts may well turn into marketing goals that can affect a salesperson's compensation in an important way. Such considerations exert a downward bias in individual forecasts.

3. *Product schizophrenia (i.e., stereotyped salesperson's optimism):* It is important for salesperson to be enthusiastic about their product and its potential uses. It is not clear that this enthusiasm is consistent with a cold-eyed appraisal of its market potential.

In summary, grass roots forecasting may not fit well with other organization objectives and thus may not be effective in an overall sense.

Consulting Consumers   Market research is a large and important topic in its own right. It includes a variety of techniques, from consumer panels through consumer surveys and on to test marketing. The goal is to make predictions about the size and structure of the market for specific goods and/or services. These predictions (forecasts) are usually based on small samples and are qualitative in the sense that the original data typically consists of subjective evaluations of consumers. A large menu of quantitative techniques exists to aid in determining how to gather the data and how to analyze it.

Market research is an important activity in most consumer product firms. It also plays an important role in the political and electoral process.

_____16.7
NOTES ON IMPLEMENTATION

Whether in the private or public sector, the need to deal with the future is an implicit or explicit part of every management action and decision. Because of this, managing the forecasting activity is a critical part of a manager's responsibility. A manager must decide what resources to devote to a particular forecast and what approach to use to obtain it.

What Resources?   The question of "what resources" hinges on two issues:

1. The importance of the forecast, or more precisely, the importance of the decision awaiting the forecast and its sensitivity to the forecast.

2. The quality of the forecast as a function of the resources devoted to it.

In other words, how much does it matter and how much does it cost; these are the same questions that management must ask and answer about many of the services it purchases.

What Methods?   In actual applications, the selection of the appropriate forecasting method for a particular situation depends on a variety of factors. Some of the features that distinguish one situation from the next are

1. The importance of the decision.
2. The availability of relevant data.
3. The time horizon for the forecast.
4. The cost of preparing the forecast.
5. The time until the forecast is needed.

6. The number of times such a forecast will be needed.

7. Stability of the environment.

Choice of Method and Importance of Decision

The importance of the decision probably plays the strongest role in determining what forecasting method to use. Curiously, *qualitative approaches* (as opposed to *quantitative*) dominate the stage at the extremes of important and not very important forecasts.

On the low end of the importance scale, think of the many decisions a supermarket manager makes on what are typically implicit forecasts: what specials to offer, what to display at the ends of the aisles, how many baggers to employ. In such cases, forecasts are simply business judgments. The potential return is not high enough to justify the expenditure of resources required for formal and extensive model development.

On the high end, the decisions are *too important* (and perhaps too complex) to be left entirely to formal quantitative models. The future of the company, to say nothing of the executive, may hinge on a good forecast and the ensuing decision. *Quantitative models may certainly provide important input. In fact, the higher the planning level, the more you can be sure that forecasting models will at least to some extent be employed.* But for very important decisions, the final forecast will be based on the judgment of the executive and his or her colleagues. The extent to which a quantitative model is employed as an input to this judgment will depend, in the final analysis, on management's assessment of the model's validity. A consensus panel (a management committee) is often the chosen vehicle for achieving the final forecast. For example, what forecasts do you think persuaded Henry Ford IV to reject Lee Iacocca's plan to move Ford into small energy-efficient cars in the late 1970s? Also, what forecasts led Panasonic to introduce a tape-based system while RCA introduced a disk-base system for the TV player market? And what about the Cuban missile crisis? The Bay of Pigs? Clearly, management's personal view of the future played an important role.

Quantitative models play a major role in producing directly usable forecasts in situations that are deemed to be of "midlevel importance." This is especially true in short-range (up to 1 month) and medium-range (1 month to 2 years) scenarios. Time-series analyses are especially popular for repetitive forecasts of midlevel importance in a relatively stable environment. The use of exponential smoothing to forecast the demand for mature products is a prototype of this type of application.

Causal models actively compete with various experts for forecasting various economic phenomena in the midlevel medium range. Situations in which a forecast will be repeated quite often, and where much relevant data are available, are prime targets for quantitative models, and in such cases many successful models have been constructed. As our earlier discussion of interest rates forecasts indicated, there is ample room in this market for the "expert" with a good record of performance. In commercial practice one finds that many management consulting groups, as well as specialized firms such as DRI, provide forecasting "packages" for use in a variety of midlevel scenarios.

As a final comment, we can make the following observations about the use of forecasting in decision making within the public sector: Just as in private industry it is often the case that the higher the level of the planning function, the more one sees the use of forecasting models employed as inputs. In such high-level situations there is a high premium on expertise, and forecasting is, in one sense, a formal extension of expert judgment. Think of the Council of Economic Advisors, the Chairman of the Federal Reserve Board, or the Director of the Central Intelligence Agency. You can be sure that forecasts are of importance in these contexts and you can be sure that there is within these environments a continuing updating and, one hopes, improvement of forecasting techniques. As always, the extent to which the results of existing models are employed is a function of the executive's overall assessment of the model itself.

KEY TERMS

CAUSAL FORECASTING. The forecast for the quantity of interest is determined as a function of other variables.

CURVE FITTING. Selecting a "curve" that passes close to the data points in a scatter diagram.

SCATTER DIAGRAM. A plot of the response variable against a single independent variable.

METHOD OF LEAST SQUARES. A procedure for fitting a curve to a set of data. It minimizes the sum of the squared deviations of the data from the curve.

POLYNOMIAL OF DEGREE n. A function of the form $y = a_0 + a_1x + a_2x^2 + \cdots + a_nx^n$. Often used as the curve in a least-squares fit.

TIME-SERIES FORECASTING. A variable of interest is plotted against time and extrapolated into the future using one of several techniques.

SIMPLE n-PERIOD MOVING AVERAGE. Average of last n periods is used as the forecast of future values; $(n - 1)$ pieces of data must be stored.

WEIGHTED n-PERIOD MOVING AVERAGE. A weighted sum, with decreasing weights, of the last n observations is used as a forecast. The sum of the weights equals 1; $(n - 1)$ pieces of data must be stored.

EXPONENTIAL SMOOTHING. A weighted sum, with decreasing weights of *all* past observations; the sum of the weights equals 1; only one piece of information need be stored.

RANDOM WALK. A stochastic process in which the variable at time t equals the variable at time $t - 1$ plus a random element.

PANEL CONSENSUS. An assembled group of experts produces an agreed-upon forecast.

DELPHI METHOD. A method of achieving a consensus among experts while eliminating factors of group dynamics.

GRASS ROOTS FORECASTING. Soliciting forecasts from individuals "close to" and thus presumably knowledgeable about the entity being forecast.

MARKET RESEARCH. A type of grass roots forecasting that is based on getting information directly from consumers.

VALIDATION. The process of using a model on past data to assess its credibility.

LINEAR REGRESSION ANALYSIS. A body of statistics concerned with fitting linear forms to data.

MAJOR CONCEPTS QUIZ

True–False

1. **T F** Quick and dirty forecasting methods are typically based on the method of least squares.

2. **T F** Minimizing total deviations (i.e., $\sum_{i=1}^{n} d_i$) is a reasonable way to define a "good fit."

3. **T F** Least-squares fits can be used for a variety of curves in addition to straight lines.

4. **T F** Regression analysis can be used to prove that the method of least squares produces the best possible fit for any specific real problem.

5. **T F** The method of least squares is used in causal models as well as in time-series models.

6. **T F** In a weighted three-period moving-average forecast the weights can be assigned in many different ways.

7. **T F** Exponential smoothing automatically assigns weights that decrease in value as the data gets older.

8. **T F** Average squared error is one way to compare various forecasting techniques.

9. **T F** "Validation" refers to the process of determining a model's credibility by simulating its performance on past data.

10. **T F** A "random walk" is a stochastic model.

11. **T F** At higher levels of management, qualitative forecasting models become more important.

12. Quick and dirty forecasting methods
   a. consider only the last k data points
   b. primarily apply to problems with one independent variable
   c. use an intuitive measure of good fit
   d. both b and c

13. Linear regression (with 1 independent variable)
   a. requires the estimation of three parameters
   b. is a special case of polynomial least squares
   c. is a quick and dirty method
   d. uses total deviation as a measure of good fit

14. An operational problem with a simple k-period moving average is that
   a. it assigns equal weight to each piece of past data
   b. it assigns equal weight to each of the last k observations
   c. it requires storage of $k - 1$ pieces of data
   d. none of the above

15. A large value of α puts more weight on
   a. recent
   b. older
   data in an exponential smoothing model

16. If the data being observed can be best thought of as being generated by random deviations about a stationary mean, a
   a. large
   b. small
   value of α is preferable in an exponential smoothing model

17. A divide-and-conquer strategy means
   a. Divide the modeling procedure into two parts: (1) Use all the data to estimate parameter values and (2) Use the parameter values from part (1) to see how well the model works.
   b. Divide the data into two parts. Estimate the parameters of the model on the first part. See how well the model works on the second part.
   c. Compare two models on the same data base.
   d. None of the above.

18. The Delphi Method
   a. relies on the power of written arguments
   b. requires resolution of differences via face-to-face debate
   c. is mainly used as an alternative to exponential smoothing
   d. none of the above

19. Conflict of interest can be a serious problem in
   a. the Delphi Method
   b. asking salespeople
   c. marketing research based on consumer data
   d. none of the above

20. Quick and dirty forecasting methods are deficient in that
   a. they require the evaluation of squares and square roots
   b. they cannot be extended to more than one independent variable
   c. they have no objective measure for obtaining a good fit
   d. both b and c

Answers

1. F	6. T	11. T	16. b
2. F	7. T	12. d	17. b
3. T	8. T	13. b	18. a
4. F	9. T	14. c	19. b
5. T	10. T	15. a	20. d

PROBLEMS

16-1. Consider the following set of data:

x	y	x	y
100	57	60	46
70	40	50	45
30	35	20	26
40	33	10	26
80	56	90	53

(a) Plot a scatter diagram of these data.

(b) Fit a straight line to the data using the method of least squares.

(c) Use the function derived in part (b) to forecast a value for y when $x = 120$.

16-2. Consider the following set of data where x is the independent and y the dependent variable:

x_i	y_i
30	35
25	26
20	25
15	5
10	9
5	1

(a) Plot the scatter diagram for these data.

(b) Fit a straight line to the data by the method of least squares.

16-3. Consider the following set of data:

x	y
1	2.00
2	1.50
3	4.50
4	4.00
5	5.50
6	4.50
7	6.00

(a) Plot a scatter diagram of the data.

(b) Fit a straight line to the data by the method of least squares. Plot the line on the scatter diagram.

(c) Fit a quadratic function to the data by the method of least squares. Plot the curve on the scatter diagram.

16-4. Fit a quadratic function to the data in Problem 16.2 by the method of least squares.

16-5. Compare the goodness of fit on the data in Problem 16-2 for the least-square linear function and the least-squares quadratic (derived in Problem 16-4) by calculating the sum of the squared deviations.

16-6. Compare the goodness of fit on the data in Problem 16-3 for the least-squares linear function and the least-squares quadratic function by calculating the sum of the squared deviations.

16-7. Further investigation reveals that the x variable in Problem 16-1 is simply 10 times the time at which an observation was recorded, and the y variable is demand. For example, a demand of 57 occurred at time 10; a demand of 26 occurred at times 1 and 2.

(a) Plot actual demand against time.

(b) Use a simple four-period moving average to forecast demand at time 11.

(c) By inspecting the data, would you expect this to be a good model or not? Why?

16-8. Consider the following data set:

TIME	1	2	3	4	5	6	7	8	9	10	11	12
DEMAND	20	34	14	7	18	30	22	9	20	35	25	13

(a) Plot this time series. Connect the points with a straight line.

(b) Use a simple four-period moving average to forecast the demand for period 13.

(c) Does this seem like a reasonable forecasting device in view of the data?

16-9. Consider the data in Problem 16-7.

(a) Use a four-period weighted moving average with the weights $\frac{4}{10}$, $\frac{3}{10}$, $\frac{2}{10}$, and $\frac{1}{10}$ to forecast demand for time 11. Heavier weights should apply to more recent observations.

(b) Do you prefer this approach to the simple four-period model suggested in Problem 16-7? Why?

16-10. Consider the data in Problem 16-8.

(a) Use a six-period weighted moving average with the weights $\frac{10}{30}$, $\frac{8}{30}$, $\frac{6}{30}$, $\frac{3}{30}$, $\frac{2}{30}$, and $\frac{1}{30}$ to forecast demand for time period 13.

(b) Do you prefer this approach to the simple four-period model suggested in Problem 16-8? Why?

16-11. Consider the data in Problem 16-7.

(a) Let $\hat{y}_1 = 22$ and $\alpha = 0.4$. Use an exponential smoothing model to forecast demand in period 11.

(b) It you were to use an exponential smoothing model to forecast this time series, would you prefer a larger (than 0.4) or smaller value for α? Why?

16-12 Consider the data in Problem 16-8.

(a) Assume that $\hat{y}_1 = 18.35$ and $\alpha = 0.3$. Use an exponential smoothing model to forecast demand in period 13.

(b) If you were to use an exponential smoothing model to forecast this time series, would you prefer $\alpha = 0.3$, a larger (than 0.3), or smaller, value of α? Why?

16-13. The president of Quacker Mills wants a subjective evaluation of the market potential of a new nacho-flavored breakfast cereal from a group consisting of (1) the vice-president of marketing, (2) the marketing manager of the western region, (3) 10 district sales managers from the western region. Discuss the advantages and disadvantages of a consensus panel and the Delphi Method for obtaining this evaluation.

16-14. The president of a midwestern university is considering a new budgeting system in which the large professional schools (business, law, and medicine) will become profit centers. She would like to get an evaluation of this plan from the deans of these schools. Would you recommend a consensus panel or the Delphi approach?

16-15. Given your current knowledge of the situation, would you recommend a causal or a time-series model to forecast next month's demand for Kellogg's Rice Crispies? Why?

16-16. Given your current knowledge of the situation, would you recommend a causal or a time-series model to forecast the number of new housing starts one year from now? Why?

16-1. In some cases it is possible to obtain better forecasts by using a trend-adjusted forecast. For example, consider the following two-step procedure:

1. Calculate $\hat{y}_t$ as before
2. Let $\hat{w}_t$ be the forecast of demand in period $t + 1$ based on data through period t, given as

$$\hat{w}_t = \hat{y}_t + \alpha[\hat{y}_t - \hat{y}_{t-1}] + (1 - \alpha)[\hat{y}_{t-1} - \hat{y}_{t-2}]$$

(a) Use the above trend-adjusted model with $\alpha = 0.4$ to forecast the sequence of demands in Problem 16-11.

(b) Use the average squared error measure to compare the simple exponential smoothing model (Problem 16-11) with the trend-adjusted model from part (a) on forecasting demand for periods 4 through 10, i.e. compare $\frac{1}{7}\sum_{t=4}^{10} (y_t - \hat{y}_{t-1})^2$ with $\frac{1}{7}\sum_{t=4}^{10} (y_t - \hat{w}_{t-1})^2$.

16-18. (a) Use the trend-adjusted model with $\alpha = 0.3$ to forecast the sequence of demands in Problem 16-12.

(b) As in Problem 16-17, compare the above result with the result from Problem That is, compare $\frac{1}{9}\sum_{t=4}^{12} (y_t - \hat{y}_{t-1})^2$ with $\frac{1}{9}\sum_{t=4}^{12} (y_t - \hat{w}_{t-1})^2$.

16-19. Discuss the merit of the measure "average squared error." In comparing two methods, is the one with a smaller average squared error *always* superior?

16-20. With reference to Problem 16-19, what other quantitative measures can you think of for comparing different forecasting methods?

—————— APPENDIX 16.1
FITTING FORECASTING MODELS,
THE DATA TABLE SPREADSHEET COMMAND

It probably occurred to you, as you gained experience with spreadsheet programs in earlier chapters, that Figure 16.17 can easily be generated with a spreadsheet program such as LOTUS 1–2–3. The symbolic spreadsheet for doing this is shown in Figure 16.26. Cell B1 of the spreadsheet contains the value of α used to generate the exponentially weighted moving average. Cells C3 through C14 contain the forecasts for January through December. Recall that Victor decided to use a value of 0.6 for α and a value of 40 for $\hat{y}_1$, the forecast for January. Consequently, 0.6 appears in cell B1 and 40 in cell C3. Cell D3 contains a formula for the weighted average of actual sales in January, the value of cell B3, and forecast sales, the value of cell C3. $B$1 is an absolute reference to the value of α in cell B1. When cell D3 is copied to cells D4 through D14, the absolute reference to cell B1 stays the same while the other cells change. For example, in copying the formula to cell D4, cells B3 and C3 change to B4 and C4. Cells E6 through E14 contain the formulas for computing the squared difference of forecast sales in column C and actual sales in column B. The @SUM in cell E15 totals these squared errors and the @AVG in cell E16 computes their average.

Once the symbolic spreadsheet has been set up, it is feasible to ask "what if" questions such as "what if we change the value of α?" We would like to be able to find the value of α that gives us the lowest average squared error. This is the value of α that provides the best fit of the historical data and so would be a reasonable choice for forecasting future sales. An inefficient way to go about this is to randomly enter different values in cell B1, recalculating the spreadsheet for each new value. A more efficient way is to set up a data table.

FIGURE 16.26
Symbolic Spreadsheet Used to Generate
Figure 16.17

	A	B	C	D	E
1	Alpha =		0.6			
2	Month	Actual Sales	$\hat{y}_t$	$\alpha y_t + (1-\alpha)\hat{y}_t$	Squared Error
3	Jan.		20	40	+ $B$1*B3 + (1 − $B$1)*C3	
4	Feb.		24	+ D3	+ $B$1*B4 + (1 − $B$1)*C4	
5	Mar.		27	+ D4	+ $B$1*B5 + (1 − $B$1)*C5	
6	Apr.		31	+ D5	+ $B$1*B6 + (1 − $B$1)*C6	(C6 − B6) ^ 2
7	May		37	+ D6	+ $B$1*B7 + (1 − $B$1)*C7	(C7 − B7) ^ 2
8	June		47	+ D7	+ $B$1*B8 + (1 − $B$1)*C8	(C8 − B8) ^ 2
9	July		53	+ D8	+ $B$1*B9 + (1 − $B$1)*C9	(C9 − B9) ^ 2
10	Aug.		62	+ D9	+ $B$1*B10 + (1 − $B$1)*C10	(C10 − B10) ^ 2
11	Sept.		54	+ D10	+ $B$1*B11 + (1 − $B$1)*C11	(C11 − B11) ^ 2
12	Oct.		36	+ D11	+ $B$1*B12 + (1 − $B$1)*C12	(C12 − B12) ^ 2
13	Nov.		32	+ D12	+ $B$1*B13 + (1 − $B$1)*C13	(C13 − B13) ^ 2
14	Dec.		29	+ D13	+ $B$1*B14 + (1 − $B$1)*C14	(C14 − B14) ^ 2
15	Total					@SUM(E6..E14)
16	Average					@AVG(E14..E6)

FIGURE 16.27
Data Table of Average Squared Error

	A	B
20		@AVG(E6..E14)
21	0	132.11
22	0.1	159.05
23	0.2	170.30
24	0.3	168.24
25	0.4	157.25
26	0.5	141.70
27	0.6	125.10
28	0.7	109.59
29	0.8	96.11
30	0.9	84.89
31	1	75.78 ← Lowest Average Squared Error

Cells A21 through A31 of Figure 16.27 contain the different values of α for which we want to calculate the average squared errors. Cell B20 contains the formula used to calculate the average squared errors. The average squared errors will appear in cells B21 through B31 when the DATA TABLE command is issued. To issue this command, type /DT1. You will be prompted to enter a data table range and an input cell. The data table range is the rectangular array of cells defined by corner cells A20 and B31. The input cell is cell B1. It appears that $\alpha = 1$ will give the lowest average squared error for this set of data. Note that when $\alpha = 1$, $\hat{y}_{t+1} = y_t$; i.e., the forecast for next month's sales is simply this month's sales.

17

HEURISTICS, MULTIPLE OBJECTIVES, AND GOAL PROGRAMMING

NATIONAL CENTER FOR DRUG ANALYSIS*

The National Center for Drug Analysis is a division of the Bureau of Drugs at FDA (the U.S. Food and Drug Administration). A major responsibility of the National Center for Drug Analysis is the analysis of drug samples in order that the FDA can perform its market surveillance function. A new recent responsibility is implementation of the Good Laboratory Practice Program. This program ensures accuracy and reliability of analytical data which the FDA obtains. Implementation of the latter program requires the allocation of employees' time to numerous activities (e.g., follow-up on quality control stipulations, etc.). The Center has only 44 person-years of staff to allocate to its total responsibilities. The need to implement the Good Laboratory Practice Program implied that not all of the Center's goals could be completely achieved. For example, a goal of analyzing 1600 drug samples per year requires about 20 person-years. A complete implementation of the Good Laboratory Practice Program would leave only 4.9 person-years for drug sample analysis. In order to deal with these competing demands on the limited resources, a goal programming approach was adopted. A formulation with 11 preemptive priorities, 25 constraints,

* Lawrence Jones and K. K. Kwak, "A Goal Programming Model for Allocating Human Resources for the Good Laboratory Practice Regulations," *Decision Sciences*, Vol. 13, No. 1, (January 1982), pp. 156–66.

and 11 decision variables has been implemented as a decision-making tool to evaluate outcomes and costs associated with implementing the Good Laboratory Practice Program. The code is interactive so that priority rankings can be adjusted, allowing management to evaluate the effects of the resource allocations obtained from different priority assignments.

APPLICATION CAPSULE

MANAGEMENT OF COLLEGE STUDENT RECRUITING ACTIVITIES*

Declining enrollments can be costly. A drop in enrollment of 50 students in a single freshman class may result in a four-year revenue loss of nearly a million dollars. But due to a decrease in the birthrate, as well as the high cost of education, college enrollments are falling. This creates a requirement for improved strategies in the recruiting of college freshmen. Since resources are limited, the recruiting effort must be efficient as well as effective.

One approach using the goal programming technique was developed and implemented to manage recruiting activities at a small college in Nebraska. The two major recruiting activities are (1) candidate identification, and (2) follow-up work. Since early in the season the emphasis is on generating a candidate list, three separate models were developed. One model, for the first two quarters, emphasizes candidate identification. Variables include numbers of local high school visits, numbers of long-distance visits, numbers of phone calls made, form letters mailed, personal letters written, and so on. The coefficients needed in the model are estimated from the college's historical data. For the first two quarters, the goal program had nine priorities and fewer than 28 decision variables. The third quarter model gives equal emphasis to candidate identification and follow-up, and in the fourth quarter, follow-up and budget balancing become more important. The overall objective is to identify the type and number of activities that must be completed each quarter in order to reach an enrollment goal for a given year. Use of the model enables recruiters to meet enrollment requirements while managing recruiting resources in order to remain within the budget. The model and its results can also be used as a tool in lobbying for more funds.

* Kenneth E. Kendall and Richard L. Luebbe, "Management of College Student Recruiting Activities Using Goal Programming," *Decision Sciences*, Vol. 12, No. 2, (April 1981), pp. 193–205.

INTRODUCTION

From time to time a manager's problem may be so complex that the mathematical model constructed to attack it cannot be solved with the traditional algorithms which are available to the analyst. This may occur because

1. The model, "correctly formulated," may be too large, too nonlinear, or logically too complex (requiring, for example, the use of many 0–1 variables in the formulation).

2. It is felt that the imposition of simplifying assumptions or approximations, which might make the problem more tractable, would destroy too much of the important real-world structure of the problem (i.e., would carry the model too far from reality to be useful).

Here is a real dilemma. The model at hand is too complex to solve. At the same time we are unwilling to simplify in any ameliorative way. What does one do in this seemingly hopeless situation?

In part to answer this question, the field of heuristic programming has developed. In the discussion above, when we employed the phrase "the problem is too complicated to *solve*" we were using the word *solve* in a rigorous mathematical sense. We meant that the mathematical model was so complicated that, although a rigorous solution exists (e.g., an optimal solution in an optimization model), it is too difficult, perhaps even impossible, to discover with existing know-how and technology. In such a case a *heuristic algorithm* might be employed.

**Heuristic
Algorithm**

A *heuristic algorithm* is one that efficiently provides good approximate solutions to a given problem. Often (but by no means always) in employing such an algorithm one may be able to measure precisely the "goodness" of the approximation. For example, in the optimization context, with some heuristic algorithms one can make a statement like "Upon termination you can be sure of being within _____% of optimality." Or, "Under certain assumptions the heuristic answer will be optimal _____% of the time."

The term *heuristic* is also frequently encountered.

Heuristic

A *heuristic* is an intuitively appealing "rule of thumb" for dealing with some aspect of a problem. A collection of heuristics, or heuristic algorithms, is referred to as a *heuristic program*. Some computer codes, for example, employ heuristics in phase 1 of the simplex method to attempt to quickly find an initial corner. Heuristics are employed to get a quick start with the transportation algorithm, and so on.

As you can infer from the definitions above, heuristics are devices which you no doubt use with frequency in everyday problem solving. In going to the bank, and wanting to minimize your time waiting, you may stand in the shortest line. Although this is by no means guaranteed to be optimal, it is a rule of thumb that often works quite well. In checking through customs you may prefer the bench occupied by a smiling young male officer, although he is certainly not guaranteed to be more lenient than others. The list goes on.

In the context of mathematical programming, heuristics are often employed in conjunction with, or as a special case of, more general or more rigorous problem-solving strategies. The important point to remember is that a heuristic procedure or algorithm is intuitively appealing but can guarantee its results, if at all, only statistically or within certain margins of uncertainty. It is employed mainly for *efficiency*—namely, to produce quickly what are hopefully good, if not optimal, results.

**Combinatorial
Optimization**

In the first part of this chapter we discuss several examples of heuristic algorithms as applied to large *combinatorial optimization* problems. The term *combinatorial opti-*

mization means there are only a finite number of feasible alternatives, and if all of these are enumerated, the optimal one can be found. The problem is that in practice this finite number often amounts to millions or even billions of possibilities and hence even on high-speed computers complete enumeration is out of the question. Although such problems can often be formulated as integer programs with 0–1 variables, they are often so large that even the IP formulation is prohibitively expensive to bring to optimality with the usual branch-and-bound or partial enumeration approach.

Goal Programming

Following the examples in the first part of the chapter we then look at problems for which the objective is to achieve acceptable levels of certain "goals." For example, consider a problem with multiple but conflicting objectives. The president of a firm wants high profits but also wants to maintain low prices in order to keep from losing clients. An executive with a fixed budget wants to invest in R&D but also wants to purchase raw materials to use in obtaining near-term profits. Such examples of multiple but conflicting objectives are typical in business applications. *Goal programming* deals with such problems. The topic is closely related to heuristic programming, for in a sense goal programming itself could be thought of as a heuristic approach to dealing with multiple objectives.

_____ 17.2
FACILITY SCHEDULING (SEQUENCING COMPUTER JOBS)

Sequence-Dependent Setup Time

Consider a single production facility through which numerous jobs must be processed—for example, a computer, a drill press, or an ice cream machine. Typically, the facility may have to shut down after processing one job in order to set up for the next. Such "downtime" is termed *setup*, or *changeover*, time. The length of the setup time may depend on the next job to be processed and the job just completed. A sequence of similar jobs (making French vanilla ice cream after New York vanilla) would be interrupted by less setup time (cleaning out the machine) than a sequence of dissimilar jobs (French vanilla after Dutch chocolate). A typical managerial problem would be to *sequence the jobs in such a way as to minimize total setup time.*

You can easily see that from the combinatorial point of view this can be a very large problem. If there are only three jobs to be processed, say jobs A, B, and C, then any of the three could be taken first, with either of the remaining two second and the third determined (i.e., the single remaining job). The possible sequences can be displayed as a tree with each branch representing one sequence. The six possibilities are shown in Figure 17.1. In general, with n jobs, there are $n! = n(n-1)(n-2)\cdots 1$ possible combinations or sequences. Only 10 jobs produces $10! = 3,628,800$ different sequences. You can see that this number of possible sequences ($n!$) increases rapidly with the size of n.

Obviously, one way to think about solving the minimization problem above is by complete enumeration. That is, generate each of the $n!$ possible sequences of jobs and

FIGURE 17.1
Tree Showing Six Possible Sequences for
Three jobs A, B, C

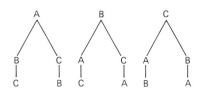

FIGURE 17.2

Setup Times in Minutes

To job / From job	A	B	C
0	27	21	32
A		35	22
B	49		46
C	46	12	

compute the total setup time associated with each sequence. Then pick the sequence associated with the smallest total time. Although this algorithm would provide a true optimum, it is not practical even for modest values of n because of the large number of sequences that would have to be enumerated.

Heuristic rules, although they will not guarantee an optimal solution, are often applied to this problem, for they will usually lead quite quickly to a satisfactory solution.

As an example, consider a computer operator who has three rather long jobs to be run on Monday afternoon. The computer is currently idle. For each of these jobs there is a setup time (searching for input tapes, hanging tapes, setting up the disk drive units and other auxiliary equipment) as specified in Figure 17.2. Since there are only

$$3! = 3 \cdot 2 = 6$$

possible sequences, they can all be enumerated. The results appear in Figure 17.3. As you can see, the optimal (minimum total setup time) sequence is $0 \rightarrow A \rightarrow C \rightarrow B$.

Let us now see how a heuristic rule might be applied to this problem. The rule we shall illustrate is called the *next best rule*, sometimes called a *greedy algorithm*. The rule goes as follows:

A Greedy Heuristic

1. At step 1 (e.g., in selecting the first job), perform the task with least initial setup time.
2. At each subsequent step, select the task with least setup time, based on the current state.

Let us now apply this rule to the data in Figure 17.2. The task with the least initial setup time is B. Hence, the first step is $0 \rightarrow B$. According to the greedy algorithm,

FIGURE 17.3

Results of Complete Enumeration

SEQUENCE	SETUP TIME	TOTAL (MIN)
$0 \rightarrow A \rightarrow B \rightarrow C$	27 + 35 + 46	108
$0 \rightarrow A \rightarrow C \rightarrow B$	27 + 22 + 12	61
$0 \rightarrow B \rightarrow C \rightarrow A$	21 + 46 + 46	113
$0 \rightarrow B \rightarrow A \rightarrow C$	21 + 49 + 22	92
$0 \rightarrow C \rightarrow A \rightarrow B$	32 + 46 + 35	113
$0 \rightarrow C \rightarrow B \rightarrow A$	32 + 12 + 49	93

given that we have just completed B, the task to be selected is C, since the setup for B → C is less than for B → A. Thus, we have 0 → B → C, and we can then finish only with A. Thus, we obtain

$$\text{greedy heuristic: } 0 \rightarrow B \rightarrow C \rightarrow A$$

$$\text{total setup time} = 21 + 46 + 46 = 113$$

Notice that this is far from optimal. In fact, in this example, the greedy heuristic, although intuitively appealing, provides the worst possible policy for our problem.[1] However, the rule is extremely easy to apply, and studies on this type of problem have shown that *statistically*, for the above type of sequencing problem, the rule is not bad. For example, one article[2] shows that the heuristic will often produce better results than could be obtained by a purely random selection of tasks. The same article shows that the following modified heuristic gives even better results:

A Better Heuristic

1. Transform the original data in Figure 17.2 by subtracting the minimum setup time in each column from all other entries in that column. This produces the data in Figure 17.4.

FIGURE 17.4
Transformed Data

	A	B	C
0	0	9	10
A		23	0
B	22		24
C	19	0	

2. Apply the greedy algorithm to this set of transformed data. Doing this, we obtain

Best first step   0 → A

Best second step   A → C

Third step   C → B

and thus the modified heuristic produces the sequence 0 → A → C → B, which was already shown to be optimal for this problem.

Although this modified heuristic will not always give the optimal solution, it is easy to implement and in practice, for large problems, it often produces quite good results.

---

[1] Although it is true that in general, for sequential decision problems, the greedy algorithm does *not* lead to an optimal solution, there are in fact a few special problems for which it does. See, for example, the problem of finding a minimal spanning tree in Chapter 9.

[2] J. W. Gavett, "Three Heuristic Rules for Sequencing Jobs to a Single Production Facility," *Management Science*, 11, (1965), pp. B166–76.

SCHEDULING WITH LIMITED RESOURCES
(WORKLOAD SMOOTHING)

Imagine a sequence of activities to be scheduled in order to complete a project. Basic models such as PERT and CPM will schedule the activities in such a way as to minimize total project completion time subject to the constraint that all precedence relationships must be respected (see Chapter 10). The resources (money, labor, machinery, etc.) needed to complete the individual activities are often considered to be available in any quantities required by any particular schedule. In reality, however, such resources may be limited, in which case this becomes another constraint.

A Simple Example As a simple example, consider the scheduling problem shown in Figures 17.5 and 17.6. Figure 17.5 shows *precedence relationships* among the various activities, that is, which activities must be completed before others can begin. For example, activity VIII cannot begin until VII is completed, and VII cannot begin until I is completed. Figure 17.6 shows the duration of each activity (in weeks) and the resources required (number of people) to complete each activity.

FIGURE 17.5
Precedence Relationships

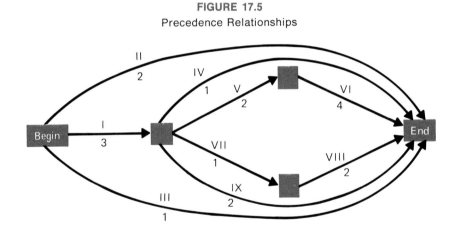

FIGURE 17.6
Requirements for Each Activity

ACTIVITY	TIME REQUIRED TO COMPLETE	PERSONNEL (PER WEEK) REQUIRED TO COMPLETE
I	3	6
II	2	3
III	1	3
IV	1	3
V	2	6
VI	4	5
VII	1	3
VIII	2	4
IX	2	3

FIGURE 17.7
Proposed Schedule of Activities

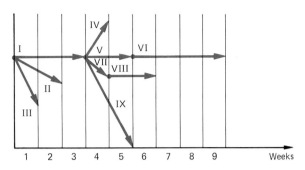

FIGURE 17.8
Personnel Loading Chart for
the Proposed Schedule

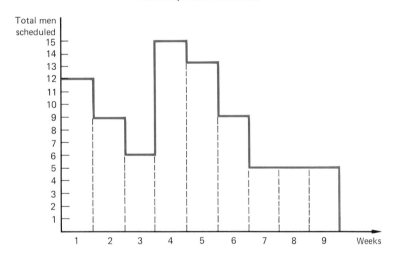

This problem is simple and thus the earliest possible completion time can be easily computed. It is 9 weeks.[3] Figure 17.7 shows a proposed activity schedule that will achieve this overall completion time. Thus, Figure 17.7 respects the precedence relationships of Figure 17.5, and at the same time shows when each activity should start and how long (in weeks) it will take. In this proposed schedule, each activity starts as early as possible. You can see that I, II, and III start immediately (at the beginning of week 1). Activities IV, V, VII, and IX start at the beginning of week 4. Activity VI starts at the beginning of week 6, and activity VIII starts at the beginning of week 5.

Now consider the personnel per week required to implement the proposed schedule. The personnel data in Figure 17.6 can be combined with the schedule in Figure 17.7 **Personnel** to produce the *personnel loading chart* shown in Figure 17.8. As you can see, the proposed **Loading** schedule makes an erratic utilization of personnel, the requirements fluctuating between **Chart** the extremes of 15 people in week 4 and only 5 in weeks 7, 8, and 9. It may be to

---

[3] If you have studied PERT, you can see that activities I, V, and VI form the *critical path*.

management's advantage to have a schedule that employs resources more smoothly. Heuristic programs are often applied to accomplish such an objective.

In order to discuss one such heuristic, let us define, for each activity, its *slack*.

Slack is the maximum amount of time an activity can be delayed without delaying overall project completion.

For example, Figure 17.7 indicates that the slack on activity VIII is 3 weeks, while activity V has no slack.

Now, using this concept, the following heuristic can be given:

Workload Smoothing Heuristic

1. Determine the maximum required resources in the proposed schedule, say m.

2. In each week, impose an upper limit of $m - 1$ for resource utilization, and, if possible, revise the proposed schedule to satisfy this constraint. The revision is systematically performed as follows:

   a. Beginning with the earliest week violating the constraint, consider the activities contributing to the overload and move forward the one with *most* slack as little as possible until it contributes to no overloading, but without delaying the completion of the entire project (which means that activities with zero slack may not be moved). If there are ties, move forward the activity that contributes *least* to the overload (i.e., utilizes the fewest personnel).

   b. The heuristic terminates when the current overload cannot be decreased.

To apply this heuristic, let us portrary the proposed plan as in Figure 17.9. In this figure, the activity label appears below each arrow. Above each arrow is the weekly personnel utilization. For example, the 6 above activity I implies that 6 people are required for each of the 3 weeks needed to complete activity I. Thus, you can read down

FIGURE 17.9
First Proposal

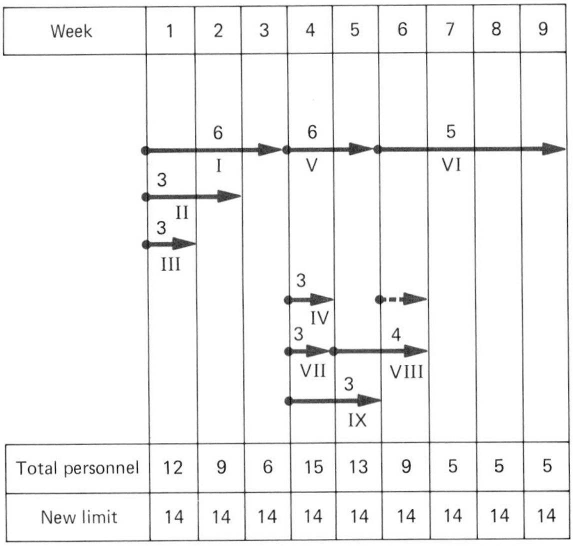

Week	1	2	3	4	5	6	7	8	9
Total personnel	12	9	6	15	13	9	5	5	5
New limit	14	14	14	14	14	14	14	14	14

the appropriate columns to obtain total personnel utilization in a given week. For example, since week 2 is intersected by activities I and II, the entry in the Total Personnel row, under the week 2 column, is 9. Similarly, the distance from the head of each unfollowed arrow at the end of a *series* of jobs to the end of week 9 indicates the slack for such an arrow. Thus, activity IV has 5 weeks of slack, while activity VIII has 3 weeks of slack, and so on. For activity VII, which is a followed arrow, we compute the slack by noting that VII is followed only by VIII. Since the slack on VIII is 3 weeks, slack on activity VII must also be 3 weeks. Also notice that activities I, V, and VI have zero slack since they cannot be moved forward at all without increasing the overall completion time of 9 weeks. In applying the foregoing heuristic we move forward only activities with positive slack, and hence activities I, V, and VI are not considered.

Applying the Heuristic
Given these observations, we may now employ the heuristic. For the first proposal, the maximum required resource is 15 in period 4. Thus, according to step 2, we impose an upper limit of 14 in each week. This is violated only in week 4. The "movable" activities contributing to the overload are IV, VII, and IX (since V need not be considered). Of these, the one which most slack is IV. Moving IV forward 1 period reduces the utilization in week 4 by 3 units to 12 people, but creates a utilization of 3 additional units in week 5, giving a total of 16 in week 5, which overloads week 5 (i.e., violates the imposed upper limit of 14). Hence, it must be moved further forward. You can see that by moving activity IV forward a total of 2 weeks (into week 6 as illustrated in Figure 17.9) no upper limit will be violated. This gives the second proposal, as shown in Figure 17.10.

FIGURE 17.10
Second Proposal

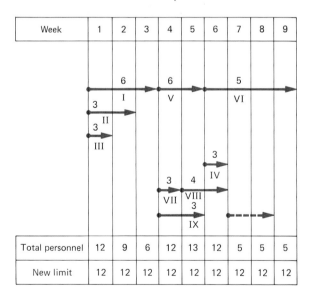

In this figure the upper limit of 13 must be reduced to 12. The only overload is caused by VIII and IX in week 5. Activity IX has the most slack and it must be advanced 3 weeks to begin in week 7, as shown. This gives the third proposal presented in Figure 17.11. Here the upper limit of 12 must be reduced to 11. There are violations in weeks 1 and 6. According to the algorithm, we first move III forward 2 weeks and then IV

FIGURE 17.11
Third Proposal

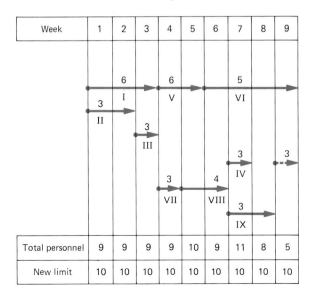

Week	1	2	3	4	5	6	7	8	9
Total personnel	12	9	6	9	10	12	8	8	5
New limit	11	11	11	11	11	11	11	11	11

forward 1 week. Continuing with the heuristic, we obtain the fourth and fifth proposals shown in Figures 17.12 and 17.13.

Heuristic Terminates

The algorithm is unable to improve beyond the fifth proposal. To see this, note that the overload on week 5 can be reduced only by moving forward activity VIII. However, advancing VIII by 1, 2, or 3 weeks would increase the total personnel in weeks 7 and 8 or 8 and 9 to 12. Step 2b of the heuristic *is* thus satisfied, and hence this schedule is the heuristic solution. This final schedule has smoothed the utilization considerably from that shown in Figure 17.8, for the maximum utilization is now 10 (in period 5) and the minimum is 8.

FIGURE 17.12
Fourth Proposal

Week	1	2	3	4	5	6	7	8	9
Total personnel	9	9	9	9	10	9	11	8	5
New limit	10	10	10	10	10	10	10	10	10

FIGURE 17.13
Fifth Proposal

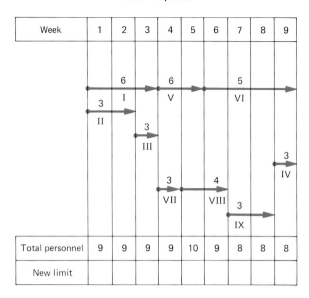

Week	1	2	3	4	5	6	7	8	9
Total personnel	9	9	9	9	10	9	8	8	8
New limit									

For this problem one might define an optimal solution to be a schedule that *minimizes the maximum utilization* of personnel. For the heuristically generated schedule (Figure 17.13) the maximum utilization is 10, occurring in week 5. An optimal schedule, according to this *minimax* criterion, is shown in Figure 17.14. Although the heuristic algorithm did not lead to optimality (in this minimax sense—and it must be admitted that the schedule in Figure 17.14 is smoother than that in Figure 17.13), our heuristic approach did quite well. In large problems (i.e., with many activities) it would not be possible to easily generate the optimal minimax schedule. It is for this reason that a heuristic is often employed to smooth requirements.

FIGURE 17.14
Optical Minimax Schedule

Week	1	2	3	4	5	6	7	8	9
Total personnel	9	9	9	9	9	9	9	8	8

This section and the preceding one have given only a very brief introduction to the important topic of heuristic algorithms. Another example, assigning facilities to locations, is discussed in Problems 2, 3, and 4 at the end of this chapter.

Acceptability of Heuristics

> **Generally speaking, from the viewpoint of a manager, a heuristic procedure may certainly be as acceptable as, and possibly (from a cost consideration) even preferable to, a "more exact" algorithm that produces an optimal solution. The dominant considerations should be the amount of insight and guidance that the model can provide, and the overall net benefit as measured by the difference "savings due to the model less cost of producing the model and its solution."**

_____ 17.4
MULTIPLE OBJECTIVES

The Problem of Multiple Objectives

In many applications, the planner has more than one objective. These different objectives may all be of equal importance or, at the very least, it may be difficult for the planner to compare the importance of one objective as opposed to another. The presence of multiple objectives is frequently referred to as the problem of "combining apples and oranges." Consider for example the corporate planner whose long-range goals are to (1) maximize discounted profits, (2) maximize market share at the end of the planning period, and (3) maximize existing physical capital at the end of the planning period. These goals are not commensurate, which means that they cannot be *directly* combined or compared. It is also clear that the goals are *conflicting*. That is, there are *trade-offs* in the sense that sacrificing the requirements on any one goal will tend to produce greater returns on the others. For example, fewer dollars spent on advertising (less marketing) allows for the building of new plants (more physical capital) and the purchase of more raw materials (more production).

The treatment of multiple objectives is a young but important area in applications. At this time the analytic methods for handling problems with multiple objectives have not been applied as often in practice as some of the other models, such as linear programming, forecasting, and inventory control. However, the concepts involved are important and some leaders in the management science community feel that they will become more important in the near future. The models have been found to be especially useful on problems in the public sector.

Approaches to the Problem

Several approaches to multiple objective problems (also called multicriteria decision making) have been developed. They are use of multiattribute utility theory, search for Pareto optimal solutions via multicriteria linear programming, heuristic search methods, and goal programming. Our discussion is limited to goal programming, a concept introduced by A. Charnes and W. W. Cooper,[4] which in some ways can be thought of as a heuristic approach to the multiple-objectives-problem. Goal programming is a powerful approach that builds on the development of linear programming presented in Chapters 2 through 6. It is an area that is now experiencing considerable interest and development and is potentially an important topic for future mangers.

_____

[4] *Management Models and Industrial Applications of Linear Programming* (New York: John Wiley & Sons, Inc., 1961).

720

Goal programming is generally applied to linear problems; it is an extension of LP that enables the planner to come as close as possible to satisfying various goals and constraints. It allows the decision maker, at least in a heuristic sense, to incorporate his or her preference system in dealing with multiple conflicting goals. It is sometimes considered to be an attempt to put into a mathematical programming context the concept of *satisficing. This term was coined to communicate the idea that individuals often do not seek optimal solutions, but rather, they seek solutions that are "good enough" or "close enough."* We shall illustrate the method of goal programming with several examples.

An Example: Designing an Education Program   Suppose that we have an educational program design model with decision variables x_1 and x_2, where x_1 is the hours of classroom work and x_2 is the hours of laboratory work. Assume that we have the following constraint on total program hours:

$$x_1 + x_2 \leq 100 \qquad \text{(total program hours)}$$

In the goal programming approach there are two kinds of constraints: (1) *system constraints* (so-called "hard constraints") that cannot be violated and (2) *goal constraints* (so-called "soft constraints") that may be violated if necessary. The above constraint on total program hours is an example of a system constraint.

Now, in the program we are designing, suppose that each hour of classroom work involves 12 minutes of small-group experience and 19 minutes of individual problem solving, whereas each hour of laboratory work involves 29 minutes of small-group experience and 11 minutes of individual problem solving. Note that the total program time is at most 60(100) or 6000 minutes. The designers have the following two *goals:* Each student should spend as close as possible to one-fourth of the maximum program time working in small groups, and one-third of the time on problem solving. These conditions are

$$12x_1 + 29x_2 \cong 1500 \qquad \text{(small-group experience)}$$
$$19x_1 + 11x_2 \cong 200 \qquad \text{(individual problem solving)}$$

where the symbol $\cong$ means that the left-hand side is desired to be "as close as possible" to the RHS. If it were possible to find a policy that exactly satisfies the small-group and problem-solving goals (that is, exactly achieves both right-hand sides), without violating the system constraint on total program hours, then this policy would solve the problem. A simple geometric analysis will show that no such policy exists. Clearly then, in order to satisfy the system constraint, at least one of the two goals will be violated.

To implement the goal programming approach, the small-group condition is rewritten as the goal constraint

$$12x_1 + 29x_2 + u_1 - v_1 = 1500 \qquad (u_1 \geq 0, v_1 \geq 0)$$

where u_1 = the amount by which total small-group experience falls short of 1500
   v_1 = the amount by which total small-group experience exceeds 1500

The variables u_1 and v_1 are called *deviation variables*. We note that by definition we want either u_1 or v_1 (or both) to be zero because it is impossible simultaneously to exceed and fall short of 1500. In order to make $12x_1 + 29x_2$ as close as possible to 1500, it suffices to make the sum $u_1 + v_1$ small.

In a similar way, the problem-solving condition is written as the goal constraint

$$19x_1 + 11x_2 + u_2 - v_2 = 2000 \qquad (u_2 \geq 0, v_2 \geq 0)$$

and in this case we want the sum of the two deviation variables $u_2 + v_2$ to be small. Our complete (illustrative) model is now written as follows:

**The Goal
Programming
Model**

$$\text{Min } u_1 + v_1 + u_2 + v_2$$

$$
\begin{array}{lll}
\text{s.t.} & x_1 + x_2 & \leq 100 & \text{(total program hours)} \\
& 12x_1 + 29x_2 + u_1 - v_1 & = 1500 & \text{(small-group experience)} \\
& 19x_1 + 11x_2 \qquad + u_2 - v_2 = 2000 & & \text{(problem solving)} \\
& x_1, x_2, u_1, v_1, u_2, v_2 \geq 0 & &
\end{array}
$$

This is an ordinary LP problem and can now be easily solved on the computer. The optimal decision variables will satisfy the system constraint (total program hours). Also, it turns out that the simplex method (for technical reasons that we shall not dwell on) will guarantee that either u_1 or v_1 (or both) will be zero and thus these variables automatically satisfy this desired condition. The same statement holds for u_2 and v_2 and in general for any pair of deviation variables.

Note that the objective function is the sum of the deviation variables. This choice of an objective function indicates that we have no preference among the various deviations from the stated goals. For example, we are indifferent between the following 3 decisions: (1) a decision that overachieves the group experience goal by 5 minutes and hits the problem-solving goal exactly, (2) a decision that hits the group experience goal exactly and underachieves the problem-solving goal by 5 minutes, and (3) a decision that underachieves each goal by 2.5 minutes. In other words, we are indifferent between the three solutions:

$$
\begin{array}{lll}
(1) \quad u_1 = 0 & (2) \quad u_1 = 0 & (3) \quad u_1 = 2.5 \\
\qquad v_1 = 5 & \qquad v_1 = 0 & \qquad v_1 = 0 \\
\qquad u_2 = 0 & \qquad u_2 = 5 & \qquad u_2 = 2.5 \\
\qquad v_2 = 0 & \qquad v_2 = 0 & \qquad v_2 = 0
\end{array}
$$

We must be indifferent because each of these three decisions yields the same value (5) for the objective function. This condition may be appropriate for this particular problem, but it certainly would not hold for all goal programming problems. Differences in units alone could produce a preference among the deviation variables. Suppose, for example, that the individual problem-solving constraint had been written in hours; that is

$$\frac{19}{60}x_1 + \frac{11}{60}x_2 + u_2 - v_2 = \frac{2000}{60}$$

It is hard to believe that the program designers would be indifferent between a 1-minute excess of small-group experience ($v_1 = 1$) and 1-hour shortfall of individual problem solving ($u_2 = 1$).

**Weighting the
Deviation
Variables**

One way of expressing a preference among the various goals is to assign different coefficients to the deviation variables in the objective function. In the program-planning example one might select

$$\text{Min } 2u_1 + 10v_1 + u_2 + 20v_2$$

as the objective function. Since u_2 (underachievement of problem solving) has the smallest coefficient, the program designers would prefer to have u_2 positive than any of the other deviation variables (positive u_2 is penalized the least). Indeed, with this objective function it is better to be 9 minutes under the problem-solving goal than to exceed by 1 minute the small-group-experience goal. To see this, note that for any solution in which $v_1 \geq 1$, decreasing v_1 by 1 and increasing u_2 by 9 would yield a smaller value for the objective function.

**Goal Interval
Constraints**

Another type of goal constraint is called a *goal interval constraint*. Suppose, for example, that in the above illustration the designers were indifferent among programs for which

$$1800 \leq [\text{minutes of individual problem solving}] \leq 2100$$

$$\text{i.e., } 1800 \leq 19x_1 + 11x_2 \leq 2100$$

In this situation the interval goal is captured with two goal constraints:

$$19x_1 + 11x_2 - v_1 \leq 2100 \qquad (v_1 \geq 0)$$

$$19x_1 + 11x_2 + u_1 \geq 1800 \qquad (u_1 \geq 0)$$

When the terms u_1 and v_1 are included in the objective function, the LP code will attempt to minimize them. We note that when, at optimality, $u_1^* = 0$ and $v_1^* = 0$ (their minimum possible values), the total minutes of problem solving ($19x_1 + 11x_2$) fall within the desired range (i.e., $1800 \leq 19x_1 + 11x_2 \leq 2100$). Otherwise it will turn out that, at optimality, 1 of the 2 variables will be positive and the other 0, which means that only 1 side of the 2-sided inequality can be satisfied.

**Absolute
Priorities**

In some cases managers do not wish to express their preferences among various goals in terms of weighted deviation variables, for the process of assigning weights may seem too arbitrary or subjective. In such cases it may be more acceptable to state preferences in terms of an *absolute priority* of the goals. Before turning to this approach, it will be useful to summarize the various ways in which goal constraints can be formulated and employed.

**Summary on
the Use of Goal
Constraints**

Each goal constraint consists of a left-hand side, say $g_i(x_1, \ldots, x_n)$, and a right-hand side, b_i. Goal constraints are written by using nonnegative *deviational variables* u_i, v_i. At optimality at least one of the pair u_i, v_i will always be zero. The variable u_i represents *underachievement*; v_i represents *overachievement*. Whenever u_i is used it is *added* to $g_i(x_1, \ldots, x_n)$. Whenever v_i is used it is *subtracted* from $g_i(x_i, \ldots, x_n)$. Only deviational variables (or a subset of deviational variables) appear in the objective function, and the objective is always "minimize." The decision variables x_i, $i = 1, \ldots, n$ do not appear in the objective. We have discussed four types of goals:

1. **Target.** Make $g_i(x_1, \ldots, x_n)$ as close as possible to b_i. To do this we write the goal constraint as

$$g_i(x_1, \ldots, x_n) + u_i - v_i = b_i \qquad (u_i \geq 0, v_i \geq 0)$$

and in the objective we minimize $u_i + v_i$. At optimality, at least one of the variables u_i, v_i will be zero.

2. **Minimize Underachievement.** To do this, we can write

$$g_i(x_1, \ldots, x_n) + u_i - v_i = b_i \qquad (u_i \geq 0, v_i \geq 0)$$

and in the objective we minimize u_i, the underachievement. Since v_i does not appear in the objective function, and is in only this constraint, it plays the role of a surplus variable, and hence the constraint can be equivalently written as

$$g_i(x_1, \ldots, x_n) + u_i \geq b_i \qquad (u_i \geq 0)$$

If the optimal u_i is positive, this constraint will be active, for otherwise u_i^* could be made smaller. This is also clear from the equality form of the constraint. That is, if $u_i^* > 0$ then, since v_i^* must equal zero, it must be true that $g_i(x_1, \ldots, x_n) + u_i^* = b_i$.

3. **Minimize Overachievement.** To do this, we can write

$$g_i(x_1, \ldots, x_n) + u_i - v_i = b_i \qquad (u_i \geq 0, v_i \geq 0)$$

and in the objective we minimize v_i, the overachievement. Since in this case u_i plays the role of only a slack variable, the constraint can be equivalently written as

$$g_i(x_1, \ldots, x_n) - v_i \leq b_i \qquad (v_i \geq 0)$$

If the optimal v_i is positive, this constraint will be active. The argument for this is analogous to that in item 2 above.

4. **Goal Interval Constraint.** In this instance, the goal is to come as close as possible to satisfying

$$a_i \leq g_i(x_1, \ldots, x_n) \leq b_i$$

In order to write this as a goal, we first "stretch out" the interval by writing

$$a_i - u_i \leq g_i(x_1, \ldots, x_n) \leq b_i + v_i \qquad (u_i \geq 0, v_i \geq 0)$$

which is equivalent to the two constraints

$$\left. \begin{array}{l} g_i(x_1, \ldots, x_n) + u_i \geq a_i \\ g_i(x_1, \ldots, x_n) - v_i \leq b_i \end{array} \right\} \leftrightarrow \begin{cases} g_i(x_1, \ldots, x_n) + u_i - \hat{v}_i = a_i & (u_i \geq 0, \hat{v}_i \geq 0) \\ g_i(x_1, \ldots, x_n) + \hat{u}_i - v_i = b_i & (\hat{u}_i \geq 0, v_i \geq 0) \end{cases}$$

In the case of a goal interval constraint we minimize $u_i + v_i$ in the objective function. The variables $\hat{v}_i$ and $\hat{u}_i$ are merely surplus and slack, respectively (not deviational variables). As usual, at optimality, at least 1 of the deviational variables u_i, v_i will be 0. In dealing with 2 constraints representing a goal interval, the constraint with the nonzero deviational variable (if there is one) will be active.

In general, goal constraints are most often expressed in the appropriate equality form using deviational variables, surplus, and slack as required. The equivalent inequality forms which we have displayed will allow us, for problems in 2 decision variables, to obtain some geometric insight into the solution procedure.

Swenson's
Media
Selection
Problem (A
Minicase
Involving
Absolute
Priorities)

In this application, we examine another possible facet of goal programming—the assignment of *absolute priorities* (as opposed to weights) to a set of goals.

Tom Swenson, a senior partner at J. R. Swenson, his father's advertising agency, has just completed an agreement with a pharmaceutical manufacturer to mount a radio and television campaign to introduce a new product, Mylonal. The total expenditures for the campaign are not to exceed $120,000. The client is interested in reaching several audiences with this campaign. To determine how well a particular campaign meets this client's needs, the agency estimates the impact of the advertisements on the audiences of interest. The impact is measured in *rated exposures*, a term that means "people reached per month." Radio and television, the two media the agency is considering using, are not equally effective in reaching all audiences. Data relevant to the Mylonal campaign are shown in Figure 17.15.

After lengthy discussions with the client, Tom accepts the following goals for this campaign. Tom feels that the order in which he has listed his goals reflects the absolute priority among them.

1. He hopes total exposures will be at least 840,000.
2. In order to maintain effective contact with the leading radio station, he hopes to spend no more than $90,000 on TV advertising.
3. He feels that the campaign should achieve at least 168,000 upper-income exposures.
4. Finally, if all other goals are satisfied, he would like to come as close as possible to maximizing the total number of exposures. He notes that if he spends all of the $120,000 on TV advertisting he would obtain $120 \times 14,000$, or 1,680,000 exposures, and this is the maximum obtainable.

This is clearly a problem with a number of constraints. It is not quite a typical mathematical programming problem, however, since Tom has a number of objectives. Nevertheless, he feels that a mathematical programming approach will help him understand and solve the problem. He thus proceeds in the typical manner. To model the problem, he introduces the notation

$$x_1 = \text{dollars spent on TV} \qquad \text{(in thousands)}$$

$$x_2 = \text{dollars spent on radio} \qquad \text{(in thousands)}$$

Since his highest-priority goal is total exposures, he feels that a reasonable way to model the problem is to use total exposures as the objective function and to treat the other goals as contraints. The formulation and computer solution of this problem are shown in Figure 17.16. Each constraint and the objective function are labeled to indicate the purpose they serve. We see that the problem is infeasible.

Clearly, since it is infeasible, there is no way to satisfy simultaneously the three goals (total expenditures, TV expenditure, and upper-income exposures) that Tom has stated as constraints. Since there are only two decision variables in this problem, the graphical approach can be used to investigate Tom's initial formulations. The analysis

FIGURE 17.15
Exposures per $1000 Expenditure

	TV	RADIO
Total	14,000	6,000
Upper Income	1,200	1,200

FIGURE 17.16
Maximizing Total Exposures

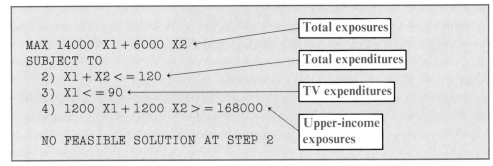

```
MAX 14000 X1 + 6000 X2 ←            [Total exposures]
SUBJECT TO                          [Total expenditures]
  2) X1 + X2 < = 120 ←
  3) X1 < = 90 ←                     [TV expenditures]
  4) 1200 X1 + 1200 X2 > = 168000 ←
                                     [Upper-income
  NO FEASIBLE SOLUTION AT STEP 2     exposures]
```

in Figure 17.17 clearly shows that there are no points that satisfy both the first (total expenditures) and the third (upper-income exposures) constraints. At this point, Tom could attempt to approach the problem somewhat differently. He might change one or more of his goals, or perhaps the objective function, and start again. In general, however, this is not a satisfactory systematic approach. In problems with many decision variables and several conflicting goals, restructuring the problem to create a new problem that has a feasible solution could prove a difficult task. More important, in this restructuring process, the essence of the real problem could be lost.

Recall that Tom is not indifferent about the various goals; indeed, he has stated an absolute priority among them. Goal programming with absolute priorities is designed to handle exactly the type of decision process Tom Swenson wants. It is a sequential process in which goals are added one at a time (in the order of decreasing priority) to an LP problem. A description of the general procedure, illustrated with Tom's advertising campaign problem, follows.

Swenson's Goal Programming Model

In order to set up his problem as a goal program, Tom notes that the first goal, if violated, will be underachieved. The second goal, if violated, will be overachieved, and so on. Employing this reasoning, he restates his goals, in descending priority, as

FIGURE 17.17
Maximizing Total Exposures:
A Graphical Approach

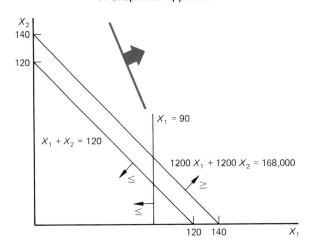

1. Minimize the underachievement of 840,000 total exposures (i.e., Min u_1, subject to the condition $14{,}000x_1 + 6000x_2 + u_1 \geq 840{,}000$, $u_1 \geq 0$).
2. Minimize expenditures in excess of $90,000 on TV (i.e., Min v_2, subject to the condition $x_1 - v_2 \leq 90$, $v_2 \geq 0$).
3. Minimize underachievement of 168,000 upper-income exposures (i.e., Min u_3, subject to the condition $1200x_1 + 1200x_2 + u_3 \geq 168{,}000$, $u_3 \geq 0$).
4. Minimize underachievement of 1,680,000 total exposures—the maximum possible (i.e., Min u_4, where $14{,}000x_1 + 6000x_2 + u_4 \geq 1{,}680{,}000$, $u_4 \geq 0$).

Note that Tom's priorities are now clearly stated in terms of either minimizing underachievement (i.e., minimizing a u_i), or minimizing overachievement (i.e., minimizing a v_i). His goals, as stated above, have been expressed as inequalities in accord with our previous discussion. This will facilitate a graphical analysis.

Given that he has correctly formulated his priorities, Tom must distinguish between (1) *system constraints* (all constraints which may not be violated) and (2) *goal constraints*. In his problem, the only system constraint is that total expenditures will be no greater than $120,000. Thus (since the units of x_1 and x_2 are thousands), we have

$$x_1 + x_2 \leq 120 \qquad \text{(S)}$$

In goal programming notation, Tom's problem can now be expressed as follows:

$$
\begin{aligned}
&\text{Min } P_1u_1 + P_2v_2 + P_3u_3 + P_4u_4 \\
&\text{s.t.} & x_1 + x_2 &\leq 120 & \text{(S)} \\
& & 14{,}000x_1 + 6000x_2 + u_1 &\geq 840{,}000 & \text{(1)} \\
& & x_1 - v_2 &\leq 90 & \text{(2)} \\
& & 1200x_1 + 1200x_2 + u_3 &\geq 168{,}000 & \text{(3)} \\
& & 14{,}000x_1 + 6000x_2 + u_4 &\geq 1{,}680{,}000 & \text{(4)} \\
& & x_1, x_2, u_1, v_2, u_3, u_4 &\geq 0
\end{aligned}
$$

Note that the objective function consists only of deviational variables and is of the *Min* form. As already stated, this is true of every goal programming formulation. In the objective function, the P_k terms serve merely to indicate priorities, with P_1 denoting highest priority, and so on. What the problem statement above means precisely is

1. Find the set of decision variables that satisfies the system constraint (S) and that also gives the Min possible value to u_1 subject to constraint (1) and $x_1, x_2, u_1 \geq 0$. Call this set of decisions FR I (i.e., "feasible region I"). Considering *only the highest goal*, all of the points in FR I are "optimal" (i.e., the best that Tom can do) and (again considering only the highest goal) he is indifferent between which of these points he selects.

2. Find the subset of points in FR I that gives the Min possible value to v_2, subject to constraint (2) and $v_2 \geq 0$. Call this subset FR II. Considering only the ordinal ranking of the two highest-priority goals, all of the points in FR II are "optimal," and in terms of these two highest-priority goals Tom is indifferent between which of these points he selects.

3. Let FR III be the subset of points in FR II that minimize u_3, subject to constraint (3) and $u_3 \geq 3$.

4. FR IV is the subset of points in FR III that minimize u_4, subject to constraint (4) and $u_4 \geq 0$. Any point in FR IV is an optimal solution to Tom's overall problem.

Since Tom's marketing problem has only two decision variables, the solution method above can be accomplished with graphical analysis. In general, the computer would be required. In the next section we show how this can be done using LP.

1. In Figure 17.18, both the computer output and the geometry reveal that the Min of u_1 s.t. (S), (1), and x_1, x_2, $u_1 \geq 0$ is $u_1^* = 0$. Although the computer prints out optimal values for x_1^* and x_2^*, these values are not of interest. The important information is that $u_1^* = 0$, which tells us that the first goal can be completely attained. Alternative optima for the current problem are provided by all values of (x_1, x_2) that satisfy the conditions

$$\text{FR I} \begin{cases} x_1 + x_2 \leq 120 \\ 14{,}000x_1 + 6000x_2 \geq 840{,}000 \\ x_1 \geq 0, x_2 \geq 0 \end{cases}$$

FIGURE 17.18
First Goal

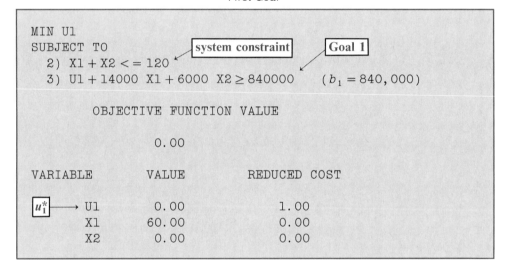

```
MIN U1
SUBJECT TO                    system constraint        Goal 1
   2)  X1 + X2 < = 120
   3)  U1 + 14000 X1 + 6000 X2 ≥ 840000      (b₁ = 840,000)


         OBJECTIVE FUNCTION VALUE

                  0.00


   VARIABLE          VALUE            REDUCED COST

      U1             0.00                1.00
      X1            60.00                0.00
      X2             0.00                0.00
```

u_1^*

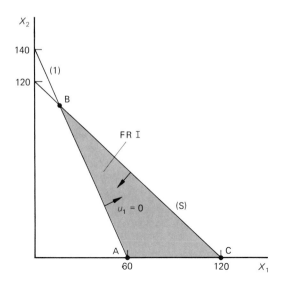

At any such point Tom's first goal is attained ($u_1^* = 0$) so that, in terms of only the first goal, these decisions are equally preferable. Thus FR I is the shaded area ABC. The line labeled (1) represents goal 1. The arrow marked $u_1 = 0$ indicates that at all points to the right of line (1) goal 1 is achieved.

The Feasible Region Becomes Smaller

2. In the computer formulation in Figure 17.19, we have entered the constraints defining FR I (rows 2 and 3), together with the new goal constraint (2), and we see that

$$\text{Min } v_2$$

s.t. x in FR I, goal (2), and $v_2 \geq 0$

FIGURE 17.19
Goal 2

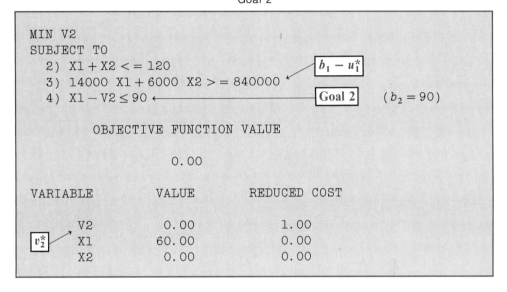

```
MIN V2
SUBJECT TO
  2) X1 + X2 <= 120                          [b₁ − u₁*]
  3) 14000 X1 + 6000 X2 >= 840000
  4) X1 − V2 ≤ 90  ←                          [Goal 2]    (b₂ = 90)

          OBJECTIVE FUNCTION VALUE

                0.00

  VARIABLE          VALUE          REDUCED COST

       V2           0.00              1.00
[v₂*]  X1          60.00              0.00
       X2           0.00              0.00
```

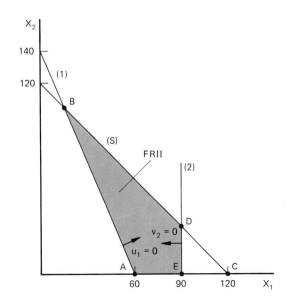

is $v_2^* = 0$. Thus, FR II is defined by

$$\text{FR II} \begin{cases} x_1 + x_2 \leq 120 \\ 14{,}000x_1 + 6000x_2 \geq 840{,}000 \\ x_1 \leq 90 \\ x_1, x_2 \geq 0 \end{cases}$$

which is the shaded area ABDE, clearly a subset of FR I.

Goal 3 Is
Not Attained

Continuing in this way, Figure 17.20 shows that FR III is the line segment BD. In this case $u_3^* = 24{,}000$. Although the first two goals were completely attained (since $u_1^* = v_2^* = 0$), the third goal cannot be completely attained because $u_3^* > 0$. At this stage,

FIGURE 17.20
GOAL 3

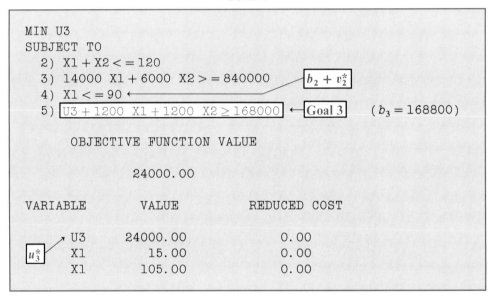

```
MIN U3
SUBJECT TO
   2)  X1 + X2 < = 120
   3)  14000 X1 + 6000 X2 > = 840000        ── b₂ + v₂*
   4)  X1 < = 90  ←
   5)  U3 + 1200 X1 + 1200 X2 ≥ 168000  ← Goal 3   ( b₃ = 168800 )

         OBJECTIVE FUNCTION VALUE

                 24000.00

   VARIABLE          VALUE          REDUCED COST

        U3          24000.00            0.00
u₃*     X1             15.00            0.00
        X1            105.00            0.00
```

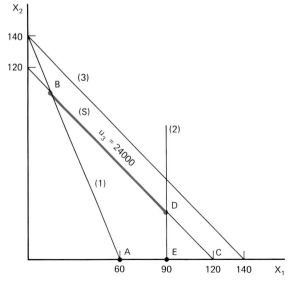

Tom is indifferent about any decision satisfying

$$x_1 + x_2 \leq 120$$

$$14,000x_1 + 6000x_2 \geq 840,000$$

$$x_1 \leq 90$$

$$1200x_1 + 1200x_2 \geq 168,000 - 24,000 = 144,000$$

which defines the line segment BD.

The Optimal Solution
Finally, Figure 17.21 shows the optimal solution at point D. Recall that the fourth goal is to minimize underachievement of the maximum possible number of exposures,

FIGURE 17.21

Optimal Solution

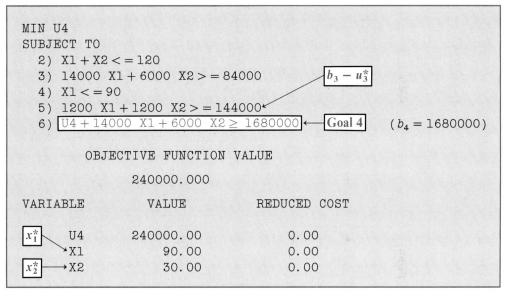

```
MIN U4
SUBJECT TO
   2)  X1 + X2 < = 120
   3)  14000 X1 + 6000 X2 > = 84000          b₃ − u₃*
   4)  X1 < = 90
   5)  1200 X1 + 1200 X2 > = 144000
   6)  U4 + 14000 X1 + 6000 X2 ≥ 1680000     Goal 4    (b₄ = 1680000)


             OBJECTIVE FUNCTION VALUE

                 240000.000

    VARIABLE          VALUE          REDUCED COST

x₁*     U4         240000.00           0.00
        X1             90.00           0.00
x₂*     X2             30.00           0.00
```

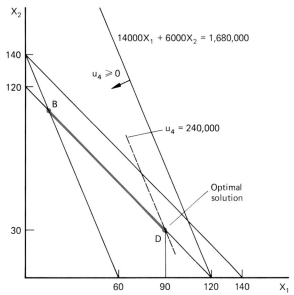

which is 1,680,000. Thus, we wish to minimize the underachievement u_4 where

$$14{,}000x_1 + 6000x_2 + u_4 \geq 1{,}680{,}000$$

In Figure 17.21 we find the unique optimum $x_1^* = 90$ and $x_2^* = 30$; that is, Tom should spend $90,000 on TV advertising and $30,000 on radio advertising. This fact is verified in the geometric analysis, where it is clear that point D ($x_1 = 90$, $x_2 = 30$) is closer to the line that describes goal 4 ($14{,}000x_1 + 6000x_2 = 1{,}680{,}000$) than any other point in FR III (i.e., than any other point on the line BD). We also note that $u_4^* = 240{,}000$. Thus, Tom achieves only $1{,}680{,}000 - 240{,}000 = 1{,}440{,}000$ exposures.

We see, then, that goal programming with absolute priorities allows a manager (like Tom) to solve a problem in which there is no solution that achieves all the goals, but where he is willing to specify an absolute ranking among the goals and successively restrict his attention to those points that come as close as possible to each goal.

Combining Weights and Absolute Priorities

It is possible to combine, to some extent, the concepts of weighted and absolute priority goals. To illustrate this fact, we return to Tom Swenson's advertising problem.

In reviewing the results of the absolute priority study, Tom and his client begin to discuss the importance of the older members of the Mylonal market. In particular, they focus on the number of exposures to individuals 50 years old or older. Again, they see that radio and TV are not equally effective in generating exposures in this segment of the population. The exposures per $1000 of advertising as follows:

	TV	RADIO
50 and over	3000	8000

A New Goal

If there were no other considerations, Tom would like as many 50-and-over exposures as possible. Since radio yields such exposures at a higher rate than TV ($8000 > 3000$), Tom sees that the maximum possible number of 50-and-over exposures would be achieved by allocating all of the $120,000 available to radio. Thus, the maximum number of 50-and-over exposures is $120 \times 8000 = 960{,}000$. Tom and his client would like to be as close as possible to this goal (minimize underachievement) once the first three goals are satisfied. Recall, however, that they also want to be as close as possible to the goal of 1,680,000 total exposures (minimize underachievement) once the first three goals are satisfied. To resolve this conflict of goals, they decide to use a weighted sum of the deviation variables as the objective in the final phase of the absolute priorities approach. It is their judgment that underachievement in the fifth goal (960,000 exposures to the 50-and-over group) is three times as serious as underachievement in the fourth goal (1,680,000 total exposures). The formulation, solution, and graphical analysis are presented in Figure 17.22.

From the computer solution we see that the optimal solution to this problem is point B ($x_1^* = 15$, $x_2^* = 105$). Recall that when the objective function was to minimize u_4, the optimal decision was point D ($x_1^* = 90$, $x_2^* = 30$). Thus, in the graphical analysis, we see that the new objective function has moved the optimal solution from one end of FR III to the other. There is no obvious graphical way to find the optimal solution to this problem; that is, there is not an obvious objective function contour to push in

FIGURE 17.22
Weighting the Final Step

```
MIN 3 U5 + U4
SUBJECT TO
  2) X1 + X2 < = 120
  3) 14000 X1 + 600 X2 > = 840000
  4) X1 < = 90
  5) 1200 X1 + 1200 X2 > = 144000
  6) U4 + 14000 X1 + 6000 X2 ≥ 1680000
  7) U5 + 3000 X1 + 8000 X2 ≥ 960000
```

u_5 = Underachieved 50 and over
u_4 = Underachieved Total Exposures

```
            OBJECTIVE FUNCTION VALUE

                 1065000.00

VARIABLE          VALUE          REDUCED COST

    U5         75000.00            0.00
    U4        840000.00            0.00
    X1            15.00            0.00
    X2           105.00            0.00
```

x_1^* → X1
x_2^* → X2

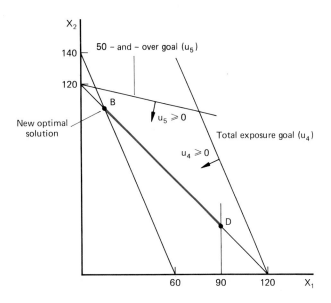

a "downhill" direction that takes us to the point $x_1 = 15$, $x_2 = 105$. It is, however, intuitively appealing to see that the optimal solution is as close as possible to the more heavily weighted goal.

This completes the analysis of Tom Swenson's advertising campaign problem. It is important to note that the general sequential LP procedure described above for goal programming with absolute priorities holds for any problem in which the system constraints and the goal constraints are formulated with linear functions. For each new

733

problem a single constraint is added to the previous model and the objective function is slightly modified. Generally speaking, a fairly large number of decision variables can be involved. The example with two variables was useful since it made it possible to present, in tandem with the computer output, geometric interpretations. This adds insight to the solution technique.

The foregoing problem is useful in indicating how conflicting and noncommensurate goals (i.e., apples and oranges) can be simultaneously considered via goal programming. Thus, it gives some insight into why goal programming is a promising and increasingly useful tool in analyzing public policy questions.

---------- 17.5
NOTES ON IMPLEMENTATION

As is true of most types of quantitative models, heuristic approaches are typically implemented with a computer program. One difference, in practice, between using heuristic procedures, as opposed to more formal models such as linear or quadratic programming, is that in the latter case the computer software already exists. In the heuristic case, however, the application is often *ad hoc*, which implies that the software must be constructed. A typical application of heuristics is, as stated earlier, the area of large combinatorial problems, for which obtaining a solution either by enumeration or by applying a formal mathematical or integer programming model would be prohibitively expensive. In all applications of heuristics there is an implicit managerial judgment that "acceptability" rather than "optimality" is an appropriate way of thinking. In other words, it is felt that "good solutions" as opposed to "optimal solutions" can be useful and satisfactory. *This philosophy is particularly well suited to problems that are rather vague in their statement, such as high-level problems with surrogate objectives or for which there may be numerous conflicting criteria of interest and for which, consequently, there is not a clear definitive single objective function.*

In practice, the use of heuristics is in some cases closely linked to the field of *artificial intelligence*, where the computer is programmed with heuristic techniques to prove theorems, play chess, and even write poems.

Perhaps the most common use of heuristics in management science has been, to date, in problems of assembly-line balancing, job-shop scheduling, and resource allocation in project management. However, recently there has been an increase in the scope of applications to such areas as media selection in marketing, political districting, and scheduling or positioning urban systems.

Interaction between Model and Decision Maker   In the implementation of all heuristic models, managerial interaction and feedback must play perhaps an even greater role than in the case of more formal modeling, for in the heuristic case the manager must assess not only the model but, implicitly, the heuristic algorithm as well. This is because, *for the same model, different heuristics will lead to different "solutions."*

This close interaction between the model and the decision maker is also manifest in goal programming when the decision maker must assign priorities to various goals, such as in the form of ordinal ranking (i.e., *absolute priorities*). Goal programming is an intuitively appealing, and in this sense a "heuristic," approach to problems with multiple objectives. In goal programming with absolute priorities, the manager must consider carefully the "relative importance" or "utility" of his or her goals. Depending on model output, the decision maker may wish to change priorities, or even the number of goals, and rerun the model. In other words, just as with LP, sensitivity analysis becomes an important aspect of implementation. Since goal programming is still more or less in its infancy, the field is developing, from a theoretical point of view, at a rapid rate, and it seems clear that this will prompt greater use of the technique, especially as sensitivity analysis becomes better understood.

In practice, computer codes do exist for solving large-scale goal programs in the batch processing mode, but typically these are not part of the standard program libraries. For problems of modest size, the interactive mode is ideally suited to the sequential technique described in this chapter.

———— 17.6
KEY TERMS

HEURISTIC. An intuitively appealing rule of thumb for dealing with some aspect of a problem.

HEURISTIC ALGORITHM. An algorithm that efficiently provides good approximate solutions to a given problem, often with estimates as to the goodness of the approximation.

HEURISTIC PROGRAM. A collection of heuristics and/or heuristic algorithms.

SETUP TIME. Time required before an activity can begin.

GREEDY ALGORITHM. An algorithm which says that the maximum improvement should be made at each step of a sequential process.

NEXT BEST RULE. Same as the greedy algorithm.

PRECEDENCE RELATIONSHIPS. Means that certain activities must be completed before others may begin.

PERSONNEL LOADING CHART. A bar chart showing the total number of personnel required per week in order to carry out a given schedule of activities.

SLACK. In the project scheduling context this refers to the maximum amount of time any given activity can be delayed without delaying completion of the overall project.

GOAL PROGRAMMING. Seeks allowable decisions which come as close as possible to achieving specified goals.

DEVIATION VARIABLES. Variables used in goal programming to measure the extent to which a specified goal is violated.

INTERVAL GOAL PROGRAMMING. A version of goal programming in which goals are specified by an interval of indifference, rather than by a specific numerical value.

MAJOR CONCEPTS QUIZ ————————————

True–False

1. **T F** Heuristic algorithms are guaranteed to be within a specified percentage of optimality at termination.

2. **T F** The optimal solution to a combinatorial optimization problem can, in principle, be found by complete enumeration.

3. **T F** An alternative heuristic in the problem of scheduling with limited resources is to move forward that activity that contributes *most* to the overload (i.e., utilizes the largest number of personnel).

4. **T F** Goal programming is the only quantitative technique designed for use on problems with multiple objectives.

5. **T F** Each step in goal programming with absolute priorities introduces a new goal and eliminates from further consideration all current candidates that do not satisfy this new goal as well as possible.

6. **T F** Consider the goal constraint $12x_1 + 3x_2 + u_1 - v_1 = 100$. Suppose that, because of other constraints in the model, the goal cannot be achieved. If u_1 is positive the goal is overachieved.

7. **T F** One way to state priorities among goals is to place weights on deviational variables.

8. **T F** Consider the goal interval constraint $180 \le 4x_1 + 12x_2 \le 250$. A correct goal formulation is

$$4x_1 + 12x_2 - v_1 \le 250$$
$$4x_1 + 12x_2 - u_1 \ge 180$$

9. **T F** If a goal interval constraint cannot be achieved (exactly satisfied) then one deviational variable will be positive and the constraint in which that variable appears will be active.

10. **T F** In goal programming a system constraint is not permitted to be violated.

11. **T F** A goal programming problem cannot be infeasible.

**Multiple
Choice**

12. If changeover time of n jobs on a single machine is sequence dependent, the problem of minimizing total setup time requires the inspection of
   a. n
   b. 1
   c. $n!$
   d. $\binom{n}{2}$
   sequences.

13. The intuitively appealing notion that motivates a *greedy* algorithm is
   a. get as close as you can to the optimal solution
   b. do the best you can at the current step
   c. minimize the number of steps required
   d. none of the above

14. In the facility scheduling problem subtracting the minimum setup time in a column from the other entries in that column
   a. is a heuristic based on the notion that it is relative costs that matter
   b. is guaranteed to yield an optimal solution if the greedy algorithm is applied
   c. makes the greedy algorithm not useful
   d. all of the above

15. If a goal programming problem includes the constraint $g_1(x_1, \ldots, x_n) + u_1 - v_1 = b_1$ and the term $6u_1 + 2v_1$ in the objective function, the decision maker
   a. prefers $g_1(x_1, \ldots, x_n)$ to be greater than, rather than smaller than, b_1
   b. prefers $g_1(x_1, \ldots, x_n)$ to be smaller than, rather than larger than, b_1
   c. is indifferent as to whether $g_1(x_1, \ldots, x_n)$ is larger than or smaller than b_1

16. Problems with multiple objectives.
   a. are difficult because it is often true that improving one objective will hurt another
   b. are difficult because the objectives may be in incommensurate units (i.e., the problem of "combining apples and oranges")
   c. can sometimes be treated with the goal programming approach
   d. all of the above

Questions 17, 18, 19 apply to the following problem:
(1) $g_1(x_1, x_2) \le b_1$ is a system constraint
(2) minimizing underachievement of $g_2(x_1, x_2) = b_2$ is top priority
(3) minimizing overachievement of $g_3(x_1, x_2) = b_3$ is next in priority

17. The first step of the solution procedure is
   a. Min u_2, s.t. $g_1(x_1, x_2) \le b_1$, $g_2 - u_2 = b_2$, $x_1, x_2, u_2 \ge 0$
   b. Min u_2, s.t. $g_1(x_1, x_2) \le b_1$, $g_2 + u_2 \ge b_2$, $x_1, x_2, u_2 \ge 0$
   c. Min u_2, s.t. $g_1(x_1, x_2) \le b_1$, $g_2 - u_2 \le b_2$, $x_1, x_2, u_2 \ge 0$

18. Let FR I denote the points (x_1, x_2) obtained in the first step of the solution procedure. The second step is
    a. Min $u_3 + v_3$, s.t. (x_1, x_3) in FR I and $g_3(x_1, x_2) + u_3 - v_3 = b_3$
    b. Min u_3, s.t. (x_1, x_2) in FR I and $g_3(x_1, x_2) + u_3 \le b_3$
    c. Min v_3, s.t. (x_1, x_2) in FR I and $g_3 - v_3 \le b_3$

19. In this model
    a. at least one goal will be achieved
    b. if the first goal is not achieved, the second goal will not be achieved
    c. none of the above

20. Consider a goal program with the constraint

$$g_1(x_1, \ldots, x_n) - v_1 \le b_1, \qquad v_1 \ge 0$$

   with v_1 in the objective function. Then
    a. The goal is to minimize overachievement
    b. if $v_1^* > 0$ then the constraint will be active
    c. neither of the above
    d. both a and b

Answers	1. F	6. F	11. F	16. d
	2. T	7. T	12. c	17. b
	3. T	8. F	13. b	18. c
	4. F	9. T	14. a	19. c
	5. T	10. T	15. a	20. d

PROBLEMS

17-1. For the minimax scheduling problem, find an alternative optimal solution to the one given in Figure 17.14.

Problems 2, 3, and 4 refer to the following example of the so-called *facilities layout problem*:

Solomon Gemorah, high-priced management consultant, has been hired to redo the layout of a small bank. There are 4 key departments to be taken into consideration: (1) Trusts, (2) Estates, (3) Accounting, (4) Savings. These 4 departments must be assigned to 4 locations. The distances between locations are given in Figure 17.23. Thus the distance from location 2 to location 4 is 2 units, from 4 to 1 is 1 unit, and so on. A measure of the 2-way "daily flows" between the 4 key departments is shown in Figure 17.24.

FIGURE 17.23
Distances Between Locations

	LOCATION			
LOCATION	1	2	3	4
1	0	1	2	1
2	1	0	1	2
3	2	1	0	1
4	1	2	1	0

FIGURE 17.24
Flows Between Departments

	DEPARTMENT			
DEPT.	1	2	3	4
1	0	20	19	14
2	20	0	12	10
3	19	12	0	14
4	14	10	14	0

The problem is to assign the 4 departments to the 4 locations (1 department per location) in such a way as to minimize the sum of the distance-weighted daily flows.[5] For example, if we make the assignment of departments to locations as follows: $1 \rightarrow 1, 2 \rightarrow 2, 3 \rightarrow 3, 4 \rightarrow 4$, then the objective value will be

weighted 2-way cost
between facilities 1 and 2 = distance × flow = $1(20)$ = 20

weighted 2-way cost
between facilities 1 and 3 = distance × flow = $2(19)$ = 38

weighted 2-way cost
between facilities 1 and 4 = distance × flow = $1(14)$ = 14

weighted 2-way cost
between facilities 2 and 3 = distance × flow = $1(12)$ = 12

weighted 2-way cost
between facilities 2 and 4 = distance × flow = $2(10)$ = 20

weighted 2-way cost
between facilities 3 and 4 = distance × flow = $1(14)$ = 14

total cost = 118

17-2. (a) Suppose Solomon assigned department 1 to location 2, department 2 to location 3, department 3 to location 4, and department 4 to location 1. What would be the distance between departments? What would be the total cost of Solomon's assignment?
(b) What is the total number of possible assignments of facilities to locations that Solomon would consider if he were to attack the problem by complete enumeration? For the general problem of assigning n facilities to n locations, what is the total possible number of assignments?

17-3. Suppose that facility 1 is assigned to location 1. Analogous to Figure 17.1, draw a tree showing the remaining possible assignments of facilities 2, 3, and 4 to locations 2, 3, and 4.

17-4. (a) How many different pairs of 2 departments can be selected from 4 departments?
(b) Start from the answer to part (a) of Problem 17-2 to improve the assignment by

---

[5] This problem can be formally expressed as a 0–1 integer program as follows. Let

$$x_{pq} = \begin{cases} 1, & \text{if facility } p \text{ is to be placed in location } q \\ 0, & \text{otherwise} \end{cases}$$

and let c_{ikjl} be the cost of placing facility i in location k and facility j in location l. Then the model is

$$\text{Min } \tfrac{1}{2} \sum_{i=1}^{n} \sum_{k=1}^{n} \sum_{j=1}^{n} \sum_{l=1}^{n} c_{ikjl} x_{ik} x_{jl}$$

$$\text{s.t.} \quad \sum_{i=1}^{n} x_{ik} = 1, \qquad k = 1, \dots, n$$

$$\sum_{k=1}^{n} x_{ik} = 1, \qquad i = 1, \dots, n$$

$$x_{ik} = 0 \text{ or } 1, \qquad \text{all } i, k$$

This problem is called the *quadratic assignment problem*.

employing the following Best Pairwise Exchange Heuristic[6], as described below:

■ **Step 1:** Find the potential improvement in the objective function associated with each pairwise exchange of departments. For example, if departments 1 and 2 are exchanged, the new assignment will be $1 \rightarrow 3$, $2 \rightarrow 2$, $3 \rightarrow 4$ and $4 \rightarrow 1$. That is, the location of departments 1 and 2 are changed, but departments 3 and 4 remain unchanged.

■ **Step 2:** Make the pairwise exchange that results in the largest improvement. Then repeat the procedure until no pairwise exchange will improve the value of the objective function.

17-5. Sam Hull is a marketing manager for a pharmaceutical company. He must assign 5 detail people to 5 hospitals. The expected sales are shown in Figure 17.25.

FIGURE 17.25

DETAIL PERSON	HOSPITAL				
	A	B	C	D	E
1	25	18	23	22	16
2	20	21	18	15	12
3	23	19	20	21	20
4	30	26	25	22	20
5	28	22	23	20	18

(a) Use a greedy heuristic to assign each detail person to each hospital so that total expected sales are maximized.

(b) Use the modified heuristic in Section 17.2: After transforming the data by subtracting the maximum sales in each column from all other entries in that column, use the greedy heuristic.

17-6. A computer chip maker tests 3 different characteristics (A, B, and C) before shipping its products. The test time, including a setup time, depends on what test has been done previously. Initially, the testing equipment is not set up for any of the 3 characteristics. Figure 17.26 shows the required time.

FIGURE 17.26

PREVIOUS TEST	TEST		
	A	B	C
O	25	30	18
A	—	45	25
B	30	—	15
C	20	40	—

[6] There are in the literature many heuristics which have been proposed for attacking the facilities assignment problem. In one study involving 12 facilities (R. Mojena, T. Vollmann, and Y. Okamotot, "On Predicting Computational Time of a Branch-and-Bound Algorithm for the Assignment of Facilities," *Decision Sciences* 7, no. 4, (1976), pp. 856–67), it is reported that achieving a true optimum with a branch and bound algorithm required 2 hours on a high-speed computer. In 7 seconds the Best Pairwise Exchange Heuristic produced a proposal that was, in terms of associated objective values, within 3% of the optimum.

(a) Use a greedy heuristic to schedule the tests. The objective is to minimize total test time.

(b) Use the modified heuristic in Section 17.2.

17-7. Erma McZeal is in charge of quality control for the city of Chicago's water supply. There are currently 3 test stations located in Lake Michigan. Letting (x_1, x_2) denote coordinates, the 3 existing locations are placed as follows:

$$\text{station 1:} \quad x_1 = 2, \quad x_1 = 10$$
$$\text{station 2:} \quad x_1 = 6, \quad x_2 = 6$$
$$\text{station 3:} \quad x_1 = 1, \quad x_2 = 3$$

Erma's job is to locate a new station in such a way as to minimize the total distance of the new station from the three existing stations. Assume that, because of existing channel marker locations, distance is measured rectangularly. In other words, if the new station is located at $(x_1 = 3, x_2 = 4)$, then it is a distance of $(3 - 2) + (10 - 4)$, or 7 units, from station 1; and so on. Let (x_1, x_2) denote the coordinates of the new station, and formulate a goal programming model to solve Erma's problem.

17-8. In Problem 17-7, suppose that station 1 handles twice the workload of station 3, and station 2 handles 4 times the workload of station 3. Suppose it is felt that the importance of locating the new station near an existing station is proportional to its workload. Reformulate the model with weights on the deviations that reflect this importance.

17-9. *Product Mix* A firm produces 2 products. Each product must be processed through 2 machines, each of which has available 240 minutes of capacity per day. Each unit of product 1 requires 20 minutes on machine 1 and 12 minutes on machine 2. Each unit of product 2 requires 12 minutes on machine 1 and 20 minutes on machine 2. In determining the daily product mix, management would like to achieve the following goals:

1. Joint total production of 12 units
2. Produce 9 units of product 2
3. Produce 10 units of product 1

Suppose that management wishes to minimize the underachievement of each of these goals and that predetermined priority weights w_1, w_2, and w_3 are to be assigned to the 3 goals, respectively. Formulate this as a goal programming problem.

17-10. In Problem 17-9, suppose that the 3 goals are in order of descending absolute priority.

(a) Use graphical analysis to find an optimal product mix.

(b) Suppose that the marginal costs associated with each unit of products 1 and 2 are, respectively, $6 and $12. Replace the third goal with "keep a daily cost under $125," where you wish to minimize overachievement. Use graphical analysis to find the new solution.

17-11. Consider the goal programming model

$$\text{Min } P_1 v_1 + P_2 v_2 + P_3 u_3 + P_4 (u_4 + v_4)$$

$$\text{s.t.} \quad x_2 + u_1 - v_1 = 100$$
$$x_1 + x_2 + u_2 - v_2 = 80$$
$$x_2 + u_3 = 40$$
$$x_1 + 2x_2 + u_4 - v_4 = 160$$
$$x_1, x_2, u_1, u_2, u_3, u_4, v_1, v_2, v_3, v_4 \geq 0$$

(a) Use the graphical method to solve the problem.

(b) Interpret the third goal $x_2 + u_3 = 40$.

(c) Replace $x_2 + u_3 = 40$ with $x_2 + u_3 \geq 40$. What is the new interpretation?

(d) Use the graphical method to solve the problem with the replacement prescribed in (c).

17-12. Consider the goal programming model

$$\text{Min } P_1 v_1 + P_2 v_2 + P_3 v_3 + P_4(u_4 + v_4)$$

$$\text{s.t.} \qquad x_2 + u_1 - v_1 = 100$$

$$x_1 + x_2 + u_2 - v_2 = 80$$

$$x_1 - v_3 = 40$$

$$x_1 + 2x_2 + u_4 - v_4 = 160$$

$$x_1, x_2, u_1, u_2, u_3, u_4, v_1, v_2, v_3, v_4 \geq 0$$

(a) Use the graphical method to solve the problem.

(b) Interpret the third goal $x_1 - v_3 = 40$.

(c) Replace $x_1 - v_3 = 40$ with $x_1 - v_3 \leq 40$. What is the new interpretation?

(d) Use the graphical method to solve the problem with the replacement prescribed in (c).

17-13. Consider the following goal program:

$$\text{Min } P_1 u_2 + P_2 v_1 + P_3 u_3$$

$$\text{s.t.} \quad x_1 + x_2 + u_1 - v_1 = 80$$

$$x_1 + u_2 - v_2 = 100$$

$$x_2 + u_3 \geq 45$$

$$x_1, x_2, u_1, v_1, u_2, v_2, u_3 \geq 0$$

(a) Solve by the graphical method.

(b) Is the first-priority goal achieved? What about the second and third? In case of under-achievement or overachievement state actual numerical amounts of the violations.

17-14. An electronics firm produces two types of tape recorders: reel-to-reel and cassette. Production of either type requires an average of 3 hours. The plant has a normal production capacity of 150 hours per week. According to the marketing department, in each week 30 cassette recorders can be sold and 25 reel-to-reel recorders can be sold. The reel-to-reel models are twice as profitable as the cassette models. Management has set the following goals, in order of decreasing importance:

1. Minimize underutilization of production capacity.
2. Minimize underachievement of demand of reel-to-reel models.
3. Minimize underachievement of demand of cassette models.
4. Maximize profit.

Formulate the goal programming model and solve it by the graphical method.

17-15. There are 6 jobs to be processed on 2 machines (cutting and grinding). Each job must go through the cutting machine before being processed on the grinding machine. Assume that the sequence in which jobs are processed is the same on both machines. Figure 17.27 shows the time (in hours) required to finish a job on each machine.

FIGURE 17.27

MACHINE	JOBS					
	A	B	C	D	E	F
Cutting	2	5	4	1	4	2
Grinding	2	5	1	1	2	1
Total	4	10	5	2	6	3

The objective is to schedule the jobs so that the time required to finish all jobs is minimized.

(a) How many alternatives should you compare for complete enumeration?

(b) What is the time required to finish all jobs if the jobs are processed in the ascending order of the total processing time? Draw a Gantt Chart for the schedule.

17-16. Given the job-scheduling exercise in Problem 17-15, can you see any improvement when you apply the following heuristic method?

- **Step 1:** List the jobs along with their processing times on the cutting and grinding machines. ·
- **Step 2:** Find the job with the smallest processing time. If the smallest time is on the cutting machine, schedule the job as early as possible; if it is on the grinding machine, schedule it as late as possible. Break ties arbitrarily.
- **Step 3:** Eliminate the job from the list.
- **Step 4:** Repeat steps 2 and 3 until all jobs have been scheduled.

17-17. The city of Chicago is considering 2 projects. Each unit of Project A costs $400, generates 20 jobs, and returns $200 at the end of the year. Each unit of Project B costs $600, generates 40 jobs, and returns $200. The city planner would like to achieve the following goals:

1. Keep total expenditure at or below $2400.
2. Generate at least 120 jobs.
3. Maximize return at end of year.

Suppose that the 3 goals are in order of descending absolute priority. Use graphical analysis to find the optimal number of units to engage in each project. Are the goals achieved? If not, what are the underachievements? What are the net expenditure and the number of jobs generated?

17-18. In Problem 17-17, replace the second goal with "minimize underachievement of generating 200 jobs." What are the underachievements and number of jobs generated? What is the net expenditure?

18

CALCULUS-BASED
OPTIMIZATION AND
AN INTRODUCTION TO
NONLINEAR PROGRAMMING

——— 18.1
INTRODUCTION

There are many problems in business and economics where the functions or mathematical relationships involved are not all linear. You may recall, for example, that the EOQ formula for replenishing inventory (Chapter 11) was derived from a nonlinear relationship. In fact, it is probably true that the real-world problems which fit the strict mold of linearity are the exception rather than the rule.

As a simple illustration, in a linear model price is usually assumed to be a given constant, say p, and quantity to be sold is a variable x which is assumed to be independent of price. Hence, revenue is given by px, and we say that revenue is proportional to price. In reality, however, price may be a variable and quantity of sales (demand) may be dependent on price. This dependency is expressed by writing sales $= f(p)$, where f is some specified (nonconstant) function of p. Thus, revenue would be given by

$$\text{revenue} = \text{price} \cdot \text{sales} = pf(p)$$

which is nonlinear in the variable p. In this case a model to find the price level that maximizes revenue would be a nonlinear model.

In general, some of the prominent (and not necessarily distinct) reasons for nonlinearity are (1) nonproportional relationships [in the example above, revenue is not proportional to price, for, depending on the specific form of $f(p)$, price may increase and revenue decrease]; (2) nonadditive relationships (e.g., when two chemicals are added

743

744

CHAPTER 18
Calculus-Based
Optimization and
an Introduction to
Nonlinear
Programming

together the resulting volume need not be the sum of the two added volumes); and (3) efficiencies or inefficiencies of scale (e.g., when too many workers try to plant beans on the same acre of ground they begin to get into each other's way and the yield per worker will decrease, as opposed to remaining constant[1]). In short, any number of physical, structural, biological, economic, and logical relationships may be responsible for the appearance of nonlinearity in a model.

It must be stated at the outset that, although nonlinear phenomena are common, nonlinear models are considerably more difficult to solve than linear models. Combine this with the fact that linear models, in many contexts, provide *good approximations* to nonlinear models, and you can understand the popularity of linear models, such as LP.

As we know, a model is not the real world. It is an abstract representation of reality. The important point for the modeler is to know when a linearized version provides an *adequate* representation of the nonlinear world. The answer to such a judgmental question comes with experimentation and much experience, and even then only imperfectly and often without consensus. In this chapter we want to address those situations where nonlinear programming models are deemed to be required. Our objective is to provide some understanding of the tools and concepts necessary to deal with nonlinear programming models.

The chapter is organized as follows: The first few sections review the facts concerning *unconstrained* optimization in one decision variable and then in several. Then we give a descriptive and geometric introduction to constrained nonlinear optimization. We then focus on problems with equality constraints, emphasizing the role of Lagrange multipliers and their interpretation in a pricing context. In Section 18.7 we loosely define the concept of concave and convex programs and discuss in a qualitative way the kinds of nonlinear problems that can be routinely solved. The chapter concludes with some notes on implementation of NLP (nonlinear programming), including a brief discussion of the nature of some of the algorithms used to solve NLP problems.

_____ 18.2
UNCONSTRAINED OPTIMIZATION IN ONE DECISION VARIABLE

We here review the problem of optimizing a nonlinear function of a single variable. This is a good starting point because some of the concepts involved will carry over to more general problems.

An Application: Marginal Analysis in Perfume Production

Let us begin with a simple example of a one-dimensional (i.e., single-variable) optimization model:

A perfume manufacturer sells all that it produces, and normally in a year produces between 2000 and 7000 ounces of product. Based on historical data the manufacturer has determined that within the range of its normal production the following equation provides a reasonable estimate of revenue (dollars) in terms of output (ounces of perfume):

$$\text{revenue} = -\frac{1}{500} x^2 + 20x = R(x)$$

In this equation the variable x denotes ounces of output. The marginal cost (cost per ounce) of producing the perfume is estimated to be $4 per ounce. The yearly fixed cost

---

[1] Note that this leads to a nonproportional relationship between total yield and number of workers.

745

CHAPTER 18
Calculus-Based
Optimization and
an Introduction to
Nonlinear
Programming

of production is $10,000. Based on these data, at what level should the firm produce in order to maximize yearly profit?

Let us begin to see how we would go about solving this problem. We are told that the objective is to maximize profit, which is $R(x) - C(x)$ where $R(x)$ is revenue and $C(x)$ is total cost. The revenue function is given. Also, since fixed cost is $10,000 and per unit cost is $4, we deduce that

$$\text{total cost} = 4x + 10{,}000 = C(x)$$

Hence, it follows that

$$\text{profit} = \text{revenue} - \text{total cost} = P(x)$$

$$= R(x) - C(x)$$

$$= \frac{-x^2}{500} + 20x - (4x + 10{,}000)$$

$$= \frac{-x^2}{500} + 16x - 10{,}000$$

The profit, revenue, and total cost functions, since they are all functions of a single variable, can be graphically represented, as shown in Figure 18.1. You can read from the graphic displays in Figure 18.1 that profit is maximized at a production level of approximately 4000 ounces. Our first goal in this chapter is to show how the correct answer to this problem can be precisely obtained by an analytic, as opposed to the more approximate graphic, approach shown in the figure.

**The General
One-
Dimensional
Case**

Henceforth we assume that all variables are continuous (as opposed to discrete as in Chapter 8). Moreover, because we will need to employ differential calculus, *all functions considered will be assumed to be as many times continuously differentiable as required.* Thus, when speaking of second derivatives, for example, it will be assumed that they

FIGURE 18.1
Perfume Data

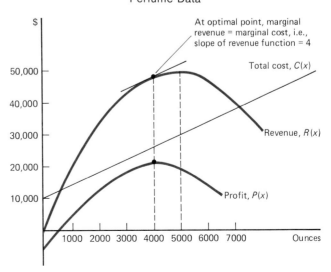

exist and are continuous. It is also assumed that the reader has had some exposure to the differentiation of a function of several variables. Finally, let us state at the outset that when the sense of optimization is important, our preference will always be for the "maximization" flavor. If the real problem is to "minimize," then, as was the case with LP, the negative of the objective function can be maximized. That is, a minimizer of $f(x)$ is a maximizer of $-f(x)$.

Tests for Local Maxima and Minima

Figure 18.2 shows graphs of several "interesting" functions of a single variable. In this figure, points A through I are referred to as *inflection points*, also called *stationary points*, or *critical points*. These are, *by definition, points at which the first derivative vanishes* (has the value zero). Points A, C, E, F, and H are called *local (or relative) maximizers* of the function and the function values at these points are *local (or relative) maxima*. More tersely we shall say, for example, that the function has a local Max at A. Points E, F, and H are also *global maximizers* and the function values at these points are called *global maxima* (we say, for example, that the function has a global Max at E). It is important to emphasize that point A in Figure 18.2 is a local, but not global, maximizer. The function graphed in (i) has no global Max. If a function does have a global maximum, that value (that is, the value of the function at a global maximizer) must, by definition, be unique, although a global maximizer (that is, the maximizing value of the independent variable, x) need not be. For example, consider the function graphed in (iii) of Figure 18.2. The global Max is the numerical value 10, but there is not a unique global maximizer. The points F and H are two different global maximizers.

Also in Figure 18.2, points B, D, and G are called *local (or relative) minimizers* and the function values at these points are *local (or relative) minima* (we say that the function has a local Min at B). There are no global minima in Figure 18.2.

Figure 18.2 reflects the following criterion:

FIRST DERIVATIVE TEST: **If a function f has a local Max or local Min at a point x^*, then $f'(x^*) = (0)$ (i.e., the first derivative vanishes at x^*).**

FIGURE 18.2
Functions of a Single Variable

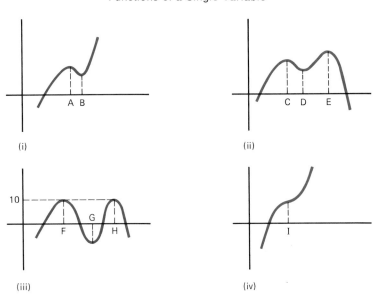

747

CHAPTER 18
Calculus-Based
Optimization and
an Introduction to
Nonlinear
Programming

This is called a *necessary condition* for optimality, which means that *it must prevail* at an optimal point. Assuming that the function is twice differentiable, we can also state a *sufficient condition* for a local optimum (a sufficient condition for an event is one that guarantees its occurrence).

SECOND DERIVATIVE TEST: **If a point x is such that $f'(x) = 0$ and $f''(x) < 0$, then x is a local maximizer of f. If $f'(x) = 0$ and $f''(x) > 0$, then x is a local minimizer of f.**

Concave and Convex Functions

A function f is said to be *strictly concave* at a point if $f''(x) < 0$ at that point. It is a *strictly concave function* if $f''(x) < 0$ for all x and a *concave* function if $f''(x) \leq 0$ for all x. Note that, according to this definition, a linear function is a special case of a concave function (because for a linear function $f''(x) = 0$ for all x). A function g is said to be *convex* at a point x if $g''(x) > 0$ at that point. The function is *strictly convex* if $g''(x) > 0$ for all x and *convex* if $g''(x) \geq 0$ for all x. Note that a linear function is also convex. It is the only function that is both concave and convex.

As an illustration, consider the function $f(x) = 9 - (x - 3)^2$, which is plotted in Figure 18.3. We note that $f'(x) = -2(x - 3)$ and $f''(x) = -2$. Since $f''(x) < 0$ for all x, we observe that f is strictly concave.

Now consider the function $g(x) = (x + 4)^2$, which is also plotted in Figure 18.3. We note that $g'(x) = 2(x + 4)$ and $g''(x) = 2$. Thus, since $g''(x) > 0$ for all x, the function g is strictly convex.

The two functions in Figure 18.3 indicate the general shape of concave and convex functions. It is useful to think of a convex function as being U-shaped and a concave function as having the opposite shape. With these intuitive notions we return to Figure 18.2 and note that *at points A, C, E, F, and H*:

1. The first derivative is zero ($f'(x) = 0$).
2. The function is strictly concave ($f''(x) < 0$) and thus the sufficient conditions for a local maximum are satisfied.

Similarly, *at points B, D, and G*

1. The first derivative is zero ($f'(x) = 0$).
2. The function is strictly concave ($f''(x) < 0$) and thus the sufficient conditions for a local maximum are satisfied.

FIGURE 18.3
Concave and Convex Functions

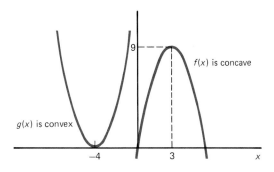

748

CHAPTER 18
Calculus-Based
Optimization and
an Introduction to
Nonlinear
Programming

Inspection of Figure 18.3 suggests the following important facts:

For a concave function [i.e., $f''(x) \leq 0$ for all x] a local Max is also a global Max. For a strictly concave function the global maximizer is unique. For a convex function [i.e., $f''(x) \geq 0$ for all x] a local Min is a global Min. For a strictly convex function the global minimizer is unique.

Let us now apply this theory to the perfume production problem.

Analytic Solution to the Perfume Problem

Recall that the objective here is to maximize profit, where the profit function is given by

$$P(x) = R(x) - C(x) = \frac{-x^2}{500} + 16x - 10,000$$

Differentiating, we obtain

$$P'(x) = \frac{-2x}{500} + 16 \quad \text{and} \quad P''(x) = \frac{-2}{500}$$

Setting $P'(x)$ equal to zero we obtain $(-2x/500 + 16 = 0)$ and solving for x gives us $x^* = 4000$. Since $P''(x) = -\frac{2}{500}$, it is true that $P''(4000) < 0$, which means, by the *second derivative test*, that $x^* = 4000$ is a local maximizer. However, we can go a step further than this. Since $P''(x) < 0$ for all x, we know from the discussion above that P is a strictly concave function and hence $x^* = 4000$ is a *unique global maximizer*. In concluding this example, we can note that since

$$P(x) = R(x) - C(x)$$

it follows that

$$P'(x) = R'(x) - C'(x)$$

We also know that for the optimal value of x (i.e., x^*), $P'(x^*) = 0$. This implies that $R'(x^*) - C'(x^*) = 0$, or $R'(x^*) = C'(x^*)$. The value $R'(x)$ is called the marginal revenue at the point x. The point $C'(x)$ is called the marginal cost at the point x. Thus, as shown in Figure 18.1, we have obtained the well-known result from economic theory that *profit is maximized when marginal revenue equals marginal cost*. In this example, since $C'(x) = 4$, we see that profit is maximized when marginal revenue $= 4$.

Now consider this example.

Example 1 Define

$$f(x) = x^3 + 2x^2 + 2$$

Then

$$f'(x) = 3x^2 + 4x$$

749

CHAPTER 18
Calculus-Based
Optimization and
an Introduction to
Nonlinear
Programming

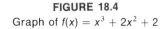

FIGURE 18.4
Graph of $f(x) = x^3 + 2x^2 + 2$

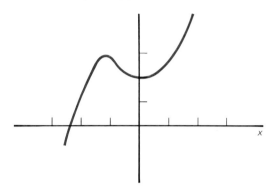

Setting $f'(x)$ equal to zero and solving for x gives

$$3x^2 + 4x = 0$$
$$x(3x + 4) = 0$$
$$x = 0 \text{ or } -\tfrac{4}{3}$$

This gives two stationary points (i.e., points at which $f' = 0$) for the function f. Computing the second derivative gives

$$f''(x) = 6x + 4$$

Evaluating this function at the two stationary points yields

$$f''(0) = 6(0) + 4 = 4 > 0$$
$$f''(-\tfrac{4}{3}) = 6(-\tfrac{4}{3}) + 4 = -8 + 4 = -4 < 0$$

This shows that the function f has a local Min at zero and a local Max at $-\tfrac{4}{3}$. The graph is shown in Figure 18.4.

The above discussion is intended as a review and to provide an initial appreciation for the important role of concavity and convexity in nonlinear optimization. We shall return to this topic in subsequent sections.

_____ 18.3
UNCONSTRAINED OPTIMIZATION IN TWO DECISION VARIABLES

Let us now consider the case of two decision variables, x_1 and x_2. Thus, we consider a function $f(x_1, x_2)$. For the case of two decision variables (that is, two independent variables) we must use partial derivatives to describe local or global optima. We shall use the notation f_{x_i} for first partial derivative, $f_{x_i x_i}$ for second partial derivative, and so on. Any point at which all first partial derivatives vanish is called a *stationary point*. We

750

CHAPTER 18
Calculus-Based
Optimization and
an Introduction to
Nonlinear
Programming

have the following *necessary condition* for optimality:

At a local Max or Min both partial derivatives must equal zero (i.e., $f_{x_1} = f_{x_2} = 0$). That is, a local maximizer or a local minimizer is always a stationary point.

However, as we saw for functions of a single variable, not all stationary points provide maxima and minima. Thus, we may wish to employ the so-called second-order (meaning that second derivatives are involved) sufficient condition for optimality, which in the several-variable case is somewhat more complicated than the necessary condition. The rule is

---

Suppose that $x^* = (x_1^*, x_2^*)$ is a stationary point of f. Define

$$D = D(x_1^*, x_2^*) = [f_{x_1 x_1}(x_1^*, x_2^*)][f_{x_2 x_2}(x_1^*, x_2^*)] - [f_{x_1 x_2}(x_1^*, x_2^*)]^2$$

Case (a): If $f_{x_1 x_1}(x_1^*, x_2^*) > 0$ and $D > 0$, then (x_1^*, x_2^*) is a local minimizer.
Case (b): If $f_{x_1 x_1}(x_1^*, x_2^*) < 0$ and $D > 0$, then (x_1^*, x_2^*) is a local maximizer.
Case (c): If $D < 0$, then (x_1^*, x_2^*) is a so-called saddle point, which is neither a local minimizer nor maximizer. Indeed, at such a point the function will attain a local Max with respect to one of the variables and a local Min with respect to the other, thereby having a saddle shape at that point.
Case (d): If $D = 0$, further analysis (beyond the scope of the present discussion) is required to determine the nature of the stationary point.

Note, in the above conditions, that if $f_{x_1 x_1}(x_1^*, x_2^*) = 0$ then $D \leq 0$ and we are in either Case (c) or Case (d).

**Importing
Coconut Oil:
Profit
Maximization**

Hoot Spa imports coconut oil from his home town in Jamaica. He uses this oil to produce two kinds of tanning creme: Sear and Char. The price per pound at which he will be able to sell these products depends on how much of each he produces. In particular, if Hoot produces x_1 pounds of Sear and x_2 pounds of Char, he will be able to sell all he produces at the following prices (in dollars):

$$\text{price per pound of Sear} = 80 - 3x_1$$

and

$$\text{price per pound of Char} = 60 - 2x_2$$

The cost of manufacturing x_1 pounds of Sear and x_2 pounds of Char is

$$\text{cost of manufacturing the two cremes} = 12x_1 + 8x_2 + 4x_1 x_2$$

751
CHAPTER 18
Calculus-Based
Optimization and
an Introduction to
Nonlinear
Programming

Assuming that he can sell all he produces, Hoot wishes to determine how many pounds of each creme he should schedule for production so as to maximize his profit.

We observe that

$$\text{revenue received for Sear} = x_1(80 - 3x_1)$$

$$\text{revenue received for Char} = x_2(60 - 2x_2)$$

$$\text{total revenue received} = x_1(80 - 3x_1) + x_2(60 - 2x_2)$$

$$\text{profit received} = x_1(80 - 3x_1) + x_2(60 - 2x_2) - (12x_1 + 8x_2 + 4x_1x_2)$$

$$= 80x_1 - 3x_1^2 + 60x_2 - 2x_2^2 - 12x_1 - 8x_2 - 4x_1x_2$$

$$= P(x_1x_2)$$

$$= \text{profit function}$$

Deriving the Necessary Conditions To find the optimal production schedule we first locate the stationary points of the profit function. Taking first partial derivatives of $P(x_1, x_2)$ yields

$$P_{x_1} = 80 - 6x_1 - 12 - 4x_2$$

$$P_{x_2} = 60 - 4x_2 - 8 - 4x_1$$

Hence, solving the *necessary* optimality conditions $P_{x_1} = 0$ and $P_{x_2} = 0$ gives

$$6x_1 + 4x_2 = 68$$

$$4x_1 + 4x_2 = 52$$

The solution to these simultaneous equations is

$$x_1^* = 8 \text{ pounds} \quad \text{and} \quad x_2^* = 5 \text{ pounds}$$

Checking the Sufficient Conditions To see whether this solution actually gives a local maximum, we check the second-order conditions. The second partials of $P(x_1, x_2)$ are

$$P_{x_1x_1} = -6, \qquad P_{x_2x_2} = -4, \qquad P_{x_1x_2} = -4$$

Hence,

$$D = P_{x_1x_1}P_{x_2x_2} - P_{x_1x_2}^2 = (-6)(-4) - (-4)^2 = 8 > 0$$

Since $P_{x_1x_1} = -6 < 0$ and $D > 0$, it follows from Case (b) above that we have a local maximum. In fact (using methods beyond our scope), it can be demonstrated that $P(x_1x_2)$ is a strictly concave function and hence the solution $(x_1^* = 8, x_2^* = 5)$ is in fact a unique global maximizer of the profit. Thus, Hoot should produce 8 pounds of Sear and 5 pounds of Char in order to maximize his profit.

We now turn our attention to a second example.

Example 2 Define

$$f(x_1, x_2) = 5x_1^2 + 10x_2^2 + 10x_1x_2 - 22x_1 - 32x_2 + 20$$

752
CHAPTER 18
Calculus-Based
Optimization and
an Introduction to
Nonlinear
Programming

Let us find all local maximizers and minimizers of this function. To acheive this, we first set both first partials equal to zero and find all solutions. This gives all stationary points of the function, and among these points will be the points we are seeking. Proceeding, then, we obtain

$$f_{x_1} = 10x_1 + 10x_2 - 22 = 0$$
$$f_{x_2} = 20x_2 + 10x_1 - 32 = 0$$

Solving these two equations in two unknowns yields

$$x_1^* = 1.2, \qquad x_2^* = 1.0$$

Thus, there is only one stationary point. To determine its nature we first compute the second partials at (x_1^*, x_2^*):

$$f_{x_1x_1} = 10, \qquad f_{x_2x_2} = 20, \qquad f_{x_1x_2} = 10$$

Since

$$f_{x_1x_1} = 10 > 0$$

and

$$D = (f_{x_1x_1})(f_{x_2x_2}) - (f_{x_1x_2})^2 = (10)(20) - 10^2 = 100 > 0$$

Case (a) applies, and the point (1.2, 1.0) is a local minimizer of the function.

Thus, we have seen that, just as for functions of a single variable, there is a first-order (first derivative) and second-order (involving second derivatives) test that can be applied to locate unconstrained local optima. These tests are called *first-order optimality conditions* and *second-order optimality conditions*. Note that the first-order conditions are necessary; the second-order conditions are sufficient. Also note that the second-order conditions subsume the first-order ones (that is, the second-order conditions assume that x_1^*, x_2^* is a stationary point).

In the absence of knowledge that the function is either concave or convex, a local (as opposed to global) optimizer is the most that one can generally hope to find, as illustrated (in one dimension) by (i) in Figure 18.2. The first derivative test (the necessary condition) says that the local optima are contained among the stationary points of the function. The second derivative test (the sufficient condition) allows us to distinguish between local maximizers and minimizers and points which are neither.

Let us now move on to the most general case, a function of n variables.

_____ 18.4
UNCONSTRAINED OPTIMIZATION IN *n* DECISION VARIABLES: THE COMPUTER APPROACH

Similarities between single-variable optimization and two-variable optimization continue to hold for functions of more than two decision variables. The first similarity is the necessary optimality conditions, which require that all first partial derivatives are zero. In other words, for a differentiable function of n variables, each local optimizer is a

753

CHAPTER 18
Calculus-Based
Optimization and
an Introduction to
Nonlinear
Programming

stationary point. The other similarity is that, to guarantee that a stationary point is, for example, a local maximizer, second-order sufficiency conditions must be invoked. Although these two types of optimality conditions have theoretic interest, they have, for many nonlinear problems in more than two variables, limited *practical relevance*. The reasons are

1. Setting the first partial derivatives equal to zero gives a system of n equations in n unknowns. Unless this system is linear (i.e., the original function was quadratic) it is not easy to find solutions. It may well be impossible to do by hand.
2. The second-order sufficiency conditions are quite complicated, requiring the evaluation of determinants of certain entries in the matrix of second partial derivatives. Indeed, even in the case of one or two decision variables, if the function f is sufficiently complicated, it may not be possible to hand-solve the optimality conditions, and hence this approach is not generally viable.

For these reasons, computer codes have been developed to find local optima of nonlinear functions of n variables (where n is any integer ≥ 1). Often such codes are based on hill-climbing (or hill-descent) behavior. That is, for a maximization problem, as initial point is chosen, and then an uphill direction is determined. Intuitively, the algorithm moves from the initial point, along the straight line in the uphill direction, to the highest point that can be attained on that line. Then a new uphill direction is defined and the procedure is continued. The algorithm terminates when the first partials are sufficiently close to zero. Such a point, then, will always be a "local peak." Other local maxima are searched for by initiating the computer code at a different point.

The description above reveals the main role of the first-order necessary conditions in applications. They are used indirectly, in the sense that they serve as a *termination criterion* for the "hill-climbing" computer codes which search for local optima. The second-order sufficiency conditions, for the general problem in n variables, are mainly of theoretic interest, and go beyond the introductory nature of this chapter.

In concluding this section we mention one other practical approach that one sometimes takes in maximizing a *concave function*. Recall that for a concave function, any stationary point is a global maximizer (for a convex function, any stationary point is a global minimizer). Thus, if we can write out the first derivatives, we can then solve the n equations in n unknowns. Special computer codes exist to solve such systems. Whereas in the general case a solution could be a local maximizer or minimizer or neither, in the concave case we are guaranteed that any solution is a global maximizer. This approach is generally limited to the case of a concave or convex function. Moreover, it is limited by the requirement that the first-order partial derivatives can be explicitly written. For some problems this may not be possible.

_____ 18.5
NONLINEAR OPTIMIZATION WITH CONSTRAINTS: A DESCRIPTIVE GEOMETRIC INTRODUCTION

This chapter, up to this point, has focused on *unconstrained* optimization. More typically, in a management-oriented decision-making setting, we are interested in optimizing an objective function subject to constraints. These constraints are in the form of mathematical equalities and/or inequalities, just as in the case of linear programming, except

754

CHAPTER 18
Calculus-Based
Optimization and
an Introduction to
Nonlinear
Programming

that in this chapter linearity is not assumed. Thus, the *general mathematical programming model*, in symbolic terms, can be written as

$$
\begin{array}{ll}
\text{Max } f(x_1, x_2, \ldots, x_n) & \text{(objective)} \\
\text{s.t.} \quad \left.\begin{array}{l}
g_1(x_1, \ldots, x_n) = b_1 \\
g_2(x_1, \ldots, x_n) = b_2 \\
\quad\vdots \qquad\qquad \vdots \\
g_m(x_1, \ldots, x_n) = b_m
\end{array}\right\} & m \text{ equality constraints} \\
\left.\begin{array}{l}
h_1(x_1, \ldots, x_n) \leq r_1 \\
h_2(x_1, \ldots, x_n) \leq r_2 \\
\quad\vdots \qquad\qquad \vdots \\
h_k(x_1, \ldots, x_n) \leq r_k
\end{array}\right\} & k \text{ inequality constraints}
\end{array}
$$

(P_0)

Graphical Analysis   Just as with LP, we can use two-dimensional geometry to gain insight into this problem. For example, let us use graphical analysis to solve the specific problem

$$
\begin{array}{ll}
\text{Max } x_1 - x_2 \\
\text{s.t.} \quad -x_1^2 + x_2 \geq 1 \\
\qquad\quad x_1 + x_2 \leq 3 \\
\qquad -x_1 + x_2 \leq 2 \\
x_1 \geq 0, \qquad x_2 \geq 0
\end{array}
$$

Note that everything in this model is linear except for the first constraint. A model is called nonlinear if at least one of the constraint functions or the objective function or both are nonlinear. Therefore, the model above is properly termed a *nonlinear program*. In order to use the graphic approach to solve this problem, we proceed just as we did in LP. First we plot the set of points that simultaneously satisfy *all* the constraints. **The Feasible** This is called, just as in LP, the *constraint set*, or the *feasible region*. This set represents **Region** the allowable decisions. In order to find an allowable decision that maximizes the objective function, we find the "most uphill" (i.e., highest-valued) *contour* of the objective function that still touches the constraint set. The point at which it touches will be an optimal solution (often more simply referred to as a solution) to the problem. Figure 18.5 shows the graphical solution to the problem presented above.

Noncorner   You can see in Figure 18.5 that the nonlinear constraint puts curvature into the **Optima** boundary of the constraint set. The feasible set is no longer a polyhedron (i.e., a flat-sided figure defined by linear inequalities), as is the case with LP, and the optimal solution does not lie on a corner. Recall that in the LP case the graphical analysis allowed us to identify the active constraints at an optimal corner and then the *exact solution* was obtained by solving two equations in two unknowns. In general this does not work in the nonlinear case. As shown in Fig. 18.5, there is only one active constraint. We defer to Section 18.6 a discussion of what can be done, in a case like this, to obtain the exact solution algebraically.

755

CHAPTER 18
Calculus-Based
Optimization and
an Introduction to
Nonlinear
Programming

FIGURE 18.5
Graphical Solution to the Nonlinear Model

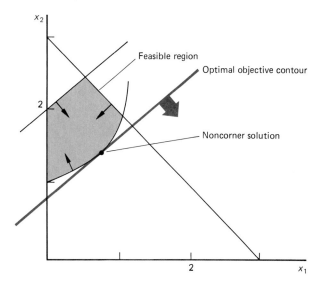

Another example of an NLP is shown in Figure 18.6, which shows a *hypothetical* nonlinear inequality constrained maximization model. In this figure the constraints are all linear, and hence the constraint set is a polyhedron. The objective function, however, is nonlinear, and again it is seen that the solution does not occur at a corner. Of course, a solution *could* appear at a corner, but the important point is that this property is not guaranteed, as it is in the linear model.

This fact has significant algorithmic implications. It means that in the nonlinear case, we cannot use a "corner-searching" method such as the simplex algorithm for finding a solution. This enormously complicates the solution procedure. The topic of solution procedures will be taken up in Sections 18.6, 18.7, and 18.8.

FIGURE 18.6
Noncorner Solution

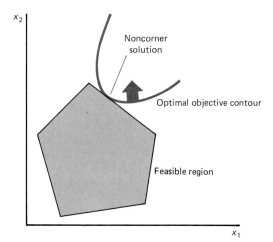

There are several instructive parallels between LP and NLP. For example, the following four statements hold *in either type of model*:

1. Increasing (decreasing) the RHS on a $\leq$ ($\geq$) constraint loosens the constraint. This cannot contract, and may expand, the constraint set.
2. Increasing (decreasing) the RHS on a $\geq$ ($\leq$) constraint tightens the constraint. This cannot expand, and may contract, the constraint set.
3. Loosening a constraint cannot hurt, and may help, the optimal objective value.
4. Tightening a constraint cannot help, and may hurt, the optimal objective value.

Another concept that is common to both LP and NLP is the notion of changes in the OV as a right-hand side changes, with all other data held fixed. This topic was discussed, for LP, in Chapter 5, where we defined the *dual variable* on a specified constraint to be *the rate of change in OV as the RHS of that constraint increases*. In the NLP context this rate of change is often called the *Lagrange multiplier* as opposed to the dual variable, but the meaning is the same. There is, however, one important property of dual variables associated with LP that Lagrange multipliers in the NLP context will not generally share. Recall that in an LP the dual variable (or dual price) is constant for a range of values for the RHS of interest. It can be easily illustrated that in the NLP context this property does not generally hold true. As an illustration, consider the following simple NLP:

$$\text{Max } x^2$$

$$\text{s.t.} \quad x \leq b$$

$$x \geq 0$$

In order to maximize x^2, we want to make x as large as possible. Thus, the optimal solution is $x^* = b$, and the optimal value of the objective function, which we call the OV, is $(x^*)^2 = b^2$. Thus you can see that the OV is a function of b. That is

$$\text{OV}(b) = b^2$$

From basic calculus we know that the rate of change of this function as b increases is the derivative of OV(b), namely $2b$. In other words, the Lagrange multiplier is *not* constant for a range of values of the RHS, b. It varies continuously with b.[2]

Another important difference between LP and NLP has to do with *global, versus local, solutions*. In an LP, it is always true that there cannot be a local solution that is not also global. This is not generally true for general nonlinear programming problems. In other words, such problems may have local, as well as global, solutions. This is illustrated by the hypothetical Max model in Figure 18.7. In this figure, the point identified as "Local" is termed a *local constrained maximizer* because the value of the objective function at this point is no smaller than at its *neighboring* feasible points. The point identified as "Global" is termed a *global constrained maximizer* because the value of the

---

[2] It may be briefly noted that this same example also serves to illustrate that the optimal value for a NLP *Max* problem can exhibit increasing marginal returns. This can *never* happen in LP (i.e., the OV for an LP *Max* model *always* exhibits nonincreasing marginal returns).

757

CHAPTER 18
Calculus-Based
Optimization and
an Introduction to
Nonlinear
Programming

FIGURE 18.7
Local and Global Solutions

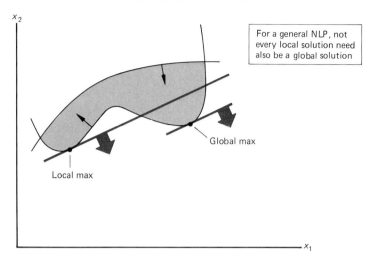

objective function at this point is no smaller than at *all other* feasible points. As was the case with unconstrained optimization, certain convexity and concavity conditions must be satisfied to gaurantee that a local constrained optimizer is also global. These properties will be defined in Section 18.7. In the absence of these properties it is generally not possibly to know whether a given solution is a local or a global maximizer.

_____ 18.6
EQUALITY-CONSTRAINED MODELS AND LAGRANGE MULTIPLIERS

Many problems in business and economics are of the form

$$\text{Maximize (or Minimize)} \ f(x_1, \ldots, x_n)$$
$$\text{s.t. } g_i(x_1, \ldots, x_n) = b_i, \qquad i = 1, \ldots, m \qquad (m < n) \tag{P_1}$$

that is, the goal is to maximize or minimize an objective function in n variables subject to a set of m $(m < n)$ *equality* constraints. Here are two examples:

Example 3   A manufacturer can make a product on either of two machines. Let x_1 denote the quantity made on machine 1, and x_2 the quantity on machine 2. Let

$$a_1 x_1 + b_1 x_1^2 = \text{cost of producing on machine 1}$$
$$a_2 x_2 + b_2 x_2^2 = \text{cost of producing on machine 2}$$

Determine the values of x_1 and x_2 that minimize total cost subject to the requirement that total production is some specified value, say R. The formulation of this problem is

$$\text{Min } a_1 x_1 + b_1 x_1^2 + a_2 x_2 + b_2 x_2^2$$
$$\text{s.t. } x_1 + x_2 = R$$

758

CHAPTER 18
Calculus-Based
Optimization and
an Introduction to
Nonlinear
Programming

Example 4 Let p_1, p_2, and p_3 denote given prices of three goods and let B denote the available budget (i.e., B is a specified constant). Let s_1, s_2, and s_3 be given constants and let $x_1^{s_1} + x_2^{s_2} + x_3^{s_3}$ denote the "utility derived" from consuming x_1 units of good 1, x_2 units of good 2, and x_3 units of good 3. Determine the consumption mix that maximizes utility subject to the budget constraint. The formulation of this problem is

$$\text{Max } x_1^{s_1} + x_2^{s_2} + x_3^{s_3}$$

$$\text{s.t. } \quad p_1 x_1 + p_2 x_2 + p_3 x_3 = B$$

In both of these examples the physical interpretations require the decision variables to be nonnegative. We shall assume that the parameters in the two models (a_i and b_i, $i = 1$, 2 in Example 3; and p_i, s_i, $i = 1$, 2, 3 and B in Example 4) are such that the optimal solutions will for sure turn out to be nonnegative, and hence nonnegativity constraints need not be explicitly included. Such conditions, if appended, would convert the models to more difficult problems with both equality *and* inequality conditions.

The Case with Two Variables Before analyzing the above general problem (P$_1$) let us consider the special case of two decision variables and one equality constraint. Thus, we treat the problem

$$\text{Max } f(x_1, x_2)$$

$$\text{s.t. } \quad g(x_1, x_2) = b \qquad \text{(P}_2\text{)}$$

Example 5 As a particular example of (P$_2$), consider the problem

$$\text{Max } x_1 - x_2$$

$$\text{s.t. } \quad -x_1^2 + x_2 = 1$$

The geometric analysis is shown in Figure 18.8. The graphical analysis shows that at the optimal solution the contour of the objective function is tangent to the equality constraint. It also suggests that the optimal solution is approximately $x_1^* = 0.5$ and $x_2^* = 1.25$. We shall now show how to solve this problem analytically. To do this, we make use of the tools of differential calculus. The formal solution procedure is called the *Lagrangian technique*. This procedure includes four steps that are specified below for problem (P$_2$):

Implementing the Lagrangian Technique

■ **Step 1: Form Lagrangian** Form a *new* function called the *Lagrangian*. This function involves a new variable, which we shall denote as λ, and which is called a *Lagrange multiplier*. The function, *for a maximization model*, is

$$L(x_1, x_2, \lambda) = f(x_1, x_2) + \lambda(b - g(x_1, x_2))$$

■ **Step 2: Take partial derivatives** Compute the partial derivatives of the Lagrangian with respect to x_1, x_2, *and* λ, and set these partial derivatives equal to zero to obtain

$$L_{x_1} = f_{x_1} - \lambda g_{x_1} = 0 \qquad (18.1)$$

$$L_{x_2} = f_{x_2} - \lambda g_{x_2} = 0 \qquad (18.2)$$

$$L_\lambda = b - g = 0 \qquad (18.3)$$

759

CHAPTER 18
Calculus-Based
Optimization and
an Introduction to
Nonlinear
Programming

FIGURE 18.8
Graphical Solution

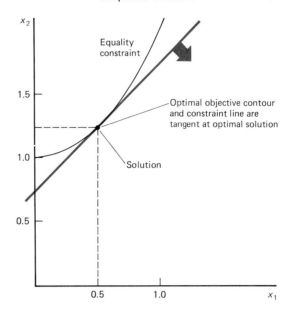

■ **Step 3: Find all solutions** Find the values x_1^*, x_2^*, λ^* that satisfy the equations derived in step 2. These equations are the first-order necessary optimality conditions for (P_2).

■ **Step 4: Check sufficiency conditions** For each triple $(x_1^*, x_2^*, \lambda^*)$ determined in step 3, check whether x_1^*, x_2^* yields a constrained maximizer or constrained minimizer of f. Often this will be apparent from economic or physical considerations. Mathematically, this check can be performed as follows. Evaluate, at the point (x_1^*, x_2^*), the expression

$$D^* = -(g_{x_2})^2 L_{x_1 x_1} - (g_{x_1})^2 L_{x_2 x_2} + 2 g_{x_1} g_{x_2} L_{x_1 x_2} \qquad (18.4)$$

If $D^* > 0$, then (x_1^*, x_2^*) is a local constrained maximizer. If $D^* < 0$, then (x_1^*, x_2^*) is a local constrained minimizer. If $D^* = 0$, no conclusion can be drawn.

Solving Example 5 Let us now apply these steps to Example 5, that is, to the problem

$$\text{Max } x_1 - x_2$$

$$\text{s.t.} \quad -x_1^2 + x_2 = 1$$

■ **Step 1: Form Lagrangian** The problem is already in the form of a *Max model*. Thus, the Lagrangian is

$$L(x_1, x_2, \lambda) = f(x_1, x_2) + \lambda(b - g(x_1, x_2)) = x_1 - x_2 + \lambda(1 + x_1^2 - x_2)$$

■ **Step 2: Take partial derivatives**

$$L_{x_1} = 1 + 2\lambda x_1 = 0$$

$$L_{x_2} = -1 - \lambda = 0$$

$$L_\lambda = 1 + x_1^2 - x_2 = 0$$

760

CHAPTER 18
Calculus-Based
Optimization and
an Introduction to
Nonlinear
Programming

■ **Step 3: Find all solutions** The unique solution to the above system of three equations in three unknowns x_1, x_2, λ is obtained by noting, from the second equation, that $\lambda^* = -1$. Substituting into the first equation and solving for x_1 gives $x_1^* = \frac{1}{2}$. Then the third equation gives $x_2^* = (x_1^*)^2 + 1 = 1\frac{1}{4}$. We have thus obtained

$$\lambda^* = -1, \qquad x_1^* = \tfrac{1}{2}, \qquad x_2^* = \tfrac{5}{4}$$

■ **Step 4: Check sufficiency conditions**

$$D^* = -1(2\lambda^*) - 4(x_1^*)^2(0) + 2(-2x_1^*)(1)(0)$$

$$= 2$$

Since $D^* > 0$, the solution is a constrained maximizer.

Note that the solution in step 3 is consistent with that obtained in the geometric analysis of Figure 18.8.

Solving a Class of Problems

Example 6 Let us use the foregoing necessary conditions to find the solution to the problem

$$\text{Min } a_1 x_1 + a_2 x_2 + b_1 x_1^2 + b_2 x_2^2 + c_1 x_1 x_2$$

$$\text{s.t. } x_1 + x_2 = R \tag{18.5}$$

This example will illustrate how the Lagrangian technique can be used to solve a whole class of problems. In other words, we will derive an expression for the optimal values of the decision variables (x_1^*, x_2^*) in terms of the parameters $(a_1, a_2, b_1, b_2, c_1,$ and $R)$. Having done so, we can use these general expressions to find solutions quickly and easily for any problem that is of the general form of problem (18.5). Indeed, our next example will illustrate this fact. We now turn to problem (18.5). Since the problem is in minimization form, we first convert it to Max form as follows:

$$\text{Max } -a_1 x_1 - a_2 x_2 - b_1 x_1^2 - b_2 x_2^2 - c_1 x_1 x_2$$

$$\text{s.t. } x_1 + x_2 = R$$

■ **Step 1: Form Lagrangian** The Lagrangian for the Max problem is

$$L(x_1, x_2, \lambda) = -a_1 x_1 - a_2 x_2 - b_1 x_1^2 - b_2 x_2^2 - c_1 x_1 x_2 + \lambda(R - x_1 - x_2)$$

■ **Step 2: Take partial derivatives** Taking first partial derivatives yields

$$L_{x_1} = -a_1 - 2b_1 x_1 - c_1 x_2 - \lambda = 0$$

$$L_{x_2} = -a_2 - 2b_2 x_2 - c_1 x_1 - \lambda = 0$$

$$L_\lambda = R - x_1 - x_2 = 0$$

■ **Step 3: Find all solutions** Solve for x_1^*, x_2^*, and λ^*. From the first two equations

$$a_1 + 2b_1 x_1 + c_1 x_2 = a_2 + 2b_2 x_2 + c_1 x_1$$

Thus, assuming that $2b_1 - c_1 \neq 0$,

$$x_1(2b_1 - c_1) = (a_2 - a_1) + x_2(2b_2 - c_1)$$

761

CHAPTER 18
Calculus-Based
Optimization and
an Introduction to
Nonlinear
Programming

or

$$x_1 = \frac{(a_2 - a_1) + x_2(2b_2 - c_1)}{(2b_1 - c_1)}$$

Substituting this expression into the third equation yields

$$R - \frac{(a_2 - a_1) + x_2(2b_2 - c_1)}{(2b_1 - c_1)} - x_2 = 0$$

or

$$R(2b_1 - c_1) - (a_2 - a_1) - x_2(2b_2 - c_1) - x_2(2b_1 - c_1) = 0$$

Thus, assuming that $b_1 + b_2 - c_1 \neq 0$,

$$x_2^* = \frac{(a_1 - a_2) + R(2b_1 - c_1)}{2(b_1 + b_2 - c_1)} \tag{18.6}$$

Once a numerical value of x_2^* is determined, the third equation easily yields

$$x_1^* = R - x_2^* \tag{18.7}$$

Then the value of λ_1^* is obtained by substituting x_1^* into the first equation. This yields

$$\lambda_1^* = -a_1 - 2b_1 R + x_2^*(2b_1 - c_1)$$

To determine if x_1^*, x_2^* is a local maximizer, we must check the "sufficiency conditions." The first step is to evaluate the expression for D^* given in (19.4). To perform this task we first note that $g_{x_2} = 1$, $g_{x_1} = 1$, $L_{x_2 x_2} = -2b_2$, $L_{x_1 x_1} = -2b_1$, and $L_{x_1 x_2} = -c_1$. Substituting these values into (19.4) yields

$$D^* = -(1)^2(-2b_1) - (1)^2(-2b_2) + 2(1)(1)(-c_1)$$
$$= 2(b_1 + b_2 - c_1)$$

Thus, if $b_1 + b_2 - c_1 > 0$, we know that x_1^*, x_2^* is a local maximizer of the function

$$-a_1 x_1 - a_2 x_2 - b_1 x_1^2 - b_2 x_2^2 - c_1 x_1 x_2$$

which means x_1^*, x_2^* is a local minimizer of

$$a_1 x_1 + a_2 x_2 + b_1 x_1^2 + b_2 x_2^2 + c_1 x_1 x_2$$

We will now apply these general results to a specific problem.

An Application: Optimal Marketing Expenditures

A restaurant's average daily budget for advertising is $100, which is to be allocated to newspaper ads and radio commercials. Suppose that we let

x_1 = average number of dollars per day spent on newspaper ads

x_2 = average number of dollars per day spent on radio commercials

762

CHAPTER 18
Calculus-Based
Optimization and
an Introduction to
Nonlinear
Programming

In terms of these quantities, the restaurant's total annual cost of running the advertising department has been estimated to be

$$\text{cost} = C(x_1, x_2) = 20{,}000 + 20x_1^2 + x_1x_2 + 12x_2^2 - 440x_1 - 300x_2$$

Find the budget allocation that will minimize this total annual cost.

The model to be solved is

$$\text{Min } 20{,}000 + 20x_1^2 + x_1x_2 + 12x_2^2 - 440x_1 - 300x_2$$

$$\text{s.t. } x_1 + x_2 = 100$$

We first note that the first term in the objective function (20,000) is a constant that does not depend on the values of the decision variables. Thus, we can ignore it in determining the optimal value of the decision variables. We thus wish to select x_1^*, x_2^* in order to

$$\text{Min } -440x_1 - 300x_2 + 20x_1^2 + 12x_2^2 + x_1x_2$$

$$\text{s.t. } x_1 + x_2 = 100$$

Observe that this problem is a specific case of the general class of problems given by (18.5). It follows that we can use the general equations (18.6) and (18.6) to determine x_2^* and x_1^*, respectively. To do so we first observe that $a_1 = -440$, $a_2 = -300$, $b_1 = 20$, $b_2 = 12$, $c_1 = 1$, and $R = 100$. Thus, substituting in

$$x_2^* = \frac{(a_1 - a_2) + R(2b_1 - c_1)}{2(b_1 + b_2 - c_1)} \tag{18.6}$$

we obtain, after performing the indicated calculations, $x_2^* = 60.645$. Now turning to (19.7) we obtain $x_1^* = R - x_2^* = 100 - 60.645 = 39.355$. To consider the sufficiency conditions we simply note that $b_1 + b_2 - c_1 = 31 > 0$. Thus, $(x_1^* = 60.645, x_2^* = 39.355)$ is a local constrained minimizer of the objective function. In Problem 18-11, you are asked to argue that this is indeed a global minimizer.

The General Case

We now turn to the general equality constrained problem, P_1. In this case there are m constraints, and we introduce m new variables, one for each constraint. These m new variables are called *Lagrange multipliers*. Put the problem into the maximization form. Then the Lagrangian function is

$$L(x_1, x_2, \ldots, x_n, \lambda) = f(x_1, \ldots, x_n) + \sum_{i=1}^{m} \lambda_i[b_i - g_i(x_1, \ldots, x_n)]$$

For problem P_1 we can now state a *necessary condition* for $(x_1^*, \ldots, x_n^*)$ to be optimal. In order to do this, rather technical regularity conditions must be imposed on the constraint functions $g_i(x_1, \ldots, x_n)$ at the point $(x_1^*, \ldots, x_n^*)$.[3] These conditions, called a

---

[3] For example, it suffices to assume that the m vectors (each vector n-dimensional) $(\partial g_i/\partial x_1, \ldots, \partial g_i/\partial x_n)$, all evaluated at $(x_1^*, \ldots, x_n^*)$, are linearly independent. Although it was not explicitly mentioned, the optimality conditions for P_2 also require that the regularity condition must hold.

constraint qualification, are usually satisfied, and hence are more of theoretical than practical importance. Moreover, a precise discussion of these conditions would lead well beyond the scope of this text. Therefore, as is usually done in practice, *we shall assume that a suitable regularity condition is satisifed* at $(x_1^*, \ldots, x_n^*)$. Under this assumption

A General Statement of the First Order Conditions

If $(x_1^*, \ldots, x_n^*)$ is a **local constrained maximizer** in (P_1), then there are m numbers $\lambda_1^*, \ldots, \lambda_m^*$ such that $x_1^*, \ldots, x_n^*, \lambda_1^*, \ldots, \lambda_m^*$ are a solution to the following system of $n + m$ equations in the $n + m$ unknowns $x_1, \ldots, x_n$, $\lambda_1, \ldots, \lambda_m$.

$$\frac{\partial f}{\partial x_1} - \sum_{i=1}^{m} \lambda_i \frac{\partial g_i}{\partial x_1} = 0 \qquad (L_{x_1} = 0)$$

$$\frac{\partial f}{\partial x_2} - \sum_{i=1}^{m} \lambda_i \frac{\partial g_i}{\partial x_2} = 0 \qquad (L_{x_2} = 0)$$

$$\vdots$$

$$\frac{\partial f}{\partial x_n} - \sum_{i=1}^{m} \lambda_i \frac{\partial g_i}{\partial x_n} = 0 \qquad (L_{x_n} = 0)$$

$$g_1(x_1, \ldots, x_n) = b_1 \qquad (L_{\lambda_1} = 0)$$

$$g_2(x_1, \ldots, x_n) = b_2 \qquad (L_{\lambda_2} = 0)$$

$$\vdots$$

$$g_m(x_1, \ldots, x_n) = b_m \qquad (L_{\lambda_m} = 0)$$

This necessary condition is a direct generalization of the two-variable case, Problem (P_2), discussed above. In other words, each local constrained optimizer (maximizer or minimizer) must be a solution to the system of equations obtained by setting the $n + m$ partial derivatives of the Lagrangian equal to zero.

In theory, a global solution to Problem (P_1) could be obtained by finding *all solutions* to the equations above (the necessary conditions) and then finding, among those, one that produces the largest objective value. Alternatively, one could seek a local solution to (P_1) by finding *a solution* to the equations above and then applying a complicated sufficiency test to see whether that solution is a local constrained maximizer. However, it is misleading to suggest that either of these approaches is, in general, a useful practical technique for solving problems of the form (P_1). The situation is analogous to what we encountered in the unconstrained case with n variables. There we saw that, although in special cases the necessary conditions could be explicitly solved, these conditions are more typically employed as a termination criterion in computer codes. In the current context, it is also true that special-purpose computer codes exist for solving the general problem (P_1). The Lagrangian conditions are first-order necessary conditions for a point to be optimal in (P_1). Rather than solving these conditions directly, the codes take other approaches. To describe this in detail would go beyond the scope of this chapter. It suffices to say that the Lagrangian conditions provide *a termination criterion*

764

CHAPTER 18
Calculus-Based
Optimization and
an Introduction to
Nonlinear
Programming

for such codes. The point to remember is that for all NLP models it is generally true that the necessary conditions are (1) of theoretic interest (i.e., they reveal properties of the real-world model being studied) and (2) used as a termination criterion in computer codes designed to solve the problem.

For (P_1), as for most NLP models, second-order sufficiency conditions also exist. However, these are entirely of theoretic interest and too complicated to discuss in the general cases.

Having now discussed the general problem with equality constraints, the next level of difficulty would be to add inequality constraints to the model to obtain the general constrained model (P_0). Necessary optimality conditions for this problem are the so-called Karush–Kuhn–Tucker Conditions, of which the Lagrange multiplier conditions in step 2 above are a special case. Again, because of the introductory level of this chapter, a discussion of the inequality constrained model cannot be taken further. This is, more appropriately, a topic covered in a course on nonlinear programming.

Economic Interpretation of Lagrange Multipliers

Lagrange multipliers have an interesting and important economic interpretation. Indeed, as stated in Section 18.5, the Lagrange multipliers in NLP have the same interpretation as the dual variables in LP. In other words, the optimal value of the ith Lagrange multiplier λ_i^* is the instantaneous *rate of change* in the OV, the optimal value of the objective function, as the ith RHS, b_i, is increased, with all other data unchanged. Another way of saying this, in economic terminology, is that λ_i^* reflects the marginal value of the ith resource. Thus, the units of λ_i^* are

$$\frac{\text{units of objective function}}{\text{units of RHS of constraint } i}$$

Recall Example 3, where a manufacturer wished to minimize total production cost, the objective in dollars, subject to the restriction that the total production, say in tons, had to equal R. The Lagrange multiplier then has units of dollars per ton and its value is the instantaneous marginal cost of producing the Rth unit.

In order to illustrate specifically the foregoing interpretation of λ^*, for a Max model, consider again the problem posed by Example 5, which was solved with geometric analysis in Figure 18.8. In this case, however, let the parameter b denote the RHS. Thus, the problem is

$$\text{Max } x_1 - x_2$$
$$\text{s.t.} \quad -x_1^2 + x_2 = b$$

The Lagrangian is

$$x_1 - x_2 + \lambda(b + x_1^2 - x_2)$$

and the equations to be solved (for x_1, x_2 and λ) are

$$L_{x_1} = 1 + 2\lambda x_1 \quad = 0$$
$$L_{x_2} = -1 - \lambda \quad = 0$$
$$L_{\lambda} = b + x_1^2 - x_2 = 0$$

765

CHAPTER 18
Calculus-Based
Optimization and
an Introduction to
Nonlinear
Programming

The solution is

$$\lambda^* = -1, \qquad x_1^* = \tfrac{1}{2}, \qquad x_2^* = b + \tfrac{1}{4} \qquad (18.8)$$

To observe the interpretation of λ^*, we will first find an expression for the optimal value of the objective as a function of b. Let $OV(b)$ be this function. By definition $OV(b) = x_1^* - x_2^*$. Thus, by substitution,

$$OV(b) = \tfrac{1}{2} - [b + \tfrac{1}{4}] = \tfrac{1}{4} - b$$

To determine the rate of change in $OV(b)$ as a function of b we take the first derivative. We see that

$$\frac{d}{db} OV(b) = -1$$

But $\lambda^* = -1$, and hence, as stated above, λ^* is the rate of change in the OV with respect to b.

In concluding this section, we mention that, just as is true with LP, a dual to Problem P_1 can be defined. This dual is a different optimization problem, which can be expressed in only the variables $\lambda_1, \ldots, \lambda_m$, and the Lagrange multipliers will be the optimal solution to the dual problem. This topic of *nonlinear duality theory* is studied in more advanced courses in NLP.

_____ **18.7**
DIFFERENT TYPES OF NLP PROBLEMS AND SOLVABILITY

The algorithms for solving general NLP problems are markedly different from the simplex approach. In LP we saw that for a problem that has an optimal solution, we could always be assured that there would in fact be at least one optimal corner solution. This is a critically important characteristic of LP models, for we saw that the corners of the feasible region can be defined by linear equations in such a way that a simple pivoting operation allows us to move from one corner to any adjacent corner at which the objective value either improves or remains at the same value. Using this technique, the simplex algorithm provides a fail-safe method for attacking LP problems. None of these comments apply to the general NLP problem (P_0), or even to the special case (P_1) involving only equality constraints.

In contrast to the LP case there is not a single preferred algorithm for solving nonlinear programs. Without difficulty one can easily find 10 or 15 methods in the literature. Some of these, such as *penalty function methods* or *reduced gradient methods*, are applicable to general NLP models. But nonlinear programming is a very broad topic and many interesting special types of problems are identified in the literature. Indeed, many of the solution methods found in the literature are designed to solve special types of NLP problems. For example, some algorithms are designed exclusively for *quadratic programming problems*, others for problems with a *nonlinear objective function and linear constraints*, and so on.

Rather than confronting you with a compendium of the numerous types of algorithms for solving NLP problems, we shall look at the other end of the stick, giving at least a brief description of a few major classes of nonlinear programs that one might

766

CHAPTER 18
Calculus-Based
Optimization and
an Introduction to
Nonlinear
Programming

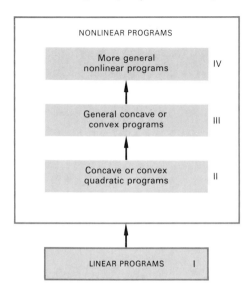

FIGURE 18.9
Increasing Computational Difficulty

encounter in practical applications. That is, we can "break down" this very general class of problems into more-special cases, defined by the nature of the objective function and the constraint functions, and then discuss how easily solvable these special cases are. Indeed, from the managerial perspective these are important issues, to know what type of NLP one may be facing, and the prospects for finding a solution. It will be seen that these prospects are heavily dependent on the type of problem.

We might begin this overview with the observation that nonlinear models are divided into two classes: (1) those that can be solved and (2) those that one can try to solve. The models that can be solved must typically conform to certain qualifications of structure and size. The hierarchy of increasing computational difficulty is shown in Figure 18.9. In this figure, the increasing Roman numerals reflect increasing computational difficulty. Let us now consider these several classes of nonlinear programs in somewhat more detail.

Nonlinear Programs that Can Be Solved: Concave and Convex Programs

To define these problems it is necessary to introduce a new technical term, a *convex set of points*. Loosely speaking, this is a set of points without any "holes" or "indentations." More formally, a convex set is any set that has the following property:

Consider all possible pairs of points in the set, and consider the line segment connecting any such pair. All such line segments must lie entirely within the set.

Figure 18.10 shows two-dimensional sets of points that do not satisfy this property and hence are *not* convex sets, together with sets that are convex. The polygon in the first of these two figures may remind you of the constraint sets that occur in LP problems. This is appropriate since any constraint set for a linear program is a convex set. *The nonlinear programs that we can be reasonably sure of solving must also have convex constraint sets.*

767

CHAPTER 18
Calculus-Based
Optimization and
an Introduction to
Nonlinear
Programming

FIGURE 18.10

Convex and Nonconvex Sets of Points

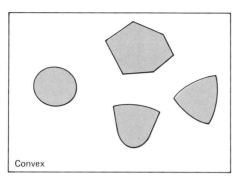

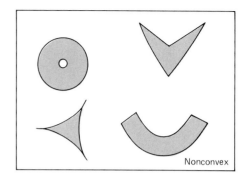

Convex

Nonconvex

Concave and Convex Functions

The next question to be asked then is: What kinds of nonlinear programs have convex constraint sets? It is useful to be able to use the notion of concave and convex functions in answering this question. These functions were discussed in some detail for the case of one variable in Section 18.2. If the function has two independent variables, a *concave function* is shaped like an upside-down bowl. In general, a concave function, by definition, has the property that the line segment connecting any two points on the graph of the function never enters the space above the graph (if it always lies strictly under the graph then the function is *strictly concave*). Similarly, if the function has two variables, a *convex function* is shaped like a bowl. In general, a convex function, by definition, has the property that the line segment connecting any two points on the graph of the function never enters the space below the graph (if it always lies strictly above the graph then the function is *strictly convex*). The same ideas hold for functions that have a single variable, or more than two variables. It should also be remarked that a linear function is considered to be both concave and convex (the above-mentioned line segments always lie in the graph).

Now suppose that we have a nonlinear program with only inequality constraints.

> **If the constraint function associated with each $\leq$ constraint is convex and the constraint function associated with each $\geq$ constraint is concave, the constraint set will be a convex set.**

These facts are illustrated in Figure 18.11, which shows a convex function g of a single variable, given by $g(x) = x^2 + 1$. You can see that the set of x values for which $g(x) \leq 2$ is convex (i.e., this is the set $-1 \leq x \leq 1$), whereas the set of x values for which $g(x) \geq 2$ is not convex (i.e., this is the set $x \leq -1, x \geq 1$). This set is not convex because it is possible to find two points in the set (say $x = +2$ and $x = -2$) such that the straight line that connects them passes through points (e.g., the point $x = 0$) that are not in the set.

Thus we see that in this example $g(x)$ is convex and the set defined by the inequality $g(x) \leq 2$ is convex, whereas the set defined by the inequality $g(x) \geq 2$ is not convex. A similar demonstration could be constructed to show that if $g(x)$ is concave, then the set defined by the inequality $g(x) \geq 2$ is convex, whereas the set defined by the inequality $g(x) \leq 2$ is not convex (this is related to the fact that the negative of a concave function is convex, and vice versa). We thus have a test at our disposal that will enable us to verify that certain NLPs have a convex constraint set. This test certainly will not

768

CHAPTER 18
Calculus-Based
Optimization and
an Introduction to
Nonlinear
Programming

FIGURE 18.11

Constraint Sets $g(x) \leq 2$ and $g(x) \geq 2$

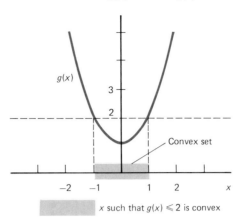

x such that $g(x) \leqslant 2$ is convex

enable us to determine if the constraint set for *any* NLP is convex. In particular, in the case of problems involving one or more *nonlinear equality* constraints, there is great difficulty in characterizing whether the constraint set is convex. Concerning the discussion in this subsection, it is worth noting that the term "concave" applies only to functions, whereas the term "convex" can apply to either a function or a set of points, depending on the context.

Now that you understand the meaning of a convex set, it is easy, at least formally, to define a concave or convex program:

A concave program is a Max model with a concave objective function and a convex constraint set.

A convex program is a Min model with a convex objective function and a convex constraint set.

Convexity and Global Optima

The rationale for this characterization has to do with the fact that in the maximization context, just as in elementary calculus with one variable, concave objective functions are very convenient to work with in terms of the mathematical properties associated with the upside-down bowl shape. Convex objective functions (bowl-shaped) are convenient in the minimization context. Finally, the convexity of the constraint set endows the problem with other attractive mathematical properties that can be exploited both theoretically and computationally. A most important characteristic of concave (or convex) programming problems is that for such problems *any local constrained optimizer is a global constrained optimizer.* This fact has obvious computational implications.

Figure 18.9 indicates that the easiest type of nonlinear program is a concave or convex quadratic program. These problems, by definition, have linear (equality or inequality) constraints. The objective function must be quadratic and concave if it is a Max model and quadratic and convex if it is a Min model. It turns out that a variation of the simplex method can be used to solve such problems, and in practice this is reasonably efficient. It is not uncommon to solve quadratic programs with hundreds of constraints and several thousand variables. Financial models such as those used in portfolio analysis are often quadratic programs, so this class of models is of some applied importance.

In Figure 18.9 the next level of difficulty involves the general (nonquadratic) concave or convex program. There are numerous mathematical approaches and corresponding algorithms for solving such problems. For example, suppose that the problem to be solved is a Max model. One typical approach proceeds as follows:

A Solution Procedure

1. Find an initial feasible point "inside" the constraint set (not on the boundary).
2. Find an uphill direction and move along this straight line until either reaching a maximum along the line or until hitting some boundary of the constraint set.
3. Modify the direction of motion so as to continue uphill while remaining in the feasible region.
4. Terminate the algorithm when a point satisfying the necessary optimality conditions is found.

In this type of algorithm, as well as most others that apply to nonlinear programs that are not quadratic, there is considerable use of advanced calculus, and hence it is not possible in this development to get into much detail. Suffice it to say that *for general concave or convex programs, as opposed to linear programs, the number of nonlinear variables (i.e., those that enter into the problem nonlinearly) seems to be at least as significant as the number of constraints as an indicator of problem difficulty.* Without making use of additional special structure, it could be a major task to solve a "general" (i.e., no special structure) concave or convex program with more than 100 variables. However, we hasten to add that most large real world problems do indeed have special structure, such as sparse matrices. We saw in Chapter 9, concerning network models, that special structure was used to devise especially efficient algorithms. The same is true for nonlinear programs. Since constraints on space prevent us from exploring this further, suffice it to say that in various applications (such as refinery scheduling or power distribution) nonlinear programs with many thousands of variables have been solved.

Nonlinear Programs That We Try to Solve

Finally, we consider problems in the next, and highest, level of difficulty. These problems are often called *highly nonlinear*, which usually means that the convexity and concavity properties discussed in this chapter are absent. To attack such problems, it is common practice to use the same algorithm one would use for general concave and convex programs. The results are different, however. Any NLP algorithm will generally terminate at a point at which the necessary (i.e., first-order) optimality conditions are satisfied. For a concave or convex program, such a point is guaranteed to be a global optimizer (indeed, if the objective function is *strictly* concave, or *strictly* convex, we are guaranteed that such a point is a *unique* global optimizer). But for general nonlinear programs this need not be true, as illustrated for a problem in one variable in Figure 18.12. The objective function f, which is to be maximized, is neither concave nor convex. The solution to the problem is given by x^*, but the algorithm may terminate at any of the points x_1, x_3, or x^* (for they will satisfy the necessary conditions) and, in general, the analyst has no way to determine which of these cases he or she has actually obtained. To date, no one has been smart enough to invent algorithms that overcome this possibility.

Thus it appears that our capabilities in this realm are rather limited, and you may well wonder, since we seem to have no assurance that what we are getting really provides a global constrained optimum, why we even attempt to solve these general highly nonlinear problems. The answer (and justification) is surprisingly unpedantic and empirical.

770

CHAPTER 18
Calculus-Based
Optimization and
an Introduction to
Nonlinear
Programming

FIGURE 18.12
Nonconcave Constrained Max Problem

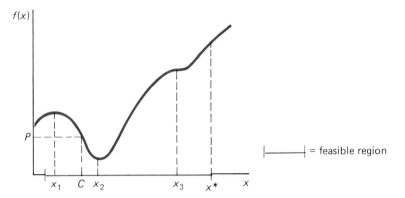

The firm may be currently employing the policy designated as C in Figure 18.12, with an associated profit of P. If our algorithm can produce a *better* solution, whether it be x_1, x_3, or x^*, then the use of the algorithm might well be justified. This is consistent with the overall theme that in practice there is nothing so pure as a truly optimal solution. *The goal in quantiative modeling is always to assist in the search for better decisions. The general considerations are the cost of improvement (the cost of the modeling effort and obtaining the solution) versus the benefit rendered by the solution.* In this spirit, whether the model is convex or concave, the tools of management science may well provide management with useful information.

In concluding, let us address one additional practical aspect: How can we tell whether a nonlinear program in many variables is concave, convex, or neither? In other words, how do we know whether the objective function and the constraints have the right mathematical form? There are several answers to this question:

1. Sometimes there are mathematical tests that can be applied to the problem functions to determine whether they are concave, convex, or neither.

2. Sometimes economic intuition is used to assert that such-and-such a phenomenon reflects diminishing marginal returns or increasing marginal costs, and hence the associated function is concave or convex.

3. In many real problems nothing is done to address the question. One simply attempts to solve the problem and then inquires as to the practical usefulness of the terminal point (the purported "solution" produced by the algorithm). For a problem that is thought or known to be nonconvex or nonconcave, one frequently restarts the algorithm from a different initial point with the hope of producing a better terminal point.

——— 18.8
NOTES ON IMPLEMENTATION

The practice of nonlinear programming is in some ways even more of an art than the practice of LP. Concerning LP, almost every computer library will have as part of its standard repertoire an LP software package. Also, every LP code is, in major respects, the same, since they are variants of the simplex method. Nonlinear programming codes

771

CHAPTER 18
Calculus-Based
Optimization and
an Introduction to
Nonlinear
Programming

are less easy to come by. They are generally not a standard part of computer libraries. Moreover, it would not be difficult to identify as many as 10 or 15 quite different algorithmic procedures for solving NLP problems. To find the best method for a given problem, indeed even to understand the differences between various approaches, the user, at least in this respect, must be more of an expert with mathematics. Another delicate aspect of NLP practice is the existence, from a mathematical viewpoint, of so many different types of nonlinear problems with different theoretical properties (whereas there is only one type of LP). Associated with this fact is the need to reckon with the issue of local versus global solutions to the model. The user must know enough about the mathematical structure of his or her model to have at least a feeling for the quality of the solution (e.g., local versus global) produced by the code, and often he or she must experiment in order to locate improved solutions.

Although most NLP codes will print out dual prices (i.e., the optimal values of the Lagrange multipliers) along with the solution, additional sensitivity analysis is generally not available. Thus, from the manager's point of view, the NLP output contains less information than an LP output provides.

Probably the most used codes in practice are GRG (a reduced gradient method) and SUMT (a penalty function method). These codes can be obtained from commercial sources for modest fees. Getting them to run on your local computer installation is, unfortunately, in some cases more a tragic comdey than a straightforward rational endeavor.

Although NLP applies to a wide spectrum of problems, the most common applications probably occur in situations where the model has special structure. For example, there may be linear constraints but a nonlinear objective function, and so on. In such cases there is hope of solving reasonably large-scale models—provided that the code makes efficient use of the problem's special structure.

What do we mean by "large scale" in NLP? Again, this is much less clearly defined than it is for LP. For a concave or convex quadratic program, we can aspire to several thousand constraints and unlimited variables. This power derives from the fact that for such a model a variant of the simplex method is employed. However, for more general nonlinear problems, without special structure which is used to advantage, one would probably hesitate to attack a problem with more than 100 variables, regardless of how few the constraints.

As a final note, NLP applications are probably clustered in such areas as engineering design, nonlinear estimation, electrical power transmission, physical applications such as oil drilling, and finally, optimal scheduling and equipment utilization when nonlinear costs are involved.

———— **18.9**
KEY TERMS

INFLECTION POINT.   A point at which the first derivative (or first partials) is zero.

STATIONARY POINT.   Same as inflection point.

CRITICAL POINT.   Same as inflection point.

LOCAL MAXIMIZER (MINIMIZER).   A point at which a function takes on a local maximum (minimum) value. If x^* is a local maximizer, then $f(x) \leq f(x^*)$ for all x in a neighborhood of (i.e., all x sufficiently near) x^*.

RELATIVE MAXIMIZER (MINIMIZER).   "Relative" is synonymous with "local."

GLOBAL MAXIMIZER (MINIMIZER).   A point at which a function takes on a global maximum (minimum) value. If x^* is a global maximizer, then $f(x) \leq f(x^*)$ for all x.

LOCAL (OR RELATIVE) MAXIMA (MINIMA).   The function values at local maximizers (minimizers).

772

CHAPTER 18
Calculus-Based
Optimization and
an Introduction to
Nonlinear
Programming

GLOBAL MAXIMUM (MINIMUM). The function value at a global maximizer (minimizer).

NECESSARY OPTIMALITY CONDITION. A condition that must be satisfied by an optimal point.

CONCAVE FUNCTION. A function with "umbrella" curvature (wherever there is curvature)—shows diminishing marginal returns.

CONVEX FUNCTION. A function with "upside-down umbrella" curvature (wherever there is curvature)—shows increasing marginal returns.

SUFFICIENT OPTIMALITY CONDITION. A condition which, when satisfied by a given x, guarantees that x is optimal.

LAGRANGE MULTIPLIER. The optimal value of the ith Lagrange multiplier, λ_i^*, is the rate of change of the OV as the ith RHS increases.

LOCAL CONSTRAINED MAXIMIZER. The value of the objective function at such a point is greater than or equal to its value at all neighboring feasible points.

GLOBAL CONSTRAINED MAXIMIZER. The value of the objective function at such a point is greater than or equal to its value at all other feasible points.

CONSTRAINT QUALIFICATION. A regularity condition that the constraints in an NLP must satisfy in order for the necessary optimality conditions to be valid.

LAGRANGIAN FUNCTION. A function that employs the objective function and the constraint functions in a given NLP.

KARUSH-KUHN-TUCKER CONDITIONS. The necessary optimality conditions for a general inequality and equality constrained NLP problem.

CONCAVE PROGRAM. A Max model with a concave objective function and a convex constraint set.

CONVEX PROGRAM. A Min model with a convex objective function and a convex constraint set.

CONVEX SET. The partial line segment connecting any two points in the set is entirely contained in the set.

QUADRATIC PROGRAM. A model with a quadratic objective function and linear (equality and/or inequality) constraints.

MAJOR CONCEPTS QUIZ

True–False

1. **T F** Economy of scale is a nonlinear relationship.
2. **T F** An applied problem involving a nonlinear relationship cannot be modeled as an LP.
3. **T F** If the necessary conditions for a local Max occur, a local Max occurs.
4. **T F** If a local Min occurs, the necessary conditions for a local Min occur.
5. **T F** If a local Min is a global Min, it is the only point where the sufficient conditions for a local Min hold.
6. **T F** A straight line is neither a concave nor a convex function.
7. **T F** In an NLP or an LP, tightening a constraint cannot help, and it might hurt.
8. **T F** For a Max model, a Lagrange multiplier has the same interpretation as the dual price that appears on the computer output for LP problems earlier in the text, although in general it is not constant over an RHS interval.
9. **T F** A quadratic programming problem is always a special type of concave or convex programming problem.
10. **T F** An NLP is always either a concave or a convex programming problem.
11. **T F** The constraint set defined by the following inequalities is convex:

$$9x + \ 4 \le 36$$
$$4x + 12 \le 20$$

12. **T F** In practice, to find a local Max of a function of several variables, one first finds all stationary points. One then evaluates the function at these points to determine which of them are local maximizers.

13. **T F** Although nonlinear programs are more difficult than LPs, in terms of finding an optimal solution it is nevertheless true that a corner-searching technique can be applied.

14. **T F** One problem in NLP is distinguishing between local and global solutions.

Multiple Choice

15. Suppose that f is a function of a single variable. The condition $f''(x^*) > 0$
    a. is a necessary condition for a local Min
    b. is a sufficient condition for a local Min
    c. says that f is strictly convex at x^*
    d. none of the above

16. Suppose that f is a function of a single variable. The condition $f'(x^*) = 0$ is
    a. a necessary condition for x^* to be a local Max
    b. a necessary condition for x^* to be a local Min
    c. a necessary condition for x^* to be a global Min
    d. all of the above

17. In nonlinear models differential calculus is needed
    a. to avoid multiple (local) solutions
    b. to express optimality conditions
    c. both a and b
    d. neither a nor b

18. A point x^* with the property that $f''(x^*) > 0$ (where f is a function of a single variable) satisfies the sufficient conditions for x^* to be
    a. a local Max
    b. a local Min
    c. neither a nor b

19. Which of the following is true of a concave function?
    a. One can attempt to find a global maximizer by using a hill-climbing computer code.
    b. One can attempt to find a global maximizer by setting the first partials to zero and solving the resulting system of equations on the computer.
    c. Any local maximizer is also a global maximizer.
    d. All of the above.

20. Which of the following is true?
    a. For a general NLP, optimality conditions are directly used in solving NLP problems. That is, computer codes exist to directly solve these conditions, and this produces an NLP solution.
    b. For a general NLP, optimality conditions are indirectly used in solving NLP problems. That is, computer codes exist to directly attack the NLP, employing, for example, a "hill-climbing" approach. The optimality conditions provide a termination criterion for such algorithms.
    c. Optimality conditions are only of theoretic interest.

21. For concave programming problems
    a. the second-order conditions are more useful
    b. any local optimum is a global optimum as well
    c. both the constraint set and the objective function must be concave

22. Convexity
    a. is a description that applies both to sets of points and to functions
    b. is an important mathematical property used to guarantee that local solutions are also global
    c. is useful in unconstrained as well as constrained optimization
    d. all of the above

23. Which of the following is *not* generally true of a Lagrange multiplier?
    a. It has an economic interpretation similar to that of dual variable.

774

CHAPTER 18
Calculus-Based
Optimization and
an Introduction to
Nonlinear
Programming

b. It is the rate of change of OV as the RHS of a constraint is increased.

c. It is valid (i.e., constant) over an RHS range.

d. It enters into the first-order optimality conditions.

24. Which of the following is *not* true?

a. Even when global solutions cannot be guaranteed, optimization can still be a useful tool in decision making.

b. In LP, we need never worry about local solutions (i.e., every local solution is also global).

c. Since we can only guarantee that local solutions are global when the appropriate convexity (or concavity) properties exist, these are the only types of NLP problems that yield useful information.

Answers			
1. T	7. T	13. F	19. d
2. F	8. T	14. T	20. b
3. F	9. F	15. c	21. b
4. T	10. F	16. d	22. d
5. F	11. T	17. b	23. c
6. F	12. F	18. c	24. c

PROBLEMS

18-1. (a) Maximize the function $f(x) = -8x^2 - 14x - 32$.

(b) What is the sign of the second derivative of this function at the maximizing value of x?

(c) Maximize this function over the interval $1 \le x \le 10$.

(d) Can you tell whether this function is concave or convex?

18-2. (a) Minimize the function $f(x) = 6x^2 - 12x + 30$.

(b) What is the sign of the second derivative of this function at the minimizing value of x?

(c) Minimize this function over the interval $2 \le x \le 12$.

(d) Can you tell whether this function is concave or convex?

18-3. Lotta Crumb, manager of Crumb Baking Services, is considering the offer of a distributor who sells an instant croissant mix. The total cost of x pounds of the mix is given by

$$\text{total cost} = x^3 - 50x^2 + 2x$$

What quantity of this mix will minimize *total cost per pound*?

18-4. Homer Will Burst is inventory manager for the regional warehouse of a fast-food chain. The following function is used by Homer to give the monthly cost of purchasing and holding its inventory of deluxe frozen dinners, where q is the size of each order:

$$\text{monthly cost} = \frac{20,000,000}{q} + 5q + 19,000 = f(q)$$

(a) Determine the order quantity q^* that minimizes the annual inventory cost.

(b) What is the minimum annual cost?

(c) Verify the nature of the stationary point i.e., is it a local or global optimizer?

18-5. Consider the function

$$f(x_1, x_2) = -2x_1^4 + 12x_1^2 - 2x_1^2 x_2 - x_2^2 + 4x_2 - 60$$

Determine whether the points below yield local minima, local maxima, or saddle points.

775

CHAPTER 18
Calculus-Based
Optimization and
an Introduction to
Nonlinear
Programming

(a) $(x_1 = 0, x_2 = 2)$

(b) $(x_1 = 2, x_2 = -2)$

(c) $(x_1 = -2, x_2 = -2)$

18-6. Solve the constrained optimization problem

$$\text{Max} \quad -x_1^2 - 2x_2^2 + 8x_1 + 12x_2 - 34$$

$$\text{s.t.} \quad -2x_1 - 4x_2 = -8$$

18-7. *Linear Regression Analysis* In the linear regression model, historical data points (x_i, y_i), $i = 1, \ldots, n$, are given. The linear model is an estimating equation (also called the regression line) $y = ax + b$, where a and b are chosen so as to minimize the sum of squared deviations

$$S(a, b) = \sum_{i=1}^{n} [y_i - (ax_i + b)]^2$$

(a) Use this approach to determine the estimating equation for the following data:

x	8	6	12
y	6	14	-18

(b) Use the same approach to determine the estimating equation for the following data:

x	10	12.6	14.9	17.4	20.1
y	25	20	15	10	5

18-8. (a) Solve the following problem:

$$\text{Min} \quad x_1^2 + x_2^2 - 12x_1 - 10x_2 - 61$$

$$\text{s.t.} \quad 20x_1 + 30x_2 = 60$$

(b) For this problem, what is the rate of change of OV with respect to the RHS of the constraint?

18-9. Consider the problem

$$\text{Max} \quad -3x_1^2 + 42x_1 - 3x_2^2 + 48x_2 - 339$$

$$\text{s.t.} \quad 4x_1 + 6x_2 = 24$$

(a) Solve the problem.

(b) Estimate the change in OV if the RHS of the constraint were to increase from 24 to 25.

18-10. Consider the problem

$$\text{Max} \quad -2x_1^2 + 20x_1 - 2x_1x_2 - x_2^2 + 14x_2 - 58$$

$$\text{s.t.} \quad x_1 + 4x_2 = 8$$

(a) Solve the problem.

(b) Estimate the change in OV if the RHS of the constraint were to decrease from 8 to 7.

18-11. Show that the solution found in the "Optimal Marketing Expenditures" example (Section 19.6) is actually a global (as opposed to local) optimum.

More Challenging Problems

18-12. In Example 4, let $s_1 = s_2 = s_3 = c$, where c is a specified constant such that $0 < c < 1$. Solve Example 4 for the utility-maximizing values, x_1^*, x_2^*, x_3^*, and for λ^*.

18-13. Solve Example 4 for the optimal x_i^*'s and λ^* with $s_i = \frac{1}{2}$, $i = 1, 2, 3$.

18-14. Assuming that all the data are positive, give the general solution to Example 3. Also state the second-order sufficiency condition in terms of the data.

18-15. Consider the function

$$f(x_1, x_2) = a_1 x_1 + a_2 x_2 + b_1 x_1^2 + b_2 x_2^2 + c_1 x_1 x_2 + d$$

Give a general solution to the problem of minimizing $f(x_1, x_2)$, as follows: Assume that $c_1^2 \neq 4b_1 b_2$, $c_1 \neq 0$. Solve explicitly for the optimizing value of x_2^*. Solve for x_1^* in terms of x_2^*. Express the second-order sufficiency conditions in terms of the data.

ANSWERS TO ODD-NUMBERED PROBLEMS

Chapter 1

1-1. Here is an example: "How much should we spend for national defense?" One reason this is such a hard problem is that there is no generally accepted model. As discussed in this text, for this specific problem the objective function is particularly problematic. No one yet has found a model for this problem that is widely acceptable in terms of objective, assumptions, etc. Other examples are provided by situations with significant social and/or political considerations.

1-3. Here are three suggestions: 1. Possible savings from using the model do not justify the expenses of implementing it. 2. Poor communication between the model builder and the potential user might lead the potential user to have a lack of understanding of the model and a lack of confidence in its ability to produce useful results. 3. The modeler's "selective representation of reality" may not be close enough to the manager's perception of the problem (i.e., the manager may believe that the model does not deal with the real problem).

1-5. Other suggestions are: 1. Maximize cash flow. 2. Maximize market share. 3. Maximize monopolistic stature. 4. Maximize number of employees. 5. "Perpetuate itself" as much as possible.

1-7. This statement simply does not make sense. Clearly, increasing output will also increase costs. One can attempt to maximize output for a given cost (i.e., with a $\leq$ or $=$ constraint on cost) or minimize cost for a given output (i.e., with a $\geq$ or $=$ constraint on output) but not to minimize cost and maximize output simultaneously.

1-9. When the data are not known with precision the notion of a constraint is a more fuzzy concept. For example, in an engineering model of a rocket flight to the moon the sixth or tenth decimal place of accuracy in a right-hand side may be important in the sense that changing the number in the last decimal place may change the output obtained from running the model. In a social or economic model with less precise data, the required right-hand-side accuracy may be much less. The use of a model in such situations, where some of the data are imprecise, can be justified if changes in the data, within the range of imprecision, produce insignificant changes in the model's output.

Chapter 2

2-1. (a) (8) (b) (2) (c) (3) (d) (4) (e) (1) (f) (6) (g) (7) (h) (5)

2-3. Let A = number of product 1 produced
B = number of product 2 produced
Then the model is

$$\text{Max } 12A + 4B$$
$$\text{s.t.} \quad A + 2B \leq 800$$
$$A + 3B \leq 600$$
$$2A + 3B \leq 2000$$
$$A \geq 0, \qquad B \geq 0$$

2-5. Let G = number of Gofer stocks to be bought
C = number of Can Oil stocks to be bought
S = number of Sloth P. stocks to be bought
The LP model is

$$\text{Max } 7G + 3C + 3S$$
$$\text{s.t.} \quad 60G + 25C + 20S \leq 100{,}000$$
$$G \leq 1{,}000$$
$$C \leq 1{,}000$$
$$S \leq 1{,}500$$
$$G \geq 0, \qquad C \geq 0, \qquad S \geq 0$$

2-7. Let A_1, A_2 = quarts of A to be used in Red Baron and Diablo, respectively. Also, let B_1, B_2 = quarts of B to be used in Red Baron and Diablo, respectively. Then the LP model is

$$\text{Max } 3.35(A_2 + B_2) + 2.85(A_1 + B_1) - 1.6(A_1 + A_2) - 2.59(B_1 + B_2)$$

s.t. $\dfrac{A_1}{A_1 + B_1} \leq 0.75$

$\dfrac{A_2}{A_2 + B_2} \geq 0.25,$ $\qquad \dfrac{B_2}{A_2 + B_2} \geq 0.5$

$A_1 + A_2 \leq 40$

$B_1 + B_2 \leq 30$

$A_1, A_2, B_1, B_2 \geq 0$

or in linear form

$0.25A_1 - 0.75B_1 \leq 0$

$0.75A_2 - 0.25B_2 \geq 0$

$-0.5A_2 + 0.5B_2 \geq 0$

2-9. Let A_i = thousands of pounds of type i fertilizer to be bought. The LP model is

$$\text{Min } 10A_1 + 8A_2 + 7A_3$$

s.t. $0.025A_1 + 0.01A_2 + 0.005A_3 \geq .010$

$0.01A_1 + 0.005A_2 + 0.01A_3 \geq .007$

$0.005A_1 + 0.01A_2 + 0.005A_3 \geq .005$

$A_1, A_2, A_3 \geq 0$

2-11. x_1 = pounds of product 1 produced
x_2 = pounds of product 2 produced

$$\text{Max } 4x_1 + 3x_2$$

s.t. $3x_1 + 2x_2 \leq 10$

$x_1 + 4x_2 \leq 16$

$5x_1 + 3x_2 \leq 12$

$x_1 \geq 0, \qquad x_2 \geq 0$

2-13. Let U, D = quantities of Umidaire or Depollinator to be produced. The LP model is

$$\text{Min } 240U + 360D$$

s.t. $U \geq 500$

$450U + 700D = 240U + 360D + 390,000$

$U \geq 0, \qquad D \geq 0$

2-15. Let T, C, M, MU = dollars invested in Treasury bonds, common stock, money market, and municipal bonds, respectively. The LP model is

$$\text{Max } 0.08T + 0.06C + 0.12M + 0.09MU$$

s.t. $T \leq 5 \times 10^6$

$C \leq 7 \times 10^6$

$M \leq 2 \times 10^6$

$MU \leq 4 \times 10^6$

$C + T \geq 3 \times 10^6$

$M + MU \leq 4 \times 10^6$

$C + T + M + MU = 10^7$

$T, C, M, MU \geq 0$

2-17. Let A_{ij} = number of packages sent to wholesaler j from station i, $i = 1, 2$, $j = 1, 2, 3, 4, 5$. The LP formulation is

$$\text{Min } 5.25(A_{11} + A_{12} + A_{13} + A_{14} + A_{15}) + 5.70(A_{21} + A_{22} + A_{23} + A_{24} + A_{25})$$

$$+ 0.06A_{11} + 0.04A_{12} + 0.12A_{13} + 0.09A_{14} + 0.05A_{15}$$

$$+ 0.15A_{21} + 0.09A_{22} + 0.05A_{23} + 0.08A_{24} + 0.08A_{25}$$

$$\text{s.t. } A_{11} + A_{12} + A_{13} + A_{14} + A_{15} \leq 20{,}000$$

$$A_{21} + A_{22} + A_{23} + A_{24} + A_{25} \leq 12{,}000$$

$$A_{11} + A_{21} = 4{,}000$$

$$A_{12} + A_{22} = 6{,}000$$

$$A_{13} + A_{23} = 2{,}000$$

$$A_{14} + A_{24} = 10{,}000$$

$$A_{15} + A_{25} = 8{,}000$$

All variables nonnegative

2-19. Let A_i = acres of A to be planted on farm i
B_i = acres of B to be planted on farm i
C_i = acres of C to be planted on farm i
$i = 1, 2, 3, 4$

The LP problem is

$$\text{Max } 500(A_1 + A_2 + A_3 + A_4) + 200(B_1 + B_2 + B_3 + B_4) + 300(C_1 + C_2 + C_3 + C_4)$$

$$\text{s.t. } A_1 + B_1 + C_1 \leq 500$$

$$A_2 + B_2 + C_2 \leq 900$$

$$A_3 + B_3 + C_3 \leq 300$$

$$A_4 + B_4 + C_4 \leq 700 \qquad A_1 + A_2 + A_3 + A_4 \leq 700$$

$$2A_1 + 4B_1 + 3C_1 \leq 1700 \qquad B_1 + B_2 + B_3 + B_4 \leq 800$$

$$2A_2 + 4B_2 + 3C_2 \leq 3000 \qquad C_1 + C_2 + C_3 + C_4 \leq 300$$

$$2A_3 + 4B_3 + 3C_3 \leq 900$$

$$2A_4 + 4B_4 + 3C_4 \leq 2200$$

$$\frac{A_1 + B_1 + C_1}{500} = \frac{A_2 + B_2 + C_2}{900} = \frac{A_3 + B_3 + C_3}{300} = \frac{A_4 + B_4 + C_4}{700}$$

All variables nonnegative

2-21. Number the days 1 through 7 starting with Monday. Let w_i be the number of waitresses who start their work week on day i.

$$\text{Min } \sum_{i=1}^{7} w_i$$

$$\text{s.t. } 6(w_1 + w_4 + w_5 + w_6 + w_7) \geq 150$$

$$6(w_1 + w_2 + w_5 + w_6 + w_7) \geq 200$$

$$6(w_1 + w_2 + w_3 + w_6 + w_7) \geq 400$$

$$6(w_1 + w_2 + w_3 + w_4 + w_7) \geq 300$$

$$6(w_1 + w_2 + w_3 + w_4 + w_5) \geq 700$$

$$6(w_2 + w_3 + w_4 + w_5 + w_6) \geq 800$$

$$6(w_3 + w_4 + w_5 + w_6 + w_7) \geq 300$$

$$w_i \geq 0, \qquad i = 1, 2, \ldots, 7$$

Note that minimizing the total number of waitresses is equivalent to minimizing total cost, which is $5r \sum_{i=1}^{7} w_i$, where r is the daily wage.

2-23. A_i = hours of job A handled in shop i

B_i = hours of job B handled in shop i

C_i = hours of job C handled in shop i

D_i = hours of job D handled in shop i, $i = 1, 2, 3$

$$\text{Min } 89(A_1 + B_1 + C_1 + D_1) + 81(A_2 + B_2 + C_2 + D_2) + 84(A_3 + B_3 + C_3 + D_3)$$

$$\text{s.t. } A_i + B_i + C_i + D_i \leq 160, \qquad i = 1, 2, 3$$

$$\frac{A_1}{32} + \frac{A_2}{39} + \frac{A_3}{46} = 1$$

$$\frac{B_1}{151} + \frac{B_2}{147} + \frac{B_3}{155} = 1$$

$$\frac{C_1}{72} + \frac{C_2}{61} + \frac{C_3}{57} = 1$$

$$\frac{D_1}{118} + \frac{D_2}{126} + \frac{D_3}{121} = 1$$

$$A_i, B_i, C_i, D_i \geq 0, \qquad \text{all } i$$

2-25. The model is

$$\text{Max } p_1 x_1 + p_2 x_2$$

$$\text{s.t. } \quad 3x_1 + 12x_2 \leq 300 \qquad \text{(limitation on kerosene)}$$

$$9x_1 + 6x_2 \leq 450 \qquad \text{(limitation on benzene)}$$

$$15x_1 + 9x_2 \geq 600 \qquad \text{(demand on starter fluid)}$$

$$6x_1 + 24x_2 \geq 225 \qquad \text{(demand on lighter fluid)}$$

$$x_1 \geq 0, \qquad x_2 \geq 0$$

2-27. Let X_j denote the pounds of food j in the "ideal daily diet." Then the model

$$\text{Min } \sum_{j=1}^{116} c_j x_j$$

$$\text{s.t. } \sum_{j=1}^{116} a_{ij} x_j \geq N_i, \qquad i = 1, \ldots, 16$$

$$x_j \geq 0, \qquad \text{all } j$$

This statement of the problem ignores a technological constraint. In other words, how can we be assured that a human being will be able to process the "ideal daily diet" chosen by the model. For example, suppose that 1 pound of raw alfalfa contained exactly $\frac{1}{2000}$ of the daily requirement of each of the 16 essential nutrients. Then 2000 pounds (1 ton) of alfalfa would satisfy the constraints. With the "right" cost coefficients this could be the optimal solution. Obviously, it is not technologically (physically) possible.

2-29.

$$\text{Min } 20P_1 + 20P_2 + \cdots + 22P_9 + .2(I_1 + I_2 + \cdots + I_9)$$

$$\text{s.t. } I_1 = P_1 - 1000$$

$$I_2 = I_1 + P_2 - 900$$

$$\vdots$$

$$I_9 = I_8 + P_9 - 500$$

$$I_t, P_t > = 0 \qquad t = 1, \ldots, 9$$

2-31. (a)

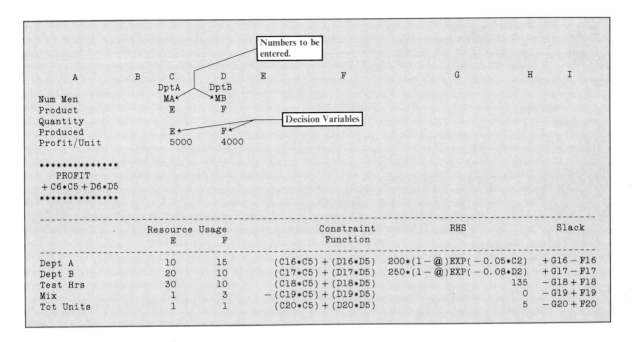

2-31. (b) The plan with E = 6 and F = 9 is infeasible. It requires more time in both Dept. A and B than is available. (c) The optimal production policy is E = 5.59 and F = 7.40. (d) Decreasing returns to scale.

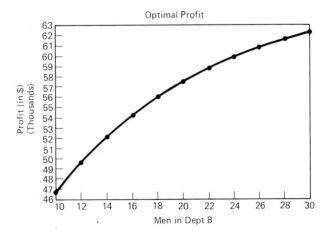

2-33. (a)

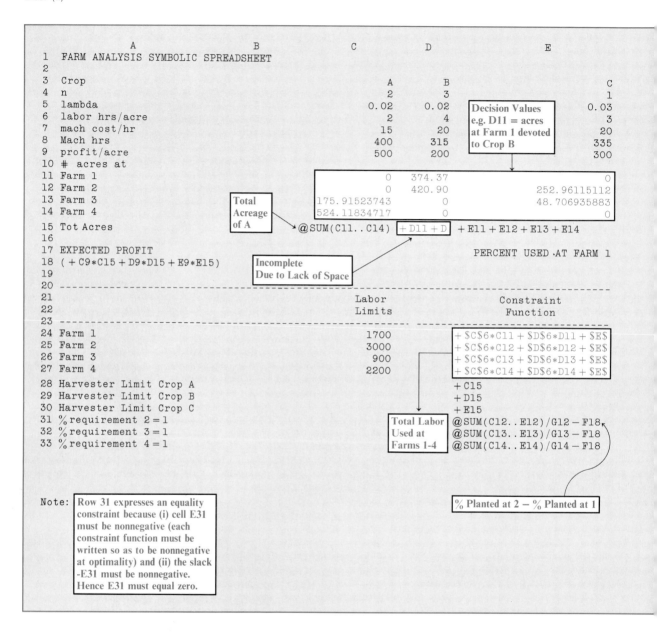

	A	B	C	D	E
1	FARM ANALYSIS SYMBOLIC SPREADSHEET				
2					
3	Crop		A	B	C
4	n		2	3	1
5	lambda		0.02	0.02	0.03
6	labor hrs/acre		2	4	3
7	mach cost/hr		15	20	20
8	Mach hrs		400	315	335
9	profit/acre		500	200	300
10	# acres at				
11	Farm 1		0	374.37	0
12	Farm 2		0	420.90	252.96115112
13	Farm 3		175.91523743	0	48.706935883
14	Farm 4		524.11834717	0	0
15	Tot Acres		@SUM(C11..C14)	+D11+D	+E11+E12+E13+E14

Total Acreage of A → @SUM(C11..C14)

Decision Values e.g. D11 = acres at Farm 1 devoted to Crop B

17 EXPECTED PROFIT   PERCENT USED ·AT FARM 1
18 (+C9*C15 + D9*D15 + E9*E15)

Incomplete Due to Lack of Space → +D11+D

```
19
20 ---------------------------------------------------------------------
21                                        Labor          Constraint
22                                        Limits         Function
23 ---------------------------------------------------------------------
24 Farm 1                                 1700           +$C$6*C11 + $D$6*D11 + $E$
25 Farm 2                                 3000           +$C$6*C12 + $D$6*D12 + $E$
26 Farm 3                                 900            +$C$6*C13 + $D$6*D13 + $E$
27 Farm 4                                 2200           +$C$6*C14 + $D$6*D14 + $E$
28 Harvester Limit Crop A                                +C15
29 Harvester Limit Crop B                                +D15
30 Harvester Limit Crop C                                +E15
31 % requirement 2 = 1                                   @SUM(C12..E12)/G12 − F18
32 % requirement 3 = 1                                   @SUM(C13..E13)/G13 − F18
33 % requirement 4 = 1                                   @SUM(C14..E14)/G14 − F18
```

Total Labor Used at Farms 1-4

% Planted at 2 − % Planted at 1

Note: Row 31 expresses an equality constraint because (i) cell E31 must be nonnegative (each constraint function must be written so as to be nonnegative at optimality) and (ii) the slack -E31 must be nonnegative. Hence E31 must equal zero.

	F	G	H

Fixed Co-op Investment
                19000
Utilized Investment
+ C7*C8 + D7*D8 + E7*E8

Acres Used

+ C11 + D11 + E11

+ C12 + D12 + E12

+ C13 + D13 + E13

+ C14 + D14 + E14

Acres Avail	Unused Acres
500	+ G11 − F11
900	+ G12 − F12
300	+ G13 − F13
700	+ G14 − F14

@SUM(C11..E11)/G11

	RHS	Slack	Surplus

+ C24

+ C25 ← Labor Hours Available

+ C26

+ C27

+ $C$4*($C$8 − 1/$C$5*(1 − @EXP(− $C$5*$C$8)))

+ $D$4*($D$8 − 1/$D$5*(1 − @EXP(− $D$5*$D$8)))

+ $E$4*($E$8 − 1/$E$5*(1 − @EXP(− $E$5*$E$8)))

Total Acreage of Each
Crop Which Can Be
Harvested

+ F24 − E24

+ F25 − E25

+ F26 − E26

+ F27 − E27

+ F28 − E28

+ F29 − E29

+ F30 − E30

− E31

− E32

− E33

```
         FARM ANALYSIS OPTIMIZED SPREADSHEET

          A        B        C        D        E        F        G        H
 1  FARM ANALYSIS SPREADSHEET
 2
 3  Crop                    A        B        C
 4  n                     2.00     3.00     1.00
 5  lambda                0.02     0.02     0.03          Fixed Co-op Investment
 6  labor hrs/acre        2.00     4.00     3.00               19000.00
 7  mach cost/hr         15.00    20.00    20.00          Utilized Investment
 8  Mach hrs            400.00   315.00   335.00               19000.00
 9  profit/acre         500.00   200.00   300.00
10  # acres at                                     Acres Used Acres Avail Unused Acres
11  Farm 1               0.00   374.37     0.00      374.37     500.00      125.63
12  Farm 2               0.00   420.91   252.96      673.87     900.00      226.13
13  Farm 3             175.92     0.00    48.71      224.62     300.00       75.38
14  Farm 4             524.12     0.00     0.00      524.12     700.00      175.88
15  Tot Acres          700.03   795.28   301.67
16
17  EXPECTED PROFIT     ┌─────────────┐  PERCENT USED AT FARM 1
18       599572.32      │Optimal Values│            0.75
                        │of Decision Variables│
20  ----------------------------------------------------------------------------------
21                      Labor    Constraint
22                      Limits   Function          RHS       Slack     Surplus
23  ----------------------------------------------------------------------------------
24  Farm 1               1700      1497.48      1700.00      202.52
25  Farm 2             3000.00     2442.50      3000.00      557.50
26  Farm 3              900.00      497.95       900.00      402.05
27  Farm 4             2200.00     1048.24      2200.00     1151.76
28  Harvester Limit Crop A          700.03       700.03        .00
29  Harvester Limit Crop B          795.28       795.28        .00
30  Harvester Limit Crop C          301.67       301.67        .00
31  % requirement 2=1                  .00                     .00
32  % requirement 3=1                  .00                     .00
33  % requirement 4=1                  .00                     .00
```

2-33. (c) Management can select any set of hours, say T1, T2, and T3, such that $15T1 + 20T2 + 20T3 \leq 19,000$.

Chapter 3 3-1.

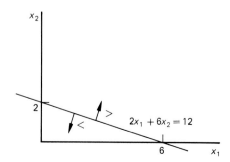

3-3. (a) Same as 3-1(d) (b) Below (c) Corresponds to 1(d)

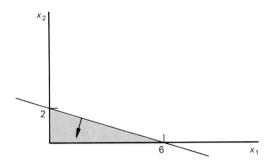

3-5. A = amps
P = preamps
Assembly: $12A + 4P \leq 60$
performance: $4A + 8P \leq 40$

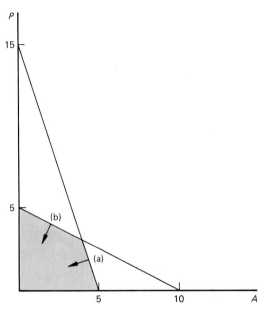

3-7.

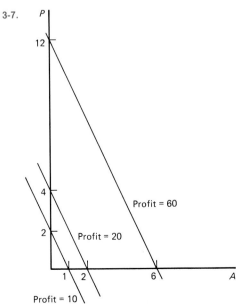

3-9. (a) $A^* = 4$, $P^* = 3$ (b) OV $= 10A^* + 5P^* = \$55$ (c) Active constraints are assembly and high-performance testing. (d) Inactive are

$$A \leq 6, \qquad \text{slack} = 2$$
$$P \leq 4, \qquad \text{slack} = 1$$

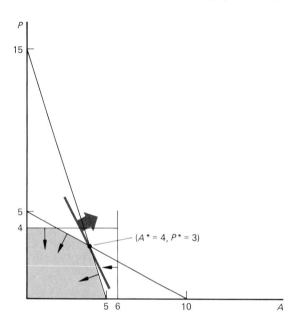

3-11. No

3-13. Makes it infeasible

3-15.

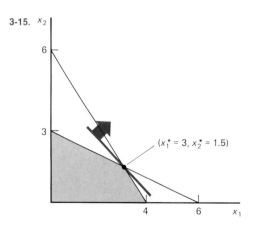

(a) $x_1^* = 3$, $x_2^* = 1.5$, OV $= 4.5$ (b) $x_1^* = 0$, $x_2^* = 3$ (c) Four extreme points: $(0, 0)$, $(4, 0)$, $(3, 1.5)$, $(0, 3)$

3-17. (a) $x_1^* = 6\frac{2}{3}$, $x_2^* = 2\frac{2}{3}$, OV $= 30\frac{2}{3}$
(b) First constraint: slack $= 18\frac{2}{3}$
Second constraint: 0 slack
Third constraint: 0 surplus

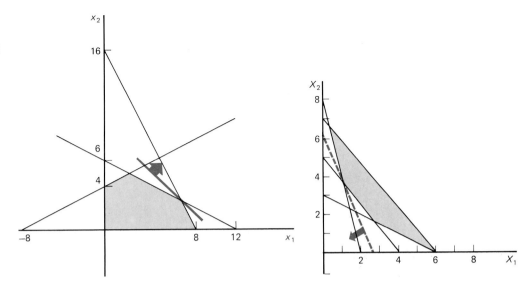

3-19. (a) $x_1^* = 1\frac{1}{11}$, $x_2^* = 3\frac{7}{11}$, OV $= 12\frac{8}{11}$
 (b) Active constraints are second and third; inactive constraints are first and fourth.
 (c) Zero associated with second and third
  First constraint: surplus is $7\frac{1}{11}$
  Fourth constraint: slack is $12\frac{6}{11}$
 (d) 4 (e) $(x_1^* = 1\frac{1}{11}, x_2^* = 3\frac{7}{11})$, $(x_1^* = 2\frac{2}{3}, x_2^* = 1\frac{2}{3})$

3-21. (a) $E^* = 118.4$, $F^* = 152.6$, OV $= 223{,}686$ (b) $E + F \leq 290$ (c) -18.496 (d) 0.1599 (e) 1667

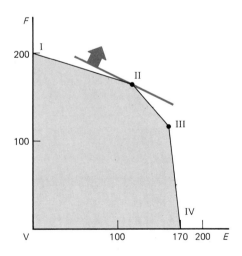

Chapter 4   **4-1.** (a) New solution is $E^* = \frac{48}{7}$, $F^* = \frac{16}{7}$. (b) New OV $= 38{,}857\frac{1}{7}$.

4-3. Since the relative profitability of F has increased, it is desirable to produce relatively more F. Because of the limitations on resources, this can only be done by also producing less E.

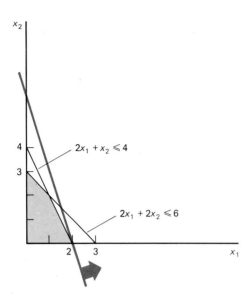

4-5. Becomes infeasible

4-7. (a) $x_1^* = 2$, $x_2^* = 0$ (b) Increase coefficient of x_2 to 15.
(c) 2; $(x_1^* = 2, x_2^* = 0)$ and $(x_1^* = 1, x_2^* = 2)$. (d) Can be infinitely increased. Can be decreased by 2 units.
(e) A change in either direction will change the optimal solution.
(f) The first constraint is active. The second is inactive.
(g) The optimal solution changes to $(x_1^* = \frac{1}{3}, x_2^* = 2\frac{2}{3})$ and the OV changes accordingly.
(h) No effect (i) Satisfies, satisfy

4-9. The first is tighter; (2, 1) satisfies both; (3, 0) satisfies the second, not the first.

4-11. The second

4-13. More, loosening

4-15. Enlarge, smaller, unchanged

4-17. The first constraint. No.

4-19. No. It may not be redundant for other values of the parameters in the model.

4-21. No.

4-23. (a) and (d) match with (2) and (5); (b) and (e) match with (1) and (4); (c) matches with (3).

Chapter 5 **5-1.**

$$\text{Max } 3x_1 - 4x_2$$
$$\text{s.t.} \quad 8x_1 + 12x_2 + s_1 \qquad\qquad = 49$$
$$14x_1 - 6x_2 \quad\;\; + s_2 \qquad\; = 29$$
$$3x_1 + 14x_2 \qquad\qquad - s_3 = 12$$
$$x_1 + \quad x_2 \qquad\qquad\qquad = 2$$
$$x_1, x_2, s_1, s_2, s_3 \geq 0$$

5-3. (a) 0 (b) 6 (c) −5

5-5. 14

5-7. (a) OV increases by 750. (b) OV decreases by 3000. (c) Between −∞ and 11.50

5-9. Zero

5-11. The current solution is degenerate

5-13. (a) Same as before ($E^* = 4.5$, $F^* = 7.0$) (b) OV decreases by 4500.

5-15. (a) \$91.11 (b) Optimal solution unchanged, but OV decreases by 20.8.
(c) No. Cost increases by \$25.96.

5-17. There are alternative optima.

5-19.

$$\text{Max } 3x_1 + 17x_2$$

$$\text{s.t. } 18x_1 + 6x_2 \leq 4$$

$$12x_1 + 2x_2 \leq 13$$

$$x_1 \leq 0, \quad x_2 \text{ unconstrained in sign}$$

5-21. (a) 1500 (b) 120 (c) The dual

5-23. Special structure

5-25. (a) Rate of improvement in the OV as the RHS increases
(b) Rate of change in the OV as the RHS increases

5-27. Let $z_1 = x_1$; $z_2 = y_1$; $z_3 = y_2$; $z_4 = x_3$ to obtain

$$\text{Max } 4z_1 + z_2 - z_3$$

$$\text{s.t. } 3z_1 + 2z_2 - 2z_3 - z_4 + z_5 = 0$$

$$z_1 - 3z_2 + 3z_3 \quad - z_6 = 14$$

$$z_i \geq 0, \quad i = 1, 2, 3, 4, 5, 6$$

5-29. (a) 128 hours on 1 and 2, 76.8 hours on 3. (b) Dollars per minute (c) 60 cents
(d) \$1.38 per pound

5-31. The decrease of 1500 makes the optimal objective function contour coincident to the fourth
constraint line (see Figure 5.9). The decrease of 19,000 makes it coincident to the market balance
line (see Figure 5.10).

5-33. D_2 will have two more equations in unconstrained variables, but these two extra equations will
give the sign conditions in D_1.

Chapter 6

6-1. (a) (4) (b) (6) (c) (1) (d) (7) (e) (9) (f) (11) (g) (5) (h) (8) (i) (3) (j) (2) (k) (10)

6-3. (a)

$$3x_1 + x_3 + s_1 - 2s_2 = 100$$

$$x_1 + x_2 \quad + s_2 = 200$$

$$-5x_1 - 2s_1 + 4s_2 + s_3 = 400$$

$$x_i \geq 0, \quad i = 1, 2, 3$$

$$s_j \geq 0, \quad j = 1, 2, 3$$

(b) $\{x_2, x_3, s_3\}$ (c) $\{x_1, s_1, s_2\}$

(d)

BASIC COEFFICIENT	BASIC VARIABLE	20 x_1	30 x_2	25 x_3	0 s_1	0 s_2	0 s_3	VALUE
25	x_3	3	0	1	1	−2	0	100
30	x_2	1	1	0	0	1	0	200
0	s_3	−5	0	0	−2	④	2	400
z_j		105	30	25	25	−20	0	
$c_j - z_j$		−85	0	0	−25	20	0	8500

(e) No. s_2 should enter and s_3 should exit.

(f)

BASIC COEFFICIENT	BASIC VARIABLE	20	30	25	0	0	0	
		x_1	x_2	x_3	s_1	s_2	s_3	VALUE
25	x_3	$\frac{1}{2}$	0	1	0	0	$\frac{1}{2}$	300
30	x_2	$\frac{9}{4}$	1	0	$\frac{1}{2}$	0	$-\frac{1}{4}$	100
0	s_2	$-\frac{5}{4}$	0	0	$-\frac{1}{2}$	1	$\frac{1}{4}$	100
	z_j	80	30	25	15	0	5	
	$c_j - z_j$	-60	0	0	-15	0	-5	10,500

The optimal solution is $x_3 = 300$, $x_2 = 100$, $s_2 = 100$.

6-5. (a)

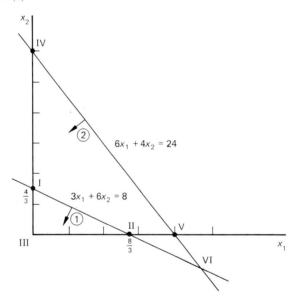

The equality form of the LP is

$$\text{Max } 5x_1 + 6x_2$$
$$\text{s.t.} \quad 3x_1 + 6x_2 + s_1 = 8$$
$$6x_1 + 4x_2 + s_2 = 24$$

Then we have at most $\binom{4}{2} = 6$ possible basic solutions

(b) I, II and III in figure above are possible.

6-7. (a) $\binom{4}{2} = 6$ (b) No (c) At least 1, at most 6

6-9.

BASIC COEFFICIENT	BASIC VARIABLE	40 x_1	60 x_2	50 x_3	0 s_1	0 s_2	0 s_3	VALUE
0	s_1	10	4	2	1	0	0	950
0	s_2	2	②	0	0	1	0	410
0	s_3	1	0	2	0	0	1	610
z_j		0	0	0	0	0	0	
$c_j - z_j$		40	60	50	0	0	0	0

BASIC COEFFICIENT	BASIC VARIABLE	40 x_1	60 x_2	50 x_3	0 s_1	0 s_2	0 s_3	VALUE
0	s_1	6	0	②	1	-2	0	130
60	x_2	1	1	0	0	$\frac{1}{2}$	0	205
0	s_3	1	0	2	0	0	1	610
z_j		60	60	0	0	30	0	
$c_j - z_j$		-20	0	50	0	-30	0	12,300

BASIC COEFFICIENT	BASIC VARIABLE	40 x_1	60 x_2	50 x_3	0 s_1	0 s_2	0 s_3	VALUE
50	x_3	3	0	1	$\frac{1}{2}$	-1	0	65
60	x_2	1	1	0	0	$\frac{1}{2}$	0	205
0	s_3	-5	0	0	-1	②	1	480
z_j		210	60	50	25	-20	0	
$c_j - z_j$		-170	0	0	-25	20	0	15,550

BASIC COEFFICIENT	BASIC VARIABLE	40 x_1	60 x_2	50 x_3	0 s_1	0 s_2	0 s_3	VALUE
50	x_3	$\frac{1}{2}$	0	1	0	0	$\frac{1}{2}$	305
60	x_2	$\frac{9}{4}$	1	0	$\frac{1}{4}$	0	$-\frac{1}{4}$	85
0	s_2	$-\frac{5}{2}$	0	0	$-\frac{1}{2}$	1	$\frac{1}{2}$	240
z_j		160	60	50	15	0	10	
$c_j - z_j$		-120	0	0	-15	0	-10	20,350

The optimal solution is $x_2 = 85$, $x_3 = 305$, $x_1 = 0$.

6-11.

BASIC COEFFICIENT	BASIC VARIABLE	25 x_1	50 x_2	0 s_1	0 s_2	0 s_3	VALUE
0	s_1	2	2	1	0	0	1000
0	s_2	3	0	0	1	0	600
0	s_3	1	③	0	0	1	600
	z_j	0	0	0	0	0	
	$c_j - z_j$	25	50	0	0	0	0

BASIC COEFFICIENT	BASIC VARIABLE	25 x_1	50 x_2	0 s_1	0 s_2	0 s_3	VALUE
0	s_1	$\frac{4}{3}$	0	1	0	$-\frac{2}{3}$	600
0	s_2	③	0	0	1	0	600
50	x_2	$\frac{1}{3}$	1	0	0	$\frac{1}{3}$	200
	z_j	$\frac{50}{3}$	50	0	0	$\frac{50}{3}$	
	$c_j - z_j$	$\frac{25}{3}$	0	0	0	$-\frac{50}{3}$	10,000

BASIC COEFFICIENT	BASIC VARIABLE	25 x_1	50 x_2	0 s_1	0 s_2	0 s_3	VALUE
0	s_1	0	0	1	$-\frac{4}{9}$	$-\frac{2}{3}$	$\frac{1000}{3}$
25	x_1	1	0	0	$\frac{1}{3}$	0	200
50	x_2	0	1	0	$-\frac{1}{9}$	$\frac{1}{3}$	$\frac{400}{3}$
	z_j	25	50	0	$\frac{25}{9}$	$\frac{50}{3}$	
	$c_j - z_j$	0	0	0	$-\frac{25}{9}$	$-\frac{50}{3}$	35,000/3

The optimal solution is: $x_1 = 200$, $x_2 = \frac{400}{3}$.

6-13.

BASIC COEFFICIENT	BASIC VARIABLE	6 x_1	8 x_2	16 x_3	0 s_1	0 s_2	M a_1	M a_2	VALUE
M	a_1	②	1	0	-1	0	1	0	5
M	a_2	0	1	2	0	-1	0	1	4
	z_j	$2M$	$2M$	$2M$	$-M$	$-M$	M	M	
	$c_j - z_j$	$6-2M$	$8-2M$	$16-2M$	M	M	0	0	$9M$

BASIC COEFFICIENT	BASIC VARIABLE	6 x_1	8 x_2	16 x_3	0 s_1	0 s_2	M a_1	M a_2	VALUE
6	x_1	1	$\frac{1}{2}$	0	$-\frac{1}{2}$	0	$\frac{1}{2}$	0	$\frac{5}{2}$
M	a_2	0	1	②	0	-1	0	1	4
	z_j	6	$3 + M$	$2M$	-3	$-M$	3	M	
	$c_j - z_j$	0	$5 - M$	$16 - 2M$	3	M	$M - 3$	0	$4M + 15$

BASIC COEFFICIENT	BASIC VARIABLE	6 x_1	8 x_2	16 x_3	0 s_1	0 s_2	M a_1	M a_2	VALUE
6	x_1	1	$\frac{1}{2}$	0	$-\frac{1}{2}$	0	$\frac{1}{2}$	0	$\frac{5}{2}$
16	x_3	0	⓵$\frac{1}{2}$	1	0	$-\frac{1}{2}$	0	$\frac{1}{2}$	2
	z_j	6	11	16	-3	-8	3	8	
	$c_j - z_j$	0	-3	0	3	8	$M - 3$	$M - 8$	47

BASIC COEFFICIENT	BASIC VARIABLE	6 x_1	8 x_2	16 x_3	0 s_1	0 s_2	VALUE
6	x_1	1	0	-1	$-\frac{1}{2}$	$\frac{1}{2}$	$\frac{1}{2}$
8	x_2	0	1	2	0	-1	4
	z_j	6	8	10	-3	-5	
	$c_j - z_j$	0	0	6	3	5	35

The optimal solution is: $x_1 = \frac{1}{2}$, $x_2 = 4$, $x_3 = 0$.

6-15.

BASIC COEFFICIENT	BASIC VARIABLE	6 x_1	1 x_2	3 x_3	-2 x_4	0 s_1	0 s_2	M a_1	M a_2	VALUE
0	s_1	1	1	0	0	1	0	0	0	42
M	a_1	2	3	-1	-1	0	-1	1	0	10
M	a_2	1	0	2	1	0	0	0	1	30
	z_j	$2M$	$3M$	M	0	0	$-M$	M	M	
	$c_j - z_j$	$6 - 2M$	$1 - 3M$	$3 - M$	-2	0	M	0	0	$40M$

6-17. $x_1 = 7.27$, $x_2 = 0$, $x_3 = 6.36$, $x_4 = 0$

6-19.

Variable	AI	AD
x_1	0	∞
x_2	∞	5.0
x_3	5.5	0
x_4	∞	5.0

Constraint		
1	∞	14.3
2	16.9	∞
3	70.0	40.0

Chapter 7

7-1. (a) (i) Northwest corner rule:

$$x_{A1} = 45, \qquad x_{B1} = 45, \qquad x_{B2} = 5, \qquad x_{C2} = 25, \qquad x_{C3} = 20, \qquad x_{D3} = 30$$

$$\text{cost} = \$1390$$

(ii) Vogel's approximation method:

$$x_{A3} = 45, \qquad x_{B1} = 15, \qquad x_{B2} = 30, \qquad x_{B3} = 5, \qquad x_{C1} = 45, \qquad x_{D1} = 30$$

$$\text{cost} = \$785$$

(b) VAM yields a better solution. This is what we expect.

7-3. (a) and (b) optimal solution:

$$x_{A3} = 45, \qquad x_{B1} = 15, \qquad x_{B2} = 30, \qquad x_{B3} = 5, \qquad x_{C1} = 45, \qquad x_{D1} = 30$$

$$\text{cost} = \$785$$

(c) No additional cost (d) 70

7-5. 85

7-7. $x_{A2} = 150$, $x_{A3} = 250$, $x_{B2} = 300$, $x_{C1} = 150$, $x_{C2} = 50$, OV $= 7600$

7-9. $x_{A2} = 200$, $x_{B1} = 100$, $x_{C1} = 100$, $x_{C2} = 100$, $x_{C3} = 100$, OV $= 2500$

7-11.

ORIGIN	DESTINATION					SUPPLY
	1	2	3	4	DUMMY	
A	20	19	22	24	0	800
B	26	24	28	23	0	600
C	33	25	29	28	0	700
DEMAND	300	500	400	600	300	2100

7-13. A1, B4, C3, D2, OV $= 68$

7-15. A4, B3, C1, D2, OV $= 320$

Chapter 8

8-1. (a) Max $A + 3C$ (b) $A = 1.25$, $C = 5.5$
s.t. $A \leq 7$
  $4C \leq 22$
  $2A + 3C \leq 19$
  $A, C \geq 0$ and integer
(c) $A = 2$, $C = 5$ (d) $A = 1$, $C = 5$; Yes (e) \$1

8-3. Lower bound. LP relaxation is ILP problem without integer constraints.

8-5. Upper bound. LP relaxation is ILP problem without integer constraints.

8-7. $x_i = \$$ invested in stock i
$\quad y_i = 1 \quad$ invest in stock i
$\quad\quad\quad 0 \quad$ do not

$$\text{Max} \sum_{i=1}^{20} r_i x_i$$

$$\text{s.t.} \sum_{i=1}^{20} x_i \le 100{,}000$$

$$x_i \le 20{,}000 y_i \qquad i = 1, \dots, 20$$

$$x_i \ge 5{,}000 y_i \qquad i = 1, \dots, 20$$

$$y_i = 0, 1; \qquad x_i \ge 0, \text{ all } i$$

8-9. x_{ij} = megawatts produced by generator i in period j
$\quad y_i = 1 \quad$ if generator i is started
$\quad\quad = 0 \quad$ if generator i is not started

$$\text{Min } 3000 y_A + 2000 y_B + 1000 y_C + 5 x_{A1} + 5 x_{A2} + 4 x_{B1} + 4 x_{B2} + 7 x_{C1} + 7 x_{C2}$$

$$\text{s.t.} \quad x_{A1} + x_{B1} + x_{C1} \ge 2900$$

$$x_{A2} + x_{B2} + x_{C2} \ge 3900$$

$$x_{A1} \le 2100 y_A$$

$$x_{A2} \le 2100 y_A$$

$$x_{B1} \le 1800 y_B$$

$$x_{B2} \le 1800 y_B$$

$$x_{C1} \le 3000 y_C$$

$$x_{C2} \le 3000 y_C$$

$$x_{ij} \ge 0 \qquad i = A, B, C; \qquad j = 1, 2$$

$$y_i = 0 \text{ or } 1 \qquad i = A, B, C$$

8-11. $y_i = 1 \quad$ make investment i
$\quad\quad = 0 \quad$ do not make investment i

$$\text{Max} \sum_{i=1}^{7} R_i y_i$$

$$\text{s.t.} \qquad y_2 \le y_1$$

$$y_3 \le y_2$$

$$y_2 \le y_4$$

$$y_5 \le (1 - y_1)$$

$$y_5 \le (1 - y_2)$$

$$y_6 \le 2 - y_2 - y_3$$

$$2 y_7 \le y_2 + 1 - y_3$$

$$\sum_{i=1}^{7} C_i y_i \le M$$

$$y_i = 0 \text{ or } 1 \qquad i = 1, \dots, 7$$

8-13. (1) Solution to LP relaxation: $A = 1.25$, $C = 5.5$, OV $= 17.75$.
$\quad$ (2) Branch on A
$\quad\quad$ (a) Problem 2: add constraint $A \ge 2$
$\quad\quad\quad$ Optimal solution to LP relaxation $A = 2$, $C = 5$, OV $= 17$

(b) Problem 3: add constraint $A \leq 1$
   Optimal solution to LP relaxation $A = 1$, $C = 5.5$, OV $= 17.5$
(3) Branch on C in Problem 3
   (a) Problem 4: add constraint $C \geq 6$
      Problem infeasible
   (b) Problem 5: add constraint $C \leq 5$
      Optimal solution to LP relaxation $A = 1$, $C = 5$, OV $= 16$
Optimal solution: $A = 2$, $C = 5$, OV $= 17$

8-15.

RHS(b_2)	OPTIMAL VALUE
24	18
$20 \leq b_2 < 24$	17
$16 \leq b_2 < 20$	15
$12 \leq b_2 < 16$	14
$8 \leq b_2 < 12$	12
$4 \leq b_2 < 8$	10
$0 \leq b_2 < 4$	7

8-17. (a) $x_1 = \frac{8}{3}$, $x_2 = \frac{5}{3}$ (b) (1, 5), (1, 4), (2, 4), (2, 3), (3, 3), (3, 2), (4, 2), (4, 1), (5, 1) (c) (4, 1) (d) (3, 2) (e) No.
(f) One more.

8-19.   Min 170XA1 + 40XA2 + 70XA3 + 160XA4 + 100XC1 + 240XC2 + 140XC3 + 60XC4

   s.t.   XA1 + XC1 = 100

               XA2 + XC2 = 90

               XA3 + XC3 = 110

               XA4 + XC4 = 60

      XA1 + XA2 + XA3 + XA4 $\leq$ 200

      XC1 + XC2 + XC3 + XC4 $\leq$ 300

                  $X_{ij} \geq 0$ $i = $ A, C; $j = 1, \ldots, 4$

8-21.   Min $300X_1 + 670Y_1 + 950Z_1 + \cdots + 145X_5 + 322Y_5 + 458Z_5$

      s.t. $C_1 = 800 + 10X_1 + 50Y_1 + 100Z_1$

            $C_t = C_{t-1} + 10X_t + 50Y_t + 100Z_t$ $t = 2, \ldots, 5$

            $C_1 >= 880, \ldots, C_5 >= 1280$

            $C_t >= 0;$ $X_t, Y_t, Z_t >= 0$ and integer $t = 1, \ldots, 5$

8-23. Let s_i be a 0–1 variable that is 1 if the supplier makes a direct shipment to location i and is 0
otherwise, $i = 1, \ldots, 10$. Add to the objective function $Rs_1 + \ldots + Rs_{10} + Rt$. Include the constraints
$x_i <= d_i s_i$ and s_i is 0 or 1, $i = 1, \ldots, 10$.

8-25. No. There are six positive variables counting slack and surplus variables, but only five constraints.

8-27. The allowable decrease is $.75 - .369 = .381$.

8-29. Max $.089X + .21Y + .23Z$

   s.t. $.0108075X^2 + .0583917Y^2 + .0942268Z^2 + .0248144XY + .0261502XZ + .1108528YZ <= V$

                  $X + Y + Z = 1$

         $X <= .75,$ $Y <= .75,$ $Z <= .75$

                  $X, Y, Z >= 0$

9-1.

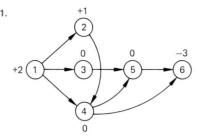

	ARCS (i, j)							
NODE	(1, 2)	(1, 3)	(1, 4)	(2, 4)	(3, 5)	(4, 5)	(4, 6)	(5, 6)	SUPPLIES
1	1	1	1						2
2	−1			1					1
3		−1			1				0
4			−1	−1		1	1		0
5					−1	−1		1	0
6							−1	−1	−3

9-3.

$$-x_{21} + x_{14} = 0$$
$$x_{21} + x_{24} + x_{25} = 2$$
$$x_{36} = 8$$
$$-x_{14} - x_{24} + x_{47} = -1$$
$$-x_{25} - x_{65} + x_{57} = 0$$
$$-x_{36} + x_{65} = 0$$
$$-x_{47} - x_{57} = -9$$

9-5.

	ARCS (i, j)					
NODE	(1, 2)	(1, 3)	(2, 3)	(2, 4)	(3, 4)	SUPPLIES
1	1	1				2
2	−1		1	1		0
3		−1	−1		1	2
4				−1	−1	−4

9-7. The heavy lines below represent a shortest path tree and minimum spanning tree.

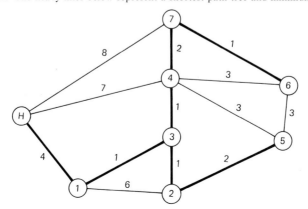

But the two algorithms do not necessarily produce the same tree. For example, consider the network

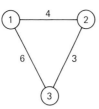

The minimum spanning tree is

whereas the shortest-path tree (from 1) is

9-9.

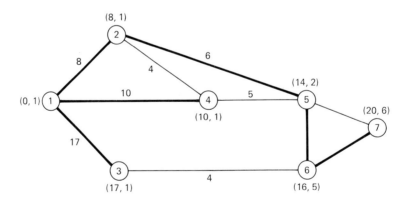

9-11.

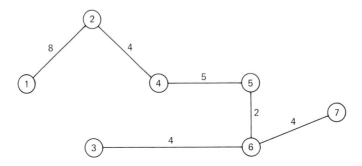

9-13.

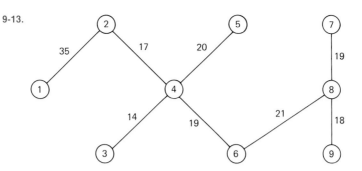

9-15.

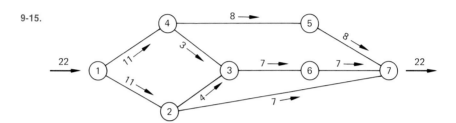

9-17.

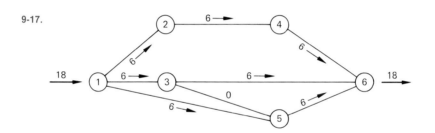

9-19. All arcs (i, j), $i = 1, \ldots, S$, $j = S + 1, \ldots, S + D$ are permitted, where $i = 1, \ldots, S$ denotes origins and $j = S + 1, \ldots, S + D$ denotes destinations. There are SD arcs and $n = S + D$ nodes. For $j = 1, \ldots, S$, there is no arc (k, j), hence $\Sigma_k x_{kj} = 0$. Also, $L_j = S_j =$ supply at j, for $j = 1, \ldots, S$. For $j = S + 1, \ldots, S + D$, there is no arc (j, k). Hence $\Sigma_k x_{jk} = 0$. Also, $L_j = -D_j = -$(demand at j), for $j = S + 1, \ldots, S + D$. Thus, we get the supply and demand equations. Also, let $u_{ij} = \infty$, all (i, j).

9-21. Put a supply of 1 at the origin, a demand of 1 at the destination, and make all other nodes transshipment points.

9-23. (a) 17 (b) 9 (c) 5, 4, and 10 (d) 8, 6, and 11

(e)

From \ To	3	6	9	SUPPLY
1	5	4	10	200
5	8	6	11	150
Demands	50	250	50	

(f) $50(5) + 150(4) + 100(6) + 50(11) = 2000$

10-1.

ACTIVITY	IMMEDIATE PREDECESSORS
2	—
1	2
3	1
4	3
6	4
5	1
8	1
7	8
10	8, 5
9	6, 7, 10

10-3.

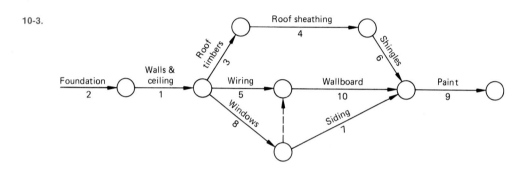

10-5.

ACTIVITY NUMBER	ACTIVITY	ES	EF	LS	LF	SLACK
2	Foundation	0	3	0	3	—
1	Walls and Ceiling	3	8	3	8	—
3	Roof Timbers	8	10	8	10	—
4	Roof Sheathing	10	13	10	13	—
6	Roof Shingles	13	21	13	21	—
5	Electrical Wiring	8	12	14	18	6
8	Windows	8	10	14	16	6
10	Inside Wall Board	12	15	18	21	6
7	Siding	10	15	16	21	6
9	Paint	21	23	21	23	—

Critical path: 2–1–3–4–6–9

10-7. (a)

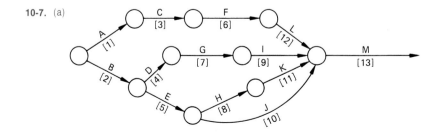

ACTIVITY	EARLIEST START	EARLIEST FINISH	LATEST START	LATEST FINISH	SLACK
A	0	1	4	5	4
B	0	2	0	2	—
C	1	4	5	8	4
D	2	6	6	10	4
E	2	7	2	7	—
F	4	10	8	14	4
G	6	13	10	17	4
H	7	15	7	15	—
I	13	22	17	26	4
J	7	17	16	26	9
K	15	26	15	26	—
L	10	22	14	26	4
M	26	39	26	39	—

Critical path: B–E–H–K–M.
(b) Savings = 9 days.

10-9.

ACTIVITY NUMBER	ACTIVITY	μ	σ
2	Foundation	$\dfrac{2 + 4(3) + 4}{6} = 3$	$\dfrac{4 - 2}{6} = \frac{1}{3}$
1	Walls and Ceiling	$\dfrac{3 + 4(5) + 7}{6} = 5$	$\dfrac{7 - 3}{6} = \frac{2}{3}$
3	Roof Timbers	$\dfrac{1 + 4(2) + 3}{6} = 2$	$\dfrac{3 - 1}{6} = \frac{1}{3}$
4	Roof Sheathing	$\dfrac{1 + 4(2) + 9}{6} = 3$	$\dfrac{9 - 1}{6} = 1\frac{1}{3}$
6	Roof Shingles	$\dfrac{4 + 4(8) + 12}{6} = 8$	$\dfrac{12 - 4}{6} = 1\frac{1}{3}$
5	Electrical Wiring	$\dfrac{4 + 4(4) + 4}{6} = 4$	$\dfrac{4 - 4}{6} = 0$
8	Windows	$\dfrac{1 + 4(2) + 3}{6} = 2$	$\dfrac{3 - 1}{6} = \frac{1}{3}$
7	Exterior Siding	$\dfrac{1 + 4(3) + 17}{6} = 5$	$\dfrac{17 - 1}{6} = 2\frac{2}{3}$
10	Inside Wall Board	$\dfrac{2 + 4(3) + 4}{6} = 3$	$\dfrac{4 - 2}{6} = \frac{1}{3}$
9	Paint	$\dfrac{2 + 4(2) + 2}{6} = 2$	$\dfrac{2 - 2}{6} = 0$

10-11. P (completion time ≤ 12) = 0
P (completion time ≤ 25) = 0.83
Probability critical path completed within 25 days $\geq$ probability project completed within 25 days.

10-13. (a)

ACTIVITY NUMBER	ACTIVITY	NORMAL TIME	NORMAL COST	CRASH TIME	CRASH COST	MAXIMUM CRASH DAYS	COST PER CRASH DAY
2	Foundation	3	$20	2	$30	1	$\dfrac{30 - 20}{3 - 2} = \$10$
1	Walls and Ceiling	5	50	3	72	2	$\dfrac{72 - 50}{5 - 3} = \$11$
3	Roof Timbers	2	15	1	30	1	$\dfrac{30 - 15}{2 - 1} = \$15$
4	Roof Sheathing	3	8	1	20	2	$\dfrac{20 - 8}{3 - 1} = \$6$
6	Roof Shingles	8	13	4	21	4	$\dfrac{21 - 13}{8 - 4} = \$2$
5	Wiring	4	30	4	30	0	$0

ACTIVITY NUMBER	ACTIVITY	NORMAL TIME	NORMAL COST	CRASH TIME	CRASH COST	MAXIMUM CRASH DAYS	COST PER CRASH DAY
8	Windows	2	45	1	52	1	$\dfrac{52 - 45}{2 - 1} = \$7$
7	Siding	5	65	1	45	4	$\dfrac{65 - 45}{5 - 1} = \$5$
10	Inside Wall Board	3	22	2	34	1	$\dfrac{34 - 22}{3 - 2} = \$12$
9	Paint	2	40	2	40	0	$0

(b) $308 (c) $30; it is impossible

10-15.

$$MIN \ 10CFOUND + 11CWALLS + 15CRTIMB + 6CRSHEA + 2CSHING$$
$$+ 7CWIND + 5CSIDIN + 12CWALB$$

s.t.

$$ESWAL + CFOUND \geq 3$$
$$ESRTIM + CWALLS - ESWALL \geq 5$$
$$ESWIR + CWALLS - ESWALL \geq 5$$
$$ESWIN + CWALLS - ESWALL \geq 5$$
$$ESRSHE + CRTIMB - ESRTIM \geq 2$$
$$ESSHIN + CRSHEA - ESRSHE \geq 3$$
$$ESPAIN + CSHING - ESSHIN \geq 8$$
$$ESWALB - ESWIR \geq 2$$
$$ESPAIN + CWALB - ESWALB \geq 3$$
$$ESWALB + CWIND - ESWIND \geq 2$$
$$ESSID + CWIND - ESWIND \geq 2$$
$$ESPAIN + CSIDIN - ESSID \geq 5$$
$$EFPAIN - ESPAIN = 2$$
$$CFOUND \leq 1$$
$$CWALLS \leq 2$$
$$CRTIMB \leq 1$$
$$CRSHEA \leq 2$$
$$CSHING \leq 4$$
$$CWIND \leq 1$$
$$CSIDIN \leq 4$$
$$CWALB \leq 1$$
$$EFPAIN + X \leq 23$$

All variables nonnegative

The last equation represents the constraint on the total time required to complete.

$$23 = normal \ time \ to \ complete$$
$$X = desired \ reduction$$

ACTIVITY NUMBER	ACTIVITY	DAY									
		1	2	3	4	5	6	7	8	9	10
2	Foundation	6.67	6.67	6.67							
1	Walls and Ceiling				10	10	10	10	10		
3	Roof Timbers									7.50	7.50
4	Roof Sheathing										
6	Roof Shingles										
5	Wiring									7.50	7.50
8	Windows									22.50	22.50
10	Wall Board										
7	Siding										
9	Paint										
Daily Project Cost		6.67	6.67	6.67	10	10	10	10	10	37.50	37.50
Total Project Cost		6.67	13.34	20.00	30.00	40.00	50.00	60.00	70.00	107.5	145

Latest Start

ACTIVITY NUMBER	ACTIVITY	DAY									
		1	2	3	4	5	6	7	8	9	10
2	Foundation	6.67	6.67	6.67							
1	Walls and Ceiling				10	10	10	10	10		
3	Roof Timbers									7.50	7.50
4	Roof Sheathing										
6	Roof Shingles										
5	Wiring										
8	Windows										
10	Wall Board										
7	Siding										
9	Paint										
Daily Project Cost		6.67	6.67	6.67	10	10	10	10	10	7.50	7.50
Total Project Cost		6.67	13.34	20	30	40	50	60	70	77.50	85

DAY

11	12	13	14	15	16	17	18	19	20	21	22	23
2.67	2.67	2.67										
			1.63	1.63	1.63	1.63	1.63	1.63	1.63	1.63		
7.50	7.50											
		7.33	7.33	7.33								
13	13	13	13	13								
											20	20
23.17	23.17	23	21.96	21.96	1.63	1.63	1.63	1.63	1.63	1.63	20	20
168.17	191.34	214.34	236.3	258.26	259.89	261.52	263.15	264.78	266.41	268.04	288.04	308.04

DAY

11	12	13	14	15	16	17	18	19	20	21	22	23
2.67	2.67	2.67										
			1.63	1.63	1.63	1.63	1.63	1.63	1.63	1.63		
				7.50	7.50	7.50	7.50					
				22.50	22.50							
								7.33	7.33	7.33		
						13	13	13	13	13		
											20	20
2.67	2.67	2.67	1.63	31.63	31.63	22.13	22.13	21.96	21.96	21.96	20	20
87.67	90.34	93.01	94.64	126.27	157.90	180.03	202.16	224.12	246.08	268.04	288.04	308.04

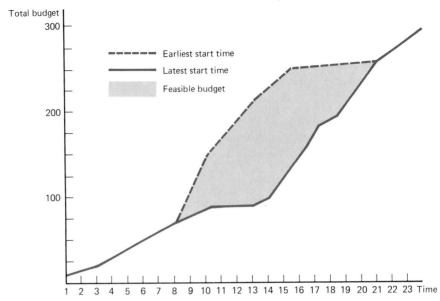

10-19. (a)

ACTIVITY NUMBER	ACTIVITY	PERCENT COMPLETE	BUDGET	BUDGETED COST	ACTUAL COST	COST OVERRUN
2	Foundation	100	20	20	22	2.
1	Walls and Ceiling	100	50	50	46	(4)
3	Roof Timbers	100	15	15	15	0
4	Roof Sheathing	100	8	8	10	2
6	Roof Shingles	25	13	3.25	4.50	1.25
5	Wiring	100	30	30	20	(10)
8	Windows	100	45	45	22.50	(22.50)
10	Inside Wall Board	100	22	22	20	(2)
7	Siding	100	65	65	40	(25)
9	Paint	0	40	0	0	0
Totals			308.00	258.25	200	(58.25)

(b)

ACTIVITY NUMBER	ACTIVITY	PERCENT COMPLETE	BUDGET	BUDGETED COST	ACTUAL COST	COST OVERRUN
2	Foundation	100	20	20	22	2
1	Walls and Ceiling	100	50	50	46	(4)
3	Roof Timbers	100	15	15	15	0
4	Roof Sheathing	100	8	8	10	2
6	Roof Shingles	25	13	3.25	4.50	1.25
5	Wiring	25	30	7.50	20	12.50
8	Windows	50	45	22.50	22.50	20
10	Inside Wall Board	0	22	0	20	20
7	Siding	0	65	0	40	40
9	Paint	0	40	0	0	0
Totals			308.00	113.75	200	73.75

10-21. $26 - 15\frac{2}{3} = 10\frac{1}{3}$

Chapter 11

11-1. (a) 7000 (b) $420 (c) $1300 (d) $1720 (e) 183,720
(f) Larger, since annual ordering cost exceeds annual holding cost

11-3. $Q^* = 3020.76$, $N^* = 3.02$

11-5. (a) $48,989.80 (b) 48.99 (c) 0.020 year = 5.10 days

11-7. (a) $18,974 (b) 12.65 (c) 0.079 year

11-9. (a) 50 dozen (b) 50 orders/year (c) 0.02 year = 5 days (d) 20 days (e) 200 dozen (f) 200 dozen

11-11. (a) $Q^* = 12,000$; $T^* = 0.01$ year = 24 days; $N^* = 10$; ATC = $121,800
(b) 0.5% discount: $121,432
     0.7% discount: $121,754
(c) Order 20,000

11-13. (a) $Q^* = 96$; $N^* = 24$; $T^* = 8.33$ days; AHO(Q^*) = 4800 (b) C_b = $40
(c) $Q^* = 144$; $S^* = 80$; $N^* = 16$; $T^* = 12.5$ days; AHOB(Q^*) = $3200 (d) Backlog

11-15. (a) $Q^* = 1000$; $N^* = 25$; $T^* = 10$ days; $S^* = 750$; AHOB* = 1250
(b) On hand = -50; on order = 0; position = -50 (c) 700 books (d) Yes

11-17. (a) $Q = 1800$ gallons; $T = 75$ days; production run = 37.5 days; maximum inventory
level = 900 gallons (b) AHO = 9750

11-19. $0.107

11-21. (a) Engines 245, spark plug sets 120, carburetors 155, throats 5, butterfly valves 55.

(b)

DAY	11	13	16	17	22
ACTION	Order Throats	Order Butterfly Valves	Assemble Carburetors	Order Spark Plugs	Assemble Engines

Chapter 12

12-1. $r = 10$, $Q^* = 30$

12-3. (a) 0.052 (b) 0.058

12-5. (a) (iii); Q affects the number of orders per year. It has no effect on the probability of a stockout during an inventory cycle. (b) (ii); increasing Q decreases cycles per year and thus decreases the number of opportunities to stockout.

12-7. $r = 107.78$, $Q^* = 500$

12-9. $7.78

12-11. (a) $Q^* = 574.70$ (b) 0.60 (c) $Q^* = 728.3$ (d) $g = $625.00

Chapter 13

13-1. (a) $\lambda = 0.5$ barges per hr (b) 2 hrs (c) 0.5 barges per hr

13-3. (a) $\mu = 15$ people per hr (b) 0.067 hrs per person (c) 15 people per hr

13-5. (a) $L = 2$ (b) $L_q = 1.33$ (c) $W = 0.2$ hr/person (d) $W_q = 0.133$ hr/person (e) $P_0 = 0.333$

13-7. (2) is wrong, for λ should be N/8.

13-9.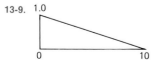

13-11. $W = L/\lambda = [\lambda/(\mu - \lambda)]/\lambda = 1/(\mu - \lambda)$

13-13. $L = 1.25$

13-15. Since $\lambda > \mu$ the queue grows without limit.

13-17. (a) $P_0 = 0.111$ (b) $L = 0.888$ (c) $W_q = 0.0444$ (d) $W = 0.144$ (e) $L = 2.88$

13-19. A three server queue with Poisson arrivals (exponential interarrival times) and deterministic service time.

13-21. $TC(5) = \$184$ per hour

13-23. $C_S/C_W = 1.63$

13-25. (a) $P_3 = 0.034$ (b) 0.409 (c) 5.91

Chapter 14

14-1. Computerized war games, military exercises, training exercises.

14-3 (a)

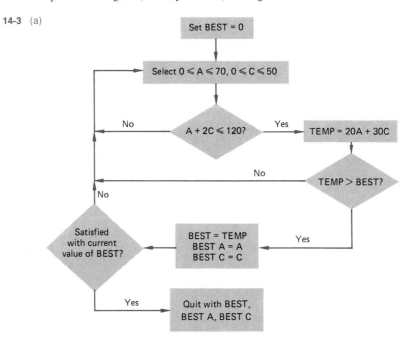

(b) A = 40, C = 30, **BEST** = 1700
A = 50, C = 30, **BEST** = 1900

14-5. False. Simplex is guaranteed to find optimum.

14-7.

EVENT	RANDOM NUMBER
Increase	00–29
Remain the Same	30–79
Decrease	80–99

14-9. 115.55

14-11. RN = 06, $W = 6.0$, RN = 60, $W = 38.6$; RN = 80, $W = 47.7$

14-13.

	RN									
	90	49	6	60	92	77	38	39	84	47
Demand	13	10	8	11	13	11	10	10	12	10
Pans Left	0	0	2	0	0	0	0	0	0	0
Pans Short	3	0	0	1	3	1	0	0	2	0

(a) Average cost $= \dfrac{7(2) + 10(10)}{10} = 11.4$ (b) Number of stockouts = 5

14-15.

NUMBER OF BRAKE JOBS	RELATIVE FREQUENCY	RANDOM NUMBERS
5	0.1	00–09
6	0.3	10–39
7	0.3	40–69
8	0.2	70–89
9	0.1	90–99

	RN									
	20	82	74	8	1	69	36	35	52	99
Demand	6	8	8	5	5	7	6	6	7	9

14-17.

TIME BETWEEN ARRIVALS	RANDOM NUMBERS
5	00–24
10	25–74
15	75–99

CUSTOMER	R.N.	INTERARRIVAL TIME	ARRIVAL TIME	SERVICE STARTS	SERVICE ENDS	WAIT
1	None Needed		0	0	8	No
2	97	15	15	15	23	No
3	02	5	20	23	31	Yes
4	80	15	35	35	43	No
5	66	10	45	45	53	No
6	96	15	60	60	68	No
7	65	10	70	70	78	No
8	50	10	80	80	88	No
9	29	10	90	90	98	No
10	58	10	100	100	108	No
11	51	10	110	110	118	No
12	04	5	115	118	126	Yes
13	86	15	130	130	138	No
14	24	5	135	138	146	Yes
15	39	10	145	146	154	Yes
16	47	10	155	155	163	No

Four customers have to wait.

(d)

	STATES OF NATURE			
	1	2	3	4
1	0	3	3	21
2	8	0	8	15
3	13	0	3	5
4	15	0	0	0

(e) 3

15-3. (a) 4 (b) 4 (c) Maximizing expected net dollar return and minimizing expected regret always lead to the same optimal decision.

15-5. (a) Accept government contract (b) Accept government contract

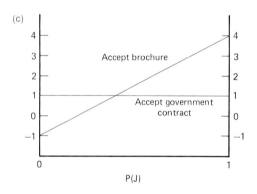

(d) 0.4 (e) Bid on brochure (f) Accept government contract (g) 1000 (h) Expected value of perfect information

15-7. (a) Accept government contract; 1000 (b) No. The risk-averse nature of the utility function will decrease the attractiveness of bidding relative to accepting the government contract. (c) 0.73 (d) ER(bid) = 666.7; $U(666.7) = 0.70$ (e) EU(bid) = 0.66 (f) No. Not in general.

15-9. (a) $U(30) \geq 0.6$ (b) $U(50) \geq 0.85$ (c) $U(10) \leq 0.55$

15-11. $P(\text{ordering error}\,|\,\text{late}) = 0.6$
$P(\text{delivery error}\,|\,\text{late}) = 0.4$
Therefore, look for ordering error.

15-13. (a) $P(\tfrac{1}{2}) = 0.225$ (b) $P(A\,|\,\tfrac{1}{2}) = 0.44$ (c) ER = \$188.50

15-15. (a) Optimal strategy: If "sun" forecast, go ahead. If "rain" forecast, cancel. (b) Expected value of sample information = \$5250 − \$3750 = \$1500

15-17. $P(\text{bad risk}\,|\,\text{credit}) = 0.024$

15-19.

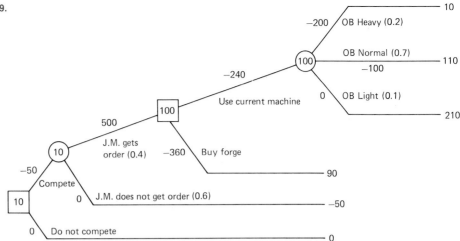

Optimal strategy: 1. Compete. 2. If order is received, use current machines.

15-21. $.3(200) + .6(1000) + .1(3000) = 960 > 900$, sell to the movie company. $.3(900) + .6(1000) + .1(3000) - 960 = 210$, at most $210,000.

15-23. Marple should make the component.

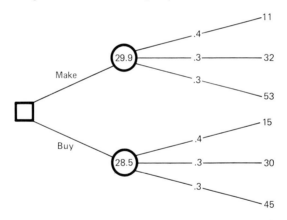

15-25. (a)

	DEMAND		
ORDER	0	1	2
0	0	100	200
1	10	10	110
2	20	20	20

(b)

ORDER	EXPECTED COST
0	$100(\frac{8}{36}) + 200(\frac{4}{36}) = \$44.44$
1	$10(\frac{24}{36}) + 10(\frac{8}{36}) + 110(\frac{4}{36}) = \$21.11$
2	$\$20$

Hospital should order 2 units each month.

15-27. (a)

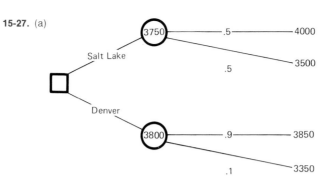

(b) Denver.

15-29. (a)

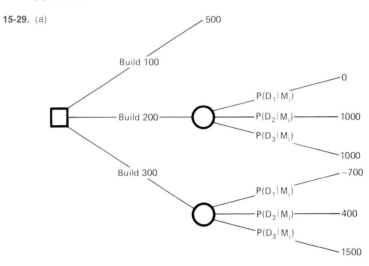

Note that there are three different trees depending on whether the measurement of demand is M_1, M_2, or M_3.

(b)

	$P(D_i \mid M_j)$			
	D_1	D_2	D_3	$P(M_j)$
M_1	.55	.40	.05	.38
M_2	.19	.62	.19	.32
M_3	.10	.50	.40	.30

	Expected Payoff		
	M_1	M_2	M_3
Build 100	500	500	500
Build 200	450	810	900
Build 300	−150	400	730

If M_1, then Build 100, else if M_2 or M_3 Build 200.
(c) EVSI = 719,000 − 700,000 = $19,000.
EVSI/EVPI = $\frac{19000}{250000}$ = .076, the survey is not very efficient.

16-1. (a)

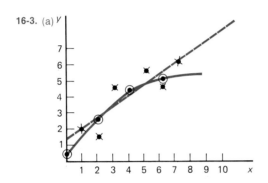

(b) Relevant data:

$$\sum x_i = 550, \qquad \sum y_i = 420$$
$$\sum x_i y_i = 26,120, \qquad \sum x_i^2 = 38,500$$
$$y = 21.87 + .366x$$

(c) $y = 21.87 + 0.36(120) = 65.79$

16-3. (a)

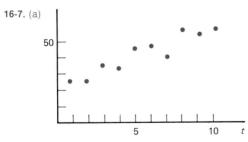

(b) Relevant data:

$$\sum x_i = 28, \qquad \sum y_i = 28, \qquad \sum x_i y_i = 131, \qquad \sum x_i^2 = 140$$
$$\sum x_i^3 = 784, \qquad \sum x_i^4 = 4676, \qquad \sum x_i^2 y_i = 706$$

$y = 1.29 + 0.68x$
(c) $y = 0.428 + 1.250x - 0.071x^2$

16-5. Sum of squared deviations: linear, 214.08, quadratic, 99.72

16-7. (a)

(b) $\hat{y}_{11} = 51.50$ (c) No. There seems to be a linear trend in the data and a simple moving average underestimates future demand if there is a trend.

16-9. (a) $\hat{y}_{11} = 53.9$ (b) Yes. Since there seems to be a trend, a weighted moving average with decreasing weights will underestimate demand less than a simple average. Still not as good as explicitly including the trend.

16-11. (a) $\hat{y}_{11} = 52.24$ (b) Larger. Since there seems to be a trend, we would like to put more weight on recent observations.

16-13. The anonymity of the source of each evaluation is an advantage of the Delphi Method. This is important in this case, since some of the participants are in subordinate positions. The cost and time involved are serious disadvantages of the Delphi Method as compared to the consensus panel.

16-15. Time series. The horizon is short. It is a mature product.

16-17. (a)

t	3	4	5	6	7	8	9	10
$\hat{\omega}_t$	31.0	33.6	39.6	45.2	42.4	49.0	53.9	55.1

(b) Simple average squared error = 97.6; trend-adjusted = 58.8.

16-19. No. Average squared error is sensitive to large but perhaps infrequent errors. Example: you might prefer errors of 0, 0, 0, 11 to $+5$, -5, $+5$, -5, but the average squared error is greater in the first case.

Chapter 17

17-1. (Start III at beginning of week 1 and II at beginning of week 2) and/or (Start IX at beginning of week 5 and VII at beginning of week 7) are three alternative optima.

17-3. Let (i, j) mean i is assigned to j. Then the tree is

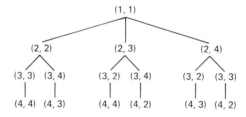

17-5. (a) Assign 4 to A. Delete row 4, column A. Assign 1 to C. Delete row 1, column C. Assign 5 to B. Delete row 5 and column B. Assign 3 to D, and assign 2 to E. Total Sales = 108.
(b) Transformed Data

	A	B	C	D	E
1	-5	-8	-2	0	-4
2	-10	-5	-7	-7	-8
3	-7	-7	-5	-1	0
4	0	0	0	0	0
5	-2	-4	-2	-2	-2

Assign 4 to A, 1 to D, 3 to E, 5 to C, 2 to B. Total Sales = 116.

17-7.
$$\text{Min} \sum_{i=1}^{12} u_i$$

$$\text{s.t.} \quad x_1 + u_1 - u_2 = 2$$
$$x_2 + u_3 - u_4 = 10$$
$$x_1 + u_5 - u_6 = 6$$
$$x_2 + u_7 - u_8 = 6$$
$$x_1 + u_9 - u_{10} = 1$$
$$x_2 + u_{11} - u_{12} = 3$$
$$u_i \geq 0, \qquad i = 1, \ldots, 12$$

17-9.

$$\text{Min } w_1u_1 + w_2u_2 + w_3u_3$$

$$20x_1 + 12x_2 \leq 240$$

$$12x_1 + 20x_2 \leq 240$$

$$x_1 + x_2 + u_1 - v_1 = 12$$

$$x_2 + u_2 - v_2 = 9$$

$$x_1 + u_3 - v_3 = 10$$

$$x_1, x_2 \geq 0, \qquad u_i, v_i \geq 0, i = 1, 2, 3$$

17-11. (a) $x_1^* = 40$, $x_2^* = 40$. (b) Minimize underachievement, no overachievement allowed. (c) Minimize underachievement, overachievement allowed. (d) $x_1^* = 0$, $x_2^* = 80$

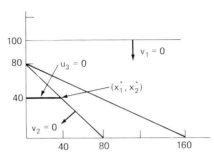
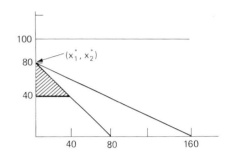

17-13. (a) $x_1^* = 100$, $x_2^* = 0$
(b) yes; $v_1^* = 20$ overachieved by 20;
       $u_3^* = 45$ underachieved by 45.

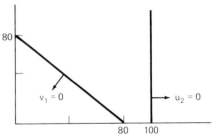

17-15. (a) $6! = 6 \times 5 \times 4 \times 3 \times 2 = 720$
(b) Sequence of jobs $= D - F - A - C - E - B$
Gantt Chart
Cutting

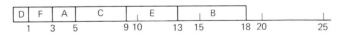

Grinding

Total processing time: 23 hours

17-17. Formulation:

$$\text{Min } P_1v_1 + P_2u_2 + P_3(-200A - 200B)$$

$$\text{s.t. } 400A + 600B + u_1 - v_1 = 2400$$

$$20A + 40B + u_2 - v_2 = 120$$

$$A, B, u_1, u_2, v_1, v_2 \geq 0$$

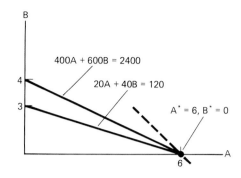

Optimal Solution: $A^* = 6$, $B^* = 0$.
The goals are exactly achieved with the optimal solution.
Net expenditure $= 6(400 - 200) = 1200$.
\# of jobs generated $= 120$.

Chapter 18

18-1. (a) $x^* = -\frac{7}{8}$ (b) Negative (c) $x = 1$ (d) Concave, because $f'' < 0$ for all x

18-3. $x^* = 25$

18-5. (a) Saddle point; (b) local maximizer; (c) local maximizer

18-7. (a) $a^* = -5.428$, $b^* = 47.714$ (b) $a^* = -2$, $b^* = 45$

18-9. (a) $x_1^* = 3$, $x_2^* = 2$ (b) about 6, the value of λ^*

18-11. The stationary point is unique. Since it is a local Min it must be global.

18-13.

$$\lambda^* = \frac{1}{2}\sqrt{\frac{1}{B}\sum_{i=1}^{3}\frac{1}{p_i}}, \qquad x_i^* = \frac{B}{p_i^2 \sum_{i=1}^{3}(1/p_i)}$$

18-15.

$$x_2^* = \frac{a_1 c_1 - 2b_1 a_2}{4b_1 b_2 - c_1^2}, \qquad x_1^* = \frac{-a_2 - 2b_2 x_2^*}{c_1}$$

$$b_1 > 0 \text{ and } 4b_1 b_2 - c_1^2 > 0 \Rightarrow \text{local min}$$

$$b_1 < 0 \text{ and } 4b_1 b_2 - c_1^2 > 0 \Rightarrow \text{local max}$$

$$4b_1 b_2 - c_1^2 < 0 \Rightarrow \text{saddle point}$$

SELECTED ANSWERS TO MAJOR CONCEPTS QUIZZES

Chapter 2

  2. An LP, by definition, is a constrained optimization model.

  5. Positive or equal to zero.

 11. b is obvious; because of b, a is also true.

 19. The accuracy constraint is $(.02)300X_1 + (.01)200X_2 + (.04)350X_3 \le .02(300X_1 + 200X_2 + 350X_3)$ which is equivalent to c.

 20. 8 hours of operation may produce more than 2000 inspections.

 21. (i) # inspections ≥ 2000, (ii) errors $\le 2\%$, (iii) $X_1 + X_2 + X_3 = 8$ and 3 more constraints: $X_i \le 4$, $i = 1, 2, 3$

 22. $X_1 = 4$, $X_2 = 4$ is feasible.

 23. b. False because, for example $X_2 = 1$, $X_3 = 7$ is cheaper than $X_3 = 8$ and either policy is feasible when the accuracy requirement and the 4-hour limitation are dropped.

 26. B is cheaper.

Chapter 3

  2. The intersection may be infeasible.

  3. Need not use *all*.

  6. May be unbounded.

 11. The optimal solution could be at the origin with no constraints active.

Chapter 4

  2. *Less* confidence.

  3. Quantitative information is produced.

  8. Can affect the feasible region if tightened enough.

 15. c is false if the corresponding decision variable has optimal value of zero.

 17. Should not be dropped if the model is to be run with more than one set of data.

Chapter 5

  1. Slack and surplus must be nonnegative.

  5. Rate of *improvement*.

  6. Dual price is constant over the range.

 10. Inactive constraints.

 12. Can vary only 1 parameter.

19. a is false because the variables are free in sign.

21. Less than because x is nonoptimal.

22. P_0 need not be feasible.

Chapter 7

2. Opportunity cost.

4. $u_i + v_j = c_{ij}$

7. Costs need not be integers.

Chapter 8

4. Upper bound.

6. Replace "all corners" with "all integer points" and the statement is true.

7. There is also an upper bound constraint $x_j \leq 1$ for each variable.

10. $x_2 \leq x_1$

11. For a transportation problem, the optimal solution produced by the simplex algorithm is integer valued.

15. Rounded solution by definition is integer, is always ≥ 0, and OV is not as good as OV for LP relaxation.

16. $x_k + x_m \leq 0$ means neither k nor m can be selected.

IP Section

23. If t is positive, so is z because of constraint $z - tD \geq 0$.

If z is positive, so is t because of constraint $z - t \sum_{i=1}^{10} d_i \leq 0$. Hence, e is correct.

24. False. It may be necessary to ship from the warehouse to location k where $35 + C_k > 50$ so that the delivery to the warehouse will be at least D units.

25. This is false because of the last argument in 24.

27. True, in order to get the discount.

29. True, because of 27.

QP Section

31. The constraint functions must be linear.

32. Must have quadratic objective.

33. LP is a special QP.

34. The feasible region is the same as for an LP.

36. Could have an optimum at a degenerate corner.

37. Loosening increases the set of feasible solutions.

40. It doesn't hold for an LP.

42. Because the constraint $x + y + z = 1$ defines a plane in 3-dimensional space.

43. See the example in Figure 8.24.

Chapter 9   3. There may be alternate routes between sources and sinks that do not use the arc with zero capacity.

9. The disjoint sets must be a partition with one set containing the source and the other set containing the sink.

Chapter 10   3. It connects the terminal nodes of activities 2 and 3.

4. Should read "The latest start time ..."

6. Should read ... latest finish time plus activity time.

7. Should read "A tactical ..."

8. With random times paths other than the critical path can determine the completion time for the project.

12. See Figure 10.28.

15. There is no specific indication of precedent relationships on a Gantt chart.

21. c is not correct since we only need to know the standard deviation of activities on the critical path.

Chapter 11   1. The opportunity cost segment of the holding cost is determined by the return that could be earned by investing the money tied up in inventory.

3. It is inversely proportional.

6. ... the expected demand ...

7. Not allowing backlogging imposes a constraint which cannot help the optimal value.

11. Only the total holding cost per unit must be known.

13. If price increases the holding cost typically increases and thus the optimal order quantity will decrease.

14. $N^* = \dfrac{D}{Q^*} = \dfrac{D}{\sqrt{\dfrac{2DC_o}{C_h}}} = \sqrt{\dfrac{DC_h}{2C_o}}$

15. Since $Q_D^* > B$ we can achieve the lowest point on the ATC curve calculated with discounted price. Since this must be less than the best we can do with the regular price we order Q_D^*.

16. $S^* = Q^* \left(\dfrac{C_h}{C_h + C_b} \right)$ thus S^* is directly proportional to the square root of D.

17. If the production rate equalled the rate of demand you would only set up once and produce all the time. As the rate increases you do not produce all of the time thus you set up more often. The result also can be seen from the expression for N^*.

Chapter 12   1. Larger holding costs lead to more frequent orders.

4. ... as the distribution changes, the amount of inventory required to guarantee the same probability of a stockout will change.

5. By determining the number of occasions at which the system is in a position to stock out.

6. They provide information to guide managerial judgement.

Chapter 13

1. It includes those being served.

3. It is specified by a single parameter, λ.

6. Since expected time in queue decreases, waiting time and thus waiting cost would generally decrease.

7. True, if sentence reads ... mean service time ... mean interarrival time ...

9. True, if the words service and arrival are interchanged.

13. λ represents the rate at which arrivals join the queue.

Chapter 14

3. Although the parameters remain the same, the simulated events, typically generated with random numbers, will usually change.

5. The expected cost is unknown.

6. To get correct probabilities it may be necessary to treat some outcomes as no trial.

9. The common error is to make the simulator too complicated and "lifelike."

11. c is not correct and thus the answer must be e.

16. a is not correct since in many cases the choice of system parameters is determined by the environment.

20. b is incorrect since you may wish to vary the numbers of trials to obtain greater precision in estimating the average return for some decisions.

Chapter 15

3. The assumption of what "is known" about the probabilities of the various states determines the criterion.

5. This is known as using the Laplace Criterion.

6. The concept is that the random outcome is known before the decision must be made.

8. It is concave.

9. Folding backwards.

12. Return is not known with certainty and thus cannot be maximized.

13. Since probabilities are not known, the expected return cannot be computed.

15. c is incorrect because EVPI is the expected return from knowing a particular type of information.

Chapter 16

1. They are typically based on curves fitted by eye.

2. This definition allows positive and negative deviations to cancel each other.

4. Regression analysis can be used to prove that the method of least squares produces the best fit for a particular model.

20. Quick and dirty as defined here is fitting a curve "by eye." This is impractical with more than one independent variable.

Chapter 17

1. Some, but not all, heuristic algorithms have this property.

4. Other approaches include multiattribute utility theory and heuristic search procedures.

6. Since u_1 is positive this value had to be added to $12x_1 + 3x_2$ to reach 100. Thus, the goal is underachieved.

8. The 2nd constraint should be $4x_1 + 12x_2 + u_1 \geq 180$ since we want $u_1 > 0$ when the goal is violated.

9. The constraint is active because we choose the smallest deviational variable that makes the problem feasible.

10. Only goal constraints can be violated.

11. The set of system constraints could be infeasible.

15. Since the coefficient of u_1 is greater than the coefficient of v_1 we would prefer to subtract something from $g_1(x_1, \ldots, x_n)$ to make it equal to b_1. Thus we prefer to have $g_1(x_1, \ldots, x_n)$ greater than b_1.

17. a. is incorrect since if after the system constraint is applied the only feasible values for g_2 are $< b_2$, this constraint makes the problem infeasible. b. is OK. Note if $g_2 > b_2$ then u_2 can $= 0$. c. is incorrect. If $g_2 < b_2$ then u_2 can $= 0$. There is no motivation to make $g_2 \geq b_2$

18. a. is incorrect. The objective implies indifference between over and underachievement. b. is incorrect. If after the first two constraints the only feasible values of g_3 are > 0 this constraint makes the problem infeasible c. OK. Note if $g_3 < b_3$ then $v_3 = 0$ is OK.

Chapter 18

2. It may be possible to estimate the nonlinear relationship with linear expressions.

9. Not every quadratic function is concave or convex.

12. This is a conceptual prescription which is generally non-implementable.

15. b. is incorrect because the sufficient condition includes $f'(x^*) = 0$.

18. See answer above.

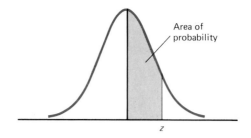

Area of probability

TABLE T.1
AREAS FOR THE STANDARD NORMAL DISTRIBUTION

Entries in the table give the AREA under the curve between the mean and z standard deviations above the mean. For example, for $z = 1.25$ the area under the curve between the mean and z is 0.3944.

z	0.00	0.01	0.02	0.03	0.04	0.05	0.06	0.07	0.08	0.09
0.0	0.0000	0.0040	0.0080	0.0120	0.0160	0.0199	0.0239	0.0279	0.0319	0.0359
0.1	0.0398	0.0438	0.0478	0.0517	0.0557	0.0596	0.0636	0.0675	0.0714	0.0753
0.2	0.0793	0.0832	0.0871	0.0910	0.0948	0.0987	0.1026	0.1064	0.1103	0.1141
0.3	0.1179	0.1217	0.1255	0.1293	0.1331	0.1368	0.1406	0.1443	0.1480	0.1517
0.4	0.1554	0.1591	0.1628	0.1664	0.1700	0.1736	0.1772	0.1808	0.1844	0.1879
0.5	0.1915	0.1950	0.1985	0.2019	0.2054	0.2088	0.2123	0.2157	0.2190	0.2224
0.6	0.2257	0.2291	0.2324	0.2357	0.2389	0.2422	0.2454	0.2486	0.2518	0.2549
0.7	0.2580	0.2612	0.2642	0.2673	0.2704	0.2734	0.2764	0.2794	0.2823	0.2852
0.8	0.2881	0.2910	0.2939	0.2967	0.2995	0.3023	0.3051	0.3078	0.3106	0.3133
0.9	0.3159	0.3186	0.3212	0.3238	0.3264	0.3289	0.3315	0.3340	0.3365	0.3389
1.0	0.3413	0.3438	0.3461	0.3485	0.3508	0.3531	0.3554	0.3577	0.3599	0.3621
1.1	0.3643	0.3665	0.3686	0.3708	0.3729	0.3749	0.3770	0.3790	0.3810	0.3830
1.2	0.3849	0.3869	0.3888	0.3907	0.3925	0.3944	0.3962	0.3980	0.3997	0.4015
1.3	0.4032	0.4049	0.4066	0.4082	0.4099	0.4115	0.4131	0.4147	0.4162	0.4177
1.4	0.4192	0.4207	0.4222	0.4236	0.4251	0.4265	0.4279	0.4292	0.4306	0.4319
1.5	0.4332	0.4345	0.4357	0.4370	0.4382	0.4394	0.4406	0.4418	0.4429	0.4441
1.6	0.4452	0.4463	0.4474	0.4484	0.4495	0.4505	0.4515	0.4525	0.4535	0.4545
1.7	0.4554	0.4564	0.4573	0.4582	0.4591	0.4599	0.4608	0.4616	0.4625	0.4633
1.8	0.4641	0.4649	0.4656	0.4664	0.4671	0.4678	0.4686	0.4693	0.4699	0.4706
1.9	0.4713	0.4719	0.4726	0.4732	0.4738	0.4744	0.4750	0.4756	0.4761	0.4767
2.0	0.4772	0.4778	0.4783	0.4788	0.4793	0.4798	0.4803	0.4808	0.4812	0.4817
2.1	0.4821	0.4826	0.4830	0.4834	0.4838	0.4842	0.4846	0.4850	0.4854	0.4857
2.2	0.4861	0.4864	0.4868	0.4871	0.4875	0.4878	0.4881	0.4884	0.4887	0.4890
2.3	0.4893	0.4896	0.4898	0.4901	0.4904	0.4906	0.4909	0.4911	0.4913	0.4916
2.4	0.4918	0.4920	0.4922	0.4925	0.4927	0.4929	0.4931	0.4932	0.4934	0.4936
2.5	0.4938	0.4940	0.4941	0.4943	0.4945	0.4946	0.4948	0.4949	0.4951	0.4952
2.6	0.4953	0.4955	0.4956	0.4957	0.4959	0.4960	0.4961	0.4962	0.4963	0.4964
2.7	0.4965	0.4966	0.4967	0.4968	0.4969	0.4970	0.4971	0.4972	0.4973	0.4974
2.8	0.4974	0.4975	0.4976	0.4977	0.4977	0.4978	0.4979	0.4979	0.4980	0.4981
2.9	0.4981	0.4982	0.4982	0.4983	0.4984	0.4984	0.4985	0.4985	0.4986	0.4986
3.0	0.4986	0.4987	0.4987	0.4988	0.4988	0.4989	0.4989	0.4989	0.4990	0.4990

Reprinted with permission from Richard I. Levin and Charles A. Kirkpatrick, *Quantitative Approaches to Management*, 3rd Edition, McGraw-Hill, Inc., New York, NY, 1975.

INDEX

Absolute priorities, 723
Active and inactive, graphical interpretations, 118
Active constraints, 117
Activity, 439
Activity, definition of, 439
Activity list, 439
Activity time (PERT):
    expected time, 453
    most probable time, 453
    optimistic time, 452
    pessimistic time, 453
    standard deviation, 454
Activity times:
    crashing, 457–63
    estimation, 454
    variability, 452
Adding constraints, 145
Adjacent extreme points, 231
Algorithm:
    branch and bound, 354
    critical path, 445–49
    Hungarian, 310
    Maximal flow, 418
    minimal spanning time, 413
    MODI, 297
    northwest corner, 285
    shortest route, 407
    simplex, 221
    stepping-stone, 291
    Vogel's approximation, 285
Algorithms, 1
All integer linear program, 339
All integer model (ILP), 339
Allowable objective function coefficient ranges:
    computer output, 170
    geometry, 165
    simplex computation, 275
Allowable RHS range:
    computer output, 170
    geometry, 168
    simplex computation, 271
Alternative optima, 170, 258
Alternative optima (LP):
    degenerate solution, 173
    geometric interpretation, 121
    nondegenerate solution, 172
    simplex algorithm, 259
Annual holding and ordering cost, 496
Appliance angle problem, 528
Applications capsules:
    A Network Model at Air Products and Chemicals, Inc., 400
    Allocating a Scarce Resource, 30
    An Inventory of Trucks, 152
    Coordinating Decisions for Increased Profit, 488
    Designing a Complex Interconnected System, 614
    Management of College Student Recruiting Activities, 709
    National Center for Drug Analysis, 708
    Naval Ship Production, 575
    Scheduling Training at American Airlines, 336
Applications; queuing models:
    hermatology lab, 556

repairman, 565
selecting number of WATS lines, 561
Arborist, 666
Arc:
    capacity, 402
    network model, 401
    nondirected, 406
    PERT diagram, 441
Arrival process, 552
Artificial variables, 248
Assigning sales representatives, diagnostic assignment, 396
Assignment problem, 306
    computer solution, 309
    Hungarian method, 310
    max problem, 315
    relation to transportation problem, 307
    social theorem, 353
    unacceptable assignments, 319
    unequal supply and demand, 313
Astro and Cosmo:
    definition, 55
    simplex solution, 165
Average squared error, 687

Backlogging:
    cost, 508
    definition, 490
    in EOQ model, 508
    example, 511
Backward pass, 446
Barnum, P. T., 26
Basic feasible solution, 227
Basic queuing model:
    assumptions, 552
    characteristics, 554
Basic solutions in LP, 224
Basic variables, 225
    degenerate corner, 227
    nonbasic variables, 225
    nondegenerate corner, 227
Bayes Theorem, 638
Bender's Decomposition, 366
Beta distribution, 453
Binary integer linear programs, 339
Binding constraint, 118
Binomial distribution, 531
Blending problem, 56
Box-Jenkins approach, 695
Branch:
    decision trees, 633
    network model, 401
    PERT diagram, 441
Branch and bound:
    decision tree, 355
    general approach, 354
    graphical interpretation, 357
    ILP example, 354
    role of LP relaxation, 354
    summary, 361
Branch and bound algorithm, 354
Break-even analysis:
    definition, 6
    longer books example, 64
Budget allocation:
    integer programming, 344
Bumles, Inc. minicase, 68

Capacitated transshipment model:
    general formulation, 404
    importance, 405
    Seymour Miles, 401
Capital budgeting: ILP model, 345
Carried load, 564
Carr, Lisa, 412
Cases:
    An Application of Spreadsheet Analysis to Foreign Exchange Markets, 97
    Kiwi Computer, 210
    Municipal Bond Underwriting, 392
    Production Planning at Bumles, 214
    Red Brand Canners (computer solution), 206
    Red Brand Canners (formulation), 93
    Saw Mill River Feed and Grain Company, 208
    To Drill or Not to Drill, 668
Casual forecasting, 673
Charnes, A., 720
Circular node, 633
Combinatorial optimization, 710
Communication links, 413
Comparison between LP and NLP, 756
Complete enumeration: integer programming, 343
Computer (PERT), 449
Computer, role of, 2
Concave function, 747
Conditional probability, 633
Connected node, 413
Consensus panel, 698
Constrained optimization, 18, 32
Constraint function, definition, 21
Constraint set, 112
Constraints, 20
    bottlenecks, 22
    cost of search, 22
    laws of nature, 22
Continuous review, 592
Contour, 108
Contours, 107
Controlling project costs, 467
Convex function, 747
Cooper, W. W., 720
Cost (inventory models):
    holding, 490
    ordering, 490
    stockout, 490
CPM and time-cost trade-offs:
    crash cost, 458
    crash time, 458
    LP formulation, 460
    normal cost, 458
    normal time, 457
CPM (Critical Path Method (see also PERT), 438
Crash cost (CPM), 458
Crash time (CPM), 458
Crashing the project (CPM), 459
Crawler Tread:
    computer solution, 175
    definition, 49
Crawler Tread and a new angle, diagnostic assignment, 217
Critical path, 443

Critical points, 746
Curve fitting, 673, 684
Cut, 423
Cut capacity, 423
Cycle time, 498

Dantzig, George, 221
Dantzig, Tobias, 188
Decision analysis, 651
Decision Models, 7
    classification, 8
    definition, 7
Decision theory, 615
Decision trees, 631
    creation of, 633
    definition, 631
    folding back, 634
    market research study example, 638
    market research study, continued, 641
    optimal strategy, 648
Decision variable, definition, 21
Decisions against nature, 615
Decisions:
    under certainty, 616
    under risk, 617
    under uncertainty, 620
Degeneracy, 161
Degeneracy in transportation problems, 301
Degenerate corner, 161
Degenerate problems, 258
Degenerate solution:
    definition, 168
    geometry, 168
Deleting constraints, 145
Delphi method, 698
Demand function, 5
Destinations, 280
Deviation variables, 721
Diagnostic assignments:
    assigning sales representatives, 396
    Crawler Tread and a new angle, 217
    inventory turns, 547
    Johnson's Metal, 669
    scheduling tanker arrivals, 610
Different types of models, 3
Dual price, 166
Dual problem, 184
    computational significance, 194
    economic significance, 191
    theory, 188
    transformation rules, 184
Dual theorem of linear programming, 190
Dual variables:
    computation in simplex, 269
    relation to dual price, 194
Dummy activity, 442

Earliest finish time, 445
Earliest start time:
    definition, 445
    rule, 445
Economic analysis of queuing systems, 559
Economic order quantity, 495
Enter rule, 236
Enter variable, 236
EOQ (Economic Order Quantity):
    annual holding and ordering costs, 499
    with backlogging, 508
    managerial considerations, 504
    model, 459
    optimal cycle time, 499
    optimal number of orders, 499
    order quantity formula, 499

production lot size model, 512
quantity discounts, 505
sensitivity, 502
when-to-order rule, 500
Equipment replacement, 412
Erlang loss distribution, 562
Exit rule, 241
Exit variable, 239
Expected return, 618
Expected value of perfect information, 624
Expected value of sample information, 644
Exponential distribution, 552, 567
    lack of memory property, 567
    relation to Poisson, 567
    role in queuing models, 552
    small service times, 567
Exponential smoothing, 689
    ramp, 692
    seasonal demand, 694
    sudden change, 692
Extreme points, 221
Extreme points and optimal solutions, 120

Facility scheduling, 711
Factorial, 225
Feasible budgets for total project costs, 467
Feasible set, 112
Feasible solutions in LP, 224
Financial and production planning, 319
Financial planning example, 62
Finite calling population, 565
First derivative test, 746
Flow balance equation, 403
Flow capacity, 419, 423
    arc, 402
    path, 419
Flying Tiger Line, 365
Folding back, 634
Forecasting (qualitative), 698
    consensus panel, 698
    Delphi method, 698
    grass roots, 699
    market research, 700
Forecasting (quantitative), 672
    causal models, 673
    curve fitting, 673
    least squares, 676
    moving averages, 684
    random walk, 695
    time series, 684
Formulation of models, 52
Forward pass, 446

Game theory, 615
Gantt Chart, 440,
Gantt, Henry L., 440
GASP II, 598
Generating random events, 576
GINO, 369
Global maximizer, 746
Global Oil, 668
Goal programming, 721
    absolute priorities, 723
    combining weights and absolute priorities, 732
    definition, 721
    designing an educational program, 721
    goal interval constraint, 723
    graphical analysis and computer implementation, 728
    media selection example, 725
Goldstein, Rebecca, 438
GPSS (General Purpose Systems Simulator), 569

Graphical method:
    ILP (all-integer model), 341
    LP max, 109
    LP min, 122
Graphical solution method, 110
Grass roots forecasting, 699
Gravity model, 4
Great Pyramid, 437
Greedy algorithm (heuristic), 712
Greedy algorithm (networks):
    graphic method, 413
    tabular method, 415
Guidelines on model formulation, 52

Herodotus, 437
Heuristic algorithms, 710
    facility scheduling, 711
    work-load scheduling, 714
Hierarchies, 24
Historical data, 697
Holding costs, 490
Hungarian method, 310
Hunt-Wesson Foods, 365

Immediate predecessors, 439
IMPACT, 541
Implementation of modeling, 16
Important constraint, 143
Inactive constraints, 116
Inconsistency, 126
Inequality constraints, definition, 34
Infeasible problems, 257
Infeasible problem, 124
    definition, 126
    geometry in LP, 126
    signal in simplex, 257
Infinite calling population, 565
Inflection points, 746
INFOREM, 541
Integer linear programming, 337
    0–1 variables, 339, 344
    all-integer model, 339
    branch and bound, 354
    compared to enumeration, 344
    dependent decisions, 347
    graphical interpretation, 339
    importance of integer variables, 337
    k of n alternatives, 347
    logical conditions, 347
    lot size constraints, 348
    LP relaxation, 342
    mixed integer linear program, 339
    Protrac example, 340
    rounded solution, 337, 342
Integer property, 406
Integrality conditions, 39
Intermediate goods, 515
Internal Revenue Service, 406
Intuitive modeling, 25
Inventory position, 500
Inventory turns, diagnostic assignment, 547
Inventory:
    definition, 489
    reasons for holding, 489
IP (Integer Programming) formulations:
    capital budgeting, 345
    warehouse locations, 354
Iso-cost, 108
Iso-profit, 108
Iso-quant, 108
Iteration, 222
    pivot, 222, 242
    transformed equations, 229

Jackson, Monte, 550
Joseph, 618

Karush-Kuhn-Tucker conditions, 764
Keeney, Ralph, 650
Kelly-Springfield Tire Company, 365
Kendall, D. G., 559
King Khufu, 437
Kowalski, Victor, 489

Lack of memory property, 567
Lagrange multipliers:
    economic interpretation, 764
    one constraint, 757
    the general case, 762
Laplace criterion, 620
Latest finish time:
    definition, 446
    rule, 447
Latest start time, 446
Lead time, 500
Lead-time demand, 530
Lead-time offsetting, 518
Lean-year programming, 618
Least-squares, 676
    linear fit, 678
    quadratic fit, 679
Limitations, 32
LINDO:
    IP solution, 346
    LP solution, 170
Linear function, 93
Linear least squares, 676
Linear programming, computer solution, 163
Linear programming, computer solution, 183
Linear regression, 682
Little's flow equation, 554
Local minimizer, 746
Logical conditions in ILP:
    dependent decisions, 347
    k of n alternatives, 347
    lot size constraints, 348
Longer boats break-even example, 65
Loosening a constraint, 140
Lot size constraints, 348
Lotus 1-2-3, 9
LP formulations:
    assignment, 309
    Astro/Cosmo, 55
    blending, 49, 56
    breakeven analysis, 309
    crashing a CPM project, 460
    Crawler Tread, 49
    financial and production planning, 319
    financial planning, 62
    goal programming, 728
    guidelines, 52
    longer boats, 72
    media selection, 323
    product mix, 34
    Protrac, 33
    Winston-Salem, 62
    work force schedule, 57
LP relaxation, 339
LP (Linear Programming):
    basic solution, 224
    basic variables, 225
    degenerate corner, 228
    feasible solution, 224
    not all variables non-negative, 206
    optimal solution, 223
    solution, 223
LP–NLP comparisons, 756

Managerial role, 1, 2, 16
Market equilibrium, 5
Market research, 700
Markowitz, H. M., 598
Material requirements planning (MRP), 515
Mathematical programming, 20
Matrix generator, 47
Max flow/min cut theorem, 423
Maximal-flow algorithm, 419
Maximal-flow problem, 417
Maximax, 622
Maximin, 621
McConnel, Peggy, 536
Mean arrival rate, 552
Mean interarrival time, 552
Mean service rate, 552
Media selection problem, 323
Mencken, H. L., 26
Minimax, 622
Minimax regret, 622
Minimum spanning tree, 413
Mixed integer linear program, 339
Model:
    as an abstraction, 3
    decision models, 7
    formal, 13, 44
    implementation, 16
    intuitive, 25
    role of numbers, 6
    spreadsheet, 14, 44
    uses at different levels of firm, 17
    what if, 2
Model building, 14
Model formulation, 53
MODI (Modified Distribution) method:
    allocation, 299
    determine index, 297
    example, 297–99
    marginal cost of unused cells, 303
Monte Carlo method, 581
Most probable time, 454
Moving averages, 684
    exponential smoothing, 689
    simple n-period, 684
    weighted n-period, 686
MRP (Material Requirements Planning), 515
    additional requirements, 517
    time phasing, 517
Multiperiod inventory models, 65
Multiple-channel queue, 557
Multiple objectives, 720
Multiple optima, 121
Multiserver queue, 556
M/G/s; blocked customers cleared, 561
M/M/s, 565

Necessary condition, 747
Negative exponential distribution, 552
Negative variables in LP, 206
Nest feathering, 24
Network diagram, 401
    network problem, 401
    PERT, 441
Network model, 401
Newsboy problem, 537, 624
    decision under risk, 618
    general result, 538
    normal demand, 539
    value of perfect information, 624
    uniform demand, 538
New York blackout, 437
NLP (Non Linear Programming) problems:
    concave or convex quadratic, 766
    general concave or convex, 767
    highly nonlinear, 769

Node:
    decision tree, 633
    network diagram, 402
    PERT diagram, 441
Node-arc incidence matrix, 403
Nondirected arc, 406
Nonlinear objective in LP, 324
Nonlinear optimization:
    constrained, 753
    equality constrained, 757
    unconstrained, 744
Nonnegativity, 35
Normal cost (CPM), 459
Normal distribution:
    lead-time demand, 533
    newsboy problem, 539
    simulation of, 588
    table, 822
Normal time (CPM), 457
Northwest corner rule, 285

Oak Products, Inc., 8
Objective function, 20, 32
Opportunity costs of simplex tableau, 233
Opposite corner rule, 242
Optimal decision, 19
Optimal objective value (OV), 116
Optimality, 19
Optimality criterion (simplex), 247
Optimistic time, 453
Ordering costs, 490

Parameters, 147
Parametric analysis, 23, 135
Path, 406
Payoff function, 21
Payoff table, 616
PC applications:
    decision trees, 666
    forecasting, 706
    network problems, 432
    PERT/CPM, 483
    simulation, 607
Permanent label, 407
PERT and CPM:
    activity list, 439
    activity times, 453
    dummy activity, 442
    earliest start time, 445
    event, 441
    immediate predecessor, 439
    latest finish time, 447
    network diagram, 441
    PERT/Cost, 463
    probability of completing the project on
        time, 454
    slack, 449
    summary, 455
PERT (Program Evaluation Review
    Technique), 438
PERT/Cost, 463
    budget demands, earliest start, 465
    budget demands, latest start, 466
    feasible budgets, 467
Pessimistic time, 453
Phase, 248
Phase I, 190
Pivot element, 242
Pivoting operation, 243
Plotting inequalities, 107
Plotting objective function contours, 113
Poisson distribution, 552, 568

Polynomial regression, 681
Portfolio model, 376
Portfolio selection, 373
    definition of return, 378
    definition of risk, 374
    efficient frontier, 380
Positive variables at corners, 160
Post-optimality analysis, 135
Primal problem, 188
Pritsker, A. Alan B., 598
Probability of completing a project on time, 454
Probability of stocking out, 530
Production lot size, 512
PROFIT, 541
Project cost management (PERT/Cost), 563
Project crashing (CPM), 463
PROTRAC:
    capital budgeting problem, 345
    combined model, 319
    formulation, 33
    graphical solution, 110
    ILP modification, 340
    inventory simulation, 592
    sensitivity analysis (computer solution), 163
    sensitivity analysis (graphical), 134
    simplex algorithm, 253
PROTRAC, Inc.,
    branch and bound, 354
    combined model, 319
    ILP modification, 340
    lot size constraints, 348
    simplex solution, 253

QSB, 432, 483
Quadratic function, 367
Quadratic least squares, 679
Quadratic programming, 367
    application to portfolio selection, 373
    sensitivity analysis analysis, 370
    consensus panel, 698
    Delphi method, 698
    expert judgement, 698
    grass roots, 699
    market research, 699
Quantity discounts, 505
Queue discipline, 553, 568
Queuing problem, 550
Queuing:
    basic model, 551
    blocked customers cleared, 561
    economic analysis, 559
    multiple-channel, 559
    repairman problem, 565
Quick and dirty, 674

Random number:
    definition, 586
    example of use, 588
    table, 587
Random walk, 694
    with a drift, 695
Raw data, 44
Red Brand Canners, case:
    computer analysis, 206
    formulation, 107
Reduced cost, 173
Reduced decision tree, 634
Redundant constraint, 141
Regret, 622
Relative maximizer, 746
Relaxation, in IP, 342
Reorder point-reorder quantity model, 528

Reorder point:
    definition, 528
    with normal lead-time demand, 533
    with uniform lead-time demand, 530
Repairman problem, 565
Requirements, 32
Restrictions, 31
Revised simplex method, 259
Risk, 627
    averse, 627
    indifferent, 627
    seeking, 628
Role of this book, 1
Rounded solution to ILP, 343
Route, 407

Safety stock, 504, 535
    definition, 535
    expected annual cost, 535
Saw Mill River Feed and Grain Company, 208
Scatter diagram, 673
Scheduling tanker arrivals, diagnostic assignment, 610
Second derivative test, 747
Security force scheduling, 57
Sensitivity analysis (LP):
    computing allowable changes in the objective function coefficients, 275
    computing optimal dual variables, 270
    introduction, 134
    objective function coefficient (computer solution), 170
    RHS (computer solution), 165
    RHS (graphical), 136
Sensitivity (decision analysis), 635
Sensitivity (EOQ), 502
Sequential decision problem, 646
Service process, 552
Shortest-route algorithm, 404
    shortest-path tree, 411
    labeling procedure, 407
Shortest-route problem:
    network, 407
Simplex method:
    alternative optima, 259
    artificial variables, 248
    Astro/Cosmo example, 223
    basic feasible solutions, 224
    characterization of adjacent extreme points, 231
    computing allowable changes in objective function coefficients, 275
    computing allowable changes in RHS, 271
    computing opportunity costs, 233
    degenerate problems, 258
    dual variables, 270
    dummy destinations, 301
    enter rule, 247
    enter variable, 240
    exchange operation, 232
    exit rule, 241
    exit variable, 244
    full tableau representation, 237
    infeasible problems, 257
    initial tableau, 232
    max problems, 300
    nonbasic columns, 234
    optimality criterion, 247
    phase I, 221
    sensitivity analysis, 269
    solution to original equations, 224
    stopping rule, 247
    summary, 222

    transformed equations, 229
    unbounded problems, 257
SIMSCRIPT, 598
Simulation, 577
    computer analysis, 590
    design questions, 596
    documentation, 598
    group dynamics, 598
    preliminary analytic analysis, 593
    sampling questions, 597
Simulation examples:
    a fair die, 588
    initial conditions, 595
    inventory control, 592
    Wiles problem, 589
Simulation languages, 598
Single-channel queue, 551
Sink, 417
Slack and surplus variables, 154
Slack variable, 118
Slack (PERT), 449
Solution to original equations in LP, 224
Source, 417
Spreadsheet applications, 14
    Bumles, Inc., minicase, 68
    forecasting, 706
    modified PROTRAC E and F, 44
    Oak Products, Inc., 8
    PROTRAC E and F, 39
    security force scheduling, 59
    Wiles' housewares simulation, 607
Spreadsheet models:
    cells, 39
    components of, 39
    debugging, 48
    formulas, 41
    labels, 39
    optimized, 43
    symbolic spreadsheet, 42
    value spreadsheet, 42
Square node, 633
Standard equality constraint form, 153, 156
    geometric representation, 158
Stationary points, 746
Steady state, 553
Steco:
    EOQ model, 495
    introduction, 489
    inventory, deterministic demand, 488–514
    inventory, probabilistic demand, 528–36
    moving averages, 515
    MRP, 515
    production lot size, 512–14
    warehouse location, 349
Stepping-stone method:
    determine allocation, 294
    evaluating unused routes, 294
    example, 291–96
Stime, Gloria, 418
Stocking out:
    average number per year, 511
    probability each cycle, 511
    probability of more than one per year, 531
Stockout costs, 490
Stopping rule (simplex), 247
Strategic analysis in PERT, 450
Substitution coefficients, 235
Sufficient condition, 747
Sum of squared deviations, 680
Sunk vs. variable cost, 53
Supply function, 4
Surplus variable, 118
Surrogate objectives, 23

Table of random numbers, 587
Tableau, 234
    full representation, 237
    initial, 232
    updating, 241
Tactical analysis in PERT, 450
Taxonomy of queuing models, 559
Temporary label, 407
Terminal positions, 634
Termination criteria, 753
Tightening a constraint, 140
Time-cost trade-offs, 457
    crashing, 459
    PERT/Cost, 463
Time phasing, 517
Time-series, 683
To Drill or Not to Drill, case, 668
Tower of Babel, 437
Transformed equations in LP, 230
Transportation problem:
    computer solution, 282
    eliminating unacceptable routes, 300
    generacy, 301
    integer properties, 305
    MODI, 297
    northwest corner rule, 280
    special algorithms, 305
    special properties, 305

stepping-stone method, 291
supply exceeds demand, 300
Vogel's approximation method, 285
Transshipment nodes, 403
Tree, 408
Truncated Poisson distribution, 562
Turns, 547
Two-bin system, 540

Unbounded constraint set, 125
Unbounded problem, 124
Unbounded problems:
    definition, 125
    geometry in LP, 125
    signal in simplex, 258
Unconnected nodes, 413
Unconstrained optimization:
    n decision variables, 752
    one-decision variable, 744
    two-decision variables, 749
Urban Development Planning Commission, 418
Use of modeling, 16
Utility, 626
    creating a function, 630
    function, 627
    rationale, 626

risk averse, 627
risk indifferent, 628
risk seeking, 628
use of function, 628

Validation study, 686
VAM (Vogel's approximation method), 285
Vertices, 221
VINO, 12, 43
Vogel's approximation method:
    allocation rule, 287
    comparison with NW corner rule, 289
    example, 285–90
Vogel's approximation method, penalty costs, 287
von Ribbentrop, Joachim, 671

Warehouse location, 515
What if, 8
What'sBest, 12, 43
When-to-order rule, 500
Winston-Salem Development Corporation, 64
WISDOM, 541
Work-load smoothing, 714

Zero-one integer linear programs, 339
Zero-one variables, 339